Lecture Notes in Computer Science 13584

Founding Editors

Gerhard Goos, Germany
Juris Hartmanis, USA

Editorial Board Members

Elisa Bertino, USA
Wen Gao, China

Bernhard Steffen🆔, Germany
Moti Yung🆔, USA

Advanced Research in Computing and Software Science

Subline of Lecture Notes in Computer Science

Subline Series Editors

Giorgio Ausiello, *University of Rome 'La Sapienza', Italy*
Vladimiro Sassone, *University of Southampton, UK*

Subline Advisory Board

Susanne Albers, *TU Munich, Germany*
Benjamin C. Pierce, *University of Pennsylvania, USA*
Bernhard Steffen🆔, *University of Dortmund, Germany*
Deng Xiaotie, *Peking University, Beijing, China*
Jeannette M. Wing, *Microsoft Research, Redmond, WA, USA*

More information about this series at https://link.springer.com/bookseries/558

Panagiotis Kanellopoulos · Maria Kyropoulou ·
Alexandros Voudouris (Eds.)

Algorithmic
Game Theory

15th International Symposium, SAGT 2022
Colchester, UK, September 12–15, 2022
Proceedings

 Springer

Editors
Panagiotis Kanellopoulos ⓘ
University of Essex
Colchester, UK

Maria Kyropoulou ⓘ
University of Essex
Colchester, UK

Alexandros Voudouris ⓘ
University of Essex
Colchester, UK

ISSN 0302-9743   ISSN 1611-3349 (electronic)
Lecture Notes in Computer Science
ISBN 978-3-031-15713-4   ISBN 978-3-031-15714-1 (eBook)
https://doi.org/10.1007/978-3-031-15714-1

© The Editor(s) (if applicable) and The Author(s), under exclusive license
to Springer Nature Switzerland AG 2022
This work is subject to copyright. All rights are reserved by the Publisher, whether the whole or part of the material is concerned, specifically the rights of translation, reprinting, reuse of illustrations, recitation, broadcasting, reproduction on microfilms or in any other physical way, and transmission or information storage and retrieval, electronic adaptation, computer software, or by similar or dissimilar methodology now known or hereafter developed.
The use of general descriptive names, registered names, trademarks, service marks, etc. in this publication does not imply, even in the absence of a specific statement, that such names are exempt from the relevant protective laws and regulations and therefore free for general use.
The publisher, the authors, and the editors are safe to assume that the advice and information in this book are believed to be true and accurate at the date of publication. Neither the publisher nor the authors or the editors give a warranty, expressed or implied, with respect to the material contained herein or for any errors or omissions that may have been made. The publisher remains neutral with regard to jurisdictional claims in published maps and institutional affiliations.

This Springer imprint is published by the registered company Springer Nature Switzerland AG
The registered company address is: Gewerbestrasse 11, 6330 Cham, Switzerland

Preface

This volume contains the papers and extended abstracts presented at the 15th International Symposium on Algorithmic Game Theory (SAGT 2022), held during September 12–15, 2022, in Colchester, UK. The purpose of SAGT is to bring together researchers from computer science, economics, mathematics, operations research, psychology, physics, and biology to present and discuss original research at the intersection of algorithms and game theory.

This year, we received a record number of 83 submissions which were rigorously peer-reviewed by the Program Committee (PC). Each paper was reviewed by at least 3 PC members, and evaluated on the basis of originality, significance, and exposition. The PC eventually decided to accept 34 papers to be presented at the conference, for an acceptance ratio of 41%.

The works accepted for publication in this volume cover most of the major aspects of algorithmic game theory, including auction theory, mechanism design, markets and matchings, computational aspects of games, resource allocation problems, and computational social choice. To accommodate the publishing traditions of different fields, authors of accepted papers could ask that only a one-page abstract of the paper appeared in the proceedings. Among the 34 accepted papers, the authors of three papers selected this option.

Furthermore, due to the generous support by Springer, we were able to provide a Best Paper Award. The PC decided to give the award to the paper "Financial Networks with Singleton Liability Priorities" by Stavros Ioannidis, Bart de Keijzer, and Carmine Ventre. The program also included three invited talks by distinguished researchers in algorithmic game theory, namely Ioannis Caragiannis (Aarhus University, Denmark), Aggelos Kiayias (University of Edinburgh and IOHK, UK), and Sigal Oren (Ben-Gurion University of the Negev, Israel). In addition, SAGT 2022 featured two tutorial talks: one given by Aris Filos-Ratsikas (University of Liverpool, UK) and Alexandros Hollender (University of Oxford, UK) and the other one by Rohit Vaish (Indian Institute of Technology Delhi, India). We would like to thank all the authors for their interest in submitting their work to SAGT 2022, as well as the PC members and the external reviewers for their great work in evaluating the submissions. We also want to thank Meta, IOHK, Google, Springer, the Artificial Intelligence Journal, and CSEE at the University of Essex for their generous financial support.

We are grateful to the University of Essex for hosting the conference. Finally, we would like to thank Springer for their work on the proceedings, as well as the Easy-Chair conference management system for facilitating the peer-review process.

July 2022

Panagiotis Kanellopoulos
Maria Kyropoulou
Alexandros A. Voudouris

Organization

Program Committee

Georgios Amanatidis	University of Essex, UK
Vittorio Bilò	University of Salento, Italy
Georgios Birmpas	Sapienza University of Rome, Italy
Bart de Keijzer	King's College London, UK
Argyrios Deligkas	Royal Holloway, University of London, UK
Paul Dütting	Google Research, Switzerland
Alon Eden	Harvard University, USA
Edith Elkind	University of Oxford, UK
Jiarui Gan	University of Oxford, UK
Jugal Garg	University of Illinois at Urbana-Champaign, USA
Yiannis Giannakopoulos	Friedrich-Alexander-Universität Erlangen-Nürnberg, Germany
Laurent Gourves	Université Paris Dauphine-PSL, France
Tobias Harks	University of Augsburg, Germany
Alexandros Hollender	University of Oxford, UK
Ayumi Igarashi	National Institute of Informatics, Japan
Panagiotis Kanellopoulos (Co-chair)	University of Essex, UK
Pieter Kleer	Tilburg University, The Netherlands
Maria Kyropoulou (Co-chair)	University of Essex, UK
Philip Lazos	IOHK and Sapienza University of Rome, Italy
Stefanos Leonardos	Singapore University of Technology and Design, Singapore
Bo Li	Hong Kong Polytechnic University, Hong Kong
Pasin Manurangsi	Google Research, USA
Reshef Meir	Technion – Israel Institute of Technology, Israel
Themistoklis Melissourgos	University of Essex, UK
Baharak Rastegari	University of Southampton, UK
Alkmini Sgouritsa	University of Liverpool, UK
Piotr Skowron	University of Warsaw, Poland
Warut Suksompong	National University of Singapore, Singapore
Tami Tamir	Reichman University, Israel
Rohit Vaish	Indian Institute of Technology Delhi, Israel
Carmine Ventre	King's College London, UK
Adrian Vetta	McGill University, Canada
Cosimo Vinci	University of Salerno, Italy

Alexandros Voudouris (Co-chair)	University of Essex, UK
Anaëlle Wilczynski	Université Paris-Saclay, France
Jie Zhang	University of Southampton, UK

Organizing Committee

Panagiotis Kanellopoulos	University of Essex, UK
Maria Kyropoulou	University of Essex, UK
Alexandros Voudouris	University of Essex, UK

Steering Committee

Elias Koutsoupias	University of Oxford, UK
Marios Mavronicolas	University of Cyprus, Cyprus
Dov Monderer	Technion–Israel Institute of Technology, Israel
Burkhard Monien	University of Paderborn, Germany
Christos Papadimitriou	Columbia University, USA
Giuseppe Persiano	University of Salerno, Italy
Paul Spirakis (Chair)	University of Liverpool, UK

Additional Reviewers

Michael Albert
Alessandro Aloisio
Thomas Archbold
Gennaro Auricchio
Xiaohui Bei
Gili Bielous
Davide Bilò
Ruben Brokkelkamp
Johannes Brustle
Martin Bullinger
Andrés Cristi
Ágnes Cseh
Théo Delemazure
Jack Dippel
Roy Fairstein
Alireza Fallah
Angelo Fanelli
John Fearnley
Aris Filos-Ratsikas
Kaito Fujii
Federico Fusco
Felipe Garrido Lucero

Badih Ghazi
Abheek Ghosh
Hugo Gilbert
Alexander Grosz
Kasper Høgh
Stavros Ioannidis
Michał Jaworski
Yasushi Kawase
Bojana Kodric
Sonja Kraiczy
Piotr Krysta
Ron Kupfer
Pascal Lenzner
Weian Li
Yingkai Li
Xinhang Lu
Jayson Lynch
Faraaz Mallick
Francisco Javier Marmolejo Cossio
Marios Mavronicolas
Gianpiero Monaco
Aniket Murhekar

Caspar Oesterheld
Georgios Papasotiropoulos
Grzegorz Pierczyński
Nicos Protopapas
John Qin
Shaul Rosner
Zhang Ruilong
Soumendu Sarkar
Rahul Savani
Daniel Schmand
Marc Schroder
Nikolaj Ignatieff Schwartzbach
Eklavya Sharma
Yiheng Shen
Alexander Skopalik
George Skretas
Krzysztof Sornat

Ankang Sun
Zhaohong Sun
Seiji Takanashi
Xizhi Tan
Wei Tang
Nicholas Teh
Taiki Todo
Alexandros Tsigonias-Dimitriadis
Artem Tsikiridis
Andries van Beek
Estelle Varloot
Giovanna Varricchio
Yllka Velaj
Jonny Wagner
Yutong Wu
Konstantin Zabarnyi
Hanrui Zhang

Abstracts of Invited Talks

New Fairness Concepts for Allocating Indivisible Items

Ioannis Caragiannis

Department of Computer Science, Aarhus University, Denmark
iannis@cs.au.dk

Fair division is a very popular research area, with roots in antiquity and many important real-world applications today. In the model that has received much attention in the EconCS research community, a set of indivisible items has to be allocated to a set of agents. Each agent has a valuation function for the items that help her evaluate bundles of items and compare different bundles.

Fairness in allocations is usually interpreted in two ways. The first interpretation is comparative; to evaluate an allocation as fair, each agent compares the bundle of items allocated to her to bundles of items allocated to other agents. The well-known fairness concept of envy-freeness and its relaxations are typical examples of fairness notions defined this way. In particular, the concept of envy-freeness up to any item (abbreviated as EFX) is a very compelling one. An allocation is EFX if every agent prefers her bundle to the bundle allocated to any other agent after removing any single item from the latter.

The second interpretation is in more absolute terms. In this category, each agent defines a threshold value based on her view of the allocation instance (the set of items, the number of agents, her valuation function, etc.) and evaluates as fair those allocations in which she gets a bundle of value that exceeds the threshold. Variations of proportionality are the typical examples here, with max-min fair share (MMS) being the fairness concept that has attracted the lion's share of attention.

Despite intensive research efforts, it is still unknown whether EFX allocations always exist for sufficiently broad valuation functions and instances with more than three agents. Furthermore, even if such allocations always exist, polynomial-time algorithms to find them do not seem to be within reach. The situation with MMS is rather worse. Today we know that MMS allocations may not exist, and the research has focused on finding the best possible "fairness approximation".

In this talk, we present two new fairness notions that are inspired by EFX. The first one, called epistemic EFX (EEFX), is comparative and is defined as follows. An allocation is EEFX if, for every agent, there is a redistribution of the items not allocated to the agent so that the EFX conditions for her are satisfied. The second one, called minimum EFX value (MXS), is absolute and requires that each agent gets a value that is at least as high as the minimum value the agent gets among all allocations where the

EFX conditions for her are satisfied. We argue about the importance of these fairness concepts, showing that allocations that satisfy them always exist and can be computed efficiently.

The talk is based on joint work with Jugal Garg, Nidhi Rathi, Eklavya Sharma, and Giovanna Varricchio.

Decentralizing Information Technology: The Advent of Resource Based Systems

Aggelos Kiayias

School of Informatics, University of Edinburgh and IOG, Edinburgh, UK
akiayias@inf.ed.ac.uk

Abstract. The growth of the Bitcoin network during the first decade of its operation to a global system is a singular event in the deployment of Information Technology systems. Can this approach serve as a broader paradigm for Information Technology services beyond the use case of digital currencies? We investigate this question by introducing the concept of resource based systems and their four fundamental characteristics: (i) resource-based operation, (ii) tokenomics, (iii) decentralized service provision, and (iv) rewards sharing. We explore these characteristics, identify design goals and challenges and investigate some crucial game theoretic aspects of reward sharing that can be decisive for their effective operation.

Algorithmic Game Theory Meets Behavioral Economics

Sigal Oren

Ben-Gurion University of the Negev, Israel
sigal3@gmail.com

A recent line of work strives to bridge the gap between Algorithmic Game Theory and Behavioral Economics. This can be approached from two opposite directions: (1) Utilizing tools from theoretical computer science and algorithmic game theory to obtain and analyze more rigorous models for cognitive biases and (2) Enriching well-studied settings in Algorithmic Game Theory by considering players that exhibit cognitive biases. In this talk, we will discuss two recent papers taking the second approach. The first considers biased agents facing optimal stopping problems and the second tackles a fundamental assumption of Algorithmic Mechanism Design: Truthfulness.

Optimal Stopping with Behaviorally Biased Agents. We explore the implications of two central human biases studied in behavioral economics, *reference points* and *loss aversion*, in optimal stopping problems. In such problems, people evaluate a sequence of options in one pass, either accepting the option and stopping the search or giving up on the option forever. Here we assume that the best option seen so far sets a reference point that shifts as the search progresses, and a biased decision-maker's utility incurs an additional penalty when they accept a later option that is below this reference point. Our results include tight bounds on the performance of a biased agent in this model relative to the best option obtainable in retrospect as well as tight bounds on the ratio between the performance of a biased agent and the performance of a rational one.

Mechanism Design with Moral Bidders. A rapidly growing literature on lying in behavioral economics and psychology shows that individuals often do not lie even when lying maximizes their utility. In this work, we attempt to incorporate these findings into the theory of mechanism design. We consider bidders that have a preference for truth-telling, and will only lie if their benefit from lying is sufficiently larger than the loss of the others. To accommodate such bidders, we introduce α-moral mechanisms, in which the gain of a bidder from misreporting his true value, compared to truth-telling, is at most α fraction of the loss that the others incur due to misreporting. We develop a theory of moral mechanisms in the canonical setting of single-item auctions. Our main results explore the circumstances under which an auctioneer can take advantage of the players' preference for truth-telling.

Based on joint works with Jon Kleinberg and Robert Kleinberg (GEB'22) and with Shahar Dobzinski (ITCS'22).

Contents

Congestion and Network Creation Games

Data Sharing and Learning

Social Choice and Stable Matchings

Abstracts

Invited Talk

Decentralizing Information Technology: The Advent of Resource Based Systems

Aggelos Kiayias[(⊠)]

School of Informatics, University of Edinburgh and IOG, Edinburgh, UK
akiayias@inf.ed.ac.uk

Abstract. The growth of the Bitcoin network during the first decade of its operation to a global system is a singular event in the deployment of Information Technology systems. Can this approach serve as a broader paradigm for Information Technology services beyond the use case of digital currencies? We investigate this question by introducing the concept of resource based systems and their four fundamental characteristics: (i) resource-based operation, (ii) tokenomics, (iii) decentralized service provision, and (iv) rewards sharing. We explore these characteristics, identify design goals and challenges and investigate some crucial game theoretic aspects of reward sharing that can be decisive for their effective operation.

1 Introduction

A paradigm shift took place during the last decade in the way the consensus problem is looked at in Computer Science. Three decades after the seminal work of Lamport, Shostak and Pease [31], Satoshi Nakamoto with the Bitcoin blockchain protocol [26] put forth a novel way to solve the consensus problem. Traditionally, Byzantine consensus was considered to be the problem of reaching agreement between a set of processors, some of which may arbitrarily deviate from the protocol and try to confuse the ones who follow the protocol. Over time, significant research was invested into establishing the exact bounds in the *number* of deviating parties as well as the intrinsic complexity bounds of the problem in terms of round and message complexity.

The approach did not address the question who assigns identities to the processors or sets up the network that connects them, or how the processors agree about the identities of all those present in the particular protocol instance. These were tasks left to a system setup phase that, for all purposes, seemed sufficient to be a centralized operation carried out by a trusted party. The success of the Internet however and the development of peer-to-peer networks in the early 2000's set the stage for challenging this assumption. At the same time, Sybil attacks [11] posed a significant obstacle to apply known consensus protocol techniques to this new setting.

Given the above landscape, Nakamoto's solution is unexpected. The blockchain protocol design circumvents entirely the issue of identity and provides a solution for consensus that "takes advantage of information being easy to spread but hard

ⓒ The Author(s), under exclusive license to Springer Nature Switzerland AG 2022
P. Kanellopoulos et al. (Eds.): SAGT 2022, LNCS 13584, pp. 3–19, 2022.
https://doi.org/10.1007/978-3-031-15714-1_1

to stifle" [27]. In the Bitcoin blockchain, it is the computational power that different participants contribute to the protocol execution that facilitates convergence to a unique view. And as long as the deviating parties are in the minority of computational power, Nakamoto's blockchain protocol can be shown to converge to an unambiguous view that incorporates new inputs in a timely manner, as proven formally in [17] and subsequently refined in [18,29].

The bitcoin blockchain however is much more than just a consensus protocol; it provides a service—transferring digital currency between principals—and also provides incentives to those who engage in service provision in the form of "mining" the digital currency following a regular schedule. In this way, agreeing to a joint view is not the primary objective but rather a precondition for the service to materialize. Participants need to agree on the ledger of digital asset ownership.

Becoming a system maintainer in Bitcoin does not require anything else other than possessing the software and necessary hardware to run the protocol. Remarkably, there is no need to be approved by other participants as long as the underlying peer to peer network allows diffusing messages across all peers without censorship.

Given the successful growth of the Bitcoin network at a worldwide level, a fundamental question arises: does its architecture suggest a novel way of deploying information technology (IT) services at a global scale? So far, in IT, we have witnessed two major ways of scaling systems to such level. In the "centralized" approach, we have organizations such as Google, Facebook and Amazon that offer world-wide operations with reasonably high quality of service. The downsides of the centralized approach is —naturally— centralization itself and the fact that long term common good may not necessarily align properly with company shareholder interest. In such settings, regulatory arbitrage may deprive the public any leverage against the service operator. A second approach is the "federated" one. In this case, we have the coordination of multiple organizations or entities with a diverse set of interests to offer the service in cooperation. Examples of such federated organization have been very successful and far reaching as they include the Internet itself. Nevertheless, for federated organization to scale, significant efforts should be invested to make sure the individual systems interoperate and the incentives of their operators remain aligned.

Viewed in this light, the decentralized approach offered by Nakamoto's Bitcoin system provides an alternative pathway to a globally scalable system. In this paper, we abstract Nakamoto's novel approach to system deployment under a general viewpoint that we term "resource-based systems." Preconditioned on the existence of an open network, a resource based system capitalizes on a particular resource that is somehow dispersed across a wide population of *resource holders* and bootstraps itself to a sufficient level of quality of service and security out of the self-interest of resource holders who engage with each other via the system's underlying protocol. Depending on the design, the resulting system may scale more slowly and be less performant than a centralized system, but it offers security and resilience characteristics that can be attractive for a number of applications especially for global scale IT.

In the next section we introduce the four fundamental characteristics of resource based systems and then we expand on each one in a separate section describing the challenges that resource based system designers must overcome in order to make them successful. We also identify a configuration in the effective operation of a resource based system that arises in the form of a centralized equilibrium. We discuss the ramifications of this result and conclude with some examples of resource based systems and directions for future research.

2 Fundamental Characteristics of Resource Based Systems

Consider a service described as a program $\mathscr{F}$ that captures all the operations that users wish to perform. A resource-based realization of $\mathscr{F}$ is a system that exhibits the following four fundamental characteristics, cf. Fig. 1

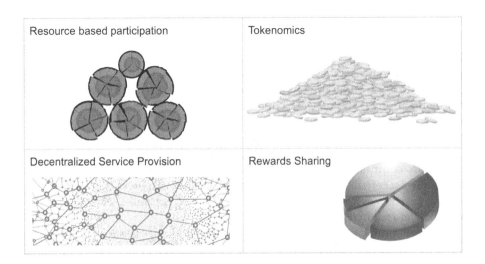

Fig. 1. The four characteristic components of resource-based systems

- *Resource-based participation.* There exists a fungible resource that can be acquired by anyone interested in doing so, possibly at a cost. Entities in possession of units of the resource can exercise it to participate in the maintenance of the service, possibly incurring further costs.
- *Tokenomics.* The system issues a digital asset or currency that is used to tokenize the collective efforts of the maintainers and reward them. Such digital "coins" are maintained in cryptographic wallets and should be argued to be of sufficient utility to make system maintenance an attractive endeavor as a joint effort.
- *Decentralized service provision.* A user interacts with the service by submitting a transaction which is circulated in the network of maintainers provided it meets some well formedness guarantee. This may require the commitment of a sufficient amount of digital currency or other user expenditure to prevent spamming. The maintainers collectively take the required actions of $\mathscr{F}$ needed for the

submitted transactions in a consistent and expedient fashion while the system records their efforts in a robust manner.
- *Rewards Sharing.* The digital assets that the system makes available to maintainers are distributed to the active maintainers in a regular and fair manner so that the system's safety and liveness properties emanate from their incentive driven participation. Any property violation should be a deviation from an equilibrium state that reduces the utility of the perpetrators, hence ensuring the stable operation of the system.

Based on the above, implementing a given system functionality $\mathscr{F}$ by a resource based protocol requires the design of a protocol with suitable cryptographic and game theoretic characteristics. In the next four sections we delve into each characteristic in some more detail.

3 Resource-Based Participation

In classic distributed systems, system maintenance is offered by nodes that are authorized to do so either by common agreement (e.g., via a list of public-keys that identify them) or by the network connections that are assumed to exist between them (cf. [16] for an overview). Such configurations are commonly referred to in cryptographic modeling as setup assumptions.

Contrary to this, in the decentralized setting of resource-based protocols, participation to contribute to the protocol execution is attained via demonstrating the possession of a certain resource. This comes in the form of a *proof of resource*, commonly referred to as "proof-of-X" (PoX) in Bitcoin nomenclature, where X signifies the particular resource in question.

It is worth noting that this approach generalizes both the classic distributed setting, since the resource in question could be the possession of one of the authorized identities, as well as the centralized setting—in a trivial manner.

The two most widely cited such schemes are proof-of-work (PoW) and proof-of-stake (PoS). The case of PoW is exemplified in the Bitcoin blockchain protocol [26] and is essentially a proof of possession of computational power. Given the characteristics of the PoW algorithm, a specific logic or architecture may be more advantageous and as a result, maintainers may benefit from special purpose implementations. In such case, the PoW algorithm will not be a proof of general computational power, but rather a proof of ability to execute the particular algorithm utilized in the PoW scheme. This issue has brought forth significant criticism against the implementation of PoW utilized in the Bitcoin protocol (the hashcash algorithm [3] instantiated by the hash function SHA256) and subsequently a number of other PoW algorithms were developed and deployed in alternative blockchain protocols (these include scrypt, see [32], and ethash, see [34], which motivated research in memory-hardness with algorithms such as argon2 [5]).

Independently of the properties of the implementation, a common characteristic of PoW is that running the algorithm requires energy expenditure (needed to power the hardware executing the algorithm logic). This aspect, combined with the fact that the source of energy cannot be discriminated, lead to concerns about the use of non-renewable sources in the Bitcoin blockchain.

Contrary to PoW, a PoS scheme proves possession of a virtual resource (e.g., the possession of a certain amount of digital currency). A significant distinction in this class of algorithms is that issuing a PoS has cost independent of the amount of "stake" in possession of the prover, while PoW typically incurs a linear cost in terms of computational power. Examples of PoS schemes are Ouroboros [23] and Algorand [19].

Beyond stake and work, other types of resources, both virtual and physical, have been proposed and utilized. These include "proof of space", whereby the prover demonstrates possession of storage capacity, cf. [12], and "proof of elapsed time", supported by Intel SGX cf. [28], whereby the prover demonstrates that certain wait time has elapsed, just to name two examples.

An important property of PoX's in the way they are integrated within the underlying system is the fact that the freshness of the proof needs to be ensured. This is invariant of the specific resource used. In particular, it should be impossible to "replay" an old proof that refers to resources possessed at a previous point in time. This point is crucial since resources are transferable between participants and hence any proof should reflect the present state of resource allocation.

A second property that is also essential is that the verification of a PoX should be performed with low complexity, ideally independent of the level of resources involved in the generation of the proof. The reasoning behind this requirement is that verification is something that needs to be performed network wide, possibly even by entities that do not possess any units of the resource used in PoX, as such entities may still need to verify the state of the system.

4   Tokenomics

The key concept behind resource-based system tokenomics is the *tokenization* of the efforts of the system maintainers in the form of a *digital asset* that subsequently can be utilized in some way by the maintainers to influence the utility they extract from the system. The essential objective is that —collectively— maintainers' utility remains positive, hence maintenance costs can be covered and the system is viable. The necessary economics argument needed here gives rise to the term "tokenomics" as a portmanteau word derived from "token" and "economics."

The approach to achieve the tokenomics objective suggested by Nakamoto's design and built upon and extended in numerous follow up blockchain projects is *market based.* The underlying digital asset of the system becomes a native digital currency that is required for accessing the service. The system also facilitates the exchange of the digital currency between parties and hence a market is created for the IT service. Moreover, its availability for public trading allows speculators to estimate the value of the service in the near term and far future.

At system launch, it is possible to have a pre-distribution of digital coins. For instance, digital coins can be "airdropped" to token holders of a pre-existing digital currency. In other cases, digital coins can be made available to investors in a "presale" stage whereby software developers of the platform may use to fund the development of the software pre-launch, cf. [7] for an exposition of some of the relevant economics considerations in this setting.

A key characteristic of the digital currency is that it should be easily transferable between parties. The coin can be listed on "cryptocurrency" exchanges and hence its value can be determined vis-à-vis other currencies (or commodities or other instruments) that potential system users may possess and willing to trade. Users should be able to keep the digital coin on a "wallet", an application running on a user's device. This means that a user should apply a cryptographic key in order to exercise ownership of the digital coins and issue a transaction. While users of the system have the option to perform the necessary key management themselves, they can also opt to delegate the custody of their digital assets to third parties.

After system launch, additional coins can become available and distributed following a certain ruleset to the system maintainers. Such ruleset is public knowledge and algorithmically enforced during system maintenance. Depending on the system, the rate of new coin availability can be constant per unit of time (as e.g., in Ethereum originally), or follow some function per unit of time (as e.g., in the case of Bitcoin, which has a finite total supply and hence relies on a geometric series to distribute coins to maintainers). In some cases, the number of new coins that become added to the circulating supply depend on the behavior of the maintainers, e.g., in the case of Cardano, higher coin "pledges" by the participants increase the rate that coins become available. While the ruleset is algorithmic, as it is enforced in the system's "ledger rules", it can be changed by modifying the software that supports the system, assuming there is wide consensus between the system maintainers to adopt the update (see [9] for a formal treatment of updates in blockchains). An example of such update was for instance the "London update" of Ethereum which made the total supply of coins a variable function that depends on the transactions processed by the system.

In some cases, an amount of coins is reserved to a development fund or "treasury" that the system can subsequently utilize to fund further research and development. This is exemplified in systems like Decred[1] and Cardano's Project catalyst[2] and also explored from first principles, see e.g., [35]. Such treasury can also receive funding in perpetuity by taxing the system users.

The ability to trade the system's coin enables the assessment of the system's potential value given its public tokenomics characteristics and its utility. A plunge in value of the system's coin suggest a loss of faith in the system's utility and can lead to system instability due to weak participation in system maintenance or the total abandonment of maintenance and the inevitable "death" of the system. Examples of system instability are for instance the 51% attacks observed against a number of systems (e.g., Ethereum classic in [33]) while there are thousands of cryptocurrency projects that have been abandoned.[3] Trading also enables reinvesting rewards towards the acquisition of additional resources for protocol participation leading to

---

[1] See https://docs.decred.org/research/overview/.

[2] See https://projectcatalyst.org.

[3] See for instance, https://www.coinopsy.com/dead-coins/.

interesting compounding effects, see e.g. [15,20] for some interesting investigations in this direction.

While speculation can drive the price of the system's digital currency up, the real value of the token lies with the underlying functionality of the system. Ultimately, users should wish to obtain the token in order to transact with the system and engage in the functionality it offers. Given this, speculators may choose to acquire the token at an early time prior to the system's utility becoming fully realized in the hope of selling the token for profit at a future time.

To conclude, the key requirement for the above market-based tokenomics approach to achieve the essential objective identified in the beginning of this section is the following: the demand curve for the system token, as a function of time, when projected over the supply as determined by the digital currency schedule, should produce a price for the system token that offsets the collective cost of maintenance for a sufficient level of quality of service. This ensures that system maintenance, at least in the way it is encoded by the system software, is an attractive endeavor to engage in. As a final note, it is worth noting that the market-based approach, even though currently dominant in deployed resource based systems, may not be necessary for successful system tokenomics. In theory other mechanisms could also work, e.g., a reputation-based approach. As long the system is able to influence the utility of system mainainers to a sufficient degree so that quality of service is maintained, the tokenomics objective would have been met.

5   Decentralized Service Provision

Now we come to the key question how to offer the prescribed service functionality $\mathscr{F}$ (cf. Sect. 2) while users have no specific point of contact to reach. Users package their desired input to a transaction and release that transaction to the open network under a suitable encoding. The software running in the system maintainer side should receive such transaction and in the right circumstances propagate its encoding further. The system maintainers should act on this input in a timely manner and collectively the system should reach a state where the desired output is produced.

There are two important properties that the decentralized implementation of the service should provide: safety and liveness.

In terms of safety, the condition that is sought is that the system should exhibit consistency in the way it processes requests. In other words, despite being realized by a fluctuating population of system maintainers, the resulting effect of applying a certain valid input should never be incongruous to the effect that the same input would have if it was applied to $\mathscr{F}$. A safety violation for instance, would be that a user submits two mutually exclusive inputs, i.e., inputs that cannot be both applied to the state of $\mathscr{F}$ and subsequently some users observe the first input as being actioned upon by the system while others observe similarly the second input.

The liveness property refers to the ability of the system to react in a timely manner to users' input. Liveness, may be impacted both by congestion or even denial of service (DoS) attacks, where the system's capacity gets depleted as well as by censorship attacks where system maintainers choose to ignore the user's input. The expected responsiveness of the system may be affected by demand, but ideally, the system should have the capability to scale up with increasing demand so that quality of service is maintained.

Given the decentralized nature of the implementation, it would be impossible to argue the above properties in all circumstances. Instead, what is sought is to argue that under reasonable resource restrictions the properties hold in the Byzantine sense – i.e., an adversary cannot violate them unless it controls a significant amount of resources. It is worth pointing out that while this is necessary, it is not sufficient; we would also want that given a reasonable modeling of the participants' utility functions, the desired system behavior is an equilibrium or even a dominant strategy, given a plausible class of demand curves for service provision. Such strategic considerations however will have to wait for the next Section on reward sharing.

While system maintainers utilize their resources to support service provision, it should be feasible for clients of the system's functionality $\mathcal{F}$ to engage in a "light weight" fashion with the system, i.e., while spending the minimum effort possible both in terms of communication as well as computational complexity and resource expenditures.

Mitigating DoS attacks can be a crucial consideration in resource-based systems given their open and distributed nature. For instance, it should be hard for malicious actor to generate a significant load of "spam" transactions and saturate the system's capacity. Collecting fees to process transactions in a native digital currency of the resource based system is a standard way that can help mitigate such DoS attacks while it also helps generating revenue for the maintainers that is proportional to the transactions processed.

A final important component of the system implementation is the ability of the system to collectively record at regular intervals relevant *performance metrics* for the system maintainers that engage with it. While not needed for providing the service to the clients, metrics are important so that the system records the efforts of maintainers so they can be rewarded appropriately. The performance metrics operation should be *robust* in the sense that, ideally, the metrics are resilient in the Byzantine sense: a set of maintainers, perhaps appropriately restricted, should not be able to manipulate the recorded performance of a targeted system maintainer. The Bitcoin blockchain uses a non-robust performance metric (the number of blocks produced by a system maintainer) which has given rise to attacks (cf. selfish-mining [14]). Other blockchain protocols in the PoW and PoS setting developed robust metrics, see [23,30], enabling better game theoretic argumentation—e.g., proving the protocol an equilibrium in [23].

6   Rewards Sharing

In this section we come to the topic of "rewards sharing" that focuses on how individual system maintainers are being compensated and the strategic considerations that arise from that. We will expand on this topic a bit more compared to the previous sections giving a formal treatment and a theorem. As mentioned in Sect. 4 the system may make digital coins available to the maintainers following a specific schedule.

Additionally, maintainers may claim transaction fees that are provided by the users who engage with the system.

The operation of rewards sharing can be "action based" in the sense of rewarding directly specific actions (e.g., as in the setting of the Bitcoin blockchain where a miner who produces a block can obtain a certain amount of bitcoin as well as the fees of the transactions that are included in the block), or "epoch based" where the actions of all maintainers are examined in regular intervals and then rewards are apportioned accordingly (e.g. in the case of the Cardano blockchain such epochs last 5 days). The distinction between action or epoch based is not very essential for the exposition of this section.

Let Ω be the finite universe of all resource units. Resource units can be exchanged between participants and some participants may hold a larger amount of resource units than others. The nature of a resource unit depends on the specific details of the system; it can be a hardware unit with software that is capable of performing fast certain operations; it can be storage device; or, it can be a virtual unit controlled by a cryptographic key and maintained in a ledger. We will assume for simplicity that Ω is constant and hence it refers to all resource units in existence. Note that if some are unavailable they will just not engage in the protocol and can be assigned to a non-participating entity (e.g., an entity with infinite cost of participation).

We consider that at system launch each resource unit is labelled by its current owner and, overloading notation, we will use Ω for the set of such labelled units. The *operator partition* of Ω is a partition $O_1, \ldots, O_n$ that aggregates the units of all (prospective) operators in separate sets, where n is the number of distinct operators (note that our interpretation of an "operator" will be liberal and can correspond to any set of resources that can act independently and engage in the protocol; in particular the same principal entity possessing a set of resources can correspond to many operators).

Operators need not engage with the system as maintainers directly. Instead they can form "resource pools" where many of them together operate a system maintenance node. In such configurations it is common that one of the contributors is the actual operator and the others invest in the system operation—however other arrangements are also possible. Such pooling arrangements can take the form of a contract between various resource holders enabling them to operate in tandem as an organization with members having different responsibilities. The Bitcoin system over the years has exhibited significant pooling behavior and there were times that a single pool reached or even exceeded the critical threshold of controlling 51% of the total active resources.

We will use functions of the form $c : 2^{\Omega} \to \mathbb{R} \cup \{\bot, \infty\}$ to express the cost that maps a set of units to the numerical cost expenditure that is incurred when the owners of these resource units engage in the system over a fixed period of time. Note that we only require c to have a non $\bot$ value for sets of the operator partition of Ω, and sets resulting by the joining of these sets. We use $c(O) = \infty$ to signify resource units that may be impossible to use (e.g., because they are inaccessible), and by convention if $c(O) = \infty$ then $c(O \cup O') = \infty$.

A pooling configuration $\mathscr{P}$ is a family of mutually disjoint sets $P_1, \ldots, P_m \subseteq \Omega$ accompanied by a reward splitting strategy for each pool that describes how to distribute rewards to the resource holders who participate (if they are more than one). It is important to note that rewards sharing at the protocol level only goes up to the level of the pool; beyond that, by the nature of resource based systems, it can be infeasible for the system to distinguish between a pool of a single resource holder compared to one where many join their resources.

Pooling configurations are an important subject of study in resource based systems since they impact the "decentralization" of the underlying system. A stable centralized pooling configuration, e.g., one where all operators have joined a single pool, Ω, indicates that the resource based system can be retired and substituted by a centralized system supported by an organization reflecting the constituent membership of the single pool. In such circumstances, the benefits of using a resource based system entirely dissipate. As a result, it is of interest to understand in what settings such centralized pooling configurations may arise.

Before we proceed, it is useful to introduce a metric for resource sets. We will use that metric to signify the influence that any single pool can exert on the protocol. We denote the measure $\sigma : 2^\Omega \to \mathbb{R}$ of the resources of a pool P by $\sigma(P)$. We require that $\sigma(\Omega) = 1, \sigma(\emptyset) = 0$ and $\sigma(P \cup Q) = \sigma(P) + \sigma(Q) - \sigma(P \cap Q)$.

Rewards sharing in resource based systems is controlled by a function ρ; without loss of generality we count the rewards distributed in a fixed period of time (the same period over which we also consider costs). Let $\rho(P, \mathscr{P})$ be the rewards provided to a given pool P by the system given a pooling configuration $\mathscr{P}$. A reward function $\rho(\cdot)$ is called *simple* if $\rho(P, \mathscr{P}) = \rho(P, \mathscr{P}')$ for any pooling configurations $\mathscr{P}, \mathscr{P}'$ that contain P. For simple reward functions we can write $\rho(P)$ to denote the rewards that are provided to P. Note moreover that $\rho(\emptyset) = 0$. A reward function is continuous if it holds that for every $P \subseteq \Omega, \epsilon > 0$ there is a $\delta > 0$ such that for any P', $|\sigma(P) - \sigma(P')| < \delta \implies |\rho(P) - \rho(P')| < \epsilon$. In the exposition of this section we consider only continuous simple reward functions.

The reward function ρ is a critical component of a resource based system. We put forth the following set of axioms regarding the reward function ρ. As we will see, these axioms have certain implications regarding the pooling configurations that may arise in the system.

- Resource fungibility. For any P, Q, $(\sigma(P) = \sigma(Q)) \to (\rho(P) = \rho(Q))$. This means that the system does not distinguish between particular resource units with respect to rewards.
- Sybil resilience. It holds that $\rho(P_1 \cup P_2) \geq \rho(P_1) + \rho(P_2)$ for any disjoint sets $P_1, P_2 \subseteq \Omega$. This reflects the desideratum that an operator controlling some resources will not gain anything by splitting their resources into two pools.
- Egalitarianism. It holds $\rho(P) \leq \rho(Q) + \rho(R)$ for any disjoint sets P, Q, R such that $\sigma(P) = \sigma(Q) + \sigma(R)$. This reflects the desideratum that a "rich" operator controlling resources P does not obtain more rewards than two "poorer" operators controlling in aggregate the same amount of resources.

Given the above axioms, we will prove that a centralized pooling configuration can be a Nash equilibrium in the strong sense, i.e., even taking into account arbitrary coalitions [2]. We need two more properties to be defined first.

Definition 1. *Consider a pooling configuration* $\mathscr{P}$. *A pool* $P \in \mathscr{P}$ *is called: (i)* viable, *if and only if* $\rho(P) \geq c(P)$, *(ii)* cost efficient, *if and only if* $c(P)/\sigma(P) \leq c(P')/\sigma(P')$, *for any* $P' \subseteq P$, *i.e., its cost per unit of resource is no worse than any of its subsets.*

We are now ready to state and prove the following theorem.

Theorem 1. *If* Ω *is viable and cost efficient, then there is a centralized pooling configuration that is a Strong Nash equilibrium.*

Proof. Consider first any pooling configuration $\mathscr{P}$ and $P \in \mathscr{P}$ such that it is viable and cost efficient. The rule to distribute rewards within P is the following. Any subset S of P corresponding to a participant receives rewards equal to $\sigma(S)(\rho(P) - c(P))/\sigma(P)$, i.e., a "fair" share of the total rewards available. We observe next the following lower bound:

$$\sigma(S)(\rho(P) - c(P)) \geq \sigma(S)\rho(P) - \sigma(P)c(S) \geq \sigma(P)\rho(S) - \sigma(P)c(S) = \sigma(P)(\rho(S) - c(S)) \tag{1}$$

The first inequality follows from the cost efficiency of P, which implies $c(S)/\sigma(S) \geq c(P)/\sigma(P)$.

For the second inequality we need to prove $\rho(P)/\sigma(P) \geq \rho(S)/\sigma(S)$, i.e., the rewards per unit of resource is no worse for P compared to S. We will prove something stronger. For any $x \in [0,1]$ we define $\hat{\rho}(x)$ to be equal to the value $\rho(P)$ for some P with $\sigma(P) = x$. The function $\hat{\rho}$ is well defined due to resource fungibility. Furthermore, observe that $\hat{\rho}$ is superadditive due to Sybil resilience, and subadditive due to Egalitarianism. It follows that $\hat{\rho}$ satisfies Cauchy's functional equation and as a result, due to the continuity of $\hat{\rho}(\cdot)$, it holds that $\hat{\rho}(x) = \gamma x$, for some $\gamma \in \mathbb{R}$. From this we derive that $\rho(S)/\sigma(S) = \gamma = \rho(P)/\sigma(P)$.

We conclude by observing that the profit of S, is equal to $\rho(S) - c(S)$, and hence it is no better than the rewards received as part of the pool P which equals to $\sigma(S)(\rho(\Omega) - c(\Omega))/\sigma(P)$. This implies that any set of participants will be no better off operating their own pool separating from the "mother" pool P. We note the same can be also shown in case they decide to run multiple separate pools. The statement of the theorem follows immediately by recalling $\sigma(\Omega) = 1$. $\square$

We remark that the above theorem easily generalizes to a setting where instead of Ω we have a cost-efficient set P and for any $O \subseteq \Omega \setminus P$ it holds that $c(O) = \infty$. In such case, the strong Nash equilibrium will be the pool P.

It follows from the above arguments that it is of interest to detect large cost efficient resource sets. To this end, we examine an important class of cost functions, that we call "operator-linear." First, let $O_1, \ldots, O_n$ be the operator partition of Ω. The cost function is operator linear if it holds that (i) for all $i = 1, \ldots, n$, $c(O_i) = c_i + d_i \cdot \sigma(O_i)$, and (ii) for any $P = \cup_{j=1}^m O_{i_j}$, it holds the cost of P is defined by the following function

$$c(P) = d_{i_1} \cdot \sigma(O_{i_1}) + \ldots d_{i_m} \cdot \sigma(O_{i_m}) + \min\{c_{i_1}, \ldots, c_{i_m}\}.$$

This class of cost functions captures, at a certain level of abstraction, both proof of work and proof of stake systems where pooling is organized so that the operator becomes the resource holder with the smaller individual fixed cost. For proof of stake, given the cost incurred for processing is independent of the resources held, one can set $d_i = 0$ for all $i = 1, \ldots, n$. For proof of work, we observe the linear dependency in the amount of resources held that can be reflected by choosing a suitable value for d_i derived from electricity costs and equipment characteristics used for performing the proof of work operation. We now prove the following proposition.

Proposition 1. *Given an operator-linear cost function, Ω is cost efficient, as long as $\Delta \leq \min\{c_1, \ldots, c_n\}$, where $\Delta = \max\{d_i - d_j \mid i, j \in [n]\}$.*

Proof. We want to prove that $c(\Omega) \leq c(S)/\sigma(S)$ for any $S \subseteq \Omega$. Let us denote by $x_i = \sigma(O_i), c_i = c(O_i)$, where $O_1, \ldots, O_n$ is the operator partition of Ω. Without loss of generality we assume that S includes the operators $O_1, \ldots, O_k$ for some $k \leq n$. We also denote by $\tilde{c}_j = \min\{c_1, \ldots, c_j\}$. We will prove that

$$(\tilde{c}_n + \sum_{i=1}^{n} d_i x_i) \cdot \sum_{i=1}^{k} x_k \leq \tilde{c}_k + \sum_{j=1}^{k} d_j x_j$$

We observe that based on the condition in the proposition's statement, we have that $\Delta \cdot \sum_{j=1}^{k} x_j \leq \tilde{c}_k$ which implies that $\sum_{j=1}^{k} (d_i - d_j) x_j x_i \leq \tilde{c}_k x_i$. Summing for all $i = k+1, \ldots, n$, we have that

$$\sum_{i=k+1}^{n} \sum_{j=1}^{k} (d_i - d_j) x_i x_j \leq \tilde{c}_k \sum_{i=k+1}^{n} x_i \Rightarrow \sum_{i=k+1}^{n} \sum_{j=1}^{k} d_i x_i x_j \leq \sum_{i=k+1}^{n} \sum_{j=1}^{k} d_j x_i x_j + \tilde{c}_k \sum_{i=k+1}^{n} x_i$$

We add now in both sides of the inequality the terms $\sum_{i,j=1}^{k} d_i x_i x_j$ and $\tilde{c}_k \sum_{i=1}^{k} x_i$ and by the observation $\tilde{c}_n \leq \tilde{c}_k$, we have the inequality

$$\tilde{c}_n \sum_{i=1}^{k} x_i + \sum_{i=1}^{n} \sum_{j=1}^{k} d_i x_i x_j \leq \sum_{i=1}^{n} \sum_{j=1}^{k} d_j x_i x_j + \tilde{c}_k \sum_{i=1}^{n} x_i$$

From this we obtain $(\tilde{c}_n + \sum_{i=1}^{n} d_i x_i) \sum_{i=1}^{k} x_i \leq \tilde{c}_k + \sum_{j=1}^{k} d_j x_j$ that demonstrates $c(\Omega) \leq c(S)/\sigma(S)$.   □

Based on the above, we obtain that if Ω is viable and the conditions of Proposition 1 are satisfied, the system will have a strong Nash equilibrium that centralizes to one operator. This applies to both proof of stake as well as proof of work in the case when differences in electricity costs are small across operators.

On the other hand, in settings where cost efficiency does not hold, the joining of two resource sets can become undesirable for one of the two operators. A weaker property for cost functions that captures "economies of scale" and dictates that $c(P_1 \cup P_2) \leq c(P_1) + c(P_2)$, (reflecting the property that merging two pools results in no higher costs compared to the two pools operating alone), is insufficient by itself to imply a centralized pooling configuration.

Even in the case of operator-linear cost functions however, careful design of the reward function and analysis of Nash dynamics can show that better equilibria arise and can be reachable by the participants. For instance, if costs for "off-chain" pooling are high, the rewards sharing schemes developed and analyzed in [6] can be seen to converge to highly participatory decentralized equilibria for constant cost functions, a special case of operator linear cost functions.

7   A High-Level Blueprint for a Stake-Based System

Given the four characteristics outlined in the previous sections, we will provide an illustration how to apply those to develop and deploy a *stake-based* system. We assume as preconditions that the developer has already a classical distributed protocol implementation of the service $\mathcal{F}$ for, say, k parties and has an understanding of the service maintenance costs and user demand.

Adopting a stake-based approach, the resource will be digital coins. The developer mints an initial supply of such coins and disperses them over an existing population of recipients. This can be achieved by e.g., "airdropping" such digital coins to cryptocurrency holders of an existing blockchain platform. Due to this distribution event, the recipients become the stakeholders of the system.

A tokenomics schedule that takes into account the expected demand is determined and programmed into a smart contract $\mathcal{S}$. This contract will acknowledge the initial supply of coins as well as the schedule under which any new coins will be made available to the maintainers – the entities running the k-party protocol. Following market-based tokenomics the contract will also manage incoming transaction fees.

Decentralized service provision is comprised of four parts. One is the k-party protocol that implements $\mathcal{F}$; the second is a proof-of-stake blockchain protocol that offers "dynamic availability" (e.g., such as Ouroboros, [4,23]) – i.e., a protocol that can handle a wide array of participation patterns without the requirement to be able to predict closely the active participation level). Inputs to the protocol will be recorded on chain, an action that will incur transaction costs to be withheld by $\mathcal{S}$. The chain will also maintain the contract $\mathcal{S}$. The third part is a "proof-of-service" sub-system that should enable any system maintainer running the k-party protocol to demonstrate their efforts in a robust way. The verifier of such proofs will be the smart contract $\mathcal{S}$ which will determine a performance factor for each maintainer. Finally, the fourth part is an algorithm that will parse the blockchain at regular intervals and determine the k parties to run the k-party protocol for $\mathcal{F}$. This can be done e.g., by weighted sampling [13], taking into account the stake supporting each operator.

For rewards sharing, we need a mechanism to incentivize the stakeholders to organize themselves into at least k well functioning nodes that will execute the multiparty protocol for $\mathcal{F}$ when selected. To achieve this we can deploy the reward sharing scheme of [6] over the underlying PoS blockchain; for that scheme it is shown how incentive driven engagement by the stakeholders can determine a set of k nodes at equilibrium. The reward scheme will be coded into the contract $\mathcal{S}$ and will reward the stakeholders at regular intervals using the available supply from the tokenomics schedule and the transaction fees collected. The performance factor of each operator will influence the rewards, adjusting them in proportion to the operator's efforts.

The developer will produce an implementation of the above system and will make it available for download. A launch date for the system will be set as well as an explanation for its purpose. The initial set of k operators can be sampled by observing some publicly observable random source. At this point, the developer's engagement can stop. The stakeholders —the recipients of the newly minted digital coin— can examine the proposition that the system offers and choose whether to engage or not. If a minimum number of them (according to the dynamic availability properties of the underlying blockchain protocol) chooses to engage out of their own self-interest the system will come to life bootstrapping itself.

8   Concluding Remarks

In this paper, we put forth a new paradigm for deploying Information Technology services inspired by the operation of the Bitcoin system. We identified four characteristics of resource based systems: (i) resource-based operation, (ii) tokenomics, (iii) decentralized service provision, and (iv) rewards sharing, and we elaborated on their objective and associated design challenges. We also presented a high-level blueprint showing how the paradigm can materialize in the form of a stake-based system.

In more details, we identified the cryptographic and distributed protocol design challenge which asks for a suitable PoX algorithm integrated with a protocol that facilitates decentralized service provision and the requirement of robust performance metrics. We also pointed to the economics and game theoretic considerations related to tokenomics and reward sharing.

We explored at some length game theoretic aspects of pooling behavior and proved that a centralized equilibrium can be a strong Nash equilibrium for a wide variety of reward and cost functions. This result is in the same spirit but more general than previous negative results presented in [1,24,25] as it does not rely on the distribution of resources across owners, or a specific "economies of scale" assumption that dictates a superlinear relation between rewards and costs, or the specific reward scheme used in Bitcoin, respectively.

On a more positive note, existence of "bad equilibria" does not prohibit the existence of other equilibria with better decentralization profiles. Furthermore, centralized pooling configurations require coordination between agents that may prove difficult and costly to achieve. In this respect, "bimodal" systems, see [21], where users can perform two (or more) actions to engage in system maintenance (e.g., propose themselves as operators as well as vote others as operators) examples of which include [6,8], show promise in this direction. Furthermore, being able to investigate the Nash dynamics of the system as e.g., performed in [6] is crucial to demonstrate that the system reaches desirable equilibria expediently and moreover it can be also possible to demonstrate that bad equilibria can be avoided. It is also worth pointing out that even if a resource based system manages to scale but eventually centralizes, the invested efforts may still not be completely in vain: the resulting constituent membership of the centralized pool organization may take over as a centralized (or even distributed) system and offer the service.

The characteristics put forth in this paper are, in many respects, the minimum necessary. Other desirable features can be argued such as the existence of multiple, open source software codebases that realize the system's protocol as well as the existence of a governance sub-system that facilitates operations such as software updates not only for correcting the inevitable software bugs but also ensuring the system adapts to run time conditions that were unanticipated during the initial design. The problem of software updates in the decentralized setting is complex and more research is required, cf. [9] for some first steps in terms of formally defining the problem in the context of distributed ledgers, as well as the systematization of knowledge work of [22].

The resource based paradigm is still nascent. Nevertheless, we can identify some early precursors that include smart contract systems—e.g., Ethereum and Cardano, the name service of Namecoin, or the cross border payment system of Ripple. More recently, the Nym network [10] exemplified the paradigm in a novel context—that of mix-nets and privacy-preserving communications. Extending the paradigm to additional use cases will motivate further advances in cryptography, distributed systems and game theory and eventually has the potential to change the landscape of global information technology.

Acknowledgements. I am grateful to Matthias Fitzi, Dimitris Karakostas, Aikaterini Panagiota Stouka and Giorgos Panagiotakos for helpful comments and discussions.

References

1. Arnosti, N., Matthew Weinberg, S.: Bitcoin: a natural oligopoly. In: Blum, A. (ed.) 10th Innovations in Theoretical Computer Science Conference, ITCS 2019, San Diego, California, USA, 10–12 January 2019. LIPIcs, vol. 124, pp. 5:1–5:1. Schloss Dagstuhl - Leibniz-Zentrum für Informatik (2019)
2. Aumann, R.J.: Acceptable points in general cooperative n-person games. In: Contributions to the Theory of Games. Annals of Mathematics Studies, vol. IV, pp. 287–324 (1959)
3. Back, A.: Hashcash (1997). http://www.cypherspace.org/hashcash
4. Badertscher, C., Gazi, P., Kiayias, A., Russell, A., Zikas, V.: Ouroboros genesis: composable proof-of-stake blockchains with dynamic availability. In: Lie, D., Mannan, M., Backes, M., Wang, X. (eds.) Proceedings of the 2018 ACM SIGSAC Conference on Computer and Communications Security, CCS 2018, Toronto, ON, Canada, 15–19 October 2018, pp. 913–930. ACM (2018)
5. Biryukov, A., Dinu, D., Khovratovich, D., Josefsson, S.: Argon2 memory-hard function for password hashing and proof-of-work applications. RFC 9106, pp. 1–21 (2021)
6. Brünjes, L., Kiayias, A., Koutsoupias, E., Stouka, A.-P.: Reward sharing schemes for stake pools. In: IEEE European Symposium on Security and Privacy, EuroS&P 2020, Genoa, Italy, 7–11 September 2020, pp. 256–275. IEEE (2020)
7. Catalini, C., Gans, J.S.: Initial coin offerings and the value of crypto tokens. Working Paper 24418 (2018). https://www.nber.org/papers/w24418
8. Cevallos, A., Stewart, A.: A verifiably secure and proportional committee election rule. In: AFT 2021: 3rd ACM Conference on Advances in Financial Technologies (2021)

9. Ciampi, M., Karayannidis, N., Kiayias, A., Zindros, D.: Updatable blockchains. In: Chen, L., Li, N., Liang, K., Schneider, S. (eds.) ESORICS 2020. LNCS, vol. 12309, pp. 590–609. Springer, Cham (2020). https://doi.org/10.1007/978-3-030-59013-0_29

10. Diaz, C., Halpin, H., Kiayias, A.: The Nym network: the next generation of privacy infrastructure (2021). https://nymtech.net/nym-whitepaper.pdf

11. Douceur, J.R.: The Sybil attack. In: Druschel, P., Kaashoek, F., Rowstron, A. (eds.) IPTPS 2002. LNCS, vol. 2429, pp. 251–260. Springer, Heidelberg (2002). https://doi.org/10.1007/3-540-45748-8_24

12. Dziembowski, S., Faust, S., Kolmogorov, V., Pietrzak, K.: Proofs of space. In: Gennaro, R., Robshaw, M. (eds.) CRYPTO 2015. LNCS, vol. 9216, pp. 585–605. Springer, Heidelberg (2015). https://doi.org/10.1007/978-3-662-48000-7_29

13. Efraimidis, P.S., Spirakis, P.: Weighted random sampling. In: Encyclopedia of Algorithms, pp. 2365–2367 (2016)

14. Eyal, I., Sirer, E.G.: Majority is not enough: bitcoin mining is vulnerable. In: Financial Cryptography (2014)

15. Fanti, G., Kogan, L., Oh, S., Ruan, K., Viswanath, P., Wang, G.: Compounding of wealth in proof-of-stake cryptocurrencies. In: Goldberg, I., Moore, T. (eds.) FC 2019. LNCS, vol. 11598, pp. 42–61. Springer, Cham (2019). https://doi.org/10.1007/978-3-030-32101-7_3

16. Garay, J., Kiayias, A.: SoK: a consensus taxonomy in the blockchain era. In: Jarecki, S. (ed.) CT-RSA 2020. LNCS, vol. 12006, pp. 284–318. Springer, Cham (2020). https://doi.org/10.1007/978-3-030-40186-3_13

17. Garay, J., Kiayias, A., Leonardos, N.: The bitcoin backbone protocol: analysis and applications. In: Oswald, E., Fischlin, M. (eds.) EUROCRYPT 2015. LNCS, vol. 9057, pp. 281–310. Springer, Heidelberg (2015). https://doi.org/10.1007/978-3-662-46803-6_10

18. Garay, J., Kiayias, A., Leonardos, N.: The bitcoin backbone protocol with chains of variable difficulty. In: Katz, J., Shacham, H. (eds.) CRYPTO 2017. LNCS, vol. 10401, pp. 291–323. Springer, Cham (2017). https://doi.org/10.1007/978-3-319-63688-7_10

19. Gilad, Y., Hemo, R., Micali, S., Vlachos, G., Zeldovich, N.: Algorand: scaling byzantine agreements for cryptocurrencies. In: Proceedings of the 26th Symposium on Operating Systems Principles, Shanghai, China, 28–31 October 2017, pp. 51–68. ACM (2017)

20. Karakostas, D., Kiayias, A., Nasikas, C., Zindros, D.: Cryptocurrency egalitarianism: a quantitative approach. In: Danos, V., Herlihy, M., Potop-Butucaru, M., Prat, J., Piergiovanni, S.T. (eds.) International Conference on Blockchain Economics, Security and Protocols, Tokenomics 2019, Paris, France, 6–7 May 2019. OASIcs, vol. 71 pp. 7:1–7:21. Schloss Dagstuhl - Leibniz-Zentrum für Informatik (2019)

21. Kiayias, A.: Blockchain reward sharing - a comparative systematization from first principles. IOHK Blog (2020). https://iohk.io/en/blog/posts/2020/11/30/blockchain-reward-sharing-a-comparative-systematization-from-first-principles/

22. Kiayias, A., Lazos, P.: SoK: blockchain governance. CoRR, abs/2201.07188 (2022)

23. Kiayias, A., Russell, A., David, B., Oliynykov, R.: Ouroboros: a provably secure proof-of-stake blockchain protocol. In: Katz, J., Shacham, H. (eds.) CRYPTO 2017. LNCS, vol. 10401, pp. 357–388. Springer, Cham (2017). https://doi.org/10.1007/978-3-319-63688-7_12

24. Kiayias, A., Stouka, A.-P.: Coalition-safe equilibria with virtual payoffs. In: AFT 2021: 3rd ACM Conference on Advances in Financial Technologies (2021)

25. Kwon, Y., Liu, J., Kim, M., Song, D., Kim, Y.: Impossibility of full decentralization in permissionless blockchains. In: Proceedings of the 1st ACM Conference on Advances in Financial Technologies, AFT 2019, Zurich, Switzerland, 21–23 October 2019, pp. 110–123. ACM (2019)

26. Nakamoto, S.: Bitcoin: a peer-to-peer electronic cash system (2008). http://bitcoin.org/bitcoin.pdf

27. Nakamoto, S.: Bitcoin open source implementation of P2P currency (2009). http://p2pfoundation.ning.com/forum/topics/bitcoin-open-source
28. Olson, K., Bowman, M., Mitchell, J., Amundson, S., Middleton, D., Montgomery, C.: Sawtooth: an introduction (2018). https://www.hyperledger.org/wp-content/uploads/2018/01/Hyperledger_Sawtooth_WhitePaper.pdf
29. Pass, R., Seeman, L., Shelat, A.: Analysis of the blockchain protocol in asynchronous networks. In: Coron, J.-S., Nielsen, J.B. (eds.) EUROCRYPT 2017. LNCS, vol. 10211, pp. 643–673. Springer, Cham (2017). https://doi.org/10.1007/978-3-319-56614-6_22
30. Pass, R., Shi, E.: FruitChains: a fair blockchain. In: Schiller, E.M., Schwarzmann, A.A. (eds.) Proceedings of the ACM Symposium on Principles of Distributed Computing, PODC 2017, Washington, DC, USA, 25–27 July 2017, pp. 315–324. ACM (2017)
31. Pease, M.C., Shostak, R.E., Lamport, L.: Reaching agreement in the presence of faults. J. ACM **27**(2), 228–234 (1980)
32. Percival, C., Josefsson, S.: The scrypt password-based key derivation function. RFC 7914, pp. 1–16 (2016)
33. Voell, Z.: Ethereum classic hit by third 51 CoinDesk (2020). https://www.coindesk.com/markets/2020/08/29/ethereum-classic-hit-by-third-51-attack-in-a-month/
34. Wood, G.: Ethereum: a secure decentralised generalised transaction ledger. Ethereum Project Yellow Paper **151**, 1–32 (2014)
35. Zhang, B., Oliynykov, R., Balogun, H.: A treasury system for cryptocurrencies: enabling better collaborative intelligence. In: 26th Annual Network and Distributed System Security Symposium, NDSS 2019, San Diego, California, USA, 24–27 February 2019. The Internet Society (2019)

Auctions, Markets and Mechanism Design

How Bad is the Merger Paradox?

Liad Blumrosen[1] and Yehonatan Mizrahi[2(✉)]

[1] School of Business Administration, The Hebrew University, Jerusalem, Israel
blumrosen@gmail.com
[2] School of Computer Science and Engineering, The Hebrew University,
Jerusalem, Israel
yehonatan.mizrahi@mail.huji.ac.il

Abstract. The merger paradox is a classic, counter-intuitive result from the literature of Industrial Organization saying that merging firms typically experience a decline in their overall profit compared to their total pre-merger profit. This phenomenon is more striking in small oligopolistic markets, where mergers increase market concentration and may hence trigger a substantial increase in prices. In this paper, we investigate the severity of the merger paradox in Cournot oligopoly markets. Namely, we study the worst-case magnitude of this profit loss in quantity-setting market games. We consider convex, asymmetric production costs for the firms, and we show that the profit loss can be substantial even in small markets. That is, two merging firms can lose half of their pre-merger profit, but no more than half in markets with concave demand functions. On the positive side, we show that in markets with affine demand two firms can never lose more than 1/9 of their profit when merging, and this bound is tight. We also study the asymptotic loss in larger markets, where it is easy to show that the profit loss can be arbitrarily large when multiple firms merge; we give bounds that characterize the profit loss from a merger as a function of the market size and the number of merging firms.

Keywords: Cournot Oligopoly · Approximation · Nash Equilibrium · Mergers and Acquisitions · Industrial Organization · Market Structure

1 Introduction

Evaluating the benefits from mergers of firms is an important challenge both for managers and for regulators worldwide. A merger of firms is a costly, often irreversible, process and therefore managers should make sure that the merger is indeed a profitable business move. Mergers increase concentration in markets, and antitrust authorities all over the world try to predict the effect of such mergers on the market power of firms and on the consumer surplus. This paper belongs to a line of work that aims to improve our understanding of the potential outcome of mergers. In this paper, we take a worst-case approach to this problem. We do not assume any probabilistic assumptions or knowledge of

© The Author(s), under exclusive license to Springer Nature Switzerland AG 2022
P. Kanellopoulos et al. (Eds.): SAGT 2022, LNCS 13584, pp. 23–40, 2022.
https://doi.org/10.1007/978-3-031-15714-1_2

prior distributions. We give results that hold for all possible demand and cost functions under standard assumptions. Several recent papers applied algorithmic thinking for analyzing competition in markets, see, e.g., [1–3,5,20,22,24,33].

Finding the right model for portraying competition in markets has always been one of the greatest challenges in economics. When competition is modeled as a price-setting game (á la Bertrand [4]), it is well known that the outcome tends to be highly competitive and that mergers are beneficial both for the merging firms and for the other firms (e.g., [8]). Another popular way to model competition is by quantity-setting games, where the basic model is known as the Cournot oligopoly model [6] – which is arguably the most influential model of competition, both for theoretical and applied modeling (e.g., [19]). Cournot models are especially useful in homogeneous-good environments where quantity decisions are set in advance, like in the airline industry, computer chips, cars, etc. Cournot models markets as a game, where firms simultaneously determine the output they produce, and the price is determined by the total output of all firms via the demand curve. An equilibrium in the Cournot model is a Nash equilibrium – a situation where no firm would benefit from unilaterally changing its production level. The solution to the Cournot model has many desirable properties, e.g., it lies somewhere between the Cartelistic and the competitive outcome and the equilibrium price decreases as the number of competitors increases [23].

Our paper focuses on the analysis of mergers in the Cournot oligopoly model. When some of the firms in the market merge, this creates a new game where the merged firm determines its production level as one entity. The benefits for the merging firms are quite straightforward – mergers create more concentrated markets with higher prices for consumers. Moreover, firms produce more efficiently in the merged firm and thus their manufacturing costs drop.[1] This intuition makes the following classic result, called the *Merger Paradox*, quite surprising: According to the Merger Paradox, not only that there exist scenarios where the profit of the merged firm will be smaller than the total profit of the firms before merger, this is actually the typical case. Beyond the theoretical analysis (see references below), the merger paradox was also tested empirically, where it was shown that the market values of some companies declined after merging (see, e.g., [13,17] and the references within).

We will show settings where two merged firms can lose up to half of their profit by deciding to merge, but our main result shows that for affine demand curves (and convex, asymmetric cost functions) the profit loss of $1/9$ is the worst example.

The intuition for the merger paradox is quite easy in large markets. If we have a market with 1000 symmetric firms and two of them merge, the effect of the merger on the concentration in the market is negligible, but the two firms that had a pre-merger market share of $\frac{1}{1000}$ *each*, now hold a market share of

---

[1] Examples of profitable mergers are relatively common. For instance, consider a market with three firms, where one of the firms plays a small role in it, in terms of its market share – a merger of the other two results in a market which relatively resembles a monopoly, hence being beneficial for the merging firms.

$\frac{1}{999}$ *together*! In fact, in Cournot's original setting with many firms, at least 80% of the firms should be included in the merger to guarantee its profitability (e.g., [26]). It is hard, however, to find such an intuition for smaller markets. If two out of three firms merge, one may expect that after merging, the two firms in the market will have a much stronger market power that will lead to a substantial increase in prices. Still, even mergers of two out of three symmetric firms will often lead to a profit loss for the merged firm.

The merger paradox builds on some other subtleties, and it seems to be confusing at first glance. For example, how can the merging firms lose when they can still produce at exactly the same pre-merger level? The answer is that the merger creates a new game with a new incentive structure and this production level will no longer be a best response to the quantity produced by the other, unmerged, firms; the merged company will actually have the incentive to cut back the produced quantity. The other firms understand the new incentive structure as well, and the post-merger equilibrium may be completely different.[2] In addition, there is evidence in the literature that other factors which are not taken into account in the Cournot model make mergers more profitable. One such factor is *Coordinated Effects* (see the survey [9]), saying that mergers change the market structure in a way that makes it easier for the remaining firms to collude, and makes the collusion more effective, either legally or illegally.

In this paper we quantify the magnitude of the merger paradox. We give a worst-case analysis of the potential loss from mergers, and we give tight bounds for the maximal possible loss. For the most popular and important mergers, of two firms, we show that the this profit loss can be high in general, but relatively-mild when the demand functions are affine.

1.1 Our Results

We consider the classic Cournot model of n competing firms that produce and sell a single, divisible, homogeneous good. Each firm F_i has a cost function $C_i(\cdot)$ for producing identical units of the good. We assume the standard assumptions that the cost functions are non-decreasing and convex – that is, that the marginal production cost is positive and increasing. When two firms merge, they can produce in the factory of the first firm (i.e., according to C_1), or in the factory of the second firm (C_2), or split the production between the two factories in order to reduce costs (as in standard cartel models). The market demand is represented by a demand function $P(\cdot)$. We give results for two families of demand functions: concave demand and affine demand. Concave demand is a general sufficient condition for the existence and uniqueness of equilibrium in the Cournot market ([30]), and thus analyzing the Cournot model without this assumption presumably requires a different approach than the one we take in our analysis. The case of affine demand functions is a special case which is well-studied in the literature (see e.g., [11, 26, 28, 29]).

---

[2] Sometimes merged firms choose, or are even forced, to create a "firewall" between the merged divisions – however, this custom is infrequently used and it is hard to be maintained in the long run [15].

As mentioned earlier, the merger paradox is mostly interesting for small markets. Therefore, our main results are given for mergers of two out of three firms. We also discuss their extensions to larger markets. Our first result shows that when two firms merge, there are settings where they lose half of their pre-merger profit, even in small markets. We also show that for all markets with concave demand functions such firms lose at most half.

Theorem 1: (Informal) *In a market with concave demand and three firms with convex costs, two merging firms can lose up to half of their pre-merger profits. This bound is tight.*

We extend the above results to larger markets. We show that if k out of n firms merge, they lose at most a factor of $1 - \frac{1}{k}$ of their pre-merger profit, and we show that this bound is asymptotically tight in large markets, from which it follows that the profit loss from mergers can be arbitrarily large. As mentioned, in large markets it is quite straightforward that the profit loss of two merging firms is almost half (see the above intuition about the merger of 2 out of 1000 symmetric firms); the above result proves that this holds even in small markets.

Our main result is for markets with affine demand, where we show that the profit loss is mild for all convex cost functions:

Theorem 2: (Informal) *In a market with affine demand and three firms with convex costs, two merging firms can lose up to $\frac{1}{9}$ of their pre-merger profits. This bound is tight.*

The asymptotic bound for merging k out of n firms which was mentioned above also holds for the case of affine demand, hence even with affine demand the profit loss from mergers can be arbitrarily large.

We will now describe the technical gist of our main result. The simplest form of the merger paradox concerns mergers with no cost synergies, that is, situations where the merging firms have symmetric, constant marginal costs (as in the above example). In this simple case, the firms do not save any production costs due to the merger. Thus, it crystallizes the tradeoff between the increased market concentration on one hand and the decrease in the relative market weight of the merged firms on the other hand (e.g., the transition from 2 out of 3 firms to 1 of 2). We first show that in this simple case, two merging firms will always lose 1/9 of their profit from merging (ignoring some degenerate cases). If the firms have *asymmetric* constant marginal costs (i.e., linear cost functions), then by merging they can produce at the factory with the lower marginal costs and therefore gain additional benefits from merging. One would hope that we can directly reduce any profile of cost-functions to the linear-cost case, and show this way that the worst-case loss is indeed 1/9 for all convex costs. Unfortunately, the treatment of some of the cases shows that this simple reduction does not work. We bypass this problem by reducing it to the analysis of a linear-cost market that relaxes the assumption of equilibrium production levels.

We conclude with a new paradoxical example regarding the Cournot model, which unlike the above results is unrelated to mergers. This example considers technological improvements that reduce production costs of the firms. It is known [30] that if the technology of one firm is improved, such that its marginal cost for every additional unit decreases, then the profit of this firm must increase in the new Cournot equilibrium. However, we note that if the costs of two firms in the market improved as above, it might be the case that the total profit of the two firms in the new Cournot solution *decreases*. We show that this profit loss is mild for linear costs, but a further analysis of this surprising phenomenon is left for future work. Due to space limitations, this result appears in the full version of our paper.

1.2 Related Work

The merger paradox is originated in the work by Salant, Switzer and Reynolds [26], who showed how the merger paradox appears in Cournot's original setting from [6]. [26] showed that in all markets with linear costs, any merger of less than 80% of the firms will lead to unprofitable mergers. [16] modeled the multi-firm merger decision as a multi-stage game, and identified its sub-game perfect equilibria where the owner of the group of firms may be better off by letting some of the firms compete against the others. [21] showed how allowing the merged firm to be a market (Stackelberg) leader can mitigate the merger paradox. More papers devised models that yield beneficial mergers (e.g., [7,10]).

Probably the closest papers to our work are papers by Tsitsiklis and Xu [31,32]. They compare the Cournot outcome to the optimal outcome both in terms of profit [31] and social efficiency [32]. Our approach in this paper is similar to [31,32] as we also take a worst-case approximation approach and we prove our main result via a reduction to the case of linear cost functions. However, [31,32] compare the Cournot outcome to the post-merger outcome only in the case of a complete merger – where all the market participants merge to a monopoly (and clearly improve their profit). Also, our results require different techniques. As an example, we reduce the general case to a generalized variant of markets with linear costs, as attempts of applying a straightforward reduction prove futile. As another example, we deploy a concrete computation of the equilibria in the reduced markets. Since many comparative statics results regarding a monopoly formation do not hold in our case – the use of these computations is crucial for our analysis. An earlier paper by Johari and Tsitsiklis [14] showed the Cournot outcome achieves at least 2/3 of the maximal social efficiency for markets with concave demand using the Price of Anarchy approach [12,18,25].[3]

2 Model

We consider a game with n firms, denoted by $F_1, \ldots, F_n$. Each firm F_i chooses a quantity $x_i \in [0, \infty)$ to be supplied by it. The *inverse demand function*, denoted

---

[3] We note that our framework is fundamentally different from Price-of-Anarchy models. Price of Anarchy analysis compares an equilibrium outcome to some unrealistic optimal solution. Our approach is to compare two practical alternatives for decision makers: markets with or without mergers. For managers, who need to decide whether to merge or not, and for regulators who need to approve mergers – these are two realistic situations they need to carefully understand.

by $P(X)$, represents the price per unit the consumers are willing to pay, given that the total production of the firms is $X = \sum_{j=1}^{n} x_j$. The *cost function* of F_i, denoted $C_i(x)$, represents its cost for producing quantity x. The *profit* of F_i is

$$\Pi_i(x_1, \ldots, x_n) = P(x_1 + \ldots + x_n) \cdot x_i - C_i(x_i) \tag{1}$$

The Nash equilibrium point of such game is termed a *Cournot equilibrium point*. That is, a Cournot equilibrium is a vector $x = (x_1, \ldots, x_n)$ such that

$$\forall i \in [n], \forall x_i' \in [0, \infty) \quad \Pi_i(x_i, x_{-i}) \geq \Pi_i(x_i', x_{-i}) \tag{2}$$

where we use the standard notation x_{-i} to denote the vector of strategies of all firms except for F_i.

We provide two assumptions on $P(\cdot)$ and the functions $C_i(\cdot)$, that will be used throughout this paper:

Assumption 1: The function $P(\cdot)$ is differentiable, strictly decreasing and concave on the part where it is positive. Moreover, it is non-negative with $P(0) > 0$.
Assumption 2: The functions $C_i(\cdot)$ are all continuously differentiable, non-decreasing and convex. Moreover, they all maintain that $C_i(0) = 0$.

For brevity, we refer to Assumption 1 as the "concave demand function" assumption and similarly to Assumption 2 as the "convex cost functions" assumption, although the rest of the details are also in force. Note that concavity of the inverse demand function implies the concavity of its inverse, namely the demand function, which we also occasionally refer to instead. The convexity assumption imposed on the cost functions is rather standard in economics literature, and follows from the law of diminishing returns, which states that increasing a factor of production (e.g., labor, capital) by one unit, ceteris paribus, results in lower output per incremental input unit [27]. The concavity assumption on $P(\cdot)$, in turn, ensures the existence and uniqueness of the equilibrium point, as well as some other properties we mention later. While it only provides a sufficient condition for uniqueness, there is a rich and well established literature with various results, many of which are used in the sequel, that use this assumption. Some of our results and our analysis are particularly concerned with the special case of affine demand functions.[4]

The purpose of this paper is to compare the profits of firms in equilibrium in two states, before some of the firms merge and afterwards. We consider a merger of any subset of firms in our analysis, and provide bounds on the ratio of those two profits. This motivates the assumption by which $\forall i \; C_i(0) = 0$, that ensures we avoid comparing positive profits (or costs) to negative ones, resulting in negative bounds.

Assuming that the firms $F_1, \ldots, F_k$ merged, we denote the merged firm by $F_{1,\ldots,k}$. We think of that firm as having multiple factories, such that each factory

---

[4] Note that affine functions also have negative values. The use of such functions is still legitimate, though, as the firms do not produce quantities for which the functions are negative, as we show in our proofs.

i corresponds to the firm F_i before merging. Therefore, a strategy $\widetilde{x}_{1,\ldots,k}$ of the merged firm can be represented by a (not necessarily unique) vector of quantities $(\widetilde{x}_1, \ldots, \widetilde{x}_k)$, such that $\widetilde{x}_i$ is the quantity produced by factory i, and interpreted as $\widetilde{x}_{1,\ldots,k} = \widetilde{x}_1 + \ldots + \widetilde{x}_k$. We define the cost function of the merged firm as

$$\widetilde{C}_{1,\ldots,k}(x) = min\left\{\sum_{j=1}^{k} C_j(x_j) \mid \sum_{j=1}^{k} x_j = x, \ \forall j \in [k] \ x_j \geq 0\right\} \tag{3}$$

This function is well defined as the minimum is taken on a continuous function over a compact set.

Further notations used throughout this paper include the following. Any market M with n firms has two states, as already mentioned, before any merging occurred and afterwards. Its Cournot equilibrium (which exists and is unique under Assumption 1 and Assumption 2, as we mention later), before any merging took place, is denoted by $x^M = (x_1^M, \ldots, x_n^M)$. The profit and cost functions are denoted with the superscript M. For example, $\Pi_2^M(x^M)$ is the profit of F_2 in equilibrium before merging. For brevity, we also denote the profit of F_i in equilibrium by Π_i^M instead of $\Pi_i^M(x^M)$, and omit the superscript M when it is clear. The Cournot equilibrium in M in its second state, after $F_1, \ldots, F_k$ merged for some predefined k, is denoted by $\widetilde{x}^M = (\widetilde{x}_{1,\ldots,k}^M, \widetilde{x}_{k+1}^M, \ldots, \widetilde{x}_n^M)$. The profit and cost functions are denoted similarly, with the same shorthand notations applied. For example, $\widetilde{\Pi}_{k+1}^M = \widetilde{\Pi}_{k+1}^M(\widetilde{x}^M)$ is the profit of F_{k+1} in equilibrium after $F_1, \ldots, F_k$ merged. When we do not mention with which of the two states an equilibrium is affiliated, the pre-merger state or the post-merger state, we refer to the former.

With those notations, we say that $F_1, \ldots, F_k$ lose a fraction of η of their total pre-merge profits (assuming they lose profits at all) if $\widetilde{\Pi}_{1,\ldots,k} = (1 - \eta) \cdot (\Pi_1 + \ldots + \Pi_k)$. As we are normally interested in cases that cause loss of profits by merging, the pre-merger profits are positive in those, i.e., $\Pi_1 + \ldots + \Pi_k > 0$. Therefore, the *fraction of loss* is merely $\eta = 1 - \frac{\widetilde{\Pi}_{1,\ldots,k}}{\Pi_1 + \ldots + \Pi_k}$.

2.1 Known Properties of Cournot Markets

In this subsection, we mention a few known and existing properties from the literature that are guaranteed to hold in markets satisfying the aforementioned assumptions. These properties are presented in the following lemmas, which all assume Assumption 1 and Assumption 2. The first two of those lemmas are well known in economics literature and textbooks (see, e.g., [30,31] and the references within). The other three are from a work by Szidarowsky and Yakowitz [30].

Lemma 1. *The following are necessary and sufficient conditions for a vector* $x = (x_1, \ldots, x_n)$ *to be a Cournot equilibrium, which exists and is unique in markets with a concave demand and convex costs. For each $i \in [n]$:*

$$\text{If } x_i > 0: \ C_i'(x_i) = P(x_1 + \ldots + x_n) + x_i \cdot P'(x_1 + \ldots + x_n) \tag{4}$$
$$\text{If } x_i = 0: \ C_i'(x_i) \geq P(x_1 + \ldots + x_n) + x_i \cdot P'(x_1 + \ldots + x_n) \tag{5}$$

If all firms produce according to Eq. (4), the corresponding equilibrium is called an *internal Cournot equilibrium*. If, however, some firm violates it, we say that the equilibrium is a *corner solution* for that firm.

Lemma 2. *If firms $F_1, .., F_k$ merge in a market with a concave demand and convex costs, for some $k \leq n$, the function $\widetilde{C}_{1,..,k}(\cdot)$ maintains Assumption 2 in the post-merger market. Moreover, if each factory F_i produces a quantity of $\widetilde{x}_i$ units after merging, then for each $i \in [k]$:*

$$\text{If } \widetilde{x}_i > 0: \quad C_i'(\widetilde{x}_i) = \widetilde{C}_{1,..,k}'(\widetilde{x}_1 + \ldots + \widetilde{x}_k) \tag{6}$$

$$\text{If } \widetilde{x}_i = 0: \quad C_i'(\widetilde{x}_i) \geq \widetilde{C}_{1,..,k}'(\widetilde{x}_1 + \ldots + \widetilde{x}_k) \tag{7}$$

Lemma 3. *If some firms merge, each of the other firms produces in equilibrium, in markets with a concave demand and convex costs, at least the amount it produced before that merging. That is, if $x = (x_1, \ldots, x_n)$ is the Cournot equilibrium before $F_1, \ldots, F_k$ merged, for some $k \leq n$, and $\widetilde{x} = (\widetilde{x}_{1,\ldots,k}, \widetilde{x}_{k+1}, \ldots, \widetilde{x}_n)$ is the equilibrium afterwards, then $\widetilde{x}_i \geq x_i$ for each $i \geq k + 1$.*

Lemma 4. *If some firm F_i improves its cost function $C_i(\cdot)$ to $\widehat{C}_i(\cdot)$, in the sense that for each $x \geq 0$ it holds that $C_i'(x) \geq \widehat{C}_i'(x)$, then both $F_i's$ production level and its profit in equilibrium can only increase in markets with a concave demand and convex costs. The production level and the profit of each of the other firms can only decrease in that case.*

Another important lemma proved in [30] states that if some firm leaves the market, the other firms can only benefit, and when some firm joins the market, the other firms' profits can only decrease. To emphasize the connections between the lemmas in this section, we provide a new proof for this lemma, which is shorter, and is based on a reduction from the analysis of omitting a firm to the analysis of replacing an existing firm's cost function. This new proof can be found in the full version of our paper.

Lemma 5. *If some firm F_i leaves the market, then the profit of each of the other firms in equilibrium is at least as it was before F_i left, in markets with a concave demand and convex costs. On the other hand, if some firm joins the market, the profit of the others can only decrease in equilibrium.*

3   Markets with Concave Demand

Our main result in this section is that the merger paradox may be severe when two firms merge, namely, two firms can lose half of their profit by merging. While this is intuitive in large markets, we show that this may happen even when two out of three firms merge. On the other hand, we show that this is indeed the worst case for markets with concave demand; in such markets, two merging firms will lose *at most half* of their pre-merger profit. We also give asymptotic results for mergers of k firms out of n, and in particular we show that in some markets, the losses incurred by merging can be arbitrarily high.

We start by proving the following lemma that shows that the profit of the merged firm is at least the profit of each of the merging firms, prior to merging. The lemma is a key ingredient in our analysis. We state and prove the lemma for the general case of k merging firms out of a total of n firms in a market with concave demand.

Lemma 6. *Consider a market with a concave demand function and $n \geq 3$ firms, each having a convex cost function. When $F_1, \ldots, F_k$ merge, for some $k \leq n$, the profit of the merged firm in equilibrium is at least the profit of F_i in equilibrium before merging, for any $i \in [k]$.*

Proof. Denote the market by M_1. By Lemma 2, M_1 in its post-merger state maintains Assumption 1 and Assumption 2. So, by Lemma 1, the Cournot equilibrium in M_1 before $F_1, \ldots, F_k$ merge exists and is unique, and so is the Cournot equilibrium in M_1 afterwards. We show that

$$\widetilde{\Pi}_{1,\ldots,k}^{M_1} \geq max\left\{\Pi_1^{M_1}, \Pi_2^{M_1}, \ldots, \Pi_k^{M_1}\right\} \tag{8}$$

Let $i \in [k]$. Denote by M_2 the market in which F_i replaces its cost function by $\widetilde{C}_{1,\ldots,k}^{M_1}(\cdot)$. It has a unique Cournot equilibrium. We show the inequality $\Pi_i^{M_2} \geq \Pi_i^{M_1}$. Consider the factories $F_1, \ldots, F_k$ that constitute the merged firm $F_{1,\ldots k}$. By Lemma 2, for each non-negative $x_1, \ldots, x_k$ and x such that $x = \sum_{i=1}^k x_i$, and such that each factory F_i produces x_i units, each of $C_1'^{M_1}(x_1), \ldots, C_k'^{M_1}(x_k)$ is at least $\widetilde{C}_{1,\ldots,k}'^{M_1}(x)$. Since $C_i^{M_1}(\cdot)$ is convex, its slope is increasing in its input, so $x \geq x_i$ implies that $C_i'^{M_1}(x) \geq C_i'^{M_1}(x_i) \geq \widetilde{C}_{1,\ldots,k}'^{M_1}(x)$. So, by Lemma 4, it indeed follows that

$$\Pi_i^{M_2} \geq \Pi_i^{M_1} \tag{9}$$

Now, denote by M_3 the market in which we omit each F_j for $j \in [k] \setminus \{i\}$ from M_2. It also has a unique Cournot equilibrium. Thus, by Lemma 5:

$$\Pi_i^{M_3} \geq \Pi_i^{M_2} \tag{10}$$

Note that M_1, in its state after merging, is exactly M_3 (before any merging occurred). Combining Inequality (9) and Inequality (10), we obtain that

$$\widetilde{\Pi}_{1,\ldots,k}^{M_1} = \Pi_i^{M_3} \geq \Pi_i^{M_1} \tag{11}$$

As it holds for each $i \in [k]$, this proves inequality (8). ∎

Armed with this lemma, we are ready to present our first theorem and analyze the loss of profits by merging in markets with concave demand. The theorem is an immediate consequence of Lemma 6.

Theorem 1. *Consider a market with a concave demand function and $n \geq 3$ firms, each having a convex cost function. When k of the firms merge, for $k < n$,* *they may lose in equilibrium at most a fraction of $1 - 1/k$ of their total pre-merger equilibrium profits. The bound is asymptotically tight. That is, for every $n > k \geq 2$, there exists such a market with n firms, in which k of them merge, and lose a fraction of $(1 - 1/k) \cdot (1 - o(1))$ of their total pre-merger profits, where the asymptotic notation is a function of n.*

Proof. We first note that the merging firms can lose at most $1 - 1/k$ of their profits by colluding, which is an immediate consequence of Lemma 6. Assume that $F_1, \ldots, F_k$ merge. By Lemma 2, the market in its state after merging also maintains Assumption 1 and Assumption 2. So, by Lemma 1, the equilibrium in the market before merging exists and is unique, and so is the equilibrium in it afterwards.

By Lemma 6, the profit of the merged firm in equilibrium is at least the profit of F_i in equilibrium, for every $i \in [k]$, before they merged. Thus:

$$\widetilde{\Pi}_{1,\ldots,k} \geq max\{\Pi_1, \Pi_2, \ldots, \Pi_k\} \geq \frac{1}{k} \cdot (\Pi_1 + \Pi_2 + \ldots + \Pi_k) \qquad (12)$$

So the merging firms indeed lose a fraction of $1 - \frac{\widetilde{\Pi}_{1,\ldots,k}}{\Pi_1 + \Pi_2 + \ldots + \Pi_k} \leq 1 - \frac{1}{k}$ of their total pre-merger profits as a consequence of that merging.

Regarding the tightness, as those examples occur even in markets with affine demand functions, they are presented in Proposition 2 in the next section. In those examples, the k firms lose a fraction of exactly $max\{1 - \frac{(n+1)^2}{k(n+2-k)^2}, 0\} = (1 - \frac{1}{k}) \cdot (1 - o(1))$ of their total pre-merger profits.

We mention that when the number of merging firms is $\Theta(n)$, rather than a fixed constant (n is the total number of firms) – the merging firms may lose an arbitrarily high fraction of their profits. This is formally shown in Sect. 4.

We stress that there are examples that realize the bound from Theorem 1, up to an arbitrarily small constant, even in markets consisting of a small number of firms, i.e., not only asymptotically. These examples exhibit the potential severity of the merger paradox in general markets, even when all firms have simple linear cost functions. The full statement of the corresponding proposition and its proof can be found in the full version of our paper.

4   Markets with Affine Demand

This section presents our main theorem, improving the bound from Theorem 1 for the case of affine demand functions. As earlier mentioned, the loss of two merging firms can be substantial in general. However, in this section we show that when the demand function is affine this loss is mild; in such markets, two merging firms will always lose at most $1/9$ of their pre-merger profits, with any profile of convex cost functions. The tightness of the bound and extensions to larger markets are also discussed.

Our main result of this paper is the following:

Theorem 2. *Consider a market with an affine demand function and three firms with convex cost functions. When two of the firms merge, they may lose at most a fraction of $1/9$ of their total pre-merger profits in equilibrium. Moreover, there exists such a market, in which the two merging firms lose exactly a fraction of $1/9$ of their total profits by merging.*

4.1 Warm Up – Affine Demand, Linear Costs

This subsection is concerned with a subset of the above markets, namely those in which the cost functions are all linear. The aforementioned tight bound is proved for those markets. The proof for general markets, given in the following subsection, is obtained via a reduction to the analysis of markets with linear costs, and specifically to a variant of the analysis from the current subsection.

The following proposition presents a tight bound of $1 - \frac{(n+1)^2}{2n^2}$ on the fraction of profit losses of two firms out of $n \geq 3$ in markets with linear costs. For simplicity, this proposition focuses on the internal equilibria case. Its proof can be found in the full version of our paper.

Proposition 1. *Consider a market with an affine demand function and $n \geq 3$ firms with linear cost functions, in which two of the firms merge. Assume that all firms produce positive quantities in that market, pre-merging and post-merging. Then, the merging firms may lose at most a fraction of $1 - \frac{(n+1)^2}{2n^2}$ of their total pre-merger profits in equilibrium. Moreover, for every $n \geq 3$, there exists such a market, in which the merging firms lose exactly a fraction of $1 - \frac{(n+1)^2}{2n^2}$ of their total profits by merging.*

Similarly, it can be shown that in the setting of Proposition 1, whenever the merging firms have the same cost function, excluding some degenerate cases, the loss of profits is exactly $1 - \frac{(n+1)^2}{2n^2}$. This is regardless of the market share of the merging firms, compared to that of the non-merging firms. The full statement of this observation and its proof can also be found in the full version of our paper.

4.2 Main Result

In order to handle the case of general cost functions, as earlier stressed, we reduce the problem to the analysis of a simpler market, namely a market with linear cost functions. Note that one might intuitively argue that linear markets would straightforwardly form the worst-case example in terms of losses due to merging, since in the symmetric case, there are no cost synergies. That is, in this case, the merged firm does not improve its cost function as compared to the cost functions of the firms that constitute it. However, mergers in the linear case could potentially lead to a higher increase in prices, as compared to the general case, which balances the former effect.

As previously emphasized, our focus is on the case of two merging firms out of three. The following lemma shows a reduction from the analysis of the general case, to the case in which the *non-merging* firm has a linear cost function. We show that for every market with general convex cost functions in which two firms merge, there exists a (possibly different) market such that the non-merging firm has a linear cost function, and in which the two merging firms attain a *higher* fraction of loss.

Lemma 7. *Consider a market with an affine demand function and three firms with convex cost functions. Assume that when two of them merge, they lose a fraction of η of their total pre-merger profits. Then, there exists a linear function, such that replacing the cost functions of the non-merging firm by it, yields a market in which the merging firms lose a fraction of at least η of their total pre-merger profits due to merging.*

Proof. Assume that F_1 and F_2 merge, and denote the original market by M. By Lemma 2, M in its state after merging maintains Assumption 1 and Assumption 2, similarly to its pre-merger state. So, by Lemma 1, the Cournot equilibrium in M before F_1 and F_2 merge exists and is unique, and so is the Cournot equilibrium in M afterwards.

Denote by LIN_1 the market obtained from M by replacing $C_3^M(\cdot)$ with the linear function $C_3^{\text{LIN}_1}(x) = c_3 \cdot x$, where $c_3 = C_3'^M(x_3^M)$. By Lemma 1, x^M is also a unique Cournot equilibrium in the market LIN_1, since it preserves the necessary and sufficient conditions in the lemma. Since the cost functions of F_1 and F_2 in LIN_1 are identical to those of M, the profits of these two firms are equal in both markets.

$$\Pi_1^M + \Pi_2^M = \Pi_1^{\text{LIN}_1} + \Pi_2^{\text{LIN}_1} \tag{13}$$

Similarly, denote by LIN_2 the market obtained from M by replacing $C_3^M(\cdot)$ with the linear function $C_3^{\text{LIN}_2}(x) = \tilde{c}_3 \cdot x$, where $\tilde{c}_3 = \tilde{C}_3'^M(\tilde{x}_3^M)$ (recall that $\tilde{x}_3^M$ is the quantity F_3 produces in equilibrium after F_1 and F_2 merged). By the same reasoning as above, $\tilde{x}^M$ is also the unique post-merger Cournot equilibrium in the market LIN_2. Similarly to the above argument, the profit of the merged firm is equal in both markets. That is,

$$\tilde{\Pi}_{1,2}^M = \tilde{\Pi}_{1,2}^{\text{LIN}_2} \tag{14}$$

Now, Lemma 3 assures that $\tilde{x}_3^M \geq x_3^M$, and since C_3^M is convex, i.e., its slope is increasing in its input, it follows that $\tilde{c}_3 \geq c_3$. Therefore, applying Lemma 4 on LIN_1 and LIN_2 results in

$$\Pi_1^{\text{LIN}_2} + \Pi_2^{\text{LIN}_2} \geq \Pi_1^{\text{LIN}_1} + \Pi_2^{\text{LIN}_1} \tag{15}$$

Thus, F_1 and F_2 lose the following fraction of their profits by merging in the market LIN_2:

$$1 - \frac{\widetilde{\varPi}_{1,2}^{\text{LIN}_2}}{\varPi_1^{\text{LIN}_2} + \varPi_2^{\text{LIN}_2}} \geq 1 - \frac{\widetilde{\varPi}_{1,2}^{\text{LIN}_2}}{\varPi_1^{\text{LIN}_1} + \varPi_2^{\text{LIN}_1}} = \tag{16}$$

$$= 1 - \frac{\widetilde{\varPi}_{1,2}^{M}}{\varPi_1^{\text{LIN}_1} + \varPi_2^{\text{LIN}_1}} = \tag{17}$$

$$= 1 - \frac{\widetilde{\varPi}_{1,2}^{M}}{\varPi_1^{M} + \varPi_2^{M}} = \eta \tag{18}$$

The inequality follows from (15), the first equality follows from (14) and the second from (13). Therefore, the statement in the lemma indeed holds.

We turn to prove **Theorem** 2, the main result of our paper:

Proof. We show first that two merging firms lose at most a fraction of $1/9$ of their profits in any such market. Denote that market by M and its inverse demand function by $P(X) = b - a \cdot X$ for some $a, b > 0$. Assume that F_1 and F_2 merge. By Lemma 2, the cost function of the merged firm adheres to Assumption 1. Therefore, M maintains Assumption 1 and Assumption 2 in both of its states, pre-merger and post-merger, and by Lemma 1, it has a unique Cournot equilibrium x^M before F_1 and F_2 merge, and a unique Cournot equilibrium $\widetilde{x}^M$ afterwards.

Assume, for now, that x^M and $\widetilde{x}^M$ are both are internal Cournot equilibria, an assumption we later relax. Assume w.l.o.g. that the non-merging firm F_3 has a linear cost function, i.e., $C_3^M(x) = c_3 \cdot x$ for some $c_3 \geq 0$. We can safely assume that, since Lemma 7 guarantees that if it has a non-linear cost function, replacing it by some specific linear function yields a market in which F_1 and F_2 lose a (weakly) higher fraction of profits by merging, and we can analyze the latter.

Our objective is showing that $\widetilde{\varPi}_{1,2}^{M} \geq \frac{8}{9} \cdot \left(\varPi_1^{M} + \varPi_2^{M} \right)$.

Step 1: First, we express $\widetilde{\varPi}_{1,2}^{M}$ as the profit of a (merged) firm in a market in which *all* firms have linear cost functions, plus some non-negative value defined later. Concretely, consider the market LIN_1 obtained from M by replacing the functions $C_1^M(x)$ and $C_2^M(x)$ by the function $C^{\text{LIN}_1}(x) = \widetilde{c} \cdot x$, where $\widetilde{c} = \widetilde{C}_{1,2}'^M(\widetilde{x}_{1,2}^M)$. Namely, $\widetilde{c}$ is the slope of the line tangent to the cost function of the merged firm, at the point it produces in equilibrium. Note that $\widetilde{C}_{1,2}^{\text{LIN}_1}(\cdot) \equiv C^{\text{LIN}_1}(\cdot)$, from the definition of the cost function of a merged firm given in Eq. (3). To see this, note that from linearity:

$$\forall x, x' \geq 0 \quad C^{\text{LIN}_1}(x) + C^{\text{LIN}_1}(x') = C^{\text{LIN}_1}(x + x') \tag{19}$$

Therefore, by Lemma 1, $\widetilde{x}^M$ is also a unique Cournot equilibrium in the market LIN_1 in its post-merger state, since it preserves the necessary and sufficient conditions in the lemma. Denote by $\widetilde{x}_i^M$ the amount that factory F_i produces in $\widetilde{x}^M$, for $i = 1, 2$. Since M and LIN_1 have the same unique post-merger eq., then

$$\widetilde{\Pi}_{1,2}^M = \widetilde{\Pi}_{1,2}^{\mathrm{LIN}_1} + \widetilde{C}_{1,2}^{\mathrm{LIN}_1}(\widetilde{x}_{1,2}^M) - \widetilde{C}_{1,2}^M(\widetilde{x}_{1,2}^M) = \tag{20}$$

$$= \widetilde{\Pi}_{1,2}^{\mathrm{LIN}_1} + C^{\mathrm{LIN}_1}(\widetilde{x}_1^M + \widetilde{x}_2^M) - C_1^M(\widetilde{x}_1^M) - C_2^M(\widetilde{x}_2^M) = \tag{21}$$

$$= \widetilde{\Pi}_{1,2}^{\mathrm{LIN}_1} + \widetilde{c} \cdot \widetilde{x}_1^M - C_1^M(\widetilde{x}_1^M) + \widetilde{c} \cdot \widetilde{x}_2^M - C_2^M(\widetilde{x}_2^M) \tag{22}$$

The 2nd inequality is by the definition of $\widetilde{x}_1^M$ and $\widetilde{x}_2^M$, and from the mentioned fact that $\widetilde{C}_{1,2}^{\mathrm{LIN}_1}(\cdot) \equiv C^{\mathrm{LIN}_1}(\cdot)$. The 3rd is due to the linearity of $C^{\mathrm{LIN}_1}(\cdot)$.

As mentioned, we show that (22) equals $\widetilde{\Pi}_{1,2}^{\mathrm{LIN}_1}$ plus some non-negative constant, i.e., that

$$\widetilde{c} \cdot \widetilde{x}_1^M - C_1^M(\widetilde{x}_1^M) + \widetilde{c} \cdot \widetilde{x}_2^M - C_2^M(\widetilde{x}_2^M) \geq 0 \tag{23}$$

For $i = 1, 2$, denote $z_i = \widetilde{c} \cdot \widetilde{x}_i^M - C_i^M(\widetilde{x}_i^M)$. If $\widetilde{x}_i^M = 0$, then $z_i = 0$. Otherwise, by Lemma 2, $\widetilde{c}$ is the slope of the line tangent to C_i^M at $\widetilde{x}_i^M$.

Recall that any convex function lies above any line tangent to it. That is, if $C(\cdot)$ is convex and differentiable, then for every $x, x_0 \geq 0$:

$$C(x) \geq C'(x_0) \cdot (x - x_0) + C(x_0) \tag{24}$$

Applying Inequality (24) to the convex $C_i^M(\cdot)$ by plugging $x = 0$ and $x_0 = \widetilde{x}_i^M$ we obtain that

$$0 = C_i^M(0) \geq \widetilde{c} \cdot (-\widetilde{x}_i^M) + C_i^M(\widetilde{x}_i^M) \tag{25}$$

Putting it differently, $z_i \geq 0$ for $i = 1, 2$, and

$$\widetilde{\Pi}_{1,2}^M = \widetilde{\Pi}_{1,2}^{\mathrm{LIN}_1} + z_1 + z_2 \tag{26}$$

Step 2: Now, we deploy another replacement of the cost functions of F_1 and F_2, similar to the one presented above. The difference is that this time, it guarantees that the *pre-merger* Cournot equilibrium in the resulting market is identical to that of M, instead of the *post-merger* one. For that, consider a different market, LIN_2, obtained from M by replacing the functions $C_1^M(x)$ and $C_2^M(x)$ by the functions $C_1^{\mathrm{LIN}_2}(x) = c_1 \cdot x$ and $C_2^{\mathrm{LIN}_2}(x) = c_2 \cdot x$ respectively, where $c_i = C_i'^M(x_i^M)$ for $i = 1, 2$. Note that x^M is also a unique Cournot equilibrium in the market LIN_2, as it preserves the necessary and sufficient conditions given in Lemma 1. Plugging $x = x_1^M$ and $x_0 = \widetilde{x}_1^M$ in Inequality (24) yields

$$C_i^M(x_i^M) \geq \widetilde{c} \cdot (x_i^M - \widetilde{x}_i^M) + C_i^M(\widetilde{x}_i^M) = \widetilde{c} \cdot x_i^M - z_i \tag{27}$$

So, for $i = 1, 2$:

$$\Pi_i^M(x^M) = \Pi_i^{\mathrm{LIN}_1}(x^M) + C^{\mathrm{LIN}_1}(x_i^M) - C_i^M(x_i^M) = \tag{28}$$

$$= \Pi_i^{\mathrm{LIN}_1}(x^{\mathrm{LIN}_2}) + C^{\mathrm{LIN}_1}(x_i^M) - C_i^M(x_i^M) = \tag{29}$$

$$= \Pi_i^{\mathrm{LIN}_1}(x^{\mathrm{LIN}_2}) + \widetilde{c} \cdot x_i^M - C_i^M(x_i^M) \leq \tag{30}$$

$$\leq \Pi_i^{\mathrm{LIN}_1}(x^{\mathrm{LIN}_2}) + z_i \tag{31}$$

The first equality follows from the definition of LIN_1 and the profit functions. The second from $x^M = x^{\mathrm{LIN}_2}$ as we just mentioned. The third from the definition of C^{LIN_1}, and the inequality follows from Inequality (27).

Step 3: The computations in Step 1 and Step 2 imply that

$$\frac{\widetilde{\Pi}_{1,2}^M}{\Pi_1^M + \Pi_2^M} = \frac{\widetilde{\Pi}_{1,2}^{\mathrm{LIN}_1} + z_1 + z_2}{\Pi_1^M + \Pi_2^M} \tag{32}$$

$$\geq \frac{\widetilde{\Pi}_{1,2}^{\mathrm{LIN}_1} + z_1 + z_2}{\Pi_1^{\mathrm{LIN}_1}(x^{\mathrm{LIN}_2}) + \Pi_2^{\mathrm{LIN}_1}(x^{\mathrm{LIN}_2}) + z_1 + z_2} \tag{33}$$

where the equality follows from Eq. (26) and the inequality from Eq. (31).

Note that since we regularly assume that $\Pi_1^M + \Pi_2^M > 0$ (as otherwise the statement in the theorem becomes trivial), then Inequality (31) also implies that the denominator in (33) is positive. Denote the numerator of (33) by $x \geq 0$ and the denominator by $y \geq 0$. If $x/y \geq 1$ then we are done, as there are no losses due to merging in that case. In particular, if $y - z_1 - z_2 < 0$, that ratio is at least 1, as $x - z_1 - z_2 = \widetilde{\Pi}_{1,2}^{\mathrm{LIN}_1} \geq 0 > y - z_1 - z_2$.

So, assume that $y - z_1 - z_2 \geq 0$ and that $y > x$. Note that in general, $y - z_1 - z_2 > x - z_1 - z_2 \geq 0$ and $z_1 + z_2 \geq 0$ imply that $\frac{x}{y} \geq \frac{x - z_1 - z_2}{y - z_1 - z_2}$.

Therefore the term in (33) is at least $\frac{\widetilde{\Pi}_{1,2}^{\mathrm{LIN}_1}}{\Pi_1^{\mathrm{LIN}_1}(x^{\mathrm{LIN}_2}) + \Pi_2^{\mathrm{LIN}_1}(x^{\mathrm{LIN}_2})}$. This ratio presents a scenario which is a variant of Proposition 1 from Sect. 4 regarding the ratio of profits in markets with linear cost functions. This variant concerns, this time, hybrid linear markets that take into account only the equilibrium productions for the post-merger state, ignoring those of the pre-merger state. In the full version of our papers, we fully analyze this type of hybrid markets, and the ratio is shown to be at least 8/9 by that lemma, as required.

So, we conclude that the statement holds for the internal equilibria case. The treatment of the corner cases in fully discussed in the full version of our paper. Note that the tightness of the bound immediately follows from Proposition 1, by plugging $n = 3$, so we are done.

4.3 Arbitrarily High Losses Due to Merging

In the previous subsections, we gave bounds on the fraction of loss of two merging firms. This subsection discusses the case of a larger number of merging firms, i.e., more than two, and shows that when the total number of firms tends to infinity, the fraction of loss due to merging approaches 1, even in simple markets with affine demand functions and linear cost functions. This also covers the cliffhanger from the previous section, namely the tightness of the statement in Theorem 1.

This is formally stated and proved in the following proposition, which generalizes the tightness proof in Proposition 1, and in the corollary that follows. Note that the closed form representation of the production levels and the profits in markets with linear costs used below, can be found and are proved in the full version of our paper.

Proposition 2. *For every $n > k \geq 2$, there exists a market with n firms, in which k of them merge, and consequently lose a fraction of $max\{1 - \frac{(n+1)^2}{k(n+2-k)^2}, 0\}$ of their pre-merger profits.*

Proof. Take M to have the inverse demand function $P(X) = 1 - X$ with n identical firms, each having the cost function $C(\cdot) \equiv 0$. The candidate for the pre-merger production level of each of the firms is

$$x_i = \frac{1 - (n+1) \cdot 0 + \sum_{j=1}^{n} 0}{(n+1) \cdot 1} = \frac{1}{n+1} > 0, \quad \text{for all } i \in [n] \qquad (34)$$

As for the market in its post-merger state, note that by the definition in Eq. (3), it holds that $\widetilde{C}_{1,\ldots,k}(\cdot) \equiv C_k(\cdot)$, as for all $x_1, \ldots, x_k \geq 0$:

$$C_1(x_1) + \ldots + C_k(x_k) = C_k(x_1) + \ldots + C_k(x_k) = C_k(x_1 + \ldots + x_k) \qquad (35)$$

The first equality follows from the fact that the firms are identical, and the second equality follows from the linearity of C_k.

So, the analysis of M in its post-merger state is identical to the analysis of M, with $n - k + 1$ firms instead of n. Thus, the candidate for the post-merger production level of each firm is (for all $i \in [n] \setminus [k]$):

$$\widetilde{x}_{1,\ldots,k} = x_i = \frac{1 - (n+2-k) \cdot 0 + \sum_{j=2}^{n} 0}{(n+2-k) \cdot 1} = \frac{1}{(n+2-k)} > 0 \qquad (36)$$

Since those candidates are all positive, those are the actual production levels in the two equilibria. In addition,

$$\Pi_i = 1 \cdot \left(x_i^M\right)^2 = 1 \cdot \left(\frac{1}{n+1}\right)^2, \quad \text{for all } i \in [n] \setminus [k] \qquad (37)$$

$$\widetilde{\Pi}_{1,\ldots,k} = 1 \cdot \left(\widetilde{x}_{1,\ldots,k}^M\right)^2 = 1 \cdot \left(\frac{1}{n+2-k}\right)^2 \qquad (38)$$

This implies that $\frac{\widetilde{\Pi}_{1,\ldots,k}}{\Pi_1 + \Pi_2 + \ldots + \Pi_k} = \frac{(n+1)^2}{k(n+2-k)^2}$, as required.

Corollary 1. *For every $\epsilon > 0$, there exist $n > k \geq 2$ and a market with n firms, such that when k of them merge, they lose a fraction of $1 - \epsilon$ of their total pre-merger profits.*

Proof. Let $\epsilon > 0$. Fix some even $n > max\{\frac{32}{\epsilon}, 4\}$ and $k = \frac{1}{2}n$.

By the previous proposition, there exists a market with n firms, in which k of them merge, and lose the following fraction of their pre-merger profits:

$$1 - \frac{(n+1)^2}{k(n+2-k)^2} = 1 - \frac{(n+1)^2}{\frac{1}{2}n \cdot (n+2-\frac{1}{2}n)^2} = \qquad (39)$$

$$= 1 - \frac{8(n+1)^2}{n(n+4)^2} \geq \qquad (40)$$

$$\geq 1 - \frac{8(2n)^2}{n \cdot n^2} = 1 - \frac{32}{n} \geq 1 - \epsilon \qquad (41)$$

and the result holds.

Acknowledgements. This research was supported by the Israel Science Foundation grant number 2570/19 and by the Asper center in the Hebrew University Business School.

References

1. Babaioff, M., Blumrosen, L., Nisan, N.: Networks of complements. In: Chatzigiannakis, I., Mitzenmacher, M., Rabani, Y., Sangiorgi, D. (eds.) 43rd International Colloquium on Automata, Languages, and Programming, ICALP 2016, 11–15 July 2016. LIPIcs, vol. 55, pp. 140:1–140:14 (2016)
2. Babaioff, M., Blumrosen, L., Nisan, N.: Selling complementary goods: dynamics, efficiency and revenue. In: Chatzigiannakis, I., Indyk, P., Kuhn, F., Muscholl, A. (eds.) 44th International Colloquium on Automata, Languages, and Programming, ICALP 2017, Warsaw, Poland, 10–14 July 2017. LIPIcs, vol. 80, pp. 134:1–134:14 (2017)
3. Babaioff, M., Lucier, B., Nisan, N.: Bertrand networks. In: ACM Conference on Electronic Commerce (ACM-EC) (2013)
4. Bertrand, J.L.F.: Theorie mathematique de la richesse sociale. J. de Savants **67**, 499–508 (1883)
5. Bimpikis, K., Ehsani, S., Ilkiliç, R.: Cournot competition in networked markets. In: Proceedings of the Fifteenth ACM Conference on Economics and Computation, EC 2014, p. 733 (2014)
6. Cournot, A.A.: Recherches sur les principes mathematiques de la theori des Richesses (1838)
7. Creane, A., Davidson, C.: Multidivisional firms, internal competition, and the merger paradox. Can. J. Econ./Revue canadienne d'Economique **37**(4), 951–977 (2004)
8. Deneckere, R., Davidson, C.: Incentives to form coalitions with Bertrand competition. Rand J. Econ. **16**(4), 473–486 (1985)
9. Fabra, N., Motta, M.: Guidelines for the analysis of coordinated effects in mergers. Policy Report commissioned by the World Bank for the Latin American Antitrust Authorities (2013)
10. Fan, C., Wolfstetter, E.G.: The merger-paradox: a tournament-based solution. Econ. Lett. **127**(C), 35–38 (2015)
11. Fiat, A., Koutsoupias, E., Ligett, K., Mansour, Y., Olonetsky, S.: Beyond myopic best response (in Cournot competition). Games Econ. Behav. **113**, 38–57 (2019)
12. Papadimitriou, C.: Algorithms, games, and the internet. In: Proceedings of the 33rd Annual ACM Symposium on Theory of Computing, pp. 749–753 (2001)
13. Jarrell, G.A., Poulsen, A.B.: The returns to acquiring firms in tender offers: evidence from three decades. Financ. Manag. **18**(3), 12–19 (1989)
14. Johari, R., Tsitsiklis, J.N.: Efficiency loss in Cournot games: technical Report 2639. MIT Laboratory for Information and Decision Systems, Cambridge, MA, USA (2005)
15. ADUDO Justice: Merger remedies manual (2020). https://www.justice.gov/atr/page/file/1312416/download
16. Kamien, M.I., Zang, I.: The limits of monopolization through acquisition. Q. J. Econ. **105**(2), 465–499 (1990)
17. Kling, G.: Does the merger paradox exist even without any regulations? Evidence from Germany in the pre-1914 period. Empirica **33**(5), 315–328 (2006)

18. Koutsoupias, E., Papadimitriou, C.: Worst-case equilibria. In: Proceedings of the 16th Annual Symposium on Theoretical Aspects of Computer Science, pp. 404–413 (1999)
19. Kreps, D.M., Scheinkman, J.A.: Quantity precommitment and Bertrand competition yield Cournot outcomes. Bell J. Econ. **14**, 326–337 (1983)
20. Lee, E., Buchfuhrer, D., Andrew, L., Tang, A., Low, S.: Progress on pricing with peering. In: Proceedings of the 45th Annual Allerton Conference on Computing, Communications and Control, Allerton 2007, pp. 286–291 (2007)
21. Levin, D.: Horizontal mergers: the 50-percent benchmark. Am. Econ. Rev. **80**(5), 1238–1245 (1990)
22. Lin, W., Pang, J.Z., Bitar, E., Wierman, A.: Networked Cournot competition in platform markets: access control and efficiency loss. SIGMETRICS Perform. Eval. Rev. **45**(2), 15–17 (2017)
23. Mas-Collel, A., Whinston, W., Green, J.: Microeconomic Theory. Oxford University Press (1995)
24. Nadav, U., Piliouras, G.: No regret learning in oligopolies: Cournot vs. Bertrand. In: Proceedings of the Third International Conference on Algorithmic Game Theory, SAGT 2010, pp. 300–311 (2010)
25. Roughgarden, T., Tardos, E.: How bad is selfish routing? J. ACM **49** (2002). https://doi.org/10.1145/506147.506153
26. Salant, S.W., Switzer, S., Reynolds, R.J.: Losses from horizontal merger: the effects of an exogenous change in industry structure on Cournot-Nash equilibrium. Q. J. Econ. **98**(2), 185–199 (1983)
27. Samuelson, P.A., Nordhaus, W.D.: Microeconomics. Edisi 17, 30–31. McGraw-Hill, New York (2001)
28. Shubik, M., Levitan, R.: Market Structure and Behavior (2013). https://doi.org/10.4159/harvard.9780674433403
29. Singh, N., Vives, X.: Price and quantity competition in a differentiated duopoly. RAND J. Econ. **15**(4), 546–554 (1984). https://www.jstor.org/stable/2555525
30. Szidarovszky, F., Yakowitz, S.: Contributions to Cournot oligopoly theory. J. Econ. Theory **28**(1), 51–70 (1982)
31. Tsitsiklis, J.N., Xu, Y.: Profit loss in Cournot oligopolies. Oper. Res. Lett. **41**(4), 415–420 (2013)
32. Tsitsiklis, J.N., Xu, Y.: Efficiency loss in a Cournot oligopoly with convex market demand. J. Math. Econ. **53**, 46–58 (2014). Special Section: Economic Theory of Bubbles (I)
33. Zhang, B., Johari, R., Rajagopal, R.: Competition and efficiency of coalitions in Cournot games with uncertainty. IEEE Trans. Control Netw. Syst. **6**(2), 884–896 (2019)

Greater Flexibility in Mechanism Design Through Altruism

Ruben Brokkelkamp[1](✉)(iD), Sjir Hoeijmakers[1], and Guido Schäfer[1,2](iD)

[1] Networks and Optimization Group, Centrum Wiskunde & Informatica (CWI),
Amsterdam, The Netherlands
{ruben.brokkelkamp,g.schaefer}@cwi.nl
[2] Institute for Logic Language and Computation, University of Amsterdam,
Amsterdam, The Netherlands

Abstract. We study the problem of designing truthful mechanisms for players that are (partially) altruistic. Our approach is to extend the standard utility model by encoding other-regarding preferences of the players into the utility functions. By doing so we leave the original domain where VCG mechanisms can be applied directly.

We derive a characterization of the class of truthful mechanisms under the new model, crucially exploiting the specific form of the other-regarding preferences. We also derive sufficient conditions for truthfulness, which we then exploit to derive mechanisms for two specific models of altruism and with respect to two natural social welfare objectives. As it turns out, altruistic dispositions lead to the positive effect that the designer needs to extract smaller payments from the players to ensure truthfulness. Further, we investigate the effect of redistribution mechanisms that can redistribute the payments among the players. Also here, it turns out that altruism has a positive effect in the sense that the payments needed to guarantee truthfulness can be further reduced.

Finally, we illustrate our theoretical results by applying them to well-studied mechanism design problems such as the public project problem and the multi-unit auction problem. Among other results, we show that the problem of funding a public project can be resolved by our mechanism even for moderate altruistic dispositions, while this is impossible in the standard utility setting.

1 Introduction

Most models in mathematical economics are based on the *self-interest hypothesis*, which assumes that human beings make decisions following purely selfish motives. Certainly, this hypothesis applies in many economic settings, oftentimes simplifies analysis and allows us to make strong predictions on the outcome of economic situations. However, especially when they concern behavior of individuals, these predictions often reflect more what the outcomes 'should' be according to this assumption rather than what they actually are. This has become all the clearer in the past decades through the advent of behavioral economics. Various

© The Author(s), under exclusive license to Springer Nature Switzerland AG 2022
P. Kanellopoulos et al. (Eds.): SAGT 2022, LNCS 13584, pp. 41–59, 2022.
https://doi.org/10.1007/978-3-031-15714-1_3

empirical studies have shown that this assumption oftentimes just 'fails' (see, e.g., [1, 9, 19]).

Mechanism design, in particular, is a branch that heavily relies on this assumption. On a high level, the goal here is to counter the negative effects of self-interested decision-making in a group context. When a group of individuals has to take a decision (or someone has to make a choice on behalf of a group), simply asking each member of the group individually how much they like each alternative might motivate them to over- or understate their actual preferences. A mechanism provides incentives to the involved individuals so that they will reveal their true preferences such that the best decision for the group as a whole can be made. Basically, the self-interest of the participants is used to make them act in the interest of the group after all. Of course, this comes at a cost: often, payments need to be made by (or to) the participants. Mechanism design is the study of finding the 'best' mechanisms that incur the least 'damage' to the group (or the person making the decision) according to certain criteria.

If individuals were fully altruistic in that their preferences are aligned with the group's interests, there would be no need for mechanism design. But what happens if they reside in the large spectrum between 'full altruism' and 'pure selfishness', i.e., when they care about others but not as much as about themselves? It seems a reasonable guess that nearly all human beings fall into this category and this constitutes the main motivation for our investigations in this paper. The main question that we address here is: How does partially altruistic behavior of the involved individuals impact the payments in mechanism design?

Our Contributions. The main contributions of this paper are as follows:

1. We introduce a general utility model incorporating other-regarding preferences of players. Our approach is to adapt the standard utility model by adding to each player's utility an extra term which represents their dispositions towards the other players.
2. By adding these other-regarding preferences, the utilities of the players become interdependent. As a consequence, the general class of VCG mechanisms cannot straightforwardly be applied to our setting. However, we are able to derive a characterization of truthful mechanisms in our new utility model with other-regarding preferences. The key in deriving our characterization is to exploit the specific form of the disposition functions.
3. Unfortunately, this characterization does not provide us with a "recipe" of how to obtain truthful mechanisms. We, therefore, establish a sufficient condition for truthfulness. We also derive sufficient and necessary conditions for when the resulting mechanisms satisfy the no positive transfer (NPT) and individual rationality (IR) property. This also serves as a design template for our mechanisms.
4. We then address the question of how the payments can be redistributed among the players (while maintaining truthfulness) such that the overall payments are minimized. In general, we cannot expect that such redistribution mechanism are strongly budget-balanced (i.e., the sum of the payments equals

zero). We, therefore, use a relation of *individual dominance* between mechanisms, introduced by Guo et al. [16], and provide a characterization of such redistribution mechanisms for our new utility model.

5. We then consider two specific models of altruism that are captured by our utility model with other-regarding preferences in combination with two natural social welfare objectives. We derive truthful mechanisms satisfying NPT and IR for all four settings. As it turns out, the altruistic dispositions of the players provide us with some additional flexibility in choosing the payments. A common property is that as the degree of altruism of a player increases, the designer needs to pay them less to have them reveal their private valuations.

6. We demonstrate the usefulness of our mechanisms by applying them to some fundamental problems in mechanism design: For the bilateral trade problem, we show that our truthful mechanism can be run without any subsidy (if the involved players are sufficiently altruistic), while this is impossible when using VCG payments. For the public project problem, we show that our mechanism allows us to overcome some pathological deficiencies that are unavoidable in the standard setting. In fact, even a modest degree of altruism turns out to be sufficient to resolve the problem positively. Finally, we show that any mechanism that does not take altruism into account can be converted into a mechanism that does, and at the same time, uses lower payments, where the gain is proportional to the altruism levels of the players.

Altogether, our results provide some evidence that altruism can only help in the mechanism design setting considered here. This is in contrast to some previous works (although in a purely strategic setting) showing that altruism may also have a negative impact on equilibrium outcomes [5,6,10].

Related Work. There are different types of other-regarding preferences. In this work we focus mainly on altruism (and spite), other types are reciprocity [20] and inequity aversion [14]. For more information on the different types of other-regarding preferences, we refer to [13].

Although the role of altruism in algorithmic game theory has sparked some interest in recent years (see for instance [2,5,6,10,12,26], literature on incorporating altruism (or its counterpart spite) in mechanism design has been relatively scarce up to this point. We provide a few references that go into this direction.

Brandt and Weiß [4] show that when spiteful bidders are present, the second-price auction fails in that it loses its favorable property of truthfulness. They do not present a truthful alternative themselves but provide a motivation to research implications of spite (and altruism) in mechanism design and to search for such a truthful alternative. Tang and Sandholm [27] also consider single-item auctions and spiteful bidders and direct themselves to finding revenue-maximizing mechanisms. They model spite and altruism using a *player-oriented model*, which is a special case of our utility model with other-regarding preferences. In their proposed revenue-optimal mechanism, a player's own valuation for the object to be auctioned may directly influence their payment. Also, bidders may have to pay even if the auctioneer keeps the item, whereas on the other hand losers are sometimes subsidized by the mechanism. Kucuksenel [21] also models altruism according to the player-oriented model but studies its implications in the Bayesian setting. He characterizes a class of mechanisms that are *interim efficient*: they lead to outcomes that cannot be unanimously improved upon by the players utility-wise. Cavallo [8] proposes a regret-based model of altruism. In this model, players are α-altruistic if they are willing to sacrifice up to α of their potential utility if that improves the aggregate egoistic utility. He also treats a 'proportional' variant, in which α is not a fixed value but a percentage of the potential utility of a player. In his paper, he uses redistribution to come up with strongly budget-balanced mechanisms (i.e., no net payments are made to or by the mechanism) for the single-item allocation setting when players are at least 'mildly' altruistic.

A simple yet effective way to redistribute a large portion of the surplus on the payments can be done by the Bailey-Cavallo redistribution function [3,7]. Other ways to redistribute payments are studied by Guo and Conitzer [17,18] and Moulin [23]. Once you start redistributing, a natural question is what redistribution functions are best in some sense. Guo et al. [16] define partial orders on non-deficit Groves mechanisms and give characterizations of the maximal elements.

2   Preliminaries

We are given a finite set $N = \{1, \ldots, n\}$ of $n \geq 1$ players and a finite set A of alternatives to choose from. Each player $i \in N$ has a *private valuation function* $v_i : A \to \mathbb{R}$ which specifies their preferences over the set of alternatives A, independently of the other players' preferences. Note that the valuation function v_i is considered to be *private* information, i.e., only known to player i themselves. Given an alternative $a \in A$, we say that $v_i(a)$ is the *valuation* of player i for alternative a. We define V_i as the set of all possible valuation functions of player i. Unless stated otherwise, we assume that $V_i \subseteq \mathbb{R}^A$ is unrestricted and commonly known. Define $V = V_1 \times \cdots \times V_n$.

We use the following standard notation. Given an n-dimensional vector $\vec{x} = (x_1, \ldots, x_n)$ of objects (i.e., reals, sets, functions) and a player $i \in N$, we define $\vec{x}_{-i} = (x_1, \ldots, x_{i-1}, x_{i+1}, \ldots, x_n)$ as the same vector with the i-th component removed. We also slightly abuse notation and write $(x_i, \vec{x}_{-i})$ instead of $\vec{x}$. Similarly, we use V_{-i} to refer to $V_1 \times \cdots \times V_{i-1} \times V_{i+1} \times \cdots \times V_n$.

Suppose there is a central *designer* (e.g., principal, government) who wants to determine a socially desirable outcome, taking the preferences of the players into account. Each player $i \in N$ expresses their preferences over the available alternatives by reporting a valuation function $b_i \in V_i$ (not necessarily equal to their private valuation function v_i). The designer then utilizes a mechanism to decide on an outcome. A *(direct revelation) mechanism* $M = (f, \vec{p})$ is specified by a *social choice function* $f : V \to A$ and a vector of *payment functions* $\vec{p} = (p_1, \ldots, p_n)$ with $p_i : V \to \mathbb{R}$ for all $i \in N$. Given the reported valuation functions $\vec{b} = (b_1, \ldots, b_n)$, the mechanism determines an alternative $f(\vec{b})$ and for each player $i \in N$ a payment $p_i(\vec{b})$ to be made to the designer. We write $\vec{b}(f(\vec{b})) = (b_1(f(\vec{b})), \ldots, b_n(f(\vec{b})))$.

We assume that each player wants to maximize a given utility function. In the *standard utility model*, each player $i \in N$ has a quasi-linear utility function defined as $u_i^s(\vec{b}) = v_i(f(\vec{b})) - p_i(\vec{b})$. The goal of the designer is to determine an alternative that maximizes a given *design objective* $D : V \times A \to \mathbb{R}$, i.e., $f(\vec{b}) \in \arg\max_{a \in A} D(\vec{b}, a)$. A commonly used design objective is to maximize the *social welfare*, i.e., the sum of the valuations of all players; formally, $D^{sw}(\vec{b}, a) = \sum_{i \in N} b_i(a)$. For any design objective considered in this paper, we assume that we can decompose $D(\vec{b}, a) = \sum_{i \in N} d_i(b_i, a)$ for functions $d_i : V_i \times A \to \mathbb{R}$. Then, we write $D_{-i}(\vec{b}, a) = D_{-i}(\vec{b}_{-i}, a) = \sum_{j \in N \setminus \{i\}} d_j(\vec{b}_j, a)$.

A mechanism $M = (f, \vec{p})$ is *truthful* if for every player $i \in N$, for any vector of reported valuations $\vec{b} \in V$, we have that $u_i(v_i, \vec{b}_{-i}) \geq u_i(b_i, \vec{b}_{-i})$. In other words, a truthful mechanism ensures that for each player i it is always at least as good to report their private valuation v_i than any other valuation, independent of what the other players report. Another desirable property of a mechanism is that it never makes payments to the players. A mechanism M satisfies the *no positive transfers (NPT)* property if for every player $i \in N$ and all $\vec{b} \in V$ we have that $p_i(\vec{b}) \geq 0$. Sometimes, we only require that the sum of payments is non-negative, i.e., $\sum_{i \in N} \vec{p}_i(\vec{b}) \geq 0$ for all $\vec{b} \in V$, then we call the mechanism *non-deficit*. Finally, every player should be guaranteed to receive a non-negative utility if they report their valuations truthfully. A mechanism M satisfies the *individual rationality (IR)* property if for every player $i \in N$ and for all reported valuations $\vec{b}_{-i} \in V_{-i}$ of the other players, $u_i(v_i, \vec{b}_{-i}) \geq 0$.

Definition 1. *A mechanism $M = (f, \vec{p})$ is called a* Vickrey-Clarke-Groves (VCG) *mechanism if the following two conditions are satisfied:*

1. $f(\vec{b}) \in \arg\max_{a \in A} \sum_{i \in N} b_i(a)$;
2. *for every player $i \in N$ there is a function $h_i : V_{-i} \to \mathbb{R}$ such that*

$$p_i(\vec{b}) = h_i(\vec{b}_{-i}) - \sum_{j \neq i} b_j(f(\vec{b})).$$

VCG mechanisms allow for different instantiations of functions h_i to define the payments of the players. However, if the valuation functions are non-negative and one additionally insists on satisfying both NPT and IR then there remains a unique payment rule due to Clarke (1971): A VCG mechanism $(f, \vec{p})$ implements the *Clarke pivot rule* if for every player $i \in N$ we have that $h_i(\vec{b}_{-i}) = \sum_{j \neq i} b_j(a^{-i})$, where $a^{-i} \in \arg\max_{a \in A} \sum_{j \neq i} b_j(a)$ is an alternative that maximizes the social welfare if player i would not be present.

The following is due to [11,15,28].

Proposition 1. *Every VCG mechanism is truthful. The VCG mechanism that uses the Clarke pivot rule satisfies NPT. Further, if all valuation functions of the players are non-negative, then it also satisfies IR.*

Due to page limitations, some proofs are omitted here and can be found in the full version of the paper.

3   Modeling Other-Regarding Preferences

3.1   Utility Model with Other-Regarding Preferences

We propose a general utility model capturing that players may care about other players (both in the positive and negative sense).

Definition 2. *Suppose we are given a function* $g_i : \mathbb{R}^{n-1} \times \mathbb{R}^n \to \mathbb{R}$ *for every player* $i \in N$ *modeling their* other-regarding *preferences. The utility* $u_i^{g_i}$ *of player* $i \in N$ *in the* utility model with other-regarding preferences *is then defined as*

$$u_i^{g_i}(\vec{b}) = v_i(f(\vec{b})) - p_i(\vec{b}) + g_i(\vec{b}_{-i}(f(\vec{b})), \vec{p}(\vec{b})).$$

Observe that the function g_i does not depend on the private valuations of the other players (which would be infeasible). This reflects the intuition that the other-regarding preferences of a player originate from *beliefs* about the experiences of others rather than from their true experiences.[1]

In Definition 2, the other-regarding preferences may depend on the payments. This makes it very general, but in proofs, this poses an extra challenge. Therefore, for some results below, we restrict to other-regarding preferences that are *payment independent*.

Definition 3. *The other-regarding preferences* g_i *are* payment independent *if they only depend on* $\vec{b}_{-i}(f(\vec{b}))$ *for all* $i \in N$.

We will see in Sect. 5 that there are natural models where the other-regarding preferences do not depend on the payments.

3.2   Characterization of Truthful Mechanisms

We give a characterization of truthful mechanisms in the utility model with other-regarding preferences.

Theorem 1. *A mechanism* $M = (f, \vec{p})$ *is truthful in the utility model with other-regarding preferences if and only if it satisfies the following two conditions:*

1. *For every player* $i \in N$ *the difference between the other-regarding preferences* g_i *and the payment* p_i *only depends on the chosen alternative* $f(\vec{b})$ *and* $\vec{b}_{-i}$ *(but not on* b_i *itself), i.e., there is a function* $\mu_i : A \times V_{-i} \to \mathbb{R}$ *such that*

$$p_i(\vec{b}) - g_i(\vec{b}_{-i}(f(\vec{b})), \vec{p}(\vec{b})) = \mu_i(f(\vec{b}), \vec{b}_{-i}).$$

2. *The alternative chosen by* M *satisfies for every player* $i \in N$ *that*

$$f(b_i, \vec{b}_{-i}) \in \arg \max_{a \in A(\vec{b}_{-i})} (b_i(a) - \mu_i(a, \vec{b}_{-i})),$$

where $A(\vec{b}_{-i}) = \{ f(b_i', \vec{b}_{-i}) \mid b_i' \in V_i \}$ *refers to the image of* $f(\cdot, \vec{b}_{-i})$.

---

[1] Intuitively, the function g_i of player i can be viewed as being dependent on the reported valuation functions $\vec{b}_{-i}$ of the other players and the payment functions $\vec{p}$. Formally, however, g_i only depends on the respective *values* of these functions under the outcome $(f(\vec{b}), \vec{p}(\vec{b}))$ determined by the mechanism $M = (f, \vec{p})$ when run on $\vec{b}$.

Proof. We first prove the if part. Consider a player $i \in N$ and fix $\vec{b}_{-i} \in V_{-i}$ arbitrarily. Define $\bar{a} = f(v_i, \vec{b}_{-i})$ and $a = f(b_i, \vec{b}_{-i})$ as the alternatives chosen by M when i reports their private valuation function v_i truthfully and when i reports an arbitrary valuation function b_i, respectively.

By the first condition of the statement, we have
$$u_i^{g_i}(v_i, \vec{b}_{-i}) = v_i(\bar{a}) - \mu_i(\bar{a}, \vec{b}_{-i}) \quad \text{and} \quad u_i^{g_i}(b_i, \vec{b}_{-i}) = v_i(a) - \mu_i(a, \vec{b}_{-i}). \quad (1)$$

By the second condition, the alternative $\bar{a}$ chosen by M for $(v_i, \vec{b}_{-i})$ satisfies
$$v_i(\bar{a}) - \mu_i(\bar{a}, \vec{b}_{-i}) \geq v_i(a) - \mu_i(a, \vec{b}_{-i}). \quad (2)$$

Combining (1) and (2) proves truthfulness.

Now, we prove the only-if part of the first condition. Consider a player $i \in N$ and fix an arbitrary $\vec{b}_{-i} \in V_{-i}$. Given some $b_i \in V_i$, for notational convenience we define $m_i(b_i, \vec{b}_{-i})$ as a shorthand for
$$m_i(b_i, \vec{b}_{-i}) = p_i(b_i, \vec{b}_{-i}) - g_i(\vec{b}_{-i}(f(b_i, \vec{b}_{-i})), \vec{p}(b_i, \vec{b}_{-i}))$$

The utility of player i can then be written as $u_i^{g_i}(b_i, \vec{b}_{-i}) = v_i(f(b_i, \vec{b}_{-i})) - m_i(b_i, \vec{b}_{-i})$. Suppose there are two valuation functions $b_i, b_i' \in V_i$ of player i such that $f(b_i, \vec{b}_{-i}) = f(b_i', \vec{b}_{-i})$ and $m_i(b_i, \vec{b}_{-i}) < m_i(b_i', \vec{b}_{-i})$. Then by identifying the private valuation function v_i of i with b_i', we obtain
$$u_i^{g_i}(v_i, \vec{b}_{-i}) = v_i(f(b_i', \vec{b}_{-i})) - m_i(b_i', \vec{b}_{-i})$$
$$< v_i(f(b_i, \vec{b}_{-i})) - m_i(b_i, \vec{b}_{-i}) = u_i^{g_i}(b_i, \vec{b}_{-i}),$$

which contradicts the truthfulness of M. Thus $m_i(b_i, \vec{b}_{-i}) = m_i(b_i', \vec{b}_{-i})$ whenever $f(b_i, \vec{b}_{-i}) = f(b_i', \vec{b}_{-i})$. This proves the existence of a function μ_i only depending on $f(\vec{b})$ and $\vec{b}_{-i}$ as claimed.

Finally, we prove the only-if part of the second condition. Again, consider a player $i \in N$ and fix an arbitrary $\vec{b}_{-i} \in V_{-i}$. Suppose there is some $b_i \in V_i$ such that $f(b_i, \vec{b}_{-i})$ is not a maximizer of the expression. Let $a' \in A(\vec{b}_{-i})$ be such a maximizer, i.e.,
$$a' \in \arg \max_{a \in A(\vec{b}_{-i})} (b_i(a) - \mu_i(a, \vec{b}_{-i})).$$

By the definition of $A(\vec{b}_{-i})$, we have $a' = f(b_i', \vec{b}_{-i})$ for some $b_i' \in V_i$. By identifying the private valuation function v_i of i with b_i and defining $\bar{a} = f(b_i, \vec{b}_{-i})$, we obtain
$$u_i^{g_i}(v_i, \vec{b}_{-i}) = b_i(\bar{a}) - \mu_i(\bar{a}, \vec{b}_{-i}) < b_i(a') - \mu_i(a', \vec{b}_{-i}) = u_i^{g_i}(b_i', \vec{b}_{-i}),$$

which contradicts the truthfulness of M. $\square$

Generally, it might be difficult to model the other-regarding preferences of the players exactly as we might not know them. However, this is not necessary to obtain a truthful mechanism if the other-regarding preferences are payment independent: the same mechanism is truthful with respect to different other-regarding preferences (as long as they are payment independent).

Corollary 1. *Let g_i, g_i' be other-regarding preferences that are payment independent. Suppose we have a truthful mechanism with respect to g_i'. Then the mechanism is also truthful with respect to g_i.*

3.3   Design Template

Theorem 1 gives a characterization of truthful mechanisms but does not provide us with a "recipe" of how to obtain such mechanisms for a given design objective D.

Theorem 2. *Fix a design objective D. A mechanism $M = (f, \vec{p})$ is truthful in the utility model with other-regarding preferences if the following two conditions are satisfied:*

1. *$f(\vec{b}) \in \arg\max_{a \in A} D(\vec{b}, a)$.*
2. *For every player $i \in N$ there exist functions $h_i, \gamma_i : V_{-i} \to \mathbb{R}$ such that*

$$p_i(\vec{b}) = h_i(\vec{b}_{-i}) + g_i(\vec{b}_{-i}(f(\vec{b})), \vec{p}(\vec{b})) - \gamma_i(\vec{b}_{-i}) \cdot D_{-i}(\vec{b}_{-i}, f(\vec{b})).$$

As in the standard utility setting, we would like to ensure that our mechanisms satisfy NPT and IR. In light of Theorem 2, it is now easy to specify which choices of the functions h_i are feasible for this.

Proposition 2. *Let $M = (f, \vec{p})$ be a mechanism as defined in Theorem 2. Then M satisfies NPT if and only if for every player $i \in N$, $h_i(\vec{b}_{-i}) \geq \gamma_i(\vec{b}_{-i}) \cdot D_{-i}(\vec{b}_{-i}, f(\vec{b})) - g_i(\vec{b}_{-i}(f(\vec{b})), \vec{p}(\vec{b}))$. Further, M satisfies IR if and only if for every player $i \in N$, $h_i(\vec{b}_{-i}) \leq \gamma_i(\vec{b}_{-i}) \cdot D_{-i}(\vec{b}) + v_i(f(\vec{b}))$.*

The above proposition shows that, in principle, there is a leeway of choosing h_i of size $v_i(f(\vec{b})) + g_i(\vec{b}_{-i}(f(\vec{b})), \vec{p}(\vec{b}))$; however, recall that h_i may only depend on $\vec{b}_{-i}$ and we might thus be unable to exploit the full range. Further, Proposition 2 shows that if the valuation functions can be negative, then we cannot guarantee both NPT and IR. In fact, the same holds if $g_i(\vec{b}_{-i}(f(\vec{b})), \vec{p}(\vec{b}))$ is allowed to be negative.

It is not always necessary to know the other-regarding preferences exactly when designing an individually rational mechanism. If we are dealing with payment-independent other-regarding preferences the following proposition shows that if we design an individually rational mechanism while underestimating the other-regarding preferences, it is also individually rational with respect to the real other-regarding preferences.

Proposition 3. *Let g_i, g_i' be other-regarding preferences that are payment independent such that $g_i(\vec{b}_{-i}(f(\vec{b}))) \geq g_i'(\vec{b}_{-i}(f(\vec{b})))$ for all $\vec{b}$. Let $M = (f, \vec{p})$ be a mechanism as in Theorem 2 with respect to g_i' for player i that is individually rational. The mechanism with respect to g_i is also truthful and individually rational.*

4   Minimizing Payments

One way to incur the least "damage" on the set of participating players is to minimize the payments that are paid to the central designer (e.g., principal, government). In fact, in various settings it is plausible to assume that the players would prefer to redistribute the payments among themselves, rather than giving it away to an external entity. In this section, we study redistribution mechanisms and derive characterization results of such mechanisms. These results will be used in Sect. 6.3 to show that altruism allows us to design mechanisms in which less payments need to be paid to the designer.

Insisting on both IR and NPT, and requiring a mechanism that follows the recipe from Theorem 2, Proposition 2 restricts us to payment functions that satisfy

$$h_i(\vec{b}_{-i}) \geq \gamma_i(\vec{b}_{-i}) \cdot D_{-i}(\vec{b}_{-i}, f(\vec{b})) - g_i(\vec{b}_{-i}(f(\vec{b})), \vec{p}(\vec{b})).$$

In Theorem 2, the payments depend on the other-regarding preferences that, in turn, can depend on the payments. To avoid issues with recursive definitions we assume the other-regarding preferences are payment independent.

If the other-regarding preferences are payment independent, we can easily find the payment functions that minimize the sum of payments $\sum_{i \in N} p_i(b) = \sum_{i \in N} h_i(\vec{b}_{-i}) + g_i(\vec{b}_{-i}(f(\vec{b}))) - D_{-i}(\vec{b}_{-i}, f(\vec{b}))$ while making sure NPT still holds:

$$h_i(\vec{b}_{-i}) = \sup_{b_i'} \gamma_i(\vec{b}_{-i}) \cdot D_{-i}(\vec{b}_{-i}, f(b_i', \vec{b}_{-i})) - g_i(\vec{b}_{-i}(f(\vec{b}))). \tag{3}$$

Here, we define $\vec{b}' = (b_i', \vec{b}_{-i})$ and use this notation throughout this section; b_i' will be clear from the context.

There is no need to insist on NPT in general. There are settings in which it is desirable to keep as much money within the group of participants as possible and it is not a problem if some participants receive money from the mechanism. As an example, consider some housemates with a shared car who have to decide who gets to use the car on a particular day.

Unfortunately, it is impossible to have a *strongly budget-balanced*, i.e., the sum of payments is 0, mechanism in many settings [22,24]. As we cannot aim for 0, we would like to minimize the amount we cannot redistribute. Not insisting on NPT enlarges the set of payment functions we can use. However, we do not want to subsidize the mechanism, and thus we keep the requirement that the mechanism should be non-deficit, i.e., $\sum_i \vec{p}_i(\vec{b}) \geq 0$ for all $\vec{b}$.

Guo et al. [16] characterized Groves mechanisms that are undominated in terms of the amount of money flowing from the mechanism to the auctioneer. We extend this to the mechanisms with other-regarding preferences.

A non-deficit mechanism with payment vector $\vec{p}$ *collectively dominates* a non-deficit mechanism with payment vector $\vec{p}'$ if for all $\vec{b} : \sum_i \vec{p}_i(\vec{b}) \leq \sum_i \vec{p}_i'(\vec{b})$ and there is at least one $\vec{b}$ for which this inequality is strict. Getting characterizations for payments that are collectively undominated is difficult. We can, however, relax the requirement a bit.

Definition 4. *A non-deficit mechanism with payment vector $\vec{p}$ is said to indi-vidually dominate a non-deficit mechanism with payment vector $\vec{p'}$ if for all $\vec{b}$ and all i, $\vec{p}_i(\vec{b}) \leq \vec{p'}_i(\vec{b})$ and there is at least one $\vec{b}$ and i for which $\vec{p}_i(\vec{b}) < \vec{p'}_i(\vec{b})$.*

Individual domination defines a partial order on mechanisms. The maximal elements in this order are interesting because they are the mechanisms in which no player can improve without making another player worse off.

Using mechanisms that follow the recipe in Theorem 2, we closely follow Guo et al. [16] to characterize when a mechanism is non-deficit and when it is individually undominated.

Lemma 1. *A mechanism $M = (f, \vec{p})$ with $\vec{p}_i = h_i(\vec{b}_{-i}) + g_i(\vec{b}_{-i}(f(\vec{b}))) - \gamma_i(\vec{b}_{-i})D_{-i}(\vec{b}_{-i}, f(\vec{b}))$ is non-deficit if and only if for all i and $\vec{b}_{-i}$*

$$h_i(\vec{b}_{-i}) \geq \sup_{b'_i} \sum_j \left(\gamma_j(\vec{b}'_{-j})D_{-j}(\vec{b}'_{-j}, f(\vec{b}')) - g_j(\vec{b}'_{-j}(f(\vec{b}'))) \right) - \sum_{j \neq i} h_j(\vec{b}'_{-j}). \quad (4)$$

Theorem 3. *A mechanism $M = (f, \vec{p})$ with $\vec{p}_i = h_i(\vec{b}_{-i}) + g_i(\vec{b}_{-i}(f(\vec{b}))) - \gamma_i(\vec{b}_{-i})D_{-i}(\vec{b}_{-i}, f(\vec{b}))$ is individually undominated if and only if for all i and $\vec{b}_{-i}$*

$$h_i(\vec{b}_{-i}) = \sup_{b'_i} \sum_j \left(\gamma_j(\vec{b}'_{-j})D_{-j}(\vec{b}'_{-j}, f(\vec{b}')) - g_j(\vec{b}'_{-j}(f(\vec{b}'))) \right) - \sum_{j \neq i} h_j(\vec{b}'_{-j}). \quad (5)$$

5   A Case Study: Altruism

5.1   Two Altruism Models and Design Objectives

We consider two models of altruism that are instantiations of the utility model with other-regarding preferences. We assume that each player $i \in N$ is equipped with an *altruism level* $\alpha_i \in [0, 1]$, which interpolates between a 'purely selfish' ($\alpha_i = 0$) and a 'fully altruistic' ($\alpha_i = 1$) attitude[2].

Definition 5. *Given an altruism level $\alpha_i \in [0, 1]$ for every player $i \in N$, in the welfare-oriented model, the utility $u_i^w : V \to \mathbb{R}$ of player $i \in N$ is defined as:*

$$u_i^w(\vec{v}) = v_i(f(\vec{b})) - p_i(\vec{b}) + \alpha_i \sum_{j \neq i} b_j(f(\vec{b})).$$

In the welfare-oriented model, each player i receives a fraction of α_i of the reported valuations of all other players. Note that i fully cares about their own payment. Altruism here corresponds to a willingness to contribute to the creation of value in the form of valuations of alternatives.

---

[2] Note that although our focus here is on altruism levels in the range $[0, 1]$, many results given below can be extended in a straightforward way to other cases such as spiteful players ($\alpha_i < 0$) or players that care about others more than about themselves ($\alpha_i > 1$).

Definition 6. *Given an altruism level $\alpha_i \in [0, 1]$ for every player $i \in N$, in the omnistic model, the utility $u_i^o : V \to \mathbb{R}$ of a player $i \in N$ is given by:*

$$u_i^o(\vec{b}) = v_i(f(\vec{b})) - p_i(\vec{b}) + \alpha_i \left(p_i(\vec{b}) + \sum_{j \neq i} b_j(f(\vec{b})) \right).$$

In the omnistic model, each player i cares about every other player in the same way as in the welfare-oriented model. The difference, however, is that player i perceives their payment p_i to the designer as being discounted by a fraction of $(1 - \alpha_i)$ (although they pay p_i eventually). Put differently, i enjoys a fraction of α_i of the payment p_i that the designer receives from them. This is also the reason why we call this the 'omnistic' model (omnes = all/everybody).

We derive mechanisms for these models with respect to the following two design objectives:

$$D^{sw}(\vec{b}, a) = \sum_{i \in N} b_i(a) \quad \text{and} \quad D^{ow}(\vec{b}, a) = \sum_{i \in N} \left(1 + \sum_{k \neq i} \alpha_k \right) b_i(a).$$

The design objective D^{sw} is the classical social welfare objective. In our context, it captures situations where the designer only cares about the sum of the individual valuations of the players, disregarding the positive perceptions that they receive from other players. Intuitively, here the utility functions serve merely as a means to model the positive attitudes of players towards others.

The design objective D^{ow} models situations in which the designer takes both the individual valuations of the players and their positive other-regarding preferences towards others into account. Note that this objective is equal to the sum of all valuations that the players receive (directly or indirectly). We refer to it as the *omnistic welfare* objective.

5.2   Mechanisms for Altruistic Players

We derive truthful mechanisms for the welfare-oriented and omnistic model (referred to as w and o for short) with respect to both the social and omnistic welfare objective. In order to keep the presentation concise, we introduce the following generic definition of adjusted VCG mechanisms. The respective payment functions $\vec{p}$ are stated in Table 1.

Definition 7. *Let $m \in \{w, o\}$ refer to an altruism model as defined above and let $D \in \{D^{sw}, D^{ow}\}$ be a design objective. A mechanism $M^{m,D} = (f, \vec{p})$ is called an altruism-adjusted VCG mechanism (AAVCG) with respect to altruism model m and design objective D if the following two conditions are satisfied:*

1. *$f(\vec{b}) \in \arg\max_{a \in A} D(\vec{b}, a)$.*
2. *For every player $i \in N$ and some function $h_i : V_{-i} \to \mathbb{R}$, the payment function $p_i(\vec{b})$ is defined as in Table 1.*

Table 1. Definition of the payment function of the AAVCG mechanisms and its altruism-adjusted Clarke pivot rule, depending on the altruism model and design objective. The parameter c_i can be fixed arbitrarily in the range $[0, \alpha_i]$

(m, D)	payment function and altruism-adjusted Clarke pivot rule
(w, D^{sw})	$p_i(\vec{b}) = h_i(\vec{b}_{-i}) - (1 - \alpha_i) \sum_{j \neq i} b_j(f(\vec{b}))$ $h_i(\vec{b}_{-i}) = (1 - \alpha_i + c_i) \sum_{j \neq i} b_j(a^{-i})$ $a^{-i} \in \arg\max_{a \in A} \sum_{j \neq i} b_j(a)$
(o, D^{sw})	$p_i(\vec{b}) = \frac{1}{1 - \alpha_i} h_i(\vec{b}_{-i}) - \sum_{j \neq i} b_j(f(\vec{b}))$ $h_i(\vec{b}_{-i}) = (1 - \alpha_i + c_i) \sum_{j \neq i} b_j(a^{-i})$ $a^{-i} \in \arg\max_{a \in A} \sum_{j \neq i} b_j(a)$
(w, D^{ow})	$p_i(\vec{b}) = h_i(\vec{b}_{-i}) - \sum_{j \neq i} \left(\frac{1 + \sum_{k \neq j} \alpha_k}{1 + \sum_{k \neq i} \alpha_k} - \alpha_i \right) b_j(f(\vec{b}))$ $h_i(\vec{b}_{-i}) = \sum_{j \neq i} \left(\frac{1 + \sum_{k \neq j} \alpha_k}{1 + \sum_{k \neq i} \alpha_k} - \alpha_i + c_i \right) b_j(a^{-i})$ $a^{-i} \in \arg\max_{a \in A} \sum_{j \neq i} \left(1 + \sum_{k \neq j, i} \alpha_k - \alpha_i \sum_{k \neq i} \alpha_k \right) b_j(a)$
(o, D^{ow})	$p_i(\vec{b}) = h_i(\vec{b}_{-i}) - \frac{1}{1 - \alpha_i} \sum_{j \neq i} \left(\frac{1 + \sum_{k \neq j} \alpha_k}{1 + \sum_{k \neq i} \alpha_k} - \alpha_i \right) b_j(f(\vec{b}))$ $h_i(\vec{b}_{-i}) = \frac{1}{1 - \alpha_i} \sum_{j \neq i} \left(\frac{1 + \sum_{k \neq j} \alpha_k}{1 + \sum_{k \neq i} \alpha_k} - \alpha_i + c_i \right) b_j(a^{-i})$ $a^{-i} \in \arg\max_{a \in A} \sum_{j \neq i} \left(1 + \sum_{k \neq j, i} \alpha_k - \alpha_i \sum_{k \neq i} \alpha_k \right) b_j(a)$

Similarly, we give a generic definition of an altruism-adjusted Clarke pivot rule for these mechanisms. The respective definitions of the functions h_i are stated in Table 1.

Definition 8. *We say that an AAVCG mechanism $M^{m,D} = (f, \vec{p})$ with respect to altruism model m and design objective D implements the altruism-adjusted Clarke pivot rule if for every player $i \in N$ there is some $c_i \in [0, \alpha_i]$ such that the function h_i is as defined in Table 1.*

With the help of Theorem 2 and Proposition 2, we can show that the four AAVCG mechanisms as specified in Table 1 are truthful and satisfy NPT and IR.

Theorem 4. *Every AAVCG mechanism $M^{m,D} = (f, \vec{p})$ with respect to altruism model m and design objective D is truthful. Further, $M^{m,D}$ satisfies NPT and IR if it implements the altruism-adjusted Clarke pivot rule.*

5.3   Discussion

We discuss a few main properties of the mechanisms introduced above.

First, note that the two AAVCG mechanisms for the social welfare objective reduce to the standard VCG mechanism (Definition 1) if the players are entirely selfish, i.e., $\alpha_i = 0$ for all i. This is to be expected because, in this case, both the welfare-oriented model and the omnistic model reduce to the standard utility model.

Further, these mechanisms nicely capture the intuition that altruism counters the negative effect of egoistic predispositions: As the altruism level of a player i increases, the designer needs to pay them less to have them want to reveal the truth about their valuation functions. And in fact, as we would expect the players require no extra incentive at all when they are fully altruistic ($\alpha_i = 1$ for all i).

Observe that the altruism-adjusted Clarke pivot gives rise to a family of mechanisms (parametrized by $c_i \in [0, \alpha_i]$ for all i). The size of this set grows with the altruism levels α_i of the players. This flexibility can be exploited to extract smaller payments from the players.

The altruism-adjusted Clarke pivot rule has a particularly nice representation in the omnistic model with respect to the social welfare objective, i.e., for every $c_i \in [0, \alpha_i]$

$$p_i(\vec{b}) = \left(1 + \frac{c_i}{1 - \alpha_i}\right) \sum_{j \neq i} b_j(a^{-i}) - \sum_{j \neq i} b_j(f(\vec{b})), \tag{6}$$

where a^{-i} is as defined in Table 1.

Note that by choosing $c_i = 0$ for every i, the resulting AAVCG mechanism reduces to the standard VCG mechanism with Clarke pivot rule. In particular, this means that for this setting the standard VCG mechanism (not taking care of any other-regarding preferences) is truthful.

6   Impact of Altruism

First, we apply our altruism-adjusted VCG mechanism derived in the previous section to two classical problems in mechanism design: bilateral trade and funding a public project. Then, we show that mechanisms that ignore altruism can be converted into ones that do take the altruistic motives of the players into account, reducing the payments that leave the group of participants in the process.

6.1   Bilateral Trade

A buyer is interested in some object and values it at v_b, while some seller has the object and values it at v_s. We want a mechanism such that the players reveal their true preferences. In a mechanism design context, this is modeled as follows: (i) The set of alternatives is $A = \{trade, no\text{-}trade\}$. (ii) The buyer has valuation function v_b defined as $v_b(trade) = v_b$ and $v_b(no\text{-}trade) = 0$. (iii) The seller has valuation function v_s defined as $v_s(trade) = -v_s$ and $v_b(no\text{-}trade) = 0$.

If we require that there are no payments when there is no trade, VCG gives us that if the trade happens, i.e., $v_b \geq v_s$, then we charge the buyer v_s, and the seller gets v_b. But $v_b > v_s$ implies that the mechanism needs to be subsidized.

In contrast, suppose the buyer has an altruism level of $-\alpha_b$ and the seller of α_s, then using the welfare-oriented model, we should charge the buyer $(1+\alpha_b)v_s$ and the seller gets $(1 - \alpha_s)v_b$. Hence, if

$$(1 + \alpha_b)v_s \geq (1 - \alpha_s)v_b,$$

the mechanism runs without the need of subsidizing it.

6.2   Funding a Public Project

In the *public project problem*, a contractor (e.g., a government) considers undertaking a public project (e.g., building a bridge) at a commonly known cost C. Each player $i \in N$ (e.g., citizen) reports a value b_i that the realization of the project is worth to them (not necessarily equal to their private value v_i). Given the bids $\vec{b} = (b_1, \ldots, b_n)$, the contractor determines whether the project is realized and what the contribution $p_i(\vec{b})$ of every player $i \in N$ is. Here the project is realized if and only if it can be *funded* by the players, i.e., $\sum_{i \in N} p_i(\vec{b}) \geq C$.

This models a very realistic situation. It would be desirable that the theory of mechanism design provides us with a mechanism that ensures that the project is undertaken when it should be undertaken, i.e., when the actual value created by the realization of the project is at least C; formally, $\sum_{i \in N} v_i \geq C$. This is precisely what a truthful mechanism maximizing social welfare would achieve. Unfortunately, the only instances of the public project problem that can be solved in the standard mechanism design setting are trivial ones.

Formally, the *public project problem* in a mechanism design context can be defined as follows (after Clarke (1971)): (i) The set of alternatives is $A = \{\text{yes}, \text{no}\}$. (ii) The set of players consists of $N = \{1, \ldots, n\}$ and a special player 0, representing the contractor. (iii) Player $i = 0$ has a singleton valuation set $V_i = \{v_i\}$ with $v_i(\text{yes}) = -C$ for some $C \in \mathbb{R}^+$ and $v_i(\text{no}) = 0$. (iv) Every player $i \in N$ has a valuation set V_i such that for every $v_i \in V_i$ we have $v_i(\text{yes}) = w_i$ for some $w_i \in \mathbb{R}^+$ and $v_i(\text{no}) = 0$. (v) The design objective is the social welfare D^{sw}.

Note that player $i = 0$ is essentially a dummy player as they do not have any choice other than reporting their valuation function truthfully. Also, their valuation is $-C$ (reflecting that the realization of the project incurs a cost to them). In particular, they cannot be asked to contribute anything to the project.

Why Standard Mechanism Design Fails. The VCG mechanism with the Clarke pivot rule is known to be the only truthful mechanism that satisfies individual rationality (given the social welfare design objective); see, e.g., Nisan et al. (2007, Chap. 9). In order to understand how this mechanism determines the payments in the public project problem, we need the following concept: Given the reports $(b_i)_{i \in N}$, a player $i \in N$ is called *pivotal* if $\sum_j b_j \geq C$ but $\sum_{j \neq i} b_j < C$; otherwise, i is *non-pivotal*. In other words, a pivotal player is essential to make the project fundable.

The following proposition characterizes when a project is funded:

Proposition 4 ([25])**.** *Using the VCG mechanism with the Clarke pivot rule, the public project in the standard utility model is funded if and only if*

1. $b_i \geq C$ *for some* $i \in N$ *and* $b_j = 0$ *for all* $j \in N$, $j \neq i$, *or*
2. $\sum_{i \in N} b_i = C$.

As a consequence, a public project is only funded if there is exactly one player who benefits from it, or if there is no benefit at all but just a break-even between the value created and the investment costs incurred.

We next show how altruism helps to escape the above dilemma. More specifically, we consider the omnistic model and use the VCG mechanism with the altruism-adjusted Clarke pivot rule (6) with $c_i = \alpha_i$ for all i.

Proposition 5. *Let* N_p *be the set of pivotal players, and* N_n *the set of non-pivotal players. Using the VCG mechanism with the altruism-adjusted Clarke pivot rule (choosing* $c_i = \alpha_i$ *for all* i)*, the public project in the omnistic model is funded if and only if*

$$\sum_{i \in N_p} \left(C - \sum_{j \neq i} b_j \right) + \sum_{i \in N_n} \frac{\alpha_i}{1 - \alpha_i} \left(\sum_{j \neq i} b_j - C \right) \geq C.$$

What does Proposition 5 tell us? First of all, we see that the project is more likely to be fully funded when it is more profitable for the group to undertake it. For the pivotal players, the higher the contribution of the other players, the higher $C - \sum_{j \neq i} b_j$ and for the non-pivotal players it is clear that the more profitable the project is the higher $\sum_{j \neq i} b_j - C$. This relation is rather satisfying, especially if one compares it with the results for the standard utility model (where, paradoxically, the larger the net benefits of the project are, the less likely it is that it will be funded).

Secondly, we observe that altruism of non-pivotal players *always* has a positive effect on the likelihood of funding the project, and this effect is amplified when the altruism levels of the (non-pivotal) players with small valuation are large. This effect becomes even more apparent if one considers uniform altruism levels ($\alpha_i = \alpha$ for all i) and only non-pivotal players. The condition of Proposition 5 simplifies to

$$\alpha \left(\sum_{j \in N} b_j - C \right) \geq \frac{C}{n - 1}.$$

Also, note that the number of players n is positively related to the likelihood of funding the project.

6.3   Minimizing Payments

In this section, we assume that all other-regarding preferences are payment independent. Given a mechanism where we do not take altruism into account but where players are actually altruistic, we will transform it into a mechanism with a smaller total payment. Consider welfare-oriented other-regarding preferences. Let every player i have an altruism level of α_i. Define $\alpha = \min_i \alpha_i$. Suppose we have some non-deficit mechanism satisfying the requirements of Theorem 2 with $\gamma = 1$ without taking the other-regarding preferences into account, i.e., $g_i = 0$ (one can think of standard VCG). Hence, we have $h_i(\vec{b}_{-i})$ such that for $p_i(v) = h_i(\vec{b}_{-i}) - D_{-i}(\vec{b}_{-i}, f(\vec{b}))$ the mechanism is non-deficit. Lemma 1 implies that

$$h_i(\vec{b}_{-i}) \geq \sup_{b_i'} \sum_j D_{-j}(\vec{b}_{-j}', f(\vec{b}')) - \sum_{j \neq i} h_j(\vec{b}_{-i}'). \tag{7}$$

Let $g_i(\vec{b}_{-i}(f(\vec{b}))) = \alpha_i \sum_{j \neq i} b_j(f(\vec{b}))$. And let $g_i'(\vec{b}_{-i}(f(\vec{b}))) = \alpha \sum_{j \neq i} b_j(f(\vec{b}))$. First note that $g_i'(\vec{b}_{-i}(f(\vec{b}))) = \alpha \cdot D_{-i}(\vec{b}_{-i}, f(\vec{b}))$ and also observe that by choice of α it holds that $g_i'(\vec{b}_{-i}(f(\vec{b}))) \leq g_i(\vec{b}_{-i}(f(\vec{b})))$. This will allow us to later invoke Proposition 3.

We manipulate Eq. (7) by multiplying both sides by $(1 - \alpha)$

$$(1 - \alpha)h_i(\vec{b}_{-i}) \geq \sup_{b_i'} \sum_j (1 - \alpha)D_{-j}(\vec{b}_{-j}', f(\vec{b}')) - \sum_{j \neq i}(1 - \alpha)h_j(\vec{b}_{-i}')$$

$$= \sup_{b_i'} \sum_j D_{-j}(\vec{b}_{-j}', f(\vec{b}')) - g_j'(\vec{b}_{-j}'(f(\vec{b}'))) - \sum_{j \neq i}(1 - \alpha)h_j(\vec{b}_{-i}').$$

Thus, substituting $(1 - \alpha)h_i$ by h_i', shows that h_i' satisfies Lemma 1 and so the mechanism with respect to h_i' is non-deficit.

Because $g_i' \leq g_i$ Proposition 3 tells us that our mechanism is also IR and truthfulness follows from Theorem 2.

We take a look at the payments. First, observe that

$$p_i'(\vec{b}) = h_i'(\vec{b}_{-i}) + g_j'(\vec{b}_{-i}(f(\vec{b}))) - D_{-j}(\vec{b}_{-i}, f(\vec{b}))$$

$$= (1 - \alpha)h_i(\vec{b}_{-i}) - (1 - \alpha)D_{-j}(\vec{b}_{-i}, f(\vec{b})) = (1 - \alpha)p_i(\vec{b}).$$

And hence if $\alpha > 0$, every player pays or receives a factor $(1 - \alpha)$ less, and also the total payment $\sum_i p_i'(\vec{b}) = (1 - \alpha) \sum_{-i} p_i(\vec{b})$ is reduced by a factor $(1 - \alpha)$.

Example 1 (Multi-Unit Auction). Consider a multi-unit auction with k identical goods. Each player can win at most 1 item.

Standard VCG without other-regarding preferences charges the highest losing bid to all players. We can capture this in the welfare-oriented model with the classical social welfare objective by setting $\alpha_i = 0$ for all $i \in N$ and $h_i(\vec{b}_{-i}) = \sum_{j=1}^k [\vec{b}_{-i}]_j$, where $[\vec{x}]_j$ denotes the j-th highest entry in $\vec{x}$. Let $\alpha = \min_{i \in N} \alpha_i$

where α_i is the altruism level of player i. If we require NPT, we can take $c_i = 0$ for all i to minimize payments and obtain

$$h_i(\vec{b}_{-i}) = (1 - \alpha) \sum_{j=1}^{k} [\vec{b}_{-i}]_j.$$

As also the second part of the payment (see Table 1) is multiplied by $(1 - \alpha)$ the total payments are a factor $(1 - \alpha)$ lower.

Not insisting on NPT (but still requiring the mechanism to be non-deficit) allows us to do better. Already in the standard VCG setting we can apply the Bailey-Cavallo redistribution function [3,7]. This corresponds to $h_i(\vec{b}_{-i}) = \sum_{j=1}^{k} [\vec{b}_{-i}]_j - \frac{k}{n}[\vec{b}_{-i}]_{k+1}$, significantly reducing the sum of payments to $\sum_i \vec{p}_i(\vec{b}) = \sum_{j=1}^{k} [\vec{b}]_j - k \cdot [\vec{b}]_{k+1}$. Applying the theory from this subsection we know that we can take

$$h_i(\vec{b}_{-i}) = (1 - \alpha)\left(\sum_{j=1}^{k} [\vec{b}_{-i}]_j - \frac{k}{n}[\vec{b}_{-i}]_{k+1} \right).$$

and still have a non-deficit, individually rational, and truthful mechanism saving a factor $(1 - \alpha)$ on the payments:

$$\sum_{i \in N} \vec{p}_i(\vec{b}) = (1 - \alpha)\left(\sum_{j=1}^{k} [\vec{b}]_j - k \cdot [\vec{b}]_{k+1} \right).$$

It is even true that the last mechanism is individually undominated. Taking $b_i' = [\vec{b}_{-i}]_{k+1}$ in the supremum of Eq. (5) will result in equality. For example for $k = 1$ and $i = 1$ we have $\sum_j D_{-j}(\vec{b}_{-1}, [\vec{b}_{-1}]_2) = (1 - \alpha)(n - 1)[\vec{b}_{-1}]_1$ and $\sum_{j \neq 1} h_j(\vec{b}_{-j}') = (1 - \alpha)\left((n - 2)[\vec{b}_{-j}']_1 + \frac{[\vec{b}_{-j}']_2}{n}\right)$. Note that $[\vec{b}_{-j}']_1 = [\vec{b}_{-1}]_1$ and $[\vec{b}_{-j}']_2 = [\vec{b}_{-1}]_2$. Taking the difference is equal to $h_1(\vec{b}_{-1})$. This equality can be verified for all k and i.

7   Conclusion

We introduced a general utility model that incorporates other-regarding preferences and characterized the respective truthful mechanisms. We also proposed two specific altruism models and showed that they can be used to explain how the classic mechanism design problems of bilateral trade and public project become feasible. Clearly, several other other-regarding preferences are conceivable, and we hope that our framework provides an easy tool to come up with truthful mechanisms for such alternative settings. By extending the results of Guo et al. [16], we derived a characterization of individually undominated mechanisms in our model. Moreover, we showed that any VCG mechanism not taking altruism into account can be converted into a truthful mechanism that does take altruism into account with lower payments.

An interesting question for future work is to investigate whether one can come up with mechanisms that are strongly budget-balanced. As a starting point, one might want to exploit the insights obtained in [8] to leverage the flexibility that altruism provides for this purpose. Finally, on a conceptual level, we hope there will be more research into how altruism can be incorporated into mechanism design.

Acknowledgements. Part of this work was done when Sjir Hoeijmakers was at CWI.

References

1. Andreoni, J., Miller, J.: Giving according to GARP: an experimental test of the consistency of preferences for altruism. Econometrica **70**(2), 737–753 (2002)
2. Apt, K.R., Schäfer, G.: Selfishness level of strategic games. J. Artif. Intell. Res. **49**, 207–240 (2014)
3. Bailey, M.J.: The demand revealing process: to distribute the surplus. Public Choice **91**(2), 107–126 (1997)
4. Brandt, F., Weiß, G.: Antisocial agents and Vickrey auctions. In: Meyer, J.-J.C., Tambe, M. (eds.) ATAL 2001. LNCS (LNAI), vol. 2333, pp. 335–347. Springer, Heidelberg (2002). https://doi.org/10.1007/3-540-45448-9_25
5. Buehler, R., et al.: The price of civil society. In: Chen, N., Elkind, E., Koutsoupias, E. (eds.) WINE 2011. LNCS, vol. 7090, pp. 375–382. Springer, Heidelberg (2011). https://doi.org/10.1007/978-3-642-25510-6_32
6. Caragiannis, I., Kaklamanis, C., Kanellopoulos, P., Kyropoulou, M., Papaioannou, E.: The impact of altruism on the efficiency of atomic congestion games. In: Wirsing, M., Hofmann, M., Rauschmayer, A. (eds.) TGC 2010. LNCS, vol. 6084, pp. 172–188. Springer, Heidelberg (2010). https://doi.org/10.1007/978-3-642-15640-3_12
7. Cavallo, R.: Optimal decision-making with minimal waste: strategyproof redistribution of VCG payments. In: Proceedings of the Fifth International Joint Conference on Autonomous Agents and Multiagent Systems, pp. 882–889 (2006)
8. Cavallo, R.: Efficient auctions with altruism (2012). http://www.eecs.harvard.edu/cavallo/papers/cavallo-altru.pdf
9. Charness, G., Rabin, M.: Understanding social preferences with simple tests. Q. J. Econ. **117**(3), 817–869 (2002)
10. Chen, P.-A., de Keijzer, B., Kempe, D., Schäfer, G.: The robust price of anarchy of altruistic games. In: Chen, N., Elkind, E., Koutsoupias, E. (eds.) WINE 2011. LNCS, vol. 7090, pp. 383–390. Springer, Heidelberg (2011). https://doi.org/10.1007/978-3-642-25510-6_33
11. Clarke, E.H.: Multipart pricing of public goods. Public Choice 17–33 (1971)
12. De Marco, G., Morgan, J.: Altruistic behavior and correlated equilibrium selection. Int. Game Theory Rev. **13**(04), 363–381 (2011)
13. Fehr, E., Fischbacher, U.: Why social preferences matter-the impact of non-selfish motives on competition, cooperation and incentives. Econ. J. **112**(478), C1–C33 (2002)
14. Fehr, E., Schmidt, K.M.: A theory of fairness, competition, and cooperation. Q. J. Econ. **114**(3), 817–868 (1999)
15. Groves, T.: Incentives in teams. Econometrica: J. Econometric Soc. 617–631 (1973)

16. Guo, M., Markakis, V., Apt, K., Conitzer, V.: Undominated groves mechanisms. J. Artif. Intell. Res. **46**, 129–163 (2013)
17. Guo, M., Conitzer, V.: Worst-case optimal redistribution of VCG payments in multi-unit auctions. Games Econom. Behav. **67**(1), 69–98 (2009)
18. Guo, M., Conitzer, V.: Optimal-in-expectation redistribution mechanisms. Artif. Intell. **174**(5–6), 363–381 (2010)
19. Kahneman, D.: Thinking, Fast and Slow. Macmillan (2011)
20. Kozlovskaya, M., Nicolò, A.: Public good provision mechanisms and reciprocity. J. Econ. Behav. Organ. **167**, 235–244 (2019)
21. Kucuksenel, S.: Behavioral mechanism design. J. Public Econ. Theory **14**(5), 767–789 (2012)
22. Mas-Colell, A., Whinston, M.D., Green, J.R., et al.: Microeconomic Theory, vol. 1. Oxford University Press, New York (1995)
23. Moulin, H.: Almost budget-balanced VCG mechanisms to assign multiple objects. J. Econ. Theory **144**(1), 96–119 (2009)
24. Myerson, R.B., Satterthwaite, M.A.: Efficient mechanisms for bilateral trading. J. Econ. Theory **29**(2), 265–281 (1983)
25. Nisan, N., Roughgarden, T., Tardos, E., Vazirani, V.: Algorithmic Game Theory. Cambridge University Press, Cambridge (2007)
26. Rahn, M., Schäfer, G.: Bounding the inefficiency of altruism through social contribution games. In: Chen, Y., Immorlica, N. (eds.) WINE 2013. LNCS, vol. 8289, pp. 391–404. Springer, Heidelberg (2013). https://doi.org/10.1007/978-3-642-45046-4_32
27. Tang, P., Sandholm, T.: Optimal auctions for spiteful bidders. In: Twenty-Sixth AAAI Conference on Artificial Intelligence (2012)
28. Vickrey, W.: Counterspeculation, auctions, and competitive sealed tenders. J. Financ. **16**(1), 8–37 (1961)

Lookahead Auctions with Pooling

Michal Feldman[1,3], Nick Gravin[2], Zhihao Gavin Tang[2(✉)], and Almog Wald[1]

[1] Tel Aviv University, Tel Aviv, Israel
michal.feldman@cs.tau.ac.il
[2] ITCS, Shanghai University of Finance and Economics, Shanghai, China
{nikolai,tang.zhihao}@mail.shufe.edu.cn
[3] Microsoft Research, Herzliya, Israel

Abstract. A Lookahead Auction (LA), introduced by Ronen, is an auction format for the sale of a single item among multiple buyers, which is considered simpler and more fair than the optimal auction. Indeed, it anonymously selects a provisional winner by a symmetric ascending-price process, and only then uses a personalized posted price. A LA auction extracts at least 1/2 of the optimal revenue, even under a correlated value distribution. This bound is tight, even for 2 buyers with independent values. We introduce a natural extension of LA, called *lookahead with pooling* (LAP). A LAP auction proceeds as LA, with one difference: it allows the seller to *pool* together a range of values during the ascending-price stage, and treat them the same; thus, it preserves the simplicity and fairness of LA. Our main result is that this simple pooling operation improves the revenue guarantees for independent buyers from 1/2 to 4/7 of the optimal revenue. We also give a complementary negative result, showing that for arbitrary correlated priors LAP cannot do better than 1/2 approximation.

Keywords: Auction Design · Revenue Maximization · Lookahead Auctions

1 Introduction

Optimal auction design is important both theoretically and practically, and has been extensively studied in both economics and computer science over the last few decades [7]. The scenario of a single item auction is the most fundamental setting, and serves as the basis for the design and analysis of auctions [9].

In a single item auction, an item is sold to one of n bidders. Each bidder has a value v_i drawn from an underlying distribution F_i. The value v_i is i's private information, while F_i is known to all. A common way to sell items is through auctions. An auction receives as input the bidder values, and determines an allocation rule (who gets the item) and a payment rule (how much each bidder pays) based on the reported values. The utility of a bidder is her value for the item (if she wins) minus the payment she makes.

An auction is *dominant-strategy incentive compatible* (DSIC) if it is in the best interest of every bidder to bid her true value v_i, for any value profile of the

© The Author(s), under exclusive license to Springer Nature Switzerland AG 2022
P. Kanellopoulos et al. (Eds.): SAGT 2022, LNCS 13584, pp. 60–77, 2022.
https://doi.org/10.1007/978-3-031-15714-1_4

other bidders. An auction is *individually rational* (IR) if the utility of all bidders is non-negative. The seller's *revenue* is the payment collected by the auction. An auction is said to be optimal if it maximizes the expected revenue among all DSIC and IR mechanisms.

Myerson [9] gave a full characterization of the revenue-optimal auction in the case where agent values are independent. Specifically, he showed that an auction is DSIC if and only if its allocation rule is monotone (i.e., the allocation of bidder i is non-decreasing in her value), and the payment is then determined uniquely (up to normalization) by the allocation rule. Given value v_i drawn from F_i, the *virtual value* of bidder i is defined as $\varphi_i(v_i) = v_i - \frac{1-F_i(v_i)}{f_i(v_i)}$, where f_i is the derivative of F_i. The main observation of [9] is that maximizing the expected revenue is equivalent to maximizing the *virtual welfare*, i.e., the sum of virtual values.

The simplest case is one where bidder values are identically and independently distributed according to a *regular* distribution, meaning that the virtual value is monotonically non-decreasing in the value. In this case, the optimal auction is essentially a second-price auction with a reserve price. However, as we move slightly beyond this scenario, the optimal auction becomes less intuitive and less natural. For example, if valuations are non-identically distributed, then the winner may not necessarily be the bidder who placed the highest bid. Moreover, for non-regular distributions, some ironing process takes place, which further complicates the auction from a bidder's perspective.

Thus, the optimal auction suffers from some undesirable properties, including asymmetry among bidders and lack of simplicity, which makes it hard to apply in practice. Indeed, even in the simplest case of a single-item auction, practical applications tend to prefer simpler and more natural auction formats over the optimal auction. This observation has given rise to a body of literature known as "simple versus optimal auctions" [8] that studies the trade offs between simplicity and optimality in auction design. The goal is to design simple auctions that provide good approximation guarantees to the optimal revenue.

Lookahead Auctions. The *lookahead* (LA) auction is a simple auction format that has been introduced by Ronen [11]. Ronen showed that the LA auction format gives at least a half of the optimal revenue, even if agent values are distributed according to a correlated joint distribution (i.e., where distributions are not independent, in contrast to the setting studied by Myerson).

In a LA auction, the item can only go to the highest-value bidder i^*, but this bidder does not always win the item. Instead, she is offered the item for a price that equals the revenue-optimal price for the distribution F_{i^*}, given the bids of all other bidders and the fact that i^* has the highest value, and buys it if her value exceeds the price.

The LA auction can equivalently be described as follows: increase the price continuously until a single agent remains. Then, sell the item to the remaining bidder at a price that depends only on the non-top bidders. This is a natural "ascending price" process, which is common in practical auctions. One can easily observe that this auction is DSIC. Indeed, non-top bidders are never allocated, thus have no incentive to lie; and the top bidder is offered a price that does not depend on her bid, thus has no incentive to lie either. Clearly, it is also IR since the provisional winner buys the item only if her value exceeds the price.

Moreover, unlike the optimal auction, which may treat different bidders very differently, the LA auction may be perceived as more fair. Indeed, the process of identifying the provisional winner is symmetric; differential treatment is applied only for that bidder and only for determining the price. See [4] for further discussion on symmetry and discrimination in auctions.

The $1/2$ approximation provided by the LA auction format is tight, even for independent values. Namely, there exists an instance with two independently distributed bidders where no LA auction gives more than half of the optimal revenue. Improvements are possible by a variant of the LA auction called the k-LA auction [2,5,11], which finds the optimal revenue that can be obtained by the top k bidders (see more on this in Sect. 1.2).

A clear advantage of the LA auction is its simplicity. As it turns out, however, LA entails a revenue loss that may account for up to 50% of the optimal revenue. The question that leads us in this paper is whether there is a different way to trade off simplicity for optimality, in a way that would give better revenue guarantees.

To this end, we introduce a variant of the LA auction, which we call *lookahead with pooling* (LAP). LAP is essentially a LA auction with the option of "pooling" some types together. In particular, we allow the mechanism to pool together an interval of values and treat them as the same type. I.e., the mechanism is allowed to allocate the item to any of the bidders within the same interval, similar to ironing in the Myerson's auction when it is applied to a single bidder. LAP preserves many of the merits of LA, including simplicity and fairness, while providing better approximation guarantees. In particular, while LA cannot give a better approximation than $1/2$, even for a simple scenario with two independent bidders, LAP gives a better approximation for any number of independent bidders.

The following example demonstrates how pooling works, and gives some intuition as to how it increases the revenue compared to LA.

Example 1. Consider a setting with 2 bidders, where $v_1 = 1$, and

$$v_2 = \begin{cases} 1 + \varepsilon, & \text{with probability } 1 - \varepsilon \\ 1/\varepsilon, & \text{otherwise} \end{cases}$$

The optimal revenue is 2, which is obtained by offering a price of $1/\varepsilon$ to bidder 2, and offering a price of 1 to bidder 1 in case bidder 2 rejects. The maximum revenue that can be obtained by LA is $1 + \varepsilon$, since LA always sells to bidder 2 and $v \cdot \mathbf{Pr}[v_2 \geq v] \leq 1 + \varepsilon$ for every v. However, LAP can do better by pooling together the interval $[1, 1/\varepsilon]$. I.e., we do not differentiate different values within the interval of $[1, 1/\varepsilon]$. One can also interpret it as a discrete jump of the "ascending price" from 1 to $1/\varepsilon$. By doing so, the first bidder must drop after the price jump. If the second bidder also drops, our mechanism sells the item at a price of 1 to a random uniformly chosen bidder; if the second bidder survives, our mechanism sells the item at a price of $\frac{1+\varepsilon}{2\varepsilon}$. The prices are set to guarantee the truthfulness of our mechanism. See Sect. 2 for a more detailed discussion. In summary, the seller's revenue is 1 with probability $1 - \varepsilon$ and $\frac{1+\varepsilon}{2\varepsilon}$ with probability ε, giving a revenue of $1.5 - \varepsilon/2$. One can verify that this is the optimal LAP. This example also shows that LAP cannot give a better approximation than 3/4, even for settings with two independent bidders.

1.1   Our Results

Our main result is an improved bound on the approximation ratio of LAP auctions for the case of independent bidders.

Theorem: For any setting with an arbitrary number of independent bidders, LAP achieves a $\frac{4}{7}$-approximation to the optimal revenue.

Interestingly, the LAP auction that provides this guarantee is a special case of 2-LA (i.e., k-LA for $k = 2$), which exhibits more symmetry than a general 2-LA. (In general, LAP may not be k-LA, it just so happens that the LAP we use adheres to a 2-LA format.) We complement our main result with a negative result, showing that for correlated values, LAP does not improve over the approximation ratio achievable by LA, namely 1/2.

Theorem: There exists an instance with two correlated bidders, where no LAP mechanism achieves better than $\frac{1}{2} + o(1)$ approximation to the optimal revenue.

1.2   Related Work

Dobzinski, Fu and Kleinberg [5] extended the lookahead auction to k-lookahead auctions for correlated bidders, and proved an approximation ratio of $\frac{2k-1}{3k-1}$. Subsequently, Chen, Hu, Lu and Wang [2] improved the approximation ratio to $\frac{e^{1-1/k}}{e^{1-1/k}+1}$. Dobzinski and Uziely [6] showed that any DSIC single-item auction that is forbidden to allocate item to the lowest bidder has a constant factor gap of $1 - \frac{1}{e}$ compared to the optimal auction, even when the number of bidders n goes to infinity. Their result implies that k-lookahead auctions with $k \to \infty$ does not approach the revenue of the optimal auction. Bei, Gravin, Lu and Tang [1] considered single-item auction in the correlation robust framework. Among other auction formats, they study lookahead auctions and obtain computational and approximation results in the correlation-robust framework.

While single-item auctions with independent values are well understood, scenarios with correlated values are much less understood. Cremer and McLean [3] introduce a mechanism that extracts full surplus in revenue for settings with a correlated joint distribution. However, this auction is considered highly non-practical, and satisfies only *interim* IR, as opposed to ex-post IR, meaning that IR holds only in expectation over others' values.

Papadimitriou and Pierrakos [10] study the computational complexity of optimal deterministic single-item auctions with a general joint prior distribution. They provide an inapproximability result for $n \geq 3$ bidders (and an efficient auction for 2 bidders). This is another indication of the complexity of correlated distributions.

2 Preliminaries

A set N of n potential buyers participate in a *single item* auction. Each buyer $i \in N$ has a private value v_i for obtaining the item. By the revelation principle, we restrict our attention to truthful sealed bid auctions: that is, each bidder i submits a sealed bid b_i to the auctioneer who upon receiving all bids $\mathbf{b} = (b_1, \ldots, b_n)$ decides on the allocation $\mathbf{x}(\mathbf{b}) = (x_1, \ldots, x_n)$ and payments $\mathbf{p}(\mathbf{b}) = (p_1, \ldots, p_n)$. Each allocation function $x_i(\mathbf{b}) \in [0,1]$ indicated the probability that bidder i gets the item and since at most one bidder can win the item, we have $\sum_{i \in N} x_i(\mathbf{b}) \leq 1$.

Throughout most of the paper, we assume that all values v_i are *independently* drawn from *known* prior distributions $v_i \sim F_i$ and $\mathbf{v} = (v_1, \ldots, v_n) \sim \mathbf{F} = F_1 \times \ldots \times F_n$. We assume that each F_i is a continuous distribution supported on a bounded interval $[0, B]$. We use F_i to refer to the cumulative distribution function (CDF) of the distribution $F_i(t) = \mathbf{Pr}_{v_i}[v_i \leq t]$ and use $f_i(t)$ to denote its probability density function at t. We will also consider the case of interdependent prior $\mathbf{F}$ in which case we write $\mathbf{v} \sim \mathbf{F}$.

We are interested in dominant-strategy incentive compatible (DSIC) and individually rational (IR) mechanisms. As standard, we assume that bidders maximize their *quasi-linear* utility $u_i(v_i, \mathbf{b}) = v_i \cdot x_i(\mathbf{b}) - p_i(\mathbf{b})$. A mechanism is DSIC if for every bidder i, valuation profile $\mathbf{v}$ and a deviation v_i' of bidder i

$$u_i(v_i, (\mathbf{v}_{-i}, v_i)) = v_i \cdot x_i(\mathbf{v}) - p_i(\mathbf{v}) \geq u_i(v_i, (\mathbf{v}_{-i}, v_i')) = \qquad \text{(DSIC)}$$
$$v_i \cdot x_i(\mathbf{v}_{-i}, v_i') - p_i(\mathbf{v}_{-i}, v_i'),$$

where we use standard notation $\mathbf{v}_{-i} = (v_1, \ldots, v_{i-1}, v_{i+1}, \ldots, v_n)$ and we similarly denote $\mathbf{b}_{-i} = (b_1, \ldots, b_{i-1}, b_{i+1}, \ldots, b_n)$. A mechanism is IR if for every bidder i and valuation profile $\mathbf{v}$,

$$u_i(v_i, \mathbf{v}) = v_i \cdot x_i(\mathbf{v}) - p_i(\mathbf{v}) \geq 0 \qquad \text{(IR)}$$

Our goal is to maximize the expected revenue $\text{Rev} \overset{\text{def}}{=} \mathbf{E}_{\mathbf{v}}[\sum_{i \in N} p_i(\mathbf{v})]$ of the seller (auctioneer) over truthful mechanisms (DSIC + IR).

Myerson's Lemma. Myerson [9] characterized DSIC mechanisms and described revenue maximizing auction for independent prior distribution[1] $\mathbf{F}$:

---

[1] Myerson's results hold even for a weaker requirement of Bayesian Incentive Compatibility (BIC) for the agents when the prior distributions are independent.

- A mechanism $(\mathbf{x}, \mathbf{p})$ is DSIC if and only if
  (a) $x_i(v_i, \mathbf{v}_{-i})$ is monotonically non-decreasing in v_i for each bidder i and valuations $\mathbf{v}_{-i}$.
  (b) The payment is fully determined by the allocation rule, and is given by

$$p_i(\mathbf{v}) = v_i \cdot x_i(\mathbf{v}) - \int_0^{v_i} z \cdot x_i(z, \mathbf{v}_{-i}) \, dz.$$

- The optimal mechanism selects the bidder with maximal non-negative virtual value $\varphi_i(v_i)$ and the expected revenue is

$$\mathrm{OPT} = \mathbf{E}_\mathbf{v} \left[\max_{i \in N} (\varphi_i^+(v_i)) \right],$$

where $\varphi_i^+(v_i) \stackrel{\text{def}}{=} \max\{\varphi_i(v_i), 0\}$ and $\varphi_i(v_i) \stackrel{\text{def}}{=} v_i - \frac{1 - F_i(v_i)}{f_i(v_i)}$ is the virtual value for *regular* distribution F_i (for irregular distribution F_i an ironed virtual value is used instead).

A distribution F is called *regular* if the virtual value function $\varphi_i(v_i)$ is non-decreasing in v_i. For the case of irregular distribution F, Myerson defined an *ironing* procedure on the *revenue curves* that allows to transform irregular distribution into a regular one.

Revenue Curves and Ironing. Consider a bidder with value drawn from distribution F. Given a price p, the buyer buys the item with probability $1 - F(p)$, leading to an expected revenue of $p \cdot (1 - F(p))$. Let $q(p) \stackrel{\text{def}}{=} 1 - F(p)$ denote the selling probability at price p, and call it the *quantile* of p. It is convenient to plot the revenue in quantile space, i.e., as a function of the quantile $q \in [0, 1]$. We get $R(q) = q \cdot F^{-1}(1 - q)$ which is called the *revenue curve* of F. In other words, $R(q)$ is the revenue of a selling strategy that sells with ex-ante probability q. Without loss of generality, one may assume that $R(0) = R(1) = 0$. The corresponding value of a quantile q is $v(q) = F^{-1}(1 - q)$ and the derivative of $R(q)$ at q is the virtual value $\varphi(v) = v - \frac{1 - F(v)}{f(v)}$ of v. Thus, for regular distributions, the revenue curve is concave. For irregular distributions we additionally apply ironing procedure to the revenue curve.

One way to achieve an ex-ante selling probability of q is to set a price $p = F^{-1}(1 - q)$. However, achieving an ex-ante selling probability q is possible also by randomizing over different prices. For example, we may randomize between two quantiles q_1 and q_2, choosing the price corresponding to q_1 with probability α, and the price corresponding to q_2 with probability $1 - \alpha$. Choosing q_1, q_2, α such that $\alpha \cdot q_1 + (1 - \alpha) \cdot q_2 = q$ also gives quantile q. The revenue obtained by this randomized pricing is $\alpha \cdot R(q_1) + (1 - \alpha) \cdot R(q_2)$.

If F is a regular distribution, then the revenue curve $R(q)$ is concave, and the maximum possible revenue for an ex-ante selling probability q is achieved by a deterministic price of $p = F^{-1}(1 - q)$.

If, however, F is irregular, then $R(q)$ is not a concave function. Let $\bar{R}(q)$ denote the maximum revenue achievable for a quantile q (possibly by a random pricing). $\bar{R}(q)$ corresponds to the concave envelope of the revenue curve $R(q) = q \cdot F^{-1}(1-q)$. I.e., $\bar{R}(q) = \max_{\alpha, q_1, q_2}\{\alpha \cdot R(q_1) + (1-\alpha)R(q_2) \mid \alpha \cdot q_1 + (1-\alpha) \cdot q_2 = q\}$. The *ironed virtual value* is defined as the derivative of the concave function $\bar{R}(q)$ at q (similar to the virtual value in the regular case, which is equal to the derivative of $R(q)$ at q). Note that the concave envelope $\bar{R}(q)$ of a single-parameter function $R(q)$ uses at most 2 points of $R(q)$: we find a few disjoint intervals $[a_1, b_1], \ldots, [a_k, b_k]$ and let $\bar{R}(q)$ be the linear combination of the endpoints $(a_j, R(a_j)), (b_j, R(b_j))$ for the region $q \in [a_j, b_j]$; and $\bar{R}(q) = R(q)$ for all other q. Thus the ironed virtual value along each such interval $[a_j, b_j]$ is a constant (the derivative of a linear function $\bar{R}(q)$). This means that for an irregular distribution $F_i = F$ for bidder i, all values $v_i \in [p(a_j), p(b_j)]$ within an ironed interval $q \in [a_j, b_j]$ are treated in the same way by the revenue optimal auction.

Ex-ante Optimal Revenue. A common way to derive an upper bound on the optimal revenue is by the *ex-ante* relaxation. Given concave revenue curves $R_1, \ldots, R_n$ (of regular distributions, or ironed ones $\bar{R}_1, \ldots, \bar{R}_n$), the ex-ante optimal revenue is given by the following program (referred to as the ex-ante program):

$$\max_{\mathbf{x}} \sum_{i \in N} R_i(x_i) \qquad \text{s.t.} \sum_{i \in N} x_i \leq 1, \quad \forall i \in N \ x_i \geq 0$$

Let $\mathbf{x}^* = (x_1^*, \ldots, x_n^*)$ denote the optimal solution to this program. The optimal ex-ante revenue is an upper bound on the optimal revenue. We refer the reader to [8] for more details.

Lookahead Auctions. A Lookahead Auction (LA) introduced by Ronen [11] is a DSIC and IR mechanism that can only allocate to the highest bidder. Every such auction consists of two stages: (i) the seller starts with a $c = 0$ cutoff price and keeps continuously increasing it until all but one bidder i^* drop from the competition, (ii) once only i^* remains active, the seller sets a final take-it-or-leave price $p(i^*, \mathbf{v}_{-i^*}) \geq c$ for i^*. The best LA achieves $1/2$-approximation (i.e., at least a half of the optimal revenue), even for the case of correlated prior distribution $\mathbf{F}$, and the approximation ratio $1/2$ is tight even for independent priors $\mathbf{F} = \prod_{i \in N} F_i$. The following LA maximizes revenue for the case of independent priors.

Definition 1 (Lookahead auction (LA)). *Continuously and uniformly raise the cutoff price c for all bidders $i \in N$ until only one bidder i remains with $v_i \geq c$. Then, offer a final take-it-or-leave price $p \geq c$ to bidder i based on F_i and c, where the price p is chosen to maximize the expected revenue $p = \text{argmax}_{r \geq c}(r \cdot \mathbf{Pr}[v_i \geq r \mid v_i \geq c])$.*

We next introduce a new variant of LA, called *lookahead with pooling* (LAP). Similar to the treatment of irregular distributions in Myerson's auction, we consider the effect of ironing on the LA auction format. Namely, we allow the auctioneer, in addition to the standard continuous increments, to perform discrete jumps of the cutoff price c from some c^o to some $c^+ > c^o$ (i.e., *pool together* all types $v \in [c^o, c^+)$) at any moment of the auction. Consider such a jump, and let S denote the set of currently active bidders who (simultaneously) drop as a result of this jump. If S contains all currently active bidders, then the item is allocated to a random bidder $i \in S$ for a price of $p_i = c^o$. If all but one active bidder i^* drop, then bidder i^* is offered a *menu* of two options: (i) get the item $x_{i^*} = 1$ at a high price $p_i = p \cdot \frac{|S|-1}{|S|} + c^o \cdot \frac{1}{|S|}$, where $p = \mathrm{argmax}_{r \geq c^+}(r \cdot \mathbf{Pr}[v_i \geq r \mid v_i \geq c^+])$, or (ii) double back on the high bid (claim $c^o \leq v_{i^*} < c^+$) and get $x_{i^*} = \frac{1}{|S|}$ (S is the set of active bidders at $c = c^o$) at a low price of $p_i = c^o$; note that the other bidders $i \in S$ get nothing $x_i = 0$ in this case. This family is called lookahead with pooling (LAP).

We give below the formal definition of LAP for the general case of possibly correlated prior distribution. Similarly to LA, a LAP auction maintains a cutoff price c at every point in time, and raises it as the auction proceeds.

Definition 2 (Lookahead auction with Pooling (LAP)). *At each point in time, raise the cutoff price c uniformly for all bidders in one of two possible ways: (a) continuously, as in LA; or (b) in a discrete jump from the current cutoff c^o to some $c^+ > c^o$, as long as the set of remaining buyers $S(c) \overset{def}{=} \{i \mid v_i \geq c\}$ consists of more than one bidder, i.e., $|S(c)| \geq 2$. Finally, after the last increment, either no bidder, or a single bidder accepts the cutoff price. If the last remaining bidder i was determined in a continuous phase (a) of raising c, then $\{i\} = S(c)$ and we proceed as in LA (offer i the revenue maximizing take-it-or-leave price $p = \mathrm{argmax}_{r \geq c}(r \cdot \mathbf{Pr}[v_i \geq r \mid v_i \geq c])$). If we stop after a discrete jump (b) from c^o to $c^+ > c^o$ (i.e., $|S(c^+)| \leq 1$), then*

- *If $S(c^+) = \emptyset$, then the item is sold to a bidder i chosen uniformly at random from $S(c^o)$ at a price c^o (i.e., for every $i \in S(c^o)$ $x_i = \frac{1}{|S(c^o)|}, p_i = x_i \cdot c^o = \frac{c^o}{|S(c^o)|}$).*
- *If $|S(c^+)| = 1$, then the single bidder i in $S(c^+)$ may choose one of the following two options:*
  1. *Get the item at a price $p_i = c^o \cdot x_i$ with probability $x_i = \frac{1}{|S(c^o)|}$. (As if $S(c^+) = \emptyset$.)*
  2. *Get the item with probability $x_i = 1$ at a price $p_i = \frac{1}{|S(c^o)|} \cdot c^o + \frac{|S(c^o)|-1}{|S(c^o)|} \cdot r$, where $r = \mathrm{argmax}_{t \geq c^+} (t \cdot \mathbf{Pr_v}[v_i \geq t \mid v_i \geq c^+, \mathbf{v}_{-i}])$.[2]*

For the case of independent prior $\mathbf{F} = \prod_{i \in N} F_i$, we have

$$r = \underset{t \geq c^+}{\mathrm{argmax}} \left(t \cdot \mathbf{Pr}\left[v_i \geq t \mid v_i \geq c^+\right] \right).$$

The following theorem shows that LAP is truthful. The proof is deferred to Appendix A.

Theorem 1. *Any LAP auction is DSIC and IR.*

---

[2] Equivalent description: post a random take-it-or-leave price c^o to i with probability $\frac{1}{|S(c^o)|}$, with remaining probability post the revenue maximizing price r to i for the posterior distribution of v_i given $\mathbf{v}_{-i}$ and that $v_i \geq c^+$.

3   **LAP** for Independent Valuations

In this section we prove our main result (Theorem 2). We first prove the theorem under the assumption that all value distributions F_i are regular. In Subsect. 3.1, we show how to extend this result to irregular distributions.

Theorem 2. *For any instance with (any number of) independent bidders, LAP achieves a $\frac{4}{7}$-approximation to the optimal revenue.*

Proof. To prove our main theorem, we first consider a hypothetical scenario with two real bidders and one dummy bidder. The dummy bidder has a known value v, and the two real bidders have independent values $v_1, v_2 \geq v$. This scenario naturally appears if we keep continuously increasing the cutoff price c in a LAP until exactly two bidders remain in $S(v) = \{i : v_i \geq v\}$. In this case, the LAP can only sell to the two "real" bidders and it also has to adhere to the LAP format. On the other hand, it is natural to upper bound the benchmark (the optimal mechanism for all n bidders) with the optimal mechanism that can allocate to the two real bidders and also the dummy bidder with deterministic value v. The following lemma (Lemma 1) shows the existence of a LAP auction for the two-bidder scenario that gives a $\frac{4}{7}$-approximation with respect to the three-bidder scenario.

Lemma 1. *There is a LAP mechanism M for the instance with two bidders A, B with independent values of at least v that obtains a $\frac{4}{7}$ approximation against the best revenue that can be obtained in an instance with bidders A, B and an additional bidder C with deterministic value v.*

We first show how Lemma 1 implies Theorem 2, and then prove the lemma. Our LAP mechanism proceeds as follows:

1. Increase continuously the cutoff price c until exactly two bidders $i, j \in N$ remain.
2. Apply the LAP mechanism M that is guaranteed by Lemma 1 to i, j, with v equal to the last cutoff price c.

We use $M(F_A, F_B, v)$ to denote the revenue generated by M when the value distributions of A and B bidders are F_A, F_B, conditioned on the fact that their values are at least v. We have the following.

$$\text{OPT} = \mathop{\mathbf{E}}_{\mathbf{v}} \left[\max_\ell \varphi_\ell^+(v_\ell) \right] = \sum_{i \neq j \neq k} \mathop{\mathbf{E}}_{v_k} \left[\mathbf{Pr}\left[v_i, v_j \geq v_k \right] \cdot \prod_{m \neq i,j,k} \mathbf{Pr}\left[v_m < v_k \right] \cdot \right.$$

$$\left. \mathop{\mathbf{E}}_{\mathbf{v}_{-k}} \left[\max_\ell \varphi_\ell^+(v_\ell) \Big| v_i, v_j \geq v_k, v_m < v_k, \forall m \neq i,j,k \right] \right] \leq \sum_{i,j,k} \mathop{\mathbf{E}}_{v_k} \left[\mathbf{Pr}\left[v_i, v_j \geq v_k \right] \cdot \right.$$

$$\left. \prod_{m \neq i,j,k} \mathbf{Pr}\left[v_m < v_k \right] \cdot \mathop{\mathbf{E}}_{v_i, v_j} \left[\max_\ell \left(\varphi_i^+(v_i), \varphi_j^+(v_j), v_k \right) \Big| v_i, v_j \geq v_k \right] \right]$$

$$\leq \sum_{i,j,k} \mathop{\mathbf{E}}_{v_k} \left[\mathbf{Pr}\left[v_i, v_j \geq v_k\right] \cdot \prod_{m \neq i,j,k} \mathbf{Pr}\left[v_m < v_k\right] \cdot \frac{7}{4} \cdot \mathsf{M}\left(F_i|_{v_i \geq v_k}, F_j|_{v_j \geq v_k}, v_k\right) \right]$$

$$= \frac{7}{4} \cdot \mathsf{LAP}$$

The first equality follows from Myerson's theorem. For the second equality, we divide the value space according to the third highest value v_k and the identity i, j of the remaining bidders. In other words, v_k is the value of the price c when our LAP mechanism switches to the second step. For the first inequality, we use the fact that the virtual value is no larger than the value, i.e., $\varphi_m^+(v_m) \leq v_m \leq v_k$. For the second inequality, we apply Lemma 1 with respect to bidders i, j and value v_k. Notice that by Myerson's theorem, $\mathbf{E}[\max(\varphi_i^+(v_i), \varphi_j^+(v_j), v_k)]$ is exactly the optimal revenue when there is an additional bidder of deterministic value v_k. The final equality follows from the definition of our mechanism.

Remark 1. The reduction from our main theorem to Lemma 1 directly applies to irregular distributions. Notice that for regular distributions, the virtual values with respect to F_i and $F_i|_{v_i \geq v}$ are the same for all values $v_i \geq v$. We implicitly use this fact in the second inequality above. For irregular distributions, the inequality continues to hold in the right direction, i.e. the virtual value function only increases when we restrict the distribution to $v_i \geq v$.

We next prove our main lemma.

Proof of Lemma 1: Consider the *ex-ante relaxation* for the 3-bidder scenario, with variables x_1, x_2, x_3 denoting the respective allocation probabilities and $R_A(x_1), R_B(x_2)$, and $R_C(x_3)$ denoting the respective revenues obtained from the three bidders A, B, and C.

$$\operatorname*{maximize}_{x_1, x_2, x_3} : R_A(x_1) + R_B(x_2) + R_C(x_3) \quad \text{s.t. } x_1 + x_2 + x_3 \leq 1 \qquad (1)$$

We shall design a $\frac{4}{7}$-approximate LAP mechanism against this stronger benchmark. For regular distributions, $R_A(x_1) = x_i \cdot F_A^{-1}(1-x_1)$, $R_B(x_2) = x_2 \cdot F_B^{-1}(1-x_2)$, and $R_C(x_3) = v \cdot x_3$. Without loss of generality, we assume that $v = 1$. Then, $R_C(x_3) = x_3 \leq 1 - x_1 - x_2$. We reformulate the program as follows.

$$\max_{x_1, x_2} \ x_1 \cdot F_A^{-1}(1-x_1) + x_2 \cdot F_B^{-1}(1-x_2) + (1 - x_1 - x_2) \quad \text{s.t. } x_1 + x_2 \leq 1 \ (2)$$

Let x_1^*, x_2^* be the optimal solution to the ex-ante program (2), and $p_1^* = F_A^{-1}(1 - x_1^*), p_2^* = F_B^{-1}(1 - x_2^*)$ be the corresponding prices. Let $r_1^* = R_A(x_1^*) = x_1^* \cdot p_1^*$ and $r_2^* = R_B(x_2^*) = x_2^* \cdot p_2^*$. It holds that

$$\text{OPT}_{\text{ex-ante}} = r_1^* + r_2^* + 1 - x_1^* - x_2^*. \qquad (3)$$

Without loss of generality, we assume that $p_1^* \leq p_2^*$. We introduce below three LAP mechanisms that apply different pooling strategies. Each of these mechanisms uses pooling at most once during the course of the mechanism (and increases the cutoff price continuously at all other times).

1. Continuously increase the cutoff price to p_1^*:
   - if only bidder A survives, we post a price p_1^* to A;
   - if only bidder B survives, we post a price p_2^* to B;
   - if both A and B survive, pool $[p_1^*, p_2^*]$.
2. Continuously increase the cutoff price without any pooling.
3. Either pool $[1, p_1^*]$ or pool $[1, p_2^*]$, whichever gives a higher expected revenue.

Let Rev_1, Rev_2, Rev_3 be the respective revenues of the three LAP mechanisms above.

Claim. $\mathsf{Rev}_1 \geq r_1^* + r_2^* - \frac{r_2^* \cdot x_1^* + r_1^* \cdot x_2^*}{2}$, $\mathsf{Rev}_2 \geq \max\{r_1^*, r_2^*\}$, and $\mathsf{Rev}_3 \geq \max\left\{1 + \frac{r_1^* - x_1^*}{2}, 1 + \frac{r_2^* - x_2^*}{2}\right\}$.

Proof. We calculate the revenue of the first mechanism.

$$\mathsf{Rev}_1 \geq \Pr[v_1 \geq p_1^*, v_2 < p_1^*] \cdot p_1^* + \Pr[v_1 < p_1^*, v_2 \geq p_2^*] \cdot p_2^*$$
$$+ \left(\Pr[v_1 \geq p_1^*, v_2 \geq p_1^*] \cdot p_1^* + \Pr[v_1 \geq p_1^*, v_2 \geq p_2^*] \cdot \frac{p_2^* - p_1^*}{2} \right)$$
$$= \Pr[v_1 \geq p_1^*] \cdot p_1^* + \Pr[v_1 < p_1^*, v_2 \geq p_2^*] \cdot p_2^* + \Pr[v_1 \geq p_1^*, v_2 \geq p_2^*] \cdot \frac{p_2^* - p_1^*}{2}$$
$$= x_1^* \cdot p_1^* + (1 - x_1^*) \cdot x_2^* \cdot p_2^* + x_1^* \cdot x_2^* \cdot \frac{p_2^* - p_1^*}{2} = r_1^* + r_2^* - \frac{r_2^* x_1^* + r_1^* x_2^*}{2}.$$

In the first inequality, the first two terms correspond to the revenue achieved when only one bidder survives after price p_1^*. In the third case when both bidders survive, we have a guaranteed revenue of p_1^* and an additional revenue of at least $\frac{p_2^* - p_1^*}{2}$ if $v_2 \geq p_2^*$.[3]

The second mechanism achieves revenue greater than or equal to the revenues of the following two mechanisms: post price p_1^* to A, or post price p_2^* to B. I.e., $\mathsf{Rev}_2 \geq \max\{r_1^*, r_2^*\}$.

For the third mechanism, if we pool $[1, p_1^*]$, then the revenue is at least

$$1 + \Pr[v_1 \geq p_1^*] \cdot \frac{p_1^* - 1}{2} = 1 + x_1^* \cdot \frac{p_1^* - 1}{2} = 1 + \frac{r_1^* - x_1^*}{2}.$$

The case for pooling $[1, p_2^*]$ is similar. Therefore, $\mathsf{Rev}_3 \geq \max\left\{1 + \frac{r_1^* - x_1^*}{2}, 1 + \frac{r_2^* - x_2^*}{2}\right\}$.

According to the above claim and Eq. (3), it suffices to verify that

$$\max\left\{r_1^* + r_2^* - \frac{r_2^* \cdot x_1^* + r_1^* \cdot x_2^*}{2}, r_1^*, r_2^*, 1 + \frac{r_1^* - x_1^*}{2}, 1 + \frac{r_2^* - x_2^*}{2}\right\}$$

$$\geq \frac{4}{7} \cdot (r_1^* + r_2^* + 1 - x_1^* - x_2^*) \,(4)$$

---

[3] Observe that if both bidders survive after the pooling $[p_1^*, p_2^*]$, then the expected revenue we get is at least p_2^*. Indeed, in this case we continuously increase the cutoff price and can post a sub-optimal price to the winner that is equal to the last cutoff price of c. This gives us a guaranteed payment of $c > p_2^*$.

From now on, we shall treat this as an algebraic inequality and use the following properties: 1) $x_1^* + x_2^* \leq 1$, 2) $r_1^* \geq x_1^*, r_2^* \geq x_2^*$ 3) $v \geq 1$. Observe the symmetry of r_1^*, x_1^* and r_2^*, x_2^*. We shall assume w.l.o.g. that $1 \leq r_1^* \leq r_2^*$. We prove the inequality by a case analysis.

Lemma 2. *If $r_1^* \geq 1$, then*

$$\max\left\{ r_1^* + r_2^* - \frac{r_2^* \cdot x_1^* + r_1^* \cdot x_2^*}{2}, r_2^* \right\} \geq \frac{2}{3} \cdot (r_1^* + r_2^* + 1 - x_1^* - x_2^*).$$

Proof. First, note that scaling down r_1^* and r_2^* by the same factor until $r_1^* = 1$ would only make the inequality tighter, since $x_1^* + x_2^* \leq 1$. Thus, we can assume that $r_1^* = 1$. Moreover, increasing x_1^* and decreasing x_2^* by the same amount may only decrease the left hand side of the inequality (the constraint $r_1^* \geq x_1^*$ is satisfied as $r_1^* \geq 1 \geq x_1^* + x_2^*$). Hence, it suffices to check the case when $x_2^* = 0$, i.e., we are left to show

$$\max\left\{ 1 + r_2^* - \frac{r_2^* \cdot x_1^*}{2}, r_2^* \right\} \geq \frac{2}{3} \cdot (2 + r_2^* - x_1^*)$$

Case 1: $x_1^* \cdot r_2^* \geq 2$. We show that $r_2^* \geq \frac{2}{3} \cdot (2 + r_2^* - x_1^*)$. Indeed,

$$\frac{2 + r_2^* - x_1^*}{r_2^*} \leq \frac{2 + r_2^* - 2/r_2^*}{r_2^*} \leq \frac{3}{2},$$

where the last inequality is equivalent to $(r_2^* - 2)^2 \geq 0$.

Case 2: $x_1^* \cdot r_2^* < 2$. We show that $1 + r_2^* - \frac{r_2^* \cdot x_1^*}{2} \geq \frac{2}{3} \cdot (2 + r_2^* - x_1^*)$. We have

$$\frac{2 + r_2^* - x_1^*}{1 + r_2^* - \frac{1}{2}r_2^* x_1^*} \leq \frac{3}{2} \iff 1 + \frac{3}{2}r_2^* x_1^* - r_2^* - 2x_1^* \leq 0.$$

The last inequality is linear in x_1^* for any r_2^*. We can continuously change x_1^* towards one of the extremes: $x_1^* = 0$, or $x_1^* = 1$, whichever maximizes $1 + \frac{3}{2}r_2^* x_1^* - r_2^* - 2x_1^*$. Note that if the desired inequality holds for the updated x_1^*, then it must also hold for the original x_1^*. During this continuous change of x_1^* we may get $x_1^* \cdot r_2^* = 2$. In this case we stop and obtain the desired result due to the case 1 (note that $1 + r_2^* - \frac{1}{2}x_1^* \cdot r_2^* = r_2^*$ when $x_1^* \cdot r_2^* = 2$). Otherwise, we reach one of the extremes $x_1^* = 0$, or $x_1^* = 1$ and still have $x_1^* \cdot r_2^* < 2$. For $x_1^* = 0$, the last inequality becomes $1 \leq r_2^*$, which is true. For $x_1^* = 1$, the last inequality becomes $1 + \frac{3}{2}r_2^* \leq r_2^* + 2 \iff r_2^* \leq 2$, which holds by virtue of case 2 (recall $x_1^* = 1$).

Lemma 3. *If $r_1^* < 1$, then*

$$\max\left\{ r_1^* + r_2^* - \frac{r_2^* \cdot x_1^* + r_1^* \cdot x_2^*}{2}, r_2^*, 1 + \frac{r_1^* - x_1^*}{2}, 1 + \frac{r_2^* - x_2^*}{2} \right\}$$

$$\geq \frac{4}{7} \cdot (r_1^* + r_2^* + 1 - x_1^* - x_2^*).$$

Proof. Note that it is w.l.o.g. to assume that $x_2^* = 0$. Indeed, by decreasing r_2^* $(r_2^* \geq x_2^*)$ and x_2^* by the same amount, only the first two terms $r_1^* + r_2^* - \frac{r_2^* \cdot x_1^* + r_1^* \cdot x_2^*}{2}$ and r_2^* decrease (the first term decreases, because $\frac{x_1^* + r_1^*}{2} \leq 1$, as $1 > r_1^* \geq x_1^*$) and nothing else changes. Substituting $x_2 = 0$, it suffices to show that:

$$\max\left\{r_1^* + r_2^* - \frac{r_2^* \cdot x_1^*}{2}, r_2^*, 1 + \frac{r_1^* - x_1^*}{2}, 1 + \frac{r_2^*}{2}\right\} \geq \frac{4}{7} \cdot (r_1^* + r_2^* + 1 - x_1^*).$$

Case 1: $r_2^* \leq 2$. We have

$$\frac{7}{4} \cdot \max\left\{r_1^* + r_2^* - \frac{r_2^* \cdot x_1^*}{2}, 1 + \frac{r_1^* - x_1^*}{2}, 1 + \frac{r_2^*}{2}\right\}$$

$$\geq \frac{3}{4} \cdot \left(r_1^* + r_2^* - \frac{r_2^* \cdot x_1^*}{2}\right) + \frac{1}{2} \cdot \left(1 + \frac{r_1^* - x_1^*}{2}\right) + \frac{1}{2} \cdot \left(1 + \frac{r_2^*}{2}\right)$$

$$\geq \frac{3}{4} \cdot (r_1^* + r_2^* - x_1^*) + \frac{1}{2} \cdot \left(1 + \frac{r_1^* - x_1^*}{2}\right) + \frac{1}{2} \cdot \left(1 + \frac{r_2^*}{2}\right) = r_1^* + r_2^* + 1 - x_1^*$$

Case 2: $r_2^* > 2$. We have

$$\frac{3}{2} \cdot \max\left\{r_1^* + r_2^* - \frac{r_2^* \cdot x_1^*}{2}, r_2^*\right\} \geq \left(r_1^* + r_2^* - \frac{r_2^* \cdot x_1^*}{2}\right) + \frac{1}{2} \cdot r_2^*$$

$$\geq r_1^* + r_2^* + \frac{1}{2}r_2^*(1 - x_1^*) \geq r_1^* + r_2^* + 1 - x_1^*$$

Combining Lemmas 2 and 3, we conclude the proof of the main lemma. □

3.1   Extension to Irregular Distributions

In this section we extend the proof of Theorem 2 to irregular distributions. It suffices to show that Lemma 1 holds for irregular distributions. We follow the same analysis by solving the ex-ante relaxation.

$$\underset{x_1, x_2}{\text{maximize}} : \bar{R}_A(x_1) + \bar{R}_B(x_2) + 1 - x_1 - x_2 \quad \text{s.t. } x_1 + x_2 \leq 1, \tag{5}$$

where $\bar{R}_A(x_1)$ and $\bar{R}_B(x_2)$ denote the ironed revenue curves of bidders A and B, respectively.

Denote the optimal solution by x_1^*, x_2^*. The only difference compared to the regular case is that the values $\bar{R}_A(x_1^*), \bar{R}_B(x_2^*)$ might not correspond to a single posted price $p_1^* = F_A^{-1}(1 - x_1^*)$, or $p_2^* = F_B^{-1}(1 - x_2^*)$. In fact, if both $\bar{R}_A(x_1^*), \bar{R}_B(x_2^*)$ correspond to posted prices p_1^* and p_2^*, respectively, then the proof of Lemma 1 for regular distributions applies intact.

Recall that each of $\bar{R}_A(x_1^*)$ and $\bar{R}_B(x_2^*)$ corresponds to a randomization of two prices if and only if x_i^* lies on the ironed region of the corresponding revenue curve $R_A(x_1)$ or $R_B(x_2)$.

Consider the case when both x_1^*, x_2^* lie strictly inside the ironed regions of their respective revenue curves $\bar{R}_A(\cdot), \bar{R}_B(\cdot)$. Then their derivatives $\bar{R}_A'(\cdot)$ and

$\bar{R}'_B(\cdot)$ must be locally a constant around x_1^*, or respectively around x_2^*. Moreover, $\bar{R}'_B(x_1^*) = \bar{R}'_B(x_2^*)$, since otherwise,

$$\max\left(\bar{R}_A(x_1^* + \varepsilon) + \bar{R}_B(x_2^* - \varepsilon), \bar{R}_A(x_1^* - \varepsilon) + \bar{R}_B(x_2^* + \varepsilon)\right) > \bar{R}_A(x_1^*) + \bar{R}_B(x_2^*),$$

holds for a sufficiently small $\varepsilon > 0$, violating the optimality of x_1^*, x_2^*. Consequently, we can keep increasing x_1^* and decreasing x_2^* at the same rate until one of them hits the end of their respective ironed interval, and the objective function $\bar{R}_A(x_1^*) + \bar{R}_B(x_2^*)$ remains unchanged. Therefore, we can assume that only one of x_1^*, x_2^* lies inside the ironed region. Without loss of generality, we assume that it is x_1^*.

Furthermore, we may assume that $x_1^* + x_2^* = 1$. Indeed, otherwise we can increase x_1^* (when $\bar{R}'_A(x_1^*) > 1$), or decrease x_1^* (when $\bar{R}'_A(x_1^*) \leq 1$) until x_1^* escapes from its ironed region, or we get $x_1^* + x_2^* = 1$.

Finally, it remains to consider the case where $\bar{R}_A(x_1^*)$ corresponds to a randomization of two prices, $\bar{R}_B(x_2^*)$ corresponds to a single price, and $x_1^* + x_2^* = 1$. Let $x_1^* = \alpha \cdot x_{11}^* + (1 - \alpha) \cdot x_{12}^*$, and $p_{11}^* = F_A^{-1}(1 - x_{11}^*), p_{12}^* = F_A^{-1}(1 - x_{12}^*)$ be the corresponding prices. Let $r_{11}^* \overset{\text{def}}{=} x_{11}^* \cdot p_{11}^*, r_{12}^* \overset{\text{def}}{=} x_{12}^* \cdot p_{12}^*$ and $r_1^* \overset{\text{def}}{=} \bar{R}_A(x_1^*) = \alpha \cdot x_{11}^* \cdot p_{11}^* + (1 - \alpha) \cdot x_{12}^* \cdot p_{12}^*$. Let $r_2^* \overset{\text{def}}{=} \bar{R}_B(x_2^*) = x_2^* \cdot p_2^*$. Then we have

$$\text{OPT}_{\text{ex-ante}} = r_1^* + r_2^* = \alpha \cdot r_{11}^* + (1 - \alpha) \cdot r_{12}^* + r_2^*$$

We use one of the following two LAP mechanisms from the proof of Lemma 1 with only slight modifications.

1. Continuously increase the cutoff price to p_1^*:
   - if only bidder A survives, we post a price p_1^* to A;
   - if only bidder B survives, we post a price p_2^* to B;
   - if both A and B survive, pool $[p_1^*, p_2^*]$.
2. Continuously increase the cutoff price without any pooling.

We modify the above mechanisms by setting p_1^* to be p_{11}^* or p_{12}^*, whichever gives a higher expected revenue. Denote the revenue of the two mechanisms by $\text{Rev}_1, \text{Rev}_2$. Following the same derivations as in Claim 3, we get that

$$\text{Rev}_1 \geq \max\left\{r_{11}^* + r_2^* - \frac{r_2^* \cdot x_{11}^* + r_{11}^* \cdot x_2^*}{2}, r_{12}^* + r_2^* - \frac{r_2^* \cdot x_{12}^* + r_{12}^* \cdot x_2^*}{2}\right\};$$

$$\text{Rev}_2 \geq \max\left\{r_{11}^*, r_{12}^*, r_2^*\right\}.$$

Consequently, we have

$$\text{Rev}_1 \geq \alpha \cdot \left(r_{11}^* + r_2^* - \frac{r_2^* \cdot x_{11}^* + r_{11}^* \cdot x_2^*}{2}\right) + (1 - \alpha) \cdot$$

$$\cdot \left(r_{12}^* + r_2^* - \frac{r_2^* \cdot x_{12}^* + r_{12}^* \cdot x_2^*}{2}\right) = r_1^* + r_2^* - \frac{r_2^* \cdot x_1^* + r_1^* \cdot x_2^*}{2};$$

$$\text{Rev}_2 \geq \max\left\{\alpha \cdot r_{11}^* + (1 - \alpha) \cdot r_{12}^*, r_2^*\right\} = \max\left\{r_1^*, r_2^*\right\} \geq x_1^* \cdot r_2^* + x_2^* \cdot r_1^*.$$

Finally, we have

$$\mathsf{LAP} \geq \frac{2}{3}\left(\mathsf{Rev}_1 + \frac{1}{2}\cdot\mathsf{Rev}_2\right) \geq \frac{2}{3}\left(r_1^* + r_2^* - \frac{r_2^*\cdot x_1^* + r_1^*\cdot x_2^*}{2} + \right.$$

$$\left.\frac{x_1^*\cdot r_2^* + x_2^*\cdot r_1^*}{2}\right) = \frac{2}{3}\left(r_1^* + r_2^*\right) = \frac{2}{3}\mathsf{OPT} > \frac{4}{7}\mathsf{OPT}.$$

This concludes the proof of Lemma 1 for irregular distributions.

4   LAP for Correlated Values

In this section we show that when the value distributions are correlated, then LAP cannot achieve better performance than LA, even in the case of $n = 2$ bidders. We construct a correlated distribution with the following unnatural *"cryptographic"* feature: the seller can precisely recover the value of the lower bidder from the bid of the higher bidder, while the lower bid reveals almost no useful information about the top value. We construct the distribution of pairs of values $(v_1 \leq v_2)$ as follow.

– $v_1 \sim F_1$, where $\mathbf{Pr}[v_1 > x] = \frac{1}{x}$ is a discrete equal revenue distribution supported on the interval $[1, \frac{1}{\varepsilon_1}]$ for a small $\varepsilon_1 > 0$.
– $v_2 = v_1 \cdot (\xi_2 + \varepsilon^3)$, where $\varepsilon > 0$ is a negligibly small number, $\xi_2 \sim F_2$ and F_2 is a discrete equal revenue distribution with the support $[1, \frac{1}{\varepsilon_2}]$ for a small $\varepsilon_2 > 0$. We assume that $\varepsilon_1 \ll \varepsilon_2$.
– The supports of the discrete distributions $v_1 \sim F_1, \xi_2 \sim F_2$ consists of numbers that are multiples of $\varepsilon < \varepsilon_1$. This allows us to recover v_1 from the value of v_2 alone. Indeed, notice that $v_2 = n_1\varepsilon \cdot (n_2\varepsilon + \varepsilon^3)$ for integer $n_1, n_2 < \frac{1}{\varepsilon^2}$. Then $\frac{v_2}{\varepsilon^2} = n_1 \cdot n_2 + \varepsilon^2 \cdot n_1$ and its fractional part $\left\{\frac{v_2}{\varepsilon^2}\right\} = v_1 \cdot \varepsilon$. On the other hand, we can ignore the tiny term of ε^3 in v_2, i.e., just think of $v_2 = v_1 \cdot \xi_2$ without any noticeable change to the posterior distribution $F_2(v_2|v_1)$.

Theorem 3. *No LAP mechanism achieves better than $\frac{1}{2} + o(1)$ approximation to the optimal revenue for the above instance of correlated distribution.*

Proof. To simplify the presentation we will ignore in the analysis small terms that appear due to the discretization by ε. Assume to the contrary that there is a LAP mechanism with better than $\frac{1}{2} + o(1)$ approximation to the optimum. This mechanism keeps increasing the lowest threshold for both bidders in leaps $[s_1, t_1], [s_2, t_2], \ldots$ until at least one bidder drops, in which case it offers a new final price to the surviving bidder, if a single one survives, or sells the item at the latest offered price to one of the bidders picked uniformly at random, if none of them survived. Here we assume that for every i, the LAP proceeds in one jump from s_i to t_i and then increases the price continuously from t_i to s_{i+1}.

  The optimum mechanism can offer to the second bidder the highest possible price of $\frac{v_1}{\varepsilon_2}$ and if he rejects, offer a price of v_1 (which the seller can identify from the second bidder) to the first bidder. Thus the optimum gets the expected revenue of $(1 - \varepsilon_2)v_1 + \frac{v_1}{\varepsilon_2}\varepsilon_2 = (2 - o(1))v_1$ for each fixed value of v_1, which in expectation gives[4]

$$\text{OPT} \approx \int_1^{1/\varepsilon_1} \frac{1}{t^2} \cdot (2 - \varepsilon_2) \cdot t \, dt = (2 - \varepsilon_2) \ln(1/\varepsilon_1),$$

Next, we analyse the performance of LAP in different cases of values v_1, v_2. We will argue that in almost all cases LAP's revenue is not more than the revenue of an LA which is a 2-approximation to OPT (LA can only sell to the second bidder and thus for each value of v_1 the best revenue it can get is v_1).

First, if v_1 falls into any interval (t_i, s_{i+1}), then LAP will certainly loose the lowest bidder. The best revenue it can get from $v_2 = v_1 \cdot \xi_2$ will be v_1. I.e., in expectation it is $\int_{t_i}^{s_{i+1}} \frac{1}{t^2} \cdot t \, dt$.

Second, if $v_1 \in [s_i, t_i]$ for $t_i < \frac{1}{\varepsilon_1}$. Then there are two possibilities for the top bid v_2: (i) $v_2 < t_i$, in which case LAP sells equally likely to one of the bidders at price s_i; (ii) $v_2 \geq t_i$, in which case the LAP can only sell to the highest bidder and its allocation and payment rules are bounded by the incentive constraint from case (i). In case (i) the revenue is s_i, while in (ii) case with half probability the item must be sold to the first bidder at a low price of s_i (due to the incentive constraint for the top bidder) and with the remaining probability it can be sold at the best price of t_i (since F_2 is the equal revenue distribution). Hence, the total revenue of LAP in this case is

$$\mathsf{LAP}([s_i, t_i]) = \int_{s_i}^{t_i} \frac{1}{t^2} \cdot \left(s_i \cdot \frac{t_i - t}{t_i} + \left(\frac{s_i}{2} + \frac{t_i}{2} \right) \cdot \frac{t}{t_i} \right) dt = 1 - \frac{s_i}{t_i} + \frac{t_i - s_i}{2t_i} \ln \frac{t_i}{s_i}. \tag{6}$$

Denoting by $x \overset{\text{def}}{=} \frac{s_i}{t_i} \in (0, 1]$ we get (6) $= 1 - x - \frac{1-x}{2} \ln x \leq -\ln(x)$ (the latter inequality can be verified using Taylor expansion of $\ln(1 - y)$ where $y = 1 - x$). Thus (6) $\leq \int_{s_i}^{t_i} \frac{1}{t^2} \cdot t \, dt = \mathsf{LA}([s_i, t_i])$.

Finally, if $v_1 \in [s_i, t_i]$ for $t_i > \frac{1}{\varepsilon_1}$, then LAP cannot get more revenue than v_1 from the second bidder and the payment from the lower bidder is not more than s_i. The total expected revenue of LAP in this case is

$$\mathsf{LAP}([s_i, 1/\varepsilon_2]) \leq \int_{s_i}^{1/\varepsilon_1} \frac{1}{t^2} \cdot (s_i + t) \, dt \leq 1 + \mathsf{LA}([s_i, 1/\varepsilon_1]).$$

In conclusion we get that $\mathsf{LAP} \leq 1 + \mathsf{LA} \leq 1 + \text{OPT}(\frac{1}{2} + o(1)) \leq \text{OPT}(\frac{1}{2} + o(1))$, since $\text{OPT} = (2 - \varepsilon_1) \ln(1/\varepsilon_2)$.

This cryptographic construction makes our correlated distribution not quite realistic. The point we illustrate here is that the class of general correlated distribution even for $n = 2$ bidders is just unrealistically general.

---

[4] We write $\approx$ (and not "="), as the distributions in our construction are discrete instead of the continuous equal revenue distribution. We write the integral and not the summation over the discrete values to simplify our presentation and calculations. This is w.l.o.g., as $\varepsilon_1, \varepsilon_2 \to 0$ and the integral above arbitrarily closely approximates the respective summation. We apply the same approximation principle in our derivations below.

A   Truthfulness of **LAP**

Proof of Theorem 1: If i is a bidder with $x_i(\mathbf{v}) > 0$, then she always has an option either not to buy the item, or to pay $c^o \leq v_i$ whenever she gets the item in a lottery, i.e., $p_i \leq x_i \cdot v_i$. Thus $u_i = v_i \cdot x_i - p_i \geq 0$ and **LAP** is IR.

Next we show that any **LAP** is DSIC. We assume that all bidders bid truthfully and argue that no bidder i can improve their utility by bidding $b_i \neq v_i$.

We consider the bidders who dropped strictly before the last increment (either continuous or discrete from c^o to c^+) of the cut-off price c. Let $c' \geq v_i$ be the value of the cut-off price, when bidder i has dropped. If $b_i < c'$, then nothing changes for the bidder i, as $x_i = 0$. If $b_i > c'$ and i gets a different allocation $x_i > 0$, then i has to pay at least $p_i \geq c' \cdot x_i$ which gives a non-positive utility to bidder i.

Next, consider the case when **LAP** stops at the cut-off price c' while continuously increasing c. Then only one bidder i^* whose value $v_{i^*} \geq c'$ may receive the item. Let $c^+ < c'$ be the value of the cut-off price right after the last discrete jump of c ($c^+ = 0$ if there were no discrete jumps). We have already discussed above that any bidder i with $v_i < c'$ cannot get positive utility. The bidder $i \neq i^*$ with $v_i = c'$ drops the last from S. Les us consider her possible bids: (i) she would loose and get $x_i = 0$ by bidding $b_i < c^+$ or $b_i \in [c^+, c']$; (ii) she would have to pay $p_i > c' \cdot x_i = v_i \cdot x_i$ by bidding any $b_i > c'$. Consider all possible bids of i^*: (i) i^* looses to i by bidding $b_{i^*} < c^+$ or by dropping earlier at any earlier cut-off price c; (ii) i^* gets the same take-it-or-leave-price $p(\mathbf{v}_{-i^*})$ with any bid $b_{i^*} \geq c'$. In summary, any bidder $i \in N$ cannot increase their utility by bidding $b_i \neq v_i$ if **LAP** stops while continuously increasing c.

We are only left to consider the case when **LAP** stops (and potentially allocates the item) within a discrete increment of c from c^o to $c^+ > c^o$. We also only need to consider the bidders in $S(c^o)$, since any other bidder drops before the last increment of c.

Observe that any bidder $i \in S(c^o)$ ($v_i \geq c^o$) would loose a chance to win the item if they bid $b_i < c^o$, so such deviation results in 0 utility for them.

Next, let i be any bidder with $c^o \leq v_i < c^+$. Any bid $c^o \leq b_i < c^+$ leads to the same outcome and payment for i as $b_i = v_i$.

If i bids $b_i \geq c^+$, then either two bidders will get to the next stage $c > c^+$ (in this case i will need to pay at least $c^+ > v_i$), or only i accepts the cut-off price $c = c^+$ (then i would take the first option out of two, which will give her the same allocation of $x_i = \frac{1}{|S(c^o)|}$ and payment $p_i = \frac{c^o}{|S(c^o)|}$ as if $b_i = v_i$). Finally, there could be at most one bidder i^* with value $v_{i^*} \geq c^+$. Note that bidding any $b_{i^*} \geq c^+$ results in the same choice of two options for i^*, while bidding below c^o results in $x_{i^*} = 0$. Any bid $c^o \leq b_{i^*} < c^+$ leads to an allocation probability $\frac{1}{|S(c^o)|}$, i.e., i^* would be restricted to choosing the first option.

We conclude that truthful bidding is a dominant strategy of every bidder. $\square$

References

1. Bei, X., Gravin, N., Lu, P., Tang, Z.G.: Correlation-robust analysis of single item auction. In: SODA, pp. 193–208. SIAM (2019)
2. Chen, X., Hu, G., Lu, P., Wang, L.: On the approximation ratio of k-lookahead auction. In: Chen, N., Elkind, E., Koutsoupias, E. (eds.) WINE 2011. LNCS, vol. 7090, pp. 61–71. Springer, Heidelberg (2011). https://doi.org/10.1007/978-3-642-25510-6_6
3. Crémer, J., McLean, R.P.: Full extraction of the surplus in Bayesian and dominant strategy auctions. Econometrica **56**(6), 1247–1257 (1988). http://www.jstor.org/stable/1913096
4. Deb, R., Pai, M.M.: Discrimination via symmetric auctions. Am. Econ. J. Microecon. **9**(1), 275–314 (2017). http://www.jstor.org/stable/26157031
5. Dobzinski, S., Fu, H., Kleinberg, R.D.: Optimal auctions with correlated bidders are easy. In: Fortnow, L., Vadhan, S.P. (eds.) Proceedings of the 43rd ACM Symposium on Theory of Computing, STOC 2011, San Jose, CA, USA, 6–8 June 2011, pp. 129–138. ACM (2011). https://doi.org/10.1145/1993636.1993655
6. Dobzinski, S., Uziely, N.: Revenue loss in shrinking markets. In: EC, pp. 431–442. ACM (2018)
7. Hartline, J.: Mechanism design and approximation. http://jasonhartline.com/MDnA/. Accessed 7 May 2020
8. Hartline, J.D., Roughgarden, T.: Simple versus optimal mechanisms. In: Chuang, J., Fortnow, L., Pu, P. (eds.) Proceedings 10th ACM Conference on Electronic Commerce (EC-2009), Stanford, CA, USA, 6–10 July 2009, pp. 225–234. ACM (2009). https://doi.org/10.1145/1566374.1566407
9. Myerson, R.: Optimal auction design. Math. Oper. Res. **6**(1), 58–73 (1981)
10. Papadimitriou, C.H., Pierrakos, G.: On optimal single-item auctions. In: STOC, pp. 119–128. ACM (2011)
11. Ronen, A.: On approximating optimal auctions. In: Wellman, M.P., Shoham, Y. (eds.) Proceedings 3rd ACM Conference on Electronic Commerce (EC-2001), Tampa, FL, USA, 14–17 October 2001, pp. 11–17. ACM (2001). https://doi.org/10.1145/501158.501160

Budget Feasible Mechanisms for Procurement Auctions with Divisible Agents

Sophie Klumper[1,2(✉)] ![ORCID] and Guido Schäfer[1,3] ![ORCID]

[1] Networks and Optimization Group, Centrum Wiskunde en Informatica (CWI),
Amsterdam, The Netherlands
{s.j.klumper,g.schaefer}@cwi.nl
[2] Department of Mathematics, Vrije Universiteit Amsterdam,
Amsterdam, The Netherlands
[3] Institute for Logic, Language and Computation, University of Amsterdam,
Amsterdam, The Netherlands

Abstract. We consider budget feasible mechanisms for procurement auctions with additive valuation functions. For the divisible case, where agents can be allocated fractionally, there exists an optimal mechanism with approximation guarantee $e/(e-1)$ under the small bidder assumption. We study the divisible case without the small bidder assumption, but assume that the true costs of the agents are bounded by the budget. This setting lends itself to modeling economic situations in which the goods represent time and the agents' true costs are not necessarily small compared to the budget. Non-trivially, we give a mechanism with an approximation guarantee of 2.62, improving the result of 3 for the indivisible case. Additionally, we give a lower bound on the approximation guarantee of 1.25. We then study the problem in more competitive markets and assume that the agents' value over cost efficiencies are bounded by some $\theta \geq 1$. For $\theta \leq 2$, we give a mechanism with an approximation guarantee of 2 and a lower bound of 1.18. Finally, we extend these results to settings with different agent types with a linear capped valuation function for each type.

Keywords: Mechanism design · Procurement auction · Budget feasible mechanism · Divisible agents · Knapsack auction · Additive valuations

1 Introduction

We consider procurement auctions in which the auctioneer has a budget that limits the total payments that can be paid to the agents. In this setting, we are given a set of agents $A = [n]$ offering some service (or good), where each agent $i \in A$ has a privately known cost c_i and a publicly known valuation v_i. The auctioneer wants to do business with these agents and needs to decide with which agents $S \subseteq A$ to do so. In order for each agent $i \in S$ to comply, the auctioneer

© The Author(s), under exclusive license to Springer Nature Switzerland AG 2022
P. Kanellopoulos et al. (Eds.): SAGT 2022, LNCS 13584, pp. 78–93, 2022.
https://doi.org/10.1007/978-3-031-15714-1_5

will have to make a payment p_i to this agent i. The auctioneer has a total budget B available for these payments. The goal of the auctioneer is to find a subset of agents $S \subseteq A$ that (approximately) maximizes the total value, while the total of the payments is at most B; such payments are said to be *budget feasible*. As the costs of the agents are assumed to be private, agents may misreport their actual costs to their own advantage. The goal is to design a mechanism that computes this subset and budget feasible payments, such that the agents have no incentive to misreport their actual costs (i.e., the agents are truthful).

Basically, there are two standard approaches in the literature to study this problem: (i) in the *Bayesian setting* it is assumed that the distributions of the agents' true costs are known, and (ii) in the *prior-free setting* it is assumed that nothing is known about these distributions. In this paper, we focus on the prior-free setting as it may not be possible to extract representative distributions of the agents' true costs.

Notably, most previous studies focus on the *indivisible case*, where the services (or goods) offered by the agents need to be allocated integrally. In contrast, the *divisible case*, where the agents can also be allocated fractionally, received much less attention and has been studied only under the so-called *small bidder assumption*, i.e., when the agents' costs are much smaller than the available budget. While this assumption is justified in certain settings (e.g., for large markets), it is less appropriate in settings where the agents' costs may differ vastly or be close to the budget. This motivates the main question that we address in this paper: Can we derive budget feasible truthful mechanisms with attractive approximation guarantees if the agents are divisible?

Singer [1] initiated the study of budget feasible mechanisms in the prior-free setting with indivisible agents and designed a deterministic mechanisms with an approximation guarantee of 5. Later, Chen et al. [2] improved this to $2 + \sqrt{2}$. Almost a decade later, Gravin et al. [3] improved the approximation guarantee to 3 and showed that no mechanism can do better than 3 (when compared to the fractional optimal solution). All three papers also provide additional results such as randomized algorithms with improved approximation guarantees and mechanisms for the more general setting of submodular functions.

To the best of our knowledge, the divisible case of knapsack procurement auctions has not been studied so far. When an agent is offering a service, which can be interpreted as offering time, it is suitable to model this as a divisible good. As an example, consider the situation where an auctioneer has a budget available and wants to organize a local comedy show. Agents are offering to perform and for each agent the auctioneer has a valuation, which reflects the amusement when this agent performs. The agents have costs related to their performance which could consist of the invested time in their performance, attributes needed, travel costs, etc. In this example it makes sense for the auctioneer to have the option to select agents fractionally. After selecting one agent, the budget left might only be enough to let some agent perform half of what they are offering. Or the auctioneer might want to have at least three performances and must select agents fractionally to achieve this due to the budget constraint.

As mentioned, the prior-free setting with divisible goods has been studied by Anari et al. [4] under the small bidder assumption. More formally, if $c_{\max} = \max_{i \in A}\{c_i\}$ and $r = c_{\max}/B$, then the results are analysed for $r \to 0$. Anari et al. [4] give optimal mechanisms for both the divisible (deterministic) and indivisible (randomized) case, both with an approximation guarantee of $e/(e-1)$. They also mention that in the divisible case, no truthful mechanism with a finite approximation guarantee exists without the small bidder assumption. This can already be shown by an instance with budget B and one agent with value v and true cost $c > B$. An optimal fractional solution can achieve a value of $v\frac{B}{c}$. Therefore any truthful mechanism must allocate the agent fractionally in order to achieve some positive value and thus a finite approximation guarantee. Additionally, it must be that $p \leq B$, with p the payment of the agent, for the mechanism to be budget feasible. As we do not know c or any bound on c, there is no way to bound p and satisfy budget feasibility in this instance and at the same time achieve the same approximation guarantee in any other possible instance.

However, if we assume that the true costs of the agents are bounded by the budget, there is still a lot we can do without the small bidder assumption and there are settings in which it makes sense to have this assumption. If we revisit our example of an auctioneer wanting to organize a local comedy show, an internationally famous comedian with a true cost exceeding the budget will most likely not be one of the agents offering to perform. On the other hand, there might be a national well-known comedian offering to perform. This comedian might have a true cost that is smaller than the budget, but not much smaller than the available budget, which is what the small bidder assumption requires.

Our Contributions. For the knapsack procurement auction with divisible goods and true costs bounded by the budget, we give a mechanism with an approximation guarantee of 2.62 in Sect. 3. Additionally, we proof that no mechanism can achieve an approximation guarantee better than 1.25. Although the divisible case gives more freedom in designing an allocation rule, improving the approximation guarantee compared to the indivisible case is non-trivial. In particular, it remains difficult to bound the threshold bids and the complexity of the payment rule increases compared to the indivisible case. Additionally, if an agent is allocated fractionally one needs to determine this fraction exactly while remaining budget feasible. A natural method is to determine this fraction based on the agents' declared costs, but then one must limit the influence that this method gives to the agents.

Proving the above mentioned lower bound of 1.25 on the approximation guarantee requires that the true costs of the agents differ significantly ($\epsilon \ll B$), a property that is used more often when proving lower bounds. Therefore, in Sect. 4, we introduce a setting in which the agents' efficiencies (i.e., value over cost ratios) are bounded by some $\theta \geq 1$. It is reasonable to assume that the efficiencies of the agents is somewhat bounded, as agents will cease to exist if they cannot compete with the other agents in terms of efficiency. Another interpretation of this setting is some middle ground between the prior-free and the Bayesian setting. It might be impossible to find representative distributions of

Table 1. Overview of the results obtained in this paper.

Assumptions		Origin	Approximation Guarantee	
			Upper bound	Lower bound
Indivisible		[1]	5	2
		[2]	≈ 3.41	≈ 2.41
		[3]	3	3^*
Divisible	none**	Sects. 3 and 5	≈ 2.62	1.25
$(c_i \leq B \ \forall i)$	$\theta \leq 2^{**}$	Sects. 4 and 5	2	≈ 1.18

*Compared to the optimal fractional solution
**Also holds for multiple linear capped valuation functions

the agents' true costs and address the problem in the Bayesian setting, but the auctioneer could have information about the minimum and maximum efficiencies in the market by previous experiences or market research. We give a mechanism with an approximation guarantee of 2 when the efficiencies are bounded by a factor $\theta \leq 2$. For this case we also prove a lower bound of 1.18 on the approximation guarantee and generalize this for different values of θ.

In Sect. 5, we extend our results to a model in which agents may have different types. This new model allows us to capture slightly more complex settings. If we revisit the example of hosting a comedy show, this translates to each agent having a certain type of comedy that they preform. In order to set up a nice diverse program, the auctioneer wishes the jokes of a certain type to be limited. The auctioneer knows that, if at some point in time too many jokes of the same type are told, no additional value is added to the show. This is modeled by a linear capped valuation function for each type. We prove that for linear capped valuation functions, the mechanisms of Sect. 3 and 4 can be slightly altered to achieve the same approximation guarantees (Table 1).

Related Work. As mentioned earlier, settings with different valuation functions have been studied for the indivisible case. In the case of submodular valuation functions, Singer [1] gave a randomized mechanism with an approximation guarantee of 112. Again, Chen et al. [2] improved this to 7.91 and gave a deterministic exponential time mechanism with an approximation guarantee of 8.34. Later Jalaly and Tardos [5] improved this to 5 and 4.56 respectively. For subadditive valuation functions, Dobzinski et al. [10] gave a randomized and deterministic mechanism with an approximation guarantee of $O(\log^2 n)$ and $O(\log^3 n)$ respectively. Bei et al. [11] improved this to $O(\log n/(\log \log n))$ with a polynomial time randomized mechanism and gave a randomized exponential time mechanism with an approximation guarantee of 768 for XOS valuation functions. Leonardi et al. [7] improved the latter to 436 by tuning the parameters of the mechanism.

Related settings have also been studied for the indivisible case. Leonardi et al. [7] consider the problem with an underlying matroid structure, where each element corresponds to an agent and the auctioneer can only allocate an independent set. Chan and Chen [8] studied the setting in which agents offer multiple units of their good. They regard concave additive and subadditive valuation functions. The setting in which the auctioneer wants to get a set of heterogeneous tasks done and where each task requires the performing agent to have a certain skill has been studied by Goel et al. [6]. They give a randomized mechanism with an approximation guarantee of 2.58, which is truthful under the small bidder assumption. Jalaly and Tardos [5] match this result with a deterministic mechanism. The results of Goel et al. [6] can be extended to settings in which tasks can be done multiple times and agents can perform multiple tasks. Related to this line of work is also the strategic version of matching and coverage, in which edges and subsets represent strategic agents, that Singer [1] also studied. Chen et al. [2] also studied the knapsack problem with heterogeneous items, were items are divided in groups and at most one item from each group can be allocated. Amanatidis et al. [12] give randomized and deterministic mechanisms for a subclass of XOS problems. For the mechanism design version of the budgeted max weighted matching problem, they give a randomized (deterministic) mechanism with an approximation guarantee of 3 (4) and they generalize their results to problems with a similar combinatorial structure.

2   Preliminaries

We are given a (finite) set of agents A offering some service (or good), where each agent $i \in A$ has a privately known non-negative cost c_i and a non-negative valuation v_i. Each agent $i \in A$ declares a non-negative cost b_i, which they might use to misreport their actual cost c_i. Given the declared costs $\mathbf{b} = (b_i)_{i \in A}$, valuations $\mathbf{v} = (v_i)_{i \in A}$ and a budget $B > 0$, the problem is to design a mechanism that computes an allocation vector $\mathbf{x} = (x_i)_{i \in A}$ and a payment vector $\mathbf{p} = (p_i)_{i \in A}$[1]. The allocation vector $\mathbf{x}$ should satisfy $x_i \in [0, 1]$ for all $i \in A$, where x_i denotes the fraction selected of agent i. An element p_i of the payment vector $\mathbf{p}$ corresponds to the payment of agent i. We want to (approximately) maximize the value of the allocation vector and the total of the payments to be within the budget. We assume that the true costs $\mathbf{c} = (c_i)_{i \in A}$ are bounded by the budget, i.e., $c_i \leq B$ for all $i \in A$. We also assume that the costs incurred by the agents are linear, i.e., given allocation vector $\mathbf{x}$ the cost incurred by agent i is equal to $c_i x_i$. Therefore the utility u_i of agent $i \in A$ is equal to $u_i = p_i - c_i x_i$. The auctioneer has an additive valuation function, i.e., given allocation vector $\mathbf{x}$ the value derived by the auctioneer is $v(\mathbf{x}) = \sum_{i \in A} v_i x_i$. The goal of each player $i \in A$ is to maximize their utility u_i, and as the costs of the agents are assumed to be private, they may misreport their actual costs to achieve this. If the agents are not strategic, i.e., the costs are publicly known, the above setting naturally corresponds to the fractional knapsack problem.

We seek mechanisms that satisfy the following properties:

---

[1] It is important to realize that the mechanism only has access to the declared costs $\mathbf{b}$, as the actual costs $\mathbf{c}$ are assumed to be private information of the agents.

1. *Truthfulness:* for every agent i reporting their true cost is a dominant strategy: for any declared costs b_i and $\mathbf{b}_{-i}$ it holds that $p_i - x_i c_i \geq p'_i - x'_i c_i$, where (x_i, p_i) and (x'_i, p'_i) are the allocations and payments of agent i with respect to the declared costs $(c_i, \mathbf{b}_{-i})$ and $(b_i, \mathbf{b}_{-i})$.
2. *Individual rationality:* for every agent i it holds that $p_i \geq x_i b_i$, so under a truthful report agent i has non-negative utility.
3. *Budget feasibility:* the total payment is at most the budget: $\sum_{i \in A} p_i \leq B$.
4. *Approximation guarantee:* a mechanism has an approximation guarantee of $\gamma \geq 1$ if, for any declared costs $\mathbf{b}$, it outputs an allocation $\mathbf{x}$ such that $\gamma \cdot v(\mathbf{x}) \geq$ opt, where opt is the value of the optimal fractional solution with respect to $\mathbf{b}$.
5. *Computational efficiency:* the allocation and payment vector can be computed in polynomial time.

Given declared costs $\mathbf{b} = (b_i)_{i \in A}$, let $x_i(\mathbf{b})$ be the fraction selected of agent $i \in A$. An allocation rule is said to be *monotone non-increasing* if for each agent i, the fraction of i selected can only increase as their declared cost decreases. More formally, for all $\mathbf{b}_{-i}$ and $b_i > b'_i$: $x_i(b_i, \mathbf{b}_{-i}) \leq x_i(b'_i, \mathbf{b}_{-i})$. In order to design truthful mechanisms, we will exploit Theorem 1 and derive mechanisms that have a monotone non-increasing allocation rule.

Theorem 1. *(Archer and Tardos [9]) A monotone non-increasing allocation rule $x(\mathbf{b})$ admits a truthful payment rule that is individually rational if and only if for all i, $\mathbf{b}_{-i}$: $\int_0^\infty x_i(u, \mathbf{b}_{-i})du < \infty$. In this case we can take the payment rule $p(\mathbf{b})$ to be*

$$p_i(b_i, \mathbf{b}_{-i}) = b_i \cdot x_i(b_i, \mathbf{b}_{-i}) + \int_{b_i}^\infty x_i(u, \mathbf{b}_{-i})du \quad \forall i. \tag{1}$$

Next we introduce some additional notation that is used throughout the paper. We say that agent i *wins* if $x_i > 0$ and *loses* if $x_i = 0$. Note that $p_i = 0$ for a losing agent i if the above payment rule is used. We define the *efficiency* of an agent as the ratio of their value over (declared) cost. Agents with a high efficiency are preferable as, compared to agents with a lower efficiency, they (relatively) contribute a higher value per unit cost. If the cost of an agent i is 0, we define their efficiency as being ∞ such that i has maximum efficiency among the considered agents. Whenever we order the agents according to decreasing efficiencies, we assume that ties are broken arbitrarily but consistently. We define $\text{opt}(A, \mathbf{c})$ as the value of the optimal fractional solution regarding the set of agents A, costs $\mathbf{c} = (c_i)_{i \in A}$ and values $\mathbf{v} = (v_i)_{i \in A}$. $\text{opt}_{-i}(A, \mathbf{c})$ is defined similarly, only regarding the set of agents $A \setminus \{i\}$. For the sake of readability, we omit the valuations $\mathbf{v}$ as an argument as these are publicly known.

Given that we focus on the design of truthful mechanisms in this paper, we adopt the convention (which is standard in this context) and often use $\mathbf{c} = (c_i)_{i \in A}$ also to refer to the declared costs of the agents.

3   Linear Valuation Functions

The Mechanism. It is well-known that designing a truthful and individually rational mechanism comes down to designing a monotone allocation rule and implementing it together with the payment rule of Theorem 1. When selecting an agent i in this case, the first term of (1) is equal to cost incurred by agent i and the second term can be interpreted as the amount agent i is overpaid. It is beneficial for this second term to be as small as possible, in order to select more agents and achieve a better approximation guarantee.

We give a mechanism that realizes this by imposing a *threat*, denoted τ_i, on each agent i in the second part of the mechanism. If the declared cost of agent i exceeds this threat, i will loose. In this case, the second term of the payment formula is equivalent to $\int_{b_i}^{\tau_i} x_i(u, \mathbf{b}_{-i}) du$, and our goal thus is to choose τ_i close to the true cost c_i to not overpay too much, while remaining at least as large to avoid a negative impact on the approximation guarantee.

In order to use these threats to bound the payments, τ_i must not increase when agent i declares a higher cost. Note that bounding the payments with τ_i can still be done if τ_i decreases when agent i declares a higher cost. In our mechanism, we use the following threat τ_i for an agent i, which is independent of the declared cost of i:

$$\tau_i = v_i \frac{B}{\alpha(1 + \beta)\mathsf{opt}_{-i}(N, \mathbf{c})}.$$

Note that this threat τ_i imposes an upper bound on the *threshold bid* of agent i, i.e., the largest cost agent i can declare such that i wins.

Additionally, we define for each agent i:

$$\rho_i(N, \mathbf{c}) = \frac{v_i}{\mathsf{opt}_{-i}(N, \mathbf{c})},$$

which represents some measure of how valuable agent i individually is. Note that an agent i has no influence on their own ratio.

Our allocation rule will either select one valuable agent, or select agents in a greedy manner according to efficiencies, which naturally leads to a monotone allocation rule. Let $\alpha \in (0, 1]$ and $\beta > 0$ be some parameters which we fix later. Our mechanism is as follows:

DIVISIBLE AGENTS (DA)

1: Let $N = \{i \in A \mid c_i \le B\}$, $n = |N|$ and $i^* = \arg\max_{i \in N} \rho_i(N, \mathbf{c})$
2: **if** $\rho_{i^*}(N, \mathbf{c}) \ge \beta$ **then** set $x_{i^*} = 1$ and $x_i = 0$ for $i \in N \setminus \{i^*\}$
3: **else**
4:      Rename agents s.t. $\frac{v_1}{c_1} \ge \frac{v_2}{c_2} \ge \cdots \ge \frac{v_n}{c_n}$
5:      Compute $\mathbf{x}$ s.t. $v(\mathbf{x}) = \alpha\mathsf{opt}(N, \mathbf{c})$ with $x_i = 1$ for $i < k$, $x_k \in (0, 1]$
        and $x_i = 0$ for $i > k$, $k \le n$
6:      **for** $i \le k$ **do**
7:          **if** $c_i > \tau_i$ **then** set $x_i = 0$
8: For $i \in N$ compute payments p_i according to (1)
9: **return** $(\mathbf{x}, \mathbf{p})$

Lemma 1. *Mechanism* **DA** *is truthful and individually rational.*

Proof. We start by showing that the allocation rule is monotone non-increasing. Suppose that, given declared costs $\mathbf{c} = (c_i)_{i \in A}$, $\mathbf{x}$ is computed by the mechanism.

Suppose the mechanism selected agent i^* and suppose i^* decreases their declared cost to $c' < c_{i^*}$ and let $\mathbf{c}' = (c', \mathbf{c}_{-i^*})$. Note that the set N does not change as long as $c' \leq B$. Then $\rho_i(N, \mathbf{c}')$ of agents $i \neq i^*$ can only decrease, $\rho_{i^*}(N, \mathbf{c}')$ stays the same and therefore i^* remains fully selected. Now suppose i^* increases their declared cost c' such that $c_{i^*} < c' \leq B$. Then $\rho_i(N, \mathbf{c}')$ of agents $i \neq i^*$ can only increase and again $\rho_{i^*}(N, \mathbf{c}')$ stays the same. Therefore i^* remains fully selected if $\forall i \in N: \rho_{i^*}(N, \mathbf{c}') \geq \rho_i(N, \mathbf{c}')$, otherwise i^* loses. When i^* increases their declared cost to $c' > B$, i^* definitely loses.

Otherwise the mechanism computed $\mathbf{x}$ such that (initially) $v(\mathbf{x}) = \alpha \mathbf{opt}(N, \mathbf{c})$. Suppose some winning agent i decreases their declared cost to $c' < c_i$ and let $\mathbf{c}' = (c', \mathbf{c}_{-i})$. Then $\rho_j(N, \mathbf{c}')$ of agents $j \neq i$ can only decrease and $\rho_i(N, \mathbf{c}')$ stays the same, so the allocation vector is still computed in the second part of the mechanism. The ratio $\frac{v_i}{c'}$ increases, so i can only move further to the front of the ordering. In addition, $\mathbf{opt}(N, \mathbf{c}')$ can only increase and therefore i will be selected to the same extent or more. Note that the threat will not deselect agent i, as the value of the threat does not change and i decreases their declared cost. Now suppose i increases their declared cost c' such that $c_i < c' \leq B$. Then $\rho_j(N, \mathbf{c}')$ of agents $j \neq i$ can only increase and $\rho_i(N, \mathbf{c}')$ stays the same. If the mechanism now selects agent i^*, agent i loses. Otherwise, the ratio $\frac{v_i}{c'}$ decreases, so i can only move further to the back of the ordering. In addition, $\mathbf{opt}(N, \mathbf{c}')$ can only decrease and therefore i will be selected to the same extent or less. When i increases their declared cost to $c' > \min\{B, \tau_i\}$, i definitely loses. Therefore, the allocation rule is monotone.

Note that a winning agent i definitely loses when declaring a cost $c' > B$ and as $x_i \in [0, 1]$, we have $\int_0^\infty x_i(u, \mathbf{c}_{-i}) du \leq 1 \cdot B < \infty$. Therefore, the mechanism is truthful and individually rational by Theorem 1. □

Lemma 2. *Mechanism* **DA** *is budget feasible.*

Proof. Suppose, given declared costs $\mathbf{c} = (c_i)_{i \in A}$, $\mathbf{x}$ is computed by selecting agent i^*. We have $\sum_{i \in N} p_i = p_{i^*} \leq 1 \cdot B$, as $x_{i^*} \in [0, 1]$ and i^* definitely loses when declaring a cost $c' > B$.

Otherwise, the mechanism computed $\mathbf{x}$ by selecting k agents such that (initially) $v(\mathbf{x}) = \alpha \mathbf{opt}(N, \mathbf{c})$. By construction we know that the threshold bid for agent i is smaller than or equal to our threat τ_i. Therefore, and because the allocation rule is monotone, the payment of agent i can be bounded by $x_i \tau_i$ and

$$\sum_{i \in N} p_i = \sum_{i=1}^{k} p_i \leq \sum_{i=1}^{k} x_i v_i \frac{B}{\alpha(1 + \beta)\mathbf{opt}_{-i}(N, \mathbf{c})} \leq \sum_{i=1}^{k} x_i v_i \frac{B}{\alpha \mathbf{opt}(N, \mathbf{c})} \leq B,$$

were the second inequality follows from $\mathbf{opt}(N, \mathbf{c}) \leq \mathbf{opt}_{-i}(N, \mathbf{c}) + v_i < (1 + \beta)\mathbf{opt}_{-i}(N, \mathbf{c})$, as the mechanism did not select agent i^*. Hence, the mechanism is budget feasible. □

In order to prove the approximation guarantee, we need the following lemma.

Lemma 3. *Let* $\mathbf{x}^*$ *be a solution of* $\mathsf{opt}(A, \mathbf{c})$ *and assume agents* $i \in A$, $n = |A|$, *are ordered such that* $\frac{v_1}{c_1} \geq \cdots \geq \frac{v_n}{c_n}$. *Let* $k \leq n$ *be an integer such that* $\sum_{i=1}^{k-1} v_i x_i^* < \alpha \mathsf{opt}(A, \mathbf{c}) \leq \sum_{i=1}^{k} v_i x_i^*$, $\alpha \in (0, 1]$. *Then* $\frac{c_k}{v_k}(1 - \alpha)\mathsf{opt}(A, \mathbf{c}) \leq B$.

Proof. For convenience let $\mathsf{opt} = \mathsf{opt}(A, \mathbf{c})$. Note that we can split $\mathbf{x}^*$ into $\mathbf{x} = (x_1^*, \ldots, x_{k-1}^*, x_k, 0, \ldots, 0)$ and $\mathbf{y} = (0, \ldots, 0, x_k^* - x_k, x_{k+1}^*, \ldots, x_n^*)$ with $x_k \leq x_k^*$ such that $\mathbf{x}^* = \mathbf{x} + \mathbf{y}$, $v(\mathbf{x}) = \alpha\mathsf{opt}$ and $v(\mathbf{y}) = (1 - \alpha)\mathsf{opt}$. By feasibility of $\mathbf{x}^*$, and thus $\mathbf{y}$, and the ordering of the agents it follows that

$$B \geq \sum_{i=k}^{n} c_i y_i = \sum_{i=k}^{n} \frac{c_i}{v_i} v_i y_i \geq \frac{c_k}{v_k} \sum_{i=k}^{n} v_i y_i = \frac{c_k}{v_k}(1 - \alpha)\mathsf{opt}.$$

$\square$

Lemma 3 can be interpreted in the following way. If agents k up to some $j \in A$, $j \geq k$, together contribute a fraction of $(1 - \alpha)$ of the value of the optimal solution, then 'paying' these agents a cost per unit value of $\frac{c_k}{v_k}$ is budget feasible, as these agents actually have a greater or an equal cost per unit value.

Lemma 4. *Mechanism* **DA** *has an approximation guarantee of* $\frac{\sqrt{5}+1}{\sqrt{5}-1}$ *if* $\alpha = \frac{\sqrt{5}-1}{\sqrt{5}+1}$ *and* $\beta = \frac{1}{2}\sqrt{5} - \frac{1}{2}$.

Proof. Suppose given declared costs $\mathbf{c} = (c_i)_{i \in A}$, $\mathbf{x}$ is computed by the mechanism. If the mechanism selected agent i^*, we have

$$v_{i^*} \geq \beta\mathsf{opt}_{-i^*}(N, \mathbf{c}) \geq \beta\mathsf{opt}(N, \mathbf{c}) - \beta v_{i^*} \quad \Leftrightarrow \quad v(\mathbf{x}) \geq \frac{\beta}{1+\beta}\mathsf{opt}(N, \mathbf{c}).$$

Otherwise the mechanism computed $\mathbf{x}$ by selecting k agents such that initially $v(\mathbf{x}) = \alpha\mathsf{opt}(N, \mathbf{c})$. We want no agent $i \leq k$ to be deselected by our threat, i.e., we want $c_i \leq \tau_i$. If

$$R := \frac{\alpha(1+\beta)}{(1-\alpha)} \leq 1 \quad \text{then} \quad \frac{\alpha(1+\beta)}{(1-\alpha)}\mathsf{opt}_{-i}(N, \mathbf{c}) \leq \mathsf{opt}(N, \mathbf{c}),$$

and rearranging terms leads to

$$\tau_i = v_i \frac{B}{\alpha(1+\beta)\mathsf{opt}_{-i}(N, \mathbf{c})} \geq v_i \frac{B}{(1-\alpha)\mathsf{opt}(N, \mathbf{c})} \geq c_i,$$

where the last inequality follows from Lemma 3 and the ordering of the agents. To see that the condition of Lemma 3 is satisfied, note that there exists an optimal solution of the form $(1, \ldots, 1, a \in [0, 1], 0, \ldots, 0)$ and for equal values of α the integer k of the mechanism and Lemma 3 then correspond.

Balancing the approximation guarantees $(1 + \beta)/\beta = 1/\alpha$ subject to $R \leq 1$ leads to $\alpha = \frac{\sqrt{5}-1}{\sqrt{5}+1} \approx 0.38$, $\beta = \frac{1}{2}\sqrt{5} - \frac{1}{2} \approx 0.61$ and an approximation guarantee of $\frac{\sqrt{5}+1}{\sqrt{5}-1} \approx 2.62$.

$\square$

The mechanism **DA** is computationally efficient: it is trivial to see that all steps take polynomial time, except for the computation of the payments. The latter can also be done efficiently for each agent i because the payment function is piecewise and the number of subfunctions one needs to consider is bounded by n. Further details can be found in the full version of the paper (see [13]). From Lemmas 1, 2 and 4, we arrive at the following theorem.

Theorem 2. *Mechanism* **DA** *with* $\alpha = \frac{\sqrt{5}-1}{\sqrt{5}+1}$ *and* $\beta = \frac{1}{2}\sqrt{5} - \frac{1}{2}$ *is truthful, individually rational, budget feasible, computationally efficient and has an approximation guarantee of* $\frac{\sqrt{5}+1}{\sqrt{5}-1}$.

Lower Bound. Next we show that no truthful, individually rational, budget feasible and deterministic mechanism exists with an approximation guarantee of $(\frac{5}{4} - \epsilon_1)$, for some $\epsilon_1 > 0$. For contradiction, assume such a mechanism does exist. Consider two instances, both with budget B and two agents with equal valuations: $\mathcal{I}_1 = (B, \mathbf{v} = \mathbf{1}, \mathbf{c} = (B, B))$ and $\mathcal{I}_2 = (B, \mathbf{v} = \mathbf{1}, \mathbf{c} = (\epsilon_2, B))$. In the first instance $\mathbf{opt} = 1$, so for the approximation guarantee to hold, an allocation vector must satisfy $v(\mathbf{x}) \geq 4/(5-4\epsilon_1)$. Therefore, any such mechanism must have some agent i for which $x_i \geq 2/(5-4\epsilon_1)$ and assume w.l.o.g. that this is agent 1. In the second instance $\mathbf{opt} = 2 - \epsilon_2/B$, so for the approximation guarantee to hold, an allocation vector must satisfy $v(\mathbf{x}) \geq (2-\epsilon_2/B)(4/(5-4\epsilon_1))$. By the previous instance and individual rationality, it follows that agent 1 can guarantee itself a utility of at least $u = (B - \epsilon_2)2/(5 - 4\epsilon_1)$ by deviating to B. As agent 1 must be somewhat selected to achieve the approximation guarantee, $p_1 \geq \epsilon_2 x_1 + u$ by truthfulness. Therefore in the best case, if agent 1 is entirely selected, this leads to a budget left of at most $B' = B - \epsilon_2 - u$. By spending this all on agent 2, this leads to an allocation vector with a value of at most $2 - \epsilon_2/B - u/B$. With elementary calculations, one can show that this value is smaller than $\mathbf{opt}/(\frac{5}{4} - \epsilon_1)$ if $\epsilon_2 < (8B\epsilon_1)/(4\epsilon_1 + 1)$, resulting in a contradiction.

4   Competitive Markets

It is common for lower bound proofs to use multiple instances in order to show that a mechanism cannot satisfy all properties in each instance. In our proof, and also in the lower bound proofs by Singer [1] and Gravin et al. [3], this leads to very specific instances. One instance has agents with equal efficiency while the other instance has agents for which the difference in efficiency cannot be bounded by a finite constant. Both instances are plausible in, say, a mature market were the efficiencies of the agents are close, or a premature market were the efficiencies of the agents differ a lot.

However, it is reasonable to assume that after some time the efficiencies of the agents are somewhat bounded, as agents will cease to exist if they cannot compete with the other agents in terms of efficiency. We therefore introduce a setting in which some bound on the efficiencies of the agents is known and seek a tighter approximation guarantee for this setting. We formalize this with the following definition.

Definition 1. *A procurement auction instance* $\mathcal{I} = (B, (v_i)_{i \in A}, (c_i)_{i \in A})$ *is* θ-*competitive with* $\theta \geq 1$ *if*

$$\max_{i \in A : c_i \leq B} \frac{v_i}{c_i} \leq \theta \min_{i \in A : c_i \leq B} \frac{v_i}{c_i}. \tag{2}$$

In this setting, we will also say that the agents are θ-*competitive*. Note that if $\theta = 1$ then all agents are equally competitive. If $\theta \to \infty$ the competitiveness of the agents is unbounded, which corresponds to the original setting.

The Mechanism. Under the assumption that an instance is θ-competitive, an agent can only increase their declared cost up to some c' before becoming the agent with worst efficiency. Again, we use the payment rule of Theorem 1, and want the second term of (1) to be as small as possible. We give a mechanism that realizes this, not by directly imposing a threat, but by setting the parameters of the mechanism to specific values. This will ensure that if, in the second part of the mechanism, the declared cost of an agent exceeds some c', this agent will lose. Let $\alpha \in (0, 1]$ and $\beta > 0$ be some parameters which we fix later. Our mechanism is as follows:

DIVISIBLE θ-COMPETITIVE AGENTS (DA-θ)

1: Let $N = \{i \in A \mid c_i \leq B\}$, $n = |N|$ and $i^* = \arg\max_{i \in N} \rho_i(N, \mathbf{c})$
2: **if** $\rho_{i^*}(N, \mathbf{c}) \geq \beta$ **then** set $x_{i^*} = 1$ and $x_i = 0$ for $i \in N \setminus \{i^*\}$
3: **else**
4:     Rename agents such that $\frac{v_1}{c_1} \geq \frac{v_2}{c_2} \geq \cdots \geq \frac{v_n}{c_n}$
5:     Compute $\mathbf{x}$ s.t. $v(\mathbf{x}) = \alpha \mathsf{opt}(N, \mathbf{c})$ with $x_i = 1$ for $i < k$, $x_k \in (0, 1]$
       and $x_i = 0$ for $i > k$, $k \leq n$
6: For $i \in N$ compute payments p_i according to (1)
7: **return** $(\mathbf{x}, \mathbf{p})$

Lemma 5. *Mechanism* **DA-θ** *is truthful and individually rational.*

The proof of Lemma 5 is identical to the proof of Lemma 1 with one exception: In the second part of the mechanism, a winning agent i will definitely loose if i would have declared a cost $c' > \min\{B, \theta c_i\}$, were the reasoning of the second argument is stated in the proof of Lemma 7. In order to prove budget feasibility, we will need the following lemma which states that if some k most efficient agents together contribute a fraction of α of the value of the optimal solution, then the corresponding total cost of these agents cannot exceed a fraction of α of the budget.

Lemma 6. *Let* $\mathbf{x}^*$ *be a solution of* $\mathsf{opt}(A, \mathbf{c})$ *and assume agents* $i \in A$, $n = |A|$, *are ordered such that* $\frac{v_1}{c_1} \geq \cdots \geq \frac{v_n}{c_n}$. *Let* $v(\mathbf{x}) = \alpha \mathsf{opt}(A, \mathbf{c})$ *with* $\alpha \in (0, 1]$, *integer* $k \leq n$, $x_i = x_i^*$ *for* $i < k$, $x_k \in (0, x_k^*]$, $x_i = 0$ *for* $i > k$. *Then* $\sum_{i=1}^k c_i x_i \leq \alpha B$.

Proof. For convenience let $\mathsf{opt} = \mathsf{opt}(A, \mathbf{c})$. Define $\mathbf{y} = \mathbf{x}^* - \mathbf{x}$, then $v(\mathbf{y}) = (1 - \alpha)\mathsf{opt}$. For contradiction, suppose $c(\mathbf{x}) = \sum_{i=1}^k c_i x_i > \alpha B$. Then it must be that $c(\mathbf{y}) < (1 - \alpha)B$, as otherwise $c(\mathbf{x}^*) = c(\mathbf{x}) + c(\mathbf{y}) > B$. We have

$$\alpha B < \sum_{i=1}^{k} c_i x_i = \sum_{i=1}^{k} \frac{c_i}{v_i} v_i x_i \leq \frac{c_k}{v_k} \sum_{i=1}^{k} v_i x_i = \frac{c_k}{v_k} \alpha \mathsf{opt} \quad \Leftrightarrow \quad B < \frac{c_k}{v_k} \mathsf{opt},$$

and

$$(1 - \alpha)B > \sum_{i=k}^{n} c_i y_i = \sum_{i=k}^{n} \frac{c_i}{v_i} v_i y_i \geq \frac{c_k}{v_k} \sum_{i=k}^{n} v_i y_i = \frac{c_k}{v_k}(1 - \alpha)\mathsf{opt} \quad \Leftrightarrow \quad B > \frac{c_k}{v_k} \mathsf{opt},$$

resulting in a contradiction. □

Lemma 7. *Mechanism* **DA-**θ *is budget feasible if* $\alpha \leq \min\left\{\frac{1}{\theta}, \frac{1}{1+\beta}\right\}$.

Proof. If, given declared costs $\mathbf{c} = (c_i)_{i \in A}$, $\mathbf{x}$ is computed by selecting agent i^*, the proof is identical to Lemma 2. Otherwise the mechanism computed $\mathbf{x}$ such that $v(\mathbf{x}) = \alpha \mathsf{opt}(N, \mathbf{c})$. Suppose a winning agent i increases their declared cost to $c' > \theta c_i$ and let $\mathbf{c}' = (c', \mathbf{c}_{-i})$. If $c' > B$, agent i loses. If this is not the case, we proof that i loses if $\alpha \leq \frac{1}{1+\beta}$. As the allocation vector was initially computed in the second part of the mechanism, we have $v_i \leq \beta \mathsf{opt}_{-i}(N, \mathbf{c})$ leading to

$$\mathsf{opt}(N, \mathbf{c}') \leq \mathsf{opt}(N, \mathbf{c}) \leq \mathsf{opt}_{-i}(N, \mathbf{c}) + v_i \leq (1 + \beta)\mathsf{opt}_{-i}(N, \mathbf{c}) \quad \Leftrightarrow$$

$$\alpha \mathsf{opt}(N, \mathbf{c}') \leq \frac{1}{1 + \beta} \mathsf{opt}(N, \mathbf{c}') \leq \mathsf{opt}_{-i}(N, \mathbf{c}) \leq \sum_{j \in N, j \neq i} v_j.$$

The above inequality points out that the total valuation of agents $j \neq i$ is greater than or equal to $\alpha \mathsf{opt}(N, \mathbf{c}')$. Therefore, as agent i will be last in the ordering when increasing their cost to c', i loses if the allocation vector is computed in the second part of the mechanism. If the allocation vector is computed by selecting i^*, agent i also loses. Therefore, and by monotonicity of the allocation rule, we can bound the sum of the payments with

$$\sum_{i \in N} p_i = \sum_{i=1}^{k} p_i \leq \sum_{i=1}^{k} \theta c_i x_i \leq \theta \alpha B,$$

where the last inequality follows from Lemma 6. To see this, note that an optimal solution of the form $(1, \ldots, 1, a \in [0, 1], 0, \ldots, 0)$ exists and for equal values of α the integer k and allocation vector $\mathbf{x}$ of the mechanism and Lemma 6 then correspond. So if $\alpha \leq \frac{1}{\theta}$ and $\alpha \leq \frac{1}{1+\beta}$, the payments are budget feasible. □

It is not hard to see that the mechanism **DA-**θ is computationally efficient. We refer the reader to the full version of the paper for further details. The approximation guarantee is equal to $\max\left\{\frac{\beta+1}{\beta}, \frac{1}{\alpha}\right\}$, where the second argument is by construction and the first argument follows from exactly the same reasoning as in Lemma 4. Minimizing this max-expression subject to $\alpha \leq \min\left\{\frac{1}{\theta}, \frac{1}{1+\beta}\right\}$ (budget feasibility) leads to $\alpha = \frac{1}{2}$ and $\beta = 1$ if $\theta \in [1, 2]$. Therefore, the following theorem follows from Lemmas 5 and 7.

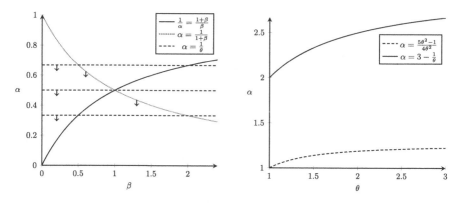

Fig. 1. Left: Plot of when the approximation guarantees are equal and parameter constraints for α (dashed and dotted). Right: Lower bound on the approximation guarantee for different values of θ for the divisible (dashed) and indivisible case.

Theorem 3. *If $\theta \in [1,2]$, mechanism **DA-θ** with $\alpha = \frac{1}{2}$ and $\beta = 1$ is truthful, individually rational, budget feasible, computationally efficient and has an approximation guarantee of 2.*

It can be seen in the left plot of Fig. 1 that if $\theta > 2$, it is optimal to set $\alpha = \frac{1}{\theta}$ and β to any number in $\left[\frac{\alpha}{1-\alpha}, \frac{1-\alpha}{\alpha}\right]$, as then α is the limiting factor in the approximation guarantee $(\frac{1}{\alpha} \geq (1 + \beta)/\beta)$ and the value of α is feasible $(\alpha \leq 1/(1 + \beta))$. So if it is known that agents are θ-competitive with $\theta < 2.62$, it is beneficial to use mechanism **DA-θ** instead of mechanism **DA**.

Lower Bound. Similar to Sect. 3, one can show that if $\theta \geq 2$ no deterministic, truthful, individually rational and budget feasible mechanism exists with an approximation guarantee of $(\frac{19}{16} - \epsilon)$, for some $\epsilon > 0$. Additionally, this instance can be adjusted to a specific value of θ to prove that no mechanism exists with an approximation guarantee of $((5\theta^2 - 1)/(4\theta^2) - \epsilon)$, for some $\epsilon > 0$. Details can be found in the full version of the paper. The general lower bound is plotted in Fig. 1 and, as in Sect. 3, converges to $\frac{5}{4}$ if $\theta \to \infty$.

For the indivisible case, one can show that if $\theta \geq 2$ no deterministic, truthful, individually rational and budget feasible mechanism exists with an approximation guarantee of $(\frac{5}{2} - \epsilon)$ compared to the fractional optimum, for some $\epsilon > 0$. This lower bound can also be adjusted to a specific value of θ and, as in Gravin et al. [3], converges to 3 if $\theta \to \infty$. Again, details can be found in the full version of the paper.

5   Agent Types with Capped Linear Valuation Functions

In this section, we extend the original setting with two extra elements: namely agent types and a capped linear valuation function for each type. In the Introduction, we described how this relates to the example in which an auctioneer wants to organize a comedy show. The two extra elements of an instance

$\mathcal{I} = (B, (v_i)_{i \in A}, (c_i)_{i \in A}, (t_i)_{i \in A}, (l_j)_{j \in T})$ of this type of procurement auction are defined as follows: Each agent $i \in A$ has a type $t_i \in T = \{1, 2, \ldots, t\}$, with $t \leq n$. If agents have the same type, they are substitutable, meaning that they are offering a similar good or service. For every type $j \in T$, the auctioneer has a valuation function $l_j : \mathbb{R}_{\geq 0} \to \mathbb{R}_{\geq 0}$, which maps the accumulative selected value of type j, to the actual value obtained by the auctioneer. We assume that there is a maximum total value of each type that the auctioneer wishes to buy, and the auctioneer will obtain no extra value if more value is selected. Additionally, selecting more than this maximum value will not have a negative impact. More formally for a type $j \in T$, $M_j \in \mathbb{R}^+$ represents this maximum value for type j, $l_j(x) = x$ for $x \leq M_j$ and $l_j(x) = M_j$ for $x \geq M_j$.

In this section, $\mathsf{opt}(A, \mathbf{c})$ now corresponds to the value of the optimal solution of the linear program stated below and $\mathsf{opt}_{-i}(A, \mathbf{c})$ corresponds to the optimal value when regarding the set of agents $A \setminus \{i\}$.

$$
\begin{aligned}
\max \quad & \sum_{j \in T} l_j(V_j) \\
\text{s.t.} \quad & \sum_{i \in A} c_i x_i \leq B \\
& \sum_{i \in A : t_i = j} v_i x_i = V_j \quad \forall j \in T \\
& V_j \leq M_j \quad \forall j \in T \\
& x_i \in [0, 1] \quad \forall i \in A
\end{aligned}
$$

Note that if an optimal solution has a value of $\sum_{j \in T} M_t$ and some remaining budget, the inequality $V_j \leq M_j$ ensures that this remaining budget is not spend on some agent that is not yet entirely selected. This has no influence on optimality and ensures that Lemmas 3 and 6 also hold in this setting. We define for each agent i:

$$
\rho_i(N, \mathbf{c}) = \frac{\min\{v_i, M_{t_i}\}}{\mathsf{opt}_{-i}(N, \mathbf{c})}.
$$

Note that an agent i still has no influence on their own ratio. Again we either select one valuable agent, or select agents in a greedy manner according to efficiencies and an optimal solution, which still naturally leads to a monotone allocation rule. Let $\alpha \in (0, 1]$ and $\beta > 0$ be some parameters which we fix later. Our mechanism is as follows:

DIVISIBLE AGENTS CAPPED VALUATION (DACV)

1: Let $N = \{i \in A \mid c_i \leq B\}$, $n = |N|$ and $i^* = \arg\max_{i \in N} \rho_i(N, \mathbf{c})$
2: **if** $\rho_{i^*}(N, \mathbf{c}) \geq \beta$ **then** set $x_{i^*} = 1$ and $x_i = 0$ for $i \in N \setminus \{i^*\}$
3: **else**
4:     Rename agents s.t. $\frac{v_1}{c_1} \geq \frac{v_2}{c_2} \geq \cdots \geq \frac{v_n}{c_n}$
5:     Compute $\mathbf{x}^*$ of $\mathsf{opt}(N, \mathbf{c})$ and set $\mathbf{x}$ s.t. $v(\mathbf{x}) = \alpha v(\mathbf{x}^*)$ with
      $x_i = x_i^*$ for $i < k$, $x_k \in (0, x_k^*]$ and $x_i = 0$ for $i > k$, $k \leq n$
6:     **for** $i \leq k$ **do**
7:         **if** $c_i > \tau_i$ **then** set $x_i = 0$
8: For $i \in N$ compute payments p_i according to (1)
9: **return** $(\mathbf{x}, \mathbf{p})$

Theorem 4. *Mechanism* **DACV** *with* $\alpha \approx 0.38$ *and* $\beta \approx 0.61$ *is truthful, individually rational, budget feasible, computationally efficient and has an approximation guarantee of* ≈ 2.62.

If the θ-competitive market assumption is added to this setting, we define mechanism **DACV-θ** as being identical to **DACV**, but with the threats (lines 6 and 7) excluded.

Theorem 5. *If* $\theta \in [1,2]$, *mechanism* **DACV-θ** *with* $\alpha = \frac{1}{2}$ *and* $\beta = 1$ *is truthful, individually rational, budget feasible, computationally efficient and has an approximation guarantee of 2.*

The proofs of Theorems 4 and 5, and the reasoning why both mechanisms are computationally efficient can be found in the full version of the paper, as they are similar to earlier proofs. Note that for both settings the lower bounds of Sects. 3 and 4 still hold. In both examples one can define that each agent has the same type t and $M_t = \sum_{i \in A} v_i$.

6   Conclusion and Future Work

We considered budget feasible mechanisms for procurement auctions in the case of divisible agents. The challenge of exploiting the divisibility of agents is to limit the consequences of selecting agents fractionally, so that budget feasibility can be ensured. To achieve this in the initial setting with an additive linear valuation function, we introduced the notion of threats and found an upper bound of 2.62 and a lower bound of 1.25 on the approximation guarantee. When introducing a notion of competitiveness between agents, we found an upper and lower bound on the approximation guarantee of 2 and 1.18 respectively. In both settings the gap between the upper and lower bound on the approximation guarantee remains and it would be interesting to see if both of these gaps can be tightened or even closed. Both results can be extended to the setting with multiple agent types and a linear capped valuation function for each type. This setting can be used to model a maximum total value of each type that the auctioneer wishes to buy.

An interesting extension of our multiple agent type setting is to consider multiple concave (non-decreasing) valuation functions (per agent type). Such functions can be used to model diminishing returns of the auctioneer, i.e., the marginal increase in value decreases as more value of a certain type is selected (but selecting more value will never have a negative impact). We have some (preliminary) results showing that our mechanisms can be adapted to this more general setting, though at the expense of worse approximation guarantees (as the number of different types t enters the approximation factor). More details can be found in the full version of the paper (see [13]).

It would be natural to also study the divisible case in settings with other valuation functions. Additionally, one could study the problem with an underlying structure, such as matroids in the indivisible case, to capture a relation between goods.

Acknowledgement. We thank Georgios Amanatidis for proposing to study budget feasible mechanisms for divisible agents when he was a postdoc at CWI. Part of this work was sponsored by the Open Technology Program of the Dutch Research Council (NWO), project number 18938.

References

1. Singer, Y.: Budget feasible mechanisms. In: Proceedings of the 51st Annual IEEE Symposium on Foundations of Computer Science, pp. 765–774. IEEE (2010)
2. Chen, N., Gravin, N., Lu, P.: On the approximability of budget feasible mechanisms. In: Proceedings of the 22nd Annual ACM-SIAM Symposium on Discrete Algorithms (SODA), pp. 685–699. SIAM (2011)
3. Gravin, N., Jin, Y., Lu, P., Zhang, C.: Optimal budget-feasible mechanisms for additive valuations. ACM Trans. Econ. Comput. (TEAC) **8**(4), 1–15 (2020)
4. Anari, N., Goel, G., Nikzad, A.: Mechanism design for crowdsourcing: an optimal 1–1/e competitive budget-feasible mechanism for large markets. In: IEEE 55th Annual Symposium on Foundations of Computer Science (FOCS), pp. 266–275. IEEE (2014)
5. Jalaly Khalilabadi, P., Tardos, É.: Simple and efficient budget feasible mechanisms for monotone submodular valuations. In: Christodoulou, G., Harks, T. (eds.) WINE 2018. LNCS, vol. 11316, pp. 246–263. Springer, Cham (2018). https://doi.org/10.1007/978-3-030-04612-5_17
6. Goel, G., Nikzad, A., Singla, A.: Mechanism design for crowdsourcing markets with heterogeneous tasks. In: Proceedings of the 2nd AAAI Conference on Human Computation and Crowdsourcing. AAAI (2014)
7. Leonardi, S., Monaco, G., Sankowski, P., Zhang, Q.: Budget feasible mechanisms on matroids. In: Eisenbrand, F., Koenemann, J. (eds.) IPCO 2017. LNCS, vol. 10328, pp. 368–379. Springer, Cham (2017). https://doi.org/10.1007/978-3-319-59250-3_30
8. Chan, H., Chen, J.: Truthful multi-unit procurements with budgets. In: Liu, T.-Y., Qi, Q., Ye, Y. (eds.) WINE 2014. LNCS, vol. 8877, pp. 89–105. Springer, Cham (2014). https://doi.org/10.1007/978-3-319-13129-0_7
9. Archer, A., Tardos, É.: Truthful mechanisms for one-parameter agents. In: Proceedings 42nd IEEE Symposium on Foundations of Computer Science (FOCS), pp. 482–491. IEEE (2001)
10. Dobzinski, S., Papadimitriou, C.H., Singer, Y.: Mechanisms for complement-free procurement. In: Proceedings of the 12th ACM Conference on Electronic Commerce (EC), pp. 273–282 (2011)
11. Bei, X., Chen, N., Gravin, N., Lu, P.: Budget feasible mechanism design: from prior-free to Bayesian. In: Proceedings of the 44th annual ACM Symposium on Theory of Computing (STOC), pp. 449–458 (2012)
12. Amanatidis, G., Birmpas, G., Markakis, E.: Coverage, matching, and beyond: new results on budgeted mechanism design. In: Cai, Y., Vetta, A. (eds.) WINE 2016. LNCS, vol. 10123, pp. 414–428. Springer, Heidelberg (2016). https://doi.org/10.1007/978-3-662-54110-4_29
13. Klumper, S., Schäfer, G.: Budget feasible mechanisms for procurement auctions with divisible agents. arXiv preprint arXiv:2206.13124 (2022)

On Improved Interval Cover Mechanisms for Crowdsourcing Markets

Evangelos Markakis$^{(\boxtimes)}$, Georgios Papasotiropoulos, and Artem Tsikiridis

Athens University of Economics and Business, Athens, Greece
markakis@gmail.com

Abstract. We study a covering problem motivated by spatial models in crowdsourcing markets, where tasks are ordered according to some geographic or temporal criterion. Assuming that each participating bidder can provide a certain level of contribution for a subset of consecutive tasks, and that each task has a demand requirement, the goal is to find a set of bidders of minimum cost, who can meet all the demand constraints. Our focus is on truthful mechanisms with approximation guarantees against the optimal cost. To this end, we obtain two main results. The first one, is a truthful mechanism that achieves a bounded approximation guarantee. This mechanism improves the state of the art, which is a mechanism with an arbitrarily large factor in worst case. The second one, concerns a class of instances that generalizes the minimum knapsack problem. Namely, we consider inputs with a constant number of tasks, for which we provide a truthful FPTAS. Finally, we also highlight connections of our problem with other well-studied optimization problems, out of which, we infer further conclusions on its (in)approximability.

1 Introduction

We consider a mechanism design problem, that emerges under certain spatial models for crowdsourcing and labour matching markets. It is instructive to start with an example, so as to introduce the main aspects of the model. Imagine a set of cities, located geographically in a consecutive order, and consider a company that has opened a store in each of these cities. In Fig. 1, we see an instance with 5 cities, named A to E. The company needs to meet a demand constraint, i.e., a lower bound on the volume of goods that need to be transported to each store, based on consumption and future planning. To achieve this goal, it chooses to hire other firms, or single individuals, that can make deliveries, via a reverse (procurement) auction (for an exposition on auctions for transportation routes, see [15]). Suppose that every participating entity, referred to as a bidder or a worker, can only cover a certain interval of contiguous cities, at a cost that she specifies, and furthermore, she can only accommodate a certain volume of goods, assumed to be the same for each city in her declared interval (among others, dependent on the transportation means that she owns). The problem boils down to selecting a set of winning bidders who can jointly cover all the demand constraints at minimum cost, and in a way that prevents the workers from misreporting their true preferences.

© The Author(s), under exclusive license to Springer Nature Switzerland AG 2022
P. Kanellopoulos et al. (Eds.): SAGT 2022, LNCS 13584, pp. 94–112, 2022.
https://doi.org/10.1007/978-3-031-15714-1_6

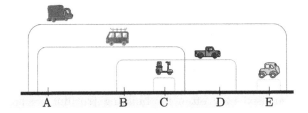

Fig. 1. An example with 5 tasks (A to E) and 5 workers.

In the crowdsourcing jargon, we can view the store in each city as a task with a demand requirement. For instance, in labeling/classification tasks, the demand could correspond to the number of people who should execute the task in order to acquire a higher confidence on the outcome. In other cases, it could be interpreted as a (not necessarily integral) volume coverage requirement.

Table 1. Contribution and costs of the workers of Fig. 1.

vehicle	contribution	cost
truck	8	10
van	6	5
pickup	5	4
motorbike	1	2
car	3	4

Coming back to the example of Fig. 1, say that the demand of cities A to E are given by the vector $(6, 2, 9, 1, 3)$. The contribution per task, as well as the cost of the workers are given by Table 1. The interval covered by each worker is visible in Fig. 1. Obviously, hiring all the workers is a feasible solution. Selecting the workers with the van, the pickup and the car also forms a feasible solution since the demands of all cities are indeed satisfied. Notice that the optimal solution is to hire the workers with the truck and the motorbike at a total cost of 12.

From an algorithmic viewpoint, there has been already significant progress on the problem. As it can be easily seen to be NP-hard, the main results on this front include constant factor approximation algorithms, with further improvements for special cases. However, in the context of mechanism design, one needs to consider strategic aspects as well. Bidders may attempt to report higher costs in order to achieve higher payments, or they can lie about the subset of tasks they can actually fulfil. It would be therefore desirable to have mechanisms that, on the one hand, achieve competitive approximation guarantees, and on the other, deter bidders from misreporting. To our knowledge, the currently best result on this direction is by [18], where however the approximation ratio of their truthful mechanism is unbounded in terms of the number of tasks and workers (and depends on numerical parameters of each instance). It has remained open since then, if truthfulness can be compatible with bounded approximation guarantees.

Contribution

We focus on truthful mechanisms and their approximation guarantees against the optimal cost. To this end, we provide two main results. The first one, in

Sect. 3, is a truthful Δ-approximation mechanism, where Δ is the maximum number of workers that are willing to work on the same task (the maximum being taken over all tasks). This mechanism, improves significantly the state of the art, coming to a guarantee that is polynomially bounded in terms of the input size. Apart from the improvement, we note also that our result is based on the local-ratio technique from approximation algorithms [4], a technique that has not been used very often for building truthful mechanisms (for an exception, see [20]). Moving on, our second result, in Sect. 4, concerns the class of instances with a constant number of tasks, which generalizes MIN-KNAPSACK, an NP-hard variant of KNAPSACK that corresponds to the single-task case of our problem. For this class we provide a truthful FPTAS, by mainly exploiting and adapting the framework of [8]. In doing so, we also identify a flaw in a previous attempt for designing a truthful FPTAS for MIN-KNAPSACK. Finally, in Sect. 5, we discuss some further implications and extensions. Namely, we bring to light some interesting connections with well-studied optimization problems, related to unsplittable flow problems and caching. By exploiting known results for these problems, we rule out a FPTAS for the general case, and also identify a special case where a PTAS is likely to exist.

Related Work

As already discussed, the work most related to ours is [18], which introduced the model in the context of crowdsourcing. They provide a truthful optimal mechanism when the workers have an identical contribution, whereas for the general case, they present a truthful approximate mechanism, the ratio of which is dependent on the contribution parameters of the workers. Furthermore, [41] studies the case of unit-demand tasks and unit-contribution workers and identifies a truthful optimal mechanism. For the same setting, they also propose a mechanism when workers can submit multiple bids, for which they attain a logarithmic factor. Additionally, in [42] the authors studied the prominent special case of a single task (MIN-KNAPSACK) and provided a randomized, truthful-in-expectation mechanism that achieves an approximation factor of 2.

Regarding the purely algorithmic problem, without the constraint of truthfulness, it has appeared under the name of (0-1)RESOURCE ALLOCATION, and a 4-approximation was presented in [10]. The currently best known algorithm achieves a factor of 3, in [33]. For the MIN-KNAPSACK problem, a PTAS is implied by [17] and a FPTAS is given in [29].

There are quite a few problems that can be viewed as generalizations of what we study here, such as *general scheduling problem* [2], *multidimensional min-knapsack, column restricted covering integer programs* [11]. Moreover, several problems in discrete optimization can be seen as related variants, but are neither extensions nor special cases of ours. Indicatively: *bandwidth allocation* [12], *multiset multicover* [7,38], *geometric knapsack* [23], *capacitated network design* [9], *admission control* [36].

Finally, for general spatio-temporal models appearing in the crowdsourcing literature, we refer to two recent surveys [25,39], which cover to a big extent the relevant results.

2   Preliminaries

In this section, we first define formally the problem that we study, together with some additional necessary notation. In the sequel, we discuss the relevant definitions for the design of truthful mechanisms. We note that all the missing proofs from the following sections can be found in the full version of our work.

Problem Statement

We are interested in the optimization problem defined below. For motivating applications, we refer the reader to Section 1.2 in [18].

Cost Minimization Interval Cover (CMIC): Consider a set of tasks, say $\{1, \ldots, m\}$, that are ordered in a line, and a set of available bidders $\mathcal{N} = \{1, \ldots, n\}$. We will interchangeably use the term bidder or worker in the sequel. An instance of CMIC is determined by a tuple $(\mathbf{b}, \mathbf{q}, \mathbf{d})$, where:

- The vector $\mathbf{b} = (b_1, \ldots, b_n)$ is the bidding profile. For each bidder $j \in \mathcal{N}$, $b_j = (c_j, [s_j, f_j])$, where $[s_j, f_j] = I_j$ is the interval of contiguous tasks $\{s_j, s_j + 1, \ldots, f_j\} \subseteq [m]$, that j is able to contribute to, and $c_j \in \mathbb{R}_{\geq 0}$ is the cost incurred to her, if she is selected to contribute. We can assume positive costs since workers of zero cost are trivially included in the solution. We often denote $\mathbf{b}$ as $(\mathbf{c}, \mathbf{I})$ where $\mathbf{c}$ is the cost vector and $\mathbf{I}$ is the vector of the intervals.
- The vector $\mathbf{q} = (q_1, \ldots, q_n)$ is the contribution vector, so that $q_j \in \mathbb{R}_{>0}$ denotes the contribution that bidder j can make to the tasks that belong to $[s_j, f_j]$.
- The vector $\mathbf{d} = (d_1, \ldots, d_m)$ specifies the demand $d_j \in \mathbb{R}_{>0}$ of a task j.

The goal is to select a set of bidders $S \subseteq \mathcal{N}$ of minimum cost, that satisfies

$$\sum_{i \in \mathcal{N}_j(\mathbf{I}) \cap S} q_i \geq d_j, \ \forall j \in [m], \tag{1}$$

where for $j \in [m]$, $\mathcal{N}_j(\mathbf{I}) := \{i \in \mathcal{N} \mid j \in [s_i, f_i]\}$, i.e. is the set of bidders who can contribute to task j.

The problem belongs to the broad family of problems described by covering integer programs. It may also seem reminiscent of multicover variants of the SET COVER problem on an interval universe. We note however that in CMIC, each worker is allowed to be picked at most once, and moreover, the coverage requirement is not necessarily integral, which is a substantial difference.

Given a feasible solution $S \subseteq \mathcal{N}$, we refer to its total cost, $\sum_{i \in S} c_i$, as the derived *social cost*. Throughout all our work, we focus on deterministic allocation algorithms that use a consistent deterministic tie-breaking rule. Given an instance $P = (\mathbf{b}, \mathbf{q}, \mathbf{d})$, and an allocation algorithm A, we denote by $\mathcal{W}_A(\mathbf{b})$ the set of bidders selected by A, when $\mathbf{q}, \mathbf{d}$ are clear from the context[1]. In the same spirit, we let also $C(A, \mathbf{b}) := \sum_{i \in \mathcal{W}_A(\mathbf{b})} c_i$ be the *social cost* derived by algorithm A on input P. Finally, we use $OPT(\mathbf{b})$ to denote the cost of an optimal solution.

---

[1] It is convenient to highlight the dependence on $\mathbf{b}$, especially when arguing about truthful mechanisms in the remaining sections.

Truthful Mechanisms

We move now to the strategic scenario, where bids can be private information. A mechanism for a reverse auction, like the ones we study here, is a tuple $M = (A, \boldsymbol{\pi})$, consisting of an *allocation algorithm* A and a *payment rule* $\boldsymbol{\pi}$. Initially, each bidder $j \in \mathcal{N}$ is asked to submit a bid $b_j := (c_j, [s_j, f_j])$, which may differ from her actual cost and interval. Then, given a bidding profile $\mathbf{b} = (\mathbf{c}, \mathbf{I})$, the allocation algorithm $A(\mathbf{b})$ selects the set of winning bidders, i.e., this is a binary setting where the allocation decision for each bidder is whether she is included in the solution or not. Finally, the mechanism computes a vector of payments $\boldsymbol{\pi}(\mathbf{b})$, so that $\pi_i(\mathbf{b})$ is the amount to be paid to bidder i by the auctioneer. Naturally, we will consider that non-winning bidders do not receive any payment.

Note that we consider the contribution q_j, for $j \in \mathcal{N}$, to be public information, available to the auctioneer. The reason is that such a parameter could be estimated by past statistical information on the performance or capacity of the worker. As an example, we refer to [18], where for labeling tasks, it is explained how q_j can be computed as a function of a worker's quality (i.e., the probability for a worker to label correctly), that can be available in a crowdsourcing platform with rating scores or reviews for the workers.

Our setting corresponds to what is usually referred to as a pseudo-2-parameter environment (or almost-single-parameter [5]), since each bidder has two types of private information, the monetary cost and the interval. And in particular, our model can be seen as a special case of *single-minded* bidders, who are interested in a single subset each, but for reverse auctions. As in [18], when the true type of a worker i is $(c_i, [s_i, t_i])$, and she declares her true interval or any non-empty subset of it, then she enjoys a utility of $\pi_i - c_i$, if she is selected as a winner by the mechanism (with π_i being her payment). If she declares any other interval that contains any task $j \notin [s_i, t_i]$, and she is selected as a winner, then the bidder has a utility of $-\infty$, or equivalently has an infinite cost. This simply models the fact that the worker may not be capable of executing or does not desire to be assigned to any task outside her true interval (and therefore would have no incentive for such deviations).

The previous discussion allows us to exploit the sufficient conditions proposed by [31] (for forward auctions), to obtain truthful mechanisms, as an extension of the seminal result by [34]. For reverse auctions, the same framework is also applicable, implying that as long as an allocation algorithm is exact (each selected bidder is assigned her declared interval), the crucial property we need to enforce is *monotonicity*. Monotonicity of an algorithm means that if a winning bidder declares a more competitive bid, she should still remain a winner. To be more precise, we define first the following partial order on possible bids.

Definition 1. *Let* $b_i = (c_i, [s_i, f_i])$ *and* $b'_i = (c'_i, [s'_i, f'_i])$ *be two bids of bidder* $i \in \mathcal{N}$. *We say that* $b'_i \succeq b_i$, *if* $c_i \geq c'_i$ *and* $[s_i, f_i] \subseteq [s'_i, f'_i]$.

Definition 2. *An allocation algorithm* A *is monotone if for every bidding profile* $\mathbf{b}$, *for any bidder* $i \in \mathcal{W}_A(\mathbf{b})$ *and any bid* $b'_i \succeq b_i$, *it holds that* $i \in \mathcal{W}_A(b'_i, \mathbf{b}_{-i})$.

Theorem 1 (cf. [31], Theorem 9.6). *In settings with single-minded bidders, given a monotone and exact algorithm A, there exists an efficiently computable payment rule π, such that $\mathcal{M} = (A, \pi)$ is a truthful mechanism.*

Finally, we stress that all our proposed algorithms are exact by construction, which means that bidders will only be assigned to the set of tasks which they asked for, as in [8], and hence we only need to care about monotonicity.

3   An Improved Truthful Approximation Mechanism

As already stated in Sect. 1, the currently best algorithm for CMIC has an approximation ratio of 3 [33], based on refining the 4-approximation algorithm by [10]. However, as the next proposition shows, these algorithms are not monotone[2]. More generally, it has been noted in [18] that primal-dual algorithms with a "delete phase" at the end, are typically non-monotone, without, however, providing an example. For the sake of completeness, in the full version of our work, we provide a concrete example that proves the following statement:

Proposition 1. *The current state of the art constant factor approximation algorithms for CMIC by [10,33] are not monotone.*

So far, the only truthful mechanism that has been identified [18], achieves an approximation ratio of $2 \cdot \max_{i \in \mathcal{N}}\{q_i\}$. Note that this approximation ratio is dependent on the contribution parameters of the workers, which can become arbitrarily large, and not bounded by any function of n and m. The main result of this section is the following theorem, established via a greedy, local-ratio algorithm, which reduces the gap between truthful and non-truthful mechanisms. In particular, this gap is related to the maximum number of workers that contribute to any given task, which for an instance $((\mathbf{c}, \mathbf{I}), \mathbf{q}, \mathbf{d})$ of CMIC, is $\Delta(\mathbf{I}) := \max_{j=1,\dots,m} |\mathcal{N}_j(\mathbf{I})|$. We denote it simply by Δ when $\mathbf{I}$ is clear from context. Obviously, Δ is always upper bounded by the number of workers, n.

Theorem 2. *There exists a truthful, polynomial-time mechanism, that achieves a Δ-approximation for the CMIC problem.*

The rest of the section is devoted to the proof of Theorem 2. The main component of the proof is an approximation-preserving reduction to a particular job scheduling problem for a single machine [3], defined as follows:

Loss Minimization Interval Scheduling (LMIS): We are given a limited resource whose amount may vary over a time period, which WLOG, is defined by the integral time instants $\{1, \dots, m\}$. We are also given a set of activities $\mathcal{J} = \{1, \dots, n\}$, each of which requires the utilization of the resource, for an interval of time instants. An instance of LMIS is determined by a tuple $(\mathbf{p}, \mathbf{T}, \mathbf{r}, \mathbf{D})$, where:

---

[2] For a similar reason, the 40-approximation for CMIC by [11], which uses as a subroutine a primal-dual algorithm involving a "delete phase", is non-monotone as well.

- The vector $\mathbf{p} = (p_1, \ldots, p_n)$ specifies a penalty $p_j \in \mathbb{R}_{>0}$, for each activity $j \in \mathcal{J}$, reflecting the cost that is incurred by not scheduling the activity.
- For each activity $j \in \mathcal{J}$, we are given an interval[3] $T_j = [s_j, f_j]$, such that $s_j, f_j \in \{1, \ldots, m\}$ are the start and finish times of j respectively. Let $\mathbf{T} = (T_1, \ldots, T_n)$, be the vector of all activity intervals.
- The vector $\mathbf{r}$ contains, for each activity $j \in \mathcal{J}$, the width $r_j \in \mathbb{R}_{>0}$, reflecting how much resource the activity requires, i.e., this means that activity j requires r_j units of resource at every integral time instant of its interval T_j.
- The vector $\mathbf{D} = (D_1, \ldots, D_m)$ specifies the amount of available resource $D_i \in \mathbb{R}_{>0}$, at each integral time instant $i \in [m]$.

Let $\mathcal{J}_i(\mathbf{T}) := \{j \in \mathcal{J} \mid i \in T_j\}$. The goal in LMIS is to select a set of activities $S \subseteq \mathcal{J}$ to schedule, that meet the resource constraint

$$\sum_{j \in S \cap \mathcal{J}_i(\mathbf{T})} r_j \leq D_i, \quad i = 1, \ldots, m, \tag{2}$$

and such that $\sum_{j \in \mathcal{J} \setminus S} p_j$ is minimized, i.e., we want to minimize the sum of the penalties for the non-scheduled activities.

Our work highlights an interesting connection between LMIS and CMIC. This can be seen via the reduction provided by algorithm $\hat{A}$ below, where for an instance $((\mathbf{c}, \mathbf{I}), \mathbf{q}, \mathbf{d})$, we let $\mathbf{Q}(\mathbf{I}) = (Q_1(\mathbf{I}), \ldots, Q_m(\mathbf{I}))$ and $Q_j(\mathbf{I}) := \sum_{i \in \mathcal{N}_j(\mathbf{I})} q_i, \forall j \in [m]$.

Algorithm 1: $\hat{A}(\mathbf{b})$

▷ **Input:** A bidding profile $\mathbf{b} = (\mathbf{c}, \mathbf{I})$ of a CMIC instance $((\mathbf{c}, \mathbf{I}), \mathbf{q}, \mathbf{d})$

---

1 Construct the LMIS instance $(\mathbf{p}, \mathbf{T}, \mathbf{r}, \mathbf{D}) = (\mathbf{c}, \mathbf{I}, \mathbf{q}, \mathbf{Q}(\mathbf{I}) - \mathbf{d})$, with $\mathcal{J} = \mathcal{N}$.
2 Run an approximation algorithm for the LMIS instance, and let S be the set of scheduled activities.
3 **return** $\mathcal{N} \setminus S$

Theorem 3. *Algorithm $\hat{A}$ converts any α-approximation algorithm for LMIS to an α-approximation algorithm for CMIC.*

Theorem 3 is based on the lemma below, which shows the connection between the feasible solutions of the two problems.

Lemma 1. *Consider a CMIC instance $P = ((\mathbf{c}, \mathbf{I}), \mathbf{q}, \mathbf{d})$. Let also P' be the LMIS instance defined by $(\mathbf{p}, \mathbf{T}, \mathbf{r}, \mathbf{D}) = (\mathbf{c}, \mathbf{I}, \mathbf{q}, \mathbf{Q}(\mathbf{I}) - \mathbf{d})$, with $\mathcal{J} = \mathcal{N}$. Then, for every feasible solution S of P, it holds that $\mathcal{J} \setminus S$ is a feasible solution for P' with the same cost, and vice versa.*

---

[3] Originally, the problem was defined using a semi-closed interval for each activity, but it is easy to see that defining it using a closed one instead, is equivalent and more convenient for our purposes.

Approximation Guarantee and Monotonicity of $\hat{A}$

If we only cared about the approximation ratio of $\hat{A}$, it would suffice to use as a black box any algorithm for LMIS. And in fact, the best known algorithm for LMIS achieves a 4-approximation, and was obtained in [3], using the local-ratio framework. Plugging in this algorithm however, does not ensure that we will end up with a truthful mechanism for CMIC. Instead, we will consider an appropriate modification of the algorithm by [3], which enforces monotonicity of $\hat{A}$, but at the price of a higher approximation ratio. This is presented as Algorithm 2 below.

We introduce first a notion that will be useful both for the statement of Algorithm 2 and for our analysis. Consider an instance $(\mathbf{p}, \mathbf{T}, \mathbf{r}, \mathbf{D})$ of LMIS. Given a set of jobs $S \subseteq \mathcal{J}$, and a time instant $i = 1, \dots, m$, we define

$$R_i(S, \mathbf{T}, \mathbf{D}) := \sum_{\ell \in S \cap \mathcal{J}_i(\mathbf{T})} r_\ell - D_i.$$

The quantity $R_i(S, \mathbf{T}, \mathbf{D})$ measures how much (if at all), the resource constraint of Eq. (2), for the i-th time instant is violated when scheduling all the activities in S. Accordingly, define $R^*(S, \mathbf{T}, \mathbf{D}) := \max_{i=1,\dots,m} R_i(S, \mathbf{T}, \mathbf{D})$. Note that a schedule S is feasible if and only if $R^*(S, \mathbf{T}, \mathbf{D}) \leq 0$.

Algorithm 2 constructs a feasible schedule S as follows: Initially, it checks if the entire set of activities $S = \mathcal{J}$ constitutes a feasible schedule. If not, the algorithm iteratively removes one activity per iteration from S, in a greedy fashion, until S becomes feasible. The algorithm determines the time instant t^* with the most violated feasibility constraint, by computing $R^*(S, \mathbf{T}, \mathbf{D})$, and considers all activities from S whose interval contains t^*. Then, it removes from S one of these activities that minimizes a certain ratio, dependent on the current penalties and resource requirements, while it simultaneously decreases the penalty of all other activities that contain t^*.

Algorithm 2: LMIS-LR$(\mathbf{p}, \mathbf{T}, \mathbf{r}, \mathbf{D})$

$\triangleright$ **Input:** An instance $(\mathbf{p}, \mathbf{T}, \mathbf{r}, \mathbf{D})$ of LMIS

---

1 Initialize $S = \mathcal{J}, k = 0$, and $\mathbf{p}_k = (p_{i,k})_{i \in [n]} = \mathbf{p}$.

2 **while** $R^*(S, \mathbf{T}, \mathbf{D}) > 0$ **do**

3 $\quad$ Let $t^* \in [m]$ be a maximizer of $R^*(S, \mathbf{T}, \mathbf{D})$.

4 $\quad$ $S_k = S \cap \mathcal{J}_{t^*}(\mathbf{T})$

5 $\quad$ $\varepsilon_k = \min\limits_{i \in S_k} \dfrac{p_{i,k}}{\min\{R^*(S, \mathbf{T}, \mathbf{D}), r_i\}}$

6 $\quad$ For $i = 1, \dots, m$ let

$$p_{i,k+1} = \begin{cases} p_{i,k} - \varepsilon_k \min\{R^*(S, \mathbf{T}, \mathbf{D}), r_i\}, & \text{if } i \in S_k, \\ p_{i,k}, & \text{o/w.} \end{cases}$$

7 $\quad$ Let $j^* \in S_k$ be a minimizer of ε_k.

8 $\quad$ Set $S = S \setminus \{j^*\}$, and $k = k + 1$.

9 **return** S

Remark 1. A variation of Algorithm 2 for LMIS is stated in [3]. The main difference is that the algorithm of [3] has an additional step to ensure that the solution returned is maximal. The extra step helps in improving the approximation ratio, but it destroys the hope for monotonicity of $\hat{A}$. This can be demonstrated using the same example that we used for the primal-dual algorithms of Proposition 1. Furthermore, we note that the algorithm of [3] is presented using the local-ratio jargon. We have chosen to present Algorithm 2 in a self-contained way for ease of exposition but for its analysis, we do make use of the local-ratio framework.

Theorem 4. *Algorithm 2 achieves a Δ-approximation for the* LMIS *problem, where $\Delta = \max_{j=1,\ldots,m} |\mathcal{N}_j(\mathbf{I})|$, and the analysis of its approximation is tight.*

It remains to be shown that $\hat{A}$, with Algorithm 2 as a subroutine, becomes a monotone allocation algorithm for CMIC. For establishing the monotonicity, according to Definition 2, we have to examine the ways in which a winning worker i can deviate from the truth with a bid $b_i' \succeq b_i$, where b_i is her initial bid. By Definition 1, this means that under b_i', a lower or equal cost and a larger or the same interval are declared, compared to b_i. But to argue about $\hat{A}$, we first have to understand how such deviations from the truth affect the outcome of Algorithm 2, when it is called by $\hat{A}$. Lowering the cost at a CMIC instance corresponds to lowering the penalty of an activity at the LMIS instance that $\hat{A}$ constructs. The lemma below examines precisely what happens when we lower the penalty of a non-scheduled activity in a LMIS instance.

Lemma 2. *For an instance $(\mathbf{p}, \mathbf{T}, \mathbf{r}, \mathbf{D})$ of* LMIS*, let S be the schedule returned by Algorithm 2, and $j \in \mathcal{J} \setminus S$. Then, for any $p_j' \leq p_j$, it holds that $j \in \mathcal{J} \setminus S'$, where S' is the schedule returned by Algorithm 2 for $((p_j', \mathbf{p}_{-j}), \mathbf{T}, \mathbf{r}, \mathbf{D})$.*

The next lemma examines enlarging the interval of an activity. This needs a different argument from the previous lemma because the deviation causes an activity to participate in more time instants.

Lemma 3. *For an instance $(\mathbf{p}, \mathbf{T}, \mathbf{r}, \mathbf{D})$ of* LMIS*, let S be a schedule returned by Algorithm 2 and $j \in \mathcal{J} \setminus S$. For any interval $T_j' \supseteq T_j$, consider the instance $P' = (\mathbf{p}, (T_j', \mathbf{T}_{-j}), \mathbf{r}, \mathbf{D}')$, where $\mathbf{D}' = (D_1', \ldots, D_m')$ such that:*

$$D_\ell' = \begin{cases} D_\ell + r_j, & \text{if } \ell \in T_j' \setminus T_j, \\ D_\ell, & \text{o/w.} \end{cases}$$

Then, $j \in \mathcal{J} \setminus S'$, where S' is the schedule returned by Algorithm 2 for P'.

Combining Lemma 2 and Lemma 3 we get the following:

Theorem 5. *Algorithm $\hat{A}$ is monotone, when using Algorithm 2 as a black box for solving* LMIS*.*

Proof. Fix a bidding profile $\mathbf{b}$ and a winning worker $i \in \mathcal{W}_{\hat{A}}(\mathbf{b})$. Let $b_i = (c_i, [s_i, f_i])$, and consider an arbitrary deviation of i, say $b_i'' = (c_i', [s_i', f_i'])$, such that $b_i'' \succeq b_i$. We need to show that $i \in \mathcal{W}_{\hat{A}}(b_i'', \mathbf{b}_{-i})$ and we will do this in two steps. First, we consider the deviation $b_i' = (c_i', [s_i, f_i])$. Since b_i' differs from b_i only with respect to the declared cost and the bids of the remaining workers remain the same, we can directly use Lemma 2 to conclude that $i \in \mathcal{W}_{\hat{A}}(b_i', \mathbf{b}_{-i})$. Having established that i is still a winner under $(b_i', \mathbf{b}_{-i})$, consider now the deviation from b_i' to b_i''. Note that $(b_i'', \mathbf{b}_{-i})$ differs from $(b_i', \mathbf{b}_{-i})$ only with respect to the declared interval of bidder i. Recall also that Algorithm $\hat{A}$ calls Algorithm 2 with input the tuple $(\mathbf{c}, \mathbf{I}, \mathbf{q}, \mathbf{Q}(\mathbf{I}) - \mathbf{d})$. This means that under b_i'', the vector $\mathbf{Q}(\mathbf{I}) - \mathbf{d}$ in the constructed LMIS instance changes only for time instants that belong to $[s_i', f_i'] \setminus [s_i, f_i]$ (where we simply add q_i). But then, this can be handled by Lemma 3, and obtain that $i \in \mathcal{W}_{\hat{A}}(b_i'', \mathbf{b}_{-i})$.

To conclude, it is trivial that Algorithm $\hat{A}$ runs in polynomial time, when using Algorithm 2 for solving LMIS, and hence, the monotonicity of $\hat{A}$, together with Theorems 3 and 4 complete the proof of Theorem 2.

4   A Truthful FPTAS for a Small Number of Tasks

At what follows, we investigate whether we can have truthful mechanisms with a better approximation ratio for special cases of restricted problem size. An instance of CMIC with a constant number of workers can be optimally solved in polynomial time by a brute force algorithm, which, together with the VCG payment scheme, results in a truthful mechanism. On the other hand, the story is different when we have a small number of tasks, since CMIC is NP-hard even for one task [18]. Building upon this negative result, we provide a truthful mechanism that achieves the best possible approximation factor, for the case of a constant number of tasks, and our main result of this section is the following:

Theorem 6. *There exists a truthful FPTAS for* CMIC, *when the number of tasks is constant.*

We would like first to pay attention to the special case of a single task, which corresponds to the MIN-KNAPSACK problem, the minimization version of KNAPSACK, where items have costs (instead of values) and there is a covering requirement (instead of a capacity constraint) for the selected items. The work of [8], which proposes a truthful FPTAS for the classic maximization version of KNAPSACK, claims (without providing a proof) that the analogous result holds for MIN-KNAPSACK too. To our knowledge, the only published work that explicitly attempts to extend [8] and describe a truthful FPTAS for MIN-KNAPSACK is [13]. However, we found that the analysis of truthfulness there is flawed and we refer to our full version for a counterexample, establishing the following claim.

Proposition 2. *The FPTAS for* MIN-KNAPSACK, *proposed by* [13], *is not monotone.*

Therefore, our Theorem 6 helps to resolve any potential ambiguities for MIN-KNAPSACK. Finally, for two or more tasks, we are not aware of any truthful mechanism attaining any bound better than the one provided by Theorem 2.

Remark 2. As in other approaches for constructing a truthful FPTAS, e.g. [8], we also make the assumption from here onwards, that $c_i \geq 1$ for every worker i, i.e., the workers will not be allowed to declare a cost lower than 1. In the full version of our work, we prove that we can adjust the assumption to $c_i \geq \delta$ for any arbitrarily small δ, but for convenience, here we stick to $\delta = 1$.

Furthermore, we bring in some additional notation that we use in this section. Given a bidding profile $\mathbf{b}$, let $c_{sum}(\mathbf{b}) := \sum_{i \in \mathcal{N}} c_i$. Similarly let $c_{min}(\mathbf{b})$ (resp. $c_{max}(\mathbf{b})$), be the minimum (resp. maximum) cost by the bidders.

4.1   A Pseudopolynomial Dynamic Programming Algorithm

The first step towards designing the FPTAS, is a pseudopolynomial dynamic programming algorithm that returns the optimal solution for the case of a constant number of tasks. For simplicity, we focus on describing the algorithm for the case of two tasks. The generalization is rather obvious (and discussed briefly at the end of this subsection).

Given an instance with two tasks, let d_1, d_2 be the demand requirements of the tasks. Note that $\mathcal{N}$ can be partitioned into three sets, W_0, W_1, W_2, since we can have at most three types of workers: W_0 is the set of workers who can contribute to both tasks, and for $\ell \in \{1, 2\}$, W_ℓ is the set of workers who are capable of contributing only to task ℓ.

We define a 3-dimensional matrix $Q[\ell, i, c]$, where for $\ell = 0, 1, 2$, for $i = 0, 1, \ldots n$, and for $c = 0, 1, \ldots, c_{sum}(\mathbf{b})$, $Q[\ell, i, c]$ denotes the maximum possible contribution that can be jointly achieved by any set of workers in $W_\ell \cap \{1, \ldots, i\}$ with a total cost of exactly c. For our purposes, we assume[4] that for $i \in [n]$, each c_i is an integer, so that c also takes only integral values. Our algorithm is based on computing the values of the cells of Q and we claim that this can be done by exploiting the following recursive relation:

$$Q[\ell, i, c] = \begin{cases} 0, & \text{if } i = 0 \\ Q[\ell, i-1, c], & \text{if } i > 0 \text{ and either } i \notin W_\ell \text{ or } c_i > c \\ \max\{Q[\ell, i-1, c], Q[\ell, i-1, c-c_i] + q_i\}, & \text{o/w} \end{cases} \quad (3)$$

Observe that for a feasible solution S, the workers who contribute to the demand of task 1 (resp. 2) are those from $S \cap W_0$ and $S \cap W_1$ (resp. $S \cap W_0$ and $S \cap W_2$). Hence, for $\ell \in \{1, 2\}$, it should hold that $\sum_{j \in S \cap W_0} q_j + \sum_{j \in S \cap W_\ell} q_j \geq d_\ell$. Our algorithm then can work as follows: After computing the values of Q, according to Eq. (3), return the set of workers that minimize $c^{(0)} + c^{(1)} + c^{(2)}$, subject to $Q[0, n, c^{(0)}] + Q[\ell, n, c^{(\ell)}] \geq d_\ell$, for $\ell \in \{1, 2\}$. This can be done by enumerating all possible options, for breaking down the final cost as a sum of 3 values, $c^{(0)}$, $c^{(1)}$ and $c^{(2)}$. The formal statement can be found below.

---

[4] It becomes clear in the next subsection, that the dynamic programming procedure is only needed for integral cost values.

Algorithm 3: DP(**b**) (presented for two tasks)

▷ **Input:** A bidding profile **b** = (**c**, **I**) of a CMIC instance (**b**, **q**, **d**) with $m = 2$

1 **for** $\ell \in \{0, 1, 2\}$ **do**
2 | **for** $i \in \{0, 1, \ldots, n\}$ **do**
3 | | **for** $c \in \{0, 1, \ldots, c_{sum}(\mathbf{b})\}$ **do**
4 | | | Compute $Q[\ell, i, c]$ using Equation (3)

5 **return** the set of workers that minimize $c^{(0)} + c^{(1)} + c^{(2)}$, s.t.
$Q[0, n, c^{(0)}] + Q[\ell, n, c^{(\ell)}] \geq d_\ell, \forall \ell \in \{1, 2\}$ (or $+\infty$, if (**b**, **q**, **d**) has no solution)

The optimality of the DP algorithm is straightforward from the preceding discussion. Furthermore, its running time is pseudopolynomial, since the size of the table Q is $3 \cdot (|\mathcal{N}| + 1) \cdot (c_{sum}(\mathbf{b}) + 1)$ and to find the optimal solution we need to check at most $\binom{c_{sum}(\mathbf{b})}{3}$ different combinations for the decomposition of the total cost in three terms, as described earlier. It is easy to extend these ideas, for more tasks given the interval structure of the problem, i.e., the first dimension of Q will have a range of $O(m^2)$ and the enumeration part of the algorithm will require an order of $\binom{c_{sum}}{m^2}$ steps. Finally, we note that since this is an optimal mechanism and we use a deterministic, consistent tie-breaking rule, it will trivially be monotone.

Henceforth, we will be referring to this pseudopolynomial dynamic programming algorithm for any constant number of tasks, as the DP algorithm.

Theorem 7. *Given an instance of* CMIC *on a profile* **b**, *with a constant number of tasks and integer costs, Algorithm DP(**b**) is optimal, monotone, and runs in pseudopolynomial time, i.e. polynomial in the input size and in* c_{sum}.

4.2   The FPTAS

In order to convert the DP algorithm to a truthful FPTAS, we adapt the framework of [8]. To that end, we define, for every integer k, an algorithm $A_k(\mathbf{b}, \epsilon)$, that uses the DP algorithm as a subroutine, on a subset of the initial set of bidders, with rounded costs, as follows:

Algorithm 4: $A_k(\mathbf{b}, \epsilon)$

▷ **Input:** A bidding profile **b** = (**c**, **I**) of a CMIC instance (**b**, **q**, **d**), $\epsilon \in (0, 1)$

Let $\mathcal{L}_k(\mathbf{c}) = \{i \in \mathcal{N} : c_i \leq 2^{k+1}\}$
1 $a_k = \frac{n}{\epsilon 2^k}$.
2 **for** $i \in \mathcal{L}_k(\mathbf{c})$ **do**
3 | $\bar{c}_i = \lceil a_k \cdot c_i \rceil$
4 $\bar{\mathbf{b}} = (\bar{c}_i, [s_i, f_i])_{i \in \mathcal{L}_k(\mathbf{c})}$
5 **return** DP($\bar{\mathbf{b}}$)

Lemma 4. *Let* $0 < \epsilon < 1$. *For a bidding profile* **b** *and* $k \geq 0$, *the algorithm* $A_k(\mathbf{b}, \epsilon)$ *runs in time polynomial in the input size and in* $\frac{1}{\epsilon}$, *and if* $2^k \leq OPT(\mathbf{b}) < 2^{k+1}$, *it computes a solution of cost at most* $(1 + \epsilon)OPT(\mathbf{b})$.

Using Lemma 4, we can achieve the desired approximation by checking all possible values for k. However, to provide a polynomial-time mechanism, we can only test polynomially many such values, and hope that we compute the same outcome as if we were able to test all such algorithms. We will show that Algorithm 5, that tests all values up to a certain threshold, is what we need.

Algorithm 5: $A_{\mathrm{FPTAS}}(\mathbf{b}, \epsilon)$

▷ **Input:** A bidding profile $\mathbf{b} = (\mathbf{c}, \mathbf{I})$ of a CMIC instance $((\mathbf{c}, \mathbf{I}), \mathbf{q}, \mathbf{d})$, $\epsilon \in (0, 1)$

1 **for** $k = 0, \ldots, \lceil \log\left(\frac{nc_{max}(\mathbf{b})}{\epsilon}\right) \rceil$ **do**

2   Run $A_k(\mathbf{b}, \epsilon)$ and store the winning set and its cost.

3 **return** the set of workers that achieve the minimum cost among the above, breaking ties in favor of the algorithm with the lowest index

---

Let $k^*(\mathbf{b}) := \lceil \log\left(\frac{nc_{max}(\mathbf{b})}{\epsilon}\right) \rceil$ (or simply k^* when the bidding profile is clear from the context). To see that the algorithm is well-defined, recall that $c_{max}(\mathbf{b}) \geq 1$ and since also $\frac{n}{\epsilon} \geq 1$, we have that $k^* \geq 0$. To establish that this is indeed a FPTAS, we prove in the following lemma that one cannot find a better solution by running an algorithm A_k for a value of k higher than k^*. In combination with Lemma 4, this directly establishes that A_{FPTAS} is a FPTAS for CMIC.

Lemma 5. *Given an instance of* CMIC *and an* $\epsilon \in (0, 1)$, *it holds that* $\mathcal{W}_{A_k(\mathbf{b})} = \mathcal{W}_{A_{k^*}(\mathbf{b})}$, *for every* $k > k^*(\mathbf{b})$.

Monotonicity of A_{FPTAS}

To establish monotonicity, we will make use of the following operator:

Definition 3. *Let* $\mathcal{A} = \{A_0, A_1, \ldots\}$ *be the set of all allocation algorithms* A_k. *For a profile* $\mathbf{b}$ *and a finite collection of algorithms* $S \subseteq \mathcal{A}$, *let* $MIN(S, \mathbf{b}) :=$ $\arg\min_{A \in S} C(A, \mathbf{b})$, *with ties broken in favor of the lowest index.*

Given a bidding profile $\mathbf{b}$, the algorithm A_{FPTAS} can be expressed as $MIN\{A_0, \ldots, A_{k^*(\mathbf{b})}\}$. Hence, the next step is to determine when is the MIN operator monotone. The framework of [8] defines a set of sufficient conditions, for maximization objectives. We adapt these properties below, and we note that they are sufficient conditions for minimization problems as well.

Definition 4. *A monotone allocation algorithm* A *is bitonic w.r.t. the social cost function* C *if for any bidding profile* $\mathbf{b}$ *and any worker* i, *the following hold:*

1. $i \in \mathcal{W}_A(\mathbf{b}) \Rightarrow C(A, \mathbf{b}) \geq C(A, (b_i', \mathbf{b}_{-i})) \quad \forall b_i' \succeq b_i$
2. $i \notin \mathcal{W}_A(\mathbf{b}) \Rightarrow C(A, \mathbf{b}) \geq C(A, (b_i', \mathbf{b}_{-i})) \quad \forall b_i' \preceq b_i$

Lemma 6. *For* $k \geq 0$, *Algorithm 4 is monotone and bitonic w.r.t. the social cost function* C.

Lemma 6 will be used in conjunction with the following Lemma.

Lemma 7. *(implied by [8]) For a bidding profile* **b**, *$MIN(\{A_0, \ldots, A_\ell\}, \mathbf{b})$ is monotone if $A_0, \ldots, A_\ell$ are monotone algorithms that are additionally bitonic w.r.t. the social cost function C.*

Before we proceed, we would like to comment on a subtle point regarding the MIN operator. We stress that the set of algorithms A_k that are called by A_{FPTAS}, depends on the input profile **b**. There is no a priori fixed set of algorithms that are run in every profile, but instead, this is determined by the quantity $k^*(\mathbf{b})$. As a result, Lemma 7 does not suffice on its own. For the monotonicity of A_{FPTAS}, we also need to consider the case that a winning worker declares a lower cost that changes $c_{max}(\mathbf{b})$, and decreases the number of algorithms that A_{FPTAS} runs. This is where Lemma 5 comes to rescue, as explained in the proof of Theorem 8, and this is where the flaw in [13] is located (i.e., the algorithm of [13] does not perform enough iterations).

Given the above discussion, by performing a suitable case analysis and by using Lemmas 6 and 7, we can prove the following theorem, which also completes the proof of Theorem 6 and concludes this section.

Theorem 8. *For the domain of bidding profiles* **b**, *such that $c_{min}(\mathbf{b}) \geq 1$, the algorithm A_{FPTAS} is monotone.*

5   Further Implications and Extensions

Apart from truthful mechanisms, it would be interesting to also consider CMIC from the purely algorithmic angle. In particular, the existence of a FPTAS (or other types of approximation schemes) could be possible beyond the case studied in Sect. 4. Furthermore, it is natural to examine whether the mechanisms presented in the previous sections could be used in more general crowdsourcing scenarios. The following subsections shed more light towards these two questions.

5.1   Relation to Unsplittable Flow Problems and (In)approximability

At what follows, we first establish a connection between CMIC and other relevant algorithmic problems, namely UFP, weighted UFP-COVER, and FAULT-CACHING. These problems concern (a) the selection of subpaths of a path-graph so as to satisfy a demand (resp. capacity) constraint on every edge, at a minimum (resp. maximum) total cost and (b) the minimization of the total cache misses in a fault model with a cache of fixed size and requests for non-uniform size pages. We refer to the full version of the work for the definitions of the problems. Such connections are interesting in their own right, and are summarized in the following theorem.

Theorem 9. CMIC *is equivalent to weighted* UFP-COVER. *Furthermore* UFP *and* FAULT-CACHING *are special cases of* CMIC.

We can now exploit some known results about these problems and obtain analogous implications for CMIC. The following table lists the most important results that concern the polynomial solvability and the approximability of (weighted) UFP-COVER, UFP and FAULT-CACHING that also apply for CMIC, due to Theorem 9. As an example, we can now rule out a FPTAS for the general case of CMIC (and in fact for its simpler cases, as stated in the first two lines of Table 2), unless P=NP. We note that before our work, there were no results about the hardness of CMIC, other than the obvious NP-hardness result in [18]. We comment further on Table 2 in Sect. 6.

Table 2. Results concerning the (in)approximability of CMIC implied by Theorem 9 together with existing works on UFP-COVER, UFP and FAULT-CACHING. We have used the symbols $\star, \odot, \diamond$ to denote the complexity assumptions $P \neq NP$, $W[1] \neq FPT$ and $QP \neq NP$ respectively. For the $W[1]$-hardness result, it is assumed that UFP-COVER is parameterized by the cardinality of the optimal solution.

Restriction	Result for	Reduction
$d_i = 1 \quad \forall i \in [m]$ $q_i \in \{1, 2, 3\} \quad \forall i \in \mathcal{N}$ $c_i \in \mathbb{Z}$	strongly NP-hard $\overset{[40]}{\Longrightarrow}$ $\nexists$ FPTAS*	UFP [6]
$d_i = 1 \quad \forall i \in [m]$ $c_i = 1 \quad \forall i \in \mathcal{N}$	strongly NP-hard $\overset{[40]}{\Longrightarrow}$ $\nexists$ FPTAS*	FAULT-CACHING [14]
$c_i = 1 \quad \forall i \in \mathcal{N}$	$W[1]$-hard $\overset{[21]}{\Longrightarrow}$ $\nexists$ EPTAS$^\odot$	UFP-COVER [16]
q_i : quasi-poly $\quad \forall i \in \mathcal{N}$	QPTAS $\overset{[1]}{\Longrightarrow}$ $\nexists$ APX-hardness$^\diamond$	weighted UFP-COVER [26]

5.2   Generalization to Non-interval Structures

The focus of our work has been largely on highlighting the difference on the approximation ratio between truthful and non-truthful algorithms. We conclude our work by showing that one can get tighter results, when moving to more general scenarios. A direct generalization of CMIC is to drop the linear arrangement of the tasks, and allow each worker $j \in \mathcal{N}$ to declare an arbitrary subset of tasks $I_j \subseteq [m]$. The rest of the input remains the same (costs, contributions and demands), and we refer to this problem as Cost Minimization Demand Cover (CMDC). Notice that CMDC with $q_i = 1$ for every worker i, and $d_j = 1$ for every task j, is nothing but the famous SET COVER problem.

Further extensions of CMDC have been studied under various names in a series of works regarding covering IPs (e.g., [28,38]) and approximation algorithms that match the factor of Algorithm 1 exist (e.g. [9,22,30,37]). However, the focus of these works was not about monotonicity and it is unclear if any of these algorithms are monotone (in fact some of them are certainly non-monotone).

Towards obtaining a monotone algorithm, a careful inspection of the proofs of Sect. 3, suffices to deduce that Algorithm 1 can be used for this more general setting as well (after defining first the appropriate generalization of LMIS) and it continues to yield the Δ factor for CMDC. Furthermore, under this setting, Algorithm 1 yields essentially a tight result, according to the following Proposition. The proof of Proposition 3 is straightforward due to the hardness results for k-UNIFORM HYPERGRAPH VERTEX COVER [19,27], which is a special case of SET COVER, and therefore a special case of CMDC.

Proposition 3. *For the class of instances where Δ is constant, CMDC is $\Delta-1-\epsilon$ inapproximable, unless $P = NP$, and $\Delta-\epsilon$ inapproximable assuming the Unique Games Conjecture.*

Finally, we note that the algorithms of Sect. 4 can in principle also be applied for CMDC with no loss in the approximation factor, but at the expense of a much higher running time (doubly exponential in m, which still remains polynomial, as long as the number of tasks is a constant).

6   Discussion and Open Problems

From a mechanism design viewpoint, the most important question for future research is to design truthful mechanisms with better approximation guarantees for CMIC, as there is still a large gap between the non-truthful 3-approximation and our truthful Δ-approximation of Sect. 3. Moreover, exploring the approximability of well-motivated special cases of CMIC, other than the restriction on a constant number of tasks that we examined in Sect. 4, is also an intriguing topic (Table 2 in Sect. 5.1 suggests such possible restrictions). In the context of crowdsourcing, some of these special cases are also meaningful to study in a 2-dimensional model, where workers can cover circular areas of a given radius, or other geometric shapes. Apart from positive results, we believe it is very interesting to investigate the existence of lower bounds on the worst case performance of polynomial time truthful mechanisms. After all, it is conceivable that there may be a strict separation on the approximability by monotone and non-monotone algorithms, as, e.g., for combinatorial public project problems [35].

From a purely algorithmic viewpoint, we would like to point out some interesting open-problems for CMIC, that emerge from the results of Table 2. In particular, it has been known by [18], that we have polynomial solvability when all the workers have the same contribution parameter. On the contrary, by the first row of Table 2, we have a hardness result when the workers can be partitioned in three distinct groups by their contribution. It still remains open to determine what happens when we have two distinct groups for the contribution of the workers. Interestingly the last row of Table 2 implies that the existence of a PTAS is likely (at least for the case of quasi-polynomially bounded contributions) and, yet, such a PTAS still remains to be found. Finally, even though the problem is W[1]-hard (parameterized by the number of workers in the optimal solution) for unit costs, it belongs to FPT for unit costs and integral numerical values [24,32], and hence an EPTAS may well exist for this case.

Acknowledgement. This research was supported by the Hellenic Foundation for Research and Innovation. The first two authors were supported by the "1st Call for HFRI Research Projects to support faculty members and researchers and the procurement of high-cost research equipment" (Project Num. HFRI-FM17-3512) and the third author by the HFRI PhD Fellowship grant (Fellowship Num. 289).

References

1. Bansal, N., Chakrabarti, A., Epstein, A., Schieber, B.: A quasi-PTAS for unsplittable flow on line graphs. In: Proceedings of the 38th ACM Symposium on Theory of Computing, pp. 721–729 (2006)
2. Bansal, N., Pruhs, K.: The geometry of scheduling. SIAM J. Comput. **43**(5), 1684–1698 (2014)
3. Bar-Noy, A., Bar-Yehuda, R., Freund, A., Naor, J., Schieber, B.: A unified approach to approximating resource allocation and scheduling. J. ACM **48**(5), 1069–1090 (2001)
4. Bar-Yehuda, R., Bendel, K., Freund, A., Rawitz, D.: The local ratio technique and its application to scheduling and resource allocation problems. In: Golumbic, M.C., Hartman, I.B.A. (eds.) Graph Theory, Combinatorics and Algorithms, pp. 107–143. Springer, Cham (2005). https://doi.org/10.1007/0-387-25036-0_5
5. Blumrosen, L., Nisan, N.: Algorithmic Game Theory. Introduction to Mechanism Design. Cambridge University Press, Cambridge (2007)
6. Bonsma, P., Schulz, J., Wiese, A.: A constant-factor approximation algorithm for unsplittable flow on paths. SIAM J. Comput. **43**(2), 767–799 (2014)
7. Bredereck, R., Faliszewski, P., Niedermeier, R., Skowron, P., Talmon, N.: Mixed integer programming with convex/concave constraints: fixed-parameter tractability and applications to multicovering and voting. Theor. Comput. Sci. **814**, 86–105 (2020)
8. Briest, P., Krysta, P., Vöcking, B.: Approximation techniques for utilitarian mechanism design. SIAM J. Comput. **40**(6), 1587–1622 (2011)
9. Carr, R.D., Fleischer, L.K., Leung, V.J., Phillips, C.A.: Strengthening integrality gaps for capacitated network design and covering problems. In: Proceedings of the 11th ACM-SIAM Symposium on Discrete Algorithms, pp. 106–115 (2000)
10. Chakaravarthy, V.T., Kumar, A., Roy, S., Sabharwal, Y.: Resource allocation for covering time varying demands. In: Demetrescu, C., Halldórsson, M.M. (eds.) ESA 2011. LNCS, vol. 6942, pp. 543–554. Springer, Heidelberg (2011). https://doi.org/10.1007/978-3-642-23719-5_46
11. Chakrabarty, D., Grant, E., Könemann, J.: On column-restricted and priority covering integer programs. In: Eisenbrand, F., Shepherd, F.B. (eds.) IPCO 2010. LNCS, vol. 6080, pp. 355–368. Springer, Heidelberg (2010). https://doi.org/10.1007/978-3-642-13036-6_27
12. Chen, B., Hassin, R., Tzur, M.: Allocation of bandwidth and storage. IIE Trans. **34**(5), 501–507 (2002)
13. Chen, J., Ye, D., Ji, S., He, Q., Xiang, Y., Liu, Z.: A truthful FPTAS mechanism for emergency demand response in colocation data centers. In: Proceedings of the IEEE International Conference on Computer Communications-INFOCOM (2019)
14. Chrobak, M., Woeginger, G.J., Makino, K., Xu, H.: Caching is hard-even in the fault model. Algorithmica **63**(4), 781–794 (2012)
15. Cramton, P., Shoham, Y., Steinberg, R., et al.: Combinatorial auctions. Technical report, University of Maryland (2006)

16. Cristi, A., Mari, M., Wiese, A.: Fixed-parameter algorithms for unsplittable flow cover. Theory of Computing Systems (2021)
17. Csirik, J.: Heuristics for the 0-1 min-knapsack problem. Acta Cybernetica (1991)
18. Dayama, P., Narayanaswamy, B., Garg, D., Narahari, Y.: Truthful interval cover mechanisms for crowdsourcing applications. In: Proceedings of the 14th International Conference on Autonomous Agents and Multiagent Systems (2015)
19. Dinur, I., Guruswami, V., Khot, S., Regev, O.: A new multilayered PCP and the hardness of hypergraph vertex cover. SIAM J. Comput. **34**(5), 1129–1146 (2005)
20. Elkind, E., Goldberg, L.A., Goldberg, P.W.: Frugality ratios and improved truthful mechanisms for vertex cover. In: Proceedings of the 8th ACM Conference on Electronic Commerce (2007)
21. Feldmann, A., Karthik, C., Lee, E., Manurangsi, P.: A survey on approximation in parameterized complexity: hardness and algorithms. Algorithms **13**(6) (2020)
22. Fujito, T., Yabuta, T.: Submodular integer cover and its application to production planning. In: Persiano, G., Solis-Oba, R. (eds.) WAOA 2004. LNCS, vol. 3351, pp. 154–166. Springer, Heidelberg (2005). https://doi.org/10.1007/978-3-540-31833-0_14
23. Gálvez, W., Grandoni, F., Ingala, S., Heydrich, S., Khan, A., Wiese, A.: Approximating geometric Knapsack via L-packings. ACM Trans. Algorithms **17**(4), 1–67 (2021)
24. Gavenciak, T., Knop, D., Koutecký, M.: Integer programming in parameterized complexity: three miniatures. In: 13th International Symposium on Parameterized and Exact Computation, pp. 21:1–21:16 (2019)
25. Gummidi, S.R.B., Xie, X., Pedersen, T.B.: A survey of spatial crowdsourcing. ACM Trans. Database Syst. **44**(2), 1–46 (2019)
26. Höhn, W., Mestre, J., Wiese, A.: How unsplittable-flow-covering helps scheduling with job-dependent cost functions. Algorithmica (2018)
27. Khot, S., Regev, O.: Vertex cover might be hard to approximate to within $2 - \varepsilon$. J. Comput. Syst. Sci. **74**(3), 335–349 (2008)
28. Kolliopoulos, S., Young, N.: Approximation algorithms for covering/packing integer programs. J. Comput. Syst. Sci. **71**(4), 495–505 (2005)
29. Kothari, A., Parkes, D., Suri, S.: Approximately-strategyproof and tractable multiunit auctions. Decis. Support Syst. **39**(1), 105–121 (2005)
30. Koufogiannakis, C., Young, N.: Greedy δ-approximation algorithm for covering with arbitrary constraints and submodular cost. Algorithmica (2013)
31. Lehmann, D., O'Callaghan, L.I., Shoham, Y.: Truth revelation in approximately efficient combinatorial auctions. J. ACM **49**(5), 577–602 (2002)
32. Lenstra, H.: Integer programming with a fixed number of variables. Math. Oper. Res. **8**, 538–548 (1983)
33. Mondal, S.: Improved algorithm for resource allocation problems. Asia-Pac. J. Oper. Res. **35**(01), 1–23 (2018)
34. Myerson, R.: Optimal auction design. Math. Oper. Res. **6**(1), 58–73 (1981)
35. Papadimitriou, C., Schapira, M., Singer, Y.: On the hardness of being truthful. In: Proceedings of the 49th Foundations of Computer Science, pp. 250–259 (2008)
36. Phillips, C.A., Uma, R., Wein, J.: Off-line admission control for general scheduling problems. J. Sched. **3**(6), 365–381 (2000)
37. Pritchard, D., Chakrabarty, D.: Approximability of sparse integer programs. Algorithmica **61**(1), 75–93 (2011)
38. Rajagopalan, S., Vazirani, V.: Primal-dual RNC approximation algorithms for (multi)-set (multi)-cover and covering integer programs. In: Proceedings of the 34th Foundations of Computer Science (1993)

39. Tong, Y., Zhou, Z., Zeng, Y., Chen, L., Shahabi, C.: Spatial crowdsourcing: a survey. VLDB J. **29**(1), 217–250 (2019). https://doi.org/10.1007/s00778-019-00568-7
40. Vazirani, V.: Approximation Algorithms. Springer, Cham (2001). https://doi.org/10.1007/978-3-662-04565-7
41. Xu, J., Xiang, J., Yang, D.: Incentive mechanisms for time window dependent tasks in mobile crowdsensing. IEEE Trans. Wirel. Commun. **14**, 6353–6364 (2015)
42. Zhang, L., Ren, S., Wu, C., Li, Z.: A truthful incentive mechanism for emergency demand response in colocation data centers. In: Proceedings of the IEEE International Conference on Computer Communications-INFOCOM (2015)

Explicitly Simple Near-Tie Auctions

Reshef Meir[(✉)] and Riccardo Colini-Baldeschi

Meta, Core Data Science, London, UK
reshef24@gmail.com

Abstract. We consider the problem of truthfully auctioning a single item, that can be either fractionally or probabilistically divided among several winners when their bids are sufficiently close to a tie.

While Myerson's Lemma states that any monotone allocation rule can be implemented, truthful payments are computed by integrating over each profile, and may be difficult to comprehend and explain. We look for payment rules that are given explicitly as a simple function of the allocated fraction and the others' bids. For two agents, this simply coincides with (non-negative) Myerson's payments. For three agents or more, we characterize the near-tie allocation rules that admit such explicit payments, and provide an iterative algorithm to compute them. In particular we show that any such payment rule must require positive payments to some of the bidders.

Keywords: Mechanism design · Diversity · Simplicity

1 Introduction

Consider a single-item auction with several participants, and suppose the leading bids are \$100 and \$94. While the first two bids are almost tied, the outcome for the bidders is very different: The first one gets the item (and pays for it), whereas the second one gets nothing. Awarding the item to the second highest bidder with some probability (say 0.25), or dividing it $3/4$ and $1/4$ (when possible) would not have a serious impact on the social welfare, but it would greatly increase the satisfaction of the runner-up. However, when gaps are larger (say, bids are \$100 and \$43), we may prefer to allocate everything to a single winner. Two questions arise from this example:

1. What would be reasonable allocation rules that partially award the non-highest bidder(s)?
2. Given such allocation rules, can we implement those rules with truthful dominant strategies?

A particular case of interest, that includes the above example, is a class of allocation rules we call *near-tie*. Near-tie allocation rules differentiate between two scenarios: (i) a 'Default' case, where the item is allocated to the highest bidder, and (ii) a 'near-Tie' case that is triggered when bids are sufficiently close, thus diversifying the allocation between the highest bidders.

Clearly, increasing the diversity in the set of winning bidders comes at a cost of both welfare and revenue (as we already know that truthful welfare-optimal auctions will

© The Author(s), under exclusive license to Springer Nature Switzerland AG 2022
P. Kanellopoulos et al. (Eds.): SAGT 2022, LNCS 13584, pp. 113–130, 2022.
https://doi.org/10.1007/978-3-031-15714-1_7

only allocate to the highest bidder). However, in many theoretical and practical cases there are additional properties that need to be evaluated and traded-off with welfare and revenue. For example, awarding some fraction of the item to high-enough bidders would (beyond diversification amongst the set of winners) disincentivize fraudulent behavior (e.g., bid leakage [6,11]), increase egalitarian welfare, and increase bidder retention. Some additional examples from the literature include item utilization [14]; Egalitarian welfare [27]; No-Envy [21,22]; and bidder dropout [12,17].

So far, we have discussed how we can design allocation rules that can allocate the item to *high-enough* bidders and why they are important, but, going back to our second question, can we implement them in truthful dominant strategies?

The classic "Myerson Lemma" [18] already gives a positive answer to this question. Indeed, Myerson fully characterizes the set of dominant strategy incentive-compatible allocation and payment rules: any monotone allocation rule can be implemented (including 'near-tie' rules); and implementation is unique under the requirements of individual rationality and no positive transfers.

Unfortunately, the payment rule characterized by the Myerson Lemma is quite complex and can be problematic for implementation in practical scenarios [16,19]. Moreover, complex mechanisms can directly affect the ability of bidders to best-respond and, in turn, impact their truthful implementation [13,20].

In this work, we suggest describing the payment rule explicitly using linear functions of the bids, inspired by the common use of *model trees* to represent functions in AI [7,23]. Informally, in an *explicitly simple* payment rule, the decision tree is only required to decide the allocation, which itself completely determines the payment as a single linear combination of bids. In contrast, a complex rule would require a long list of cases (a larger subtree) with a distinct linear payment function in each case. We believe this description is a natural extension of linear payment functions, which are common in the auction literature.

Using the explicit complexity framework, we focus first on the basic Myerson payment rule (i.e. without positive transfers), showing that it is only explicitly simple in very restricted cases. We then turn to study and characterize other payment rules that are explicitly simple while maintaining our requirement of strategyproofness and individual-rationality.

1.1 Contribution

○ We show that basic Myerson's payments are explicitly simple if, and only if, the item is divided amongst the two leading bidders.
○ We characterize the conditions under which a near-tie auction for n agents has an explicitly simple implementation.
○ We prove that when the item is divided amongst 3 or more agents, any explicit implementation (except in a very specific case we identify) *must require* positive transfers to agents.

The second result shows that it is possible to implement any partition of the item where a near-tie *reduces* the portion of the leading agent and *benefits* all others. We further provide an iterative algorithm that calculates the explicit formula for the payment of each agent as a linear function of the other bids. For all other cases, we show there is no explicit implementation of near-tie auctions (of the kind we study).

Some proofs and details appear only in the full version on Arxiv.

1.2   Related Literature

Welfare, revenue, and Myerson.   Auctions are typically designed to maximize social welfare and/or revenue. In the case of a single item allocation, welfare maximization is straight forward—the item should be given to the agent with the highest value, and this can be implemented by a second price auction which allocates the item to the highest bidder. A general formula for optimizing revenue (given agents' value distributions) was developed by Myerson, who suggested to transform agents' valuations into 'virtual values' and then optimal strategyproof auction is maximizing these virtual values [18]. In the case of a single-item auction, this always means selecting the single agent with the maximal virtual value, provided that it is not negative. The simplest example of an optimal auction is a second price auction with a reserve price for i.i.d. agents. Note that the revenue-maximizing auction may not be efficient in terms of welfare since, given the reserve price, it may decide to not allocate the auctioned item. The tradeoff between social welfare and revenue has naturally attracted much attention in the literature, see e.g. [5].

Beyond Welfare and Revenue.   There may be other considerations on top of welfare and revenue that guide the allocation and/or the choice of the payment rule. Some examples from the literature include item utilization [14]; Egalitarian welfare [27]; redistribution [2,9]; Equal rights lower bound [10]; No-Envy [21,22]; and bidder dropout [12,17].

These issues may be of importance on their own, but also indirectly affect welfare and revenue in the long term, by decreasing competition among bidders (in the case of bidders dropping out) or by intervention of regulation authorities.

Crucially, some of these models are special cases of Myerson's, meaning the desired class of rules must be contained in the set Myerson characterized. Yet, the additional required properties mean that Myerson's lemma, on its own, does not provide the answer (although it may play a part in the solution). Our paper joins this line of work. We further note that some of these papers present negative results, highlighting conditions under which an auction cannot be both truthful and obtain the desired criterion.

Diverse Allocations.   There are different motivations in literature that justify the study of mechanisms that allocate the items to non-highest bidders, either through fractional or probabilistic allocation rules. The bottom line of this literature is that giving to the non-highest bidders a positive probability of winning the auction will increase participation and satisfaction within the bidders, resulting in better long-term welfare and revenue results. One such example is starvation/bidder dropout. Lee et al. [12] observe that:

> "Applying traditional auction mechanisms ... may result in an inevitable starvation for resources for certain customers ... customers may decide to drop out of the future auction rounds, thereby decreasing the long-term demand."

In their paper, they consider auctions in a sequential setting with a particular dropout model, and suggest an optimal solution. In contrast, we propose to diversify the set of winners as a heuristic solution that is also likely to mitigate the problem of bidder dropout.

Another interesting scenario is represented by the *contests* literature. In a contest, partitioning the item/prize is often desirable as this may incentivize low-chance participants to invest more effort. We note that in contrast to auctions, the probabilistic allocation of a prize in contests is not a design decision, but rather an assumption on the relation between effort and outcome in a given environment. A designer may however decide on the size of the prize and/or decide to partition it up front into several prizes. The common wisdom in contests (Clark and Riis [3]) is that:

> "an income maximizing contest administrator obtains the most rent seeking contributions when he makes available a single, large prize"

However, this is not always true. Eden [4] assumes the designer can decide on a smaller shared prize in case of a tie between two or more contestants, and artificially increase the chance of a tie (e.g. by deciding that sufficiently close grades are tied). It turns out that under some conditions, such a 'noisy tie' can induce more effort from contestants, in equilibrium.

Representation and Simplicity. Various authors have argued that mechanisms should be simple to understand or interact with, with different interpretations of what this simplicity means. E.g., Nuñez [20] writes:

> "The idea of transparency is based on the cognitive ability of each player to understand the consequences of his actions. The more transparent a mechanism, the less cognitively complex for an agent to compute his best responses."

One important argument Nuñez cites for transparency, is that agents may differ in their ability to understand the mechanism, where some cannot even figure out their best responses. Indeed, in the auction literature, 'simple mechanisms' are often such with a succinct description, e.g. by few posted prices [24, 25].

Milgrom [15] considers a different notion of simplicity by comparing the strategy spaces of the participants and the resulting equilibria. A mechanism A is simpler than B if its strategy space is contained and it does not introduce new equilibria.

Our notion of explicit mechanisms is motivated more by the arguments of Nuñez that refer to the mechanism itself, than by the ones by Milgrom which consider the simplicity of the strategy space, as in our case the strategy is just reporting the private value. The representation we suggest is inspired by *model trees* [23], which have ample uses in AI, including for learning valuations [8].

2 Preliminaries

We consider a setting with a set of n bidders $N = \{1, \ldots, n\}$ that compete for a single item. Each bidder $i \in N$ has a non-negative value denoted by $v_i \in \mathbb{R}_{\geq 0}$. We will assume that bidders are sorted in non-increasing order of their values, e.g., $v_1 \geq v_2 \geq \ldots \geq v_n$. We refer to i as the *position* or *rank* of the bidder with value v_i.

A *bid profile* $b \in \mathbb{R}_{\geq 0}^n$ is a vector of n non-negative bids, e.g., $b = (b_1, \ldots, b_n)$. Except when explicitly stated otherwise (and then different notation is used), we assume that bids are sorted in a non-increasing order, and all of our definitions are anonymous. I.e. they depend only on the values of bids and their relative position, and not on bidders' identity. We denote by $\mathcal{B}^n$ the set of all (sorted) bid profiles of length n.

Allocation. An allocation function is a function $x : \mathcal{B}^n \to \mathbb{R}_{\geq 0}^n$ mapping bid profiles to allocations. When allocating a single item we have the constraint that $\sum_{j \in N} x_j(b) \leq 1$.

Denote $\Delta(n) := \{p \in \mathbb{R}_{\geq 0}^n : \sum_{i \leq n} p_i = 1\}$. Unless explicitly stated otherwise, we restrict attention to allocation functions that are:

Pareto Efficient if $\forall b \in \mathcal{B}^n, \sum_{j \in N} x_j(b) = 1$, thus the range of x is $\Delta(n)$;
Monotone $b_j' \geq b_j$ means $x_j(b_j', b_{-j}) \geq x_j(b_j, b_{-j})$;
Homogeneous of degree 0 $\forall c \in \mathbb{R}_{\geq 0}$, and any profile b, $x(c \cdot b) = x(b)$.

Note that anonymity is also implied as the profile contains no information on agents' identity, and we can make sure there are no ties (see Footnote 2).

In order to conveniently capture the dependency between bids and allocations as in the opening example, we divide the allocation function into two stages: first, a function $\tilde{s}$ mapping the bid profile into one of finitely many states S; then, at each state $s \in S$, there is a fixed allocation $p^{(s)} \in \Delta(n)$.

Definition 1. *A* Partitioned Single-item Allocation *(PSA)* x *is described by a tuple* $(S, \tilde{s}, \bar{p})$ *such that:*

○ $\tilde{s} : \mathcal{B}^n \to S$;
○ $\bar{p} = (p^{(s)})_{s \in S}$, *where each* $p^{(s)} \in \Delta(n)$;
○ $x(b) = p^{(\tilde{s}(b))}$ *for any profile* b.

Thus $p_i^{(s)}$ is the fraction (or probability) of the item that the i'th highest bidder gets at state s. The set of distributions $\bar{p} = (p^{(s)})_{s \in S}$ is called a *partial PSA*.

Two-state PSAs. In this work we focus mainly on *two-state* PSAs, that is when the set S is partitioned in only two subsets, e.g., $S = \{D, T\}$ (alluding to **D**efault and **T**ies). In the following, we define relevant sub-classes of two-state PSAs:

○ A two-state PSA is *separated* if there is $k \in \{1, \ldots, n-1\}$ s.t. $p_j^{(D)} > p_j^{(T)}$ if and only if $j \leq k$ (i.e., the top ranked agents prefer D and the others prefer T);
○ A separated PSA is *single-top* if $k = 1$. Otherwise it is *multi-top*;
○ A single-top PSA is *near-tie* if $p_1^{(D)} = 1$.

We provide two examples of near-tie PSAs.

Example I. In the example from the introduction we have two states $S = \{D, T\}$, with $p^{(D)} = (1, 0, 0, \ldots)$ and $p^{(T)} = (0.75, 0.25, 0, \ldots)$. The 'near-tie' state T is declared whenever the second bid exceeds half of the highest bid, i.e., $\tilde{s}(b) = T$ iff $b_2 > 0.5 b_1$.

Example II. This will be our running example, with $n = 3$. The winner gets the full item if her bid exceeds twice the sum of the two other bids. Otherwise, the leader gets half the item and the two other agents equally split the remaining half. Formally, we have two states $S = \{D, T\}$, with $p^{(T)} = (0.5, 0.25, 0.25)$ and $p^{(D)} = (1, 0, 0)$. All profiles where $b_1 > 2b_2 + 2b_3$ are mapped to $s = D$ and all other profiles are mapped to $s = T$.

We denote by $\mathcal{B}(s)$ the set of all profiles b s.t. $\tilde{s}(b) = s$, thus $\{\mathcal{B}(s)\}_{s \in S}$ is a partition of $\mathcal{B}^n$. Informally, we say that two states s', s'' are *adjacent* if the sets $\mathcal{B}(s'), \mathcal{B}(s'')$ "touch" one another.

Definition 2. *A* payment rule *is a set of functions* PAY $= (\text{PAY}_j)_{j \leq n}$, *where* $\text{PAY}_j(b) \in \mathbb{R}_{\geq 0}$ *is the price j pays for the full item. An* auction *is a pair* (x, PAY).

As with x and p, the index $j \leq n$ refers to the *position* of the agent, not to their identity. That is, $\text{PAY}_1(b)$ is the payment assigned to the highest bidder.

The utility of j with value v_j under auction (x, PAY) with bids b is $x_j(v_j, b) := p_j(b)[v_j - \text{PAY}_j(b)]$. Under truthful bidding we can assume $v_j = b_j$.

Manipulations. Suppose that agent j bids $b'_j \neq v_j$. This may alter her position to some $j' \neq j$. Thus $b' = (b_{-j}, b'_j)$ may induce a different ranking over agents. We use $u'_j(v_j, b')$ for the counterfactual utility of the agent whose real rank is j but may not be ranked j in the reported profile b'. Formally, consider a profile b_{-j} and a (possibly untruthful) bid b'_j. Denote by j' the new rank of b'_j in profile $b' = (b_{-j}, b'_j)$. Then

$$u'_j(v_j, b') := u_{j'}(v_j, b') = x_{j'}(b')[v_j - \text{PAY}_{j'}(b')],$$

that is, the utility that the agent ranked at position j' in profile b' would get, if their value had been v_j. A manipulation for j at profile b is a bid b'_j s.t. $u'_j(v_j, b') > u_j(v_j, b)$.

Local Manipulations. In general, an agent may report a bid $b_j \neq v_j$ such that the state changes, or her rank increases or decreases (by one step or more), or both. However if the bid change is sufficiently small, then the changes are 'local': either a single step up or down in rank; *or* a change to an adjacent state. A formal definition of local moves and manipulations is in the full version. An auction is:

○ *Individually rational* (IR) if $u_j(v_j, b) \geq 0$ for all $j \leq n, b \in \mathcal{B}^n$;
○ *[Locally] Strategyproof* ([L]SP) if there are no [local] manipulations;
○ *No Positive Transfers* (NPT) if $\text{PAY}_j(b) \geq 0$ for all $j \leq n, b \in \mathcal{B}^n$;

We say that an auction *implements [in NPT]* PSA x if it holds IR [,NPT] and SP.

2.1 The Myerson Lemma

According to the Myerson lemma [18], for any monotone PSA x there is a unique auction that is SP, IR and NPT. For a discrete allocation rule, the *Total Myerson Payment* is derived by integrating over all increments in allocation as the bid is increasing.

$$TMP_{\underline{c}}(b) = \begin{cases} 0 & \text{if } b_{\underline{c}} < 0.5 \\ \frac{1}{2} \cdot \frac{1}{4} = \frac{1}{8} & \text{if } b_{\underline{c}} \in (0.5, 3) \\ \frac{1}{8} + 3 \cdot \frac{1}{4} = \frac{7}{8} & \text{if } b_{\underline{c}} \in (3, 8) \\ \frac{7}{8} + 8 \cdot \frac{1}{2} = 4\frac{7}{8} & \text{if } b_{\underline{c}} > 8 \end{cases}$$

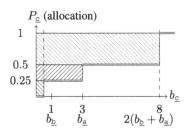

Fig. 1. The total Myerson payment in Example II, under specific bids. The cutoff points are all points where allocation changes: $y_3 = 3$ is a tie profiles (in $y_2 = 1$ there is no change); and $y_1 = 0.5, y_4 = 8$ are the boundary profiles, where the state changes from D to T (when $\underline{c}$ is ranked third) and then from T to D (when $\underline{c}$ is ranked first). The contribution of each cutoff point to the TMP appears in the same color in the formula on the left and in the diagram on the right.

To be consistent with Myerson's definitions, we use $\underline{k}$ for the *name* of an agent, rather than her position.

Formally, we denote by $x_{\underline{k}}^-(b) := \lim_{\varepsilon \to 0} x_{\underline{k}}(b_{-\underline{k}}, b_{\underline{k}} - \varepsilon)$ the left limit $x_{\underline{k}}$ at b, as a function of $b_{\underline{k}}$.[1] Similarly, $x_{\underline{k}}^+(b)$ is the right limit. Thus $x_{\underline{k}}^-(b), x_{\underline{k}}^+(b)$ differ whenever the allocation to $\underline{k}$ changes. Let:

$$\mathrm{TMP}_{\underline{k}}(b_{\underline{k}}, b_{-\underline{k}}) := \sum_{\ell=1}^{L(b_{\underline{k}})} y_\ell [x_{\underline{k}}^+(y_\ell, b_{-\underline{k}}) - x_{\underline{k}}^-(y_\ell, b_{-\underline{k}})], \tag{1}$$

where $y_1, \ldots, y_{L(b_{\underline{k}})}$ are all points in the range $[0, b_{\underline{k}}]$ where the allocation $x_{\underline{k}}$ changes.

Lemma 1 (Myerson's Lemma [18]). *Let x be a PSA.*

1. *x can be implemented if and only if it is monotone;*
2. *A payment rule implements x if and only if the payment of each agent $\underline{k}$ can be written as $p_{\underline{k}}^0(b_{-\underline{k}}) + \mathrm{TMP}_{\underline{k}}(b)$ for some function $p_{\underline{k}}^0 : \mathcal{B}^{n-1} \to \mathbb{R}$;*
3. *The unique payment rule implementing x in NPT is $\mathrm{TMP} = (\mathrm{TMP}_{\underline{k}})_{\underline{k} \in N}$.*

Example. Suppose we fix in our Example II two of the bids at $(b_{\underline{a}} = 3, b_{\underline{b}} = 1)$. The payment rule $\mathrm{TMP}_{\underline{c}}$ for the third agent bidding $b_{\underline{c}}$ is then computed in Fig. 1. E.g. under bidding profile $b = (3, 1, 6)$ agent c will be ranked first, get $x_{\underline{c}}(b) = x_1(b) = \frac{1}{2}$ of the item and will pay $\frac{7}{8}$. Note that in our notation this means the per-unit price for the leading bidder is $\mathrm{PAY}_1(b) = \frac{3}{4}$.

The reason we can always translate $\mathrm{TMP}_{\underline{k}}$ (which is based on agent's index) to PAY_j (which is based on agent's position) is that the Myerson's auction is anonymous. We only need to switch the indices according to the rank of $\underline{k}$, and divide by the allocation (since the total payment of j is $x_j \mathrm{PAY}_j$).

We refer to all payment rules of the form $(p_{\underline{k}}^0(b_{-\underline{k}}) + \mathrm{TMP}_{\underline{k}}(b))_{\underline{k} \in N}$ as the *Myerson class*, to the payment rule PAY induced from TMP (i.e. with $p^0 \equiv 0$) as *Myerson's payments*, and to (x, PAY) as *Myerson's auction*.

---

[1] For a PSA, $x_{\underline{k}}$ is a step function. In the general case Myerson's lemma uses an integral over $x_{\underline{k}}$ rather than a sum.

2.2   Explicit Representation

A payment function PAY_j is *linear* if it is a linear combination of $b_{-j} = (b_i)_{i \neq j}$.

Some common auction rules are linear, specifying in a clear way how much the winner (or winners) will pay, as a function of the other bids. The immediate example is of course second-price auction, but this true more generally e.g. for GSP and VCG ad-auctions, where every winner pays the next bid, or a fixed linear combination of all lower bids [26].

Ideally, we would like to have a similar explicit description for the payments rules we derive for PSAs. However, while the Myerson lemma enables us to compute the payment for every profile, it is not clear if it has such an explicit formula that can be presented up front: e.g. the solution in Fig. 1 requires multiple cases, and this is for just a single profile $b_{-\underline{c}} = (1, 3)$. For other bids, we will get a different conditional description of the payment. Such a payment rule is not particularly convenient to work with, or to explain to naïve participants.

In contrast, we can think of an *explicit representation* of a payment rule as a decision tree for every agent position: the first level of the tree decides the allocation (state). In a simple payment rule, this level would be enough to specify a linear payment rule. A more complicated rule will require a larger subtree at every state, with a single linear payment function in each leaf.

Definition 3. *An* explicit representation *of a payment function* PAY_j *is a tuple* $(Z_j, \tilde{z}_j, \bar{P}_j)$ *such that:*

- $\tilde{z}_j : \mathcal{B}^n \to Z$;
- $\bar{\mathrm{PAY}}_j = (\mathrm{PAY}_j^{(z)})_{z \in Z}$ *where each* $\mathrm{PAY}_j^{(z)}$ *is linear;*
- $\mathrm{PAY}_j(b) = \mathrm{PAY}_j^{(\tilde{z}(b))}(b_{-j})$ *for any profile b.*

W.l.o.g each Z_j is a refinement of S, since except in degenerate cases, each state will require a different payment. Hence we refer to S and Z as *states* and *substates*, respectively. We denote by $Z_j(s) \subseteq Z_j$ the set of substates that compose the state s (namely, all payment formulae that may be used under a certain allocation).

Tree/Tabular form. The tree representation of PAY_j sets $\tilde{s}(b)$ in the first level, and $\tilde{z}_j(b)$ in the second level (all substates of $z \in Z_j(s)$ are direct children of s). Then at every leaf $z \in Z_j$ there is the linear payment rule:

$$\mathrm{PAY}_j^{(z)}(b_{-j}) = \sum_{i<j} t_j^{(z)[i]} b_i + \sum_{i>j} t_j^{(z)[i-1]} b_i. \tag{2}$$

Note that we use a subscript j for the rank, and a superscript (z) for the substate. Then, $t_j^{(z)} = (t_j^{(z)[i]})_{i=1}^{n-1}$ where $t_j^{(z)[i]} \in \mathbb{R}$ is the weight that agent j assigns to the i'th highest bid in b_{-j} in substate $z \in Z_j$. We do not assume weights are positive or normalized.

Therefore every payment rule is described by $n \times \max_j |Z_j| \times (n-1)$ real numbers, which we can conveniently put in a table. See Fig. 2.

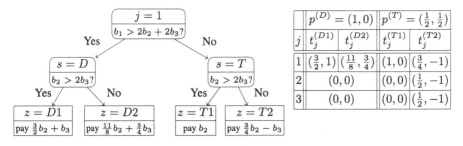

Fig. 2. Myerson's payments for Example II in tree form (left, position 1 only) and in tabular form (right). Note that: (1) the states are the same for all positions $j \in \{1, 2, 3\}$ but the substates need not be the same; and (2) the payment is per-unit, e.g. in substate $T1$ the highest bidder gets a fraction $p_1^{(T)} = \frac{1}{2}$ of the item and pays $p_1^{(T)} b_2 = \frac{1}{2} b_2$ in total.

An Explicit Representation of Myerson's Payment Rule. It is not hard to see that Myerson's payments can always be written explicitly as a finite tree form: the number of cutoff points must be finite, since by monotonicity, a bidder at rank j can pass through each substate at most once when increasing her bid. Moreover, at every leaf, $\text{TMP}_k(b)$ is a sum of terms of the form $x_k(\cdot) y_\ell$, where $x_k(\cdot) = p_j^{(z)}$ for the appropriate rank and substate (i.e. a constant), and y_ℓ is a linear combination of bids, as in Fig. 1. Thus for all profiles b where $\tilde{z}_j(b) = z$, $\text{TMP}_j(b_j, b_{-j})$ is a weighted combination of b_{-j}, where $w_j^{(z)} \in \mathbb{R}^{n-1}$ is some fixed weight vector.

Note that we still need to 'translate' Myerson's expression to our notation, which requires switching from agents' names to positions (as we do in the paragraph above), and also from total payment to payment per item unit. For this last part, we set $t_j^{(z)} := w_j^{(z)} / p_j^{(z)}$, as the total payment holds $\text{TMP}_j(b) = p_j^{(z)} \cdot \text{PAY}_j^{(z)}(b)$.

Measuring Explicit Complexity. Given a PSA $x = (S, \tilde{s}, \bar{p})$, we define the *explicit complexity* of a payment rule that implements x as $\max_{j \le n, s \in S} |Z_j(S)|$, namely the size of the largest subtree. If the explicit complexity is 1, we say that PAY is *explicitly simple*.

The explicit complexity of Myerson's payments for Example II is 2 since some states are further divided into two substates. See Fig. 2 . Intuitively, this is since the red rectangle in Fig. 1 exists only on some profiles, and thus we get different linear combinations (different substates of s).

By the Myerson lemma, if there exists an explicitly simple payment rule, it must belong in the Myerson class, i.e. there are some functions $(p_k^0)_{k \in N}$ that modify each agents' payment. However it is not clear a-priori under what conditions such functions exist, how to find them, and what would be the resulting (simple) tabular form. Characterizing these conditions will be our primary goal in this work.

Single State PSAs. We argue that the problem of complexity only arises in non-trivial PSAs, i.e. when there is more than one state.

Consider a single-state auction (i.e. where each agent gets a fixed fraction of the item according to her rank). According to Eq. (1), the agent ranked k'th goes through exactly $L(b_k) = n - k$ cutoff points—one for every agent she passes on the way up. This induces a fixed payment function which is a weighted combination of all lower bids—namely the good old VCG payment.

As we already saw above, this does no longer hold even for two states.

3 Complexity of the Myerson Payment Rule

In this section we show that Myerson's rule is explicitly simple for two agents (regardless of the allocation rule), but becomes substantially more complex as the number of agents grows.

3.1 Two Agents

Theorem 1. *Every 2-agent PSA has a unique explicitly simple NPT implementation, which is the Myerson payment rule.*

Proof Sketch. Myerson's lemma states the unique payment rule that is SP, IR and NPT. Thus all that is left is to provide an explicitly simple representation to Myerson payment rule as $(t_1^{(s)}, t_2^{(s)})_{s=1,\dots,c}$.

We order states such that $s = 1$ is the state closest to a tie, and $s = c$ applies when the gap is widest. Let $\beta^{(s)} := \frac{b_2^{(s)}}{b_1^{(s)}}$ at the boundary profile $b^{(s)}$ between states $s, s+1$. We calculate the weights, starting with the lower agent 2.

At any profile $b \in \mathcal{B}(s)$ where $b_1 > b_2$, we have $\mathrm{TMP}_j(b) = p_j^{(s)}\mathrm{PAY}_j(b) = p_j^{(s)}t_j^{(s)}b_{-j}$. We then apply Eq. (1) and get

$$
t_2^{(s)} = \frac{1}{b_1 p_2^{(s)}}\mathrm{TMP}_{\underline{b}}(b) = \frac{1}{b_1 p_2^{(s)}} \sum_{\ell=1}^{L(b_{\underline{b}})} y_\ell [x_{\underline{b}}^+(y_\ell, b_{\underline{a}}) - x_{\underline{b}}^-(y_\ell, b_{\underline{a}})]
$$

$$
= \frac{1}{b_1 p_2^{(s)}} \sum_{s'=c-1}^{s} (\beta^{(s')}b_1)[p_2^{(s')} - p_2^{(s'+1)}]
$$

where the second transition is since the allocation increment points y_ℓ are exactly the boundary profiles where $b_{\underline{b}} = \beta^{(s')}b_{\underline{a}}$. Thus,

$$
t_2^{(s)} = \sum_{s'=c-1}^{s} \beta^{(s')}\frac{p_2^{(s')} - p_2^{(s'+1)}}{p_2^{(s)}} = \frac{p_2^{(s+1)}}{p_2^{(s)}}t_2^{(s+1)} + \beta^{(s)}(1 - \frac{p_2^{(s+1)}}{p_2^{(s)}}).
$$

We then continue to compute weights for agent 1 from the tie state $s = 1$ to $s = c$, getting $t_1^{(1)} = \frac{p_2^{(1)}}{p_1(1)}t_2^{(1)} + (1 - \frac{p_2^{(1)}}{p_1(1)})$ and:

$$
t_1^{(s)} = \frac{p_1^{(s-1)}}{p_1^{(s)}}t_1^{(s-1)} + \frac{1}{\beta^{(s)}}(1 - \frac{p_1^{(s-1)}}{p_1^{(s)}}).
$$

$\qquad\square$

3.2   Beyond Two Agents

Proposition 1. *Consider an explicit representation of the Myerson payment rule. For a single-top PSA with n agents, $|Z_j(s)| \le n$, and this is tight even for a near-tie PSA.*

Intuitively, we show that even in near-tie PSAs, which are the simplest non-trivial allocation rules, the Myerson payment uses a linear combination of the bids whose coefficients depend on how many other bids are above/below the state cutoff point. Since there are n different options, this induces n substates with distinct linear combinations.

Proof (tightness). Consider any generic near-tie PSA (i.e. $p_1^{(T)} > p_2^{(T)} > \cdots > p_n^{(T)}$). State T is selected iff $b_1 > 2 \sum_{i>1} b_i$. Denote $p_i := p_i^{(T)}$ for short.

To calculate the TMP of the leading agent, we fix the bids of agents $2, \ldots, n$ and consider all cutoff points $y \in \mathbb{R}$. These are exactly $Y = \{b_i\}_{i>1} \cup \{b^*, b^{**}\}$, where $b^* := \frac{1}{2} b_2 - \sum_{i>2} b_i$ is the transition point from D to T, and $b^{**} = 2 \sum_{i>1} b_i$ is the transition point from T to D. Note that for any $j \ge 2$, it is easy to find a profile (in fact many profiles) s.t. b^* is strictly between b_j and b_{j+1} (where $b_{n+1} = 0$). It is also easy to find profiles where $b^* < 0$, meaning that the state is T for any bid $b' < b_2$. Thus for any $j = 2, \ldots, n+1$ we denote these profiles as 'type j' profiles.

By summing over the cutoff points Y using Eq. (1), we get that at every type j profile b, the payment of agent 1 is:

- $\mathrm{PAY}_1(b) = \frac{1}{p_1} \mathrm{TMP}_1(b) = \sum_{i=2}^{j} \frac{p_{i-1} - p_i}{p_1} b_2 + \frac{p_j}{p_1} b^*$, if $b \in \mathcal{B}(T)$;
- $\mathrm{PAY}_1(b) = \mathrm{TMP}_1(b) = \sum_{i=2}^{j} (p_{i-1} - p_i) b_2 + p_j b^* + (1 - p_1) b^{**}$, if $b \in \mathcal{B}(D)$.

since this yields a distinct formula for every j, each of the states T, D must split into n substates, so $|Z_1(T)| = |Z_1(D)| = n$, as required.   □

The reason that in Fig. 2 the sets $Z_1(T), Z_1(D)$ include only two substates each rather than 3, is that Example II is not generic, as $p_2 = p_3$.

4   Explicitly Simple Auctions

In the remainder of the paper we will focus on explicitly simple payment rules. We therefore only use the set of states S, as $Z_i = S$ for all i. In this section we derive some general properties that will be used for characterization in the later sections.

Exact Ties and Boundary Points. The definitions above look over the cases where $b_j = b_{j'}$ for some j, j'. More generally, the partition of $\mathcal{B}^n$ into $|S|$ can create complications with closed and open sets. E.g. in our running example, the profile $(b_1 = 8, b_2 = 3, b_3 = 1)$ can be treated as belonging to either state.

We will not be assuming anything on the state at the boundary profiles. As for ties, we assume the profile b implicitly contains ranking to use in case of a tie. Since this ranking is affected by the bids, an agent may 'choose' her rank in case of a tie.[2]

---

[2] This can be formally implemented, for example, if each agent j reports (in addition to b_j) a rational number r_j. In case of a tie, we rank the tied agents according to $R_j := r_j \cdot \sqrt{\psi_j}$ where ψ_j is the j'th prime. Note that $R_j, R_{j'}$ are never tied (since $\sqrt{\psi_j}$ are linearly independent over the rationals [1]), unbounded on both sides, and that for any $r_{j'} < r_{j''}$ and j there is r_j s.t. $R_{j'} < R_j < R_{j''}$.

Therefore, in the remainder of the paper it will not matter how boundary profiles are classified in the PSA x or how ties are broken. Since the payment function is defined directly on S the utilities in any profile $b \in \mathcal{B}^n$ are well defined.

4.1   Conditions for Strategyproofness

Proposition 2. *An explicit auction is strategyproof if and only if it is locally strategyproof.*

The proof is by breaking the difference between the real value and the reported bid into local steps (into an adjacent state or one rank up or down). Then prove by induction on the number of local steps.

In this section we show that to characterize strategyproofness, we essentially only need to show that all agents are indifferent on certain boundary profiles: between two adjacent states, or between two adjacent positions (i.e. in a tie).

The formal definitions and proofs are available in the full version.

An agent that is right on the boundary and can decide the state in a given profile is called *pivotal*. She *connects* the two states s', s'' if whenever she can change s' to s'', she can also bid right on the boundary.

Lemma 2 (Informal). *If j connects s', s'', then the following statements are equivalent:*

- j *does not have a local state manipulation for s', s'';*
- j *is indifferent between s', s'' at any boundary profile.*

Lemma 3 (Informal). *The following statements are equivalent for agent j and state s:*

- j *does not have a local position manipulation to $j + 1$;*
- j *is indifferent about her rank in case of a tie with $j + 1$.*

One can check that in our Example II, the agents are indifferent at any boundary point. For example at the boundary profile $b = (8, 3, 1)$ we have $u_1^{(T)} = 0.5(8 - 0.75 \cdot 3 + 0.5 \cdot 1) = 3.125$; and $u_1^{(D)} = 8 - 1.375 \cdot 3 - 0.75 \cdot 1 = 3.125$.

5   Two-State PSAs and Near-Ties

In a two-state PSA there are only two states $S = \{T, D\}$ and thus two possible outcome distributions $p^{(T)}$ and $p^{(D)}$. Due to homogeneity, the function $\tilde{s}$ must be a linear function. That is, there are constants $\bar{\alpha} = (\alpha_1, \ldots, \alpha_n) \in \mathbb{R}^n$ s.t. $\tilde{s}(b) = T$ if $\sum_{i \leq n} \alpha_i b_i > 0$ and $\tilde{s}(b) = D$ if $\sum_{i \leq n} \alpha_i b_i < 0$, with some tie-breaking rule. A two-state PSA is thus fully described by a triplet $(p^{(D)}, p^{(T)}, \bar{\alpha})$.

Note that multiplying $\bar{\alpha}$ by a positive constant does not change the rule.

$$t_n^{(D)} \leftrightarrow t_{n-1}^{(D)} \cdots t_j^{(D)} \cdots t_2^{(D)} \overset{?}{\longleftrightarrow} t_1^{(D)}$$
$$\updownarrow \qquad \updownarrow \qquad \updownarrow \qquad \updownarrow \qquad \updownarrow$$
$$t_n^{(T)} \leftrightarrow t_{n-1}^{(T)} \cdots t_j^{(T)} \cdots t_2^{(T)} \leftrightarrow t_1^{(T)}$$

Fig. 3. Every $t_j^{(s)}$ is a vector of $n-1$ weights. Every vertical arrow corresponds to an agent that connects the two states. Every horizontal arrow corresponds to adjacent agents in the respective state.

A two-state PSA $(p^{(D)}, p^{(T)}, \bar{\alpha})$ induces two types of agents: type D for which $p_j^{(D)} > p_j^{(T)}$ and type T for which it is the opposite. We denote by $N_D, N_T \subseteq N$ the two subsets of agents. Note that $\alpha_j < 0$ for $j \in N_D$ and $\alpha_j > 0$ for $j \in N_T$.[3] E.g. the cutoff rule in our running example can be defined by $\alpha_1 = -1, \alpha_2 = \alpha_3 = 2$.

Since multiplying $\bar{\alpha}$ by a positive constant does not matter, we assume w.l.o.g. that agent 1 is type D.

Separated PSAs. Recall that a two-state PSA is *separated* if $j < j'$ for all $j \in N_D, j' \in N_T$ (if all T are above all D we flip the names of the states). A non-separated PSA is *mixed*. In a separated PSA the type T agents get a larger fraction of the item (at the expense of D agents) as the gap between high and low bids becomes smaller. In the remainder of this section we only consider separated PSAs unless stated otherwise.

If only the highest bidder increases her share of the item in state D then we say this is a **single-top** PSA. Any other separated PSA is **multi-top**. In a single-top PSA, only α_1 is negative and thus we denote $\gamma := -\alpha_1 > 0$. A special case of single-top PSA is a **near-tie** PSA, after which we have named the states **D**efault (where there is a single winner) and near-**T**i.e.

Our main result in this section is characterising the set of single-top PSAs that can be implemented with explicitly simple payments, while showing that multi-top PSAs can never be.

Since we already know from Sect. 4.1 that strategyproofness is characterized by indifference at the boundary/tie profiles, we need to:

1. Identify which boundary/tie profiles are possible in each class of PSAs;
2. Understand what constraints are imposed on the payments (and possibly on the PSA) by indifference at such profiles.

5.1 Identifying All Boundary and Tie Profiles

Each vertical arrow in position j in Fig. 3 means that agent j connects the two states (meaning there is a boundary profile where she is pivotal). We can see in the figure that all agents connect both states.

We say that agents $j, j+1$ are *adjacent* in state s if there is a profile $b \in \mathcal{B}(s)$ where they are tied (recall that j refers to the agent's rank).

Each horizontal arrow in Fig. 3 shows a pair $j, j+1$ that are adjacent in the respective state. We can see in the figure that all pairs are adjacent in both states, except possibly

---

[3] We do not allow agents for which $\alpha_j = 0$, as they would change the allocation without being affected.

the pair $1, 2$ in state D. This will be the crucial difference between multi-top PSAs (where the edge always exist), and single-top PSAs, where the edge exists if and only if $\gamma \geq \alpha_2$. For proofs, see full version.

5.2 Indifference Constraints

Every arrow in the diagram shown in Fig. 3 imposes constraints on the payments, since it means that in any corresponding boundary profile (for a vertical edge) or tie profile (for a horizontal edge), the respective agent should be indifferent between the two states/ranks.

Lemma 4. $u_j^{(T)}(v_j, b_{-j}) = u_j^{(D)}(v_j, b_{-j})$ in all profiles where j is pivotal between T and D, if and only if:

$$\forall i < j, \quad t_j^{(T)[i]} = \frac{1}{p_j^{(T)}} \left[p_j^{(D)} t_j^{(D)[i]} - \frac{\alpha_i}{\alpha_j} (p_j^{(T)} - p_j^{(D)}) \right] \tag{3}$$

$$\forall i \geq j, \quad t_j^{(T)[i]} = \frac{1}{p_j^{(T)}} \left[p_j^{(D)} t_j^{(D)[i]} - \frac{\alpha_{i+1}}{\alpha_j} (p_j^{(T)} - p_j^{(D)}) \right] \tag{4}$$

The proof idea is that by equating the utilities at the boundary profile, we get an expression of the form

$$\sum_{i \neq j} F_i(p_j^{(T)}, p_j^{(D)}, t_j^{(T)}, t_j^{(D)}, \bar{\alpha}) b_i = 0$$

for some functions $F_1, \ldots, F_{n-1}$. The only way to nullify the entire expression for a generic profile b is to make sure $F_i = 0$ for all i. The solution gives Eqs. (3), (4). The proof of the next lemma uses the same idea.

Lemma 5. If $u_j^{(s)}(v_j, b_{-j}) = u_{j+1}^{(s)}(v_j, b_{-j})$ in all profiles $b \in \mathcal{B}(s)$ where $b_j = b_{j+1}$, if and only if:

$$\forall i \neq j, \quad t_j^{(s)[i]} = t_{j+1}^{(s)[i]} \frac{p_{j+1}^{(s)}}{p_j^{(s)}} \tag{5}$$

$$t_j^{(s)[j]} = 1 + (t_{j+1}^{(s)[j]} - 1) \frac{p_{j+1}^{(s)}}{p_j^{(s)}} \tag{6}$$

This means that any arrow in the diagram completely locks the values of two weight vectors to one another. Since our arrow diagram contains cycles for any $n \geq 3$, this means that the values of t are overconstrained, and we get a contradiction unless the diagram commutes: when moving from $t_j^{(D)}$ to $t_{j+1}^{(T)}$ we must get the same value whether we pick first the horizontal or the vertical edge.

Proposition 3. The diagram in Fig. 3 commutes at $j, j + 1$ if and only if

$$\frac{\alpha_{j+1}}{\alpha_j} = \frac{p_{j+1}^{(T)} - p_{j+1}^{(D)}}{p_j^{(T)} - p_j^{(D)}}. \tag{7}$$

ALGORITHM 1. COMPUTE SINGLE-TOP TWO-STATE PAYMENT RULE

Input: Partial PSA $\bar{p} = (p^{(D)}, p^{(T)})$; Tie-sensitivity parameter $\gamma \leq p_2^{(T)} - p_2^{(D)}$.
Output: An explicit auction (x, PAY).
Set $\alpha_j \leftarrow p_j^{(T)} - p_j^{(D)}$ for all $j > 1$;
Set $\alpha_1 \leftarrow -\gamma$;
(If $\gamma = \alpha_2$ then set tie-breaking towards state T);
Initialize $t_n^{(D)[i]} \leftarrow 0$ for all $i \leq n - 1$;
Set $t_n^{(T)}$ using $t_n^{(D)}$ and Eqs. (3), (4);
For each $j = n - 1, n - 2, \ldots, 1$ set $t_j^{(T)}$ using $t_{j+1}^{(T)}$ and Eqs. (5), (6);
For each $j = n - 1, \ldots, 1$ set $t_j^{(D)}$ using $t_j^{(T)}$ and Eqs. (3), (4);
Return (x, PAY) (x is defined by $\bar{p}$ and $\bar{\alpha}$, PAY is defined by t);

This means that not every Single-Top PSA is allowed: setting the allocations $p^{(T)}$ and $p^{(D)}$ also dictates $\alpha_2, \ldots, \alpha_n$. Further, setting any $t_j^{(s)}$ uniquely determines all payments, if exist. For multi-top PSAs, the allocations also dictate α_1 and we show in the full version that the induced cutoff between states is such that T is never realized (so there is only one state).

5.3 Explicitly Simple Implementation for Single-Top PSA

We can summarize the result for single-top PSAs, which is our main positive result in the paper (for a full proof see full version):

Theorem 2. *A single-top PSA has an explicitly simple implementation if and only if Eq. (7) holds for all $j > 1$.*

Moreover, given any partial single-top PSA $\bar{p} = (p^{(D)}, p^{(T)})$ and a tie-sensitivity parameter $0 \leq \gamma \leq p_2^{(T)} - p_2^{(D)}$, Algorithm 1 returns an auction that is SP, IR and consistent with $\bar{p}$ and γ.

The double arrows in Fig. 4 show the order in which Algorithm 1 sets the payments (although any order would do), and next to it the prices derived for the PSA in Example II. The reader can compare this succinct tabular form to the one derived for the Myerson payments in Fig. 2.

Proof Sketch of the Positive Direction. As stated in Sect. 5.1, setting $-\alpha_1 = \gamma \leq p_2^{(T)} - p_2^{(D)}$ guarantees that adjacency and connectedness edges are as in Fig. 3, and in particular that there is no edge (constraint) between $t_1^{(D)}, t_2^{(D)}$.

The algorithm then guarantees (due to Lemmas 5 and 4) that the respective agents are indifferent in every boundary and tie profile corresponding to each edge (note that the edge corresponding to α_1 is not part of a cycle). This guarantees SP by Lemmas 2 and 3. IR follows from strategyproofness, as no bidder can gain by becoming last, and the last bidder is guaranteed a non-negative utility (since the payment is set to 0). □

Finally, an important question is whether our explicit implementation requires positive payments to agents. For single-top PSA, we provide a full answer.

$$0 = t_n^{(D)} \quad t_{n-1}^{(D)} \quad t_j^{(D)} \quad t_2^{(D)} \quad t_1^{(D)}$$
$$\Downarrow \qquad \Uparrow \qquad \Uparrow \qquad \Uparrow \qquad \Uparrow$$
$$t_n^{(T)} \Rightarrow t_{n-1}^{(T)} \cdots t_j^{(T)} \cdots t_2^{(T)} \Rightarrow t_1^{(T)}$$

$t_j^{(s)}$	$s = D$		$s = T$
$j = 1$	$(^{11}/8, ^3/4)$	$\Leftarrow \Uparrow$	$(^3/4, -^1/2)$
$j = 2$	$(0,0)$	$\Leftarrow \Uparrow$	$(^1/2, -1)$
$j = 3$	$(0,0)$	$* \Rightarrow$	$(^1/2, -1)$

Fig. 4. Left: Adjacency and connectedness constraints in One-Top PSAs. The initialization point and the double arrows show the order of computation as preformed in Algorithm 1. Right: Explicitly simple payments for Example II, in tabular form.

Proposition 4. *Consider any SP single-top explicitly simple auction. Then either*

○ *n = 2; or*   ○ *n = 3 and $\gamma = \alpha_2$; or*   ○ *IR is violated; or*   ○ *NPT is violated.*

This means that in the first two cases, an explicitly simple implementation will coincide with Myerson's payments. In contrast, in all other cases any explicitly simple implementation must *differ* from Myerson's payments, i.e. require some non-zero $p_{\underline{k}}^0$.

E.g. for the example in Fig. 1 we can verify that the explicitly simple implementation requires $p_{\underline{c}}^0((1,3)) = -\frac{1}{8}$.

In particular the proposition characterizes when Myerson's payments (with $p_{\underline{k}}^0 \equiv 0$) are explicitly simple according to our definition. Note that we do not have a way to find the appropriate translation $p_{\underline{k}}^0$ (when exists), but we do not need one since we derived the explicit formulation directly.

5.4 Beyond the Two States Solution

Our results also extend to more than two states, as long as states are *ordered*, meaning that no three states share a boundary. See full version for details.

Intuitively, ordered states means that no profile is in the intersection of three states or more, e.g. when we can order states from 'closest to a tie' to 'farthest from a tie'. We then have a similar structure of constraints between adjacent weight vectors, which has a solution only when the allocation rule is single-top, breaking the cycles involving agent 1 (see Fig. 5). Note that this generalizes both two-agents and two-states cases.

$$0 = t_n^{(|S|)} \leftrightarrow t_{n-1}^{(|S|)} \leftrightarrow \cdots \leftrightarrow t_j^{(|S|)} \leftrightarrow \cdots \leftrightarrow t_2^{(|S|)} \qquad t_1^{(|S|)} \quad \text{(Wide gap in bids)}$$
$$\Downarrow \qquad \Uparrow \qquad \qquad \Uparrow \qquad \qquad \Uparrow \qquad \Uparrow$$
$$t_n^{(|S|-1)} \leftrightarrow t_{n-1}^{(|S|-1)} \leftrightarrow \cdots \leftrightarrow t_j^{(|S|-1)} \leftrightarrow \cdots \leftrightarrow t_2^{(|S|-1)} \qquad t_1^{(|S|-1)}$$
$$\Downarrow \qquad \Uparrow \qquad \qquad \Uparrow \qquad \qquad \Uparrow \qquad \Uparrow$$
$$\cdots \qquad\qquad\qquad\qquad\qquad\qquad\qquad\qquad\qquad \cdots$$
$$\Downarrow \qquad \Uparrow \qquad \qquad \Uparrow \qquad \qquad \Uparrow \qquad \Uparrow$$
$$t_n^{(1)} \quad \Rightarrow \quad t_{n-1}^{(1)} \quad \Rightarrow \cdots \Rightarrow \quad t_j^{(1)} \quad \Rightarrow \cdots \Rightarrow \quad t_2^{(1)} \quad \Rightarrow \quad t_1^{(1)} \quad \text{(Close to a tie)}$$

Fig. 5. Adjacency and connectedness constraints in Multi-state Ordered One-Top PSAs. The Double arrows show a possible order of computation.

6   Conclusion

We showed how certain natural allocation rules that diversify the set of winners when close to a tie, can be implemented using an explicit payment, where each agent simply pays a fixed combination of the other bids, which depends on her rank (and on whether a near-tie was declared). The designer has limited freedom: she can choose any two allocations for the two states, provided that monotonicity is maintained and that only the leading bidder loses some of the item under near-tie. Then there is only one more free parameter, which can be thought of as the 'sensitivity' of the allocation rule to near-ties. Setting this parameter uniquely defines the allocation rule and the payment.

While explicitly simple auctions for $n \geq 3$ require payments to some agents, we believe that their simple structure makes them preferable over basic (non-negative prices) Myerson payments in some situations, and that increasing buyer retention and diversity will pay off at the long run.

Natural followup directions are to study the conditions under which budget balance is guaranteed, and, more broadly, to study welfare and revenue implications when the distribution of buyer types is given. This would enable us to design good near-tie auctions that balance the different goals of the auctioneer.

Acknowledgement. The authors thank Okke Schijvers and Ella Segev for fruitful discussions.

References

1. Besicovitch, A.S.: On the linear independence of fractional powers of integers. J. London Math. Soc. **15**, 3–6 (1940)
2. Cavallo, R.: Optimal decision-making with minimal waste: strategyproof redistribution of VCG payments. In: Proceedings of the Fifth International Joint Conference on Autonomous Agents and Multiagent Systems, pp. 882–889 (2006)
3. Clark, D.J., Riis, C.: Influence and the discretionary allocation of several prizes. Eur. J. Polit. Econ. **14**(4), 605–625 (1998)
4. Eden, M.: Optimal ties in contests. Technical report, Hebrew University (2006)
5. Fiat, A., Goldberg, A.V., Hartline, J.D., Karlin, A.R.: Competitive generalized auctions. In: Proceedings of the Thirty-Fourth Annual ACM Symposium on Theory of Computing, pp. 72–81 (2002)
6. Fischer, S., Güth, W., Kaplan, T.R., Zultan, R.: Auctions with leaks about early bids: analysis and experimental behavior. Econ. Inq. **59**(2), 722–739 (2021)
7. Gama, J.: Functional trees. Mach. Learn. **55**(3), 219–250 (2004). https://doi.org/10.1023/B:MACH.0000027782.67192.13
8. Graczyk, M., Lasota, T., Trawiński, B.: Comparative analysis of premises valuation models using KEEL, RapidMiner, and WEKA. In: Nguyen, N.T., Kowalczyk, R., Chen, S.-M. (eds.) ICCCI 2009. LNCS (LNAI), vol. 5796, pp. 800–812. Springer, Heidelberg (2009). https://doi.org/10.1007/978-3-642-04441-0_70
9. Guo, M., Conitzer, V.: Worst-case optimal redistribution of VCG payments in multi-unit auctions. Games Econ. Behav. **67**(1), 69–98 (2009)
10. Hashimoto, K.: Strategy-proof rule in probabilistic allocation problem of an indivisible good and money (2015)

11. Ivanov, D., Nesterov, A.: Identifying bid leakage in procurement auctions: machine learning approach. In: Proceedings of the 2019 ACM Conference on Economics and Computation, pp. 69–70 (2019)

12. Lee, J.S., Szymanski, B.K.: A novel auction mechanism for selling time-sensitive e-services. In: Seventh IEEE International Conference on E-Commerce Technology (CEC 2005), pp. 75–82. IEEE (2005)

13. Li, S.: Obviously strategy-proof mechanisms. Am. Econ. Rev. **107**(11), 3257–87 (2017)

14. Ma, H., Meir, R., Parkes, D.C., Zou, J.: Contingent payment mechanisms for resource utilization. In: Proceedings of the 18th International Conference on Autonomous Agents and MultiAgent Systems, pp. 422–430 (2019)

15. Milgrom, P.: Simplified mechanisms with an application to sponsored-search auctions. Games Econ. Behav. **70**(1), 62–70 (2010)

16. Morgenstern, J.H., Roughgarden, T.: On the pseudo-dimension of nearly optimal auctions. In: Advances in Neural Information Processing Systems, vol. 28 (2015)

17. Murillo, J., Muñoz, V., López, B., Busquets, D.: A fair mechanism for recurrent multi-unit auctions. In: Bergmann, R., Lindemann, G., Kirn, S., Pěchouček, M. (eds.) MATES 2008. LNCS (LNAI), vol. 5244, pp. 147–158. Springer, Heidelberg (2008). https://doi.org/10.1007/978-3-540-87805-6_14

18. Myerson, R.B.: Optimal auction design. Math. Oper. Res. **6**(1), 58–73 (1981)

19. Nedelec, T., El Karoui, N., Perchet, V.: Learning to bid in revenue-maximizing auctions. In: International Conference on Machine Learning, pp. 4781–4789. PMLR (2019)

20. Núñez, M.: Towards transparent mechanisms. In: Laslier, J.-F., Moulin, H., Sanver, M.R., Zwicker, W.S. (eds.) The Future of Economic Design. SED, pp. 341–346. Springer, Cham (2019). https://doi.org/10.1007/978-3-030-18050-8_47

21. Ohseto, S.: Characterizations of strategy-proof and fair mechanisms for allocating indivisible goods. Econ. Theor. **29**(1), 111–121 (2006). https://doi.org/10.1007/s00199-005-0014-1

22. Pápai, S.: Groves sealed bid auctions of heterogeneous objects with fair prices. Soc. Choice Welfare **20**(3), 371–385 (2003). https://doi.org/10.1007/s003550200185

23. Quinlan, J.R., et al.: Learning with continuous classes. In: 5th Australian Joint Conference on Artificial Intelligence, vol. 92, pp. 343–348. World Scientific (1992)

24. Rubinstein, A.: On the computational complexity of optimal simple mechanisms. In: Proceedings of the 2016 ACM Conference on Innovations in Theoretical Computer Science, pp. 21–28 (2016)

25. Rubinstein, A., Weinberg, S.M.: Simple mechanisms for a subadditive buyer and applications to revenue monotonicity. ACM Trans. Econ. Comput. (TEAC) **6**(3–4), 1–25 (2018)

26. Varian, H.R.: Position auctions. Int. J. Ind. Organ. **25**(6), 1163–1178 (2007)

27. Yengin, D.: Characterizing welfare-egalitarian mechanisms with solidarity when valuations are private information. BE J. Theor. Econ. **12**(1) (2012)

Computational Aspects in Games

Simultaneous Contests with Equal Sharing Allocation of Prizes: Computational Complexity and Price of Anarchy

Edith Elkind, Abheek Ghosh$^{(\boxtimes)}$, and Paul W. Goldberg

Department of Computer Science, University of Oxford, Oxford, UK
{edith.elkind,abheek.ghosh,paul.goldberg}@cs.ox.ac.uk

Abstract. We study a general scenario of simultaneous contests that allocate prizes based on equal sharing: each contest awards its prize to all players who satisfy some contest-specific criterion, and the value of this prize to a winner decreases as the number of winners increases. The players produce outputs for a set of activities, and the winning criteria of the contests are based on these outputs. We consider two variations of the model: (i) players have costs for producing outputs; (ii) players do not have costs but have generalized budget constraints. We observe that these games are exact potential games and hence always have a pure-strategy Nash equilibrium. The price of anarchy is 2 for the budget model, but can be unbounded for the cost model. Our main results are for the computational complexity of these games. We prove that for general versions of the model exactly or approximately computing a best response is NP-hard. For natural restricted versions where best response is easy to compute, we show that finding a pure-strategy Nash equilibrium is PLS-complete, and finding a mixed-strategy Nash equilibrium is (PPAD∩PLS)-complete. On the other hand, an approximate pure-strategy Nash equilibrium can be found in pseudo-polynomial time. These games are a strict but natural subclass of explicit congestion games, but they still have the same equilibrium hardness results.

Keywords: contest theory · equilibrium analysis · computational complexity

1 Introduction

Contests are games where players, who are assumed to be strategic, make costly and irreversible investments to win valuable prizes [36]. Typically, the prizes have monetary value, which incentivizes the players to make the costly investments. In some scenarios, the prizes may be associated with reputation and social status. For example, many online forums and websites depend upon user-generated content to provide value to their customers, and award badges, which do not have any monetary value but provide social reputation (e.g., StackOverflow and Quora); see, e.g., [23].

© The Author(s), under exclusive license to Springer Nature Switzerland AG 2022
P. Kanellopoulos et al. (Eds.): SAGT 2022, LNCS 13584, pp. 133–150, 2022.
https://doi.org/10.1007/978-3-031-15714-1_8

In the presence of multiple simultaneous contests, each player may explicitly select one or more contests and invest efforts so as to win the associated prizes. Moreover, sometimes contest participation is implicit: players engage in various activities, and each contest awards prizes to some of the players based on their performance in a specific subset of activities.

Consider, for instance, the setting where several social media platforms or news websites compete to attract customers. The potential customers are not homogeneous: e.g., some may be interested in politics, while others focus on sports or technology. It is therefore natural to model this setting as a set of simultaneous contests, with each individual contest corresponding to a group of customers with similar preferences. The platforms can take actions that make them more attractive to potential customers. Indeed, some of the actions, such as improving the interface, or increasing the update frequency, may impact the platform's performance with respect to several customer groups. That is, we can think of platforms as engaging in several *activities*, with their performance in each contest depending on the effort they invest in these activities. Different customer groups may value different mixtures of activities in different ways: e.g., while consumers of financial and sports news care about frequent updates, those who read the gossip column are happy with daily or even weekly updates. Thus, by increasing her investment in an activity, a player may improve her performance in several—but not all—contests.

In this work, we study a formal model that can capture scenarios of this type. In our model, there are several players and several simultaneous contests, as well as a set of activities. Each player selects their effort level for each activity (and may incur a cost for doing so, or face budget constraints), and each contest j has its own success function, which specifies combinations of effort for each activity that are sufficient to succeed in j. In addition to that, we assume that each contest allocates identical prizes to all agents that meet its criteria[1]: e.g., if, to win contest j, it suffices to produce 2 units along activity ℓ, then the player who produces 3 units along ℓ and the player who produces 30 units along ℓ receive the same prize from j; however, the value of the prize in contest j may depend on the number of players who meet the criteria of j. We refer to this setting as *multi-activity games*.

From the perspective of the player, we distinguish between two models: (1) the *cost model*, which has cost functions for producing output, and (2) the *budget model*, which has generalized budget constraints (feasible subsets of the space). The cost functions and the budget constraints may be different across players, capturing the fact that some players may be able to perform better in some activities compared to others.

Our model is very general: we impose very mild and natural constraints on the contests' success functions and prize allocation rules. In particular, we assume

---

[1] The motivation for equal sharing allocation is somewhat similar to that of proportional allocation (e.g., in Tullock contests [34]), with equal sharing becoming relevant in situations where the contests use explicit rules (or criteria) to decide on an allocation.

that the total value of the prizes allocated to the winners of each contest is a monotonically non-decreasing and concave function of the number of winners; these assumptions capture the idea that the value of an award decreases as it gets awarded to a larger number of players (see, e.g., [23]). A specific instantiation of this model is a contest that has a *fixed total prize* of V, and every winner gets a share of V/k if there are k winners.

Besides our social media platform example, several other situations can be modeled using contests with equal sharing allocation of prizes, where players compete by engaging in activities valued by multiple contests. For instance, funding agencies are generally not able to *perfectly discriminate* among the applicants to select the most deserving ones. They might score candidates based on attributes such as strength of proposal, publication history, and management experience, and allocate their budget to one of the eligible candidates or distribute it among them. Because of this uniform distribution of the funding, from the perspective of an expected utility maximizing applicant, this situation can be approximated using a contest with an equal sharing allocation with a fixed total prize.

1.1 Our Results

We observe that, under mild assumptions, multi-activity games are *exact potential games* [27] (see Definition 4). This guarantees the existence of a pure-strategy Nash equilibrium (PNE). Moreover, an approximate PNE can be computed in pseudo-polynomial time. In fact, a sequence of ϵ-better/best[2] response moves converges to an ϵ-PNE, with the number of steps proportional to $1/\epsilon$ (and pseudo-polynomial in other parameters). For the budget model, for the natural definition of social welfare in these games, we observe that the price of anarchy (PoA) is at most 2 and the price of stability (PoS) can be close to 2, so both these bounds are tight.[3] However, for the cost model, for meaningful definitions of social welfare, the PoS can be infinite.

We then study the computation complexity of finding an equilibrium in these games, which is the main focus of our paper. This portion of the paper concentrates on a specific instantiation of the model, where the contests' criteria and the players' budget constraints are all linear; let us call this model the *linear model*. (Here, we discuss the results for the budget model. With similar assumptions, similar results hold for the cost model as well.) We show that, for the linear model, it is NP-hard for a player to best respond to the strategies of other players. This hardness result holds even for a game with only one player; in other words, the hardness is due to the optimization problem that a player faces while playing the game. We also prove that there exists no polynomial-time approximation scheme unless P=NP. (Here, NP-hardness for best-response

---

[2] An ϵ-better response move increases the utility of a player by at least ϵ.

[3] The price of anarchy (stability) is the ratio between the social welfare of the optimal solution and the social welfare of an equilibrium solution, in the worst case over instances of the problem, and in the worst (best) case over corresponding equilibrium solutions.

directly implies NP-hardness for equilibrium computation.) On the positive side, we obtain fixed-parameter tractability results: we show that best response is polynomial-time computable if either the number of contests or the number of activities is a constant.

The NP-hardness result for best-response motivates us to further restrict our model: we assume that a player can produce output only along a small (polynomial) number of portfolios of activities. Mathematically, a portfolio corresponds to a direction in the activity space along which a player can produce output. This restricted model captures salient features of the original model: e.g., it maintains the property that the contests can have overlapping criteria.

With a simple transformation of the activity space, the portfolio model can be converted to an equivalent model where a player produces output along a single activity only, i.e., only along the axes, where an activity in the new model corresponds to a portfolio in the old model. In our discussion, we call this new model the *single-activity model* to differentiate it from the original model, which we call the *multi-activity model*.

The positive results for the multi-activity model automatically carry over to the single-activity model. Additionally, it is computationally easy for the players to best respond in the single-activity model. However, we get a different hardness result. Even for the linear model, it is PLS-complete to compute a PNE and (PPAD∩PLS)-complete to compute a mixed-strategy Nash equilibrium (MNE). These hardness results, particularly the (PPAD∩PLS)-hardness result, are interesting because single-activity games form a strict, structured and well-motivated subclass of explicit congestion games (a contest awards a $1/k$ fraction of a fixed prize to each winner if there are k winners, but a congestion game can have a cost that is an arbitrary function of the number of winners), yet finding an MNE in these games has the same computational complexity as finding an MNE of explicit congestion games [4] (and finding a fixed-point of gradient descent [18]). We also prove some fixed-parameter tractability results with respect to the number of players and the number of contests.

The rest of this paper is organized as follows. After summarizing the related work (Sect. 1.2), in Sect. 2 we introduce the general multi-activity model. We also prove the existence of PNE, the pseudo-polynomial convergence of ϵ-best-response dynamics to ϵ-PNE, and present our PoA results. In Sect. 3 we establish the hardness of best-response in linear multi-activity models. Section 4 focuses on the single-activity model and presents our results on PLS-completeness and (PPAD∩PLS)-completeness. Some proofs are omitted due to space constraints.

1.2   Related Work

The model of simultaneous contests with equal sharing allocation of prizes has been studied before in the literature [26,36]. At a high level, our contribution is to (i) generalize the model and extend the positive results and (ii) study the complexity of computing equilibria.

The linear budget model with a fixed total prize has previously been studied by May et al. [26], to model situations such as the social media platform example discussed earlier. Their theoretical results are similar to our positive results: (i) they prove existence of PNE by showing that the game is an exact potential game; (ii) they establish a PoA bound of 2. For (i), existence of PNE, we give a simpler proof by explicitly constructing the potential function that lifts these results to our general model. Our proof also makes it transparent that the PNE exists because of the equal sharing property of the contests (the *congestion* property), and the other restrictions of the model of May et al. [26]—the linear budget constraints, the linear criteria of contests, and the fixed total prize—are not necessary for the result. Moreover, the proof clarifies that using the budget model is also non-essential, as the result holds for the cost model as well. For (ii), the PoA bound, May et al. [26] prove the result from first principles. In contrast, we use the result of Vetta [35] for submodular social welfare functions to derive the same result in our—more general—setting. In summary, we extend the positive results of [26] to a general model (and we also study computational complexity, which was not considered by May et al. [26]). May et al. [26] perform an empirical study and show that the real-life behavior of social media curators resembles the predictions of the model. Bilo et al. [7] consider a model similar to the single-activity model of our paper and show inclusion in the class PLS (but no hardness results).

Models of simultaneous contests that do not have activities (i.e., the players directly produce outputs for each contest, or, equivalently, there is a one-to-one mapping between the activities and the contests) have been extensively studied. Cost-based models where the prizes are awarded based on the players' ranks have been considered by a number of authors [2,3,5,15], including empirical work [3,15,25,38]. Colonel Blotto games, where the players have budget constraints and the prize is awarded to the highest-output player for each contest, were proposed by Borel [12], and have received a significant amount of attention in the literature (e.g., [1,6,9–11,20–22,30,30,32,33,37]). Simultaneous contests with proportional allocation have been studied by, e.g., [19,29,39].

Two very recent related papers are by Birmpas et al. [8] and Elkind et al. [16]. Both these papers do not have activities, i.e., the players produce output directly for the contests, which makes their models a bit different (simpler) than ours, but they add complexity along other dimensions. Therefore, their results are not directly comparable to ours. Birmpas et al. [8] have both budgets and costs in the same model, and they give a constant factor PoA bound by augmenting players' budgets when computing the equilibrium welfare (but not when computing the optimal welfare). Elkind et al. [16] consider a model with only one contest and in the case of incomplete information. Their focus is on mechanism design, and for one of the objectives studied in the paper, they prove that the optimal contest distributes its prize equally to all players who produce output above some threshold, similar to the contests in our paper.

The complexity class PLS (Polynomial Local Search) and the concepts of PLS-hardness and PLS-completeness were introduced by Johnson et al. [24]. PLS consists of discrete local optimization problems whose solutions are easy to verify (the cost of a given solution can be computed in polynomial time and its local neighborhood can be searched in polynomial time). Similar to NP-hard problems, PLS-hard problems are believed to be not solvable in polynomial time. Several natural problems, such as finding a locally optimal solution of Max-Cut, were shown to be PLS-complete by Schaffer [31]. The problem of finding a PNE in explicit congestion games (which always have a PNE) is also PLS-complete [17], from which it follows that better or best response dynamics take an exponential time to converge in the worst case [24].

The class PPAD (Polynomial Parity Arguments on Directed graph) was introduced by Papadimitriou [28]. Like PLS problems, PPAD problems always have solutions. For PPAD, the existence of a solution is based on a parity argument: In a directed graph where each vertex has at most one predecessor and one successor, if there exists a source vertex (i.e., a vertex with no predecessor), then there exists some other degree-1 vertex. One of the most well-known results in algorithmic game theory is that the problem of finding a mixed-strategy Nash equilibrium (MNE) is PPAD-complete [13,14].

Recent work has determined the complexity of computing an MNE of an explicit congestion game. The class PPAD∩PLS represents problems that can be solved both by an algorithm that solves PPAD problems and by an algorithm that solves PLS problems. Finding an MNE of an explicit congestion game is in PPAD∩PLS: indeed, this problem can be solved either by finding a PNE (which is also an MNE) using an algorithm for PLS problems or by computing an MNE using an algorithm for PPAD problems. Recently, Fearnley et al. [18] proved that finding a fixed-point of a smooth 2-dimensional function $f : [0,1]^2 \to \mathbb{R}$ using gradient descent is complete for the class PPAD∩PLS; based on this result, Babichenko and Rubinstein [4] proved that finding an MNE of an explicit congestion game is also (PPAD∩PLS)-complete. PLS-complete, PPAD-complete, and (PPAD∩PLS)-complete problems are considered to be hard problems with no known polynomial-time algorithms.

2   General Model, Pure Nash Equilibrium, and Price of Anarchy

In this section, we formally define the general multi-activity model, prove the existence of pure Nash equilibria, and show that the price of anarchy (PoA) is 2 for the budget variant of the model and $+\infty$ for the cost variant.

We consider a set of n players, $N = [n]$,[4] who simultaneously produce output along k activities, $K = [k]$. There are m contests, $M = [m]$, which award prizes to the players based on their outputs. The contests may have different prizes and may value the activities differently.

We study two models: in one, the players have output production costs; and in the other, the players have generalized output budgets. Player $i \in N$ chooses an output vector $b_i = (b_{i,\ell})_{\ell \in K} \in \mathbb{R}_{\geq 0}^k$.

---

[4] Let $[\ell] = \{1, 2, \ldots, \ell\}$ for any positive integer $\ell \in \mathbb{Z}_{>0}$.

- **Cost.** Player i incurs a cost of $c_i(b_i)$ for producing b_i, where $c_i : \mathbb{R}^k_{\geq 0} \to \mathbb{R}_{\geq 0}$ is a non-decreasing cost function with $c_i(\mathbf{0}) = 0$ (normalized).
- **Budget.** The player does not incur any cost for the output vector b_i, but b_i is restricted to be in a set $\mathcal{B}_i \subseteq \mathbb{R}^k_{\geq 0}$. We assume that $\mathbf{0} \in \mathcal{B}_i$, i.e., players are always allowed to not participate.[5]

Technically, the budget model is a special case of the cost model, and all the positive results for the cost model automatically carry over to the budget model. We make the distinction because when we study the restricted linear models in Sect. 3, the linear cost model and the linear budget model will have different formulations.

Let $b = (b_i)_{i \in N} = (b_{i,\ell})_{i \in N, \ell \in K}$. Each contest $j \in M$ is associated with a pair of functions $f_j : \mathbb{R}^k_{\geq 0} \to \mathbb{R}_{\geq 0}$ and $v_j : \mathbb{N} \to \mathbb{R}_{\geq 0}$. The function f_j, which is an increasing function such that $f_j(\mathbf{0}) = 0$, determines the set of winners of contest j: we say that player i *wins* contest j if $f_j(b_i) \geq 1$ and set $N_j(b) = \{i \in N \mid f_j(b_i) \geq 1\}$. Let $n_j(b) = |N_j(b)|$. The function v_j determines how the prizes are allocated: each player in $N_j(b)$ receives a prize of $v_j(n_j(b))$. The total prize allocated by contest j is then $n_j(b) \cdot v_j(n_j(b))$. We make the following assumptions about the function v_j, which are necessary for our price of anarchy bounds.

1. $v_j(\ell)$ is a non-increasing function of ℓ: $v_j(\ell) \geq v_j(\ell+1)$.
2. $\ell \cdot v_j(\ell)$ is a non-decreasing function of ℓ: $\ell \cdot v_j(\ell) \leq (\ell+1) \cdot v_j(\ell+1)$.
3. $\ell \cdot v_j(\ell)$ is a weakly concave function of ℓ, i.e., $(\ell+1) \cdot v_j(\ell+1) - \ell \cdot v_j(\ell)$ is a non-increasing function of ℓ: $(\ell+2) \cdot v_j(\ell+2) - 2 \cdot (\ell+1) \cdot v_j((\ell+1)+\ell \cdot v_j(\ell) \leq 0$. This condition says that the rate of increase in the total prize allocated by a contest j weakly decreases as the number of winners increases.

Some examples of functions v_j that satisfy these conditions are:

- $x \cdot v_j(x) = x$ or $v_j(x) = 1$. Here, the total value of the prize scales linearly with the number of winners, i.e., the prize awarded to a winner does not change as the number of winners increases.
- $x \cdot v_j(x) = 1$ or $v_j(x) = 1/x$. Here, the total value of the prize remains constant, i.e., the prize awarded to a winner decreases and is equal to the inverse of the number of winners.
- $x \cdot v_j(x) = \sqrt{x}$ or $v_j(x) = 1/\sqrt{x}$. This sits between the previous two examples. Here, the total value of the prize increases, but the prize awarded to a winner decreases as the number of winners increases.

The utility of a player i in the cost and the budget model is, respectively,

$$u_i^C(b) = \sum_{j \in M} v_j(n_j(b)) \cdot \mathbb{1}_{\{i \in N_j(b)\}} - c_i(b_i), \quad u_i^B(b) = \sum_{j \in M} v_j(n_j(b)) \cdot \mathbb{1}_{\{i \in N_j(b)\}}$$

---

[5] The budget model has an alternative interpretation—each player selects a subset of activities among a feasible set of subset of activities for that player—as discussed in Sect. 2.3.

where $\mathbb{1}_{\{\dots\}}$ is the indicator function; we omit the superscripts B and C if they are clear from the context.

We will be interested in stable outcomes of multi-activity games, as captured by their Nash equilibria.

Definition 1 (Pure-Strategy Nash Equilibrium (PNE)). *A pure strategy profile* $b = (b_i, b_{-i})$ *is a pure Nash equilibrium (PNE) if for every* $i \in N$ *and every action* b_i' *of player* i *we have* $u_i(b) \geq u_i(b_i', b_{-i})$.

Definition 2 (Mixed-Strategy Nash Equilibrium (MNE)). *A mixed strategy profile* $\mu = \times_{\ell \in [n]} \mu_\ell$ *is a mixed Nash equilibrium (MNE) if for every* $i \in N$ *and every distribution over actions* μ_i' *of player* i *we have* $\mathbb{E}_{b \sim \mu}[u_i(b)] \geq \mathbb{E}_{b_i' \sim \mu_i', b_{-i} \sim \mu_{-i}}[u_i(b_i', b_{-i})]$, *where* $\mu_{-i} = \times_{\ell \neq i} \mu_\ell$.

We now give definitions of the price of anarchy and the price of stability, which will be used to study the efficiency of equilibria in our models.

Definition 3 (Price of Anarchy (PoA) and Price of Stability (PoS)). *Let* $\mathcal{G}$ *denote a class of games and let* $\mathcal{I} \in \mathcal{G}$ *denote a particular instance of the game. For a given instance of a game* $\mathcal{I}$, *let* $Action(\mathcal{I})$ *denote the set of action profiles and* $Eq(\mathcal{I})$ *denote the set of all MNE. Let* $sw(b)$ *denote the social welfare for an action profile* $b \in Action(\mathcal{I})$. *The* price of anarchy *and the* price of stability *for class* $\mathcal{G}$ *are defined as, respectively,*

$$PoA = \max_{\mathcal{I} \in \mathcal{G}} \frac{\max_{b \in Action(\mathcal{I})} sw(b)}{\min_{\mu \in Eq(\mathcal{I})} \mathbb{E}_{b \sim \mu}[sw(b)]}; \quad PoS = \max_{\mathcal{I} \in \mathcal{G}} \frac{\max_{b \in Action(\mathcal{I})} sw(b)}{\max_{\mu \in Eq(\mathcal{I})} \mathbb{E}_{b \sim \mu}[sw(b)]}.$$

I.e., the PoA (PoS) is the ratio between the optimal social welfare and the equilibrium social welfare in the worst (best) case over possible equilibria and in the worst case over instances of the game.

2.1   Existence of Pure-Strategy Nash Equilibrium

We start by showing that multi-activity games are exact potential games. We then use the classic result of Monderer and Shapley [27] to conclude that multi-activity games always have pure Nash equilibria.

Definition 4 (Exact Potential Games). [27] *A normal form game is an exact potential game if there exists a potential function* ϕ *such that for any player* i *with utility function* u_i, *any two strategies* b_i *and* b_i' *of player* i, *and any strategy profile* b_{-i} *of the other players it holds that*

$$u_i(b_i', b_{-i}) - u_i(b_i, b_{-i}) = \phi(b_i', b_{-i}) - \phi(b_i, b_{-i}).$$

Theorem 1. [27] *Exact potential games always have a pure-strategy Nash equilibrium. Indeed, every pure strategy profile that maximizes* ϕ *is a PNE.*

We define the potential functions for the multi-activity budget and cost games as, respectively,

$$\phi^B(\mathrm{b}) = \sum_{j \in M} \sum_{\ell \in [n_j(\mathrm{b})]} v_j(\ell), \qquad \phi^C(\mathrm{b}) = \sum_{j \in M} \sum_{\ell \in [n_j(\mathrm{b})]} v_j(\ell) - \sum_{i \in N} c_i(\mathrm{b}_i); \quad (1)$$

we omit the superscripts B and C if they are clear from the context. We use these potential functions to prove the existence of PNE in multi-activity games. In Sect. 4, we shall also use them to study the complexity of computing equilibria in these games.

Theorem 2. *A multi-activity budget/cost game is an exact potential game, and hence has a pure-strategy Nash equilibrium.*

We note that the crucial property required for the proof of Theorem 2 is the equal sharing property; some of the other assumptions made in our model, e.g., that the cost functions $c_i(b_i)$ are non-decreasing, $\ell \cdot v_j(\ell)$ are non-decreasing and weakly concave, etc., are not essential for the proof. We also note that for a restricted version of the model the same result was proved by [26,36], but we believe that our proof using the potential function is simpler.

2.2 Approximate Pure-Strategy Nash Equilibrium Using Better-Response

The characterization in Theorem 2 is very useful for finding approximate equilibria of multi-activity games.

Definition 5 (ϵ-Pure-Strategy Nash Equilibrium). *A pure strategy profile* $\mathrm{b} = (\mathrm{b}_i, \mathrm{b}_{-i})$ *is an ϵ-PNE if for every $i \in N$ and every action b'_i of player i we have $u_i(\mathrm{b}'_i, \mathrm{b}_{-i}) \leq u_i(\mathrm{b}) - \epsilon$.*

Definition 6 (ϵ-Better-Response). *For a pure strategy profile* $\mathrm{b} = (\mathrm{b}_i, \mathrm{b}_{-i})$, *a player $i \in N$, and an action b'_i of player i, the move from b_i to b'_i is an ϵ-better-response move if $u_i(\mathrm{b}'_i, \mathrm{b}_{-i}) > u_i(\mathrm{b}) + \epsilon$.*

From the definitions above, it is immediate that a pure strategy profile is an ϵ-PNE if and only if it does not admit any ϵ-better-response moves. Now, as multi-activity games are exact potential games, each ϵ-better-response increases the potential by at least ϵ. As the potential function is bounded from above, a sequence of ϵ-better-response moves necessarily terminates, and the resulting profile is an ϵ-PNE.

Corollary 1. *In multi-activity games, any sequence of ϵ-better-response moves arrives to an ϵ-PNE in at most $n \cdot m \cdot (\max_j v_j(1))/\epsilon$ steps.*

Corollary 1 provides a pseudo-polynomial bound in the number of steps required for convergence to an approximate PNE, which can be meaningful in situations where the prizes (i.e., the values $v_j(1)$) are not very large. It also implies that an ϵ-PNE can be computed in pseudo-polynomial time if we can compute ϵ-better-responses efficiently.

2.3   Social Welfare, Price of Anarchy, and Price of Stability

To start, let us briefly discuss what would be a natural definition(s) of social welfare for multi-activity games.

Consider first the budget model. From the perspective of the players, social welfare naturally corresponds to the total prize allocated. This definition is also natural from the perspective of the contests. Indeed, consider the motivating example involving the social media curators (players) and subscribers (contests). The welfare of the curators corresponds to the total subscribers' attention they receive, which is equal to the total prize allocated. On the other hand, the welfare of the subscribers corresponds to the compatible curators who serve them, which again corresponds to the total prize allocated. For this definition of social welfare, we prove an upper bound of 2 on the price of anarchy (PoA) and a lower bound of $2 - o(1)$ on the price of stability (PoS), so both of these bounds are tight.

For the cost model, the formulation of social welfare can be similarly motivated, with or without subtracting the cost. If one assumes that the cost to the players is a sunk cost, then it is reasonable to subtract it from the social welfare. On the other hand, if one assumes that the cost gets transferred to the contest organizers (or the society), then it should not be subtracted. In any case, for both of these definitions, the PoS (and therefore, PoA) turns out to be infinite.

Budget Model. For the budget model, the social welfare is equal to the total prize that gets allocated:

$$sw(b) = \sum_{i \in N} u_i(b) = \sum_{i \in N} \sum_{j \in M} v_j(n_j(b)) \cdot \mathbb{1}_{\{i \in N_j(b)\}} = \sum_{j \in M} v_j(n_j(b)) \cdot n_j(b). \quad (2)$$

To prove the upper bound of 2 on PoA, we shall use the result of Vetta [35] for *submodular* social welfare functions. This result states that the PoA can be upper-bounded by 2 if the following conditions are satisfied:

1. the utility of the players and the social welfare are measured in the same units,
2. the total utility of the players is at most the social welfare,
3. the social welfare function is non-decreasing and submodular, and
4. the private utility of a player is at least as much as the *Vickrey utility* (see Definition 8).

By definition, our model satisfies the first two requirements on this list. To show that it also satisfies the last two requirements, we reinterpret it using a different notation.

In the budget game, an action by a player i effectively corresponds to a subset of the contests that i wins. The output vector produced by the player to win a given set of contests is not important as long as the set of contests that she wins remains the same.[6] Hence, we will represent the action taken

---

[6] Not important for PoA analysis, but very important for computational complexity: the budget constraint for a player i boils down to selecting a subset of contests in

by player i as a subset of elements from a set of size m, as follows: Let $\mathcal{G}$ denote a set of $n \cdot m$ elements partitioned into n size-m sets $\mathcal{G}^1, \mathcal{G}^2, \ldots, \mathcal{G}^n$, where $\mathcal{G}^i = \{g_1^i, g_2^i, \ldots, g_m^i\}$. We represent the set of feasible actions for player i by $\mathcal{A}_i \subseteq 2^{\mathcal{G}^i}$: an action $A_i \in \mathcal{A}_i$ contains g_j^i if and only if player i satisfies the criteria for contest $j \in M$. Note that $\emptyset \in \mathcal{A}_i$, because we assume that each player is allowed to not participate and produce a $\mathbf{0}$ output (which does not win her any contests). An action profile $A = (A_i)_{i \in N} \in \times_{i \in N} \mathcal{A}_i$ can be equivalently written as $\cup_{i \in N} A_i \in \cup_{i \in N} \mathcal{A}_i$ because the sets $\mathcal{A}_i$ are disjoint as per our notation.

As before, let $N_j(A) = \{i \mid g_j^i \in A\}$ denote the players who win contest j under action profile A, and let $n_j(A) = |N_j(A)|$. The utility functions and the social welfare function can be rewritten using the new set notation as follows:

$$u_i(A) = \sum_{j \in M} v_j(n_j(A)) \cdot \mathbb{1}_{\{g_j^i \in A\}}; \qquad sw(A) = \sum_{j \in M} v_j(n_j(A)) \cdot n_j(A).$$

Let us formally define submodular set functions.

Definition 7 (Submodular Functions). *A function $f : 2^\Omega \to \mathbb{R}$ is submodular if for every pair of subsets $S, T \subseteq \Omega$ such that $S \subseteq T$ and every $x \in \Omega \setminus T$ we have*

$$f(S \cup \{x\}) - f(S) \geq f(T \cup \{x\}) - f(T).$$

The next two lemmas prove that our model satisfies the conditions required to use the result of Vetta [35].

Lemma 1. *For the budget model, if the total prize allocated by a contest is a weakly concave function of the number of winners of the contest, then the social welfare function is submodular.*

Definition 8 (Vickrey Utility). *The Vickrey utility of player i at an action profile A is the loss incurred by other players due to i's participation, i.e.,*

$$u_i^{Vickrey}(A) = \sum_{q \neq i} u_q(\emptyset, A_{-i}) - \sum_{q \neq i} u_q(A_i, A_{-i}),$$

where $\emptyset$ is the action to not participate (or, equivalently, produce 0 output and not win any contests).

Lemma 2. *For the budget model, if the total prize allocated by a contest is a non-decreasing function of the number of winners of the contest, then for every profile A and every player i, the utility of i is at least as large as her Vickrey utility, i.e., $u_i(A_i, A_{-i}) \geq u_i^{Vickrey}(A)$.*

Theorem 3. *The social welfare in any mixed-strategy Nash equilibrium of a multi-activity budget game is at least $1/2$ of the optimum social welfare.*

---

some feasible set of subsets, say $\mathcal{A}_i \in 2^M$. The budget constraint is a concise way of representing this $\mathcal{A}_i$, and $\mathcal{A}_i$ may be of size exponential in the representation.

The following result complements the upper bound of 2 for PoA by giving a lower bound of 2 for PoS, which is based upon an example in [36] and ensuring that the equilibrium is unique.

Theorem 4. *There are instances of multi-activity budget games where the social welfare in every mixed-strategy Nash equilibrium approaches $1/2$ of the optimum social welfare as the number of players grows.*

Cost Model. As discussed before, we consider two definitions of social welfare for the cost model. The first definition does not subtract the costs from social welfare and corresponds to the definition given in (2). The second definition subtracts the costs from the social welfare and is equal to

$$\overline{sw}(b) = \sum_{i \in N}(u_i(b) - c_i(b)) = \sum_{j \in M} v_j(n_j(b)) \cdot n_j(b) - \sum_{i \in N} c_i(b). \qquad (3)$$

Next, we prove that the PoS can be unbounded for both definitions of social welfare in the cost model.

Theorem 5. *There are instances of multi-activity cost games where the social welfare in every mixed-strategy Nash equilibrium can be arbitrarily low compared to the optimum social welfare. This holds even if there are at most two players, two activities, and two contests.*

3 Multi-activity Games: Hardness of Best-Response

In this section, we focus on a restricted model: each contest uses a linear criterion, and the budget constraint or the cost function of each player are also linear. We call this model the *linear multi-activity model*. Formally, for an output profile $b = (b_i)_{i \in N} = (b_{i,\ell})_{i \in N, \ell \in K}$, the winners of contest j are $N_j(b) = \{i \mid \sum_{\ell \in K} w_{j,\ell} b_{i,\ell} \geq 1\}$, where $w_{j,\ell} \in \mathbb{R}_{\geq 0}$ is a non-negative weight that contest j has for activity ℓ. Similarly, the linear budget constraint of a player i is of the form $\sum_{\ell \in K} \beta_{i,\ell} b_{i,\ell} \leq 1$, where $\beta_{i,\ell} \in \mathbb{R}_{>0}$. Likewise, a linear cost function for player i is of the form $\sum_{\ell \in K} c_{i,\ell} b_{i,\ell}$, where $c_{i,\ell} \in \mathbb{R}_{>0}$.

We also impose another constraint: we assume that for each contest its total prize is fixed. That is, each contest $j \in M$ is associated with a total prize V_j, and if there are ℓ winners, each winner gets a prize V_j/ℓ.

We study the computational complexity of best-response in this linear multi-activity model. Observe that it suffices to consider this problem for $n = 1$. Indeed, consider a player $i \in N$. If there are ℓ winners other than i for a given contest j, then i gets a prize of $v_j(\ell + 1) = V_j/(\ell + 1)$ from this contest if she satisfies this contest's criteria, and 0 otherwise. By scaling the values of all contests appropriately, we reduce i's optimization problem to one where i is the only player in the game.

In the next theorem, we prove that finding a best-response exactly or approximately is NP-hard.

Theorem 6. *In the linear multi-activity model, both cost and budget, a player cannot approximate a best response beyond a constant factor in polynomial time unless* P = NP.

We note that in a single-player case finding a best response is equivalent to finding a PNE. We obtain the following corollary.

Corollary 2. *In the linear multi-activity model, both cost and budget, the problem of computing an exact or an approximate PNE is* NP*-hard.*

Theorem 6 proves that the problem of finding a best response in the linear multi-activity model does not admit a polynomial-time approximation scheme. For restricted versions of the model, a constant factor approximation can be found. For example, for the budget model, if the contests have $\{0,1\}$ weights for the activities, and the player has a budget that she can distribute across any of the activities (the hard instance constructed in Theorem 6 for the budget model satisfies these conditions), then the problem becomes a submodular maximization problem with a polynomial-time constant-factor approximation algorithm. However, we feel that a constant-factor approximation result is of limited usefulness in the context of computing a best response or a Nash equilibrium.

Next, we study the fixed-parameter tractability of the problem of computing a best response. There are three natural parameters of the model: the number of players n, the number of contests m, and the number of activities k. We have already shown that the problem is NP-hard even with only one player, $n = 1$. On the positive side, we show that the problem becomes tractable if either the number of contests m or the number of activities k is a constant.

Theorem 7. *In the linear multi-activity model, both cost and budget, a player can compute a best response in polynomial time if either the number of contests or the number of activities is bounded by a constant.*

4   Single-Activity Games: PPAD∩PLS-Completeness

In this section, we focus our attention on the single-activity model, and show that, for both cost and budget models, it is PLS-complete to find a pure Nash equilibrium and (PPAD∩PLS)-complete to find a mixed Nash equilibrium (MNE). Note that the set of MNE of a game is a super-set of the set of PNE, so finding an MNE is at least as easy as finding a PNE.

In a single-activity game, for every player i there is at most one activity ℓ for which the output $b_{i,\ell}$ may be strictly positive; for every other activity $\ell' \neq \ell$ it holds that $b_{i,\ell'} = 0$. Additionally, we assume that each contest i has a fixed total prize, which it distributes equally among all winners.

Theorem 8. *In the linear single-activity model, both cost and budget, it is* (PPAD ∩ PLS)*-complete to find a mixed-strategy Nash equilibrium.*

A recent paper by Fearnley et al. [18] proved the interesting result that finding a fixed-point of a 2-dimensional smooth function $(f : [0,1]^2 \to \mathbb{R})$ given by a circuit of addition and multiplication operators using gradient descent, 2D-GD-FIXEDPOINT, is complete for the class PPAD∩PLS. Based on this result, Babichenko and Rubinstein [4] proved that the problem of computing an MNE of an explicit congestion game, EXPCONG, is also complete for PPAD∩PLS. Babichenko and Rubinstein [4] do this by first reducing 2D-GD-FIXEDPOINT to identical interest 5-polytensor games, 5-POLYTENSOR, and then 5-POLYTENSOR to EXPCONG. In our proof for Theorem 8, we reduce 5-POLYTENSOR to the single-activity game, proving the required result.

Before moving to the proof, let us define identical interest polytensor games, κ-POLYTENSOR. Polytensor games are a generalization of the better known poly-matrix games, POLYMATRIX; specifically, POLYMATRIX = 2-POLYTENSOR.

Definition 9 (POLYMATRIX: Identical Interest Polymatrix Game). *There are n players. Player i chooses from a finite set of actions A_i. The utility of player i for action profile $(a_i, \mathrm{a}_{-i}) = \mathrm{a} = (a_j)_{j \in [n]} \in \times_{j \in [n]} A_j$ is given by $u_i(\mathrm{a}) = \sum_{j \in [n], j \neq i} u_{i,j}(a_i, a_j)$, where $u_{i,j} : A_i \times A_j \to \mathbb{R}_{\geq 0}$. The players have identical interest, i.e., $u_{i,j} = u_{j,i}$.*

The definition of κ-POLYTENSOR games is similar to that of POLYMATRIX games: instead of $u_{i,j}$ we have u_S, where $S \subseteq [n], |S| = \kappa$.

Definition 10 (κ-POLYTENSOR: Identical Interest κ-Polytensor Game). *There are n players. Player i chooses from a finite set of actions A_i. The utility of player i for action profile $\mathrm{a} = (a_j)_{j \in [n]} \in \times_{j \in [n]} A_j$ is given by $u_i(\mathrm{a}) = \sum_{S \subseteq [n], i \in S, |S| = \kappa} u_S(\mathrm{a}_S)$, where $\mathrm{a}_S = (a_j)_{j \in S}$ is the action profile of the players in S and $u_S : \times_{j \in S} A_j \to \mathbb{R}_{\geq 0}$.*

When the number of actions for each player, $|A_i|$, is bounded by m, note that the representation size of a κ-POLYTENSOR game is $O(n^\kappa m^\kappa)$. In particular, if κ is a constant and $m = poly(n)$, then κ-POLYTENSOR games admit a succinct representation.

Proof Sketch for Theorem 8. Below, we provide a reduction from 3-POLYTENSOR to the budget game for a cleaner presentation of the main steps (unlike 5-POLYTENSOR, 3-POLYTENSOR is not known to be (PPAD∩PLS)-complete). Similar steps with more calculations apply to 5-POLYTENSOR, for both cost and budget models (we provide this argument in the full version of the paper).

Take an arbitrary instance of 3-POLYTENSOR with n players; we shall use the same notation as in Definition 10. We construct a single-activity game with n players, $\sum_{i \in [n]} |A_i|$ activities, and a polynomial number of contests to be defined later.

The $\sum_{i \in [n]} |A_i|$ activities have a one-to-one association with the actions of the players. The activities are partitioned into n subsets, so that the i-th subset has size $|A_i|$ and is associated with player i; we identify these activities with the set A_i. Player i has a budget of 1 that they can use to produce output along any activity from A_i, but they have 0 budget for the activities in A_j for $j \neq i$. Effectively, as we are in a single-activity model, player i selects an activity from the activities in A_i and produces an output of 1 along it. Note that the players have disjoint sets of activities for which they can produce outputs.

All the contests we construct are associated with exactly three players and at most three activities. We shall denote a contest by $\mathcal{C}_{i,j,k}(A)$, where (i) $S = \{i, j, k\}$ are the three distinct players whose utility function in the polytensor game, u_S, will be used to specify the prize of contest $\mathcal{C}_S(A)$; (ii) the contest $\mathcal{C}_S(A)$ awards its prize to any player who produces an output of at least 1 along the activities in A; (iii) the activities in A are from $A_i \cup A_j \cup A_k$ with $|A| \leq 3$ and $|A \cap A_\ell| \leq 1$ for $\ell \in S$. We shall call a contest $\mathcal{C}_S(A)$ a Type-ℓ contest if $|A| = \ell$.

Let us focus on a fixed set of three players $S = \{i, j, k\}$. We create contests to exactly replicate the utility that these players get from u_S. If we can do this, then, by repeating the same process for every triple of players, we will replicate the entire 3-POLYTENSOR game. The utility that player i gets from u_S is $u_S(a_i, a_j, a_k)$, where a_i, a_j, and a_k are the actions of the three players. We have the following contests:

Type-3 Contests. Let us add a contest $\mathcal{C}_S(a_i, a_j, a_k)$ with prize $v_S(a_i, a_j, a_k)$ for every $(a_i, a_j, a_k) \in A_i \times A_j \times A_k$. Later, we shall specify the $v_S(a_i, a_j, a_k)$ values based on $u_S(a_i, a_j, a_k)$ values. Contest $\mathcal{C}_S(a_i, a_j, a_k)$ distributes a prize of $v_S(a_i, a_j, a_k)$ to players who produce output along the activities a_i, a_j, or a_k.

Say, the players i, j, k select the actions a_i^*, a_j^*, a_k^*. The total prize that player i gets from the contests we added is:

$$\frac{v_S(a_i^*, a_j^*, a_k^*)}{3} + \sum_{a_j \neq a_j^*} \frac{v_S(a_i^*, a_j, a_k^*)}{2} + \sum_{a_k \neq a_k^*} \frac{v_S(a_i^*, a_j^*, a_k)}{2} + \sum_{\substack{a_j \neq a_j^* \\ a_k \neq a_k^*}} v_S(a_i^*, a_j, a_k) \quad (4)$$

In expression (4), the first term is for the prize that i shares with j and k, the second term is for the prizes that i shares with k, but not with j, the third term is for the prizes that i shares with j, but not with k, and the fourth term is for the prizes that i does not share with j or k.

In expression (4), the first term $\frac{1}{3}v_S(a_i^*, a_j^*, a_k^*)$ resembles the utility that the players obtain in the polytensor game, $u_S(a_i^*, a_j^*, a_k^*)$. If we were to set $v_S(a_i^*, a_j^*, a_k^*) = 3u_S(a_i^*, a_j^*, a_k^*)$, then it would be exactly equal to it. However, we also need to take care of the additional terms in expression (4). Hence, we will add Type-1 and Type-2 contests to cancel these terms.

The expression in (4) can be rewritten as

$$\sum_{\substack{a_j \in A_j \\ a_k \in A_k}} v_S(a_i^*, a_j, a_k) - \sum_{a_j \neq a_j^*} \frac{v_S(a_i^*, a_j, a_k^*)}{2} - \sum_{a_k \neq a_k^*} \frac{v_S(a_i^*, a_j^*, a_k)}{2} - \frac{2v_S(a_i^*, a_j^*, a_k^*)}{3}.$$

Type-1 Contests. Let us add a contest $\mathcal{C}_S(a_i')$ with prize

$$\sum_{a_i \neq a_i', a_j \in A_j, a_k \in A_k} v_S(a_i, a_j, a_k)$$

for every $a_i' \in A_i$. This contest $\mathcal{C}_S(a_i')$ awards its prize to any player who produces output along activity a_i' (effectively, it awards the prize to player i if they produce output along a_i', because no other player can produce output along a_i'). Similarly, we add the contests $\mathcal{C}_S(a_j')$ and $\mathcal{C}_S(a_k')$ for $a_j' \in A_j$ and $a_k' \in A_k$, respectively. The total prize that player i gets from Type-1 and Type-3 contests is $\sum_{a_i, a_j, a_k} v_S(a_i, a_j, a_k) - \sum_{a_j \neq a_j^*} \frac{1}{2} v_S(a_i^*, a_j, a_k^*) - \sum_{a_k \neq a_k^*} \frac{1}{2} v_S(a_i^*, a_j^*, a_k) - \frac{2}{3} v_S(a_i^*, a_j^*, a_k^*)$. As $\sum_{a_i, a_j, a_k} v_S(a_i, a_j, a_k)$ does not depend upon the action a_i^* selected by i, the utility of player i is effectively

$$- \sum_{a_j \neq a_j^*} \frac{1}{2} v_S(a_i^*, a_j, a_k^*) - \sum_{a_k \neq a_k^*} \frac{1}{2} v_S(a_i^*, a_j^*, a_k) - \frac{2}{3} v_S(a_i^*, a_j^*, a_k^*).$$

Type-2 Contests. Let us add a contest $\mathcal{C}_S(a_i', a_j')$ with prize

$$\sum_{a_k \in A_k} \frac{1}{2} v_S(a_i', a_j', a_k)$$

for every $a_i' \in A_i$ and $a_j' \in A_j$. This contest $\mathcal{C}_S(a_i', a_j')$ awards its prize to players who produce output along activity a_i' or a_j'. In a similar manner, we add contests corresponding to the actions of the other 5 possible combinations of players among the three players i, j, k, e.g., $\mathcal{C}_S(a_i', a_k')$ for $a_i' \in A_i$ and $a_k' \in A_k$, and so on. The net utility that player i gets from Type-1, Type-2 and Type-3 contests is $\frac{1}{3} v_S(a_i^*, a_j^*, a_k^*)$. We set $v_S(a_i, a_j, a_k) = 3 u_S(a_i, a_j, a_k)$ for every $(a_i, a_j, a_k) \in A_i \times A_j \times A_k$, and we are done. □

In Theorem 8, we analyzed the complexity of computing an MNE. As we have shown earlier, single-activity cost and budget games always have a PNE, and therefore, it is relevant to know the complexity of computing a PNE. In the next theorem, we prove that computing a PNE is PLS-complete, and this is true even if all the players are identical. In the proof, we reduce MAX-CUT to the problem of finding a PNE in a particular class of single-activity games with identical players. For this class of single-activity games, finding an MNE is easy, which highlights that the class of single-activity games where PNE is hard (PLS-complete) to compute is strictly larger than the class of single-activity games where MNE is hard (PPAD∩PLS-complete) to compute.

Theorem 9. *In the single-activity models, both cost and budget, it is PLS-complete to find a pure-strategy Nash equilibrium. The result holds even if all players are identical.*

A direct corollary of this PLS-completeness result is that better/best-response dynamics takes an exponential number of steps to converge for some instances of the problem [24].

Regarding fixed-parameter tractability (FPT), in the full version of the paper we show that a PNE is efficiently computable for both cost and budget single-activity models if the number of players is a constant, and for the budget model if the number of contests is a constant. Providing FPT results for other cases remains open.

5   Conclusion and Future Work

In this paper, we studied a model of simultaneous contests and analyzed the existence, efficiency, and computational complexity of equilibria in these contests. Given the real-life relevance of the three-level model, player–activity–contest, it will be interesting to study it for prize allocation rules other than the equal-sharing allocation, such as rank-based allocation, proportional allocation, etc. For these contests, one may investigate the properties of the equilibria and their computational complexity. We also believe that there is much to explore regarding the computational complexity of simultaneous contests, in general.

Acknowledgement. We thank the anonymous reviewers for their valuable feedback. The second author is supported by Clarendon Fund and SKP Scholarship.

References

1. Adamo, T., Matros, A.: A Blotto game with incomplete information. Econ. Lett. **105**(1), 100–102 (2009)
2. Amann, E., Qiao, H.: Parallel contests. Technical report, Thurgauer Wirtschaftsinstitut, University of Konstanz (2008)
3. Archak, N., Sundararajan, A.: Optimal design of crowdsourcing contests. In: ICIS 2009 (2009)
4. Babichenko, Y., Rubinstein, A.: Settling the complexity of Nash equilibrium in congestion games. In: STOC 2021, pp. 1426–1437 (2021)
5. Bapna, R., Dellarocas, C., Rice, S.: Vertically differentiated simultaneous Vickrey auctions: theory and experimental evidence. Manag. Sci. **56**(7), 1074–1092 (2010)
6. Bellman, R.: On "colonel Blotto" and analogous games. SIAM Rev. **11**(1), 66–68 (1969)
7. Bilò, V., Gourvès, L., Monnot, J.: Project games. In: CIAC 2019, pp. 75–86 (2019)
8. Birmpas, G., Kovalchuk, L., Lazos, P., Oliynykov, R.: Parallel contests for crowdsourcing reviews: existence and quality of equilibria. arXiv preprint arXiv:2202.04064 (2022)
9. Blackett, D.W.: Some Blotto games. Naval Res. Logist. Q. **1**(1), 55–60 (1954)
10. Blackett, D.W.: Pure strategy solutions of Blotto games. Naval Res. Logist. Q. **5**(2), 107–109 (1958)
11. Borel, E., Ville, J.: Application de la théorie des probabilitiés aux jeux de hasard, Gauthier-Villars; reprinted in Borel, E., & Chéron, A. (1991). Théorie mathematique du bridge à la portée de tous, Editions Jacques Gabay (1938)
12. Borel, E.: La théorie du jeu et les équations intégrales à noyau symétrique gauche. Comptes rendus de l'Académie des Sciences **173**, 1304–1308 (1921)
13. Chen, X., Deng, X., Teng, S.H.: Settling the complexity of computing two-player Nash equilibria. J. ACM (JACM) **56**(3), 1–57 (2009)
14. Daskalakis, C., Goldberg, P.W., Papadimitriou, C.H.: The complexity of computing a Nash equilibrium. SIAM J. Comput. **39**(1), 195–259 (2009)
15. DiPalantino, D., Vojnovic, M.: Crowdsourcing and all-pay auctions. In: ACM EC 2009, pp. 119–128 (2009)
16. Elkind, E., Ghosh, A., Goldberg, P.: Contest design with threshold objectives. In: WINE 2021, p. 554 (2021). arXiv preprint arXiv:2109.03179

17. Fabrikant, A., Papadimitriou, C., Talwar, K.: The complexity of pure Nash equilibria. In: STOC 2004, pp. 604–612 (2004)
18. Fearnley, J., Goldberg, P.W., Hollender, A., Savani, R.: The complexity of gradient descent: CLS=PPAD∩PLS. In: STOC 2021, pp. 46–59 (2021)
19. Feldman, M., Lai, K., Zhang, L.: A price-anticipating resource allocation mechanism for distributed shared clusters. In: ACM EC 2005, pp. 127–136 (2005)
20. Gross, O., Wagner, R.: A continuous colonel Blotto game. Technical report, RAND Project Air Force Santa Monica CA (1950)
21. Hart, S.: Discrete colonel Blotto and general lotto games. Int. J. Game Theory **36**(3), 441–460 (2008)
22. Hortala-Vallve, R., Llorente-Saguer, A.: Pure strategy Nash equilibria in non-zero sum colonel Blotto games. Int. J. Game Theory **41**(2), 331–343 (2012)
23. Immorlica, N., Stoddard, G., Syrgkanis, V.: Social status and badge design. In: WWW 2015, pp. 473–483 (2015)
24. Johnson, D.S., Papadimitriou, C.H., Yannakakis, M.: How easy is local search? J. Comput. Syst. Sci. **37**(1), 79–100 (1988)
25. Lakhani, K.R., Garvin, D.A., Lonstein, E.: Topcoder (a): developing software through crowdsourcing. Harvard Business School General Management Unit Case (610–032) (2010)
26. May, A., Chaintreau, A., Korula, N., Lattanzi, S.: Filter & follow: how social media foster content curation. In: SIGMETRICS 2014, pp. 43–55 (2014)
27. Monderer, D., Shapley, L.S.: Potential games. Games Econom. Behav. **14**(1), 124–143 (1996)
28. Papadimitriou, C.H.: On the complexity of the parity argument and other inefficient proofs of existence. J. Comput. Syst. Sci. **48**(3), 498–532 (1994)
29. Pálvölgyi, D., Peters, H., Vermeulen, D.: A strategic approach to multiple estate division problems. Games Econom. Behav. **88**, 135–152 (2014)
30. Roberson, B.: The colonel Blotto game. Econ. Theor. **29**(1), 1–24 (2006)
31. Schäffer, A.A.: Simple local search problems that are hard to solve. SIAM J. Comput. **20**(1), 56–87 (1991)
32. Shubik, M., Weber, R.J.: Systems defense games: colonel Blotto, command and control. Naval Res. Logist. Q. **28**(2), 281–287 (1981)
33. Tukey, J.W.: A problem of strategy. Econometrica **17**(1), 73 (1949)
34. Tullock, G.: Efficient rent-seeking. In: Buchanan, J., Tollison, R., Tullock, G. (eds.) Toward a Theory of the Rent Seeking Society, pp. 131–146. Texas A & M University, College Station (1980)
35. Vetta, A.: Nash equilibria in competitive societies, with applications to facility location, traffic routing and auctions. In: FOCS 2002, pp. 416–425 (2002)
36. Vojnović, M.: Contest Theory: Incentive Mechanisms and Ranking Methods. Cambridge University Press, Cambridge (2015)
37. Washburn, A.: Blotto politics. Oper. Res. **61**(3), 532–543 (2013)
38. Yang, J., Adamic, L.A., Ackerman, M.S.: Crowdsourcing and knowledge sharing: strategic user behavior on Taskcn. In: ACM EC 2008, pp. 246–255 (2008)
39. Zhang, L.: The efficiency and fairness of a fixed budget resource allocation game. In: Caires, L., Italiano, G.F., Monteiro, L., Palamidessi, C., Yung, M. (eds.) ICALP 2005. LNCS, vol. 3580, pp. 485–496. Springer, Heidelberg (2005). https://doi.org/10.1007/11523468_40

Complexity of Public Goods Games on Graphs

Matan Gilboa$^{(\boxtimes)}$ and Noam Nisan

School of Computer Science and Engineering, Hebrew University of Jerusalem,
Jerusalem, Israel
matan.gilboa@mail.huji.ac.il , noam@cs.huji.ac.il

Abstract. We study the computational complexity of "public goods games on networks". In this model, each vertex in a graph is an agent that needs to take a binary decision of whether to "produce a good" or not. Each agent's utility depends on the number of its neighbors in the graph that produce the good, as well as on its own action. This dependence can be captured by a "pattern" $T : \mathbb{N} \to \{0, 1\}$ that describes an agent's best response to every possible number of neighbors that produce the good. Answering a question of [Papadimitriou and Peng, 2021], we prove that for some simple pattern T the problem of determining whether a non-trivial pure Nash equilibrium exists is NP-complete. We extend our result to a wide class of such T, but also find a new polynomial time algorithm for some specific simple pattern T. We leave open the goal of characterizing the complexity for all patterns.

Keywords: Nash Equilibrium · Public Goods · Computational Complexity

1 Introduction

We study scenarios where there is a set of agents, each of which must decide whether to make an effort to produce some "good", where doing so benefits not only himself but also others. This general type of phenomena is captured by the general notion of public goods, and we focus on cases where the public good produced by some agent does not benefit *all* other agents but rather there is some neighborhood structure between agents specifying which agents benefit from the public goods produced by others. Examples for these types of scenarios abound: anti-pollution efforts that benefit a geographical neighborhood, research efforts that benefit other researchers in related areas, vaccination efforts, security efforts, and many more.

We focus on the following standard modeling of *public goods games on networks*: We are given an undirected graph, where each node models an agent, and

---

This project has received funding from the European Research Council (ERC) under the European Union's Horizon 2020 Research and Innovation Programme (grant agreement no. 740282).

© The Author(s), under exclusive license to Springer Nature Switzerland AG 2022
P. Kanellopoulos et al. (Eds.): SAGT 2022, LNCS 13584, pp. 151–168, 2022.
https://doi.org/10.1007/978-3-031-15714-1_9

the neighbors of a node are the other agents that benefit from his production of the public good. We focus on the case where each agent has a single boolean decision to make of whether to produce the good or not, and furthermore, as in, e.g., [3–5,7,9], limit ourselves to cases where the effect of an agent's neighbors is completely characterized by the number of them that produce the good. Furthermore we focus on the cleanest, so called, *fully homogenous* case where all agents have the same costs and utility functions so all of the heterogeneity between agents is captured by the graph structure.

Formally, there is a cost c that each agent pays if they produce their good, and a utility function $u(s_i, k_i)$ describing each agent's utility, where $s_i \in \{0,1\}$ describes whether agent i produces the good and $k_i \in \mathbb{N}$ is the number of i's neighbors (excluding i) that produce the good[1]. We focus on the 'strict' version of the problem [4], where we do not allow knife's-edge cases where $u(1, k_i) - u(0, k_i) = c$. Therefore, our agent's best response to exactly k_i of its neighbors producing the good is to produce the good ($s_i = 1$) if $u(1, k_i) - u(0, k_i) > c$ and to not produce the good ($s_i = 0$) if $u(1, k_i) - u(0, k_i) < c$. Hence, we can summarize the Best-Response Pattern as $T : \mathbb{N} \to \{0,1\}$. We study the following basic problem of finding a non-trivial pure Nash equilibrium in a network.

Equilibrium in a Public Goods Game: For a given Best-Response Pattern $T : \mathbb{N} \to \{0,1\}$, given as input an undirected graph $G = (V, E)$, determine whether there exists a pure non-trivial Nash equilibrium of the public goods game on G, i.e. an assignment $s : V \to \{0,1\}$ that is not all 0, such that for every $1 \le i \le |V|$ we have that $s_i = T(\sum_{(i,j) \in E} s_j)$.

Several cases of this problem have been studied in the literature. In [1], the "convex case" where the pattern is monotone (best response is 1 if at least t of your neighbors play 1) and the "Best Shot" case (where the best response is 1 only if none of your neighbors play 1, i.e. $T(0) = 1$ and for all $k > 0$, $T(k) = 0$) were shown to have polynomial time algorithms. The general heterogeneous case where different agents may have different patterns of best responses was shown to be NP-complete in [9] as was, in [4,7], the fully-homogenous case, if we allow also knife's-edge cases, i.e. for some utility function where for some k we have $u(1, k) - u(0, k) = c$ (which lies outside our concise formalization of patterns, since in these cases, both 1 and 0 are best responses).[2] The parameterized complexity for several natural parameters of the graph was studied in [4]. In [3], it is shown that in a public goods game, computing an equilibrium where at least k agents produce the good, or at least some specific subset of agents produce it, is NP-Complete. In [5], a version of this problem[3] on *directed* graphs was studied, and a full characterization of the complexity of this problem was given for every pattern: except for a few explicitly given Best-Response Patterns, for any other

---

[1] In this paper, we use the notation $\mathbb{N}$ to also contain 0, and use $\mathbb{N}_+$ to exclude 0.

[2] An early version [8] of [9] contained an erroneous proof of NP-completeness in the fully-homogenous case for some pattern T, but a bug was found by [7] who gave an alternative proof of the NP-completeness of the case that allows $u(1, k) - u(0, k) = c$.

[3] A version without the non-triviality assumption on the equilibrium.

pattern the directed problem is NP-complete.[4] They also suggested an open problem of providing a similar characterization for the more standard undirected case and specifically asked about the complexity of the pattern where the best response is 1 iff exactly one of your neighbors plays 1. Our main result answers this question, showing that for this specific pattern the problem is NP-complete.

Theorem: For the Best-Response Pattern where each agent prefers to produce the good iff exactly one of its neighbors produces the good, i.e. $T(1) = 1$ and for all $k \neq 1$ $T(k) = 0$, the equilibrium decision problem in a public goods game is NP-complete.

When considering the strict version of the game, this is the first pattern for which the equilibrium problem is shown to be NP-complete, and in fact it is even the first proof that the general problem (where the pattern is part of the input) is NP-complete. We then embark on the road to characterizing the complexity for all possible patterns. We extend our proof of NP-completeness to large classes of patterns. We also find a new polynomial time algorithm for a new interesting case:

Theorem: For the pattern where each agent prefers to produce the good iff at most one of its neighbors produces the good, i.e. $T(0) = T(1) = 1$ and for all $k > 1$, $T(k) = 0$, the public goods game always has a pure non-trivial equilibrium, and it can be found in polynomial time.

We were not able to complete our characterization for all patterns and leave this as an open problem. In particular, we were not able to determine the complexity for the following two cases:

Open Problem 1: Determine the computational complexity of the equilibrium decision problem of a public goods game for the pattern where $T(0) = T(1) = T(2) = 1$ and for all $k > 2$, $T(k) = 0$.

Open Problem 2: Determine the computational complexity of the equilibrium decision problem of a public goods game for the pattern where $T(0) = T(2) = 1$ and for all $k \notin \{0, 2\}$, $T(k) = 0$.

We suspect that at least the first problem is computationally easy, and in fact that there exists a non-trivial pure Nash equilibrium in any graph.

The rest of this paper is organized as follows: After defining our model and notations in Sect. 2, we present our main theorem (hardness of the Single-Neighbor pattern) in Sect. 3, and provide some intuition about the problem. In Sect. 4 we construct a polynomial time algorithm for the At-Most-Single-Neighbor pattern. In Sect. 5 we characterize a number of classes of patterns for which the problem is hard, by reducing from our main theorem, where each sub-section focuses on a specific class of patterns. Our results are summarized in Table 1.

---

[4] One of the few easy cases they identify can be seen to apply also to the undirected case: where the pattern alternates between 0 and 1, i.e. $T(k)$ only depends on the parity of k, a case that can be solved as a solution of linear equations over $GF(2)$.

Table 1. A summary of our (and previous) results.

Category	Pattern	Reference
PTIME	1,0,0,0,...	[1]
	1,1,0,0,0,...	Theorem 2
	0,0,...,1,1,1,...	[1]
	1,0,1,0,1,0,...	[5]
NPC	0,1,0,0,0,...	Theorem 1
	0,?,?,...,1,0,0,0,...	Theorem 4
	1,1,?,?,...,0,?,?,...,1,0,0,0,...	Theorem 5
	1,0,..,0,1,1,?,?,...,0,0,0,...	Theorem 6
	Adding 1,0 to non-flat hard patterns	Theorem 7
Open Problems	1,1,1,0,0,0,...	
	1,0,1,0,0,0,...	

2   Model and Notation

We define a *Public Goods Game* (PGG) on an undirected graph $G = (V, E)$ with n nodes $V = \{1, ..., n\}$, each one representing an agent. The *neighborhood* of agent i, denoted $N(i)$, is defined as the set of agents adjacent to i, excluding i, i.e.: $N(i) = \{j|(j, i) \in E\}$. An edge between two agents' nodes models the fact that these agents are directly affected by each other's decision to produce or not produce the good. The strategy space, which is assumed to be the same for all agents, is $S = \{0, 1\}$, where 1 represents producing the good, and 0 represents the opposite. The strategy of agent i is denoted $s_i \in S$.

Definition 1. *If nodes i, j are adjacent, and $s_j = 1$ (i.e. agent j produces the good) we say that j is a **supporting neighbor** of i.*

For convenience, if some node v represents agent i, we sometimes write $v = 1$ or $v = 0$ instead of $s_i = 1$ or $s_i = 0$ respectively, to mark i's strategy. The utility function is assumed to be the same for all agents. Furthermore, we restrict ourselves to utility functions where an agent is never indifferent between producing and not producing the good, and so always has a single best response according to the strategies of the agents in their neighborhood. This characteristic of the utility function allows us to adopt a more convenient way to inspect a PGG model, which we call the *Best-Response Pattern*.

Definition 2. *For any PGG, we define its Best-Response Pattern (BRP), denoted by T, as an infinite boolean vector in which the kth entry represents the best response for each agent i given that exactly k neighbors of i (excluding i) produce the good:*

$$\forall k \in \mathbb{N} \ T[k] = best \ response \ to \ k \ productive \ neighbors$$

We henceforth identify PGGs by their Best-Response Pattern, rather than their utility function and cost. This concludes the definition of a PGG model. We now define a *pure Nash equilibrium*, which is our main subject of interest.

Definition 3. *A strategy profile* $s = (s_1, ..., s_n) \in S^n$ *of a Public Goods Game corresponding to a BRP T is a pure Nash equilibrium (PNE) if all agents play the best response to the strategies of the agents in their neighborhood:*

$$\forall i \in [n] \ \ s_i = T[\sum_{j \in N(i)} s_j]$$

In addition, if there exists $i \in [n]$ *s.t* $s_i = 1$, *then* s *is called a non-trivial pure Nash equilibrium (NTPNE).*

Definition 4. *For a fixed BRP T, the non-trivial pure Nash equilibrium decision problem corresponding to T, denoted by NTPNE(T), is defined as follows: The input is an undirected graph G. The output is 'True' if there exists an NTPNE in the PGG defined on G with respect to T, and 'False' otherwise. The search version of the problem asks for the NTPNE itself.*

Let us give names to the following three simplest patterns:

Definition 5. *The Best-Shot Best-Response Pattern is defined as follows:*

$$\forall k \in \mathbb{N} \ \ T[k] = \begin{cases} 1 & \text{if } k = 0 \\ 0 & \text{if } k \geq 1 \end{cases}$$

i.e.

$$T = [1, 0, 0, 0, 0, ...]$$

Definition 6. *The Single-Neighbor Best-Response Pattern is defined as follows:*

$$\forall k \in \mathbb{N} \ \ T[k] = \begin{cases} 1 & \text{if } k = 1 \\ 0 & \text{otherwise} \end{cases}$$

i.e.

$$T = [0, 1, 0, 0, 0, ...]$$

Definition 7. *The At-Most-Single-Neighbor Best-Response Pattern is defined as follows:*

$$\forall k \in \mathbb{N} \ \ T[k] = \begin{cases} 1 & \text{if } k \leq 1 \\ 0 & \text{if } k > 1 \end{cases}$$

i.e.

$$T = [1, 1, 0, 0, 0, ...]$$

The Best-Shot BRP was coined in [1], where they prove that a pure Nash equilibrium exists in any graph, and show a correspondence between PNEs and Maximal Independent Sets. We study the Single-Neighbor BRP in Sect. 3, where we prove the decision problem is NP-Complete. We study the At-Most-Single-Neighbor BRP in Sect. 4, where we prove that a pure Nash equilibrium exists in any graph.

3   Hardness of the Single-Neighbor Pattern

In this section we prove NP-completeness of $NTPNE(T)$ defined by the Single-Neighbor BRP, and provide basic intuition about its combinatorial structure. This is a linchpin of our hardness results, from which we reduce to many other patterns. We remind the reader that in the Single-Neighbor BRP, an agent prefers to produce the good iff exactly one of their neighbors produces it.

Theorem 1. *Let T be the Single-Neighbor Best-Response Pattern. Then $NTPNE$ (T) is NP-complete.*

Before the proof, we provide intuition about the Single-Neighbor problem, by examining a few simple graphs. First, we note that since $T[0] = 0$, a trivial all-zeros PNE exists in any graph. This observation is true for any such pattern[5], which is the reason we choose to focus on non-trivial PNEs. Now, take for example a simple path with two nodes. The assignment where both nodes are set to 1 is an NTPNE, since neither of them benefit from changing their strategy. But looking at a simple path with 3 nodes, it is easy to verify that there is no NTPNE. Specifically, the all-ones assignment in such a path is *not* a PNE since the middle node would rather play 0, as it already has two supporting neighbors. Generalizing this NTPNE analysis to paths of any size, we see that in order for a simple path with n nodes $x_1, ..., x_n$ to have an NTPNE, it must be that $n \equiv 2 \pmod 3$. To see why, let us examine x_1. If x_1 is assigned 0 then so is x_2, as otherwise x_1 wishes to change strategy; and since x_2 is assigned 0 then so is x_3, and so forth. Therefore, in order to get a non-trivial assignment x_1 must be assigned 1, and it must have a supporting neighbor, which must be x_2. This leads to only one possibility for an NTPNE, as shown in Fig. 1. A similar analysis shows that a cycle with n nodes has an NTPNE iff $n \equiv 0 \pmod 3$ (see Fig. 2).

Fig. 1. *NTPNE: paths with $n \equiv 2 \pmod 3$*

Another simple example is the Complete Graph, or Clique. In any Clique of size at least 2, we can construct an NTPNE by choosing any two nodes to be assigned 1, and assigning 0 to all other nodes (see Fig. 3).

---

[5] These patterns are denoted *flat* patterns, and are formally defined in Definition 10.

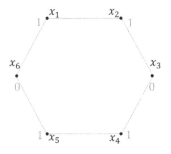

Fig. 2. *NTPNE: cycles with* $n \equiv 0$ (mod 3)

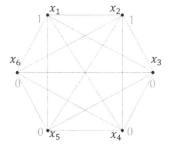

Fig. 3. *NTPNE: Clique*

So we see there are cases where there exists an NTPNE, and others where there doesn't, and so the problem is not trivial (and in fact is NP-Hard).

We now begin the proof of Theorem 1, first showing that the problem is NP-Hard. To do so, we construct a reduction from *ONE-IN-THREE 3SAT*, which is a well known NP-complete problem [6]. The input of the *ONE-IN-THREE 3SAT* problem is a CNF formula where each clause has exactly 3 literals, and the goal is to determine whether there exists a boolean assignment to the variables such that in each clause exactly one literal is assigned with *True*.

For the reduction, we introduce our Clause Gadget. For each clause (l_1, l_2, l_3) in the *ONE-IN-THREE 3SAT* instance, we construct a 9-nodes Clause Gadget as demonstrated in Fig. 4. The nodes l_1, l_2, l_3 represent the literals of the clause, respectively, and are denoted the *Literal Nodes*. Nodes a, b, c are denoted the *Inner Nodes*, and nodes x, y, z are denoted the *Peripheral Nodes*. Each Literal Node is adjacent to all other Literal Nodes, and to all Peripheral Nodes. In addition, the Literal Nodes l_1, l_2, l_3 are *paired* with the Peripheral Nodes x, y, z respectively, in the sense that they share the same Inner Node as a neighbor, and only that Inner Node (for example, l_1 and x are *paired* since they are both adjacent to a, and not to b, c). Notice that the Peripheral Nodes are *not* adjacent to each other. Additionally, note that in the final graph, only the Literal Nodes will be connected to nodes outside the Clause Gadget. The proof is constructed by a number of Lemmas.

Lemma 1. *In any PNE in a graph which includes the Clause Gadget, if one of the nodes of the Clause Gadget is assigned 1, then one of the Literal Nodes must be assigned 1.*

Proof. Assume by way of contradiction that all Literal Nodes are assigned 0. Since at least one node in the gadget is assigned 1, it must either be an Inner Node or a Peripheral Node. Notice that if an Inner Node is assigned 1, w.l.o.g $a = 1$, then its neighboring Peripheral Node x has exactly one supporting neighbor and according to the BRP must also be assigned 1, seeing that x is connected only to a and to the Literal Nodes (which are assigned 0). Similarly, if a Peripheral Node is assigned 1, w.l.o.g $x = 1$, then its neighboring Inner Node a must also be

Fig. 4. *Clause Gadget, with the NTPNE assignment of Lemma 4*

Fig. 5. *Transfer Node (blue edges not shown).* (Color figure online)

assigned 1, as otherwise x would prefer changing strategy. Therefore, there must be a pair of adjacent Inner Node and Peripheral Node that are both assigned 1. w.l.o.g $a = x = 1$. Since a is assigned 1, and already has a supporting neighbor, then all other neighbors of a (i.e. b and c) must be set to 0. This leaves us only with z, y; since neither of them have any supporting neighbors, they must be set to 0. The contradiction comes from nodes b, c, both of which prefer changing their strategy to 1, having exactly one supporting neighbor. □

Lemma 2. *In any PNE in a graph which includes the Clause Gadget, if one of the Literal Nodes of the Clause Gadget is assigned 1, then the other two Literal Nodes must be assigned 0.*

Proof. Assume by way of contradiction that two different Literal Nodes are assigned 1 (w.l.o.g $l_1 = l_2 = 1$). Since l_1 and l_2 are adjacent, they both already have a supporting neighbor, and so all their other neighbors must be set to 0. Therefore $l_3 = x = y = z = a = b = 0$. This leaves us only with node c, which must be set to 0 since all its neighbors are set to 0. The contradiction comes from nodes a, b, both of which prefer changing their strategy to 1, having exactly one supporting neighbor. □

Lemma 3. *In any PNE in a graph which includes the Clause Gadget, if one of the Literal Nodes of the Clause Gadget is assigned 1, then so is its paired Peripheral Node.*

Proof. Assume by way of contradiction that a Literal Node is set to 1 while its *paired Peripheral Node* is set to 0. w.l.o.g $l_1 = 1, x = 0$. From Lemma 2, we have that $l_2 = l_3 = 0$. Therefore, since x cannot have only one supporting neighbor and still prefer playing 0, we must set its remaining neighbor, a, to 1. Since l_1, a both have a supporting neighbor, all their other neighbors must be set to 0. Therefore $b = c = y = z = 0$. The contradiction comes from nodes b, c, both of which prefer changing their strategy to 1, having exactly one supporting neighbor. □

Lemma 4. *In any PNE in a graph which includes a Clause Gadget, if one of the nodes of the Clause Gadget is assigned 1, then there is only one possible assignment to the nodes in the gadget. Specifically, one Literal Node and its paired Peripheral Node must be set to 1, and so do the two Inner Nodes that aren't connected to them, whereas all other nodes in the gadget must be set to 0.*

Proof. Since there exists a node that is set to 1 inside the gadget, From Lemma 1 one of the Literal Nodes must be set to 1, w.l.o.g $l_1 = 1$. From Lemma 2 $l_2 = l_3 = 0$, and from Lemma 3 $x = 1$. Since l_1, x are supporting neighbors to each other, they cannot have any other neighbor set to 1, therefore $a = y = z = 0$. Since y is set to 0 and has only one supporting neighbor (l_1), we must set its remaining neighbor b to 1 as well. Symmetrically, we must set c to 1 in order to support z's assignment. It is easy to verify that indeed each node of the Clause Gadget is playing its best response given this assignment.   □

So far we have seen that the Clause Gadget indeed permits an NTPNE, and enforces the fact that each clause of the CNF formula must have exactly one literal set to 1. We now wish to enforce the fact that *all* clauses must have a literal assigned with *True*. We first construct a connection between the Clause Gadgets such that *if* some Clause Gadget has a node set to 1, then all gadgets must have one. The connection is defined as follows. Each pair[6] of Clause Gadgets is connected by one *Transfer Node*, denoted by t. The Transfer Node is adjacent to all Literal Nodes of both of the gadget to which it is connected, and only to those nodes. The connection between the Clause Gadgets is demonstrated in Fig. 5.

Lemma 5. *In any PNE in a graph which includes 2 Clause Gadgets which are connected by a Transfer Node t, t must be set to 0.*

Proof. Assume by way of contradiction that $t = 1$. Then it must have a supporting neighbor. Since t is only connected to Literal Nodes, one of those Literal Nodes must be set to 1 (w.l.o.g $l_1 = 1$). From Lemma 3, x must also be assigned with 1, which leads to a contradiction since l_1 has 2 supporting neighbors and yet plays 1.   □

Lemma 6. *In any PNE in a graph which includes at least two Clause Gadgets, which are all connected to each other by Transfer Nodes, if one of the Clause Gadgets has a node set to 1, then all of the Clause Gadgets have a node set to 1.*

Proof. Denote the gadget that has a node set to 1 by g_1, and let g_2 be some other Clause Gadget. Then g_2 is connected to g_1 via a Transfer Node t. Denote the Literal Nodes in g_1 by l_1, l_2, l_3, and the Literal Nodes in g_2 by l'_1, l'_2, l'_3. From Lemma 1 and Lemma 2 we have that one of l_1, l_2, l_3 is set to 1, while the other

---

[6] It is enough to connect all Clause Gadgets as a chain to one another (by Transfer Nodes), but for ease of proof we connect every pair of gadgets.

two are set to 0. w.l.o.g assume $l_1 = 1, l_2 = l_3 = 0$. From Lemma 5, $t = 0$, and therefore, t must have another supporting neighbor other than l_1. Since t's only neighbors are $l_1, l_2, l_3, l'_1, l'_2, l'_3$, and $l_2 = l_3 = 0$, it follows that one of l'_1, l'_2, l'_3 must be set to one, while the other two must be set to 0. From Lemma 4 we know the assignments in each Clause Gadget necessary for an NTPNE, and it is easy to verify that this assignment is still a Nash Equilibrium after adding Transfer Nodes between the gadgets.   □

Now that we have ensured all Clause Gadgets have a node set to 1 (assuming one of them does), we wish to enforce that any two identical literals in the CNF formula are assigned with the same value. To do so, we introduce another connecting node, which we call the *Copy Node*. Any two[7] Literal Nodes l_1, l'_1 (from different Clause Gadgets, or possibly from the same one) which represent the same variable in the original CNF formula, will be connected via a Copy Node denoted by k, as shown in Fig. 6. Each Copy Node has exactly two neighbors, which are l_1, l'_1.

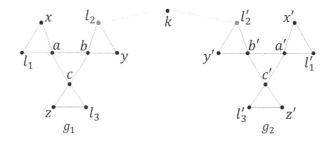

Fig. 6. *Copy Node (blue edges not shown).* (Color figure online)

Lemma 7. *In any PNE in a graph which includes two Literal Nodes l_1, l'_1 in two Clause Gadgets g_1, g_2 respectively, where l_1, l'_1 are connected by a Copy Node k, k must be set to 0.*

Proof. Since k is connected only to Literal Nodes, the proof of Lemma 5 applies to this claim as well.   □

Lemma 8. *In any PNE in a graph which includes two Literal Nodes l_1, l'_1 in two Clause Gadgets g_1, g_2 respectively, where l_1, l'_1 are connected by a Copy Node k, l_1 and l'_1 must have the same assignment.*

Proof. Assume by way of contradiction that (w.l.o.g) $l_1 = 1, l'_1 = 0$. From Lemma 7, k must be set to 0. But since l_1, l'_1 are the only neighbors of k, k has only one supporting neighbor, and therefore k must be set to 1, in contradiction.   □

---

[7] It is enough to connect all literals representing the same variable as a chain to one another (by Copy Nodes), but for ease of proof we connect every pair of them.

The next property of a *ONE-IN-THREE 3SAT* assignment we need to enforce, is that a variable x and its negation $\bar{x}$ must be set to different values. Since the Copy Nodes already ensure that a variable appearing several times will always get the same value, it is enough to make sure for each variable that one instance of it is indeed different from one instance of its negation. To do so, we introduce another connecting node, called the *Negation Node*. For each variable x, where both x and $\bar{x}$ appear in the CNF formula, we choose one instance of x and one instance of $\bar{x}$ from different clauses.[8] Denote the Literal Nodes representing $x, \bar{x}$ by l_1, l_1' respectively, and denote the other two Literal Nodes residing with l_1' in the same Clause Gadget by l_2', l_3'. We connect a Negation Node n to l_1 as well as to l_2', l_3', as demonstrated in Fig. 7. For convenience, we say that l_1, l_1' are connected by n even though n is only adjacent to one of them.

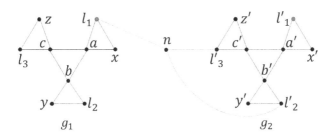

Fig. 7. *Negation Node (blue edges not shown).* (Color figure online)

Lemma 9. *In any PNE in a graph which includes two Literal Nodes l_1, l_1' in two different Clause Gadgets g_1, g_2 respectively, where l_1, l_1' are connected by a Negation Node n, then n must be set to 0.*

Proof. Since n is connected only to Literal Nodes, the proof of Lemma 5 applies to this claim as well. □

Lemma 10. *In any PNE in a graph which includes two Literal Nodes l_1, l_1' in two different Clause Gadgets g_1, g_2 respectively, where l_1, l_1' are connected by a Negation Node n, and each of g_1, g_2 has at least one node set to 1, then l_1, l_1' must be assigned with different values.*

Proof. Denote by l_2', l_3' the other two Literal Nodes residing with l_1' in the same Clause Gadget. Divide into cases. Case 1: If $l_1 = 1$, then n must have another supporting neighbor (since n itself is set to 0, from Lemma 9). Thus, either l_2' or l_3' must be set to 1, and from Lemma 2 we have that $l_1' = 0$, as needed. Case 2: If $l_1 = 0$, assume by way of contradiction $l_1' = 0$. Since g_2 has some node set to 1, then from Lemmas 1 and 2 we have that either l_2' or l_3' are set to 1, and only one of them. Thus, n has exactly one supporting neighbor, and therefore n must be set to 1, in contradiction to Lemma 9. □

---

[8] We assume a variable and its negation never appear together in the same clause, as the problem without this assumption is easily reducible to the problem with it.

We have shown that our construction enforces all properties of a valid *ONE-IN-THREE 3SAT* solution. But notice that most of the proofs rely on the assumption that every Clause Gadget has at least one node set to 1. It is left to prove that there cannot be any NTPNE where all of the Clause Gadgets are all-zero.

Lemma 11. *In any NTPNE in the graph constructed throughout the proof of Theorem 1, all Clause Gadgets have at least one node set to 1.*

Proof. Since we have an NTPNE, there must be some non-zero node, denoted by v. From Lemmas 5, 7, and 9 we have that all Transfer Nodes, Copy Nodes and Negation Nodes must be set to 0, and therefore v must be a part of a Clause Gadget.[9] From Lemma 6 we conclude that all Clause Gadgets must have a node set to 1.   □

These Lemmas lead us to the conclusion that indeed any satisfying assignment to the *ONE-IN-THREE 3SAT* problem matches an NTPNE in the constructed graph, and vice versa, which directly implies that the NTPNE problem is NP-Hard. This result is formulated by the claim in Theorem 1, which we can now prove.

Proof. (Theorem 1) Clearly the problem is in NP, as given any graph and a binary assignment to the nodes, we can verify that the assignment is an NTPNE in polynomial time. It is left to prove the problem is NP-Hard. Given a ONE-IN-THREE 3SAT instance, we construct a graph as described previously. If there exists a satisfying assignment to the variables of the ONE-IN-THREE 3SAT instance, then we can assign 1 to all Literal Nodes which represent variables that are assigned 'True', and to the necessary nodes within each gadget according to Lemma 4, and set all other nodes to 0. Since we saw that the assignment described in Lemma 4 forms an NTPNE, and that all connecting nodes (i.e. Transfer, Copy and Negation Nodes) do not affect this NTPNE given that they are all set to 0, we will get an NTPNE. In the other direction, if there exists an NTPNE in the constructed graph, From Lemmas 1, 2, 6, 8, 10, 11 we have that this NTPNE corresponds to a satisfying assignment to the ONE-IN-THREE 3SAT instance, where every Literal Node set to 1 will translate to assigning 'True' to its matching variable, and every Literal Node set to 0 will translate to assigning 'False' to its matching variable.   □

The proof itself gives a slightly more general result: The degree of the constructed graph is bounded[10] by 13. Therefore, our proof does not require any information about the 15th entry of the BRP onward, and thus extends to any NTPNE(T) where T agrees with the first 14 entries of the SN-BRP.

---

[9] Lemmas 5, 7, and 9 do not assume that the Clause Gadgets have a node set to 1, and therefore are valid to use here.

[10] The reader who has read the details of the proof may verify that, in the version where the gadgets are chained as mentioned in footnotes 6 and 7, a Literal Node is attached to 6 nodes within its Clause Gadget, and at most 2 Transfer Nodes, 2 Copy Nodes and 3 Negation Nodes.

Corollary 1. *Let T be a BRP such that:*

1. T[1]=1
2. $\forall k \in \{0, 2, 3, ..., 13\}$ $T[k] = 0$

Then NTPNE(T) is NP-complete.

4   Algorithm for the At-Most-Single-Neighbor Pattern

In this section, we focus on one of the most basic cases of a *monotone* Best-Response Pattern, which is the *At-Most-Single-Neighbor BRP*. We remind the reader that in the At-Most-Single-Neighbor BRP, an agent prefers to produce the good iff at most one of their neighbors produces it. In addition, we formally define a *monotone* Best-Response Pattern as follows:

Definition 8. *A BRP T is called monotonically increasing (resp. decreasing) if for all $k \in \mathbb{N}$, $T[k] \leq T[k+1]$ (resp. $T[k] \geq T[k+1]$).*

The most basic (and well studied) case of a monotonically-decreasing BRP is the Best-Shot BRP. In [1], it is shown that in any PGG corresponding to the Best-Shot BRP, an NTPNE always exists. Thus, the decision problem in this case is trivially solvable in polynomial time. In this section, we show a similar result for the At-Most-Single-Neighbor BRP: we prove that an NTPNE exists in any PGG corresponding to this BRP, and present a polynomial time algorithm to find one. An important notion in Graph Theory, which will be of use during our proof, is the *Maximum Independent Set*. Given a Graph $G = (V, E)$, an Independent Set (Henceforth IS) is a subset of nodes $S \subseteq V$ such that no two nodes in S are adjacent. A *Maximal Independent Set* is an IS S such that for any node v outside S it holds that $S \cup \{v\}$ is not an IS. A *Maximum Independent Set* S is a Maximal IS, such that for any Maximal IS S' it holds that $|S| \geq |S'|$. Using this notion, we constructively prove that an NTPNE of the At-Most-Single-Neighbor BRP exists in any graph, by providing a non-polynomial time algorithm to find one. We later alter the algorithm to work in polynomial time.

Algorithm 1. At-Most-Single-Neighbor: Non-Polynomial Time Algorithm

---
    Input graph $G = (V, E)$
    Output NTPNE for the At-Most-Single-Neighbor PGG on G
1: find a maximum IS $S \subseteq V$, and assign all its nodes with 1.
2: for each $v \in V \setminus S$, if v has exactly one supporting neighbor at the moment of its assignment, then $v = 1$. Otherwise $v = 0$.

Theorem 2. *Let T be the At-Most-Single-Neighbor BRP. Given any graph G as an input, Algorithm 1 outputs an NTPNE of the PGG defined on G corresponding to T, and thus an NTPNE always exists. Therefore, the decision problem NTPNE(T) is trivially solvable in polynomial time.*

Proof. A Maximum IS always exists in any graph, and therefore stage 1 of the algorithm, though not efficient, is well defined. Assume by way of contradiction that the assignment given by the algorithm is not a PNE. Then there must be some node u that is not playing the best response to its neighbors assignments. Divide into two cases:

Case 1: If u is playing 0, then at the time of its assignment u must have had at least two supporting neighbors, otherwise the algorithm would have assigned it with 1. Since the algorithm never changes a node's assignment from 1 to 0, we have that also at the end of the run u has at least two supporting neighbors, and therefore u is playing its best response, in contradiction.

Case 2: If u is playing 1, then it must be that u has at least two supporting neighbors, otherwise u is playing its best response. Let x, y be two supporting neighbors of u. Divide into two sub-cases:

Sub-Case 2.1: If $u \in S$, then $x, y \in V \backslash S$ (otherwise we have a contradiction to S being an IS), and therefore u had received its assignment before x, y did. Any node not in S is only assigned with 1 by the algorithm if it has exactly one supporting neighbor at the time of the assignment, and therefore x, y only had u as a supporting neighbor at the time of the assignment. Specifically, x, y are not adjacent to any other node in S, because all nodes in S were already assigned 1 by the time x, y were assigned. Therefore, we have that $S' := (S \setminus \{u\}) \cup \{x, y\}$ is also an IS. Since $|S'| > |S|$, we have a contradiction to the fact that S is a Maximum IS.

Sub-Case 2.2: If $u \notin S$, then at least one of x, y must have gotten its assignment after u, otherwise the algorithm would have assigned u with 0. w.l.o.g assume x got its assignment after u, and in particular $x \in V \backslash S$. Since x was assigned 1, it had exactly one supporting neighbor at the time of the assignment, hence u was its only supporting neighbor at the time of the assignment. Since $u \notin S$, we have that x is not adjacent to any node in S, which means that $S \cup \{x\}$ is an IS, in contradiction to S being a maximal IS.

Therefore, all nodes play their best response, and so the assignment is an NTPNE.[11]

Theorem 2 shows that the decision problem is easy in this case, using the fact that a Maximum IS always exists in any graph. However, finding a Maximum IS is an NP-Hard problem, and so Algorithm 1 does not run in polynomial time. Nevertheless, it does provide a base for our following refined algorithm, which runs in polynomial time and finds an NTPNE in any given graph.

Theorem 3. *Let T be the At-Most-Single-Neighbor BRP. Given any graph G as an input, Algorithm 2 runs in polynomial time and outputs an NTPNE of the PGG defined on G corresponding to T.*

---

[11] Since $T[0] = 1$, any PNE must be an NTPNE.

Algorithm 2. At-Most-Single-Neighbor: Polynomial Time Algorithm

---

    Input graph $G = (V, E)$
    Output NTPNE for the At-Most-Single-Neighbor PGG on G
1: find a Maximal IS $S \subseteq V$.
2: perform stage 2 of Algorithm 1 using S
3: **if** the assignment is a PNE **then**
4:     return
5: **else**
6:     let u be a node which isn't playing its best response
7:     $S \leftarrow S \setminus \{u\}$
8:     **for** x s.t $(x, u) \in E$ **do**
9:         **if** x is not adjacent to any node in S **then**
10:             $S \leftarrow S \cup \{x\}$
11: go back to stage 2

Proof. Correctness: We show that if at the beginning of iteration S is a Maximal IS, then at the end of it S increases by at least 1, and remains a Maximal IS. Therefore, after at most $|V|$ iterations, either the algorithm finds an NTPNE and stops, or S increases enough to become a Maximum IS, and therefore by Theorem 2 the algorithm outputs an NTPNE.

S **Increases by At Least 1 After Each Iteration:** At the beginning of the iteration S is a Maximal IS, but not necessarily a Maximum IS. Inspect the different cases of the proof of Theorem 2, when assuming that the assignment is not a PNE. Notice that all the cases from the proof of Theorem 2 were contradicted by the fact that S is a *Maximal* IS (which is true for the current theorem as well), except for Sub-Case 2.1, which was contradicted by the fact that S is a *Maximum* IS. Therefore, if the assignment given by stage 2 of Algorithm 1 is not a PNE, the conditions of case 2.1 of the proof of Theorem 2 must hold. Thus, we are guaranteed that any node not playing its best response must be in S, and must have at least two neighbors which satisfy the condition of stage 9 in Algorithm 2. Therefore, in each iteration of the Algorithm 2 S gains at least 2 new nodes in the loop of stage 8, and loses exactly one node (which is u), and therefore the size of S overall increases by at least 1.

S **Remains a Maximal IS After Each Iteration:** Since S is a maximal IS at the beginning of the iteration, any node not in S is adjacent to at least one node in S. In each iteration we only remove a single node u from S, hence only u and nodes that were adjacent to u might (possibly) not be adjacent to any node in S. After iterating over all of u's neighbors and adding whichever possible to S, we have that all of u's neighbors are either in S or adjacent to some node in S. Regarding u itself, we have already shown that at least 2 of its neighbors must be added to S. Thus we have that S remains a Maximal IS at the end of the iteration. This concludes the correctness of the algorithm.

Run-Time: Stage 1 can be achieved in $O(|V|)$, greedily. Stages 2, 3 and 8–10 all require iterating over all nodes, and for each node iterating over all its neighbors, i.e. $O(|V|^2)$. Therefore, each iteration of the algorithm runs in $O(|V|^2)$. As explained in the Correctness part of the proof, the number of iterations of the algorithm is bounded by $|V|$. Hence the overall run time of the algorithm is polynomial w.r.t the input.

5   More Hard Patterns

Theorem 1 provides a base to discover more classes of BRPs for which the decision problem is hard, which we present in this section. We focus specifically on non-monotone patterns, with a finite number of 1's, except for in Sect. 5.4 where we do not assume this. All proofs of this section can be found in the full version of this paper [2].

Definition 9. *A BRP T is called finite if it has a finite number of 1's, i.e.*

$$\exists N \in \mathbb{N} \ s.t \ \forall n > N \ T[n] = 0$$

5.1   Flat Patterns

In this section we generalize the result of the Single-Neighbor BRP to any t-Neighbors BRP (where an agent's best response is 1 iff exactly t of their neighbors play 1), and in fact to an even more general case: we show that any BRP that is *flat* (i.e. starting with 0), non-monotone and finite, models an NP-complete decision problem.

Definition 10. *A BRP T is called flat[12] if $T[0] = 0$.*

Theorem 4. *Let T be a BRP which satisfies the following conditions:*

1. *T is flat*
2. *T is non-monotone*
3. *T is finite*

Then NTPNE(T) is NP-complete.

5.2   Sloped Patterns

In this section, we show that the decision problem remains hard when the assumption of flatness is replaced with the assumption that the BRP begins with a finite number of 1's, and at least two. That is, we prove hardness of any non-monotone, finite, *sloped* BRP.

Definition 11. *A BRP T is called sloped if $T[0] = T[1] = 1$.*

Theorem 5. *Let T' be a BRP which satisfies the following conditions:*

1. *T' is sloped*
2. *T' is non-monotone*
3. *T' is finite*

Then NTPNE(T') is NP-complete under Turing reduction.

---

[12] Coined by Papadimitriou and Peng in [5].

5.3   Sharp Patterns Followed by Two 1's

Among all non-monotone, finite BRPs, we have shown hardness of those which are flat, and those which are sloped. It is left to address the decision problem for non-monotone, finite BRPs which start with $1, 0$.

Definition 12. *A BRP T is called sharp if $T[0] = 1$ and $T[1] = 0$.*

In this section, we focus on patterns which start with 1, followed by any positive, finite number of 0's, and then $1, 1$. We prove that such BRPs present hard decision problems.

Theorem 6. *Let T' be a BRP which satisfies the following conditions:*

1. *T' is finite*
2. *T' is sharp*
3. *$\exists m \geq 2$ s.t:*
   (a) $\forall 1 \leq k < m$ $T'[k] = 0$
   (b) $T'[m] = T'[m+1] = 1$

Then NTPNE(T') is NP-complete under Turing reduction.

5.4   Adding 1, 0 to Non-flat Patterns

In this section, we show that any non-flat pattern for which the decision problem is hard remains hard when $1, 0$ is added to the beginning of it. Notice that adding $1, 0$ at the beginning of a non-flat pattern yields another non-flat pattern, and so, by using this result recursively we can add any finite number of $1, 0$ to a non-flat hard pattern, and it will remain hard. So far, the only non-flat patterns we have shown to be hard are the ones from Theorems 5 and 6. Notice that adding $1, 0$ to a pattern of the form of 5 simply gives a pattern of the form of 6, which we have already proved is hard. Thus, until other non-flat patterns are proved hard, the new class of patterns that are shown to be hard in this section is summarized by the form:

$$T = [\ \underbrace{1, 0, 1, 0, 1, 0, ...}_{finite\ number\ of\ '1,0'}\ , \underbrace{1, 0, 0, 0, ..., 1, 1, ?, ?, ..., 0, 0, 0, ...}_{pattern\ from\ Theorem\ 6}]$$

If other non-flat patterns are proved hard, this result could be applied to them as well. We begin with a new definition:

Definition 13. *Let T, T' be two BRPs. We say that T' is shifted by m from T if:*

$$\forall k \in \mathbb{N}\ \ T'[k+m] = T[k]$$

We say that T' is positively-shifted by m from T if in addition:

$$\forall k < m\ \ T'[k] = 1$$

Theorem 7. *Let T be a non-flat BRP s.t NTPNE(T) is NP-complete. Let T'
be a BRP satisfying the following conditions:*

1. *T' is shifted by 2 from T.*
2. *T' is sharp*

Then NTPNE(T') is NP-complete.

References

1. Bramoullé, Y., Kranton, R.: Public goods in networks. J. Econ. Theory **135**(1), 478–494 (2007)
2. Gilboa, M., Nisan, N.: Complexity of public goods games on graphs. arXiv:2207.04238v1 (2022)
3. Kempe, D., Yu, S., Vorobeychik, Y.: Inducing equilibria in networked public goods games through network structure modification. arXiv preprint arXiv:2002.10627 (2020)
4. Maiti, A., Dey, P.: On parameterized complexity of binary networked public goods game. arXiv preprint arXiv:2012.01880 (2020)
5. Papadimitriou, C., Peng, B.: Public goods games in directed networks. In: 2021 Proceedings of the 22nd ACM Conference on Economics and Computation, pp. 745–762 (2021)
6. Schaefer, Thomas J.: The complexity of satisfiability problems. In: Proceedings of the Tenth Annual ACM Symposium on Theory of Computing, pp. 216–226 (1978)
7. Yang, Y., Wang, J.: A refined study of the complexity of binary networked public goods games. arXiv preprint arXiv:2012.02916 (2020)
8. Yu, S., Zhou, K., Brantingham, J., Vorobeychik, Y.: Computing equilibria in binary networked public goods games. In: Proceedings of the AAAI Conference on Artificial Intelligence, vol. 34, no. 02, pp. 2310–2317 (2020)
9. Yu, S., Zhou, K., Brantingham, J., Vorobeychik, Y.: Computing equilibria in binary networked public goods games. arXiv:1911.05788v3 (2021)

PPAD-Complete Pure Approximate Nash Equilibria in Lipschitz Games

Paul W. Goldberg[ORCID] and Matthew Katzman[✉][ORCID]

Department of Computer Science, University of Oxford, Oxford, England
{paul.goldberg,matthew.katzman}@cs.ox.ac.uk

Abstract. Lipschitz games, in which there is a limit λ (the Lipschitz value of the game) on how much a player's payoffs may change when some other player deviates, were introduced about 10 years ago by Azrieli and Shmaya. They showed via the probabilistic method that n-player Lipschitz games with m strategies per player have *pure ϵ-approximate Nash equilibria*, for $\epsilon \geq \lambda\sqrt{8n\log(2mn)}$. Here we provide the first hardness result for the corresponding computational problem, showing that even for a simple class of Lipschitz games (Lipschitz polymatrix games), finding pure ϵ-approximate equilibria is PPAD-complete, for suitable pairs of values $(\epsilon(n), \lambda(n))$. Novel features of this result include *both* the proof of PPAD hardness (in which we apply a population game reduction from unrestricted polymatrix games) and the proof of containment in PPAD (by derandomizing the selection of a pure equilibrium from a mixed one). In fact, our approach implies containment in PPAD for any class of Lipschitz games where payoffs from mixed-strategy profiles can be deterministically computed.

Keywords: Equilibrium computation · Lipschitz games · Population games · PPAD

1 Introduction

The basic setting of game theory models a finite game as a finite set of *players*, each of whom chooses from a finite set of allowed *actions* (or *pure strategies*). Such a game maps any choice of actions by the players to *payoffs* for the players. It follows that if players are allowed to randomize over their actions, there is a well-defined notion of expected payoff for each player. Nash's famous theorem [26] states that there exist randomized (or "mixed") strategies for the players so that no player can improve their expected payoff by unilaterally deviating to play some alternative strategy. In this paper we make a standard assumption that all payoffs lie in the range $[0, 1]$, and we take an interest in ϵ-approximate Nash equilibria, in which no single player can improve their expected payoff by more than some small additive $\epsilon > 0$ by deviating.

In a λ-*Lipschitz game*, a deviation by any single player can change any other player's payoffs by at most an additive λ. This property of a multiplayer game is of course analogous to the notion of Lipschitz continuity in mathematical

© The Author(s), under exclusive license to Springer Nature Switzerland AG 2022

P. Kanellopoulos et al. (Eds.): SAGT 2022, LNCS 13584, pp. 169–186, 2022.
https://doi.org/10.1007/978-3-031-15714-1_10

analysis. As shown by Azrieli and Shmaya [2], for $\lambda \leq \epsilon/\sqrt{8n\log(2mn)}$, any n-player, m-action, λ-Lipschitz game has an ϵ-approximate Nash equilibrium *in pure strategies*. This is shown by taking a mixed-strategy Nash equilibrium, known to exist by [26], and showing that when pure strategies are sampled from it, there is a positive probability that it will be ϵ-approximate. As observed in [2], solutions based on *mixed* strategies are often criticized as being unrealistic in practice, and pure-strategy solutions are more plausible. However the existence proof of [2] is non-constructive, raising the question of how hard they are to discover.

Here we study the problem of *computing* approximate pure equilibria of Lipschitz games. In a Lipschitz *polymatrix* game, the effect of any one player A's action on the payoffs of any other player B is both bounded and independent of what the remaining players are doing. For each of B's available actions, B's payoff is just the sum of a collection of contributions (each at most λ) associated with the action of each other player, plus some constant shift. For these simple games, we identify values of λ and ϵ (as functions of n) for which this problem is PPAD-complete, and thus unlikely to have a polynomial-time algorithm. Containment in PPAD holds for more general subclasses of Lipschitz games; in essence, any for which one can deterministically and efficiently compute payoffs associated with mixed-strategy profiles. However, for Lipschitz games whose payoff function is computed by a general circuit (or more abstractly, a payoff oracle for pure-strategy profiles), we just have containment in a randomized analogue of PPAD.

1.1   Background, Related Work

A key feature of the problem of computing a mixed Nash equilibrium (either an exact one, or an ϵ-approximate one for some $\epsilon > 0$) is that due to the guaranteed existence [26] of a solution that once found can be easily checked, it cannot be NP-hard unless NP = co-NP [24]. Beginning with [7,9], the complexity class PPAD (defined below) emerged as the means of identifying whether a class of games is likely to be hard to solve. Until recently, PPAD-completeness has mostly been used to identify computational obstacles to finding mixed equilibria rather than pure ones. In the setting of Bayes-Nash equilibrium, Filos-Ratsikas et al. [15] obtain a PPAD-completeness result for pure-strategy solutions of a class of first-price auctions. Closer to the present paper is a PPAD-completeness result of Papadimitriou and Peng [28] for a class of public goods games with divisible goods, where the continuous action-space of the players can represent probabilities in the solution of a corresponding 2-player game. Here instead we approximate continuous values (those taken at the gates of an arithmetic circuit for which we seek a fixed point) by the actions of a subset of the players, interpreting a given estimate as the fraction of players in such a subset who play some strategy.

Lipschitz Games. Lipschitz games are a well-studied topic formally introduced by Azrieli and Shmaya in [2] as a natural class of games that admit approximate pure Nash equilibria. Such games arise in many common situations such as financial markets and various types of network games.

These games are assumed to have a large number of players, and introduce the (Lipschitz) restriction that every player can have at most a bounded impact on the payoffs of any other player. They exhibit many fascinating properties, such as various metrics of fault tolerance (explored in [21]) and ex-post stability of equilibria (studied in [12]).

Following their introduction, further work on equilibria of Lipschitz games by Daskalakis and Papadimitriou [11] shows that for *anonymous* Lipschitz games, pure approximate equilibria can be computed in polynomial time via reduction to MAXFLOW, even for an approximation factor *independent* of the number of players (i.e. $\epsilon = O(\lambda m)$ for λ-Lipschitz, m-action games). When such games are restricted to 2 actions, there is an algorithm that can find such equilibria making polynomially-many *approximate* queries [20] (where the query may be off by some additive error), and even a randomized algorithm running in polynomial time using only *best-response* queries [3]. Cummings *et al.* [8] exploit a concentration argument to generalize [11] and identify pure approximate equilibria in *aggregative games*.

In [16], Goldberg and Katzman study Lipschitz games from the perspective of *query complexity*, in which an algorithm has black-box access to the game's payoff function. They identify lower bounds on the number of payoff queries needed to find an equilibrium. This leaves open the problem of computing an equilibrium of a Lipschitz game that has a *concise* representation: if a game is known to be concisely representable, then its query complexity is low [19]. Here we show that for concisely-representable Lipschitz games, there remains a computational obstacle. Prior to [16], [18] gave a query-based algorithm for computing $1/8$-approximate Nash equilibria in $1/n$-Lipschitz games; there may be scope to improve on the constant of $1/8$, but the present paper indicates a limit to further progress.

Polymatrix Games. Another line of work explores the computational properties of equilibria in *polymatrix* games introduced in [22]. [6] and [10] show that, for *coordination-only* polymatrix games (games in which each pair of players wants to agree) finding pure Nash equilibria is PLS-complete while finding mixed Nash equilibria is contained in CLS. Furthermore, [29] shows that the problem of finding ϵ-approximate Nash equilibria of *general* polymatrix games is PPAD-complete for some constant $\epsilon > 0$. To complement this lower bound, [14] provide an upper bound in the form of an algorithm running in time polynomial in the number of players to find an ϵ-approximate Nash equilibrium of such games for any constant $\epsilon > 0.5$ *independent of the number of actions*. Polymatrix games are known to be hard to solve even for sparse win-lose matrices [23], and for tree polymatrix games [13].

Here we extend the PPAD-hardness results of [29] to games having the Lipschitz property in addition to being polymatrix and binary-action. We show PPAD containment for the problem of finding approximate *pure* Nash equilibria of this class.

1.2   Our Contributions

In its most general form, the problem we address is, for $\lambda \leq \epsilon/\sqrt{8n \log 4mn}$:

> Given as input an n-player, m-action game, find either an ϵ-approximate
> pure Nash equilibrium, or a witness that the game is not λ-Lipschitz for
> the above λ (a witness consists of two pure-strategy profiles whose payoffs
> show the game is not λ-Lipschitz).

We will consider m, ϵ, and λ to be parameters of the problem statement rather
than provided in the input, however the problem is similar if these are instead
passed in as input.

Notice that the two alternative kinds of solutions (an equilibrium *or* a witness
against the λ-Lipschitz property) avoids a promise problem: there is no hard-
to-check promise that a given game is Lipschitz. The problem statement can be
taken to apply in general to any class of games whose payoff functions are efficiently computable (e.g. circuit games [30]). Efficient computability of payoffs is
also a sufficient condition to guarantee that solutions are easy to check, allowing
us to check the validity of either kind of solution. In the special case of Lipschitz
polymatrix games of interest here, they can be presented in a straightforward
format for which we can check the λ-Lipschitz property.

A PPAD-completeness result consists of containment in PPAD as well as
PPAD-hardness. In the context of *mixed-strategy* Nash equilibrium computation,
the following property of a class of games is sufficient for containment in PPAD:

> Given a mixed-strategy profile, it is possible to deterministically compute
> the payoffs with additive error $O(\epsilon)$, in time polynomial in the representa-
> tion size of the game, and $1/\epsilon$.

This property is shared by most well-studied classes of multiplayer games, such
as graphical games or polymatrix games. It does not hold for unrestricted Lipschitz games[1], but it of course holds for Lipschitz polymatrix games. In this
paper we obtain PPAD containment for *pure-strategy* approximate equilibria.
The approach of [2] places the problem in "randomized PPAD". We establish
containment in PPAD via a *deterministic* approach to selecting a pure approximate equilibrium (Lemma 2). Our approach requires λ to be a smaller-growing
function of ϵ and n than that of [2], however there *is* overlap between the (ϵ, λ)
régime where the problem is contained in (deterministic) PPAD and the one
where the problem is hard for PPAD.

PPAD-hardness applies to the binary-action case where each player has two
pure strategies $\{1, 2\}$. We reduce from the polymatrix games of [29], by considering an induced *population game* (details in Sect. 3.2), which has the Lipschitz
property.

---

[1] For Lipschitz games presented in terms of unrestricted circuits that compute payoffs
from pure-strategy profiles, one cannot deterministically and efficiently compute
approximate payoffs to mixed-strategy profiles unless P = RP. For games abstractly
presented via a payoff query oracle, this is unconditionally not possible to achieve
(regardless of any complexity class collapses).

For any fixed number of actions $m \geq 2$, PPAD-completeness (Theorem 2 and Corollary 1) holds for carefully-chosen functions $\epsilon(n)$ and $\lambda(n)$. In particular, $\lambda(n)$ needs to be sufficiently small relative to $\epsilon(n)$ in order for our derandomization approach to achieve containment in PPAD (described in Sect. 3.1, Theorem 3). At the same time $\lambda(n)$ needs to be large enough that we still have hardness for PPAD (Sect. 3.2, Theorem 4). Theorem 2 and Corollary 1 identify $\epsilon(n)$, $\lambda(n)$ for which both of these requirements hold.

2   Preliminaries

We use the following basic notation throughout.

- Boldface letters denote vectors; the symbol $\mathbf{a}$ is used to denote a pure profile, and $\mathbf{p}$ is used when the strategy profiles may be mixed.
- $[n]$ and $[m]$ denote the sets $\{1, \dots, n\}$ of players and $\{1, \dots, m\}$ of actions, respectively. Furthermore, $i \in [n]$ will always refer to a player, and $j \in [m]$ will always refer to an action.

2.1   Basic Game Theoretic and Complexity Concepts

We first introduce standard concepts of strategy profiles, payoffs, regret, and pure/mixed equilibria, followed by the complexity class PPAD. We mostly consider binary-action games (where $m = 2$) with actions labelled 1 and 2 (for more general results considering $m > 2$, see the discussion in Sect. 4).

Types of Strategy Profile

- A *pure* action profile $\mathbf{a} = (a_1, \dots, a_n) \in [m]^n$ is an assignment of one action to each player. We use $\mathbf{a}_{-i} = (a_1, \dots, a_{i-1}, a_{i+1}, \dots, a_n) \in [m]^{n-1}$ to denote the set of actions played by players in $[n] \setminus \{i\}$.
- A (possibly *mixed*) strategy profile $\mathbf{p} = (p_1, \dots, p_n) \in (\Delta([m]))^n$, where $\Delta([m])$ is the probability simplex over $[m]$. When $m = 2$, let p_i be the probability with which player i plays action 2. Generally $p_{i,j}$ is the probability that player i allocates to action j. The set of distributions for players in $[n] \setminus \{i\}$ is denoted $\mathbf{p}_{-i} = (p_1, \dots, p_{i-1}, p_{i+1}, \dots, p_n)$. When $\mathbf{p}$ contains just 0-1 values, $\mathbf{p}$ is equivalent to some action profile $\mathbf{a} \in [m]^n$.
- A random realization of a mixed strategy profile $\mathbf{p}$ is a pure strategy profile $\mathbf{a}$ such that, for every player i, $a_i = j$ with probability $p_{i,j}$.

Notation for Payoffs Given player i, action j, and pure action profile $\mathbf{a}$,

- $u_i(j, \mathbf{a}_{-i})$ is the payoff that player i obtains for playing action j when all other players play the actions given in $\mathbf{a}_{-i}$.
- $u_i(\mathbf{a}) = u_i(a_i, \mathbf{a}_{-i})$ is the payoff that player i obtains when all players play the actions given in $\mathbf{a}$.
- Similarly for mixed-strategy profiles: $u_i(j, \mathbf{p}_{-i}) = \mathbb{E}_{\mathbf{a}_{-i} \sim \mathbf{p}_{-i}}[u_i(j, \mathbf{a}_{-i})]$ and $u_i(\mathbf{p}) = \mathbb{E}_{\mathbf{a} \sim \mathbf{p}}[u_i(\mathbf{a})]$.

Solution Concepts

Definition 1 (Best Response). *Given a player i and a strategy profile $\mathbf{p}$, define the* best response

$$\mathrm{br}_i(\mathbf{p}) = \arg\max_{j\in[m]} u_i(j, \mathbf{p}_{-i}).$$

In addition, for $\epsilon > 0$, any action j' satisfying

$$u_i(\mathbf{p}) - u_i(j', \mathbf{p}_{-i}) \leq \epsilon$$

*is labelled an ϵ-*best response.

Definition 2 (Regret). *Given a player i and a strategy profile $\mathbf{p}$, define the* regret

$$\mathrm{reg}_i(\mathbf{p}) = \max_{j\in[m]} u_i(j, \mathbf{p}_{-i}) - u_i(\mathbf{p})$$

to be the difference between the payoffs of player i's best response to $\mathbf{p}_{-i}$ and i's strategy p_i.

Definition 3 (Equilibria). *We consider the following three types of Nash equilibrium:*

- *An ϵ-approximate Nash equilibrium (ϵ-ANE) is a strategy profile $\mathbf{p}^*$ such that, for every player $i \in [n]$, $\mathrm{reg}_i(\mathbf{p}^*) \leq \epsilon$.*
- *An ϵ-well supported Nash equilibrium (ϵ-WSNE) is an ϵ-ANE $\mathbf{p}^*$ for which every action j in the support of p_i^* is an ϵ-best response to $\mathbf{p}_{-i}^*$.*
- *An ϵ-approximate pure Nash equilibrium (ϵ-PNE) is a pure action profile $\mathbf{a}$ such that, for every player $i \in [n]$, $\mathrm{reg}_i(\mathbf{a}) \leq \epsilon$.*

The Complexity Class PPAD We assume the reader is familiar with the classes of problems P and NP and the concepts of asymptotic behavior (for an introduction to these concepts, see e.g. [1]). Below we provide the detailed definition of PPAD, introduced in [27].

PPAD is defined by a problem that is complete for the class, the END OF LINE problem.

Definition 4 (END OF LINE). *Define* END OF LINE *to be the problem taking as input a graph $G = (V, E)$, where the vertex set V is the exponentially-large set $\{0, 1\}^n$, and E is encoded by two circuits P and S, where G contains directed edge (u, v) if and only if $S(u) = v$ and $P(v) = u$. Every vertex has both in-degree and out-degree at most one, and $0^n \in V$ has indegree 0, outdegree 1. The problem is to output another vertex v with total degree 1.*

Definition 5 (PPAD). PPAD *is the set of problems many-one reducible to* END OF LINE *in polynomial time. A problem belonging to* PPAD *is* PPAD-*complete if* END OF LINE *reduces to that problem.*

Here we do not use END OF LINE directly; we reduce from another pre-existing PPAD-complete problem.

2.2 Lipschitz Polymatrix Games

In this section we define the classes of games we consider, followed by the associated problem we solve. We will first define binary-action Lipschitz games, before extending the definition to more actions.

Definition 6 (Lipschitz Games [2]**).** *For any value $\lambda \in (0,1]$, a binary-action λ-Lipschitz game is a game in which a change in strategy of any given player can affect the payoffs of any other player by at most an additive λ, i.e. for every player i and pair of action profiles $\mathbf{a}, \mathbf{a}'$ with $a_i = a_i'$,*

$$|u_i(\mathbf{a}) - u_i(\mathbf{a}')| \leq \lambda ||\mathbf{a}_{-i} - \mathbf{a}'_{-i}||_0$$

(equivalently, the ℓ_1 norm can be used, and is more relevant when it comes to mixed strategies). Note that, under the definition of payoffs to mixed strategies presented above, because mixed strategies of binary-action games are still represented as vectors (of scalars), this can be easily extended to mixed profiles $\mathbf{p}, \mathbf{p}'$ with $p_i = p_i'$:

$$|u_i(\mathbf{p}) - u_i(\mathbf{p}')| \leq \lambda ||\mathbf{p}_{-i} - \mathbf{p}'_{-i}||_1.$$

The above definition, while presented in a different way, is mathematically equivalent to that given by [2] (just provided here in a form more relevant to the current work).

In order to extend the definition above to $m > 2$ actions, we will require a measure of distance for probability distributions:

Definition 7 (Total Variation Distance). *The total variation distance between distributions $\mathcal{D}_1$ and $\mathcal{D}_2$ over discrete sample space $\mathcal{X}$ (each represented by m-dimensional vectors) is*

$$d_{\text{TV}}(\mathcal{D}_1, \mathcal{D}_2) = \frac{1}{2}||\mathcal{D}_1 - \mathcal{D}_2||_1 = \frac{1}{2} \sum_{x \in \mathcal{X}} \left| \Pr_{x' \sim \mathcal{D}_1}(x' = x) - \Pr_{x' \sim \mathcal{D}_2}(x' = x) \right|.$$

Definition 8. *For $m > 2$, the pure action definition remains the same as in the $m = 2$ case. However, now that mixed strategies are represented by vectors of distributions, the Lipschitz property becomes*

$$|u_i(\mathbf{p}) - u_i(\mathbf{p}')| \leq \lambda \sum_{i'=1}^{n} d_{\text{tv}}(p_{i'}, p'_{i'})$$

where d_{tv} is the total variation distance between two distributions (i.e. an extension of the ℓ_1 norm definition above).

Remark 1. We will rely on the total variation distance implicitly throughout the remainder of this work. It follows from Definition 8 that when a player i moves probability ρ from one action to another in a mixed strategy profile, every other player's payoffs may be affected by at most an additive $\lambda\rho$. In addition, because the payoff function u_i is λ-Lipschitz in this sense, the regret function reg_i is 2λ-Lipschitz in the same way, as the payoff of player i's best response can increase with a slope of at most λ while the payoff of player i's current strategy can decrease with a slope of at most λ.

Here, we define *polymatrix* games, introduced in [22]:

Definition 9 (Polymatrix Games). *A polymatrix game is an n-player, m-action game in which each pair of players i_1, i_2 plays a bimatrix game and receives as payoff the sum of their $n - 1$ payoffs from each separate bimatrix game. If player i_1 plays action j_1 and player i_2 plays action j_2, we denote the payoff to player i_1 from this bimatrix game as $\beta_{i_1, i_2, j_1, j_2}$.*

Note that, as defined, such a game is λ-Lipschitz for any

$$\lambda \geq \max_{i, i' \in [n], j, j_1', j_2' \in [m]} \left| \beta_{i, i', j, j_1'} - \beta_{i, i', j, j_2'} \right|.$$

At most $n^2 m^3$ queries to the payoff function are required to ensure this inequality holds. Furthermore, if i plays j, i's payoff is a linear function of the indicator variables of the other player-strategy pairs. $\beta_{i, i', j, j'}$ represents a small contribution, possibly negative, that i' makes to i (when i plays j) by playing j'. To be valid, all total payoffs must lie in $[0, 1]$, which can be checked from a game presented via the quantities $\beta_{i, i', j, j'}$ by performing the following additional checks for every $i \in [n], j \in [m]$:

$$\sum_{i' \neq i} \max_{j' \in [m]} \beta_{i, i', j, j'} \leq 1$$

$$\sum_{i' \neq i} \min_{j' \in [m]} \beta_{i, i', j, j'} \geq 0$$

There are $2\,nm$ such calculations, each of which requires $O(nm)$ operations, so an invalid game can be uncovered in polynomial time.

Remark 2. Lipschitz polymatrix games are a strict subset of Lipschitz games and require only $O(n^2 m^2)$ queries to learn completely and can thus be concisely represented in $O(n^2 m^2)$ space (by providing the value of each $\beta_{i_1, i_2, j_1, j_2}$).

We now define the main problem we consider in this work.

Definition 10. *Define (m, ϵ, λ)-PURELPG to be the problem of finding ϵ-PNEs of n-player, m-action, λ-Lipschitz polymatrix games, or alternatively finding a witness that the game is not λ-Lipschitz (note once more that m, ϵ, and λ are parameters of the problem while n is provided as input). Furthermore, define (m, ϵ, λ)-MIXEDLPG to be the equivalent problem for mixed equilibria.*

Remark 3. Note that, while we will often fix the number of actions m, both ϵ and λ are often functions of the number of players n. We generally think of these as being decreasing functions of n.

We are interested in the complexity of the problem, for various pairs of functions $\epsilon(n)$, $\lambda(n)$.

Remark 4. One basic observation we make is that, for any $a \in (0,1)$, (m, ϵ, λ)-PURELPG reduces to $(m, a\epsilon, a\lambda)$-PURELPG, by rescaling payoffs.

We extend the following result of [29] to pure equilibria in *Lipschitz* polymatrix games:

Theorem 1. ([29]). *There exists some constant $\epsilon > 0$ such that given a binary-action polymatrix game, finding an ϵ-ANE is PPAD-complete.*

3   Results

The result we achieve is as follows:

Theorem 2 (Main Result). *For every constant $m \geq 2$, there exists some constant $\epsilon > 0$ such that, for all functions $\lambda(n) = \Theta(n^{-3/4})$, (m, ϵ, λ)-PURELPG is PPAD-complete.*

In fact, for any constant $\alpha \in (\frac{2}{3}, 1)$, Theorem 2 holds for $\lambda(n) = \Theta(n^{-\alpha})$. In order to prove Theorem 2, we will need to show both containment in PPAD and PPAD-hardness under these settings of the parameters.

3.1   Containment in PPAD

Theorem 3. *For all functions $\epsilon(n), \lambda(n)$ satisfying*

$$\lambda(n) = \frac{1}{\text{poly}(n)}, \qquad \epsilon = \lambda(n)\omega(n^{2/3})$$

(m, ϵ, λ)-PURELPG $\in$ PPAD.

In particular, we prove this when $\epsilon(n) \geq 6\lambda(n)\sqrt[3]{n^2 m \log 3m}$. We will include the proof for $m = 2$ (see Sect. 4 for a discussion of the more general proof). The proof of this theorem is broken down further into two smaller steps, along the lines of [2]. First, we will exhibit sufficient settings of the parameters such that *mixed* approximate Nash equilibria of Lipschitz polymatrix games can be found in PPAD. Second, with the parameters set as in the statement of Theorem 3, we describe a derandomization technique for deriving a *pure* approximate equilibrium from the mixed one in polynomial time. More formally:

Lemma 1. *Whenever $\lambda(n) = \frac{1}{\text{poly}(n)}$, $(2, \frac{\lambda}{8}, \lambda)$-MIXEDLPG $\in$ PPAD.*

Proof (Sketch). As in the standard proof placing the problem of finding approximate Nash equilibria in PPAD (e.g. Theorem 3.1 of [9]), since ϵ is an inverse polynomial in n, the key requirement is the existence of an efficient deterministic algorithm answering mixed payoff queries. Because the payoffs to a player i in polymatrix games are linear in the actions of every other player, any mixed payoff query can be answered in time $O(n^2 m^2)$ (or simply $O(n^2)$ when keeping the number of actions fixed). Thus $(2, \frac{\lambda}{8}, \lambda(n))$-MIXEDLPG $\in$ PPAD. $\square$

Lemma 2. (Main Technical Lemma). *For functions $\epsilon(n), \lambda(n)$ satisfying $\epsilon(n) \geq \lambda \sqrt[3]{70n^2}$, an ϵ-PNE of an n-player, binary-action, λ-Lipschitz polymatrix game G can be derived from an $\frac{\lambda}{8}$-ANE of G in polynomial time.*

Proof. Throughout this proof we implicitly use the assumption that payoffs from mixed strategy profiles can be computed in polynomial time. We will consider the (signed) discrepancy

$$d_i(\mathbf{p}) = u_i(2, \mathbf{p}_{-i}) - u_i(1, \mathbf{p}_{-i})$$

(d_i is a 2λ-Lipschitz function via the same argument as Remark 1).

Take some $\frac{\lambda}{8}$-ANE $\mathbf{p}^*$ of G. The reduction is performed in three steps:

(1) Constructing from $\mathbf{p}^*$ a well-supported Nash equilibrium $\mathbf{p}^{(0)}$. This step is required because we will use a player's discrepancy as a linear proxy for regret, and general approximate equilibria may allow players to allocate small probabilities to bad actions, thus decoupling the two measures (in contrast with exact equilibria, in which any mixed strategy by definition implies no discrepancy between the actions). Well-supported equilibria do not suffer from this same decoupling.
(2) Iteratively converting $\mathbf{p}^{(0)}$ into a pure action profile $\mathbf{a}$ that is "close" to an equilibrium. To achieve this step, we will bound the rate at which the sum of all players' discrepancies is allowed to increase, ensuring that few players experience large regret.
(3) Correcting $\mathbf{a}$ to obtain an approximate pure equilibrium $\mathbf{a}^*$. Because of the guarantees from the previous step, we can achieve this by allowing every player with high regret to change to their best response.

Step 1: Mixed equilibrium to WSNE In this first step we construct WSNE $\mathbf{p}^{(0)}$ from $\mathbf{p}^*$. The idea here is to ensure that all players fall into one of the following two categories:

- Players with discrepancy that is small in absolute value
- Players playing pure strategies

In order to do this, consider any player i such that $|d_i(\mathbf{p}^*)| > \frac{\lambda}{2}\sqrt{n}$ (without loss of generality we can assume the discrepancy is negative, i.e. action 1 is significantly better). Then

$$\text{reg}_i(\mathbf{p}^*) = -p_i^* d_i > p_i^* \frac{\lambda}{2}\sqrt{n}$$

so, since $\mathbf{p}^*$ is an approximate equilibrium,

$$p_i^* < \frac{1}{4\sqrt{n}}.$$

If every such player (at most n) changes to playing their pure best response, then every player's discrepancy will increase by at most $2n\lambda p_i^*$ (recall that discrepancy is 2λ-Lipschitz), so in this new profile, no player playing a mixed strategy can experience discrepancy greater than

$$\frac{\lambda}{2}\sqrt{n} + 2n\lambda\frac{1}{4\sqrt{n}} = \lambda\sqrt{n}$$

while no player playing a pure strategy can experience regret greater than

$$0 + 2n\lambda\frac{1}{4\sqrt{n}} = \frac{\lambda}{2}\sqrt{n}.$$

Thus this new profile is a $\lambda\sqrt{n}$-WSNE, and for any player i playing a mixed strategy, $d_i(\mathbf{p}^*) \leq \lambda\sqrt{n}$. Call this $\lambda\sqrt{n}$-WSNE $\mathbf{p}^{(0)}$.

Step 2: WSNE to pure profile In this step, we iteratively define intermediate strategy profiles $\mathbf{p}^{(i)}$ and intermediate sets of players $S^{(i)}$ who have, at any point, experienced small discrepancy (defined below to ensure that players not in $S^{(i)}$ cannot have high regret in profile $\mathbf{p}^{(i)}$). Informally, for every player i, $\mathbf{p}^{(i)}$ is a strategy profile in which players $1, \ldots, i$ are playing pure strategies and players $i+1, \ldots, n$ may not be. Furthermore, the set $S^{(i)}$ is the set of players who, in at least one of the profiles $\mathbf{p}^{(0)}, \ldots, \mathbf{p}^{(i)}$ have experienced discrepancy at most $\lambda\sqrt{n}$. These will be iteratively computed to ultimately arrive at $\mathbf{a} = \mathbf{p}^{(n)}$: a pure action profile that is in some sense "close" to an approximate pure equilibrium.

Counterintuitively, this will not always involve assigning each player to play their best response. Instead, we will instruct each player to play the pure strategy that allows us to bound the effect on the other players. Roughly, we identify below a measure of badness C that is quadratic in the probability p assigned by a player to strategy 2 as opposed to strategy 1. In setting p to 0 or 1, we minimize the linear term in this measure, choosing 0 or 1 depending on the sign of the derivative with respect to p, and the measure increases by the relatively small second-order term.

More formally, take $\mathbf{p}^{(0)}$ as above and define

$$S^{(0)} = \{i' : |d_{i'}(\mathbf{p}^{(0)})| \leq \lambda\sqrt{n}\}$$

(i.e. a superset of the players playing mixed strategies in $\mathbf{p}^{(0)}$) while

$$S^{(i)} = S^{(i-1)} \cup \{i' : |d_{i'}(\mathbf{p}^{(i)})| \leq \lambda\sqrt{n}\}$$

(adding at each step the set of players playing pure strategies in $\mathbf{p}^{(0)}$ but experiencing small discrepancy for the first time at step i; note that, due to the Lipschitz property, no player's discrepancy can change sign without that player joining $S^{(i)}$, so any player not in $S^{(i)}$ must be playing their pure best response). Furthermore, define the sum of squared discrepancies cost function (which considers only the players in $S^{(i)}$):

$$C(\mathbf{p}^{(i)}) = \sum_{i' \in S^{(i)}} d_{i'}^2(\mathbf{p}^{(i)}).$$

Note that C only considers players in the set $S^{(i)}$, as it is meant to be a proxy for how far we are from equilibrium, and players in $[n] \setminus S^{(i)}$ have high discrepancies but are playing their best responses and hence should not contribute to this distance to equilibrium.

It is difficult to minimize C itself, and regardless C is already only a proxy for the true objective we must minimize to achieve an approximate pure equilibrium. However, since $d_{i'}$ is a multi-linear function (in fact, in the case of polymatrix games, linear), we can write

$$d_{i'}(\mathbf{p}^{(i)}) = c + \ell p_i$$

where c is some constant dependent only on $\mathbf{p}_{-i}^{(i)}$ and ℓ is a coefficient with absolute value at most 2λ (the Lipschitz parameter of $d_{i'}$). Squaring this, and keeping in mind that $\mathbf{p}_{-i}^{(i-1)} = \mathbf{p}_{-i}^{(i)}$, we can expand (for every $i' \in S^{(i-1)}$):

$$d_{i'}^2(\mathbf{p}^{(i)}) - d_{i'}^2(\mathbf{p}^{(i-1)}) = \alpha(p_i^{(i)} - p_i^{(i-1)}) + \ell^2((p_i^{(i)})^2 - (p_i^{(i-1)})^2)$$

for some value $\alpha_i = 2c\ell$ dependent only on $\mathbf{p}_{-i}^{(i)}$. Taking the sum over all players $i' \in S^{(i)}$, this yields

$$C(\mathbf{p}^{(i)}) - C(\mathbf{p}^{(i-1)}) = A(p_i^{(i)} - p_i^{(i-1)}) + \Lambda((p_i^{(i)})^2 - (p_i^{(i-1)})^2) + K_i$$

where

- A may be negative or non-negative.
- $\Lambda \leq 4\lambda^2 n$ (and obviously $(p_i^{(i)})^2 - (p_i^{(i-1)})^2 \leq 1$).
- K_i represents the one-time contribution of at most $\lambda^2 n$ each from any player in $S^{(i)} \setminus S^{(i-1)}$ whose discrepancy will be counted in this and all future costs. While we can't say anything about each individual K_i (since we don't know when exactly every player's discrepancy will dip to this level), we note that there are at most n such contributions of $\lambda^2 n$, i.e.:

$$\sum_{i \in [n]} K_i \leq \lambda^2 n^2$$

(this bound is the reason we needed to start from a WSNE).

If $p_i^{(i-1)} \in \{0, 1\}$, then set $\mathbf{p}^{(i)} = \mathbf{p}^{(i-1)}$ (if a player is already playing a pure strategy, we can avoid adding to C at all on their turn). Otherwise, since we can efficiently compute A and decide whether it is negative or not, we can select $p_i^{(i)}$ such that $A(p_i^{(i)} - p_i^{(i-1)}) \leq 0$ (one such option for $p_i^{(i)} \in \{0, 1\}$ must exist). This bounds

$$C(\mathbf{p}^{(i)}) - C(\mathbf{p}^{(i-1)}) \leq 4\lambda^2 n + K_i$$

and a quick induction achieves

$$C(\mathbf{p}^{(n)}) \leq 4\lambda^2 n^2 + \sum_{i \in [n]} K_i \leq 4\lambda^2 n^2 + \lambda^2 n^2 = 5\lambda^2 n^2.$$

Furthermore, $\mathbf{a} = \mathbf{p}^{(n)}$ is a pure action profile.

Step 3: Pure profile to pure equilibrium Here we distinguish between players in $S^{(n)}$ and players not in $S^{(n)}$.

The players not in $S^{(n)}$ must be playing their best response in $\mathbf{a}$. This is because they were playing their best response in $\mathbf{p}^{(0)}$, and their discrepancy never approached 0 or changed sign, so their best response must never have changed. In particular, therefore, none of these players suffer any regret.

We now consider the players in $S^{(n)}$. Note that we have bounded the sum of the squares of the discrepancies of the players in this set to be at most $5\lambda^2 n^2$. We can now also bound the number of players with regrets that are too high and fix them. To begin this final step, define $\delta = \lambda\sqrt[3]{20n^2}$ and consider the number of players $i \in S^{(n)}$ such that $d_i(\mathbf{a}) > \delta$. This will be at most $\frac{C(\mathbf{a})}{\delta^2}$. So have every player with *regret* at least δ in profile $\mathbf{a}$ (a subset of those with high *discrepancy*) simultaneously switch actions. Then, once more invoking Remark 1, the maximum regret any player (in $S^{(n)}$ or otherwise) can experience is

$$\delta + 2\lambda\frac{C(\mathbf{a})}{\delta^2} = \delta + \frac{10\lambda^3 n^2}{\delta^2} < \lambda\sqrt[3]{70n^2}.$$

In other words, the action profile $\mathbf{a}^*$ obtained after these players switch actions is a $\lambda\sqrt[3]{70n^2}$-PNE. This completes the proof of Lemma 2. □

Finally, because a violation of the Lipschitz property can be uncovered in a quick check before commencing the above algorithm simply by ensuring all the coefficients are smaller than λ, and [5] show that PPAD is closed under Turing reductions, Theorem 3 clearly follows from combining the two Lemmas above.

3.2   Hardness for PPAD

The Induced Population Game. This section introduces the approach that will be used to show PPAD-hardness. The technique involves artificially converting a general game into a Lipschitz game by treating every player i as instead a collection of many different players, each with a say in i's ultimate strategy. This reduction was used by [2] in an alternative proof of Nash's Theorem, and by [4] to upper bound the support size of ϵ-ANEs. More recently, [16] used a query-efficient version of this reduction to lower-bound the query complexity of computing ϵ-PNEs of general Lipschitz games.

Definition 11. *Given a game G with payoff function $\mathbf{u}$, we define the population game induced by G, $G' = g_G(L)$ with payoff function $\mathbf{u}'$ in which every player i is replaced by a population of L players (v_ℓ^i for $\ell \in [L]$), each playing G against the aggregate behavior of the other $n - 1$ populations. More precisely, for $\mathbf{p}'$ a mixed profile of G',*

$$u'_{v_\ell^i}(\mathbf{p}') = u_i\left(p'_{v_\ell^i}, \mathbf{P}_{-i}\right)$$

where

$$p_{i'} = \frac{1}{L} \sum_{\ell=1}^{L} p'_{v_\ell^{i'}}$$

for all $i' \neq i$.

Remark 5. Note that, regardless of the Lipschitz parameter of G, the induced population game $G' = g_G(L)$ is $\frac{1}{L}$-Lipschitz.

Population games date back even to Nash's thesis [25], in which he uses them to justify the consideration of mixed equilibria as a solution concept. To date, the reduction to the induced population game has been focused on proofs of existence. We show that the reduction can also be used to obtain the first PPAD-hardness result for a *pure* Nash equilibrium problem for a class of non-Bayesian games with discrete action spaces.

Remark 6. Note that any ϵ-PNE of $g_G(L)$ induces a $\frac{1}{L}$-uniform[2] ϵ-WSNE (and thus ϵ-ANE) of G in which each player in G plays the aggregate behavior of their population.

Proof of Hardness. In Theorem 4, we only consider binary-action games (clearly the hardness results can be extended to games with more actions).

Theorem 4. *There exists some constant $\epsilon > 0$ such that $(2, \epsilon, \epsilon n^{-4/5})$-PURELPG is PPAD-hard.*

Remark 7. While we show this Theorem for $\lambda = \epsilon n^{-4/5}$, the same proof holds for $\lambda = \epsilon n^{-\alpha}$ for any $\alpha \in (\frac{1}{2}, 1)$. Note that if $\alpha \leq \frac{1}{2}$ the pure equilibrium guarantee of [2] does not hold.

Proof. (Proof of Theorem 4). By Theorem 1, there is a constant $\epsilon > 0$ such that it is PPAD-hard to find ϵ-ANEs of polymatrix games (we may assume $\frac{1}{\epsilon} \in \mathbb{N}$). We reduce the problem of computing an ϵ-ANE of polymatrix game G to finding an ϵ-PNE of Lipschitz polymatrix game G' as follows. Consider the induced population game $G' = g_G(L)$ for $L = n^4/\epsilon^5$. This game has $N = (n/\epsilon)^5$ players and is $\epsilon N^{-4/5}$-Lipschitz. Thus (for large enough n) it is guaranteed to have an ϵ-PNE. Furthermore, G' is still a polymatrix game, as the payoff to any player v_ℓ^i is simply the sum of the payoffs from $N - L$ games played with the players $v_\ell^{i'}$ for $i' \neq i$.

Now, because the payoffs of any pure action profile of G' can be derived from payoffs of mixed strategy profiles of G (which can be computed in polynomial time), this entire reduction occurs in polynomial time. Thus there is a constant $\epsilon > 0$ such that, for $\lambda(n) = \epsilon n^{-4/5}$, $(2, \epsilon, \lambda)$-PURELPG is PPAD-hard. □

Combining Theorems 3 and 4 yields Theorem 2. In fact, by scaling the payoffs in Theorem 2 as described in Remark 4, we obtain:

---

[2] a k-uniform mixed strategy is one in which each action of each player is assigned a probability that is a discrete multiple of k.

Corollary 1. *Fix some constant* $\alpha \in \left(\frac{2}{3}, 1\right)$. *For any constant* $m \geq 2$, *non-increasing function* $\epsilon(n) = \frac{1}{poly(n)}$, *and* $\lambda(n) = \Theta(\epsilon n^{-\alpha})$, (m, ϵ, λ)-PURELPG *is* PPAD-*complete.*

4   Upper Bound for Additional Actions

Clearly increasing the number of actions does not affect the PPAD-hardness of this problem:

Lemma 3. (Extension of Lemma 1). *For any fixed* $m \geq 2, \lambda(n) = \frac{1}{poly(n)}$, $\left(m, \left(\frac{m-1}{m}\right)^2 \lambda, \lambda\right)$-MIXEDLPG $\in$ PPAD.

However, the proof of containment is made significantly more complex:

Lemma 4. (Extension of Lemma 2). *For functions* $\epsilon(n), \lambda(n)$ *satisfying*

$$\epsilon(n) \geq 6\lambda(n) \sqrt[3]{n^2 m \log 3m}$$

an $\epsilon(n)$-*PNE of an* n-*player,* m-*action,* λ-*Lipschitz polymatrix game* G *can be derived from an* $\left(\frac{m-1}{m}\right)^2 \lambda$-*ANE of* G *in polynomial time.*

The complete proof of Lemma 4 can be found in the full version of this paper. We present an abridged form below.

Proof (Sketch). Similar to the proof of Lemma 2, we will need to convert an approximate *mixed* equilibrium $\mathbf{p}^*$ to a *pure* one $\mathbf{a}^*$, and we will do so in the same three steps.

The primary generalization required is the transition from considering discrepancy to considering variance. Whereas in Lemma 2 there was a well-defined notion of discrepancy that, when squared, could be expressed as quadratic in the probabilities assigned to the actions of a given player, such a concept does not easily translate to games with more actions. In order to rely on similar techniques, we will instead consider the variance of *a subset of* each player's actions. The exact subset is described in [17], and throughout this proof sketch will be referred to as the "relevant" set, as it will contain the set of actions that may become relevant in our analysis of the algorithm.

In essence, player i's "relevant" set starts out containing the player's low-regret actions in $\mathbf{p}^*$ and gains actions that can be added to it at some point without decreasing the average payoff of the actions in the set. Fortunately, this has the effect of both including all the actions we might care to consider, and adding them in such a way that the variance remains under control.

Step 1: Mixed equilibrium to WSNE Taking

$$\epsilon_0 = \left(\frac{m-1}{m}\right)^2 \lambda, \qquad \epsilon_1 = 2\sqrt{2n\lambda\epsilon_0}$$

we can begin with an ϵ_0-ANE and convert it to an ϵ_1-WSNE as done in the proof of Lemma 2.

Step 2: WSNE to pure profile Here we define the concepts

Notation	Definition
$S_i^{(i')}$	Player i's **relevant set** of actions (defined below) after step i'
$m_i^{(i')}$	$\left\|S_i^{(i')}\right\|$, i.e. the number of relevant actions player i has after step i'
$\mathbf{u}_i(S, t)$	the length-$\|S\|$ restriction of player i's payoff vector after step t to the actions in set S
$\mu_i(S, t)$	the average value of $\mathbf{u}_i(S, t)$, i.e. the payoff to player i after step t for playing the uniform mixed strategy over all actions in player set S
$\sigma_i^2(S, t)$	the variance of the values in $\mathbf{u}_i(S, t)$
$\text{reg}_i(j, t)$	the regret player i experiences for playing action j after step t

where $S_i^{(i'+1)}$ is the superset of $S_i^{(i')}$ obtained by repeatedly adding player i's highest-paying action to $S_i^{(i'+1)}$ and recalculating the value of $\mu_i(S_i^{(i'+1)}, i'+1)$ until doing so would decrease its value. We split

$$\sum_{i=1}^{n} \sigma_i^2\left(S_i^{(n)}, n\right)$$
$\qquad$ Sum of variances of final relevant sets

$$= \sum_{i=1}^{n} \sigma_i^2\left(S_i^{(0)}, 0\right)$$
$\qquad$ Sum of variances of initial relevant sets

$$+ \sum_{i=1}^{n}\sum_{i'=1}^{n} \sigma_i^2\left(S_i^{(i')}, i'\right) - \sigma_i^2\left(S_i^{(i'-1)}, i'\right)$$
$\qquad$ Variance increase from adding to relevant set

$$+ \sum_{i=1}^{n}\sum_{i'=1}^{n} \sigma_i^2\left(S_i^{(i'-1)}, i'\right) - \sigma_i^2\left(S_i^{(i'-1)}, i'-1\right)$$
$\qquad$ Variance increase of actions in relevant set

and bound each of these three terms. This makes up the bulk of the proof, and results in an upper bound of

$$\sum_{i=1}^{n} \sigma_i^2\left(S_i^{(n)}, n\right) < 8n^2\lambda^2\log 3m.$$

Step 3: Pure profile to pure equilibrium The final step again follows along the lines of Lemma 2, allowing every player with large enough regret to change to their best response, we are able to complete the proof of Lemma 4.   □

5   Discussion

Our PPAD-hardness result is rather strongly negative, since Lipschitz polymatrix games are quite a restricted subset of either Lipschitz or polymatrix games in general. There may be scope to broaden the (ϵ, λ) values for which Lipschitz games are hard to solve. On the other hand, there are more positive results for computing approximate Nash equilibria of Lipschitz games, with further scope for progress.

In particular, Theorem 3 is unable to place the problem of finding ϵ-PNEs of λ-Lipschitz polymatrix games in PPAD for the total range of values guaranteed by [2] (while they guarantee existence for $\epsilon \geq \lambda\Omega(\sqrt{n \log n})$, the above successfully computes equilibria when $\epsilon \geq \lambda\Omega\left(n^{2/3}\right)$). It would be of future interest to determine if this is a characteristic of our choice of algorithm/analysis, or an indication of a barrier to the complete derandomization of computing these equilibria.

Furthermore, it may even be the case that Lipschitz *polymatrix* games, like anonymous Lipschitz games [11], guarantee pure equilibria for a smaller value of ϵ. It would be interesting to determine how close to a complete derandomization we are able to achieve. There are obvious obstacles to finding a deterministic lower bound asymptotically stronger than that of [2], as such a discovery would resolve the P vs. BPP question.

References

1. Arora, S., Barak, B.: Computational Complexity - A Modern Approach. Cambridge University Press, Cambridge (2009). http://www.cambridge.org/catalogue/catalogue.asp?isbn=9780521424264
2. Azrieli, Y., Shmaya, E.: Lipschitz games. Math. Oper. Res. **38**(2), 350–357 (2013). https://doi.org/10.1287/moor.1120.0557
3. Babichenko, Y.: Best-reply dynamics in large binary-choice anonymous games. Games Econ. Behav. **81**, 130–144 (2013). https://doi.org/10.1016/j.geb.2013.04.007
4. Babichenko, Y.: Small support equilibria in large games. CoRR abs/1305.2432 (2013). https://arxiv.org/abs/1305.2432
5. Buss, S.R., Johnson, A.S.: Propositional proofs and reductions between NP search problems. Ann. Pure Appl. Log. **163**(9), 1163–1182 (2012)
6. Cai, Y., Daskalakis, C.: On minmax theorems for multiplayer games. In: Randall, D. (ed.) Proceedings of the Twenty-Second Annual ACM-SIAM Symposium on Discrete Algorithms, SODA, pp. 217–234. SIAM (2011). https://doi.org/10.1137/1.9781611973082.20
7. Chen, X., Deng, X., Teng, S.: Settling the complexity of computing two-player Nash equilibria. J. ACM **56**(3), 14:1-14:57 (2009)
8. Cummings, R., Kearns, M., Roth, A., Wu, Z.S.: Privacy and truthful equilibrium selection for aggregate games. In: Markakis, E., Schäfer, G. (eds.) WINE 2015. LNCS, vol. 9470, pp. 286–299. Springer, Heidelberg (2015). https://doi.org/10.1007/978-3-662-48995-6_21
9. Daskalakis, C., Goldberg, P.W., Papadimitriou, C.H.: The complexity of computing a Nash equilibrium. Commun. ACM **52**(2), 89–97 (2009). https://doi.org/10.1145/1461928.1461951
10. Daskalakis, C., Papadimitriou, C.H.: Continuous local search. In: Randall, D. (ed.) Proceedings of the Twenty-Second Annual ACM-SIAM Symposium on Discrete Algorithms, SODA, pp. 790–804. SIAM (2011). https://doi.org/10.1137/1.9781611973082.62

11. Daskalakis, C., Papadimitriou, C.H.: Approximate Nash equilibria in anonymous games. J. Econ. Theor. **156**, 207–245 (2015)
12. Deb, J., Kalai, E.: Stability in large Bayesian games with heterogeneous players. J. Econ. Theor. **157**, 1041–1055 (2015)
13. Deligkas, A., Fearnley, J., Savani, R.: Tree Polymatrix Games are PPAD-hard. In: 47th International Colloquium on Automata, Languages, and Programming, ICALP. LIPIcs, vol. 168, pp. 38:1–38:14 (2020)
14. Deligkas, A., Fearnley, J., Savani, R., Spirakis, P.: Computing approximate Nash equilibria in polymatrix games. Algorithmica **77**(2), 487–514 (2015). https://doi. org/10.1007/s00453-015-0078-7
15. Filos-Ratsikas, A., Giannakopoulos, Y., Hollender, A., Lazos, P., Poças, D.: On the complexity of equilibrium computation in first-price auctions. In: EC 2021: The 22nd ACM Conference on Economics and Computation, pp. 454–476. ACM (2021)
16. Goldberg, P.W., Katzman, M.J.: Lower bounds for the query complexity of equilibria in Lipschitz games. In: Caragiannis, I., Hansen, K.A. (eds.) SAGT 2021. LNCS, vol. 12885, pp. 124–139. Springer, Cham (2021). https://doi.org/10.1007/ 978-3-030-85947-3_9
17. Goldberg, P.W., Katzman, M.J.: PPAD-complete pure approximate Nash equilibria in Lipschitz games (2022)
18. Goldberg, P.W., Marmolejo Cossío, F.J., Wu, Z.S.: Logarithmic query complexity for approximate Nash computation in large games. Theory Comput. Syst. **63**(1), 26–53 (2019)
19. Goldberg, P.W., Roth, A.: Bounds for the query complexity of approximate equilibria. ACM Trans. Economics and Comput. **4**(4), 24:1-24:25 (2016)
20. Goldberg, P.W., Turchetta, S.: Query complexity of approximate equilibria in anonymous games. J. Comput. Syst. Sci. **90**, 80–98 (2017)
21. Gradwohl, R., Reingold, O.: Fault tolerance in large games. Games Econ. Behav. **86**, 438–457 (2014)
22. Janovskaja, E.: Equilibrium points in polymatrix games. Lith. Math. J. **8**, 381–384 (1968). https://doi.org/10.15388/LMJ.1968.20224
23. Liu, Z., Li, J., Deng, X.: On the approximation of Nash equilibria in sparse win-lose multi-player games. In: Thirty-Fifth AAAI Conference on Artificial Intelligence, AAAI, pp. 5557–5565. AAAI Press (2021)
24. Megiddo, N., Papadimitriou, C.H.: On total functions, existence theorems and computational complexity. Theor. Comput. Sci. **81**(2), 317–324 (1991)
25. Nash, J.: Non-cooperative games. Ph.D. thesis, Princeton University (1950)
26. Nash, J.: Non-cooperative games. Ann. Math. **286–295**, 286–295 (1951)
27. Papadimitriou, C.H.: On the complexity of the parity argument and other inefficient proofs of existence. J. Comput. Syst. Sci. **48**(3), 498–532 (1994)
28. Papadimitriou, C.H., Peng, B.: Public goods games in directed networks. In: EC 2021: The 22nd ACM Conference on Economics and Computation, pp. 745–762. ACM (2021)
29. Rubinstein, A.: Inapproximability of Nash equilibrium. SIAM J. Comput. **47**(3), 917–959 (2018). https://doi.org/10.1137/15M1039274
30. Schoenebeck, G., Vadhan, S.P.: The computational complexity of Nash equilibria in concisely represented games. ACM Trans. Comput. Theory **4**(2), 4:1-4:50 (2012). https://doi.org/10.1145/2189778.2189779

Seniorities and Minimal Clearing
in Financial Network Games

Martin Hoefer🆔 and Lisa Wilhelmi$^{(\boxtimes)}$🆔

Institute for Computer Science, Goethe University Frankfurt,
Frankfurt/Main, Germany
{mhoefer,wilhelmi}@em.uni-frankfurt.de

Abstract. Financial network games model payment incentives in the
context of networked liabilities. In this paper, we advance the understanding of incentives in financial networks in two important directions:
minimal clearing (arising, e.g., as a result of sequential execution of payments) and seniorities (i.e., priorities over debt contracts).

We distinguish between priorities that are chosen endogenously or
exogenously. For endogenous priorities and standard (maximal) clearing, the games exhibit a coalitional form of weak acyclicity. A strong
equilibrium exists and can be reached after a polynomial number of
deviations. Moreover, there is a strong equilibrium that is optimal for
a wide variety of social welfare functions. In contrast, for minimal clearing there are games in which no optimal strategy profile exists, even for
standard utilitarian social welfare. Perhaps surprisingly, a strong equilibrium still exists and, for a wide range of strategies, can be reached after
a polynomial number of deviations. In contrast, for exogenous priorities,
equilibria can be absent and equilibrium existence is NP-hard to decide,
for both minimal and maximal clearing.

Keywords: Financial networks · Clearing problem · Equilibrium
computation

1 Introduction

The complex interconnections between financial institutions are a major source
of systemic risk in modern economies. This has become clear over the last decade
when the financial crisis unfolded. Ever since the crash of 2008, governments,
regulators, and financial institutions have been making unprecedented efforts to
maintain functioning and stability of the financial system (and more generally,
the global economy). Perhaps surprisingly, however, little is known about the
inherent challenges arising in this domain. What are sources of systemic risk
in financial networks? What is the (computational) complexity of the resulting decision and optimization problems? Questions of this type are not well-
understood, even in seemingly simple cases when the network is composed of

This research was supported by the Deutsche Forschungsgemeinschaft (DFG),
Grant/Award Numbers: 3831/7-1, 3831/6-1.

© The Author(s), under exclusive license to Springer Nature Switzerland AG 2022
P. Kanellopoulos et al. (Eds.): SAGT 2022, LNCS 13584, pp. 187–204, 2022.
https://doi.org/10.1007/978-3-031-15714-1_11

elementary debt contracts. Perhaps the most fundamental operation in these networks, and the basis for most analyses of systemic risk, is *clearing*, i.e., the settling of debt. Clearing is non-trivial in a network context because institutions typically depend on other institutions to satisfy their own obligations. Recent work in theoretical computer science has started to carve out interesting effects arising in this context [1, 12–15, 17–19]. Despite these advances, incentives and economic implications in the clearing process are not well-understood.

In the majority of the literature, clearing is interpreted as a mechanical process where payments are prescribed to banks by a central entity following a fixed set of rules (e.g., *proportional* payments w.r.t. amount of debt). In reality, however, financial institutions have to be expected to act strategically within the limits of their contractual and legal obligations. Therefore, in this paper, we consider financial network games (or *clearing games*) [1], a novel game-theoretic framework based on the classic network model by Eisenberg and Noe [4]. In these games, institutions strategically choose to allocate payments in order to clear as much of their debt as possible. We strive to understand the existence, structure and computational complexity of *stable payments*, i.e., Nash and strong equilibria. Our focus lies on two aspects that received little or no attention in the algorithmic literature so far: seniorities and minimal clearing.

The *seniority* of a debt contract is the priority that this contract enjoys in the payment order of the bank. When a bank has contracts of different seniority, it first needs to pay all debt of highest priority before spending money on obligations with lower priority. Clearing games with "endogenous" priorities, in which banks strategically choose the order of payment at the time of clearing, have been subject of interest very recently [1,9]. Arguably, however, in financial markets such priorities are often exogenous, i.e., determined in advance and not subject to strategic choice at the time of clearing. Exogenous priorities are considered regularly across the literature [3,7,10], but their impact on equilibria in clearing games has not yet been considered. We are interested in the effect of limiting the strategic interaction of banks with exogenous priorities (potentially with ties), which imply strategic choices constrained by the seniority structure.

Clearing states represent solutions of a fixed point problem. The classic network model with proportional payments [4] usually guarantees a *unique* clearing state – only a few cases allow multiple clearing states to exist. In that case, the network is assumed to settle on a maximum clearing state, in which as much of the debt as possible is paid [6,16]. This is justified when a central authority has structural insight into the network and the ability to steer the clearing process.

When banks choose payment functions strategically, the system allows multiple clearing states, and the choice of clearing state becomes significant. Moreover, an orchestrated clearing effort steering the process to a maximal fixed point is not immediately available, at least on a global scale, which can be seen by rather heterogeneous regulatory efforts to counter several financial crises over the last decade. Instead, clearing may occur in a decentralized, local, and sequential fashion, where institutions repay debt (partially) as soon as they have liquid assets available. In such an environment, clearing steers towards the *minimal* fixed point of the payment function [2]. Therefore, we focus on the *minimal clearing state*, i.e., the set of consistent payments that clear the least debt. The properties of minimal clearing are much less understood in the literature.

Results and Contribution. We analyze equilibrium existence and computational complexity of pure Nash equilibria in financial clearing games with different priority and clearing properties. We distinguish between exogenous (or *fixed*) and endogenous (or *non-fixed*) priorities. Priorities are captured as priority orderings, possibly with *thresholds* defining installments for each contract. This includes, as a special case, a priority *partition* of contracts, i.e., an ordering with ties in which debt contracts are being cleared. For strategic payments to contracts with the *same* priority, we consider a very general approach. We analyze both *minimal* as well as standard maximal clearing.

Formally, we define a framework of games based on a notion of so-called threshold-$\mathcal{M}$ strategies. The thresholds capture the priority structure. The set $\mathcal{M}$ specifies a set of functions for the payments to parts with the same priority. Most of our results apply to a very general set of threshold-$\mathcal{M}$ strategies for all suitable choices of $\mathcal{M}$, which is equivalent to all monotone payment strategies. Popular and natural choices for $\mathcal{M}$ are strategies resulting in proportional or ranking-based payments. We will use them for exposition throughout the paper.

After defining the model in Sect. 2, we consider non-fixed thresholds and maximal clearing. Recent work [1,9] proves non-existence and NP-hardness results for deciding existence of a Nash equilibrium. In contrast, we show in Sect. 3.1 that clearing games with threshold-$\mathcal{M}$ strategies have a coalitional form of weak acyclicity, for every suitable set $\mathcal{M}$. From every initial state, there is a sequence of coalitional deviations leading to a strong equilibrium. The sequence has length polynomial in the network size. In particular, every strategy profile with a Pareto-optimal clearing state is a strong equilibrium. This shows that the strong price of stability is 1 for many natural social welfare functions. This is a substantial extension of results [1] for edge-ranking strategies with thresholds.

For non-fixed thresholds and minimal clearing, all payments have to be traced back to initial (external) assets. Our first observation in Sect. 3.2 is that these games might not admit a socially optimal strategy profile, even for the arguably most basic notion of utilitarian social welfare. Maybe surprisingly, we prove existence of strong equilibria in games with threshold-$\mathcal{M}$ strategies and minimal clearing, for every suitable set $\mathcal{M}$. The games are coalitional weakly acyclic if the strategies satisfy a property we call *reduction consistency*. Then, from every initial state, there is a finite sequence of coalitional deviations leading to a strong equilibrium. The sequence has length polynomial in the network size.

Non-existence of social optima results from a compact set of strategies and a continuity problem. If we instead restrict attention to finite strategy sets (finitely many thresholds and finite $\mathcal{M}$), a social optimum trivially exists. However, we show that an optimal profile can be NP-hard to compute, even when a strong equilibrium can be obtained in polynomial time.

For fixed thresholds, we obtain a set of non-existence and NP-hardness results. They apply even when (1) some banks have fixed priorities in the form of partitions, (2) for every suitable strategy set $\mathcal{M}$, and (3) for both maximal and minimal clearing. In particular, for games with fixed thresholds it can be NP-hard to compute an optimal strategy profile, there exist games without a Nash equilibrium, and deciding existence of a Nash equilibrium can be NP-hard. Notably, the results do *not* follow directly from previous work in [1,9] – in previous constructions the decision about the correct *priorities* is the main problem.

Due to space restrictions, we omit some proofs and discussions and refer the ready to the full version [8].

Related Work. We build upon the network model for systemic risk by Eisenberg and Noe [4] to study properties of clearing states for proportional payments. This model has received significant attention in the literature over the last 20 years (see, e.g., [6,7,16] and references therein). Some recent additions to the literature include the effects of portfolio compression, when cyclic liabilities are removed from the network [17,20].

The Eisenberg-Noe model has been extended, e.g., by augmenting the model with credit-default swaps (CDS) [18,19]. Computational aspects of this model has attracted some interest recently, when banks can delete or add liabilities, donate to other banks, or change external assets [12]. The model also can give rise to standard game-theoretic scenarios such as Prisoner's Dilemma. Moreover, there has been interest in debt swapping among banks as an operation to influence the clearing properties [13].

We study seniorities and minimal clearing. For this model, an iterative algorithm that converges to a minimal clearing state is given in [11]. Similarly, decentralized processes that monotonically increase payments based on currently available funds converge to a minimal clearing state [2]. Somewhat related is work on sequential defaulting in [15], where a clearing state is computed by sequentially updating the recovery rate of banks. However, this process can converge to different clearing states depending on the order of updates. Properties of the Eisenberg-Noe model with proportional payments can be extended to liabilities with different seniorities in the sense of priority orderings over debt contracts [5]. Seniorities of this kind have been analyzed in several works, e.g., in [3,7,10]. Notably, all works discussed so far assume a mechanical clearing process, with the vast majority focusing on proportional payments.

Closely related to our work are recent game-theoretic approaches to clearing, where banks determine payments strategically. Financial network games without seniorities are proposed in [1], where the authors focus on ranking-based payment strategies, especially edge-ranking (priority order over debt contracts) and coin-ranking (priority order over single units of payment). Properties of clearing states in these games have also been analyzed (in a non-strategic context) in [2]. More recent work [9] extended the results to strategies that consist of a mixture of edge-ranking and proportional payments, and to networks with CDS.

2   Clearing Games

Clearing Games. A clearing game is defined as follows. The financial network is modeled as a directed graph $G = (V, E)$. Each node $v \in V$ is a financial institution, which we call a *bank*. Each directed edge $e = (u, v) \in E$ has an edge weight $c_e > 0$ and indicates that u owes v an amount of c_e. We denote the set of incoming and outgoing edges of v by $E^-(v) = \{(u, v) \in E\}$ and $E^+(v) = \{(v, u) \in E\}$, respectively. We use $c_v^+ = \sum_{e \in E^+(v)} c_e$ to denote the *total liabilities*, i.e., the total amount of money owed by v to other banks, and $c_v^- = \sum_{e \in E^+(v)} c_e$ to denote the total amount of money owed by other banks to v. Each bank v has *external assets* $b_v \geq 0$, which can be seen as an external inflow of money. To aid the study of computational complexity, we assume all numbers in the input, i.e., all b_v and c_e, are integer numbers in binary encoding.

Each bank v chooses a *strategy* $\mathbf{a}_v = (a_e)_{e \in E^+(v)}$, where $a_e : \mathbb{R} \to [0, c_e]$ is a payment function for edge e. Given any amount $y_v \in [b_v, b_v + c_v^-]$ of total assets (external b_v plus money incoming over E^-), bank v allocates a payment $a_e(y_v)$ to edge e. We follow [1] and assume the strategies fulfill several basic properties: (1) each $a_e(y_v)$ is monotone in y_v, (2) every bank spends all incoming money until all debt is paid, i.e., $\sum_{e \in E^+(v)} a_e(y_v) = \min\{y_v, c_v^+\}$, (3) no bank can generate additional money, i.e., $\sum_{e \in E^+(v)} a_e(y_v) \leq y_v$.

Given a strategy profile $\mathbf{a} = (\mathbf{a}_v)_{v \in V}$ of the game, we assume a money flow on each edge emerges. The above conditions (1)–(3) give rise to a set of fixed-point conditions, which can be satisfied by several possible flows. More formally, a *feasible flow* $\mathbf{f} = (f_e)_{e \in E}$ is such that $f_{(u,v)} = a_{(u,v)}(f_u)$ for every $(u, v) \in E$, where $f_v = b_v + \sum_{e \in E^-(v)} f_e$. The set of feasible flows for a strategy profile $\mathbf{a}$ forms a complete lattice [1,2]. The *clearing state* of $\mathbf{a}$ is the feasible flow realized in strategy profile $\mathbf{a}$. We are interested in games, where the clearing state is either the supremum (termed *max-clearing*) or the infimum (*min-clearing*).

Given a strategy profile $\mathbf{a}$ and the resulting clearing state $\mathbf{f}$, we assume that each bank v wants to maximize the total assets, i.e., the utility is $u_v(\mathbf{a}, \mathbf{f}) = u_v(\mathbf{f}) = b_v + \sum_{e \in E^-(v)} f_e$. Equivalently, each bank strives to maximize its equity, given by total assets minus total liabilities $b_v + \sum_{e \in E^-(v)} f_e - c_v^+$.

Previous work has focused on priority-based strategies such as coin- or edge-ranking [1] or a mix of edge-ranking and proportional payments [9]. In an *edge-ranking* strategy, each bank chooses a permutation π_v over all edges in $E^+(v)$. Money is used to pay towards edges in the order of π_v. Formally, number the edges of $E^+(v)$ such that $e_1 \succ_{\pi_v} e_2 \succ_{\pi_v} \ldots \succ_{\pi_v} e_{|E^+(v)|}$. v pays to e_1 until the payment is c_{e_1}, then to e_2 until the payment is c_{e_2}, then $\ldots$, or stops earlier if it runs out of funds.

Thresholds. Strategies with thresholds have been briefly touched upon in [1]. A threshold τ_e for edge e splits edge e into a high-priority installment e^h and a low-priority one e^l. The weights for these parts are $c_{e^h} = \tau_e$ and $c_{e^l} = c_e - \tau_e$. In the following, we assume that the two parts are each represented by an auxiliary edge where $e^{(1)}$ has weight $c_{e^{(1)}} = \tau_e$ and $e^{(2)}$ has weight $c_{e^{(2)}} = c_e - \tau_e$. Bank

v then first tries to pay the auxiliary edge $e^{(1)}$ representing the high-priority installment, for all edges e in $E^+(v)$, according to some monotone strategy. Once these are fully paid, the low-priority auxiliary edges $e^{(2)}$ are paid according to some (potentially different) monotone strategy with the remaining funds.

Towards multiple thresholds $\tau_e^{(i)}$ per edge, bank v first pays auxiliary edge $e^{(1)}$ of all edges in $E^+(v)$ using a monotone strategy $\mathbf{a}_v^{(1)}$. Once these are fully paid, it uses a monotone strategy $\mathbf{a}_v^{(2)}$ to pay the auxiliary edges $e^{(2)}$, and so on, until all auxiliary edges are paid or v runs out of funds. By assumption, at least one suitable choice exists for $\mathbf{a}_v^{(i)}$, for every possible threshold vector.

Let us formally define general classes of threshold-based strategies. A *suitable* set $\mathcal{M}$ of monotone strategies contains, for every vector $\boldsymbol{\tau}_v = (\tau_e)_{e \in E^+(v)}$ of thresholds with $\tau_e \in [0, c_e]$, at least one strategy $\mathbf{a} \in \mathcal{M}$ with $a_e(T_v) = \tau_e$ for every $e \in E^+(v)$, where $T_v = \sum_{e \in E^+(v)} \tau_e$. For any integer $k \geq 2$, a *threshold-$\mathcal{M}$ strategy* $(\boldsymbol{\tau}_v^{(1)}, \ldots, \boldsymbol{\tau}_v^{(k-1)}, \mathbf{a}_v^{(1)}, \ldots, \mathbf{a}_v^{(k)})$ is given by (1) $k-1$ vectors of thresholds $\boldsymbol{\tau}_v^{(i)} = (\tau_e^{(i)})_{e \in E^+(v)}$ with $\tau_e^{(i)} \in [0, c_e]$ and $\tau_e^{(i)} \geq \tau_e^{(i-1)}$, for all $i = 1, \ldots, k-1$ and all $e \in E^+(v)$, and (2) k monotone strategies $\mathbf{a}_v^{(i)} \in \mathcal{M}$, for $i = 1, \ldots, k$. Thresholds $\tau_e^{(i)}$ split edge e into k auxiliary edges $e^{(i)}$ with $c_{e^{(i)}} = \tau_e^{(i)} - \tau_e^{(i-1)}$, for $i = 1, \ldots, k$, where we assume $\tau_e^{(0)} = 0$ and $\tau_e^{(k)} = c_e$.

Formally, let $T_v^{(i)} = \sum_{e \in E^+(v)} \tau_e^{(i)}$, i.e., the sum of weights of all edges $e^{(1)}$ to $e^{(i)}$, and $t_v^{(i)} = \sum_{e \in E^+(v)} c_{e^{(i)}} = T_v^{(i)} - T_v^{(i-1)}$, i.e., the sum of weights of all $e^{(i)}$ The monotone strategy $\mathbf{a}_v^{(i)} \in \mathcal{M}$ satisfies $a_e^{(i)}(0) = 0$ and $a_e^{(i)}(t_v^{(i)}) = \tau_e^{(i)} - \tau_e^{(i-1)} = c_{e^{(i)}}$ for all $e \in E^+(v)$. The total payment to edge e in the threshold-$\mathcal{M}$ strategy is then $a_e(x) = \sum_{i=1}^k a_e^{(i)}(\min\{x - T_v^{(i-1)}, t_v^{(i)}\}) = \tau_e^{(i')} + a_e^{(i'+1)}(x - T_v^{(i')})$, where $i' = \arg\max_{i<k}\{T_v^i \leq x\}$.

Examples. We discuss several natural examples for $\mathcal{M}$. A *threshold edge-ranking strategy* $\mathbf{tr}_v = ((\boldsymbol{\tau}_v^{(i)})_{i \in [k-1]}, (\pi_v^{(j)})_{j \in [k]})$ is a threshold-$\mathcal{M}$ strategy, where $\mathcal{M}$ encompasses all edge-ranking strategies. Here $\pi_v^{(j)}$ are permutations over $e^{(j)}$ for all edges e in $E^+(v)$. Bank v pays first towards each auxiliary edge $e^{(1)}$, in the order of the ranking $\pi_v^{(1)}$, until the payment to the edge reaches $c_{e^{(1)}}$ (or it runs out of funds). Once it pays $c_{e^{(1)}}$ to every edge, it uses additional money to increase the payment on $e^{(2)}$ to $c_{e^{(2)}}$, in the order of $\pi_v^{(2)}$ (or stops upon running out of funds), and so on.

Threshold edge-ranking strategies are a significant generalization of edge-ranking strategies. In particular, we show below that clearing games with threshold edge-ranking strategies always have strong equilibria, while for edge-ranking strategies even pure Nash equilibria can be absent [1].

In a *threshold proportional* strategy $\mathbf{tp}_v = ((\boldsymbol{\tau}_v^{(i)})_{i \in [k-1]}, (\mathbf{a}_v^{(j)})_{j \in [k]})$, the set $\mathcal{M}$ encompasses all proportional payment strategies. Bank v pays the marginal debt on auxiliary edges $e^{(i)}$ of class i using proportional payments in this class:

$$a_e^{(j)}(x) = x \cdot \frac{c_{e^{(j)}}}{\sum_{e \in E^+(v)} c_{e^{(j)}}} = x \cdot \frac{\tau_e^{(j)} - \tau_e^{(j-1)}}{t_v^{(j)}} \ ,$$

in the order of $j = 1, \ldots, k$. Fixing any set of thresholds $(\tau_v^{(i)})_{i \in [k-1]}$, proportional strategies $\mathbf{a}_v^{(j)} \in \mathcal{M}$ are uniquely determined for every $j = 1, \ldots, k$ (while for edge-ranking strategies there are $(E^+(v))!$ many choices for each $\mathbf{a}_v^{(j)}$).

Thresholds and Partitions. An interesting special case of a threshold-$\mathcal{M}$ strategy is a *partition*-$\mathcal{M}$ strategy, in which all thresholds are $\tau_e^{(i)} \in \{0, c_e\}$. Then each auxiliary edge has weight $c_{e^{(i)}} \in \{0, c_e\}$. The result is a partition ranking over the contracts, where for partition $E^{(i)}$ of priority i we make payments based on the strategy $a_v^{(i)}$. Conversely, every threshold-$\mathcal{M}$ strategy $(\tau_v^{(1)}, \ldots, \tau_v^{(k-1)}, \mathbf{a}_v^{(1)}, \ldots, \mathbf{a}_v^{(k)})$ can be interpreted as a partition-$\mathcal{M}$ strategy over auxiliary edges $e^{(i)}$ for all $e \in E^+(v)$.

Observation 1. *Every threshold-$\mathcal{M}$ strategy can be interpreted as a partition-$\mathcal{M}$ strategy where each edge $e \in E^+(v)$ is replaced by k auxiliary edges.*

Let us illustrate the relationship between strategy profiles and the associated clearing states. For simplicity, we assume edge-ranking strategy profiles (where all thresholds $\tau_e = c_e$). The following example builds an intuition for the differences between minimal and maximal clearing states of a given strategy profile. Further, it illustrates the great benefit that the players derive from collaboration.

Example 1. Consider the game depicted in Fig. 4a. Note that the behavior of players v_3, v_4 and v_5 is fully predetermined, since they either have no liabilities or pay all assets towards their single outgoing edge. Hence, it is sufficient to focus on the (non-trivial) strategy choices of players v_1 and v_2. In Fig. 1b and 1c we show the resulting maximal and minimal clearing states for all four strategy profiles, depending on the edge rankings chosen by v_1 and v_2. In the following, we discuss the clearing states for two profiles.

Consider strategy profile $\mathbf{a}$ (depicted as the second from the left in Fig. 1), where player v_1 first fully pays off edge (v_1, v_4) and afterwards (v_1, v_2), whereas player v_2 completely pays off edge (v_2, v_3) before paying edge (v_2, v_5). Formally, the strategies are $\pi_{v_1}^{(1)} = ((v_1, v_4), (v_1, v_2))$ and $\pi_{v_2}^{(1)} = ((v_2, v_3), (v_2, v_5))$. Each player v_i, for $i \in \{1, 2\}$, directs all payments towards her highest-ranked edge until all debt is settled. All remaining money is used to pay off the other edge. Let us first consider the resulting minimal clearing state. Player v_1 holds external assets of 1 and is obligated to spend these. By her strategy choice, she just pays off her debt of 1 towards v_4. The resulting payments satisfy all fixed-point conditions and represent the minimal clearing state for $\mathbf{a}$. To construct the maximal clearing state, we examine if there are higher feasible payments. Note that players v_1, v_2 and v_3 with edges $(v_1, v_2), (v_2, v_3)$ and (v_3, v_1) form a cycle in terms of the (most preferred) payments. Suppose the payment along the cycle is increased by 1. The fixed-point conditions remain satisfied. It is easy to see that no larger feasible payments can exist. The maximal clearing state is attained.

Now consider the second strategy profile $\mathbf{a}'$ (depicted as the third from the left in Fig. 1), where the order of payments is reversed for both players. Here the strategies are $\pi_{v_1}^{(1)} = ((v_1, v_2), (v_1, v_4))$ and $\pi_{v_2}^{(1)} = ((v_2, v_5), (v_2, v_3))$. In this

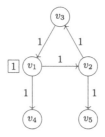

(a) Game of Example 1. v_1 has external assets of 1, all edges have a weight of 1.

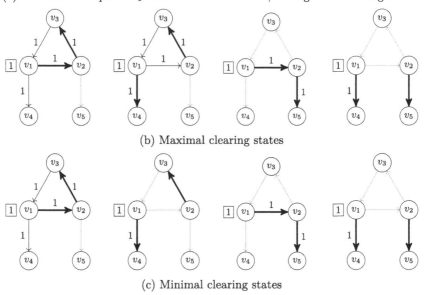

(b) Maximal clearing states

(c) Minimal clearing states

Fig. 1. Image (a) depicts a clearing game whereas images in (b) and (c) represent the maximal and minimal clearing states resulting from all four edge-ranking strategy profiles. Edge labels denote flows over the edge, there is no flow on edges without labels. Thick edges indicate the preferred outgoing edge in the strategy of the node.

case, v_1 pays off her liabilities towards v_2 using her external assets, whereupon v_2 passes the incoming payments on to the sink v_5. Again, the resulting payments are feasible and form the minimal clearing state. In contrast to **a**, for **a'** the clearing state is unique, i.e., the minimal clearing state equals the maximal clearing state. To observe this, consider the cycle including v_1, v_2 and v_3. The edge (v_1, v_2) is already fully saturated and, hence, payments along the cycle cannot by increased. Instead, player v_1 would pass all additional incoming payments to v_4, which excludes the possibility of a feasible increase of payments. ∎

3   Clearing Games with Seniorities

3.1   Max-Clearing

In this section, we consider computational problems in clearing games with max-clearing. Subclasses of our games have been studied in the literature before. In particular, for edge-ranking strategies, non-existence of Nash equilibrium and NP-hardness of deciding equilibrium existence follow directly from [1]. Similar results can be shown for proportional strategies when thresholds are $\tau_e^{(i)} \in \{0, c_e\}$, i.e., for *partition* proportional strategies considered in [9]. We instead focus on threshold variants and start with an observation about the clearing state.

Proposition 1. *A maximum clearing state can be computed in polynomial time for games with threshold edge-ranking or threshold proportional strategies.*

Given a strategy profile $\mathbf{a}$ and the corresponding clearing state $\mathbf{f}$, consider a set $C \subseteq V$ of players and a deviation $\mathbf{a}'_C = (\mathbf{a}'_v)_{v \in C}$. Let $\mathbf{a}' = (\mathbf{a}'_C, \mathbf{a}_{-C})$ be the resulting strategy profile after deviation, and let $\mathbf{f}'$ be the clearing state. The pair $(\mathbf{a}, \mathbf{a}')$ is a *coalitional improvement step* if $u_v(\mathbf{a}', \mathbf{f}') > u_v(\mathbf{a}, \mathbf{f})$ for all $v \in C$, i.e., every player strictly improves her utility upon deviation. Furthermore, a strategy profile $\mathbf{a}$ with corresponding clearing state $\mathbf{f}$ forms a *strong equilibrium*, if there exists *no coalitional improvement step* $(\mathbf{a}, \mathbf{a}')$, for any coalition $C \subseteq V$.

For the main result in this section, we show that for every game with threshold-$\mathcal{M}$ strategies and every initial strategy profile, there is a sequence of coalitional improvement steps ending in a strong equilibrium. We term this property *coalitional weakly acyclic*.

Theorem 2. *Every max-clearing game with threshold-$\mathcal{M}$ strategies is coalitional weakly acyclic. For every initial strategy profile, there is a sequence of coalitional improvement steps that ends in a strong equilibrium. The sequence requires a number of steps that is polynomial in $|E|$.*

Consider any *flow-monotone* welfare function $z(\mathbf{f})$ for the set of banks (for a formal definition see [8]). For every such objective function, we can show that an optimal strong equilibrium exists, i.e., the *strong price of stability* is 1. Moreover, there is an optimal strong equilibrium with a consistency property.

Corollary 1. *In every max-clearing game with threshold-$\mathcal{M}$ strategies, the strong price of stability is 1 for every flow-monotone welfare function. There is an optimal strong equilibrium with the same clearing state for every choice of $\mathcal{M}$.*

3.2   Min-Clearing

Let us turn to games with min-clearing. In a minimal clearing state, all flow is initiated by external assets. In particular, consider an iterative process where

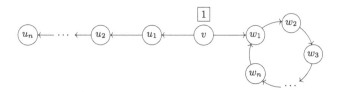

Fig. 2. A min-clearing game without a social optimum for utilitarian social welfare, for all threshold-$\mathcal{M}$ strategies. All edges have unit weight and the external assets of v are $b_v = 1$.

players initially pay off debt only utilizing their external assets. This creates an initial flow. Then, in the next round, players may use additional incoming assets to pay off further debt, and so on. For a given strategy profile, the iteration of this process will monotonically increase the flow towards a minimal clearing state (see also [2] for more formal arguments of this fact). Indeed, this idea can be applied in a structured fashion for threshold edge-ranking games to compute a minimal clearing state in polynomial time.

Proposition 2. *A minimal clearing state can be computed in polynomial time for games with threshold edge-ranking strategies.*

In contrast, observations in [11, Chapter 3] suggest that the minimal clearing state for proportional payments can not be computed with a bounded number of steps, even without thresholds (or $\tau_e^{(i)} = c_e$ for all $i \le k$). Furthermore, the non-existence of pure Nash equilibria for partition edge-ranking and proportional strategies shown in [1, Proposition 13] and [9, Theorem 4] transfers to min-clearing – it can be verified that there are *unique* feasible flows for any strategy profile arising in the games without pure equilibria.

We first observe that Corollary 1 cannot be extended to min-clearing games. The main problem is that there might be no social optimum, even for utilitarian social welfare $z(\mathbf{f}) = \sum_{v \in V} u_v(\mathbf{a}, \mathbf{f})$.

Example 2. Consider threshold-$\mathcal{M}$ strategies in the game depicted in Fig. 2, for any suitable set $\mathcal{M}$. Player v is the only player with a non-trivial strategy choice. Also v is the only player with external assets and, hence, all money flow must be originated by v. We, therefore, want to find a strategy for v that maximizes social welfare. If v pays all external assets either towards u_1 or w_1, the social welfare is $1 + n$ in both cases. Now assume v splits assets and picks a strategy with threshold ϵ on (v, w_1) and $1 - \epsilon$ on (v, u_1). Then payments correspond to thresholds. The payment of ϵ is repeatedly passed through the cycle until all players w_i have completely paid off their liabilities. The payment of $1 - \epsilon$ is passed on along the path to u_n. The social welfare $1 + n + \epsilon + n \cdot (1 - \epsilon) = 1 + 2n - \epsilon \cdot (n - 1)$ is monotonically increasing when $\epsilon \to 0$. However, at $\epsilon = 0$ no flow is initiated on the cycle, and the social welfare drops to $1 + n$. Consequently, there is no social optimum for this instance. ∎

Interestingly, we can obtain positive results towards existence of strong equilibria. With min-clearing, observe that a profitable coalitional improvement step $(\mathbf{a}, \mathbf{a}')$ requires at least one player $v \in C$ with strictly positive assets with respect to $\mathbf{a}$. Otherwise, due to min-clearing, no flow among the agents in C can evolve.

Lemma 1. *Every strategy profile in a min-clearing game with Pareto-optimal clearing state is a strong equilibrium.*

For a wide range of strategies, we can extend our result and show that, for every initial strategy profile, there exists a sequence of coalitional improvement steps that end in a strong equilibrium. We consider games in which the set of strategies $\mathcal{M}$ has a consistency property. Consider a strategy $\mathbf{a}_v \in \mathcal{M}$ for a player v. Suppose we reduce all thresholds to $\hat{\tau}_e = a_e(x)$ for each $e \in E^+(v)$ and some value $0 \le x \le T_v = \sum_{e \in E^+(v)} \tau_e$. Then there should be another strategy $\hat{\mathbf{a}}_v \in \mathcal{M}$ such that $\hat{\mathbf{a}}$ results in assignments for each $y \le x$ that are consistent with $\mathbf{a}$. For a formal definition see [8].

For every game with such strategies, we construct sequences of coalitional improvement steps similar to max-clearing by increasing the flow along a cycle. However, the proof construction for max-clearing (see Lemma 6 in [8]) does not directly apply. Intuitively, when changing the strategies along a cycle, too much flow could end up being assigned to edges outside the cycle, and hence the intended flow along the cycle is not obtained in a minimal clearing state.

Theorem 3. *Every min-clearing game with reduction consistent threshold-$\mathcal{M}$ strategies is coalitional weakly acyclic. For every initial strategy profile, there is a sequence of coalitional improvement steps that ends in a strong equilibrium. The sequence requires a number of steps that is polynomial in $|E|$.*

Proof. Existence of a strong equilibrium follows by Lemma 1. It remains to show that for any profile $\mathbf{a}$ with clearing state $\mathbf{f}$ which is not Pareto-optimal there is a coalitional improvement step $(\mathbf{a}, \mathbf{a}')$ such that (1) the clearing state $\mathbf{f}'$ in $\mathbf{a}'$ Pareto-dominates $\mathbf{f}$ and (2) $\mathbf{f}'$ saturates at least one more edge than $\mathbf{f}$.

Given strategy profile $\mathbf{a}$, consider clearing state $\mathbf{f}$. By assumption, there is another strategy profile $\tilde{\mathbf{a}}$ with minimal clearing state $\tilde{\mathbf{f}}$ that Pareto dominates $\mathbf{f}$. Since all feasible flows in clearing games can be interpreted as circulation flows [1, Proposition 2], the difference $\delta_e = \tilde{f}_e - f_e \ge 0$ is again a (non-zero) circulation flow. Consider the set of edges with circulation flow $E_{>0} = \{e \in E \mid \delta_e > 0\}$ and the set of incident nodes $V_{\ge 0} = \{u, v \in V \mid e = (u, v) \in E_{>0}\}$. There must be at least one node $v^* \in V_{>0}$ such that $u_{v^*}(\tilde{\mathbf{a}}, \tilde{\mathbf{f}}) > \sum_{e \in E^+(v^*)} \delta_e$. Otherwise, $\tilde{f}_e = \delta_e$ for all $e \in E_{>0}$, and we could obtain a smaller clearing state in $\tilde{\mathbf{a}}$ setting $\tilde{f}_e = 0$ for all $e \in E_{\ge 0}$. Note that node v^* must have $u_{v^*}(\mathbf{a}, \mathbf{f}) = u_{v^*}(\tilde{\mathbf{a}}, \tilde{\mathbf{f}}) - \sum_{e \in E^+(v^*)} \delta_e > 0$. As such, $\mathbf{f}$ must admit a cycle K such that $f_e < c_e$ for all $e \in E(K)$ and K contains node v^* with $u_{v^*}(\mathbf{a}, \mathbf{f}) > 0$.

We construct a coalitional improvement step as follows. First, compute the set $A = \{v_i \in V \mid u_{v_i}(\mathbf{a}, \mathbf{f}) > 0\}$ of players with strictly positive utility. Next, choose a node $v_i \in A$ and determine all simple cycles containing v_i via depth-first search over the set $E' = \{e \in E \mid f_e < c_e\}$ of non-saturated edges. If no cycle containing v_i is found[1], proceed to the next player from A. Otherwise, let K' denote any one of the cycles found. We first perform an intermediate step for all players v in $V(K')$, and determine the highest index l such that $f_e \leq \tau_e^{(l)}$, for every outgoing edge $e \in E^+(v)$. Then, all players $v \in V(K')$ deviate to a threshold-$\mathcal{M}$ strategy with thresholds $\hat{\tau}_e^{(i)} = \tau_e^{(i)}$, for $i < l$ and $\hat{\tau}_e^{(l)} = f_e$, for all $e \in E^+(v)$. Choose all strategies $\hat{\mathbf{a}}_v^{(1)}, \hat{\mathbf{a}}_v^{(2)}, \ldots, \hat{\mathbf{a}}_v^{(l+1)} \in \mathcal{M}$ such that the resulting flow $\hat{f}_e$ equals the initial flow f_e for each edge. Because all strategies $\mathbf{a}_v$ are reduction consistent there exists at least one such strategy. We now modify the strategy $\hat{\mathbf{a}}$ to increase circulation on K'. Let $\delta = \min_{e \in E(K')} c_e - \hat{f}_e$ be the minimal residual capacity of all edges in the cycle. For every $v_j \in V(K')$ and edge $e_j \in E(K')$, For every edge $e_j \in E(K')$ in the cycle, define the thresholds as $\hat{\tau}_{e_j}^{(l+1)} = \hat{\tau}_{e_j}^{(l)} + \delta$ for $l > 0$ and $\hat{\tau}_{e_j}^{(1)} = \delta$. Regarding all other edges $e' \in E^+(v_j) \backslash \{e_j\}$, we set $\hat{\tau}_{e'}^{(l+1)} = \hat{\tau}_{e'}^{(l)}$ for $l > 0$ and $\hat{\tau}_{e'}^{(1)} = 0$. Further, define $\hat{\mathbf{a}}_e^{(l+1)} = \hat{\mathbf{a}}_e^{(l)}$ and arbitrarily choose $\hat{\mathbf{a}}_e^{(1)}$ for all $e \in E^+(v_j)$. Let $\mathbf{a}'$ denote the resulting strategy profile. Clearly, every player $v_i \in A$ still has strictly positive assets with respect to $\mathbf{a}'$. Thus, at least one player $v_j \in V(K')$ initiates flow on cycle K'. By construction of the first vector of thresholds $\tau_v^{(1)}$, the flow on K' is first raised to δ. Afterwards, each player has the same assets available as with respect to $\mathbf{a}$. From the next step on, players distribute their payments exactly as before for $\mathbf{a}$. Since $\delta > 0$, all players in the cycle strictly profit from the deviation while the flow on all other edges remains unchanged. Moreover, the pair $(\mathbf{a}'_{V(K')}, \mathbf{a}_{-V(K')})$ forms a coalitional improvement step for coalition $V(K')$.   □

The improvement step saturates one more edge in the clearing state. Hence, any sequence of such steps is limited in length by $|E|$. Note that each improvement step adds one vector of thresholds to the strategy of every player. In contrast, for max-clearing games the strong equilibrium can be obtained using only a single set of thresholds for each player. It is an interesting open problem if a similar property can be shown for min-clearing games with reduction consistent strategies. Moreover, it is unclear whether a sequence of improvement steps ending in a strong equilibrium exists for strategies without said property.

The sequence of coalitional improvement steps to a strong equilibrium can even be performed for threshold proportional strategies, when given an initial profile *along with its minimal clearing state*. For constructing the improvement step, it is sufficient to recognize whether there is a non-saturated cycle with at least one player having strictly positive assets. We obtain $\mathbf{a}'$ as described above, and we obtain the minimal clearing state of $\mathbf{a}'$ adaptively by increasing the flow along the cycle until the first edge becomes saturated.

The non-existence of a social optimum in Example 2 arises from a continuity problem. For every flow f_e on edge $e = (v, w_1)$ there exists some flow $\mathbf{f}'$ with $f'_e < f_e$ and strictly higher welfare. A simple way to resolve this problem is to restrict attention to a finite set of strategies for each player, i.e., a finite set

---

[1] At least one cycle must exist for at least one $v_i \in A$ by the discussion above.

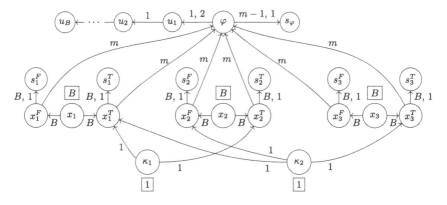

Fig. 3. Example construction of a game in the proof of Theorem 5. Black edge labels indicate edge weights while blue labels indicate seniorities. (Color figure online)

of possible threshold vectors and a finite set $\mathcal{M}$ of strategies for same-priority installments. Then, an optimal strategy profile always exists. A natural example enjoying this discretization are *coin-ranking* strategies studied in [1], where flow is split into "coins", i.e., units of 1. Considering min-clearing games with coin-ranking strategies, strong equilibria exist and can be computed efficiently (for a detailed discussion see [8]) whereas computing optimal strategy profiles with respect to social welfare is NP-hard.

Theorem 4. *For min-clearing games with threshold edge-ranking strategies and unit thresholds, it is* NP*-hard to compute a strategy profile that maximizes utilitarian social welfare.*

4   Clearing Games with Fixed Seniorities

In this section, we consider clearing games with fixed seniorities, i.e., when thresholds are fixed exogenously. In this case, a player with fixed thresholds is only allowed to choose appropriate strategies $a_e^{(i)}$. We will concentrate on the simpler case of fixed *partition* strategies. A bank with a fixed partition strategy is obligated to pay debt of edges completely in a given order with ties. A strategic choice arises only in case of ties, i.e., for edges of the same priority, where the bank can strategically choose $a_e^{(i)}$ to pay for the edges with seniority i.

In the remainder of this section, we consider games in which some agents have fixed partition-$\mathcal{M}$ strategies, while others are free to choose threshold-$\mathcal{M}$ strategies, for any suitable set $\mathcal{M}$. For the fixed partitions, we specify the priority class of an edge. Our results imply that the positive properties for threshold-$\mathcal{M}$ strategies do not persist if partitions are fixed for some players. Notably, these conditions are not implied by existing constructions in [1,9].

We start by proving NP-hardness for computation of the optimal strategy profile in both min- and max-clearing games.

Theorem 5. *Consider max-clearing and min-clearing games with threshold-$\mathcal{M}$ strategies and $k \geq 2$. For fixed seniorities, it is NP-hard to compute an optimal strategy profile with respect to social welfare.*

Proof. We prove the statement by reduction from 3-SATISFIABILITY. For a given instance, let φ denote the Boolean formula with variables $x_1, x_2, \ldots, x_n$ and clauses $\kappa_1, \kappa_2, \ldots, \kappa_m$. We construct a clearing game with an acyclic graph $G = (V, E)$, hence, all flow originates from external assets. For this reason, in this game minimal and maximal clearing states coincide for every strategy profile. We construct the game as follows.

First, we define a gadget for every variable x_i consisting of the players x_i, x_i^T, x_i^F, s_i^T and s_i^F. Player x_i holds external assets of $B \gg m$, where B is polynomial in n and m. Further, x_i owes assets of B to both x_i^T and x_i^F, i.e., $(x_i, x_i^T), (x_i, x_i^F) \in E$. Additionally, we add the edges (x_i^T, s_i^T) and (x_i^F, s_i^F) with seniority 1 and weight B each. For every clause κ_j, we include player κ_j with external assets of 1. If variable x_i appears as $\neg x_i$ (or x_i) in clause κ_j, the unit-weight edge (κ_j, x_i^F) (or (κ_j, x_i^T)) is added to E. Further, we add player φ and edges (x_i^T, φ) and (x_i^F, φ) with edge weight m and seniority 2 for every i. Player φ has liabilities of $m-1$ to sink s_φ with seniority 1 and liabilities of 1 with seniority 2 to a linear graph consisting of $u_1, u_2, \ldots, u_B$. An example construction for the instance $(x_1 \vee x_2) \wedge (x_1 \vee \neg x_2 \vee x_3)$ is depicted in Fig. 3.

Intuitively, when player x_i pays off all assets towards x_i^T (or x_i^F), we interpret the literal x_i (or $\neg x_i$) in φ to be assigned with TRUE. The players x_i^T and x_i^F are obligated to first pay off all debt towards a sink. Therefore, one of these players can make payments outside the gadget only if the literal associated with her is true. We call such a player *unlocked*. Note that by the choice of B, it is impossible to unlock both x_i^T and x_i^F with flow of $B + m$ which is the maximal flow achieved when all κ_j pay their assets towards the same gadget. Assume κ_j to settle the debt to an unlocked player. By definition, she can forward the payments from κ_j to φ. In contrast, a *locked* player would forward the payments to the respective sink. Whenever player φ receives incoming flow of k, at least k players κ_j pass their assets to an unlocked player. Thus, the assets of φ can be interpreted as the number of satisfied clauses. Thus, whenever there is strictly positive flow along the linear graph, all clauses are interpreted as satisfied.

For every formula φ, the number of nodes and edges in the constructed game is linear in the number of variables n and number of clauses m. Hence, the construction can be performed in polynomial time.

We state that there exists a satisfying assignment of φ if and only if the social welfare of the optimal strategy profile is $(3n+1)B + 4m - 1$. First, assume there exists a satisfying assignment of φ. We then define a strategy profile **a** along the lines of this assignment. For every variable x_i that is assigned TRUE, x_i prioritizes the edge (x_i, x_i^T), i.e., $\tau^{(1)}_{(x_i, x_i^T)} = 1$ and $\tau^{(1)}_{(x_i, x_i^F)} = 0$. In the case, when x_i is assigned FALSE we proceed analogously and prioritize the edge towards x_i^F. For each clause κ_j, choose one arbitrary clause-fulfilling literal l_j and prioritize the edge (κ_j, l_j) as described before. Then in each variable gadget, the social welfare of at least $3B$ is achieved. Also, every κ_j pays her assets towards an

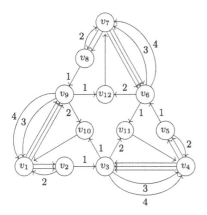

$v_7 : (1)$

v_1 \ v_4	(1)	(2)
(1)	2,2,2	2,3,2
(2)	3,2,2	3,0,1

$v_7 : (2)$

v_1 \ v_4	(1)	(2)
(1)	2,2,3	2,3,0
(2)	0,2,3	1,1,1

(a) A max-clearing game with threshold-$\mathcal{M}$ strategies for players v_1, v_4 and v_7 and fixed partition-$\mathcal{M}$ strategies for the remaining players (blue edge labels). The game has no pure Nash equilibrium.

(b) The game among players v_1, v_4 and v_7 has only two meaningful strategies for each player. Entries of the tables denote utility of v_1, v_4 and v_7, respectively.

Fig. 4. Max-clearing game without pure Nash equilibrium.

unlocked player, leading to incoming flow of m for φ. Thus, φ can settle all debts leading to assets of $m - 1$ for s_φ and assets of 1 for every player u_i in the path graph. In total, the social welfare is $(3n + 1)B + 4m - 1$.

For the other direction, assume there exists a strategy profile **a** yielding social welfare of $(3n + 1)B + 4m - 1$. In the constructed game, n players each hold external assets of B, which are paid in full via x_i^T and x_i^F to sinks s_i^T and s_i^F. This generates social welfare of $3Bn$. The social welfare can only be increased by another B, if flow of 1 exists on the path graph $u_1, \ldots, u_B$. Since this flow must be initiated by φ, her incoming flow must be at least m. Thus, every κ_j pays her external assets via an unlocked player towards φ.   □

For clearing games and threshold-$\mathcal{M}$ strategies, the strategy profile with Pareto-optimal clearing state has been shown to be a strong equilibrium and, in case of max-clearing, even efficiently computable. By fixing seniorities, however, we do not only impact the computational complexity of the optimal strategy profile but also the existence of stable states. In fact, the subsequent theorem shows that there are max-clearing games with threshold-$\mathcal{M}$ strategies without pure Nash equilibria.

Proposition 3. *For threshold-$\mathcal{M}$ strategies with any $k \geq 2$, there exists a max-clearing game with fixed seniorities that has no pure Nash equilibrium.*

Proof. Consider the game depicted in Fig. 4a where no player owns external assets and all edges have unit weights. The labels of the edges indicate the seniorities. Note that only players v_1, v_4 and v_7 have a meaningful strategy choice, since the behavior of all others is essentially determined.

Player v_1 has liabilities to v_2 and v_9 of same priority, thus her strategy choices can be divided into three distinct categories: (1) She directs all payments towards v_2 until her liabilities towards v_2 are completely payed off, (2) she directs all payments towards v_9 until her liabilities towards v_9 are completely payed off, or (3) she splits her payments between the two in some arbitrary way. A strategy from the last category is never profitable for the player, since part of her payments are either retained by v_{10} or passed on from v_9 to v_{12}. On the other hand, if the player uses all her assets to pay off one debt, she can exploit the cycles and increase her assets depending on the strategies of the other players. Therefore, we restrict ourselves to categories (1) and (2). By symmetry, the same arguments apply to strategies of v_4 and v_7. The utilities of all resulting strategy profiles are illustrated in Fig. 4b. For each combination of strategies, at least one player strictly benefits from a unilateral deviation. □

In the game analyzed in the previous proof, it is never profitable for any player v_1, v_4 or v_7 to split her payments to different agents. A player always prefers to direct all money flow towards one player. Thus, the choices of $a_e^{(i)}$ are inconsequential and only one threshold per edge is needed.

We can adjust the game in the proof of Proposition 3 to reduce each fixed partition to only *two* priority classes. To see this, consider a player $v \in \{v_3, v_6, v_9\}$ whose outgoing edges are divided into four seniority classes. We can add an auxiliary player w and redirect all edges with seniority higher than 1 towards w. In particular, replace every edge (v, u) with seniority j, with edges (v, w) with seniority 2 and (w, u) with seniority $j - 1$. Then proceed to node w. In each step, the required number of seniority classes is reduced by one. We obtain an equivalent game where every fixed partition for a node contains only two classes.

The next result revisits the discussed game and proves that deciding existence of an equilibrium for a given max-clearing game with fixed seniorities is NP-hard.

Theorem 6. *For a given max-clearing game with fixed seniorities and threshold-$\mathcal{M}$ strategies with any $k \geq 2$, it is NP-hard to decide whether a pure Nash equilibrium exists.*

Proof. Consider the game with no Nash equilibrium described in proof of Proposition 3. In this game, we can generate an equilibrium by paying additional assets of 1 to player v_1. Then, v_1 can pay off her total liabilities when v_4 chooses strategy (2) and v_7 chooses (1). When playing according to this strategy profile, no player has an incentive to deviate unilaterally. The additional assets are generated by the construction described in proof of Theorem 5. Recall, that we constructed a game for a given instance φ of 3-SATISFIABILITY. The player u_B has assets of 1 if and only if there exists a satisfying assignment of φ. Hence by adding the edge (u_B, v_1), the statement follows. □

Both results regarding max-clearing can be extended to min-clearing games. For non-existence of Nash equilibria, a game is constructed where three players are able to freely choose their strategies while the behavior of all other players is fully determined by seniorities.

Proposition 4. *For threshold-$\mathcal{M}$ strategies with any $k \geq 2$, there exists a min-clearing game with fixed seniorities that has no pure Nash equilibrium.*

Theorem 7. *For a given min-clearing game with fixed seniorities and threshold-$\mathcal{M}$ strategies with any $k \geq 2$, it is NP-hard to decide whether a pure Nash equilibrium exists.*

References

1. Bertschinger, N., Hoefer, M., Schmand, D.: Strategic payments in financial networks. In: Proceedings of 11th Symposium on Innovations in Theoretical Computer Science (ITCS), pp. 46:1–46:16 (2020)
2. Csóka, P., Jean-Jacques Herings, P.: Decentralized clearing in financial networks. Manag. Sci. **64**(10), 4681–4699 (2018)
3. Diamond, D.: Seniority and maturity of debt contracts. J. Financ. Econ. **33**(3), 341–368 (1993)
4. Eisenberg, L., Noe, T.: Systemic risk in financial systems. Manag. Sci. **47**(2), 236–249 (2001)
5. Elsinger, H.: Financial networks, cross holdings, and limited liability. Working Paper 156, Oesterreichische Nationalbank (Austrian Central Bank) (2009)
6. Elsinger, H., Lehar, A., Summer, M.: Risk assessment for banking systems. Manag. Sci. **52**(9), 1301–1314 (2006)
7. Fischer, T.: No-arbitrage pricing under systemic risk: accounting for cross-ownership. Math. Financ. **24**(1), 97–124 (2014)
8. Hoefer, M., Wilhelmi, L.: Seniorities and minimal clearing in financial network games. arXiv preprint arXiv:2205.15628 (2022)
9. Kanellopoulos, P., Kyropoulou, M., Zhou, H.: Financial network games. In: Proceedings of 2nd ACM International Conference on AI in Finance (ICAIF) (2021, to appear)
10. Krieter, F., Rau, D.: Limited liabilities within a (re-)insurance group. Working Paper 5694 (2021)
11. Kusnetsov, M.: Clearing models for systemic risk assessment in interbank networks. Ph.D. thesis, London School of Economics and Political Science (2018)
12. Papp, P.A., Wattenhofer, R.: Network-aware strategies in financial systems. In: Proceedings of 47th International Colloquium on Automata, Languages and Programming (ICALP), pp. 91:1–91:17 (2020)
13. Papp, P.A., Wattenhofer, R.: Debt swapping for risk mitigation in financial networks. In: Proceedings of 22nd Conference on Economics and Computation (EC), pp. 765–784 (2021)
14. Papp, P.A., Wattenhofer, R.: Default ambiguity: finding the best solution to the clearing problem. In: Feldman, M., Fu, H., Talgam-Cohen, I. (eds.) WINE 2021. LNCS, vol. 13112, pp. 391–409. Springer, Cham (2022). https://doi.org/10.1007/978-3-030-94676-0_22
15. Papp, P.A., Wattenhofer, R.: Sequential defaulting in financial networks. In: Proceedings of 12th Symposium on Innovations in Theoretical Computer Science (ITCS), pp. 52:1–52:20 (2021)
16. Rogers, L., Veraart, L.: Failure and rescue in an interbank network. Manag. Sci. **59**(4), 882–898 (2013)

17. Schuldenzucker, S., Seuken, S.: Portfolio compression in financial networks: incentives and systemic risk. In: Proceedings of 21st Conference on Economics and Computation (EC), p. 79 (2020)
18. Schuldenzucker, S., Seuken, S., Battiston, S.: Finding clearing payments in financial networks with credit default swaps is PPAD-complete. In: Proceedings of 8th Symposium on Innovations in Theoretical Computer Science (ITCS), pp. 32:1–32:20 (2017)
19. Schuldenzucker, S., Seuken, S., Battiston, S.: Default ambiguity: credit default swaps create new systemic risks in financial networks. Manag. Sci. **66**(5), 1981–1998 (2020)
20. Veraart, L.: When does portfolio compression reduce systemic risk? (2020). sSRN 10.2139/ssrn.3688495

Financial Networks with Singleton Liability Priorities

Stavros D. Ioannidis, Bart de Keijzer, and Carmine Ventre[✉]

King's College London, London, UK
{stavros.ioannidis,bart.de_keijzer,carmine.ventre}@kcl.ac.uk

Abstract. Financial networks model debt obligations between economic firms. Computational and game-theoretic analyses of these networks have been recent focus of the literature. The main computational challenge in this context is the clearing problem, a fixed point search problem that essentially determines insolvent firms and their exposure to systemic risk, technically known as recovery rates. When Credit Default Swaps, a derivative connected to the 2008 financial crisis, are part of the obligations *and* insolvent firms pay the same proportion of all their debts, computing a weakly approximate solution is PPAD-complete [29], whereas computing a strongly approximate solution is FIXP-complete [17]. This paper addresses the computational complexity of the clearing problem in financial networks with derivatives, whenever priorities amongst creditors are adopted. This practically relevant model has been only studied from a game-theoretic standpoint. We explicitly study the clearing problem whenever the firms pay according to a singleton liability priority list and prove that it is FIXP-complete. Finally, we provide a host of NP-hardness results for the computation of priority lists that optimise specific objectives of importance in the domain.

1 Introduction

The financial services industry has been very creative, with the constant introduction of new products designed as investment and/or risk management tools. This makes the web of liabilities between the different institutions in the market hard to track and oversee. It is, in fact, this inherent complex structure of the evolving modern financial system that has led to several somewhat unforeseen and deeply damaging crises, such as the Great Financial Crisis (GFC) of 2008. There is, therefore, the need to mathematically model and study this network of obligations among interconnected financial agents in order to understand the impact of new products, regulations or even single contracts.

The main computational challenge in this context is the *clearing problem* introduced in [6]: Given the banks' funds and the face values of all the liabilities in the network, compute for each bank its exposure to systemic risk, in the form of what is known as its *clearing recovery rate*. It turns out that the

---

C. Ventre—Partially supported by the UKRI grant EP/V00784X/1.

© The Author(s), under exclusive license to Springer Nature Switzerland AG 2022
P. Kanellopoulos et al. (Eds.): SAGT 2022, LNCS 13584, pp. 205–222, 2022.
https://doi.org/10.1007/978-3-031-15714-1_12

complexity of this problem is closely related to the class of financial products populating the network. In fact, in financial networks where firms only subscribe simple debt contracts, clearing recovery rates can be computed in polynomial time [6,25]. Whilst this setup makes up for an easy modeling of networks as directed graphs with nodes standing for financial institutions and edges representing debt obligations, this representation is too simplistic in that it does not capture more advanced products, based on other existing contracts like mortgages, loans, interest rates etc. These complex contracts are called *derivatives*. The addition of one such derivative, namely, *Credit Default Swaps (CDSes)*, introduced to financial networks in [28], makes the model more intriguing from a computational perspective. A CDS involves three parties i, j, k, where k must pay an amount of money to j on the condition that i cannot pay off all of its obligations. Since adding CDSes to a financial network may generate irrational clearing recovery rates [17,28], our interest turns to finding approximate clearing recovery rates; it is proved that weakly (or "almost") approximate recovery rates are PPAD-complete to compute [29] and strong (or "near") approximate solutions are FIXP-complete to compute [17].

In this paper, we look at this problem from the perspective of the financial regulator. We ask whether rules that determine how insolvent banks pay off their debts can fundamentally change the computational hardness landscape above. The most-studied payment scheme is the *proportional payment scheme* where each bank pays off its debts proportionally to its recovery rate. However, defining priority classes amongst creditors and pay proportionally in each class (with funds available at the current priority level) is another widely adopted measure used in practice in the industry. For example, some regulatory regimes require employees to be prioritised over other creditors whereas some advanced derivatives (such as, the renown Collateralized Debt Obligations leading to the GFC) define their payoff via *tranching* (effectively a priority list) of the underlying securities. Whilst priority payments have been studied under a game-theoretic framework [3,18,21], nothing is known about the complexity of the clearing problem with this payment scheme in presence of financial derivatives.

Our Contribution. We study the clearing problem in financial networks with derivatives under the *priority list* payment scheme. Specifically, we examine financial networks consisting of both debt and CDS contracts and address the complexity of computing a *clearing recovery rate vector* whenever each bank has to pay its debts in the following way. For each bank, we define a partition of its liabilities in priority classes. With the funds available at a certain priority (i.e., after having paid all the liabilities with higher priority), the liabilities at the current priority are paid proportionally – in particular, this means that these are paid in full if the funds are sufficient. This notion generalises the proportional payment scheme studied in related literature (i.e., consider the case in which the partition contains one part) and the class of *singleton priorities*, where each part is a singleton. We call this problem CDS-PRIORITY-CLEARING. Note that without CDSes, CDS-PRIORITY-CLEARING is known to be in P, both for proportional [6] and priority [18] payment schemes.

We observe here that whenever the partition defined by the priority list contains at least of part of size 2 or more then CDS-PRIORITY-CLEARING is FIXP-complete. FIXP [8] is a complexity class that captures the fixed point computations of total search problems. In our context, it is important to observe that FIXP is defined in terms of fixed-point functions defined upon the algebraic basis $A = \{+, -, *, /, \max, \min, \sqrt[k]{}\}$. It is not hard to see that the FIXP-completeness follows from the recent reduction given in [17] where all gadgets adopted have maximum out-degree 2.[1] Therefore, the only case left open is when all the parts of the priority list are singletons. We focus our attention on this setup in our work. We then call CDS-PRIORITY-CLEARING the problem of finding recovery rates for singleton priorities, i.e., each bank has an ordering of its liabilities according to which its debts are paid off.

Our first contribution gives technical evidence that the financial regulator cannot change the complexity of computing clearing recovery rates, by enforcing priority payments. Specifically, we prove that CDS-PRIORITY-CLEARING is at least as hard as the *square root sum* (SQRT-SUM) problem [8,11,20,30] and that it is complete for FIXP. We then give the full picture of the complexity for the clearing problem, under all payment schemes proposed in the literature. Whilst the proof of FIXP-completeness adopts known approaches [17], our reduction introduces new financial network gadgets with priority payments for the operations in A. In particular, our new multiplication gadget highlights the flexibility of financial networks in handling arithmetic operations.

Whilst the regulator cannot ease the computational complexity of the problem, we wonder whether one can efficiently compute the banks' priority lists to optimise certain objective functions of financial interest. These include maximising the equity of a specific bank, maximising the liquidity in the system, and minimising the number of activated CDSes. As our second main contribution, we present a set of NP-hardness results showing a parallel with the known hardness of computing similarly "optimal" solutions with proportional payments [22].

Related Work. Clearing problems have been studied a lot in the literature [1,5–7,12,14–16,25]. Analysis of financial networks with CDSes as well as their properties is a popular topic in the area [17,21,23,24,27–29]. A game-theoretic approach to financial networks, the edge ranking game as well as other financial network games are listed in [3,18,19,22]. The FIXP-complexity class was defined first in [8,17,31], which established the FIXP-completeness of various fundamental fixed point computation problems. There are various further recent papers that show FIXP-completeness of a range of problems, including [9,10,13,17].

2   Model and Preliminaries

Financial Networks and Payment Schemes. A financial network consists of a set of financial entities (which we refer to as *banks* for convenience), interconnected through a set of financial contracts. Let $N = \{1, \ldots, n\}$ be the set

---

[1] We defer a formal treatment of this and the omitted proofs herein to the full version.

of n banks. Each bank $i \in N$ has *external assets*, denoted by $e_i \in \mathbb{Q}_{\geq 0}$. We let $e = (e_1, \ldots, e_n)$ be the vector of all external assets. We consider two types of liabilities among banks: *debt contracts* and *credit default swaps (CDSes)*. A debt contract requires one bank i (debtor) to pay another bank j (creditor) a certain amount $c_{i,j} \in \mathbb{Q}_{\geq 0}$. A CDS requires a debtor i to pay a creditor j on condition that a third bank called the *reference bank* R is in default, meaning that R cannot fully pay its liabilities. Formally, we associate each bank i with a *recovery rate* $r_i \in [0,1]$, that indicates the proportion of liabilities i is able to pay. Having $r_i = 1$ means that bank i can fully pay its liabilities, while $r_i < 1$ indicates that i is in default. In case a reference bank R of a CDS is in default, the debtor i of that CDS pays the creditor j an amount of $(1 - r_R)c_{i,j}^R$, where $c_{i,j}^R \in \mathbb{Q}_{\geq 0}$ is the face value of the CDS. The value $c_{i,j}$ ($c_{i,j}^R$, resp.) of a debt contract (CDS, resp.) is also called the *notional* of the contract. Finally, we let c be the collection of all contracts' notionals. We do not allow any bank to have a debt contract with itself, and assume that all three banks in any CDS are distinct.

The financial system $\mathcal{F}$ can therefore be represented as the triplet (N, e, c). Given $\mathcal{F}$, we let $\mathcal{DC}_{\mathcal{F}}$ denote the set of all pairs of banks participating in a debt contract in $\mathcal{F}$. Similarly, $\mathcal{CDS}_{\mathcal{F}}$ denotes the set of all triplets participating in a CDS in $\mathcal{F}$. (We drop $\mathcal{F}$ from the notation when it is clear from the context.) The *contract graph* of $\mathcal{F} = (N, e, c)$ is defined as a coloured directed multigraph $G_{\mathcal{F}} = (V, A)$, where $V = N$ and $A = (\cup_{k \in N} A_k) \cup A_0$ where $A_0 = \{(i,j) \mid i,j \in N \wedge c_{i,j} \neq 0\}$ and $A_k = \{(i,j) \mid i,j \in N \wedge c_{i,j}^k \neq 0\}$. Each arc $(i,j) \in A_0$ is coloured blue and each $(i,j) \in A_k$ orange. For all $(i,j,R) \in \mathcal{CDS}$ we draw a dotted orange line from node R to arc $(i,j) \in A_R$, denoting that R is the reference bank of the CDS between i and j. [2] Finally, we label each arc with the notional of the corresponding contract, and each node with the external assets of the corresponding bank.

All banks are obliged to pay off their liabilities according to a set of prespecified rules, which we refer to as a payment scheme. If a bank has sufficient assets, then the payment scheme is trivial and prescribes to simply make payments that correspond exactly to each of the bank's liabilities. If there are insufficient assets, on the other hand, the payment scheme will determine for each of the outgoing contracts how much of it is paid off. The most studied payment scheme is the *proportional payment scheme*, where each bank i submits an r_i proportion of each liability, leaving a $(1 - r_i)$ fraction of each liability unpaid. In this paper we study payments resulting from another rule, called the *singleton liability priority lists* payment scheme. More specifically, given a financial system $\mathcal{F} = (N, e, c)$, for each bank i we define a total order over the arcs going out of i in $G_{\mathcal{F}}$. We denote the singleton liability priority list of i as $P_i = (i_1 \mid i_2 \mid \ldots \mid i_{\text{outdeg}(i)})$, where i_k stands for the k-th element in the order, or kth *priority* of node i, and outdeg(i) denotes the out degree of node i in $G_{\mathcal{F}}$. The payments under this scheme are now formed through an iterative process where each bank pays off its liabilities, one after the other, preserving the ordering in its priority list. We denote by c_{i_k} the contract notional of the i_kth priority and denote by $\mathcal{P} = (P_1, \ldots, P_n)$ the profile

---

[2] This means that $G_{\mathcal{F}}$ is a directed hypergraph with arcs of size 2 and 3.

of singleton liability priority lists. We denote a financial system $\mathcal{F}$ endowed with a singleton liability priority profile $\mathcal{P}$ as $(\mathcal{F}, \mathcal{P})$. The next example illustrates the model.

Example 1. The financial system of Fig. 1 consists of six banks, $N = \{1, 2, 3, 4, 5, 6\}$. Banks 2 and 5 have external assets $e_2 = e_5 = 1 - c$, for some constant $c \in (0, 1)$, while all other banks have zero external assets. The set of debt contracts is $\mathcal{DC} = \{(2, 3), (5, 4)\}$ and the set of CDS contracts is $\mathcal{CDS} = \{(2, 1, 5), (5, 6, 2)\}$. All contract notionals are set to 1. For example, $c_{2,3} = c_{2,1}^5 = 1$. Node 2 has two candidate singleton liability priority lists, one is $P_2^1 = ((2, 3) \mid (2, 1, 5))$, where $2_1 = (2, 3)$ with contract notional $c_{2_1} = c_{2,1} = 1$ and $2_2 = (2, 1, 5)$ with contract notional $c_{2_2} = c_{2,1}^5 = 1$. The other one is $P_2^2 = ((2, 1, 5) \mid (2, 3))$ where $2_1 = (2, 1, 5)$ with $c_{2_1} = c_{2,1}^5 = 1$ and $2_2 = (2, 3)$ with $c_{2_2} = c_{2,3} = 1$. Symmetrically one can derive the lists for node 5.

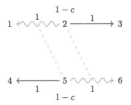

Fig. 1. Example of a financial network

We are interested in computing for a pair $(\mathcal{F}, \mathcal{P})$, for each bank i, the proportion of liabilities that it is able to pay. This proportion is captured by the *recovery rate*, mentioned earlier: For each bank i we associate a variable $r_i \in [0, 1]$, that indicates the proportion of liabilities that bank i can pay. Recall that, to define the liability generated from a CDS contract, we need the recovery rate of the reference banks. Consequently in order to define all liabilities of banks in a financial system, we need to be presented with an a-priori recovery rate vector $r = (r_1, \cdots, r_n)$. So given a $(\mathcal{F}, \mathcal{P})$ and assuming a vector $r \in [0, 1]^n$, we define the liabilities, the payments that each bank submits and the assets for each bank as follows. We denote by $l_{i_k}(r)$ the k-th *liability priority* of node i. If $i_k = (i, j) \in \mathcal{DC}$ for some $j \in N$, then $l_{i_k}(r) = c_{i,j}$ and if $i_k = (i, j, R) \in \mathcal{CDS}$ for some $j, R \in N$, then $l_{i_j}(r) = (1 - r_R)c_{i,j}^R$. The liability of bank $i \in N$ to a bank $j \in N$ is denoted by $l_{i,j}(r)$ and it holds that

$$l_{i,j}(r) = c_{i,j} + \sum_{k \in N}(1 - r_k)c_{i,j}^k. \tag{1}$$

We denote by $l_i(r)$ the total liabilities of node i, and it holds that

$$l_i(r) = \sum_{j=1}^{\text{outdeg}(i)} l_{i_j}(r) = \sum_{j \neq i} l_{i,j}(r) = \sum_{j \in N \setminus \{i\}}\left(c_{i,j} + \sum_{k \in N \setminus \{i,j\}}(1 - r_k)c_{i,j}^k\right).$$

Node i can fully pay its kth priority only if he has sufficient assets left after paying off the liabilities corresponding to priorities $i_1, \ldots, i_{k-1}$. We denote by $p_{i_k}(r)$ the payment of node i to its k-th priority, and by $a_i(r)$ its assets, which are defined as the external assets it possesses plus all incoming payments submitted from its debtors (see below for a more formal definition). Under our singleton priority lists payment scheme:

$$p_{i_j}(r) = \max\left\{0, \min\left\{l_{i_j}(r), a_i(r) - \sum_{j' < j} l_{i_{j'}}(r)\right\}\right\}. \tag{2}$$

Moreover, we denote by $p_{i,j}(r)$ the payment of node i to node j under recovery rate vector r: Let $C_j = \{i_j \mid i_j \text{ is a contract with node } j \text{ as the creditor}\}$, then $p_{i,j}(r) = \sum_{i_j \in C_j} p_{i_j}(r)$. The total payment made by a node is the sum of its individual payments to its priorities which is equal to the total sum of its payments to its creditors. Also, the payment of node i needs to be equal to the proportion of its total liabilities it can pay off. Therefore, the following equations hold.

$$p_i(r) = \sum_{j=1}^{\text{outdeg}(i)} p_{i_j}(r) = \sum_{j \in N} p_{i,j}(r) = r_i l_i(r). \tag{3}$$

The assets of a bank i are denoted as $a_i(r)$ and are the total amount of money it possesses summing its external assets and all incoming payments made by its debtors. It holds that

$$a_i(r) = e_i + \sum_{j \neq i} p_{j,i}(r). \tag{4}$$

We are interested in computing a specific recovery rate vector in $[0,1]^n$, such that (3) holds (i.e., $p_i(r) = r_i l_i(r)$ for all $i \in N$), under the singleton liability priority list payment rule (just defined formally by (2) and (4)). Formally:

Definition 1 (Clearing recovery rate vectors (CRRVs)). *Given a financial system and a singleton liability priority profile $(\mathcal{F}, \mathcal{P})$, a recovery rate vector r is called clearing if and only if for all banks $i \in N$,*

$$r_i = \min\left\{1, \frac{a_i(r)}{l_i(r)}\right\} \text{ if } l_i(r) > 0, \text{ and } r_i = 1 \text{ if } l_i(r) = 0. \tag{5}$$

We illustrate the notions of the dynamics and the CRRVs by reconsidering Example 1 and computing them for some priority profile $\mathcal{P}$.

Example 1 (continued). Let $c = 1/4$ in Fig. 1. Let $\mathcal{P} = (P_2 = ((2,3) \mid (2,1,5)), P_5 = ((5,4) \mid (5,6,2)))$. Both nodes 2 and 5 receive no payment from any other node thus their assets are defined as $a_2 = e_2 = 1-c$ and $a_5 = e_5 = 1-c$. For node 2, given P_2, we get that $l_{2_1} = l_{2,1} = c_{2_1} = c_{2,3} = 1$ and $l_{2_2} = l_{2,1} = (1-r_5)c_{2,1}^5 = (1-r_5)$, thus the total liabilities for node 2 are $l_2 = l_{2_1} + l_{2_2} = 2 - r_5$. For node 5 we get that $l_{5_1} = l_{5,4} = c_{5_1} = c_{5,4} = 1$ and $l_{5_2} = l_{5,6} = c_{5_2} = (1-r_2)c_{5,6}^2 = 1-r_2$, thus the total liabilities for node 5 are $l_5 = l_{5_1} + l_{5_2} = 2 - r_2$. Let us compute the CRRV. By (5) it must be $r_2 = \min\{1, a_2(r)/l_2(r)\} = \min\{1, 1 - c/2 - r_5\}$ and

$r_5 = \min\{1, a_5(r)/l_5(r)\} = \min\{1, (1-c)/(2-r_2)\}$. After solving this system we get that $r_2 = r_5 = 1 - \sqrt{c}$ and since we assumed $c = 1/4$ we finally get that $r_2 = r_5 = 1/2$. For the payments of node 2, we know that $a_2 = 3/4$ and it first prioritises node 3 for which it has a liability of 1, thus it cannot fully pay off that liability and submits all of its assets to node 3, namely $p_{2_1} = p_{2,3} = 3/4$ and $p_{2_2} = p_{2,1} = 0$. The payments of node 5 are symmetrical.

Our Search Problem. We define CDS-PRIORITY-CLEARING to be the search problem that asks for a clearing recovery rate vector r given a pair $(\mathcal{F}, \mathcal{P})$. The term CDS refers to the fact that $\mathcal{F}$ may contain CDS contracts (the problem becomes polynomial time computable without CDSes [18]) and the term PRIORITY indicates that banks pay according to singleton liability priority list $\mathcal{P}$. Similarly to [17,29], we assume that $\mathcal{F}$ is non-degenerate (see below for a discussion).

Definition 2. *A financial system is non-degenerate if and only if the following two conditions hold. Every debtor in a CDS either has positive external assets or is the debtor in at least one debt contract with a positive notional. Every bank that acts as a reference bank in some CDS is the debtor of at least one debt contract with a positive notional.*

Given an instance $I \in$ CDS-PRIORITY-CLEARING we transform (1) into a function defined on arbitrary recovery rate vectors $r = (r_1, \cdots, r_n)$ as:[3]

$$f_I(r)_i = \frac{a_i(r)}{\max\{a_i(r), l_i(r)\}}. \tag{6}$$

From (6) we ascertain that r is a clearing recovery rate vector for I if and only if r is a fixed point of f_I, namely $r = f_I(r)$. Thus, solving CDS-PRIORITY-CLEARING comes down to computing the fixed points of f_I. We define CDS-PRIORITY-CLEARING to contain only non-degenerate financial networks, for the analytical convenience that non-degeneracy provides (note that a division by 0 never occurs in $f_I(r)_i$ for these instances). It is not hard to see that f_I has fixed points, see, e.g., [21]. Moreover, there exist instances of $(\mathcal{F}, \mathcal{P})$ that admit multiple CRRVs.

Irrationality. As is the case for the proportional payments, the singleton liability priority list model contains instances that admit irrational CRRVs. Observation 1 below provides such an example while Observations 2 and 3 present examples of how the priority profile affects the payments in the network. These examples also provide insights on an important difference between the two payment scheme: In the proportional model, whenever the CRRV is irrational then the clearing payment vector must be irrational as well. That is not the case in the singleton liability priority payment scheme, where irrationality of a CRRV need not cause any irrationality in the payments.

---

[3] Strictly speaking, $f_I(r)_i$ is defined only for nodes i that are not sinks in the contract graph. Sink nodes have recovery rate 1, cf. (5). Their exclusion simply allows to bypass potential divisions by 0 in f_I (e.g., take node 1 in Fig. 1 when $c = 1$) while preserving its continuity. For notational simplicity, we will implicitly assume that we compute $f_I(r)_i$ iff i is not a sink.

Observation 1. *There exist instances of* $(\mathcal{F}, \mathcal{P})$ *that have irrational CRRVs. For instance, we know that* $r_2 = r_5 = 1 - \sqrt{c}$ *in Example 1. Thus, it is clear that for many choices of* $c \in (0, 1)$ *(e.g.,* $c = 1/2$*) the CRRV is irrational.*

Observation 2. *There exist a pair* $(\mathcal{F}, \mathcal{P})$ *with an irrational CRRV and irrational payments. Take again Example 1 and fix* $c = 1/3$*. We have* $e_2 = e_5 = 2/3$*,* $l_{2,3} = l_{5,6} = 2/3$ *and* $r_2 = r_5 = 1 - \sqrt{1/3}$*. Now consider the singleton liability priority lists* $P_2 = ((2, 1, 5) \mid (2, 3))$ *and* $P_5 = ((5, 6, 2) \mid (5, 4))$*. Since node 2 prioritises the* $(2, 1, 5)$ *contract, it has to pay an amount of* $1 - \sqrt{1/3}$ *to node 1. Given that its total assets are* $2/3$*, it can fully pay this liability and so* $p_{2,1} = 1 - \sqrt{1/3}$ *and what is left is being paid to node 3. Symmetrically, one can compute that* $p_{5,6} = 1 - \sqrt{1/3}$*.*

Observation 3. *There exist a pair* $(\mathcal{F}, \mathcal{P})$ *with an irrational CRRV and rational payments. Consider Example 1 once more and fix* $c = 1/2$*. This yields* $e_2 = e_5 = 1/2$*,* $l_{2,3} = l_{5,6} = 1/2$ *and* $r_2 = r_5 = 1 - \sqrt{1/2}$*. Consider the singleton liability priority lists* $P_2 = ((2, 1, 5) \mid (2, 3))$ *and* $P_5 = ((5, 6, 2) \mid (5, 4))$*. Since node 2 prioritises the* $(2, 1, 5)$ *contract, it has to pay a amount of* $1 - \sqrt{1/2}$ *to node 1 but only possesses total assets of* $1/2$*. Thus it cannot fully pay this liability, meaning that* $p_{2,1} = 1/2$*. Symmetrically, we can compute that* $p_{5,6} = 1/2$*.*

A Primer on FIXP. A useful framework for studying the complexity of fixed point computation problems is defined in [8]. Both exact and approximate computation of the solutions to such problems are considered. We begin by defining the notion of approximation we are interested in. Let F be a continuous function that maps a compact convex set to itself and let $\epsilon > 0$ be a small constant. An ϵ-*approximate fixed point* of F is a point x is within a distance ϵ near a fixed point of F, i.e., $\exists x' : F(x') = x' \wedge \|x' - x\|_\infty < \epsilon$. This notion is also known as *strong approximation*.[4] We now introduce the problems we are focusing on. A *fixed point problem* Π is defined as a search problem such that for every instance $I \in \Pi$ there is an associated continuous function $F_I : D_I \to D_I$ —where $D_I \subseteq \mathbb{R}^n$ (for some $n \in \mathbb{N}$) is a convex polytope described by a set of linear inequalities with rational coefficients that can be computed from I in polynomial time—such that the solutions of I are the fixed points of F_I.

Definition 3. *The class* FIXP *consists of all fixed point problems* Π *for which for all* $I \in \Pi$ *the function* $F_I : D_I \to D_I$ *can be represented by an algebraic circuit* C_I *over the basis* $\{+, -, *, /, \max, \min, \sqrt[k]{\cdot}\}$*, using rational constants, such that* C_I *computes* F_I*, and* C_I *can be constructed from* I *in time polynomial in* $|I|$*.*

The class FIXP$_a$ *is defined as the class of search problems that are the strong approximation version of some fixed point problem that belongs to* FIXP*.*

---

[4] A *weak* ϵ *-approximate fixed point* of a continuous function F is a point x such that its image is within distance ϵ of x, i.e., $\|x - F(x)\|_\infty < \epsilon$. Under *polynomial continuity*, a mild condition on the fixed point problem under consideration, a strong approximation is also weak [8].

The class Linear-FIXP *is defined analogously to* FIXP, *but under the smaller arithmetic basis where only the gates* $\{+, -, \max, \min\}$ *and multiplication by rational constants are used.*

These classes admit complete problems. The completeness results in [8] in fact show that it is without loss of generality to consider a restricted basis $\{+, *, \max\}$ ($\{+, \max\}$) for FIXP (Linear-FIXP), and to assume that $D_I = [0,1]^n$.[5] Hardness of a search problem Π for FIXP is defined through the existence of a polynomial time computable function $\rho : \Pi' \to \Pi$, for all $\Pi \in$ FIXP, such that the solutions of I can be obtained from the solutions of $\rho(I)$ by applying a (polynomial-time computable) linear transformation on a subset of $\rho(I)$'s coordinates. This type of reduction is known as a *polynomial time SL-reduction*.

It is known that $\text{FIXP}_a \subseteq$ PSPACE and Linear-FIXP = PPAD [8]. An informal understanding of the hardness of FIXP vis-a-vis PPAD is as follows. PPAD captures a type of computational hardness stemming from an essentially combinatorial source. FIXP introduces on top of that a type of numerical hardness that emerges from the introduction of multiplication and division operations: These operations give rise to irrationality in the exact solutions to these problems, and may independently also require the computation of rational numbers of very high precision or very high magnitude.

3   Hardness of CDS-PRIORITY-CLEARING

We are interested in identifying the complexity of CDS-PRIORITY-CLEARING. Recall that in Example 1, we presented an instance which under proper coefficients admits only irrational clearing recovery rate vectors, which means that either one should study this problem with respect to complexity classes compatible real-valued solutions, or one should redefine the goal of the problem along the lines of finding a rational-valued approximation to a potentially irrational solution.

As an initial step, we first show that determining whether $r_i < 1$ for a specific bank i is at least as hard as solving the *square root sum* (SQRT-SUM) problem. An instance of SQRT-SUM consists of $n + 1$ integers $d_1, d_2, ..., d_n, k$ and asks whether $\sum_{i=1}^{n} \sqrt{d_i} \leq k$. It is known that SQRT-SUM is solvable in PSPACE but it is unknown whether it is in P, or even in NP. In [30] it is shown that it can be solved in polynomial time in the unit-cost RAM model [2,26,30].

Lemma 1. *For a given pair* $(\mathcal{F}, \mathcal{P})$, *deciding whether a specific bank is in default is* SQRT-SUM-*hard.*

Proof. We prove the lemma by reducing from SQRT-SUM to CDS-PRIORITY-CLEARING. Let $(d_1, ..d_n, k)$ be an instance of SQRT-SUM. Firstly, we note that in [4] it is shown that checking whether $\sum_{i=1}^{n} \sqrt{d_i} = k$ can be done in polynomial time. We check whether equality holds for our input first and proceed without loss of generality to the proof without minding equality.

---

[5] We will make use of these facts in the proof of Theorem 1, below.

We construct a financial system $\mathcal{F}$ as follows, first we construct n financial subnetworks which we refer to as *square root gadgets* and denote by $g_{i,\sqrt{\cdot}}$ the ith square root gadget. Whenever referring to a node k, belonging in a square root gadget $g_{i,\sqrt{\cdot}}$, we use the notation k_i. The square root gadget $g_{i,\sqrt{\cdot}}$ consists of the financial network we presented in Fig. 1, augmented with two additional nodes x_i, y_i, and the CDS contract $(x_i, y_i, 2_i)$. We let the external assets of nodes 2_i and 5_i be $e_{2_i} = e_{5_i} = 1 - d_i$. We let $e_{x_i} = 1$ and $e_{y_i} = 0$ and the CDS contract $(x_i, y_i, 2_i)$ has a notional of 1: $c^{2_i}_{x_i, y_i} = 1$. The n square root gadgets are all connected to a single node τ with $e_\tau = 0$, by n debt contracts $\{(y_i, \tau) : i \in [n]\}$. There is one further node τ' to which τ is connected through debt contract (τ, τ') with notional $c_{\tau,\tau'} = k$. The construction is illustrated in Fig. 2.

We claim that this resulting financial system has a clearing recovery rate vector r with $r_\tau = 1$ if and only if $\sum_{i=1}^{n} \sqrt{d_i} \geq k$. From the analysis of Example 1, it follows that under any clearing recovery rate vector r, the recovery rate of node 2_i is $r_{2_i} = 1 - \sqrt{d_i}$ for all $i \in [n]$. Since node 2_i is always in default (assuming all $d_i \neq 0$) the CDS $(x_i, y_i, 2_i)$ is activated and since node x_i can fully pay its liabilities, node y_i receives a payment of $1 - r_{2_i} = \sqrt{d_i}$. This implies that τ receives a total payment of $\sum_{i \in [n]} \sqrt{d_i}$. Since τ has only one liability of k, it holds that $r_\tau = 1$ if and only if the total payment that τ receives exceeds k, i.e., if and only if $\sum_{i \in [n]} \sqrt{d_i} \geq k$, and this proves the claim.   □

(a) The i square root gadget $g_{i,\sqrt{\cdot}}$ (b) The constructed financial system

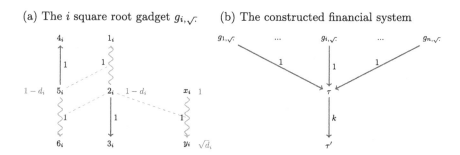

Fig. 2. The financial system constructed from a given Square Root Sum instance

Next we show that CDS-PRIORITY-CLEARING and its strong approximation variant are FIXP and FIXP$_a$ complete, respectively. Our hardness reduction does not start from a particular FIXP-hard problem. Rather, we show that we can take an arbitrary algebraic circuit and encode it in a direct way in the form of a financial system accompanied by a specific singleton liability profile. Hence, our polynomial time hardness reduction works from any arbitrary fixed point problem in FIXP. The reduction is constructed by devising various financial network gadgets which enforce that certain banks in the system have recovery rates that are the result of applying one of the operators in FIXP's arithmetic base to the recovery rates of two other banks in the system: In other words, we can design our financial systems and singleton liability priorities such that the interrelation between the recovery rates mimics a computation through an arbitrary algebraic circuit.

Theorem 1. CDS-PRIORITY-CLEARING *is FIXP-complete, and its strong approximation version is* $FIXP_a$*-complete.*

Proof (sketch). Containment of CDS-PRIORITY-CLEARING in FIXP is immediate: The clearing vectors for an instance $I = (N, e, c) \in$ CDS-PRIORITY-CLEARING are the fixed points of the function f_I defined coordinate-wise by $f_I(r)_i = \frac{a_i(r)}{\max\{l_i(r), a_i(r)\}}$ as in (6). The functions $l_i(r)$ and $a_i(r)$ are defined in (1) and (4), from which it is clear that f_I can be computed using a polynomial size algebraic circuit with only $\{\max, +, *\}$, and rational constants. Note that non-degeneracy of I prevents division by 0, so that the output of the circuit is well-defined for every $x \in [0, 1]^n$. This shows that CDS-PRIORITY-CLEARING is in FIXP and that its strong approximation version is in $FIXP_a$.

For the FIXP-hardness of the problem, let Π be an arbitrary problem in FIXP. We describe a polynomial-time reduction from Π to CDS-PRIORITY-CLEARING. Let $I \in \Pi$ be an instance, let $F_I : [0, 1]^n \rightarrow [0, 1]^n$ be I's associated fixed point function, and let C_I be the algebraic circuit corresponding to F_I. Our reduction is analogous to the proof in [17], where the variant of the problem with proportional payments is shown to be FIXP-hard: The proof consists of a "pre-processing" step (in which the algebraic circuit is transformed into a specific form) followed by a transformation into a financial network, where a set of financial subnetwork gadgets are interconnected, and each such gadget corresponds to an arithmetic gate in the algebraic circuit. The pre-processing step of this reduction is entirely equal to that of [17]: This step transforms C_I into a circuit C_I' that satisfies that all the signals propagated by all gates in C_I' and all the used rational constants in C_I' are contained in the interval $[0, 1]$. The transformed circuit C_I' may contain two additional type of gates: Division gates and gates that compute the absolute value of the difference of two operands. We will refer to the latter type of gate as an *absolute difference gate*. The circuit C_I' does not contain any subtraction gates, and will not contain max and min gates either. The reader interested in the details of this pre-processing step is referred to [17].

The second part of the proof (the transformation step) differs from [17] in that a different set of gadgets needs to be used. For notational convenience, we may treat C_I' as the function F_I, hence we may write $C_I'(x) = y$ to denote $F_I(x) = y$.

Each of our gadgets has one or two *input banks* that correspond to the input signals of one of the types of arithmetic gate, and there is an *output bank* that corresponds to the output signal of the gate. For each of the gadgets, it holds that the output bank must have a recovery rate that equals the result of applying the respective arithmetic operation on the recovery rates of the input banks. Each gadget represents an arithmetic gate of the circuit, and the output banks of a gadget are connected to input banks of other gadgets such that there is a direct correspondence with the infrastructure of the arithmetic circuit. For precise details on this correspondence, we refer the reader to the proof in [17].

For defining our gadgets, we use our graphical notation for convenience. As stated, our gadgets each have one or two input banks, and one output bank, where the output bank is forced to have a clearing recovery rate that is obtained by applying a arithmetic operation on the recovery rate of the input banks, so as to simulate the arithmetic basis on which the algebraic circuit C'_I is built.

As a simple example of one of these gadgets we define a straightforward addition gadget, named g_+, depicted in Fig. 3a. This gadget directly accounts for the addition operation in the arithmetic basis. In our figures, input banks are denoted by black arrows incoming from the left, and output banks correspond to black arrows pointing out of the bank. The black arrows represent connections to other gadgets, and these connections are always realised by a debt contract of unit cost, and are always from the output node of a gadget to an input node of another gadget. Another slightly more complex gadget example is the *positive subtraction* gadget, displayed in Fig. 3b, taking two inputs r_1, r_2 and producing as output the value $\max\{0, r_1 - r_2\}$. This gadget is in turn used to form the absolute difference gadget, which can be constructed by combining two positive subtraction gadgets with an addition gadget (as $|r_1 - r_2| = \max\{0, r_1 - r_2\} + \max\{0, r_2 - r_1\}$). It is also used in the construction of our multiplication gadget.

In the figures representing our gadgets, some of the nodes have been annotated with a formula in terms of the recovery rates of the input banks of the gadget, subject to the resulting values being in the interval $[0, 1]$. This can be seen for example in the output node of our addition gadget in Fig. 3a. Such a formula represents the value that a clearing recovery rate must satisfy for the respective node. It is straightforward to verify that the given formulas are correct for each of our gadgets.

Since all signals inside C'_I are guaranteed to be in $[0, 1]$ for all input vectors, our financial system gadgets can readily be used and connected to each other to construct a financial system that corresponds to C'_I, i.e., such that the clearing recovery rates of the input and output banks of each of the gadgets must correspond to each of the signals inside the circuit C'_I.

The remaining gadgets are omitted. Some of our gadgets are composed of auxiliary gadgets, where in particular, the construction of the division gadget is rather involved, and a separate discussion of how this gadget is constructed is deferred to the full version of the paper. Another notably non-trivial gadget is the multiplication gadget, where the main challenge in its construction is to ensure that non-degeneracy holds and that the expressions for the intermediate recovery rates inside the gadget are all contained in $[0, 1]$.   □

4   Hardness of Deciding the Best Priority Profile

In a financial network, each node i can be assigned one of outdeg(i)! singleton liability priority lists. Consequently the number of candidate priority profiles for a system is exponentially large in terms of its input size. Next, we consider the setting where a financial authority is able to determine which priority list each bank should get assigned, and is interested in assigning these in such a way that

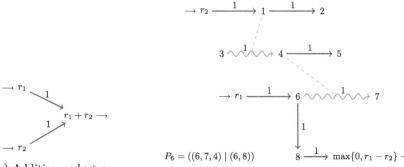

(a) Addition gadget g_+.

(b) Positive subtraction gadget $g_{\text{pos}-}$. Generates the value $\max\{0, r_1 - r_2\}$ from the input recovery rates r_1 and r_2. In this gadget node 6 pays according to the priority list $P_6 = ((6,7,4) \mid (6,8))$ thus it submits to node 8 the amount of $r_1 - r_2$ in case $r_1 > r_2$ and 0 otherwise

Fig. 3. Example gadgets from our reduction.

a specific objective is optimised for. We show that this problem is NP-hard for a set of natural choices of objective functions:

1. Minimising the number of defaulting nodes.
2. Minimising the number of not fully paid liabilities.
3. Minimising the number of activated CDSes in the financial system.
4. Maximising the equity of a specific node.
5. Maximising the liquidity in the financial system.

We here only prove Statements 1, 2 and 4.

Lemma 2. *Finding a priority list profile that minimises the number of defaulting banks and finding a priority list profile that minimises the number of not fully paid liabilities are both NP-hard problems.*

Proof. We prove the lemma via a reduction from the satisfiability problem (SAT), where we are given a boolean formula in conjunctive normal form, and have to determine whether there is a truth assignment to the variables that renders the formula true. Let $F = \bigwedge_{i=1}^{n} C_i$ be a SAT instance, where $C_1, \ldots, C_n$ are the clauses, and let V_F be the set of all variables that in F. We create a financial network from F as follows. For each variable $x \in V_F$ we construct a gadget that is refereed to as the x-subnetwork. Each x-subnetwork consists of four nodes, labeled as $i_x, x, \neg x, j_x$, where $e_{i_x} = 1$ and $e_x = e_{\neg x} = e_{j_x} = 0$, and of four debt contracts, $\mathcal{DC} = \{(i_x, x), (i_x, \neg x), (x, j_x), (\neg x, j_x)\}$ all with contract notionals equal to one. Moreover, the constructed financial network has n further nodes, labeled as $C_1, \ldots, C_n$, that correspond to each clause in F with $e_{C_1} = \cdots = e_{C_n} = 0$, and one terminal node labeled as τ, towards which each C_i

holds a debt contract of notional one, i.e. $c_{C_i, \tau} = 1$. Finally for each variable x of F, we construct two nodes labeled as k_x and $k_{\neg x}$ respectively, where e_{k_x} and $e_{k_{\neg x}}$ are equal to the number of occurrences of literals x and $\neg x$ in F, respectively. Whenever a literal l belongs to a clause C_i we construct the CDS $(k_l, C_i, \neg l)$ with $c^{\neg l}_{k_l, C_i} = 1$. An example of a network induced from $F = (x \vee y) \wedge (y \vee \neg y)$ is given in Fig. 4. We now map a truth assignment $T : V_F \mapsto \{true, false\}$ to a priority list profile $\mathcal{P}_T$ as follows: If $T(x) = true$, node i_x prioritises node x, and otherwise it prioritises node $\neg x$. All k_l nodes posses enough external assets to fully pay their debts under any priority list, so we can take an arbitrary list for those nodes, and all remaining nodes have at most one liability. Conversely, from a priority list profile $\mathcal{P}$ we induce the truth assignment $T_\mathcal{P}$ as follows: if i_x prioritises x then $T(x) = true$ otherwise $T(x) = false$.

Let $T : V_F \mapsto \{true, false\}$ be any truth assignment and consider the priority list profile $\mathcal{P}_T$. In each x-subnetwork, node i_x can fully pay only its first priority, thus in each x-subnetwork there exist two defaulting nodes regardless of the choice of priority list of i_x, meaning that the minimum number of defaulting nodes in the induced financial system is $2|V_F|$. Similarly, each x-subnetwork has two not fully paid liabilities regardless of the choice of priority lost of i_x. The only additional defaulting nodes might be the nodes $C_1, \ldots, C_n$, and the only additional not fully paid liabilities might be on the n debt contracts in which one of $C_1, \ldots, C_n$ is the debtor. Let us inspect which of the latter set of nodes are defaulting and which of the latter liabilities are not fully paid under $\mathcal{P}_T$. If clause C_i is a clause that is not satisfied under T, then none of the CDSes involving node C_i are activated, and node C_i does not have any assets under $\mathcal{P}_T$. Since C_i has to pay 1 to τ, node C_i will be in default, and C_i's liability of 1 will not be paid. If clause C_i is a clause that is satisfied under T, then at least one CDS involving node C_i is activated, and since the reference bank in this CDS has recovery rate 0, node C_i will receive the CDS's full notional of 1, with which it can fully pay its liability of 1. Hence, in the latter case, node C_i is not in default.

Hence, for a truth assignment T, under $\mathcal{P}_T$, the number of banks in default and the number of not fully paid liabilities is are both equal to $2|V_F|$ plus the number of unsatisfied clauses. Since we argued above that restricting to the profiles $\{\mathcal{P}_T \mid T$ is a truth-assignment for $F\}$ is without loss of generality, from finding the profile of priority lists minimising the number of defaulting banks or minimising the number of not fully paid liabilities in the constructed financial network, one can infer whether the formula F is satisfiable, which proves our claim. □

Lemma 3. *Finding a priority list profile that maximises the equity of a specific node is NP-hard.*

Proof. We prove the lemma via a reduction from KNAPSACK. Let us be given a knapsack instance with a knapsack of capacity B, a set $S = \{a_1, \ldots, a_n\}$ of objects having profit $profit(a_i)$ and size $size(a_i)$. Without loss of generality, we assume that $size(a_i)$, for all $a_i \in S$ as well as B are integer numbers. We

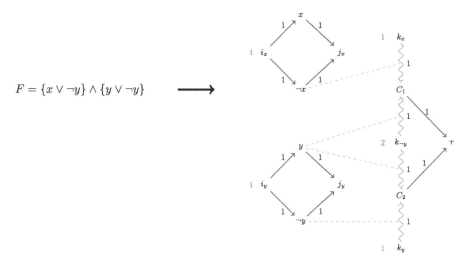

$$F = \{x \vee \neg y\} \wedge \{y \vee \neg y\}$$

Fig. 4. The financial system corresponding to the formula $F = \{x \vee \neg y\} \wedge \{y \vee \neg y\}$.

construct a financial network $\mathcal{F} = (N, e, c)$ as follows: We introduce a node 0 with external assets $e_0 = B$ and for each object $a_j \in S$ we introduce a corresponding node j and let node 0 hold a debt contract towards each node j with notional $c_{0,j} = \text{size}(a_j)$. Moreover we introduce a node τ with $e_\tau = 0$, and a node T with $e_T = 0$, which we refer to as the *terminal node*. We add a debt contract of notional $\text{size}(a_j)$ from each node j to node τ. For each node j we moreover introduce a *j-subnetwork*, consisting of:

- two nodes y_j and x_j with $e_{y_j} = 1, e_{x_j} = 0$,
- a CDS contract (y_j, x_j, j) with notional $c_{y_j,x_j}^j = \max_{a_j \in S}\{size(a_j)\}$,
- a node z_j towards which x_j holds a debt contract of notional $c_{x_j,z_j} = 1$.
- a node k_j with $e_{k_j} = \text{profit}(a_j)$ and an outgoing CDS (k_j, T, x_j) with notional $\text{profit}(a_j)$.

The construction of the j-subnetwork is illustrated in Fig. 5.

Assume an optimal solution to the original Knapsack instance and let OPT be the set of the objects a_j contained in it. We know that $\sum_{a_i \in \text{OPT}} \text{size}(a_i) \leq B$ and that $\sum_{a_i \in \text{OPT}} \text{profit}(a_i)$, is the maximum profit that can fit in the knapsack. We define the set $N = \{1, \ldots, n\}$, and $N_{\text{OPT}} = \{j \mid a_j \in \text{OPT}\}$ to be the set containing all nodes in $\mathcal{F}$ that correspond to objects contained in the optimal solution. Fix the singleton liability priority list for node 0 to be $\mathcal{P}_0 = (\{N_{\text{OPT}}\} \mid \{N \setminus N_{\text{OPT}}\})$, meaning that node 0 first prioritises all creditors in N_{OPT} in an arbitrary order and afterwards all other creditors in $N \setminus N_{\text{OPT}}$ again in an arbitrary order. Next we prove that under this profile, node T receives its maximum total assets. Observe that $\forall j \in N_{\text{OPT}}$, $p_{0j} = \text{size}(a_j)$ since $\sum_{j \in N_{\text{OPT}}} c_{0j} = \sum_{a_j \in \text{OPT}} \text{size}(a_j) \leq B = e_0$. Since every j node that corresponds to an object $a_j \in \text{OPT}$ receives $\text{size}(a_j)$, it can fully pay node τ, so $r_j = 1$. For all creditors $m \in N \setminus N_{\text{OPT}}$ it holds that $p_{0m} < \text{size}(a_m)$

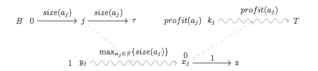

Fig. 5. The j subnetwork of the constructed financial system

So, $\forall j \in N_{\text{OPT}} : r_j = 1$ while $\forall m \in N \setminus N_{\text{OPT}} : r_m < 1$. Next we prove that for each $j \in N_{\text{OPT}}$, $p_{k_j,T} = \text{profit}(a_j)$ and for each $m \in N \setminus N_{\text{OPT}}$, $p_{k_m,T} = 0$. Take a $j \in N_{\text{OPT}}$, we know that $r_j = 1$, which implies that the CDS (y_j, x_j, j) is not activated thus $r_{x_j} = 0$ which in turn activates the CDS (k_j, T, x_j) where node k_j pays $\text{profit}(a_j)$ to node T. On the other side, for a $m \in N \setminus N_{\text{OPT}}$, it holds that $r_m < 1$, which means that the CDS (y_m, x_m, m) is activated and generates a liability of $\max_{a_i \in S}\{\text{size}(a_i)\} \cdot (1 - r_m)$ for node y_m. We prove that this liability is at least 1: For an object $a_m \notin \text{OPT}$, r_m indicates the proportion of $\text{size}(a_m)$ that fits in the available knapsack area unoccupied by the objects in OPT. Obviously for $a_m \notin \text{OPT}$, $\text{size}(a_m) > B - \text{size}(\text{OPT})$, otherwise $a_m \in \text{OPT}$ and $r_m \cdot \text{size}(a_m) + \text{size}(\text{OPT}) = B$. Since by assumption B and $\text{size}(a_j)$ for all $a_j \in S$ are integers, it holds that $\forall a_m \notin \text{OPT}$, $r_m \leq (\max_{a_k \in S}\{\text{size}(a_k)\} - 1)/(\max_{a_k \in S}\{\text{size}(a_k)\}$, so the liability for y_m is:

$$l^m_{y_m,x_m} = \max_{a_k \in S}\{\text{size}(a_k)\}(1 - r_m)$$

$$\geq \max_{a_k \in S}\{\text{size}(a_k)\}\left(1 - \frac{\max_{a_k \in S}\{\text{size}(a_k)\} - 1}{\max_{a_k \in S}\{\text{size}(a_k)\}}\right) = 1.$$

So eventually, $\forall m \in N \setminus N_{\text{OPT}}$, $p_{y_m,x_m} = 1$. Now $r_{x_m} = 1$ thus the CDS (k_m, T, x_m) is not activated meaning that $p_{k_m,T} = 0$. From the above observations we conclude that the equity of T is $\sum_{j \in N_{\text{OPT}}} \text{profit}(a_j)$: node T receives money from all nodes that correspond to objects contained in OPT. We claim that this is the maximum equity node T can receive. If there exist a higher equity for T, then this must be generated from another profile $\mathcal{P}'_0$ that corresponds to a solution to the original Knapsack instance with higher profit than the optimal one which is a contradiction.

For the opposite direction assume $\mathcal{P}_0$ to be the profile of node 0 that maximises T's equity. Let $A = \{a_j \mid p_{0j} = \text{size}(a_j)\}$ be the set of objects that corresponds to creditor nodes that node 0 can fully pay. Obviously A can be computed in polynomial time from $\mathcal{P}_0$. We claim that A is the optimal solution to the original Knapsack instance. Assume that there exists another set A' such that $\sum_{a_j \in A'} \text{size}(a_j) \leq B$ and $\sum_{a_j \in A'} \text{profit}(a_j) > \sum_{a_j \in A} \text{profit}(a_j)$. Now node 0 could rearrange its priorities by prioritising all creditors j for which $a_j \in A'$. Doing so, node 0 can fully pay all nodes j for which $a_j \in A'$ since $\sum_{a_j \in A'} \text{size}(a_j) \leq B = e_0$ and node T receives $\sum_{a_j \in A'} \text{profit}(a_j) > \sum_{a_j \in A} \text{profit}(a_j)$, a contradiction to the original assumption that $\sum_{a_j \in A} \text{profit}(a_j)$ is the maximum equity for node T. $\qquad\square$

5   Conclusions and Future Work

Financial networks have emerged as a fertile research area in both computational complexity and algorithmic game theory. It is paramount to understand systemic risk in finance from both these perspectives. In this paper, we join both streams of work by settling questions around the computational complexity of systemic risk for priority payments, a scheme so far only studied from the game-theoretic point of view. In an interesting parallel with the state of the art for proportional payments, we prove that computing clearing recovery rates is FIXP-complete whereas it is NP-hard to compute the priority lists optimising several measures of financial health of the system.

Our work paves the way for studying payment schemes in financial networks in more detail. Is there a payment scheme for financial networks with derivatives that makes the computation of systemic risk easy and/or that induces "nice" equilibria? We also wonder the extent to which the flexibility of working with financial networks can lead to a deeper understanding of FIXP; e.g., are there payment schemes that can be proved complete for variants of FIXP defined upon a different basis?

References

1. Acemoglu, D., Ozdaglar, A., Tahbaz-Salehi, A.: Systemic risk and stability in financial networks. Am. Econ. Rev. **105**(2), 564–608 (2015)
2. Bertoni, A., Mauri, G., Sabadini, N.: A characterization of the class of functions computable in polynomial time on random access machines. In: STOC, pp. 168–176. ACM (1981)
3. Bertschinger, N., Hoefer, M., Schmand, D.: Strategic payments in financial networks. In: ITCS. LIPIcs, vol. 151, pp. 46:1–46:16 (2020)
4. Borodin, A., Fagin, R., Hopcroft, J.E., Tompa, M.: Decreasing the nesting depth of expressions involving square roots. J. Symb. Comput. **1**(2), 169–188 (1985)
5. Cifuentes, R., Ferrucci, G., Shin, H.S.: Liquidity risk and contagion. J. Eur. Econ. Assoc. **3**(2–3), 556–566 (2005)
6. Eisenberg, L., Noe, T.H.: Systemic risk in financial systems. Manag. Sci. **47**(2), 236–249 (2001)
7. Elliott, M., Golub, B., Jackson, M.O.: Financial networks and contagion. Am. Econ. Rev. **104**(10), 3115–3153 (2014)
8. Etessami, K., Yannakakis, M.: On the complexity of nash equilibria and other fixed points. SIAM J. Comput. **39**(6), 2531–2597 (2010)
9. Filos-Ratsikas, A., Giannakopoulos, Y., Hollender, A., Lazos, P., Poças, D.: On the complexity of equilibrium computation in first-price auctions. In: EC, pp. 454–476 (2021)
10. Filos-Ratsikas, A., Hansen, K.A., Høgh, K., Hollender, A.: Fixp-membership via convex optimization: games, cakes, and markets. In: FOCS, pp. 827–838 (2021)
11. Garey, M.R., Graham, R.L., Johnson, D.S.: Some NP-complete geometric problems. In: STOC, pp. 10–22 (1976)
12. Glasserman, P., Young, H.P.: How likely is contagion in financial networks? J. Bank. Finance **50**, 383–399 (2015)

13. Goldberg, P.W., Hollender, A.: The hairy ball problem is PPAD-complete. J. Comput. Syst. Sci. **122**, 34–62 (2021)
14. Heise, S., Kühn, R.: Derivatives and credit contagion in interconnected networks. Eur. Phys. J. B **85**(4), 1–19 (2012)
15. Hemenway, B., Khanna, S.: Sensitivity and computational complexity in financial networks. Algorithmic Finance **5**(3–4), 95–110 (2016)
16. Hu, D., Zhao, J.L., Hua, Z., Wong, M.C.S.: Network-based modeling and analysis of systemic risk in banking systems. MIS Q. 1269–1291 (2012)
17. Ioannidis, S.D., De Keijzer, B., Ventre, C.: Strong approximations and irrationality in financial networks with derivatives. In: ICALP (2022)
18. Kanellopoulos, P., Kyropoulou, M., Zhou, H.: Financial network games. CoRR, abs/2107.06623 (2021)
19. Kanellopoulos, P., Kyropoulou, M., Zhou, H.: Forgiving debt in financial network games. CoRR, abs/2202.10986 (2022)
20. Papadimitriou, C.H.: The euclidean traveling salesman problem is np-complete. Theor. Comput. Sci. **4**(3), 237–244 (1977)
21. Papp, P.A., Wattenhofer, R.: Network-aware strategies in financial systems. In: ICALP, vol. 168, pp. 91:1–91:17 (2020)
22. Papp, P.A., Wattenhofer, R.: Debt swapping for risk mitigation in financial networks. In: EC, pp. 765–784 (2021)
23. Papp, P.A., Wattenhofer, R.: Default ambiguity: finding the best solution to the clearing problem. In: Feldman, M., Fu, H., Talgam-Cohen, I. (eds.) WINE 2021. LNCS, vol. 13112, pp. 391–409. Springer, Cham (2022). https://doi.org/10.1007/978-3-030-94676-0_22
24. Papp, P.A., Wattenhofer, R.: Sequential defaulting in financial networks. In: ITCS, vol. 185, pp. 52:1–52:20 (2021)
25. Rogers, L.C.G., Veraart, L.A.M.: Failure and rescue in an interbank network. Manag. Sci. **59**(4), 882–898 (2013)
26. Schönhage, A.: On the power of random access machines. In: Maurer, H.A. (ed.) ICALP 1979. LNCS, vol. 71, pp. 520–529. Springer, Heidelberg (1979). https://doi.org/10.1007/3-540-09510-1_42
27. Schuldenzucker, S., Seuken, S.: Portfolio compression in financial networks: incentives and systemic risk. In: EC, p. 79 (2020)
28. Schuldenzucker, S., Seuken, S., Battiston, S.: Clearing payments in financial networks with credit default swaps. In: EC, p. 759 (2016)
29. Schuldenzucker, S., Seuken, S., Battiston, S.: Finding clearing payments in financial networks with credit default swaps is PPAD-complete. In: ITCS, vol. 67, pp. 32:1–32:20 (2017)
30. Tiwari, P.: A problem that is easier to solve on the unit-cost algebraic RAM. J. Complex. **8**(4), 393–397 (1992)
31. Yannakakis, M.: Equilibria, fixed points, and complexity classes. In: STACS, vol. 1, pp. 19–38 (2008)

Automated Equilibrium Analysis
of 2 × 2 × 2 Games

Sahar Jahani[(✉)] and Bernhard von Stengel

London School of Economics and Political Science, London WC2A 2AE, UK
{s.jahani,b.von-stengel}@lse.ac.uk

Abstract. The set of all Nash equilibria of a non-cooperative game
with more than two players is defined by equations and inequalities
between nonlinear polynomials, which makes it challenging to compute.
This paper presents an algorithm that computes this set for the simplest
game with more than two players with arbitrary (possibly non-generic)
payoffs, which has not been done before. We give new elegant formulas
for completely mixed equilibria, and compute visual representations of
the best-response correspondences and their intersections, which define
the Nash equilibrium set. These have been implemented in Python and
will be part of a public web-based software for automated equilibrium
analysis. For small games, which are often studied in economic models,
a complete Nash equilibrium analysis is desirable and should be feasible.
This project demonstrates the difficulties of this task and offers pathways
for extensions to larger games.

Keywords: Equilibrium enumeration · Nash equilibrium ·
Three-player game

1 Introduction

Game theory provides mathematical models for multiagent interactions. The
primary solution concept is Nash equilibrium and its refinements (e.g., perfect
equilibrium, [12]) or generalizations such as correlated equilibrium (which arises
from regret-based learning algorithms). Already for two-player games, finding
just one Nash equilibrium is PPAD-hard [3,5]. However, this "intractability" of
the Nash equilibrium concept applies to *large* games. Many games that are used
as economic models are small, with less than a few dozen payoff parameters,
and often given in extensive form as game trees. It would be desirable to have
a *complete* analysis of *all* Nash equilibria of such a game, in order to study
the implications of the model. Such a complete analysis is known for two-player
games. Their Nash equilibria can be represented as unions of "maximal Nash
subsets" [14]. These are maximally "exchangeable" Nash equilibrium sets, that
is, products of two polytopes of mixed strategies that are mutual best responses.
Their non-disjoint unions form the topologically connected components of Nash
equilibria, and are computed by the *lrsnash* algorithm of Avis, Rosenberg, Savani,

© The Author(s), under exclusive license to Springer Nature Switzerland AG 2022
P. Kanellopoulos et al. (Eds.): SAGT 2022, LNCS 13584, pp. 223–237, 2022.
https://doi.org/10.1007/978-3-031-15714-1_13

and von Stengel [1], which works well for games with up to about twenty strategies per player.

For games with more than two players, the set of all Nash equilibria cannot be described in such a way, because it is determined by equations and inequalities between nonlinear polynomials. The Gambit software package [10] provides access to polynomial solvers in order to compute Nash equilibria for generic games. "Generic" means that the payoffs do not represent edge cases, for example when (11) below reads as "$0 = 0$". The edge cases can be encoded as the zeros of a suitable polynomial in the game parameters and form a set of measure zero. Generic games have only finitely many equilibrium points. Non-generic games can have infinite set of equilibria.

However, rather remarkably, there is to our knowledge no algorithm that computes (in some description) the entire set of Nash equilibria for even the simplest game with more than two players if the game is non-generic, which naturally occurs for games in extensive form, such as "Selten's horse" [12]; see Sect. 4.3 below.

This paper describes an algorithm that computes the entire set of Nash equilibria for arbitrary $2 \times 2 \times 2$-games, that is, three-player games where every player has two strategies. These are the simplest games with more than two players that do not have a special structure (such as being a polymatrix game arising from pairwise interactions, see [8]). While this seems like a straightforward task, it is already challenging in its complexity.

One contribution of this paper is to reduce this complexity by carefully preserving the symmetry among the players, and a judicious use of intermediate parameters (Eq. (6) in Sect. 4) derived from the payoffs. We determine a quadratic equation (see (11)) that has a regular structure using determinants (not known to us before), which also implies that a generic $2 \times 2 \times 2$ game has at most two completely mixed equilibria (shown much more simply than in [4] or [9]). The standard approach to manipulating such complicated algebraic expressions is to use a computer algebra system [6].

As a "binary" game with only two pure strategies per player, the equilibria of a $2 \times 2 \times 2$ game can be visualized in a cube, but this needs some 3D graphics to be accessible (our graphics can be "moved in 3D"). We think that good visualizations of the geometry of equilibrium solutions of a game are important for understanding them, and their possible structure (both for applications of and research in game theory).

We present our algorithm in two parts: Identifying partially mixed equilibria (on the faces or edges of the cube) which arise from two-player equilibria where the third player plays a pure strategy that remains optimal; this part has a straightforward generalization to larger numbers of strategies for the three players, and may be practically very useful, certainly for a preliminary analysis. The second part is to look for completely mixed equilibria, which is challenging and does not generalize straightforwardly. A substantial part of the code, which we cannot describe in full because it involves a large number of case distinctions, deals systematically with the degenerate cases (which do arise in game trees even when payoffs are generic).

2   General Form of the Game

The following table describes the general form of a three-player game in which each player has two strategies:

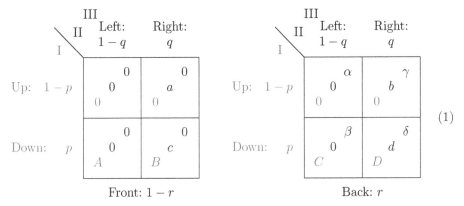

$$(1)$$

This game is played by player I, II, III choosing (simultaneously) their second strategy with probability p, q, r, respectively. Player I chooses a row, either Up or Down (abbreviated U and D), player II chooses a column, either Left or Right (abbreviated L and R), and player III chooses a panel, either Front or Back (abbreviated F and B). The strategy names are also chosen to remember the six faces of the three-dimensional unit cube of mixed-strategy profiles (p, q, r), shown in Fig. 1.

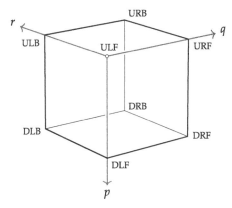

Fig. 1. Cube of mixed-strategy probabilities (p, q, r) drawn as in (1) down, right, and backwards.

Each of the eight cells in (1) has a payoff triple (T, t, τ) to the three players, with the payoffs to player I, II, III in upper case, lower case, and Greek letters, respectively. The payoffs in (1) are staggered and shown in color to distinguish them more easily between the players.

The payoffs have been normalized so that each player's first pure strategy has payoff zero throughout. (Zero is the natural "first" number, as in 0 and 1 for the two strategies of each player, or for the payoffs.) This normalization is obtained by subtracting a suitable constant from the player's payoffs for each combination of opponent strategies (e.g., each column for player I). This does not affect best responses [13, p. 239f]. With this normalization, the first strategy of each player gives always expected payoff zero.

For each player's second strategy, the expected payoffs are as follows:

player I : $S(q,r) = (1-q)(1-r)\,A\,+\,q(1-r)\,B\,+\,(1-q)r\,C\,+\,qr\,D,$
player II : $s(r,p) = (1-r)(1-p)\,a\,+\,r(1-p)\,b\,+\,(1-r)p\,c\,+\,rp\,d,$
player III : $\sigma(p,q) = (1-p)(1-q)\,\alpha\,+\,p(1-q)\,\beta\,+\,(1-p)q\,\gamma\,+\,pq\,\delta,$

$$(2)$$

so the three players can be treated symmetrically. The cyclic shift among p, q, r in (2), and corresponding choice of where to put b and c and β and γ in (1), will lead to more symmetric solutions.

The mixed-strategy profile (p, q, r) is a *mixed equilibrium* if each player's mixed strategy is a *best response* against the other players' strategies. That best response is a pure (deterministic) strategy, unless the two pure strategies have *equal* expected payoffs [11]. Hence, p is a best response of player I to (q, r) if the following conditions hold:

$$
\begin{aligned}
p = 0 \quad &\Leftrightarrow\ S(q,r) \le 0 \\
p \in [0,1] &\Leftrightarrow\ S(q,r) = 0 \\
p = 1 \quad &\Leftrightarrow S(q,r) \ge 0\,.
\end{aligned}
\tag{3}
$$

Similarly, q is a best response of player II to (r, p) and r is a best response of player III to (p, q) if and only if

$$
\begin{aligned}
q = 0 \quad &\Leftrightarrow s(r,p) \le 0 & r = 0 \quad &\Leftrightarrow \sigma(p,q) \le 0 \\
q \in [0,1] &\Leftrightarrow s(r,p) = 0 & r \in [0,1] &\Leftrightarrow \sigma(p,q) = 0 \\
q = 1 \quad &\Leftrightarrow s(r,p) \ge 0 & r = 1 \quad &\Leftrightarrow \sigma(p,q) \ge 0.
\end{aligned}
\tag{4}
$$

For each player I, II, or III, the triples (p, q, r) that fulfill the respective conditions for p, q, or r in (3) or (4) define the *best-response correspondence* of that player, a subset of the cube $[0, 1]^3$. The set of Nash equilibria is the intersection of these three sets. The best-response correspondence for player I, for example, has one of the following forms, as shown in Fig. 2:

(a) If $A = B = C = D = 0$, then $S(q,r) = 0$ for all $q, r \in [0, 1]$ and player I's best-response correspondence is the entire cube $[0, 1]^3$.

(b) If $A, B, C, D < 0$, then $S(q, r) < 0$ for all $(q, r) \in [0, 1]^2$ and strategy U strictly dominates D, so that player I will always play U, and the game reduces to a two-player game between players II and III. The same happens when $A, B, C, D > 0$, in which case D strictly dominates U. In these two cases the best-response correspondence of player I is the upwards "U face" or downwards "D face" of the cube (as in Fig. 2(b)), respectively.

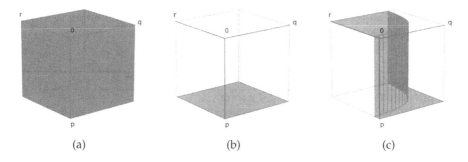

Fig. 2. Different forms of best-response correspondence.

(c) In all other cases, the best response of player I to (q, r) is sometimes U and sometimes D. The best-response correspondence of player I is then a surface that consists of subsets of the U or D face according to (3), which are connected by vertical parts, as in Fig. 2(c) where player I is indifferent between U and D. Figure 3 shows a generic example.

The Nash equilibria of a game can be divided to two categories, based on which strategies are used:

- *partially mixed equilibria* in which at least one player plays a pure strategy (including pure equilibria where all the players play pure strategies). These equilibria are on the faces of the cube.
- *completely mixed equilibria* in which none of the players plays a pure strategy. These equilibria are in the interior of the cube.

In order to find all the equilibria in these games, we can divide the procedure into two parts:

(i) Find the *partially mixed* (including pure) equilibria.
(ii) Find the *completely mixed* equilibria.

We use different methods for each part. The union of the answers will be the set of all equilibria of the game.

3   Partially Mixed Equilibria

In an equilibrium, each player's strategy is a best response to the other players' strategies. In a partially mixed equilibrium, at least one player plays a pure strategy. All partially mixed equilibria are thus identified via six subgames. In each subgame we fix the strategy s_i of one player $i = 1, 2, 3$ to be 0 or 1. Fixing one player's strategy gives a 2×2 game for which we compute all equilibria. Then, for each equilibrium component of the subgame, given by the profile s_{-i} of strategies of the other two players, we check if it is the best response for the fixed player i and if it is, this means it is a partially mixed equilibrium (PMNE) of the game. Algorithm 1 gives a simplified pseudo-code.

Algorithm 1. Finding partially mixed equilibria

Input: payoff matrix of a $2 \times 2 \times 2$ game
Output: its set of partially mixed Nash equilibria
PMNE $\leftarrow \emptyset$
for each player i **do**
  for $s_i \in \{0, 1\}$ **do**
    SG $\leftarrow 2 \times 2$ game when player i plays s_i
    cand $\leftarrow$ all Nash equilibria of SG   ▷ using lrsNash algorithm
    for each $s_{-i} \in$ cand **do**   ▷ strategy pair of the other two players
      if $U_i(s_i, s_{-i}) \geq U_i(1 - s_i, s_{-i})$ **then**   ▷ U_i is player i's utility function
        add (s_i, s_{-i}) to PMNE
  return PMNE

Algorithm 1 also applies when cand is an infinite set of equilibria of the 2×2 subgame. Such a set can contain line segments or be equal to the whole facet of the cube. Then the output of Algorithm 1 is the intersection of the best-response surface of player i with cand. This intersection is computed as follows: Equilibrium segments of a 2×2 game can be only horizontal or vertical; then the strategy of one player is constant throughout the segment and just one variable changes. Furthermore, the intersection of an entire facet of the cube with the best-response surface has parameterized borders that are lines or hyperbola arcs (see Sect. 4.2).

4 Completely Mixed Equilibria

In this section, we assume that all the partially mixed equilibria are found using the previous algorithm. Here, we focus on finding the completely mixed equilibria. First, we find these equilibria algebraically by solving the best-response equations. Second, we display each player's best-response correspondence as a surface, and the intersection of these surfaces will also show the equilibria.

4.1 Finding the Completely Mixed Equilibria Algebraically

We focus on player I using (3); the consideration for players II and III is analogous. We will show that the indifference equation $S(q, r) = 0$, which by (3) is necessary for player I to be able to mix ($0 < p < 1$), defines either a line or a (possibly degenerated) hyperbola, using possibly both branches.

Generically, the intersection of the three best-response surfaces is a finite set of points. However, certain kinds of degeneracy may occur, which leads to infinite components of Nash equilibria.

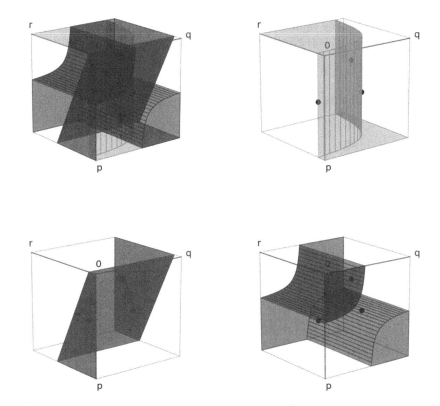

Fig. 3. Example of best-response surfaces of a game with two completely mixed equilibria and one partially mixed equilibrium, marked as black dots. (The actual display can be 3D-animated and handled interactively.)

For our algebraic approach, we rewrite (2) as

$$
\begin{aligned}
S(q,r) &= A + Kq + Lr + Mqr \\
s(r,p) &= a + kr + lp + mrp \\
\sigma(p,q) &= \alpha + \kappa p + \lambda q + \mu pq
\end{aligned}
\tag{5}
$$

with

$$
\begin{aligned}
K &= B - A, & L &= C - A, & M &= A - B - C + D, \\
k &= b - a, & l &= c - a, & m &= a - b - c + d, \\
\kappa &= \beta - \alpha, & \lambda &= \gamma - \alpha, & \mu &= \alpha - \beta - \gamma + \delta.
\end{aligned}
\tag{6}
$$

The expressions in (5) are linear in each of p, q, r, and we consider when they are equal to zero, which defines the indifference surfaces:

$$
\begin{aligned}
A + Kq + (L + Mq)r &= 0 \\
a + lp + (k + mp)r &= 0 \\
\alpha + \kappa p + (\lambda + \mu p)q &= 0.
\end{aligned}
\tag{7}
$$

We first eliminate r by multiplying the first equation in (7) with $(k + mp)$ and the second with $-(L + Mq)$ and adding them, which gives

$$(A + Kq)(k + mp) - (L + Mq)(a + lp) = 0 \tag{8}$$

or, using determinants,

$$\begin{vmatrix} A & L \\ a & k \end{vmatrix} + \begin{vmatrix} A & L \\ l & m \end{vmatrix} p + \begin{vmatrix} K & M \\ a & k \end{vmatrix} q + \begin{vmatrix} K & M \\ l & m \end{vmatrix} pq = 0. \tag{9}$$

In the same way, we eliminate q by multiplying the last equation in (7) with $\begin{vmatrix} K & M \\ a & k \end{vmatrix} + \begin{vmatrix} K & M \\ l & m \end{vmatrix} p$ and (9) with $-(\lambda + \mu p)$ and addition, which gives

$$\left(\begin{vmatrix} K & M \\ a & k \end{vmatrix} + \begin{vmatrix} K & M \\ l & m \end{vmatrix} p \right) (\alpha + \kappa p) - \left(\begin{vmatrix} A & L \\ a & k \end{vmatrix} + \begin{vmatrix} A & L \\ l & m \end{vmatrix} p \right) (\lambda + \mu p) = 0 \tag{10}$$

or (verified by expanding each 3×3 determinant in the last column)

$$\begin{vmatrix} A & L & \alpha \\ K & M & \lambda \\ a & k & 0 \end{vmatrix} + \left(\begin{vmatrix} A & L & \alpha \\ K & M & \lambda \\ l & m & 0 \end{vmatrix} + \begin{vmatrix} A & L & \kappa \\ K & M & \mu \\ a & k & 0 \end{vmatrix} \right) p + \begin{vmatrix} A & L & \kappa \\ K & M & \mu \\ l & m & 0 \end{vmatrix} p^2 = 0. \tag{11}$$

Unless it states $0 = 0$, the quadratic equation (11) has at most two solutions for p, which have to belong to $[0, 1]$ to represent a mixed equilibrium strategy of player I. Substituted into the linear equation (9) for q and the second equation in (7) for r, this then determines q and r uniquely unless one of the equations has no or infinitely many solutions. If q and r belong to $[0, 1]$, these determine mixed equilibria. They are completely mixed if p, q, r are all strictly between 0 and 1. Moreover, a generic $2 \times 2 \times 2$ game has therefore at most two completely mixed equilibria (as proved in much more complicated ways by [4] and [9]).

The system (5) can be solved in exactly the same manner to derive a quadratic equation for q, where in (5), we only need to move the first equation into last position and change A, a, α to a, α, A respectively, and similarly for the other letters. Then (11) becomes

$$\begin{vmatrix} a & l & A \\ k & m & L \\ \alpha & \kappa & 0 \end{vmatrix} + \left(\begin{vmatrix} a & l & A \\ k & m & L \\ \lambda & \mu & 0 \end{vmatrix} + \begin{vmatrix} a & l & K \\ k & m & M \\ \alpha & \kappa & 0 \end{vmatrix} \right) q + \begin{vmatrix} a & l & K \\ k & m & M \\ \lambda & \mu & 0 \end{vmatrix} q^2 = 0. \tag{12}$$

Similarly, the quadratic equation for r states

$$\begin{vmatrix} \alpha & \lambda & a \\ \kappa & \mu & l \\ A & K & 0 \end{vmatrix} + \left(\begin{vmatrix} \alpha & \lambda & a \\ \kappa & \mu & l \\ L & M & 0 \end{vmatrix} + \begin{vmatrix} \alpha & \lambda & k \\ \kappa & \mu & m \\ A & K & 0 \end{vmatrix} \right) r + \begin{vmatrix} \alpha & \lambda & k \\ \kappa & \mu & m \\ L & M & 0 \end{vmatrix} r^2 = 0. \tag{13}$$

As before, in the generic case, any of the up to two solutions q to (12) determines r and p. Similarly, any of the up to two solutions r to (13) determines p and q.

If p, q, r are the solutions to (11), (12), (13) in a completely mixed equilibrium, they may be irrational numbers. They can be output as approximate floating-point numbers or symbolically with square roots as algebraic numbers (assuming rational payoffs as inputs).

The conditions (11), (12), (13) are all necessary when each player is required to be indifferent between his pure strategies. However, they may hold trivially in the form $0 = 0$, which may indicate infinite solution sets; an example is (11) for case (a) when $A = K = L = M = 0$. Furthermore, even if (11) has two real solutions p, say, then for one or both choices of p the third equation in (7) may state $0 = 0$ and then q is not determined; one would expect that this implies that (12) states $0 = 0$ as well. A further source of infinite solutions may be that some solutions for p, q, or r are 0 or 1, because then the respective player plays a pure strategy and does not have to be indifferent. This should come up in the analysis of the partially mixed equilibria in the previous section.

Other than these quadratic equations, we can acquire more information about the game by studying the relation between any two variables. Using (5), we can write each variable as a function of the other variable. So, from $S(q, r) = 0$ we will have:

$$q = \frac{-Lr - A}{Mr + K} = f_q(r), \qquad\qquad r = \frac{-Kq - A}{Mq + L} = f_r(q). \qquad (14)$$

Similarly, we have four more equations derived from the other two equations. These equations will help us identify the mixed equilibria when the quadratic equations have infinite solutions and do not give us any information. An example for this case is the game shown in Fig. 4. In this game, we have $0 = 0$ for (11) and (12). Also, (13) cannot be formed because we have to multiply by 0 to eliminate other variables; hence, we have to look at the relation between the variables. Here, r cannot be written as a function of other variables (division by 0), and for the other relations we have

$$p = f(q) = \tfrac{-8q+7}{-8q+8}, \qquad\qquad q = f(p) = \tfrac{-8p+7}{-8p+8},$$

$$p = f(r) = \quad\tfrac{1}{2}, \qquad\qquad q = f(r) = \quad\tfrac{3}{4}.$$

These relations show that there is a line of equilibria in the r direction where $p = \tfrac{1}{2}$ and $q = \tfrac{3}{4}$, as one can see on each player's best-response surface in Fig. 4.

4.2   Displaying Best-Response Surfaces

To see how the best-response surfaces look like, we focus on player I's expected payoff equation; for the other players it is similar. With (6) and (5), the condition $S(q, r) = 0$ states

$$S(q, r) = A + Kq + Lr + Mqr = 0. \qquad (15)$$

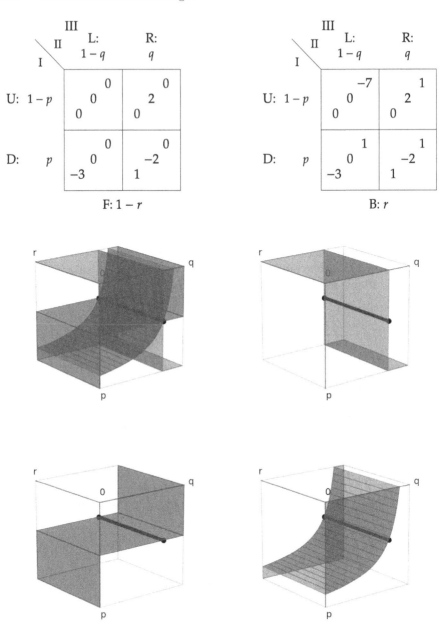

Fig. 4. Example of a game with a line of mixed equilibria when the quadratic equations have infinitely many solutions.

(a) First, we exclude the case when $(A, B, C, D) = (0, 0, 0, 0)$ because it means the player is completely indifferent between the two strategies in every point. Then every point in $[0, 1] \times [0, 1] \times [0, 1]$ will be part of the best-response correspondence. In the next step we compute the intersection of the best-response correspondences of the other two players, so we do not need to take this first player into account.

We continue by studying different cases for $S(q, r) = 0$ when at least one of A, B, C, D is not 0.

(b) The *linear case* applies if $M = A - B - C + D = 0$, that is,

$$A + Kq + Lr = 0. \tag{16}$$

If $K = L = 0$ then $A = B = C = D$ and either $A = 0$ and (a) applies, or $A \neq 0$ and either U or D is dominant (and (16) has no solution), so assume $(K, L) \neq (0, 0)$. If $K = 0$ then the line is defined by a constant for r, namely $r = -A/L$, and if $L = 0$ then the line is defined by a constant for q, namely $q = -A/K$. Otherwise, (16) expresses a standard linear relationship between q and r. In all cases, it is a line in the $q \times r$ plane which is extended vertically in the p-axis direction. According to (3), on this plane, Player I is indifferent between the first and second strategy. For the points on each side of the plane, (3) determines that the best response is $p = 0$ or $p = 1$.

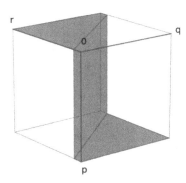

(c) Now, suppose $M \neq 0$. Then (15) is equivalent to

$$\frac{A}{M} + \frac{K}{M}q + \frac{L}{M}r + qr = 0. \tag{17}$$

Adding $\frac{KL}{M^2} - \frac{A}{M}$ on both sides of this equation and using (6) gives

$$\left(q + \frac{L}{M}\right)\left(r + \frac{K}{M}\right) = \frac{KL - AM}{M^2} = \frac{BC - AD}{M^2}. \tag{18}$$

If $BC - AD = 0$, then (18) states that $q = -\frac{L}{M}$ or $r = -\frac{K}{M}$. This defines two perpendicular lines, each similar to a line in case (b). This is a degenerate hyperbola, with a best-response surface like the blue surface in Fig. 5 in the q direction, or as in this picture:

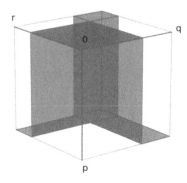

If $BC - AD \neq 0$, then these two lines are the asymptotes of a hyperbola defined by (18). Depending on the values of A, B, C, D, it is possible that the $[0,1] \times [0,1]$ rectangle contains two parts of the arcs of hyperbola or a part of one of the arcs (see the green and red best-response surface in Fig. 3), or just a point on it, or none at all (but then the game has a dominated strategy). For the points (q, r) that are not located on the hyperbola, player I's pure best response is determined according to the inequalities $S(q, r) < 0$ and $S(q, r) > 0$ in (3). Note that when (15) with "<" or ">" instead of "=" is replaced by the corresponding inequality in (17), its direction is reversed if $M < 0$.

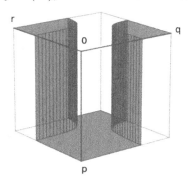

4.3   A Well-Known Example

The extensive-form game in Fig. 5 is a famous example from Selten [12, Fig. 1]. The game tree is in the shape of a horse, so this game is also known as "Selten's horse". The strategic form of this game is displayed on the right. It is known that this game has two segments of partially mixed equilibria and no completely mixed equilibria. Below that the best-response correspondences are displayed, with the Nash equilibria marked in black. There are two segments of equilibria, which include the pure equilibria (U, R, F) and (D, R, B).

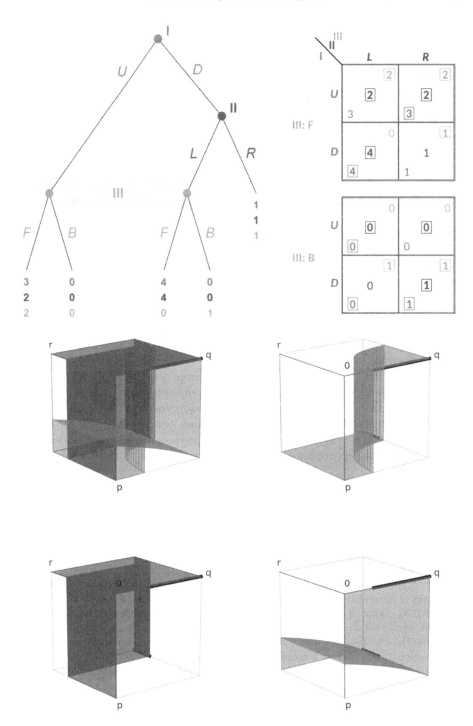

Fig. 5. A famous example: "Selten's horse", see Sect. 4.3.

5   Conclusions

The computational complexity of finding Nash equilibria is often concerned with asymptotic properties such as PPAD-hardness. Many concrete games are small and would profit from a complete analysis of all its Nash equilibria. This has been done for two-player games, but is significantly more difficult for general games with more than two players. Solvers based on solving polynomial equations and inequalities often fail in degenerate cases, which can have an infinite number of equilibria [10].

Our contribution is a "proof of principle" that the complete equilibrium set can be computed and displayed in full no matter how degenerate the game is. We apply it only to the simplest multiplayer game, namely three players with two strategies each, which had not been done before. We also streamlined the corresponding algebraic expressions using determinants in (11), (12), (13) and exploiting the symmetry of the setup. We did exploit the fact that the mixed-strategy profiles can be displayed in a three-dimensional cube. Our experience with the implementation is that one needs to deal with a large number of case distinctions for the possible degenerate cases.

Another insight is that computing partially mixed equilibria is a fruitful approach. For larger games, this means reducing the number of strategies for some players. This can already give information about equilibria with relatively little extra effort.

For larger games, it seems advisable to proceed incrementally in the same manner: Computing partially mixed equilibria, and using algebraic solvers such as done by Datta [6] under the assumption of nondegeneracy. The main question in this context is what kind of multiplayer games people really want to solve. Using models such as polymatrix games, which are based on pairwise interactions [2,7,8], may be the appropriate next step in this direction.

Acknowledgements. We thank the anonymous referees for helpful comments.

References

1. Avis, D., Rosenberg, G.D., Savani, R., von Stengel, B.: Enumeration of Nash equilibria for two-player games. Econ. Theor. **42**(1), 9–37 (2010)
2. Cai, Y., Candogan, O., Daskalakis, C., Papadimitriou, C.: Zero-sum polymatrix games: a generalization of minmax. Math. Oper. Res. **41**(2), 648–655 (2016)
3. Chen, X., Deng, X., Teng, S.H.: Settling the complexity of computing two-player Nash equilibria. J. ACM **56**(3), Article 14 (2009)
4. Chin, H., Parthasarathy, T., Raghavan, T.: Structure of equilibria in N-person non-cooperative games. Internat. J. Game Theory **3**(1), 1–19 (1974)
5. Daskalakis, C., Goldberg, P.W., Papadimitriou, C.H.: The complexity of computing a Nash equilibrium. SIAM J. Comput. **39**(1), 195–259 (2009)
6. Datta, R.S.: Finding all Nash equilibria of a finite game using polynomial algebra. Econ. Theor. **42**(1), 55–96 (2010)
7. Govindan, S., Wilson, R.: Computing Nash equilibria by iterated polymatrix approximation. J. Econ. Dyn. Control **28**(7), 1229–1241 (2004)

8. Howson, J.T., Jr.: Equilibria of polymatrix games. Manag. Sci. **18**(5, Part I), 312–318 (1972)
9. McKelvey, R.D., McLennan, A.: The maximal number of regular totally mixed Nash equilibria. J. Econ. Theory **72**(2), 411–425 (1997)
10. McKelvey, R.D., McLennan, A.M., Turocy, T.L.: Gambit: software tools for game theory, version 16.0.1 (2016). http://www.gambit-project.org
11. Nash, J.: Non-cooperative games. Ann. Math. **54**(2), 286–295 (1951)
12. Selten, R.: Reexamination of the perfectness concept for equilibrium points in extensive games. Internat. J. Game Theory **4**(1), 25–55 (1975)
13. von Stengel, B.: Game Theory Basics. Cambridge University Press, Cambridge (2022)
14. Winkels, H.M.: An algorithm to determine all equilibrium points of a bimatrix game. In: Moeschlin, O., Pallaschke, D. (eds.) Game Theory and Related Topics, North-Holland, Amsterdam, pp. 137–148 (1979)

Congestion and Network Creation Games

An Improved Bound for the Tree Conjecture in Network Creation Games

Jack Dippel[(✉)] and Adrian Vetta

McGill University, Montreal, QC H3A 0G4, Canada
jack.dippel@mail.mcgill.ca, adrian.vetta@mcgill.ca
https://www.cs.mcgill.ca/jdippe/, https://www.math.mcgill.ca/vetta/

Abstract. We study Nash equilibria in the network creation game of Fabrikant et al. [11]. In this game a vertex can buy an edge to another vertex for a cost of α, and the objective of each vertex is to minimize the sum of the costs of the edges it purchases plus the sum of the distances to every other vertex in the resultant network. A long-standing conjecture states that if $\alpha \geq n$ then every Nash equilibrium in the game is a spanning tree. We prove the conjecture holds for any $\alpha > 3n - 3$.

Keywords: Network creation games · Tree conjecture · Algorithmic game theory

1 Introduction

In the *network creation game*, there is a set $V = \{1, 2, \ldots, n\}$ of agents (vertices). A vertex can buy (build) an edge for a fixed cost of α. Thus, a strategy for vertex v is a set of incident edges E_v that it buys. A strategy profile $\mathcal{E} = \{E_1, E_2, \ldots, E_n\}$ of the agents induces a graph $G = (V, E)$, where $E = E_1 \cup E_2 \cup \cdots \cup E_n$. The objective of each vertex is to minimize its total cost which is the sum of its building cost and its connection cost. The *building cost* for vertex v is $\alpha \cdot |E_v|$, the cost of all the edges it buys. The *connection cost* is $\sum_{u:u \neq v} d_G(u, v)$, the sum of the distances in G of v to every other vertex. That is

$$c_v(\mathcal{E}) = \alpha \cdot |E_v| + \sum_{u:u \neq v} d_G(u, v)$$

Our focus is on Nash equilibria of the game.

A strategy profile $\mathcal{E} = \{E_1, E_2, \ldots, E_n\}$ is a Nash equilibrium if E_v is a best response to $\mathcal{E}_{-v} = \{E_u\}_{u \neq v}$, for every vertex v. That is, no agent can reduce its total cost by buying a different set of edges, given the strategies of the other agents are fixed. By default, $d_G(u, v) = \infty$ if there is no path from u to v in the network. It immediately follows that every Nash equilibrium G is a connected graph. The main result in this paper is that if $\alpha > 3n - 3$ then every Nash equilibrium in the network creation game is a spanning tree.

© The Author(s), under exclusive license to Springer Nature Switzerland AG 2022
P. Kanellopoulos et al. (Eds.): SAGT 2022, LNCS 13584, pp. 241–257, 2022.
https://doi.org/10.1007/978-3-031-15714-1_14

1.1 Background

Motivated by a desire to study network formation in the internet, Fabrikant et al. [11] introduced the *network creation game* in 2003. They proved the *price of anarchy* for the game is $O(\sqrt{\alpha})$, and conjectured that it is a constant. More specifically, they showed that any Nash equilibrium that is a spanning tree has total cost at most 5 times that of the optimal network (a star). They then conjectured that, for α greater than some constant, every Nash equilibrium is a spanning tree. This was the original *tree conjecture* for network creation games.

Subsequently, there has been a profusion of work on the tree conjecture. Albers et al. [1] proved that the tree conjecture holds for any $\alpha \geq 12n \log n$. However, they also showed that the conjecture is false in general. Moreover, Mamageishvili et al. [13] proved the conjecture is false for $\alpha < n$. This has lead to a *revised tree conjecture*, namely that every Nash equilibrium is a tree if $\alpha \geq n$. Indeed, Mihalák and Schlegel [14] proved the conjecture holds when $\alpha \geq cn$ for a large enough constant c, specifically for $c > 273$. This constant has subsequently been improved in a series of works. Mamageishvili et al. [13] proved the revised tree conjecture for $\alpha \geq 65n$ and Àlvarez and Messegué [3] improved the bound to $\alpha \geq 17n$. The current best bound for the revised tree conjecture was given by Bilò and Lenzner [7]. They proved every Nash equilibria in the network creation game is a spanning tree if $\alpha > 4n - 13$.

As stated, our contribution is to further improve the bound. In particular, we prove the revised tree conjecture holds for any $\alpha > 3n - 3$. Our proof exploits the concept of a *min-cycle*, introduced by Lenzner in [12].

We remark that numerous extensions and variations of the network creation game have also been studied; we refer the interested reader to [2,5,6,8–10].

2   Preliminaries

In this section, we present structural properties of Nash equilibria in the network creation game and introduce the main strategic tools that will subsequently be used to quantitatively analyze equilibria. We begin with some basic notation. Given a subgraph H of a graph G, we let $d_H(v, u)$ denote the distance between v and u in H. In particular, $d(u, v) = d_G(u, v)$ is the distance from v to u in the whole graph. We let $D(v) = \sum_{u:u \neq v} d_G(u, v)$ be the sum of the distances from v to every other vertex; that is, $D(v)$ is the connection cost for vertex v. The shortest path tree rooted at v is denoted T_v. For any vertex u we denote the subtree of T_v rooted at u by $T_v(u)$; similarly for any edge $e \in T_v$, we denote the subtree of T_v below e by $T_v(e)$.

Recall that G is an undirected graph. Thus, once built, an edge (u, v) of G can be traversed in either direction. However, it will sometimes be useful to also view G as a directed graph. Specifically, (u, v) is oriented from u to v if the edge was bought by u and is oriented from v to u if the edge was bought by v.

2.1   Min-Cycles

Of primary importance is the concept of a min-cycle, introduced by Lenzner [12] and used subsequently by Àlvarez and Messegué [3] and by Bilò and Lenzner [7]. A cycle C is a *min-cycle* if $d_C(u, v) = d_G(u, v)$, for every pair of vertices $u, v \in V(C)$. We will require the following two known min-cycle lemmas, short proofs of which we present for completeness. The first lemma states that min-cycles arise in any graph.

Lemma 1 [12]. *For all cycles containing edge e, those with minimal length are min-cycles.*

Proof. Consider a minimal length cycle C containing an edge e. Suppose for the sake of contradiction that there are two vertices $u, v \in C$ such $d_G(u, v) < d_C(u, v)$. Without loss of generality, suppose the shortest path between u and v, labelled P, lies entirely outside C. Note that C contains two paths between u and v. Let Q be the path of C from u to v that contains e. Then $P \cup Q$ is a cycle containing e that is strictly smaller than C, a contradiction.

Notice that Lemma 1 applies to any graph G regardless of whether or not it is a Nash equilibrium. The second lemma states that, given the orientations of the edges, every min-cycle in a Nash equilibrium is directed. To prove this, we require one definition and an observation. Given a min-cycle C, we say that edge $\bar{e} \in C$ is *opposite* $v \in C$ if it is at least as far from v as any other edge in C. Note that if C has odd cardinality then there is a unique edge opposite to $v \in C$; if C has even cardinality then there are two edges opposite to $v \in C$. Our observation is then:

Remark 1. For any vertex v in a min-cycle C and any edge e opposite v in C, there is a shortest path tree T_v which does not contain e.

Proof. If C has even cardinality then there is a unique vertex $u \in C$ farthest from v. The two paths in C from v to u have the same length. Thus, either of the edges in C incident u (thus, opposite v) may be excluded from some T_v by including the other edge.

    If C has odd cardinality then there are two vertices $u_1, u_2 \in C$ furthest from v. Then the edge (u_1, u_2) is opposite v and is not in any T_v.

Lemma 2 [7]. *Let $\alpha > 2(n - 1)$. Then every min-cycle in a Nash equilibrium G is directed.*

Proof. Let C be a min-cycle that is *not* directed. Then there is a vertex v that buys two edges of the cycle, say e_1 and e_2. Take an edge $\bar{e}$ opposite v in C, and let $u \in C$ be the vertex which buys $\bar{e}$. By Remark 1, a shortest path tree T_v rooted at v need not contain $\bar{e}$. Thus u can sell $\bar{e}$ and buy the edge uv without increasing the distance from v to any other vertex. It follows, by the Nash equilibrium conditions, that

$$D(u) \leq D(v) + n - 1 \tag{1}$$

On the other hand, the edges e_1 or e_2 are not needed in a shortest path from u to any other vertex $w \in C \setminus \{v\}$. It follows that v can sell *both* e_1 and e_2 and instead buy the edge vu without increasing the distance from u to any other vertex. It follows, by the Nash equilibrium conditions, that

$$D(v) \leq D(u) + n - 1 - \alpha \qquad (2)$$

Together (1) and (2) give

$$D(v) \leq D(v) + 2(n-1) - \alpha < D(v)$$

This contradiction implies that C must be a directed cycle.

Given Lemma 2, we may use the following specialized notation for min-cycles. We will label the vertices of a min-cycle as $C = \{v_0, v_1, \dots, v_k = v_0\}$, where $k = |C|$. As the min-cycle is directed, we may also assume v_i buys the edge $e_i = v_i v_{i+1}$, for each $0 \leq i \leq |C| - 1$. Recall there are two paths on C between any pair of vertices v_i and v_j. The path that follows the orientation of the edges in the directed cycle is called the *clockwise path* from v_i to v_j and that path that goes against the orientation of the cycle is called the *anti-clockwise path*.

To conclude our discussion on min-cycles, we present two trivial, but very useful, observations. First we remark that every min-cycle is *chordless*.

Remark 2. Every min-cycle C is chordless.

Proof. This follows immediately from the definition of a min-cycle.

The Remark 2 implies that any vertex $v_i \in C$ has exactly two neighbours on C, namely v_{i-1} and v_{i+1}. Any other neighbour of v_i must lie outside of C. For the second observation, define $k_{\max}$ to be the maximum length of a min-cycle in a biconnected component.[1]

Remark 3. Let $e = (u, v)$ be an edge in a biconnected component H of G. Then

$$d_{G \setminus e}(u, v) \leq d_G(u, v) + k_{\max} - 2$$

Proof. Since H is biconnected, e lies in a cycle. Thus, by Lemma 1, e lies in a min-cycle C. Because there are two paths between u and v on C (the clockwise and anti-clockwise paths), the removal of $e = (u, v)$ increases the distance between u and v by at most $(|C| - 1) - 1 \leq k_{\max} - 2$. The observation follows.

The applicability of Remark 3 is evident. It can be used to upper bound the increase in connection costs arising from the sale of an edge. At a Nash equilibrium, this upper bound must be at least α, the amount saved in construction costs by the sale.

---

[1] A *biconnected component* $H \subseteq G$ is a maximal set such that there are two vertex-disjoint paths between any pair of vertices in H.

2.2 Basic Strategic Options or a Vertex

To prove a Nash equilibrium G is a tree we must show G contains no cycles. In particular, it suffices to show G contains no biconnected components. This leads to the following basic idea used in our proof. We take a vertex v in a biconnected component H of a Nash equilibrium G. By the Nash equilibrium conditions, any strategy change by v cannot decrease its total cost. Thus the resultant change in cost is non-negative. In particular, each potential strategy change induces an *inequality constraint*. Further, a collection of potential strategy changes induces a set of inequalities. By case analysis, we will show that it is always possible to find a collection of strategy changes for which linear combinations of the corresponding inequality constraints induce the constraint $\alpha \le 3n - 3$. It follows that if $\alpha > 3n - 3$ then G is not a Nash equilibrium. Consequently, every Nash equilibrium for $\alpha > 3n - 3$ has no biconnected components and is, thus, a spanning tree.

In fact, nearly every strategy change we use in the paper will take one of three general forms. Therefore, it will be helpful to present these three general forms here.

Lemma 3 (Strategy I). *Let H be a biconnected component in a Nash equilibrium G with $u, v \in H$. Assume v buys edge $vw \in H$. If $w \notin T_u(v)$, for some $T_u(v)$, then the strategy change where v swaps vw for vu induces the inequality*

$$0 \; \le \; D(u) + (n-1) - D(v) - (d(u,v) + 1) \cdot (|T_u(v)| - 1) \qquad (3)$$

Proof. This strategy change is illustrated in Fig. 1. The basic idea is that by adding the edge vu the vertex v can now use the shortest path tree T_u. The distance from v to any vertex x would then be at most $1 + d(u, x)$, inducing a communication cost of at most $D(u) + (n-1)$ instead of its current communication cost of $D(v)$.

By selling vw the construction cost for vertex v does not change. But there is a problem. What if vw is used in the shortest path tree T_u? Since $w \notin T_u(v)$, the only way this can occur is if wv is the final edge on the path P from u to v in T_u. That is, the edge wv is only needed by u in order to connect to the vertices in $T_u(v)$. But it can now connect to those vertices simply by using the edge uv instead of the path P. In particular, by swapping vw for vu: (i) the distance from u to any other vertex x cannot increase, and (ii) the distance from u to any vertex $x \in T_u(v)$ decreases by $|P| - 1 = d(u, v) - 1$. Moreover, v does not need to use the edge vu in order to connect to the vertices in $T_u(v)$. Thus the total change in cost is at most

$$\sum_{x \notin T_u(v)} \big(1 + d(u,x)\big) + \sum_{x \in T_u(v)} \big(d(u,x) - |P|\big) - D(v)$$

$$= D(u) + \big(n - |T_u(v)|\big) - |P| \cdot |T_u(v)| - D(v)$$

$$\le D(u) + \big(n - 1\big) - (|P| + 1) \cdot (|T_u(v)| - 1) - D(v)$$

$$= D(u) + \big(n - 1\big) - \big(d(u,v) + 1\big) \cdot (|T_u(v)| - 1) - D(v)$$

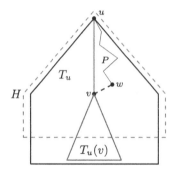

Fig. 1. Strategy I

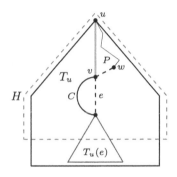

Fig. 2. Strategy II

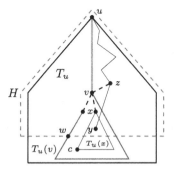

Fig. 3. Strategy III

But, by the Nash equilibrium conditions, this change in cost must be non-negative. The claimed inequality (3) then holds.

Lemma 4 (Strategy II). *Let H be a biconnected component in a Nash equilibrium G with $u, v \in H$. Assume v buys edges $vw, e \in H$. If $w \notin T_u(v)$, for some $T_u(v)$, then the strategy change where v swaps both vw and e for vu induces the inequality*

$$0 \leq D(u) + (n-1) - D(v) - (d(u,v)+1) \cdot (|T_u(v)|-1) + (k_{\max}-2) \cdot |T_u(e)| - \alpha \quad (4)$$

Proof. This strategy change is illustrated in Fig. 2. The first four terms of (4) follow as in the argument of Lemma 3. What remains to be considered is the additional effect of selling edge e. The $-\alpha$ term arises in the construction cost because v is now buying one less edge than before. Since e is in a biconnected component H, it is in a min-cycle C by Lemma 1. By Lemma 2, C is directed. Hence, $vw \notin C$. The term $(k_{\max}-2) \cdot |T_u(e)|$ then follows by applying Remark 3.

Note we can always choose e s.t. $T_u(e) \subseteq T_u(v) \setminus v$. Therefore, instead of (4), we will often use the following simplified bound:

$$0 \leq D(u) + n - 1 - D(v) + (k_{\max} - d(u,v) - 3) \cdot (|T_u(v)| - 1) - \alpha \quad (5)$$

Lemma 5 (Strategy III). *Let H be a biconnected component in a Nash equilibrium G with $u, v \in H$. Assume v buys a quantity ℓ of edges of H. Let w be the vertex in any $T_u(v) \cap H$ furthest from u. Then the strategy change where v swaps all its edges for vu induces the inequality*

$$0 \ \leq \ D(u) + (n-1) - D(v) + 2d(v, w) \cdot (|T_u(v)| - 1) - (\ell - 1) \cdot \alpha \quad (6)$$

Proof. This strategy change is illustrated in Fig. 3. Again, the first three terms of (6) follow as in Lemma 3. The final term arises because v buys $(\ell - 1)$ fewer edges after the strategy change. It remains to explain the fourth term, namely $2d(v, w) \cdot |T_u(v)|$. Let L be the set of ℓ edges that v sells. This change may cause the distances from u to vertices in $T_u(v)$ to increase.

To quantify this effect, we first prove that for any pair of vertices a, b with edges $va, vb \in L$, the subtrees $T_u(a)$ and $T_u(b)$ have no edge between them. Suppose, for a contradiction, that vertex $t \in T_u(a)$ buys an edge to vertex $s \in T_u(b)$. By Lemma 3, we have

$$0 \leq D(v) + n - 1 - D(t) - (d(t, v) + 1) \cdot (|T_v(t)| - 1)$$
$$\leq D(v) + n - 1 - D(t) \quad (7)$$

On the other hand, by Lemma 4, we have

$$0 \leq D(t) + n - 1 - D(v) - (d(t, v) + 1) \cdot (|T_t(v)| - 1) + (k_{\max} - 2) \cdot |T_t(vb)| - \alpha$$
$$\leq D(t) + n - 1 - D(v) - \alpha \quad (8)$$

The second inequality holds because $|T_t(vb)| = 0$. To see this, note that the shortest path from t to v need not use vb as $t \in T_u(a)$. Furthermore, the path from t to b consisting of the edge ts plus the subpath from s to b in $T_u(b)$ is at most as long as the path from t to b using the subpath from t to v in $T_u(v)$ plus the edge vb; otherwise it would be the case that $s \in T_u(a)$. Thus the shortest path from t to any vertex need not use vb and so $|T_t(vb)| = 0$. Summing (7) and (8) gives $\alpha < 2(n-1)$, a contradiction.

Next, take $vx \in L$. Since H is biconnected, there is an edge yz with $y \in T_u(x)$ and $z \notin T_u(x)$ where $z \neq v$ and possibly $y = x$. Furthermore, as proven above, $z \notin T_u(b)$ for any $vb \neq vx \in L$. Therefore the distance from z to u does not increase when v sells its edges. In addition, the distance between any vertex in $T_u(x)$ and x is the same as before vx was sold. We also have $d(x, y) \leq d(v, w) - 1$, by our choice of w, because $y \in T_u(v)$ and $y \neq v$.

We claim $d(u, z) \leq d(u, v) + d(v, w)$. If not, assume $d(u, z) \geq d(u, v) + d(v, w) + 1$. Then we could choose $T_u(v)$ such that $z \in T_u(v)$, contradicting our choice of w. Therefore, for any vertex $c \in T_u(x)$, originally we have $d(c, u) = d(u, v) + d(v, c)$. But, after the change in strategy of vertex v, there is a path from c to u, via x, y, z, of length at most

$$d(c, x) + d(x, y) + d(y, z) + d(z, u)$$
$$\leq (d(v, c) - 1) + (d(v, w) - 1) + 1 + (d(u, v) + d(v, w))$$
$$= (d(c, v) + d(v, u)) - 1 + 2d(v, w)$$
$$< d(c, u) + 2d(v, w) \quad (9)$$

Thus the length of the shortest path from u to c increases by less than $2d(v, w)$. This gives the fourth term (6).

This completes the description of the three main strategic options that we will study. We remark that we will apply these strategies to vertices on a min-cycle. This is valid because every biconnected component contains a min-cycle.

Remark 4. Any biconnected component H of cardinality at least two contains a min-cycle C.

Proof. As H has cardinality at least two it contains an edge $e = (u, v)$. Note that e cannot be a cut edge or H is not biconnected. Thus by Lemma 1, e is in a min-cycle C. It immediately follows that $C \subseteq H$.

3   Equilibria Conditions

In this section, we derive further structural properties that must be satisfied at a Nash equilibrium.

3.1   Biconnected Components

We have already derived some properties of min-cycles in a Nash equilibrium G. Recall, that we wish to prove the non-existence of biconnected components in a Nash equilibrium. So, more generally, we will now derive properties satisfied by any biconnected component H in a Nash equilibrium.

The girth of a graph G, denoted γ, is the length of its smallest cycle.[2] The following lemma that lower bounds the girth of an equilibrium will subsequently be useful.

Lemma 6. *Let $\alpha > 2(n-1)$. Then the girth of any Nash equilibrium G satisfies* $\gamma(G) \geq \frac{2\alpha}{n-1} + 2$.

Proof. Take a minimum length cycle $C = v_0, v_1 \ldots, v_{k-1}, v_k = v_0$ in G.

By Lemma 1, C is a min-cycle. Therefore, By Lemma 2, C is a directed cycle. So, as stated, we may assume $e_i = v_i v_{i+1}$ is bought by v_i, for each $0 \leq i \leq k-1$. Now, for each vertex $u \in V$, we define a set $L_u \subseteq \{0, 1, \ldots, k-1\}$ as follows. We have $i \in L_u$ if and only if *every* shortest path from $v_i \in C$ to u uses the edge e_i. (In particular, $u \in T_{v_i}(e_i)$ for every shortest path tree T rooted at v_i.)

We claim $|L_u| \leq \frac{|C|-1}{2}$ for every vertex u. If not, take a vertex u with $|L_u| > \frac{|C|-1}{2}$. Let $d(v_i, u)$ be the shortest distance between u and $v_i \in C$. Next give v_i a label $\ell_i = d(v_i, u) - d(v_{i+1}, u)$. Observe that $\ell_i \in \{-1, 0, 1\}$. Furthermore, the labels sum to zero as

$$\sum_{i=0}^{|C|-1} \ell_i = \sum_{i=0}^{|C|-1} (d(v_i, u) - d(v_{i+1}, u)) = \sum_{i=0}^{|C|-1} d(v_i, u) - \sum_{i=1}^{|C|} d(v_i, u) = 0$$

---

[2] The girth is infinite if G is a forest.

Now take a vertex v_i in C that uses e_i in *every* shortest path to u; that is, $i \in L_u$. Then $\ell_i = 1$ and $\ell_{i-1} \geq 0$. In particular, if $|L_u| > \frac{|C|-1}{2}$ then there are $> \frac{|C|-1}{2}$ positive labels and $> 1 + \frac{|C|-1}{2}$ non-negative labels. Hence, there are $< |C| - \left(1 + \frac{|C|-1}{2}\right) = \frac{|C|-1}{2}$ negative labels. But then the sum of the labels is strictly positive, a contradiction.

Now, for each i, let T_{v_i} be a shortest path tree rooted at v_i such that the size of $T_{v_i}(e_i)$ is minimized. As $|L_u| \leq \frac{|C|-1}{2}$ for every vertex u, there exists a v_i with $|T_{v_i}(e_i) \setminus C| \leq \frac{n-|C|}{2}$. On the other hand, clearly $|T_{v_j}(e_j) \cap C| \leq \frac{|C|-1}{2}$ for every v_j. It follows that $|T_{v_i}(e_i)| \leq \frac{n-1}{2}$. But then if v_i sells e_i its cost increases by at most $(|C| - 2) \cdot |T_{v_i}(e_i)| - \alpha \leq (|C| - 2) \cdot \frac{n-1}{2} - \alpha$. This must be non-negative by the Nash equilibrium conditions, this implies that $\frac{2\alpha}{n-1} + 2 \leq |C|$ as desired.

We remark that Lemma 6 actually holds for all α. We omit the proof of this fact as we only need the result for the case of $\alpha > 2(n-1)$.

Lemma 7. *In a min cycle* C, $T_{v_{\lfloor \frac{k}{2} \rfloor}}(v_0) = T_{v_{\lceil \frac{k}{2} \rceil}}(v_0)$ *for some choice of* $T_{v_{\lfloor \frac{k}{2} \rfloor}}(v_0)$ *and* $T_{v_{\lceil \frac{k}{2} \rceil}}(v_0)$.

Proof. For even k, $\lfloor \frac{k}{2} \rfloor = \lceil \frac{k}{2} \rceil$, and the result is trivial. For odd k, suppose $T_{v_{\lfloor \frac{k}{2} \rfloor}}(v_0) \neq T_{v_{\lceil \frac{k}{2} \rceil}}(v_0)$. Without loss of generality, let $x \in T_{v_{\lfloor \frac{k}{2} \rfloor}}(v_0) \setminus T_{v_{\lceil \frac{k}{2} \rceil}}(v_0)$. Therefore there is a shortest path P from x to $v_{\lfloor \frac{k}{2} \rfloor}$ which goes through v_0. Hence, there must be a path of the same length from x to $v_{\lceil \frac{k}{2} \rceil}$. Thus either x may belong to $T_{v_{\lceil \frac{k}{2} \rceil}}(v_0)$ for a different choice of $T_{v_{\lceil \frac{k}{2} \rceil}}(v_0)$, or there is a path Q between x and $v_{\lceil \frac{k}{2} \rceil}$ that is strictly shorter than P and does not use v_0. But then $Q \cup v_{\lceil \frac{k}{2} \rceil} v_{\lfloor \frac{k}{2} \rfloor}$ is a path from x to $v_{\lfloor \frac{k}{2} \rfloor}$ of length at most $|P|$ which does not use v_0. This implies we can choose $T_{v_{\lfloor \frac{k}{2} \rfloor}}(v_0)$ such that $x \notin T_{v_{\lfloor \frac{k}{2} \rfloor}}(v_0)$. It follows that we may choose $T_{v_{\lfloor \frac{k}{2} \rfloor}}(v_0) = T_{v_{\lceil \frac{k}{2} \rceil}}(v_0)$, as desired.

Given a biconnected component H and a vertex $v \in H$, let $S_H(v)$ be the set of vertices in G that are closer to v than to any other vertex of H.

Lemma 8. *For any pair of vertices* u *and* v *in a biconnected component* H, *we have* $S_H(u) \cap S_H(v) = \emptyset$.

Proof. For a contradiction, take $x \in S_H(u) \cap S_H(v)$. Note that $x \in S_H(x)$ and $x \notin S_H(v)$ for any $v \neq x \in H$. Thus, it must be that $x \notin H$. We may assume that x is the closest vertex to u and v in $S_H(u) \cap S_H(v)$. In particular, there are shortest paths P from x to u and Q from x to v that are disjoint except for their source x. But then $H \cup P \cup Q$ is biconnected, contradicting the maximality of H.

Lemma 9. *Let* $\alpha > 2(n-1)$. *Then any min-cycle* C *of a biconnected component* H *has a vertex* $v \in C$ *which buys an edge* $e \in H \setminus C$.

Proof. First, assume that $C = H$. By Lemma 6, $C = \{v_0, v_1, \ldots, v_k = v_0\}$ has length $\frac{2\alpha}{n-1} + 2 > 6$ as $\alpha > 2(n-1)$. By Lemma 2, v_i buys the edge $e_i = v_i v_{i+1}$ for $0 \leq i \leq k-1$. Without loss of generality, let $v_1 = argmin_{v \in C} |S_H(v)|$. Then suppose v_0 sells e_0 and buys $v_0 v_2$. This reduces its costs by at least $|S_H(v_2)| + |S_H(v_3)| - |S_H(v_1)| > 0$, contradicting the Nash equilibrium conditions.

Second, assume $C \neq H$. Take an edge $f \in H \setminus C$ incident to a vertex of C. As H is biconnected, f is in a cycle D which, by Lemma 1, we may assume is a min-cycle. Furthermore, by Lemma 2, D is directed. But D contains f and so intersects C. Therefore, there must be a vertex of C which buys an edge $e \in D \setminus C$ as desired.

3.2 The Key Lemma

The following lemma will be critical in proving the main result.

Lemma 10. *Let $\alpha > 2(n-1)$. In a maximum length min-cycle C of a biconnected component H, there exist two vertices $u, v \in C$ with $d(u,v) \geq \frac{k_{\max}}{3}$ which buy edges $f, g \notin C$ respectively.*

Proof. Take a maximum length min-cycle C. By Lemma 9, we may assume v_0 buys an edge f outside C. Suppose, for the sake of contradiction, only vertices in $W = \{v_0, \ldots v_{\lceil \frac{k_{\max}}{3} \rceil - 1}\}$ buy an edge outside C. Let $X = \{v_{\lceil \frac{k_{\max}}{3} \rceil}, \ldots v_{\lfloor \frac{k_{\max}}{2} \rfloor}\}$. Since $\alpha > 2(n-1)$, Lemma 6 implies that the girth $\gamma(G) \geq 7$, which means both X and W are non-empty. We now break the proof up into three cases:

Case 1: There exists $x \in X$ with $deg_H(x) \geq 3$
As $x \notin W$ there is an edge $d \in H$ incident to x that is bought by a vertex outside C. Since d is in H it is not a cut-edge. Let D be a minimum length cycle D containing d. Thus D is a directed min-cycle by Lemma 1 and Lemma 2.

Since D is directed it contains a vertex $w \in W$ which buys an edge of $D \setminus C$. Take w to be the last vertex of C before x in D. Let $\overrightarrow{D}_{wx}$ be the clockwise path in D from w to x and let $\overleftarrow{D}_{wx}$ be the anticlockwise path. Next observe that the clockwise path P from w to x in C is shorter than the anticlockwise part. Thus, because C is a min-cycle, P is a shortest path from w to x. But then $|P \cup \overrightarrow{D}_{wx}| \leq |D|$. Furthermore, $P \cup \overrightarrow{D}_{wx}$ is a cycle containing d. So $P \cup \overrightarrow{D}_{wx}$ is also a minimum length cycle containing d. But then it must be a directed cycle; this contradicts the fact that P and $\overrightarrow{D}_{wx}$ are both paths directed from w to x.

Case 2: $deg_H(v_{\lfloor \frac{k_{\max}}{2} \rfloor + 1}) \geq 3$
Note that $v_{\lfloor \frac{k_{\max}}{2} \rfloor + 1} \notin W$. So there is some vertex $u \in H \setminus C$ which buys an edge $d = uv_{\lfloor \frac{k_{\max}}{2} \rfloor + 1}$. By Lemma 1 and Lemma 2, d is in a directed min cycle $D \neq C$. Therefore, some vertex $w \in W$ must buy an edge $f \in D \setminus C$. If $w \neq v_0$ then exactly the same argument as in Case 1 can be applied. Thus, the only possibility remaining is $w = v_0$. However, by Remark 1 applied to C, the shortest path tree $T_{v_{\lfloor \frac{k_{\max}}{2} \rfloor + 1}}$ rooted at $v_{\lfloor \frac{k_{\max}}{2} \rfloor + 1}$ need not contain the edge e_0. Similarly, as D has

length at most that of C, the shortest path tree $T_{v_{\lfloor \frac{k_{\max}}{2} \rfloor + 1}}$ need not contain the edge f either.

Now apply Strategy II. Noting that $T_{v_{\lfloor \frac{k_{\max}}{2} \rfloor + 1}}(f) = \emptyset$, we have that (4) gives

$$D(v_{\lfloor \frac{k_{\max}}{2} \rfloor + 1}) - D(v_0) + n - 1 - \alpha \geq 0 \tag{10}$$

On the other hand, suppose we apply Strategy I with $v_{\lfloor \frac{k_{\max}}{2} \rfloor + 1}$ selling $e_{\lfloor \frac{k_{\max}}{2} \rfloor + 1}$ and buying $v_{\lfloor \frac{k_{\max}}{2} \rfloor + 1} v_0$. By (3), we have

$$D(v_0) - D(v_{\lfloor \frac{k_{\max}}{2} \rfloor + 1}) + n - 1 \geq 0 \tag{11}$$

Together, (10) and (11) imply $\alpha \leq 2(n - 1)$, a contradiction.

Case 3: Else

So $deg_H(v) = 2$ for every vertex $v \in X \cup v_{\lfloor \frac{k_{\max}}{2} \rfloor + 1}$. In particular, we have $deg_H(v_{\lfloor \frac{k_{\max}}{2} \rfloor}) = deg_H(v_{\lfloor \frac{k_{\max}}{2} \rfloor + 1}) = 2$. We now consider four strategy changes.

(i) $v_{\lfloor \frac{k_{\max}}{2} \rfloor - 1}$ sells $e_{\lfloor \frac{k_{\max}}{2} \rfloor - 1}$ and buys $v_{\lfloor \frac{k_{\max}}{2} \rfloor - 1} v_{\lfloor \frac{k_{\max}}{2} \rfloor + 1}$.

As $deg_H(v_{\lfloor \frac{k_{\max}}{2} \rfloor}) = 2$, the only vertices now further from $v_{\lfloor \frac{k_{\max}}{2} \rfloor - 1}$ are those in $S_H(v_{\lfloor \frac{k_{\max}}{2} \rfloor})$. Their distances have increased by exactly 1. On the other hand, this strategy change decreases the distance from $v_{\lfloor \frac{k_{\max}}{2} \rfloor - 1}$ to $S_H(v_{\lfloor \frac{k_{\max}}{2} \rfloor} + 1)$ by 1. Therefore, the Nash equilibrium conditions imply

$$|S_H(v_{\lfloor \frac{k_{\max}}{2} \rfloor} + 1)| \leq |S_H(v_{\lfloor \frac{k_{\max}}{2} \rfloor})| \tag{12}$$

(ii) $v_{\lfloor \frac{k_{\max}}{2} \rfloor}$ sells $e_{\lfloor \frac{k_{\max}}{2} \rfloor}$ and buys $v_{\lfloor \frac{k_{\max}}{2} \rfloor} v_{\lfloor \frac{k_{\max}}{2} \rfloor + 3}$.

As $deg_H(v_{\lfloor \frac{k_{\max}}{2} \rfloor} + 1) = 2$, the only vertices now further from $v_{\lfloor \frac{k_{\max}}{2} \rfloor}$ are those in $S_H(v_{\lfloor \frac{k_{\max}}{2} \rfloor} + 1)$. Their distances have increased by exactly 2. On the other hand, the vertices in $T_{v_{\lfloor \frac{k_{\max}}{2} \rfloor}}(v_0)$ are now closer to $v_{\lfloor \frac{k_{\max}}{2} \rfloor}$. If $k_{\max}$ is odd then they are exactly 1 closer and if $k_{\max}$ is even then they are exactly 2 closer. Therefore, the Nash equilibrium conditions imply

$$|T_{v_{\lfloor \frac{k_{\max}}{2} \rfloor}}(v_0)| \leq 2 \cdot |S_H(v_{\lfloor \frac{k_{\max}}{2} \rfloor + 1})| \qquad \text{if } k_{\max} \text{ odd} \tag{13}$$

$$|T_{v_{\lfloor \frac{k_{\max}}{2} \rfloor}}(v_0)| \leq |S_H(v_{\lfloor \frac{k_{\max}}{2} \rfloor + 1})| \qquad \text{if } k_{\max} \text{ even} \tag{14}$$

(iii) $v_{\lceil \frac{k_{\max}}{2} \rceil}$ sells $e_{\lceil \frac{k_{\max}}{2} \rceil}$ and buys $v_{\lceil \frac{k_{\max}}{2} \rceil} v_0$.

This is an instance of Strategy I with a slight twist for odd k. First note that $T_{v_0}(v_{\lceil \frac{k_{\max}}{2} \rceil}) = S_H(v_{\lceil \frac{k_{\max}}{2} \rceil})$. For even k we then obtain the following bound from (3).

$$0 \leq D(v_0) + n - 1 - D(v_{\lceil \frac{k_{\max}}{2} \rceil}) - \left(\left\lfloor \frac{k_{\max}}{2} \right\rfloor + 1 \right) \cdot (|S_H(v_{\lceil \frac{k_{\max}}{2} \rceil})| - 1)$$

However, we can improve upon this for odd k. Note that $S_H(v_{\lfloor \frac{k_{\max}}{2} \rfloor})$ is $(\lfloor \frac{k_{\max}}{2} \rfloor - 1)$ closer to $v_{\lfloor \frac{k_{\max}}{2} \rfloor}$ than v_0 was before the switch. Thus for odd k we use the bound

$$0 \le D(v_0) + n - 1 - D(v_{\lceil \frac{k_{\max}}{2} \rceil}) - \left(\left\lfloor \frac{k_{\max}}{2} \right\rfloor + 1 \right) \cdot (|S_H(v_{\lceil \frac{k_{\max}}{2} \rceil})| - 1)$$

$$- \left\lfloor \frac{k_{\max}}{2} \right\rfloor \cdot |S_H(v_{\lfloor \frac{k_{\max}}{2} \rfloor})|$$

These two separate inequalities for odd and even k can be turned into the following bound for all k using the inequalities (12), (13) and (14).

$$0 \le D(v_0) - D(v_{\lceil \frac{k_{\max}}{2} \rceil}) + n - 1 - \left\lfloor \frac{k_{\max}}{2} \right\rfloor \cdot (|T_{v_{\lceil \frac{k_{\max}}{2} \rceil}}(v_0)| - 1) \qquad (15)$$

(iv) v_0 sells e_0 and a and buys $v_0 v_{\lceil \frac{k_{\max}}{2} \rceil}$.
This is just a straightforward application of Strategy II. Here (5) yields

$$0 \le D(v_{\lceil \frac{k_{\max}}{2} \rceil}) - D(v_0) + n - 1$$

$$+ \left(k_{\max} - \left\lfloor \frac{k_{\max}}{2} \right\rfloor - 3 \right) \cdot (|T_{v_{\lceil \frac{k_{\max}}{2} \rceil}}(v_0)| - 1) - \alpha$$

$$\le D(v_{\lceil \frac{k_{\max}}{2} \rceil}) - D(v_0) + n - 1 + (\lfloor \frac{k_{\max}}{2} \rfloor) \cdot (|T_{v_{\lceil \frac{k_{\max}}{2} \rceil}}(v_0)| - 1) - \alpha \qquad (16)$$

Finally, summing (15) and (16) gives $0 \le 2(n-1) - \alpha$. But this contradicts the assumption that $2(n-1) < \alpha$. This completes the proof; there exist two vertices $v_1, v_2 \in C$ with $d(v, u) \ge \frac{k_{\max}}{3}$ which buy edges $f, g \notin C$ respectively.

4   The Tree Conjecture Holds for $\alpha > 3(n-1)$

In this section, we put all the pieces together to obtain the following result.

Theorem 1. *For $\alpha > 3(n-1)$, any Nash equilibrium G is a tree.*

Proof. Let C be a maximum length min-cycle of a biconnected component H. By Lemma 10, there are two vertices $r_1, r_2 \in C$ with $d(r_1, r_2) \ge \frac{k_{\max}}{3}$ that buy edges $e_1, e_2 \in \{C\}$ $f_1, f_2 \in H \setminus \{C\}$, respectively. Let P_1 be the shorter of the two paths in C between r_1 and r_2. Without loss of generality, let P_1 be directed from r_1 to r_2. Finally, take a vertex $r_3 \in H \cap T_{r_1}(r_2)$ that is as deep as possible in $T_{r_1}(r_2)$. It must buy an edge $f_3 \in H \setminus T_{r_1}(r_2)$ because all vertices in H are in directed min-cycles by Lemma 1 and Lemma 2.

We now consider six cases for which we propose a set of strategy changes. None of these strategies decrease the agent's cost only if $\alpha \le 3(n-1)$. This fact implies no biconnected component H can exist when $\alpha > 3(n-1)$, giving the theorem.

Case 1: $D(r_1) \ge D(x)$ for some $x \in T_{r_1}(r_2)$
In this case, we consider two strategy changes:

1. r_1 sells e_1 and buys $r_1 x$
2. r_1 sells e_1 and f_1 and buys $r_1 x$

The first change is an instance of Strategy I. Thus from (3), we have the bound:

$$0 \leq D(x) - D(r_1) + n - 1 - (|P_1| + d(r_2, x) + 1) \cdot (|T_x(r_1)| - 1) \quad (17)$$

The second change is an instance of Strategy II. Thus from (5), we have the bound:

$$0 \leq D(x) - D(r_1) + n - 1 + (k_{\max} - |P_1| - d(r_2, x) - 3) \cdot (|T_x(r_1)| - 1) - \alpha \quad (18)$$

The linear combination $2 \times (17) + 1 \times (18)$ gives

$$
\begin{aligned}
0 \leq 3 \cdot &\left(D(x) - D(r_1) + n - 1 - (|P_1| + d(r_2, x)) \right. \\
&+ \tfrac{1}{3}(k_{\max} - 5) \big) \cdot (|T_x(r_1)| - 1) - \alpha \\
\leq 3 \cdot &\left(n - 1 - (|P_1| + d(r_2, x)) \cdot (|T_x(r_1)| - 1) \right) + k_{\max} \cdot (|T_x(r_1)| - 1) - \alpha \\
\leq 3 \cdot &\left(n - 1 - \tfrac{1}{3}k_{\max} \cdot (|T_x(r_1)| - 1) \right) + k_{\max} \cdot (|T_x(r_1)| - 1) - \alpha \\
\leq 3&(n - 1) - \alpha
\end{aligned}
$$

Here the second inequality holds as $D(r_1) \geq D(x)$. It follows that for $\alpha > 3(n - 1)$, we may now assume $D(r_1) < D(x)$ for every $x \in T_{r_1}(r_2)$.

Case 2: $d(r_2, r_3) \geq \tfrac{1}{3}k_{\max}$

In this case, we consider three strategy changes:

1. r_1 sells e_1 and buys $r_1 r_3$
2. r_1 sells e_1 and f_1 and buys $r_1 r_3$
3. r_3 sells f_3 and buys $r_1 r_3$

The first change is an instance of Strategy I. Thus from (3), we have the bound:

$$0 \leq D(r_3) - D(r_1) + n - 1 - (|P_1| + d(r_3, r_2) + 1) \cdot (|T_{r_3}(r_1)| - 1) \quad (19)$$

The second change is an instance of Strategy II. Thus from (5), we have the bound:

$$0 \leq D(r_3) - D(r_1) + n - 1 + (k_{\max} - |P_1| - d(r_3, r_2) - 3) \cdot (|T_{r_3}(r_1)| - 1) - \alpha \quad (20)$$

The third change is an instance of Strategy I. Thus from (3), we have the bound:

$$
\begin{aligned}
0 \leq {} & D(r_1) - D(r_3) + n - 1 - (|P_1| + d(r_3, r_2) + 1) \cdot (|T_{r_1}(r_3)| - 1) \\
\leq {} & D(r_1) - D(r_3) + n - 1 \quad (21)
\end{aligned}
$$

The linear combination $\tfrac{1}{2} \times (19) + 1 \times (20) + \tfrac{3}{2} \times (21)$, all D terms cancel and we're left with

$$
\begin{aligned}
0 \leq {} & \tfrac{3}{2} \cdot \left(n - 1 + n - 1 - (|P_1| + d(r_3, r_2)) + \tfrac{2}{3}(k_{\max} - 3.5) \right) \cdot (|T_{r_1}(r_3)| - 1) - \alpha \\
= {} & 3(n - 1) - \tfrac{3}{2} \cdot (|P_1| + d(r_3, r_2)) \cdot (|T_{r_1}(r_3)| - 1) + k_{\max} \cdot (|T_{r_1}(r_3)| - 1) - \alpha \\
\leq {} & 3(n - 1) - k_{\max} \cdot (|T_{r_1}(r_3)| - 1) + k_{\max} \cdot (|T_{r_1}(r_3)| - 1) - \alpha \\
\leq {} & 3(n - 1) - \alpha
\end{aligned}
$$

Here the third inequality holds as $d(r_2, r_3) \geq \frac{1}{3}k_{\max}$. It follows that for $\alpha > 3(n-1)$, we may now assume that $d(r_2, r_3) < \frac{1}{3}k_{\max}$.

Case 3: $(|T_{r_1}(r_2)| - 1) \leq \frac{n-1}{d(r_3, r_2)}$

In this case, we consider one new strategy change:

1. r_2 sells e_2 and f_2 and buys $r_1 r_2$

This strategy change is an instance of Strategy III. Thus from (6), we have the bound:

$$\begin{aligned}
0 &\leq D(r_1) - D(r_2) + n - 1 + 2d(r_3, r_2) \cdot (|T_{r_1}(r_2)| - 1) - \alpha \\
&< n - 1 + 2d(r_3, r_2) \cdot (|T_{r_1}(r_2)| - 1) - \alpha \\
&\leq n - 1 + 2(n - 1) - \alpha \\
&\leq 3(n - 1) - \alpha
\end{aligned}$$

Here the strict inequality holds as $D(r_1) < D(r_2)$; the second inequality holds by the assumption $(|T_{r_1}(r_2)| - 1) \leq \frac{n-1}{d(r_3, r_2)}$. Thus, for $\alpha > 3(n-1)$, we may now assume that $(|T_{r_1}(r_2)| - 1) > \frac{n-1}{d(r_3, r_2)}$.

Case 4: $D(r_1) - D(r_3) \leq -(2 - \frac{|P_1|}{d(r_3, r_2)}) \cdot (n - 1)$

In this case, we reconsider one strategy change:

1. r_3 sells f_3 and buys $r_1 r_3$

Recall $d(r_2, r_3) < \frac{1}{3}k_{\max}$. Then because $|P_1| \geq \frac{1}{3}k_{\max}$, u is closer to every vertex of $|T_{r_1}(r_2)|$ than r_1 by at least $|P_1| - d(r_3, r_2)$. Thus, the equilibrium conditions imply that

$$\begin{aligned}
0 &\leq D(r_1) - D(r_3) + n - 1 - (|P_1| - d(r_3, r_2)) \cdot (|T_{r_1}(r_2)| - 1) \\
&\leq -(2 - \tfrac{|P_1|}{d(r_3, r_2)}) \cdot (n - 1) + n - 1 - (|P_1| - d(r_3, r_2)) \cdot (|T_{r_1}(r_2)| - 1) \\
&< -(2 - \tfrac{|P_1|}{d(r_3, r_2)}) \cdot (n - 1) + n - 1 - (|P_1| - d(r_3, r_2)) \cdot \tfrac{n-1}{d(r_3, r_2)} \\
&= 0
\end{aligned}$$

Thus, for $\alpha > 3(n - 1)$, we may now assume $D(r_1) - D(r_3) > -\left(2 - \frac{|P_1|}{d(r_3, r_2)}\right) \cdot (n - 1)$ or, equivalently, $D(r_3) - D(r_1) < \left(2 - \frac{|P_1|}{d(r_3, r_2)}\right) \cdot (n - 1)$.

Case 5: $(|T_{r_3}(r_1)| - 1) \geq \frac{\left(3 - \frac{|P_1|}{d(r_3, r_2)}\right) \cdot (n-1)}{(|P_1| + d(r_3, r_2))}$

In this case, we reconsider one strategy change:

1. r_1 sells e_1 and buys $r_1 r_3$

This is an instance of Strategy I. Thus from (3), we have the bound:

$$0 \le D(r_3) - D(r_1) + n - 1 - \left(|P_1| + d(r_3, r_2) + 1\right) \cdot \left(|T_{r_3}(r_1)| - 1\right)$$
$$< \left(2 - \frac{|P_1|}{d(r_3, r_2)}\right) \cdot (n - 1) + n - 1 - \left(|P_1| + d(r_3, r_2)\right) \cdot \left(|T_{r_3}(r_1)| - 1\right)$$
$$\le \left(3 - \frac{|P_1|}{d(r_3, r_2)}\right) \cdot (n - 1) - \left(|P_1| + d(r_3, r_2)\right) \cdot \frac{\left(3 - \frac{|P_1|}{d(r_3, r_2)}\right) \cdot (n-1)}{\left(|P_1| + d(r_3, r_2)\right)}$$
$$= 0$$

Thus, for $\alpha > 3(n-1)$, we may now assume $\left(|T_{r_3}(r_1)| - 1\right) < \frac{\left(3 - \frac{|P_1|}{d(r_3, r_2)}\right) \cdot (n-1)}{\left(|P_1| + d(r_3, r_2)\right)}$.

Case 6: Else

For this final case, define $\gamma = \frac{d(r_3, r_2)}{|P_1|}$. Since $d(r_2, r_3) < \frac{1}{3} k_{\max} \le |P_1|$, it follows that $\gamma \in (0, 1)$. We now consider one strategy change:

1. r_1 sells e_1 and f_1 and buys $r_1 r_3$

This is an instance of Strategy II. Thus from (5), we have the bound:

$$0 \le D(r_3) - D(r_1) + n - 1 + (k_{\max} - (|P_1| + d(r_2, r_3) + 3)) \cdot (|T_{r_3}(r_1)| - 1) - \alpha \quad (22)$$

Substituting in $D(r_3) - D(r_1) < \left(2 - \frac{|P_1|}{d(r_3, r_2)}\right) \cdot (n - 1)$ and $(|T_{r_3}(r_1)| - 1) < \frac{(3 - \frac{|P_1|}{d(r_3, r_2)}) \cdot (n-1)}{(|P_1| + d(r_3, r_2))}$ gives

$$0 < \left(3 - \frac{|P_1|}{d(r_3, r_2)}\right) \cdot (n - 1)$$
$$+ (k_{\max} - (|P_1| + d(r_2, r_3) + 3)) \cdot \frac{(3 - \frac{|P_1|}{d(r_3, r_2)}) \cdot (n-1)}{(|P_1| + d(r_3, r_2))} - \alpha$$
$$= (k_{\max} - 3) \cdot \frac{(3 - \frac{|P_1|}{d(r_3, r_2)})}{(|P_1| + d(r_3, r_2))} \cdot (n - 1) - \alpha$$
$$\le \frac{k_{\max}}{|P_1|} \cdot \frac{3 - \frac{1}{\gamma}}{1 + \gamma} \cdot (n - 1) - \alpha$$
$$\le 3(n - 1) \cdot \frac{3 - \frac{1}{\gamma}}{1 + \gamma} - \alpha$$
$$\le 3(n - 1) - \alpha$$

The third inequality holds as $\frac{1}{3} k_{\max} \le |P_1|$. For the last inequality, we claim that $\frac{3 - \frac{1}{\gamma}}{1 + \gamma} \le 1$, for any γ. To see this, note that $(\gamma - 1)^2 \ge 0$. Rearranging gives $\gamma^2 + \gamma \ge 3\gamma - 1$ and the claim holds.

This completes the case analysis. If $\alpha > 3(n - 1)$ there are no cases where a biconnected component of G can exist. Thus any Nash equilibrium G must be a tree for $\alpha > 3(n - 1)$.

5 Conclusion

In this paper, we have shown that the revised tree conjecture holds for $\alpha > 3(n-1)$. Moreover, we have confirmed that min-cycles are a powerful tool in tackling the conjecture. Specifically, examining the strategic options of vertices on maximum length min-cycles is a promising technique for contradicting the existence of cycles in Nash equilibria. This is particularly the case for the range $\alpha > 2(n-1)$, where we know that all min-cycles must be directed. Indeed, all the results presented in this paper, except for the main theorem, hold for the range $\alpha > 2(n-1)$. This suggests improved bounds can be obtained using these methods.

Acknowledgements. We are grateful to the reviewers for comments and suggestions that helped improve this paper.

References

1. Albers, S., Eilts, S., Even-Dar, E., Mansour, Y., Roditty, L.: On Nash equilibria for a network creation game. ACM Trans. Econ. Comput. **2**, 1–27 (2014)
2. Alon, N., Demaine, E., Hajiaghayi, M., Leighton, T.: Basic network creation games. SIAM J. Discret. Math. **27**, 656–668 (2013)
3. Alvarez, C., Messegue, A.: Network creation games: structure vs anarchy. arXiv:1706.09132
4. Àlvarez, C., Messegué, A.: On the price of anarchy for high-price links. In: Caragiannis, I., Mirrokni, V., Nikolova, E. (eds.) WINE 2019. LNCS, vol. 11920, pp. 316–329. Springer, Cham (2019). https://doi.org/10.1007/978-3-030-35389-6_23
5. Bilò, D., Gualà, L., Leucci, S., Proietti, G.: Network creation games with traceroute-based strategies. In: Halldórsson, M.M. (ed.) SIROCCO 2014. LNCS, vol. 8576, pp. 210–223. Springer, Cham (2014). https://doi.org/10.1007/978-3-319-09620-9_17
6. Bilo, D., Guala, L., Leucci, S., Proietti, G.: Locality-based network creation games. ACM Trans. Parallel Comput. **3**, 210–223 (2014)
7. Bilò, D., Lenzner, P.: On the tree conjecture for the network creation game. Theory Comput. Syst. **64**(3), 422–443 (2019). https://doi.org/10.1007/s00224-019-09945-9
8. Cord-Landwehr, A., Lenzner, P.: Network creation games: think global – act local. In: Italiano, G.F., Pighizzini, G., Sannella, D.T. (eds.) MFCS 2015. LNCS, vol. 9235, pp. 248–260. Springer, Heidelberg (2015). https://doi.org/10.1007/978-3-662-48054-0_21
9. Chauhan, A., Lenzner, P., Melnichenko, A., Molitor, L.: Selfish network creation with non-uniform edge cost. In: Bilò, V., Flammini, M. (eds.) SAGT 2017. LNCS, vol. 10504, pp. 160–172. Springer, Cham (2017). https://doi.org/10.1007/978-3-319-66700-3_13
10. Demaine, E., Hajiaghayi, M., Mahini, H., Zadimoghaddam, M.: The price of anarchy in cooperative network creation games. ACM Trans. Econ. Comput. **8**, 1–20 (2012)
11. Fabrikant, A., Luthra, A., Maneva, E., Papadimitriou, C., Shenker, S.: On a network creation game. In: Proceedings of 22nd Symposium on Principles of Distributed Computing (PODC), pp. 347–351 (2003)

12. Lenzner, P.: On selfish network creation. Humboldt-Universität zu Berlin (2014)
13. Mamageishvili, A., Mihalak, M., Muller, D.: Tree Nash equilibria in the network creation game. Internet Math. **11**, 472–486 (2015)
14. Mihalak, M., Schlegel, J.: The price of anarchy in network creation games is (mostly) constant. Theoret. Comput. Sci. **53**, 53–72 (2013)

A Common Generalization of Budget Games and Congestion Games

Fuga Kiyosue[1] and Kenjiro Takazawa[2]([✉]) [iD]

[1] SCSK Corporation, Tokyo, Japan
[2] Hosei University, Tokyo 184-8584, Japan
takazawa@hosei.ac.jp

Abstract. Budget games are introduced by Drees, Feldotto, Riechers, and Skopalik (2015) as a model of noncooperative games arising from resource allocation problems. Budget games have several similarities to congestion games, one of which is that the matroid structure of the strategy space is essential for the existence of a pure Nash equilibrium (PNE). Despite these similarities, however, the theoretical relation between budget games and congestion games has been unclear. In this paper, we reveal the common structure of budget games and congestion games by providing a generalized model of budget games, called generalized budget games (g-budget games, for short). We show that the model of g-budget games includes weighted congestion games and player-specific congestion games under certain assumptions. We further show that g-budget games also include offset budget games, a generalized model of budget games by Drees, Feldotto, Riechers, and Skopalik (2019). We then prove that every matroid g-budget game has a PNE, which extends the result for budget games. We finally present a linear-time procedure to find a PNE in a certain class of singleton g-budget games.

Keywords: Noncooperative game · Pure Nash equilibrium · Matroid

1 Introduction

Analysis of the existence of pure Nash equilibria (PNE) has been a central topic in the study of algorithmic game theory [12]. A classical and important class of noncooperative games is *congestion games* [11]. Congestion games, which generalize selfish routing games, provide a model of the behavior of players choosing an optimal strategy while avoiding congestion. A prominent feature of congestion games is that every congestion game is a potential game [11], and conversely, every potential game is represented by a congestion game [9]. A potential game has a property that a strategy profile minimizing the potential function is a PNE.

Recently, Drees, Feldotto, Riechers, and Skopalik [2,3] introduced *budget games*, which offer a model of noncooperative games arising from resource allocation problems, and have some similarity to congestion games. A sketch of

The second author is partially supported by JSPS KAKENHI Grant Number JP20K11699, Japan.

© The Author(s), under exclusive license to Springer Nature Switzerland AG 2022
P. Kanellopoulos et al. (Eds.): SAGT 2022, LNCS 13584, pp. 258–274, 2022.
https://doi.org/10.1007/978-3-031-15714-1_15

budget games is as follows (see Sect. 2.2 for details). Each resource is associated with a *budget*, which is a positive number and is allocated to the players as utility. Each player has a *demand* on each resource, and obtains the whole demand from a resource if the total demand on the resource does not exceed its budget. Otherwise, the budget is allocated among the players in proportion to their demands. Namely, if the total demand on a resource exceeds its budget, then the budget is allocated to each player in the inverse proportion to the total demand. Therefore, budget games have the same property as congestion games that more players on one resource result in less utility (more cost).

Drees et al. [3] presented several theorems on the existence of PNE in some kinds of restricted budget games. For instance, they proved that a *matroid budget game*, in which the strategy space of each player is a base family of a matroid, has a PNE (Theorem 1). They also presented an instance of a budget game which is not a matroid budget game and does not have a PNE. These results suggest that the matroid structure is essential for budget games to possess a PNE. Related work also appears in [2,4].

The importance of the matroid structure is also appreciated for congestion games. Ackermann, Röglin, and Vöcking [1] proved that *weighted congestion games* and *player-specific congestion games* have a PNE if the strategy space of each player is a base family of a matroid. Weighted congestion games are generalized to *congestion games with monotone cost functions* [14], and player-specific congestion games are generalized to *polymatroid congestion games* [8]. The matroid structure plays a key role to the existence of PNE in both of these two models as well. Further relations of matroids and congestion games are investigated by Fujishige et al. [5,6].

Despite these similarities, the theoretical relation between budget games and congestion games has been unclear. The objective of this paper is to provide a comprehensive understanding of budget games and congestion games. To achieve this objective, we provide a generalized model of budget games, called *generalized budget games* (*g-budget games*, for short). The model is established by figuring out the essential property for a matroid budget game to have a PNE. Specifically, we generalize the allocation of utility so that it may not be the inverse proportion to the total demands but is represented by a monotone nonincreasing set function defined on the power set of the players (see Sect. 3.1 for precise description).

This generalization indeed sheds light on the relation between budget games and congestion games. We show that weighted congestion games and player-specific congestion games under certain assumptions are included in the model of g-budget games (Theorems 8 and 9), revealing the common structure of budget games and congestion games. We further show that g-budget games also include *offset budget games* [3], a generalized model of budget games addressing an offset on each resource.

We then prove that every matroid g-budget game has a PNE (Theorem 11), which extends the result of Drees et al. [3] for budget games. This demonstrates that g-budget games inherits the good property of budget games. Furthermore, applied to offset budget games, this result provides a new class of offset budget games possessing a PNE. Previous results on PNE in offset budget games [3] only discusses singleton games, in which every strategy consists of one resource, and games with two resources. Our result first provides a PNE theorem for offset budget games without the restriction on the size of the strategies and the number of resources.

Finally, for a certain class of singleton g-budget games, we show that a PNE can be computed in linear time, extending a result for singleton budget games [3]. We also make a remark on the computation method described in [3].

We remark that the model of g-budget games is still a special case of congestion games with monotone cost functions [14]. However, g-budget games retain the simplicity of budget games, which can be found in the potential function and the upper bound on the convergence time to a PNE. We will discuss this issue in Sect. 6.

The organization of the rest of the paper is as follows. We describe the previous models and results in Sect. 2. In Sect. 3, we introduce our model of g-budget games and show the classes of previous models included in g-budget games. Section 4 is devoted to a proof of the existence of a PNE in matroid g-budget games. In Sect. 5, we address singleton g-budget games. Section 6 concludes the paper with some discussion.

2 Preliminaries

In this paper, we denote the set of the integers by $\mathbb{Z}$ and that of the real numbers by $\mathbb{R}$. Subscripts $+$ and $++$ mean that the set has only nonnegative and positive numbers, respectively. For instance, $\mathbb{Z}_+$ denotes the set of nonnegative integers and $\mathbb{R}_{++}$ that of positive real numbers.

2.1 Matroids

For a finite set R and its subset family $\mathcal{S} \subseteq 2^R$, the pair $(R, \mathcal{S})$ is called a *matroid* if it satisfies the following axiom:

(i) $\mathcal{S} \neq \emptyset$, and
(ii) if $S, S' \in \mathcal{S}$ and $r \in S \setminus S'$, then there exists $r' \in S' \setminus S$ such that $(S \setminus \{r\}) \cup \{r'\} \in \mathcal{S}$.

The set family $\mathcal{S}$ is referred to as a *base family*, and each set $S \in \mathcal{S}$ as a *base*. It follows from the axiom that all bases have the same size, that is, $|S| = |S'|$ for every $S, S' \in \mathcal{S}$.

Optimization over matroids has long history and rich literature (see, e.g., [10,13]). The following lemma is an example of a nice structure of matroids, which will be used in subsequent sections. For a vector $w \in \mathbb{R}^R$ and a subset $R' \subseteq R$, let $w(R')$ denote $\sum_{r \in R'} w_r$.

Lemma 1 (see, e.g., [10,13]). *Let $(R, \mathcal{S})$ be a matroid, $S \in \mathcal{S}$ be its base, and $w \in \mathbb{R}^R$ be a weight vector. If there exists some base $S' \in \mathcal{S}$ such that $w(S') > w(S)$, then there exist $s \in S$ and $s' \in R \setminus S$ such that $(S \setminus \{s\}) \cup \{s'\} \in \mathcal{S}$ and $w((S \setminus \{s\}) \cup \{s'\}) > w(S)$.*

2.2 Previous Models

All models in this paper consist of the set of the players $N = \{1, \ldots, n\}$ and the set of the resources R. A strategy of each player is a subset of R, and the strategy space of a player $i \in N$ is denoted by $\mathcal{S}_i \subseteq 2^R$. If $(R, \mathcal{S}_i)$ is a matroid for every player $i \in N$, then the model is referred to as a *matroid game*. In particular, if $\mathcal{S}_i$ consists of singletons for each $i \in N$, i.e., every strategy is a single resource, then it is called a *singleton game*.

A *strategy profile* is a collection $\mathbf{S} = (S_1, \ldots, S_n)$ of a strategy $S_i \in \mathcal{S}_i$ of every player $i \in N$. For a strategy profile $\mathbf{S} = (S_1, \ldots, S_n)$ and a resource $r \in R$, let $N_r(\mathbf{S}) \subseteq N$ denote the set of players choosing r in their strategies, i.e.,

$$N_r(\mathbf{S}) = \{i \in N \mid r \in S_i\}.$$

In a strategy profile $\mathbf{S}$, a player $i \in N_r(\mathbf{S})$ obtains *utility* (or *cost*) $u_{i,r}(\mathbf{S})$ from r, and her total utility $u_i(\mathbf{S})$ is

$$u_i(\mathbf{S}) = \sum_{r \in S_i} u_{i,r}(\mathbf{S}).$$

The objective of a player is to maximize her total utility (or minimize her total cost) by choosing an appropriate strategy. A *pure Nash equilibrium* (*PNE*) is a strategy profile in which no player has an incentive to change her strategy, which is formally defined as follows. Let $\mathbf{S} = (S_1, \ldots, S_n)$ be a strategy profile and $i \in N$ be a player. Let $\mathbf{S}_{-i}$ denote the collection of the strategies of the players other than i, that is, $\mathbf{S}_{-i} = (S_1, \ldots, S_{i-1}, S_{i+1}, \ldots, S_n)$. An *improving move* of a player i in $\mathbf{S}$ is to change her strategy from S_i to another strategy $S_i' \in \mathcal{S}_i$ such that $u_i(\mathbf{S}_{-i}, S_i') > u_i(\mathbf{S}_{-i}, S_i)$. In particular, if $|S_i \setminus S_i'| = |S_i' \setminus S_i| = 1$, then such an improving move is referred to as a *lazy move*. If no player has an improving move, then the strategy profile $\mathbf{S}$ is called a PNE. In other words, a PNE is a strategy profile $\mathbf{S}$ in which $u_i(\mathbf{S}) \geq u_i(\mathbf{S}_{-i}, S_i')$ holds for every strategy $S_i' \in \mathcal{S}_i$ and every player $i \in N$.

Budget Games. A budget game [2,3] is represented by a tuple

$$(N, R, (\mathcal{S}_i)_{i \in N}, (b_r)_{r \in R}, (d_r(i))_{i \in N, r \in R}). \tag{1}$$

For each resource $r \in R$, a positive number $b_r \in \mathbb{R}_{++}$ stands for its *budget*. A positive number $d_r(i) \in \mathbb{R}_{++}$ stands for the *demand* of a player $i \in N$ on a resource $r \in R$. The tuple (1) is often abbreviated as $(N, R, (\mathcal{S}_i), (b_r), (d_r(i)))$.

The utility $u_{i,r}(\mathbf{S})$ is defined by the budget and demands in the following manner. Basically, the budget b_r of a resource $r \in R$ is allocated to the players in $N_r(\mathbf{S})$ according to their demands on r. For a subset $N' \subseteq N$, let $d_r(N') = \sum_{i \in N'} d_r(i)$. If $b_r \geq d_r(N_r(\mathbf{S}))$, that is, the budget b_r is large enough to manage its total demand $d_r(N_r(\mathbf{S}))$, then every player $i \in N_r(\mathbf{S})$ obtains her whole demand $d_r(i)$. If $b_r < d_r(N_r(\mathbf{S}))$, then the budget b_r is distributed among the players in $N_r(\mathbf{S})$ in proportion to their demands. In summary, in a strategy profile $\mathbf{S} = (S_1, \ldots, S_n)$, the utility $u_{i,r}(\mathbf{S})$ that a player $i \in N$ obtains from a resource $r \in S_i$ is defined as

$$u_{i,r}(\mathbf{S}) = \min \left\{ d_r(i), \ b_r \cdot \frac{d_r(i)}{d_r(N_r(\mathbf{S}))} \right\}$$

$$= d_r(i) \cdot \min \left\{ 1, \ \frac{b_r}{d_r(N_r(\mathbf{S}))} \right\}. \tag{2}$$

Drees et al. [3] proved that a budget game G has a PNE if G obeys two assumptions: G is a matroid budget game; and G is *with fixed demands*. A budget game $G = (N, R, (S_i), (b_r), (d_r(i)))$ is *with fixed demands* if, for each player $i \in N$, her demands on the resources are identical, i.e., $d_r(i) = d(i)$ holds for some constant $d(i) \in \mathbb{R}_{++}$ for every $r \in R$.

Theorem 1 ([3]). *A matroid budget game $G = (N, R, (S_i), (b_r), (d_r(i)))$ with fixed demands has a PNE, which can be attained from an arbitrary strategy profile by a finite number of lazy moves.*

The importance of the matroid structure is explained in two ways. First, in order to discuss the existence of PNE in a matroid budget game, it is not necessary to consider all improving moves but only lazy moves. This fact follows from Lemma 1, which will be formally described as Theorem 10 in Sect. 4.

Second, the matroid structure is indeed necessary, because Drees et al. [3] constructed a non-matroid budget game with fixed demands that does not have a PNE.

Theorem 2 ([3]). *There exists a budget game with fixed demands that does not possess a PNE.*

Offset Budget Games. Drees et al. [3] introduced *offset budget games*, which is a generalized model of budget games. An offset budget game is represented by a tuple

$$(N, R, (S_i)_{i \in N}, (b_r)_{r \in R}, (d_r(i))_{i \in N, r \in R}, (\alpha_r)_{r \in R}), \tag{3}$$

where $\alpha_r \in \mathbb{R}_+$ stands for the *offset* of a resource $r \in R$. As before, the tuple (3) is often abbreviated as $(N, R, (S_i), (b_r), (d_r(i)), (\alpha_r))$.

The unique difference from a budget game is that the utility function $u_{i,r}$ is defined by

$$u_{i,r}(\mathbf{S}) = d_r(i) \cdot \min \left\{ 1, \ \frac{b_r}{d_r(N_r(\mathbf{S})) + \alpha_r} \right\}.$$

for each strategy profile $\mathbf{S}$. Clearly, a budget game is a special case of an offset budget game where $\alpha_r = 0$ for each $r \in R$.

Drees et al. [3] proved the following theorems on PNE in certain classes of offset budget games. Let $G = (N, R, (S_i), (b_r), (d_r(i)), (\alpha_r))$ be an offset budget game with $N = \{1, \ldots n\}$. The players are *ordered* if

$$d_r(i) \geq d_r(j) \tag{4}$$

holds for each $i, j \in N$ with $i < j$ and each $r \in R$. For an offset budget game G with ordered players, G has *increasing demand ratios* if

$$\frac{d_r(i)}{d_{r'}(i)} \geq \frac{d_r(j)}{d_{r'}(j)}$$

holds for every $i, j \in N$ with $i < j$ and every $r, r' \in R$ with $d_r(i) \geq d_{r'}(i)$.

Theorem 3 ([3]). *Singleton offset budget games with ordered players and increasing demand ratios always have a PNE.*

Theorem 4 ([3]). *Matroid offset budget games with two resources always have a PNE.*

Congestion Games. A *weighted congestion game* [1] is represented by a tuple

$$(N, R, (\mathcal{S}_i)_{i \in N}, (l_r)_{r \in R}, (w_i)_{i \in N}).$$

Here, $l_r : \mathbb{R}_+ \to \mathbb{R}_+$ denotes the *latency function* of a resource $r \in R$, which is monotone nondecreasing. Also, $w_i \in \mathbb{R}_{++}$ denotes the weight of a player $i \in N$. For simplicity, we often use a shorter notation $(N, R, (\mathcal{S}_i), (l_r), (w_i))$.

In a strategy profile $\mathbf{S} = (S_1, \ldots, S_n)$, every player in $N_r(\mathbf{S})$ must pay the same cost for using r, which depends on the congestion on r. The congestion is defined as the total weight $w(N_r(\mathbf{S}))$ of the players choosing r, and hence every player in $N_r(\mathbf{S})$ pays a cost $l_r(w(N_r(\mathbf{S})))$ for using r. Thus, the total cost $c_i(\mathbf{S})$ paid by a player i is equal to

$$c_i(\mathbf{S}) = \sum_{r \in S_i} l_r(w(N_r(\mathbf{S}))).$$

Again, the matroid structure of $\mathcal{S}_i$ ($i \in N$) is essential for the existence of PNE. Ackermann et al. [1] proved that a weighted matroid congestion game always have a PNE, while it is not the case with general weighted congestion games.

Theorem 5 ([1]). *A weighted matroid congestion game has a PNE, which can be attained from an arbitrary strategy profile by a finite number of lazy moves. Also, there exists a weighted congestion game that does not have a PNE.*

A *player-specific congestion game* [1] is represented by

$$(N, R, (\mathcal{S}_i)_{i \in N}, (l_{i,r})_{i \in N, r \in R}),$$

or $(N, R, (\mathcal{S}_i), (l_{i,r}))$ for short. Here, each player has her specific latency function $l_{i,r} : \mathbb{Z}_+ \to \mathbb{R}_+$ for each resource $r \in R$. The argument of $l_{i,r}$ is the number of players choosing r, and hence the total cost $c_i(\mathbf{S})$ paid by a player i in a strategy profile $\mathbf{S} = (S_1, \ldots, S_n)$ is defined as

$$c_i(\mathbf{S}) = \sum_{r \in S_i} l_{i,r}(|N_r(\mathbf{S})|).$$

As well as the above models, the matroid structure of the strategy space is essential for player-specific congestion games to have a PNE.

Theorem 6 ([1]). *A player-specific matroid congestion game has a PNE, which can be attained from an arbitrary strategy profile by a finite number of lazy moves. Also, there exists a player-specific congestion game that does not have a PNE.*

The model of *congestion games with monotone cost functions* [14] generalizes weighted congestion games. In this model, the latency function $l_r \colon 2^N \to \mathbb{R}_+$ is a monotone nondecreasing set function for each $r \in R$. Thus, the total cost paid by a player $i \in N$ in a strategy profile $\mathbf{S}$ is described as

$$c_i(\mathbf{S}) = \sum_{r \in S_i} l_r(N_r(\mathbf{S})).$$

Theorem 5 extends to congestion games with monotone cost functions.

Theorem 7 ([14]). *A matroid congestion game with monotone cost functions has a PNE, which can be attained from an arbitrary strategy profile by a finite number of lazy moves.*

We close this section by mentioning the relations among the above models. Budget games have similarities to both weighted congestion games and player-specific congestion games in the following sense. The demands in budget games roughly correspond to the weights in weighted congestion games, because both of them represent the impact of a player on the resources. Also, the fact that a player in a budget game can have distinct demands on the resources roughly corresponds to the model of player-specific congestion games, in which the players have distinct latency functions on one resource.

Despite these similarities, however, these models do not coincide. The utility function (2) in budget games cannot represent the general form of latency functions of weighted/player-specific congestion games. Conversely, a weighted congestion game cannot represent budget games, in which different players may obtain different utilities from the same resource, and the model of player-specific congestion games also does not include budget games because the latency functions only take the number of players as argument and thus cannot take the demands into account.

3   Our Model: Generalized Budget Games

In this section, we introduce our model of *generalized budget games*, or *g-budget games* for short. We then explain some special cases of the previous models included in g-budget games.

3.1   Model

We generalize the core part $b_r/d_r(N_r(\mathbf{S}))$ of the utility function (2) of a budget game so that it may not be the inverse proportion. In order to inherit the property that more players result in less utility, we adopt a strictly decreasing set function defined on the power set of the players. A set function $f \colon 2^N \to \mathbb{R}$ is strictly decreasing if $f(X) > f(Y)$ for each $X \subset Y \subseteq N$. Similarly, a set function $g: 2^N \to \mathbb{R}$ is strictly increasing if $f(X) < f(Y)$ for each $X \subset Y \subseteq N$.

Now a generalized budget game is represented by a tuple

$$(N, R, (\mathcal{S}_i)_{i \in N}, (f_r)_{r \in R}, (d_r(i))_{i \in N, r \in R}),$$

where $f_r: 2^N \to \mathbb{R}_+$ is a strictly decreasing set function for each resource $r \in R$. Again, it is often abbreviated as $(N, R, (\mathcal{S}_i), (f_r), (d_r(i)))$. In a strategy profile $\mathbf{S} = (S_1, \ldots, S_n)$, a player $i \in N$ obtains utility $u_{i,r}(\mathbf{S}) \in \mathbb{R}_+$ from a resource $r \in S_i$, which is determined by the function f_r as

$$u_{i,r}(\mathbf{S}) = d_r(i) \cdot \min\{1, \, f_r(N_r(\mathbf{S}))\}.$$

Note that the term $b_r/d_r(N_r(\mathbf{S}))$ in (2) is replaced with $f_r(N_r(\mathbf{S}))$.

This generalization retains the characterizing feature of budget games: if the set $N_r(\mathbf{S})$ of players choosing a resource r is small, then each player $i \in N_r(\mathbf{S})$ obtains her whole demand $d_r(i)$ on r; and as $N_r(\mathbf{S})$ becomes larger, the utility decreases after $f(N_r(\mathbf{S}))$ becomes smaller than one, corresponding to strategy profiles in budget games with $d_r(N_r(\mathbf{S}))$ larger than b_r.

3.2 Special Cases

Clearly, a budget game $G = (N, R, (\mathcal{S}_i), (b_r), (d_r(i)))$ is a special case of a generalized budget game $(N, R, (\mathcal{S}_i), (f_r), (d_r(i)))$, where the set function $f_r: 2^N \to \mathbb{R}_+$ is defined by

$$f_r(N') = \frac{b_r}{d_r(N')} \quad (N' \subseteq N) \tag{5}$$

for each $r \in R$. It is also straightforward to see that an offset budget game can be represented as a generalized budget game. Given an offset budget game $(N, R, (\mathcal{S}_i), (b_r), (d_r(i)), (\alpha_r))$, define the set function f_r by

$$f_r(N') = \frac{b_r}{d_r(N') + \alpha_r} \quad (N' \subseteq N) \tag{6}$$

for each $r \in R$. It is clear that the set function f_r determined by (5) or (6) is strictly decreasing, and hence determines a generalized budget game.

Weighted congestion games and player-specific congestion games under certain assumptions are also included in generalized budget games. Let $G = (N, R, (\mathcal{S}_i), (l_r), (w_i))$ be a weighted congestion game, and suppose that the size of the strategies of each player is identical. Namely, for each $i \in N$, there exists an integer $\rho_i \in \mathbb{Z}_+$ such that

$$|S_i| = \rho_i \quad \text{for each } S_i \in \mathcal{S}_i. \tag{7}$$

Note that this is the case with matroid congestion games.

Now, such a weighted congestion game G is represented as a generalized budget game $G' = (N, R, (\mathcal{S}_i), (f_r), (d_r(i))$ in the following way. Let $d_r(i) = 1$ for each $i \in N$ and each $r \in R$, and let L be a positive number such that

$$L \geq \max_{r \in R}\{l_r(w(N))\}.$$

Namely, $L \in \mathbb{R}_{++}$ is at least the maximum cost possible on one resource. Then, define the function $f_r : 2^N \to \mathbb{R}_+$ for each resource $r \in R$ by

$$f_r(N') = 1 - \frac{l_r(w(N'))}{L} \quad (N' \subseteq N). \tag{8}$$

We have that f_r is strictly decreasing if the latency function l_r is strictly increasing. We have thus obtained a generalized budget game $G' = (N, R, (\mathcal{S}_i), (f_r), (d_r(i)))$ with fixed demands.

In this generalized budget game G', the utility $u_i(\mathbf{S})$ of a player $i \in N$ in a strategy profile $\mathbf{S} = (S_1, \ldots, S_n)$ is equal to

$$\sum_{r \in S_i} u_{i,r}(\mathbf{S}) = \sum_{r \in S_i} d_r(i) \cdot \min\{1, f_r(N_r(\mathbf{S}))\}$$

$$= \sum_{r \in S_i} \left(1 - \frac{l_r(w(N_r(\mathbf{S})))}{L}\right)$$

$$= \rho_i - \frac{c_i(\mathbf{S})}{L}.$$

Thus, the minimization of cost $c_i(\mathbf{S})$ in the weighted congestion game G amounts to the maximization of utility $u_i(\mathbf{S})$ in the generalized budget game G'.

Theorem 8. *A weighted congestion game $(N, R, (\mathcal{S}_i), (l_r), (w_i))$ can be represented by a generalized budget game with fixed demands if the latency function l_r is strictly increasing for each resource $r \in R$ and the size of the strategies of a player i is identical for each $i \in N$.*

Player-specific congestion games can also be represented by a generalized budget game in the following way. Let $G = (N, R, (\mathcal{S}_i), (l_{i,r}))$ be a player-specific congestion game. Suppose that there exists constant numbers $\delta_{i,r} \in \mathbb{R}_+$ ($i \in N$, $r \in R$) and strictly increasing functions $\tilde{l}_r : \mathbb{Z}_+ \to \mathbb{R}_+$ ($r \in R$) such that

$$l_{i,r}(k) = \delta_{i,r} \cdot \tilde{l}_r(k) \quad (k = 1, \ldots, n) \tag{9}$$

for each $i \in N$ and each $r \in R$. Intuitively, (9) means that $\tilde{l}_r$ is a master of the cost functions for all players, and it is multiplied by $\delta_{i,r}$, which specifies the cost function for $i \in N$ and $r \in R$ and is a constant with respect to the number k of players choosing r. Suppose further that there exists a constant $D_i \in \mathbb{R}_+$ with

$$\sum_{r \in S_i} \delta_{i,r} = D_i \quad (S_i \in \mathcal{S}_i) \tag{10}$$

holds for each $i \in N$, meaning that the sum of the multipliers $\delta_{i,r}$ of a strategy is constant for each player. This assumption (10) is satisfied if $(R, \mathcal{S}_i)$ is the direct sum of matroids on the subsets of R, all of whose elements r have the same value of $\delta_{i,r}$.

Then, define a g-budget game $G' = (N, R, (\mathcal{S}_i), (f_r), (d_r(i)))$ as follows. Let $L \in \mathbb{R}_{++}$ be a sufficiently large number satisfying

$$L \geq \max_{i \in N, r \in R} \left\{ \tilde{l}_r(n) \right\}$$

and let $d_r(i) = \delta_{i,r}$ $(i \in N,\, r \in R)$. The function $f_r : 2^N \to \mathbb{R}_+$ is defined by

$$f_r(N') = 1 - \frac{\tilde{l}_r(|N'|)}{L} \tag{11}$$

for each $r \in R$.

The utility $u_i(\mathbf{S})$ of a player $i \in N$ in a strategy profile $\mathbf{S} = (S_1, \ldots, S_n)$ is equal to

$$\sum_{r \in S_i} u_{i,r}(\mathbf{S}) = \sum_{r \in S_i} d_r(i) \cdot \min\{1,\, f_r(N_r(\mathbf{S}))\}$$

$$= \sum_{r \in S_i} \delta_{i,r} \cdot \left(1 - \frac{\tilde{l}_r(|N_r(\mathbf{S})|)}{L} \right)$$

$$= D_i - \frac{1}{L} \sum_{r \in S_i} l_{i,r}(|N_r(\mathbf{S})|)$$

$$= D_i - \frac{1}{L} \cdot c_i(\mathbf{S}).$$

Now the minimization of the cost $c_i(\mathbf{S})$ in the g-budget game G' exactly corresponds to the maximization of the utility $u_i(\mathbf{S})$ in the player-specific congestion game G.

Theorem 9. *A player-specific congestion game* $(N, R, (\mathcal{S}_i), (l_{i,r}))$ *can be represented by a generalized budget game if there exists constant numbers* $\delta_{i,r} \in \mathbb{R}_+$ *$(i \in N, r \in R)$, $D_i \in \mathbb{R}_+$ $(i \in N)$, and strictly increasing functions* $\tilde{l}_r : \mathbb{Z}_+ \to \mathbb{R}_+$ *$(r \in R)$ satisfying (9) and (10).*

Remark 1. It is possible to remove the assumptions (7) and (10) by allowing the utility functions in g-budget games to be negative. Namely, we remove the term 1 from the right-hand side of (8) and (11).

We can also include weighted/player-specific congestion games whose latency functions are not strictly increasing but nondecreasing, by allowing the function f_r in g-budget games to be nonincreasing, i.e., $f_r(X) \geq f_r(Y)$ for $X \subset Y \subseteq N$. However, this relaxation loses some simplicity of budget games mentioned in Sect. 6. We thus model generalized budget games by using strictly increasing functions f_r $(r \in R)$. It is also possible to recognize this model of g-budget games as a special class of congestion games with monotone cost functions [14] retaining that simplicity.

4   PNE in Matroid g-Budget Games

The goal of this subsection is to extend Theorem 1 to generalized budget games. We first show that it is not necessary to consider all improving moves, and suffices to consider only lazy moves in order to discuss pure Nash equilibria in a matroid g-budget game. This property was pointed out for weighted matroid congestion games by Ackermann, Röglin and Vöcking [1], and extended to a more generalized model of matroid congestion games with monotone cost function [14]. For budget games, Drees et al. [3] mentioned that matroid budget games also possess this property. As for matroid g-budget games, this property directly follows from the argument in [1,14], while we present its full proof to have this paper self-contained.

Theorem 10. *Let $(N, R, (\mathcal{S}_i), (f_r), (d_r(i)))$ be a matroid g-budget game and let $\mathbf{S} = (S_1, \ldots, S_n)$ be its strategy profile. If a player $i \in N$ has an improving move in $\mathbf{S}$, then i has a lazy move in $\mathbf{S}$.*

Proof. Let $\mathbf{S} = (S_1, \ldots, S_n)$ be a strategy profile, and suppose that a player $i \in N$ has an improving move. If i changes her strategy to $\tilde{S}_i \in \mathcal{S}_i$ with $\mathbf{S}_{-i}$ fixed, then her total utility becomes

$$u_i(\mathbf{S}_{-i}, \tilde{S}_i) = \sum_{r \in \tilde{S}_i} u_{i,r}(\mathbf{S}_{-i}, \tilde{S}_i)$$

$$= \sum_{r \in \tilde{S}_i} d_r(i) \cdot \min\{1, f_r(N_r(\mathbf{S}_{-i}, \tilde{S}_i))\}$$

$$= \sum_{r \in \tilde{S}_i} d_r(i) \cdot \min\{1, f_r(N_r(\mathbf{S}_{-i}) \cup \{i\})\},$$

where $N_r(\mathbf{S}_{-i})$ denotes the set of players choosing r in the strategy profile $\mathbf{S}$ except for i. Note that $d_r(i) \cdot \min\{1, f_r(N_r(\mathbf{S}_{-i}) \cup \{i\})\}$ is a constant when i and $\mathbf{S}_{-i}$ are fixed.

Here, define a weight vector $w \in \mathbb{R}^R$ by

$$w_r = d_r(i) \cdot \min\{1, f_r(N_r(\mathbf{S}_{-i}) \cup \{i\})\} \quad (r \in R).$$

It then follows that

$$u_i(\mathbf{S}_{-i}, \tilde{S}_i) = w(\tilde{S}_i),$$

that is, the maximization of the total utility of i amounts to finding a maximum weight base $S_i^* \in \mathcal{S}_i$ with respect to the weight vector w. In particular, if i has an improving move in $\mathbf{S}$, it means that S_i is not a maximum weight base. Then, by Lemma 1, there exist resources $r \in S_i$ and $r' \in R \setminus S_i$ such that $(S_i \setminus \{r\}) \cup \{r'\} \in \mathcal{S}_i$ and $w((S_i \setminus \{r\}) \cup \{r'\}) > w(S_i)$, implying that i has an lazy move from S_i to $(S_i \setminus \{r\}) \cup \{r'\}$.   □

We then show that each lazy moves strictly increases some *potential function* defined on the strategy profiles. For a strategy profile $\mathbf{S} = (S_1, \ldots, S_n)$, its potential function $\phi(\mathbf{S})$ is defined in the following manner. For each $r \in R$, define the *utility per demand* $c_r(\mathbf{S}) \in \mathbb{R}_+$ by

$$c_r(\mathbf{S}) = \frac{u_{i,r}(\mathbf{S})}{d_r(i)} = \min\{1, f_r(N_r(\mathbf{S}))\}, \tag{12}$$

where i is an arbitrary player in $N_r(\mathbf{S})$. Now the potential function $\phi(\mathbf{S})$ is a sequence $(c_r(\mathbf{S}))_{r \in R}$, where the utilities per demand are ordered in nondecreasing order.

Among the potential functions, we introduce a lexicographic order $<_{\text{lex}}$ as follows. Let $\mathbf{S}$ and $\mathbf{S}'$ be two strategy profiles, and denote $\phi(\mathbf{S}) = (c_{r_1}(\mathbf{S}), \ldots, c_{r_m}(\mathbf{S}))$ and $\phi(\mathbf{S}') = (c_{q_1}(\mathbf{S}), \ldots, c_{q_m}(\mathbf{S}))$, where $\{r_1, \ldots, r_m\} = \{q_1, \ldots, q_m\} = R$. Then, $\phi(\mathbf{S}) <_{\text{lex}} \phi(\mathbf{S}')$ if there exists an integer ℓ with $1 \leq \ell \leq m$ such that $c_{r_{\ell'}}(\mathbf{S}) = c_{q_{\ell'}}(\mathbf{S}')$ for each $\ell' < \ell$ and $c_{r_\ell}(\mathbf{S}) < c_{q_\ell}(\mathbf{S}')$.

Theorem 11. *Let $G = (N, R, (\mathcal{S}_i), (f_r), (d_r(i)))$ be a matroid g-budget game with fixed demands. Then, G has a PNE and it is attained by a finite number of lazy moves from an arbitrary strategy profile.*

Proof. Let $\mathbf{S} = (S_1, \ldots, S_n)$ be a strategy profile that is not a PNE. It follows from Theorem 10 that there exists a player $i \in N$ who has a lazy move. Suppose that the player i performs a lazy move to choose a new strategy $S_i' = (S_i \setminus \{r\}) \cup \{r'\}$, and let $\mathbf{S}' = (\mathbf{S}_{-i}, S_i')$ denote the resulting strategy profile. We show that $\phi(\mathbf{S}) <_{\text{lex}} \phi(\mathbf{S}')$, i.e., the potential function ϕ strictly increases by a lazy move. Then the proof follows from the finiteness of the potential function ϕ.

It follows from the definition of a lazy move that

$$u_{i,r}(\mathbf{S}) < u_{i,r'}(\mathbf{S}'). \tag{13}$$

Here $G = (N, R, (\mathcal{S}_i), (f_r), (d_r(i)))$ is a g-budget game with fixed demands, and in particular $d_r(i) = d_{r'}(i)$. Thus, it follows from (12) and (13) that

$$c_r(\mathbf{S}) < c_{r'}(\mathbf{S}'), \tag{14}$$

and further

$$c_r(\mathbf{S}) = f_r(N_r(\mathbf{S})) < 1. \tag{15}$$

We have that $i \in N_r(\mathbf{S})$ and $N_r(\mathbf{S}') = N_r(\mathbf{S}) \setminus \{i\}$. Hence,

$$f_r(N_r(\mathbf{S})) < f_r(N_r(\mathbf{S}')), \tag{16}$$

because f_r is strictly decreasing. It then follows from (15) and (16) that

$$c_r(\mathbf{S}') = \min\{1, f_r(N_r(\mathbf{S}'))\} > f_r(N_r(\mathbf{S})) = c_r(\mathbf{S}). \tag{17}$$

Therefore, from (14) and (17), we obtain $\phi(\mathbf{S}) <_{\text{lex}} \phi(\mathbf{S}')$, completing the proof. $\square$

Theorem 11 implies that the special classes of g-budget games listed in Sect. 3.2 have PNE if it can be represented by matroid g-budget games with fixed demands. In particular, we obtain a new class of offset budget games possessing a PNE.

Corollary 1. *Let $G = (N, R, (\mathcal{S}_i), (b_r), (d_r(i)), (\alpha_r))$ be a matroid offset budget game with fixed demands. Then, G has a PNE and it is attained by a finite number of lazy moves from an arbitrary strategy profile.*

As mentioned in Sect. 2.2, previous results on PNE in offset budget games only discusses singleton games and games with two resources. Therefore, Corollary 1 first provides a PNE theorem for offset budget games without the restriction on the size of the strategies and the number of resources.

Implication of Theorem 11 for congestion games will be discussed in Sect. 6.

5   Singleton g-Budget Games

In this section, we address singleton g-budget games, a special class of matroid g-budget games. If a singleton g-budget game G is with fixed budget, it follows from Theorem 11 that G possesses a PNE. Here we prove that a PNE can be found in $O(n)$ time if the players are ordered.

For singleton budget games with fixed demands, a previous result [3, Theorem 3] presents a method to compute a PNE in $O(n)$ time. However, we point out by showing a condition where the computation method fails. Despite this incompleteness, we show that the statement itself is correct, by presenting a method to compute a PNE in a singleton g-budget game with fixed demands and ordered players in $O(n)$ time, which implies a proof for singleton budget games.

We describe our computation method in Sect. 5.1, and then mention the detail of the previous result in Sect. 5.2.

5.1   Computing a PNE in Linear Time

Let $(N, R, (\mathcal{S}_i), (f_r), (d_r(i)))$ be a g-budget game with $N = \{1, \ldots n\}$. We generalize the definition (4) of ordered players in offset budget games to g-budget games. In a g-budget game $(N, R, (\mathcal{S}_i), (f_r), (d_r(i)))$, the players are *ordered* if

$$f_r(N' \cup \{i\}) \le f_r(N' \cup \{j\}) \tag{18}$$

holds for each $N' \subset N$, $i, j \in N \setminus N'$ with $i < j$, and each $r \in R$. Intuitively, (18) implies that, if $i < j$, player i has larger effect (make the utility smaller) than player j for each resource $r \in R$.

It is straightforward to see that (18) generalizes the definition (4) of ordered players for offset budget games. Given an offset budget game $(N, R, (\mathcal{S}_i), (b_r), (d_r(i)), (\alpha_r))$ with ordered players, construct a g-budget game $(N, R, (\mathcal{S}_i), (f_r), (d_r(i)))$ by defining the function f_r by (6) for each $r \in R$. Then, (18) immediately follows from (4).

Theorem 12. *Let $G = (N, R, (S_i), (f_r), (d_r(i)))$ be a singleton g-budget game with fixed demands and $N = \{1, \ldots n\}$ ordered. Then, a PNE in G can be computed in $O(n)$ time.*

Proof. Construct a strategy profile in the following manner. Each player starts with the empty strategy, and chooses her resource with the largest utility in the order of $1, \ldots, n$. We prove that the resulting strategy profile is a PNE.

For $i \in N$, let $\mathbf{S}_i$ denote the collection $(S_1, \ldots, S_i)$ of the strategies of players $1, \ldots, i$. In $\mathbf{S}_i$, denote a subset of players choosing a resource $r \in R$ by $N_r(\mathbf{S}_i)$, that is, $N_r(\mathbf{S}_i) = \{j \mid 1 \le j \le i, r \in S_j\}$.

Fix a player i, and suppose that i has chosen a resource r. This means that the resource r is optimal for i in $\mathbf{S}_i$:

$$u_{i,r}(\mathbf{S}_i) \ge u_{i,r'}(\mathbf{S}_i \cup \{i\}) \quad (r' \in R). \tag{19}$$

We show that this still holds in $\mathbf{S} = \mathbf{S}_n$ by induction.

Let j be a player with $j > i$. It is clear if j chooses a resource r' other than r: the choice of j can only decrease the utility of r'. Suppose that j chooses the same resource r as i. Since G is with fixed demands, this means that

$$\min\{1, f_r(N_r(\mathbf{S}_j))\} \ge \min\{1, f_{r'}(N_{r'}(\mathbf{S}_j \cup \{j\}))\} \quad (r' \in R). \tag{20}$$

If $f_r(N_r(\mathbf{S}_j)) = 1$, then r is still optimal for i in $\mathbf{S}_j$, and thus we are done. Suppose $f_r(N_r(\mathbf{S}_j)) < 1$. It then follows from (20) that

$$f_{r'}(N_{r'}(\mathbf{S}_j \cup \{j\})) \le f_r(N_r(\mathbf{S}_j)) < 1$$

for each $r' \in R$. Here, if i changes her strategy from r to another resource r', then her utility becomes

$$\min\{1, f_{r'}(N_{r'}(\mathbf{S}_j)) \cup \{i\})\}.$$

Now since the players are ordered and $i < j$, we obtain that

$$f_{r'}(N_{r'}(\mathbf{S}_j) \cup \{i\}) \le f_{r'}(N_{r'}(\mathbf{S}_j) \cup \{j\}) \le f_r(N_r(\mathbf{S}_j)).$$

Since G is with fixed demands, this implies that i has no incentive to change her strategy, completing the proof. $\qquad\square$

5.2   Remark on the Reverse Player Order

For a singleton budget game with fixed demands, Drees et al. [3, Theorem 3] constructively claimed that a PNE can be computed in $O(n)$ time. However, we point out a condition where the construction fails.

The construction by Drees et al. [3, Theorem 3] is as follows. Each player starts with the empty strategy, and chooses her resource with the largest utility in the nondecreasing order of the demands $d(\cdot)$. The authors claimed that the optimality of a player's choice is not affected by the subsequent players, but this is not the case with the following example.

Example 1. Let $G = (N, R, (\mathcal{S}_i), (b_r), (d_r(i)))$ be a singleton budget game with fixed demands, where

$$N = \{1, 2\}, \quad R = \{r, r'\}, \quad \mathcal{S}_1 = \mathcal{S}_2 = \{\{r\}, \{r'\}\},$$
$$d_r(1) = d_{r'}(1) < d_r(2) = d_{r'}(2).$$

Denote $d(1) = d_r(1) = d_{r'}(1)$ and $d(2) = d_r(2) = d_{r'}(2)$. Suppose that the following condition is satisfied:

$$\min\left\{1, \frac{b_{r'}}{d(2)}\right\} \leq \min\left\{1, \frac{b_r}{d(1) + d(2)}\right\} < \min\left\{1, \frac{b_{r'}}{d(1)}\right\}. \tag{21}$$

The latter inequality in (21) implies that

$$\frac{b_r}{d(1) + d(2)} < 1,$$

and then the former inequality in (21) implies that

$$\frac{b_{r'}}{d(2)} \leq \frac{b_r}{d(1) + d(2)}.$$

We thus obtain $b_{r'} < b_r$.

This means that player 1 can choose r as her strategy. Then, consider the choice of player 2. If player 2 chooses r or r', then her utility is

$$d(2) \cdot \min\left\{1, \frac{b_r}{d(1) + d(2)}\right\} \quad \text{or} \quad d(2) \cdot \min\left\{1, \frac{b_{r'}}{d(2)}\right\},$$

respectively. From the former inequality in (21), we can assume that player 2 chooses r. Then, the utility of player 1 becomes

$$d(1) \cdot \min\left\{1, \frac{b_r}{d(1) + d(2)}\right\},$$

which is smaller than $d(1) \cdot \min\{1, b_{r'}/d(1)\}$ by the latter inequality in (21). This means that player 1 loses the optimality of her choice due to the subsequent player 2.

Note that, if we apply the proof of Theorem 12 to singleton budget games with fixed demands, the players are ordered in the nonincreasing order of $d(i) = d_r(i)$ ($r \in R$). This order is the reversal of the order in [3, Theorem 3].

To conclude, we establish the following as a corollary of Theorem 12.

Corollary 2. *A PNE in a singleton budget game with fixed demands can be computed in $O(n)$ time.*

6   Discussion

For weighted matroid congestion games, Ackermann, Röglin, and Vöcking [1] already proved the existence of PNE, without the assumption that $l_r \colon \mathbb{R}_+ \to \mathbb{R}_+$ is strictly decreasing (Theorem 5). Takazawa [14] extended this result so that $l_r \colon 2^N \to \mathbb{R}_+$ is a nonincreasing set function (Theorem 7). Thus, the statement of Theorem 11 itself is not new for congestion games.

However, the potential function ϕ used in the proof of Theorem 11 is simpler than those used in [1,14]. In the proof of Theorem 11, the potential function $\phi(\mathbf{S})$ is in the form $(c_r(\mathbf{S}))_{r \in R}$, whereas the potential function used in [1] is a collection of a pair $(l_r(N_r(\mathbf{S})), |N_r(\mathbf{S})|)$ for every $r \in R$. This suggests that g-budget games have some simpler structure than congestion games, resulting from the fact that the function f_r in g-budget games is strictly decreasing, whereas the latency function l_r in congestion games is nonincreasing.

As an advantage of this simpler potential function, we can obtain a better upper bound on the number of lazy moves until converging to a PNE in g-budget games. Let $C_r \in \mathbb{Z}_{++}$ denote the number of distinct values of f_r or l_r for each $r \in R$. In general, the number of lazy moves is bounded by the number of potential functions. Thus, we obtain a bound $\prod_{r \in R} C_r$ for g-budget games, whereas the bound for weighted congestion games is $n^n \cdot \prod_{r \in R} C_r$.

One direction of future research is to discuss the lower bound on the number of improving moves for g-budget games. It would be of interest to provide a counterpart of the following theorem for g-budget games.

Theorem 13. ([1]).   *There exists a constant $c \in \mathbb{R}_{++}$ such that, for every integer $k \in \mathbb{Z}_{++}$, there exists a weighted singleton congestion game $(N, R, (\mathcal{S}_i), (l_r), (w_i))$ with $|N| \leq ck^2$, $|R| \leq ck$, $\max_{r \in R} C_r \leq ck^3$ requiring 2^k improving moves until converging to a PNE.*

The potential argument suggests another direction of further research. Harks, Klimm, and Möhring [7] introduced a framework of strategic games with the *lexicographical improvement property*, which guarantees the existence of a strong equilibrium, and presented a class of *bottleneck congestion games*, which have that property. Detailed investigation on the relation of g-budget games to lexicographical improvement property, in particular the role of the matroid structure, would be worthwhile.

Acknowledgements. The authors are grateful to the anonymous referees for their helpful comments.

References

1. Ackermann, H., Röglin, H., Vöcking, B.: Pure Nash equilibria in player-specific and weighted congestion games. Theor. Comput. Sci. **410**(17), 1552–1563 (2009). https://doi.org/10.1016/j.tcs.2008.12.035

2. Drees, M., Feldotto, M., Riechers, S., Skopalik, A.: On existence and properties of approximate pure Nash equilibria in bandwidth allocation games. In: Hoefer, M. (ed.) SAGT 2015. LNCS, vol. 9347, pp. 178–189. Springer, Heidelberg (2015). https://doi.org/10.1007/978-3-662-48433-3_14

3. Drees, M., Feldotto, M., Riechers, S., Skopalik, A.: Pure Nash equilibria in restricted budget games. J. Comb. Optim. **37**(2), 620–638 (2018). https://doi.org/10.1007/s10878-018-0269-7

4. Drees, M., Riechers, S., Skopalik, A.: Budget-restricted utility games with ordered strategic decisions. In: Lavi, R. (ed.) SAGT 2014. LNCS, vol. 8768, pp. 110–121. Springer, Heidelberg (2014). https://doi.org/10.1007/978-3-662-44803-8_10

5. Fujishige, S., Goemans, M.X., Harks, T., Peis, B., Zenklusen, R.: Congestion games viewed from M-convexity. Oper. Res. Lett. **43**(3), 329–333 (2015). https://doi.org/10.1016/j.orl.2015.04.002

6. Fujishige, S., Goemans, M.X., Harks, T., Peis, B., Zenklusen, R.: Matroids are immune to Braess' paradox. Math. Oper. Res. **42**(3), 745–761 (2017). https://doi.org/10.1287/moor.2016.0825

7. Harks, T., Klimm, M., Möhring, R.H.: Strong equilibria in games with the lexicographical improvement property. Int. J. Game Theory **42**(2), 461–482 (2013). https://doi.org/10.1007/s00182-012-0322-1

8. Harks, T., Klimm, M., Peis, B.: Sensitivity analysis for convex separable optimization over integral polymatroids. SIAM J. Optim. **28**(3), 2222–2245 (2018). https://doi.org/10.1137/16M1107450

9. Monderer, D., Shapley, L.S.: Potential games. Games Econ. Behav. **14**, 124–143 (1996). https://doi.org/10.1006/game.1996.0044

10. Murota, K.: Discrete Convex Analysis. Society for Industrial and Applied Mathematics, Philadelphia (2003)

11. Rosenthal, R.W.: A class of games possessing pure-strategy Nash equilibria. Int. J. Game Theory **2**, 65–67 (1973). https://doi.org/10.1007/BF01737559

12. Roughgarden, T.: Twenty Lectures on Algorithmic Game Theory. Cambridge University Press, Cambridge (2016)

13. Schrijver, A.: Combinatorial Optimization—Polyhedra and Efficiency. Springer, Heidelberg (2003)

14. Takazawa, K.: Generalizations of weighted matroid congestion games: pure Nash equilibrium, sensitivity analysis, and discrete convex function. J. Comb. Optim. **38**(4), 1043–1065 (2019). https://doi.org/10.1007/s10878-019-00435-9

Cost-Sharing Games with Rank-Based Utilities

Shaul Rosner[(✉)] and Tami Tamir[iD]

School of Computer Science, Reichman University, Herzliya, Israel
shaul.rosner@post.idc.ac.il, tami@idc.ac.il

Abstract. Studies in behavioural science show that individuals are often concerned primarily about their *relative* welfare, rather than their absolute well-being. In this paper we define and study a variant of congestion game that reflects this phenomenon. In a *cost-sharing game with rank-based utilities* (CSRB-game, for short), the players are partitioned into *competition sets*, and the goal of every player is to minimize its cost *relative to its competitors*. Specifically, the primary goal of a player is to minimize the *rank* of its cost among its competitors, while minimizing the cost itself is a secondary objective.

We show that CSRB-games are significantly different from classical cost-sharing games, and that competition may lead to a poor outcome. In particular, singleton CSRB-games need not have a pure Nash equilibrium, and even when a NE exists, natural dynamics may not converge to a NE, and the price of stability is linear in the number of players. We then analyze several natural restricted classes of singleton CSRB-games, for which we present positive results. We provide tight characterization of classes for which a NE exists and can be computed efficiently, and bound the equilibrium inefficiency, based on the competition structure, the number of players and resources, the uniformity of resources' costs, and the strategy space of competing players.

Keywords: Cost-sharing games · Competition · Rank-based utilities · Equilibrium existence and inefficiency

1 Introduction

Many resource-allocation environments, such as job-scheduling applications as well as communication or transportation networks, lack a central authority and are often managed by multiple strategic users, whose individual payoff is affected by the assignment of other users. As a result, game theory has become an essential tool in the analysis of resource-allocation services. In the corresponding game, every user corresponds to a selfish player who selects the resources aiming to maximize its own utility. Of particular interest are cost-sharing games, in which the players who use a resource share its activation cost. These games

Supported by the Israel Science Foundation (ISF). Grant No. 1036/17.

© The Author(s), under exclusive license to Springer Nature Switzerland AG 2022
P. Kanellopoulos et al. (Eds.): SAGT 2022, LNCS 13584, pp. 275–292, 2022.
https://doi.org/10.1007/978-3-031-15714-1_16

fit numerous applications such as network formation, or infrastructure maintenance.

In traditional cost-sharing games, the goal of a player is to minimize its cost.
In this paper we consider a different model that fits environments with strong
competition among the players. Formally, in a cost-sharing game with rank-
based utilities (CSRB-game, for short), the players form *competition sets*, and
a player's main goal is to do well *relative to its competitors*. The welfare of a
player is not measured by a predefined cost or utility function, but relative to
the performance of its competitors. The primary goal of a player is to minimize
the *rank* of its cost among its competitors, while minimizing the cost itself is a
secondary objective.

Our model is motivated by studies in behavioural science, where it is shown
that individuals are concerned primarily about their relative welfare, rather than
their absolute well-being. For example, workers care more about their relative
salary than they do about their actual salary [7]; students' motivation to study is
increased when their grade is based on their position in class [8]; and happiness
depends not just on absolute, but mainly on relative consumption [9]. Rank-
based utilities arise in many real-life scenarios. For example, in cryptocurrency
mining, one needs to be the first miner to build a block. It is less important how
long it takes a miner to build a block, as long as she is the first to do so. Similarly,
when buying event tickets from online vendors, the time spent in the queue is
far less important than what tickets are available when it is your turn to buy.
Participants' ranking is crucial also in auctions with a limited number of winners,
transplant queues, sport leagues, and even submission of papers to competitive
conferences. In all of these settings, the participants' rank is more important
than their actual performance. Moreover, studies in consumer psychology show
that relative performance is crucial also in settings in which participants aim at
minimizing their cost, as in cost-sharing games. In particular, even high-income
consumers are looking for deals, and individuals' satisfaction is determined by
the relative quality of the products they buy, and the relative cost they have paid
[27]. Similarly, competing businesses with shared goals, such as drug companies
or internet providers, are willing to increase their expenses in order to bypass
their competitors [29].

We analyze the effect of competition on the stability of cost-sharing games.
We identify classes of instances for which a stable solution exists and can be
computed efficiently, we study the equilibrium inefficiency, and the convergence
of best-response dynamics. We distinguish between different classes of instances,
and give tight analysis for each class. The games are classified based on the
competition structure, the number of players and resources, the uniformity of
resources' costs, and the strategy space of competing players.

2   Model and Preliminaries

A *cost-sharing game with rank based utilities* (henceforth referred to as a cost-
sharing RB-game, or CSRB-game) is given by $G = \langle \mathcal{N}, E, \{A_j\}_{j \in \mathcal{N}}, \{c_i\}_{i \in E}, S \rangle$,
where $\mathcal{N}$ is a set of n *players*, E is a set of m *resources*, $A_j \subseteq 2^E$ is the *strategy*

space of player j, c_i is the *activation cost* of resource i, and S is a partition of the players into *competition sets*. Specifically, $S = \{S_1, \ldots, S_c\}$ such that $c \leq n$, $\cup_{\ell=1}^{c} S_\ell = \mathcal{N}$, and for all $\ell_1 \neq \ell_2$, we have $S_{\ell_1} \cap S_{\ell_2} = \emptyset$. For every player $j \in S_\ell$, the other players in S_ℓ are denoted the *competitors* of j. We denote the number of players in competition set S_ℓ by $n_\ell = |S_\ell|$.

A profile of a CSRB-game G is a tuple $p = \langle p_1, p_2, \ldots, p_n \rangle \in (A_1 \times A_2 \times \ldots \times A_n)$ of strategies selected by the players. For a resource $i \in E$, the *load* on i in p, denoted $L_i(p)$, is the number of players using resource i in p. When p is clear from the context, we omit it. As common in the classical analysis of cost-sharing games, we assume that the activation cost of a resource is evenly split among the players using it. Formally, the cost of player j in profile p is $C_j(p) = \sum_{i \in p_j} \frac{c_i}{L_i(p)}$.

Unlike classical cost-sharing games, in which the goal of a player is to minimize its cost, in CSRB-games the goal of a player is to do well relative to its competitors. That is, every profile induces a ranking of the players according to their cost, and the goal of each player is to have a lowest possible rank in its competition set. Formally, for a profile p, and competition set S_ℓ, let $C_{S_\ell}^p = \langle C_{\ell_1}^p, \ldots, C_{\ell_{n_\ell}}^p \rangle$ be a sorted vector of the costs of the players in S_ℓ. That is, $C_{\ell_1}^p \leq \ldots \leq C_{\ell_{n_\ell}}^p$, where $C_{\ell_1}^p$ is the minimal cost of a player from S_ℓ in p, etc. The *rank* of Player $j \in S_\ell$ in profile p, denoted $rank_j(p)$ is the position of its cost in $C_{S_\ell}^p$. If several players in a competition set have the same cost, then they all have the same rank, which is the corresponding median value. For example, if $n_\ell = 4$ and $C_{S_\ell}^p = \langle 7, 8, 8, 13 \rangle$ then the players' ranks are $\langle 1, 2.5, 2.5, 4 \rangle$, and if all players in S_ℓ have the same cost then they all have rank $(n_\ell + 1)/2$. Note that, independent of the profile, $\sum_{j \in S_\ell} rank_j(p) = n_\ell(n_\ell + 1)/2$.

The primary objective of every player is to minimize its rank. The secondary objective is to minimize its cost. Formally, Player j prefers profile p' over profile p if $rank_j(p') < rank_j(p)$ or $rank_j(p') = rank_j(p)$ and $C_j(p') < C_j(p)$. Note that classic games are a special case of RB-games in which the competition sets are singletons; thus, for every player j, in every profile, p, we have $rank_j(p) = 1$, and the secondary objective, of minimizing the cost, is the only objective.

A strategy is a *best response* (BR) for Player j if it optimizes j's objective, as defined above, given the strategies of all other players. Best-Response Dynamics (BRD) is a local-search method where in each step some player is chosen and plays its best improving deviation (if one exists), given the strategies of the other players. Note that a best improving deviation is one that results in the lowest rank, with cost as only a secondary objective. A strategy is a *better-response* for Player j if it improves its current utility, that is, reduces its rank or keep its rank and reduce its cost. While beneficial, a better-response deviation may not be the best possible one for the deviating player.

The focus in game theory is on the *stable* outcomes of a given setting. The most prominent stability concept is that of a Nash equilibrium (NE): a profile in which no player can improve its objective by unilaterally deviating from its current strategy, assuming that the strategies of the other players do not change. Formally, a profile p is a NE if, for every $j \in \mathcal{N}$, p_j is a BR for Player j.

The *social cost* of a profile p, denoted $cost(p)$ is the total activation cost of all resources with a positive load in p, that is, $cost(p) = \sum_{i|L_i(p)>0} c_i$. Clearly, this is also the total players' cost. A *social optimum* of a game G is a profile that attains the lowest possible social cost. We denote by $OPT(G)$ the cost of a social optimum profile; i.e., $OPT(G) = \min_p cost(p)$.

It is well known that decentralized decision-making may lead to sub-optimal solutions from the point of view of society as a whole. We quantify the inefficiency incurred due to self-interested behavior according to the *price of anarchy* (PoA) [19,22] and *price of stability* (PoS) [1,25] measures. The PoA is the worst-case inefficiency of a pure Nash equilibrium, while the PoS measures the best-case inefficiency of a pure Nash equilibrium. Formally,

Definition 1. *Let $\mathcal{G}$ be a family of games, and let G be a game in $\mathcal{G}$. Let $\Upsilon(G)$ be the set of pure Nash equilibria of the game G. Assume that $\Upsilon(G) \neq \emptyset$.*

- *The* price of anarchy *of G is the ratio between the* maximal *cost of a PNE and the social optimum of G. That is, $PoA(G) = \max_{s \in \Upsilon(G)} cost(s)/OPT(G)$. The* price of anarchy *of the family of games $\mathcal{G}$ is $PoA(\mathcal{G}) = \sup_{G \in \mathcal{G}} PoA(G)$.*
- *The* price of stability *of G is the ratio between the* minimal *cost of a PNE and the social optimum of G. That is, $PoS(G) = \min_{s \in \Upsilon(G)} cost(s)/OPT(G)$. The* price of stability *of the family of games $\mathcal{G}$ is $PoS(\mathcal{G}) = \sup_{G \in \mathcal{G}} PoS(G)$.*

We conclude this introduction with two examples that highlight the differences between CSRB-games and classical cost-sharing games, and introduce some of the challenges in analyzing them. Consider a singleton CSRB-game G_1 with players $N = \{j_1, j_2, j_3\}$, and resources $E = \{a, b, c\}$ having activation-costs $\{24, 11, 23\}$, respectively. Since G_1 is a singleton game, the players strategies can be given as a set of resources, so the players' strategy spaces are $A_1 = \{a\}, A_2 = \{a, b\}, A_3 = \{a, c\}$. Assume that the players in G_1 form a single competition set, that is, $c = 1$ and $S_1 = \mathcal{N}$. Figure 1 presents three profiles of this game. Each player is represented by a rectangle whose height is proportional to the players' cost. Every player is labeled by its rank (bottom) and cost (top). The profile p_1^* is the social optimum. In classical cost-sharing games, p_1^* is also a NE. However, in a CSRB-game, j_2 has a beneficial *cost-increasing* deviation. By migrating to resource b, profile p_1' is obtained. In this profile, the cost of j_2 is 11, while the cost of each of its competitors is 12. Note that p_1' is not a NE either, as j_3 would benefit by a cost-increasing deviation to resource c. By deviating to profile p_1'', the rank of j_3 is decreased from 2.5 to 2. The profile p_1'' is the only NE of this game.

Consider next a game G_2 with the same set of players and resources as in G_1, only that the players form two competition sets, $S_1 = \{j_1, j_2\}$ and $S_2 = \{j_3\}$. Figure 2 presents two profiles of this game; competing players have the same color. In G_2, as in G_1, p_2^* is the social optimum and also a NE in classical cost-sharing games. Again, j_2 would benefit from a deviation to resource b. However, the resulting profile, p_2' is a NE. Having no competitors, the only objective of j_3 is to minimize its cost.

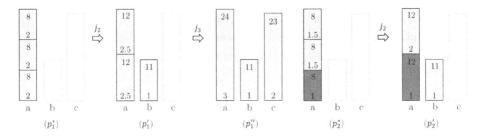

Fig. 1. Three profiles of the game G_1, in which $S_1 = N$. The profile p_1^* is the social optimum, the profile p_1'' is the only NE.

Fig. 2. Two profiles of the game G_2, in which $S_1 = \{j_1, j_2\}$ and $S_2 = \{j_3\}$. The profile p_2' is the only NE.

2.1 Our Results

We show that competition dramatically impacts the stability of cost-sharing environments that are controlled by selfish users. Cost-sharing games with rank-based utilities are significantly different from classical cost-sharing games; their analysis is unintuitive, and known tools and techniques fail even on simple instances. On the other hand, for some important natural classes of instances we present positive results, by introducing an original potential function, or an efficient algorithm for computing a NE. We also provide tight bounds on their equilibrium inefficiency, which are lower than the bound for general CSRB-games.

Most of our results refer to *singleton games*, in which every player needs to select a single resource. Formally, $A_j \subseteq E$ and $p_j \in A_j$. Our results for singleton games are summarized in Table 1.

We first show that singleton cost-sharing RB-games need not have a NE. This is valid for instances with as few as four players or as few as three resources. We also show that deciding whether a game instance has a NE is an NP-complete problem. Moreover, even when a NE exists, BRD may not converge to one, and the *price of stability* is linear in the number of players. For small games with at most three players or two resources, we show that a NE exists and can be computed efficiently. However, even such small games are not potential games and natural dynamics may not converge.

Striving for positive results, we consider specific classes of singleton CSRB-games, that reflect real-life situations and applications. The class $\mathcal{G}_{fair}$ consists of CSRB-games in which competing players have the same strategy space. Formally, a CSRB-game G is *fair* if, for every $1 \leq \ell \leq c$, all players in S_ℓ have

Table 1. Our main results for singleton games. (i) Time complexity of identifying whether a NE exists and computing one if exists. (ii) Yes for $m = 2$, or $n \le 3$. (iii) n for no-competition. (iv) Yes for $m \le 3$.

Instance	NE guaranteed	Complexity$^{(i)}$	PoA	PoS
General	No$^{(ii)}$	NP-complete	n	$n - O(1)$
Symmetric	Yes	Linear	$n - 1^{(iii)}$	1
Unit costs	Yes	Polynomial	n	1
Fair	Yes	Polynomial	$n - 1$	$O(H(c))$
Full competition	No$^{(iv)}$	NP-complete	n	$n - O(1)$

the same strategy space. This class reflects a natural phenomenon: competition tends to arise among similar entities. In sport competitions, the participants are categorized by their sex and age group, or by their weight. Companies that provide cell-phone services compete with each other, and the competition among them is stronger than their competition with, say, a company that sells soft drinks. Similarly, students care more about their relative performance in class, and less about their performance relative to their roommates who study different subjects.

For the class $\mathcal{G}_{fair}$ we define the notion of *fair-BRD* – a supervised application of best-response dynamics, in which competing players get a chance to deviate out of a resource one after the other. We show that any application of fair-BRD converges to a NE. Technically, we show that fair games possess the Lexicographical Improvement Property (LIP), defined in [14]. Thus, there exists a generalized strong ordinal potential function, such that the potential strictly increases in every iteration of fair-BRD. The LIP holds for the sorted vector of the resources' $\frac{c_i}{L_i(p)+1}$ values. We also provide an $O(n + (c + m) \log m)$-time algorithm for directly computing a NE, and show that it returns a NE whose social cost is at most $c \cdot OPT$. The equilibrium inefficiency of $\mathcal{G}_{fair}$ is significantly lower than the general linear bound and the PoS is logarithmic in the number of competition sets.

The class $\mathcal{G}_{unit}$ consists of singleton CSRB-games in which all resources have the same activation cost. W.l.o.g., $G \in \mathcal{G}_{unit}$ if for every $i \in E$ it holds that $c_i = 1$. The strategy space as well as the partition into competition sets may be arbitrary. We show that every game in $\mathcal{G}_{unit}$ has a NE, and BRD converges to a NE. Our proof uses a non-trivial 2-dimensional potential function. For a given profile p, the first component of the potential function is the sum of squares of the resources' loads in p, and the second component is the sum of squares of the loads generated by each competition set on each of the resources. We show that every beneficial migration of a player either increases the first component, or keeps its value and decreases the value of the second component. In regards to the equilibrium inefficiency, we show that $PoA(\mathcal{G}_{unit}) = n$, that is, as high as the general case; however, every instance has an optimal solution that is stable, thus, $PoS(\mathcal{G}_{unit}) = 1$.

The class $\mathcal{G}_{sym}$ consists of symmetric CSRB-games – in which all players have the same strategy space. The partition into competition sets can be arbitrary. We show that symmetric CSRB-games are simple: a NE exists, the PoS is 1, and in fact, in the presence of some competition, that is, when $c < n$, the PoA is $n - 1$, which is a bit lower than the PoA in classical symmetric games. Our positive results for this class are for general strategies, and not necessarily singleton games.

The class $\mathcal{G}_{FC}$ consists of CSRB-games with *full competition*. That is, instances in which all players compete with each other and form a single competition set. The players may have arbitrary strategy space. Unfortunately, even with this simple competition structure, all our negative results are valid. The only exception is that every singleton game $G \in \mathcal{G}_{FC}$ played on three resources has a NE, while with arbitrary competition structure, there are singleton CSRB-games played on three resources that have no NE.

2.2   Related Work

Congestion games [19,23] consist of a set of resources and a set of players who need to use these resources. Players' strategies are subsets of resources. In *cost-sharing games*, each resource has an activation cost that is shared by the players using it, according to some sharing mechanism. With unit-weight players and uniform cost-sharing, this is a potential game, a NE exists and the PoS is logarithmic in the number of players [1].

In *singleton* congestion games, also known as *resource selection* games, players' strategies are a single resource. Singleton congestion games are studied in [16], where it is shown that an optimal equilibrium can be found efficiently, and BRD converges to a NE. The logarithmic bound on the price of stability is valid also for singleton cost-sharing games. On the other hand, singleton games with player-specific costs, or games with resource-dependent weights, need not have a pure NE, and the PoS may be as high as the number of players [1,3,20]. The paper [26] studies the complexity of equilibria in a wide range of cost-sharing games. Specifically, it shows that even a strong NE can be computed efficiently in singleton cost-sharing games. Another line of research studies the effect of different cost-sharing mechanisms on the equilibrium inefficiency [6,12,13,15].

A closely related model to ours is given in [2], and is referred to as a *social context game with rank competition*. The competition structure in their model is arbitrary and defined by a network. Also, congestion has negative effect, unlike our work that studies cost-sharing games. For the case of disjoint competition sets, that is, when the network is a collection of disjoint cliques, the paper shows that a NE may not exist and is guaranteed to exist in a game with identical resources. More in-depth analysis of job scheduling games under the same ranking model is given in [24]. The paper [17] considers a model with arbitrary competition structure, in which players' utility combine their payoff and ranking.

General ranking games are studied in [5], where it is shown that computing a NE is NP-complete in most cases. In [11] a player's utilization combines its rank with the effort expended to achieve it. Like our work, these works show that the analysis of games with rank-based utilities tends to be very different from the analysis of classical games. Our model, however, is more general since all the above works relate to a single ranking of all the players, that is, all the players belong to the same competition set. Note that our model enables various levels and structures of competition; in particular, the classical cost-sharing model is a special case of our model (when $c = n$, meaning every player is in a separate competition set).

Additional related models, studied mainly in behavioral game theory, consider environments in which players' objective involves social preferences that may be based on emotions such as empathy, envy, or inequality aversion, e.g., [4,10,28].

3   General Singleton CSRB-Games

In a general singleton cost-sharing games with rank-based utilities, resources have arbitrary costs, and players have arbitrary strategies and arbitrary partition into competition sets. We show that a NE may not exist even in a simple game with three resources, with only two of the players not restricted to a single strategy.

Theorem 2. *A singleton CSRB-game may not have a NE.*

Proof. We describe a singleton CSRB-game, G_6, that has no NE. Let $E = \{a, b, c\}$ having activation costs $\{54, 75, 26\}$, respectively. There are 6 players in two competition sets. The first competition set includes one player that is restricted to use resource b. The second competition set includes 5 players. Two players are restricted to use resource a and one player is restricted to use resource b. Only two players, to be denoted j_1 and j_2, have a choice. Specifically, $A_1 = \{a, b\}$, and $A_2 = \{b, c\}$. Therefore, the game has four possible profiles, depending on the strategies of these two players. Figure 3 presents the four profiles, and shows the costs and ranks of each of the players. Rectangle heights correspond to the player's costs. The dark rectangle represents the only player in the first competition set. The five lighter rectangles represent the players in the second competition set, out of which, each of the two 'dynamic' players has a unique pattern. In profile p_1 the 5 players of S_2 have costs $\langle 18, 18, 18, 25, 25 \rangle$ and therefore ranks $\langle 2, 2, 2, 4.5, 4.5 \rangle$. Profile p_2 is obtained from profile p_1 when player j_2 migrates from resource b to resource c. Doing so, j_2 increases its cost from 25 to 26, but reduces its rank from 4.5 to 4. Moving from p_2 to p_3, j_1 migrates from resource a to resource b. Doing so, j_1 increases its cost from 18 to 25, but reduces its rank from 2 to 1.5. It is easy to verify that the other deviations are also beneficial, thus no NE exists.   □

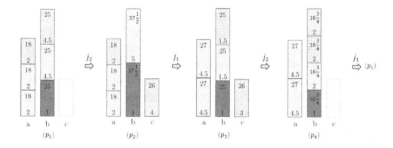

Fig. 3. The four profiles of the cost-sharing CSRB-game G_6 that has no NE.

The players in G_6 form two competition sets. In Sect. 3.2 we show that a NE may not exist even in a game with a single competition set and only four players. A natural question is whether it is possible to efficiently decide whether a singleton CSRB-game has a NE. We answer this question negatively.

Theorem 3. *Given an instance of a singleton CSRB-game G, it is NP-complete to decide whether G has a NE profile.*

Our next negative result shows that even if a CSRB-game has a NE, then natural dynamics may not converge. The proof is based on extending the game G_6 described in Theorem 2.

Theorem 4. *In a singleton CSRB-game, BRD may not converge to a NE, even if a NE exists.*

Equilibrium Inefficiency: As common in cost-sharing games, we analyze the equilibrium inefficiency of CSRB-games with respect to the objective of minimizing the total activation cost of the non-empty resources. For classical cost-sharing game, the Price of Anarchy is known to be n for n players, and the Price of Stability is known to be logarithmic. The upper bound for the PoA is easily shown to be also valid for CSRB-games. That is, for every singleton CSRB-game G, $PoA(G) \leq n$. On the other hand, we show that the PoS of CSRB-games is $n - O(1)$. The idea in the proof is to modify and scale the game G_6 to a game that has a unique expensive NE profile. A no-NE game similar to G_6 is induced whenever the expensive profile is not selected by all players.

Theorem 5. *There exists a singleton CSRB-game G with n players, such that $PoS(G) \geq n - 7$.*

Proof. Given $n > 7$ we describe a game with n players, and a PoS of $n - 7$. The game G is based on an extension of the game G_6 described in Theorem 2. Let $k = n - 4$. G_6 is played over $k + 3 = n - 1$ resources, three resources a, b, c with activation costs $\frac{3k}{k+2} - \epsilon, k, 1 - \epsilon$ respectively for $\epsilon > 0$, and k resources $\{e_i\}$ for $i = 1, \ldots, k$ each having activation cost k.

We turn to describe the competition sets and the players' strategies. Each of the first $k-1$ competition sets includes a single player. Formally, for $1 \leq i \leq k-1$, we have $S_i = \{i\}$ and $A_i = \{e_i, b\}$. The k-th competition set includes 5 players, which behave similarly to the players in G_6. j_1 can select a or b, j_2 can select b or c, two players are restricted to use resource a, and one player can select b or e_k. Note that each of the players that can be assigned to b, besides j_1 and j_2, has a unique alternative resource of cost k.

In the social optimum profile, all players that can choose b do so. Resource a must also be activated, thus, $OPT(G) = k + \frac{3k}{k+2} - \varepsilon$. The social optimum is not stable since the game G_6 is induced, and one of the players j_1 and j_2 will always have a beneficial deviation, as described in Theorem 2. Moreover, in every profile in which any of the players that can choose b do so, it is beneficial for all players that can choose b to choose it. In the resulting game, j_1 and j_2 have the same behaviour as in the game G_6.

We conclude that the only NE of G is when no player chooses b, meaning there are 3 players on resource a and one player on each of resources c and e_i for $i = 1, \ldots, k$. This is a NE as a migration to b is not beneficial as b is a highest cost resource and has no players assigned to it, meaning that deviating to b is never rank-reducing. The cost of this NE is $k^2 + \frac{3k}{k+2} + 1 - 2\varepsilon$, implying that $PoS(G) = \frac{k^2 + \frac{3k}{k+2} + 1 - 2\epsilon}{k + \frac{3k}{k+2} - \varepsilon}$, which is at least $k - 3 = n - 7$.   □

3.1   Symmetric CSRB-Games

For symmetric games we present positive results. Our results are valid for all symmetric games, not only singleton games. Recall that in a symmetric game, all the players have the same strategy space, $A_{all} \subseteq 2^E$. The partition into competition sets is arbitrary. Unsurprisingly, the analysis of this class is simple.

Theorem 6. *For every CSRB-game $G \in \mathcal{G}_{sym}$, the profile p^* in which all players are assigned to the strategy with lowest activation cost in A_{all} is a NE.*

Next, we bound the equilibrium inefficiency of the class $\mathcal{G}_{sym}$. Theorem 6 implies that every social optimum profile is also a NE, therefore, $PoS(\mathcal{G}_{sym}) = 1$.

In classical symmetric cost-sharing games, the PoA is known to be n. Since CSRB-games are a superset of classical games (when there is no competition and each player is a singleton competition set), this is also the PoA for CSRB-games. However, with the presence of any competition, that is, whenever $c < n$, the PoA is a bit smaller.

Theorem 7. *For every game $G \in \mathcal{G}_{sym}$ with $c < n$, $PoA(G) \leq n - 1$. Additionally, for every $c < n$, there exists a game $G \in \mathcal{G}_{sym}$ with c competition sets such that $PoA(G) = n - 1$.*

3.2 Small Number of Resources or Players

In light of our negative results for general instances, it is interesting to study games with a small number of resources or players, and identify the largest parameters for which a NE is guaranteed to exist. We present a tight answer for this question.

We first describe a CSRB-game $G_4 \in \mathcal{G}_{FC}$ with $n = 4$ and $m = 4$ that has no NE. This game is then shown to be the smallest negative example with respect to both the number of players, and, in case of full competition, the number of resources.

Theorem 8. *There exists a CSRB-game $G_4 \in \mathcal{G}_{FC}$ with $n = 4$ and $m = 4$ that has no NE.*

Proof. Consider the game $G_4 \in \mathcal{G}_{FC}$ with $E = \{a, b, c, d\}$, having activation costs $(10, 11, 16, 18)$ respectively. There are four players in one competition set. One player is restricted to use resource c, and one player is restricted to use resource d. Denote by j_1, j_2 the two remaining players. Let $A_1 = \{a, c\}$, and $A_2 = \{b, d\}$.

The four possible profiles of G_4 are presented in Fig. 4. Let p_1 be the profile in which j_1 selects resource a and j_2 selects resource b. Starting from p_1, j_2 can decrease its rank from 2 to 1.5 by migrating from b to d. From the resulting profile, p_2, j_1 can migrate from a to c, decreasing its rank from 3 to 1.5. The resulting profile, p_3, is not a NE either, as j_2 has a beneficial deviation from d to b. Note that this is a cost-increasing deviation, however, it decreases j_2's rank from 3.5 to 3. From the resulting profile, p_4, j_1 can migrate from c to a and decrease its rank from 1.5 to 1. This deviation is also cost-increasing. Since these are the only four possible profiles of G_4, we conclude that the game has no NE.   □

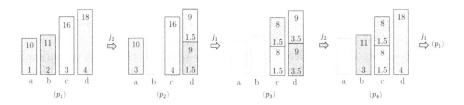

Fig. 4. The four profiles of the cost-sharing RB-game $G_4 \in \mathcal{G}_{FC}$ that has no NE.

Due to space constraints we do not complete the picture. However, we state, with proof omitted, that G_4 is the smallest possible no-NE game. With regard to the number of players, any singleton CSRB-game with at most 3 players has a NE. With regard to the number of resources, every game on two resources has a NE. For $m = 3$, the competition structure affects the stability of the game. Specifically, the game G_6 described in Theorem 2 implies that in general, a game on three resources may not have a NE. However, that instance has two competition sets. With full competition, that is, for the class $\mathcal{G}_{FC}$, a NE is guaranteed to exist in any game with $m = 3$. On the other hand, while a NE is guaranteed to exist, there exists a game $G \in \mathcal{G}_{FC}$ played on three resources for which better-response dynamics does not converge. Finally, for $m \geq 4$, the game G_4 demonstrates that a NE may not exist even for games with full competition. Moreover, using a construction similar to the one used in the proof of Theorem 5, we can show that $PoS(\mathcal{G}_{FC}) = O(n)$.

4 CSRB-Games with Unit-Cost Resources

In this section we study the class $\mathcal{G}_{unit}$, which includes singleton cost-sharing games with rank-based utilities and unit-cost resources. The partition into competition sets may be arbitrary, as well as the players' strategy space.

Theorem 9. *Every CSRB-game $G \in \mathcal{G}_{unit}$ has a NE, and BRD on G converges to a NE.*

Proof. We show that the game is an ordinal potential game [21], implying that every sequence of improvement steps is guaranteed to converge to a NE. Given a profile p, let $\alpha(p)$ be the sum of squares of the resources' loads in p, that is $\alpha(p) = \sum_i L_i(p)^2$. Let $\beta(p)$ be the sum of the squares of the loads generated by each competition set on each of the resources, that is $\beta(p) = \sum_i \sum_\ell (\# \text{ players from } S_\ell \text{ assigned to } i \text{ in profile } p)^2)$.

Our potential function is $\Phi(p) = (\alpha(p), \beta(p))$. We show that every beneficial migration of a player either increases the value of α, or does not change the value of α and decreases the value of β. Consider a profile p and assume that player j has a beneficial deviation from resource a to resource b. Let p' be the resulting profile. For the sake of conciseness, for any resource i, we use L_i and L_i' to denote the load on resource i in profile p and p' respectively.

We first show that a beneficial deviation cannot be cost-increasing. Assume by contradiction that a beneficial deviation is cost-increasing, thus, $L_b' < L_a$. Among the players assigned to a and b in profile p, L_a players have the same cost as player j and L_b players have higher cost, as otherwise the deviation is not cost increasing. Since $L_b' = L_b + 1$ and $L_b' < L_a$, in p' among the players assigned to a and b, $L_a' = L_a - 1$ players have the same or lower cost than player j and L_b' players have the same cost as player j. Players on other resources do not change their cost, and can only improve their rank relative to j. Therefore, the rank of player j could not decrease and the deviation cannot be beneficial.

If the deviation is cost-decreasing, then $L_b' > L_a$, thus, $L_a \leq L_b' - 1 = L_b$. We have, $L_a'^2 + L_b'^2 = (L_a - 1)^2 + (L_b + 1)^2 = L_a^2 + L_b^2 - 2L_a + 2L_b + 2 \geq L_a^2 + L_b^2 + 2 > L_a^2 + L_b^2$. Therefore, $\alpha(p') > \alpha(p)$. If a deviation is cost-maintaining then $L_b' = L_a$

and $\alpha(p') = \alpha(p)$. We show that the value of β decreases. A cost-maintaining deviation is beneficial if and only if the number of players from same competition set as j, with the same cost as j in p', is lower than in p. Since the only resources that change are a and b, this is equivalent to the number of j's competitors assigned to b in p' being lower than the number of j's competitors assigned to a in p. Thus, the total contribution of a and b to β is reduced. We conclude that Φ is a potential function as required.   □

We note that the above potential function fails on games with arbitrary resource activation costs since with arbitrary activation costs, a cost-increasing deviation may be beneficial (e.g., j_1 changing its strategy from a to b in the game G_6).

We turn to analyze the equilibrium inefficiency of the class $\mathcal{G}_{unit}$. For general games, we showed in Theorem 5 that the PoS is $\Omega(n)$. For games with unit-cost resources, while the PoA remains as high as the number of players, we can show that for every instance, there is an optimal solution that is stable. Thus,

Theorem 10. $PoA(\mathcal{G}_{unit}) = n$ and $PoS(\mathcal{G}_{unit}) = 1$.

5   Fair CSRB-Games

In this section we consider fair CSRB-games. A game is *fair* if, for every $1 \le \ell \le c$, all players in S_ℓ have the same strategy space, to be denoted A_ℓ. We denote this class of games by $\mathcal{G}_{fair}$. For a game $G \in \mathcal{G}_{fair}$, let P_{fair} be the set of profiles where for every competition set S_ℓ, all players in S_ℓ are assigned to the same resource. Note that every game in G_{sym} is also in G_{fair}.

Proposition 11. *For any game* $G \in \mathcal{G}_{fair}$, *if p is a NE profile then $p \in P_{fair}$.*

We now define a restricted class of BRD sequences, in which once a player deviates, its competitors on the source resource get a chance to deviate.

Definition 12. *A fair-BRD is a sequence of best response deviations in which after a player $j \in S_\ell$ deviates out of resource a, then all other players in S_ℓ that are assigned to a get a chance to deviate sequentially.*

Consider a fair-BRD sequence in a game $G \in \mathcal{G}_{fair}$, starting from an arbitrary initial profile p^0. We denote by *an iteration of fair-BRD* a sequence of deviations in which competing players sequentially leave the same resource. Let $p^0, p^1, \ldots$ be the sequence of profiles in the beginning of every iteration. For every resource $i \in E$, let $\delta_i(p^z) = \frac{c_i}{L_i(p^z)+1}$; for the profile p^z let $\delta(p^z) = (\delta_1(p^z), \ldots, \delta_m(p^z))$, sorted in non-decreasing order.

We show that any application of fair-BRD converges to a NE. We do this by showing that fair-games possess the Lexicographical Improvement Property (LIP), defined in [14]. Thus, there exists a generalized strong ordinal potential function, such that the potential strictly increases in every iteration of fair-BRD. Note that the LIP property is defined for coordinated deviations, while we apply it only for fair-BRD consisting of unilateral deviations.

Definition 13. *A vector* $(x_1, x_2, \ldots, x_m)$ *is larger than* $(y_1, y_2, \ldots, y_m)$ *lexicographically if for some* i, $x_i > y_i$ *and* $x_k = y_k$ *for all* $k < i$. *A profile* p' *is larger than* p *lexicographically if the vector* $\delta(p')$ *is larger lexicographically than* $\delta(p)$. *We denote this relationship by* $p' \succ p$.

The following simple observation will also be used in our proof: In a fair-BRD, if a player leaves resource i, then all players from its competition set that are currently assigned to i, will also leave resource i. We are now ready to show that the δ-vector increases lexicographically in every iteration of fair-BRD. Formally,

Lemma 14. *For every game* $G \in \mathcal{G}_{fair}$, *and* $z > 0$, *it holds that* $p^z \succ p^{z-1}$.

Using the lemma, we conclude:

Corollary 15. *For every game* $G \in \mathcal{G}_{fair}$, *any application of fair-BRD converges to a NE.*

Moreover, we present an algorithm for computing a NE profile directly. In classical singleton cost-sharing games, a NE can be computed by a simple algorithm, presented in [26], that greedily assigns players on a resource with minimal potential cost-per-player. This algorithm fails in CSRB-games since the resulting assignment is not stable against cost-increasing rank-decreasing deviations. Our algorithm differs in two ways. First, it uses a different greedy criterion for the resource selection, and second, the selected resource is assigned only a subset, possibly empty, of the players that can be assigned to it. We note that since a fair CSRB-game may be free of competition (when $S = N$), our algorithm fits both CSRB-games and classical games.

Theorem 16. *If* $G \in \mathcal{G}_{fair}$, *then a NE can be computed in time* $O(n + (c + m) \log m)$.

Proof. We present a greedy algorithm for computing a NE. Let Γ denote the set of resources that were not previously processed by the algorithm.

Algorithm 1. Computing a NE in a CSRB-game $G \in \mathcal{G}_{fair}$

1: $\Gamma = E$
2: $\forall i \in \Gamma$, let $F(i) = \{j | A_j \cap \Gamma = \{i\}\}$
3: **while** $\Gamma \neq \emptyset$ **do**
4:     Let $i_0 = \arg\max_{i \in \Gamma} \frac{c_i}{|F(i)|+1}$
5:     Assign $F(i_0)$ to i_0, remove i_0 from Γ, and update $F(i)$ for every $i \in \Gamma$
6: **end while**

Note that after each iteration some resource is removed from Γ. Therefore, the algorithm halts within m iterations. The values $\frac{c_i}{|F(i)|+1}$ for every resource i, are kept in a priority queue of size $m = |E|$. Every competition set is added exactly once to some $F(i)$, therefore there are exactly c update operations and exactly m delete operations.

For any resource i, the set $F(i)$ can be the empty, and can only increase during the algorithm, as it holds the set of players that have i as their only strategy in Γ. Since Γ is only reduced during the algorithm, players can only be added to $F(i)$. Let p be the resulting profile. Note that $p \in P_{fair}$, since for every competition set S_ℓ, and every set $F(i)$, all the players in S_ℓ are either all or none in $F(i)$. Also note that in some iterations, $F(i)$ may be empty for some or for all resources. A resource i for which $F(i) = \emptyset$ may still be selected in step 4, and no player would be assigned to it in p.

Assume for contradiction that p is not a NE. Let $j \in S_\ell$ be a player that has a beneficial deviation from some resource a to some resource b. For every resource i, let $F_a(i)$ and $F_b(a)$ be $F(i)$ immediately before the assignment of a and b, respectively. Let $f_a(i)$ and $f_b(i)$ denote their respective sizes. In the algorithm, a player is only assigned to a resource once it is its only remaining strategy. Since both a and b are in A_j, we conclude that b must be assigned before a. Note that $f_b(i)$ is the load on b in p. Since $F_b(a) \subseteq F_a(a)$ and $S_\ell \subseteq F_a(a) \setminus F_b(a)$, it holds that $f_a(a) \geq f_b(a) + |S_\ell|$. If j has no competitors, that is, $|S_\ell| = 1$, then $f_a(a) \geq f_b(a) + 1$, implying that $\frac{c_a}{f_a(a)} \leq \frac{c_a}{f_b(a)+1}$. For the deviation of j to be beneficial, it must be cost decreasing, that is, $\frac{c_a}{f_a(a)} > \frac{c_b}{f_b(b)+1}$. Combining the above inequalities, we get that $\frac{c_b}{f_b(b)+1} < \frac{c_a}{f_a(a)} \leq \frac{c_a}{f_b(a)+1}$, contradicting the choice of b as i_0 in the corresponding iteration.

If j has competitors, that is, $|S_\ell| \geq 2$, then $f_a(a) \geq f_b(a) + 2$, meaning $f_a(a) - 1 \geq f_b(a) + 1$, implying that $\frac{c_a}{f_a(a)-1} \leq \frac{c_a}{f_b(a)+1}$. For the deviation of j to be beneficial, it must be that $\frac{c_a}{f_a(a)-1} > \frac{c_b}{f_b(b)+1}$. Therefore, $\frac{c_b}{f_b(b)+1} < \frac{c_a}{f_a(a)-1} \leq \frac{c_a}{f_b(a)+1}$. Again, we get a contradiction to the choice of b as i_0. We conclude that p is a NE. □

We show that the social cost of the returned NE is at most $c \cdot OPT$.

Theorem 17. *For any game* $G \in \mathcal{G}_{fair}$, *Algorithm 1 returns a NE whose social cost is at most* $c \cdot OPT$. *Also, for every* c, *there is a game* $G \in \mathcal{G}_{fair}$ *with* c *competition sets such that Algorithm 1 returns a NE whose social cost is* $c \cdot OPT$.

Proof. Let p^* be a social optimum profile. W.l.o.g., for every competition set, S_ℓ, all players of S_ℓ are assigned to the same resource in p^*, to be denoted p_ℓ^*. Let p be the profile produced by the algorithm. For every competition set ℓ, all players in S_ℓ have the same strategy space, A_ℓ, and are therefore added together to some $F(i)$, when $\{i\} = A_\ell \cap \Gamma$. By the algorithm, all the players in S_ℓ will end up assigned to resource i, that is, $p_\ell = i$.

The cost of p is $\sum_i c_i$ for all non-empty resources i. For every non-empty resource, i, let S_ℓ^i be the first competition set that is added to $F(i)$. Let $i^* = p_\ell^*$. Either $i^* = i$, or i^* is processed by the algorithm before i. Therefore, in the iteration in which i^* is processed, $\frac{c_{i^*}}{|F(i^*)|+1} \geq \frac{c_i}{|F(i)|+1}$. Since the players in S_ℓ^i are the first players to be added to $F(i)$, we have that $|F(i)| = 0$ in this iteration, thus, $c_i \leq c_{i^*}$. We conclude that for each non-empty resource i, $c_i \leq c_{i^*} \leq OPT$. Since there are at most c non-empty resources, $cost(p) \leq c \cdot OPT$.

For the lower bound, consider a game $G \in \mathcal{G}_{fair}$ with n players with an arbitrary partition into c competition sets. There are $c + 1$ resources in G, resource a_0 has activation cost $1 + \epsilon$, and for every $1 \leq \ell \leq c$ there is a resource a_ℓ with $c_\ell = 1$. The strategy space of players in competition set S_ℓ is $A_\ell = \{a_0, a_\ell\}$. In the social optimum profile all players are assigned to a_0, that is, $cost(p^*) = 1 + \epsilon$. However, in the first iteration of the algorithm $F(i) = 0$ for every i, meaning $i_0 = a_0$ and a_0 is removed from Γ. Afterwards, for every $1 \leq i \leq c$, resource a_i is the only remaining strategy in Γ for players in S_i, meaning that $p_\ell = a_\ell$. We get that $cost(p) = c$, while $OPT = 1 + \epsilon$. □

We turn to analyze the equilibrium inefficiency of the class $\mathcal{G}_{fair}$. The PoA analysis of symmetric games presented in Theorem 7, can be extended to fair games. However, the PoS is logarithmic in the number of competition sets. Specifically, we bound the price of stability by $O(H(c))$, where $H(c)$ is the harmonic sum $1 + \frac{1}{2} + \frac{1}{3} + \ldots + \frac{1}{c}$.

We omit the proof and sketch its structure: Given a game G, in order to reach a NE of cost at most $O(H(c)) \cdot OPT$, we perform fair better-response deviations, starting from a social optimum profile in P_{fair}, in an equivalent *competition free* game G', and apply the analysis of the PoS in [1] on G'. G' is identical to G, except that we add dummy resources and a dummy player that enable a 'simulation' of beneficial cost-increasing rank-decreasing deviations. Since in every NE profile of G, for every competition set S_ℓ all players in S_ℓ are assigned to the same resource, the harmonic sum length depends on c and not on n.

Theorem 18. $PoA(\mathcal{G}_{fair}) = n - 1$ and $PoS(\mathcal{G}_{fair}) = O(H(c))$.

6   Conclusions and Open Problems

In this paper we extend the vast literature on congestion games by studying cost-sharing games with rank-based utilities. According to studies in social science, social status is of great importance for selfish agents in many environments. Games in which players' welfare is based on their relative status are extensively studied by economists, but, as far as we know, have not received much attention in the AGT community.

In our model, the players are divided into competition sets and the primary objective of every player is to perform well relative to its competitors. While in general, cost-sharing games with rank-based utilities are not potential games, and have high equilibrium inefficiency, there are several important classes of games for which we provide positive results.

Analyzing a behavioral phenomenon (competition among agents) using theoretical tools is challenging mainly due-to the seemingly irrational agents' behaviour. In particular, the fact that cost-increasing deviations may be beneficial and cost-decreasing deviations may be harmful, prevents the use of known techniques used in the analysis of classical cost-sharing games.

Rank-based utilities are relevant to many environments and their study can add an interesting twist to many games, in particular congestion games with negative congestion effect or cost-sharing games with an arbitrary, not necessarily fair, sharing rule. It is also possible to extend the cost-sharing model to non-singleton games.

A different possible direction for future work is to consider other models of competition Specifically, players may belong to more than a single competition set, players may have their individual (private or declared) set of competitors, and may have different motivation to compete. In its most general form, the competition may be described by a directed graph whose vertices correspond to players and an edge from j_1 to j_2 indicates that j_1 consider j_2 as its competitor. A similar, undirected network, is introduced in [2]. Moreover, players may have a different 'competition threshold' indicating by how much they are ready to hurt their welfare in order to hurt their competitors.

References

1. Anshelevich, E., Dasgupta, A., Kleinberg, J., Tardos, E., Wexler, T., Roughgarden, T.: The price of stability for network design with fair cost allocation. SIAM J. Comput. **38**(4), 1602–1623 (2008)
2. Ashlagi, I., Krysta, P., Tennenholtz, M.: Social context games. In: Papadimitriou, C., Zhang, S. (eds.) WINE 2008. LNCS, vol. 5385, pp. 675–683. Springer, Heidelberg (2008). https://doi.org/10.1007/978-3-540-92185-1_73
3. Avni, G., Tamir, T.: Cost-sharing scheduling games on restricted unrelated machines. Theoret. Comput. Sci. **646**, 26–39 (2016)
4. Bolton, G.E., Ockenfels, A.: ERC: a theory of equity, reciprocity, and competition. Am. Econ. Rev. **90**(1), 166–193 (2000)
5. Brandt, F., Fischer, F., Harrenstein, P., Shoham, Y.: Ranking games. Artif. Intell. **173**(2), 221–239 (2009)
6. Chen, H., Roughgarden, T.: Network design with weighted players. Theor. Comput. Syst. **45**(2), 302–324 (2009)
7. Dhillon, A., Herzog-Stein, A.: Games of status and discriminatory contracts. Games Econ. Behav. **65**(1), 105–123 (2009)
8. Dubey, P., Geanakoplos, J.: Grading exams: 100,99,98, . . . or a, b, c? Games Econ. Behav. **69**(1), 72–94 (2010). Special Issue In Honor of Robert Aumann
9. Easterlin, R.A.: Does economic growth improve the human lot? Some empirical evidence. In: Nations and Households in Economic Growth, pp. 89–125. Academic Press (1974)
10. Fehr, E., Schmidt, K.M.: A theory of fairness, competition, and cooperation. Q. J. Econ. **114**(3), 817–868 (1999)
11. Goldberg, L.A., Goldberg, P.W., Krysta, P., Ventre, C.: Ranking games that have competitiveness-based strategies. Theoret. Comput. Sci. **476**, 24–37 (2013)
12. Gkatzelis, V., Kollias, K., Roughgarden, T.: Optimal cost-sharing in general resource selection games. Oper. Res. **64**(6), 1230–1238 (2016)
13. Harks, T., Klimm, M.: On the existence of pure Nash equilibria in weighted congestion games. Math. Oper. Res. **37**(3), 419–436 (2012)
14. Harks, T., Klimm, M., Möhring, R.H.: Strong equilibria in games with the lexicographical improvement property. Int. J. Game Theory **42**(2), 461–482 (2013)

15. Harks, T., Miller, K.: The worst-case efficiency of cost sharing methods in resource allocation games. Oper. Res. **59**(6), 1491–1503 (2011)
16. Ieong, S., McGrew, R., Nudelman, E., Shoham, Y., Sun, Q.: Fast and compact: a simple class of congestion games. In: Proceedings of the 20th National Conference on Artificial Intelligence, AAAI 2005, vol. 2 (2005)
17. Immorlica, N., Kranton, R., Stoddard, G.: Striving for social status. In: Proceedings of the 13th ACM Conference on Electronic Commerce, p. 672 (2012)
18. Kann, V.: Maximum bounded 3-dimensional matching is MAX SNP-complete. Inf. Process. Lett. **37**, 27–35 (1991)
19. Koutsoupias, E., Papadimitriou, C.: Worst-case equilibria. Comput. Sci. Rev. **3**(2), 65–69 (2009)
20. Milchtaich, I.: Congestion games with player-specific payoff functions. Games Econ. Behav. **13**(1), 111–124 (1996)
21. Monderer, D., Shapley, L.S.: Potential games. Games Econ. Behav. **14**, 124–143 (1996)
22. Papadimitriou, C.H.: Algorithms, games, and the internet. In: Proceedings of 33rd ACM Symposium on Theory of Computing, pp. 749–753 (2001)
23. Rosenthal, R.W.: A class of games possessing pure-strategy Nash equilibria. Int. J. Game Theory **2**, 65–67 (1973)
24. Rosner, S., Tamir, T.: Race scheduling games. In: Harks, T., Klimm, M. (eds.) SAGT 2020. LNCS, vol. 12283, pp. 257–272. Springer, Cham (2020). https://doi.org/10.1007/978-3-030-57980-7_17
25. Schulz, A.S., Stier Moses, N.: On the performance of user equilibria in traffic networks. In: Proceedings of the 14th ACM-SIAM Symposium on Discrete Algorithms, SODA 2003, pp. 86–87 (2003)
26. Syrgkanis, V.: The complexity of equilibria in cost sharing games. In: Saberi, A. (ed.) WINE 2010. LNCS, vol. 6484, pp. 366–377. Springer, Heidelberg (2010). https://doi.org/10.1007/978-3-642-17572-5_30
27. Weaver, K., Daniloski, K., Schwarz, N., Cottone, K.: The role of social comparison for maximizers and satisficers: wanting the best or wanting to be the best? J. Consum. Psychol. **25**(3), 372–388 (2015)
28. Winter, E., Méndez-Naya, L., García-Jurado, I.: Mental equilibrium and strategic emotions. Manage. Sci. **63**(5), 1302–1317 (2017)
29. The UNCTAD secretariat: The role of competition in the pharmaceutical sector and its benefits for consumers (2015). https://unctad.org/system/files/official-document/tdrbpconf8d3_en.pdf

On Tree Equilibria in Max-Distance Network Creation Games

Qian Wang[✉]

CFCS, Peking University, Beijing, China
charlie@pku.edu.cn

Abstract. We study the Nash equilibrium and the price of anarchy in the max-distance network creation game. The network creation game, first introduced and studied by Fabrikant et al. [18], is a classic model for real-world networks from a game-theoretic point of view. In a network creation game with n selfish vertex agents, each vertex can build undirected edges incident to a subset of the other vertices. The goal of every agent is to minimize its creation cost plus its usage cost, where the creation cost is the unit edge cost α times the number of edges it builds, and the usage cost is the sum of distances to all other agents in the resulting network. The max-distance network creation game, introduced and studied by Demaine et al. [15], is a key variant of the original game, where the usage cost takes into account the maximum distance instead. The main result of this paper shows that for $\alpha > 19$ all equilibrium graphs in the max-distance network creation game must be trees, while the best bound in previous work is $\alpha > 129$ [25]. We also improve the constant upper bound on the price of anarchy to 3 for tree equilibria. Our work brings new insights into the structure of Nash equilibria and takes one step forward in settling the tree conjecture in the max-distance network creation game.

Keywords: Network creation game · Tree equilibrium · Price of anarchy

1 Introduction

Many important networks in the real world, e.g. the Internet or social networks, have been created in a decentralized, uncoordinated, spontaneous way. Modeling and analyzing such networks is an important challenge in the fields of computer science and social science. Fabrikant et al. [18] studied the process of building these networks from a game-theoretic perspective by modeling it as a network creation game, which formalizes the cost function for each agent in the network as its creation cost plus its usage cost. Each agent, as a vertex, can choose to build an edge to any other agent at a prefixed constant cost α. The creation cost is α times the number of edges it builds. The usage cost is the sum of the distances from this agent to all the others in the original game, while later variants of this

© The Author(s), under exclusive license to Springer Nature Switzerland AG 2022
P. Kanellopoulos et al. (Eds.): SAGT 2022, LNCS 13584, pp. 293–310, 2022.
https://doi.org/10.1007/978-3-031-15714-1_17

game define the usage cost differently. Each agent aims to minimize its total cost by choosing a suitable subset of other agents to connect, which makes it a complex game on the graph. This sum-distance network creation game and its variants are increasingly applied in various areas and have recently been used to study payment channel networks on the blockchain [6, 7, 26].

In the max-distance network creation game introduced by Demaine et al. [15], the usage cost of an agent is defined as the maximum distance from this agent to other agents. This variant covers a great portion of applications in practice. On the one hand, we can naturally think of it as a model with the assumption of risk aversion. Each agent always considers the worst case in which it needs to communicate with the farthest agent, while each agent considers the average case in the sum-distance network creation game. On the other hand, as interactions between agents can often be parallel in decentralized networks, such as social networks, the max-distance game could be a more realistic model than the sum-distance game if considering the non-additive time cost. For example, a post shared by one person on Facebook can be seen by multiple friends at the same time. Suppose that a person posts a nice photo and wants a group of people to see it as soon as possible. Some of them may not be his friends, but everyone who sees it is willing to share on his or her timeline. Then the person will care more about the maximum social distance rather than the sum of social distances to them.

No matter which cost function is chosen, the selfish agents in networks only make local decisions based on their own interests, so the equilibrium graph often fails to achieve global optimality, i.e., the lowest social cost. Thus, characterizing the structure of the equilibrium graph and calculating the price of anarchy (PoA) [22] are the key parts of the research, where the price of anarchy is defined to be the ratio between the social cost of a worst Nash equilibrium and the optimal social cost [18].

It has been proved that if all equilibrium graphs are trees, the price of anarchy will be constant in either sum-distance setting or max-distance setting [10, 18, 25]. This result will help to analytically justify the famous small-world phenomenon [21, 27], which suggests selfishly built networks are indeed very efficient. Therefore, researchers pay special attention to the distinguishment between the tree structure and the non-tree structure in the network creation game. Intuitively, when the unit cost α for building an edge is high enough, a tree is likely to be an equilibrium graph due to the fact that each agent can already reach other agents and will have no incentive to build additional edges.

For the sum-distance network creation game, Fabrikant et al. [18] conjectured that every equilibrium graph is a tree for $\alpha > A$ where A is a constant. Although this tree conjecture was disproved by Albers et al. [1], the reformulated tree conjecture is well accepted as that in the sum-distance network creation game, every equilibrium graph is a tree for $\alpha > n$, where n is the number of agents. A series of works have contributed to this threshold from $12n \log n$ [1] to $273n$ [25], $65n$ [24], $17n$ [3], and to $4n - 13$ [10]. Recently, a preprint by Dippel and Vetta [16] claimed an improved bound of $3n - 3$.

For the max-distance network creation game, there is no work formally stating an adapted tree conjecture. However, by evaluating the difference between the usage costs (sum-distance and max-distance), we can roughly conjecture that every equilibrium graph is a tree for $\alpha > A$ where A is a constant. Mihalák and Schlegel [25] proved A is at most 129 and gave the example that for $\alpha \leq 1$, a non-tree equilibrium graph could be constructed.

The main contribution of this paper is to prove A is at most 19, i.e. for $\alpha > 19$, every equilibrium graph is a tree in the max-distance network creation game (Theorem 1). We bring new insights into the structure of Nash equilibria and take one step forward in settling the tree conjecture in the max-distance network creation game. Our proof for the first time combines two orthogonal techniques, the classic degree approach [3,24,25] and the recent min-cycle approach [3,10]. Moreover, we prove the upper bound on the price of anarchy is 3 for tree equilibria (Theorem 2), so that we not only enlarge the range of α for which the price of anarchy takes a constant value, but also further tighten this constant upper bound from 4 [25] to 3. The best known bounds on the price of anarchy are available in Table 1. Our results can be interpreted as that the efficiency of decentralized networks is in fact better than previously known and demonstrated.

Table 1. Summary of the known bounds on the PoA.

2   Related Work

Fabrikant et al. [18] first introduced and studied the (sum-distance) network creation game. They proved a general upper bound of $O(\sqrt{\alpha})$ on the PoA. Then they found that numerous experiments and attempted constructions mostly yielded Nash equilibria that are trees with only a few exceptions, and postulated the tree conjecture that there exists a constant A, such that for $\alpha > A$, all Nash equilibria are trees. Moreover, if all Nash equilibria are trees, the price of anarchy is upper bounded by a constant 5.

However, the tree conjecture was soon disproved by Albers et al. [1] by leveraging some interesting results on finite affine planes. They on the other hand showed that for $\alpha \geq 12n\lceil \log n \rceil$, every Nash equilibrium forms a tree and the price of anarchy is less than 1.5. They also gave a general upper bound of $O(1 + (\min\{\alpha^2/n, n^2/\alpha\})^{1/3})$ on the price of anarchy for any α. Demaine et al. [15] further proved in the range $O(n^{1-\epsilon})$, the price of anarchy is constant and also improved the constant values in some ranges of α. For α between $n^{1-\epsilon}$ and $12n\log n$, they gave an upper bound of $2^{O(\sqrt{\log n})}$.

By the work Demaine et al. [15], it is believed that for $\alpha \geq n$, every Nash equilibrium is a tree, as the reformulated tree conjecture. Mihalák and Schlegel

[25] used a technique based on the average degree of biconnected components and significantly improved this range from $\alpha \geq 12n\lceil \log n \rceil$ to $\alpha > 273n$, which is asymptotically tight. Based on the same idea, Mamageishvili et al. [24] improved this range to $\alpha > 65n$ and Alvarez and Messegué [3] further improved it to $\alpha > 17n$. Recently, Biló and Lenzner [10] improved the bound to $\alpha > 4n - 13$, using a technique based on critical pairs and min cycles, which is orthogonal to the known degree approaches. Dippel and Vetta [16] proved an improved bound of $3n - 3$ through a more detailed case-by-case discussion. By the above results, we immediately have that the price of anarchy is constant for $\alpha = O(n^{1-\epsilon})$ and $\alpha > 3n-3$. Moreover, Àlvarez and Messegué [4] proved that the price of anarchy is constant for $\alpha > n(1+\epsilon)$ by bounding the size of any biconnected component of any non-tree Nash equilibrium, but his newer result has no implication on the tree conjecture.

The max-distance network creation game, as a key variant of the original game, was introduced by Demaine et al. [15]. They showed that the price of anarchy is at most 2 for $\alpha \geq n$, $O(\min\{4^{\sqrt{\log n}}(n/\alpha)^{1/3}\})$ for $2\sqrt{\log n} \leq \alpha \leq n$, and $O(n^{2/\alpha})$ for $\alpha < 2\sqrt{\log n}$. Mamageishvili et al. [24] showed that the price of anarchy is constant for $\alpha > 129$ and $\alpha = O(n^{-1/2})$ and also proved that it is $2^{O(\sqrt{\log n})}$ for any α. Specifically, they showed that in the max-distance network creation game, for $\alpha > 129$ all equilibrium graphs are trees. In this work, we combine the classic degree approach [3,24,25] and the recent min-cycle approach [3,10] to show that for $\alpha > 19$ all equilibrium graphs are trees and the price of anarchy is constant. Compared to Mihalák and Schlegel [25], we also improve the constant upper bound on the price of anarchy from 4 to 3 for tree equilibria.

It has been proved that computing the optimal strategy of a single agent in the network creation game with either cost function is NP-hard [18,25], making it impractical to verify whether a non-tree equilibrium graph exists through experimentation.

There are other variants of the network creation game, such as weighted network creation game proposed by Albers et al. [1], bilateral network creation game studied by Corbo and Parkes [13], Demaine et al. [15]. For more studies on these variants, as well as exact or approximation algorithms for computing equilibria in network creation games, we refer readers to [1,2,5,8,9,11–15,17,19, 20,23].

3   Game Model

In a network creation game, there are n agents denoted by $\{1, 2, \ldots, n\}$. The strategy of agent i is specified by a subset s_i of $\{1, 2, \ldots, n\}\backslash\{i\}$, which corresponds to the set of neighbor agents to which agent i creates links. Together, a strategy profile of this network is denoted by $s = (s_1, s_2, \ldots, s_n)$. The cost of creating a link is a constant $\alpha > 0$ and the goal of every agent is to minimize its total cost. We only consider the pure Nash equilibrium in this work.

To define the cost function, we consider a graph $G_s = \langle V, E_s \rangle$, where $V = \{v_1, v_2, \ldots, v_n\}$ represents n agents and E_s is determined by the strategy profile s, i.e. the links they create. G_s has an edge $(u, v) \in E_s$ if either $u \in s_v$ or $v \in s_u$. Note all edges are undirected and unweighted. The distance between $u, v \in V$ is denoted by $d_{G_s}(u, v)$, the length of a shortest u-v-path in G_s. If u and v are not in the same connected component of G_s, $d_{G_s}(u, v) = +\infty$. The cost incurred by agent v is defined as

$$c_{G_s}(v) = \alpha|s_v| + D_{G_s}(v),$$

where $D_{G_s}(v) = \max_{u \in V} d_{G_s}(u, v)$. And the social cost is

$$\text{Cost}(G_s) = \sum_{v \in V} c_{G_s}(v) = \alpha|E_s| + \sum_{v \in V} D_{G_s}(v).$$

A strategy profile s is a Nash equilibrium, if for every agent v and for every s' which is different with s only on v's strategy, $c_{G_s}(v) \leq c_{G_{s'}}(v)$. In other words, no one has the incentive to deviate from its strategy as long as all other agents stick to their strategies. We call a graph G_s an equilibrium graph if s is a Nash equilibrium. Note that any equilibrium graph must be a connected graph, otherwise every agent will have an infinite cost. We also note that no edge is paid by both sides at equilibrium, otherwise either side can cancel its payment to get a lower cost.

We call a graph G_{s^*} an optimal graph if s^* minimizes the social cost such that $\text{Cost}(G_{s^*}) = \min_{s \in S} \text{Cost}(G_s)$, where S is the whole strategy space. The price of anarchy in this game is defined to be the ratio between the cost of a worst Nash equilibrium and the optimal social cost [18], i.e.,

$$\text{PoA} = \frac{\max_{s \in \mathcal{N}} \text{Cost}(G_s)}{\text{Cost}(G_{s^*})},$$

where $\mathcal{N}$ is the set of all Nash equilibria.

In the following context, we will mostly omit the reference to the strategy profile s. If we need to represent two or more graphs induced by different strategy profiles, we will use G, G', or $G_1, G_2, \ldots$ instead.

Next, we introduce some commonly used notations in graph theory. We use $V(G)$ and $E(G)$ to denote the vertex set and edge set of a graph G. We use $|\cdot|$ to denote the size of a vertex or edge set, e.g. $|V(G)|$. We also denote the length of a cycle C by $|C|$. We denote the diameter of G by $diam(G) = \max_{v \in V} D_G(v)$ and denote the radius of G by $rad(G) = \min_{v \in V} D_G(v)$. A vertex is called a central vertex if $D_G(v) = rad(G)$. A cut vertex v of G is a vertex whose removal from G increases the number of connected components. A biconnected graph is a graph with no cut vertex. A biconnected component H of G is a maximal biconnected subgraph with more than two vertices. Different from the standard definition of the biconnected component, we rule out the trivial subgraph with only two vertices and one edge for convenience. In this way, if there is no biconnected component in G, G must be a tree. The average degree of a biconnected component H is $deg(H) = \frac{1}{|V(H)|}\sum_{v \in V(H)} deg_H(v)$, where $deg_H(v)$ counts the number of edges connecting v in H.

4   Equilibrium Graphs

This section demonstrates the main results of this paper. We show that in the max-distance network creation game, for $\alpha > 19$ all equilibrium graphs are trees and the price of anarchy is less than 3. The main idea is to find the contradiction about the average degree of biconnected components. For any biconnected component H, we have $deg(H) \geq 2 + \frac{1}{5}$ when $\alpha > 5$ (Subsect. 4.2), but meanwhile, we also have $deg(H) < 2 + 2/\lceil (\alpha - 1)/2 \rceil$ when $\alpha > 2$ (Subsect. 4.3). Hence if $\alpha > 19$, a contradiction implies there is no biconnected component in G, thus a tree (Subsect. 4.4). Finally, we give a upper bound of 3 on the price of anarchy if all Nash equilibria are trees.

4.1   Cycles in the Equilibrium Graph

In this subsection, we give a basic characterization of cycles in equilibrium graphs. We show that in every equilibrium graph, all min cycles, if any, are directed (Lemma 3) and all cycles are at least of length $2\alpha - 1$ (Lemma 5). To prove these, we first prepare Lemma 1, which is the most important lemma of this work, running through the whole paper.

Lemma 1. *Let G be an equilibrium graph and a, b are two distinct vertices of G such that a buys an edge (a, a_1). If there exists a shortest path tree T of G rooted at b such that either (a, a_1) is not an edge of T or a_1 is the parent of a in T, then $D_G(a) \leq D_G(b) + 1$. Furthermore, if a is buying also another edge $(a, a_2), a_2 \neq a_1$, and (a, a_2) is not an edge of T, then $D_G(a) \leq D_G(b) + 1 - \alpha$.*

Proof. Consider the strategy change in which vertex a swaps the edge (a, a_1) with the edge (a, b) and removes any other edge it owns but not contained in T, if any. Let G' be the graph obtained after the swap. Observe that no vertex gets further to b, $d_{G'}(b, x) \leq d_G(b, x)$ for every $x \in V$, so $D_{G'}(a) \leq D_{G'}(b) + 1 \leq D_G(b) + 1$. Since a does not apply this strategy change, we have $D_G(a) \leq D_G(b) + 1$. Furthermore, if a also saves its creation cost α by removing (a, a_2), we have $D_G(a) \leq D_{G'}(a) - \alpha \leq D_G(b) + 1 - \alpha$. See Fig. 1. □

Lemma 2 ([15]). *Every equilibrium graph has no cycle of length less than $\alpha + 2$.*

Proof. Suppose for contradiction there is a cycle C in the equilibrium graph with length less than $\alpha + 2$. Let (v, u) be an edge of C. By symmetry, we can assume v buys it. If v removes this edge it decreases its creation cost by α and increases its usage cost by at most $|C| - 2 < \alpha$. So v has the incentive to remove this edge and this cannot be an equilibrium graph, a contradiction. □

Definition 1 (Min Cycle). *Let G be a non-tree graph and let C be a cycle of G. Then C is a min cycle if for every two vertices $x_1, x_2 \in V(C)$, $d_C(x_1, x_2) = d_G(x_1, x_2)$.*

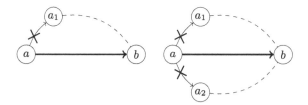

Fig. 1. On the shortest path tree T rooted at b, a_1 is the parent of a or (a, a_1) is a non-tree edge. The same goes for a_2. If a swaps (a, a_1) with (a, b), the cost increases from $D_G(a)$ to at most $D_G(b) + 1$. If a further removes (a, a_2), the cost increases from $D_G(a)$ to at most $D_G(b) + 1 - \alpha$.

Definition 2 (Directed Cycle). *Let G be a non-tree graph and let C be a cycle of length k in G. Then C is a directed cycle if there is an ordering $u_0, \ldots, u_{k-1}$ of its k vertices such that, for every $i = 0, \ldots, k-1$, $(u_i, u_{(i+1) \bmod k})$ is an edge of C which is bought by vertex u_i.*

Definition 3 (Antipodal Vertex). *Let C be a cycle of length k and let u, v be two vertices of C. Then u is an antipodal vertex of v if $d_C(u, v) \geq \lfloor \frac{k}{2} \rfloor$.*

Lemma 3. *For $\alpha > 2$, if G is a non-tree equilibrium graph, then every min cycle in an equilibrium graph is directed.*

Proof. Suppose for contradiction, there is a min cycle C in G that is not directed. That means C contains a vertex v which buys both its incident edges in C, say (v, v_1) and (v, v_2).

If C is an odd-length cycle, then v has two distinct antipodal vertices $u, u_1 \in C$. By symmetry we can assume u buys the edge (u, u_1). By Lemma 2, we have $|C| \geq \alpha + 2 > 4 \implies |C| \geq 5$. Hence v, v_1, v_2, u, u_1 are different vertices. By Lemma 1 (where $a = u, a_1 = u_1, b = v$), we have $D_G(u) \leq D_G(v) + 1$. Also by Lemma 1 (where $a = v, a_1 = v_1, a_2 = v_2, b = u$), we have $D_G(v) \leq D_G(u) + 1 - \alpha$. By summing up both the left-hand and the right-hand side of the two inequalities, we have $\alpha \leq 2$ which is a contradiction.

If C is an even-length cycle, then v has one antipodal vertex $u \in C$. Denote the vertex adjacent to u in C (from any side) by u_1. If u buys the edge (u, u_1), the same analysis as above will lead to $\alpha \leq 2$, a contradiction. If u_1 buys the edge (u_1, u), we can check v and u_1 also satisfies the condition in Lemma 1 (where $a = v, b = u_1$). Therefore we have $D_G(u_1) \leq D_G(v) + 1$ and $D_G(v) \leq D_G(u_1) + 1 - \alpha$, which also leads to $\alpha \leq 2$, a contradiction. □

Lemma 4. *If G is a non-tree equilibrium graph and H is a biconnected component of G, then for every edge e of H, there is a min cycle C of H that contains the edge e.*

Proof. Since H is biconnected, there exists at least a cycle containing the edge e. Among all cycles in H that contain the edge e, let C be a cycle of minimum length. We claim that C is a min cycle. For the sake of contradiction, assume that C is not a min cycle. This implies that there are two vertices $u, v \in V_C$ such that $d_H(u, v) < d_C(u, v)$ and the shortest path P' between u and v in H is disjoint with C. Let P_1 and P_2 be two disjoint paths between u and v in C, with length l_1 and l_2, $l_1 + l_2 = |C|$. By symmetry we can assume P_1 contains e. Then P and P_1 form a new cycle C' with length $l' + l_1 = d_H(u, v) + l_1 < d_C(u, v) + l_1 \leq l_1 + l_2 = |C|$. Therefore we can find a cycle containing e but strictly shorter than C, a contradiction. □

Corollary 1. *For $\alpha > 2$, if G is a non-tree equilibrium graph and H is a biconnected component of G, then for every vertex $v \in V(H)$, v buys at least one edge in H.*

Proof. Consider any edge of vertex v, say (v, u). By Lemma 4, (v, u) is contained in a min cycle C. Then by Lemma 3, we know v buys at least one edge in C if $\alpha > 2$. □

Lemma 5. *Every equilibrium graph has no cycle of length less than $2\alpha - 1$.*

Proof. For $\alpha \leq 2$, by Lemma 2, the length of any cycle is at least $\alpha + 2 > 2\alpha - 1$, so we assume $\alpha > 2$ from now on.

Since for every cycle in the graph, we can find a min cycle shorter than it, it is sufficient to prove that every equilibrium graph has no min cycle of length less than $2\alpha - 1$. Suppose for contradiction there is a min cycle C in the equilibrium graph, whose length is less than $2\alpha - 1$. By Lemma 3, C is a directed cycle. Let (v, v_1) be an edge of C bought by v.

If C is an even-length cycle, we denote the antipodal vertex by u and u buys the edge (u, u_1). Observe that the antipodal vertex of u_1 is v_1. If C is an odd-length cycle, we denote the antipodal vertices by u, u_1 and u buys the edge (u, u_1). Observe that the antipodal vertices of u_1 are v and v_1. Thus, in both cases, we can find a shortest path tree T rooted at u_1 such that (v, v_1) is not contained in T, and $d_G(v, u_1) = \lfloor \frac{|C|-1}{2} \rfloor$. In this directed cycle C, u_1 also buys the edge (u_1, u_2) and u_2 is the parent of u_1 in the shortest path tree rooted at v. By Lemma 1 (where $a = u_1, a_1 = u_2, b = v$), we have $D_G(u_1) \leq D_G(v) + 1$.

Consider the strategy change in which v removes the edge (v, v_1) and G' is the graph after the removal. For every vertex x, $d_{G'}(v, x) \leq d_{G'}(v, u_1) + d_{G'}(u_1, x) \leq \frac{|C|-1}{2} + d_G(u_1, x) < \alpha - 1 + D_G(u_1) \leq D_G(v) + \alpha$. Hence by applying this change, it decreases its creation cost by α and increases its usage cost by strictly less than α, which is a contradiction. □

4.2   Lower Bound for Average Degree

This subsection proves a lower bound of $2 + \frac{1}{5}$ on the average degree of biconnected components (Lemma 9). The key idea is to show that any 2-degree path is no longer than 3 (Lemma 8) so that the number of 2-degree vertices can be actually bounded.

Lemma 6. *For $\alpha > 2$, if G is a non-tree equilibrium graph and H is a biconnected component of G, then for every vertex $v \in V(H)$, $D_G(v) \leq rad(G) + 2$.*

Proof. Let T be the shortest path tree rooted at some central vertex v_0 such that $D_G(v_0) = rad(G)$. Let T_H be the intersection of H and T, i.e.,

$$T_H = H \cap T = \langle V(H), E(H) \cap E(T) \rangle.$$

Observe that T_H is still a tree. By Corollary 1, every vertex $v \in V(H)$ buys at least one edge in this biconnected component. Suppose v buys the edge (v, u) in H.

If (v, u) is a non-tree edge or u is the parent of v, consider the strategy change in which v swaps the edge (v, u) to (v, v_0). Since v does not apply this change, we have $D_G(v) \leq D_{G'}(v) \leq D_{G'}(v_0) + 1 \leq D_G(v_0) + 1 = rad(G) + 1$.

If v is the parent of u, we can always find such a vertex s which is a descendant of v and is also a leaf vertex of T_H. By Corollary 1, s buys at least one edge in H. Since it is already the leaf vertex of T_H, it could only buy a non-tree edge or a leading-up edge. Thus we have $D_G(s) \leq rad(G) + 1$. Then we consider the strategy change in which v swaps the edge (v, u) to (v, s). Note in the shortest path tree rooted at s, u is the parent of v. Since v does not apply this change, we have $D_G(v) \leq D_{G'}(v) \leq D_{G'}(s) + 1 \leq D_G(s) + 1 \leq D_G(v_0) + 2 = rad(G) + 2$. □

Let H be an arbitrary biconnected component of the equilibrium graph G. We define a family of sets $\{S(v)\}_{v \in V(H)}$ such that

$$S(v) = \{w \in V \mid v = \arg \min_{u \in V(H)} d_G(u, w)\}.$$

Every vertex w in V is assigned to its closest vertex v in $V(H)$. By the definition, we have

- $\cup_{v \in V(H)} S(v) = V$;
- for $u, v \in V(H)$, $S(u) \cap S(v) = \emptyset$;
- and for $v \in V(H)$, $S(v) \cap V(H) = \{v\}$.

The following Lemma 7 shows for every vertex $v \in V(H)$, the furthest vertex never lies in $S(v)$, nor in $S(u)$ when u is near to v.

Lemma 7. *For $\alpha > 2$, if G is a non-tree equilibrium graph and H is a biconnected component of G, then for every vertex $v \in V(H)$ and every vertex $w \in S(v)$, $d_G(v, w) \leq D_G(v) + 2 - \alpha$.*

Proof. By Lemma 4, v is contained in a min cycle C. By Lemma 5, $|C| \geq 2\alpha - 1$. Hence there exists a vertex $u \in V(H)$ such that $d_G(v, u) \geq \frac{|C| - 1}{2} \geq \alpha - 1$. By Lemma 1, we know $D_G(u) \leq D_G(v) + 1$. As H is a biconnected component, every shortest u-w-path contains v. Therefore, $d_G(v, w) = d_G(u, w) - d_G(u, v) \leq D_G(u) - (\alpha - 1) \leq D_G(v) + 2 - \alpha$. □

Lemma 8. *For $\alpha > 5$, if G is a non-tree equilibrium graph and H is a biconnected component of G, then every path $x_0, x_1, \ldots, x_k, x_{k+1}$ in H with $deg_H(x_i) = 2$ for $1 \leq i \leq k$, satisfies $k \leq 3$. Moreover, if $k = 3$, we have $D_G(x_0) = rad(G)$ and $D_G(x_{k+1}) \neq rad(G)$.*

Proof. Since $deg_H(x_i) = 2$ for $1 \leq i \leq k$, this path should be contained in some min cycle, which means it is a directed path by Lemma 3. W.l.o.g. we assume x_i buys the edge (x_i, x_{i+1}) for $0 \leq i \leq k$.

Suppose for contradiction there exists such a path with $k \geq 4$. By Lemma 6, we have $D_G(x_i) \in [rad(G), rad(G) + 2]$ for $0 \leq i \leq 3$. Therefore there exists $0 \leq j \leq 2$ such that $D_G(x_j) \geq D_G(x_{j+1})$. Consider the strategy change in which x_j swaps the edge (x_j, x_{j+1}) to (x_j, x_{j+3}) and G' is the graph after the swap. We will split the vertices V into three parts (see Fig. 2) and show for vertex w in any part, $d_{G'}(x_j, w) < D_G(x_j)$ for $\alpha > 5$, so that $D_{G'}(x_j) < D_G(x_j)$, a contradiction with equilibrium.

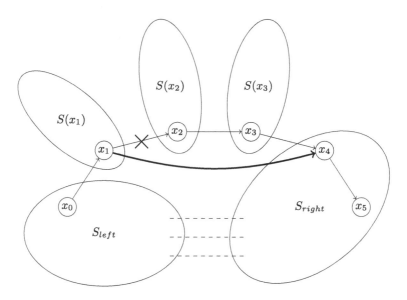

Fig. 2. Here is an example of the partition when $k = 4$ and $j = 1$. Consider x_1 swaps (x_1, x_2) with (x_1, x_4). First, by Lemma 7, we know x_1 is very near to $S(x_1)$, $S(x_2)$ and $S(x_3)$ in G while the swap only increases the distances a little. Then, by the definition of S_{right}, the swap makes x_1 strictly nearer to S_{right}. Finally, thanks to $D_G(x_1) \geq D_G(x_2)$, x_1 can actually get strictly nearer to S_{left} by taking a detour through x_4.

(a) **Set $S(x_j) \cup S(x_{j+1}) \cup S(x_{j+2})$:** By Lemma 7, for every vertex $w \in S(x_j)$, $d_{G'}(x_j, w) = d_G(x_j, w) \leq D_G(v) + 2 - \alpha \leq rad(G) + 4 - \alpha < rad(G) \leq D_G(x_j)$. By Lemma 7, for every vertex $w \in S(x_{j+t})$, $t = 1, 2$, $d_{G'}(x_j, w) \leq d_{G'}(x_j, x_{j+3}) + d_{G'}(x_{j+3}, x_{j+t}) + d_{G'}(x_{j+t}, w) = 1 + (3 - t) + d_G(x_{j+t}, w) \leq D_G(x_{j+t}) - t + 6 - \alpha < D_G(x_j)$.

(b) **Set S_{right} where for every w there exists a shortest x_j-w-path contains x_{j+3}:** For every vertex $w \in S_{right}$, $d_{G'}(x_j, w) \leq d_{G'}(x_j, x_{j+3}) + d_{G'}(x_{j+3}, w) = 1 + d_G(x_{j+3}, w) = d_G(x_j, w) - 2 < D_G(x_j)$.

(c) **Set S_{left} where for every w there is no shortest x_j-w-path contains x_{j+3}:** For every vertex $w \in S_{left}$ satisfying $d_G(x_j, w) < D_G(x_j)$, easy to see $d_{G'}(x_j, w) = d_G(x_j, w) < D_G(x_j)$. For every vertex $w \in S_{left}$ satisfying $d_G(x_j, w) = D_G(x_j)$, we claim there exists a shortest x_{j+1}-w-path contains x_{j+3}. Otherwise, $D_G(x_{j+1}) \geq d_G(x_{j+1}, w) = d_G(x_{j+1}, x_j) + d_G(x_j, w) = D_G(x_j) + 1 > D_G(x_j) \geq D_G(x_{j+1})$, a contradiction. Thus $d_{G'}(x_j, w) \leq d_{G'}(x_j, x_{j+3}) + d_{G'}(x_{j+3}, w) = 1 + d_G(x_{j+3}, w) = d_G(x_{j+1}, w) - 1 \leq D_G(x_{j+1}) - 1 < D_G(x_j)$.

Combining them together, we have $D_{G'}(x_j) < D_G(x_j)$, contradicted with the equilibrium.

When $k = 3$, if $D_G(x_0) \geq D_G(x_1)$ or $D_G(x_1) \geq D_G(x_2)$, we can find a similar contradiction, so we must have $D_G(x_0) = rad(G), D_G(x_1) = rad(G) + 1, D_G(x_2) = rad(G) + 2$. As x_2 does not choose to swap (x_2, x_3) to (x_2, x_4), we have $D_G(x_2) \leq D_G(x_4) + 1$, hence $D_G(x_{k+1}) = D_G(x_4) \geq rad(G) + 1$. □   □

Corollary 2. *For $\alpha > 5$, if G is a non-tree equilibrium graph and H is a biconnected component of G, then for every vertex $v \in V(H)$, v satisfies one of the following conditions:*

(a) there exists a vertex $u \in N_1(v)$ such that $deg_H(u) \geq 3$;
(b) $deg_H(u) = 2$ for $u \in N_1(v)$ and $deg_H(u) \geq 3$ for $u \in N_2(v) \backslash N_1(v)$,

where $N_k(v) = \{u \in H \mid d_H(u, v) \leq k\}$.

Proof. Suppose for contradiction there exists a vertex v_0 satisfies none of the conditions. Since v_0 does not satisfy condition (a), we have a path v_3, v_1, v_0, v_2, v_4 such that $deg_H(v_i) = 2$ for $0 \leq i \leq 2$. Since v_0 does not satisfy condition (b), we have $deg_H(v_3) = 2$ or $deg_H(v_4) = 2$. In either case, we get a 2-degree path with length $k \geq 4$, contradicted with Lemma 8. □

Lemma 9. *For $a > 5$, if G is a non-tree equilibrium graph, then for every biconnected component H of G, $deg(H) \geq 2 + \frac{1}{5}$.*

Proof. We assign every vertex $w \in H$ satisfying condition (a) in Corollary 2 to its closest vertex v with $deg_H(v) \geq 3$, breaking ties arbitrarily. If $deg_H(w) \geq 3$, it is assigned to itself. Then we get a family of star-like vertex sets $\{V_i\}_{i=1}^m$, each of which is formed by a star-center vertex v_i of degree at least 3 and $|V_i| - 1$ vertices of degree 2 assigned to v_i. The total degree of them is $\sum_{i=1}^m deg_H(v_i) + 2 \sum_{i=1}^m (|V_i| - 1)$. Note we have $|V_i| - 1 \leq deg_H(v_i)$.

Consider that the left vertices in H form a vertex set V_0, every element of which satisfies condition (b) in Corollary 2. The total degree of V_0 is $2|V_0|$. Each vertex in V_0 corresponds to a 2-degree path with $k = 3$. Lemma 8 implies that any vertex cannot simultaneously be the start point of a 2-degree path with $k = 3$ and the end point of another such path. Thus, every star-center vertex v_i is linked to at most $(deg_H(v_i) - 1)$ such paths because v_i should be contained in some directed min cycle by Lemma 3 and Lemma 4. Then we have $2|V_0| \leq \sum_{i=1}^m (deg_H(v_i) - 1)$.

The average degree of H is

$$
\begin{aligned}
deg(H) &= \frac{\sum_{i=1}^{m} deg_H(v_i) + 2\sum_{i=1}^{m}(|V_i| - 1) + 2|V_0|}{\sum_{i=1}^{m} |V_i| + |V_0|} \\
&= 2 + \frac{\sum_{i=1}^{m} deg_H(v_i) - 2m}{\sum_{i=1}^{m} |V_i| + |V_0|} \\
&\geq 2 + \frac{\sum_{i=1}^{m} deg_H(v_i) - 2m}{\sum_{i=1}^{m}(deg_H(v_i) + 1) + \frac{1}{2}\sum_{i=1}^{m}(deg_H(v_i) - 1)} \\
&\geq 2 + \frac{3m - 2m}{\frac{3}{2} \cdot 3m + \frac{1}{2}m} \\
&= 2 + \frac{1}{5}.
\end{aligned}
$$

$\square$

4.3   Upper Bound on Average Degree

This subsection proves that the average degree of any biconnected component is less than $2 + 2/\lceil(\alpha - 1)/2\rceil$ (Lemma 11). We consider the shortest path tree T rooted at some central vertex v_0. Let T_H be the intersection of H and T, i.e., $T_H = H \cap T = \langle V(H), E(H) \cap E(T)\rangle$. Then the average degree of a biconnected component H can be written as

$$
deg(H) = \frac{2(|E(T_H)| + |E(H)\backslash E(T_H)|)}{|V(T_H)|}.
$$

Observe that T_H is still a tree, so we have $|E(T_H)| = |V(T_H)| - 1$. Thus, to obtain the upper bound on average degree, we only need to bound the number of non-tree edges.

We call a vertex u a shopping vertex if u buys a non-tree edge. First observe that for $\alpha > 1$, every shopping vertex u buys exactly one non-tree edge, otherwise by Lemma 1, $D_G(u) \leq D_G(v_0) + 1 - \alpha < rad(G)$, a contradiction. The following Lemma 10 aims to show that every pair of shopping vertices is not so close to each other on the tree, by which we can prove the number of shopping vertices has an upper bound.

Lemma 10. *For $\alpha > 2$, if G is a non-tree equilibrium graph and H is a biconnected component of G, then for every two shopping vertices $u_1, u_2 \in V(H)$, $\max\{d_{T_H}(u_1, x), d_{T_H}(u_2, x)\} \geq \frac{\alpha - 1}{2}$, where x is the lowest common ancestor of u_1 and u_2 in T_H.*

Proof. Let (u_1, v_1) and (u_2, v_2) be the non-tree edge bought by u_1 and u_2. Consider the path P between u_1 and u_2 in T_H and we extend it with (u_1, v_1) and (u_2, v_2). Then we get a path $x_0 = v_1, x_1 = u_1, x_2, \ldots, x_j, \ldots, x_{k-1}, x_k = u_2, x_{k+1} = v_2$, where x_j is the lowest common ancestor of u_1 and u_2 in T_H, $j \in \{1, 2, \ldots, k\}$.

Since x_1 buys (x_1, x_0) and x_k buys (x_k, x_{k+1}), there has to be a vertex x_i, $1 \leq i \leq k$, such that x_i buys both (x_i, x_{i-1}) and (x_i, x_{i+1}). Consider the strategy change in which x_i removes both the edges (x_i, x_{i-1}) and (x_i, x_{i+1}) and buys the edge (x_i, v_0) and let G' be the graph after the strategy change. This change decreases the creation cost by α and increases the usage cost from $D_G(x_i)$ $(\geq D_G(v_0))$ to at most $D_{G'}(v_0)+1$. In the rest of proof, we are going to show that if $\max\{d_{T_H}(u_1, x_j), d_{T_H}(u_2, x_j)\} < \frac{\alpha-1}{2}$, then we have $D_{G'}(v_0) - D_G(v_0) + 1 < \alpha$, so that x_i has the incentive to apply this strategy, which means G cannot be an equilibrium graph.

Suppose $d_{T_H}(u_1, x_j) < \frac{\alpha-1}{2}$ and $d_{T_H}(u_2, x_j) < \frac{\alpha-1}{2}$. First, we observe that v_1 and v_2 are not the descendants of any vertex x_t for $t = 1, 2, \ldots, k$. If v_1 is the descendant of x_t for some t, u_1, v_1 and x_t forms a cycle. Note that v_1 is at most one level deeper than u_1 in T, so the length of the cycle is at most $d_{T_H}(u_1, x_t) + d_{T_H}(v_1, x_t) + 1 \leq 2(d_{T_H}(u_1, x_j) + 1) < \alpha + 1$, contradicted with Lemma 2 (or Lemma 5). The same goes for v_2.

Second, we observe that only the vertices in P and their descendants in T may have increased distance to v_0 by this strategy change of x_i. By the previous analysis we know v_0-v_1-path and v_0-v_2 path are not affected, so v_0 can reach these vertices by taking a detour through v_1 or v_2. Let y be one of the vertices in P or a descendant of any vertex in P and denote the nearest vertex to y in P by x_{t^*}, i.e. $x_{t^*} = \arg\min_{x_t} d_{T_H}(y, x_t)$. W.l.o.g., we assume $1 \leq i \leq j$.

- $1 \leq i < j$: If $i < t^* \leq k$, since v_0-x_j-x_{t^*}-path is not affected, $d_{G'}(v_0, y) \leq d_G(v_0, y)$. If $t^* = i$, the edge (x_i, v_0) makes the v_0-x_i-y-path even shorter. If $1 \leq t^* < i$, v_0 can reach y by taking a detour through $v_1(= x_0)$ (see Fig. 3).

$$
\begin{aligned}
d_{G'}(v_0, y) &\leq d_{G'}(v_0, x_0) + d_{G'}(x_0, x_{t^*}) + d_{G'}(x_{t^*}, y) \\
&= d_G(v_0, x_0) + d_G(x_0, x_{t^*}) + d_G(x_{t^*}, y) \\
&\leq (d_G(v_0, u_1) + 1) + (1 + d_G(u_1, x_{t^*})) + d_G(v_0, y) - d_G(v_0, x_{t^*}) \\
&= d_G(v_0, y) + 2d_G(u_1, x_{t^*}) + 2 \\
&\leq d_G(v_0, y) + 2d_G(u_1, x_j) \\
&< d_G(v_0, y) + \alpha - 1.
\end{aligned}
\tag{1}
$$

- $i = j$: If $t^* = i$, the edge (x_i, v_0) makes the v_0-x_i-y-path even shorter. If $t^* \neq i$, v_0 can reach y by taking a detour through v_1 or v_2. In either case we can get $d_{G'}(v_0, y) < d_G(v_0, y) + \alpha - 1$ by the inequality similar to Equation (1).

Combining them together we have $D_{G'}(v_0) < D_G(v_0) + \alpha - 1$, which finishes the proof. $\square$

Corollary 3. *For $\alpha > 2$, if G is a non-tree equilibrium graph and H is a biconnected component of G, then for every two shopping vertices $u_1, u_2 \in V(H)$, $d_{T_H}(u_1, u_2) \geq \frac{\alpha-1}{2}$.*

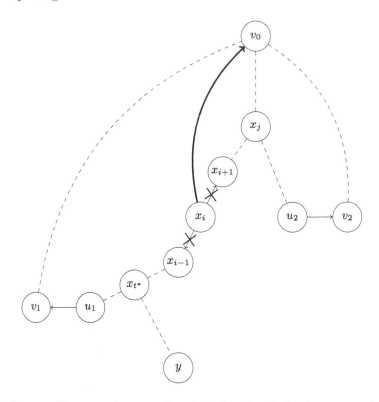

Fig. 3. Here we illustrate the case when $1 \le t^* < i < j$. In the new graph G', v_0 can reach y through v_1, u_1 and x_{t^*}. Note that v_1 is at most one level deeper than u_1. From $v_0 \to x_j \to x_{t^*} \to y$ to $v_0 \to v_1 \to x_{t^*} \to y$, the distance is increased by up to $2d_G(v_1, x_{t^*}) \le 2d_G(u_1, x_j) < \alpha - 1$.

Lemma 11. *For $\alpha > 2$, if G is a non-tree equilibrium graph, then for every biconnected component H of G, $deg(H) < 2 + 2/\lceil (\alpha - 1)/2 \rceil$.*

Proof. For each shopping vertex u, we define such a vertex set $A(u)$ that for every vertex $w \in A(u)$, $w = u$ or w is an ancestor of u in T_H, and $d_{T_H}(u, w) < \frac{\alpha - 1}{2}$. $|A(u)| = \lceil \frac{\alpha - 1}{2} \rceil$ for every shopping vertex u.

If for every pair of shopping vertex u_1, u_2, $A(u_1) \cap A(u_2) = \emptyset$, the number of shopping vertices could be bounded by $|V(H)|/\lceil (\alpha - 1)/2 \rceil$, then the desired result can be obtained by

$$deg(H) = \frac{2(|E(T_H)| + |E(H) \backslash E(T_H)|)}{|V(T_H)|} < 2 + \frac{2}{\lceil (\alpha - 1)/2 \rceil}.$$

Suppose for contradiction there are two shopping vertices u_1, u_2, such that $A(u_1) \cap A(u_2) \ne \emptyset$. Denote the lowest common ancestor of u_1 and u_2 by x. By the definition of A, we must have $x \in A(u_1) \cap A(u_2)$. However by Lemma 10, $\max\{d_{T_H}(u_1, x), d_{T_H}(u_2, x)\} \ge \frac{\alpha - 1}{2}$, which means x cannot belong to $A(u_1)$ and $A(u_2)$ simultaneously. This contradiction completes the proof. □

4.4   Tree Nash Equilibria and Price of Anarchy

Combining the lemmas from the above two subsections, we are ready to give our main result on tree Nash equilibria in Theorem 1. Then we will give the upper bound on the price of anarchy for tree equilibria in Theorem 2.

Theorem 1. *For $\alpha > 19$, every equilibrium graph is a tree.*

Proof. $\alpha > 19 \implies \lceil \frac{\alpha-1}{2} \rceil \geq 10$. By Lemma 11, if G is a non-tree equilibrium graph, for every biconnected component H of G, we have $deg(H) < 2 + \frac{1}{5}$, contradicted with Lemma 9. $\square$

Lemma 12 ([15]). *For $\alpha \leq \frac{2}{n-2}$, the complete graph is a social optimum. For $\alpha \geq \frac{2}{n-2}$, the star is a social optimum.*

Lemma 13 ([15]). *For $\alpha < \frac{1}{n-2}$, the price of anarchy is 1. For $\alpha < \frac{2}{n-2}$, the price of anarchy is at most 2.*

Theorem 2. *If all Nash equilibria are trees, the price of anarchy is less than 3.*

Proof. The claim is trivial when $n \leq 2$, or when $\alpha < \frac{2}{n-2}$ by Lemma 13. We therefore assume $n \geq 3$, and $\alpha \geq \frac{2}{n-2}$. Let G be a tree equilibrium graph and T be the shortest path tree rooted at some central vertex v such that $D_G(v) = rad(G) = \lceil \frac{diam(G)}{2} \rceil$ (observe we can find such a central vertex in a tree graph). Let u be a deepest leaf vertex of T such that $d_G(u,v) = rad(G)$ and $D_G(u) = diam(G)$. Consider the strategy change in which u additionally buys the edge (u,v) and G' is the graph after the change. Then $D_{G'}(u) \leq D_{G'}(v) + 1 \leq D_G(v) + 1$. The usage cost decreases by at least $D_G(u) - D_{G'}(u) \geq \lfloor \frac{diam(G)}{2} \rfloor - 1$ and therefore $\alpha > \lfloor \frac{diam(G)}{2} \rfloor - 1 \implies diam(G) \leq 2\alpha + 3$.

We define $N_k^=(v) = \{u \in G \mid d_G(v,u) = k\}$ and the total cost is

$$\text{Cost}(T) = (n-1)\alpha + \sum_{u \in V} D_G(u)$$

$$\leq (n-1)\alpha + \sum_{i=0}^{rad(G)} |N_i^=(v)|(rad(G) + i)$$

$$= (n-1)\alpha + n \cdot rad(G) + \sum_{i=1}^{rad(G)} |N_i^=(v)| \cdot i.$$

Observe that $|N_k^=(v)| \geq 2$ for $k = 1, 2, \ldots, rad(G) - 1$. To get the upper bound on $\text{Cost}(T)$, we can consider the worst case where $|N_k^=(v)| = 2$ for $k = 1, 2, \ldots, rad(G) - 1$ and $N_{rad(G)}^=(v) = V \setminus \bigcup_{k=0}^{rad(G)-1} N_k^=(v)$. By Lemma 12, a star is a social optimum, so we get

$$
\begin{aligned}
\text{PoA} &= \frac{\max_T \text{Cost}(T)}{\text{Cost}(G^*)} \\
&\leq \frac{(n-1)\alpha + n \cdot rad(G) + rad(G)(rad(G)-1) + (n - 2rad(G) + 1)rad(G)}{(n-1)\alpha + 2n - 1} \\
&= \frac{(n-1)\alpha + 2n \cdot rad(G) - (rad(G))^2}{(n-1)\alpha + 2n - 1} \\
&= 1 + \frac{2(n-1)(rad(G)-1) - (rad(G)-1)^2}{(n-1)\alpha + 2n - 1} \\
&< 1 + \frac{2(rad(G)-1)}{\alpha + 2} \\
&< 1 + \frac{diam(G)-1}{\alpha + 2} \\
&< 3.
\end{aligned}
$$

□

Corollary 4. *For $\alpha > 19$, the price of anarchy is less than 3.*

5   Conclusion

In this paper, we study the max-distance network creation game. We use the technique based on the average degree of the biconnected component and also combine the analysis of min cycles. We show that for $\alpha > 19$ there will be a contradiction if there exists a biconnected component in the equilibrium graph. Therefore, every equilibrium graph is a tree for $\alpha > 19$ in the max-distance network creation game and the price of anarchy in this range is a constant. Moreover, we improve the upper bound on the price of anarchy for tree equilibria to 3.

It would be interesting to determine the optimal bound in future work. By saying the optimal bound, we refer to both the minimal unit edge cost α for every equilibrium graph to be a tree, and the tightest constant upper bound on the price of anarchy. It can be seen from our proof that most lemmas only require $\alpha > 2$ or $\alpha > 5$, which implies there is still a lot of room for improvement of these bounds. Another direction of future work is to study how to combine the degree approach and the min-cycle approach to obtain better bounds in the sum-distance network creation game.

References

1. Albers, S., Eilts, S., Even-Dar, E., Mansour, Y., Roditty, L.: On Nash equilibria for a network creation game. ACM Trans. Econ. Comput. (TEAC) **2**(1), 1–27 (2014)
2. Alon, N., Demaine, E.D., Hajiaghayi, M.T., Leighton, T.: Basic network creation games. SIAM J. Discret. Math. **27**(2), 656–668 (2013)
3. Alvarez, C., Messegué, A.: Network creation games: structure vs anarchy. arXiv preprint arXiv:1706.09132 (2017)
4. Àlvarez, C., Messegué, A.: On the price of anarchy for high-price links. In: Caragiannis, I., Mirrokni, V., Nikolova, E. (eds.) WINE 2019. LNCS, vol. 11920, pp. 316–329. Springer, Cham (2019). https://doi.org/10.1007/978-3-030-35389-6_23
5. Andelman, N., Feldman, M., Mansour, Y.: Strong price of anarchy. Games Econom. Behav. **65**(2), 289–317 (2009)
6. Avarikioti, G., Scheuner, R., Wattenhofer, R.: Payment networks as creation games. In: Pérez-Solà, C., Navarro-Arribas, G., Biryukov, A., Garcia-Alfaro, J. (eds.) DPM/CBT -2019. LNCS, vol. 11737, pp. 195–210. Springer, Cham (2019). https://doi.org/10.1007/978-3-030-31500-9_12
7. Avarikioti, Z., Heimbach, L., Wang, Y., Wattenhofer, R.: Ride the lightning: the game theory of payment channels. In: Bonneau, J., Heninger, N. (eds.) FC 2020. LNCS, vol. 12059, pp. 264–283. Springer, Cham (2020). https://doi.org/10.1007/978-3-030-51280-4_15
8. Baumann, N., Stiller, S.: The price of anarchy of a network creation game with exponential payoff. In: Monien, B., Schroeder, U.-P. (eds.) SAGT 2008. LNCS, vol. 4997, pp. 218–229. Springer, Heidelberg (2008). https://doi.org/10.1007/978-3-540-79309-0_20
9. Bilò, D., Gualà, L., Leucci, S., Proietti, G.: The max-distance network creation game on general host graphs. Theor. Comput. Sci. **573**, 43–53 (2015)
10. Bilò, D., Lenzner, P.: On the tree conjecture for the network creation game. Theory of Computing Systems **64**(3), 422–443 (2019). https://doi.org/10.1007/s00224-019-09945-9
11. Chauhan, A., Lenzner, P., Melnichenko, A., Molitor, L.: Selfish network creation with non-uniform edge cost. In: Bilò, V., Flammini, M. (eds.) SAGT 2017. LNCS, vol. 10504, pp. 160–172. Springer, Cham (2017). https://doi.org/10.1007/978-3-319-66700-3_13
12. Chauhan, A., Lenzner, P., Melnichenko, A., Münn, M.: On selfish creation of robust networks. In: Gairing, M., Savani, R. (eds.) SAGT 2016. LNCS, vol. 9928, pp. 141–152. Springer, Heidelberg (2016). https://doi.org/10.1007/978-3-662-53354-3_12
13. Corbo, J., Parkes, D.: The price of selfish behavior in bilateral network formation. In: Proceedings of the Twenty-Fourth Annual ACM Symposium on Principles of Distributed Computing, pp. 99–107 (2005)
14. Cord-Landwehr, A., Hüllmann, M., Kling, P., Setzer, A.: Basic network creation games with communication interests. In: Serna, M. (ed.) SAGT 2012. LNCS, pp. 72–83. Springer, Heidelberg (2012). https://doi.org/10.1007/978-3-642-33996-7_7
15. Demaine, E.D., Hajiaghayi, M., Mahini, H., Zadimoghaddam, M.: The price of anarchy in network creation games. ACM Transactions on Algorithms (TALG) **8**(2), 1–13 (2012)
16. Dippel, J., Vetta, A.: An improved bound for the tree conjecture in network creation games. arXiv preprint arXiv:2106.05175 (2021)
17. Ehsani, S., et al.: A bounded budget network creation game. ACM Trans. Algorithms (TALG) **11**(4), 1–25 (2015)

18. Fabrikant, A., Luthra, A., Maneva, E., Papadimitriou, C.H., Shenker, S.: On a network creation game. In: Proceedings of the Twenty-Second Annual Symposium on Principles of Distributed Computing, pp. 347–351 (2003)
19. Halevi, Y., Mansour, Y.: A network creation game with nonuniform interests. In: Deng, X., Graham, F.C. (eds.) WINE 2007. LNCS, vol. 4858, pp. 287–292. Springer, Heidelberg (2007). https://doi.org/10.1007/978-3-540-77105-0_28
20. Kawald, B., Lenzner, P.: On dynamics in selfish network creation. In: Proceedings of the Twenty-Fifth Annual ACM Symposium on Parallelism in Algorithms and Architectures, pp. 83–92 (2013)
21. Kleinberg, J.: The small-world phenomenon: an algorithmic perspective. In: Proceedings of the Thirty-second Annual ACM Symposium on Theory of Computing, pp. 163–170 (2000)
22. Koutsoupias, E., Papadimitriou, C.: Worst-case equilibria. In: Meinel, C., Tison, S. (eds.) STACS 1999. LNCS, vol. 1563, pp. 404–413. Springer, Heidelberg (1999). https://doi.org/10.1007/3-540-49116-3_38
23. Lenzner, P.: On dynamics in basic network creation games. In: Persiano, G. (ed.) SAGT 2011. LNCS, vol. 6982, pp. 254–265. Springer, Heidelberg (2011). https://doi.org/10.1007/978-3-642-24829-0_23
24. Mamageishvili, A., Mihalák, M., Müller, D.: Tree Nash equilibria in the network creation game. Internet Math. **11**(4–5), 472–486 (2015)
25. Mihalák, M., Schlegel, J.C.: The price of anarchy in network creation games is (mostly) constant. Theor. Comput. Syst. **53**(1), 53–72 (2013). https://doi.org/10.1007/978-3-642-16170-4_24
26. Papadis, N., Tassiulas, L.: Blockchain-based payment channel networks: challenges and recent advances. IEEE Access **8**, 227596–227609 (2020)
27. Watts, D.J.: Networks, dynamics, and the small-world phenomenon. Am. J. Sociol. **105**(2), 493–527 (1999)

On the Impact of Player Capability on Congestion Games

Yichen Yang[(⊠)], Kai Jia[(⊠)], and Martin Rinard[(⊠)]

Department of Electrical Engineering and Computer Science,
Massachusetts Institute of Technology, Cambridge, USA
{yicheny,jiakai,rinard}@csail.mit.edu

Abstract. We study the impact of player capability on social welfare in congestion games. We introduce a new game, the ***D***istance-bounded ***N****etwork* ***C****ongestion game (DNC)*, as the basis of our study. DNC is a symmetric network congestion game with a bound on the number of edges each player can use. We show that DNC is PLS-complete in contrast to standard symmetric network congestion games which are in P. To model different player capabilities, we propose using programs in a Domain-Specific Language (DSL) to compactly represent player strategies. We define a player's capability as the maximum size of the programs they can use. We introduce two variants of DNC with accompanying DSLs representing the strategy spaces. We propose four *capability preference* properties to characterize the impact of player capability on social welfare at equilibrium. We then establish necessary and sufficient conditions for the four properties in the context of our DNC variants. Finally, we study a specific game where we derive exact expressions of the social welfare in terms of the capability bound. This provides examples where the social welfare at equilibrium increases, stays the same, or decreases as players become more capable.

Keywords: Congestion game · Player capability · Social welfare

1 Introduction

Varying player capabilities can significantly affect the outcomes of strategic games. Developing a comprehensive understanding of how different player capabilities affect the dynamics and overall outcomes of strategic games is therefore an important long-term research goal in the field. Central questions include characterizing, and ideally precisely quantifying, player capabilities, then characterizing, and ideally precisely quantifying, how these different player capabilities interact with different game characteristics to influence or even fully determine individual and/or group dynamics and outcomes.

We anticipate a range of mechanisms for characterizing player capabilities, from simple numerical parameters through to complex specifications of available player behavior. Here we use programs in a domain-specific language (DSL) to

Y. Yang and K. Jia—Equal contribution.

© The Author(s), under exclusive license to Springer Nature Switzerland AG 2022
P. Kanellopoulos et al. (Eds.): SAGT 2022, LNCS 13584, pp. 311–328, 2022.
https://doi.org/10.1007/978-3-031-15714-1_18

compactly represent player strategies. Bounding the sizes of the programs available to the players creates a natural capability hierarchy, with more capable players able to deploy more diverse strategies defined by larger programs. Building on this foundation, we study the effect of increasing or decreasing player capabilities on game outcomes such as social welfare at equilibrium. To the best of our knowledge, this paper presents the first systematic analysis of the effect of different player capabilities on the outcomes of strategic games.

We focus on network congestion games [8,23]. All congestion games have pure Nash equilibria (PNEs) [19,22]. Congestion games have been applied in many areas including drug design [18], load balancing [27], and network design [14]. There is a rich literature on different aspects of congestion games including their computational characteristics [1], efficiency of equilibria [7], and variants such as weighted congestion games [6] or games with unreliable resources [17].

We propose a new network congestion game, the **D**istance-bounded **N**etwork **C**ongestion game (DNC), as the basis of our study. A network congestion game consists of some players and a directed graph where each edge is associated with a delay function. The goal of each player is to plan a path that minimizes the delay from a source vertex to a sink vertex. The delay of a path is the sum of the delays on the edges in the path, with the delay on each edge depending (only) on the number of players choosing the edge. The game is symmetric when all players share the same source and sink. Fabrikant et al. [8] shows that finding a PNE is in P for symmetric games but PLS-complete for asymmetric ones. DNC is a symmetric network congestion game in which each player is subject to a *distance bound*—i.e., a bound on the number of edges that a player can use.

We establish hardness results for DNC. We show that with the newly introduced distance bound, our symmetric network congestion game becomes PLS-complete. We also show that computing the best or worst social welfare among PNEs of DNC is NP-hard.

We then present two games for which we define compact DSLs for player strategies. The first game is a DNC variant with **D**efault **A**ction (DNCDA). In this game, each node has a default outgoing edge that does not count towards the distance bound. Hence a strategy can be compactly represented by specifying only the non-default choices. We establish that DNCDA is as hard as DNC. The other game is Gold and Mines Game (GMG), where there are gold and mine sites placed on parallel horizontal lines, and a player uses a program to compactly describe the line that they choose at each horizontal location. We show that GMG is a special form of DNCDA.

We propose four *capability preference* properties that characterize the impact of player capability on social welfare. In this paper, we only consider social welfare of pure Nash equilibria. We call a game *capability-positive* (resp. *capability-negative*) if social welfare does not decrease (resp. increase) when players become more capable. A game is *max-capability-preferred* (resp. *min-capability-preferred*) if the worst social welfare when players have maximal (resp. minimal) capability is at least as good as any social welfare when players have less (resp. more) capability. Note that max-capability-preferred (resp. min-capability-preferred) is a weaker property than capability-positive (resp. capability-negative). Due to the hardness of DNCDA, we analyze a restricted version (DNCDAS) where all edges share the same delay function. We identify necessary and sufficient conditions on the delay function for each capability preference property to hold universally for all configurations in the context of DNCDAS and GMG (Table 1).

Finally, we study a specific version of GMG where we derive exact expressions of the social welfare in terms of the capability bound and payoff function parameterization. We present examples where the social welfare at equilibrium increases, stays the same, or decreases as players become more capable.

Summary of Contributions

- We present a framework for quantifying varying player capabilities and studying how different player capabilities affect the dynamics and outcome of strategic games. In this framework, player strategies are represented as programs in a DSL, with player capability defined as the maximal size of available programs.
- We propose four *capability preference* properties to characterize the impact of player capability on social welfare of pure Nash equilibria: *capability-positive*, *max-capability-preferred*, *capability-negative*, and *min-capability-preferred*.
- We introduce the *distance-bounded network congestion game (DNC)*, a new symmetric network congestion game in which players can only choose paths with a bounded number of edges. We further show that DNC is PLS-complete. Moreover, computing the best or worst social welfare among equilibria of DNC is NP-hard.
- We introduce two variants of DNC, DNC with default action (DNCDA) and Gold and Mines Game (GMG), with accompanying DSLs to compactly represent player strategies. We then establish necessary and sufficient conditions for the capability preference properties in DNCDAS and GMG.
- We study a special version of GMG where we fully characterize the social welfare at equilibrium. This characterization provides insights into the factors that affect whether increasing player capability is beneficial or not.

Additional Related Work. There has been research exploring the results of representing player strategies using formal computational models. Tennenholtz [25] proposes using programs to represent player strategies and analyzes program equilibrium in a finite two-player game. Fortnow [9] extends the results, representing strategies as Turing machines. Another line of research uses various kinds of automata to model a player's strategy in non-congestion games [3], such as repeated prisoner's dilemma [20,24]. Automata are typically used to model bounded rationality [15,21] or certain learning behavior [5,11]. Neyman [16] presents asymptotic results on equilibrium payoff in repeated normal-form games when automaton sizes meet certain conditions. There has also been research exploring structural strategy spaces in congestion games. Ackermann and Skopalik [2] considers a player-specific network congestion game where each player has a set of forbidden edges. Chan and Jiang [4] studies computing mixed

Nash equilibria in a broad class of congestion games with strategy spaces compactly described by a set of linear constraints. Unlike our research, none of the above research defines a hierarchy of player capabilities or characterizes the effect of the hierarchy on game outcomes.

2   Distance-Bounded Network Congestion Game

It is well-known that computing PNEs in symmetric network congestion games belongs to P while the asymmetric version is PLS-complete [8]. We present a symmetric network congestion game where we limit the number of edges that a player can use. We show that this restriction makes the problem harder—the new game is PLS-complete, and finding the best or worst Nash equilibrium in terms of global social welfare is NP-hard.

Definition 1. *An instance of the **D**istance-bounded **N**etwork **C**ongestion game* (DNC) *is a tuple* $G = (\mathcal{V}, \mathcal{E}, \mathcal{N}, s, t, b, (d_e)_{e \in \mathcal{E}})$ *where:*

- $\mathcal{V}$ *is the set of vertices in the network.*
- $\mathcal{E} \subset \mathcal{V} \times \mathcal{V}$ *is the set of edges in the network.*
- $\mathcal{N} = \{1, \ldots, n\}$ *is the set of players.*
- $s \in \mathcal{V}$ *is the source vertex shared by all players.*
- $t \in \mathcal{V}$ *is the sink vertex shared by all players.*
- $b \in \mathbb{N}$ *is the bound of the path length.*
- $d_e : \mathbb{N} \mapsto \mathbb{R}$ *is a non-decreasing delay function on edge* e.

We also require that the network has no negative-delay cycles, i.e., for each cycle $\mathcal{C}$, *we require* $\sum_{e \in \mathcal{C}} \min_{i \in \mathcal{N}} d_e(i) = \sum_{e \in \mathcal{C}} d_e(1) \geq 0$.
We only consider pure strategies (i.e., deterministic strategies) in this paper. The strategy space of a single player contains all $s - t$ *simple paths whose length does not exceed* b:

$$\mathcal{L}_b \overset{def}{=} \left\{ (p_0, \ldots, p_k) \ \middle| \ \begin{array}{l} p_0 = s, \ p_k = t, \ (p_i, p_{i+1}) \in \mathcal{E}, k \leq b, \\ p_i \neq p_j \text{ for } i \neq j \end{array} \right\}$$

In a DNC, as in a general congestion game, a player's goal is to minimize their delay. Let $s_i \overset{def}{=} (p_{i0}, \cdots, p_{ik_i}) \in \mathcal{L}_b$ denote the strategy of player i where $i \in \mathcal{N}$. A *strategy profile* $\boldsymbol{s} = (s_1, \ldots, s_n) \in \mathcal{L}_b^n$ consists of strategies of all players. Let $E_i \overset{def}{=} \{(p_{ij}, p_{i,j+1}) \mid 0 \leq j < k_i\}$ denote the corresponding set of edges on the path chosen by player i. The *load* on an edge $e \in \mathcal{E}$ is defined as the number of players that occupy this edge: $x_e \overset{def}{=} |\{i \mid e \in E_i\}|$. The delay experienced by player i is $c_i(\boldsymbol{s}) \overset{def}{=} \sum_{e \in E_i} d_e(x_e)$. A strategy profile $\boldsymbol{s}$ is a *pure Nash equilibrium (PNE)* if no player can improve their delay by unilaterally changing strategy, i.e., $\forall i \in \mathcal{N} : c_i(\boldsymbol{s}) = \min_{s' \in \mathcal{L}_b} c_i(\boldsymbol{s}_{-i}, s')$. All players experience infinite delay if the distance bound permits no feasible solution (i.e., when $\mathcal{L}_b = \emptyset$). *Social welfare* is defined as the negative total delay of all players where a larger welfare value means on average players experience less delay: $W(\boldsymbol{s}) \overset{def}{=} - \sum_{i \in \mathcal{N}} c_i(\boldsymbol{s})$.
We now present a few hardness results about DNC.

Lemma 1. *DNC belongs to* PLS.

Proof. DNC is a potential game where local minima of its potential function correspond to PNEs [22]. Clearly there are polynomial algorithms for finding a feasible solution or evaluating the potential function. We only need to show that computing the best response of some player i given the strategies of others is in P. For each $v \in \mathcal{V}$, we define $f(v, d)$ to be the minimal delay experienced by player i over all paths from s to v with length bound d. It can be recursively computed via $f(v, d) = \min_{u \in \mathcal{V}:(u, v) \in \mathcal{E}} (f(u, d - 1) + d_{(u, v)}(x_{(u, v)} + 1))$ where $x_{(u, v)}$ is the load on edge (u, v) caused by other players. The best response of player i is then $f(t, b)$. If there are cycles in the solution, we can remove them without affecting the total delay because cycles must have zero delay in the best response. □

Theorem 1. *DNC is* PLS-*complete.*

Proof. We have shown that DNC belongs to PLS. Now we present a PLS-reduction from a PLS-complete game to finish the proof.

The *quadratic threshold game* [1] is a PLS-complete game in which there are n players and $n(n + 1)/2$ resources. The resources are divided into two sets $\mathcal{R}^{\text{in}} = \{r_{ij} \mid 1 \leq i < j \leq n\}$ for all unordered pairs of players $\{i, j\}$ and $\mathcal{R}^{\text{out}} = \{r_i \mid i \in \mathcal{N}\}$. For ease of exposition, we use r_{ij} and r_{ji} to denote the same resource. Player i has two strategies: $S_i^{\text{in}} = \{r_{ij} \mid j \in \mathcal{N}/\{i\}\}$ and $S_i^{\text{out}} = \{r_i\}$.

Extending the idea in Ackermann et al. [1], we reduce from the quadratic threshold game to DNC. To simplify our presentation, we assign positive integer weights to edges. Each weighted edge can be replaced by a chain of unit-length edges to obtain an unweighted graph.

Figure 1 illustrates the game with four players. We create $n(n+1)/2$ vertices arranged as a lower triangle. We use v_{ij} to denote the vertex at the ith row (starting from top) and j^{th} column (starting from left) where $1 \leq j \leq i \leq n$. The vertex v_{ij} is connected to $v_{i,j+1}$ with an edge of length i when $j < i$ and to $v_{i+1,j}$ with a unit-length edge when $i < n$. This design ensures that the shortest path from v_{i1} to v_{ni} is the right-down path. The resource r_{ij} is placed at the off-diagonal vertex v_{ij}, which can be implemented by splitting the vertex into two vertices connected by a unit-length edge with the delay function of r_{ij}. Note that this implies visiting a vertex v_{ij} incurs a distance of 1 where $i \neq j$. We then create vertices s_i and t_i for $1 \leq i \leq n$ with unit-length edges (s_i, v_{i1}) and (v_{ni}, t_i). We connect s_i to t_i with an edge of length w_i, which represents the resource r_i. Let b be the distance bound. We will determine the values of w_i and b later. The source s is connected to s_i with an edge of length $b - w_i - 1$. Vertices t_i are connected to the sink t via unit-length edges.

We define the following delay functions for edges associated with s or t:

$$d_{(s, s_i)}(x) = \mathbb{1}_{x \geq 2} \cdot (|\mathcal{N}| + 1)R \qquad d_{(t_i, t)}(x) = (|\mathcal{N}| - i)R$$

$$\text{where } R = \left(\sum_{r \in \mathcal{R}^{\text{in}} \cup \mathcal{R}^{\text{out}}} \max_{i \in \mathcal{N}} d_r(i) \right) + 1$$

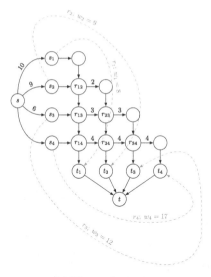
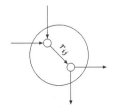

(a) The graph structure   (b) Splitting the vertex containing
                                           resource r_{ij}

Fig. 1. The DNC instance corresponding to a four-player quadratic threshold game. The distance bound $b = 19$. Non-unit-length edges have labels to indicate their lengths. Dashed gray edges correspond to the S_i^{out} strategies.

We argue that player i chooses edges (s, s_i) and (t_i, t) in their best responses. Since R is greater than the maximum possible sum of delays of resources in the threshold game, a player's best response must first optimize their choice of edges linked to s or t. If two players choose the edge (s, s_i), one of them can improve their latency by changing to an unoccupied edge $(s, s_{i'})$. Therefore, we can assume the ith player chooses edge (s, s_i) WLOG. Player i can also decrease their latency by switching from (t_j, t) to (t_{j+1}, t) for any $j < i$ unless their strategy is limited by the distance bound when $j = i$.

Player i now has only two strategies from s_i to t_i due to the distance bound, corresponding to their strategies in the threshold game: (i) following the right-down path, namely $(s_i, v_{i1}, \cdots, v_{ii}, v_{i+1,i}, \cdots, v_{ni}, t_i)$, where they occupy resources corresponding to S_i^{in} (ii) using the edge (s_i, t_i), where they occupy the resource $S_i^{\text{out}} = \{r_i\}$. Clearly PNEs in this DNC correspond to PNEs in the original quadratic threshold game.

Now we determine the values of w_i and b. The shortest paths from s_i to t_i should be either the right-down path or the edge (s_i, t_i). This implies that $w_i = a_i + b_i + c_i$ where $a_i = i(i-1) + 1$ is the total length of horizontal edges, $b_i = n + 1 - i$ is the total length of vertical edges, and $c_i = n - 1$ is the total length of edges inside v_{ij} for resources r_{ij}. Hence $w_i = i(i-2) + 2n + 1$. The bound b should accommodate player n who has the longest path and is set as $b = w_n + 2 = n^2 + 3$.

Theorem 2. *Computing the best social welfare (i.e., minimal total delay) among PNEs of a DNC is NP-hard.*

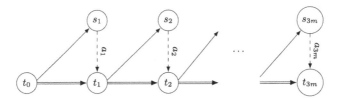

Fig. 2. Illustration of the DNC instance corresponding to a 3-partition problem. Double-line edges are slow edges, dashed edges are fast edges, and other edges have no delay. Non-unit-length edges have labels to indicate their lengths. Deciding whether the total delay can be bounded by $6m - 3$ is NP-complete.

Proof. We reduce from the strongly NP-complete 3-partition problem [10].

In the *3-partition problem*, we are given a multiset of $3m$ positive integers $S = \{a_i \in \mathbb{Z}^+ \mid 1 \leq i \leq 3m\}$ and a number T such that $\sum a_i = mT$ and $T/4 < a_i < T/2$. The question Q_1 is: Can S be partitioned into m sets $S_1, \cdots, S_m$ such that $\sum_{a_i \in S_j} a_i = T$ for all $1 \leq j \leq m$? Note that due to the strong NP-completeness of 3-partition, we assume the numbers use unary encoding so that the DNC graph size is polynomial.

As in the proof of Theorem 1, we assign a weight $w_e \in \mathbb{Z}^+$ to each edge e. The DNC instance has two types of edges with non-zero delay: fast edge and slow edge, with delay functions $d_{\text{fast}}(x) = \mathbb{1}_{x \geq 1} + 2\mathbb{1}_{x \geq 2}$ and $d_{\text{slow}}(x) = 2$.

As illustrated in Fig. 2, for each integer a_i, we create a pair of vertices (s_i, t_i) connected by a fast edge with $w_{(s_i, t_i)} = a_i$. We create a new vertex t_0 as the source while using t_{3m} as the sink. For $0 \leq i < 3m$, we connect t_i to t_{i+1} by a unit-length slow edge and t_i to s_{i+1} by a unit-length edge without delay. There are m players who can choose paths with length bounded by $b = T + 3m$.

We ask the question Q_2: Is there a PNE in the above game where the total delay is no more than $m(6m-3)$? Each player prefers an unoccupied fast edge to a slow edge but also prefers a slow edge to an occupied fast edge due to the above delay functions. Since $T/4 < a_i < T/2$, the best response of a player contains either 2 or 3 fast edges, contributing $6m - 2$ or $6m - 3$ to the total delay in either case. Best social welfare of $m(6m - 3)$ is only achieved when every player chooses 3 fast edges, which also means that their choices together constitute a partition of the integer set S in Q_1. Therefore, Q_2 and Q_1 have the same answer.

Remark. The optimal global welfare of any "centralized" solution (where players cooperate to minimize total delay instead of selfishly minimizing their own delay) achieves $m(6m - 3)$ if and only if the original 3-partition problem has a solution. Hence we also have the following theorem:

Theorem 3. *Computing the optimal global welfare of pure strategies in DNC is* NP-*hard.*

Theorem 4. *Computing the worst social welfare (i.e., maximal total delay) among PNEs of a DNC is* NP-*hard.*

Proof. We build on the proof of Theorem 2. We create a new vertex s as the source and connect s to t_0 and s_i where $1 \leq i \leq 3m$:

$$w_{(s,t_0)} = 1 \qquad\qquad d_{(s,t_0)}(x) = \mathbb{1}_{x \geq m+1} \cdot R$$
$$w_{(s,s_i)} = T + i - a_i + 1 \quad d_{(s,s_i)}(x) = \mathbb{1}_{x \geq 2} \cdot R \qquad \text{where } R = 9m + 2$$

The delay functions on fast and slow edges are changed to $d_{\text{fast}}(x) = 2\mathbb{1}_{x \geq 2} + 2\mathbb{1}_{x \geq 3}$ and $d_{\text{slow}}(x) = 3$.

There are $4m$ players in this game with a distance bound $b = T + 3m + 1$. Since R is greater than the delay on any path from s_i or t_0 to the sink, we can assume WLOG that player i choose (s, s_i) where $1 \leq i \leq 3m$, and players $3m+1, \cdots, 4m$ all choose (s, t_0). The first $3m$ players generate a total delay of $D_0 = d_{\text{slow}} \cdot 3m(3m-1)/2 = 9m(3m-1)/2$ where player i occupies one fast edge and $3m-i$ slow edges. Each of the last m players occupies 2 or 3 fast edges in their best response. Occupying one fast edge incurs 4 total delay because one of the first $3m$ players also uses that edge. Therefore, the each of last m players contributes $9m+2$ or $9m+3$ to the total delay. We ask the question Q_3: Is there a PNE where the total delay is at least $D_0 + m(9m+3)$? From our analysis, we can see that Q_3 and Q_1 have the same answer.

2.1   Distance-Bounded Network Congestion Game with Default Action

As we have discussed, we formulate capability restriction as limiting the size of the programs accessible to a player. In this section, we propose a variant of DNC where we define a DSL to compactly represent the strategies. We will also show that the size of a program equals the length of the path generated by the program, which can be much smaller than the number of edges in the path. The new game, called *distance-bounded network congestion game with default action* (DncDa), requires that each vertex except the source or sink has exactly one outgoing zero-length edge as its default action. All other edges have unit length. A strategy in this game can be compactly described by the actions taken at *divergent points* where a unit-length edge is followed.

Definition 2. *An instance of* DncDa *is a tuple* $G = (\mathcal{V}, \mathcal{E}, \mathcal{N}, s, t, b, (d_e)_{e \in \mathcal{E}}, (w_e)_{e \in \mathcal{E}})$ *where:*

- $w_e \in \{0, 1\}$ *is the length of edge* e.
- *All other symbols have the same meaning as in Definition 1.*

Moreover, we require the following properties:

- *A default action, denoted as* DA($\cdot$), *can be defined for every non-source, non-sink vertex* $v \in \mathcal{V}/\{s, t\}$ *such that:*

$$\left(v, \text{DA}(v)\right) \in \mathcal{E}, \quad w_{(v, \text{DA}(v))} = 0,$$
$$\forall u \in \mathcal{V}/\{\text{DA}(v)\} : (v, u) \in \mathcal{E} \implies w_{(v,u)} = 1$$

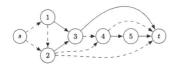

```
if (u == s) { return 2; } else {
    if (u == 3) { return 4; } else {
        return DA(u);
    }
}
```

(a) Example graph structure. Solid arrows are default edges and dashed arrows are unit-length edges.

(b) The shortest program to represent the strategy $(s, 2, 3, 4, 5, t)$.

Fig. 3. An example of the DNCDA game and a program to represent a strategy.

- *Edges from the source have unit length:* $\forall v \in \mathcal{V} : (s, v) \in \mathcal{E} \implies w_{(s, v)} = 1$
- *The subgraph of zero-length edges is acyclic. Equivalently, starting from any non-source vertex, one can follow the default actions to reach the sink.*

The strategy space of a single player contains all $s - t$ simple paths whose length does not exceed b:

$$\mathcal{L}_b \stackrel{def}{=} \left\{ (p_0, \ldots, p_k) \,\middle|\, \begin{array}{l} p_0 = s, \ p_k = t, \ (p_i, p_{i+1}) \in \mathcal{E}, \sum_{i=0}^{k-1} w_{(p_i, p_{i+1})} \le b, \\ p_i \ne p_j \ for \ i \ne j \end{array} \right\}$$

Note that the strategy spaces are strictly monotonically increasing up to the longest simple $s-t$ path. This is because for any path p whose length is $b \ge 2$, we can remove the last non-zero edge on p and follow the default actions to arrive at t, which gives a new path with length $b - 1$. Formally, we have:

Property 1. Let $\bar{b}$ be the length of the longest simple $s - t$ path in a DNCDA instance. For $1 \le b < \bar{b}$, $\mathcal{L}_b \subsetneq \mathcal{L}_{b+1}$

We define a Domain Specific Language (DSL) with the following context-free grammar [12] to describe the strategy of a player:

```
Program  →   return DA(u);
         |   if (u == V) {return V;} else {Program}
      V  →   v ∈ V
```

A program p in this DSL defines a computable function $f_p : \mathcal{V} \mapsto \mathcal{V}$ with semantics similar to the C language where the input vertex is stored in the variable u, as illustrated in Fig. 3. The strategy corresponding to the program p is a path $(c_0, \ldots, c_k)$ from s to t where:

$$c_0 = s \qquad c_{i+1} = f_p(c_i) \ for \ i \ge 0 \ and \ c_i \ne t \qquad k = i \ if \ c_i = t$$

We define the capability of a player as the maximum size of programs that they can use. The size of a program is the depth of its parse tree. Due to the properties of DNCDA, the shortest program that encodes a path from s to t specifies the edge chosen at all divergent points in this path. The size of this program equals the length of the path. Hence the distance bound in the game configuration specifies the capability of each player in the game. To study the game outcome under different player capability constraints, we study DNCDA instances with different values of b.

We state hardness results for DNCDA. Their proofs are similar to those for DNC except that we need to redesign the edge weights to incorporate default action. The proofs are given in the full version of this paper [26].

Theorem 5. DNCDA *is PLS-complete.*

Theorem 6. *Computing the best social welfare (i.e., minimal total delay) among PNEs of a* DNCDA *is NP-hard.*

Theorem 7. *Computing the worst social welfare (i.e., maximal total delay) among PNEs of a* DNCDA *is NP-hard.*

Theorem 8. *Computing the optimal global welfare of pure strategies in* DNCDA *is NP-hard.*

3   Impact of Player Capability on Social Welfare in DNCDA

We first introduce four capability preference properties for general games. Given a game with a finite hierarchy of player capabilities, we use $\mathcal{L}_b$ to denote the strategy space when player capability is bounded by b. Assuming the maximal capability is $\bar{b}$ (which is the longest $s - t$ simple path in DNCDA), we have $\mathcal{L}_b \subsetneq \mathcal{L}_{b+1}$ for $1 \leq b < \bar{b}$ (see Property 1). We use Equil$(b) \subseteq \mathcal{L}_b^n$ to denote the set of all PNEs at the capability level b. We define $W_b^+ \overset{\text{def}}{=} \max_{s \in \text{Equil}(b)} W(s)$ to be the best social welfare at equilibrium and $W_b^- \overset{\text{def}}{=} \min_{s \in \text{Equil}(b)} W(s)$ the worst social welfare.

Definition 3. *A game is capability-positive if social welfare at equilibrium cannot decrease as players become more capable, i.e.,* $\forall 1 \leq b < \bar{b}$, $W_b^+ \leq W_{b+1}^-$.

Definition 4. *A game is max-capability-preferred if the worst social welfare at equilibrium under maximal player capability is at least as good as any social welfare at equilibrium under lower player capability, i.e.,* $\forall 1 \leq b < \bar{b}$, $W_b^+ \leq W_{\bar{b}}^-$.

Note that max-capability-preferred is a weaker condition than capability-positive. We then define analogous properties for games where less capable players lead to better outcomes:

Definition 5. *A game is capability-negative if social welfare at equilibrium cannot increase as players become more capable, i.e.,* $\forall 1 \leq b < \bar{b}$, $W_{b+1}^+ \leq W_b^-$.

Definition 6. *A game is min-capability-preferred if the worst social welfare at equilibrium under minimal player capability is at least as good as any social welfare at equilibrium under higher player capability, i.e.,* $\forall b \geq 2$, $W_b^+ \leq W_1^-$.

Our goal is to identify games that guarantee these properties. Since solving equilibria for general DNCDA is computationally hard (Sect. 2.1), we focus on a restricted version of DNCDA where all edges share the same delay function; formally, we consider the case $\forall e \in \mathcal{E} : d_e(\cdot) = d(\cdot)$ where $d(\cdot)$ is non-negative and non-decreasing. We call this game *distance-bounded network congestion game with default action and shared delay (*DNCDAS*).* We aim to find conditions on $d(\cdot)$ under which the properties hold *universally* (i.e., for all network configurations of DNCDAS). Table 1 summarizes the results.

Table 1. Necessary and sufficient conditions on the delay or payoff functions such that the capability preference properties hold universally.

	DNCDAS (Sect. 3)	GMG (Sects. 4 and 5)
Resource layout	On a directed graph	On parallel horizontal lines
Strategy space	Paths from s to t	Piecewise-constant functions
Delay (payoff)	Non-negative non-decreasing	$r_g(\cdot)$ positive, $r_m(\cdot)$ negative
capability-positive	$d(\cdot)$ is a constant function	$r_g(\cdot), r_m(\cdot)$ are constant functions
max-capability-preferred	$d(\cdot)$ is a constant function	$w(x) = xr_g(x)$ attains maximum at $x = n$
capability-negative	$d(\cdot)$ is the zero function	Never
min-capability-preferred	$d(\cdot)$ is the zero function	Never

Theorem 9. DNCDAS *is universally capability-positive if and only if $d(\cdot)$ is a constant function.*

Proof. If $d(\cdot)$ is a constant function, the total delay achieved by a strategy is not affected by the load condition of each edge (thus not affected by other players' strategies). So each player's strategy in any PNE is the one in $\mathcal{L}_b$ that minimizes the total delay under the game layout. Denote this minimum delay as $\delta(b)$. For any $b \geq 1$, we have $\mathcal{L}_b \subseteq \mathcal{L}_{b+1}$, so $\delta(b) \geq \delta(b+1)$. And for any $s \in \text{Equil}(b)$, $W(s) = -n\delta(b)$. Hence $W_b^+ \leq W_{b+1}^-$.

If $d(\cdot)$ is not a constant function, we show that there exists an instance of DNCDAS with delay function $d(\cdot)$ that is not capability-positive. Define $v = \min\{x \mid d(x) \neq d(x+1)\}$. It follows that $d(v') = d(v)$ for all $v' \leq v$. We consider the cases $d(v) = 0$ and $d(v) > 0$ separately.

Case 1: $d(v) > 0$ Denote $\rho = \frac{d(v+1)}{d(v)}$. Since $d(\cdot)$ is non-decreasing, $\rho > 1$. We construct a game with the network layout in Fig. 4a with $n = v+1$ players. We will show that $W_1^+ > W_2^-$.

First, it is easy to see that the PNEs when $b = 1$ are a players take the upper path and $v + 1 - a$ players take the lower path, where $1 \leq a \leq v$. All PNEs achieves a social welfare of $W_1 = -(v+1)(N_1 + N_2 + 3)d(v)$.

We set $N_1 = \lfloor \frac{1}{\rho-1} \rfloor$ and $N_2 = \lfloor (N_1 + 2)\rho \rfloor - 1$. When $b = 2$, one PNE is that all players choose the path from upper left to lower right using the crossing edge in the middle due to our choice of N_1 and N_2. Its social welfare $W_2 = -(v+1)(2N_1+3)d(v+1)$. One can check that $W_1 > W_2$, hence $W_1^+ > W_2^-$.

Case 2: $d(v) = 0$ We construct a game with the network layout in Fig. 4b where there are $2v$ players. With $b = 1$, half of the players choose the upper path and the others choose the lower path, which has a social welfare $W_1 = 0$. With $b = 2$, a PNE is: (i) v players take the path $(s, N_1$ edges, lower right N_2 edges, $t)$

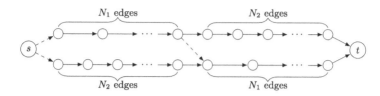

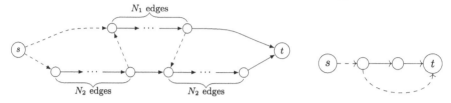

(b) Counterexample for capability-positive in the case $d(v) = 0$. Edges between filled nodes have non-zero delay in an equilibrium when $b = 2$.

(c)   Counterexample   for capability-negative.

Fig. 4. Counterexamples when $d(\cdot)$ does not meet the conditions. Dashed arrows denote unit-length edges and solid arrows denote zero-length edges (default action). Every edge shares the same delay function $d(\cdot)$.

(ii) the other v players take the path (s, lower left N_2 edges, N_1 edges, t). We choose N_1 and N_2 to be positive integers that satisfy $\frac{N_2+1}{N_1} > \frac{d(2v)}{d(v+1)}$. The social welfare $W_2 = -2vN_1d(2v) < W_1$. Hence $W_1^+ > W_2^-$.

Remark. The proof for the sufficient condition also holds when different edges have different delay functions. So the following statement is also true: DNCDA is universally capability-positive if all edges have constant delay functions.

Theorem 10. DNCDAS *is universally max-capability-preferred if and only if* $d(\cdot)$ *is a constant function.*

Proof. The "if" part follows from Theorem 9 since a capability-positive game is also max-capability-preferred. The constructed games in the proof of Theorem 9 also serve as the counterexamples to prove the "only if" part.

Theorem 11. DNCDAS *is universally capability-negative if and only if* $d(\cdot)$ *is the zero function.*

Proof. If $d(\cdot) = 0$, then all PNEs have welfare 0, which implies capability-negative. If $d(\cdot)$ is not the zero function, denote $v = \min\{x \mid d(x) \neq 0\}$. We construct a game with the network layout shown in Fig. 4c with $n = v$ players. When $b = 1$, all players use the only strategy with a social welfare $W_1 = -3vd(v)$. When $b = 2$: if $v = 1$, the player will choose both dashed paths and achieves $W_2 = -2d(1)$; if $v \geq 2$, the players will only experience delay on the first edge by splitting between the default path and the shortcut dashed path, which achieves a welfare $W_2 = -vd(v)$. In both cases, the game is not capability-negative since $W_1^- \leq W_1 < W_2 \leq W_2^+$.

The same argument can also be used to prove the following result:

Theorem 12. DNCDAS *is universally min-capability-preferred if and only if* $d(\cdot)$ *is the zero function.*

4   Gold and Mines Game

In this section, we introduce a particular form of DNCDA called Gold and Mines Game (GMG). It provides a new perspective on how to define the strategy space hierarchy in congestion games. It also enables us to obtain additional characterizations of how social welfare at equilibrium varies with player capability. Intuitively, as shown in Fig. 5, a GMG instance consists of a few parallel horizontal lines and two types of resources: gold and mine. Resources are placed at distinct horizontal locations on the lines. A player's strategy is a piecewise-constant function to cover a subset of resources. The function is specified by a program using if-statements.

Definition 7. *An instance of GMG is a tuple* $G = (\mathcal{E}, K, \mathcal{N}, r_g, r_m, b)$ *where:*

- $\mathcal{E}$ *is the set of resources. Each resource* $e \in \mathcal{E}$ *is described by a tuple* (x_e, y_e, α_e), *where* (x_e, y_e) *denotes the position of the resource in the x-y plane, and* $\alpha_e \in \{gold, mine\}$ *denotes the type of the resource. Each resource has a distinct value of x, i.e.* $x_e \neq x_{e'}$ *for all* $e \neq e'$.
- $K \in \mathbb{N}$ *is the number of lines the resources can reside on. All resources are located on lines* $y = 0$, $y = 1$, ..., $y = K - 1$, *i.e.* $\forall e, y_e \in \{0, 1, \ldots, K - 1\}$.
- $\mathcal{N} = \{1, \ldots, n\}$ *denotes the set of players.*
- $r_g : \mathbb{N} \mapsto \mathbb{R}^+$ *is the payoff function for gold.* r_g *is a positive function.*
- $r_m : \mathbb{N} \mapsto \mathbb{R}^-$ *is the payoff function for mine.* r_m *is a negative function.*
- $b \in \mathbb{N}$ *is the level in the strategy space hierarchy defined by the domain-specific language* $\mathcal{L}$ *(defined below). The strategy space is then* $\mathcal{L}_b$.

The strategy s_i of player i is represented by a function $f_i(\cdot)$ that conforms to a domain-specific language $\mathcal{L}$ with the following grammar:

```
Program  →  return C;  |  if (x < t) {return C;}  else  {Program}
C        →  0  |  1  |  ...  |  K - 1
t        ∈  ℝ
```

This DSL defines a natural strategy space hierarchy by restricting the number of if-statements in the program. A program with $b - 1$ if-statements represents a piecewise-constant function with at most b segments. We denote $\mathcal{L}_b$ as the level b strategy space which includes functions with at most $b - 1$ if-statements.

Player i *covers* the resources that their function f_i passes: $E_i = \{e \mid f_i(x_e) = y_e\}$. The load on each resource is the number of players that covers it: $x_e = |\{i \mid e \in E_i\}|$. Each player's payoff is $u_i = \sum_{e \in E_i} r_e(x_e)$, where r_e is either r_g or r_m depending on the resource type. The social welfare is $W(s) = \sum_{i \in \mathcal{N}} u_i$.

Note that GMG can be represented as a DNCDA (details available in the full version of this paper [26]). As a result, the problem of computing a PNE in a GMG belongs to **PLS**.

5 Impact of Player Capability on Social Welfare in GMG

We revisit the question of how player capability affects the social welfare at equilibrium in the context of GMG. We consider the same capability preference properties as in Sect. 3. The results are summarized in Table 1.

Theorem 13. *GMG is universally capability-positive if and only if both $r_g(\cdot)$ and $r_m(\cdot)$ are constant functions.*

The idea of the proof is similar to that of Theorem 9. The construction of the counterexamples for the "only if" part requires some careful design on the resource layout. The proof is presented in the full version of this paper [26].

Theorem 14. *Define welfare function for gold as $w_g(x) \stackrel{def}{=} x \cdot r_g(x)$. GMG is universally max-capability-preferred if and only if w_g attains its maximum at $x = n$ (i.e. $\max_{x \le n} w_g(x) = w_g(n)$), where n is the number of players.*

Proof. We first notice that there is only one PNE when $b = \bar{b}$, which is all players cover all gold and no mines. This is because r_g is a positive function and r_m is a negative function, and since all x_e's are distinct, each player can cover an arbitrary subset of the resources when $b = \bar{b}$. So $W_{\bar{b}} = nM_g r_g(n)$ where M_g is the number of gold in the game.

If $\max_{x \le n} w_g(x) = w_g(n)$, we show that $W_{\bar{b}}$ is actually the maximum social welfare over all possible strategy profiles of the game. For any strategy profile s of the game, the social welfare

$$W(s) = \sum_{i \in \mathcal{N}} \sum_{e \in E_i} r_e(x_e) = \sum_{e \in \mathcal{E}} x_e \cdot r_e(x_e) \le \sum_{e \in \mathcal{E}_g} n \cdot r_g(n) = nM_g r_g(n) = W_{\bar{b}}.$$

Therefore, the game is max-capability-preferred.

If $\max_{x \le n} w_g(x) > w_g(n)$, denote $n' = \arg\max_{x \le n} w_g(x)$, $n' < n$. We construct a game with the corresponding $r_g(\cdot)$ that is not max-capability-preferred. The game has n players, $K = n$ lines, and each line has one gold. The only PNE in Equil$(\bar{b})$ is all players cover all gold, which achieves a social welfare of $W_{\bar{b}} = n \cdot w_g(n)$. When $b = n'$, one PNE is each player covers n' gold, with each gold covered by exactly n' players. This can be achieved by letting player i cover the gold on lines $\{y = (j \mod n)\}_{j=i}^{i+n'-1}$. To see why this is a PNE, notice that any player's alternative strategy only allows them to switch to gold with load larger than n'. For all $x > n'$, since $w_g(n') \ge w_g(x)$, $r_g(n') > r_g(x)$. So such change of strategy can only decrease the payoff of the player. The above PNE achieves a social welfare $W_{n'} = n \cdot w_g(n') > W_{\bar{b}}$, so the game is not max-capability-preferred.

Theorem 15. *For any payoff functions $r_g(\cdot)$ and $r_m(\cdot)$, there exists an instance of GMG where min-capability-preferred does not hold (therefore capability-negative does not hold either).*

Fig. 5. Resource layout for the alternating ordering game. Each dot (resp. cross) is a gold (resp. mine). The dashed lines represent a PNE when $b = 2$ (with $-2 + \rho < \mu < -\rho$).

Proof. It is trivial to construct such a game with mines. Here we show that for arbitrary $r_g(\cdot)$, we can actually construct a game with only gold that is not min-capability-preferred.

Let $r_{\min} = \min_{x \leq n} r_g(x)$ and $r_{\max} = \max_{x \leq n} r_g(x)$. We construct a game with $K = 2$ lines and $N + 1$ gold where $N > \frac{r_{\max}}{r_{\min}}$. In the order of increasing x, the first N gold is on $y = 0$ and the final gold is on $y = 1$. When $b = 1$, for an arbitrary player, denoting the payoff of choosing $y = 0$ (resp. $y = 1$) as r_0 (resp. r_1). Then $r_0 = \sum_{e \in \mathcal{E}_0} r_g(x_e) \geq \sum_{e \in \mathcal{E}_0} r_{\min} = N r_{\min} > r_{\max} \geq r_1$, where $\mathcal{E}_0$ is the set of resources on $y = 0$. So all the players will choose $y = 0$ in the PNE. The social welfare is $W_1 = nN r_g(n)$. When $b = 2$, all the players will choose to cover all the gold in the PNE. So the social welfare is $W_2 = n(N+1)r_g(n) > W_1$. Therefore, the game is not min-capability-preferred.

6   Case Study: Alternating Ordering Game

In this section, we present a special form of GMG called the alternating ordering game. We derive exact expressions of the social welfare at equilibrium with respect to the capability bound. The analysis provides insights on the factors that affect the trend of social welfare over player capability.

Definition 8. *The alternating ordering game is a special form of the GMG, with $n = 2$ players and $K = 2$ lines. The layout of the resources follows an alternating ordering of gold and mines as shown in Fig. 5. Each line has M mines and $M + 1$ gold. The payoff functions satisfy $0 < r_g(2) < \frac{r_g(1)}{2}$ (reflecting competition when both players occupy the same gold) and $r_m(1) = r_m(2) < 0$. WLOG, we consider normalized payoff where $r_g(1) = 1, r_g(2) = \rho, 0 < \rho < \frac{1}{2}, r_m(1) = r_m(2) = \mu < 0$.*

Let's consider the cases $b = 1$ and $b = 2$ to build some intuitive understanding. When $b = 1$, the PNE is that each player covers one line, which has social welfare $W_1 = 2M + 2M\mu + 2$. When $b = 2$ (and $-2 + \rho < \mu < -\rho$), one PNE is shown in Fig. 5, where the players avoid one mine but cover one gold together, which has social welfare $W_2 = W_1 - 1 - \mu + 2\rho$. Whether the social welfare at $b = 2$ is better depends on the sign of $2\rho - \mu - 1$. In fact, we have the following general result:

Theorem 16. *If $-2 + \rho < \mu < -\rho$, then for any level b strategy space $\mathcal{L}_b$, all PNEs have the same social welfare*

$$W_{\text{Equil}}(b) = \begin{cases} (2M + 1)(1 + \mu) + 2(1 - \rho) + (2\rho - \mu - 1)b & \text{if } b \leq 2M + 1 \\ (4M + 4)\rho & \text{if } b \geq 2M + 2 \end{cases}.$$

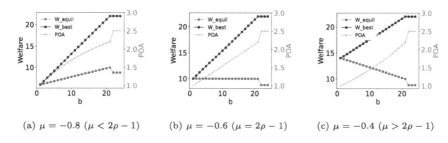

(a) $\mu = -0.8$ $(\mu < 2\rho - 1)$ (b) $\mu = -0.6$ $(\mu = 2\rho - 1)$ (c) $\mu = -0.4$ $(\mu > 2\rho - 1)$

Fig. 6. W_{Equil}, W_{best}, POA varying with b. $M = 10, \rho = 0.2$.

The full proof is lengthy and involves analyses of many different cases (presented in the full version of this paper [26]). We present the main idea here.

Proof idea. We make three arguments for this proof: (i) Any function in a PNE must satisfy some specific form indicating where it can switch lines (ii) Any PNE under $\mathcal{L}_b$ must consist of only functions that use exactly b segments (iii) For any function with b segments that satisfies the specific form, the optimal strategy for the other player always achieves the same payoff.

Remark. $-2 + \rho < \mu < -\rho$ is in fact a necessary and sufficient condition for all PNEs having the same social welfare for any b and M [26].

Depending on the sign of $2\rho - \mu - 1$, $W_{\mathrm{Equil}}(b)$ can increase, stay the same, or decrease as b increases until $b = 2M + 1$. $W_{\mathrm{Equil}}(b)$ always decreases at $b = 2M + 2$ and stays the same afterwards. Figure 6 visualizes this trend. Figure 7 summarizes how the characteristics of the PNEs varies in the ρ-μ space.

Price of Anarchy. The price of anarchy (POA) [13] is the ratio between the best social welfare achieved by any centralized solution and the worst welfare at equilibria: $\mathrm{POA}(b) = \frac{W_{\mathrm{best}}(b)}{W_{\mathrm{Equil}}(b)}$. We can show that the best centralized social welfare is $W_{\mathrm{best}}(b) = 2M + 2 + \mu \cdot \max(2M + 1 - b, 0)$ [26]. Hence

$$\mathrm{POA}(b) = \begin{cases} 1 + \frac{(1-2\rho)(b-1)}{2M+2+2M\mu+(2\rho-\mu-1)(b-1)} & \text{if } b \leq 2M + 1 \\ \frac{1}{2\rho} & \text{if } b \geq 2M + 2 \end{cases},$$

$\mathrm{POA}(b)$ increases with b up to $b = 2M + 2$, then stays the same (Fig. 6).

Interpretation. There are two opposing factors that affect whether increased capability is beneficial for social welfare or not. With increased capability, players can improve their payoff in a non-competitive way (e.g. avoiding mines), which is always beneficial for social welfare; they can also improve payoff in a competitive way (e.g. occupying gold together), which may reduce social welfare. The joint effect of the two factors determines the effect of increasing capability.

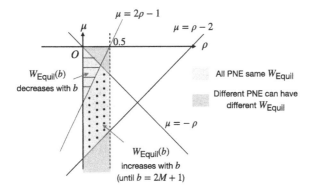

Fig. 7. Characteristics of PNEs over the ρ-μ landscape.

References

1. Ackermann, H., Röglin, H., Vöcking, B.: On the impact of combinatorial structure on congestion games. J. ACM (JACM) **55**(6), 1–22 (2008)
2. Ackermann, H., Skopalik, A.: Complexity of pure Nash equilibria in player-specific network congestion games. Internet Math. **5**(4), 323–342 (2008)
3. Almanasra, S., Suwais, K., Rafie, M.: The applications of automata in game theory. In: Intelligent Technologies and Techniques for Pervasive Computing, pp. 204–217. IGI Global (2013)
4. Chan, H., Jiang, A.X.: Congestion games with polytopal strategy spaces. In: IJCAI, pp. 165–171 (2016)
5. Chiong, R., Kirley, M.: Co-evolutionary learning in the N-player iterated prisoner's dilemma with a structured environment. In: Korb, K., Randall, M., Hendtlass, T. (eds.) ACAL 2009. LNCS (LNAI), vol. 5865, pp. 32–42. Springer, Heidelberg (2009). https://doi.org/10.1007/978-3-642-10427-5_4
6. Christodoulou, G., Gairing, M., Giannakopoulos, Y., Poças, D., Waldmann, C.: Existence and complexity of approximate equilibria in weighted congestion games. In: ICALP (2020)
7. Correa, J.R., Schulz, A.S., Stier-Moses, N.E.: On the inefficiency of equilibria in congestion games. In: Jünger, M., Kaibel, V. (eds.) IPCO 2005. LNCS, vol. 3509, pp. 167–181. Springer, Heidelberg (2005). https://doi.org/10.1007/11496915_13
8. Fabrikant, A., Papadimitriou, C., Talwar, K.: The complexity of pure Nash equilibria. In: Proceedings of the Thirty-Sixth Annual ACM Symposium on Theory of Computing, pp. 604–612 (2004)
9. Fortnow, L.: Program equilibria and discounted computation time. In: Proceedings of the 12th Conference on Theoretical Aspects of Rationality and Knowledge, TARK 2009, New York, NY, USA, pp. 128–133. Association for Computing Machinery (2009). ISBN 9781605585604
10. Garey, M., Johnson, D.: Computers and Intractability: A Guide to the Theory of NP-Completeness. Mathematical Sciences Series. W. H. Freeman (1979). ISBN 9780716710448

11. Ghnemat, R., Oqeili, S., Bertelle, C., Duchamp, G.H.: Automata-based adaptive behavior for economic modelling using game theory. In: Aziz-Alaoui, M., Bertelle, C. (eds.) Emergent Properties in Natural and Artificial Dynamical Systems. Understanding Complex Systems, pp. 171–183. Springer, Heidelberg (2006). https://doi.org/10.1007/3-540-34824-7_9

12. Hopcroft, J., Motwani, R., Ullman, J.: Introduction to Automata Theory, Languages, and Computation. Always Learning. Pearson Education (2014). ISBN 9781292039053

13. Koutsoupias, E., Papadimitriou, C.: Worst-case equilibria. In: Meinel, C., Tison, S. (eds.) STACS 1999. LNCS, vol. 1563, pp. 404–413. Springer, Heidelberg (1999). https://doi.org/10.1007/3-540-49116-3_38

14. Le, S., Wu, Y., Toyoda, M.: A congestion game framework for service chain composition in NFV with function benefit. Inf. Sci. **514**, 512–522 (2020)

15. Neyman, A.: Bounded complexity justifies cooperation in the finitely repeated prisoners' dilemma. Econ. Lett. **19**(3), 227–229 (1985)

16. Neyman, A.: Cooperation, repetition, and automata. In: Hart, S., Mas-Colell, A. (eds.) Cooperation: Game-Theoretic Approaches. NATO ASI Series, vol. 155, pp. 233–255. Springer, Heidelberg (1997). https://doi.org/10.1007/978-3-642-60454-6_16

17. Nickerl, J., Torán, J.: Pure Nash equilibria in a generalization of congestion games allowing resource failures. In: Caragiannis, I., Hansen, K.A. (eds.) SAGT 2021. LNCS, vol. 12885, pp. 186–201. Springer, Cham (2021). https://doi.org/10.1007/978-3-030-85947-3_13

18. Nikitina, N., Ivashko, E., Tchernykh, A.: Congestion game scheduling for virtual drug screening optimization. J. Comput. Aided Mol. Des. **32**(2), 363–374 (2018)

19. Nisan, N., Roughgarden, T., Tardos, E., Vazirani, V.: Algorithmic Game Theory. Cambridge University Press, Cambridge (2007). ISBN 9780521872829

20. Papadimitriou, C.H.: On players with a bounded number of states. Games Econ. Behav. **4**(1), 122–131 (1992). ISSN 0899-8256

21. Papadimitriou, C.H., Yannakakis, M.: On complexity as bounded rationality. In: Proceedings of the Twenty-Sixth Annual ACM Symposium on Theory of Computing, pp. 726–733 (1994)

22. Rosenthal, R.W.: A class of games possessing pure-strategy Nash equilibria. Int. J. Game Theory **2**(1), 65–67 (1973)

23. Roughgarden, T.: How unfair is optimal routing? In: Symposium on Discrete Algorithms: Proceedings of the Thirteenth Annual ACM-SIAM Symposium on Discrete Algorithms, vol. 6, pp. 203–204 (2002)

24. Rubinstein, A.: Finite automata play the repeated prisoner's dilemma. J. Econ. Theory **39**(1), 83–96 (1986). ISSN 0022-0531

25. Tennenholtz, M.: Program equilibrium. Games Econ. Behav. **49**(2), 363–373 (2004). ISSN 0899-8256

26. Yang, Y., Jia, K., Rinard, M.: On the impact of player capability on congestion games. arXiv preprint arXiv:2205.09905 (2022)

27. Zhang, F., Wang, M.M.: Stochastic congestion game for load balancing in mobile-edge computing. IEEE Internet Things J. **8**(2), 778–790 (2020)

Data Sharing and Learning

Learning Approximately Optimal Contracts

Alon Cohen[1,3], Argyrios Deligkas[2], and Moran Koren[3(✉)]

[1] Google Research, Mountain View, USA
alonco@tauex.tau.ac.il
[2] Royal Holloway, University of London, Egham, UK
Argyrios.Deligkas@rhul.ac.uk
[3] Tel Aviv University, Tel Aviv, Israel
me@mkoren.org

Abstract. In principal-agent models, a principal offers a contract to an agent to preform a certain task. The agent exerts a level of effort that maximizes her utility. The principal is oblivious to the agent's chosen level of effort, and conditions her wage only on possible outcomes. In this work, we consider a model in which the principal is unaware of the agent's utility and action space: she sequentially offers contracts to identical agents, and observes the resulting outcomes. We present an algorithm for learning the optimal contract under mild assumptions. We bound the number of samples needed for the principal obtain a contract that is within ϵ of her optimal net profit for every $\epsilon > 0$. Our results are robust even when considering risk averse agents. Furthermore, we show that when there only two possible outcomes, or the agent is risk neutral, the algorithm's outcome approximates the optimal contract described in the classical theory.

1 Introduction

Recent technological advances have changed the relationship between firms and employees dramatically. The rapid change in employees' required skill set combined with the availability of off-shore, qualified, cheap hiring alternatives drove employers to adopt employees on a short-term, task specific bases. This hiring model, dubbed *dynamic workforce* or *gig-economy*, has been growing exponentially over the decade. In [8] it was found that 20–30% of US workers are employed independently, at least partly, and predicts this trend will continue with popularity of the "Lean Startup" business model, and the appearance of platforms such as "Amazon Mechanical Turk".

The aforementioned labor market changes have a profound effect on the information available to firms when it comes to making hiring decisions. In the traditional workspace, hiring is often a long-term, expensive procedure. Nowadays hiring is cheap and short-termed. As a result, an employer has less information on the character and quality of her employees, thus lacking the knowledge on how to best align their incentives with those of the firm. In this work we study

ⓒ The Author(s), under exclusive license to Springer Nature Switzerland AG 2022

P. Kanellopoulos et al. (Eds.): SAGT 2022, LNCS 13584, pp. 331–346, 2022.
https://doi.org/10.1007/978-3-031-15714-1_19

a model more suitable to the new "dynamic workforce", and, using this model, we try to learn the best wages an employer should offer to her employees.

Economists use the term *agency problems* to describe models like the above. In such models one party, the *principal*, offers a *contract* to another party, the *agent*, to perform a task [25]. In his seminal paper, Ross [30] introduced the term *principal–agent* to capture these models. In the basic model, the outcome of the task is chosen randomly from a distribution determined by the *level of effort* invested by the agent. A higher effort level induces a distribution in which the probability of a better outcome is higher than in lower effort levels. On the other hand, a higher level causes the agent greater disutility. Ross [30] assumes that the principal is *risk-neutral* while the agent is *risk-averse*, therefore the incentives of both parties are *not* fully aligned.[1] Hence, the effort level that is optimal from the perspective of the principal, is not necessarily the optimal one for the agent. To bridge this gap, the principal offers the agent a contract in which the agent is rewarded for any additional effort. The lion's share of previous work assume that the principal, while oblivious to the agent's choice, has full information about the agent's utility structure *and* the set of levels of effort she can choose from *and* the probability distribution associated with every level of effort [17,18,21,22,30]. These assumptions seem confining, especially when considering the motivating scenario of a dynamic workplace.

Holmstrom, in his Nobel Prize lecture [22], identified this gap in theory as one of the main challenges in current research. A first attempt to bridge this gap was [9]. Carroll [9] presented a model where a principal has only partial knowledge on the agent's action space. He assumed that the agent is risk neutral and thus, if the principal have known the agent's complete action space, the optimal contract would have been linear. In this setting, the principal can guarantee the net profit from best linear contract pertaining the actions she knows. That is her actual net profit will never be lower. An early attempt to approach the agency problem from the lens of theoretical computer science was made in [20]. In the model of [20], there are several types of agents, each one with her own utility function, set of effort levels and effort costs, and probability distributions over the outcomes; all of which unknown to the principal. They considered a repeated setting with T rounds, where in every round the type of the agent is chosen i.i.d. from an unknown probability distribution. Their goal was to find, before round T, the optimal contract from a predefined finite set S. They followed a multi-armed bandit approach [29] and derived an algorithm that finds an approximately-optimal contract. However, the contract they find is approximately-optimal *only* with respect to the best contract in S. They provide no theoretical guarantees on approximating the optimal contract overall, but only for the case of one effort level for the agent, i.e. reject the contract or

---

[1] When given the choice between participating in some lottery X or receiving $E(X)$ with probability one, a risk-averse agent will strictly prefer the latter while a risk-neutral agent is indifferent. In the Von Neumann Morgenstern utility theory, if an agent is risk-averse, then she has a concave utility function; if she is risk-neutral, then her utility is linear.

accept it, known as *posted-price auctions*.[2] In [14], the authors study a similar scenario in which the principal knows only the expected output generated by each contract, that is, the agent's action set is unknown to the principal. As in [9], they assume that the agent's utility is linear and that limited liability holds (i.e., no negative payments) and show that the worst-case expected profit for the principal is guaranteed by a linear contract. In addition, they provide tight approximation guarantees for linear contracts. In this paper we follow a similar route to [20] and [14]. We assume the principal has *zero* information about the agent; we assume unknown utility for the agent, unknown set of effort levels and their associated costs, and unknown probability distribution for any effort level. The only knowledge the principal has is the set of outcomes and their corresponding profits. Our model extends the setting of [20] as we assume that the contract set as continuous. We extend the setting of [9] and [14] in two folds: (1) Our set of *monotone-smooth* contracts is richer than the set of linear contracts. (2) We do not assume any functional form of agent utilities, we only assume that agents are risk averse (concave utility). In the next section we illustrate the importance of this generalization in this context.

1.1   The Challenge of Learning Contracts with Risk Averse Agents

In contract theory, we study the tension between a principal and an agent. This tension is the result of misalignment between the incentives of both players. On the one hand, the principal wishes to maximize her profit, and is indifferent towards the cost the agent endures during effort; on the other hand, the agent is assumed to be risk averse, and wishes to minimize the volatility of her expected wage (ceteris paribus). In the classical PA model, the principal knows the full structure of the agent's decision problem, and can offer a contract that serves her best yet minimizing the aforementioned misalignment with the agent. To illustrate this, we show an example where the agent may choose between three levels of effort and there are two possible outcomes. As we wish to illustrate a general point, we will keep the exact utility function and cost structure implicit and just mention that the utility is concave and higher costs induce "better" output distributions. The following figure depicts the space of contracts from which the principal may offer, and the resulting effort level the agent chooses, given each possible contract. Note that unlike [20], the space of contracts is continuous. By [27], the optimal contract can be found in any of the interaction points $\{A, B, C\}$. To see why this is the case, note, for example, that when offered the contract in point A, the agent is indifferent between accepting and rejecting the contract, and between investing medium effort or high effort. Thus, based on the model assumptions, she will choose to invest the high level of effort. Not only that, but this is the contract where the highest level of effort is achieved for the lowest possible expected pay. Similarly, the contract B, is

---

[2] As they highlight, it is not generally clear whether the best contract from S can provide a good theoretical guarantees for the general problem of dynamic contract design.

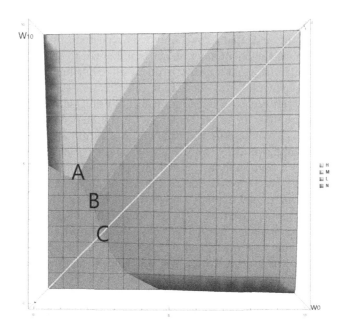

Fig. 1. The agent's optimal choice in a PA model with two possible outputs, three levels of effort:e_H, e_M, e_L, N is the rejection zone, and a concave utility.

the "cheapest" contract under which the agent chooses the middle effort level. Note that contract B is both cheaper, and yields lower expected output than contract A. When examining the principal-optimal contract, it is unclear which of the effects dominates. Therefore, in the general case, the optimal contract can be in any of A, B, C. When the principal is fully aware of the agent's incentive structure (i.e., her utility and effort-cost pairs), finding the optimal contract is straightforward (Fig. 1).

If we consider an uninformed the principal, she can attempt to learn an optimal contract using the following pesudo-algorithm: (1) create a discretized version of the contract space (2) Find the contract on the grid which yields the optimal profit. Naively, using this approach, we will find a contract that is at most ε away either A, B or C. Note that this does not preclude the possibility that the contract that we find is ε away from point A, but the absolute optimal contract is actually contract B. In extreme cases, the difference in the principal's profit between the algorithms' result and the theoretically optimal one can be arbitrarily high (see for example $u(w) = 1 - \frac{1}{w}$). Furthermore, using a finer grid may lead to different contract which is arbitrarily away, thus convergence of the process in not guaranteed. In this paper, we provide a set of contracts, and algorithm, and an appropriate discretization for which the process converges to a single maximal contract. In addition, we detail two cases, for which the resulting contract is the absolute possible best.

Further Related Work. As we have already explained, the majority of works so far has focused on the full information setting and its variants: [6] studies a model with many agents; [5] studies a setting with externalities for the agent; [13,15] study principal-agent models with combinatorial structures over the actions of the agent, or the possible outcomes. Additionally, in [15], the authors also discuss a black-box model and present sample-complexity results. More recently, a new line of work on Bayesian settings for the principal-agent model has emerged [2,10,11,19] where the agent type comes from a known probability distribution.

Our work lies in the intersection of principal-agent models and multi-armed bandit theory; [20] provide an excellent overview of literature in the field. [31–33] study a repeated setting where the principal interacts with the agent for multiple periods. [12] empirically compare several learning algorithms in a setting similar to [20].

The Lipschitz Bandit problem [1] is a generalization of the multi-armed bandit problem in which the set of arms comes from some compact space, and the expected reward of each arm is a Lipschitz function of the arm. It has received much attention from the bandit theory community over the years [4,7,23,24,26].

Our Contributions. In this work we make several contributions to both economic and computer science theory.

- We contribute to the study of agency problems by extending the literature to a setting where the principal is oblivious to the agent decision problem structure.
- We study this setting in a the context of risk averse agents. An extension which is the driving force of the canonical theoretical principal-agent model. To the best of our knowledge, our paper is first in the introduction of agent risk aversion into the theoretical study of data driven decision problems.
- We introduce a novel set of contracts we call *monotone-smooth* contracts; a large subset of monotone contracts set studied in [20].
- We complement this definition with a suitable discretization of the contract space. Unlike [20], we show that for any monotone-smooth contract there exists a contract in the discretized space for which the principal's expected net profit is ϵ-approximated. As far as we are aware, this is the first work to do so.
- Moreover, our result does not assume any specific agent utility function, but rather only mild assumptions. This allows to apply machineries from multi-armed bandit theory to find a contract ϵ-optimal against any monotone-smooth contract.
- Finally, we present two fundamental cases in which economic theory suggests the learned contract of our algorithm is ϵ-optimal against *any* contract the principal may offer. The first case in when there are only two possible outcomes. The second case is when there are many outcomes and the agent is risk neutral.

2   Preliminaries

In what follows, $[m^\star] := \{0, 1, \ldots, m\}$ and $[m] := \{1, \ldots, m\}$ for every natural m.

We study principal-agent problems with k outcomes and n effort levels. Let $0 < \pi(1) < \pi(2) < \cdots < \pi(k)$ denote the value the principal gets under outcome $i \in [k]$. We assume that $\pi(k) = H$, hence the values are bounded.

A *contract* $w = (w(1), \ldots, w(k))$ specifies a positive payment to the agent for every outcome; namely, $w(i)$ is the wage the principal pays the agent for outcome i.

Upon receiving a contract, the agent chooses an effort level $e \in [n^*]$. Every effort level is associated with a probability distribution f_e over the set of outcomes and a cost $c(e)$; $f_e(j)$ is the probability of realizing outcome j when the agent chooses the effort level e. In effort level 0, the agent rejects the contract, her utility is zero under any contract, and by convention the value for the principal is zero. We assume that the effort levels are ordered, i.e., $1 \prec \ldots \prec n$ (the order will be formally defined in Assumption 1). We follow the literature and assume that the agent has a von Neumann-Morgenstern utility. For a contract $w = (w(1), \ldots, w(k))$ the agent chooses effort level of $\hat{e}(w)$ as to maximize her utility, defined as

$$U(w, e) = \sum_{j=1}^{k} f_e(j) \cdot u(w(j)) - c(e),$$

where u is a monotonically-increasing concave function. Hence, $\hat{e}(w) = \arg\max_{e \in [n^*]} U(w, e)$.

The principal is risk-neutral; when she offers contract w to the agent, her expected net profit from the contract is,

$$V(w) = \sum_{j=1}^{k} f_{\hat{e}(w)}(j) \cdot \left(\pi(j) - w(j) \right).$$

To ensure that higher effort levels yield higher expected profit for the principal, the literature commonly lays down some assumptions about the outcome distributions.

Assumption 1 (First-order Stochastic Dominance (FOSD)). *A probability distribution associated with higher effort* first order stochastically dominates *a probability distribution associated with lower effort. Formally, if $e \succ e'$, then for every $j \in [k]$ it holds that $\sum_{i=j}^{k} f_e(i) \geq \sum_{i=j}^{k} f_{e'}(i)$.*

Note that the assumption is equivalent to the following. For every pair of effort levels $e \succ e'$ and for every sequence of real numbers $a(1) \leq \cdots \leq a(k)$,

$$\sum_{i=1}^{k} f_e(i) \cdot a(i) \geq \sum_{i=1}^{k} f_{e'}(i) \cdot a(i) . \tag{1}$$

Additionally, to break ties between effort levels we assume the following.

Assumption 2. *The agent will choose the higher effort when indifferent between two or more levels of effort.*

In this work, the principal is faced with a stream of agents. The agents are all different but identical—they share a common utility function, effort levels, costs from effort, and outcome distributions associated with each effort level. The principal proceeds in rounds $t = 1, 2, \ldots$. On round t, the principal offers a contract w_t to the agent associated with this round. The agent privately chooses effort level $\hat{e}(w_t)$ unknown to the principal. The principal observes only the outcome i_t independently drawn from $f_{\hat{e}(w_t)}$, and consequently gets a net profit of $\pi(i_t) - w_t(i_t)$.

In what follows, for $\epsilon > 0$, the goal of the principal is to find an ϵ-optimal contract in the minimum number of rounds. A contract w is ϵ-*optimal* if $V(w) \geq V(w') - \epsilon$ for every $w' \in W$, for a set of contracts W to be defined in the sequel.

2.1 Multi-armed Bandit

In the multi-armed bandit problem [29], a decision maker sequentially collects rewards from a given set of arms. In each round, the decision maker chooses a single arm, and observes an independent sample from a reward distribution associated with that arm. In our case, the goal of the decision maker is, after a predetermined number of rounds, to select an ϵ-optimal arm; that is, an arm whose expected reward is at most ϵ less than the expected reward of any arm.

When the set of arms is finite, of size N, and the rewards are bounded in $[0, B]$, the seminal work of [16] presents an algorithm called MEDIANELIMINATION with the following guarantee.

Theorem 1 ([16]). *The* MEDIANELIMINATION(ϵ, δ) *returns an ϵ-optimal arm with probability at least $1 - \delta$ after $O((NB^2/\epsilon^2) \cdot \log(1/\delta))$ rounds.*

In our problem, each contract can be seen as an arm. The expected reward of each arm is exactly the principal's utility associated with this contract. It is then expected that the principal would simply execute MEDIANELIMINATION on the space of contracts to obtain an ϵ-optimal one. However, the space of contracts is not finite which is crucial for MEDIANELIMINATION to run. In the sequel we show how to overcome this difficulty by discretizing the space of contracts, and running MEDIANELIMINATION over the discretization.

3 Main Technical Result

In this section we present our algorithm and analyze its sample complexity, but before doing so let us first define the space of contracts W that we can learn. The algorithm is presented in Sect. 3.2.

3.1 Learnable Contracts

Let $w_0 > 0$ be a minimum wage for any outcome.

Definition 1 (B-bounded contract). *A contract w is B-bounded if $w_0 \leq w(i) \leq B$ for every $i \in [k]$.*

For a bounded contract, together with the assumption that the principal's profits are bounded, ensures that the principal's expected net profit $V(w)$ can be estimated statistically.

Definition 2 (Monotone-smooth contract). *A contract w is monotone-smooth if for every $i \in [k-1]$ it holds that $0 \le w(i+1) - w(i) \le \pi(i+1) - \pi(i)$.*

For a monotone-smooth contract, Eq. (1) ensures that, keeping the contract fixed, the principal's utility cannot decrease if the agent increases her effort level. In the sequel, this property allows us to bound the difference in the principal's utility between two similar contracts.

We define W as follows.

$$W = \{w : w \text{ is monotone-smooth and } H\text{-bounded}\} \ .$$

We are aware that this set seems restrictive at first glance, yet we argue that in some important special cases, the principal's optimal net profit is achieved by a contract from this set. For example, when there are only two outcomes or the utility of the agent is linear (see Sect. 4).

3.2 Algorithm

Let $w^\star \in W$ be an optimal contract in W, that is $V(w^\star) \ge V(w)$ for all $w \in W$. The goal of our algorithm is to find an ϵ-optimal contract w, namely a contract for which $V(w^\star) \le V(w) + \epsilon$ within a predetermined number of rounds. We conjecture that it cannot be done in general therefore we make the following simplifying assumption.

Assumption 3 (Bounded Risk-Aversion). *The agent's utility from wage u is twice continuously-differentiable. Moreover, there exists a reference utility function r that is a monotonically increasing, twice-differentiable, concave function such that $u''(w)/u'(w) \ge r''(w)/r'(w)$ for all $w > 0$. This is equivalent to $w \mapsto u'(w)/r'(w)$ being monotone-nondecreasing in w.*

Intuitively, this assumption ensures that making small changes to a contract does not produce behavior by the agent that is drastically different than if the agent's utility would have been r instead of u.[3]

Our algorithm works as follows. The principal initially constructs a cover W_η of W, and then run MEDIANELIMINATION on W_η. Indeed, the main technical difficulty in this paper is in defining W_η properly so that the following result holds.

---

[3] An alternative, slightly less general, version of Assumption 3 is: Assume there exists a finite $\eta > 1$ such that $-xu''(w)/u'(w) > \eta$ for all $w > 0$. Note that the element on the left is the cannonical Arrow-Pratt relative risk aversion measure of the agent [3,28], and the element of the right corresponds with the Arrow-Pratt relative risk aversion measure of the Isoelastic utility function $r(w) = \frac{w^{\eta-1}-1}{\eta-1}$.

Theorem 2. *Suppose that Assumptions 1 to 3 hold. Let $\eta < r'(2H) \cdot H/k$. There exists a contract space W_η such that for every contract $w \in W$, there is a contract $w' \in W_\eta$ for which $V(w) \le V(w') + k\eta/r'(2H)$. Moreover, the size of W_η is at most $M = ((r(2H) - r(w_0))/\eta)^k$, and W_η can be constructed in time $O(M)$.*

The proof of the theorem is found in Sect. 3.3. Finally, we have our main result.

Theorem 3. *Suppose that Assumptions 1 to 3 hold. Let $\eta = \epsilon \cdot r'(2H)/2k$. Executing* MEDIANELIMINATION$(\epsilon/2, \delta)$ *on the set W_η produces the following guarantee. With probability at least $1 - \delta$, the algorithm outputs an ϵ-optimal contract after*

$$O\left(\left(\frac{4kH(r(2H) - r(w_0))}{\epsilon}\right)^{k+2} \cdot \log(1/\delta)\right)$$

rounds.

Proof. By Theorem 2 and by the choice of η, there is a $w' \in W_\eta$ for which $V(w') \le V(w^\star) + \epsilon/2$. By Theorem 1, with probability $1 - \delta$, MEDIANELIMINATION returns a contract $\hat{w} \in W_\eta$ such that $V(\hat{w}) \le V(w') + \epsilon/2$. Combining both results we get

$$V(\hat{w}) \le V(w') + \epsilon/2 \le V(w^\star) + \epsilon/2 + \epsilon/2 = V(w^\star) + \epsilon \ ,$$

as required. Moreover, MEDIANELIMINATION is done in the following number of rounds:

$$O\left(\frac{|W_\eta|H^2}{(\epsilon/2)^2} \log(1/\delta)\right) = O\left(\left(\frac{4kH(r(2H) - r(w_0))}{\epsilon}\right)^{k+2} \cdot \log(1/\delta)\right) \ .$$

$\square$

3.3   Discretization of the Contract Space

In this section we prove Theorem 2. We start by defining the notion of a coarse contract. To that end, we utilize the inverse function of r (that exists everywhere since r is increasing) which we denote by r^{-1}.

Definition 3 (η-coarse contract). *A contract W is η-coarse if there exists natural numbers $l_0, l_1, \ldots, l_{k-1}$ such that $w(1) = r^{-1}(r(w_0) + \eta \cdot l_0)$, and for $i \in [k-1]$, $w(i+1) = r^{-1}(r(w(i)) + \eta \cdot l_i)$.*

That is, in a coarse contract the ratios between wages of consecutive outcomes come from a discrete set of options. We define:

$$W_\eta = \{w : w \text{ is } \eta\text{-coarse and } 2H\text{-bounded}\} \ .$$

We prove the following.

Lemma 1. *The size of W_η is at most $M = ((r(2H) - r(w_0))/\eta)^k$. Moreover, W_η can be constructed in time $O(kM)$.*

Proof. The wage of outcome i has the form $r^{-1}(r(w_0) + \eta \cdot l)$ for a natural number l, and satisfies $w(i) \le 2H$. Therefore, the number of choices for $w(i)$ is at most $(r(2H) - r(w_0))/\eta$. Since there are k outcomes, there must be at most M such contracts. To construct W_η we can go over all of its elements one-by-one, which takes $O(M)$ time.   □

Finally let $w \in W$, we need to show that there is $w' \in W_\eta$ such that $V(w) \le V(w') + 2kH\eta$. We construct $w' \in W_\eta$ as follows. We let $l_0 = \lceil (r(w(1)) - r(w_0))/\eta \rceil$, and for $i \in [k-1]$, $l_i = \lceil (r(w(i+1)) - r(w(i)))/\eta \rceil$. Since r^{-1} is also monotonically-increasing, we have that $w'(1) \ge w(1)$ as well as $r(w'(i+1)) - r(w'(i)) \ge r(w(i+1)) - r(w(i))$ for $i \in [k-1]$ by construction. Clearly, w' is η-coarse and $w'(i) \ge w_0$, yet it remains to show that $w'(i) \le 2H$. For that, we have the following lemma.

Lemma 2. *We have for all $i \in [k-1]$, $r(w'(i)) \le r(w(i)) + \eta i$.*

Proof. By construction, for each $i \in [k-1]$ we have $r(w'(i+1)) - r(w'(i)) \le r(w(i+1)) - r(w(i)) + \eta$. From this we entail that $r(w'(i)) - r(w'(1)) \le r(w(i)) - r(w(1)) + (i-1) \cdot \eta$. Since also by construction $r(w'(1)) \le r(w(1)) + \eta$, we get that $r(w'(i)) \le r(w(i)) + i \cdot \eta$ as required.   □

With the lemma at hand, and by assumption that $\eta < r'(2H) \cdot H/k$ we obtain

$$w'(k) \le r^{-1}(r(w(k)) + \eta \cdot k) \le r^{-1}(r(H) + r'(2H) \cdot H) \le 2H \ ,$$

using the concavity of r. Therefore we have $w' \in W_\eta$.

We now show that, compared to w, under w' the agent's effort cannot decrease. Then, we use this fact to bound the difference in the principal's utility between w and w'.

In order to prove our first claim, we will make use of the following lemma.

Lemma 3 (Grossman and Hart [18]). *Let w^1 and w^2 be contracts. Then,*

$$\sum_{i=1}^{k} \left(f_{\hat{e}(w^1)}(i) - f_{\hat{e}(w^2)}(i) \right) \cdot \left(u(w^1(i)) - u(w^2(i)) \right) \ge 0.$$

Lemma 4. *The effort level the agent chooses can only increase from w to w'.*

Proof. First, notice that since the wages only increase, had the agent accepted the contract w, i.e., chose an effort level different than 0, she would also accept contract w'. So, let $e' = \hat{e}(w')$ and $e = \hat{e}(w)$ be the effort levels the agent chooses under contracts w' and w respectively.

If we apply Lemma 3 with w and w', we obtain

$$\sum_{i=1}^{k} \left(f_{e'}(i) - f_e(i) \right) \cdot \left(u(w'(i)) - u(w(i)) \right) \ge 0 \ .$$

Assume for now that $u(w'(i)) - u(w(i))$ is monotone nondecreasing in i. Given this, we will show by contradiction that $e' \succ e$. So, for the sake of contradiction assume that $e' \prec e$. From the fact that f_e dominates $f_{e'}$, Eq. (1) implies that

$$\sum_{i=1}^{k} \big(f_{e'}(i) - f_e(i)\big) \cdot \big(u(w'(i)) - u(w(i))\big) \leq 0 .$$

Thus,

$$\sum_{i=1}^{k} \big(f_{e'}(i) - f_e(i)\big) \cdot u(w(i)) = \sum_{i=1}^{k} \big(f_{e'}(i) - f_e(i)\big) \cdot u(w'(i)). \tag{2}$$

Therefore, by optimality of e and e' under contracts w and w' respectively, we obtain

$$\sum_{i=1}^{k} \big(f_{e'}(i) - f_e(i)\big) \cdot u(w(i)) \leq c(e') - c(e), \text{ and}$$

$$\sum_{i=1}^{k} \big(f_{e'}(i) - f_e(i)\big) \cdot u(w'(i)) \geq c(e') - c(e).$$

Combining Eq. (2) with the two inequalities above, we obtain that

$$U(w', e') = \sum_{i=1}^{k} f_{e'}(i) \cdot u(w'(i)) - c(e') = \sum_{i=1}^{k} f_e(i) \cdot u(w'(i)) - c(e) = U(w', e) .$$

This means that the agent is indifferent between effort levels e and e' under contract w'. Since, by Assumption 2, the agent chooses the highest effort in this case, we must have $e \prec e'$—a contradiction.

Hence, in order to prove the lemma it suffices to prove that $u(w'(i)) - u(w(i))$ is monotone nondecreasing in i. This is equivalent to showing that $u(w'(i+1)) - u(w'(i)) \geq u(w(i+1)) - u(w(i))$. Denote $c = r(w'(i)) - r(w(i))$. By construction, $r(w'(i+1)) - r(w(i+1)) \geq c$. Consequently, since u is monotone nondecreasing, it suffices to show

$$u(r^{-1}(r(w(i+1)) + c)) - u(r^{-1}(r(w(i)) + c)) \geq u(w(i+1)) - u(w(i)).$$

Thus, the proof boils down to showing $c \mapsto u(r^{-1}(r(w(i+1)) + c)) - u(r^{-1}(r(w(i)) + c))$ is monotone nondecreasing in c. Taking the derivative with respect to c, we need to show

$$\frac{u'(r^{-1}(r(w(i+1)) + c))}{r'(r^{-1}(r(w(i+1)) + c))} - \frac{u'(r^{-1}(r(w(i)) + c))}{r'(r^{-1}(r(w(i)) + c))} \geq 0.$$

However, the above holds since the agent is BRA (Assumption 3), and as $r^{-1}(r(w(i+1))) + c \geq r^{-1}(r(w(i))) + c$ due to both r and r^{-1} being monotone-increasing. $\qquad \square$

We can now bound the loss the principal suffers when she offers w' instead of w.

Lemma 5. *It holds that $V(w) \leq V(w') + k\eta/r'(2H)$.*

Proof. Since we focus on scenarios where the optimal contract is monotone-smooth, we get that the net profit of the principal at the optimal contract, $\pi(i) - w(i)$, is nondecreasing in i. Furthermore, from Eq. (1), keeping w fixed, the principal only benefits from an increase of the agent's effort level. Denote $e = \hat{e}(w)$ and $e' = \hat{e}(w')$. From Lemma 4 we know that $e' \succ e$. We have,

$$V(w) = \sum_{i=1}^{k} f_e(i) \cdot \big(\pi(i) - w(i)\big)$$

$$\leq \sum_{i=1}^{k} f_{e'}(i) \cdot \big(\pi(i) - w(i)\big)$$

$$= V(w') + \sum_{i=1}^{k} f_{e'}(i) \cdot \big(w'(i) - w(i)\big). \tag{3}$$

Now by Lemma 2, $w'(i) \leq r^{-1}(r(w(i)) + \eta \cdot i)$ for all $i \in [k]$. Note that r^{-1} is convex. Then, as $\eta < r'(2H) \cdot H/k$, we obtain

$$w'(i) - w(i) \leq r^{-1}(r(w(i)) + \eta \cdot i) - w(i)$$

$$\leq \frac{\eta \cdot i}{r'(2H) \cdot H} \left(r^{-1}\big(r(w(i)) + r'(2H) \cdot H\big) - w(i)\right)$$

$$\leq \frac{\eta \cdot i}{r'(2H) \cdot H} \left(r^{-1}\big(r(H) + r'(2H) \cdot H\big) - H\right)$$

$$\leq \frac{\eta \cdot i}{r'(2H) \cdot H} (2H - H)$$

$$\leq \frac{\eta \cdot k}{r'(2H)},$$

where the second and third inequalities are by the convexity of r^{-1}, and the fourth inequality is by the concavity of r. Combining the latter with Eq. (3), we get $V(w) \leq V(w') + \eta \cdot k/r'(2H)$. □

4 Applications

In this section we highlight two cases that received attention in the past. For each of them, when Assumptions 1 to 3 hold, the optimal contract will be in the set W, and thus by learning an ε-optimal contract in W, we approximate the best contract the principle could have offered the agent had she known her utility function, effort levels and costs, and the distributions they induce over outcomes.

Two Outcomes. Firstly, we focus on the case where there are only two outcomes and show that the optimal contract is in W.

Lemma 6. *When there are only two outcomes, the optimal contract is monotone-smooth and $2H$-bounded.*

Proof. By [18], the optimal contract in the two outcome case is of the shape: $w(2) = w(1) + a(\pi(2) - \pi(1))$ for some $a \in [0,1]$. By plugging this expression into the inequality in Definition 2, we get that the optimal contract is monotone-smooth. To see that the optimal contract is $2H$-bounded, let e denote her chosen effort level. Since the principal's utility at the optimal contract is nonnegative, $f_e(1)w(1) + f_e(2)w(2) \leq f_e(1)\pi(1) + f_e(2)\pi(2) \leq H$, and in particular $w(1) \leq H$. Now, $w(2) = w(1) + a(\pi(2) - \pi(1)) \leq H + 1 \cdot H = 2H$. $\square$

Thus, by Theorem 3, applied to our discretized contract space, MEDIANE-LIMINATION finds an ϵ-optimal contract under Assumptions 1 to 3. Note, the FOSD assumption (Assumption 1) is standard in the literature, hence our result essentially requires only the bounded risk-averse assumption (Assumption 3).

Risk Neutral Agent. [9] studies a setting in the agent is risk-neutral, and the principal has only partial knowledge of the agent's action space. Had the principal known the complete action space of the agent, the optimal contract would have been linear. In this setting, the principal can derive the optimal *linear* contract with respect to only the known actions of the agent. [9] show that her profit from the actual action taken by the agent (which can be one that the principal is unaware of) can only be higher than the principal's expectations.

In the following lemma we show that when the agent is risk-neutral, the optimal theoretical contract is in W, and thus our algorithm learns a contract that approximates it.

Lemma 7. *If the agent is risk-neutral then the optimal contract is H-bounded and monotone-smooth.*

Proof. When the agent is risk neutral, the optimal contract is of the shape $w(i) = \pi(i) - \alpha$ for some constant $\alpha \in \mathbb{R}_+$ (Proposition 14.B.2 on page 482 in [27]). As $\pi(i+1) > \pi(i)$, this contract is monotone-smooth. And as $\pi(k) \leq H$ it is also H-bounded. $\square$

5   Conclusions

In this paper we studied the principal-agent problem when the principal has zero information about the agent. We introduced the class of monotone-smooth contracts and showed that when the optimal contract is monotone-smooth and the agent is bounded risk-averse, then we can learn an approximately optimal contract. We complemented this result with a multi-armed bandit algorithm that finds an approximately optimal contract and we provided bounds on the number of samples it needs. Then, we applied our algorithm to two fundamental scenarios. The first one is when the output space of the task is binary and the second one is when the agent is risk-neutral. Economic theory suggests that the optimal contract *is* monotone-smooth. Thus the net profit of the principal generated by the resulting contract approximates the optimal net profit she can achieve in general. To the best of our knowledge these are the first positive results even regarding approximately optimal contracts.

Several intriguing questions remain. It is interesting to understand whether the assumption of bounded risk-aversion is needed to guarantee learning of monotone-smooth contracts. The answer to this question is not obvious even when there are only two outcomes. Furthermore, we wish to find other conditions and assumptions that allow learning. In our model, we assume that the agents are identical. Can we learn ϵ-optimal contracts if there are many different types of agents? We conjecture that we *can* under the suitable assumptions, like the setting of [20]. On the other hand, we furthermore conjecture that a there exist cases in which learning is *not* possible at all. Lower bounds, or even partial characterizations of such cases would be of great interest.

References

1. Agrawal, R.: The continuum-armed bandit problem. SIAM J. Control. Optim. **33**(6), 1926–1951 (1995)
2. Alon, T., Dütting, P., Talgam-Cohen, I.: Contracts with private cost per unit-of-effort. In: Proceedings of the 22nd ACM Conference on Economics and Computation, pp. 52–69 (2021)
3. Arrow, K.J.: Aspects of the Theory of Risk-Bearing. Yrjö Jahnsson Foundation, Helsinki (1965)
4. Auer, P., Ortner, R., Szepesvári, C.: Improved rates for the stochastic continuum-armed bandit problem. In: Bshouty, N.H., Gentile, C. (eds.) COLT 2007. LNCS (LNAI), vol. 4539, pp. 454–468. Springer, Heidelberg (2007). https://doi.org/10.1007/978-3-540-72927-3_33
5. Babaioff, M., Feldman, M., Nisan, N.: Mixed strategies in combinatorial agency. J. Artif. Intell. Res. **38**, 339–369 (2010)
6. Babaioff, M., Feldman, M., Nisan, N., Winter, E.: Combinatorial agency. J. Econ. Theory **147**(3), 999–1034 (2012)
7. Bubeck, S., Stoltz, G., Yu, J.Y.: Lipschitz bandits without the lipschitz constant. In: Kivinen, J., Szepesvári, C., Ukkonen, E., Zeugmann, T. (eds.) ALT 2011. LNCS (LNAI), vol. 6925, pp. 144–158. Springer, Heidelberg (2011). https://doi.org/10.1007/978-3-642-24412-4_14
8. Bughin, J., et al.: Independent work: choice, necessity, and the gig economy. Technical report, McKinsey & Company 2016 (2016). https://www.mckinsey.com/~/media/McKinsey/GlobalThemes/EmploymentandGrowth/IndependentworkChoicenecessityandthegigeconomy/Independent-Work-Choice-necessity-and-the-gig-economy-Full-report.ashx
9. Carroll, G.: Robustness and linear contracts. Am. Econ. Rev. **105**(2), 536–563 (2015). https://doi.org/10.1257/aer.20131159
10. Castiglioni, M., Marchesi, A., Gatti, N.: Bayesian agency: linear versus tractable contracts. Artif. Intell. **307**, 103684 (2022)
11. Castiglioni, M., Marchesi, A., Gatti, N.: Designing menus of contracts efficiently: the power of randomization. arXiv preprint arXiv:2202.10966 (2022)
12. Conitzer, V., Garera, N.: Learning algorithms for online principal-agent problems (and selling goods online). In: Proceedings of the 23rd International Conference on Machine Learning, pp. 209–216. ACM (2006)

13. Dütting, P., Ezra, T., Feldman, M., Kesselheim, T.: Combinatorial contracts. In: 62nd IEEE Annual Symposium on Foundations of Computer Science, FOCS 2021, Denver, CO, USA, 7–10 February 2022, pp. 815–826. IEEE (2021). https://doi.org/10.1109/FOCS52979.2021.00084

14. Dütting, P., Roughgarden, T., Talgam-Cohen, I.: Simple versus optimal contracts. In: Karlin, A., Immorlica, N., Johari, R. (eds.) Proceedings of the 2019 ACM Conference on Economics and Computation, EC 2019, Phoenix, AZ, USA, 24–28 June 2019, pp. 369–387. ACM (2019). https://doi.org/10.1145/3328526.3329591

15. Dütting, P., Roughgarden, T., Talgam-Cohen, I.: The complexity of contracts. SIAM J. Comput. 50(1), 211–254 (2021). https://doi.org/10.1137/20M132153X

16. Even-Dar, E., Mannor, S., Mansour, Y.: Action elimination and stopping conditions for the multi-armed bandit and reinforcement learning problems. J. Mach. Learn. Res. 7(Jun), 1079–1105 (2006)

17. Gershkov, A., Perry, M.: Dynamic contracts with moral hazard and adverse selection. Rev. Econ. Stud. 79(1), 268–306 (2012). https://doi.org/10.1093/restud/rdr026. https://academic.oup.com/restud/article-lookup/doi/10.1093/restud/rdr026

18. Grossman, S.J., Hart, O.D.: An analysis of the principal-agent problem. Econometrica 51(1), 7–45 (1983). https://doi.org/10.2307/1912246

19. Guruganesh, G., Schneider, J., Wang, J.R.: Contracts under moral hazard and adverse selection. In: Proceedings of the 22nd ACM Conference on Economics and Computation, pp. 563–582 (2021)

20. Ho, C.J., Slivkins, A., Vaughan, J.W.: Adaptive contract design for crowdsourcing markets: bandit algorithms for repeated principal-agent problems. J. Artif. Intell. Res. 55, 317–359 (2016). https://doi.org/10.1145/2600057.2602880

21. Holmstrom, B.: Moral hazard and observability. Bell J. Econ. 10(1), 74 (1979). https://doi.org/10.2307/3003320. https://www.jstor.org/stable/3003320?origin=crossref

22. Holmström, B.: Pay for performance and beyond. Am. Econ. Rev. 107(7), 1753–1777 (2017). https://doi.org/10.1586/14737167.7.4.351. https://www.tandfonline.com/doi/full/10.1586/14737167.7.4.351

23. Kleinberg, R., Slivkins, A., Upfal, E.: Bandits and experts in metric spaces. arXiv preprint arXiv:1312.1277 (2013)

24. Kleinberg, R.D.: Nearly tight bounds for the continuum-armed bandit problem. In: Advances in Neural Information Processing Systems, pp. 697–704 (2005)

25. Laffont, J.J., Martimort, D.: The Theory of Incentives: The Principal-Agent Model. Princeton University Press, Princeton (2009)

26. Magureanu, S., Combes, R., Proutiere, A.: Lipschitz bandits: regret lower bounds and optimal algorithms. arXiv preprint arXiv:1405.4758 (2014)

27. Mas-Colell, A., Whinston, M.D., Green, J.R.: Microeconomic Theory. Oxford University Press, Oxford (1995)

28. Pratt, J.W.: Risk aversion in the small and in the large. Econometrica 32(1/2), 122 (1964). https://doi.org/10.2307/1913738. https://www.jstor.org/stable/1913738?origin=crossref

29. Robbins, H.: Some aspects of the sequential design of experiments. In: Lai, T.L., Siegmund, D. (eds.) Herbert Robbins Selected Papers, pp. 169–177. Springer, Heidelberg (1985)

30. Ross, S.A.: The economic theory of agency?: the principal's problem. Am. Econ. Rev. 63(2), 134–139 (1973)

31. Sannikov, Y.: Contracts: the theory of dynamic principal-agent relationships and the continuous-time approach, vol. 1, pp. 89–124 (2011)
32. Sannikov, Y.: A continuous- time version of the principal: agent problem. Rev. Econ. Stud. **75**(3), 957–984 (2008). https://www.jstor.org/stable/20185061
33. Williams, N.: On dynamic principal-agent problems in continuous time. Technical report, UCLA Department of Economics (2004)

Coopetition Against an Amazon

Ronen Gradwohl[1(✉)] and Moshe Tennenholtz[2]

[1] Department of Economics and Business Administration, Ariel University,
Ariel, Israel
roneng@ariel.ac.il
[2] Faculty of Industrial Engineering and Management, The Technion, Haifa, Israel
moshet@ie.technion.ac.il

Abstract. This paper studies cooperative data-sharing between competitors vying to predict a consumer's tastes. We design optimal data-sharing schemes both for when they compete only with each other, and for when they additionally compete with an Amazon—a company with more, better data. We show that simple schemes—threshold rules that probabilistically induce either full data-sharing between competitors, or the full transfer of data from one competitor to another—are either optimal or approximately optimal, depending on properties of the information structure. We also provide conditions under which firms share more data when they face stronger outside competition, and describe situations in which this conclusion is reversed.

1 Introduction

A key challenge to firms competing in today's electronic marketplace is competition against Big Tech companies that have considerably more data and so better predictive models. One way in which smaller firms may overcome this hurdle is to engage in coopetitive strategies—namely, to cooperate with other small firms that is its competitors. Such coopetitive strategies have increasingly become a field of study by both academics and practitioners (see, for example, [8] and [4]), but they largely focus on industrial applications such as healthcare, IT, and service industries. In this paper, we study coopetition between e-commerce companies, and focus on the possibility of data sharing as a way to deal with their data imbalance vis-à-vis Big Tech.

Such coopetitive data-sharing can be undertaken by the firms themselves or by external service-providers. To facilitate the former, the newly burgeoning area of federated machine learning has as its goal the design of mechanisms that generate predictive models for firms based on such shared data [41]. The assumption underlying federated learning is that these firms actually want predictive

The full version of this paper is available at https://arxiv.org/abs/2005.10038 [18]. Gradwohl gratefully acknowledges the support of National Science Foundation award number 1718670. The work by Moshe Tennenholtz was supported by funding from the European Research Council (ERC) under the European Union's Horizon 2020 research and innovation programme (grant number 740435).

© The Author(s), under exclusive license to Springer Nature Switzerland AG 2022
P. Kanellopoulos et al. (Eds.): SAGT 2022, LNCS 13584, pp. 347–365, 2022.
https://doi.org/10.1007/978-3-031-15714-1_20

models based on all shared data, but in competitive scenarios this need not be the case. Although each firm certainly desires its own model to be as predictive as possible, it most likely does not wish the same for its competitors. So when is full data-sharing, leading to maximally predictive models for *all* firms, optimal? When is partial or no sharing better? And do these answers differ when firms compete against an Amazon?

In addition to using federated machine learning, coopetitive data-sharing can also be facilitated by an external service-provider. While tools for data sharing are prevalent—and include platforms such as Google Merchant and Azure Data Share—they are currently undergoing even further development. For example, in its European Strategy for Data, the European Commission plans the following: "In the period 2021–2027, the Commission will invest in a High Impact Project on European data spaces and federated cloud infrastructures. The project will fund infrastructures, data-sharing tools, architectures and governance mechanisms for thriving data-sharing and Artificial Intelligence ecosystems" [11]. But just as with federated learning, the potential benefits from data sharing may arise under partial, rather than full, sharing. For instance, one industry white paper urges service providers to "...analyze the combined, crowdsourced data and generate benchmark analyses and comparative performance reports. Each participating client gains insights that it could not otherwise access, and each benefits from the service-host provider's ability to *slice and dice* the aggregated data and share the results that are relevant to each client" [30]. What is the optimal way for such service providers to combine, slice and dice, and share e-commerce firms' data in order to facilitate successful coopetition against an Amazon?

Regardless of how coopetitive data-sharing is achieved—via federated learning or through a service provider—the answer to whether or not firms desire maximally predictive models for all depends on how these predictions are eventually used. If the firms involved act in completely unrelated markets, then of course full data-sharing is optimal—it yields a maximally predictive model for a firm, and that firm is not harmed by others' better predictions. This is no longer true if the firms are competitors, since then a firm may be harmed by an improvement in its competitors' predictions. In this case, whether or not the tradeoff is worthwhile depends on the details of the market.

In this paper we focus on one such market, which is motivated by recommender systems for online advertising and Long Tail retail. In our model, there are many types of consumers, and firms use their data to infer and take a tailored action for each consumer type. In the online advertising market, for example, firms use their data to personalize advertisements in order to maximize the probability that a consumer clicks on their ad. Data sharing is common in this market, and platforms such as Google Merchant and Azure Data Share specifically facilitate such sharing across clients in order to improve personalization and increase clickthrough rates.

For another concrete application, consider retailers in a Long Tail market—a market with an enormous number of low-demand goods that collectively make up substantial market share—interested in finding consumers for their products.

Success in such markets crucially relies on retailers' abilities to predict consumers' tastes in order to match them to relevant products [1,37]. On their own, smaller firms can be destroyed by giants with vastly greater amounts of data and thus a clear predictive advantage. In cooperation with other small firms, however, this data imbalance may be mitigated, possibly granting smaller firms a fighting chance.

In this paper we study such cooperation between competing firms, and design data-sharing schemes that are optimal—ones that maximize total firm profits subject to each firm having the proper incentives to participate. More specifically, we study two settings, one without and the other with an Amazon. In the former, in which smaller firms compete only with one another, we show that coopetition is beneficial to the extent that firms can share data to simultaneously improve their respective predictions. In the optimal data-sharing scheme firms benefit from sharing because it allows them to better predict the tastes of consumers for whom no firm predicts well on its own.

In the latter setting, in which smaller firms compete with one another but also with an Amazon, sharing data about consumers for whom no firm predicts well can be beneficial, but is not optimal. We show that, in the optimal scheme, firms share data with others and weaken their own market positions on some market segments, in exchange for receiving data from others and strengthening their market positions on other segments.

The following simple example illustrates our model and previews some of our results. The example is framed as retailers offering goods to consumers who may make a purchase, but can also be interpreted as advertisers displaying advertisements to consumers who may click on the ads. In either case, suppose the market consists of two goods, g_0 and g_1, that consumers may desire. Each consumer is described by a feature vector in $\{0,1\} \times \{0,1\}$ that determines that consumer's taste: Consumers of types 00 and 11 are only interested in g_0, whereas consumers of types 01 and 10 are only interested in g_1. A priori, suppose the distribution of consumers in the market is such that an α fraction are of type 00, a β fraction of type 01, a γ fraction of type 10, and a δ fraction of type 11.

When a consumer shows up to the market, a retailer may offer him one of the goods (as a convention, we use masculine pronouns for consumers and feminine pronouns for retailers/players). If the retailer has data about the consumer's type, she will offer the good desired by that consumer. Assume that when a consumer is offered the correct good he makes the purchase, and that this leads to a profit of 1 to the retailer. If there are two retailers offering this good to the consumer he chooses one at random from whom to make the purchase. A retailer whose good is not chosen gets profit 0.

Suppose now that there are two retailers pursuing the same consumer, but that they do not fully know the consumer's type. Instead, the first retailer only knows the first bit of the consumer's type, and the second retailer only knows the second bit. This situation is summarized in Fig. 1, where the first retailer knows the row bit and the second knows the column bit. Which goods should the competing retailers offer the consumer? For this example, suppose for simplicity

(a) Desired good   (b) Prior probability

Fig. 1. Data sharing: An example

that $\alpha > 2\beta \geq 2\gamma > 4\delta$. Then each of the retailers has a dominant strategy: If the bit they know is 0, offer g_0, and if the bit they know is 1, offer g_1.

To see that this is a dominant strategy, consider for example the row retailer, and suppose she learns that a consumer's row bit is 0. She thus knows that the correct good is g_0 with probability $\alpha/(\alpha+\beta)$ and g_1 with probability $\beta/(\alpha+\beta)$. Her utility, however, depends also on the good offered by the column retailer. The row retailer's worst-case utility from offering g_0 is $\alpha/(2\alpha+2\beta)$, which occurs when the column player also offers g_0. Her best case utility from offering g_1 is $\beta/(\alpha+\beta)$. Since we assumed $\alpha > 2\beta$, offering g_0 is best for the row player regardless of the other retailer's offer, and is thus dominant. The analyses for the case in which the row retailer's bit is 1, as well as for the column retailer's strategy, are similar.

The result from deployment of these dominant strategies is that consumers of type 00 will be offered the correct good by both retailers, and will thus choose one at random. Consumers of types 01 and 10 will be offered the correct good by only one of the retailers, whereas consumers of type 11 will not make a purchase as they will not be offered the correct good. The expected profit of the first retailer will thus be $\alpha/2 + \gamma$, and of the second retailer $\alpha/2 + \beta$.

Does data sharing improve retailers' profits? Suppose retailers could share their respective information with one another, so that both always knew the consumer's type. This would lead to both always offering the correct good, and hence to expected profits of $1/2$ for each. However, this would be detrimental to the second retailer whenever $\alpha/2 + \beta > 1/2$, since her profits with data sharing would be lower than without. Such cooperation is thus not *individually rational* – the second retailer will not want to cooperate with the first.

Instead, suppose there is a *mediator*—a trusted third-party that may represent either a service provider or a cryptographic protocol (such as a federated learning algorithm) run by the two retailers. Given such a mediator, consider the following data-sharing scheme: both retailers share their data with the mediator, who then passes along the data to all retailers *only* if the consumer's type is 11. If the consumer is not of type 11 then each retailer has her original data, and additionally infers that the consumer's type is not 11 (for otherwise she would have learned that the type is 11).

How does this scheme affect retailers' strategies? Clearly, when retailers learn that the consumer's type is 11, both offer g_0. What happens if a retailer learns that the consumer's type is not 11? Consider the row retailer. If her bit is 0, then learning that the consumer's type is not 11 does not provide any new information, and so she still has the same dominant strategy of offering g_0. If her bit is 1, however, then she learns that the consumer's type must be 10. But note that in this case, her best strategy is to offer g_1, which is the same as her dominant strategy absent a mediator. Thus, the mediator changes the row retailer's behavior *only* when the consumer is of type 11. A similar analysis and conclusion hold for the column retailer.

Since retailers offer the same goods with and without data sharing in all cases except when the consumer is of type 11, this scheme changes retailer's profits only in this latter case. In particular, it leads to an additional (ex ante) profit of $\delta/2$ for each retailer beyond her original profit—with probability δ the consumer is of type 11, in which case the retailers split the additional surplus of 1—and is thus beneficial to both. We show that such a scheme is, in fact, not only individually rational but also optimal.

Suppose now that the two retailers are also competing against an Amazon for the consumer. Since the Amazon is a giant it has more data, and, in particular, we assume that it has complete information about each consumer's type. In this three-way competition, the original dominant strategies of our two smaller retailers do not perform as well: They lead to profits of $\alpha/3+\gamma/2$ and $\alpha/3+\beta/2$ to the first and second retailer, respectively, since when they offer the correct good the consumer now chooses amongst up to 3 retailers. The mediator described above, which reveals information when the type is 11, leads to higher profits, since now there is an additional $\delta/3$ to each of the smaller retailers. However, that mediator is no longer optimal, and the retailers can actually do better.

To see this, observe that, conditional on consumer type 01, the total profit to the small retailers is $\beta/2$, since only the second makes the correct offer g_1 and then competes with the Amazon. In contrast, if both retailers were to know the type and offer the correct good, then their total profit would be $2\beta/3$, namely $\beta/3$ each. This is harmful to the second retailer as it involves a loss of profit, but a gain for the first and the sum. But the second retailer can be compensated by getting data from the first elsewhere, for instance on consumer type 10.

For simplicity of this example, suppose that $\beta = \gamma$, and consider a mediator that facilitates full data-sharing, in which both retailers learn each other's data and thus have complete information about consumers' types. Here, the profit of each is $1/3 > \alpha/3 + \beta/2 = \alpha/3 + \gamma/2$, so both gain from this data sharing. Furthermore, the total profit of the retailers is $2/3$, which is the maximal utility they can obtain when competing against an Amazon. Thus, this data-sharing scheme is individually rational and optimal. Observe that it leads to higher retailer welfare than the optimal scheme absent a mediator.

Full data-sharing is not always individually rational, however. If β is much greater than γ, then the second retailer is not sufficiently compensated by the first for sharing data about consumer 01. The second retailer will consequently be harmed by such data sharing, and so the scheme will not be individually rational. However, in Theorem 2 we show that there is a different data-sharing scheme that is individually rational and optimal, in which the first retailer shares all her data and the second shares some of her data. Overall, we show that such data-sharing coopetition against an Amazon is beneficial to the small retailers.

Contribution. Our model is more general than the simple example above, and involves many goods and many types of consumers. For the example it was useful to think of each consumer as having a feature vector describing his type, but in the model we take a more general approach that allows for a wider class of information structures. Furthermore, in general the retailers will not have dominant strategies, either with or without a mediator. Instead, we suppose that, absent a mediator, players play an arbitrary Bayesian Nash equilibrium, and construct mediators that lead to higher expected utilities in equilibrium.

In Sect. 3, we design optimal mediators for coopetitive data-sharing. In addition to maximizing total retailer profits, all our mediators are individually rational—retailers attain higher utilities when they use the mediators—and incentive compatible—in equilibrium, each retailer's best strategy is to follow the mediators' recommendations. Interestingly, we show that, despite the complexity of the environment, simple schemes are optimal. In particular, instead of relying on the details of retailers' data or on their strategies in equilibrium sans data-sharing (as in the introductory example above), optimal mediators consist of threshold rules that probabilistically induce either full data-sharing between retailers, or the full transfer of data from one retailer to another.

The analysis in Sect. 3 retains one of the assumptions present in the example above—that the joint data of the small retailers is sufficient to uniquely identify each consumer's type. In Sect. 4 we drop this assumption, leading to a new set of challenges. This is because, when the assumption holds, there is no conflict between welfare maximization and equilibrium, and so the main hurdle in designing optimal mediators is the individual rationality constraint. Without the assumption, however, participants' incentive compatibility constraints impose a limit on the total welfare that can be achieved. Surprisingly, however, we show that variants of the simple mediators from Sect. 3 are approximately optimal here as well. We also show that our approximation factor is tight.

Finally, in Sect. 5 we delve into the intriguing question of whether players share more data in the presence of an Amazon or in its absence. First, under the assumption that the joint data of the small retailers is sufficient to uniquely identify each consumer's type, we show that if data sharing is strictly beneficial in the absence of an Amazon, then it is also strictly beneficial in its presence. This confirms the intuition that players are more likely to share data when facing stronger outside competition. However, we also show that this conclusion may be reversed when the assumption does not hold—namely, that sometimes data sharing can be strictly beneficial in the absence of an Amazon, but *not* in its presence. We argue that this counterintuitive result hinges on whether or not players' equilibrium considerations conflict with welfare maximization.

The rest of the paper proceeds as follows. First we survey the related literature, and then, in Sect. 2, develop the formal model. This is followed by our main analyses in Sects. 3, 4, and 5, and concluding notes in Sect. 6. Due to space constraints, all proofs are deferred to the full version [18].

Related Literature. Most broadly, our paper contributes to a burgeoning literature on competition in prediction and machine learning. Within this literature, papers such as [3,32], and [12] study different models of learning embedded in settings where participants compete with others in their predictions. They take participants' data as given, and point to the effect competition has on optimal learning algorithms. Our focus, in contrast, is on the effect of data sharing on competitive prediction.

Because of its focus on data sharing, our paper is also related to the more established literature on strategic information-sharing, a literature that focuses on a number of distinct applications: oligopolistic competition [9,38], financial intermediation [15,23,36], supply chain management [21,39], price discrimination [24,29], and competition between data brokers [20,22]. Much of this literature revolves around the question of whether it is beneficial for participating firms to pool all their data, or whether they would prefer to pool only some or none at all. As [6] demonstrate, however, more finely tuned data sharing can be beneficial even when full or partial pooling is not, and so the existing schemes do not exhaust the potential benefits of data sharing. In this paper we analyze precisely such finely tuned sharing.

A different paper that does consider more finely tuned sharing is that of [42], who study an infinitely repeated setting in which firms compete for market share. Their main result is the construction of a data sharing scheme that Pareto improves all participants' welfare. Like our results, their scheme also only reveals partial information to participants. Unlike our approach, however, [42]'s scheme relies on the repeated nature of the interaction, and uses folk-theorem-type arguments to show that cooperation can be sustained. A similarly related paper is [19], which analyzes finely tuned sharing in a Hotelling duopoly model. Neither of the papers above considers the possible presence of an Amazon.

In terms of modeling and techniques, our paper falls into the literature on information design. Information design, recently surveyed by [10] and by [7], is the study of how the allocation of information affects incentives and hence behavior, with a focus on the extent and limits of purely informational manipulation. The information design problem encompasses work on communication in games and on Bayesian persuasion. When the mediator is assumed to have only the information held by the players, or only the information they are willing to share with him, the problem maps to the one studied in the literature on communication in games. The goal of these studies is to characterize the equilibrium outcomes achievable when players are allowed to communicate prior to playing a fixed game, and where communication is captured by players' interaction with a mediator. [35] and [14] provide useful overviews. Our paper builds on this model by endowing the mediator with the specific aim of maximizing players' utilities.

A different setting, called Bayesian persuasion [26], is one in which only the mediator (here called the sender) has payoff-relevant information, and in which he can commit to a particular information structure prior to observing that information. Initial work on Bayesian persuasion focused on the case of a single sender and a single player [26], but more recent research also consists of settings with multiple senders (such as [16]) and multiple players.

A closely related strand of the literature, recently surveyed by [5], focuses on the sale of information by a data broker. Most of this work differs from our paper in that it focuses on a market with one-sided information flow, with information going only from one party to another, whereas we study a market where information flow is bidirectional across firms.

Our paper is also related to a set of papers that focuses on designing mediators to achieve various goals, such as to improve the incentives of players, make equilibria robust to collusion, or implement correlated equilibria while guaranteeing privacy [27, 33, 34].

Finally, our work is related to research in machine learning on how competition affect predictions and data purchase (see, e.g., [13, 17, 28]). It is also conceptually related to research on federated learning, and in particular on cross-silo federated learning [25]. This framework consists of a set of agents with individual data whose goal is to jointly compute a predictive model. A recent emphasis within federated learning is on incentivizing the agents to participate, sometimes through monetary transfers [43] and sometimes by providing different models to different agents [31]. Our paper differs, in that agents are assumed to utilize the resulting models in some competition, and this subsequent competition drives agents' incentives to participate. Our work is thus orthogonal to that surveyed by [43]: we do not focus on the algorithmic aspects of computing a joint model, but rather on the benefits of participating even when others are competitors.

2   Model and Preliminaries

There is a set G of goods and a population of consumers interested in obtaining one of them. Each consumer has one of a finite set of types, $\omega \in \Omega$, that describes the good $g_\omega \in G$ in which he is interested. There are three players who compete for consumers: two regular players indexed 1 and 2, and an Amazon, a player indexed 0. We will separate the analysis to two settings: first, when the Amazon player 0 is not present and players 1 and 2 compete only with one another; and second, when they additionally compete with Amazon. The model and definitions here apply to both settings.

Player 0 (if present) has complete information of the consumer's type. In Sect. 3 we assume that players 1 and 2 have *jointly complete information*—that, when combined, their respective data uniquely identifies each consumer's type—but that each player on her own may only be partially informed.

To model this informational setting, we represent players' data using the information partition model of [2]: Each player i is endowed with a partition Π_i of Ω, where Π_i is a set of disjoint, nonempty sets whose union is Ω. For each $\omega \in \Omega$ we denote by $P_i(\omega)$ the unique element of Π_i that contains ω, with the interpretation that if the realized type of consumer is ω, each player i only learns that the type belongs to the set $P_i(\omega)$.

Framing the example from the introduction within this model would associate Ω with $\{0, 1\}^2$ and the partitions $P_1(00) = P_1(01) = \{00, 01\}$, $P_1(10) = P_1(11) = \{10, 11\}$, $P_2(00) = P_2(10) = \{00, 10\}$, and $P_2(01) = P_2(11) = \{01, 11\}$.

In this model, player 0's complete information means that $P_0(\omega) = \{\omega\}$ for all $\omega \in \Omega$, and players 1 and 2's jointly complete information means that $P_1(\omega) \cap P_2(\omega) = \{\omega\}$ for all $\omega \in \Omega$. We further assume that, before obtaining any information, all players have a common prior π over Ω.

To model data sharing between players 1 and 2 we suppose there is a mediator that gathers each player's information and shares it with the other in some way. Formally, a mediator is a function $\mathcal{M} : 2^\Omega \times 2^\Omega \mapsto \Delta(M^2)$, where M is an arbitrary message space. The range is a distribution over pairs of messages, where the first (resp., second) is the message sent to player 1 (resp., player 2).

We begin with an informal description of the game: Players offer consumers a good, and consumers choose a player from whom to acquire the good. Consumers are *single-minded*: For each ω there is a unique $g_\omega \in G$ such that the consumer will only choose a player who offers good g_ω. If there is more than one such player, the consumer chooses uniformly at random between them. One interpretation of this consumer behavior is that he chooses by "satisficing"—making a random choice among options that are "good enough" [40], where g_ω represents these good-enough options. See [3] for a similar approach.

We assume that prices and costs are fixed, and normalize a player's utility to 1 if she is chosen and to 0 otherwise. So, for example, in the online advertising application of our model, consumers are assumed to click on a random ad amongst those ads that are most relevant; once they click, the expected profit to the advertiser (conversion rate times profit from a sale) is 1. The normalization to 1 is actually without loss of generality. If we had a different profit p_ω for each consumer type ω, then we could change every p_ω to 1, modify the prior probability $\pi(\omega)$ of type ω to $p_\omega \cdot \pi(\omega)$, and then renormalize the prior to be a proper distribution. This would leave all of our analysis intact.

The following is the order of events, given a fixed mediator $\mathcal{M}$. It applies both to the case in which there are only two players $\{1, 2\}$ and to the case in which there is an additional Amazon player, indexed 0.

1. Each of players 1 and 2 chooses whether or not to opt into using the mediator.
2. If one or both players $\{1, 2\}$ did not opt into using the mediator, then each player i obtains her *base value*, the utility v_i (described below).
3. If both players $\{1, 2\}$ opted into using the mediator, then:
   (a) A consumer of type ω is chosen from Ω with prior distribution π.
   (b) If present, player 0 learns $P_0(\omega)$.
   (c) Messages (M_1, M_2) are chosen from the distribution $\mathcal{M}(P_1(\omega), P_2(\omega))$, and each $i \in \{1, 2\}$ learns their own $P_i(\omega)$ and M_i.
   (d) Each player simultaneously chooses a good to offer the consumer, and then the consumer chooses a player from whom to obtain the good.

There are several ways to interpret the base values v_1 and v_2. Our main interpretation is that these are the expected utilities of the players in the game without data sharing. To formalize this, consider the *unmediated* game $\Gamma = (\Omega, \mathcal{P}, G^{|\mathcal{P}|}, (P_i(\cdot))_{i \in \mathcal{P}}, (u_i)_{i \in \mathcal{P}}, \pi)$, where $\mathcal{P}$ is the set of participating players, and is either $\{1, 2\}$ or $\{0, 1, 2\}$, G is the set of actions, $P_i(\cdot)$ is the information of player i (which consists of the partition element of the realized type), u_i is i's utility function (described below), and π is the common prior over Ω. Given this Bayesian game, let $v = (v_1, v_2)$ be the expected utilities in some *Bayesian Nash equilibrium (BNE)* of Γ—a profile (s_1, s_2) in which s_i is the best strategy for each player i conditional on her information and the assumption that the other player plays the strategy s_j.

Although this is the main interpretation of the base values, our model and results permit additional and more general interpretations as well. One additional interpretation is to suppose each v_i is the minimax value of player i in the unmediated game. In this second interpretation, we could imagine player j "punishing" player i if the latter does not opt into using the mediator, by playing a strategy that minimizes the latter's payoff (off the equilibrium path). A third, more general interpretation is that the base values also depend on factors outside of the specific game, such as firm size, customer base, and so on, in addition to the primitives of the game Γ.

In our constructions of mediators in Sects. 3 and 4, the interpretation of v will not matter—our mediators will be optimal given any such values, regardless of whether they are derived endogenously as the equilibrium utilities of the game absent a mediator, or whether they arise exogenously from factors outside of the specific game. However, in Sect. 5, in which we compare data sharing across two different environments—with and without a mediator—we will stick with the main interpretation of base values as equilibrium payoffs absent a mediator. This is because, when we compare two different environments, the payoffs players could attain without a mediator will differ across these environments.

Now, as noted above, data sharing is modeled as a mediator $\mathcal{M} : 2^\Omega \times 2^\Omega \mapsto \Delta(M^2)$. Without loss of generality we invoke the revelation principle and assume that $M = G$, the set of possible goods. We interpret the messages of the mediator as recommended actions to the players, one recommendation for each player.

Formally, if both players 1 and 2 opt into using the mediator $\mathcal{M}$, then all play the mediated Bayesian game $\Gamma^{\mathcal{M}} = (\Omega, \mathcal{P}, G^{|\mathcal{P}|}, \mathcal{I}^{\mathcal{M}}, (u_i)_{i \in \mathcal{P}}, \pi)$. $\mathcal{P}$ is the set of participating players, and is either $\{1, 2\}$ or $\{0, 1, 2\}$. The function $\mathcal{I}^{\mathcal{M}} : \Omega \mapsto \Delta(T^{|\mathcal{P}|})$ denotes the information of players in the game for each state, where $T = 2^\Omega \times M$ is the set of possible pieces of information a player may have—a partition element and a message from the mediator. For player 0, this information consists of the realized type of consumer only, and so $\mathcal{I}^{\mathcal{M}}(\cdot)_0 = (P_0(\cdot), \emptyset)$ (where the $\emptyset$ means player 0 gets no message from the mediator). For players 1 and 2, the information consists of both the partition element of the realized type of consumer and the action recommended to her by the mediator, and so $\mathcal{I}^{\mathcal{M}}(\cdot)_i = (P_i(\cdot), \mathcal{M}(P_1(\cdot), P_2(\cdot))_i)$.

Next, each player's set of actions in the mediated game is G, and her utility function $u_i = u_i : \Omega \times G^{|\mathcal{P}|} \mapsto \mathbb{R}$. The latter is equal to 0 if player i's action $g \neq g_\omega$, and otherwise it is equal to $1/k$, where k is the total number of players who play action g_ω. The nonzero utility corresponds to utility 1 if a consumer chooses the player's good, which occurs if a player offers the consumer the correct good and the consumer chooses uniformly amongst all players that do so. We often write $E[u_i(\cdot)]$ when the expectation is over the choice of ω, in which case we omit the dependence of u_i on ω for brevity. Finally, (mixed) strategies of players in Γ are functions $s_i : T \mapsto \Delta(G)$. We also denote by $s_i(\omega) = s_i(\mathcal{I}_i(\omega))$.

An important note about the mediator is in order. We assume that when players opt into participating, they *truthfully* reveal all their data $P_i(\omega)$ to him. Players' strategic behavior is relevant in their choice of opting in or not, and then in whether or not they follow the mediator's recommendation in their interaction with the consumer. While truthful reporting is clearly restrictive, it is a natural assumption in our context—for instance, when service providers act as mediators, they are typically also the ones who host retailers' data in the cloud, and so already have the (true) data on their servers. Similarly, federated machine learning algorithms assume that participants share their true data.

Individual Rationality, Incentive Compatibility, and Optimality. A first observation is that player 0, if present, has a dominant strategy: $s_0(\omega) = g_\omega$. We will thus take that player's strategy as fixed throughout.

We will be interested in designing mediators that players actually wish to utilize, and so would like them to satisfy two requirements: first, that players want to follow the mediator's recommendations, and so that following these recommendations forms an equilibrium; and second, that players prefer their payoffs with the mediator over their payoffs without (the base values). Formally:

- $\mathcal{M}$ is *incentive compatible (IC)* if the strategy profile $\bar{s}$ in which players 1 and 2 always follow $\mathcal{M}$'s recommendation is a BNE of $\Gamma^{\mathcal{M}}$.
- $\mathcal{M}$ is *individually rational (IR)* if the expected utility of each player $i \in \{1, 2\}$ under $\bar{s}$ in $\Gamma^{\mathcal{M}}$ is (weakly) greater than v_i.

Observe that if a mediator is both IC and IR, then in equilibrium players will opt in and then follow the mediator's recommendations. Finally, as we are interested in the extent to which data sharing benefits players 1 and 2, we will study *optimal* mediators, namely, ones in which the sum of these two players' utilities is maximal subject to the IC and IR constraints. To this end, denote by $W(\mathcal{M})$ the sum of players 1 and 2's expected utilities under $\bar{s}$ in $\Gamma^{\mathcal{M}}$. Then:

Definition 1. *Mediator $\mathcal{M}$ is* optimal *if $W(\mathcal{M}) \geq W(\mathcal{M}')$ for any other $\mathcal{M}'$ that is IC and IR.*

3   Jointly Complete Information

The analysis of the optimal mediator under jointly complete information when there is no Amazon is fairly straightforward and appears in [18].

In this section we suppose there is an Amazon, and first ask: under what base values v does there exist an IR, IC mediator? To begin, observe that for any mediator $\mathcal{M}$ and any type ω the total welfare of players 1 and 2 is at most $2/3$ (since Amazon always knows the type, offers the correct good, and gets at least $1/3$ of the surplus), so it must be the case that $W(\mathcal{M}) \leq 2/3$. Thus, if $v_1 + v_2 > 2/3$, then there does not exist any IR mediator.

However, even if $v_1 + v_2 \leq 2/3$, there may still not exist a mediator that is both IR and IC. In the example from the introduction, for instance, in the simple case with an Amazon and where $\alpha > 2\beta \geq 2\gamma > 4\delta$, the row retailer can guarantee herself a payoff of $(\alpha + \gamma)/3$ by ignoring the mediator and playing her dominant actions. This implies that the most the column retailer can obtain is $2/3 - (\alpha + \gamma)/3$. Any mediator that leads to a higher payoff to the column retailer must therefore fail to satisfy the IC constraints. The result below consists of bounds on the base values under which an IR, IC mediator exists.

Theorem 1. *Suppose $v_i \geq v_j$. Then an IR, IC mediator exists only if $v_i \leq E\left[u_i(g_\omega, s'_j(\omega))\right]$ and $v_j \leq 1 - 2v_i$.*

For the rest of this section, call a pair v that satisfies the conditions in Theorem 1 a *feasible* v. We now turn to our main result for the section, the construction of an optimal mediator. At the same time, we show that the conditions in Theorem 1 are not only necessary but also sufficient. We begin with a definition.

Definition 2. *A mediator $\mathcal{M}$ is* fully revealing *to player i if the mediator's recommendation to player i always coincides with the optimal good: $\bar{s}_i(\omega) = g_\omega$ for every ω. A mediator facilitates* full data-sharing *if it is fully revealing to both players $\mathcal{P}\backslash\{0\}$.*

Fix the set of players to be $\mathcal{P} = \{0, 1, 2\}$. Consider the strategy s'_j of player j that, for every $P_j(\omega)$, chooses one of the goods that is most likely to be correct: $s'_j(\omega) \in \arg\max_{g \in G} \Pr[g = g_\omega | P_j(\omega)]$. Note that s'_j is a best-response to a player $i \neq j$ who always chooses the correct good g_ω. Furthermore, let α_j be the overall probability that s'_j chooses the correct good: $\alpha_j = \Pr\left[s'_j(\omega) = g_\omega\right]$.

Now, suppose $v_i \geq v_j$. Then if $v_i \leq 1/3$, then the mediator will facilitate full data-sharing, and so each player will offer the correct good in every state. If $v_i > 1/3$ then player i will obtain all the information and player j will obtain only partial information: she will get recommendation g_ω with probability less than 1, and otherwise will get recommendation $s'_j(\omega)$. In Mediator 1 below we maximize the probability of recommendation g_ω subject to the IR constraints, and do this in a way that following the recommendations is a BNE.

Mediator 1. Mediator for $\mathcal{P} = \{0, 1, 2\}$ with jointly complete information

```
1:  procedure M_A^v(V, W)          ▷ V = P_1(ω) and W = P_2(ω) for realized ω ∈ Ω
2:      ω ← V ∩ W
3:      i ← arg max_{k∈{1,2}} v_k
4:      j ← 3 - i
5:      if v_i ≤ 1/3 then return (g_ω, g_ω)          ▷ Full data-sharing
6:      else
7:          g_j ← s'_j(ω)
8:          Choose γ ∈ [0, 1] uniformly at random.
9:          if γ < (3-6v_i-α_j)/(1-α_j) then
10:             return (g_ω, g_ω)
11:         else if i = 1 then return (g_ω, g_j)
12:         else return (g_j, g_ω)
```

Theorem 2. *For any feasible v, $\mathcal{M}_A^v$ (Mediator 1) is IR, IC, and optimal.*

We also characterize all optimal mediators:

Theorem 3. *For any feasible v and any optimal IR mediator $\mathcal{M}$, one of the following holds: (i) $\mathcal{M}$ is fully revealing to both players 1 and 2; or (ii) $\mathcal{M}$ is fully revealing to one of the players, and the IR constraint binds for that player (i.e., she is indifferent between $\mathcal{M}$ and her base value).*

4   No Jointly Complete Information

We now drop the assumption that players 1 and 2 have jointly complete information. Formally, for a given type ω let $S(\omega) = P_1(\omega) \cap P_2(\omega)$, and call each such $S(\omega)$ a *segment*. The assumption of jointly complete information states that all segments are singletons, and in this section we consider the more general setting in which segments may contain more than one type of consumer.

This setting presents new challenges, as there is now a new conflict between optimal strategies and welfare. As an example, consider some segment $S = \{\omega^1, \omega^2\}$ for which $\Pr[\omega^1] = 4 \cdot \Pr[\omega^2]$. Then, conditional on segment S, both players have a dominant strategy, namely, to offer $g = g_{\omega^1}$. To see this, observe that a player's utility from offering g_{ω^1} is at least $\Pr[\omega^1]/2$ regardless of the other's action, the utility from offering g_{ω^2} is at most $\Pr[\omega^2]$, and by assumption $\Pr[\omega^1]/2 = 2\Pr[\omega^2] > \Pr[\omega^2]$. This leads to total welfare $\Pr[\omega^1]$. However, if players were to separate rather than pool—one offering g_{ω^1} and the other g_{ω^2}—then the total welfare would be $\Pr[\omega^1] + \Pr[\omega^2]$, which is higher. Note that this conflict between optimal strategies and welfare does not occur when players have jointly complete information, since then the pooling action, which is dominant, is also welfare-maximizing. Finally, although we illustrated this conflict for the setting without an Amazon, it is of course also present with an Amazon.

This conflict between optimal strategies and welfare maximization makes the design of mediators significantly more challenging. Nonetheless, we will show that *simple* mediators—in particular, variants of the ones from Sect. 3 for the setting with jointly complete information—are *approximately* optimal. Furthermore, we will show that these simple mediators are not only approximately optimal relative to the optimal IR, IC mediator, but rather that they are approximately optimal relative to a higher benchmark—namely, the welfare that can be achieved by *any* mediator, even one that is not IR or IC. Then, to complement our results, we will show that the approximation factors our mediators achieve are tight or nearly-tight, and that no other IR and IC mediator can in general achieve a better approximation factor relative to that same benchmark.

We begin with some notation. For any given segment $S(\omega)$, denote by g_ω^1 the good g that has the highest probability $\Pr[g = g_\omega | S(\omega)]$ in $S(\omega)$, and by g_ω^2 the good with the second highest probability, under the prior π. If there are several such goods, fix two such goods arbitrarily. Next, let $\phi_\omega^1 = \Pr[g_\omega^1 = g_\omega | S(\omega)]$ be the probability of g_ω^1 conditional on $S(\omega)$, and $\phi_\omega^2 = \Pr[g_\omega^2 = g_\omega | S(\omega)]$ be the respective probability of g_ω^2. We will also use the notation that, for a given segment $S \in \{S(\omega) : \omega \in \Omega\}$, the goods g_S^1 and g_S^2 are the goods with the highest and second-highest probabilities in S, with ϕ_S^1 and ϕ_S^2 their respective conditional probabilities. Finally, let ϕ^1 be the total (unconditional) weight of goods g_S^1 over all segments S, and ϕ^2 be the total weight of goods g_S^2: Formally, for each $k \in \{1, 2\}$, let $\phi^k = \sum_{S \in \{S(\omega) : \omega \in \Omega\}} \phi_S^k \cdot \Pr[S]$.

We will focus on the setting with an Amazon. We note that, while we drop the assumption that players 1 and 2 have jointly complete information, we still assume that the Amazon player 0 has complete information. That is, even though in any given segment S players 1 and 2 do not know which type $\omega \in S$ is realized, player 0 does know, and offers each such type the correct good g_ω.

We proceed as follows. We begin in with the design of an optimal mediator for a particular setting of parameters, namely, for the case in which $\phi_S^1 \leq \frac{3}{2} \cdot \phi_S^2$ for every segment S. We then turn to our main analysis, for the case in which $\phi_S^1 > \frac{3}{2} \cdot \phi_S^2$ for every segment S. There we design the approximately optimal simple mediator mentioned above, and analyze the tightness of the approximation factor. Finally, we show how to combine the two mediators in order to obtain an approximately optimal mediator for the general setting.

Optimal Mediator for $\phi_S^1 \leq \frac{3}{2} \cdot \phi_S^2$. We begin with the simpler case in which $\phi_S^1 \leq \frac{3}{2} \cdot \phi_S^2$ for every segment S. This case is simpler because here, conditional on any given segment, there is no conflict between optimal strategies and welfare maximization. In particular, both involve separating, with one player offering g_S^1 and the other offering g_S^2:

Claim 1. *Conditional on any segment S, if $\phi_S^1 \leq \frac{3}{2} \cdot \phi_S^2$ then the separating strategy profile is both welfare maximizing and an equilibrium.*

Given the lack of conflict between welfare maximization and equilibrium shown in Claim 1, the construction of the optimal mediator is straightforward: it facilitates full data-sharing between the players, and recommends the actions that lead to a separating equilibrium. Details appear in [18], where we construct the optimal Mediator $\mathcal{M}_1^v$ for this setting.

Approximately Optimal Mediator for $\phi_S^1 > \frac{3}{2} \cdot \phi_S^2$. Suppose now that $\phi_S^1 > \frac{3}{2} \cdot \phi_S^2$ for every segment S. This case is more complicated since, for any segment, optimal strategies and welfare maximization may conflict:

Claim 2. *Conditional on any segment S, if $\phi_S^1 > \frac{3}{2} \cdot \phi_S^2$ then pooling on g_S^1 is the dominant strategy. If $\phi_S^1 \leq 3 \cdot \phi_S^2$ then separating is welfare-maximizing, whereas if $\phi_S^1 > 3 \cdot \phi_S^2$ then pooling is welfare-maximizing.*

Our goal is to design a mediator that is approximately optimal relative to a particular benchmark. We denote the benchmark OPT, which is the maximal welfare attainable by any mediator, even disregarding the IR and IC constraints. We show that $\mathcal{M}_2^v$, a variant of mediator $\mathcal{M}_A^v$ for the case of jointly complete information, is IR, IC, and obtains welfare at least $\frac{3}{4} \cdot$ OPT. We also show that this approximation factor is tight. Due to space constraints, the mediator is formally described in [18].

Theorem 4. *Let $v_i \geq v_j$, and suppose $v_i \leq E\left[u_i(g^1_\omega, s'_j(\omega))\right]$ and $v_j \leq \phi^1/2 - v_i$. Then the mediator $\mathcal{M}^v_2$ is IR, IC, and has welfare $W(\mathcal{M}^v_2) \geq \frac{3}{4} \cdot \text{OPT}$.*

In [18] we show that the approximation factor of 3/4 is tight, by giving an example wherein there does not exist an IR mediator, not even one that is not IC, that achieves a factor higher than 3/4. We also show that even without the IR constraints, there does not exist an IC mediator that achieves an approximation factor higher than 4/5.

Approximately Optimal Mediator for the General Setting. Each of the two mediators in the previous two sections is IR, IC, and approximately-optimal under a particular setting of parameters, but not in the other. The mediators can be combined in order to yield an IR, IC, and approximately optimal mediator for any parameter setting. The idea is straightforward: to run $\mathcal{M}^v_1$ on segments S for which $\phi^1_S \leq \frac{3}{2} \cdot \phi^2_S$, and to run $\mathcal{M}^v_2$ on segments S for which $\phi^1_S > \frac{3}{2} \cdot \phi^2_S$. Details are deferred to [18].

5 Do Players Share More with or Without an Amazon?

In this section we consider the intriguing question of whether players optimally share more data in the presence of an Amazon or in its absence. While it seems intuitive that players would share more data when facing stronger outside competition, we show here that this is not necessarily the case. We also show that the reason the intuition fails is related to the possible conflict between equilibrium and welfare maximization identified in Claim 2.

Because we are interested in comparing data sharing across two different environments—without and with an Amazon—we focus on our main interpretation of the base values v, namely, that they correspond to the equilibrium expected utilities absent a mediator. Of course, because the two environments differ, so will these equilibrium expected utilities. We will thus be interested in comparing the benefit of data sharing relative to firms' no-sharing equilibrium utilities v^{noA} absent an Amazon with the benefit of data sharing relative to firms' no-sharing equilibrium utilities v^A in the presence of an Amazon.

Conditions for Sharing with Jointly Complete Information. We first show that, under jointly complete information, when players can strictly benefit from data sharing in the absence of an Amazon, they can also strictly benefit from data sharing in the presence of an Amazon.

Theorem 5. *Fix an unmediated game $\Gamma = \left(\Omega, \mathcal{P}, G^2, (P_i(\cdot))_{i \in \mathcal{P}}, (u_i)_{i \in \mathcal{P}}, \pi\right)$ in which there is jointly complete information and no Amazon, and let (v_1, v_2) be the expected utilities in a BNE of Γ for which $v_1 + v_2$ is maximal. Also, let $\Gamma' = \left(\Omega, \mathcal{P}, G^3, (P_i(\cdot))_{i \in \mathcal{P}}, (u_i)_{i \in \mathcal{P}}, \pi\right)$ be the same unmediated game, except with an Amazon, and let (v'_1, v'_2) be the expected utilities in some BNE of Γ'. Then if there exists an IR, IC mediator $\mathcal{M}$ in the game without an Amazon such that*

$W(\mathcal{M}) > v_1 + v_2$, there also exists an IR, IC mediator $\mathcal{M}'$ in the game with an Amazon such that $W(\mathcal{M}') > v_1' + v_2'$.

The converse of Theorem 5 is not true—there are examples where players strictly benefit from data sharing in the presence of an Amazon but not in its absence. A simple example is the game described in Fig. 1 in the Introduction, with parameters $\alpha > \beta = \gamma > \delta = 0$. In the absence of an Amazon, the unique equilibrium yields maximal welfare of 1, since at least one consumer always offers the correct good. Thus, data sharing cannot strictly improve welfare. In the presence of an Amazon, however, data sharing can be strictly beneficial.

Data-Sharing with No Jointly Complete Information. We now show that without jointly complete information the intuition above is not complete: while there are settings in which players benefit more from sharing data in the presence of an Amazon, there are also settings in which players benefit from data sharing in the absence of an Amazon but *not* in the presence of an Amazon. More specifically, in [18] we describe a setting where:

- In the absence of an Amazon, the optimal welfare is achieved when players share no data and not when they fully share data;
- In the presence of an Amazon, the optimal welfare is achieved when players fully share data and not when they share no data.

In contrast, in [18] we also describe a setting where:

- In the absence of an Amazon, the optimal welfare is achieved when players fully share data and not when they share no data;
- In the presence of an Amazon, the optimal welfare is achieved when players share no data and not when they fully share data.

The main driving force behind the difference is whether or not there is a conflict between equilibrium and welfare maximization, as formalized in Claim 2. The first situation is one where $\phi_S^1 \geq 3 \cdot \phi_S^2$ for every segment S. In this case, under full data sharing, it is a dominant strategy for players to pool on g_S^1 (both with and without an Amazon). In the presence of an Amazon, such pooling is also welfare maximizing, by Claim 2. In the absence of an Amazon, however, separating is always welfare maximizing. Thus, full data sharing leads to the optimal welfare in the former case, but not in the latter.

In contrast, the second situation is one where $\phi_S^1 \in (\frac{3}{2}\phi_S^2, 2\phi_S^2)$. In this case, under full data sharing, in the absence of an Amazon it is an equilibrium for players to separate, whereas in the presence of an Amazon it is dominant for players to pool (again, by Claim 2). Furthermore, in both settings, separating is welfare maximizing. Thus, full data sharing leads to the optimal welfare in the absence of an Amazon, but not in its presence.

6   Conclusion

In this paper we proposed a simple model to study coopetitive data sharing between firms, and designed optimal data-sharing schemes. In [18] we extend the model to also permit monetary transfers between the firms, and show that this loosens the IR constraint. In particular, under jointly complete information, full data-sharing is then often optimal. However, when there is no jointly complete information, full data-sharing may violate the IC constraint, and in this case our mediators (even without transfers) are close to optimal.

In [18] we also extend our model to more than two players. We leave a full analysis for future work, but prove some preliminary results: optimal mediators for jointly complete information, and necessary and sufficient conditions under which full data-sharing is optimal.

References

1. Anderson, C.: The Long Tail: Why the Future of Business is Selling Less of More. Hachette Books (2006)
2. Aumann, R.J.: Agreeing to disagree. Ann. Stat. **4**(6), 1236–1239 (1976)
3. Ben-Porat, O., Tennenholtz, M.: Regression equilibrium. In: Proceedings of the 2019 ACM Conference on Economics and Computation, pp. 173–191 (2019)
4. Bengtsson, M., Kock, S.: "Coopetition" in business networks - to cooperate and compete simultaneously. Ind. Mark. Manag. **29**(5), 411–426 (2000)
5. Bergemann, D., Bonatti, A.: Markets for information: an introduction. Ann. Rev. Econ. **11**, 85–107 (2019)
6. Bergemann, D., Morris, S.: Robust predictions in games with incomplete information. Econometrica **81**(4), 1251–1308 (2013)
7. Bergemann, D., Morris, S.: Information design: a unified perspective. J. Econ. Lit. **57**(1), 44–95 (2019)
8. Brandenburger, A.M., Nalebuff, B.J.: Co-Opetition. Crown Business (2011)
9. Clarke, R.N.: Collusion and the incentives for information sharing. Bell J. Econ. **14**(2), 383–394 (1983)
10. Dughmi, S.: Algorithmic information structure design: a survey. ACM SIGecom Exch. **15**(2), 2–24 (2017)
11. European Commission: A European strategy for data (2020). http://eur-lex.europa.eu/legal-content/EN/TXT/?qid=1593073685620&uri=CELEX: 52020DC0066. Accessed 13 May 2021
12. Feng, Y., Gradwohl, R., Hartline, J., Johnsen, A., Nekipelov, D.: Bias-variance games. arXiv preprint arXiv:1909.03618 (2019)
13. Feng, Y., Gradwohl, R., Hartline, J., Johnsen, A., Nekipelov, D.: Bias-variance games. In: Proceedings of the 2022 ACM Conference on Economics and Computation (2022)
14. Forges, F.: Five legitimate definitions of correlated equilibrium in games with incomplete information. Theory Decis. **35**(3), 277–310 (1993). https://doi.org/10.1007/BF01075202
15. Gehrig, T., Stenbacka, R.: Information sharing and lending market competition with switching costs and poaching. Eur. Econ. Rev. **51**(1), 77–99 (2007)

16. Gentzkow, M., Kamenica, E.: Competition in persuasion. Rev. Econ. Stud. **84**(1), 300–322 (2016)
17. Ginart, T., Zhang, E., Kwon, Y., Zou, J.: Competing AI: how does competition feedback affect machine learning? In: International Conference on Artificial Intelligence and Statistics, pp. 1693–1701. PMLR (2021)
18. Gradwohl, R., Tennenholtz, M.: Coopetition against an Amazon. arXiv preprint arXiv:2005.10038 (2022)
19. Gradwohl, R., Tennenholtz, M.: Pareto-improving data-sharing. In: ACM Conference on Fairness, Accountability, and Transparency (2022)
20. Gu, Y., Madio, L., Reggiani, C.: Data brokers co-opetition. Available at SSRN 3308384 (2019)
21. Ha, A.Y., Tong, S.: Contracting and information sharing under supply chain competition. Manag. Sci. **54**(4), 701–715 (2008)
22. Ichihashi, S.: Competing data intermediaries. Manuscript (2020). http://shota2.github.io/research/data.pdf
23. Jappelli, T., Pagano, M.: Information sharing, lending and defaults: cross-country evidence. J. Bank. Finance **26**(10), 2017–2045 (2002)
24. Jentzsch, N., Sapi, G., Suleymanova, I.: Targeted pricing and customer data sharing among rivals. Int. J. Ind. Organ. **31**(2), 131–144 (2013)
25. Kairouz, P., et al.: Advances and open problems in federated learning. arXiv preprint arXiv:1912.04977 (2019)
26. Kamenica, E., Gentzkow, M.: Bayesian persuasion. Am. Econ. Rev. **101**(6), 2590–2615 (2011)
27. Kearns, M., Pai, M., Roth, A., Ullman, J.: Mechanism design in large games: incentives and privacy. In: Proceedings of the 5th Conference on Innovations in Theoretical Computer Science, pp. 403–410 (2014)
28. Kwon, Y., Ginart, A., Zou, J.: Competition over data: how does data purchase affect users? arXiv preprint arXiv:2201.10774 (2022)
29. Liu, Q., Serfes, K.: Customer information sharing among rival firms. Eur. Econ. Rev. **50**(6), 1571–1600 (2006)
30. Loshen, D.: Leveraging cloud-based analytics for crowd-sourced intelligence (2014). http://gigaom.com/report/leveraging-cloud-based-analytics-for-crowdsourced-intelligence/. Accessed 6 June 2020
31. Lyu, L., et al.: Towards fair and privacy-preserving federated deep models. IEEE Trans. Parallel Distrib. Syst. **31**(11), 2524–2541 (2020)
32. Mansour, Y., Slivkins, A., Wu, Z.S.: Competing bandits: learning under competition. In: 9th Innovations in Theoretical Computer Science Conference (ITCS 2018) (2018)
33. Monderer, D., Tennenholtz, M.: k-implementation. J. Artif. Intell. Res. **21**, 37–62 (2004)
34. Monderer, D., Tennenholtz, M.: Strong mediated equilibrium. Artif. Intell. **173**(1), 180–195 (2009)
35. Myerson, R.B.: Game Theory: Analysis of Conflict. Harvard University Press, Cambridge (1991)
36. Pagano, M., Jappelli, T.: Information sharing in credit markets. J. Finance **48**(5), 1693–1718 (1993)
37. Pathak, B., Garfinkel, R., Gopal, R.D., Venkatesan, R., Yin, F.: Empirical analysis of the impact of recommender systems on sales. J. Manag. Inf. Syst. **27**(2), 159–188 (2010)
38. Raith, M.: A general model of information sharing in oligopoly. J. Econ. Theory **71**(1), 260–288 (1996)

39. Shamir, N., Shin, H.: Public forecast information sharing in a market with competing supply chains. Manag. Sci. **62**(10), 2994–3022 (2016)
40. Simon, H.A.: Rational choice and the structure of the environment. Psychol. Rev. **63**(2), 129 (1956)
41. Yang, Q., Liu, Y., Chen, T., Tong, Y.: Federated machine learning: concept and applications. ACM Trans. Intell. Syst. Technol. (TIST) **10**(2), 1–19 (2019)
42. de Zegher, J.F., Lo, I.: Crowdsourcing market information from competitors. Available at SSRN 3537625 (2020)
43. Zhan, Y., Zhang, J., Hong, Z., Wu, L., Li, P., Guo, S.: A survey of incentive mechanism design for federated learning. IEEE Trans. Emerg. Top. Comput. **10**(2), 1035–1044 (2021)

Data Curation from Privacy-Aware Agents

Roy Shahmoon[⊠], Rann Smorodinsky, and Moshe Tennenholtz

Technion - Israel Institute of Technology, Haifa 3200003, Israel
shroy@campus.technion.ac.il, {rann,moshet}@technion.ac.il

Abstract. A data curator would like to collect data from privacy-aware agents. The collected data will be used for the benefit of all agents. Can the curator incentivize the agents to share their data truthfully? Can he guarantee that truthful sharing will be the unique equilibrium? Can he provide some stability guarantees on such equilibrium? We study necessary and sufficient conditions for these questions to be answered positively and complement these results with corresponding data collection protocols for the curator. Our results account for a broad interpretation of the notion of privacy awareness. The full version of this paper is available at https://arxiv.org/abs/2207.06929.

Keywords: Mechanism design · Privacy · Unique equilibrium

1 Introduction

Consider a society of agents who would like to compute some aggregate statistic of their online activity. For example, their average daily consumption of online games, the median number of messages they send, or their daily spend on Amazon. To do so they share information with some central authority. The way agents share information is by downloading an add-on to their browser which collects and reports the data. They can choose to download an add-on which accurately reports the data (hereinafter, the 'accurate' add-on), an add-on which completely mis-represents the data, or anything in between.

The agents have privacy concerns and so may not be willing to download the accurate add-on. A data curator (also referred to as the 'center'), who possesses some data as well, collects the agents' data and uses it to make some computations which she will then share privately back with the agents. We ask whether the curator can propose a scheme for sharing her computations which will induce the agents to download the accurate add-on. Technically, we are interested in schemes where there is a **unique** equilibrium in which agents down the accurate add-on.

More abstractly, we study a setting where N agents and a data curator plan ahead of time how to share information in order to compute a function of

The work by Roy Shahmoon and Moshe Tennenholtz was supported by funding from the European Research Council (ERC) under the European Union's Horizon 2020 research and innovation programme (grant agreement 740435).

© The Author(s), under exclusive license to Springer Nature Switzerland AG 2022
P. Kanellopoulos et al. (Eds.): SAGT 2022, LNCS 13584, pp. 366–382, 2022.
https://doi.org/10.1007/978-3-031-15714-1_21

the information. If the agents have no privacy concerns then the curator can simply ask the agents for their information, compute the function and distribute the outcome back. We are interested in the setting where agents actually have privacy concerns. We capture the agents concerns by a privacy cost function. This cost is a function of how accurate is the information they reveal. In our simple setting, the private information of the agents is binary and privacy cost is modelled as an arbitrary increasing function of the probability they will disclose the actual value of this private bit.[1]

The game between the agents and the curator takes place ahead of time, before any of the information becomes known to the agents. Each agent submits an information disclosure protocol which, in our binary setting, is parameterized by two numbers - the probabilities of disclosing the actual bit for each of the two possible outcomes.

The curator also submits her protocol, which discloses which information she will share back with each of the agents depending on actual vector of protocols (the vector of pairs of probabilities). The timeline of the game is as follows. The curator proposes a protocol for sharing information and then the N agents submit their own protocols simultaneously. Only then the private information is revealed to the agents and from then on information passes back and forth between the agents and the curator according to the protocols that they have all designed in advance. Note that agents play no active role in the last stage as they cannot effect the protocols during run-time.

Our objective is to identify necessary and sufficient conditions on the parameters of the problem that will allow the curator to propose a protocol which, in turn, will 'guarantee' that the agents, in-spite of having privacy concerns, will reveal their information accurately (in the jargon of our first paragraph - will download the accurate add-on) and consequently the function will be computed accurately by all. In other words, where complete information revelation is a unique equilibrium.[2]

The curator's protocol induces a game among the agents. We will deem the protocol as successful if, in its unique equilibrium, agents reveal their information accurately and the correct value of the function becomes known to all.

Indeed we identify such conditions. First, we define the notion of a (privacy-) fanatic agent as an agent whose gain from knowing the value of the function is overshadowed by the dis-utility from disclosing her private information (Definition 4). We show that a necessary and sufficient condition for the existence of a successful protocol is that no agent is fanatic (Corollary 3).

Second, to guarantee the uniqueness of the aforementioned equilibrium we argue that the curator must herself have private information which is part of the input and, furthermore, this information must not be negligible. We refer

---

[1] In fact, for our results we do not require monotonicity but rather that privacy cost is highest when the bit is fully revealed and lowest when no information is disclosed.

[2] Requiring a unique equilibrium makes our problem technically more challenging and conceptually more compelling than merely requiring equilibrium existence, as we demonstrate in the paper.

to curators whose information is negligible as 'helpless' (Definition 3) and prove that a necessary and sufficient condition for the existence of a successful protocol which equilibrium is unique, is for the agents not to be fanatic and for the curator not to be helpless (Corollary 3, Lemma 5).

In addition, we go ahead and construct a protocol, which we refer to as the *competitive protocol*. The **unique equilibrium** of this protocol is one where agents forego their privacy concerns and information is passed on accurately. Our protocol is optimal in the following sense. Assume that for some parameters of the problem there exists a protocol possessing an equilibrium that supports the accurate computation of the function. Then, indeed, on these parameters our protocol has this exact property (Theorem 3).

This protocol has a disturbing caveat. Its single equilibrium is not in dominant strategies. In fact, off equilibrium it may be the case that a cooperative agent is guaranteed nothing. We then go on and introduce an alternative optimal protocol with a unique cooperative equilibrium, which provides some natural guarantees to cooperative agents, independently of the behavior of others.

Related Work

Our work employs strategies that are conditional commitments. In this regard our work is related to work on multi-sender single-receiver conditional commitments. The setting of conditional ex-ante commitments which was initially introduced for a single sender [13] has been extended to the context of multiple senders [10]. In particular, it is shown that a greater competition tends to increase the amount of information revealed. Our main protocol also exploits competition among data owners to facilitate data contribution.

Among work in (mediated) multi-party computation the work most related to ours is by Smorodinsky and Tennenholtz [17], later extended by Aricha and Smorodinsky [3]. In this line of research the authors address the question of multiparty computation where agents would like to free-ride on others' contribution. An important aspect of their article is that they address the agents sequentially (and not simultaneously as in our work). Another difference is that while in our model the agents wouldn't like to share their values due to privacy concerns, the agents in their model incur a cost for retrieving their values. Thus, in their model the agents' cost is discrete (by approaching the value or not) but in ours it's continuous (by sharing partial data). Similarly to our work, they aim to find a mechanism which overcomes the free-riding phenomenon and convinces the agents to send true values for correct calculation of the social function.

Another genre of mediated multi-party computation focuses on getting exclusive knowledge of the computation result rather than considering privacy considerations. The first work on that topic, referred to as non-cooperative computation (NCC) [16], considers a setting where each agent wishes to compute some social function by declaring a value to a center, who reports back the results to the agents after applying the function. In the extensions of the basic model the authors also give a greater flexibility to the center. The results of the paper show conditions which classify the social functions as deterministic NCC, probabilistic NCC and subsidized NCC in both correlated and independent values settings. In addition, Ashlagi, Klinger and Tennenholtz [4] extend the study of NCC functions to the context of group deviations. Notice that in our work, the incentives of the agents are correctness and privacy, in contrast to the NCC setting which focuses on correctness and exclusivity (the desire that other agents do not compute the function correctly) as main incentives. However, McGrew, Porter and Shoham [14] extended the framework of [16], focusing on cryptographic situations. The utility of the agents in their paper is lexicographic and relies on four components: correctness, privacy (similarly to our model), exclusivity and Voyeurism (the wish to know other agents' private inputs). They show properties of the social functions (such as reversibility or domination) that affect the existence of an incentive-compatible mechanism in each ordering of the utility. The utility function we consider is not lexicographic. In fact, their work does not consider different privacy levels, and refers to privacy only through whether agent j knows agent i's value with certainty. There is also no importance in their work for hiding value from the center. Besides the above central differences, in our model the center possesses her own private value (in contrast to theirs) and we also allow the center much more flexibility in the protocol (not necessarily returning the result of the social function's calculation).

Much work has been devoted to variants of the non-mediated multi-party computation problem. For example, Halpern and Teague [12] approach the problems of secret sharing and multiparty computation. In their paper, the agents would like to know the social function's value but also prefer exclusivity. They focus on finding conditions on the running time of the multiparty computation. Specifically, they show that there is no mechanism with a commonly-known upper bound on running time for the multiparty computation of any non-constant function. In contrast to our work, the mediator is replaced by cryptographic techniques and there is no explicit interest in privacy. The emphasis is mainly on removing the reliable party (as developed in [1,2]).

Another setting with some similarity to ours is by Ronen and Wahrmann [15] who introduced the concept of prediction games. Their setting is quite similar to ours (there are agents and a center; the goal is to compute some social function), but there are significant differences: First, the agents' costs are discrete, not continuous (the agents incur a cost by accessing the information, without privacy concerns). Second, the agents are approached serially (not simultaneously). Third and most important, the center rewards the agents in retrospect, according to the correctness of the social function's calculation. While in our model the center sacrifices her information and can ensure it for truthful agents, in theirs she pays the agents according to the social function's calculation, meaning that an agent's utility is directly affected by other agents. In addition, in their model the center can't verify the agents' honesty in contrast to our model (where the agents are obligated to the strategy they pick). This model does not focus on privacy. Similarly, models of information elicitation, and in particular ones that consider the decisions to be made following the aggregation of information [6] are relevant to our work. These however focus on the use of monetary transfers for eliciting information about uncertain events, rather than on non-monetary mechanisms for function computation based on distributed inputs and conditional commitments, nor they refer to privacy.

The papers [5,7,11] address a remotely related domain of data markets for privacy, where a data analyst wishes to pay as little as possible for data providers in order to obtain an accurate estimation of some statistic. Our setting relates to mechanism design without money, where the center may use her private information in order to incentivize the agents to reveal their secrets.

Notice that our notion of privacy differs from the one used in the context of differential privacy [8,9]. The rich literature on differential privacy attempts at protocols where agents' private secrets should not be revealed to other agents, while our setting cares about costs incurred by having private secret conveyed to a mediator. The latter is in the sense of federated learning [18], where we assume computations will be done from time to time and the mediator is the powerful organizer that we care about having our information revealed to it.

2 The Model

In our multi party computation setting we assume a society of N agents and a center (denoted as agent 0), each has a private information (taking the form of a binary bit). By revealing these secrets the agents derive dis-utility (due to privacy concerns). The center has no privacy concerns and she is the only agent who can communicate with the others and facilitate the desired computation of a binary social function $g : \{0,1\}^{N+1} \to \{0,1\}$. The flow of the game is as follows:

1. First, the center declares a communication protocol between herself and a set of agents. The protocol is a function that receives the agents' strategies (conditional commitments) and decides how to operate accordingly.
2. Then, each agent commits to a strategy which takes the form of a distribution over a set of messages as a function of a private bit, and sends it to the center. Commitments are made simultaneously. Notice that the center is obligated to the protocols and the agents are obligated to their strategies.
3. Afterwards, agents receive their bits simultaneously, random messages are drawn according to the aforementioned strategies and then communicated to the center.
4. Finally, the center's responses are generated according to the vector of agents' inputs and each agent receives her own response. Based on this response each agent guesses the true value of the social function and derives a (non-negative) profit if and only if the guess is correct.

We assume that the agents are rational individuals trying to maximize their own expected utility. The center's goal is to uncover the true value of the social function. We now introduce some formal notations.

Let Ω be the sample space of the game where a typical instance is $b \times m \times f$ such that:

- $b = (b_0, \ldots, b_N) \in \{0, 1\}^{N+1}$ is a vector containing the bits of the center and the agents.
- $m = (m_0, \ldots, m_N) \in \{0, 1\}^{N+1}$ is a vector of the agents' messages to the center ($m_0 = b_0$ is the center's message to himself).
- $f = (f_1, \ldots, f_N)$ is a vector of the center's replies to each agent, such that $\forall i \in \{1, \ldots, N\} : f_i \in \{0, 1\}^{N+1}$.

Note that each message from an agent (including the center) to the center is a bit, but each reply from the center to an agent (excluding the center) is a vector containing $N + 1$ elements. These elements should be interpreted as information on the values of the agents' $N + 1$ original bits.

We assume that the bits are $i.i.d$ and distributed uniformly over $\{0, 1\}$.[3]

For each agent $i \in \{1, \ldots, N\}$ we define her strategy space (possible conditional contracts) as follows:

$$S_i = \{(p_i, q_i) |\ p_i, q_i \in [0, 1]\}$$

where

$$p_i = p(m_i = 0 | b_i = 0), q_i = p(m_i = 0 | b_i = 1).$$

A *strategy profile* $\vec{s} = (s_1, \ldots, s_N)$ is a set of the agents' strategies, such that $s_1 \in S_1, \ldots, s_N \in S_N$.

The strategy $s_i = (1, 0)$ fully reveals the agent's secret and hence is called *truthful* and denoted by s^t. Any strategy $s_i = (p_i, q_i)$ such that $p_i = q_i$ reveals nothing about the agent's secret and hence is called a *zero-information* strategy. We denote by $S^r = \{(c, c) \mid c \in [0, 1]\}$ the set of zero-information strategies.

For each agent $i \in \{1, \ldots, N\}$ and for each agent $j \in \{0, \ldots, N\}$, let $F_{i,j}$ be the center's protocol for agent i about agent j.

$$F_{i,j} : S_1 \times S_2 \times \cdots \times S_N \times m_j \to \Delta(\{0, 1\}).$$

Let $F_i = (F_{i,0}, \ldots, F_{i,N})$ be the center's protocol for agent i such that

$$F_i : S_1 \times S_2 \times \cdots \times S_N \times m_0 \times \cdots \times m_N \to \Delta(\{0, 1\})^{N+1}.$$

The protocol F_i for agent i determines the probability distribution over the messages to i as a function of all agents' conditional commitments. Notice that each message from the center to an agent is a tuple of $N+1$ bits (e.g. standing as place holders that can serve to provide information about all participant bits).[4]

Let $F = (F_1, \ldots, F_N)$. Notice that the prior distribution over the bits together with the protocol F and the strategy profile $\vec{s}$ induce a probability

---

[3] The model can be generalized to any distribution over $\{0, 1\}$ while maintaining the same results. The main change would be in the set of zero-information strategies (which is defined later in this page).

[4] We can reduce the communication complexity of the protocol by having the center return two bits (instead of $N+1$) to each agent. To do so the center simulates agents' computations for the estimate of the social function in each of the agent's possible bits. Nevertheless, we maintain the current presentation as it is more transparent.

distribution over the sample space Ω. Knowing the value of her own bit b_i, her message m_i, and the center's reply f_i, the agent computes the conditional probability $p(g(b) = 1|b_i, m_i, f_i)$ and uses it to submit her guess, a_i, over the value of g as follows:

$$a_i(b_i, m_i, f_i) = \begin{cases} 1 & \text{if } p(g = 1|b_i, m_i, f_i) > p(g = 0|b_i, m_i, f_i) \\ 0 & \text{if } p(g = 1|b_i, m_i, f_i) < p(g = 0|b_i, m_i, f_i) \\ random\{0, 1\} & \text{if } p(g = 1|b_i, m_i, f_i) = p(g = 0|b_i, m_i, f_i) \end{cases}$$

Let as denote the profit of agent i:

$$v_i(b, m_i, f_i) = \begin{cases} c_i & \text{if } a_i(b_i, m_i, f_i) = g(b) \\ 0 & \text{if } a_i(b_i, m_i, f_i) \neq g(b) \end{cases}$$

where $c_i > 0$ is an arbitrary constant.

For a given protocol F, the vector of strategies $\vec{s} = (s_1, \ldots, s_N)$ induces the expectation of v_i, denoted as $V_i(\vec{s}; F)$. Note that $V_i(\vec{s}; F)$ doesn't depend on F but only on F_i and from now on we will write $V_i(\vec{s}; F_i)$ rather than $V_i(\vec{s}; F)$.

We shall refer to the function

$$V_i(S_i, S_{-i}; F_i) : \ S_i \times S_{-i} \times F_i \to \mathbb{R}_+$$

as the *profit function* of agent i in the protocol F_i.

Let $price_i$ be the privacy cost function of agent i.

$$price_i : S_i \to \mathbb{R}_+$$

We assume that an agent incurs a zero privacy cost if and only if she plays a zero-information strategy. Furthermore, truthfulness incurs the highest price.[5] Formally:

$$\forall i \in \{1, \ldots, N\}, \forall s^\tau \in S^\tau, \forall s_i \in S_i - S^\tau : price_i(s^t) \geq price_i(s_i) > price_i(s^\tau) = 0.$$

In addition, we assume that $price_i$ is continuous.

We define the *utility function* of an agent i in the protocol F_i as:

$$U_i(S_i, S_{-i}; F_i) : \ S_i \times S_{-i} \times F_i \to u_i \in \mathbb{R}$$

$$\text{s.t.} \quad U_i(S_i, S_{-i}; F_i) = V_i(S_i, S_{-i}; F_i) - price_i(S_i).$$

Let $F = (F_1, \ldots, F_n)$ be a protocol. Recall that the agents choose a strategy before they receive their private information. We say that a strategy profile $\vec{s} = (s_1, \ldots, s_N)$ is an equilibrium in F if

$$\forall i \in \{1, \ldots, N\}, \forall s_i' \in S_i : \ U_i(s_i, s_{-i}; F_i) \geq U_i(s_i', s_{-i}; F_i)$$

Let us recall the flow of the game using the new notations:

---

[5] It seems natural to further assume that $price_i$ is an increasing function of p_i and a decreasing function of q_i but it is not necessary of our results.

- The center declares a protocol $F = (F_1, \ldots, F_N)$.
- Each agent $i \in \{1, \ldots, N\}$ chooses a strategy $s_i \in S_i$ and immediately incurs a cost of $price_i(s_i)$.
- The private bit b_i of each agent i is realized and the message $m_i = 0$ is sent to the center with the probability p_i whenever $b_i = 0$ and with the probability q_i whenever $b_i = 1$. Otherwise, the message $m_i = 1$ is sent with the complementary probabilities.
- Each agent i receives a reply $f_i \in \{0,1\}^{N+1}$ according to the distribution $F_i(\vec{s}, m) = (F_{i,0}(\vec{s}, m_0), \ldots, F_{i,N}(\vec{s}, m_N))$ where $\vec{s} = (s_1, \ldots, s_N)$.
- Finally, each agent i leverages her information $b_i, m_i, f_i, \vec{s}$ by applying Bayes rule to compute her best guess of the value of $g(b)$. If she guesses correctly she incurs a profit, otherwise she doesn't. Her overall expected utility is $U_i(\vec{s} = (s_1, \ldots, s_N); F_i) = V_i(\vec{s} = (s_1, \ldots, s_N); F_i) - price_i(s_i)$.

2.1 A Preliminary Result

After receiving the center's reply, each agent has to decide whether the true value of g is 0 or 1 based on the information she has (b_i, m_i, f_i). Therefore, the expected profit will be the maximum between the alternatives from the agent's point of view at the time of the decision.

Now, we prove that the expected profit of an agent is the following intuitive expression that will serve us later in the proof of Lemma 2:

Lemma 1.

$$V_i(\vec{s}; F_i) = c_i \cdot \underset{b_{-i}, m_{-i}}{E} [\underset{b_i, f_i, m_i}{E} [max\{p(g(b) = 0 | f_i, b_i, m_i), p(g(b) = 1 | f_i, b_i, m_i)\}]].$$

The proof appears in the full paper.

3 Informational Profitability

In this section we address the concept of "more/better" information and show its relation to an agent's profit. Our goal is to make a connection between the agent's knowledge and her profit, and particularly to compare different replies given by the center. We prove here that there are cases in which an agent prefers in expectation one response over another. Understanding the influence of the center's replies on the agents' profits is a useful technical tool for the results presented in the following section.

Let $i \in \{1, \ldots, N\}$ be an agent, let F_i^1, F_i^2 be protocols for agent i, let $\vec{s_1} = (s_1^1, \ldots, s_N^1)$, $\vec{s_2} = (s_1^2, \ldots, s_N^2)$ be strategy profiles and let m^1, m^2 be the agents' messages to the center according to $\vec{s_1}, \vec{s_2}$ respectively (note that $m_0^1 = m_0^2 = b_0$). Let f_i^1, f_i^2 be the center's replies drawn from the distributions $F_i^1(\vec{s_1}, m^1), F_i^2(\vec{s_2}, m^2)$ respectively. In addition, assume that $v^1 = (v_0^1, v_1^1, \ldots, v_N^1)$ represents in each coordinate k the probability that the kth agent has the value 1 according to i's inference from f_i^1, m_i^1, b_i. Formally:

$$\forall k \in \{0, \ldots, N\} : v_k^1 = p(b_k = 1 | f_i^1, m_i^1, b_i) = p(b_k = 1 | f_{i,k}^1, m_i^1, b_i)$$

The last equality is derived from the fact that b_k and $f^1_{i,-k}$ are independent (recall that $f^1_i = (f^1_{i,0}, \dots, f^1_{i,N})$). Similarly, assume that $v^2 = (v^2_0, v^2_1, \dots, v^2_N)$ represents in each coordinate k the probability that the kth agent has the value 1 according to i's inference from f^2_i, m^2_i, b_i. Formally:

$$\forall k \in \{0, \dots, N\} : v^2_k = p(b_k = 1 | f^2_i, m^2_i, b_i) = p(b_k = 1 | f^2_{i,k}, m^2_i, b_i)$$

Lemma 2 (Comparison Lemma). *Let $i, j \in \{1, \dots, N\}$, where $i \neq j$. Assume that $v^1_{-j} = v^2_{-j}$ and $|v^1_j - 0.5| \geq |v^2_j - 0.5|$. Then, $V_i(\vec{s_1}; F^1_i) \geq V_i(\vec{s_2}; F^2_i)$.*

Intuition:
An agent may have two different responses from the center f^1_i, f^2_i. She would like to know whether f^1_i is better or worse than f^2_i in terms of profit. Each response reveals some information about the agents' bits (v^1 or v^2) and therefore about the true value of g. Our observation relies on the distances of v^1_j, v^2_j from 0.5. Suppose that v^1_j's distance from 0.5 is greater than v^2_j's distance from 0.5, then v^1_j reveals "more" information on b_j and therefore on g as well. As an intuitive example, let $v^1_j = 0$ and let $v^2_j = 0.5$. Then, according to v^1_j we infer that $b_j = 0$. On the other hand, according to v^2_j we infer that $p(b_j = 0 | v^2_j) = p(b_j = 1 | v^2_j) = 0.5$. Hence, v^1_j is more informative than v^2_j. Therefore, one may expect that knowing v^1_j over v^2_j will also lead to a better guess on g's value. But even though the intuition is quite clear, the claim is not immediate and true only in expectation. The proof appears in the full paper.

We now approach the general case, by applying the previous lemma several times until we get the desired result.

Theorem 1 (Comparison Theorem). *Assume that $\forall k \in \{0, \dots, N\} : |v^1_k - 0.5| \geq |v^2_k - 0.5|$. Then, $V_i(\vec{s_1}; F^1_i) \geq V_i(\vec{s_2}; F^2_i)$.*

The proof appears in the full paper.

4   The Competitive Protocol

This is the main section of the paper where we present the existence of a protocol that truthfully implements in unique equilibrium the computation of social functions, as well as prove its optimality. We show that under some minor natural assumptions we achieve a protocol, titled as the *competitive protocol* with the following properties:

1. Truthfulness is its only equilibrium.
2. When the agents play according to the equilibrium, the center knows the true value of g.
3. When the agents play according to the equilibrium, they know the true value of g.

4. This protocol is optimal - if truthfulness is an equilibrium of some other protocol (for some setting and function) then it is also a unique equilibrium of the competitive protocol.

We start with a definition. The *relative price* of agent i when choosing a strategy $s_i \in S_i$ is

$$price_i^r(s_i) = \frac{price_i(s_i)}{price_i(s^t)}.$$

Therefore,

$$\forall i \in \{1, \ldots, N\}, \forall s^r \in S^r, \forall s_i \in S_i - S^r : 1 = price_i^r(s^t) \geq price_i^r(s_i) > price_i^r(s^r) = 0$$

Notice that the relative price is continuous as well as $price_i$.

Definition 1 (The competitive protocol).
If all agents play s^t they receive $m = b$. Else, the agent whose relative price is the highest (comparing to the others) receives $m = (b_0, m_1, \ldots, m_N)$ while the others receive uniformly distributed random bits. If at least two agents incur the same highest relative price then everyone receives random bits.[6,7]

$$\forall i \in \{1, \ldots, N\}, \forall s_1 \in S_1, \ldots, s_N \in S_N, \forall m_{-0} \in \{0,1\}^N :$$

$$F_i^c(s_1, \ldots, s_N, m) = \begin{cases} m & if \ s_1 = \cdots = s_N = s^t \\ m & if \ price_i^r(s_i) > \max_{j \neq i}\{price_j^r(s_j)\} \\ \overrightarrow{0.5} & otherwise \end{cases}$$

Note that the notation of $\overrightarrow{0.5}$ refers to uniformly distributed random bits.

Intuition:
First, we want to construct a protocol with truthfulness as its only equilibrium. In order to implement it successfully, we make sure that in any other strategy profile there is at least one unsatisfied agent who prefers to deviate. We try to guarantee this property by creating a competition between the agents in every situation except from the truthful equilibrium. The competition is based on the relative prices that the agents incur. An agent who pays the highest relative price gets everything the center may offer while the others get nothing useful. For instance,

---

[6] The competitive protocol satisfies the properties above in case that $N \geq 2$. If $N = 1$ then it is easy to verify that a simple protocol that shares the center's bit if and only if the agent is truthful is the only protocol that reveals the true value of the social function for both the center and the agent.

[7] A viable criticism against the proposed protocol is that it requires that the center is familiar with the agents' privacy functions. However, if the center replaces the real price function with the indicator price function - assigning the price zero whenever the agent uses a zero-information strategy and one otherwise - this criticism no longer holds, yet the new protocol will have the exact same equilibria as the original one.

assume a situation with two agents, each wants to get the center's information and pay as little as possible. If agent 1 knows agent's 2 strategy, then she knows agent's 2 relative price so she will pick a strategy with a slightly higher price in order to "win" and get the center's info. Agent 2 has the same considerations, yielding a situation that each prefers to slightly change her strategy trying to overcome the other agent. They both may be satisfied when they play truthfully and get all the information.

One may wonder why we suggest a complex protocol where there is an intuitive protocol that seems to deliver the same results. The initial idea that comes to mind is a protocol that suggests all of the center's information (b_0, m_{-0}) for truthful agents and nothing $(\overrightarrow{0.5})$ otherwise. One may believe that the strictness of the protocol is the best way to incentivize the agents to be honest. Unfortunately, this straightforward approach has a major flaw that the competitive protocol covers. The reader can notice that there is much more stable equilibrium in the straightforward protocol, which is zero-information strategies by all agents. Indeed, an agent may not be interested in paying a full privacy cost in exchange for the center's private information, by deviating to truthfulness. On the other hand, such zero-information strategy profile is highly non-stable in our protocol where a single agent can deviate by suffering a negligible cost and obtain the center's private information. As we will show, under natural conditions truthfulness is a unique equilibrium in our protocol.

4.1   Uniqueness

A main characteristic of our desired protocol is equilibrium uniqueness. We aim to show that if truthfulness is an equilibrium in the competitive protocol, then it is the only equilibrium in the protocol. As we will show, the claim is true under an intuitive assumption about the center. Our proof will make use of the following definition of protocol improvement and its property in the Lemma following it, building on the technical comparison Theorem presented in the previous section.

Suppose that F_i is a protocol and $\vec{s}$ is a strategy profile. Recall that the first coordinate of $F_i(\vec{s}, m)$ (i.e. $F_{i,0}(\vec{s}, m_0)$) may reveal information only about the center's bit. The *improvement* F_i^+ of F_i returns in the first coordinate the center's bit if s_i is not a zero-information strategy. Formally:

Definition 2. *Let $F_i = (F_{i,0}, \ldots, F_{i,N})$ be a protocol. Hence,*

$$\forall s_1 \in S_1, \ldots, s_N \in S_N, \forall m_{-0} \in \{0,1\}^N :$$

$$F_i^+(s_1, \ldots, s_N, m) = \begin{cases} F_i(s_1, \ldots, s_N, m) & \text{if } s_i \in S^r \\ (m_0, F_{i,-0}(s_1, \ldots, s_N, m_{-0})) & \text{otherwise} \end{cases}$$

For every strategy profile $\vec{s}$, F_i's improvement (F_i^+) fully reveals the center's bit $m_0 = b_0$ instead of giving $F_{i,0}(\vec{s}, m_0)$ (which may contain a partial or full information on b_0) when the agent does not play a zero-information strategy.

Now we approach two technical lemmas that their proofs appear in the full paper. Lemma 3 shows that the agents' utility from an improved protocol is at least as high as their utility from the original protocol. Lemma 4 shows that $\overrightarrow{0.5}$ is the worst reply that an agent may get.

Lemma 3. *For every agent i and her corresponding protocol F_i:*

$$\forall s_1 \in S_1, \ldots, s_N \in S_N : U_i(s_1, \ldots, s_N; F_i^+) \geq U_i(s_1, \ldots, s_N; F_i).$$

Lemma 4. *Let F_i^1, F_i^2 be protocols for agent i. Let $\vec{s_1}, \vec{s_2}$ and m^1, m^2 be the strategy profiles and the agents' messages in those protocols respectively. If $F_i^2(\vec{s_2}, m^2) = \overrightarrow{0.5}$ then $V_i(\vec{s_1}; F_i^1) \geq V_i(\vec{s_2}; F_i^2)$.*

Now we approach the assumption that we have mentioned before.

Definition 3. *We call the center helpless if for every agent i and every protocol F_i:*

$$\forall s_i \in S_i - S^r, \forall s_1^r, \ldots, s_N^r \in S^r : U_i(s_i^r, s_{-i}^r; F_i) \geq U_i(s_i, s_{-i}^r; F_i^+).$$

The center is helpless if she doesn't have the capability to prevent an equilibrium of zero-information strategies. In case of a zero-information strategy profile, all the center may offer is her bit. If there isn't any agent in this profile who prefers to deviate from a zero-information strategy in order to receive the center's information, then we call the center helpless.

Example 1. Suppose that $N = 2$ and let $g(b) = \begin{cases} b_0 & \text{if } xor(b_1, b_2) = 0 \\ \bar{b_0} & \text{if } xor(b_1, b_2) = 1 \end{cases}$.

The reader may verify that the center is helpless. In a situation of a zero-information strategy profile notice that the center's bit is not useful for the agents without information on the other agent's bit. Therefore, regardless of the center's protocol the agents won't deviate from a zero information strategy in this profile. Note that in this example the center's information is essential for the exact computation of g even though she is helpless.

Lemma 5. *The center is helpless if and only if all the protocols have the equilibria $(s_1^r, \ldots, s_N^r) \; \forall s_1^r, \ldots, s_N^r \in S^r$.*

Proof (Proof - Direction 1). Assume that the center is helpless, and let F_i be an arbitrary protocol for agent i. We show that the profile $(s_1^r, \ldots, s_N^r)$ is an equilibrium in F_i for all $s_1^r, \ldots, s_N^r \in S^r$:

$$\forall s_i \in S_i - S^r, \forall s_1^r, \ldots, s_N^r \in S^r : \; U_i(s_i^r, s_{-i}^r; F_i) \geq U_i(s_i, s_{-i}^r; F_i^+) \geq U_i(s_i, s_{-i}^r; F_i).$$

Thus, agent i doesn't want to deviate to any $s_i \in S_i - S^r$.

Proof (Proof - Direction 2). Suppose that all the protocols have the equilibria $(s_1^r, \ldots, s_N^r)$ for all $s_1^r, \ldots, s_N^r \in S^r$, and assume in contradiction that the center is not helpless. Therefore, there is an agent i and a protocol F_i such that $\exists s_i \in S_i - S^r, \forall s_1^r, \ldots, s_N^r \in S^r : U_i(s_i, s_{-i}^r; F_i^+) > U_i(s_i^r, s_{-i}^r; F_i)$. But $\forall s_1^r, \ldots, s_N^r \in S^r : U_i(s_i^r, s_{-i}^r; F_i^+) = U_i(s_i^r, s_{-i}^r; F_i)$ and therefore, $\exists s_i \in S_i - S^r, \forall s_1^r, \ldots, s_N^r \in S^r : U_i(s_i, s_{-i}^r; F_i^+) > U_i(s_i^r, s_{-i}^r; F_i^+)$ meaning that $\forall s_1^r, \ldots, s_N^r \in S^r : (s_1^r, \ldots, s_N^r)$ is not an equilibrium in F_i^+.

Corollary 1. *If the center is helpless, there isn't any protocol with truthfulness as a unique equilibrium.*

Hence, we must assume for our desired protocol that the center is not helpless. The following Lemma demonstrates the strength of the competitive protocol. Its proof appears in the full paper.

Lemma 6. *The center is helpless if and only if $\forall s_1^r, \ldots, s_N^r \in S^r : (s_1^r, \ldots, s_N^r)$ is an equilibrium in the competitive protocol.*

Corollary 2. *The profiles $\{(s_1^r, \ldots, s_N^r) | s_1^r, \ldots, s_N^r \in S^r\}$ are equilibria in the competitive protocol if and only if they are equilibria in every protocol.*

The combination of Lemma 5 and Lemma 6 induces the above conclusion. The main use of these Lemmas is to show the equilibrium uniqueness of the protocol (under not helpless center). However, we notice that Corollary 2 implies the protocol's optimality that we will show later in this paper.

Lemma 7. *The competitive protocol has only two kinds of equilibria: $(s^t, \ldots, s^t)$ or $(s_1^r, \ldots, s_N^r) \ \forall s_1^r, \ldots, s_N^r \in S^r$.*

Proof. Let g be the social function. Let $\vec{s} = (s_1, \ldots, s_N)$ be an equilibrium in the competitive protocol assuming that $\vec{s} \neq (s^t, \ldots, s^t)$, $\vec{s} \notin \{(s_1^r, \ldots, s_N^r) | s_1^r, \ldots, s_N^r \in S^r\}$.

Suppose that $\vec{s}$ contains at least two strategies (s_i and s_j) that yield the same highest relative price (comparing to the others). In those cases, the competitive protocol submits $\overrightarrow{0.5}$ to all agents. Therefore, $\forall s_i^r \in S^r$:

$$U_i(\vec{s}; F_i^c) = V_i(\vec{s}; F_i^c) - price_i(s_i) < V_i(\vec{s}; F_i^c) = V_i(s_i^r, s_{-i}; F_i^c) = U_i(s_i^r, s_{-i}; F_i^c).$$

So agent i prefers to deviate.

Now, suppose that $\vec{s} = (s_1, \ldots, s_N)$ contains only one strategy s_i that yields the highest relative price. Therefore agent i receives $(b_0, m_1, \ldots, m_N)$. Let j be the agent who incurs the second highest relative price. She receives $\overrightarrow{0.5}$. Thus, if $s_j \in S^r$ then according to the intermediate value theorem (on $price_i^r$) there is $s_i' \in S_i$ such that i prefers to deviate from s_i to s_i' and pay less but still receive $(b_0, m_1, \ldots, m_N)$. Else, if $s_j \notin S^r$ then j prefers to deviate to some $s_j' \in S^r$ (same considerations as before).

Thus, we get that $\vec{s}$ is not an equilibrium.

Note that deviating to $s_j' \in S^r$ is not necessarily j's best response but it's sufficient for refuting the conjecture that $\vec{s}$ is an equilibrium.

Lemma 7 is the core of the uniqueness proof. The competition between the agents and the main idea behind the construction of the competitive protocol is reflected in its proof.

Theorem 2 (Uniqueness). *If the center is not helpless and truthfulness is an equilibrium in the competitive protocol, then it is the only equilibrium.*

Proof (Proof - Uniqueness). Suppose that truthfulness is an equilibrium in the competitive protocol. According to Lemma 6 we get that $\forall s_1^r, \ldots, s_N^r \in S^r$: $(s_1^r, \ldots, s_N^r)$ is not an equilibrium in the protocol. Therefore, according to Lemma 7 we get that truthfulness is the only equilibrium.

4.2   Existence

In the previous sub-section we addressed the uniqueness of the competitive protocol, assuming that truthfulness is an equilibrium. Now, we approach the conditions in which truthfulness is indeed an equilibrium in this protocol. We start with a technical Lemma which implies that when the agents in the competitive protocol are truthful, then any agent i who deviates prefers to play a zero-information strategy over any $s_i \neq s^t \in S_i$.

Lemma 8.

$$\forall i \in \{1, \ldots, N\}, \forall s_i^r \in S^r, \forall s_i \neq s^t \in S_i - S^r : U_i(s_i^r, (s^t, \ldots, s^t); F_i^c) > U_i(s_i, (s^t, \ldots, s^t); F_i^c).$$

The proof appears in the full paper.

We now approach the constraint on the existence of a truthful equilibrium in the competitive protocol. We will use the following notations:

Let F_i^{max} be a protocol such that:

$$\forall s_1 \in S_1, \ldots, s_N \in S_N, \forall m_{-0} \in \{0,1\}^N : F_i^{max}(s_1, \ldots, s_N, m) = (b_0, m_{-0}).$$

Let F_i^{min} be a protocol such that:

$$\forall s_1 \in S_1, \ldots, s_N \in S_N, \forall m_{-0} \in \{0,1\}^N : F_i^{min}(s_1, \ldots, s_N, m) = \overrightarrow{0.5}.$$

Definition 4. *We call agent i fanatic if*

$$\forall s_1 \in S_1, \ldots, s_N \in S_N : price_i(s^t) > V_i(s^t, \ldots, s^t; F_i^{max}) - V_i(s_1, \ldots, s_N; F_i^{min}).$$

A fanatic agent is an agent who won't be truthful at any rate. That is, her cost for truthfulness ($price_i(s^t)$) in greater than her profit from a full information about the social function g ($F_i^{max}(s^t, \ldots, s^t, m = b)$) comparing to the information that she can infer by herself from her bit b_i.

In service of proving existence, we present the following two lemmas. Their proofs appear in the full paper.

Lemma 9. *If there is a fanatic agent then there isn't any protocol with a truthful equilibrium.*

Lemma 10. *If truthfulness is not an equilibrium in the competitive protocol then there is a fanatic agent.*

Notice that Lemma 10 proves the opposite direction of Lemma 9. If there isn't any protocol with a truthful equilibrium, then in particular the competitive protocol doesn't have a truthful equilibrium, and according to Lemma 10 there is a fanatic agent. Therefore we get:

Corollary 3. *There is a fanatic agent if and only if there isn't any protocol with a truthful equilibrium.*

Similarly, Lemma 9 proves that if there is a fanatic agent then there isn't any protocol with a truthful equilibrium, and in particular there is no truthful equilibrium in the competitive protocol. Combining with Lemma 10 we get:

Corollary 4. *Truthfulness is an equilibrium in the competitive protocol if and only if there isn't a fanatic agent.*

4.3 Optimality

Here we present a main result of the paper. We prove that if there is at least one protocol with a truthful equilibrium (not necessarily unique) then the competitive protocol has a truthful equilibrium as well.

Theorem 3 (Optimality). *If there is a protocol with a truthful equilibrium, then truthfulness is an equilibrium in the competitive protocol.*

Proof (Proof - Optimality). Assume in contradiction that the profile $(s^t, \ldots, s^t)$ is not an equilibrium in the competitive protocol. Thus, according to Lemma 8, there is an agent i such that $\forall s_i^r \in S^r : U_i(s_i^r, (s^t, \ldots, s^t); F_i^c) > U_i(s^t, \ldots, s^t; F_i^c)$.

Let A_i be a protocol with a truthful equilibrium. We notice that

$$\forall k \in \{0, \ldots, N\} : |p(b_k = 1|F_i^{max}(s^t, \ldots, s^t), m_i = b_i, b_i) - 0.5| = |p(b_k = 1|b) - 0.5|$$
$$= 0.5 \geq |p(b_k = 1|A_i(s^t, \ldots, s^t), m_i = b_i, b_i) - 0.5|.$$

Therefore, according to the comparison theorem $V_i(s^t, \ldots, s^t; F_i^{max}) \geq V_i(s^t, \ldots, s^t; A_i)$. Thus, $U_i(s^t, \ldots, s^t; F_i^{max}) \geq U_i(s^t, \ldots, s^t; A_i)$.

In addition, according to the definition of F_i^{min} and Lemma 4 we get that $V_i(s_i^r, (s^t \ldots, s^t); A_i) \geq V_i(s_i^r, (s^t \ldots, s^t); F_i^{min})$, and therefore $U_i(s^r, (s^t \ldots, s^t); A_i) \geq U_i(s^r, (s^t \ldots, s^t); F_i^{min})$.

Recall that A_i has a truthful equilibrium. Thus, $\forall s_i^r \in S^r : U_i(s^t, \ldots, s^t; A_i) \geq U_i(s_i^r, (s^t \ldots, s^t); A_i)$. Hence, $\forall s_i^r \in S^r : U_i(s^t, \ldots, s^t; F_i^{max}) \geq U_i(s_i^r, (s^t \ldots, s^t); F_i^{min})$. But recall that in the competitive protocol $U_i(s^t, \ldots, s^t; F_i^c) = U_i(s^t, \ldots, s^t; F_i^{max})$ and $\forall s_i^r \in S^r : U_i(s_i^r, (s^t \ldots, s^t); F_i^c) = U_i(s_i^r, (s^t \ldots, s^t); F_i^{min})$, yielding that in the competitive protocol $\forall s_i^r \in S^r : U_i(s^t, \ldots, s^t; F_i^c) \geq U_i(s_i^r, (s^t \ldots, s^t); F_i^c)$ which is a contradiction.

Thus, $(s^t, \ldots, s^t)$ is an equilibrium in the competitive protocol as we wanted to show.

Combining with the Uniqueness Theorem we get the following conclusion:

Corollary 5 *If the center is not helpless and there is a protocol with a truthful equilibrium (not necessarily unique) then the competitive protocol induces truthfulness as a unique equilibrium.*

5   Beyond Equilibrium - Fair Competitive Protocol

In this section we extend our domain of interest beyond equilibrium. We showed that the competitive protocol is optimal when considering the notion of truthful implementation in equilibrium. Here we present a slight improvement of the competitive protocol. We show a protocol possessing the properties of the competitive protocol which also guarantees information to the agents outside of equilibrium. Recall that the competitive protocol allows only truthful equilibrium (under some natural assumptions). Consequently, it may be inflexible: for instance, if all agents except one share their information truthfully, then they all receive nothing $(\overrightarrow{0.5})$. Based on this phenomenon we have an incentive to construct a moderate protocol that preserves uniqueness and optimality but also has some guarantee for truthful agents regardless of the others' strategies.

Definition 5 (The fair competitive protocol (FCP)).
If an agent plays s^t she receives all of the center's information $m = (b_0, m_{-0})$. Otherwise, the agent with the highest relative price among the non-truthful agents receives m as long as she is not the only non-truthful agent. If at least two non-truthful agents incur the same highest relative price (among the non-truthful agents) then all the non-truthful agents receive $\overrightarrow{0.5}$. Otherwise, the agent receives $\overrightarrow{0.5}$. Formally:

$$\forall i \in \{1,\ldots,N\}, \forall s_1 \in S_1, \ldots, s_N \in S_N, \forall m_{-0} \in \{0,1\}^N :$$

$$F_i^{fc}(s_1,\ldots,s_N,m) = \begin{cases} m & \text{if } s_i = s^t \\ m & \text{if } price_i^r(s_i) > \max_{\{j|s_j \neq s^t,\ j \neq i\}} \{price_j^r(s_j)\} \text{ and } s_{-i} \neq \overrightarrow{s^t} \\ \overrightarrow{0.5} & \text{Otherwise} \end{cases}$$

It's easy to see that a truthful agent receives all the information that the center possesses regardless of the others. We show that the fair competitive protocol preserves the properties of the competitive protocol by equilibrium equivalence.

Theorem 4 (Equivalence). *The profile $\vec{s} = (s_1,\ldots,s_N)$ s.t. $s_1 \in S_1, \ldots s_N \in S_N$ is an equilibrium in the competitive protocol if and only if $\vec{s}$ is an equilibrium in the fair competitive protocol.*

The proof appears in the full paper.

References

1. Abraham, I., Dolev, D., Geffner, I., Halpern, J.Y.: Implementing mediators with asynchronous cheap talk. In: Robinson, P., Ellen, F. (eds.) Proceedings of the 2019 ACM Symposium on Principles of Distributed Computing, PODC 2019, Toronto, ON, Canada, 29 July–2 August 2019, pp. 501–510. ACM (2019)
2. Abraham, I., Dolev, D., Gonen, R., Halpern, J.Y.: Distributed computing meets game theory: robust mechanisms for rational secret sharing and multiparty computation. In: Ruppert, E., Malkhi, D. (eds.) Proceedings of the Twenty-Fifth Annual ACM Symposium on Principles of Distributed Computing, PODC 2006, Denver, CO, USA, 23–26 July 2006, pp. 53–62. ACM (2006)

3. Aricha, I., Smorodinsky, R.: Information elicitation and sequential mechanisms. Int. J. Game Theory **42**(4), 931–946 (2012). https://doi.org/10.1007/s00182-012-0346-6

4. Ashlagi, I., Klinger, A., Tenneholtz, M.: K-NCC: stability against group deviations in non-cooperative computation. In: Deng, X., Graham, F.C. (eds.) WINE 2007. LNCS, vol. 4858, pp. 564–569. Springer, Heidelberg (2007). https://doi.org/10.1007/978-3-540-77105-0_61

5. Chen, Y., Immorlica, N., Lucier, B., Syrgkanis, V., Ziani, J.: Optimal data acquisition for statistical estimation. In: Proceedings of the 2018 ACM Conference on Economics and Computation, pp. 27–44 (2018)

6. Chen, Y., Kash, I.A.: Information elicitation for decision making. In: Sonenberg, L., Stone, P., Tumer, K., Yolum, P. (eds.) 10th International Conference on Autonomous Agents and Multiagent Systems (AAMAS 2011), Taipei, Taiwan, 2–6 May 2011, vol. 1–3, pp. 175–182. IFAAMAS (2011)

7. Cummings, R., Ligett, K., Roth, A., Wu, Z.S., Ziani, J.: Accuracy for sale: aggregating data with a variance constraint. In: Proceedings of the 2015 Conference on Innovations in Theoretical Computer Science, pp. 317–324 (2015)

8. Dwork, C., McSherry, F., Nissim, K., Smith, A.: Calibrating noise to sensitivity in private data analysis. In: Halevi, S., Rabin, T. (eds.) TCC 2006. LNCS, vol. 3876, pp. 265–284. Springer, Heidelberg (2006). https://doi.org/10.1007/11681878_14

9. Dwork, C., Roth, A., et al.: The algorithmic foundations of differential privacy. Found. Trends Theor. Comput. Sci. **9**(3–4), 211–407 (2014)

10. Gentzkow, M., Kamenica, E.: Bayesian persuasion with multiple senders and rich signal spaces. Games Econ. Behav. **104**(C), 411–429 (2017)

11. Ghosh, A., Roth, A.: Selling privacy at auction. Games Econ. Behav. **91**, 334–346 (2015)

12. Halpern, J., Teague, V.: Rational secret sharing and multiparty computation. In: Proceedings of the Thirty-Sixth Annual ACM Symposium on Theory of Computing, pp. 623–632 (2004)

13. Kamenica, E., Gentzkow, M.: Bayesian persuasion. Am. Econ. Rev. **101**, 2590–2615 (2011). https://doi.org/10.3386/w15540

14. McGrew, R., Porter, R., Shoham, Y.: Towards a general theory of non-cooperative computation. In: Proceedings of the 9th Conference on Theoretical Aspects of Rationality and Knowledge, pp. 59–71 (2003)

15. Ronen, A., Wahrmann, L.: Prediction games. In: Deng, X., Ye, Y. (eds.) WINE 2005. LNCS, vol. 3828, pp. 129–140. Springer, Heidelberg (2005). https://doi.org/10.1007/11600930_14

16. Shoham, Y., Tennenholtz, M.: Non-cooperative computation: Boolean functions with correctness and exclusivity. Theoret. Comput. Sci. **343**(1–2), 97–113 (2005)

17. Smorodinsky, R., Tennenholtz, M.: Overcoming free riding in multi-party computations-the anonymous case. Games Econ. Behav. **55**(2), 385–406 (2006)

18. Yang, Q., Liu, Y., Chen, T., Tong, Y.: Federated machine learning: concept and applications. ACM Trans. Intell. Syst. Technol. (TIST) **10**(2), 1–19 (2019)

Fast Convergence of Optimistic Gradient Ascent in Network Zero-Sum Extensive Form Games

Georgios Piliouras[1], Lillian Ratliff[2], Ryann Sim[1(✉)], and Stratis Skoulakis[3]

[1] Singapore University of Technology and Design, Singapore, Singapore
ryann_sim@mymail.sutd.edu.sg
[2] University of Washington, Seattle, USA
[3] EPFL, Laussane, Switzerland

Abstract. The study of learning in games has thus far focused primarily on normal form games. In contrast, our understanding of learning in *extensive form games* (EFGs) and particularly in EFGs with many agents lags behind, despite them being closer in nature to many real world applications. We consider the natural class of *Network Zero-Sum Extensive Form Games*, which combines the global zero-sum property of agent payoffs, the efficient representation of graphical games as well the expressive power of EFGs. We examine the convergence properties of *Optimistic Gradient Ascent* (OGA) in these games. We prove that the time-average behavior of such online learning dynamics exhibits $O(1/T)$ rate of convergence to the set of Nash Equilibria. Moreover, we show that the day-to-day behavior also converges to a Nash with rate $O(c^{-t})$ for some game-dependent constant $c > 0$.

Keywords: Online learning in games · Optimistic gradient ascent · Network zero-sum games · Extensive form games

1 Introduction

Extensive Form Games (EFGs) are an important class of games which have been studied for more than 50 years [14]. EFGs capture various settings where several selfish agents sequentially perform actions which change the *state of nature*, with the action-sequence finally leading to a *terminal state*, at which each agent receives a payoff. The most ubiquitous examples of EFGs are real-life games such as Chess, Poker, Go etc. Recently the application of the *online learning framework* has proven to be very successful in the design of modern AI which can beat even the best human players in real-life games [2,25]. At the same time, online learning in EFGs has many interesting applications in economics, AI, machine learning and sequential decision making that extend far beyond the design of game-solvers [1,21].

The full version of this paper can be found at https://arxiv.org/abs/2207.08426.

© The Author(s), under exclusive license to Springer Nature Switzerland AG 2022
P. Kanellopoulos et al. (Eds.): SAGT 2022, LNCS 13584, pp. 383–399, 2022.
https://doi.org/10.1007/978-3-031-15714-1_22

Despite its numerous applications, online learning in EFGs is far from well understood. From a practical point of view, testing and experimenting with various online learning algorithms in EFGs requires a huge amount of computational resources due to the large number of states in EFGs of interest [23,29]. From a theoretical perspective, it is known that online learning dynamics may oscillate, cycle or even admit chaotic behavior even in very simple settings [17,18,20]. On the positive side, there exists a recent line of research into the special but fairly interesting class of *two-player zero-sum EFGs*, which provides the following solid claim: *In two-player zero-sum EFGs, the time-average strategy vector produced by online learning dynamics converges to the Nash Equilibrium (NE), while there exist online learning dynamics which exhibit day-to-day convergence* [6,26,27]. Since in most settings of interest there are typically multiple interacting agents, the above results motivate the following question:

Question. *Are there natural and important classes of multi-agent extensive form games for which online learning dynamics converge to a Nash Equilibrium? Furthermore, what type of convergence is possible? Can we only guarantee time-average convergence, or can we also prove day-to-day convergence (also known as last-iterate convergence) of the dynamics?*

In this paper we answer the above questions in the positive for an interesting class of multi-agent EFGs called *Network Zero-Sum Extensive Form Games*. A Network EFG consists of a graph $\mathcal{G} = (V, E)$ where each vertex $u \in V$ represents a selfish agent and each edge $(u, v) \in E$ corresponds to an extensive form game Γ^{uv} played between the agents $u, v \in V$. Each agent $u \in V$ selects her strategy so as to maximize the overall payoff from the games corresponding to her incident edges. The game is additionally called *zero-sum* if the sum of the agents' payoffs is equal to zero no matter the selected strategies.

We analyze the convergence properties of the online learning dynamics produced when all agents of a Network Zero-Sum EFG update their strategies according to *Optimistic Gradient Ascent*, and show the following result:

Informal Theorem. *When the agents of a network zero-sum extensive form game update their strategies using Optimistic Gradient Ascent, their time-average strategies converge with rate $O(1/T)$ to a Nash Equilibrium, while the last-iterate mixed strategies converge to a Nash Equilibrium with rate $O(c^{-t})$ for some game-dependent constant $c > 0$.*

Network Zero-Sum EFGs are an interesting class of multi-agent EFGs for much the same reasons that network zero-sum normal form games are interesting, with several additional challenges. Indeed, due to the prevalence of networks in computing systems, there has been increased interest in network formulations of normal form games [9], which have been applied to multi-agent reinforcement learning [28] and social networks [10].

Network Zero-Sum EFGs can be seen as a natural model of closed systems in which selfish agents compete over a fixed set of resources [4,5], thanks to their global constant-sum property[1] (the edge-games are not necessarily zero-sum).

---

[1] Equivalent to the global zero-sum property.

For example, consider the users of an online poker platform playing *Heads-up Poker*, a two-player extensive form game. Each user can be thought of as a node in a graph and two users are connected by an edge (corresponding to a poker game) if they play against each other. Note that here, each edge/game differs from another due to the differences in the dollar/blind equivalence. Each user u selects a poker-strategy to utilize against the other players, with the goal of maximizing her overall payoff. This is an indicative example which can clearly be modeled as a Network Zero-Sum EFG.

In addition, Network Zero-Sum EFGs are also attractive to study due to the fact that their descriptive complexity scales *polynomially* with the number of agents. Multi-agent EFGs that cannot be decomposed into pairwise interactions (i.e., do not have a network structure) admit an exponentially large description with respect to the number of the agents [9]. Hence, by considering this class of games, we are able to exploit the decomposition to extend results that are known for network normal form games to the extensive form setting.

Our Contributions. To the best of our knowledge, this is the first work establishing convergence to Nash Equilibria of online learning dynamics in network extensive form games with more than two agents. As already mentioned, there has been a stream of recent works establishing the convergence to Nash Equilibria of online learning dynamics in two-player zero-sum EFGs. However, there are several key differences between the two-player and the network cases. All the previous works concerning the two-player case follow a *bilinear saddle point approach*. Specifically, due to the fact that in the two-agent case any Nash Equilibrium coincides with a min-max equilibrium, the set of Nash Equilibria can be expressed as the solution to the following bilinear saddle-point problem:

$$\min_{x \in \mathcal{X}} \max_{y \in \mathcal{Y}} x^\top \cdot A \cdot y = \max_{y \in \mathcal{Y}} \min_{x \in \mathcal{X}} x^\top \cdot A \cdot y$$

Any online learning dynamic or algorithm that converges to the solution of the above saddle-point problem thus also converges to the Nash equilibrium in the two-player case.

However, in the network setting, there is no min-max equilibrium and hence no such connection between the Nash Equilibrium and saddle-point optimization. To overcome this difficulty, we establish that Optimistic Gradient Ascent in a class of EFGs known as *consistent* Network Zero-Sum EFGs (see Sect. 3) can be equivalently described as optimistic gradient descent in a *two-player symmetric game* (R, R) over a *treeplex polytope* $\mathcal{X}$. We remark that both the matrix R and the treeplex polytope $\mathcal{X}$ are constructed from the Network Zero-Sum EFG. Using the zero-sum property of Network EFGs, we show that the constructed matrix R satisfies the following 'restricted' zero-sum property:

$$x^\top \cdot R \cdot y + y^\top \cdot R \cdot x = 0 \text{ for all } x, y \in \mathcal{X} \tag{1}$$

Indeed, Property (1) is a generalization of the *classical zero-sum property* $A = -A^\top$. In general, the constructed matrix R does not satisfy $R = -R^\top$ and Property (1) simply ensures that the sum of payoffs equal to zero only when

$x, y \in \mathcal{X}$. Our technical contribution consists of generalizing the analysis of [26] (which holds for classical two-player zero-sum games) to symmetric games satisfying Property (1).

Related Work. *Network Zero-Sum Normal Form Games* [3–5] are a special case of our setting, where each edge/game is a normal form game. Network zero-sum normal form games present major complications compared to their two-player counterparts. The most important of these complications is that in the network case, there is no min-max equilibrium. In fact, different Nash Equilibria can assign different values to the agents. All the above works study linear programs for computing Nash Equilibria in network zero-sum normal form games. [4] introduce the idea of connecting a network zero-sum normal form game with an equivalent symmetric game (R, R) which satisfies Property (1). This generalizes the linear programming approach of two-player zero-sum normal form games to the network case. They also show that in network normal form zero-sum games, the time-average behavior of online learning dynamics converge with rate $\Theta(1/\sqrt{T})$ to the Nash Equilibrium.

The properties of *online learning in two-player zero-sum EFGs* have been studied extensively in literature. [29] and [15] propose no-regret algorithms for extensive form games with $O(1/\sqrt{T})$ average regret and polynomial running time in the size of the game. More recently, regret-based algorithms achieve $O(1/T)$ time-average convergence to the min-max equilibrium [6,8,11] for *two-player zero-sum EFGs*. Finally, [16] and [26] establish that Online Mirror Descent achieves $O(c^{-t})$ last-iterate convergence (for some game-dependent constant $c \in (0, 1)$) in *two-player zero-sum EFGs*.

2   Preliminaries

2.1   Two-Player Extensive Form Games

Definition 1. A two-player extensive form game Γ is a tuple $\Gamma := \langle \mathcal{H}, \mathcal{A}, \mathcal{Z}, p, \mathcal{I} \rangle$ where

- $\mathcal{H}$ denotes the states of the game that are decision points for the agents. The states $h \in \mathcal{H}$ form a tree rooted at an initial state $r \in \mathcal{H}$.
- Each state $h \in \mathcal{H}$ is associated with a set of *available actions* $\mathcal{A}(h)$.
- Each state $h \in \mathcal{H}$ admits a label $\text{Label}(h) \in \{1, 2, c\}$ denoting the *acting player* at state h. The letter c denotes a special agent called a *chance agent*. Each state $h \in \mathcal{H}$ with $\text{Label}(h) = c$ is additionally associated with a function $\sigma_h : \mathcal{A}(h) \mapsto [0, 1]$ where $\sigma_h(\alpha)$ denotes the probability that the chance player selects action $\alpha \in \mathcal{A}(h)$ at state h, $\sum_{\alpha \in \mathcal{A}(h)} \sigma_h(\alpha) = 1$.
- $\text{Next}(\alpha, h)$ denotes the state $h' := \text{Next}(\alpha, h)$ which is reached when agent $i := \text{Label}(h)$ takes action $\alpha \in \mathcal{A}(h)$ at state h. $\mathcal{H}_i \subseteq \mathcal{H}$ denotes the states $h \in \mathcal{H}$ with $\text{Label}(h) = i$.
- $\mathcal{Z}$ denotes the terminal states of the game corresponding to the leaves of the tree. At each $z \in \mathcal{Z}$ no further action can be chosen, so $\mathcal{A}(z) = \varnothing$ for all $z \in \mathcal{Z}$. Each terminal state $z \in \mathcal{Z}$ is associated with values $(u_1(z), u_2(z))$ where $p_i(z)$ denotes the payoff of agent i at terminal state z.

- Each set of states $\mathcal{H}_i$ is further partitioned into *information sets* $(\mathcal{I}_1, \ldots, \mathcal{I}_k)$ where $\mathcal{I}(h)$ denotes the information set of state $h \in \mathcal{H}_i$. In the case that $\mathcal{I}(h_1) = \mathcal{I}(h_2)$ for some $h_1, h_2 \in \mathcal{H}_1$, then $\mathcal{A}(h_1) = \mathcal{A}(h_2)$.

Information sets model situations where the *acting agent* cannot differentiate between different states of the game due to a lack of information. Since the agent cannot differentiate between states of the same information set, the available actions at states h_1, h_2 in the same information set $(\mathcal{I}(h_1) = \mathcal{I}(h_2))$ must coincide, in particular $\mathcal{A}(h_1) = \mathcal{A}(h_2)$.

Definition 2. A behavioral plan σ_i for agent i is a function such that for each state $h \in \mathcal{H}_i$, $\sigma_i(h)$ is a probability distribution over $\mathcal{A}(h)$ i.e. $\sigma_i(h, \alpha)$ denotes the probability that agent i takes action $\alpha \in \mathcal{A}(h)$ at state $h \in \mathcal{H}_i$. Furthermore it is required that $\sigma_i(h_1) = \sigma_i(h_2)$ for each $h_1, h_2 \in \mathcal{H}_i$ with $\mathcal{I}(h_1) = \mathcal{I}(h_2)$. The set of all behavioral plans for agent i is denoted by Σ_i.

The constraint $\sigma_i(h_1) = \sigma_i(h_2)$ for all $h_1, h_2 \in \mathcal{H}_i$ with $\mathcal{I}(h_1) = \mathcal{I}(h_2)$ models the fact that since agent i cannot differentiate between states h_1, h_2, agent i must act in the exact same way at states $h_1, h_2 \in \mathcal{H}_i$.

Definition 3. For a collection of behavioral plans $\sigma = (\sigma_1, \sigma_2) \in \Sigma_1 \times \Sigma_2$ the payoff of agent i, denoted by $U_i(\sigma)$, is defined as:

$$U_i(\sigma) := \sum_{z \in \mathcal{Z}} p_i(z) \cdot \underbrace{\Pi_{(h,h') \in \mathcal{P}(z)} \sigma_{\text{Label}(h)}(h, \alpha_{h'})}_{\text{probability that state } z \text{ is reached}}$$

where $\mathcal{P}(z)$ denotes the path from the root state r to the terminal state z and $\alpha_{h'}$ denotes the action $\alpha \in \mathcal{H}_i$ such that $h' = \text{Next}(h, \alpha)$.

Definition 4. A collection of behavioral plans $\sigma^* = (\sigma_1^*, \sigma_2^*)$ is called a Nash Equilibrium if for all agents $i = \{1, 2\}$,

$$U_i(\sigma_i^*, \sigma_{-i}^*) \geq U_i(\sigma_i, \sigma_{-i}^*) \quad \text{for all } \sigma_i \in \Sigma_i$$

The classical result of [19] proves the existence of Nash Equilibrium in normal form games. This result also generalizes to a wide class of extensive form games which satisfy a property called *perfect recall* [13,24].

Definition 5. A two-player extensive form game $\Gamma := \langle \mathcal{H}, \mathcal{A}, \mathcal{Z}, p, \mathcal{I} \rangle$ has **perfect recall** if and only if for all states $h_1, h_2 \in \mathcal{H}_i$ with $\mathcal{I}(h_1) = \mathcal{I}(h_2)$ the following holds: Define the sets $\mathcal{P}(h_1) \cap \mathcal{H}_i := (p_1, \ldots, p_k, h_1)$ and $\mathcal{P}(h_2) \cap \mathcal{H}_i := (q_1, \ldots, q_m, h_2)$. Then:

1. $k = m$.
2. $\mathcal{I}(p_\ell) = \mathcal{I}(q_\ell)$ for all $\ell \in \{1, \ldots, k\}$.
3. $p_{\ell+1} \in \text{Next}(p_\ell, \alpha, i)$ and $q_{\ell+1} \in \text{Next}(q_\ell, \alpha, i)$ for some action $\alpha \in \mathcal{A}(p_\ell)$ (since $\mathcal{A}(p_\ell) = \mathcal{A}(q_\ell)$).

Before proceeding, let us further explain the perfect recall property. As already mentioned, agent i cannot differentiate between states $h_1, h_2 \in \mathcal{H}_i$ when $\mathcal{I}(h_1) = \mathcal{I}(h_2)$. In order for the state h_1 to be reached, agent i must take some specific actions along the path $\mathcal{P}(h_1) \cap \mathcal{H}_i := (p_1, \ldots, p_k, h_1)$. The same logic holds for $\mathcal{P}(h_2) \cap \mathcal{H}_i := (p_1, \ldots, p_k, h_1)$. In case where agent i could distinguish $\mathcal{P}(h_1) \cap \mathcal{H}_i$ from set $\mathcal{P}(h_2) \cap \mathcal{H}_i$, then she could distinguish state h_1 from h_2 by recalling the previous states in $\mathcal{H}_i$. This is the reason for the second constraint in Definition 5. Even if $\mathcal{I}(p_\ell) = \mathcal{I}(q_\ell)$ for all $\ell \in \{1, \ldots, k\}$, agent i could still distinguish h_1 from h_2 if $p_{\ell+1} \in \text{Next}(p_\ell, \alpha, i)$ and $q_{\ell+1} \in \text{Next}(q_\ell, \alpha', i)$. In such a case, agent i can distinguish h_1 from h_2 by recalling the actions that she previously played and checking if the ℓ-th action was α or α'. This case is encompassed by the third constraint.

2.2 Two-Player Extensive Form Games in Sequence Form

A *two-player extensive form game* Γ can be captured by a two-player bilinear game where the action spaces of the agents are a specific kind of polytope, commonly known as a *treeplex* [8]. In order to formally define the notion of a treeplex, we first need to introduce some additional notation.

Definition 6. Given an two-player extensive form game Γ, we define the following:

- $\mathcal{P}(h)$ denotes the path from the root state $r \in \mathcal{H}$ to the state $h \in \mathcal{H}$.
- $\text{Level}(h)$ denotes the distance from the root state $r \in \mathcal{H}$ to state $h \in \mathcal{H}$.
- $\text{Prev}(h, i)$ denotes the lowest ancestor of h in the set $\mathcal{H}_i$. In particular,

$$\text{Prev}(h, i) = \text{argmax}_{h' \in \mathcal{P}(h) \cap \mathcal{H}_i} \text{Level}(h').$$

- The set of states $\text{Next}(h, \alpha, i) \subseteq \mathcal{H}$ denotes the highest descendants $h' \in \mathcal{H}_i$ once action $\alpha \in \mathcal{A}(h)$ has been taken at state h. More formally, $h' \in \text{Next}(h, \alpha, i)$ if and only if in the path $\mathcal{P}(h, h') = (h, h_1, \ldots, h_k, h')$, all states $h_\ell \notin \mathcal{H}_i$ and $h_1 = \text{Next}(h, \alpha)$.

Definition 7. Given a two-player extensive form game Γ, the set $\mathcal{X}_i^\Gamma$ is composed by all vectors $x_i \in [0, 1]^{|\mathcal{H}_i| + |\mathcal{Z}|}$ which satisfy the following constraints:

1. $x_i(h) = 1$ for all $h \in \mathcal{H}_i$ with $\text{Prev}(h, i) = \varnothing$.
2. $x_i(h_1) = x_i(h_2)$ if there exists $h'_1, h'_2 \in \mathcal{H}_i$ such that $h_1 \in \text{Next}(h'_1, \alpha, i)$, $h_2 \in \text{Next}(h'_2, \alpha, i)$ and $\mathcal{I}(h'_1) = \mathcal{I}(h'_2)$.
3. $\sum_{\alpha \in \mathcal{A}(h)} x_i(\text{Next}(h, \alpha, i)) = x_i(h)$ for all $h \in \mathcal{H}_i$.

A vector $x_i \in \mathcal{X}_i^\Gamma$ is typically referred to as an agent i's *strategy in sequence form*. Strategies in sequence form come as an alternative to the behavioral plans of Definition 2. As established in Lemma 1, there exists an equivalence between a behavioral plan $\sigma_i \in \Sigma_i$ and a strategy in sequence form $x_i \in \mathcal{X}_i^\Gamma$ for games with perfect recall.

Lemma 1. *Consider a two-player extensive form game Γ with perfect recall and the $(|\mathcal{H}_1| + |\mathcal{Z}|) \times (|\mathcal{H}_2| + |\mathcal{Z}|)$ dimensional matrices A_1^Γ, A_2^Γ with $[A_i^\Gamma]_{zz} = p_i(z)$ for all terminal nodes $z \in \mathcal{Z}$ and 0 otherwise. There exists a polynomial-time algorithm transforming any behavioral plan $\sigma_i \in \Sigma_i$ to a vector $x_{\sigma_i} \in \mathcal{X}_i^\Gamma$ such that*

$$U_1(\sigma_1, \sigma_2) = x_{\sigma_1}^\top \cdot A_1^\Gamma \cdot x_{\sigma_2} \qquad and \qquad U_2(\sigma_1, \sigma_2) = x_{\sigma_2}^\top \cdot A_2^\Gamma \cdot x_{\sigma_1}$$

Conversely, there exists a polynomial-time algorithm transforming any vector $x_i \in \mathcal{X}_i^\Gamma$ to a vector $\sigma_{x_i} \in \Sigma_i$ such that

$$x_1^\top \cdot A_1^\Gamma \cdot x_2 = U_1(\sigma_{x_1}, \sigma_{x_2}) \qquad and \qquad x_2^\top \cdot A_2^\Gamma \cdot x_1 = U_2(\sigma_{x_1}, \sigma_{x_2})$$

To this end, one can understand why *strategies in sequence form* are of great use. Assume that agent 2 selects a behavioral plan $\sigma_2 \in \Sigma_2$. Then, agent 1 wants to compute a behavioral plan $\sigma_1^* \in \Sigma_1$ which is the *best response* to σ_2, namely $\sigma_1^* := \operatorname{argmax}_{\sigma_1 \in \Sigma_1} U_1(\sigma_1, \sigma_2)$. This computation can be done in polynomial-time in the following manner: Agent 1 initially converts (in polynomial time) the behavioral plan σ_2 to $x_{\sigma_2} \in \mathcal{X}_2^\Gamma$, which is the respective strategy in sequence form. Then, she can obtain a vector $x_1^* = \operatorname{argmax}_{x_1 \in \mathcal{X}_1^\Gamma} x_1^\top \cdot A_1^\Gamma \cdot x_2$. The latter step can be done in polynomial-time by computing the solution of an appropriate linear program. Finally, she can convert the vector x_1^* to a behavioral plan $\sigma_{x_1^*} \in \Sigma_1$ in polynomial-time. Lemma 1 ensures that $\sigma_{x_1^*} = \operatorname{argmax}_{\sigma_1 \in \Sigma_1} U_1(\sigma_1, \sigma_2)$.

The above reasoning can be used to establish an equivalence between the Nash Equilibrium (σ_1^*, σ_2^*) of an EFG $\Gamma := \langle \mathcal{H}, \mathcal{A}, \mathcal{Z}, p, \mathcal{I} \rangle$ with the Nash Equilibrium in its sequence form.

Definition 8. A Nash Equilibrium of a two-player EFG Γ in sequence form is a vector $(x_1^*, x_2^*) \in \mathcal{X}_1^\Gamma \times \mathcal{X}_2^\Gamma$ such that

- $(x_1^*)^\top \cdot A_1^\Gamma \cdot x_2^* \geq (x_1)^\top \cdot A_1^\Gamma \cdot x_2^*$ for all $x_1 \in \mathcal{X}_1^\Gamma$
- $(x_2^*)^\top \cdot A_2^\Gamma \cdot x_1^* \geq (x_2)^\top \cdot A_2^\Gamma \cdot x_1^*$ for all $x_2 \in \mathcal{X}_2^\Gamma$

Lemma 1 directly implies that any Nash Equilibrium of an EFG $(\sigma_1^*, \sigma_2^*) \in \Sigma_1 \times \Sigma_2$ as per Definition 4 can be converted in polynomial-time to a Nash Equilibrium in the sequence form $(x_1^*, x_2^*) \in \mathcal{X}_1^\Gamma \times \mathcal{X}_2^\Gamma$ and vice versa.

2.3 Optimistic Mirror Descent

In this section we introduce and provide the necessary background for *Optimistic Mirror Descent* [22]. For a convex function $\psi : \mathbb{R}^d \mapsto \mathbb{R}$, the corresponding *Bregman divergence* is defined as

$$D_\psi(x, y) := \psi(x) - \psi(y) - \langle \nabla \psi(y), x - y \rangle$$

If ψ is γ-strongly convex, then $D_\psi(x, y) \geq \frac{\gamma}{2} \|x - y\|$. Here and in the rest of the paper, we note that $\| \cdot \|$ is shorthand for the L_2-norm.

Now consider a game played by n agents, where the action of each agent i is a vector x_i from a convex set $\mathcal{X}_i$. Each agent selects its action $x_i \in \mathcal{X}_i$ so as to minimize her individual cost (denoted by $C_i(x_i, x_{-i})$), which is continuous, differentiable and convex with respect to x_i. Specifically,

$$C_i(\lambda \cdot x_i + (1-\lambda) \cdot x_i', x_{-i}) \leq \lambda \cdot C_i(x_i, x_{-i}) + (1-\lambda) \cdot C_i(x_i', x_{-i}) \text{ for all } \lambda \in [0,1]$$

Given a step size $\eta > 0$ and a convex function $\psi(\cdot)$ (called a regularizer), *Optimistic Mirror Descent* (OMD) sequentially performs the following update step for $t = 1, 2, \ldots$:

$$x_i^t = \text{argmin}_{x \in \mathcal{X}_i} \left\{ \eta \left\langle x, F_i^{t-1}(x) \right\rangle + D_\psi \left(x, \hat{x}_i^t \right) \right\} \tag{2}$$

$$\hat{x}_i^{t+1} = \text{argmin}_{x \in \mathcal{X}_i} \left\{ \eta \left\langle x, F_i^t(x) \right\rangle + D_\psi(x, \hat{x}_i^t) \right\} \tag{3}$$

where $F_i^t(x_i) = \nabla_{x_i} C_i(x_i, x_{-i}^t)$ and $D_\psi(x, y)$ is the *Bregman Divergence* with respect to $\psi(\cdot)$. If the step-size η selected is sufficiently small, then *Optimistic Mirror Descent* ensures the *no-regret property* [22], making it a natural update algorithm for selfish agents [7]. To simplify notation we denote the projection operator of a convex set $\mathcal{X}^*$ as $\Pi_{\mathcal{X}^*}(x) := \text{argmax}_{x^* \in \mathcal{X}^*} \|x - x^*\|$ and the squared distance of vector x from a convex set $\mathcal{X}^*$ as $\text{dist}^2(x, \mathcal{X}^*) := \|x - \Pi_{\mathcal{X}^*}(x)\|^2$.

3   Our Setting

In this section of the paper, we introduce the concept of Network Zero-Sum Extensive Form Games, which are a network extension of the two player EFGs introduced in Sect. 2.

3.1   Network Zero-Sum Extensive Form Games

A *network extensive form game* is defined with respect to an undirected graph $\mathcal{G} = (V, E)$ where nodes V ($|V| = n$) correspond to the set of players and each edge $(u, v) \in E$ represents a *two-player extensive form game* Γ^{uv} played between agents u, v. Each node/agent $u \in V$ selects a behavioral plan $\sigma_u \in \Sigma_u$ which they use to play all the *two-player EFGs* on its outgoing edges.

Definition 9 (Network Extensive Form Games). A network extensive form game is a tuple $\Gamma := \langle \mathcal{G}, \mathcal{H}, \mathcal{A}, \mathcal{Z}, \mathcal{I} \rangle$ where

- $\mathcal{G} = (V, E)$ is an undirected graph where the nodes V represents the agents.
- Each agent $u \in V$ admits a set of states $\mathcal{H}_u$ at which the agent u plays. Each state $h \in \mathcal{H}_u$ is associated with a set $\mathcal{A}(h)$ of possible actions that agent u can take at state h.
- $\mathcal{I}(h)$ denotes the information set of $h \in \mathcal{H}_u$. If $\mathcal{I}(h) = \mathcal{I}(h')$ for some $h, h' \in \mathcal{H}_u$ then $\mathcal{A}(h) = \mathcal{A}(h')$.
- For each edge $(u, v) \in E$, Γ^{uv} is a two-player extensive form game with perfect recall. The states of Γ^{uv} are denoted by $\mathcal{H}^{uv} \subseteq \mathcal{H}_u \cup \mathcal{H}_v$.
- For each edge $(u, v) \in E$, $\mathcal{Z}^{uv}$ is the set of terminal states of the two-player extensive form game Γ^{uv} where $p_u^{\Gamma^{uv}}(z)$ denotes the payoffs of u, v at the terminal state $z \in \mathcal{Z}^{uv}$. The overall set of terminal states of the network extensive form game is the set $\mathcal{Z} := \cup_{(u,v) \in E} \mathcal{Z}^{uv}$.

In a network extensive form game, each agent $u \in V$ selects a behavioral plan $\sigma_u \in \Sigma_u$ (see Definition 2) that they use to play the two-player EFG's Γ^{uv} with $(u, v) \in E$. Each agent selects her behavioral plan so as to maximize the sum of the payoffs of the two-player EFGs in her outgoing edges.

Definition 10. Given a collection of behavioral plans $\sigma = (\sigma_1, \ldots, \sigma_n) \in \Sigma_1 \times \ldots \times \Sigma_n$ the payoff of agent u, denoted by $U_u(\sigma)$, equals

$$U_u(\sigma) := \sum_{v:(u,v) \in E} p_u^{\Gamma^{uv}}(\sigma_u, \sigma_v)$$

Moreover a collection $\sigma^* = (\sigma_1^*, \ldots, \sigma_n^*) \in \Sigma_1 \times \ldots \times \Sigma_n$ is called a Nash Equilibrium if and only if

$$U_u(\sigma_u^*, \sigma_{-u}^*) \geq U_u(\sigma_u, \sigma_{-u}^*) \quad \text{for all } \sigma_u \in \Sigma_u$$

As already mentioned, each agent $u \in V$ plays all the two-player games Γ^{uv} for $(u, v) \in E$ with the same behavioral plan $\sigma_u \in \Sigma_u$. This is due to the fact that the agent cannot distinguish between a state $h_1, h_2 \in \mathcal{H}_u$ with $\mathcal{I}(h_1) = \mathcal{I}(h_2)$ even if h_1, h_2 are states of different EFG's Γ^{uv} and $\Gamma^{uv'}$. As in the case of *perfect recall*, the latter implies that u cannot differentiate states h_1, h_2 even when recalling the states $\mathcal{H}_u$ visited in the past and her past actions. In Definition 11 we introduce the notion of *consistency* (this corresponds to the notion of *perfect recall* for two-player extensive form games (Definition 5)). From now on we assume that the network EFG is consistent without mentioning it explicitly.

Definition 11. A network extensive form game $\Gamma := \langle \mathcal{G}, \mathcal{H}, \mathcal{A}, \mathcal{Z}, \mathcal{I} \rangle$ is called **consistent** if and only if for all players $u \in V$ and states $h_1, h_2 \in \mathcal{H}_u$ with $\mathcal{I}(h_1) = \mathcal{I}(h_2)$ the following holds: for any $(u, v), (u, v') \in E$ the sets $\mathcal{P}^{uv}(h_1) \cap \mathcal{H}_u := (p_1, \ldots, p_k, h_1)$ and $\mathcal{P}^{uv'}(h_2) \cap \mathcal{H}_u := (q_1, \ldots, q_m, h_2)$ satisfy:

1. $k = m$.
2. $\mathcal{I}(p_\ell) = \mathcal{I}(q_\ell)$ for all $\ell \in \{1, k\}$.
3. $p_{\ell+1} \in \text{Next}^{\Gamma^{uv}}(p_\ell, \alpha, u)$ and $q_{\ell+1} \in \text{Next}^{\Gamma^{uv'}}(q_\ell, \alpha, u)$ for some action $\alpha \in \mathcal{A}(p_\ell)$.

where $\mathcal{P}^{uv}(h)$ denotes the path from the root state to state h in the two-player extensive form game Γ^{uv}.

In this work we study the special class of network *zero-sum* extensive form games. This class of games is a generalization of the network zero-sum normal form games studied in [4].

Definition 12. A behavioral plan $\sigma_u \in \Sigma_u$ of Definition 2 is called pure if and only if $\sigma_u(h, \alpha)$ either equals 0 or 1 for all actions $\alpha \in \mathcal{A}(h)$. A network extensive form game is called **zero-sum** if and only if for any collection $\sigma := (\sigma_1, \ldots, \sigma_n)$ of pure behavioral plans, $U_u(\sigma) = 0$ for all $u \in V$.

3.2   Network Extensive Form Games in Sequence Form

As in the case of two-player EFGs, there exists an equivalence between behavioral plans $\sigma_u \in \Sigma_u$ and strategies in sequence form x_u. As we shall later see, this equivalence is of great importance since it allows for the design of natural and computationally efficient learning dynamics that converge to Nash Equilibria both in terms of behavioral plans and strategies in sequence form.

Definition 13. Given a network extensive form game $\Gamma := \langle \mathcal{G}, \mathcal{H}, \mathcal{A}, \mathcal{Z}, \mathcal{I} \rangle$, the treeplex polytope $\mathcal{X}_u \subseteq [0,1]^{|\mathcal{H}_u|+|\mathcal{Z}_u|}$ is the set defined as follows: $x_u \in \mathcal{X}_u$ if and only if

1. $x_u \in \mathcal{X}_u^{\Gamma_{uv}}$ for all $(u,v) \in E$.
2. $x_u(h_1) = x_u(h_2)$ in case there exists $(u,v), (u,v') \in E$ and $h_1', h_2' \in \mathcal{H}_u$ with $\mathcal{I}(h_1') = I(h_2')$ such that $h_1 \in \text{Next}^{\Gamma_{uv}}(h_1', \alpha, u)$, $h_2 \in \text{Next}^{\Gamma_{uv'}}(h_2', \alpha, u)$ and $\mathcal{I}(h_1') = I(h_2')$.

The second constraint in Definition 13 is the equivalent of the second constraint in Definition 7. We remark that the linear equations describing the treeplex polytope $\mathcal{X}_u$ can be derived in polynomial-time with respect to the description of the network extensive form game. In Lemma 2 we formally state and prove the equivalence between behavioral plans and strategies in sequence form.

Lemma 2. *Consider the matrix A^{uv} of dimensions $(|\mathcal{H}_u|+|\mathcal{Z}^u|) \times (|\mathcal{H}_v|+|\mathcal{Z}^v|)$ such that*

$$[A^{uv}]_{h_1 h_2} = \begin{cases} p_u^{\Gamma_{uv}}(h) & \text{if } h_1 = h_2 = h \in \mathcal{Z}^{uv} \\ 0 & \text{otherwise} \end{cases}$$

There exists a polynomial time algorithm converting any collection of behavioral plans $(\sigma_1, \ldots, \sigma_n) \in \Sigma_1 \times \ldots \times \Sigma_n$ into a collection of vectors $(x_1, \ldots, x_n) \in \mathcal{X}_1 \times \ldots \times \mathcal{X}_n$ such that for any $u \in V$,

$$U_u(\sigma) = x_u^\top \cdot \sum_{v:(u,v)\in E} A^{uv} \cdot x_v$$

In the opposite direction, there exists a polynomial time algorithm converting any collection of vectors $(x_1, \ldots, x_n) \in \mathcal{X}_1 \times \ldots \times \mathcal{X}_n$ into a collection of behavioral plans $(\sigma_1, \ldots, \sigma_n) \in \Sigma_1 \times \ldots \times \Sigma_n$ such that for any $u \in V$,

$$x_u^\top \cdot \sum_{v:(u,v)\in E} A^{uv} \cdot x_v = U_u(\sigma)$$

Definition 14. A Nash Equilibrium of a network extensive form game $\mathcal{G}$ in sequence form is a vector $(x_1^*, \ldots, x_n^*) \in \mathcal{X}_1 \times \ldots \times \mathcal{X}_n$ such that for all $u \in V$:

$$(x_u^*)^\top \cdot \sum_{v:(u,v)\in E} A^{uv} \cdot x_v^* \geq x_u^\top \cdot \sum_{v:(u,v)\in E} A^{uv} \cdot x_v^* \quad \text{for all } x_u \in \mathcal{X}_u$$

Corollary 1. *Given a network extensive form game, any Nash Equilibrium* $(\sigma_1^*, \ldots, \sigma_n^*) \in \Sigma_1 \times \ldots \times \Sigma_n$ *(as per Definition 4) can be converted in polynomial-time to a Nash Equilibrium* $(x_1^*, \ldots, x_n^*) \in \mathcal{X}_1 \times \ldots \times \mathcal{X}_n$ *(as per Definition 14) and vice versa.*

The sequence form representation gives us a perspective with which we can analyze the theoretical properties of learning algorithms when applied to network zero-sum EFGs. In the following section, we utilize the sequence form representation to study a special case of Optimistic Mirror Descent known as Optimistic Gradient Ascent (OGA).

4 Our Convergence Results

In this work, we additionally study the convergence properties of *Optimistic Gradient Ascent* (OGA) when applied to *network zero-sum EFGs*. OGA is a special case of *Optimistic Mirror Descent* where the regularizer is $\psi(a) = \frac{1}{2}\|a\|^2$, which means that the Bregman divergence $D_\psi(x,y)$ equals $\frac{1}{2}\|x-y\|^2$. Since in network zero-sum EFGs each agent tries to maximize her payoff, OGA takes the following form:

$$x_u^t = \mathrm{argmax}_{x \in \mathcal{X}_u}\left\{\eta\left\langle x, \sum_{v:(u,v)\in E} A^{uv} \cdot x_v^{t-1}\right\rangle - D_\psi\left(x, \hat{x}_u^t\right)\right\} \qquad (4)$$

$$\hat{x}_u^{t+1} = \mathrm{argmax}_{x \in \mathcal{X}_u}\left\{\eta\left\langle x, \sum_{v:(u,v)\in E} A^{uv} \cdot x_v^t\right\rangle - D_\psi\left(x, \hat{x}_u^t\right)\right\} \qquad (5)$$

In Theorem 1 we describe the $\Theta(1/T)$ convergence rate to NE for the time-average strategies for any agent using OGA.

Theorem 1. *Let* $\{x^1, x^2, \ldots x^T\}$ *be the vectors produced by Eqs. (4), (5) for some initial strategies* $x^0 := (x_1^0, \ldots, x_n^0)$. *There exist game-dependent constants* $c_1, c_2 > 0$ *such that if* $\eta \leq 1/c_1$ *then for any* $u \in V$:

$$\hat{x}_u^\top \cdot \sum_{v:(u,v)\in E} A^{uv} \cdot \hat{x}_v \geq x^\top \cdot \sum_{v:(u,v)\in E} A^{uv} \cdot \hat{x}_v - \Theta\left(\frac{c_1 \cdot c_2}{T}\right) \quad \text{for all } x \in \mathcal{X}_u$$

where $\hat{x}_u = \sum_{s=1}^T x_u^s/T$.

Applying the polynomial-time transformation of Lemma 2 to the time-average strategy vector $\hat{x} = (\hat{x}_1, \ldots, \hat{x}_n)$ produced by Optimistic Gradient Ascent, we immediately get that for any agent $u \in V$,

$$U_u(\hat{\sigma}_u, \hat{\sigma}_{-u}) \geq U_u(\sigma_u, \hat{\sigma}_{-u}) - \Theta\left(c_1 \cdot c_2/T\right) \quad \text{for all } \sigma_u \in \Sigma_u$$

In Theorem 2 we establish the fact that OGA admits last-iterate convergence to NE in network zero-sum EFGs.

Theorem 2. *Let* $\{x^1, x^2, \dots x^T\}$ *be the vectors produced by Eqs. (4), (5) for* $\eta \leq 1/c_3$ *when applied to a network zero-sum extensive form game. Then, the following inequality holds:*

$$\text{dist}^2(x^t, \mathcal{X}^*) \leq 64 \text{dist}^2(x^1, \mathcal{X}^*) \cdot (1 + c_1)^{-t}$$

where $\mathcal{X}^*$ *denotes the set of Nash Equilibria,* $c_1 := \min\left\{\frac{16\eta^2 c^2}{81}, \frac{1}{2}\right\}$ *and* c_3, c *are positive game-dependent constants.*

We conclude the section by providing the key ideas towards proving Theorems 1 and 2. For the rest of the section, we assume that the network extensive form game is consistent and zero-sum. Before proceeding, we introduce a few more necessary definitions and notations. We denote as $\mathcal{X} := \mathcal{X}_1 \times \dots \times \mathcal{X}_n$ the product of treeplexes of Definition 13 and define the $|\mathcal{X}| \times |\mathcal{X}|$ matrix R as follows:

$$R_{(u:h_1),(v:h_2)} = \begin{cases} -[A^{uv}]_{h_1 h_2} & \text{if } (u,v) \in E \\ 0 & \text{otherwise} \end{cases}$$

The matrix R can be used to derive a more concrete form of the Eqs. (4), (5):

Lemma 3. *Let* $\{x^1, x^2, \dots, x^T\}$ *be the collection of strategy vectors produced by Eqs. (4), (5) initialized with* $x^0 := (x_1^0, \dots, x_n^0) \in \mathcal{X}$. *The equations*

$$x^t = \text{argmin}_{x \in \mathcal{X}} \{\eta \langle x, R \cdot x^{t-1} \rangle + D_\psi(x, \hat{x}^t)\} \tag{6}$$

$$\hat{x}^{t+1} = \text{argmin}_{x \in \mathcal{X}} \{\eta \langle x, R \cdot x^t \rangle + D_\psi(x, \hat{x}^t)\} \tag{7}$$

produce the exact same collection of strategy vectors $\{x^1, \dots, x^T\}$ *when initialized with* $x^0 \in \mathcal{X}$.

To this end, we derive a *two-player symmetric game* (R, R) defined over the polytope $\mathcal{X}$. More precisely, the x-agent selects $x \in \mathcal{X}$ so as to minimize $x^\top R y$ while the y-agent selects $y \in \mathcal{X}$ so as to minimize $y^\top R x$. Now consider the Optimistic Mirror Descent algorithm (described in Eqs. (2), (3)) applied to the above symmetric game. Notice that if $x^0 = y^0$, then by the symmetry of the game, the produced strategy vector (x^t, y^t) will be of the form (x^t, x^t) and indeed, $(x^t, \hat{x}^t)$ will satisfy Eqs. (6), (7). We prove that the produced vector sequence $\{x^t\}_{t \geq 1}$ converges to a *symmetric Nash Equilibrium*.

Lemma 4. *A strategy vector* x^* *is an* ϵ-*symmetric Nash Equilibrium for the symmetric game* (R, R) *if the following holds:*

$$(x^*)^\top \cdot R \cdot x^* \leq x^\top \cdot R \cdot x^* + \epsilon \quad \text{for all } x \in \mathcal{X}$$

Any ϵ-*symmetric Nash Equilibrium* $x^* \in \mathcal{X}$ *is also an* ϵ-*Nash Equilibrium for the network zero-sum EFG.*

A key property of the constructed matrix is the one stated and proven in Lemma 5. Its proof follows the steps of the proof of Lemma B.3 in [4].

Lemma 5. $x^\top \cdot R \cdot y + y^\top \cdot R \cdot x = 0$ *for all* $x, y \in \mathcal{X}$.

Once Lemma 5 is established, we can use to it to prove that the time-average strategy vector converges to an ϵ-symmetric Nash Equilibrium in a two-player symmetric game.

Lemma 6. *Let* $(x^1, x^2, \ldots, x^T)$ *be the sequence of strategy vectors produced by Eqs. (6), (7) for* $\eta \leq \min\{1/8\|R\|^2, 1\}$. *Then,*

$$min_{x \in \mathcal{X}} x^\top \cdot R \cdot \hat{x} \geq -\Theta \left(\frac{\mathcal{D}^2 \|R\|^2}{T} \right)$$

where $\hat{x} = \sum_{s=1}^T x^s / T$ *and* $\mathcal{D}$ *is the diameter of the treeplex polytope* $\mathcal{X}$.

Combining Lemma 5 with Lemma 6, we get that the time-average vector $\hat{x}$ is a $\Theta \left(\frac{\mathcal{D}^2 \|R\|^2}{T} \right)$-symmetric Nash Equilibrium. This follows directly from the fact that $\hat{x}^\top \cdot R \cdot \hat{x} = 0$. Then, Theorem 1 follows via a direct application of Lemma 4.

By Lemma 5, it directly follows that the set of symmetric Nash Equilibria can be written as:

$$\mathcal{X}^* = \{x^* \in \mathcal{X} : \min_{x \in \mathcal{X}} x^\top \cdot R \cdot x^* = 0\}.$$

Using this, we further establish that Optimistic Gradient *Descent* admits last-iterate convergence to the symmetric NE of the (R, R) game. This result is formally stated and proven in Theorem 3, the proof of which is adapted from the analysis of [27], with modifications to apply the steps to our setting.

Theorem 3. *Let* $\{x^1, x^2, \ldots x^T\}$ *be the vectors produced by Eqs. (6), (7) for* $\eta \leq \min(1/8\|R\|^2, 1)$. *Then:*

$$\mathrm{dist}^2(x^t, \mathcal{X}^*) \leq 64\mathrm{dist}^2(x^1, \mathcal{X}^*) \cdot (1 + C_2)^{-t}$$

where $C_2 := \min \left\{ \frac{16\eta^2 C^2}{81}, \frac{1}{2} \right\}$ *with* C *being a positive game-dependent constant.*

The statement of Theorem 2 then follows directly by combining Theorem 3 and Lemma 4. This result generalizes previous last-iterate convergence results for the setting of two-player zero-sum EFGs, even for games without a unique Nash Equilibrium.

5   Experimental Results

In order to better visualize our theoretical results, we experimentally evaluate OGA when applied to various network extensive form games. As part of the experimental process, for each simulation we ran a hyperparameter search to find the value of η which gave the best convergence rate.

Time-Average Convergence. Our theoretical results guarantee time-average convergence to the Nash Equilibrium set (Theorem 1). We experimentally confirm this by running OGA on a network version of the ubiquitous Matching Pennies game with 20 nodes (Fig. 1(a)), followed by a 4-node network zero-sum EFG (Fig. 1(b)). In particular, for the latter experiment each bilinear game between the players on the nodes is a randomly generated extensive form game with payoff values in [0, 1]. Next, we experimented with a well-studied simplification of poker known as Kuhn poker [12]. Emulating the illustrative example of a competitive online Poker lobby as described in Sect. 1, we modelled a situation whereby each agent is playing against multiple other agents, and ran simulations for such a game with 5 agents (Fig. 1(c)).

In the plots, we show on the y-axis the difference between the cumulative averages of the strategy probabilities and the Nash Equilibrium value calculated from the game. In each of the plots, we see that these time-average values go to 0, implying convergence to the NE set.

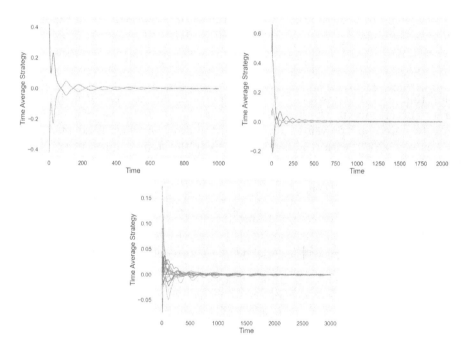

Fig. 1. Time-average convergence of OGA in network zero-sum extensive form games, where each player is involved in 2 or more different games and must select their strategy accordingly. (a) 20-node Matching Pennies game. (b) 4-node random extensive form game. (c) 5-node *Kuhn poker* game.

Last-Iterate Convergence. Theorem 2 guarantees $O(c^{-t})$ convergence in the last-iterate sense to a Nash Equlibrium for OGA. Similar to the time-average case, we ran simulations for randomly generated 3 and 4-node network extensive form games, where each bilinear game between two agents is a randomly generated matrix with values in $[0, 1]$ (Fig. 2(a–b)). Moreover, we also simulated a 5-node game of Kuhn poker in order to generate Fig. 2(c). In order to generate the plots, we measured the log of the distance between each agent's strategy at time t and the set of Nash Equilibria (computed *a priori*), given by $\log(\text{dist}^2(x^t, \mathcal{X}^*))$. As can be seen in Fig. 2, OGA indeed obtains fast convergence in the last-iterate sense to a Nash Equilibrium in each of our experiments.

A point worth noting is that when the number of nodes increases, the empirical last-iterate convergence time also increases drastically. For example, in the 5-player Kuhn poker game we see that each agents' convergence time is significantly greater compared to the smaller scale experiments. However, with a careful choice of η, we can still guarantee convergence to the set of Nash Equilibria for all players.

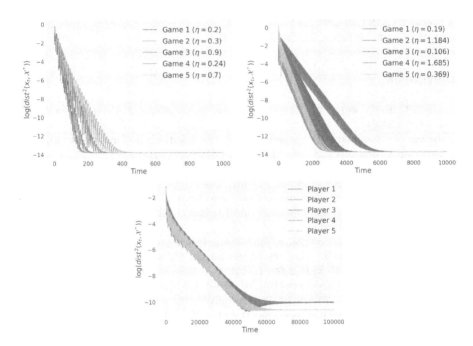

Fig. 2. Last-iterate convergence of OGA to the NE in network zero-sum extensive form games. The plots shown are: (a) 3-node randomly generated network zero-sum extensive form game. (b) 4-node random network zero-sum extensive form game. Note the significantly longer time needed to achieve convergence compared to the 3-node experiment. (c) 5-node *Kuhn poker* game.

6   Conclusion

In this paper, we provide a formulation of *Network Zero-Sum Extensive Form Games*, which encode the setting where multiple agents compete in pairwise games over a set of resources, defined on a graph. We analyze the convergence properties of *Optimistic Gradient Ascent* in this setting, proving that OGA results in both time-average and day-to-day convergence to the set of Nash Equilibria. In order to show this, we utilize a transformation from network zero-sum extensive form games to two-player symmetric games and subsequently show the convergence results in the symmetric game setting. This work represents an initial foray into the world of online learning dynamics in network extensive form games, and we hope that this will lead to more research into the practical and theoretical applications of this class of games.

Acknowledgements. This research/project is supported by the National Research Foundation Singapore and DSO National Laboratories under the AI Singapore Program (AISG Award No: AISG2-RP-2020-016), NRF2019-NRFANR095 ALIAS grant, grant PIE-SGP-AI-2020-01, NRF 2018 Fellowship NRF-NRFF2018-07 and AME Programmatic Fund (Grant No. A20H6b0151) from the Agency for Science, Technology and Research (A*STAR). Ryann Sim gratefully acknowledges support from the SUTD President's Graduate Fellowship (SUTD-PGF).

References

1. Arieli, I., Babichenko, Y.: Random extensive form games. J. Econ. Theory **166**, 517–535 (2016)
2. Brown, N., Sandholm, T.: Superhuman AI for heads-up no-limit poker: libratus beats top professionals. Science **359**(6374), 418–424 (2018)
3. Cai, Y., Candogan, O., Daskalakis, C., Papadimitriou, C.H.: Zero-sum polymatrix games: a generalization of minmax. Math. Oper. Res. **41**(2), 648–655 (2016)
4. Cai, Y., Daskalakis, C.: On minmax theorems for multiplayer games. In: Proceedings of the Twenty-Second Annual ACM-SIAM Symposium on Discrete Algorithms, pp. 217–234. SIAM (2011)
5. Daskalakis, C., Papadimitriou, C.H.: On a network generalization of the minmax theorem. In: Albers, S., Marchetti-Spaccamela, A., Matias, Y., Nikoletseas, S., Thomas, W. (eds.) ICALP 2009. LNCS, vol. 5556, pp. 423–434. Springer, Heidelberg (2009). https://doi.org/10.1007/978-3-642-02930-1_35
6. Farina, G., Kroer, C., Sandholm, T.: Optimistic regret minimization for extensive-form games via dilated distance-generating functions. In: Advances in Neural Information Processing Systems, vol. 32 (2019)
7. Hazan, E.: Introduction to online convex optimization. CoRR abs/1909.05207 (2019). http://arxiv.org/abs/1909.05207
8. Hoda, S., Gilpin, A., Peña, J., Sandholm, T.: Smoothing techniques for computing nash equilibria of sequential games. Math. Oper. Res. **35**(2), 494–512 (2010)
9. Kearns, M., Littman, M.L., Singh, S.: Graphical models for game theory. arXiv preprint arXiv:1301.2281 (2013)
10. Kempe, D., Kleinberg, J., Tardos, É.: Maximizing the spread of influence through a social network. In: Proceedings of the Ninth ACM SIGKDD International Conference on Knowledge Discovery and Data Mining, pp. 137–146 (2003)
11. Kroer, C., Farina, G., Sandholm, T.: Solving large sequential games with the excessive gap technique. In: Advances in Neural Information Processing Systems, vol. 31 (2018)

12. Kuhn, H.W.: Simplified two-person poker. In: Contributions to the Theory of Games, vol. 1, pp. 97–103 (1950)
13. Kuhn, H.W., Tucker, A.W.: Contributions to the Theory of Games, vol. 2. Princeton University Press, Princeton (1953)
14. Kuhn, H.: Extensive form games. In: Proceedings of National Academy of Science, pp. 570–576 (1950)
15. Lanctot, M., Waugh, K., Zinkevich, M., Bowling, M.: Monte Carlo sampling for regret minimization in extensive games. In: Advances in Neural Information Processing Systems, vol. 22 (2009)
16. Lee, C.W., Kroer, C., Luo, H.: Last-iterate convergence in extensive-form games. Adv. Neural. Inf. Process. Syst. **34**, 14293–14305 (2021)
17. Leonardos, S., Piliouras, G.: Exploration-exploitation in multi-agent learning: catastrophe theory meets game theory. Artif. Intell. **304**, 103653 (2022)
18. Mertikopoulos, P., Papadimitriou, C., Piliouras, G.: Cycles in adversarial regularized learning. In: Proceedings of the Twenty-Ninth Annual ACM-SIAM Symposium on Discrete Algorithms, pp. 2703–2717. SIAM (2018)
19. Nash, J.: Non-cooperative games. Ann. Math. 286–295 (1951)
20. Palaiopanos, G., Panageas, I., Piliouras, G.: Multiplicative weights update with constant step-size in congestion games: convergence, limit cycles and chaos. In: Advances in Neural Information Processing Systems, vol. 30 (2017)
21. Perolat, J., et al.: From poincaré recurrence to convergence in imperfect information games: finding equilibrium via regularization. In: International Conference on Machine Learning, pp. 8525–8535. PMLR (2021)
22. Rakhlin, A., Sridharan, K.: Online learning with predictable sequences. In: Conference on Learning Theory, pp. 993–1019. PMLR (2013)
23. Rowland, M., et al.: Multiagent evaluation under incomplete information. In: Advances in Neural Information Processing Systems, vol. 32 (2019)
24. Selten, R.: Spieltheoretische behandlung eines oligopolmodells mit nachfrageträgheit: Teil i: Bestimmung des dynamischen preisgleichwichts. Zeitschrift für die gesamte Staatswissenschaft/J. Inst. Theor. Econ. 301–324 (1965)
25. Tammelin, O., Burch, N., Johanson, M., Bowling, M.: Solving heads-up limit Texas Hold'em. In: Twenty-Fourth International Joint Conference on Artificial Intelligence (2015)
26. Wei, C.Y., Lee, C.W., Zhang, M., Luo, H.: Linear last-iterate convergence in constrained saddle-point optimization. In: International Conference on Learning Representations (2020)
27. Wei, C.Y., Lee, C.W., Zhang, M., Luo, H.: Last-iterate convergence of decentralized optimistic gradient descent/ascent in infinite-horizon competitive Markov games. In: Conference on Learning Theory, pp. 4259–4299. PMLR (2021)
28. Yang, Y., Wang, J.: An overview of multi-agent reinforcement learning from game theoretical perspective. arXiv preprint arXiv:2011.00583 (2020)
29. Zinkevich, M., Johanson, M., Bowling, M., Piccione, C.: Regret minimization in games with incomplete information. In: Advances in Neural Information Processing Systems, vol. 20 (2007)

Social Choice and Stable Matchings

Decentralized Update Selection
with Semi-strategic Experts

Georgios Amanatidis[1], Georgios Birmpas[2], Philip Lazos[4(✉)],
and Francisco Marmolejo-Cossío[3,4]

[1] Department of Mathematical Sciences, University of Essex, Colchester, UK
georgios.amanatidis@essex.ac.uk
[2] Department of Computer, Control and Management Engineering,
Sapienza University of Rome, Rome, Italy
birbas@diag.uniroma1.it
[3] School of Engineering and Applied Sciences, Harvard University, Cambridge, USA
fjmarmol@seas.harvard.edu
[4] IOHK, London, UK
{philip.lazos,francisco.marmolejo}@iohk.io

Abstract. Motivated by governance models adopted in blockchain applications, we study the problem of selecting appropriate system updates in a decentralized way. Contrary to most existing voting approaches, we use the input of a set of motivated experts of varying levels of expertise. In particular, we develop an approval voting inspired selection mechanism through which the experts approve or disapprove the different updates according to their perception of the quality of each alternative. Given their opinions, and weighted by their expertise level, a single update is then implemented and evaluated, and the experts receive rewards based on their choices. We show that this mechanism always has approximate pure Nash equilibria and that these achieve a constant factor approximation with respect to the quality benchmark of the optimal alternative. Finally, we study the repeated version of the problem, where the weights of the experts are adjusted after each update, according to their performance. Under mild assumptions about the weights, the extension of our mechanism still has approximate pure Nash equilibria in this setting.

1 Introduction

In 2009, Satoshi Nakamoto published a landmark white paper outlining the core functionality of Bitcoin [25], a decentralized blockchain-based ledger of transactions for a peer-to-peer digital currency. Indeed, a key feature of Bitcoin is precisely in its decentralized nature, whereby no single entity controls the operation of the system, a feat which is achieved by an innovative amalgamation of cryptography and carefully aligned incentives among participants in the protocol. In recent years the ecosystem for similar decentralized systems has grown drastically, and given that for each of these systems no single entity holds control,

© The Author(s), under exclusive license to Springer Nature Switzerland AG 2022
P. Kanellopoulos et al. (Eds.): SAGT 2022, LNCS 13584, pp. 403–420, 2022.
https://doi.org/10.1007/978-3-031-15714-1_23

users often find themselves in a position where they need to reach a consensus on critical decisions regarding the very platform they participate in.

A fundamental example of this governance dilemma is that of creating and implementing software updates for the underlying infrastructure of a blockchain-based solution [8]. Such drastic upgrades are known as hard forks in blockchain-based systems, and historically, there have been scenarios where cryptocurrencies have split due to opinion differences regarding the infrastructure of the blockchain (e.g., Ethereum vs. Ethereum Classic or Bitcoin vs. Bitcoin Cash). Beyond the confusion and inconvenience for the users caused by such splits, these fragmentations have very real implications for the security of blockchain-based systems, which often strongly depends on the number of users within a system. A survey on blockchain governance can be found in [19].

Software updates, as opposed to general collective decisions, are particularly interesting due to two salient features of the problem structure: 1) adequately evaluating the relative merits of software update proposals often requires a high degree of expertise 2) the overall stakes of the software update process are incredibly high. Indeed, if a proposal which is collectively chosen for uptake happens to have a fatal bug which has failed to be caught, its uptake can have catastrophic implications for the underlying system.

In this work, we focus on providing a simple on-chain methodology whereby users from a blockchain-based platform can collectively decide which software updates to implement, thereby reducing the potential for aforementioned hard fork frictions. To do so, we assume the existence of a set of users with differing levels of expertise regarding software updates. These experts are then faced with proposals for multiple potential software updates, where each expert not only formulates independent opinions on whether a given proposal will succeed or not during implementation, but may also harbor additional incentives for implementing one proposal over another. Each expert casts votes in approval or disapproval of each proposal, and as a function of these votes and the historical merit of each expert, a proposal is chosen for implementation. Ultimately, we assume the success or failure of the proposal is recorded on-chain, and as a function of each expert's votes and the outcome of the proposal, the system pays experts for their participation.

1.1   Our Contributions

Our main contributions can be summarized as follows:

- In Sect. 2 we introduce our framework for encoding expert preferences among software proposals, the notion of semi-strategic decision making among experts, and a benchmark for proposal quality which we subsequently use to measure the performance of equilibria in the semi-strategic voting setting.
- In Sect. 3, we present our approval voting inspired mechanism. We provide some sufficient conditions that limit potentially damaging deviations and show existence and Price of Anarchy (PoA) results for pure Nash equilibria. In Sects. 3.1 and 3.2, we study approximate pure Nash equilibria for semi-strategic experts and show that the PoA in this setting is exactly 2.

– Finally, in Sect. 4 we consider a repeated game setting that dynamically reflects expert performance via weight updates in rounds of approval voting (a measure of "reputation"). In this setting we show honest voting is an approximate pure Nash equilibrium and that repeated voting has a Price of Stability of at most 2.

We note that all missing proofs are deferred to the full version of this paper [1].

1.2 Related Work

In the blockchain space, Leonardos, Reijsbergen and Piliouras [24] study a related setting with a compelling motivation, where the experts are *validators* who 'vote' on accepting new blocks to the chain. They show that varying, dynamically updated weights can improve the performance in the face of malicious or abstaining validators. Due to the fact that our work focuses on creating payment mechanisms whereby a blockchain platform can elicit truthful expert opinions regarding potential software updates, it bears many similarities to existing literature in the realm of scoring rules and preference elicitation [7,18,21,29]. An thorough exposition can be found in [13]. In the context of software updates, implementing a classic scoring rule for one proposal would involve asking experts to report a probability $p \in [0,1]$ corresponding to their belief that a proposal would succeed or fail. As a function of this reported probability and the outcome of the proposal, the scoring rule pays experts in such a way that they always maximize their expected payment when reporting truthfully. The works of Chen et al. [11], Chen and Kash [10], and Othman and Sandholm [27], extend the scoring rule framework to incorporate decision-making between mutually exclusive alternatives, as is the case with our proposal setting. Indeed only one proposal is chosen, against which we must score expert performance. These results and our setting are also related with the principal-expert literature [3]: the salient difference is that in our case the 'quality' of the solution is determined by the truthful reports of the experts who *compete with their votes* to chose their favorite outcome.

Our work however also considers the very real possibility (especially in the semi-anonymous and permissionless world of blockchain platforms) that expert incentives go beyond the payment which the mechanism offers them for providing their opinions, and that they instead exhibit distinct utilities for the ultimate implementation of different proposals. This assumption is similar to the setting of Proper Decision Scoring Rules, as explored in the work of Oesterheld and Conitzer [26], as well as Restricted Investment Contracts presented in the paper of Carroll [9], where potential solutions involve experts earning rewards proportional to the principal's earnings for the alternative chosen and they each have potentially conflicting beliefs over the quality of the various proposals.

The mechanism we propose for eliciting expert beliefs builds off of a rich existing literature [23] on Approval Voting (AV) first introduced by Brams and Fishburn [4], and then extended in [12,14,15]. As in AV, experts voting consists of providing a subset of proposals which they approve (and, thus, a subset which they disapprove). Unlike typical AV, the underlying utility that experts derive from the outcome of the mechanism is tied to their beliefs regarding the success of each proposal. Furthermore, as mentioned in the work of Laslier and Sanver [22], a common technique in AV involves restricting voter actions in natural ways (i.e., admissible and sincere voting profiles from [15] for example) to restrict the set of equilibria considered in the mathematical analysis of the model. Our work introduces a novel constraint of similar nature which we dub semi-strategic voting (see Sect. 2). For semi-strategic experts we demonstrate theoretical guarantees on our mechanism's equilibria resulting from AV. Finally, it is worth mentioning that AV has additionally seen much empirical work pointing to its practical success [5,6,28].

2   Preliminaries

Let $N = \{1, 2, \ldots, n\}$ be a set of experts (typically indexed by i) and $U = \{1, 2, \ldots, k\}$ a set of proposed updates (typically indexed by j). Every update j has an associated quality $q_j \in \{0, 1\}$ indicating whether it is beneficial for the system; we call updates with $q_j = 1$ "good" and those with $q_j = 0$ "bad". These q_j values *are not initially known*: only the value of the selected proposal is revealed *after* the experts' vote has concluded. Specifically, each expert has her own prior about the q_j's. Expert i believes that q_j has a probability p_{ij} of being good. This 'opinion' p_{ij} is unaffected by what the other experts think or how they voted: no matter how some update j was selected, expert i believes that it will be good with probability p_{ij}. Every expert i has a weight $w_i \geq 0$ indicating their "power" within the system. Additionally, an expert may have some personal gain[1] when an update is implemented successfully (i.e., it is selected and it turns out to be good). We denote this external reward that expert i will receive if update j is implemented succesfully by $g_{ij} \geq 0$; this value is known to expert i, but not to the mechanism.

The strategy of each expert is a vector $\mathbf{r}_i = (r_{i1}, \ldots, r_{ik})^\mathsf{T} \in \{0, 1\}^{k \times 1}$, where r_{ij} indicates the binary vote of expert i on whether $q_j = 1$ or not. Let $\mathbf{r} = (\mathbf{r}_1, \mathbf{r}_2, \ldots, \mathbf{r}_n) \in \{0, 1\}^{k \times n}$ denote the whole *voting profile*. As is common, we write $(\mathbf{r}'_i, \mathbf{r}_{-i})$ to denote $(\mathbf{r}_1, \ldots, \mathbf{r}_{i-1}, \mathbf{r}'_i, \mathbf{r}_{i+1}, \ldots, \mathbf{r}_n)$, as well as $(r'_{ij}, \mathbf{r}_{-ij})$ to denote $((r_{i1}, \ldots, r_{i(j-1)}, r'_{ij}, r_{i(j+1)}, \ldots, r_{ik})^\mathsf{T}, \mathbf{r}_{-i})$.

A mechanism $\mathcal{M} = (x, \mathbf{f})$ consists of a (possibly randomised) selection rule x, which given $\mathbf{r}$ and $\mathbf{w} = (w_1, \ldots, w_n)$ returns $x(\mathbf{r}, \mathbf{w}) \in U \cup \{0\}$ (i.e., x could return the *dummy* proposal 0, if no proposal is selected), and an expert reward function $\mathbf{f}$, which given $\mathbf{r}, \mathbf{w}$, a winning proposal $j^\star$, and its quality $q_{j^\star}$ returns $\mathbf{f}(\mathbf{r}, \mathbf{w}, j^\star, q_{j^\star}) = (f_1(\mathbf{r}, \mathbf{w}, j^\star, q_{j^\star}), \ldots, f_n(\mathbf{r}, \mathbf{w}, j^\star, q_{j^\star})) \in \mathbb{R}^{1 \times n}$.

Given $\mathcal{M}$, the expected reward of expert i conditioned on i's own perspective $\mathbf{p}_i = (p_{i1}, \ldots, p_{ik})^\mathsf{T} \in [0, 1]^{k \times 1}$ uses an estimate of $f_i(\mathbf{r}, \mathbf{w}, j^\star, q_{j^\star})$ which depends

---

[1] For instance, an update in a DeFi protocol could alter the exchange rate calculation on assets the user might want to invest in. However, the user will only reap the benefits g_{ij} if this update is 'good', since otherwise the protocol will be rolled back to its prior state.

on the knowledge of $\mathbf{r}, \mathbf{w}$, and $p_{ij^\star}$, i.e., the probability that $j^\star$ is a good proposal according to i only:

$$\mathbb{E}\left[f_i(\mathbf{r}, \mathbf{w}, j^\star, q_{j^\star}) \mid \mathbf{p}_i\right] = p_{ij^\star} f_i(\mathbf{r}, \mathbf{w}, j^\star, 1) + (1 - p_{ij^\star}) f_i(\mathbf{r}, \mathbf{w}, j^\star, 0).$$

Thus, the expected utility of expert i conditioned on her perspective is

$$u_i^{\mathcal{M}}(\mathbf{r} \mid \mathbf{w}, \mathbf{p}_i) = \mathbb{E}\left[p_{ij^\star} \cdot g_{ij^\star} + \mathbb{E}\left[f_i(\mathbf{r}, \mathbf{w}, j^\star, q_{j^\star}) \mid \mathbf{p}_i\right]\right], \tag{1}$$

where the outer expectation is over the winning proposal $j^\star = x(\mathbf{r}, \mathbf{w})$. We adopt this approach for the utilities because when an expert declares her preference, we assume she is agnostic about the beliefs of other experts for any proposal. We also assume that all experts are *risk-neutral*.

Given the subjective evaluation of the quality of each proposal, we need a way to *aggregate* the opinions of all experts that combines robustness and explainability. To this end, we introduce a probability threshold $T \in [0,1]$ such that if expert i has $p_{ij} \geq T$ for proposal j then we consider i's honest response to be to vote in favor of j; otherwise i's honest response is to vote against j.

Our metric can be viewed as the weighted average of the probabilities *after these have been rounded to 0 or 1* with respect to the threshold T, and it has an immediate meaning which is the voting power that considers a proposal to be good enough. A natural alternative would be to use the raw probabilities p_{ij} to define some measure of estimated quality, but that would be a bit problematic: it is not reasonable to expect that experts would precisely and consistently report those, and possibly it would be considerably harder to communicate the resulting notion of "quality" to non-experts in the system. Finally, note that our estimated quality metric defined below depends on the set of experts. However, it reasonably reflects the actual quality of a proposal assuming that experts with large weights are sufficiently competent.

Definition 1 (Estimated Quality). *Given a probability threshold T, the estimated quality of proposal j is the sum of weights of experts i with $p_{ij} \geq T$. That is:*

$$\mathtt{Qual}[j] = \sum_{i \,:\, p_{ij} \geq T} w_i. \tag{2}$$

For convenience, we will refer to the optimal quality as:

$$\mathrm{OPT}(\mathbf{w}, \mathbf{p}) = \max_{j \in U} \mathtt{Qual}[j], \tag{3}$$

where $\mathbf{p} = (\mathbf{p}_1, \ldots, \mathbf{p}_n)$ is the $k \times n$ matrix that contains the $\mathbf{p}_i$s as columns.

We consider experts that are *strategic*, i.e., they strive to maximize their utility. For most of our results, we also assume they are not malicious towards the system. That is, they only choose to lie when this results in a net *increase* in their utility. If there is no strictly beneficial deviation, they remain honest. We call such experts semi-strategic.

Definition 2 (Semi-strategic Experts). *An expert i is semi-strategic if for every mechanism $\mathcal{M}$ and strategy vector $\mathbf{r}$:*

- *if $p_{ij} \geq T$ and $r_{ij} = 0$, then $u_i^{\mathcal{M}}(1, \mathbf{r}_{-ij} \mid \mathbf{w}, \mathbf{p}_i) < u_i^{\mathcal{M}}(\mathbf{r} \mid \mathbf{w}, \mathbf{p}_i)$;*
- *if $p_{ij} < T$ and $r_{ij} = 1$, then $u_i^{\mathcal{M}}(0, \mathbf{r}_{-ij} \mid \mathbf{w}, \mathbf{p}_i) < u_i^{\mathcal{M}}(\mathbf{r} \mid \mathbf{w}, \mathbf{p}_i)$.*

Note that a semi-strategic agent is not necessarily strategic. In particular, a strategic agent can always choose to misreport her vote if she is indifferent between this report and the truth.

The solution concept we use is the (multiplicatively) approximate pure Nash equilibrium. We use the multiplicative, rather than the additive, version of approximate pure Nash equilibria as we want our results to be mostly independent of scaling up or down the reward functions.[2]

Definition 3 ($(1+\varepsilon)$-Pure Nash Equilibrium). *For $\varepsilon \geq 0$, a strategy profile $\mathbf{r}$ is a multiplicatively $(1 + \varepsilon)$-approximate pure Nash equilibrium, or simply a $(1 + \varepsilon)$-PNE, for weight vector $\mathbf{w}$, if for every deviation $\mathbf{r}_i'$ we have:*

$$(1 + \varepsilon) \cdot u_i^{\mathcal{M}}(\mathbf{r} \mid \mathbf{w}, \mathbf{p}_i) \geq u_i^{\mathcal{M}}(\mathbf{r}_i', \mathbf{r}_{-i} \mid \mathbf{w}, \mathbf{p}_i). \tag{4}$$

When $\varepsilon = 0$ we simply call $\mathbf{r}$ a pure Nash equilibrium *(PNE).*

We refer to the set strategies that are $(1 + \varepsilon)$-PNE of mechanism $\mathcal{M}$ given $\mathbf{w}$ and $\mathbf{p}$ as $\mathcal{Q}_\varepsilon^{\mathcal{M}}(\mathbf{w}, \mathbf{p})$.

To measure the inefficiency of different equilibria compared to the proposal of highest quality, we use the notions *Price of Anarchy* [20] and *Price of Stability* [2], which denote the ratios between the quality of the worst or the best possible equilibrium produced by $\mathcal{M} = (x, \mathbf{f})$ and the optimal outcome, respectively. In particular, these are formally defined as:

$$\text{PoA}(\mathcal{M}) = \sup_{\mathbf{w}, \mathbf{p}} \frac{\text{OPT}(\mathbf{w}, \mathbf{p})}{\inf_{\mathbf{r} \in \mathcal{Q}_\varepsilon^{\mathcal{M}}(\mathbf{w}, \mathbf{p})} \text{Qual}[x(\mathbf{r})]}$$

and

$$\text{PoS}(\mathcal{M}) = \sup_{\mathbf{w}, \mathbf{p}} \frac{\text{OPT}(\mathbf{w}, \mathbf{p})}{\sup_{\mathbf{r} \in \mathcal{Q}_\varepsilon^{\mathcal{M}}(\mathbf{w}, \mathbf{p})} \text{Qual}[x(\mathbf{r})]}.$$

3 Approval Voting

Although our definitions allow for randomized mechanisms, as a first attempt of the problem we focus on a natural deterministic mechanism. In particular, we study the mechanism induced by *approval voting*, which we call $\mathcal{M}_{\text{AV}}$ with an appropriately selected reward function $\mathbf{f}$. Specifically, the proposal with the highest amount of weighted approval is the winner, i.e.,

$$x(\mathbf{r}, \mathbf{w}) \in \operatorname*{argmax}_j \sum_{i \,:\, r_{ij} = 1} w_i. \tag{5}$$

---

[2] This is completely precise in the case where the external rewards g_{ij} are all 0, but it is still largely true whenever the rewards of the mechanism are large compared to external rewards.

Ties can be broken arbitrarily, but in a deterministic manner, e.g., lexicographically. Hence, we might abuse the notation and use '=' with 'argmax'. It should be noted that while such naive tie-breaking rules are standard in theoretical work, in practice we expect to have a large number of experts at play with different and dynamically adjusting weights, hence a tie is very improbable anyway. Additionally, the reward given to each expert i is proportional to her weight:

$$
f_i(\mathbf{r}, \mathbf{w}, j^*, q_{j^*}) = w_i \cdot
\begin{cases}
a, & \text{if } r_{ij^*} = 1 \text{ and } q_{j^*} = 1 \\
-s, & \text{if } r_{ij^*} = 1 \text{ and } q_{j^*} = 0 \\
a', & \text{if } r_{ij^*} = 0 \text{ and } q_{j^*} = 0 \\
0, & \text{if } r_{ij^*} = 0 \text{ and } q_{j^*} = 1
\end{cases}
\tag{6}
$$

That is, $w_i \cdot a$ is the reward in case the expert approved the winning proposal and it turned out to have high quality, $w_i \cdot a'$ is the reward in case the expert disapproved the winning proposal that turned out bad, $w_i \cdot s$ is the penalty in case the expert approved the winning proposal and it turned out to be bad and we assume there is no reward or penalty if the expert disapproved the winning proposal that turned out good. Notice that the collected reward depends on the winning proposal j^* and it's quality. The other proposals are not implemented and their true nature is never revealed.

Remark 1. In the following analysis we will drop the w_i multiplier. Indeed, all rewards are equally scaled, except for the g_{ij} that do not depend on the weights. As such, to simplify notation (and without loss of generality) we consider that external rewards are scaled down appropriately by w_i for each expert i. Further, notice that as long the mechanism designer chooses the total weight to be bounded, the total payments are bounded as well.

To find out the possible pure Nash equilibria of this scheme, we start by the simplest case for $\mathcal{M}_{AV}$. Suppose everyone has already cast a vote and expert i has no way of changing the outcome (which will usually be the most likely scenario). We need to check when the expected utility of approving is higher than that of disapproving:

$$
a \cdot p_{ij^*} - s \cdot (1 - p_{ij^*}) + g_{ij^*} \cdot p_{ij^*} \geq a' \cdot (1 - p_{ij^*}) + g_{ij^*} \cdot p_{ij^*}
$$
$$
\Rightarrow \quad a \cdot p_{ij^*} - s + s \cdot p_{ij^*} \geq a' - a' \cdot p_{ij^*}
$$
$$
\Rightarrow \quad p_{ij^*} \cdot (a + s + a') \geq a' + s
$$
$$
\Rightarrow \quad p_{ij^*} \geq \frac{a' + s}{a' + s + a}.
$$

So, the a, a' and s parameters can be tuned so that approving the winning proposal is the best option only for a confidence equal or higher than a desired threshold, which we define as

$$
T = \frac{a' + s}{a' + s + a}.
\tag{7}
$$

This threshold T is used for measuring quality and allows us to define the 'honest strategy' for this voting scheme.

Definition 4. *Expert i plays her* honest strategy *if she approves the proposals for which her confidence is at least T and only those, i.e., if $r_{ij} = 1 \Leftrightarrow p_{ij} \geq T$.*

So far, we have shown that if every expert plays their honest strategy and it happens that no single expert has the power to change the outcome, then this honest strategy profile is a pure Nash equilibrium. The next result gives some insights about the possible deviations from the honest strategy, given the external rewards g_{ij}. Note that Theorem 1 does not 'protect' $\mathcal{M}_{AV}$ against all possible deviations, but only those where an expert votes for a proposal she considers bad (amongst other things) to make it win. In the remaining possible deviations an expert determines the winning proposal, not by changing her vote for it, but by disapproving a proposal she considers good. As we shall see in Theorem 3, such deviations do not hurt the overall quality significantly for semi-strategic experts. The intuition is that when the winning proposal is determined like this it necessarily has one of the highest number of honest votes and, thus, sufficiently high quality.

Theorem 1. *For any player i and voting profile $\mathbf{r}_{-i}$, let $j^\star$ be the output of $\mathcal{M}_{AV}$ if expert i votes honestly and let j' be any proposal that expert i voted against. Then, if*

$$p_{ij'} < \min \left\{ T \cdot \frac{a+s}{a+s+g_{ij'}}, \frac{a' \cdot (1-T) + s}{a+s+g_{ij'}} \right\}, \tag{8}$$

then expert i cannot increase her payoff by switching her vote in favor of proposal j' (and possibly also change any number of her votes for other proposals) to make j' the winning proposal.

Moreover, for any choice of parameters a, a', s, there are instances where an expert i can increase her payoff by switching her vote against proposal $j^\star$.

Proof. Suppose that for some outcome $\mathbf{r}$ the selected proposal is $j^\star$, but expert i could switch her vote to change the winner to another proposal j' (either by not approving $j^\star$ or by approving j', and possibly approving/disapproving other proposals as well). For each possible deviation, we consider the expected utility of expert i and show under which conditions switching the winner to j' would be a better response, given the $g_{ij'}$ and $p_{ij'}$.

- For the first group of cases, we assume that expert i considers the winning proposal $j^\star$ good enough (i.e., $p_{ij^\star} \geq T$). Therefore, we need to compare the utility of any deviation that makes j' the winner, to the utility obtained by voting 'yes' to $j^\star$. This is because voting 'no' for $j^\star$ is clearly not a best response unless the winner changes, since $p_{ij^\star} \geq T$ implies that $a \cdot p_{ij^\star} - (1 - p_{ij^\star}) \cdot s > a' \cdot (1 - p_{ij^\star})$.

- **Switches to approve j', keeps approving $j^\star$:** This deviation can only happen if the utility for switching is greater than that of voting honestly for $j^\star$.

$$a \cdot p_{ij'} - s \cdot (1 - p_{ij'}) + g_{ij'} \cdot p_{ij'} > a \cdot p_{ij^\star} - s \cdot (1 - p_{ij^\star}) + g_{ij^\star} \cdot p_{ij^\star}$$
$$\Rightarrow a \cdot p_{ij'} - s \cdot (1 - p_{ij'}) + g_{ij'} \cdot p_{ij'} > a \cdot p_{ij^\star} - s \cdot (1 - p_{ij^\star})$$
$$\Rightarrow a \cdot p_{ij'} - s \cdot (1 - p_{ij'}) + g_{ij'} \cdot p_{ij'} > a \cdot T - s \cdot (1 - T)$$
$$\Rightarrow a \cdot p_{ij'} - s + s \cdot p_{ij'} + g_{ij'} \cdot p_{ij'} > a \cdot T - s + s \cdot T$$
$$\Rightarrow p_{ij'} \cdot (a + s + g_{ij'}) > T \cdot (a + s)$$
$$\Rightarrow p_{ij'} > T \cdot \frac{a + s}{a + s + g_{ij'}},$$

using $p_{ij^\star} > T$ in the first implication.
- **Switches to approve j', switches to disapprove $j^\star$:** The incentives here are identical to the first case: in the honest outcome the reward is at least $a \cdot T - s \cdot (1 - T)$ and in the deviation it's $a \cdot p_{ij'} - s \cdot (1 - p_{ij'}) + g_{ij'} \cdot p_{ij'}$.
- **Keeps approving j', switches to disapprove $j^\star$:** The incentives are identical to the first case, but since expert i wanted to approve j' (i.e., $p_{ij'} \geq T$), no matter how high a, a' and s are set she could better off disapproving $j^\star$ in this scenario, if $p_{ij^\star} < p_{ij}$.

- For the last two cases, we consider that $p_{ij^\star} < T$. As before, any deviation that *does not* change the winner to something other than $j^\star$, needs contain a 'no' vote for $j^\star$: since $p_{ij^\star} < T$ implies that $a' \cdot p_{ij^\star} > a \cdot p_{ij^\star} - (1 - s) \cdot p_{ij^\star}$.

  - **Switches to approve j', keeps disapproving $j^\star$:** Since the honest move is to disapprove $j^\star$, we have that $p_{ij^\star} \leq T$, therefore the 'honest' payoff is at least $a' \cdot (1 - T)$.

$$a \cdot p_{ij'} - s \cdot (1 - p_{ij'}) + g_{ij'} \cdot p_{ij'} > a' \cdot (1 - p_{ij^\star}) + g_{ij^\star} \cdot p_{ij^\star}$$
$$\Rightarrow a \cdot p_{ij'} - s \cdot (1 - p_{ij'}) + g_{ij'} \cdot p_{ij'} > a' \cdot (1 - T)$$
$$\Rightarrow a \cdot p_{ij'} - s + s \cdot p_{ij'} + g_{ij'} \cdot p_{ij'} > a' \cdot (1 - T)$$
$$\Rightarrow p_{ij'} \cdot (a + s + g_{ij'}) > a' \cdot (1 - T) + s$$
$$\Rightarrow p_{ij'} > \frac{a' \cdot (1 - T) + s}{a + s + g_{ij'}}$$

- **Keeps disapproving j', switches to disapprove $j^\star$:** The rewards in the honest outcome are the same as in the first case, but the reward for deviating is different:

$$a' \cdot (1 - p_{ij'}) + g_{ij'} \cdot p_{ij'} > a \cdot p_{ij^\star} - s \cdot (1 - p_{ij^\star}) + g_{ij^\star} \cdot p_{ij^\star}$$
$$\Rightarrow a' \cdot (1 - p_{ij'}) + g_{ij'} \cdot p_{ij'} > a \cdot T - s \cdot (1 - T)$$
$$\Rightarrow a' - a' \cdot p_{ij'} + g_{ij'} \cdot p_{ij'} > a \cdot T - s + s \cdot T$$
$$\Rightarrow p_{ij'} \cdot (g_{ij'} - a') > a \cdot T - a' + s \cdot T - s$$

If $g_{ij'} > a'$, then we need

$$p_{ij'} > \frac{a \cdot T - a' + s \cdot T - s}{g_{ij'} - a'}.$$

Otherwise, we have that:

$$p_{ij'} < \frac{a \cdot T - a' + s \cdot T - s}{g_{ij'} - a'}.$$

However, since $T > 0$ and the 'no' branch of the reward function is decreasing in $p_{ij^{\star}}$ we have that $a \cdot T - (1 - T) \cdot s < a'$. Therefore, if $g_{ij'} > a'$, there is no way to set the other parameters and completely eliminate the possibility of deviating to disapproving $j^{\star}$.

Putting everything together, this mechanism can only protect from situations where the expert needs to *actively* switch her vote to approve a proposal she knows is not good enough. Following the previous cases, a necessary condition for this to happen is

$$p_{ij'} > T \cdot \frac{a + s}{a + s + g_{ij'}} \qquad \text{or} \qquad p_{ij'} > \frac{a' \cdot (1 - T) + s}{a + s + g_{ij'}}.$$

If $p_{ij'}$ is smaller than both, then there is no possibility of such a deviation and the claim holds. □

Setting $g_{ij} = 0$ yields the following corollary, showing that experts without any external rewards will never approve a perceived bad proposal.

Corollary 1. *For any expert i, it is a dominant strategy to vote against any j' such that $g_{ij'} = 0$ and $p_{ij'} < T$.*

Proof. If $g_{ij} = 0$ (i.e., the expert in question has no external motivations), the probability upper bounds from the statement of Theorem 1 take on interesting values. Specifically, there is no deviation for:

$$p_{ij'} < T \cdot \frac{a + s}{a + s} = T$$

and

$$p_{ij'} < \frac{a' \cdot (1 - T) + s}{a + s} \cdot T = \frac{a \cdot T - (1 - T) \cdot s + s}{a + s} \cdot T < T.$$

□

The previous two results show that, assuming the a, a' and s are all large enough, the experts will be reluctant to vote in favor of a proposal they already know is bad: to do so, they still need to have some faith in that proposal. It turns out that this mechanism always has pure Nash equilibria, albeit with limited guarantees, as shown in the next two propositions.

Proposition 1. *In the presence of strategic experts, the approval voting mechanism $\mathcal{M}_{AV}$ always has a PNE.*

Proof. For $i \in N$ and $j \in U$, let $\mathbf{r}^{ij}$ be the voting profile where

- $r_{ij} = 1$
- $r_{i'j'} = 0$ for any i' and $j' \neq j$.

If no expert i has positive utility for some proposal j with respect to the voting profile $\mathbf{r}^{ij}$, then clearly everyone voting 'no' to every proposal is a pure Nash equilibrium.

Assuming that the set $N_+ = \{i \in N \mid \exists j \in U : u_i^{\mathcal{M}_{AV}}(\mathbf{r}^{ij} \mid \mathbf{w}, \mathbf{p}_i) > 0\}$ is nonempty, let $i^\star = \operatorname{argmax}_{i \in N_+} w_i$. Additionally, let

$$j^\star = \operatorname*{argmax}_{j \in U} u_{i^\star}^{\mathcal{M}_{AV}}(\mathbf{r}^{i^\star j} \mid \mathbf{w}, \mathbf{p}_i).$$

It is not hard to see that the profile $\mathbf{r}^{i^\star j^\star}$ is a pure Nash equilibrium. Since the weight of every expert $i \neq i^\star$ is $w_i < w_{i^\star}$ (or $w_i = w_{i^\star}$ but i is losing to $i^\star$ in the tie-breaking), there exists no possible deviation from i that changes the winning proposal. In addition, because $j^\star$ maximizes the utility of expert $i^\star$, this is a pure Nash equilibrium. $\qquad\square$

Proposition 2. *Assuming strategic experts, the Price of Anarchy of $\mathcal{M}_{AV}$ is $\Omega(n)$, even if for all experts i and all proposals j we have that $g_{ij} = 0$.*

This equilibrium of Proposition 2, however, is unnatural: why would so many experts vote against their favorite proposal? The intuition is that the assumption about the agents being semi-strategic instead, should help us avoid such pitfalls. Unfortunately, if we assume the presence of semi-strategic agents, there are combinations of p_{ij}'s for which no PNE exists.

Proposition 3. *The mechanism $\mathcal{M}_{AV}$ does not always have PNE for semi-strategic experts, even when $g_{ij} = 0$ for all experts i and proposals j.*

Despite Proposition 3, our mechanism does have approximate PNE's for semi-strategic experts and an appropriate choice of parameters, as we show next. Moreover, these approximate equilibria always lead to choosing approximately optimal proposals.

3.1 Approximate Equilibria of $\mathcal{M}_{AV}$

Since pure Nash equilibria may not always exist when dealing with semi-strategic experts, we have to fall back to showing the existence of approximate PNE's. This can be achieved by careful tuning of the parameters a, a' and s when defining the reward function. Recall that a, a', s and T are related via Eq. (7); an equivalent equation appears in the proof of the theorem below as (9).

Theorem 2. *Suppose that for $T \in [0,1]$, we set $\varepsilon > 1$ such that:*

- *$1/(\varepsilon + 1) < T$*
- *$a = (1 + \varepsilon) \cdot a' \cdot (1 - T) > a'$*
- *$s = \frac{a \cdot (T \cdot (\varepsilon + 1) - 1)}{(1 - T) \cdot (\varepsilon + 1)}$*

In addition, let $\delta > 0$ such that for every player i and proposal j we have $g_{ij} \leq a \cdot \delta$. Then the voting profile $\mathbf{r}$ where everyone votes honestly is $(1 + \varepsilon) \cdot (1 + \delta)$-approximate pure Nash equilibrium.

Proof. As always, the honest behavior of expert i should be to approve proposal j if and only if they have $p_{ij} \geq T$. From the perspective of expert i, their reward for voting in favor of proposal j is:

$$p_{ij} \cdot a - (1 - p_{ij}) \cdot s.$$

Notice that this expression is strictly increasing in p_{ij}. Voting against proposal j yields an expected reward equal to $a' \cdot (1 - p_{ij})$, which is strictly decreasing in p_{ij}. As before, to ensure honest behavior, the two expressions need to be equal for $p_{ij} = T$:

$$T \cdot a - (1 - T) \cdot s = a' \cdot (1 - T). \tag{9}$$

Additionally, we need that a, which is the payoff for $p_{ij} = 1$ is also the maximum possible reward and satisfies $a = (1 + \varepsilon) \cdot (a \cdot T - (1 - T) \cdot s)$. Since $T \in [0,1]$, eq. (9) is actually the global minimum of the honest response reward. Therefore, the condition that a is the maximum can be replaced by $a \geq a'$, since either a or a' are the extreme points. Since T and ε are given, we can solve for the remaining values using $a' \geq 0$ as a the free parameter. Moreover, these solutions are non-negative for $1/(\varepsilon + 1) < T < 1$ (Fig. 1).

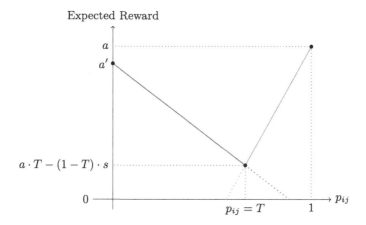

Fig. 1. The expected reward (as a function of p_{ij}) for honest voting, assuming $g_{ij} = 0$ and proposal j won. The red line is $a' \cdot (1 - p_{ij})$, corresponding to voting against j, while the green line is $a \cdot p_{ij} - (1 - p_{ij}) \cdot s$ for voting in favor of it. (Color figure online)

We are now ready to show that $\mathbf{r}$, the honest voting profile, is an approximate PNE. Let $j^\star$ be the winning proposal. Clearly, any expert who *cannot* change the outcome is playing their best response. Suppose that expert i has a beneficial deviation $\mathbf{r}'_i$ and changes the winner to j'. There are two cases:

- The expert i is honest about j' (but possibly changed his vote on some other proposals): this means that either $p_{ij'} \geq T$ and $r_{ij'} = 1$ or $p_{ij'} < T$ and $r_{ij'} = 0$. In this case, the maximum possible reward she could get is $a + g_{ij'} \leq (1 + \delta) \cdot a$. On the other hand, the minimum possible reward for an honest vote is $a' \cdot (1 - T) = a/(1 + \varepsilon)$. Therefore, this deviation can yield at most $(1 + \varepsilon) \cdot (1 + \delta)$ times the reward of the honest response.
- The expert i is dishonest about j': in this case, the reward (without g_{ij}) is at most $a' \cdot (1 - T)$, which is the minimum possible reward for honest voting. As with the previous case, the addition of $g_{ij'}$ is not great enough to motivate the expert to deviate.

Therefore, the honest profile is an $(1 + \varepsilon)$-pure Nash equilibrium.   □

Note that the existence of the approximate PNE of Theorem 2 is not guaranteed for an arbitrarily small ε. So, it is natural to ask how inefficient these equilibria are, with respect to achieving our objective of maximizing Qual. We deal with this question in the following section.

3.2   Price of Anarchy of $\mathcal{M}_{AV}$

Here we study the Price of Anarchy of the approximate pure Nash equilibria of $\mathcal{M}_{AV}$. That is, we bound the quality of a proposal returned by the mechanism in an approximate equilibrium in terms of the best possible estimated quality. Surprisingly, we show that for any ε, $(1 + \varepsilon)$-approximate PNE result in quality which is within a factor of 2 of the optimal estimated quality. Note that although the statement of Theorem 3 does not mention the g_{ij}'s explicitly, these are taken into consideration via the conditions of Theorem 1. Moreover, this bound on the Price of Anarchy is tight.

Theorem 3. *Let $\varepsilon > 0$ and suppose that a, a' and s are chosen such that:*

- *$a = (1 + \varepsilon) \cdot (1 - T) \cdot a'$.*
- *$(1 - T) \cdot a' = T \cdot a - (1 - T) \cdot s$.*

In addition, the $p_{ij} < T$ of every expert satisfy the conditions of Theorem 1. Then, the Price of Anarchy of $\mathcal{M}_{AV}$ over $(1 + \varepsilon)$-approximate pure Nash Equilibria is at most 2.

Proof. Let $\mathbf{r}$ be a $(1 + \varepsilon)$ approximate PNE whose winner is j. Further, let $j^\star$ be the proposal with highest quality and suppose that:

$$\mathtt{Qual}[j] < \frac{1}{2} \cdot \mathtt{Qual}[j^\star].$$

Each expert i belongs to one of the following categories:

– **Case 1:** $p_{ij} < T$ and $p_{ij^\star} < T$: In this case, the expert has to disapprove both proposals at the equilibrium **r**. By Theorem 1, expert i would gain no benefit by voting in favor of either j or $j^\star$. Notice that being semi-strategic is needed here; since the equilibrium is approximate, without this assumption the expert might vote in favor of j and still be close to a best response, even though this is clearly a suboptimal strategy.
– Either $p_{ij} \geq T$ or $p_{ij^\star} \geq T$:
  • **Case 2a:** In the first case, if expert i submits a 'no' vote for j and it remains the winner, this 'no' vote also clearly reduces the reward of expert i compared to a 'yes' vote. Since expert i is semi-strategic, they have to vote in favor of j.
  • **Case 2b:** In the second case, by Theorem 1 they cannot approve j. Since **r** is an equilibrium where j wins and they are semi-strategic, voting 'no' for j does not strictly increase their reward. Therefore expert i votes only in favor of $j^\star$.
– **Case 3:** $p_{ij} \geq T$ and $p_{ij^\star} \geq T$: Similarly to **Case 2**, the expert has to approve j. However, not every expert needs to vote in favor of $j^\star$. They only do so if permitted by the equilibrium condition (i.e., if the winner stays j).

We partition the experts into sets C_1, C_{2a}, C_{2b} and C_3 respectively, indexed according to the aforementioned cases. In addition, let $\rho \in [0, 1]$ be the fraction of experts in C_3 that voted for $j^\star$ as well as j. Clearly, since proposal j is the winner we have that:

$$\sum_{i \in C_{2a}} w_i + \sum_{i \in C_3} w_i \geq \sum_{i \in C_{2b}} w_i + \rho \cdot \sum_{i \in C_3} w_i$$
$$\Rightarrow \sum_{i \in C_{2a}} w_i + (1 - \rho) \cdot \sum_{i \in C_3} w_i \geq \sum_{i \in C_{2b}} w_i. \tag{10}$$

In addition, by since $j^\star$ maximizes the quality objective, we have:

$$\sum_{i \in C_{2a}} w_i + \sum_{i \in C_3} w_i < \frac{1}{2} \cdot \left(\sum_{i \in C_{2b}} w_i + \sum_{i \in C_3} w_i \right)$$
$$\Rightarrow 2 \cdot \sum_{i \in C_{2a}} w_i + \sum_{i \in C_3} w_i < \sum_{i \in C_{2b}} w_i. \tag{11}$$

Combining inequalities (10) and (11) we get:

$$\sum_{i \in C_{2a}} w_i + (1 - \rho) \cdot \sum_{i \in C_3} w_i > \sum_{i \in C_{2a}} w_i + \sum_{i \in C_3} w_i,$$

which is impossible for any $\rho \in [0, 1]$, leading to a contradiction.   □

We complement the previous theorem with a matching lower bound.

Theorem 4. *The Price of Anarchy of $\mathcal{M}_{\mathrm{AV}}$ is greater than or equal to 2.*

Proof. Consider and instance with 2 experts and 2 proposals, with the following parameters:

- Expert 1 has $p_{11} = T < p_{12} = 1$ and $w_1 = 1 + \varepsilon$.
- Expert 2 has $p_{11} = 1, p_{12} = 0$ and $w_2 = 1 - \varepsilon$.

All g_{ij} are equal to zero.

The optimal outcome is to elect proposal 1, that has quality 2. However, it is a semi-strategic deviation for expert 1 to vote *against* proposal 1, since she likes proposal 2 slightly more, even though both meet the acceptance threshold T. In this case, expert 2 has no way to change the outcome with her lower weight, leading to an exact PNE with quality $1 + \varepsilon$.   □

4   The Repeated Game

In the previous sections we described a system which incentivizes the experts to only vote 'yes' for proposals that they believe have a high chance of being good. While we have defined the reward of each expert to be proportional to her weight, this does not have any significant impact on our technical results so far. As mentioned in the introduction, however, we want the weight of an expert to serve as a proxy for that expert's demonstrated expertise level, capturing her "reputation" in the system. This, of course, makes sense in a repeated game setting, where the weights are updated after each round of proposals. We assume that every time we have a fresh set of proposals, independent of any past decisions, but the different parameters of the system (threshold T, reward parameters a, a' and s, etc.) remain the same and there is a known rule for updating the weights.

An analog of the various Folk Theorems (see, e.g., [16,17]) would not apply in our setting with the semi-strategic experts, since the notion of a "threat" used in their proofs cannot be used anymore. Nevertheless, we show below that if rewards are smoothed out appropriately, then truth-telling is an approximate pure Nash equilibrium. This, combined with Theorems 2 and 3 directly gives us a *Price of Stability* (which is the ratio between the quality of the best possible equilibrium and the optimal outcome) of 2 for this repeated game.

Let $\mathbf{w}^t = (w_1^t, w_2^t, \ldots, w_n^t)$ be the weights after round $t \geq 1$. In this context, a voting mechanism will involve two components: a reward function $\mathbf{f}^t(\mathbf{r}, \mathbf{w}^t, j, q_j)$ and a weight update rule $\mathbf{w}^{t+1} = g(\mathbf{w}^t, \mathbf{r}, j, q_j)$. The reward function will be the same to the single-shot game: $f_i^t(\mathbf{r}, \mathbf{w}^t, j, q_j) = f_i(\mathbf{r}, \mathbf{w}^t, j, q_j)$. For the sake of presentation, we will focus on a simple weight update rule here, so that the weights converge to the percentage of correct predictions; the same argument, however, could be made for *any* update rule.

In principle, we would not like the weights to fluctuate widely from round to round, since then they would not capture the empirical expertise level as intended. Suppose we define

$$\omega_i^t = \frac{\# \text{ of correct predictions}}{t}.$$

Even if we assume that each expert has an inherent expertise level π_i so that $\lim_{t\to\infty} \omega_i^t = \pi_i$, these weights can still fluctuate a lot when t is small. Having these weights as a starting point, however, for a small $\zeta > 0$, we may define $\mathbf{w}^t$ as follows:

$$w_i^0 = 1/2;$$

$$w_i^{t+1} = \begin{cases} \min\{\omega_i^t, (1+\zeta) \cdot w_i^t\}, & \text{if } t \geq 1 \text{ and } w_i^t \leq \omega_i^t \\ \max\{\omega_i^t, (1-\zeta) \cdot w_i^t\}, & \text{if } t \geq 1 \text{ and } w_i^t > \omega_i^t \end{cases}$$

Using these "delayed updates", we still have $\lim_{t\to\infty} w_i^t = \pi_i$, but the weights never change more than $100 \cdot \zeta \%$ from round to round. Note that is not necessary to start with a rule that converges in any sense.

As usual, we assume that future rewards are discounted by a *discount factor* $\gamma \in (0,1)$. That is, an amount of money x that is expected to be won τ rounds into the future, has value $\gamma^\tau x$ at the present moment for any of the experts.

Theorem 5. *Let $\xi \in (0,1)$. Also let T, ε, δ, a, a', and s be like in Theorem 2, and suppose that for every player i and any proposal j of any round t, we have $g_{ij} \leq w_i^t \cdot a \cdot \delta$. Then the sequence of voting profiles $(\mathbf{r}^t)_{t \in \mathbb{N}}$ where everyone votes honestly in each round t is $(1 + 3\varepsilon) \cdot (1 + \delta)$-approximate pure Nash equilibrium for the Repeated Update Selection game with delayed weight updates and sufficiently small discount factor γ.*

Given that repeated games introduce a large number of (approximate) pure Nash equilibria, some of which may be of very low quality, it is not possible to replicate our Price of Anarchy result from Theorem 3 here. However, that result, coupled with the fact that the sequence of voting profiles in Theorem 5 consists of approximate pure Nash equilibria of the single-shot game (Theorem 2), directly translate into the following Price of Stability result.

Corollary 2. *Under the assumptions of Theorems 5 and 3 (where the original g_{ij} is replaced by g_{ij}/w_i^t if j is an update of round t), the Repeated Update Selection game with delayed weight updates and sufficiently small discount factor γ has Price of Stability at most 2.*

5   Conclusions and Open Problems

In this work, we make the first step in combining aspects of voting and eliciting truthful beliefs at once. Typically voting applications do not involve payments dependent on votes and the chosen outcome, whereas information elicitation (using peer prediction or proper scoring rules) do not involve the experts affecting the chosen action. Using the notion of semi-strategic experts and a variant of approval voting, with appropriate rewards, we can prove the existence of approximate pure Nash equilibria and show that they produce outcomes of good quality. This is only the first step however. The natural follow-up questions would be:

- To study randomized mechanisms, which might have better guarantees. For instance, rather than always selecting the proposal with highest approval, the selection could be randomized between the top proposals that exceed a threshold.
- To allow experts a richer strategy space, including reporting their prior (i.e., the p_{ij}) directly, or even estimating how other experts might act.
- To study the trade-offs between the total rewards given and the quality of the outcome.

Either of these approaches could produce a mechanism with improved performance, at a cost of added complexity and perhaps lower robustness.

Acknowledgements. We would like to thank Nikos Karagiannidis for many enlightening meetings, helping us formulate the model in early versions of this work. This work was supported by the ERC Advanced Grant 788893 AMDROMA "Algorithmic and Mechanism Design Research in Online Markets", the MIUR PRIN project ALGADIMAR "Algorithms, Games, and Digital Markets", and the NWO Veni project No. VI.Veni.192.153.

References

1. Amanatidis, G., Birmpas, G., Lazos, P., Marmolejo-Cossío, F.J.: Decentralised update selection with semi-strategic experts. arXiv preprint arXiv:2205.08407 (2022)
2. Anshelevich, E., Dasgupta, A., Kleinberg, J.M., Tardos, É., Wexler, T., Roughgarden, T.: The price of stability for network design with fair cost allocation. SIAM J. Comput. **38**(4), 1602–1623 (2008)
3. Boutilier, C.: Eliciting forecasts from self-interested experts: scoring rules for decision makers. In: Proceedings of 11th International Conference on Autonomous Agents and Multiagent Systems, AAMAS 2012, vol. 2, pp. 737–744 (2012)
4. Brams, S.J., Fishburn, P.C.: Approval voting. Am. Polit. Sci. Rev. **72**(3), 831–847 (1978)
5. Brams, S.J., Fishburn, P.C.: Going from theory to practice: the mixed success of approval voting. In: Laslier, J.F., Sanver, M. (eds.) Handbook on Approval Voting, pp. 19–37. Springer, Heidelberg (2010). https://doi.org/10.1007/978-3-642-02839-7_3
6. Brams, S.J., Nagel, J.H.: Approval voting in practice. Public Choice **71**(1), 1–17 (1991)
7. Brier, G.W., et al.: Verification of forecasts expressed in terms of probability. Mon. Weather Rev. **78**(1), 1–3 (1950)
8. Buterin, V.: Moving beyond coin voting governance (2021). https://vitalik.ca/general/2021/08/16/voting3.html. Accessed 1 Oct 2021
9. Carroll, G.: Robust incentives for information acquisition. J. Econ. Theory **181**, 382–420 (2019)
10. Chen, Y., Kash, I.: Information elicitation for decision making (2011)
11. Chen, Y., Kash, I.A., Ruberry, M., Shnayder, V.: Eliciting predictions and recommendations for decision making. ACM Trans. Econ. Comput. (TEAC) **2**(2), 1–27 (2014)

12. Endriss, U.: Sincerity and manipulation under approval voting. Theor. Decis. **74**(3), 335–355 (2013)
13. Faltings, B., Radanovic, G.: Game theory for data science: eliciting truthful information. Synthesis Lect. Artif. Intell. Mach. Learn. **11**(2), 1–151 (2017)
14. Fishburn, P.C.: A strategic analysis of nonranked voting systems. SIAM J. Appl. Math. **35**(3), 488–495 (1978)
15. Fishburn, P.C., Brams, S.J.: Approval voting, Condorcet's principle, and runoff elections. Public Choice **36**(1), 89–114 (1981)
16. Friedman, J.W.: A non-cooperative equilibrium for supergames. Rev. Econ. Stud. **38**(1), 1–12 (1971)
17. Fudenberg, D., Maskin, E.: The Folk theorem in repeated games with discounting or with incomplete information. Econometrica **54**(3), 533–554 (1986)
18. Gneiting, T., Raftery, A.E.: Strictly proper scoring rules, prediction, and estimation. J. Am. Stat. Assoc. **102**(477), 359–378 (2007)
19. Kiayias, A., Lazos, P.: SoK: blockchain governance. arXiv preprint arXiv: 2201.07188 (2022)
20. Koutsoupias, E., Papadimitriou, C.H.: Worst-case equilibria. Comput. Sci. Rev. **3**(2), 65–69 (2009)
21. Lambert, N., Shoham, Y.: Eliciting truthful answers to multiple-choice questions. In: Proceedings of the 10th ACM Conference on Electronic Commerce, pp. 109–118 (2009)
22. Laslier, J.F., Sanver, M.R.: The basic approval voting game. In: Laslier, J.F., Sanver, M. (eds.) Handbook on Approval Voting, pp. 153–163. Springer, Heidelberg (2010). https://doi.org/10.1007/978-3-642-02839-7_8
23. Laslier, J.F., Sanver, R. (eds.): Handbook on Approval Voting. Springer, Heidelberg (2010). https://doi.org/10.1007/978-3-642-02839-7
24. Leonardos, S., Reijsbergen, D., Piliouras, G.: Weighted voting on the blockchain: improving consensus in proof of stake protocols. Int. J. Netw. Manag. **30**(5), e2093 (2020)
25. Nakamoto, S.: Bitcoin: a peer-to-peer electronic cash system. Decentralized Bus. Rev. 21260 (2008)
26. Oesterheld, C., Conitzer, V.: Decision scoring rules. In: WINE, p. 468 (2020)
27. Othman, A., Sandholm, T.: Decision rules and decision markets. In: AAMAS, pp. 625–632. Citeseer (2010)
28. Regenwetter, M., Grofman, B.: Approval voting, Borda winners, and Condorcet winners: evidence from seven elections. Manage. Sci. **44**(4), 520–533 (1998)
29. Savage, L.J.: Elicitation of personal probabilities and expectations. J. Am. Stat. Assoc. **66**(336), 783–801 (1971)

Fair Ride Allocation on a Line

Yuki Amano[1], Ayumi Igarashi[2(✉)], Yasushi Kawase[3], Kazuhisa Makino[1],
and Hirotaka Ono[4]

[1] Kyoto University, Kyoto, Japan
{ukiamano,makino}@kurims.kyoto-u.ac.jp
[2] National Institute of Informatics, Tokyo, Japan
ayumi_igarashi@nii.ac.jp
[3] University of Tokyo, Tokyo, Japan
kawase@mist.i.u-tokyo.ac.jp
[4] Nagoya University, Nagoya, Japan
ono@nagoya-u.jp

Abstract. Airport problem is a classical and well-known model of fair cost-sharing for a single facility among multiple agents. This paper extends it to the so-called assignment setting, that is, for multiple facilities and agents, each agent chooses a facility to use and shares the cost with the other agents. Such a situation can be often seen in sharing economy, such as sharing fees for office desks among workers, and taxi fare among customers of possibly different destinations on a line. Our model is regarded as a coalition formation game, based on the fair cost-sharing of the airport problem; we call our model *a fair ride allocation on a line*. As the criteria of solution concepts, we incorporate Nash stability and envy-freeness into our setting. We show that a Nash-stable feasible allocation that minimizes the social cost of agents can be computed efficiently if a feasible allocation exists. For envy-freeness, we provide several structural properties of envy-free allocations. Based on these, we design efficient algorithms for finding an envy-free allocation when either (1) the number of facilities, (2) the number of agent types, or (3) the capacity of facilities, is small. Moreover, we show that a consecutive envy-free allocation can be computed in polynomial time. On the negative front, we show the NP-hardness of determining the existence of an allocation under two relaxed envy-free concepts.

1 Introduction

Imagine a group of university students, each of whom would like to take a taxi to her/his destination. For example, Alice may want to directly go back home while Bob prefers to go downtown to meet with friends. Each of the students may ride a taxi alone or share a ride and split into multiple groups to benefit from sharing the cost. It is then natural to ask two problems: how to form coalitions and fairly divide the fee.

Many relevant aspects of the second problem have been studied in a classical model of *airport problem*, introduced by Littlechild and Owen [15]. In the airport problem, agents are linearly ordered by their demands for a facility and the cost of using the facility is determined by the agent who has the largest demand. In the context of sharing a taxi, the total cost charged to a shared taxi is determined by the last agent who drops

© The Author(s), under exclusive license to Springer Nature Switzerland AG 2022
P. Kanellopoulos et al. (Eds.): SAGT 2022, LNCS 13584, pp. 421–435, 2022.
https://doi.org/10.1007/978-3-031-15714-1_24

off from the taxi. While the problem originally refers to an application of the runway cost division, it covers a variety of real-life examples, e.g., the cost-sharing of a shared meeting room over time and an irrigation ditch [25]. In all these examples, the common property is their linear structure of the agents' demands.

The airport problem is known to be the very first successful application of the celebrated Shapley value, which has a simple and explicit expression despite the exponential nature of its definition. Littlechild and Owen [15] showed that the *sequential equal contributions rule*, which applies equal division to each segment separately, coincides with the Shapley value. Thus, the rule is the uniquely efficient solution that satisfies the basic desideratum of 'equal treatment of equals' and several other desirable properties, e.g., if two agents in the same group have the same contribution, they pay the same amount of money.[1]

However, the basic model of the airport problem does not take into account the first problem, that is, how agents should form groups. In practice, facilities to be shared have capacities, so agents need to decide not only how to divide the cost, but also how to fairly split themselves into groups. In the preceding example of ride-sharing, the way that agents form groups affects the amount of money each agent has to pay. For example, consider a simple scenario of 2 taxis with capacity 3 and 4 passengers with the same destination. One might consider that the allocation in which both taxis have 2 passengers is the unique "fair" solution, which is indeed true with respect to *envy-freeness*, though it is not with respect to *Nash stability*, as seen later. In a more complex scenario, how can we allocate passengers to taxis fairly? Which criterion of justice can we guarantee?

Envy-freeness is one of the most natural notions of fairness [12]: if we select an envy-free outcome, no agent can replace someone else to reduce her/his cost. Another relevant criterion of justice is the notion of stability (e.g., Nash stability and swap-stability), capturing resistance to agents' deviations. No user justifiably complains if there is no beneficial way of allocating her to another facility or swapping a pair of agents [3,7,8,12]. Social optimality are also fundamental notions related to efficiency. *Social optimality* means that there is no alternative allocation that decreases the total cost paid by the agents.

Our Contribution. In this paper, we extend the classical model of airport problems to the so-called assignment setting, that is, for multiple taxis and agents, each agent chooses a taxi to ride and shares the fee with the other agents riding the taxi together. In our setting, agents would like to travel from a common starting point to their destinations, which is represented by points on a line, by multiple taxis and share the travel cost. The total cost charged to passengers for each taxi is determined by the distance between the starting point and the furthest dropping point, and is shared by the agents taking it based on the sequential contributions rule, which coincides with the Shapley value. Since our model is a natural generalization of the airport problem, it can be applied in various situations such as sharing office rooms, traveling to the destinations along a highway, and boat traveling on a river; see details in Thomson [25].

We formulate the notions of stability and fairness, including envy-freeness and Nash stability, inspired by hedonic coalition formation games and resource allocation prob-

---

[1] This rule is in fact used to split the fare in a popular fair division website of Spliddit [13].

lems, and study the existence and complexity of allocations satisfying such properties. We first present basic relationships among the solution concepts; in particular, we show that in our setting, neither Nash-stability nor envy-freeness implies the other.

Concerning stability and efficiency, we show that there always exists a feasible allocation that simultaneously satisfies Nash stability and social optimality, if a given instance contains a feasible allocation. Moreover, such an allocation can be computed in linear time by a simple backward greedy strategy. This contrasts with the standard results of hedonic games in two respects. First, a stable outcome does not necessarily exist in the general setting [3]. Second, efficiency and stability are in general incompatible except for some restricted classes of games [5,7].

In contrast, there is a simple example with no envy-free feasible allocation: when three agents with the same destination split into two taxis with a capacity one and two each, the agent who becomes alone envies others. We provide three structural properties of envy-free allocations: *monotonicity*, *split property*, and *locality*. Based on these, we design efficient algorithms for finding a feasible envy-free allocation when at least one of (a) the number of taxis, (b) the number of agent types, and (c) the capacity of each taxi, is small. More precisely, in case (a), we show that the locality provides a greedy algorithm for finding an envy-free feasible allocation under a certain condition, which implies that an envy-free feasible allocation can be computed in $O(n^{3k+2})$ time, where k is the number of taxis. In case (b), when the number p of types is small, we enumerate all possible 'shapes' of envy-free allocations by utilizing the monotonicity and the split property, and then compute an envy-free feasible allocation in $O(p^p n^4)$ time by exploring semi-lattice structure of size vectors consistent with a given shape; a similar phenomenon has been observed in many other contexts of resource allocation (see, e.g., Sun and Yang [24]). Note that the algorithm is FPT with respect to p. In case (c), we focus on the setting when the capacity of each taxi is bounded by four, where we utilize an enhanced version of the split property. We construct an $O(n^6)$-time greedy algorithm for envy-free feasible allocations by combining it with the locality.

On the negative side, we show that it is NP-hard to determine the existence of an allocation under two relaxed envy-free concepts. The omitted examples and proofs are deferred to the full version of the paper [1].

Related Work. The problem of fairly dividing the cost among multiple agents has been long studied in the context of cooperative games with transferable utilities; we refer the reader to the book of Chalkiadakis *et al.* [9] for an overview. Following the seminal work of Shapley [23], several researchers have investigated the axiomatic property of the Shapley value as well as its applications to real-life problems. Chun and Park [15] analyzed the property of the Shapley value when the cost of each subset of agents is given by the maximum cost associated with the agents in that subset. Chun and Park [10] analyzed the extension of the airport problem under capacity constraints wherein the number of facilities is unlimited and the capacity of each facility is the same. They showed that a capacity-adjusted version of the sequential equal contributions rule coincides with the Shapley value of a cooperative game whose characteristic value is defined as the minimum cost of serving all the members of a coalition. Note that the payment rule in Chun and Park [10] is different from our setting: they consider a global payment rule that divides the total cost among all agents, while in our setting, the cost of each facility is divided locally among the agents assigned to the same facility. Chun et al. [11] further studied the strategic process in which agents divide the cost of the resource, showing that the division by the Shapley value is indeed a unique subgame perfect Nash equilibrium under a natural three-stage protocol.

Our work is similar in spirit to the complexity study of congestion games [16,20]. In fact, without capacity constraints, it is not difficult to see that the fair ride-sharing problem can be formulated as a congestion game. The fairness notions, including envy-freeness in particular, have been well-explored in the fair division literature. Although much of the focus is on resource allocation among individuals, several recent papers study the fair division problem among groups [14,22]. Our work is different from theirs in that agents' utilities depend not only on allocated resources, but also on the group structure.

Aziz and Savani [3], Barrot and Yokoo [5], Bodlaender et al. [6], Bogomolnaia and Jackson [7], there exists a rich body of literature studying fairness and stability. In hedonic games, agents have preferences over coalitions to which they belong, and the goal is to find a partition of agents into disjoint coalitions. While the standard model of hedonic games is too general to accommodate positive results (see Peters and Elkind [19]), much of the literature considers subclasses of hedonic games where desirable outcomes can be achieved. For example, Barrot and Yokoo [5] studied the compatibility between fairness and stability requirements, showing that top responsive games always admit an envy-free, individually stable, and Pareto optimal partition.

Finally, our work is related to the growing literature on the ride-sharing problem [2,4,11,13,18,21]. Santi et al. [21] empirically showed a large portion of taxi trips in New York City could be shared while keeping prolonged passenger travel time low. Motivated by an application to the ride-sharing platform, Ashlagi et al. [2] considered the problem of matching passengers for sharing rides in an online fashion. However, they did not study the fairness perspective of the resulting matching.

2   Model

For a positive integer $s \in \mathbb{Z}_{>0}$, we write $[s] = \{1, 2, \ldots, s\}$. For a set T and an element a, we may write $T + a = T \cup \{a\}$ and $T - a = T \backslash \{a\}$. In our setting, there are a finite set of *agents*, denoted by $A = [n]$, and a finite set of k *taxis*. The nonempty subsets of agents are referred to as *coalitions*. Each agent $a \in A$ is endowed with a destination $x_a \in \mathbb{R}_{>0}$, which is called the *destination type* (or shortly *type*) of agent a. We assume that the agents ride a taxi at the same initial location of the point 0 and they are sorted in nondecreasing order of their destinations, i.e., $x_1 \leq x_2 \leq \cdots \leq x_n$. Each taxi $i \in [k]$ has a quota q_i representing its capacity, where $q_1 \geq q_2 \geq \cdots \geq q_k \, (> 0)$ is assumed. An *allocation* $\mathcal{T} = (T_1, \ldots, T_\ell)$ is an ordered partition of A, and is called *feasible* if $\ell \leq k$ and $|T_i| \leq q_i$ for all $i \in [\ell]$. Given a monotone nondecreasing function $f \colon \mathbb{R}_{>0} \to \mathbb{R}_{>0}$, the *cost* charged to agents T_i is the value of f in the furthest destination $\max_{a \in T_i} f(x_a)$ if $|T_i| \leq q_i$, and ∞ otherwise. The cost has to be divided among the agents in T_i. Without loss of generality, we assume that the cost charged to T_i is simply the distance of the furthest destination if $|T_i| \leq q_i$, i.e., f is the identity function. In other words, we may regard that x_a is the cost itself instead of the distance.[2] Throughout, we use a succinct notation to specify examples. An allocation $\mathcal{T}$ is written as a set of arrows where the arrows correspond to coalitions $T \in \mathcal{T}$ and the black circles on the arrow T denote the set of destinations of the agents in T.

Among several payment rules of cooperative games, we consider a scenario where agents divide the cost using the well-known *Shapley value* [23], which, in our setting, coincides with the sequential contributions rule as in the airport problem [15].

Formally, for each subset T of agents and $s \in \mathbb{R}_{>0}$, we denote by $n_T(s)$ the number of agents a in T whose destinations x_a is at least s, i.e., $n_T(s) := |\{a \in T \mid x_a \geq s\}|$. For each coalition $T \subseteq A$ and positive real $x \in \mathbb{R}_{>0}$, we define

$$\varphi(T, x) = \int_0^x \frac{dr}{n_T(r)},$$

where we define $\varphi(T, x) = \infty$ if $n_T(x) = 0$. Equivalently, for a subset T of s agents whose destinations are given by $x_{i_1} \leq x_{i_2} \leq \ldots \leq x_{i_s}$, the value $\varphi(T, x_{i_j})$ is given by $x_{i_1}/s + (x_{i_2} - x_{i_1})/(s-1) + \ldots + (x_{i_j} - x_{i_{j-1}})/(s-j+1)$. See Example 1 for an illustration of the sequential contributions rule.

Example 1. Consider a taxi that forms a coalition T in Fig. 1, i.e., agents a, b, c, and d take one taxi together from a starting point to points 12, 24, 36, and 40 on a line, respectively. The total cost is 40, which corresponds to the drop-off point of d. According to the payment rule, agents a, b, c, and d pay 3, 7, 13, and 17, respectively. All the agents are in the taxi from the starting point to the drop-off point of a, so they equally divide the cost of 12, which means that a should pay $\varphi(T, x_a) = 12/4 = 3$. Between the dropping points of a and b, three agents are in the taxi, so they equally divide the cost of $24 - 12 = 12$, resulting in the cost of 4 for each of the three agents. Thus, $\varphi(T, x_b) = 12/4 + 12/3 = 3 + 4 = 7$. By repeating similar arguments, we have $\varphi(T, x_c) = 7 + (36 - 24)/2 = 13$, and $\varphi(T, x_d) = 13 + (40 - 36) = 17$.

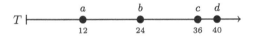

Fig. 1. The coalition in Example 1

For an allocation $\mathcal{T}$ and a coalition $T_i \in \mathcal{T}$, the *cost* of agent $a \in T_i$ is defined as $\Phi_T(a) := \varphi_i(T_i, x_a)$ where

$$\varphi_i(T_i, x) = \begin{cases} \varphi(T_i, x) & \text{if } |T_i| \leq q_i, \\ \infty & \text{if } |T_i| > q_i. \end{cases}$$

---

[2] We here emphasize that all the results for the distance cost are applicable to the case in which the cost is given by a monotone nondecreasing and polynomially computable function f of the furthest destination, by replacing the destination of a by $f(x_a)$, because $\max_{a \in T} f(x_a) = f(\max_{a \in T} x_a)$.

It is not difficult to verify that the sum of the payments in T_i is equal to the cost of taxi i. Namely, if $|T_i| \leq q_i$, we have $\sum_{b \in T_i} \varphi_i(T_i, x_b) = \max_{a \in T_i} x_a$. On the other hand, if $|T_i| > q_i$, all agents in T_i pay ∞ whose sum is equal to ∞ (i.e., the cost of taxi i). The following proposition formally states that the payment rule for each taxi coincides with the Shapley value. We note that while Littlechild and Owen [15] presented a similar formulation of the Shapley value for airport problems, our model is slightly different from theirs with the presence of capacity constraints.

Proposition 1. *The payment rule φ_i is the Shapley value.*

3   Solution Concepts

In this section, we introduce several desirable criteria that are inspired from coalition formation games and resource allocation problems [3,7,8,12].

Fairness: *Envy-freeness* requires that no agent prefers another agent. Formally, for an allocation $\mathcal{T}$, agent $a \in T_i$ *envies* $b \in T_j$ if a can be made better off by replacing herself by b, i.e., $i \neq j$ and $\varphi_j(T_j - b + a, x_a) < \varphi_i(T_i, x_a)$. A feasible allocation $\mathcal{T}$ is *envy-free (EF)* if no agent envies another agent. Without capacity constraints, e.g., $q_1 \geq n$, envy-freeness can be trivially achieved by allocating all agents to a single coalition T_1. Also, when the number of taxis is at least the number of agents, i.e., $k \geq n$, an allocation that partitions the agents into the singletons is envy-free.

Stability: We adapt the following definitions of stability concepts of hedonic games [3,6,7] to our setting. The first stability concepts we introduce are those that are immune to individual deviations. For an allocation $\mathcal{T}$ and two distinct taxis $i, j \in [k]$, agent $a \in T_i$ has a *Nash-deviation* to T_j if $\varphi_j(T_j + a, x_a) < \varphi_i(T_i, x_a)$. By the definition of function φ_j, no agent a has a Nash-deviation to T_j if adding a to T_j violates the capacity constraint, i.e., $|T_j| \geq q_j$. A feasible allocation $\mathcal{T}$ is called *Nash stable (NS)* if no agent has a Nash deviation. A feasible allocation $\mathcal{T}$ is called *contractually individually stable (CIS)* if for each $T_i \in \mathcal{T}$ and $a \in T_i$, agent a does not have a Nash deviation or the cost of some agent $a' \in T_i$ increases if a leaves T_i, i.e., $\varphi_i(T_i - a, x_{a'}) > \varphi_i(T_i, x_{a'})$.

Next, we define stability notions that capture resistance to swap deviations. For an allocation $\mathcal{T}$, agent $a \in T_i$ *can replace* $b \in T_j$ if $i = j$ or $\varphi_j(T_j - b + a, x_a) \leq \varphi_i(T_i, x_a)$ [5,17]. A feasible allocation $\mathcal{T}$ is

- *weakly swap-stable (WSS)* if there is no pair of agents a and b such that a and b envy each other;
- *strongly swap-stable (SSS)* if there is no pair of agents a and b such that a envies b and b can replace a.

Efficiency: Besides fairness and stability, another important property of allocation is efficiency. The *total cost* of an allocation $\mathcal{T}$ is defined as $\sum_{T \in \mathcal{T}} \sum_{a \in T} \varphi(T, x_a)$. Note that the total cost of a feasible allocation $\mathcal{T}$ is equal to $\sum_{T \in \mathcal{T}: T \neq \emptyset} \max_{a \in T} x_a$. A feasible allocation $\mathcal{T}$ is *socially optimal (SO)* if it minimizes the total cost over all feasible allocations.

For two allocations $\mathcal{T}$ and $\mathcal{T}'$, we say that $\mathcal{T}$ *strictly Pareto dominates* $\mathcal{T}'$ if $\Phi_{\mathcal{T}}(a) > \Phi_{\mathcal{T}'}(a)$ for all $a \in A$; $\mathcal{T}$ *weakly Pareto dominates* $\mathcal{T}'$ if $\Phi_{\mathcal{T}}(a) \geq \Phi_{\mathcal{T}'}(a)$ for all $a \in A$ with $\Phi_{\mathcal{T}}(a) > \Phi_{\mathcal{T}'}(a)$ for at least one $a \in A$. A feasible allocation $\mathcal{T}$ is *weakly Pareto optimal (WPO)* if there is no feasible allocation $\mathcal{T}'$ that strictly Pareto dominates $\mathcal{T}$; it is *strongly Pareto optimal (SPO)* if there is no feasible allocation $\mathcal{T}'$ that weakly Pareto dominates $\mathcal{T}$.

We have the inclusion relationships among these classes of outcomes shown in Fig. 2.

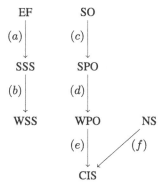

Fig. 2. Inclusion relationships among the concepts. Any two concepts without any path between them are incomparable.

Note that in general, any two concepts that do not have containment relationships in Fig. 2 are incomparable; further, all the inclusions are proper. See the full version [1] for details.

4   Stable and Socially Optimal Allocations

We start by showing that stability and social optimality can be achieved simultaneously: a feasible allocation that greedily groups agents from the furthest destinations satisfies Nash stability, strong swap-stability, and social optimality. Specifically, we design the following *backward greedy* algorithm: it constructs coalitions T_i in the increasing order of i by greedily adding agents j in the decreasing order of their destinations until T_i exceeds the capacity. We show that the outcome of the backward greedy is socially optimal and Nash stable; moreover, it satisfies strong swap stability.

Theorem 1. *If a given instance has a feasible allocation, the backward greedy computes in polynomial time a feasible allocation that is socially optimal, Nash stable, and strongly swap stable.*

Proof (Sketch). Clearly, the backward greedy computes a feasible allocation if there exists such an allocation. Let $\mathcal{T} = (T_1, \ldots, T_k)$ be a feasible allocation constructed by the algorithm, and let T_h be the last non-empty coalition in $\mathcal{T}$, i.e., $T_\kappa = \emptyset$ for $\kappa > h$. Note that $\mathcal{T}$ satisfies the Nash stability. It is enough to consider deviations to the last coalition T_h since the other coalitions are already saturated. Moreover, if agent $a \in T_i$ has a Nash deviation to T_h, she would become the last passenger to drop off but we have $|T_h| + 1 \le q_h \le q_i = |T_i|$, which implies that she cannot decrease her cost by deviating to T_h, a contradiction.

We next show that $\mathcal{T}$ is a socially optimal allocation, i.e., $\mathcal{T}$ is a feasible allocation that minimizes the total cost among feasible allocations. Recall that the total cost of a feasible allocation is simply the sum of the furthest destinations of all taxis. One can thus show that the sequence of the last drop-off points in socially optimal allocations is unique and identical to that of the allocation obtained by the backward greedy algorithm. This implies that $\mathcal{T}$ is socially optimal. The proof for strong swap stability can be found in the full version [1].   □

As a corollary of the above theorem, we can see that there exists a feasible allocation that satisfies all the notions defined in Sect. 3, except for envy-freeness, whenever a feasible allocation exists.

We remark that the backward greedy algorithm fails to find an envy-free feasible allocation even when it exists, since while the output of the algorithm always satisfies *consecutiveness*, i.e., each coalition consists of consecutive agents according to the destinations, there is an instance that has an envy-free feasible allocation but no consecutive envy-free feasible allocation (see the full version [1]).

5   Envy-Free Allocations

In this section, we consider envy-free feasible allocations for our model. Note that in contrast with Nash stability, an envy-free feasible allocation may not exist even when a feasible allocation exists as we mentioned in Sect. 1. We thus study the problem of deciding the existence of an envy-free feasible allocation and finding one if it exists. We identify several scenarios where an envy-free feasible allocation can be computed in polynomial time. We show that the problem is FPT with respect to the number of destinations, and is XP with respect to the number of taxis.[3] Further, we show that when the maximum capacity of each taxi is four, the problem is polynomial-time solvable. These restrictions are relevant in many real-life scenarios. For example, a taxi company may have a limited resource, in terms of both quantity and capacity. It is also relevant to consider a setting where the number of destinations is small; for instance, a workshop organizer may offer a few excursion opportunities to the participants of the workshop. As a negative remark, we show that two decision problems related to envy-free allocations are intractable.

We start with three basic properties of envy-free allocations that will play key roles in designing efficient algorithms for the scenarios discussed in this paper. The first one

---

[3] A problem is said to be *fixed parameter tractable* (FPT) with respect to a parameter p if each instance I of this problem can be solved in time $f(p) \cdot \text{poly}(|I|)$, and to be slice-wise polynomial (XP) with respect to p if each instance I of this problem can be solved in time $f(p) \cdot |I|^{g(p)}$.

is *monotonicity* of the size of coalitions in terms of the first drop-off point, which is formalized as follows.

Lemma 1 (Monotonicity lemma). *For an envy-free feasible allocation $\mathcal{T}$ and non-empty coalitions $T, T' \in \mathcal{T}$, we have the following implications:*

$$\min_{a \in T} x_a < \min_{a' \in T'} x_{a'} \quad \text{implies} \quad |T| \geq |T'|, \tag{1}$$

$$\min_{a \in T} x_a = \min_{a' \in T'} x_{a'} \quad \text{implies} \quad |T| = |T'|. \tag{2}$$

Proof. Let $b \in \arg\min_{a \in T} x_a$ and $b' \in \arg\min_{a' \in T'} x_{a'}$. Suppose that $b \leq b'$ and $|T| < |T'|$. Then b envies b', because $\varphi(T, x_b) = \frac{x_b}{|T|} > \frac{x_b}{|T'|} = \varphi(T' - b' + b, x_b)$. Thus $b \leq b'$ implies $|T| \geq |T'|$, proving (1) and (2). □

We next show the *split* property of envy-free feasible allocations. For a coalition T and a real s, we use notations $T_{<s}$, $T_{=s}$, and $T_{>s}$ to denote the set of agents with type smaller than s, equal to s, and larger than s, respectively. We say that *agents of type x are split in an allocation $\mathcal{T}$* if $\mathcal{T}$ contains two distinct T and T' with $T_{=x}, T'_{=x} \neq \emptyset$. The next lemma states that the agents of type x can be split in an envy-free feasible allocation only if they are the first passengers to drop off in their coalitions, and such coalitions are of the same size; further, if two taxis have an equal number of agents of split type, then no other agent rides these taxis.

An implication of the lemma is critical: we do not have to consider how to split the agents of non-first drop-off points to realize envy-free feasible allocations.

Lemma 2 (Split lemma). *If agents of type x are split in an envy-free feasible allocation $\mathcal{T}$, i.e., $T_{=x}, T'_{=x} \neq \emptyset$ for some distinct $T, T' \in \mathcal{T}$, then we have the following three statements:*

(i) *The agents of type x are the first passengers to drop off in both T and T', i.e., $T_{<x} = T'_{<x} = \emptyset$,*
(ii) *Both T and T' are of the same size, i.e., $|T| = |T'|$, and*
(iii) *If $|T_{=x}| = |T'_{=x}|$, then $T = T_{=x}$ and $T' = T'_{=x}$.*

Proof (Sketch). To show (i), let $b \in T_{=x}$ and $b' \in T'_{=x}$. By envy-freeness, both agents pay the same cost, i.e., $\varphi(T, x) = \varphi(T', x)$. Thus, if there is an agent $a \in T_{<x}$ whose type is smaller than x, agent $b' \in T'$ could reduce her cost by replacing a with herself, causing envy toward a, a contradiction. Hence, $T_{<x} = \emptyset$. By symmetry, $T'_{<x} = \emptyset$, proving (i). This implies that $\varphi(T, x) = x/|T|$ and $\varphi(T', x) = x/|T'|$. Since $\varphi(T, x) = \varphi(T', x)$ by envy-freeness, we have $|T| = |T'|$, which proves (ii). To see (iii), suppose towards a contradiction that $|T_{=x}| = |T'_{=x}|$ but there is an agent in $T \cup T'$ whose destination appears strictly after x. Let a^* be the agent with the closest destination among such agents. Without loss of generality, assume $a^* \in T$. Then, it is not difficult to see that a^* envies b, a contradiction. Hence, $|T_{=x}| = |T'_{=x}|$ implies $T = T_{=x}$ and $T' = T'_{=x}$.

The last property of envy-free allocations is *locality*, i.e., every agent a is allocated to a taxi T with minimum cost $\varphi(T, x_a)$.

Lemma 3 (Locality lemma). *For any envy-free allocation $\mathcal{T}$, coalition $T \in \mathcal{T}$, and agent $a \in T$, we have*

$$\varphi(T, x_a) \leq \varphi(T', x_a)$$

for all $T' \in \mathcal{T}$. Furthermore, the strict inequality holds if x_a is larger than the first drop-off point $\min_{a' \in T'} x_{a'}$ of T'.

Proof. To show the first statement, if there exists $T' \in \mathcal{T}$ such that $\varphi(T', x_a) < \varphi(T, x_a)$, then T' would contain an agent a' with $x_{a'} \geq x_a$, since otherwise $\varphi(T', x_a) = \int_0^{x_a} \frac{dr}{n_{T'}(r)} = \infty$; thus we have $\varphi(T, x_a) > \varphi(T', x_a) = \varphi(T' - a' + a, x_a)$, which contradicts envy-freeness of $\mathcal{T}$. To show the second statement, assume towards a contradiction that $\mathcal{T}$ contains a coalition T' such that $\min_{a' \in T'} x_{a'} < x_a$ and $\varphi(T', x_a) = \varphi(T, x_a)$. Let a' be an agent in T' such that $x_{a'} < x_a$. Then we have $\varphi(T, x_a) = \varphi(T', x_a) > \varphi(T' - a' + a, x_a)$, which again contradicts envy-freeness of $\mathcal{T}$. $\qquad\square$

5.1   Constant Number of Taxis

To begin with, we prove that an envy-free feasible allocations can be efficiently computed when there is a constant number of taxis. To this end, we exploit Locality lemma to provide a greedy algorithm for finding an envy-free feasible allocation when three parameters, the size of each coalition, the first drop-off point of each coalition, and the number of agents who first drop off at each coalition, are fixed in advance. An important observation here is that the cost of an agent a in a coalition T is solely determined by the agents of type smaller than x_a and the size of T. Formally, for a coalition $S \subseteq A$ and two positive reals x and μ, we define $\psi(S, x, \mu)$ by

$$\psi(S, x, \mu) := \int_0^x \frac{dr}{n_S(r) + \mu - |S|},$$

where $\mu \geq |S|$ is assumed. Then we have

$$\varphi(T, x) = \psi(T_{<x}, x, |T|)$$

for any coalition T and any positive real x. This yields the following reformulation of Locality lemma; namely, in an envy-free allocation, each agent rides a taxi with minimum cost in terms of $\psi(T_{<x_a}, x_a, |T|)$.

Lemma 4. *For any envy-free allocation $\mathcal{T}$, coalition $T \in \mathcal{T}$, and agent $a \in T$, we have*

$$\psi(T_{<x_a}, x_a, |T|) \leq \psi(T'_{<x_a}, x_a, |T'|)$$

for all $T' \in \mathcal{T}$. Furthermore, the strict inequality holds if $x_a > \min_{a' \in T'} x_{a'}$.

By Lemma 4, the coalition of each agent can be determined in a greedy manner from an agent with the nearest destination, if we fix the following three parameters for each taxi $i \in [k]$:

(I) the number μ_i of agents who ride taxi i,
(II) the first drop-off point s_i,
(III) the number r_i of agents who drop off at the first point.

Here we define $s_i = \infty$ if $r_i = \mu_i = 0$. Building up on Locality lemma, we design the following greedy algorithm (Algorithm 1) to compute an envy-free allocation that is consistent with a given configuration $(\mu_i, s_i, r_i)_{i \in [k]}$.

Algorithm 1: Algorithm for an envy-free allocation consistent with $(\mu_i, s_i, r_i)_{i \in [k]}$

---

1 Initialize $S_i \leftarrow \emptyset$ for each $i \in [k]$;
2 **for** $a \leftarrow 1, 2, \ldots, n$ **do**
3 $\quad$ **if** $x_a = s_i$ and $|S_i| < r_i$ for some i **then** Take such an i arbitrarily;
4 $\quad$ **else** Pick i from $\arg\min_{j \in [k]: s_j < x_a \wedge |S_j| < \mu_j} \psi(S_j, x_a, \mu_j)$;
5 $\quad$ Set $S_i \leftarrow S_i + a$;
6 **if** $(S_1, \ldots, S_k)$ is envy-free **then return** $(S_1, \ldots, S_k)$;
7 **else return** "No envy-free feasible allocation consistent with $(\mu_i, s_i, r_i)_{i \in [k]}$";

Formally, a vector $(\mu_i, s_i, r_i)_{i \in [k]}$ in $(\mathbb{Z}_{\geq 0} \times (\mathbb{R}_{>0} \cup \{\infty\}) \times \mathbb{Z}_{\geq 0})^{[k]}$ is called a *configuration* if the following four conditions hold:

1. either $(\mu_i, s_i, r_i) = (0, \infty, 0)$ or $\left(s_i \in \{x_a \mid a \in A\} \text{ and } 1 \leq r_i \leq \mu_i \leq q_i \right)$ for each $i \in [k]$,
2. $\sum_{i \in [k]} \mu_i = n$,
3. $\sum_{j \in [k]: s_j = s_i} r_i = |A_{=s_i}|$ for each $i \in [k]$, and
4. $a \leq \sum_{i \in [k]: s_i < x_a} \mu_i + \sum_{i \in [k]: s_i = x_a} r_i$ for each $a \in A$.

Here for Condition 4, we recall that for any two agents a and b, $a < b$ implies $x_a \leq x_b$. Note that (II) and (III) implies Condition 3. We will soon see that $(\mu_i, s_i, r_i)_{i \in [k]}$ is a configuration if and only if there exists a feasible allocation $\mathcal{T}$ that satisfies (I), (II), and (III), where such a $\mathcal{T}$ is called *consistent with* $(\mu_i, s_i, r_i)_{i \in [k]}$. By definition, there exist $O(n^{3k})$ many configurations, which is polynomial when k is a constant. Thus, it is sufficient to prove the following lemma.

Lemma 5. *Given a configuration $(\mu_i, s_i, r_i)_{i \in [k]}$, Algorithm 1 computes in $O(n^2)$ time an envy-free feasible allocation consistent with $(\mu_i, s_i, r_i)_{i \in [k]}$ if it exists.*

Proof. We prove that Algorithm 1 computes in polynomial time an envy-free feasible allocation consistent with $(\mu_i, s_i, r_i)_{i \in [k]}$ if it exists.

Let us first show that line 5 is executed for each agent a, i.e., it is allocated to some taxi i. If $x_a = s_i$ holds for some taxi i, then by Condition 3, the if-statement in line 3 must hold, implying that i is chosen in the line. Otherwise, by Conditions 2 and 4, at least one taxi j satisfies $s_j < x_a$ and $|S_j| < \mu_j$, which implies that i is chosen in line 4. Thus the algorithm allocates all the agents.

Let S denote $(S_1, \ldots, S_k)$ checked in line 6. It is not difficult to see that Conditions 1 and 2 imply that S is a feasible allocation satisfying (I). Moreover, Conditions 3 and

4, together with the discussion above, imply that $\mathcal{S}$ satisfies (II), (III) and Lemma 2 (i). Therefore $\mathcal{S}$ is a feasible allocation that satisfies (I), (II), (III) and Lemma 2 (i).

We finally show that, if there is an envy-free feasible allocation consistent with a given configuration $(\mu_i, s_i, r_i)_{i \in [k]}$, each agent a is allocated according to such an allocation. Since any agent a who drops off at the first drop-off point (i.e., $x_a = s_i$ holds for some taxi i) is suitably allocated by Condition 3, we only consider agents a of the other kind. By Lemma 4, there exists a unique taxi i that minimizes $\psi(S_i, x_a, \mu_i)$ among agents i with $s_i < x_a$ and $|S_i| < \mu_i$. This implies that i is properly chosen in line 4.

Therefore, it is enough to check if $\mathcal{S}$ is envy-free, since (I), (II), (III) and Lemma 2 (i) are all necessary conditions of envy-free feasible allocations, thereby completing the proof. The running time is $O(n^2)$: Indeed, in lines 2–5, there are at most n iterations and each iteration can be implemented in $O(n)$ time. In line 6, checking envy-freeness can be done in $O(kn^2) = O(n^2)$ time since for each agent a, it is possible to check in $O(n)$ time whether a envies some agent allocated to a taxi $i \in [k]$.   □

Theorem 2. *When the number k of taxis is a constant, an envy-free feasible allocation can be found in polynomial time, if it exists.*

5.2 Small Number of Types

Next, we show that an envy-free feasible allocation can be computed in FPT time with respect to the number of destination types. Recall that due to the split property, once we know the first drop-off points of each coalition, no agent of the other types will be split in an envy-free allocation. Thus, we can represent the 'shapes' of an envy-free allocation by a directed graph G where the first drop-off points can be considered as roots, followed by the agents of the other types. The main idea of our algorithm is to (1) enumerate all such G and (2) decide whether there is a size vector λ of each coalition that results in an envy-free outcome that is consistent with G. Although a naive approach to enumerate all possible size vectors gives rise to an $O(p^p n^p)$ algorithm where p is the number of destination types, we show that a more sophisticated approach results in an $O(p^p n^4)$ algorithm by utilizing structural properties of G and λ. In particular, we show that G and λ define a unique envy-free allocation (up to isomorphism), G is a star-forest, and λ forms semi-lattice. Based on these properties, we obtain the following theorem; the details can be found in the full version of our paper [1].

Theorem 3. *We can check the existence of an envy-free feasible allocation, and find one if it exists in FPT with respect to the number of types of agents.*

5.3 Constant Capacity

Finally, we consider the case when the capacity of each taxi is at most four. We design a greedy algorithm based on locality property in Lemma 4. Recall that the greedy algorithm works, once we fix (I), (II), and (III) in Sect. 5.1. If the capacity of each taxi is bounded by a constant, (I) the number μ_i of agents in taxi i can be easily treated since

we have polynomially many candidates $\mu = (\mu_1, \ldots, \mu_k)$.[4] However, it is not immediate to handle (II) and (III), i.e., how to split the agents with the first drop-off points
in taxis, even if the capacity of each taxi is bounded by four. In this section, we have a
more detailed analysis of the split property. More precisely, all possible *split patterns* of
agents with the same destination can be uniquely determined in a particular way. Based
on this, we design a polynomial time algorithm for computing an envy-free feasible
allocation when the maximum capacity is four, formalized in the following theorem.
The details of the proof can be found in the full version [1].

Theorem 4. *If $q_i \leq 4$ for all $i \in [k]$, then an envy-free feasible allocation can be
computed in polynomial time if it exists.*

5.4 Hardness Results

Having established polynomial-time algorithms for several scenarios, we turn our attention to the general problem of computing an envy-free feasible allocation. Unfortunately, it remains open whether the problem of deciding the existence of an envy-free
feasible allocation is NP-hard or polynomial-time solvable. We instead consider two
natural relaxations of envy-freeness and prove the NP-hardness of deciding the existence of such allocations.

The first one relaxes the envy-free requirement by imposing the necessary conditions in Split Lemma. More precisely, we consider the conditions (i)–(iii) in Lemma 2.
We say that a feasible allocation $\mathcal{T}$ satisfies *the split conditions* if the conditions (i)–(iii)
in Lemma 2 are satisfied for any x and distinct $T, T' \in \mathcal{T}$ such that $T_{=x}$ and $T'_{=x}$ are
non-empty. Computing such an allocation turns out to be NP-hard.

Theorem 5. *It is NP-complete to decide whether there exists a feasible allocation that
satisfies the split conditions.*

The second one generalizes the notion of envy-freeness by looking into envies
among particular ordered pairs. For a subset $S \subseteq A^2$ of the agents' ordered pairs,
an allocation is called *envy-free in S* if agent a never envies agent b for any $(a, b) \in S$.
Note that this coincides with the original envy-freeness if S is the set of all ordered
pairs of agents, i.e., $S = A^2$. This generalized envy-freeness is useful to control the
rank-wise service quality. For example, consider a frequent flyer program of an airline
company. In this case, it would be desirable to set $(a, b) \in S$ if and only if the rank of
agent a is not lower than that of agent b. Unfortunately, it is also NP-hard to find such
an allocation.

Theorem 6. *Given a subset $S \subseteq A^2$, it is NP-complete to decide whether there exists
a feasible allocation that is envy-free in S.*

We note that, the proof for the above theorem turns out to show the NP-hardness
for a more restricted variant of envy-freeness with respect to a particular subgroup of
agents: that is, given a subset C of agents, it is NP-complete to decide whether there is
a feasible allocation that does not admit an envy among all the ordered pairs in C^2.

---

[4] More precisely, assuming that the taxis are arranged in descending order of size, it suffices to
guess $\max_{i \in [k]} q_i$ changing points of their sizes. For example, if $\max_{i \in [k]} q_i \leq 4$, each of the
first k_4 taxis contains four agents, each of the next k_3 taxis contains three agents, and so on.

6   Conclusion

In this paper, we introduced a novel model of the fair ride allocation problem on a line with an initial point. We proved that the backward greedy allocation satisfies Nash stability, strong swap-stability, and social optimality. We designed several efficient algorithms to compute an envy-free feasible allocation when some parameter of our input is small. An obvious open problem is the complexity of finding an envy-free allocation for the general case. We expect that the problem becomes NP-hard even when the maximum capacity is a constant.

There are several possible extensions of our model. First, while we have assumed that agents ride at the same starting point, it would be very natural to consider a setting where the riding locations may differ. Indeed, passengers ride at different points in most of private carpooling services. Thus, extending our results to this setting would be a promising research direction. Further, besides the class of path graphs, there are other underlying structures of destinations, such as grids and planar graphs. Although we expect that the Shapley value of a cost allocation problem on a more general graph structure may become necessarily complex, it would be interesting to analyze the properties of fair and stable outcomes in such scenarios.

Acknowledgement. This work was partially supported by the joint project of Kyoto University and Toyota Motor Corporation, titled "Advanced Mathematical Science for Mobility Society," JST PRESTO Grant Numbers JPMJPR2122 and JPMJPR20C1, and JSPS KAKENHI Grant Numbers JP19K22841, JP20H00609, JP20H05967, and JP22H00513. The authors would like to thank Warut Suksompong and the SAGT reviewers for valuable feedback on earlier versions of the paper.

References

1. Amano, Y., Igarashi, A., Kawase, Y., Makino, K., Ono, H.: Fair ride allocation on a line. CoRR, abs/2007.08045 (2020)
2. Ashlagi, I., Burq, M., Dutta, C., Jaillet, P., Saberi, A., Sholley, C.: Edge weighted online windowed matching. In: Proceedings of the 20th ACM Conference on Economics and Computation (EC), pp. 729–742 (2019)
3. Aziz, H., Savani, R.: Hedonic games. In: Brandt, F., Conitzer, V., Endriss, U., Lang, J., Procaccia, A.D. (eds.) Handbook of Computational Social Choice. Cambridge University Press (2016)
4. Banerjee, S., Kanoria, Y., Qian, P.: State dependent control of closed queueing networks. In: Abstracts of the 2018 ACM International Conference on Measurement and Modeling of Computer Systems, SIGMETRICS 2018, pp. 2–4. Association for Computing Machinery, New York (2018)
5. Barrot, N., Yokoo, M.: Stable and envy-free partitions in hedonic games. In: Proceedings of the 28th International Joint Conference on Artificial Intelligence (IJCAI), pp. 67–73 (2019)
6. Bodlaender, H.L., Hanaka, T., Jaffke, L., Ono, H., Otachi, Y., van der Zanden, T.C.: Hedonic seat arrangement problems. In: Proceedings of the 19th International Conference on Autonomous Agents and Multi-Agent Systems (AAMAS), pp. 1777–1779 (2020)
7. Bogomolnaia, A., Jackson, M.O.: The stability of hedonic coalition structures. Games Econ. Behav. **38**(2), 201–230 (2002)

8. Bouveret, S., Chevaleyre, Y., Maudet, N.: Fair allocation of indivisible goods. In: Brandt, F., Conitzer, V., Endriss, U., Lang, J., Procaccia, A.D. (eds.) Handbook of Computational Social Choice. Cambridge University Press (2016)

9. Chalkiadakis, G., Elkind, E., Wooldridge, M.: Computational aspects of cooperative game theory. In: Synthesis Lectures on Artificial Intelligence and Machine Learning, vol. 5, no. 6, pp. 1–168 (2011)

10. Chun, Y., Park, B.: The airport problem with capacity constraints. Rev. Econ. Des. **20**(3), 237–253 (2016). https://doi.org/10.1007/s10058-016-0191-3

11. Chun, Y., Cheng-Cheng, H., Yeh, C.-H.: A strategic implementation of the Shapley value for the nested cost-sharing problem. J. Public Econ. Theory **19**(1), 219–233 (2017)

12. Foley, D.K.: Resource allocation and the public sector. Yale Econ. Essays **7**, 45–98 (1967)

13. Goldman, J., Procaccia, A.D.: Spliddit: unleashing fair division algorithms. SIGecom Exch. **13**(2), 41–46 (2015)

14. Kyropoulou, M., Suksompong, W., Voudouris, A.A.: Almost envy-freeness in group resource allocation. In: Proceedings of the 28th International Joint Conference on Artificial Intelligence (IJCAI), pp. 400–406 (2019)

15. Littlechild, S.C., Owen, G.: A simple expression for the Shapley value in a special case. Manag. Sci. **20**(3), 370–372 (1973)

16. Monderer, D., Shapley, L.S.: Potential games. Games Econ. Behav. **14**(1), 124–143 (1996)

17. Nguyen, N.-T., Rothe, J.: Local fairness in hedonic games via individual threshold coalitions. In: Proceedings of the 15th International Conference on Autonomous Agents and Multi-Agent Systems (AAMAS), pp. 232–241 (2016)

18. Pavone, M., Smith, S.L., Frazzoli, E., Rus, D.: Robotic load balancing for mobility-on-demand systems. Int. J. Robot. Res. **31**(7), 839–854 (2012)

19. Peters, D., Elkind, E.: Simple causes of complexity in hedonic games. In: Proceedings of the 24th International Joint Conference on Artificial Intelligence (IJCAI), pp. 617–623 (2015)

20. Rosenthal, R.W.: A class of games possessing pure-strategy Nash equilibria. Int. J. Game Theory **2**(1), 65–67 (1973)

21. Santi, P., Resta, G., Szell, M., Sobolevsky, S., Strogatz, S.H., Ratti, C.: Quantifying the benefits of vehicle pooling with shareability networks. Proc. Natl. Acad. Sci. **111**(37), 13290–13294 (2014)

22. Segal-Halevi, E., Nitzan, S.: Fair cake-cutting among families. Soc. Choice Welf. **53**(4), 709–740 (2019). https://doi.org/10.1007/s00355-019-01210-9

23. Shapley, L.S.: A value for n-person games. In: Kuhn, H.W., Tucker, A.W. (eds.) Contributions to the Theory of Games II, pp. 307–317. Princeton University Press, Princeton (1953)

24. Sun, N., Yang, Z.: A general strategy proof fair allocation mechanism. Econ. Lett. **81**(1), 73–79 (2003)

25. Thomson, W.: Cost allocation and airport problems. RCER Working Papers 537. University of Rochester - Center for Economic Research (RCER) (2007)

Stable Matching with Multilayer Approval Preferences: Approvals Can Be Harder Than Strict Preferences

Matthias Bentert, Niclas Boehmer[(✉)], Klaus Heeger, and Tomohiro Koana

Algorithmics and Computational Complexity, Technische Universität Berlin,
Berlin, Germany
{matthias.bentert,niclas.boehmer,heeger,tomohiro.koana}@tu-berlin.de

Abstract. We study stable matching problems where agents have multilayer preferences: There are ℓ layers each consisting of one preference relation for each agent. Recently, Chen et al. [EC '18] studied such problems with strict preferences, establishing four multilayer adaptations of classical notions of stability. We follow up on their work by analyzing the computational complexity of stable matching problems with multilayer *approval* preferences. We consider eleven stability notions derived from three well-established stability notions for stable matchings with ties and the four adaptations proposed by Chen et al. For each stability notion, we show that the problem of finding a stable matching is either polynomial-time solvable or NP-hard. Furthermore, we examine the influence of the number of layers and the desired "degree of stability" on the problems' complexity. Somewhat surprisingly, we discover that assuming approval preferences instead of strict preferences does not considerably simplify the situation (and sometimes even makes polynomial-time solvable problems NP-hard).

1 Introduction

Problems related to matching under preference are a popular and extensively researched topic in computer science, economics, and mathematics [25]. In the classical STABLE MARRIAGE problem, we are given two sets of agents with each agent having strict preferences over the agents from the other side. A matching of agents from one side to the other is *(Gale-Shapley) stable* if there is no so-called blocking pair, i.e., a pair of agents preferring each other to their current partner. However, in reality, agents may rank the other agents with respect to multiple criteria, with each of these criteria giving rise to a different evaluation of agents. Motivated by this, Chen et al. [15] pioneered the study of STABLE MARRIAGE where agents have multilayer preferences. In their model, there are ℓ separate layers, and in each layer, all agents provide a strict ranking of agents from the other side. Thus, each agent specifies ℓ strict rankings, one for each layer.

Multilayer preferences are a general framework which can model a wide range of situations: for instance, as mentioned above, a layer may represent a criterion according to which agents evaluate each other. Another example concerns

© The Author(s), under exclusive license to Springer Nature Switzerland AG 2022
P. Kanellopoulos et al. (Eds.): SAGT 2022, LNCS 13584, pp. 436–453, 2022.
https://doi.org/10.1007/978-3-031-15714-1_25

uncertain situations: Here, scenarios for the future each give rise to a separate layer containing the agents' preferences in this scenario. Lastly, matching fixed groups to each other (e.g., couples or classes), preferences of the different group members may be expressed in multiple layers: Each agent represents one group and the preferences in one layer represent the preferences of one (arbitrary) group member.

Chen et al. [15] considered four different multilayer adaptations of Gale-Shapley stability and showed for each that deciding the existence of a stable matching is NP-hard even for only four layers. Motivated by this, we study a simpler preference model: multilayer *approval* preferences. Here, in each layer, instead of providing a strict ranking, agents approve some agents and disapprove all others.[1] Moving from strict to approval preferences gives us more options for stability notions. We study adaptations of the three established stability notions for stable matchings with ties and single-layer preferences: *weak*, *strong*, and *super stability* [16,25]. For instance, under the most popular *weak stability* criterion, a matching is stable if there is no pair of agents that both prefer each other to their current partner. As approval preferences are easier to cast, are often used in practice, and typically lead to better axiomatic guarantees and faster algorithms, they have already been widely applied to collective-decision problems (see, e.g., [4,12,23,34]; for voting, approval preferences even constitute their own subfield). However, approval preferences have only rarely been considered in the context of matchings under preferences because stable matchings are trivial to construct for single-layer approvals.[2] Nevertheless, (multilayer) approval preferences are of high practical relevance in matching markets, as they arise, for instance, if preferences model compatibility, availability, or simply whether agents have a certain attribute or qualification (from the other agent's perspective). For instance, when matching students for a group homework, layers could represent weekdays and two agents approve each other in some layer if they are both available on this day of the week. Alternatively, layers could represent whether students deem each other qualified with respect to different criteria (e.g., being able to solve the homework, writing down the homework, presenting the homework) or whether they have completed certain relevant previous courses.

To adapt weak, strong, and super stability to multilayer preferences, we use the following four generalizations proposed by Chen et al. [15] (the meaning of "favors" and "stability" in the following definitions depends on whether we generalize weak, strong, or super stability; see Sect. 2 for details). A matching is *all-layers stable* if it is stable in every layer. The other three generalizations are each equipped with a desired degree α of stability. A matching is α-*globally stable* if there are α layers in each of which the matching is stable. (In particular, all-layers stability is equivalent to ℓ-global stability.) A matching is α-*pair stable* if for each unmatched pair of agents, there are α layers in which one of

---

[1] In our model, agents *prefer* agents they approve to agents they disapprove and to having no partner, but are *indifferent* between the later two.

[2] E.g., a weakly stable matching corresponds to a maximal matching in the undirected part of the approval graph (see Sect. 2).

the two agents "favors" the current matching to the other agent, i.e., each pair may block in at most $\ell - \alpha$ layers. Lastly, in an α-*individually stable* matching, for each unmatched pair of agents, one of them "favors" the current matching to the other agent in at least α layers. Which of these four generalizations is appropriate depends not only on the application but also on what the different layers represent: For instance, if each layer captures a potential state of an uncertain scenario, then α-global stability may be useful to maximize the probability that stability is established. In contrast, when each agent models a group and each layer contains the preferences of a group member, α-global stability seems less appealing, as a priori the preferences of different agents within one layer are completely unrelated. Here, α-individual stability is more natural, as in an α-individually stable matching, asking two currently unmatched groups whether they prefer being together, in one of them at least α agents vote against this.

Combining weak, strong, and super stability with the four multilayer generalizations of Chen et al. [15], we analyze the computational complexity of deciding the existence of a stable matching for eleven stability notions.[3] We also consider two natural preference restrictions: symmetric approvals, where agents' approvals are mutual, and bipartite approvals, where there is a bipartition of the agents and each agent only approves or disapproves agents from the other set. Symmetric approvals arise for instance if preferences encode compatibility constraints, while in many matching markets approvals are by-design bipartite, e.g., when matching applicants to jobs, students to schools, or mentees to mentors.

1.1 Related Work

Chen et al. [15] proved that deciding whether an α-globally/pair stable matching exists is NP-hard for any $2 \leq \alpha \leq \ell$ for STABLE MARRIAGE with strict preferences. For individual stability they proved that the problem is polynomial-time solvable for $\alpha = \ell$ but NP-hard for $2 \leq \alpha \leq \frac{2}{3}\ell$. Moreover, they identified two preference restrictions that lead to polynomial-time solvability: for α-global stability if, within each layer, all agents from one side have the same preferences, and for α-pair and α-individual stability with $\alpha > \lfloor \ell/2 \rfloor$ if the preferences of agents from one side do not change between different layers. In sum, our work differs from Chen et al.'s work in the following points: We consider approval instead of strict preferences (leading to eleven algorithmic questions, which are all fundamentally different from the work of Chen et al.), we do not restrict ourselves to the bipartite case, and we study several new parameterizations to achieve tractability. Notably, problems equivalent to deciding whether a STABLE MARRIAGE instance with multilayer strict preferences admits an all-layers stable matching have also been studied by Miyazaki and Okamoto [27] and Aziz et al. [2]. Following up on the work of Chen et al. [15], Wen et al. [35] also studied a bipartite matching problem where agents have multilayer strict preferences over the agents from the other side. However, different from our work and

---

[3] For individual stability, we have only two stability notions depending on the definition of when an agent "favors" another agent.

Table 1. Overview of our results for different stability notions. All algorithmic results are for arbitrary (asymmetric) approvals (except the results marked with †), while all hardness results (except the ones marked with ‡) hold for symmetric approvals. Most hardness results also hold if approvals are bipartite and each agent only approves few agents.

	weak	strong	super
all-layers	NP-h. for any $\ell \geq 2$ (T. 1)	P for sy. (Pr. 2)† NP-h. for any $\ell \geq 3$ (T. 3)‡	
global	NP-h. for any $\ell \geq \alpha \geq 2$ (Pr. 1)	NP-h. and W[1]-h. wrt. α (Pr. 3) FPT wrt. ℓ for sy. (Co. 1)† XP wrt. α for sy. (Co. 1)†	P (Pr. 4)
pair	P for $\alpha \leq \lceil \ell/2 \rceil$ (T. 2)	NP-h. for any $\ell \geq 2$ and any $0 < \alpha < \ell$ (T. 4)	NP-h. for any $1 \leq \alpha \leq \ell/2$ (T. 5) P for $\alpha \geq 2\ell/3$ for sy. (T. 6)† FPT wrt. ℓ if $\alpha > \ell/2$ for sy. (T. 6)†
individual	NP-h. for any $\ell \geq 2$ and any $\alpha > \lceil \ell/2 \rceil$ (T. 2)	−	NP-h. for any $1 \leq \alpha \leq \ell/2$ (T. 5) P for $\alpha > \ell/2$ for sy. (T. 6)†

the work of Chen et al. [15], they did not consider any type of stability notion but instead studied the problem of finding a matching that minimizes different types of "dissatisfaction scores". Moreover, Steindl and Zehavi [31,32] studied a multilayer version of the house allocation problem, where agents have multilayer preferences over a set of houses (but not the other way round) and a matching of houses to agents needs to be found. Notably, they considered an extension of Pareto optimality analogous to global stability.

More generally, multilayer preferences have started to gain increasing popularity in the area of computational social choice, e.g., in multiwinner voting [19] and fair division [22,30,33]; and in their blue sky paper Boehmer and Niedermeier [11] called for a broader application of multilayer preferences in the area. Conceptually closely related, uncertain preferences, where different preferences have different probabilities, have also been studied in the areas of stable matching [1,2] and resource allocation [3]. Lastly, while we are interested in finding a single matching for multiple preference profiles, an "opposite" problem of finding a set of (proportional) matchings given a single preference profile has been studied by Boehmer et al. [8]. They focused on agents having symmetric/bipartite approval preferences.

From a technical perspective, our problems can be phrased as finding a matching fulling certain properties in some multi-layer graph, i.e., a graph with multiple edge sets defined over the same vertex set. While there exist numerous works on multilayer graphs [7,20,24], only few studied matching-related problems and all of them are different from the ones considered here (see, e.g., [14]).

1.2 Our Contributions

We conduct an extensive study of stable matching problems with multilayer approval preferences by considering four different multilayer adaptations of three traditional stability concepts. For each resulting stability notion, we show whether deciding the existence of a stable matching is polynomial-time solvable or NP-hard; often also pinpointing the complexity for all $\alpha \leq \ell \in \mathbb{N}$. See Table 1 for an overview of our results. Lastly, in Sect. 6, we analyze two parameters measuring "similarity" in the agents' preferences and show that all our problems are fixed-parameter tractable with respect to each of the two parameters. We present three important takeaways from our results already here:

First, while constructing stable matchings for weak, strong, and super stability is simple in the one-layer setting, we show that this task is NP-hard for nine of our eleven stability notions in the general multilayer case. Our hardness results are quite strong, as we often show hardness in restrictive settings, e.g., for two-layered symmetric and bipartite approvals with each agent only approving few agents. As we have only two examples of questions which are polynomial-time solvable for symmetric approvals but become NP-hard for asymmetric approvals and no such example for bipartite approvals, our results suggest that these two seemingly strong restrictions do not influence the problems' complexity much. Nevertheless, we identify some tractable cases, e.g., when we have different forms of "similarity" in the agents' preferences (Sect. 6).

Second, from an algorithmic perspective, multilayer approval preferences are not simpler than multilayer strict preferences, rather they sometimes make problems computationally harder: Comparing the picture for Gale-Shapley stability for strict preferences and its most natural analogue weak stability for approvals, we identify two questions that are polynomial-time solvable for the former but NP-hard for the latter.[4] Moreover, for strict preferences, a stable matching is guaranteed to exist for one layer, and thus for $\alpha = 1$ all problems of Chen et al. [15] are polynomial-time solvable. In contrast, for approval preferences, there are (single-layer) instances in which there is no matching which is strongly stable or super stable. In fact, we identify several cases which are already NP-hard for $\alpha = 1$ (see Table 1). However, we also find examples where approvals are "easier" than strict preferences, e.g., finding an $\lfloor \ell/2 \rfloor$-individually stable matching is polynomial-time solvable for weak stability and approval preferences but NP-hard for Gale-Shapely stability and strict preferences [15].

Third, while our complexity picture for pair and individual stability is quite similar, it is significantly different for global stability, a contrast that is seemingly not present for strict preferences. Moreover, weak, strong, and super stability also each lead to different results, with super stability being the in some sense computationally easiest of the three (which is in line with other works on stable matchings with indifferences).

2   Preliminaries

For $i \in \mathbb{N}$, we use $[i] = \{1, 2, \ldots, i\}$. For a set S, we use $\binom{S}{2}$ to denote the set of all 2-element subsets of S.

---

[4] These are finding an ℓ-individually stable matching (Theorem 2) and finding an ℓ-pair stable matching for bipartite approvals where the preferences of agents on one side do not change (Theorem 1).

Preferences and Matchings. Let $A = \{a_1, \ldots, a_n\}$ be the set of agents and $\ell \in \mathbb{N}$ be the number of layers, i.e., each agent has ℓ layers of preferences. For $i \in [\ell]$, each agent $a \in A$ approves a subset of agents $T_a^i \subseteq A$ in layer i. We say that agent a *approves* agent a' in layer i if $a' \in T_a^i$.

A matching $M \subseteq \binom{A}{2}$ is a set of agent pairs where each agent appears in at most one pair. For a matching M and an agent $a \in A$, we say that a is *matched* in M if there is an agent a' such that $\{a, a'\} \in M$; otherwise a is *unmatched.* Further, if a is matched, we denote as $M(a)$ the partner of a in M, i.e., if $\{a, a'\} \in M$, then $M(a) = a'$. If a is unmatched, then we set $M(a) := \square$. An agent a is *happy* in matching M in layer i if $M(a) \in T_a^i$ and *unhappy* otherwise. In layer $i \in [\ell]$, an agent $a \in A$ *prefers* being matched to an agent from T_a^i to being unmatched or matched to an agent from $A \setminus T_a^i$. Moreover, a is *indifferent* between being matched to any agent in T_a^i, *indifferent* between being matched to any agent in $A \setminus T_a^i$, and *indifferent* between being matched to an agent in $A \setminus T_a^i$ and being unmatched. For the sake of brevity, we also say that $a \in A$ prefers b to c in layer i if $b \in T_a^i$ and $c \in A \setminus T_a^i$, and that a is indifferent between b and c in layer i if either $b \in T_a^i$ and $c \in T_a^i$ or $b \in A \setminus T_a^i$ and $c \in A \setminus T_a^i$. Moreover, we say that $a \in A$ is indifferent in layer i between $b \in A \setminus T_a^i$ and $\square$ (which represents being unmatched). The agents' preferences in some layer $i \in [\ell]$ can also be represented as a directed (approval) graph $G_i = (A, E_i)$ whose vertices are the agents and which contains an arc from an agent a to an agent a' if a approves a' in layer i, i.e., $E_i = \{(a, a') \in A \times A \mid a' \in T_a^i\}$. Approvals are *symmetric* if an agent a approves an agent a' in some layer i if and only if a' approves a in layer i. For symmetric approvals, the approval graph for layer $i \in [\ell]$ can be modeled as an undirected graph. Approvals are *bipartite* if the graph $G = (A, \cup_{i \in [\ell]} E_i)$ is bipartite.

Notions of Stability and Their Relationships. We consider generalizations of three different established notions of stability for the single-layer setting:

Definition 1 (weak stability). *Under* weak stability, *an agent pair* $\{a, a'\} \in \binom{A}{2}$ *blocks a matching M if a and a' prefer each other to $M(a)$ and $M(a')$, respectively.*

Definition 2 (strong stability). *Under* strong stability, *an agent pair* $\{a, a'\} \in \binom{A}{2}$ *blocks a matching M if (i) a prefers a' to $M(a)$ and (ii) a' prefers a to $M(a')$ or is indifferent between a and $M(a')$ (the roles of a and a' are interchangeable).*

Definition 3 (super stability). *Under* super stability, *an agent pair* $\{a, a'\} \in \binom{A}{2}$ *blocks a matching M if (i) a prefers a' to $M(a)$ or is indifferent between a' and $M(a)$ and (ii) a' prefers a to $M(a')$ or is indifferent between a and $M(a')$.*

A matching without a blocking pair is called stable under the respective stability notion. We do not specify under which stability notion a pair blocks a matching in some layer if it is clear from context. Note that every super stable matching is strongly stable and every strongly stable matching is weakly stable.

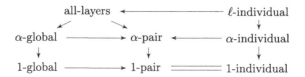

Fig. 1. Overview of the relations between different stability notions for some $\alpha \in [\ell]$ (see [15]). An arc from one notion to another implies that the first implies the second. These relationships apply to the respective adaptations of weak, strong, and super stability (there is no strong individual stability tough).

For symmetric approvals, weakly and strongly stable matchings can be nicely characterized as matchings in the undirected approval graph $G_i = (A, E_i)$: A matching M is weakly stable in layer i if and only if M restricted to E_i is a maximal matching in G_i. A matching M is strongly stable in layer i if and only if for each agent a that has a neighbor in G_i, it holds that $\{a, M(a)\} \in E_i$.

Extending the work of Chen et al. [15], we study four generalizations of the above described classic stability notions to the multilayer setting (see Fig. 1 for an overview of the relationship of the different generalizations).

Definition 4 (global and all-layers stability). *A matching M is α-globally weakly/strongly/super stable if there is a subset $S \subseteq [\ell]$ of α layers such that M is weakly/strongly/super stable in each layer from S. A matching is all-layers stable if it is ℓ-globally stable.*

Definition 5 (pair stability). *A matching M is α-pair weakly/strongly/super stable if for each pair $\{a, a'\}$ of agents there is a subset $S \subseteq [\ell]$ of at least α layers where $\{a, a'\}$ is not blocking under weak/strong/super stability.*

Definition 6 (individual stability). *A matching M is α-individually weakly (super) stable*[5] *if for each unmatched pair $\{a, a'\} \notin M$, there are α layers in which a does not approve a' or in which a is happy (in which a does not approve a' and in which a is happy). The roles of a and a' are again interchangeable.*

Individual stability can also be interpreted as follows: For each unmatched pair, at least one involved agent "favors" the current matching to the other agent from the pair in α layers (for weak stability, "favors" means prefers or is indifferent, for super stability, "favors" means prefers). By definition, every α-individually weakly/super stable matching is also α-pair weakly/super stable. The subtle difference between pair and individual stability is that for each unmatched pair, one agent needs to prevent the pair from blocking in α layers for individual stability, while the two agents together need to prevent the pair from blocking in α layers for pair stability. Note that this difference disappears for $\alpha = 1$ (1-pair weak/super stability is equivalent to 1-individual weak/super

---

[5] We call it individual "weak/super" stability since it coincides with weak/super stability for $\ell = 1$.

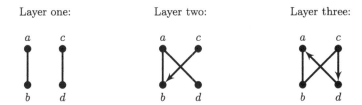

Fig. 2. Example with four agents having three-layered approval preferences over each other. An undirected edge between two agents means that they mutually approve each other in the respective layer, while a directed edge from an agent a^* to b^* means that a^* approves b^* (but b^* not a^*).

stability). In contrast, there are matchings that are all-layers weakly/super stable but not ℓ-individually weakly/super stable.[6]

Example 1. Figure 2 depicts an example with four agents and three layers. For each layer, we depict the approval graph. In the first layer, agent's approvals are symmetric but not in the other two layers. The matching $M_1 := \{\{a,b\},\{c,d\}\}$ is all-layers weakly stable, as the agents a and b are happy in all layers. Matching M_1 is 2-globally/pair strongly stable (because it is strongly stable in layers one and three) and 1-globally super stable (because it is super stable in layer one). Moreover, M_1 is 2-pair/individually super stable (as the only blocking pairs under super stability are $\{a,d\}$ in layer two and $\{b,c\}$ in layer three).

The matching $M_2 := \{\{a,d\},\{b,c\}\}$ is 2-globally/pair weakly stable (as it is weakly stable in layers two and three). However, M_2 is only 1-individually weakly stable because of the pair $\{a,b\}$. Moreover, M_2 is not α-globally/pair strongly stable and α-globally/pair/individually stable for any $\alpha > 0$, as the pair $\{a,b\}$ blocks M_2 in all layers under strong and super stability.

Given a set A of agents and their preferences $(T_a^i)_{a \in A, i \in [\ell]}$ in ℓ layers, ALL-LAYERS WEAK/STRONG/SUPER STABILITY is the problem of deciding whether there is an all-layers weakly/strongly/super stable matching. In GLOBAL WEAK/STRONG/SUPER STABILITY, we are additionally given a parameter $\alpha \in [\ell]$ and the question is to decide whether there is an α-globally weakly/strongly/super stable matching. The problems PAIR WEAK/STRONG/SUPER STABILITY and INDIVIDUAL WEAK/SUPER STABILITY are defined analogously. The proofs (or their completions) for results marked with a (★) are deferred to a full version [6].

---

[6] For example, let $A = \{a_1, a_2, a_3, a_4\}$ and $\ell = 2$ with a_1 and a_2 approving each other in the first layer and a_3 and a_4 approving each other in the second layer. Then, $M = \{\{a_1, a_2\}, \{a_3, a_4\}\}$ is all-layers super stable but not ℓ-individually super stable. Modifying the instance by letting a_1 and a_3 approve each other in both layers, M is all-layers weakly stable but not ℓ-individually weakly stable.

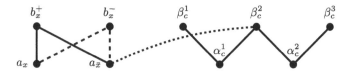

Fig. 3. Visualization of construction from Theorem 1. We depict the agents introduced for a variable x and a clause c, where $\bar{x}$ is the second literal in c. Approvals appearing only in layer 1/2 are dashed/dotted. Approvals appearing in both layers are solid.

3 Weak Stability

A weakly stable matching is guaranteed to exist in the single-layer setting: Only agents that approve each other can form a blocking pair. Thus, a maximal matching in $G = (A, \{\{a, a'\} \in \binom{A}{2} \mid a$ and a' approve each other$\})$ is weakly stable. It follows that a 1-globally/pair/individually weakly stable matching always exists and can be found in linear time.

All-Layers Stability. We start by showing that as soon as we add a second layer, ALL-LAYERS WEAK STABILITY becomes NP-hard even in very restrictive settings:

Theorem 1 (★). *For each $\ell \geq 2$, ALL-LAYERS WEAK STABILITY is NP-hard for symmetric bipartite approvals and NP-hard for (asymmetric) bipartite approvals even if agents from one side approve the same agents in both layers. Both results hold even if each agent approves at most three agents in each layer.*

Proof (construction; symmetric preferences and $\ell = 2$). We will reduce from 3-SAT, the restriction of SAT to instances where each clause contains exactly three literals. The construction is visualized in Fig. 3. Let (X, C) be an instance of 3-SAT where X is the set of variables and C the set of clauses. We construct an instance of ALL-LAYERS WEAK STABILITY with two layers and symmetric approvals. To simplify the description, we will only mention one direction of approvals, i.e., if agents a and b approve each other, then we may just write "a approves b" while omitting "b approves a". For each variable $x \in X$, we introduce a variable gadget consisting of four agents: a_x, $a_{\bar{x}}$, b_x^+, and b_x^-. In the first layer, a_x and $a_{\bar{x}}$ approve both b_x^+ and b_x^-. In the second layer, a_x and $a_{\bar{x}}$ approve b_x^+. As none of a_x, $a_{\bar{x}}$, b_x^+, and b_x^- approve other agents in the first layer, we either need to match a_x to b_x^+ and $a_{\bar{x}}$ to b_x^- (which corresponds to setting x to true) or $a_{\bar{x}}$ to b_x^+ and a_x to b_x^- (which corresponds to setting x to false) in an all-layers weakly stable matching. For each clause $c = z^1 \vee z^2 \vee z^3 \in C$, we introduce a clause gadget consisting of five agents α_c^1, α_c^2, β_c^1, β_c^2, and β_c^3. In both layers, agent α_c^1 approves agents β_c^1 and β_c^2 and agent α_c^2 approves agents β_c^2 and β_c^3. Moreover for $i \in [3]$, agent β_c^i approves a_{z^i} in the second layer. In an all-layers weakly stable matching M, for some $i \in [3]$, β_c^i will be unmatched and encodes the literal satisfying the clause: If a_{z^i} is not matched to b_x^+ in M, then β_c^i and a_{z^i} block M in the second layer. □

Since a matching is weakly stable in the case of symmetric approvals in some layer $i \in [\ell]$ if and only if it is a maximal matching in $G_i = (A, \{\{a, a'\} \mid a \in T^i_{a'}, a' \in T^i_a\})$, this also shows that finding a matching that is maximal in both layers of a two-layered graph is NP-hard. This result might be of independent interest.

Global Stability. The NP-hardness of GLOBAL WEAK STABILITY for $\alpha = \ell \geq 2$ already follows from Theorem 1. We now analyze the problem's complexity for other values of α: We have observed that GLOBAL WEAK STABILITY is linear-time solvable for $\alpha = 1$. However, by adding layers where all matchings are stable or a set of layers where a matching can be only stable in one of them, we show NP-hardness for all other values of α:

Proposition 1 (★). *For any $2 \leq \alpha \leq \ell$, GLOBAL WEAK STABILITY is NP-hard for symmetric bipartite approvals.*

Pair and Individual Stability. For $\alpha = \ell \geq 2$, Theorem 1 shows NP-hardness of PAIR WEAK STABILITY and the same construction also proves NP-hardness of INDIVIDUAL WEAK STABILITY. However, trying to extend this result to any α and ℓ, the idea of simply adding "conflicting" layers fails here, because the "stable" layers can be different for each agent/pair. Nevertheless, reducing from PAIR/INDIVIDUAL WEAK STABILITY for $\alpha = \ell = 2$ and having $\lceil \ell/2 \rceil$ copies of the first and $\lfloor \ell/2 \rfloor$ copies of the second layer, NP-hardness for any $\ell \geq 2$ and $\alpha > \lceil \ell/2 \rceil$ follows. In contrast to this, for $\alpha \leq \lceil \ell/2 \rceil$, an α-individually/pair weakly stable matching always exists:

Theorem 2 (★). *For any $\ell \geq 2$ and $\alpha \leq \lceil \ell/2 \rceil$, an α-pair/individually weakly stable matching always exists and can be found in linear time. For any $\ell \geq 2$ and $\alpha > \lceil \ell/2 \rceil$, PAIR/INDIVIDUAL WEAK STABILITY are NP-hard for symmetric bipartite approvals even if each agent approves at most three agents in each layer.*

Proof ($\alpha \leq \lceil \ell/2 \rceil$). We construct a graph G with vertex set A and an edge $\{a, a'\} \in \binom{A}{2}$ if and only if there are at least $\ell - \alpha + 1$ layers in which a approves a' and there are at least $\ell - \alpha + 1$ layers in which a' approves a. Let M be a maximal matching in G. We claim that M is α-individually weakly stable. Consider a pair $\{a, a'\}$. If $\{a, a'\} \notin E(G)$, then a does not approve a' in at least α layers or a' does not approve a in at least α layers. It follows that this pair is not blocking for α-individual weak stability. Otherwise it follows by the maximality of M that a or a' is matched by M; we assume without loss of generality that a is matched by M. Then, a is happy in M in at least $\ell - \alpha + 1 \geq \alpha$ layers, implying that a does not prefer a' to $M(a)$ in at least α layers. Thus, M is α-individually weakly stable and thereby also α-pair weakly stable.   □

Theorem 2 indicates that individual and pair stability lead to similar complexity results for weak stability, and that a low degree of stability leads to tractability for these two notions. Interestingly, the latter is in stark contrast to the results of Chen et al. [15], who showed that the problem of finding pair or individually stable matchings is polynomial-time solvable for $\alpha > \lfloor \ell/2 \rfloor$ and NP-hard for $\alpha \leq \lfloor \ell/2 \rfloor$ for strict preferences under certain constraints (note that we have results similar to Chen et al.'s for individual/pair super stability, see Theorems 5 and 6).

4   Strong Stability

In the single-layer setting, a strongly stable matching may fail to exist (consider as an example three agents all approving each other); however, deciding the existence of a strongly stable matching is polynomial-time solvable [21].

All-Layers Stability. In contrast to weak stability, for symmetric approvals ALL-LAYERS STRONG STABILITY is polynomial-time solvable.

Proposition 2. ALL-LAYERS STRONG STABILITY *for symmetric approvals can be solved in* $O(\ell n^2 + n^{2.5})$ *time.*

Proof. Recall that for some $i \in [\ell]$, $G_i = (A, E_i = \{\{a, a'\} \mid a \in T^i_{a'}, a' \in T^i_a\})$. First assume that n is even. We claim that there is an all-layers strongly stable matching if and only if there is a perfect matching in the undirected graph $H = (A, \bigcap_{i \in [\ell]} E'_i)$, where

$$E'_i := E_i \cup \{\{a, a'\} \mid a \text{ and } a' \text{ do not approve any agent in layer } i\}.$$

Note that an edge $e = \{a, a'\}$ is present in H if for every $i \in [\ell]$, either $e \in E_i$ or both a and a' have no neighbor in G_i.

Let M be a perfect matching in H. Assume towards a contradiction that there is a blocking pair $\{a, a'\}$ in some layer i. Then a and a' approve each other in layer i. Consequently, both a and a' have a neighbor in G_i and thus approve all their neighbors in (A, E'_i). As M is a perfect matching in (A, E'_i), it follows that a approves $M(a)$ and a' approves $M(a')$ in layer i, a contradiction.

Now assume that H does not admit a perfect matching. Let M be any matching. Without loss of generality, we assume that M matches all agents (note that such a matching M is not a perfect matching in H because M might include edges/pairs that are not present in H). We can assume this, as a matching can never become unstable by adding further agent pairs as agents are indifferent between being unmatched and being matched to agents they do not approve. Since M is not a perfect matching in H, matching M contains an edge $\{a, a'\} \notin E'_i$ for some $i \in [\ell]$. Consequently, a and a' do not approve each other in layer i, and one of a and a' (without loss of generality a) approves some other agent b in layer i. As approvals are symmetric, it follows that $\{a, b\}$ blocks M in layer i, implying that M is not all-layers strongly stable.

If n is odd, each matching M leaves at least one agent $a \in A$ unmatched. If a approves some agent a' in layer $i \in [\ell]$, then $\{a, a'\}$ blocks M in layer i. Thus, in an instance with an odd number of agents and a stable matching, there must be an agent a which, in each layer, does not approve any agent. If the instance does not contain such an agent, then we return that there is no stable matching. Otherwise we pick such an agent a and check whether the instance arising from the deletion of a (which has an even number of agents) has an all-layers strongly stable matching. □

For asymmetric approvals, ALL-LAYERS STRONG STABILITY becomes NP-hard. This is one of only few cases in our analysis where asymmetric and symmetric approvals computationally differ. It remains open whether ALL-LAYERS STRONG STABILITY for asymmetric (bipartite) approvals is NP-hard for two layers.

Theorem 3 (★). ALL-LAYERS STRONG STABILITY *for bipartite asymmetric approvals is NP-hard for* $\ell \geq 3$.

Global Stability. Theorem 3 also implies that GLOBAL STRONG STABILITY for asymmetric approvals is NP-hard for all $3 \leq \alpha \leq \ell$. This can be shown by adding an appropriate number of layers in which every matching is stable (e.g. layers without any approvals) and layers without any stable matching.

For symmetric approvals, on the other hand, we can solve GLOBAL STRONG STABILITY in $\binom{\ell}{\alpha} \cdot n^{O(1)}$ time: For each subset S of $[\ell]$ of size α, we check whether there is a matching stable in all layers of S using Proposition 2. This results in the following.

Corollary 1 (★). GLOBAL STRONG STABILITY *for symmetric approvals is in FPT wrt.* ℓ, *in XP wrt.* α, *and in XP wrt.* $\ell - \alpha$.

This leaves open whether GLOBAL STRONG STABILITY for symmetric approvals is in P for any α and whether it is in FPT or W[1]-hard with respect to α. Reducing from INDEPENDENT SET, we answer both questions negatively:

Proposition 3 (★). GLOBAL STRONG STABILITY *for symmetric bipartite approvals is NP-hard and W[1]-hard wrt.* α, *even if each agent approves at most two agents in each layer.*

Concerning results for arbitrary constellations of α and ℓ note that for every constant value of α or $\ell - \alpha$ the problem becomes polynomial-time solvable.

Pair Stability. In contrast to PAIR WEAK STABILITY, PAIR STRONG STABILITY is NP-hard for any $0 < \alpha < \ell$ (not just $\alpha > \lceil \ell/2 \rceil$).

Theorem 4 (★). PAIR STRONG STABILITY *for symmetric bipartite approvals is NP-hard for any* $\ell \geq 2$ *and any* $0 < \alpha < \ell$.

Notice that finding an all-layers stable matching is NP-hard for weak stability and symmetric approvals but finding a 1-pair weakly stable matching is polynomial-time solvable. The picture is reversed for strong stability and symmetric approvals.

5   Super Stability

As for strong stability, in the single-layer setting, a super stable matching might not exist, but its existence can be decided in polynomial-time [17].

All-Layers and Global Stability. We show that GLOBAL SUPER STABILITY is polynomial-time solvable (even if approvals are asymmetric). The key ingredient to this proof is the observation that each layer has at most three super stable matchings. This suggests that achieving super stability is the algorithmically easiest among our three studied stability notions.

Proposition 4 (★). GLOBAL SUPER STABILITY *can be solved in* $O(\ell n^2)$ *time.*

Pair and Individual Stability. In the following, we show a result similar to Theorem 2 which was concerned with weak stability. However, the role of $\alpha < \ell/2$ and $\alpha > \ell/2$ are reversed for super compared to weak stability. Intuitively, this comes from the fact that any matching is weakly stable if no agents approve other agents (or all agents approve each other) while no matching is super stable in these settings. We first prove that both checking for a pair or individually super stable matching is NP-hard for symmetric approvals for only two layers:

Theorem 5 (★). PAIR/INDIVIDUAL SUPER STABILITY *are NP-hard for symmetric approvals for any* $\ell \geq 2$ *and any* $\alpha \leq \ell/2$, *even if each agent approves at most four agents in each layer.*

Proof (sketch for $\ell = 2$ and $\alpha = 1$). Recall that 1-pair and 1-individually super stability are equivalent and both require that for each unmatched pair of agents there is one layer where the two agents do not approve each other and at least one of the two is happy (see Fig. 1). We reduce from the following NP-hard problem: Given a graph $G = (V, E)$ with $|V|$ even, decide whether there is a partition of $V = V' \uplus V''$ such that in $G[V']$ and in $G[V'']$ all vertices have degree one [29, Theorem 7.1].

From $G = (V, E)$, we construct an instance of PAIR/INDIVIDUAL SUPER STABILITY with two layers and $\alpha = 1$ as follows. For each vertex $v \in V$, we introduce three agents v^1, v^2, and v^*. For every edge $\{v, w\} \in E$, in the first layer, agents v^1 and w^1 approve each other and v^2 and w^2 approve each other. In the second layer, agents v^1 and v^* and agents v^2 and v^* approve each other for each $v \in V$. Moreover, we add two agents a and a' who, in both layers, do not approve any agents. The existence of these two agents implies that all other agents need to be happy in at least one layer. Thus, for each $v \in V$, either v^1 or v^2 needs to be matched to v^*. This encodes whether v is part of V' (if v^2 is matched to v^*) or V'' (if v^1 is matched to v^*). Further, this implies that for each $v \in V$ the agent from v^1 and v^2 which is not matched to v^*, say v^1, needs to be matched to an agent it approves in the first layer, i.e., some w^1 with $\{v, w\} \in E$. Moreover note that there cannot exist another agent y^1 with $\{v, y\} \in E$ and y^1 is not matched to y^*, as in this case $\{v^1, y^1\}$ blocks the matching, as both are only happy in the first layer where they approve each other. Thus in $G[V']$ and, using a similar argument also in $G[V'']$, all vertices have degree one. □

Again, for certain combinations of α and ℓ tractability can be regained.

Theorem 6 (★). *For $\alpha > \ell/2$ and symmetric approvals,* INDIVIDUAL SUPER STABILITY *is polynomial-time solvable and* PAIR SUPER STABILITY *is FPT parameterized by ℓ.* PAIR SUPER STABILITY *with symmetric approvals is polynomial-time solvable if $\alpha > 2\ell/3$.*

Notably, the FPT result for PAIR SUPER STABILITY with $\alpha > \ell/2$ and symmetric approvals excludes that this problem is NP-hard for constant ℓ and α with $\alpha > \ell/2$ and symmetric approvals (unless $P = NP$). We leave it open whether the positive results can be extended to asymmetric approvals.

6 Similarity Leads to Tractability

To circumvent the NP-hardness results from the previous sections, we start an investigation into the parameterized complexity of our problems. We focus on types of "similarity" in the agents' preferences and show for three different types that our problems become tractable when preferences are similar. Similar preferences might, for instance, occur in cases where layers correspond to objective criteria—the preferences of all agents might then be similar or even identical within a layer. We study this as uniform preferences. This type of similarity has also already been extensively studied for different stable matching problems in the context of master lists (see e. g. [9,13,18]).

Few Agent Types. We say that two agents a and a' are of the same agent type if in each layer $i \in [\ell]$, a and a' approve the "same" set of agents, i.e., $T_a^i \setminus \{a'\} = T_{a'}^i \setminus \{a\}$ and $a' \in T_a^i$ if and only if $a \in T_{a'}^i$, and are approved by the same agents, i.e., $a \in T_b^i$ if and only if $a' \in T_b^i$ for each $b \in A \setminus \{a, a'\}$ (note that the second condition is redundant in the symmetric setting). The number of agent types has proven to be a useful parameter for various stable matching problems [10,26], which is again the case here:

Theorem 7 (★). *When there are τ agent types,* GLOBAL/PAIR/INDIVIDUAL WEAK/STRONG/SUPER STABILITY *is solvable in $\mathcal{O}(2^{(\tau+1)^2} \cdot n^4 \cdot \ell)$ time.*

Uniform Approvals. Chen et al. [15] showed polynomial-time solvability for some stable matching problems with multilayer preferences if agents' preferences are uniform, i.e., when within a layer all agents have the same preferences. In our setting, this means that each agent is either approved by all or by no other agents in a layer. For symmetric approvals, the situation becomes simple: In each layer, either every pair of agents approves each other or every pair disapproves each other. Thus, for uniform symmetric approvals, all our problems are in P. For asymmetric approvals, we show that all our problems are in FPT with respect to ℓ using Theorem 7 (it is open which of our problems become polynomial-time solvable for uniform asymmetric approvals).

Corollary 2 (★). GLOBAL/PAIR/INDIVIDUAL WEAK/STRONG/SUPER STABILITY *is in FPT wrt. ℓ if in each layer each agent is either approved by all other agents or by no other agent.*

Few Agents with Changing Preferences. Lastly, we turn to situations with only few "changing" agents, i.e., agents that do not approve the same set of agents in each layer. We focus on symmetric approvals. One crucial observation here is that if a pair of non-changing agents is a blocking pair in some layer, then it is a blocking pair in all layers:

Theorem 8 (★). *Let β be the number of agents whose approval sets are not identical in all layers. For symmetric approvals,* GLOBAL/PAIR/INDIVIDUAL WEAK/STRONG/SUPER STABILITY *is in FPT wrt. β.*

Proof (sketch for weak stability). The proof works similar for global, pair, and individual stability. Let $B \subseteq A$ be the set of agents whose approval sets are not identical in all layers. For $b \in B$, let $C_b \subseteq A \setminus B$ be the set of agents from $A \setminus B$ which b approves (note that b approves each agent from C_b in all layers as approvals are symmetric). We create a set H of agents that need to be happy in all layers and a matching M as follows. We start with $H := \emptyset$ and $M := \emptyset$. For each agent $b \in B$, we guess whether b is matched to an agent from B and if so to which. If so, then we add the corresponding pair to M. If not, then we guess whether b is happy in all layers and if so, then we add b to H. Moreover, in both cases, we guess whether all agents from C_b are happy in all layers and if so, then add C_b to H. Let $B' \subseteq B$ be the set of agents currently matched in M.

We create a graph G containing the agents from $A \setminus B'$ as vertices where we connect agent $a \in A \setminus B'$ and $a' \in A \setminus B$ if a and a' approve each other in one (and thereby all) layers. We check whether there is a matching N in G that matches all agents from H. If no such matching exists, then we reject the current guess. If such a matching N exists, then we extend N arbitrarily to a maximal matching in G and set $M^* := M \cup N$. Finally, we return yes if M^* fulfills the required stability notion and otherwise reject the current guess.

Let M^* be a matching fulfilling the required stability notion. Moreover, let $\tilde{M}$ be the restriction of M^* to $G[B]$ and let $\tilde{H}$ contain each agent from B which is happy in all layers and not matched to an agent from B as well as the set C_b for each agent $b \in B$ such that all agents from C_b are happy in M^*. We claim that our algorithm returns yes for the guess resulting in $\tilde{M}$ and $\tilde{H}$. Let N be some matching that matches all agents from $\tilde{H}$ in the graph G constructed for the guess $\tilde{M}$ and $\tilde{H}$ (it is easy to see that such a matching exists, as the matching M^* restricted to G induces a matching that matches all agents from $\tilde{H}$) and that is maximal in G. Let $N^* := N \cup \tilde{M}$. We claim that the resulting matching N^* fulfills the desired weak stability notion.

Here, we only argue that no agent pair $\{a, a'\}$ with $a \in A \setminus B$ and $a' \in B$ can block N^* (and provide the arguments for the other cases in the full version [6]). Assume towards a contradiction that $\{a, a'\}$ blocks N^*. First, observe that whenever an agent $b \in B$ is happy in some layer i in M^*, then b is also happy in layer i in N^*: If $M^*(b) \in B$ for some $b \in B$, then $M^*(b) = N^*(b)$ (because of our guesses of $\tilde{M}$). Otherwise agent b is matched to an agent from $A \setminus B$ in M^*. Thus, if b is happy in some (and thereby all) layers in M^*, then by the definition of $\tilde{H}$, agent b is happy in all layers in N^*. Moreover, note that a and a' need to approve each other in at least one (and thereby all) layers to be able to form a blocking pair for N^*. As argued above, a' is happy in N^* in each layer in which it is happy in M^*. Thus, for $\{a, a'\}$ not to block M^*, there needs to be a layer where a is happy in M^* but not in N^*. This implies that a cannot be happy in all layers in N^* and thus cannot be part of $\tilde{H}$. As $a \in C_{a'}$ yet $a \notin \tilde{H}$, this implies that there is some $a^* \in C_{a'}$ that is not happy in all (and, as $a^* \in A \setminus B$, thereby not happy in any) layer in M^*. Thus, from $\{a, a'\}$ blocking N^* it follows that $\{a^*, a'\}$ blocks M^* under the considered multilayer weak stability notion, a contradiction.   □

For asymmetric approvals, obtaining even only an XP-algorithm is not possible for weak stability:

Proposition 5 (★). ALL-LAYERS WEAK STABILITY *is NP-hard for any $\ell \geq 2$ and* INDIVIDUAL WEAK STABILITY *is NP-hard for $\ell = \alpha = 2$. Both results hold for bipartite approvals, even if there is only one agent whose approval set differs between the two layers.*

We leave it open which of our problems for strong and super stability that are NP-hard for asymmetric approvals are in FPT or in XP with respect to β.

7 Conclusion

We initiated the study of stable matchings with multilayer approval preferences. We identified eleven stability notions and determined the computational complexity of deciding the existence of a stable matching for each notion. While this task turned out to be NP-hard for just two or three layers for most of the notions (even if the analogous problem for strict preferences is polynomial-time solvable), we also identified several tractable cases, e.g., when "similarity" in the agents' preferences is assumed.

For future work, note that we have posed several open questions throughout the paper, e.g., which of our problems become polynomial-time solvable if, within each layer, all agents approve the same agents. We also wonder for the two cases where we have polynomial-solvability for symmetric approvals but NP-hardness for asymmetric approvals, whether the problem is FPT with respect to the number of non-mutual approvals.

On a more conceptual note, we have argued in the introduction that multilayer preferences allow to model situations where fixed groups need to be matched to each other and each agent models a group. As groups can be of different sizes, studying situations where each agent has a different number of preference relations is also of interest. While pair and global stability seem no longer applicable, variants of individual stability still appear to be relevant.

One could also consider multilayer variants of stable matching problems with ties and incomplete lists, which would notably generalize both the models studied by us and by Chen et al. [15]. Thus, our strong intractability results already rule out the existence of efficient algorithm for many stability notions in this model.

Regarding Sect. 6, one may also consider different similarity measures, e.g. (isomorphism-based) similarity of the approval graphs of the different layers.

Lastly, studying multilayer preferences in situations where agents shall be partitioned into groups of size larger than two (also known as hedonic games [5, 28]) is a promising direction for future work.

Acknowledgements. MB was supported by the DFG project MaMu (NI 369/19). NB was supported by the DFG project MaMu (NI 369/19) and by the DFG project ComSoc-MPMS (NI 369/22). KH was supported by the DFG Research Training Group 2434 "Facets of Complexity" and by the DFG project FPTinP (NI 369/16). TK was supported by the DFG project DiPa (NI 369/21). This work was started at the research retreat of the TU Berlin Algorithmics and Computational Complexity research group held in Zinnowitz (Usedom) in September 2021.

References

1. Aziz, H., et al.: Stable matching with uncertain pairwise preferences. In: Proceedings of AAMAS-2017, pp. 344–352. ACM (2017)
2. Aziz, H., Biró, P., Gaspers, S., de Haan, R., Mattei, N., Rastegari, B.: Stable matching with uncertain linear preferences. Algorithmica **82**(5), 1410–1433 (2020)
3. Aziz, H., Biró, P., de Haan, R., Rastegari, B.: Pareto optimal allocation under uncertain preferences: uncertainty models, algorithms, and complexity. Artif. Intell. **276**, 57–78 (2019)
4. Aziz, H., Bogomolnaia, A., Moulin, H.: Fair mixing: the case of dichotomous preferences. ACM Trans. Econ. Comput. **8**(4), 18:1–18:27 (2020)
5. Aziz, H., Savani, R.: Hedonic games. In: Handbook of Computational Social Choice, pp. 356–376. Cambridge University Press, Cambridge (2016)
6. Bentert, M., Boehmer, N., Heeger, K., Koana, T.: Stable matching with multi-layer approval preferences: approvals can be harder than strict preferences. CoRR abs/2205.07550 (2022)
7. Boccaletti, S., et al.: The structure and dynamics of multilayer networks. Phys. Rep. **544**(1), 1–122 (2014)
8. Boehmer, N., Brill, M., Schmidt-Kraepelin, U.: Proportional representation in matching markets: selecting multiple matchings under dichotomous preferences. In: Proceedings of AAMAS-2022, pp. 136–144. IFAAMAS (2022)
9. Boehmer, N., Heeger, K., Niedermeier, R.: Deepening the (parameterized) complexity analysis of incremental stable matching problems. In: Proceedings of MFCS-2022. Schloss Dagstuhl - Leibniz-Zentrum für Informatik (2022, accepted for publication)
10. Boehmer, N., Heeger, K., Niedermeier, R.: Theory of and experiments on minimally invasive stability preservation in changing two-sided matching markets. In: Proceedings of AAAI-2022, pp. 4851–4858. AAAI Press (2022)
11. Boehmer, N., Niedermeier, R.: Broadening the research agenda for computational social choice: multiple preference profiles and multiple solutions. In: Proceedings of AAMAS-2021, pp. 1–5. ACM (2021)
12. Bouveret, S., Lang, J.: Efficiency and envy-freeness in fair division of indivisible goods: Logical representation and complexity. J. Artif. Intell. Res. **32**, 525–564 (2008)
13. Bredereck, R., Heeger, K., Knop, D., Niedermeier, R.: Multidimensional stable roommates with master list. In: Chen, X., Gravin, N., Hoefer, M., Mehta, R. (eds.) WINE 2020. LNCS, vol. 12495, pp. 59–73. Springer, Cham (2020). https://doi.org/10.1007/978-3-030-64946-3_5

14. Bredereck, R., Komusiewicz, C., Kratsch, S., Molter, H., Niedermeier, R., Sorge, M.: Assessing the computational complexity of multilayer subgraph detection. Netw. Sci. **7**(2), 215–241 (2019)
15. Chen, J., Niedermeier, R., Skowron, P.: Stable marriage with multi-modal preferences. In: Proceedings of EC-2018, pp. 269–286. ACM (2018)
16. Irving, R.W.: Stable marriage and indifference. Discret. Appl. Math. **48**(3), 261–272 (1994)
17. Irving, R.W., Manlove, D.F.: The stable roommates problem with ties. J. Algorithms **43**(1), 85–105 (2002)
18. Irving, R.W., Manlove, D.F., Scott, S.: The stable marriage problem with master preference lists. Discret. Appl. Math. **156**(15), 2959–2977 (2008)
19. Jain, P., Talmon, N.: Committee selection with multimodal preferences. In: Proceedings of ECAI-2020, pp. 123–130. IOS Press (2020)
20. Kivelä, M., Arenas, A., Barthelemy, M., Gleeson, J.P., Moreno, Y., Porter, M.A.: Multilayer networks. J. Complex Netw. **2**(3), 203–271 (2014)
21. Kunysz, A.: The strongly stable roommates problem. In: Proceedings of ESA-2016, pp. 60:1–60:15. Schloss Dagstuhl - Leibniz-Zentrum für Informatik (2016)
22. Kyropoulou, M., Suksompong, W., Voudouris, A.A.: Almost envy-freeness in group resource allocation. In: Proceedings of IJCAI-2019, pp. 400–406. ijcai.org (2019)
23. Lackner, M., Skowron, P.: Approval-based committee voting: axioms, algorithms, and applications. CoRR abs/2007.01795 (2020)
24. Magnani, M., Rossi, L.: The ML-model for multi-layer social networks. In: Proceedings of ASONAM-2011, pp. 5–12. IEEE Computer Society (2011)
25. Manlove, D.F.: Algorithmics of Matching Under Preferences, Series on Theoretical Computer Science, vol. 2. WorldScientific (2013)
26. Meeks, K., Rastegari, B.: Solving hard stable matching problems involving groups of similar agents. Theor. Comput. Sci. **844**, 171–194 (2020)
27. Miyazaki, S., Okamoto, K.: Jointly stable matchings. J. Comb. Optim. **38**(2), 646–665 (2019). https://doi.org/10.1007/s10878-019-00402-4
28. Peters, D.: Complexity of hedonic games with dichotomous preferences. In: Proceedings of AAAI-2016, pp. 579–585. AAAI Press (2016)
29. Schaefer, T.J.: The complexity of satisfiability problems. In: Proceedings of STOC-1978, pp. 216–226. ACM (1978)
30. Segal-Halevi, E., Suksompong, W.: Democratic fair allocation of indivisible goods. Artif. Intell. **277**, 103–167 (2019)
31. Steindl, B., Zehavi, M.: Parameterized analysis of assignment under multiple preferences. In: Rosenfeld, A., Talmon, N. (eds.) EUMAS 2021. LNCS (LNAI), vol. 12802, pp. 160–177. Springer, Cham (2021). https://doi.org/10.1007/978-3-030-82254-5_10
32. Steindl, B., Zehavi, M.: Verification of multi-layered assignment problems. In: Rosenfeld, A., Talmon, N. (eds.) EUMAS 2021. LNCS (LNAI), vol. 12802, pp. 194–210. Springer, Cham (2021). https://doi.org/10.1007/978-3-030-82254-5_12
33. Suksompong, W.: Approximate maximin shares for groups of agents. Math. Soc. Sci. **92**, 40–47 (2018)
34. Talmon, N., Faliszewski, P.: A framework for approval-based budgeting methods. In: Proceedings of AAAI-2019, pp. 2181–2188. AAAI Press (2019)
35. Wen, Y., Zhou, A., Guo, J.: Position-based matching with multi-modal preferences. In: Proceedings of AAMAS-2022, pp. 1373–1381. IFAAMAS (2022)

Collective Schedules: Axioms and Algorithms

Martin Durand and Fanny Pascual[✉]

Sorbonne Université, LIP6, CNRS, Paris, France
{martin.durand,fanny.pascual}@lip6.fr

Abstract. The collective schedules problem consists in computing a schedule of tasks shared between individuals. Tasks may have different duration, and individuals have preferences over the order of the shared tasks. This problem has numerous applications since tasks may model public infrastructure projects, events taking place in a shared room, or work done by co-workers. Our aim is, given the preferred schedules of individuals (voters), to return a consensus schedule. We propose an axiomatic study of the collective schedule problem, by using classic axioms in computational social choice and new axioms that take into account the duration of the tasks. We show that some axioms are incompatible, and we study the axioms fulfilled by three rules: one which has been studied in the seminal paper on collective schedules [17], one which generalizes the Kemeny rule, and one which generalizes Spearman's footrule. From an algorithmic point of view, we show that these rules solve NP-hard problems, but that it is possible to solve optimally these problems for small but realistic size instances, and we give an efficient heuristic for large instances. We conclude this paper with experiments.

Keywords: Computational social choice · Scheduling

1 Introduction

In this paper, we are interested in the scheduling of tasks of interest to different people, who express their preferences regarding the order of execution of the tasks. The aim is to compute a consensus schedule which aggregates as much as possible the preferences of the individuals, that we will call voters in the sequel.

This problem has numerous applications. For example, public infrastructure projects, such as extending the city subway system into several new metro lines, or simply rebuilding the sidewalks of a city, are often phased. Since workforce, machines and yearly budgets are limited, phases have to be done one after the other. The situation is then as follows: given the different phases of the project (a phase being the construction of a new metro line, or of a new sidewalk), we have to decide in which order to do the phases. Note that phases may have different duration – some may be very fast while some others may last much longer. In other words, the aim is to find a schedule of the phases, each one being considered as a task of a given duration. In order to get such a schedule, public authorities may take into account the preferences of citizens, or of citizens' representatives.

© The Author(s), under exclusive license to Springer Nature Switzerland AG 2022
P. Kanellopoulos et al. (Eds.): SAGT 2022, LNCS 13584, pp. 454–471, 2022.
https://doi.org/10.1007/978-3-031-15714-1_26

Note that tasks may not only represent public infrastructure projects, but they may also model events taking place in a shared room, or work done by co-workers (the schedule to be built being the order in which the events – or the work to be done – must follow each other).

This problem, introduced in [17], takes as input the preferred schedule of each voter (the order in which he or she would like the phases to be done), and returns one collective schedule – taking into account the preferences of the voters and the duration of the tasks. We distinguish two settings. In the first one, each voter would like each task to be scheduled as soon as possible, even if he or she has preferences over the tasks. In other words, if this were possible, all the voters would agree to schedule all the tasks simultaneously as soon as possible. This assumption – the earlier a task is scheduled the better –, will be denoted by *EB* in the sequel. It was assumed in [17], and is reasonable in many situations, in particular when tasks are public infrastructure projects. However, it is not relevant in some other situations. Consider for example workers, or members of an association, who share different works that have to be done sequentially, for example because the tasks need the same workers, or the same resource (e.g. room, tool). Each work (task) has a given duration and can imply a different investment of each worker (investment or not of a person, professional travel, staggered working hours, ...). Each worker indicates his or her favorite schedule according to his or her personal constraints and preferences. In this setting, it is natural to try to fit as much as possible to the schedules wanted by the workers – and scheduling a task much earlier than wanted by the voters is not a good thing. In this paper, our aim is to compute a socially desired collective schedule, with or without the EB assumption.

This problem generalizes the consensus ranking problem, since if all the tasks have the same unit length, the preferred schedules of the voters can be viewed as preferred rankings of tasks. Indeed, each task can be considered as a candidate (or an item), and a schedule can be considered as a ranking of the candidates (items). Computing a collective schedule in this case consists thus in computing a collective ranking, a well-known problem in computational social choice.

Related Work. Our work is at the boundary between computational social choice [6] and scheduling [7], two major domains in artificial intelligence and operational research.

As mentioned above, the collective schedule problem generalizes the collective ranking problem, which is an active field in computational social choice (see e.g. [2,5,8,12,13,16,20,21]). In this field, authors often design rules (i.e. algorithms) which return fair rankings, and they often focus on fairness in the beginning of the rankings. If the items to be ranked are recommendations (or restaurants, web pages, etc.) for users, the beginning of the ranking is indeed probably the most important part. Note that this does not hold for our problem since all the planned tasks will be executed – only their order matters. This means that rules designed for the collective ranking problem are not suitable not only because they do not consider duration for the items, but also because they focus on the beginning of the ranking. This also means that the rules we will study can be relevant for consensus ranking problems where the whole ranking is of interest.

As mentioned earlier, the collective schedule problem has been introduced in [17] for the EB setting. In this paper, the authors introduced a weighted variant of the Condorcet principle, called the PTA Condorcet principle, where PTA stands for "Processing Time Aware" (cf. page 8), and they adapted previously known Condorcet consistent rules when tasks have different processing times. They also introduced a new rule, which computes a schedule which minimizes the sum of the tardiness of tasks between the preferred schedules of the voters and the schedule which is returned. They show that the optimization problem solved by this rule is NP-hard but that it can be solved for reasonable instances with a linear program.

Up to our knowledge, there is no other work which considers the schedule of common shared tasks between voters, or agents. Multi agent scheduling problems mainly focus on cases where (usually two) agents own their *own* tasks, that are scheduled on shared machines: the aim is to find a Pareto-optimal and/or a fair schedule of the tasks of the agents, each agent being interested by her own tasks only [1,19].

We conclude this related work section by mentioning similarities between our problem and the participatory budgeting problem, which is widely studied [3]. In the participatory budgeting problem, voters give their preferences over a set of projects of different costs, and the aim is to select a socially desirable set of items of maximum cost B (a given budget). The participatory budgeting problem and the collective schedules problems have common features. They both extend a classical optimization problem when users have preferences: the participatory budgeting problem approach extends the knapsack problem when users have preferences over the items, while the collective schedules problem extends the scheduling problem when users have preferences on the order of the tasks. Moreover, when considering unit items or tasks, both problems extend famous computational social choice problems: the participatory budgeting problem generalizes the multi winner voting problem when items have the same cost, and the collective schedules problem generalizes the collective ranking problem when tasks have the same duration. For both problems, because of the costs/lengths of the items/tasks, classical algorithms used with unit items/tasks may return very bad solutions, and new algorithms are needed.

Our Contribution and Map of the Paper

- In Sect. 2, we present three rules to compute consensus schedules. We introduce the first one, that we will denote by PTA Kemeny, and which extends the well-known Kemeny rule used to compute consensus rankings in computational social choice [6]. The two other rules come from scheduling theory, and were introduced in [17]: they consist in minimizing the sum of the tardiness of tasks in the returned schedule with respect to the voters' schedules (rule ΣT), or in minimizing the sum of the deviation of tasks with respect to the voters' schedules (rule ΣD). Note that this last rule is equal to the Spearman's footrule [11] when the tasks are unitary.
- In Sect. 3, we study the axiomatic properties of the above mentioned rules by using classical social choice axioms as well as new axioms taking into

account the duration of the tasks. Table 1 summarizes our results. We also show incompatibilities between axioms: we show that a rule which is neutral, or which is based on a distance, both does not fulfill the PTA Condorcet consistency property, and can return a schedule with a sum of tardiness as far from the optimal as wanted.

- In Sect. 4, we show that the PTA Kemeny and ΣD rules solve NP-hard problems and we propose a fast heuristic which approximates the ΣD rule.
- In Sect. 5, we see that the PTA Kemeny and ΣD rules can be used for small but realistic size instances, and that the heuristic presented in the previous section returns schedules which are very close to the ones returned by ΣD. We also compare the performance of the three rules on the sum of tardiness or deviations of the tasks in the returned schedules.

Due to space constraints, some proofs are omitted. Let us now introduce formally our problem and present the three rules that we will study in the sequel.

2 Preliminaries

Definition of the Problem and Notations. Let $\mathcal{J} = \{1, \ldots, n\}$ be a set of n tasks. Each task $i \in \mathcal{J}$ has a length (or processing time) p_i. We do not consider idle times between the tasks, and preemption is not allowed: a schedule of the tasks is thus a permutation of the tasks of $\mathcal{J}$. We denote by $X^{\mathcal{J}}$ the set of all possible schedules. We denote by $V = \{1, \ldots, v\}$ the set of v voters. Each voter $k \in V$ expresses her favorite schedule $\mathcal{V}_k \in X^{\mathcal{J}}$ of the tasks in $\mathcal{J}$. The preference profile, P, is the set of these schedules: $P = \{\mathcal{V}_1, \ldots, \mathcal{V}_v\}$.

Given a schedule S, we denote by $C_i(S)$ the completion time of task i in S. We denote by $d_{i,k}$ the completion time of task i in the preferred schedule of voter k (i.e. $d_{i,k} = C_i(\mathcal{V}_k)$) – here d stands for "due date" as this completion time can be seen as a due date, as we will see in the sequel. We denote by $a \succ_S b$ the fact that task a is scheduled before task b in schedule S. This relation is transitive, therefore, if, in a schedule S, task a is scheduled first, then task b and finally task c, we can describe S as $(a \succ_S b \succ_S c)$.

An *aggregation rule* is a mapping $r : (X^{\mathcal{J}})^v \to X^{\mathcal{J}}$ that associates a schedule S – the consensus schedule – to any preference profile P. We will focus on three aggregation rules that we introduce now: ΣD, ΣT and PTA Kemeny.

Three Aggregation Rules

A) The ΣD rule. The ΣD rule is an extension of the Absolute Deviation (D) scheduling metric [7]. This metric measures the deviation between a schedule S and a set of given due dates for the tasks of the schedule. It sums, over all the tasks, the absolute value of the difference between the completion time of a task i in S and its due date. By considering the completion time $d_{i,k}$ of task i in the preferred schedule $\mathcal{V}_k$ as a due date given by voter k for task i, we express the deviation $D(S, \mathcal{V}_k)$ between schedule S and schedule $\mathcal{V}_k$ as $D(S, \mathcal{V}_k) = \sum_{i \in \mathcal{J}} |C_i(S) - d_{i,k}|$. By summing over all the voters, we obtain a metric $D(S, P)$ measuring the deviation between a schedule S and a preference profile P:

$$D(S, P) = \sum_{\mathcal{V}_k \in P} \sum_{i \in \mathcal{J}} |C_i(S) - d_{i,k}| \tag{1}$$

The ΣD rule returns a schedule S^* minimizing the deviation with the preference profile P: $D(S^*, P) = \min_{S \in \mathcal{X}^{\mathcal{J}}} D(S, P)$.

This rule was introduced (but not studied) in [17], where the authors observed that, if tasks have unitary lengths, this rule minimizes the Spearman distance, which is defined as $S(S, \mathcal{V}_k) = \sum_{i \in \mathcal{J}} |\mathbf{pos}_i(S) - \mathbf{pos}_i(\mathcal{V}_k)|$, where $\mathbf{pos}_j(S)$ is the position of item j in ranking S, i.e. the completion time of task j in schedule S if items are unitary tasks.

B) The ΣT rule. This rule, introduced in [17], extends the classical Tardiness (T) scheduling criterion [7]. The tardiness of a task i in a schedule S is 0 if task i is scheduled in S before its due date, and is equal to its delay with respect to its due date otherwise. As done for ΣD, we consider the completion time of a task i in schedule $\mathcal{V}_k$ as the due date of voter k for task i. The sum of the tardiness of the tasks in a schedule S compared to the completion times in a preference profile P is then:

$$T(S, P) = \sum_{\mathcal{V}_k \in P} \sum_{i \in \mathcal{J}} \max(0, C_i(S) - d_{i,k}) \tag{2}$$

The ΣT rule returns a schedule minimizing the sum of tardiness with P.

C) The PTA Kemeny rule. We introduce a new rule, the Processing Time Aware Kemeny rule, an extension of the well-known *Kemeny rule* [14]. The Kendall tau distance is a famous metric to measure how close two rankings are: it counts the number of pairwise disagreements between two rankings (for each pair of candidates $\{a, b\}$ it counts one if a is ranked before b in one ranking and not in the other ranking). The Kemeny rule minimizes the sum of the Kendall tau distances to the preference profile, i.e. the voter's preferred rankings.

Despite its good axiomatic properties, this rule, which does not take into account the length of the tasks, is not suitable for our collective schedules problem. Consider for example an instance with only two tasks, a short task a and a long task b. If a majority of voters prefer b to be scheduled first, then in the returned schedule it will be the case. However, in EB settings, it may be suitable that a is scheduled before b since the small task a will delay the large one b only by a small amount of time, while the contrary is not true.

We therefore propose a weighted extension of the Kemeny rule: the PTA Kemeny rule, which minimizes the sum of weighted Kendall tau distances between a schedule S and the schedules of the preference profile P. The weighted Kendall tau distance between two schedules S and $\mathcal{V}_k$ counts the weighted number of pairwise disagreements between two rankings; for each pair of tasks $\{a, b\}$ such that b is scheduled before a in $\mathcal{V}_k$ and not in S, it counts p_a. This weight measures the delay caused by task a on task b in S (whereas a caused no delay on b in $\mathcal{V}_k$). The score measuring the difference between a schedule S and P is:

$$\Delta_{PTA}(S, P) = \sum_{\mathcal{V}_k \in P} \sum_{\{a,b\} \in C^2} \mathbb{1}_{a \succ_S b, b \succ_{\mathcal{V}_k} a} \times p_a \tag{3}$$

Resoluteness. Note that each of these rules returns a schedule minimizing an optimization function, and that it is possible that several optimal schedules exist. In computational social choice, rules may be partitioned into two sets: resolute and irresolute rules. A rule is *resolute* if it always returns one single solution, and it is *irresolute* if it returns a set of solutions. Thus, rules optimizing an objective function may either be irresolute, and return all the optimal solutions, or they can be resolute and use a tie-breaking mechanism which allows to determine a unique optimal solution for each instance.

Irresolute rules have the advantage that a decision maker can choose among the optimal solutions, the one that he or she prefers. However, the set of optimal solutions can be large, and sometimes even exponential, making it difficult to compute in practice. Furthermore, in real situations, there is not always a decision maker which makes choices, and an algorithm has to return a unique solution: in this case, the rule must be resolute and needs to use a tie breaking rule that allows to decide between the optimal solutions.

In this paper, we consider that each rule returns a unique solution. However, since a good tie breaking mechanism is usually dependent on the context, we will not describe it. Instead, we will study the properties of the set of optimal solutions and see if using a tie breaking mechanism impacts the axiomatic properties of the rule – as we will see, most of the time, this will not be the case.

3   Axiomatic Properties

3.1   Neutrality and PTA Neutrality

The neutrality axiom is a classical requirement of a social choice rule. A rule is *neutral* if it does not discriminate apriori between different candidates. Note that this axiom can be fulfilled only by irresolute rules, since a resolute rule should return only one solution, even when there are only two equal length tasks a and b, and two voters: one voter who prefers that a is before b, while the other voter prefers that b is before a (the same remark holds for consensus rankings instead of consensus schedules). Therefore, in this subsection we will consider that our three rules return all the optimal solutions of the function they optimize.

Definition 1 (Neutrality). *Let r be an aggregation rule, P a preference profile, and S^* the set of solutions returned by an irresolute rule r when applied on P. Let $P_{(a \leftrightarrow b)}$ be the preference profile obtained from P by switching the positions of two candidates (tasks) a and b in all the preferences and $S^*_{(a \leftrightarrow b)}$ the set of solutions returned by r on $P_{(a \leftrightarrow b)}$. The rule r is neutral iff, for each solution S in S^*, there exists a solution $S_{(a \leftrightarrow b)}$ in $S^*_{(a \leftrightarrow b)}$, such that $S_{(a \leftrightarrow b)}$ can be obtained from S by swapping the positions of a and b.*

Proposition 1. *The ΣD rule is not neutral even if it does not apply any tie-breaking mechanism.*

As we will see later, the ΣT and the PTA Kemeny rules do not fulfill neutrality (this will be corollaries of Propositions 5 and 7).

Since neutrality leads to unsatisfactory solutions, and since we want an equal treatment between comparable tasks, we introduce the *PTA neutrality* axiom, which ensures that two tasks of equal length are considered in the same way.

Definition 2 (PTA neutrality). *Let r be an aggregation rule, P a preference profile, and $\mathcal{S}^*$ the set of solutions returned by an irresolute rule r when applied on P. Let $P_{(a\leftrightarrow b)}$ be the preference profile obtained from P by switching the positions of two tasks a and b in all the preferences and $\mathcal{S}^*_{(a\leftrightarrow b)}$ the set of solutions returned by r on $P_{(a\leftrightarrow b)}$. The rule r is PTA neutral iff, for any two tasks a and b such that $p_a = p_b$, for each solution S in $\mathcal{S}^*$, there exists a solution $S_{(a\leftrightarrow b)}$ in $\mathcal{S}^*_{(a\leftrightarrow b)}$, such that $S_{(a\leftrightarrow b)}$ can be obtained from S by swapping the positions of a and b.*

The PTA neutrality axiom extends the concept of neutrality for the cases in which tasks (candidates) have lengths (weights). This axiom ensures that two candidates with the same characteristics are treated equally. When all the tasks have the same length, the PTA neutrality axiom is equal to the neutrality axiom.

Proposition 2. *The PTA Kemeny, ΣD and ΣT rules are PTA neutral if they do not apply any tie-breaking mechanism.*

3.2   Distance

Some aggregation rules are based on the minimization of a metric. By metric, we mean a mapping between a pair of elements, most of the time a preference and a solution, and a value. Most of these rules then sum these values over the whole preference profile to evaluate the difference between a solution and a preference profile. For example, the ΣT rule returns a schedule minimizing the sum of tardiness with the preferences of the profile. If the metric is a distance (i.e. it satisfies non-negativity, identity of indiscernible, triangle inequality and symmetry), we say that the aggregation rule is "based on a distance".

Proposition 3. *The absolute deviation metric is a distance.*

Sketch of the Proof. ΣD fulfills non negativity, identity of indiscernibles, symmetry and triangle inequality because of the absolute value properties.   □

As we will see in the sequel (Propositions 6 and 8), the fact that the D metric is a distance implies that the ΣD rule is not PTA Condorcet consistent, and that it can return solutions with a sum of tardiness arbitrarily larger than the optimal sum of tardiness. Before seeing this, let us start by recalling what is the PTA Condorcet consistency property, introduced in [17].

3.3   PTA Condorcet Consistency

Definition 3 (PTA Condorcet consistency [17]). *A schedule S is PTA Condorcet consistent with a preference profile P if, for any two tasks a and b, it holds* *that a is scheduled before b in S whenever at least $\frac{p_a}{p_a+p_b} \cdot v$ voters put a before b in their preferred schedule. A scheduling rule satisfies the PTA Condorcet principle if for each preference profile it returns only the PTA Condorcet consistent schedule, whenever such a schedule exist.*

Note that if all the tasks have the same length, the PTA Condorcet consistency is equal to the well-known Condorcet consistency [9].

Proposition 4. *The PTA Kemeny rule is PTA Condorcet consistent.*

Proof. Let S be a schedule returned by the PTA Kemeny rule. For the sake of contradiction, let us suppose that, in S, there is a pair of tasks a and b such that a is scheduled before b whereas more than $\frac{p_b}{p_a+p_b} \cdot v$ voters scheduled b before a and that a PTA Condorcet schedule exists.

We study two cases. Firstly, consider the tasks a and b are scheduled consecutively in S. In that case, we call $S_{(a \leftrightarrow b)}$ the schedule obtained from S in which we swap the position of a and b. Since both schedules are identical except for the inversion of the pair $\{a, b\}$ their weighted Kendall tau scores vary only by the number of disagreements on this pair.

- We have assumed that the number v_b of voters scheduling b before a is larger than $\frac{p_b}{p_a+p_b} \cdot v$. Since in S, a is scheduled before b, the weighted disagreement of the voters on pair $\{a, b\}$ in S is larger than $\frac{p_b}{p_a+p_b} \cdot v \cdot p_a$.
- In $S_{(a \leftrightarrow b)}$, b is scheduled before a. Since $v_b > \frac{p_b}{p_a+p_b} \cdot v$, we know that the number v_a of voters scheduling a before b is smaller than $\frac{p_a}{p_a+p_b} \cdot v$. Therefore, the weighted disagreement on pair $\{a, b\}$ is smaller than $\frac{p_a}{p_a+p_b} \cdot v \cdot p_b$.

Thus the score of $S_{(a \leftrightarrow b)}$ is smaller than the one of S: S is not optimal for the PTA Kemeny rule, a contradiction.

Secondly, let us consider that a and b are not consecutive in S, and let c be the task which follows a in S. In S, it is not possible to swap two consecutive tasks to reduce the weighted Kendall tau score, otherwise the schedule could not be returned by the PTA Kemeny rule. Thus, by denoting by $S_{(a \leftrightarrow c)}$ the schedule S in which we exchange the order of tasks a and c, we get that $\Delta_{PTA}(S_{(a \leftrightarrow c)}, P) - \Delta_{PTA}(S, P) \geq 0$. This implies that $v_a \cdot p_c - v_c \cdot p_a \geq 0$ and $v_a \cdot \frac{p_c}{p_a+p_c} - v_c \cdot \frac{p_a}{p_a+p_c} \geq 0$, where $v_c = v - v_a$ is the number of voters who schedule c before a in their preferred schedule. Therefore, $v_a \geq v \cdot \frac{p_a}{p_a+p_c}$. Therefore, task a is scheduled before c in any PTA Condorcet consistent schedule. By using the same argument, we find that task c is scheduled before task d, which follows c in S, and that c has to be scheduled before d in any PTA Condorcet consistent schedule, and so forth until we meet task b. This set of tasks forms a cycle since a has to be scheduled before c in a PTA Condorcet consistent schedule, c has to be scheduled before d in a PTA Condorcet consistent schedule, ..., until we met b. Moreover b has to be scheduled before a in a PTA Condorcet consistent schedule since more than $\frac{p_b}{p_a+p_b} \cdot v$ voters scheduled b before a. The existence of this cycle means that no PTA Condorcet consistent schedule exists for the profile, a contradiction. $\square$

3.4 Incompatibilities Between Axioms and Properties

One can wonder if the PTA Kemeny rule (without breaking-tie rule) is the only rule which is PTA Condorcet consistent, neutral and which fulfills reinforcement, just like the Kemeny rule is the only Condorcet consistent neutral rule fulfilling reinforcement [24]. We will show that it is not true, since PTA Kemeny does not fulfill neutrality. We even show a more general statement: no neutral rule can be PTA Condorcet consistent. This answers an open question of [17] where the author conjectured "that rules satisfying neutrality and reinforcement fail the PTA Condorcet principle" and said that "it is an interesting open question whether such an impossibility theorem holds".

Proposition 5. *No neutral rule can be PTA Condorcet consistent.*

Proof. Let us consider an instance I with an odd number of voters $v \geq 3$, two tasks a and b, such that $p_a = 1$ and $p_b = v$, and a preference profile as follows: $v_a = \frac{v-1}{2}$ voters prefer schedule $a \succ b$ (this schedule will be denoted by A), and $v_b = \frac{v+1}{2}$ voters prefer schedule $b \succ a$ (schedule denoted by B).

By contradiction, let us suppose that r is a rule which is both neutral and PTA Condorcet consistent. Since r is PTA Condorcet consistent, it will necessarily return the only PTA Condorcet consistent schedule when applied on instance I: A (indeed at least $\frac{p_a}{p_a+p_b} \cdot v = \frac{v}{v+1} \leq 1$ voter prefer to schedule a before b).

Let $P_{(a\leftrightarrow b)}$ be the preference profile obtained from P in which the positions of a and b are swapped in all the voters' preferences. Since r is neutral, it necessarily returns schedule A in which we have inverted a and b, i.e. schedule B. However, this schedule is not PTA Condorcet consistent, whereas there exists a PTA Condorcet schedule. Indeed, schedule A is a PTA Condorcet consistent schedule for $P_{(a\leftrightarrow b)}$ since at least $\frac{p_a}{p_a+p_b} \cdot v = \frac{v}{v+1} \leq 1 \leq v_a$ voters prefer to schedule a before b, while $\frac{p_b}{p_a+p_b} \cdot v = \frac{v^2}{(v+1)}$ is larger than v_b for all values of $v \geq 3$. □

This proposition implies that the PTA Kemeny rule is not neutral, even if no tie-breaking mechanism is used, since it is PTA Condorcet consistent.

Aggregation rules based on distance metrics have several good axiomatic properties [6]. However, we show that they cannot be PTA Condorcet consistent. Propositions 6, 7, and 8 can be proven in an analogous way to Proposition 5.

Proposition 6. *Any resolute aggregation rule returning a schedule minimizing a distance with the preference profile violates the PTA Condorcet consistency property. This result holds for any tie-breaking mechanism.*

Let us now show that neutrality and distance minimization can lead to very inefficient solutions for tardiness minimization.

Proposition 7. *For any $\alpha \geq 1$, there is no neutral aggregation rule returning a set of solutions S such that all the solutions in S are α-approximate for ΣT.*

Since the ΣT rule, without tie-breaking mechanism, returns only optimal solutions for the tardiness minimization, this implies that the ΣT rule is not neutral.

Proposition 8. *For any $\alpha \geq 1$, there is no aggregation rule based on a distance minimization and always returning at least one α-approximate solution for ΣT.*

3.5 Length Reduction Monotonicity

Let us now introduce a new axiomatic property, which is close to the discount monotonicity axiom [22] for the participatory budgeting problem. A rule r satisfies the *discount monotonicity* axiom if a project cannot be penalised because it is cheaper (i.e. if a project is selected by rule r then it should also be selected by this rule if its price decreases, all else being equal). We propose a new axiom, that we call *length reduction monotonicity*, and which states that the starting time of a task in a schedule cannot be delayed if its length decreases (all else being equal). This axiom is particularly meaningful in EB settings, where all the voters would like all the tasks to be scheduled as soon as possible.

Definition 4 (Length Reduction Monotonicity). *Let S be the schedule returned by a resolute rule r on instance I. Assume that we decrease the length of a task t in I, all else being equal. Let S' be the schedule returned by r on this new instance. Rule r fulfills* length reduction monotonicity *if task t does not start later in S' than in S.*

Proposition 9. *The ΣD rule does not fulfill length reduction monotonicity for any tie-breaking mechanism.*

Proof. Let us consider an instance with 5 tasks $\{1, 2, 3, x, p\}$ with $p_1 = p_2 = p_3 = p_x = 1$ and $p_p = 10$. The preferences of the 400 voters are as follows:

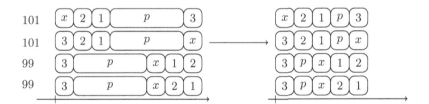

For the profile on the left, the only schedule S minimizing the absolute deviation is: $3 \succ_S p \succ_S x \succ_S 2 \succ_S 1$. For the profile on the right, the only schedule S' minimizing the absolute deviation is such that: $3 \succ_{S'} 2 \succ_{S'} x \succ_{S'} p \succ_{S'} 1$. Task p has a reduced length but it starts later in S' than in S: ΣD does not fulfill length reduction monotonicity. $\square$

3.6 Reinforcement

An aggregation rule r fulfills *reinforcement* (also known as *consistency*) [6] if, when a ranking R is returned by r on two distinct subsets of voters A and B, the same ranking R is returned by r on $A \cup B$. Since the PTA Kemeny rule sums the weighted Kendall tau score among the voters, it fulfills reinforcement.

Proposition 10. *The PTA Kemeny rule fulfills reinforcement.*

Note that the PTA Kemeny rule fulfills reinforcement and PTA Condorcet consistency, whereas the already known aggregation rules [17] for the collective schedule problem either fulfill one or the other but not both.

3.7   Unanimity

Let us now focus on the *unanimity* axiom, a well-known axiom in social choice. This axiom states that if all the voters rank candidate a higher than candidate b then, in the consensus ranking, a should be ranked higher than b. We take the same definition, replacing "rank" by "schedule":

Definition 5 (Unanimity). *Let P be a preference profile and r be an aggregation rule. The rule r fulfills* unanimity *iff when task a is scheduled before another task b in all the preferences in P, then a is scheduled before b in any solution returned by r.*

Note that this axiom is interesting through its link with precedence constraints in scheduling. Indeed, if all the voters schedule a task before another one, it may indicate that there is a dependency between the two tasks (i.e. a task must be scheduled before the other one). A rule which fulfills the unanimity axiom can then infer the precedence constraints from a preference profile.

In [17], the authors prove that the ΣT rule does not fulfill unanimity (this property is called Pareto efficiency in the paper). Let us now show that the ΣD does not fulfill this property either.

Proposition 11. *The ΣD rule does not fulfill unanimity for any tie-breaking mechanism.*

Proof. Let us consider an instance with 5 tasks $\{a, b, c, d, e\}$ such that $p_a = p_b = p_c = 10$, $p_d = p_e = 1$ and $v = 88$ voters. We consider the following preferences.

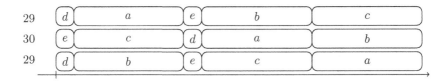

In this example, a short task e is always scheduled before a long task c in the preferences. However in the unique optimal solution S for ΣD, which is $d \succ_S c \succ_S e \succ_S a \succ_S b$, e is scheduled after c. Therefore, the ΣD rule does not fulfill unanimity.

Note that, if we reverse all the schedules in the preference profile, then the long task c is always scheduled before the short task e but has to be scheduled after the e in the optimal solution, which is S but reversed.   □

One could expect the PTA Kemeny rule to fulfill unanimity since the Kemeny rule does, and since it minimizes the pairwise disagreements with the voters. We can show that this is in fact not the case, by exhibiting a counter-example.

Proposition 12. *The PTA Kemeny rule does not fulfill unanimity for any tie-breaking mechanism.*

Note that unanimity is fulfilled if all the tasks are unit tasks. This has indeed already been shown for ΣT [17], this can easily be shown for ΣD by using an exchange argument, and this is true for PTA Kemeny since the Kemeny rule fulfills the unanimity axiom.

In our context, the unanimity axiom is not fulfilled because of the lengths of the tasks. It may indeed be better to disagree with the whole population in order to minimize the average delay or deviation, for ΣT and ΣD, or to disagree with the whole population if this disagreement has a small weight, in order to reduce other disagreements which have larger weights, for PTA Kemeny. Let us now restrict the unanimity axiom to the case where all voters agree to schedule a small task a before a large task b: we will see that the solutions returned by the PTA Kemeny rule always schedule a before b, that at least one optimal solution returned by ΣT also schedules a before b, whereas all the optimal solutions for ΣD may have to schedule b before a as we can see in the proof of Proposition 11.

Proposition 13. *Let a and b be two tasks such that $p_a \leq p_b$. If task a is always scheduled before task b in the preferences of the voters, then a is scheduled before b in any optimal schedule for the PTA Kemeny rule.*

Proof. Let us assume, by contradiction, that a schedule S such that b is scheduled before a is optimal for the PTA Kemeny rule. Let $\mathcal{S}_{(a\leftrightarrow b)}$ be the schedule obtained from S by swapping the position of a and b. Let c be a task different from a and b. If c is scheduled before b or after a in S, then the swap of a and b has no impact on the disagreements with c. If c is scheduled between a and b, then we have $b \succ_S c$ and $c \succ_S a$ and $a \succ_{\mathcal{S}_{(a\leftrightarrow b)}} c$ and $c \succ_{\mathcal{S}_{(a\leftrightarrow b)}} b$ (the order between c and the tasks other than a and b does not change between $\mathcal{S}_{(a\leftrightarrow b)}$ and S). Task a is always scheduled before task b in the preferences and $p_a \leq p_b$, therefore the overall cost of scheduling a before c is smaller than or equal to the cost of scheduling b before c. Furthermore, since a is always scheduled before b in the preferences, scheduling a before b does not create a new disagreement, whereas the cost of scheduling b before a is equal to $v \cdot p_b$. The overall cost of S is then strictly larger than the cost of $\mathcal{S}_{(a\leftrightarrow b)}$ which means that S is not optimal, a contradiction.   □

Proposition 14. *Let a and b be two tasks such that $p_a \leq p_b$. If task a is always scheduled before task b in the preferences of the voters, then a is scheduled before b in at least one optimal schedule for the ΣT rule.*

Thus, if we are looking for a single solution for ΣT, we can restrict the search to solutions fulfilling the unanimity axiom for couples of tasks for which all the voters agree that the smaller task should be scheduled first. For ΣD, we can guarantee solutions which fulfill this axiom for couples of tasks of the same length.

Proposition 15. *Let a and b be two tasks such that $p_a = p_b$. If task a is always scheduled before task b in the preferences of the voters, then a is scheduled before b in at least one optimal schedule for the ΣD rule.*

Sketch of the Proof. We compare the deviation of an optimal schedule S with b scheduled before a with the deviation of the same schedule in which the positions of a and b have been swapped. Since a and b have the same length, only their completion times change. Furthermore, since a always ends before b in the preferences, such a schedule has a deviation no larger than the deviation of S. □

We have seen that for the ΣT and PTA Kemeny rules, if a task a is scheduled before a task b and a is not longer than b, then there exists an optimal solution which schedules a before b. This is not the case for ΣD. In EB settings, we would expect well supported short tasks to be scheduled before less supported large tasks. Therefore the ΣT and PTA Kemeny rules seem well adapted for EB settings, while the ΣD rule seems less relevant in these settings.

3.8 Summary

We summarize the results shown in this section in Table 1 (a "*" means that the property has been showed in [17], the other results are shown in this paper).

Table 1. Fulfilled (✓) and unfulfilled (✗) axioms by the PTA Kemeny, ΣT and ΣD rules. Symbol $\sim$ means that the property is fulfilled by at least one optimal solution. The acronyms in the columns correspond to: neutrality (N), PTA neutrality (PTA N), reinforcement (R), PTA Condorcet consistency (PTA C), length reduction monotonicity (LRM).

Rule	N	PTA N	R	PTA C	LRM	Distance	Unanimity (a before b)		
							$p_a < p_b$	$p_a = p_b$	$p_a > p_b$
PTA K	✗	✓	✓	✓	?	✗	✓	✓	✗
ΣT	✗	✓	✓*	✗*	?	✗	$\sim$	$\sim$	✗*
ΣD	✗	✓	✓*	✗	✗	✓	✗	$\sim$	✗

4 Computational Complexity and Algorithms

In this section we study the computational complexities of the ΣD and the PTA Kemeny rules. We will then focus on resolution methods for these rules. The ΣT rule has already been proven to be strongly NP-hard [17]. In the same work, authors use linear programming to solve instances up to 20 tasks and 5000 voters, which is satisfactory since realistic instances are likely to have few tasks and a lot of voters.

The PTA Kemeny rule is NP-hard to compute since it is an extension of the Kemeny rule, which is NP-hard to compute [4]. Most of the algorithms used to compute the ranking returned by the Kemeny rule can be adapted to return the schedule returned by the PTA Kemeny rule, by adding weights on the disagreements in the resolution method. In the following section, to compute schedules returned by the PTA Kemeny rule, we will use a weighted adaptation of an exact linear programming formulation for the Kemeny rule [10].

Regarding the ΣD rule, when there are exactly two voters, the problem is easy to solve: we return one of the two schedules in the preference profile (since deviation is a distance, any other schedule would have a larger deviation to the profile because of triangle inequalities). In the general case, the problem is NP-hard, as shown below.

Theorem 1. *The problem of returning a schedule minimizing the total absolute deviation is strongly NP-hard.*

Sketch of the Proof and Remark. We prove this theorem with a polynomial time reduction from the strongly NP-hard scheduling problem $(1|no - idle|\Sigma D)$, in which a set of tasks have due dates, and the aim is to return a schedule S which minimizes the sum of the deviations between the completion time of the tasks in S and their due dates [23]. Note that the problem solved by the ΣD rule is not a generalization of this problem since in our problem the due dates given by a voter correspond to her preferred schedule, which is a feasible schedule, whereas due dates in $(1|no - idle|\Sigma D)$ are arbitrary. On the other hand, there is only one due date by task in this last problem, whereas there are v due dates by task in our problem.   □

Since computing an optimal schedule for ΣD is strongly NP-hard, we propose two resolution methods. First, we use linear programming, allowing us to solve exactly instances up to 15 tasks in less than 30 min. Second, we propose a heuristic and the use of local search to improve the solution of the heuristic.

A Heuristic for ΣD: LMT. The heuristic we propose is called LMT, which stands for "Lowest Median Time". For each task of $\mathcal{J}$, we compute its median completion time in the preferred schedules of the voters. The LMT algorithm then consists in scheduling the tasks by non decreasing median completion times.

The idea behind LMT is the following one: the closer the completion time of a task is to its median completion time, the lower is its deviation. As we will see in Sect. 5, LMT performs well in practice, even if, in the worst cases, it can lead to really unsatisfactory schedules, which can be shown by exhibiting a worst case instance.

Proposition 16. *For any $\alpha \geq 1$, LMT is not α-approximate for the total absolute deviation minimization.*

Local Search. In order to improve the solution returned by our heuristic, we propose a local search algorithm. We define the neighbourhood of a schedule S as the set of schedules obtained from S in which two consecutive tasks have been swapped. If at least one neighbour has a total deviation smaller than S, we choose the best one and we restart from it. Otherwise, S is a local optimum and we stop the algorithm. At each step, we study $(n-1)$ neighbours: the complexity is linear with the number of steps. In our experiments, by letting the algorithm reach a local optimum, we saw that the result obtained is usually very close to its local optimum at n steps and, that the local search always ends before $2n$ steps: in practice, we can bound the number of steps to $2n$ without reducing the quality of the solution.

5   Experiments

Instances. Since no database of instances for the collective schedules problem exists, we use synthetic instances. We generate two types of preference profiles: uniform (denoted below by U), in which the preferences are drawn randomly, and correlated (C) in which the preferences are drawn according to the Plackett-Luce model [15,18]. In this model, each task i has an objective utility u_i (the utilities of the tasks are drawn uniformly in the [0,1] interval). We consider that the voters pick the tasks sequentially (i.e. they choose the first task of the schedule, then the second, and so forth). When choosing a task in a subset J, each task i of J has a probability of being picked of $u_i / \sum_{j \in J} u_j$. The lengths of the tasks are chosen uniformly at random between 1 and 10 (the results do not differ when the lengths are chosen in interval [1,5]). For all the experiments, we will use linear programming (CPLEX) to compute one optimal solution for each rule. Note that for most of the instances we generated, our rules had only one optimal solution. This was the case for more than 99% of the instances for ΣT and ΣD. For PTA Kemeny, this was the case for about 90% (resp. 95%) of the instances for PTA Kemeny when the instance had 100 voters (resp. 250 voters), and for 98% of cases in correlated instances with 250 voters.

Computation Times. We run the two linear programming algorithms corresponding to the ΣD and PTA Kemeny rules. The experiments are run on a 6-core Intel i5 processor. The mean computation times can be found in Table 2.

Table 2. Mean computation times (s) for ΣD and PTA Kemeny.

Nb voters	P	ΣD			PTA Kemeny		
		$n = 4$	$n = 8$	$n = 12$	$n = 4$	$n = 8$	$n = 12$
50	U	0.01	0.28	10.4	0.004	0.02	0.05
	C	0.005	0.13	0.95	0.002	0.02	0.05
500	U	0.01	25.0	104.1	0.003	2.1	4.6
	C	0.006	13.4	47.6	0.003	1.3	3.8

These algorithms allow to solve small but realistic instances. Note that correlated instances, which are more likely to appear in realistic settings, require less computation time than uniform ones. Note also that computing an optimal schedule for PTA Kemeny is way faster than an optimal schedule for ΣD.

Performance of LMT. We now evaluate the performance of the LMT algorithm in comparison to the optimal resolution in terms of computation time and total deviation. We compute the ratio $r = D(LMT, P)/D(S^*, P)$ where S^* is a schedule returned by ΣD and LMT is a schedule returned by the LMT algorithm. We compute r before and after the local search.

The LMT algorithm alone returns solutions with a sum of deviations about 6% higher than the optimal sum of deviations. With local search, the solution improves and gets very close to the optimal solution, with on average a sum of deviation less than 1% higher than the optimal one. In terms of computation time, for 10 tasks and 100 voters, the heuristic (LMT+local search) takes 0.037 s to return its solution before the local search, and 0.63 s in total, while the linear program takes 4.5 s. This heuristic is thus a very fast and efficient alternative at rule ΣD for large instances.

Difference Between the Three Rules. We execute the three rules on 300 instances, and we compare the schedules obtained with respect to the total deviation (ΣD), the total tardiness (ΣT) and the weighted Kendall Tau score (KT). We compare each schedule obtained to the optimal schedule for the considered metric. For example, the "1.06" in column ΣT in Table 3 means that, on average, for uniform instances with 5 tasks, the schedule returned by the ΣT rule has a sum of deviation 1.06 times larger than the minimum sum of deviation.

Table 3. Performance of each rule relative to the others.

P	M	ΣD		ΣT		PTA K	
		$n = 5$	$n = 10$	$n = 5$	$n = 10$	$n = 5$	$n = 10$
U	ΣD	1	1	1.06	1.07	1.07	1.09
	ΣT	1.12	1.16	1	1	1.01	1.02
	KT	1.12	1.16	1.01	1.01	1	1
C	ΣD	1	1	1.05	1.09	1.05	1.07
	ΣT	1.06	1.08	1	1	1.001	1.001
	KT	1.07	1.07	1.002	1.01	1	1

Table 3 shows that the schedules returned by ΣT and PTA Kemeny are very close to each other (the values they obtain are very close), while the ΣD rule returns more different schedules, even if the scores obtained by the three rules do not differ from more than 16% for uniform instances and 9% for correlated instances. Note that the number of tasks does not seem to change these results. Overall, the PTA Kemeny and ΣT rules return similar schedules, in which short tasks are favored, whereas the ΣD rule seems to return schedules as close as possible to the preference profile.

Length Reduction Monotonicity (Axiom LRM). We study to what extent the length reduction monotonicity axiom is fulfilled in practice. We run the three rules on 1200 instances with 50 voters and 8 tasks. Then, we reduce the length of a random task in each of the instances, and run the three rules again. If the reduced task starts later in the schedule returned by a rule than it did before the reduction, we count one instance for which the rule violates LRM. On the 1200 instances, PTA Kemeny and ΣT always respected LRM. The ΣD rule violated LRM in 102 instances (8.5%). This percentage goes up to 12.3% on uniform instances and up to 18% on uniform instances with tasks with similar lengths.

6   Discussion and Conclusion

In this paper, we showed that some standard axioms in social choice are not adapted to the collective schedule problem, and we introduced new axioms for tasks which have duration. These axioms may also be useful in some other contexts where candidates have weights. We showed incompatibilities between axioms, showing that neutral or distance based rules are not PTA Condorcet consistent and do not approximate the sum of tardiness of the tasks.

We also studied three aggregation rules for collective schedules, from an axiomatic and an experimental viewpoint. We saw that the PTA Kemeny and the ΣT rules seem to be particularly adapted in EB settings, whereas the ΣD rule is useful in non EB settings. We conjecture that the PTA Kemeny and ΣT rules fulfill the length reduction monotonicity axiom – this is the case in our experiments but showing this from an axiomatic viewpoint is an open problem.

Acknowledgements. We acknowledge a financial support from the project THEMIS ANR-20-CE23-0018 of the French National Research Agency (ANR).

References

1. Agnetis, A., Billaut, J.C., Gawiejnowicz, S., Pacciarelli, D., Soukhal, A.: Multiagent Scheduling. Models and Algorithms. Springer, Heidelberg (2014). https://doi.org/10.1007/978-3-642-41880-8
2. Asudeh, A., Jagadish, H.V., Stoyanovich, J., Das, G.: Designing fair ranking schemes. In: Proceedings of the 2019 International Conference on Management of Data, SIGMOD 2019, pp. 1259–1276. Association for Computing Machinery (2019). https://doi.org/10.1145/3299869.3300079
3. Aziz, H., Shah, N.: Participatory budgeting: models and approaches. In: Rudas, T., Péli, G. (eds.) Pathways Between Social Science and Computational Social Science. CSS, pp. 215–236. Springer, Cham (2021). https://doi.org/10.1007/978-3-030-54936-7_10
4. Bartholdi, J., Tovey, C.A., Trick, M.A.: Voting schemes for which it can be difficult to tell who won the election. Soc. Choice Welf. **6**(2), 157–165 (1989). https://doi.org/10.1007/BF00303169
5. Biega, A.J., Gummadi, K.P., Weikum, G.: Equity of attention: amortizing individual fairness in rankings. In: The 41st International ACM SIGIR Conference on Research and Development in Information Retrieval, SIGIR 2018, pp. 405–414. Association for Computing Machinery (2018). https://doi.org/10.1145/3209978.3210063
6. Brandt, F., Conitzer, V., Endriss, U., Lang, J., Procaccia, A.D.: Handbook of Computational Social Choice. Cambridge University Press, Cambridge (2016)

7. Brucker, P.: Scheduling Algorithms, 5th edn. Springer, Heidelberg (2010)
8. Celis, L.E., Straszak, D., Vishnoi, N.K.: Ranking with fairness constraints. In: Chatzigiannakis, I., Kaklamanis, C., Marx, D., Sannella, D. (eds.) 45th International Colloquium on Automata, Languages, and Programming, ICALP. LIPIcs, vol. 107, pp. 28:1–28:15. Schloss Dagstuhl - Leibniz-Zentrum für Informatik (2018). https://doi.org/10.4230/LIPIcs.ICALP.2018.28
9. Condorcet, M.-J.-N.C.M.: Essai sur l'application de l'analyse à la probabilité des décisions rendues à la pluralité des voix (1785)
10. Conitzer, V., Davenport, A., Kalagnanam, J.: Improved bounds for computing Kemeny rankings. In: AAAI, vol. 6, pp. 620–626 (2006)
11. Diaconis, P., Graham, R.: Spearman's footrule as a measure of disarray. Stanford University, Department of Statistics (1976)
12. Dwork, C., Kumar, R., Naor, M., Sivakumar, D.: Rank aggregation methods for the web. In: Shen, V.Y., Saito, N., Lyu, M.R., Zurko, M.E. (eds.) Proceedings of the Tenth International World Wide Web Conference, WWW, pp. 613–622. ACM (2001). https://doi.org/10.1145/371920.372165
13. Geyik, S.C., Ambler, S., Kenthapadi, K.: Fairness-aware ranking in search and recommendation systems with application to linkedin talent search. In: Proceedings of the 25th ACM SIGKDD International Conference on Knowledge Discovery and Data Mining, KDD 2019, pp. 2221–2231. Association for Computing Machinery (2019). https://doi.org/10.1145/3292500.3330691
14. Kemeny, J.G.: Mathematics without numbers. Daedalus **88**(4), 577–591 (1959)
15. Luce, R.D.: Individual Choice Behavior: A Theoretical Analysis. Courier Corporation (2012)
16. Narasimhan, H., Cotter, A., Gupta, M., Wang, S.L.: Pairwise fairness for ranking and regression. In: 33rd AAAI Conference on Artificial Intelligence (2020)
17. Pascual, F., Rzadca, K., Skowron, P.: Collective schedules: scheduling meets computational social choice. In: Seventeenth International Conference on Autonomous Agents and Multiagent Systems, July 2018. https://hal.archives-ouvertes.fr/hal-01744728
18. Plackett, R.L.: The analysis of permutations. J. Roy. Stat. Soc. Ser. C (Appl. Stat.) **24**(2), 193–202 (1975). https://doi.org/10.2307/2346567. https://www.jstor.org/stable/2346567
19. Saule, E., Trystram, D.: Multi-users scheduling in parallel systems. In: 23rd IEEE International Symposium on Parallel and Distributed Processing, IPDPS, pp. 1–9. IEEE (2009). https://doi.org/10.1109/IPDPS.2009.5161037
20. Singh, A., Joachims, T.: Fairness of exposure in rankings. In: Proceedings of the 24th ACM SIGKDD International Conference on Knowledge Discovery and Data Mining, KDD 2018, pp. 2219–2228. Association for Computing Machinery (2018). https://doi.org/10.1145/3219819.3220088
21. Skowron, P., Lackner, M., Brill, M., Peters, D., Elkind, E.: Proportional rankings. In: Sierra, C. (ed.) Proceedings of the Twenty-Sixth International Joint Conference on Artificial Intelligence, IJCAI, pp. 409–415. ijcai.org (2017). https://doi.org/10.24963/ijcai.2017/58
22. Talmon, N., Faliszewski, P.: A framework for approval-based budgeting methods. In: Proceedings of the AAAI Conference on Artificial Intelligence, vol. 33, pp. 2181–2188 (2019)
23. Wan, L., Yuan, J.: Single-machine scheduling to minimize the total earliness and tardiness is strongly NP-hard. Oper. Res. Lett. **41**(4), 363–365 (2013)
24. Young, H.P., Levenglick, A.: A consistent extension of Condorcet's election principle. SIAM J. Appl. Math. **35**(2), 285–300 (1978)

Justifying Groups in Multiwinner Approval Voting

Edith Elkind[1], Piotr Faliszewski[2], Ayumi Igarashi[3], Pasin Manurangsi[4],
Ulrike Schmidt-Kraepelin[5], and Warut Suksompong[6(✉)]

[1] University of Oxford, Oxford, UK
elkind@cs.ox.ac.uk
[2] AGH University of Science and Technology, Kraków, Poland
faliszew@agh.edu.pl
[3] National Institute of Informatics, Tokyo, Japan
ayumi_igarashi@nii.ac.jp
[4] Google Research, Mountain View, USA
pasin@google.com
[5] TU Berlin, Berlin, Germany
u.schmidt-kraepelin@tu-berlin.de
[6] National University of Singapore, Singapore, Singapore
warut@comp.nus.edu.sg

Abstract. Justified representation (JR) is a standard notion of representation in multiwinner approval voting. Not only does a JR committee always exist, but previous work has also shown through experiments that the JR condition can typically be fulfilled by groups of fewer than k candidates, where k is the target size of the committee. In this paper, we study such groups—known as n/k-*justifying groups*—both theoretically and empirically. First, we show that under the impartial culture model, n/k-justifying groups of size less than $k/2$ are likely to exist, which implies that the number of JR committees is usually large. We then present efficient approximation algorithms that compute a small n/k-justifying group for any given instance, and a polynomial-time exact algorithm when the instance admits a tree representation. In addition, we demonstrate that small n/k-justifying groups can often be useful for obtaining a gender-balanced JR committee even though the problem is NP-hard.

1 Introduction

Country X needs to select a set of singers to represent it in an international song festival. Not surprisingly, each member of the selection board has preferences over the singers, depending possibly on the singers' ability and style or on the type of songs that they perform. How should the board aggregate the preferences of its members and decide on the group of singers to invite for the festival?

The problem of choosing a set of candidates based on the preferences of voters—be it singers for a song festival selected by the festival's board,

© The Author(s), under exclusive license to Springer Nature Switzerland AG 2022
P. Kanellopoulos et al. (Eds.): SAGT 2022, LNCS 13584, pp. 472–489, 2022.
https://doi.org/10.1007/978-3-031-15714-1_27

researchers selected by the conference's program committee to give full talks, or places to include on the list of world heritage sites based on votes by Internet users—is formally studied under the name of *multiwinner voting* [8]. In many applications, the voters' preferences are expressed in the form of approval ballots, wherein each voter either approves or disapproves each candidate; this is a simple yet expressive form of preference elicitation [2,10]. When selecting a committee, an important consideration is that this committee adequately represents groups of voters who share similar preferences. A natural notion of representation, which was proposed by Aziz et al. [1] and has received significant interest since then, is *justified representation (JR)*. Specifically, if there are n voters and the goal is to select k candidates, a committee is said to satisfy JR if for any group of at least n/k voters all of whom approve a common candidate, at least one of these voters approves some candidate in the committee.

A committee satisfying JR always exists for any voter preferences, and can be found by several voting procedures [1]. In fact, Bredereck et al. [4] observed experimentally that when the preferences are generated according to a range of stochastic distributions, the number of JR committees is usually very high. This observation led them to introduce the notion of an n/k-*justifying group*, which is a group of candidates that already fulfills the JR requirement even though its size may be smaller than k. Bredereck et al. found that, in their experiments, small n/k-justifying groups (containing fewer than $k/2$ candidates) typically exist. This finding helps explain why there are often numerous JR committees— indeed, to obtain a JR committee, one can start with a small n/k-justifying group and then extend it with arbitrary candidates.

The goal of our work is to conduct an extensive study of n/k-justifying groups, primarily from a theoretical perspective but also through experiments. Additionally, we demonstrate that small n/k-justifying groups can be useful for obtaining JR committees with other desirable properties such as gender balance.

1.1 Our Contribution

In Sect. 3, we present results on n/k-justifying groups and JR committees for general instances. When the voters' preferences are drawn according to the standard *impartial culture (IC)* model, in which each voter approves each candidate independently with probability p, we establish a sharp threshold on the group size: above this threshold, all groups are likely to be n/k-justifying, while below the threshold, no group is likely to be. In particular, the threshold is below $k/2$ for every value of p, thereby providing a theoretical explanation of Bredereck et al.'s findings [4]. Our result also implies that with high probability, the number of JR committees is very large, which means that the JR condition is not as stringent as it may seem. On the other hand, we show that, in the worst case, there may be very few JR committees: their number can be as small as $m - k + 1$ (where m denotes the number of candidates), and this is tight.

Next, in Sect. 4, we focus on the problem of computing a small n/k-justifying group for a given instance. While this problem is NP-hard to approximate to within a factor of $o(\ln n)$ even in the case $n = k$ (since it is equivalent to the well-known SET COVER problem in that case[1]), we show that the simple *GreedyCC* algorithm [11,12] returns an n/k-justifying group whose size is at most $O(\sqrt{n})$ times the optimal size; moreover, this factor is asymptotically tight. We then devise a new greedy algorithm, *GreedyCandidate*, with approximation ratio $O(\log(mn))$. There are several applications of multiwinner voting where the number of candidates m is either smaller or not much larger than the number of voters n; for such applications, the approximation ratio of GreedyCandidate is much better than that of GreedyCC. Further, we show that if the voters' preferences admit a *tree representation*, an optimal solution can be found in polynomial time. The tree representation condition is known to encompass several other preference restrictions [13]; interestingly, we show that it also generalizes a recently introduced class of restrictions called *1D-VCR* [9].

While small n/k-justifying groups are interesting in their own right given that they offer a high degree of representation relative to their size, an important benefit of finding such a group is that one can complement it with other candidates to obtain a JR committee with properties that one desires—the smaller the group, the more freedom one has in choosing the remaining members of the committee. We illustrate this with a common consideration in committee selection: gender balance.[2] In Sect. 5, we show that although it is easy to find a JR committee with at least one member of each gender, computing or even approximating the smallest gender imbalance subject to JR is NP-hard. Nevertheless, in Sect. 6, we demonstrate through experiments that both GreedyCC and GreedyCandidate usually find an n/k-justifying group of size less than $k/2$; by extending such a group, we obtain a gender-balanced JR committee in polynomial time. In addition, we experimentally verify our result from Sect. 3 in the IC model, and perform analogous experiments in two Euclidean models.

2   Preliminaries

There is a finite set of candidates $C = \{c_1, \ldots, c_m\}$ and a finite set of voters $N = [n]$, where we write $[t] := \{1, \ldots, t\}$ for any positive integer t. Each voter $i \in N$ submits a non-empty ballot $A_i \subseteq C$, and the goal is to select a committee, which is a subset of C of size k. Thus, an instance I of our problem can be described by a set of candidates C, a list of ballots $\mathcal{A} = (A_1, \ldots, A_n)$, and a positive integer $k \le m$; we write $I = (C, \mathcal{A}, k)$.

We are interested in representing the voters according to their ballots. Given an instance $I = (C, \mathcal{A}, k)$ with $\mathcal{A} = (A_1, \ldots, A_n)$, we say that a group of voters $N' \subseteq N$ is *cohesive* if $\cap_{i \in N'} A_i \ne \emptyset$. Further, we say that a committee W *represents* a group of voters $N' \subseteq N$ if $W \cap A_i \ne \emptyset$ for some $i \in N'$. If candidate $c_j \in W$ is approved by voter $i \in N$, we say that c_j *covers* i. We are now ready to state the justified representation axiom of Aziz et al. [1].

---

[1] In the full version of our paper [5], we extend this hardness to the case $n/k > 1$.

[2] Bredereck et al. [3] studied maximizing objective functions of committees subject to gender balance and other diversity constraints, but did not consider JR.

Definition 1 (JR). *Given an instance* $I = (C, \mathcal{A}, k)$ *with* $\mathcal{A} = (A_1, \ldots, A_n)$, *we say that a committee* $W \subseteq C$ *of size* k *provides* justified representation (JR) *for* I *if it represents every cohesive group of voters* $N' \subseteq N$ *such that* $|N'| \geq n/k$. *We refer to such a committee as a* JR *committee.*

More generally, we can extend the JR condition to groups of fewer than k candidates (the requirement that this group represents every cohesive group of at least n/k voters is with respect to the *original* parameter k). Bredereck et al. [4] called such a group of candidates an n/k-*justifying group*.

A simple yet important algorithm in this setting is *GreedyCC* [11, 12]. We consider a slight modification of this algorithm. Our algorithm starts with the empty committee and iteratively adds one candidate at a time. At each step, if there is still an unrepresented cohesive group of size at least n/k, the algorithm identifies a largest such group and adds a common approved candidate of the group to the committee. If no such group exists, the algorithm returns the current set of candidates, which is n/k-justifying by definition. It is not hard to verify that (our version of) GreedyCC runs in polynomial time and outputs an n/k-justifying group of size at most k. Sometimes we may let the algorithm continue by identifying a largest unrepresented cohesive group (of size smaller than n/k) and adding a common approved candidate of the group.

3   General Guarantees

In order to be n/k-justifying, a group may need to include k candidates in the worst case: this happens, e.g., when n is divisible by k, the first k candidates are approved by disjoint sets of n/k voters each, and the remaining $m - k$ candidates are only approved by one voter each. However, many instances admit much smaller n/k-justifying groups. Indeed, in the extreme case, if there is no cohesive group of voters, the empty group already suffices. It is therefore interesting to ask what happens in the average case. We focus on the well-studied *impartial culture (IC)* model, in which each voter approves each candidate independently with probability p. If $p = 0$, the empty group is already n/k-justifying, while if $p = 1$, any singleton group is sufficient. For each p, we establish a sharp threshold on the group size: above this threshold, all groups are likely to be n/k-justifying, while below the threshold, it is unlikely that any group is n/k-justifying.

Theorem 1. *Suppose that* m *and* k *are fixed, and let* $p \in (0, 1)$ *be a real constant and* $s \in [0, k]$ *an integer constant. Assume that the votes are distributed according to the IC model with parameter* p.

(a) *If* $p(1 - p)^s < 1/k$, *then with high probability as* $n \to \infty$, *every group of* s *candidates is* n/k-*justifying.*

(b) *If* $p(1 - p)^s > 1/k$, *then with high probability as* $n \to \infty$, *no group of* s *candidates is* n/k-*justifying.*

Here, "with high probability" means that the probability converges to 1 as $n \to \infty$. To prove this result, we will make use of the following standard probabilistic bound.

Lemma 1 (Chernoff bound). *Let $X_1, \ldots, X_t$ be independent random variables taking values in $[0, 1]$, and let $S := X_1 + \cdots + X_t$. Then, for any $\delta \in [0, 1]$,*

$$\Pr[S \geq (1 + \delta)\mathbb{E}[S]] \leq \exp\left(\frac{-\delta^2 \mathbb{E}[S]}{3}\right)$$

and

$$\Pr[S \leq (1 - \delta)\mathbb{E}[S]] \leq \exp\left(\frac{-\delta^2 \mathbb{E}[S]}{2}\right).$$

Proof (of Theorem 1). We prove part (a) and defer part (b) to the full version [5]. Let $p(1 - p)^s = 1/k - \varepsilon$ for some constant ε, and consider any group $W \subseteq C$ of size s. We claim that for any candidate $c \notin W$, with high probability as $n \to \infty$, the number of voters who approve c but do not approve any of the candidates in W is less than n/k. Since m is constant, once this claim is established, we can apply the union bound over all candidates outside W to show that W is likely to be n/k-justifying. Then, we apply the union bound over all (constant number of) groups of size s.

Fix a candidate $c \notin W$. For each $i \in [n]$, let X_i be an indicator random variable that indicates whether voter i approves c and none of the candidates in W; X_i takes the value 1 if so, and 0 otherwise. Let $X := \sum_{i=1}^{n} X_i$. We have $\mathbb{E}[X_i] = p(1 - p)^s = 1/k - \varepsilon$ for each i, and so $\mathbb{E}[X] = n(1/k - \varepsilon)$. By Lemma 1, it follows that

$$\Pr\left[X \geq \frac{n}{k}\right] \leq \exp\left(-\frac{\delta^2 n \left(\frac{1}{k} - \varepsilon\right)}{3}\right),$$

where $\delta := \min\{1, k\varepsilon/(1 - k\varepsilon)\}$ is constant. This probability converges to 0 as $n \to \infty$, proving the claim. $\qquad\square$

Theorem 1 implies that if $p < 1/k$, then the empty group is already n/k-justifying with high probability, because there is unlikely to be a sufficiently large cohesive group of voters. On the other hand, when $p > 1/k$, the threshold for the required group size s occurs when $p(1 - p)^s = 1/k$, i.e., $s = -\log_{1-p}(kp)$. For $k = 10$, the maximum s occurs at $p \approx 0.24$, where we have $s \approx 3.19$. This means that for every $p \in [0, 1]$, an arbitrary group of size 4 is likely to be n/k-justifying. Interestingly, the threshold for s never exceeds $k/2$ regardless of p.

Proposition 1. *Suppose that m and k are fixed, and let $p \in (0, 1)$ be a real constant and $s \geq k/2$ an integer constant. Assume that the votes are distributed according to the IC model with parameter p. Then, with high probability as $n \to \infty$, every group of size s is n/k-justifying.*

The proof of Proposition 1, as well as all other omitted proofs, can be found in the full version [5]. We remark that the corollary would not hold if we were to replace $k/2$ by $k/3$: indeed, for $k = 15$, the maximum s occurs at $p \approx 0.17$, where we have $s \approx 5.03 > 15/3$.

An implication of the corollary is that under the IC model, with high probability, every size-k committee provides JR. This raises the question of whether the number of JR committees is large even in the worst case. The following example shows that the answer is negative: when n is divisible by k, the number of JR committees can be as small as $m - k + 1$.

Example 1. Assume that n is divisible by k. Consider an instance $I = (C, \mathcal{A}, k)$ where

$$A_1 = \cdots = A_{\frac{n}{k}} = \{c_1\};$$
$$A_{\frac{n}{k}+1} = \cdots = A_{\frac{2n}{k}} = \{c_2\};$$

$$\vdots$$

$$A_{\frac{(k-2)n}{k}+1} = \cdots = A_{\frac{(k-1)n}{k}} = \{c_{k-1}\};$$
$$A_{\frac{(k-1)n}{k}+1} = \cdots = A_n = \{c_k, c_{k+1}, \ldots, c_m\}.$$

A JR committee must include $c_1, \ldots, c_{k-1}$; for the last slot, any of the remaining $m - k + 1$ candidates can be chosen. Hence, there are exactly $m - k + 1$ JR committees.

We complement Example 1 by establishing that, as long as every candidate is approved by at least one voter, there are always at least $m-k+1$ JR committees.[3] This matches the upper bound in Example 1 and improves upon the bound of m/k by Bredereck et al. [4, Thm. 3]. Moreover, the bound holds regardless of whether n is divisible by k.

Theorem 2. *For every instance* $I = (C, \mathcal{A}, k)$ *such that every candidate in* C *is approved by some voter, at least* $m - k + 1$ *committees of size* k *provide JR.*

4   Instance-Specific Optimization

As we have seen in Sect. 3, several instances admit an n/k-justifying group of size much smaller than the worst-case size k. However, the problem of computing a minimum-size n/k-justifying group is NP-hard to approximate to within a factor of $o(\ln n)$ even when $n = k$ (see Sect. 1.1). In this section, we address the question of how well we can approximate such a group in polynomial time.

4.1   GreedyCC

A natural approach to computing a small n/k-justifying group is to simply run (our variant of) GreedyCC, stopping as soon as the current group is n/k-justifying. However, as the following example shows, the output of this algorithm may be $\Theta(\sqrt{n})$ times larger than the optimal solution.

Example 2. Let $n = k^2$ and $m = 2k$, for some $k \geq 3$. Consider an instance $I = (C, \mathcal{A}, k)$ where

---

[3] The condition that every candidate is approved by at least one voter is necessary. Indeed, if the last approval set in Example 1 is changed from $\{c_k, c_{k+1}, \ldots, c_m\}$ to $\{c_k\}$, then there is only one JR committee: $\{c_1, c_2, \ldots, c_k\}$.

$$A_1 = \cdots = A_{k-1} = \{c_1\};$$
$$A_{(k-1)+1} = \cdots = A_{2(k-1)} = \{c_2\};$$

$$\vdots$$

$$A_{(k-2)(k-1)+1} = \cdots = A_{(k-1)^2} = \{c_{k-1}\};$$
$$A_{(k-1)^2+1} = \{c_1, c_k\};$$
$$A_{(k-1)^2+2} = \{c_2, c_k\};$$

$$\vdots$$

$$A_{k(k-1)} = \{c_{k-1}, c_k\};$$
$$A_{k(k-1)+1} = \{c_{k+1}\};$$
$$A_{k(k-1)+2} = \{c_{k+2}\};$$

$$\vdots$$

$$A_{k^2} = \{c_{2k}\}.$$

Since $c_1, \ldots, c_{k-1}$ are each approved by pairwise disjoint groups of k voters, while c_k is approved by $k-1$ voters, GreedyCC outputs the group $\{c_1, \ldots, c_{k-1}\}$. However, the singleton group $\{c_k\}$ is already n/k-justifying. The ratio between the sizes of the two groups is $(k-1) \in \Theta(\sqrt{n})$.

It turns out that Example 2 is already a worst-case scenario for GreedyCC, up to a constant factor.

Theorem 3. *For every instance* $I = (C, \mathcal{A}, k)$*, GreedyCC outputs an* n/k*-justifying group at most* $\sqrt{2n}$ *times larger than a smallest* n/k*-justifying group.*

Proof. Assume without loss of generality that $C_{\mathrm{OPT}} := \{c_1, c_2, \ldots, c_t\}$ is a smallest n/k-justifying group; our goal is to show that GreedyCC selects at most $\sqrt{2n} \cdot t$ candidates. For $j \in [t]$, we say that a candidate $c_r \in C$ (possibly $r = j$) chosen by GreedyCC *crosses* c_j if c_r is approved by some voter i who approves c_j and does not approve any candidate chosen by GreedyCC up to the point when c_r is selected. Note that each candidate selected by GreedyCC must cross some candidate in C_{OPT}—indeed, if not, the cohesive group of at least n/k voters that forces GreedyCC to select the candidate would not be represented by C_{OPT}, contradicting the assumption that C_{OPT} is n/k-justifying.

Now, we claim that for each $j \in [t]$, the candidate c_j can be crossed by at most $\sqrt{2n}$ candidates in the GreedyCC solution; this suffices for the desired conclusion. The claim is immediate if c_j is approved by at most $\sqrt{2n}$ voters, because each candidate selected by GreedyCC that crosses c_j must cover a new voter who approves c_j. Assume therefore that c_j is approved by more than $\sqrt{2n}$ voters, and suppose for contradiction that c_j is crossed by more than $\sqrt{2n}$ candidates in the GreedyCC solution. Denote these candidates by $c_{\ell_1}, \ldots, c_{\ell_s}$ in the order that GreedyCC selects them, where $s > \sqrt{2n}$. Notice that for each $i \in [s-1]$, when GreedyCC selects c_{ℓ_i}, it favors c_{ℓ_i} over c_j, which would cover at least $s - i + 1$ uncovered voters (i.e., the "crossing points" of $c_{\ell_i}, \ldots, c_{\ell_s}$ with c_j). Hence, c_{ℓ_i} itself must cover at least $s - i + 1$ uncovered voters. Moreover, c_{ℓ_s} covers at least one uncovered voter. This means that the total number of voters is at least $s + (s-1) + \cdots + 1 = s(s+1)/2 > n$, a contradiction. $\square$

Algorithm 1: GreedyCandidate

Input: An instance $(C, \mathcal{A}, k)$, where $\mathcal{A} = \{A_1, \ldots, A_n\}$
Output: An n/k-justifying group $W \subseteq C$

1   $\ell \leftarrow \lceil n/k \rceil - 1$
2   $W \leftarrow \emptyset$
3   **for** $c \in C$ **do**
4 | $B_c \leftarrow \{i \in [n] : c \in A_i\}$
5   **end**
6   **while** *there exists* $c \in C$ *such that* $|B_c| > \ell$ **do**
7 | **for** $c \in C$ **do**
8 | | $u_c \leftarrow \sum_{c' \in C}([|B_{c'}| - \ell]_+ - [|B_{c'} \setminus B_c| - \ell]_+)$
9 | **end**
10 | $c^* \leftarrow \arg\max_{c \in C} u_c$
11 | $W \leftarrow W \cup \{c^*\}$
12 | **for** $c \in C$ **do**
13 | | $B_c \leftarrow (B_c \setminus B_{c^*})$
14 | **end**
15   **end**
16   **return** W

4.2 GreedyCandidate

Next, we present a different greedy algorithm, which provides an approximation ratio of $\ln(mn) + 1$. Note that this ratio is asymptotically better than the ratio of GreedyCC in the range $m \in 2^{o(\sqrt{n})}$; several practical elections fall under this range, since the number of candidates is typically smaller or, at worst, not much larger than the number of voters (e.g., when Internet users vote upon world heritage site candidates or students elect student council members).

To understand our new algorithm, recall that GreedyCC can be viewed as a greedy covering algorithm, where the goal is to pick candidates to cover the voters. Our new algorithm instead views the problem as "covering" the candidates. Specifically, for a set of candidates $W \subseteq C$ to be an n/k-justifying group, all but at most $\ell := \lceil n/k \rceil - 1$ of the voters who approve each candidate in C must be "covered" by W. In other words, each candidate $c \in C$ must be "covered" at least $[|B_c^0| - \ell]_+$ times, where B_c^0 denotes the set of voters who approve c and we use the notation $[x]_+$ as a shorthand for $\max\{x, 0\}$. Our algorithm greedily picks in each step a candidate whose selection would minimize the corresponding potential function, $\sum_{c' \in C}[|B_{c'}| - \ell]_+$, where $B_{c'}$ denotes the set of voters who approve c' but do not approve any candidate selected by the algorithm thus far. The pseudocode of the algorithm, which we call GreedyCandidate, is presented as Algorithm 1. One can check that GreedyCandidate runs in polynomial time.

Theorem 4. *For every instance* $I = (C, \mathcal{A}, k)$, *GreedyCandidate outputs an* n/k-*justifying group that is at most* $(\ln(mn) + 1)$ *times larger than a smallest* n/k-*justifying group.*

Proof. First, note that whenever $|B_c| \leq \ell$ for all $c \in C$, every unrepresented cohesive group has size at most $\ell < n/k$, meaning that the output W of our algorithm is indeed an n/k-justifying group.

Next, let us bound the size of the output W. Assume without loss of generality that $C_{\text{OPT}} := \{c_1, c_2, \ldots, c_t\}$ is a smallest n/k-justifying group. If $t = 0$, then the while-loop immediately terminates and the algorithm outputs $W = \emptyset$. Thus, we may henceforth assume that $t \geq 1$.

For each $c \in C$, denote by B_c^i the set B_c after the i-th iteration of the while-loop (so B_c^0 is simply the set of voters who approve c). Let ψ_i denote the potential $\sum_{c' \in C} [|B_{c'}| - \ell]_+$ after the i-th iteration (so ψ_0 is the potential at the beginning). We will show that this potential decreases by at least a factor of $1 - 1/t$ with each iteration; more formally,

$$\psi_i \leq \left(1 - \frac{1}{t}\right) \cdot \psi_{i-1} \tag{1}$$

for each $i \geq 1$.

Before we prove (1), let us show how we can use it to bound $|W|$. To this end, observe that when the potential is less than 1, the while-loop terminates. This means that $\psi_{|W|-1} \geq 1$. Furthermore, we have $\psi_0 \leq \sum_{c' \in C} |B_{c'}^0| \leq mn$. Applying (1), we get

$$1 \leq \psi_{|W|-1} \leq \cdots \leq \left(1 - \frac{1}{t}\right)^{|W|-1} \cdot \psi_0 \leq e^{-\frac{|W|-1}{t}} \cdot mn,$$

where for the last inequality we use the bound $1 + x \leq e^x$, which holds for any $x \in \mathbb{R}$. Rearranging, we arrive at $|W| \leq 1 + t \ln(mn) \leq t(\ln(mn) + 1)$, as desired.

We now return to proving (1). Our assumption that C_{OPT} is an n/k-justifying group implies that $\left| B_{c'}^0 \setminus \left(\bigcup_{j=1}^t B_{c_j}^0 \right) \right| \leq \ell$ for all $c' \in C$. In each iteration, the algorithm replaces B_c by $B_c \setminus B_{c^*}$ for all c, so we also have $\left| B_{c'}^i \setminus \left(\bigcup_{j=1}^t B_{c_j}^i \right) \right| \leq \ell$ for all $c' \in C$ and i. Fix any $i \geq 1$, let $q := i - 1$, and let c^* be the candidate chosen in the i-th iteration. From the definition of c^*, we have

$$\psi_{i-1} - \psi_i = \sum_{c' \in C} \left([|B_{c'}^q| - \ell]_+ - [|B_{c'}^q \setminus B_{c^*}^q| - \ell]_+ \right)$$

$$\geq \frac{1}{t} \sum_{j=1}^t \sum_{c' \in C} \left([|B_{c'}^q| - \ell]_+ - \left[|B_{c'}^q \setminus B_{c_j}^q| - \ell \right]_+ \right)$$

$$= \psi_{i-1} - \sum_{c' \in C} \left(\frac{1}{t} \sum_{j=1}^t \left[|B_{c'}^q \setminus B_{c_j}^q| - \ell \right]_+ \right). \tag{2}$$

Consider any $c' \in C$. We claim that

$$\sum_{j=1}^t \left[|B_{c'}^q \setminus B_{c_j}^q| - \ell \right]_+ \leq (t-1) \cdot [|B_{c'}^q| - \ell]_+. \tag{3}$$

To see that (3) holds, consider the following two cases:

- $\underline{\text{Case 1}}$: $|B^q_{c'} \setminus B^q_{c_{j'}}| \leq \ell$ for some $c_{j'} \in C_{\text{OPT}}$. We may assume without loss of generality that $j' = t$. We have

$$\sum_{j=1}^{t} \left[|B^q_{c'} \setminus B^q_{c_j}| - \ell\right]_+ = \sum_{j=1}^{t-1} \left[|B^q_{c'} \setminus B^q_{c_j}| - \ell\right]_+$$

$$\leq \sum_{j=1}^{t-1} [|B^q_{c'}| - \ell]_+ = (t-1) \cdot [|B^q_{c'}| - \ell]_+ \, .$$

- $\underline{\text{Case 2}}$: $|B^q_{c'} \setminus B^q_{c_j}| > \ell$ for all $c_j \in C_{\text{OPT}}$. This means that $|B^q_{c'}| > \ell$, and

$$\sum_{j=1}^{t} \left[|B^q_{c'} \setminus B^q_{c_j}| - \ell\right]_+ = \sum_{j=1}^{t} (|B^q_{c'} \setminus B^q_{c_j}| - \ell)$$

$$= t(|B^q_{c'}| - \ell) - \sum_{j=1}^{t} |B^q_{c'} \cap B^q_{c_j}|$$

$$\leq t(|B^q_{c'}| - \ell) - (|B^q_{c'}| - \ell) = (t-1) \cdot [|B^q_{c'}| - \ell]_+ \, ,$$

where we use $\left|B^q_{c'} \setminus \left(\bigcup_{j=1}^{t} B^q_{c_j}\right)\right| \leq \ell$ for the inequality.

Hence, in both cases, (3) holds. Plugging this back into (2), we get

$$\psi_{i-1} - \psi_i \geq \psi_{i-1} - \frac{t-1}{t} \cdot \sum_{c' \in C} [|B^q_{c'}| - \ell]_+ = \frac{1}{t} \cdot \psi_{i-1}.$$

This implies (1) and completes our proof. □

Although we do not know whether an efficient $O(\ln(n))$-approximation algorithm exists, we show next that by combining Theorem 4 with a brute-force approach, we can arrive at a quasi-polynomial-time[4] algorithm that has an approximation ratio of $O(n^\delta)$ for any constant $\delta > 0$.

Theorem 5. *For any constant $\delta \in (0,1)$ there exists an $\exp(\log^{O(1)}(nm))$-time algorithm that, on input $I = (C, \mathcal{A}, k)$, outputs an n/k-justifying group that is at most $O(n^\delta)$ times larger than a smallest n/k-justifying group.*

4.3 Tree Representation

Even though computing a smallest n/k-justifying group is NP-hard even to approximate, we show in this section that this problem becomes tractable if the instance admits a *tree representation*. An instance is said to admit a tree

---

[4] Recall that a running time is said to be *quasi-polynomial* if it is of the form $\exp(\log^{O(1)} I)$, where I denotes the input size (in our case, $I = (nm)^{O(1)}$).

representation if its candidates can be arranged on a tree T in such a way that the approved candidates of each voter form a subtree of T (i.e., the subgraph of T induced by each approval set is connected). While the tree representation condition is somewhat restrictive, we remark that it is general enough to capture a number of other preference restrictions [13, Fig. 4]. In particular, we show in the full version of our paper [5] that it encompasses a recently introduced class called *1-dimensional voter/candidate range model (1D-VCR)* [9].[5]

Theorem 6. *For every instance $I = (C, \mathcal{A}, k)$ admitting a tree representation, a smallest n/k-justifying group can be computed in polynomial time.*

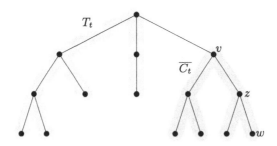

Fig. 1. Illustration for the proof of Theorem 6.

Proof. Let T be a tree representation of I, i.e., for every $i \in N$ the set A_i induces a subtree of T. Root T at an arbitrary node, and define the depth of a node in T as its distance from the root node (so the root node itself has depth 0). For each subtree $\widehat{T}$ of T, denote by $V(\widehat{T})$ the set of its nodes, and for each node $v \in V(\widehat{T})$, denote by $\widehat{T}^v$ the subtree of $\widehat{T}$ rooted at v (i.e., $\widehat{T}^v$ contains all nodes in $\widehat{T}$ whose path towards the root of $\widehat{T}$ passes v). The algorithm sets $W = \emptyset$ and proceeds as follows:

1. Select a node v of maximum depth such that there exists a set S of $\lceil n/k \rceil$ voters with the following two properties:
   (a) $A_i \subseteq V(T^v)$ for all $i \in S$;
   (b) $\bigcap_{i \in S} A_i \neq \emptyset$.
   If no such node exists, delete all candidates from C, delete the remaining tree T, and return W.
2. Add v to W, remove all voters i such that $A_i \cap V(T^v) \neq \emptyset$ from $\mathcal{A}$, and delete $V(T^v)$ from C and T^v from T. Go back to Step 1.

---

[5] Together with the results of Yang [13] and Godziszewski et al. [9], this means that the tree representation also captures the *candidate interval (CI)* and *voter interval (VI)* domains, the two most commonly studied restrictions for the approval setting, introduced by Elkind and Lackner [7].

Except for the last round, the algorithm adds one candidate to the set W in each round, so it runs for $|W| + 1$ rounds, where we slightly abuse notation and use W to refer to the final output from now on. Each round can be implemented in polynomial time—indeed, for each node v, we can consider the sets A_i that are contained in $V(T^v)$ and check whether some node in $V(T^v)$ appears in at least $\lceil n/k \rceil$ of these sets.

We now establish the correctness of the algorithm. For each round $t \in \{0, 1, \ldots, |W| + 1\}$, we define W_t to be the set of candidates selected by the algorithm up to and including round t, and T_t to be the remaining tree after round t, where round 0 refers to the point before the execution of the algorithm (so $W_0 = \emptyset$ and $T_0 = T$). We also define $\overline{C_t} := V(T) \setminus V(T_t)$ to be the set of candidates deleted up to and including round t. See Fig. 1 for an illustration.

Claim. After each round $t \in \{0, 1, \ldots, |W| + 1\}$,

(i) there exists a smallest n/k-justifying group W' of the original instance I such that $\overline{C_t} \cap W' = W_t$, and
(ii) for each $i \in N$, at least one of the following three relations holds: $A_i \subseteq \overline{C_t}$, $A_i \cap \overline{C_t} = \emptyset$, or $A_i \cap W_t \neq \emptyset$.

The proof of this claim proceeds by induction on t and is deferred to the full version [5]. As statement (i) of the claim holds in particular for $t = |W| + 1$, in which case $\overline{C_t} = C$, this concludes the proof of the theorem.   □

5   Gender Balance

In the next two sections, we demonstrate that small n/k-justifying groups can be useful for obtaining JR committees with additional properties. For concreteness, we consider a common desideratum: gender balance. Indeed, in many candidate selection scenarios, it is preferable to have a balance with respect to the gender of the committee members. Formally, assume that each candidate in C belongs to one of two types, male and female. For each committee $W \subseteq C$, we define the *gender imbalance* of W as the absolute value of the difference between the number of male candidates and the number of female candidates in W. A committee is said to be *gender-balanced* if its gender imbalance is 0.

The following example shows that gender balance can be at odds with justified representation.

Example 3. Suppose that $n = k$ is even, each voter $i \in [n-1]$ only approves a male candidate a_i, while voter n approves female candidates $b_1, \ldots, b_{n-1}$. Any JR committee must contain all of $a_1, \ldots, a_{n-1}$, and can therefore contain at most one female candidate. But there exists a (non-JR) gender-balanced committee $\{a_1, \ldots, a_{n/2}, b_1, \ldots, b_{n/2}\}$.

Example 3 is as bad as it gets: under very mild conditions, there always exists a JR committee with at least one representative of each gender.

Theorem 7. *For every instance* $I = (C, \mathcal{A}, k)$ *such that for each gender, some candidate of that gender is approved by at least one voter, there exists a JR committee with at least one member of each gender. Moreover, such a committee can be computed in polynomial time.*

In light of Theorem 7, it is natural to ask for a JR committee with the lowest gender imbalance. Unfortunately, our next result shows that deciding whether there exists a gender-balanced committee that provides JR, or even obtaining a close approximation thereof, is computationally hard.

Theorem 8. *Even when* $n = k$, *there exists a constant* $\varepsilon > 0$ *such that distinguishing between the following two cases is NP-hard:*

– *(YES) There exists a gender-balanced JR committee;*
– *(NO) Every JR committee has gender imbalance* $\geq \varepsilon k$.

It follows from Theorem 8 that one cannot hope to obtain any finite (multiplicative) approximation of the gender imbalance.

In spite of this hardness result, Proposition 1 implies that under the IC model, with high probability, there exists an n/k-justifying group of size at most $k/2$. When this is the case, one can choose the remaining members so as to make the final committee of size k gender-balanced. In the next section, we show empirically that under several probabilistic models, a small n/k-justifying group can usually be found efficiently via the greedy algorithms from Sect. 4.

6   Experiments

In this section, we conduct experiments to evaluate and complement our theoretical results. In the first experiment, we illustrate our probabilistic result for the impartial culture model (Theorem 1), and examine whether analogous results are likely to hold for two other random models. In our second experiment, we analyze how well GreedyCC and GreedyCandidate perform in finding small n/k-justifying groups. The code for our experiments is available at http://github.com/Project-PRAGMA/Justifying-Groups-SAGT-2022.

6.1   Set-up

We consider three different models for generating approval instances, all of which have been previously studied in the literature [4].[6] Each model takes as input the parameters n (number of voters), m (number of candidates), and one additional parameter, namely, either an approval probability p or a radius r.

– In the *impartial culture (IC)* model, each voter approves each of the m candidates independently with probability p. This model was already used in Theorem 1.

---

[6] In particular, we refer to the work of Elkind et al. [6] for motivation of the Euclidean models.

- In the *1D-Euclidean (1D)* model, each voter/candidate is assigned a uniformly random point in the interval $[0, 1]$. For a voter v and a candidate c, let x_v and x_c be their respective assigned points. Then, v approves c if and only if $|x_v - x_c| \leq r$.
- The *2D-Euclidean (2D)* model is a natural generalization of the 1D model where each voter/candidate is assigned a uniformly random point in the unit square $[0, 1] \times [0, 1]$. Then, a voter v approves a candidate c if and only if the Euclidean distance between their points is at most r.

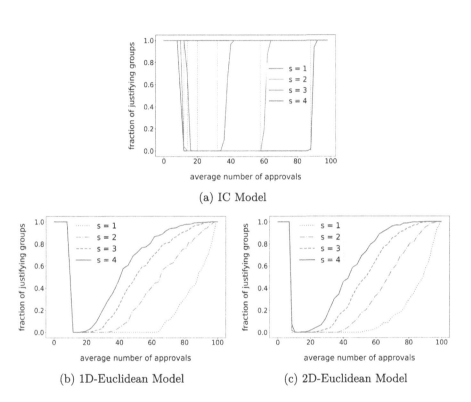

(a) IC Model

(b) 1D-Euclidean Model   (c) 2D-Euclidean Model

Fig. 2. Experimental results evaluating Theorem 1 as well as analogous settings for two Euclidean models. For each plot, the x-axis shows the average number of approvals of a voter for each parameter p (or r), and the y-axis shows the fraction of the 1000 generated elections for which a randomly selected size-s group is n/k-justifying. The dashed vertical lines indicate the transition points for large n as shown in Theorem 1.

6.2 Empirical Evaluation of Theorem 1

For our first experiment, we focus on elections with parameters $n = 5000$, $m = 100$, and $k = 10$. We chose a large number of voters as the statement of Theorem 1 concerns large values of n. For each $s \in \{1, 2, 3, 4\}$ and $p \in [0, 1)$

(in increments of 0.02), we generated 1000 elections using the IC model with parameter p. We then sampled one group of size s from each resulting election and checked whether it is n/k-justifying.

Figure 2a illustrates the fraction of generated elections for which this is the case. To make this plot comparable to analogous plots for the other two models, we label the x-axis with the average number of approvals instead of p; this number is simply $p \cdot m = 100p$. For each s, the area between the vertical dashed lines indicates the range of the interval $[0, 100]$ for which Theorem 1 shows that the probability that no size-s group is n/k-justifying converges to 1 as $n \to \infty$; this corresponds to the range of p such that $p(1-p)^s > 1/k$. For $s = 4$, Theorem 1 implies that all size-s groups are likely to be n/k-justifying for any average number of approvals in $[0, 100]$ (i.e., for any $p \in [0, 1]$) as $n \to \infty$. Hence, there are no vertical dashed lines for $s = 4$.

In Fig. 2a, we see that the empirical results match almost exactly the prediction of Theorem 1. Specifically, for $s \in \{1, 2\}$, we observe a sharp fall and rise in the fraction of n/k-justifying groups precisely at the predicted values of p. For $s = 3$, the empirical curve falls slightly before and rises slightly after the predicted points marked by the dashed lines. This is likely because the function $p(1 - p)^3$ is very close to $1/k$ in the transition areas, so $\varepsilon := 1/k - p(1 - p)^3$ as defined in the proof of Theorem 1 is very small; thus a larger value of n is needed in order for the transition to be sharp.

We carried out analogous experiments for the two Euclidean models. In particular, we iterated over $s \in \{1, 2, 3, 4\}$ and $r \in [0, 1)$ (for the 1D model) or $r \in [0, 1.2)$ (for the 2D model), again in increments of 0.02. To make the plots for different models comparable, we compute the average number of approvals induced by each value of r and label this number on the x-axis. The resulting plots, shown in Figs. 2b–2c, differ significantly from the plot for the IC model. In particular, while we see a sharp fall in the fraction of n/k-justifying groups when the average number of approvals is around 10 (for all s), there is no sharp rise as in the IC model. This suggests that a statement specifying a sharp threshold analogous to Theorem 1 for the IC model is unlikely to hold for either of the Euclidean models. Nevertheless, it remains an interesting question whether the fraction of n/k-justifying groups can be described theoretically for these models.

6.3   Performance of GreedyCC and GreedyCandidate

For our second experiment, we consider elections with parameters $n = m = 100$ and $k = 10$, and iterate over $p \in [0, 1)$ (for the IC model), $r \in [0, 1)$ (for the 1D model), and $r \in [0, 1.2)$ (for the 2D model), each in increments of 0.02. For each value of p (or r), we generated 200 elections and computed the minimum size of an n/k-justifying group (via an integer program) and the size of the n/k-justifying group returned by GreedyCC and GreedyCandidate, respectively. We aggregated these numbers across different elections by computing their average. As in the first experiment, to make the plots for different models comparable, we converted the values of p and r to the average number of approvals induced by these values. The results are shown in Fig. 3.

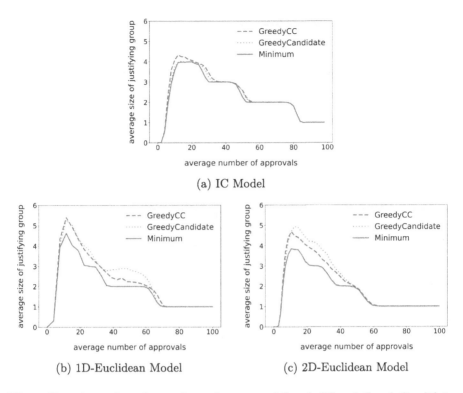

(a) IC Model

(b) 1D-Euclidean Model

(c) 2D-Euclidean Model

Fig. 3. Experimental results on the performance of GreedyCC and GreedyCandidate. For each plot, the x-axis shows the average number of approvals of a voter for each parameter p (or r), and the y-axis shows the average size of an n/k-justifying group output by GreedyCC and GreedyCandidate as well as the average size of a smallest n/k-justifying group.

In general, we observe that both GreedyCC and GreedyCandidate provide decent approximations to the minimum size of an n/k-justifying group. More precisely, the average difference between the size of a justifying group returned by GreedyCC and the minimum size is less than 1 for all three models and parameters, while for GreedyCandidate this difference is at most 1.3. The standard deviation of the size of justifying groups returned by GreedyCC and Greedy-Candidate is similar for the two Euclidean models and below 1 for all tested parameters. For the IC model, GreedyCandidate induces a smaller variance than GreedyCC. Moreover, on average, both greedy algorithms found n/k-justifying groups of size at most $k/2 = 5$ for almost all models and parameters—the only exception is the 1D model when the expected number of approvals is around 11. In absolute numbers, for this set of parameters, GreedyCC returned a justifying group of size larger than $k/2$ for 84 of the 200 instances and GreedyCandidate for 75 of the 200 instances. Interestingly, among all 32000 generated instances across all parameters, there was exactly one for which a smallest n/k-justifying group was of size larger than 5. It is also worth noting that even though Greedy-Candidate has a better worst-case guarantee than GreedyCC, this superiority is not reflected in the experiments. In particular, while GreedyCandidate performs marginally better than GreedyCC under the IC model, GreedyCC yields slightly better approximations under the Euclidean models.

We also repeated these experiments with $n = 5000$; the results are shown in our full version [5]. Notably, the plot for the IC model shows a clearer step function than Fig. 3a.

7   Conclusion and Future Work

We have investigated the notion of an n/k-justifying group introduced by Bredereck et al. [4], which allows us to reason about the justified representation (JR) condition with respect to groups smaller than the target size k. We showed that n/k-justifying groups of size less than $k/2$ typically exist, which means that the number of committees of size k satisfying JR is usually large. We also presented approximate algorithms for computing a small justifying group as well as an exact algorithm when the instance admits a tree representation. By starting with such a group, one can efficiently find a committee of size k fulfilling both JR and gender balance, even though the problem is NP-hard in the worst case.

Given the typically large number of JR committees, a natural direction is to impose desirable properties on the committee on top of JR. In addition to gender balance, several other properties have been studied by Bredereck et al. [3]. For instance, when organizing an academic workshop, one could require that at least a certain fraction of the invitees be junior researchers, or that the invitees come from a certain number of countries or continents. We expect that algorithms for computing small justifying groups will be useful for handling other diversity constraints as well.

Acknowledgments. This project has received funding from the European Research Council (ERC) under the European Union's Horizon 2020 research and innovation programme (grant agreement No 101002854), from the Deutsche Forschungsgemeinschaft under grant BR 4744/2-1, from JST PRESTO under grant number JPMJPR20C1, from the Singapore Ministry of Education under grant number MOE-T2EP20221-0001, and from an NUS Start-up Grant. We would like to thank the anonymous SAGT reviewers for their comments.

References

1. Aziz, H., Brill, M., Conitzer, V., Elkind, E., Freeman, R., Walsh, T.: Justified representation in approval-based committee voting. Soc. Choice Welfare **48**(2), 461–485 (2017). https://doi.org/10.1007/s00355-016-1019-3

2. Brams, S.J., Fishburn, P.C.: Approval Voting. Springer, New York (2007). https://doi.org/10.1007/978-0-387-49896-6

3. Bredereck, R., Faliszewski, P., Igarashi, A., Lackner, M., Skowron, P.: Multiwinner elections with diversity constraints. In: Proceedings of the 32nd AAAI Conference on Artificial Intelligence (AAAI), pp. 933–940 (2018)

4. Bredereck, R., Faliszewski, P., Kaczmarczyk, A., Niedermeier, R.: An experimental view on committees providing justified representation. In: Proceedings of the 28th International Joint Conference on Artificial Intelligence (IJCAI), pp. 109–115 (2019)

5. Elkind, E., Faliszewski, P., Igarashi, A., Manurangsi, P., Schmidt-Kraepelin, U., Suksompong, W.: Justifying groups in multiwinner approval voting. arXiv preprint arXiv:2108.12949 (2021)

6. Elkind, E., Faliszewski, P., Laslier, J.F., Skowron, P., Slinko, A., Talmon, N.: What do multiwinner voting rules do? An experiment over the two-dimensional Euclidean domain. In: Proceedings of the 31st AAAI Conference on Artificial Intelligence (AAAI), pp. 494–501 (2017)

7. Elkind, E., Lackner, M.: Structure in dichotomous preferences. In: Proceedings of the 24th International Joint Conference on Artificial Intelligence (IJCAI), pp. 2019–2025 (2015)

8. Faliszewski, P., Skowron, P., Slinko, A., Talmon, N.: Multiwinner voting: a new challenge for social choice theory. In: Endriss, U. (ed.) Trends in Computational Social Choice, chap. 2, pp. 27–47. AI Access (2017)

9. Godziszewski, M., Batko, P., Skowron, P., Faliszewski, P.: An analysis of approval-based committee rules for 2D-Euclidean elections. In: Proceedings of the 35th AAAI Conference on Artificial Intelligence (AAAI), pp. 5448–5455 (2021)

10. Kilgour, D.M.: Approval balloting for multi-winner elections. In: Laslier, J.F., Sanver, M.R. (eds.) Handbook on Approval Voting, pp. 105–124. Springer, Heidelberg (2010). https://doi.org/10.1007/978-3-642-02839-7_6

11. Lu, T., Boutilier, C.: Budgeted social choice: from consensus to personalized decision making. In: Proceedings of the 22nd International Joint Conference on Artificial Intelligence (IJCAI), pp. 280–286 (2011)

12. Nemhauser, G.L., Wolsey, L.A., Fisher, M.L.: An analysis of approximations for maximizing submodular set functions–i. Math. Program. **14**(1), 265–294 (1978)

13. Yang, Y.: On the tree representations of dichotomous preferences. In: Proceedings of the 28th International Joint Conference on Artificial Intelligence (IJCAI), pp. 644–650 (2019)

Fairness in Temporal Slot Assignment

Edith Elkind$^{(\boxtimes)}$, Sonja Kraiczy, and Nicholas Teh

Department of Computer Science, University of Oxford, Oxford, UK
{elkind,sonja.kraiczy,nicholas.teh}@cs.ox.ac.uk

Abstract. We investigate settings where projects need to be assigned to time slots based on preferences of multiple agents. We consider a variety of objectives, including utilitarian social welfare, egalitarian social welfare, Nash social welfare, Pareto optimality, equitability, and proportionality. We introduce a general-purpose randomized algorithm, which, for each of these objectives, can decide whether it is achievable for a given instance; the running time of this algorithm is in the complexity class XP with respect to the number of agents. We also provide complexity results for the case where the number of agents is large, and identify special cases that admit efficient algorithms.

1 Introduction

"Where there is an observatory and a telescope, we expect that any eyes will see new worlds at once."

—Henry David Thoreau (1817–1862)

Thoreau's words were recorded over a century ago, and yet they continue to ring true today. In July 2022, NASA's James Webb Space Telescope recorded breathtaking images of the distant cosmic cliffs and the glittering landscape of star birth in fine detail. The stunning images were made possible by the advancement of space exploring technologies, prompting widespread awe both within the scientific community and the world at large. Unsurprisingly, it is clear that no regular institution, let alone individual, could afford such highly specialized equipment for their own (research) endeavours. The new discoveries were funded by a 10 billion-dollar investment from NASA and the USA.

NASA, whose goal is to "expand knowledge for the benefit of humanity", could choose to loan its facilities (not just this telescope, but others as well) to (possibly independent) research institutes to further the exploration of space, maybe with fresh perspectives. In fact, on a smaller scale, in 2008, libraries in the US trialed the idea for loaning out telescopes, pioneered by the New Hampshire Astronomical Society. The movement has proved to be a great success, and currently, over 100 libraries across the country participates in this program. The city of Westminster in the UK also has a similar program.

Now, each institution may have their preferred schedule of equipment rental—some of them may want to see certain specific galaxies or phenomena, and due to natural conditions, they can only view them during certain time

© The Author(s), under exclusive license to Springer Nature Switzerland AG 2022
P. Kanellopoulos et al. (Eds.): SAGT 2022, LNCS 13584, pp. 490–507, 2022.
https://doi.org/10.1007/978-3-031-15714-1_28

periods. Then, the goal of NASA is to come up with a schedule for the loan of their observatories and telescopes. In doing so, multiple goals may be considered. For instance, if maximal utilization is the primary goal, then maximizing *utilitarian* welfare may be desirable, to fully utilize the telescope by filling up its schedule as much as possible. However, NASA may wish to give different institutions the opportunity to gain access to the facility and hopefully bring in new perspectives, and thus, may wish to treat different institutions fairly. Thus, other welfare objectives, such as maximizing *egalitarian* welfare, or fairness notions such as *equitability* and *proportionality* may become more relevant instead.

Other scenarios where different agents' preferences over schedules (i.e., assignments of activities to time slots) need to be aggregated into a common schedule include scheduling university lectures, conference talks or popular entertainment. Inspired by these applications, in this work, we study the problem faced by a central authority in creating a common schedule in a fair and efficient manner. In particular, we consider the computational problems associated with achieving outcomes that satisfy various welfare and fairness desiderata.

1.1   Our Contributions

We introduce a model that enables us to study welfare and fairness properties that arise in the assignment of projects to time slots when agents have approval preferences over pairs of the form (project, time slot). Throughout the paper, we assume that each project is assigned to exactly one time slot, and each time slot implements exactly one project.

To begin, we focus on the case of constant number of agents, and obtain randomized polynomial-time algorithms for all the fairness and welfare notions discussed. Also, for two agents, we show how to find an outcome that is proportional up to one slot. We then investigate the case of arbitrary number of agents. We present an efficient method for obtaining outcomes that maximize utilitarian welfare, and NP-hardness results for maximizing egalitarian welfare and for finding outcomes that are equitable or proportional. For egalitarian welfare, we obtain positive algorithmic results for an interesting special case of our problem.

1.2   Related Work

The concept of allocating projects to time slots is related to long-term (or perpetual) participatory budgeting (PB) [17,18]; however, the focus of PB is primarily on the budgetary process, rather than on distributive fairness, which affects the definitions of fairness that one considers.

Other works in the social choice literature that consider the temporal element in distributive justice include [13,14], but these works primarily focus on the dynamic setting (i.e., online reporting of preferences), and specifically on how one may obtain fair outcomes in an online fashion. Other works that look into the off-line case (albeit in different settings and considering different notions of fairness) include [3] and works in dynamic resource allocation [20].

The temporal slot assignment problem can also be re-interpreted in a spatial context, as assigning projects to plots of land (see, e.g., the work of [9]).

2   Preliminaries

We first present our basic model, and then introduce the fairness notions that we will discuss.

2.1   Model

We are given a set $N = \{1, \ldots, n\}$ of n *agents*, a set $P = \{p_1, \ldots, p_m\}$ of m distinct *projects*, and a set $T = \{t_1, \ldots, t_\ell\}$ of ℓ time slots, where $\ell \leq m$. For each time slot $r \in [\ell]$, each agent $i \in N$ specifies a subset of projects $s_{i,r} \subseteq P$: these are the projects that i approves to be implemented at time r. We write $\mathbf{s}_i = (s_{i,1}, s_{i,2}, \ldots, s_{i,\ell})$, and refer to the list $\mathbf{s}_i$ as i's *approval set*. For notational simplicity, if $s_{i,r}$ is a singleton, we sometimes omit the set notation. Equivalently, we can represent agents' preferences as graphs: for each agent $i \in N$ her *approval graph* G^i is a bipartite graph with parts P and T that contains an edge $(p_j, t_r) \in P \times T$ if and only if $p_j \in s_{i,r}$. We let $G^i_{j,r} = 1$ if $(p_j, t_r) \in G^i$, and $G^i_{j,r} = 0$ otherwise. Let μ_i be the size of a maximum matching in G^i.

An *outcome* $\mathbf{o} = (o_1, \ldots, o_\ell)$ is a list of ℓ projects such that for every $r \in [\ell]$ the project $o_r \in P$ is chosen to be built at time slot t_r. We require that for any $r, r' \in [\ell]$ with $r \neq r'$, we have $o_r \neq o_{r'}$; that is, each project is built at most once. Let Π denote the space of all possible outcomes.

The utility of an agent $i \in N$ from an outcome $\mathbf{o}$ is the number of matches between the agent's preference and the outcome: $u_i(\mathbf{o}) = |\{r \in [\ell] : o_r \in s_{i,r}\}|$. Note that an outcome maximizes agent i's utility if and only if it corresponds to a maximum matching in G^i, i.e., provides her a utility of μ_i.

Preference Restrictions. In general, our framework allows for agents to approve of any number of projects between 0 and m for each slot. From this, we can derive three natural restricted cases of our model: (1) limiting the number of approved projects for *each* slot, (2) limiting the *total* number of approved projects across all slots, and (3) limiting the *number of times* a project can be approved overall. The special case where each agent approves exactly one project for each slot and each project is approved exactly once by each agent is called the *full permutation* (FP) setting. The setting where for each $i \in N$ each project appears in at most one set $s_{i,r}$ and $|\cup_{r \in [\ell]} s_{i,r}| \leq k$ for some $k \in [m]$ is called the *k-partial permutation* (*k*-PP) setting.

2.2   Welfare and Fairness Concepts

The goal of this work is to study the algorithmic complexity of identifying good outcomes in our model. There are several ways to define what it means for an outcome to be good. In what follows, we formally define the notions of goodness that will be considered in the remainder of the paper.

Perhaps the most straightforward approach is to focus on outcomes that optimize some notion of welfare.

Definition 1 (Utilitarian Social Welfare). *An outcome* $\mathbf{o}$ *maximizes utilitarian social welfare (Max-UTIL) if for every outcome* $\mathbf{o}' \in \Pi$ *it holds that* $\sum_{i \in N} u_i(\mathbf{o}) \geq \sum_{i \in N} u_i(\mathbf{o}')$.

Definition 2 (Egalitarian Social Welfare). *An outcome* $\mathbf{o}$ *maximizes egalitarian social welfare (Max-EGAL) if for every outcome* $\mathbf{o}' \in \Pi$ *it holds that* $\min_{i \in N} u_i(\mathbf{o}) \geq \min_{i \in N} u_i(\mathbf{o}')$.

Definition 3 (Nash Social Welfare). *An outcome* $\mathbf{o}$ *maximizes Nash social welfare (Max-NASH) if for every outcome* $\mathbf{o}' \in \Pi$ *it holds that* $\prod_{i \in N} u_i(\mathbf{o}) \geq \prod_{i \in N} u_i(\mathbf{o}')$.

Another relevant notion of welfare is Pareto optimality.

Definition 4 (Pareto Optimality). *An outcome* $\mathbf{o}$ *is* Pareto optimal (PAR) *if for any outcome* $\mathbf{o}' \in \Pi$ *either* $u_i(\mathbf{o}) \geq u_i(\mathbf{o}')$ *for all* $i \in N$ *or there exists an agent* $i \in N$ *with* $u_i(\mathbf{o}) > u_i(\mathbf{o}')$.

Instead of maximizing the welfare, we may want to focus on equity: can we obtain an outcome that guarantees each agent the same utility? To capture this idea, we define the following notion of fairness.

Definition 5 (Equitability). *An outcome* $\mathbf{o}$ *is* equitable (EQ) *if for all* $i, i' \in N$ *it holds that* $u_i(\mathbf{o}) = u_{i'}(\mathbf{o})$.

Note that an equitable outcome does not always exist (this is also the case for many similar fairness properties in the social choice literature [5]). Consider the simple case of two agents, with approval sets $\mathbf{s}_1 = (p_1, p_2)$ and $\mathbf{s}_2 = (p_2, p_1)$ respectively. Then, any outcome $\mathbf{o}$ will give a utility of 2 to one agent, and 0 to the other—equal treatment of these individuals is not achievable in our model.

We will also consider another fairness property that is commonly studied in the context of fair division, namely, proportionality. Intuitively, this property demands that each agent's utility should be at least as high as her proportional fair share. In our setting, it is natural to define an agent's proportional fair share as her best-case utility $\max_{\mathbf{o} \in \Pi} u_i(\mathbf{o}) = \mu_i$, divided by the number of agents n. Thus, we define proportionality as follows.

Definition 6 (Proportionality). *An outcome* $\mathbf{o}$ *is* proportional (PROP) *if for all* $i \in N$ *it holds that* $u_i(\mathbf{o}) \geq \frac{\mu_i}{n}$.

However, the existence of PROP outcomes is not guaranteed, even in the FP setting. Indeed, consider again the two-agent instance with $\mathbf{s}_1 = (p_1, p_2)$ and $\mathbf{s}_2 = (p_2, p_1)$. A PROP outcome would have to provide each agent a utility of 1, but both possible outcomes give a utility of 2 to one agent and 0 to the other. Thus, just like for equitability, we consider an "up to k slots" relaxation.

Definition 7 (Proportionality up to k slots). *An outcome $\mathbf{o}$ is proportional up to k slots (PROPk) if, for all $i \in N$ it holds that $u_i(\mathbf{o}) \geq \frac{M_i}{n} - k$.*

In the context of proportionality, we are particularly interested in the case $k = 1$ (i.e., PROP1).

3   Welfare and Fairness with Constant Number of Agents

In this section we present positive algorithmic results for the case where the number of agents is bounded by a constant. Notably, our results hold for the most general variant of our model (i.e., arbitrary preferences).

3.1   A General-Purpose Randomized Algorithm

We present a general-purpose method that gives rise to randomized algorithms capable of solving a variety of problems efficiently (in polynomial time) if the number of agents is bounded by a constant. The problems we consider include deciding if there exists an outcome providing a certain level of utilitarian/egalitarian/Nash social welfare, Pareto optimality, equitability, proportionality, etc. Furthermore, our method can be extended to solve the search variants of these problems efficiently. To simplify presentation, we assume that the number of projects m is equal to the number of time slots ℓ, i.e., outcomes are perfect matchings between projects and time slots; towards the end of the section, we briefly discuss how to extend our results to settings where the number of available projects may exceed the number of time slots. The running time of our algorithms is polynomial in m^n, i.e., it is polynomial when n is bounded by a constant.

The key idea of our approach is to summarize the agents' preferences by means of a matrix whose entries are monomials over variables $y_1, \ldots, y_n, y_{n+1}$ (encoding the agents) and $(x_{j,r})_{j,r \in [m]}$ (encoding the project-time slot pairs); then, by evaluating the determinant of this matrix, we can determine if our instance admits a 'good' schedule.

The starting point for our construction is the Edmonds matrix, which is used to reason about matchings in bipartite graphs [21].

Definition 8 (Edmonds Matrix [21]). *Let $(x_{j,r})_{j,r \in [m]}$ be indeterminates. Given a balanced bipartite graph $G = (P \cup T, E)$ with parts $P = \{p_1, \ldots p_m\}$ and $T = \{t_1, \ldots t_m\}$, the Edmonds matrix is a matrix $\mathbf{A} \in \mathbb{R}^{m \times m}$ with entries A_{jr} defined as follows:*

$$A_{jr} = \begin{cases} x_{j,r} & \text{if } (p_j, t_r) \in E \\ 0 & \text{otherwise} \end{cases}$$

The Edmonds matrix is useful for deciding if a balanced bipartite graph contains a perfect matching [21]: it is not hard to check that its determinant is not identically zero (as a polynomial) if and only if G admits a perfect matching.

However, we cannot use the Edmonds matrix directly: indeed, the input to our problem is not a single bipartite graph, but a collection of n bipartite graphs $G^1, \ldots, G^n$. We therefore generalize Edmonds' idea as follows.

Definition 9 (Polynomial Schedule Matrix). *Let* $(y_i)_{i \in [n+1]}$ *and* $(x_{j,r})_{j,r \in [m]}$ *be indeterminates. The* polynomial schedule matrix *for* $G^1, \ldots, G^n$ *is a matrix* $\mathbf{A} \in \mathbb{R}^{m \times m}$ *with entries* A_{jr} *defined as follows:*

$$
A_{jr} = \begin{cases} y_{n+1} \cdot x_{j,r} & \text{if } G^i_{j,r} = 0 \text{ for all } i \in [n] \\ \prod_{i=1}^n y_i^{G^i_{j,r}} \cdot x_{j,r} & \text{otherwise} \end{cases}
$$

Using the Polynomial Schedule Matrix. We will now describe how to use the polynomial schedule matrix to check for existence of good outcomes. Set $\mathbf{y_N} = (y_i)_{i \in [n+1]}$, $\mathbf{x_E} = (x_{j,r})_{j,r \in [m]}$, and denote the determinant of $\mathbf{A}$ by $det(\mathbf{A}) = f(\mathbf{y_N}, \mathbf{x_E})$. The function f is a polynomial in $\mathbf{y_N}$, $\mathbf{x_E}$. It will also be convenient to think of $det(\mathbf{A})$ as a polynomial in $\mathbf{y_N}$ whose coefficients are polynomials over $\mathbf{x_E}$; when using this interpretation, we will write $det(\mathbf{A}) = g(\mathbf{y_N})$.

The function $f(\mathbf{y_N}, \mathbf{x_E})$ can be written as a sum of $m!$ monomials. Each of these monomials is of the form $(-1)^z \cdot y_1^{v_1} \ldots y_n^{v_n} y_{n+1}^{v_{n+1}} \cdot x_{j_1,r_1} \cdots \cdots x_{j_m,r_m}$, where $z \in \{0, 1\}$, $v_1, \ldots, v_{n+1}$ are non-negative integers, and $\{j_1, \ldots, j_m\} = \{r_1, \ldots, r_m\} = [m]$; for each $i \in [n]$ the value v_i is the utility that agent i derives from the schedule that assigns project p_{j_s} to time slot t_{r_s} for $s \in [m]$.

We can rephrase the reasoning above in terms of g. Specifically, we can represent $g(\mathbf{y_N})$ as a sum of at most $(m+1)^{n+1}$ monomials over $\mathbf{y_N}$, with the coefficient of each monomial being a polynomial over $\mathbf{x_E}$. Specifically, each monomial in $g(\mathbf{y_N})$ is an expression of the form $y_1^{v_1} \ldots y_n^{v_n} y_{n+1}^{v_{n+1}} \lambda(\mathbf{x_E})$, where $0 \leq v_i \leq m$ for each $i \in [n+1]$ and $\lambda(\mathbf{x_E})$ is a polynomial over $\mathbf{x_E}$; if λ is not identically zero, there are one or more outcomes providing utility v_i to agent i for $i \in [n]$ and containing v_{n+1} project-time slot pairs not approved by any of the agents.

It follows that as long as we know which monomials occur in g, we can decide whether our instance admits outcomes that satisfy each of the welfare and fairness desiderata defined in Sect. 2. In more detail[1]:

- **Egalitarian Social Welfare:** Given $v_1, \ldots, v_n \geq 0$, we can determine whether there exists an outcome $\mathbf{o}$ such that $u_i(\mathbf{o}) \geq v_i$ for each $i \in [n]$, by checking whether g contains a monomial of the form $\prod_{i=1}^{n+1} y_i^{v_i'} \lambda(\mathbf{x_E})$ such that $v_i' \geq v_i$ for all $i \in [n]$.
- **Nash Social Welfare:** The value of a Nash welfare-maximizing outcome can be computed efficiently by iterating through all monomials in g: given a monomial of the form $\prod_{i=1}^{n+1} y_i^{v_i} \lambda(\mathbf{x_E})$, we compute $\prod_{i=1}^n v_i$, and take the maximum of this quantity over all monomials that appear in g.

---

[1] We omit a discussion of utilitarian social welfare, since an outcome maximizing this measure of welfare can be computed in polynomial time for arbitrary n, m and ℓ (Theorem 1).

- **Pareto Optimality:** For each $i \in [n]$, let $v_i = u_i(\mathbf{o})$. Then if g has a term $\prod_{i=1}^{n+1} y_i^{v_i'} \lambda(\mathbf{x_E})$ with $v_i' \geq v_i$ for all $i \in [n]$ and $v_i' > v_i$ for at least one $i \in [n]$, then $\mathbf{o}$ is not Pareto optimal, otherwise it is.
- **Equitability:** Given $v \geq 0$, we can determine whether there exists an outcome $\mathbf{o}$ such that $u_i(\mathbf{o}) = v$ for each $i \in [n]$, by checking whether there exists a term $\prod_{i=1}^{n+1} y_i^v \lambda(\mathbf{x_E})$ such that $v = v_i$ for all $i \in [n]$.
- **Proportionality** can be handled similarly to egalitarian social welfare by setting $v_i = \mu_i/n$ for each $i \in [n]$.

More broadly, having access to g enables us to solve any problem where the answer depends on whether there exists an outcome that provides certain utilities to each of the agents. We will now discuss the complexity of deciding which monomials appear in g.

Evaluating g. We have argued that we can decide the existence of 'good' outcomes by evaluating $\det(\mathbf{A})$ (more specifically, by determining which monomials appear in g). However, explicitly listing all $m!$ terms of $f(\mathbf{y_N}, \mathbf{x_E})$ is computationally expensive. Instead, we will now describe a probabilistic polynomial-time algorithm that with high probability correctly identifies which monomials appear in g. Formally, we will say that a polynomial $\widehat{g}$ over $\mathbf{y_N}$ is an *over-approximation* of g if for every choice of $v_1, \ldots, v_{n+1} \in \{0, \ldots, m\}$ the following holds: if g contains a monomial of the form $\prod_{i=1}^{n+1} y_i^{v_i} \lambda(\mathbf{x_E})$ such that λ is not identically 0, then $\widehat{g}$ contains a monomial of the form $\widehat{\lambda} \cdot \prod_{i=1}^{n+1} y_i^{v_i}$ with $\widehat{\lambda} \in \mathbb{R} \setminus \{0\}$. Also, we say that $\widehat{g}$ is an *under-approximation* of g if for every choice of $v_1, \ldots, v_{n+1} \in \{0, \ldots, m\}$ the following holds: if g does not contain a monomial of the form $\prod_{i=1}^{n+1} y_i^{v_i} \lambda(\mathbf{x_E})$, then $\widehat{g}$ does not contain a monomial of the form $\widehat{\lambda} \cdot \prod_{i=1}^{n+1} y_i^{v_i}$. Our algorithm will output a polynomial $\widehat{g}$ over $\mathbf{y_N}$ such that $\widehat{g}$ is an under-approximation of g, and, with probability at least $1/2$, it is an over-approximation of g. Note that if $\widehat{g}$ is both an under-approximation and an over-approximation of g, it contains at most $(m+1)^{n+1}$ terms, and it can be used instead of g to solve all fair scheduling problems considered in this section. Moreover, the probability that $\widehat{g}$ is an over-approximation of g can be amplified using standard techniques.

To obtain $\widehat{g}$ given the matrix $\mathbf{A}$, we sample values for the variables in $\mathbf{x_E}$ from the set $\lceil dm \rceil$ for $d = 2 \cdot (m+1)^{n+1}$, and substitute them into $\mathbf{A}$, so as to obtain a matrix $\mathbf{A}'$ whose entries are polynomials in $\mathbf{y_N}$. We then set $\widehat{g} = \det(\mathbf{A}')$.

Computing the determinant is easy for real-valued matrices: e.g., one can obtain the LU decomposition [6,25] of the input matrix in time $\mathcal{O}(m^{2.376})$ time using the Coppersmith–Winograd algorithm for matrix multiplication, and then compute the determinant of the simpler matrices in the decomposition in linear-time. However, the entries of $\mathbf{A}'$ are multivariate polynomials rather than reals. We will therefore use polynomial interpolation techniques. That is, we select values $y_1', \ldots, y_{n+1}' \in \mathbb{R}$, substitute them into $\mathbf{A}'$, and compute the determinant of the resulting real-valued matrix using the LU decomposition approach. By repeating this step multiple times (selecting fresh values of $y_1', \ldots, y_{n+1}' \in \mathbb{R}$ at each iteration and computing $\widehat{g}(y_1', \ldots, y_{n+1}')$), we obtain enough information to recover $\widehat{g}$. Specifically, Zippel's deterministic method takes $\mathcal{O}(n^2 m^{n+1} t^2)$ time, where t is the true number of non-zero terms in $\widehat{g}$; whereas Zippel's probabilistic method [27] provides an improved expected running time of $\mathcal{O}(n^2 m t^2)$. An overview of methods for polynomial interpolation and their complexity can be found in [15,27].

It is clear that $\widehat{g}$ is an under-approximation of g. To show that it is an over-approximation of g with probability at least $1/2$, we use the Schwartz–Zippel lemma [21]:

Proposition 1. *Set* $d = 2 \cdot (m+1)^{n+1}$, *and let* $S = \lceil dm \rceil$. *Then picking* $x'_{j,r}$ *independently, uniformly at random from* S *gives a polynomial in* $y_1, \ldots, y_{n+1}$ *such that the coefficient of every term* $\prod_{i=1}^{n+1} y_i^{v_i}$ *that appears in* $\det(\mathbf{A})$ *is non-zero with probability at least* $1/2$.

Proof. Fix some values $v_1, \ldots, v_{n+1}$. The coefficient of $\prod_{i=1}^{n+1} y_i^{v_i}$ is a polynomial in $\mathbf{x_E}$ of degree at most m. By the Schwartz–Zippel lemma [21], the probability that this coefficient is zero is at most $\frac{m}{|S|} = \frac{1}{d}$. By the union bound, the probability that this happens for some choice of $v_1, \ldots, v_{n+1}$ is at most $\frac{1}{d} \cdot (m+1)^{n+1} = 1/2$. $\qquad\square$

The running time of our algorithm is polynomial in $(m+1)^{n+1}$, i.e., it is polynomial in m if n is bounded by a constant. Indeed, our algorithm proceeds by constructing $\mathbf{A}$, sampling values for $\mathbf{x_E}$, substituting them into $\mathbf{A}$, and evaluating the determinant of the resulting matrix using polynomial intepolation; this determinant is a multivariate polynomial that contains at most $(m+1)^{n+1}$ monomials, and, given this polynomial, the fair scheduling problems we are interested in can be solved in polynomial time.

Extension to Search Problems. We can extend our approach from decision problems to search problems. To illustrate this, we consider the problem of finding an outcome that maximizes the utilitarian welfare.

Corollary 1. *Suppose we are given a non-negative integer* v_i *for each* $i \in [n]$. *Then we can efficiently find an outcome* $\mathbf{o}$ *such that* $u_i(\mathbf{o}) \geq v_i$ *for all* $i \in [n]$, *or report that no such outcome exists.*

Proof (Sketch). Initialize the solution as $S = \varnothing$. Pick an edge $e \notin S$ from $\cup_{i=1}^n G^i$, remove it from each approval graph, and run the randomized polynomial-time algorithm on this problem instance. If a solution still exists, e was not essential, and we may continue removing edges. If there is no solution, we know e must be part of every solution that includes the edges placed in S so far; we reinstate it in the approval graphs, set $S := S \cup \{e\}$, and continue. $\qquad\square$

Extension to the case $\ell \neq m$. Throughout this section we assumed that $\ell = m$, i.e., the number of projects equals the number of time slots. For the case of $\ell \neq m$ (i.e. unbalanced bipartite graphs), we can use a similar extension of the Tutte matrix (which is a generalization of Edmonds matrix to non-bipartite graphs). Further details can be found in the full version of the paper.

3.2   PROP1 Outcomes Exist for Two Agents

In Sect. 2, we observed that some instances do not have PROP outcomes, and defined a relaxation of PROP, namely, proportionality up to k items (PROPk). We will now show that for two agents, PROP1 outcomes always exist and can be computed in polynomial time.

Proposition 2. *Let $G_1 = (V, E_1)$ and $G_2 = (V, E_2)$ be graphs on the same set of vertices V. Also, for each $i = 1, 2$, let μ_i be the size of a maximum matching in G_i. Then, we can compute, in polynomial time, a matching M in $(V, E_1 \cup E_2)$ that contains at least $\frac{\mu_1}{2} - 1$ edges from E_1 and at least $\frac{\mu_2}{2} - 1$ edges from E_2.*

Proof. For $i = 1, 2$, let $M_i \subset E_i$ be some maximum matching in G_i. We place each edge $e \in M_1 \cap M_2$ in M; note that each such edge does not share endpoints with other edges in $M_1 \cup M_2$. Let $\kappa = |M_1 \cap M_2|$, and for $i = 1, 2$, set $\mu_i' = |M_i \setminus M_{3-i}| = \mu_i - \kappa$. Consider the graph $G' = (V, (M_1 \cup M_2) \setminus (M_1 \cap M_2))$. We will say that an edge e of G' is *red* if $e \in M_1$ and *blue* if $e \in M_2$; note that each edge of G' is either red or blue. Moreover, in G' each vertex is incident on at most one red edge and at most one blue edge, so each connected component of G' is an isolated vertex, an alternating red-blue path, or an alternating red-blue cycle (which must be of even length).

Next, we construct an instance of the fair allocation problem with two agents $N = \{1, 2\}$ and divisible items. We create one item for each connected component of G'; let I be the resulting set of items. For each $C \in I$ we define the valuation of agent $i \in \{1, 2\}$ to be $v_i(C) = |E(C) \cap M_i|$. We extend the valuation function to bundles and fractional allocations in a linear fashion: if agent i obtains a bundle that contains an α_C-fraction of item C for $C \in I'$, then her valuation for this bundle is $\sum_{C \in I'} \alpha_C \cdot v_i(C)$. Note that we have $v_i(I) = \mu_i'$.

We then apply the adjusted winner procedure [4] to this instance. This procedure results in a proportional allocation that splits at most one of the items in I. For $i = 1, 2$, let I_i be the set of items that are allocated to agent i, and let C^* be the item that is split, so that agent i gets a w_i-fraction of C^*, where $w_1 + w_2 = 1$. By proportionality, the value of agent i for her bundle, given by $\sum_{C \in I_i} v_i(C) + w_i \cdot v_i(C^*)$, is at least $\mu_i'/2$. We will now transform this allocation into a matching in G'.

To this end, for each $i = 1, 2$, if the connected component C is allocated to i, we place edges $M_i \cap C$ into M. To select edges from C^*, we proceed as follows.

Suppose first that C^* is a path of length $2s$, with red edges $e_1, \ldots, e_{2s-1}$ and blue edges $e_2, \ldots, e_{2s}$. Then $v_1(C^*) = v_2(C^*) = s$. Let $t = \lfloor w_1 \cdot s \rfloor$, and place edges $e_1, \ldots, e_{2t-1}$ as well as $e_{2t+2}, \ldots, e_{2s}$ into M: by construction, these edges form a matching, which contains $t \geq w_1 \cdot s - 1$ red edges and $s - t \geq s - w_1 \cdot s = w_2 \cdot s$ blue edges.

Next, suppose that C^* is a path of length $2s - 1$, with red edges $e_1, \ldots, e_{2s-1}$ and blue edges $e_2, \ldots, e_{2s-2}$. Then $v_1(C^*) = s$, $v_2(C^*) = s - 1$. Again, let $t = \lfloor w_1 \cdot s \rfloor$, and place edges $e_1, \ldots, e_{2t-1}$ as well as $e_{2t+2}, \ldots, e_{2s-2}$ into M: by construction, these edges form a matching, which contains $t \geq w_1 \cdot s - 1$ red edges and $s - t - 1 \geq s - w_1 \cdot s - 1 = w_2 \cdot s - 1$ blue edges.

Finally, if C^* is a cycle of length $2s$, we discard one blue edge, transforming C^* into an odd-length path, and then proceed as described in the previous paragraph, i.e., select at least $w_1 \cdot s - 1$ red edges and $w_2 \cdot s - 1$ blue edges and place them in M. This completes the construction of M; it is immediate that it can be carried out in polynomial time.

For each item $C \in I_1$, we place $|E(C) \cap M_1| = v_1(C)$ red edges in M, and, when splitting C^*, we place at least $w_1 \cdot v_1(C^*) - 1$ red edges in M. By proportionality of the fractional allocation, we have $\sum_{C \in I_1} v_1(C) + w_1 \cdot v_1(C^*) \geq \mu_1'/2$; hence, we place at least $\mu_1'/2 - 1$ red edges in M. By a similar argument, we place at least $\mu_2'/2 - 1$ blue edges in M. In addition, M contains κ edges from $M_1 \cap M_2$. Hence, it contains at least $\mu_i'/2 - 1 + \kappa = (\mu_i - \kappa)/2 - 1 + \kappa \geq \mu_i/2 - 1$ edges from M_i for each $i = 1, 2$. $\qquad\square$

Corollary 2. *When $n = 2$, a PROP1 allocation exists and can be computed in polynomial time.*

Proof. Applying Proposition 2 to the approval graphs G^1 and G^2 (of agents 1 and 2 respectively) results in a PROP1 allocation. $\qquad\square$

The algorithm described in the proof of Proposition 2 runs in polynomial time. More specifically, the most computationally expensive task is computing the maximum matchings in G_1 and G_2, which takes $\mathcal{O}(\sqrt{m} \cdot |E(G_i)|)$ time for $i = 1, 2$. Constructing the graph G', finding the connected components, and defining the valuations takes $\mathcal{O}(\ell)$ time. The adjusted winner procedure is also linear in the number of items, which is at most the number of vertices in G', i.e., at most 2ℓ, so it takes $\mathcal{O}(\ell)$ time. Furthermore, given the divisible component C^*, we can decide if it is a cycle or an alternating path in linear time (by looking at the number of vertices, and the number of 1- and 2- edges each) and hence decide which of its edges to select.

4   Beyond a Constant Number of Agents

In this section, we analyze the complexity of finding good outcomes in scenarios where the number of agents may be large. We obtain an easiness result for utiliarian social welfare, and hardness results for several other solution concepts.

4.1   Utilitarian Social Welfare

The utilitarian social welfare is perhaps the most popular optimization target in multi-agent allocation problems. We start by formalizing the problem of computing an outcome that maximizes this measure of welfare.

UTILITARIAN SOCIAL WELFARE MAXIMIZATION (UTIL):
Input: A problem instance $I = (P, T, (\mathbf{s}_i)_{i \in N})$, and a parameter $\lambda \in \mathbb{N}$.
Question: Is there an outcome $\mathbf{o}$ such that $\sum_{i \in N} u_i(\mathbf{o}) \geq \lambda$?

We will now show that the problem we just defined admits an efficient algorithm; in fact, we can even compute an outcome that maximizes the utilitarian social welfare in polynomial time.

Theorem 1. UTIL *is solvable in polynomial time.*

Proof. Given an instance of UTIL, we construct a weighted complete bipartite graph with parts P and T, where the weight of the edge (p_j, t_r) equals to the number of agents that approve implementing p_j at time t_r: that is, we set $w(p_j, t_r) = |\{i \in N : p_j \in s_{i,r}\}|$. Then a maximum-weight matching in this graph corresponds to an outcome that maximizes the utilitarian social welfare. It remains to observe that a maximum-weight matching in a bipartite graph can be computed in polynomial time [24]. □

4.2 Egalitarian Social Welfare

Next, we consider the complexity of maximizing the egalitarian welfare. Again, we first formulate the associated decision problem.

EGALITARIAN SOCIAL WELFARE MAXIMIZATION (EGAL):
Input: A problem instance $I = (P, T, (s_i)_{i \in N})$, and a parameter $\lambda \in \mathbb{N}$.
Question: Is there an outcome $\mathbf{o}$ such that $u_i(\mathbf{o}) \geq \lambda$ for each $i \in N$?

It turns out that EGAL is NP-complete. In fact, this hardness result holds even in the FP setting.

Our proof proceeds by a reduction from the BINARY CLOSEST STRING PROBLEM (BCSP) [12,19]. An instance of this problem consists of ν binary strings of length ρ each, and an integer κ; it is a yes-instance if there exists a binary string y of length ρ such that the Hamming distance (i.e., number of *mismatches*) between y and each of the ν strings is at most κ (equivalently, the number of matches is at least $\rho - \kappa$), and a no-instance otherwise. This problem is known to be NP-complete [12,19].

We are now ready to establish the complexity of EGAL.

Theorem 2. EGAL *is* NP-*complete. The hardness result holds even in the FP setting.*

Proof. It is clear that EGAL is in NP: given an outcome, we can evaluate each agent's utility and compare it to λ. To establish NP-hardness, we give a reduction from BCSP.

Consider an instance of BCSP given by ν binary strings $X = \{x_1, \ldots, x_\nu\}$ of length ρ each, and an integer κ. For each $i \in [\nu]$, $j \in [\rho]$, denote the j-th bit of the string x_i by x_{ij}. To create an instance of EGAL, we introduce 2ρ projects $p_1, \ldots, p_{2\rho}$ and 2ρ time slots $t_1, \ldots, t_{2\rho}$. We will encode the bit strings as agents' preferences: for each x_{ij}, if $x_{ij} = 1$, let $s_{i,2j-1} = p_{2j-1}$ and $s_{i,2j} = p_{2j}$; if $x_{ij} = 0$, let $s_{i,2j-1} = p_{2j}$ and $s_{i,2j} = p_{2j-1}$.

Let $\lambda = 2(\rho - \kappa)$. We will now prove that there exists an outcome $\mathbf{o}$ that gives each agent a utility of at least λ if and only if there exists a binary string y of length ρ such that its Hamming distance to each string in X is at most κ (i.e., the number of matches is at least $\rho - \kappa$).

For the 'if' direction, let $y = (y_1, \ldots, y_\rho)$ be a string with at most κ mismatches to each of the strings in X. Construct an outcome $\mathbf{o}$ by setting $o_{2j-1} = p_{2j-1}$, $o_{2j} = p_{2j}$ if $y_j = 1$, and $o_{2j-1} = p_{2j}$, $o_{2j} = p_{2j-1}$ if $y_j = 0$. Consider an agent i. For each bit j such that $x_{ij} = y_j$ we have $s_{i,2j-1} = o_{2j-1}$, $s_{i,2j} = o_{2j}$. Thus, the utility of this agent is at least $2(\rho - \kappa) = \lambda$, which is what we wanted to prove.

For the 'only if' direction, suppose there exists an outcome that gives each agent a utility of λ. We will say that an outcome $\mathbf{o}$ is *proper* if for each $j \in [\rho]$ we have $\{o_{2j-1}, o_{2j}\} = \{p_{2j-1}, p_{2j}\}$. We claim that there exists a proper outcome that gives each agent a utility of λ. Indeed, suppose that this is not the case. For each outcome $\mathbf{o}$, let $z(\mathbf{o})$ be the number of time slots t_q such that $q \in \{2j-1, 2j\}$ for some $j \in [\rho]$, but $o_q \notin \{p_{2j-1}, p_{2j}\}$. Among all outcomes that give each agent a utility of λ, pick one with the minimal value of $z(\mathbf{o})$; let this outcome be $\mathbf{o}^*$. By our assumption, $\mathbf{o}^*$ is not proper, so $z(\mathbf{o}^*) > 0$. Thus, there exists a time slot t_q such that $q \in \{2j-1, 2j\}$ for some $j \in [\rho]$, but $o_q^* \notin \{p_{2j-1}, p_{2j}\}$. Then in $\mathbf{o}^*$ there is a project $p \in \{p_{2j-1}, p_{2j}\}$ that is scheduled at time slot $t_{2j'-1}$ or $t_{2j'}$ for some $j' \neq j$. Modify $\mathbf{o}^*$ by swapping p with o_q^*. Note that in $\mathbf{o}^*$, no agent derives positive utility from either of these two projects. Hence, this swap cannot decrease any agent's utility, but it decreases $z(\cdot)$ (because the project at time slot t_q is now one of p_{2j-1}, p_{2j}), a contradiction with our choice of $\mathbf{o}^*$.

Now, fix a proper outcome $\mathbf{o}$ that gives each agent a utility of λ. Let

$$y_j = \begin{cases} 1 & \text{if } o_{2j-1} = p_{2j-1} \text{ and } o_{2j} = p_{2j} \\ 0 & \text{if } o_{2j-1} = p_{2j} \text{ and } o_{2j} = p_{2j-1} \end{cases}$$

Consider a string x_i. We know that agent i's utility from $\mathbf{o}$ is at least $\lambda = 2(\rho - \kappa)$. Note that for each $j \in [\rho]$ we have either (1) $o_{2j-1} = s_{i,2j-1}$, $o_{2j} = s_{i,2j}$ or (2) $o_{2j-1} \neq s_{i,2j-1}$, $o_{2j} \neq s_{i,2j}$. Hence, there can be at most κ indices $j \in [\rho]$ for which condition (2) holds, and therefore there are at most κ mismatches between x_i and y. □

Theorem 2 indicates that even for FP instances, it is hard to decide whether each agent can be guaranteed a utility of at least λ. This motivates us to consider a less ambitious goal: can EGAL be solved efficiently if λ is bounded by a small constant?

Perhaps surprisingly, even for $\lambda = 1$ and FP instances this is unlikely to be the case: we show that EGAL is as hard as the PERFECT COMPLETE BIPARTITE PROPER RAINBOW MATCHING (PCBP-RM) problem [22], one of the many variants of the RAINBOW MATCHING problem for which an NP-hardness result is conjectured, but has not been established [1].

An instance of PCBP-RM is given by a complete bipartite graph $K_{\nu, \nu}$ (i.e., there are ν nodes on each side of the graph, and each node on one side is connected to every other node on the opposite side), where edges are properly colored (i.e., if two edges share an endpoint, they have different colors). The goal is to decide whether this instance admits a perfect rainbow matching M, i.e., a matching of size ν in which every edge has a different color.

Theorem 3. EGAL *is at least as hard as* PCBP-RM, *even when restricted to FP instances with* $\lambda = 1$.

Proof. Consider an instance of PCBP-RM with two parts V_1 and V_2, $|V_1| = |V_2| = \nu$, where for all $i, j \in [\nu]$, the i-th vertex in V_1 is connected to the j-th vertex in V_2 via an edge e_{ij}; we denote the color of this edge by $\texttt{color}(e_{ij})$. There are a total of ν unique colors $C = \{c_1, \ldots, c_\nu\}$.

We construct an instance of EGAL that contains ν agents, ν projects, and ν time slots. For each agent i and time slot t_r, we set $s_{i,r} = p_j$, where j is the index of the color of the edge e_{ir}, i.e., $\texttt{color}(e_{ir}) = c_j$.

We will now prove that there exists an outcome **o** that gives each agent a utility of at least 1 if and only if there exists a perfect rainbow matching M.

For the 'if' direction, let M be a perfect rainbow matching. We create an outcome **o** as follows. To determine the time slot for project p_j, we identify an edge of M that has color c_j; if this edge connects agent i and time slot t_r, we schedule p_j at time t_r (thereby providing utility 1 to agent i). Since M is a rainbow matching, each project is scheduled exactly once, and any two projects are assigned distinct time slots. Moreover, as M is a matching, each agent's utility is 1.

For the 'only if' direction, consider an outcome **o** that gives each agent a utility of at least 1. Observe that for each $r \in [\nu]$ and every pair of agents i, i', we have $s_{i,r} \neq s_{i',r}$. This means that for each $r \in [\nu]$, there is exactly one agent that receives a utility of 1 from o_r, i.e., the utility of each agent is exactly 1. We construct the matching M as follows: if agent i receives utility from the project scheduled at t_r, we add an edge from the i-th vertex of V_1 to the r-th vertex of V_2 to M. Note that M is a matching: each vertex in V_1 is matched, as each agent receives utiity 1 from some project, and each vertex in V_2 is matched, as each time slot provides positive utility to at most one agent. Moreover, M is a rainbow matching, as each project is scheduled exactly once. □

On a more positive note, for $\lambda = 1$ in the γ-PP setting we can characterize the complexity of EGAL with respect to the parameter γ. We do so by establishing a tight relationship between this problem and the k-SAT problem. An instance of k-SAT consists of ν Boolean variables and ρ clauses, where each clause has at most k literals; it is a yes-instance if there exists an assignment of Boolean values to the variables such that at least one literal in each clause evaluates to True, and a no-instance otherwise. This problem is NP-complete for each $k \geq 3$, but polynomial-time solvable for $k = 2$.

Theorem 4. EGAL *is* NP-*complete even when restricted to* γ-PP *instances with* $\lambda = 1$, *for any fixed* $\gamma \geq 3$.[2]

---

[2] It is important to note that this does not mean that when $\lambda = 1$, EGAL under FP is always NP-complete. We cannot use the $\gamma = m$ argument here, even if $m \geq 3$.

Proof. We describe a reduction from γ-SAT to EGAL restricted to γ-PP instances with $\lambda = 1$.

Consider an instance of γ-SAT given by ν Boolean variables $X = \{x_1, \ldots, x_\nu\}$ and ρ clauses $\mathcal{C} = \{C_1, \ldots, C_\rho\}$. In our instance of EGAL, we have a set of ρ agents $N = \{1, \ldots, \rho\}$, 2ν projects $P = \{p_1, \ldots, p_{2\nu}\}$, and 2ν time slots $T = \{t_1, \ldots, t_{2\nu}\}$. Each agent encodes a clause: for each $i \in N$, $j \in [\nu]$ we set

$$s_{i,2j-1} = \begin{cases} p_j & \text{if } C_i \text{ contains the positive literal } x_j \\ \varnothing & \text{otherwise} \end{cases}$$

and

$$s_{i,2j} = \begin{cases} p_j & \text{if } C_i \text{ contains the negative literal } \neg x_j \\ \varnothing & \text{otherwise} \end{cases}$$

As we start with an instance of γ-SAT, we have $|\cup_{r \in [2\nu]} s_{i,r}| \leq \gamma$ for each $i \in N$, i.e., we obtain a valid γ-PP instance.

We will now prove that there exists an outcome $\mathbf{o}$ that gives each agent a positive utility if and only if our instance of γ-SAT admits a satisfying assignment.

For the 'if' direction, consider a satisfying assignment $(\xi_j)_{j \in [\nu]}$. For $j \in [\nu]$, if ξ_j is set to True, let $o_{2j-1} = p_j$, $o_{2j} = p_{\nu+j}$ and if ξ_j is set to False, let $o_{2j-1} = p_{\nu+j}$, $o_{2j} = p_j$. Consider an agent $i \in [\rho]$. Since the assignment $(\xi_j)_{j \in [\nu]}$ satisfies C_i, there is a literal $\ell \in C_i$ that is satisfied by this assignment. If $\ell = x_j$ is a positive literal then ξ_j is set to True, so $o_{2j-1} = p_j$, and we have $s_{i,2j-1} = p_j$. If $\ell = \neg x_j$ is a negative literal then ξ_j is set to False, so $o_{2j} = p_j$, and we have $s_{i,2j} = p_j$. In either case, the utility of agent i is at least 1.

For the 'only if' direction, consider an outcome $\mathbf{o}$ that gives each agent a positive utility. Arguing as in the proof of Theorem 2, we can assume that for each $j \in [\nu]$ it holds that p_j is scheduled at t_{2j-1} or at t_{2j}: if this is not the case for some $j \in [\nu]$, we can move p_j to one of these slots without lowering the utility of any agent. We construct a truth assignment $(\xi_j)_{j \in [\nu]}$ by setting ξ_j to True if $o_{2j-1} = p_j$ and to False if $o_{2j} = p_j$. Now, consider a clause C_i. Since the utility of agent i is at least 1, it follows that our assignment satisfies at least one of the literals in C_i. As this holds for all clauses, the proof is complete. □

Theorem 5. EGAL *is polynomial-time solvable when restricted to 2-PP instances with $\lambda = 1$.*

Proof. Consider an instance of EGAL with $\lambda = 1$ given by n agents $N = \{1, \ldots, n\}$, m projects $P = \{p_1, \ldots, p_m\}$ and ℓ time slots $T = \{t_1, \ldots, t_\ell\}$. For each project $p_j \in P$ and time slot $t_r \in T$, create a variable x_{jr}; intuitively, we want this variable to evaluate to True if project p_j is scheduled at time slot t_r and to False otherwise.

First, we encode the fact that each project can be scheduled at most once: for each project $p_j \in P$ and each pair of time slots $t_r, t_{r'} \in T$ with $r \neq r'$ we add the clause $\neg x_{jr} \vee \neg x_{jr'}$. Let the conjunction of these clauses be C^*.

Next, we encode the fact that in each time slot we have at most one project: for each time slot $t_r \in T$ and each pair of projects $p_j, p_{j'} \in P$ with $j \neq j'$ we add the clause $\neg x_{jr} \vee \neg x_{j'r}$. Let the conjunction of these clauses be C'.

Finally, for each agent $i \in [n]$, we create a clause that requires this agent to have positive utility. Specifically, for each $i \in [n]$ we create a clause C_i as follows. If there exists a single time slot t_r such that $s_{i,r} \neq \varnothing$, we set $C_i = x_{jr}$ if $s_{i,r} = \{p_j\}$ and $C_i = x_{jr} \vee x_{j'r}$ if $s_{i,r} = \{p_j, p_{j'}\}$. If there exists two time slots t_r, $t_{r'}$ such that $s_{i,r}, s_{i,r'} \neq \varnothing$, then it has to be the case that $s_{i,r} = p_j$, $s_{i,r'} = p_{j'}$ for some $p_j, p_{j'} \in P$, so we set $C_i = x_{jr} \vee x_{j'r'}$.

It is now easy to see that there exists a truth assignment that satisfies C^*, C', and all clauses in $C_1, \dots, C_n$ if and only if there exists an outcome that guarantees positive utility to each agent. Moreover, each of the clauses in our construction is a disjunction of at most two literals. It remains to observe that 2-SAT is solvable in $\mathcal{O}(n + m)$ time [2,10,16]. □

4.3 Equitability

In Sect. 2, we have seen that not all instances admit equitable outcomes. We will now show that deciding the existence of equitable outcomes is computationally intractable.

> EQUITABILITY (EQ):
> **Input:** A problem instance $I = (P, T, (\mathbf{s}_i)_{i \in N})$, and a parameter $\lambda \in \mathbb{N}$.
> **Question:** Is there an outcome $\mathbf{o}$ such that $u_i(\mathbf{o}) = \lambda$ for each $i \in N$?

Theorem 6. EQ *is* NP-*complete. The hardness result holds even in the PP setting.*

Proof. It is clear that EQ is in NP. To show that this problem is NP-hard, we first formulate an intermediate problem to be used in our proof. Namely, we introduce the EXACT PARTIAL BINARY CLOSEST STRING PROBLEM (EXACT-P-BCSP). This problem is similar to the BCSP, but with two differences: (1) the Hamming distance between the output string and each of the input strings must be exactly κ, and (2) we allow an additional character, $*$, in the solution string. Formally, an instance of EXACT-P-BCSP consists of ν binary strings of length ρ each, and an integer κ; it is a yes-instance if there exists a string y of length ρ over the alphabet $\{0, 1, *\}$ such that the Hamming distance between y and each of the ν input strings is exactly κ (equivalently, the number of matches is exactly $\rho - \kappa$), and a no-instance otherwise.

We begin with the following lemma, whose proof is omitted due to space constraints.

Lemma 1. EXACT-P-BCSP *is* NP-*hard.*

We will now reduce EXACT-P-BCSP to EQ. Consider an instance of EXACT-P-BCSP given by ν binary strings $X = \{x_1, \ldots, x_\nu\}$ of length ρ each and an integer κ. For each $i \in [\nu]$, $j \in [\rho]$, denote the j-th bit of the i-th string by x_{ij}. We introduce 2ρ projects $p_1, \ldots, p_{2\rho}$ and 2ρ time slots $t_1, \ldots, t_{2\rho}$. We encode the bit strings in X as the agents' preferences: for each $i \in [\nu]$, $j \in [\rho]$, if $x_{ij} = 1$, let $s_{i,2j-1} = p_j$, $s_{i,2j} = \varnothing$; and if $x_{ij} = 0$, let $s_{i,2j-1} = \varnothing$, $s_{i,2j} = p_j$.

We will now prove that there exists an outcome $\mathbf{o}$ that gives each agent a utility of exactly $\rho - \kappa$ if and only if there exists a binary string y of length ρ such that the number of mismatches is exactly κ.

For the 'if' direction, let y be a solution string with exactly $\rho - \kappa$ matches to each of the strings in X. We construct an outcome $\mathbf{o}$ as follows. For each $j \in [\rho]$, if $y_j = 1$ we let $o_{2j-1} = p_j$ and if $y_j = 0$ we let $o_{2j} = p_j$; we assign the remaining projects to the remaining slots arbitrarily, with the constraint that if $y_j = *$, then p_j is not assigned to either of the time slots t_{2j-1}, t_{2j} (it is not difficult to verify that this can always be done efficiently; we omit the details). Consider an agent $i \in [\nu]$ and a time slot $j \in [\rho]$. If $x_{ij} = y_j = 1$ we have $o_{2j-1} = s_{i,2j-1}$, $s_{i,2j} = \varnothing$, if $x_{ij} = y_j = 0$ we have $o_{2j} = s_{i,2j}$, $s_{i,2j-1} = \varnothing$, and if $x_{ij} \neq y_j$ then $o_{2j-1} \notin s_{i,2j-1}$, $o_{2j} \notin s_{i,2j}$. Hence, each pair of time slots (t_{2j-1}, t_{2j}) such that $x_{ij} = y_j$ contributes exactly 1 to the utility of agent i, so $u_i(\mathbf{o}) = \rho - \kappa$.

For the 'only if' direction, consider any outcome $\mathbf{o}$ that gives each agent a utility of exactly $\rho - \kappa$. To construct the string y, for each $j \in [\rho]$ we set

$$
y_j = \begin{cases} 1 & \text{if } o_{2j-1} = p_j \\ 0 & \text{if } o_{2j} = p_j \\ * & \text{otherwise} \end{cases}
$$

Consider an agent i. Observe that her utility from the pair of time slots (t_{2j-1}, t_{2j}) is at most 1; moreover, it is 1 if and only if (1) $s_{i,2j-1} = o_{2j-1} = p_j$ or (2) $s_{i,2j} = o_{2j} = p_j$. Condition (1) holds if and only if $x_{ij} = y_j = 1$, and condition (2) holds if and only if $x_{ij} = y_j = 0$. That is, agent i's utility from (t_{2j-1}, t_{2j}) is 1 if and only if $x_{ij} = y_j$. Since we have $u_i(\mathbf{o}) = \rho - \kappa$ for each $i \in [\nu]$, this means that y has κ mismatches with every input string. $\qquad \square$

4.4 Proportionality

Finally, we consider the complexity of finding proportional outcomes.

> PROPORTIONALITY (PROP):
> **Input:** A problem instance $I = (P, T, (\mathbf{s}_i)_{i \in N})$.
> **Question:** Is there an outcome $\mathbf{o}$ such that $u_i(\mathbf{o}) \geq \mu_i/n$ for each $i \in N$?

It is easy to see that PROP does not necessarily imply UTIL or EGAL. Indeed, consider the case where $n = m = \ell$, and all agents have the same preference: $s_{i,j} = p_j$ for all $i \in [n]$, $j \in [\ell]$. Then, the only outcome that maximizes utilitarian or egalitarian social welfare is $(p_1, \ldots, p_m)$. However, any outcome with just a single project scheduled at the "correct" time slot would be a PROP outcome.

For proportionality, we obtain the following two results, whose proofs are omitted due to space constraints.

Theorem 7. PROP *is at least as hard as* PCBP-RM. *The hardness result holds even in the FP setting.*

Theorem 8. PROP *is* NP-*complete in the PP setting.*

5   Conclusion and Future Work

We considered a variety of welfare and fairness objectives in the assignment of projects to time slots based on preferences of multiple agents. In particular, we showed that when the number of agents is bounded by a constant, most of the associated decision problems are solvable in polynomial time by a randomized algorithm. When the number of agents can be arbitrary, we obtain a polynomial-time algorithm for the utilitarian welfare, and hardness results for the egalitarian welfare, equitability and proportionality; for the egalitarian welfare, we also identify special cases where optimal outcomes can be computed efficiently.

Avenues for future research include the following: (1) relaxing the capacity constraints on time slots, so that we can implement multiple (or zero) projects at each time slot; (2) considering agents with different entitlements and the associated fairness notions [7,11,26]; (3) exploring settings where agents belong to different groups and investigating group fairness and proportionality in our setting [8,23]; (4) designing strategyproof scheduling mechanisms.

References

1. Aharoni, R., Berger, E., Kotlar, D., Ziv, R.: On a conjecture of Stein. Abh. Math. Semin. Univ. Hambg. **87**(2), 203–211 (2016). https://doi.org/10.1007/s12188-016-0160-3
2. Aspvall, B., Plass, M., Tarjan, R.: A linear-time algorithm for testing the truth of certain quantified Boolean formulas. Inf. Process. Lett. **8**, 121–123 (1979)
3. Bampis, E., Escoffier, B., Mladenovic, S.: Fair resource allocation over time. In: Proceedings of the 17th International Conference on Autonomous Agents and Multi-Agent Systems (AAMAS), pp. 766–773 (2018)
4. Brams, S., Taylor, A.: Fair Division: From Cake-Cutting to Dispute Resolution. Cambridge University Press, Cambridge (1996)
5. Brandt, F., Conitzer, V., Endriss, U., Lang, J., Procaccia, A.: Handbook of Computational Social Choice. Cambridge University Press, Cambridge (2016)
6. Bunch, J.R., Hopcroft, J.E.: Triangular factorization and inversion by fast matrix multiplication. Math. Comput. **28**(125), 231–236 (1974)
7. Chakraborty, M., Igarashi, A., Suksompong, W., Zick, Y.: Weighted envy-freeness in indivisible item allocation. ACM Trans. Econ. Comput. **9**(3), 18:1–18:39 (2021)

8. Conitzer, V., Freeman, R., Shah, N., Vaughan, J.W.: Group fairness for the allocation of indivisible goods. In: Proceedings of the 33rd AAAI Conference on Artificial Intelligence (AAAI), pp. 1853–1860 (2019)

9. Elkind, E., Patel, N., Tsang, A., Zick, Y.: Keeping your friends close: land allocation with friends. In: Proceedings of the 29th International Joint Conference on Artificial Intelligence (IJCAI), pp. 318–324 (2020)

10. Even, S., Itai, A., Shamir, A.: On the complexity of time table and multicommodity flow problems. In: Proceedings of the 16th Symposium on Foundations of Computer Science (FOCS), pp. 184–193 (1975)

11. Farhadi, A., et al.: Fair allocation of indivisible goods to asymmetric agents. J. Artif. Intell. Res. **64**, 1–20 (2019)

12. Frances, M., Litman, A.: On covering problems of codes. Theory Comput. Syst. **30**, 113–119 (2007)

13. Freeman, R., Zahedi, S.M., Conitzer, V.: Fair and efficient social choice in dynamic settings. In: Proceedings of the 26th International Joint Conference on Artificial Intelligence (IJCAI), pp. 4580–4587 (2017)

14. Freeman, R., Zahedi, S.M., Conitzer, V., Lee, B.C.: Dynamic proportional sharing: a game-theoretic approach. Proc. ACM Meas. Anal. Comput. Syst. **2**(1), 1–36 (2018)

15. Gasca, M., Sauer, T.: Polynomial interpolation in several variables. Adv. Comput. Math. **12**(4), 377–410 (2000)

16. Krom, M.: The decision problem for a class of first-order formulas in which all disjunctions are binary. Math. Log. Q. **13**(1–2), 15–20 (1967)

17. Lackner, M.: Perpetual voting: fairness in long-term decision making. In: Proceedings of the 34th AAAI Conference on Artificial Intelligence (AAAI), pp. 2103–2110 (2020)

18. Lackner, M., Maly, J., Rey, S.: Fairness in long-term participatory budgeting. In: Proceedings of the 30th International Joint Conference on Artificial Intelligence (IJCAI), pp. 299–305 (2021)

19. Lanctot, K., Li, M., Ma, B., Wang, S., Zhang, L.: Distinguishing string selection problems. Inf. Comput. **185**(1), 41–55 (2003)

20. Lodi, A., Olivier, P., Pesant, G., Sankaranarayanan, S.: Fairness over time in dynamic resource allocation with an application in healthcare. arXiv preprint arXiv:2101.03716 (2022)

21. Motwani, R., Raghavan, P.: Randomized Algorithms. Cambridge University Press, Cambridge (1995)

22. Perarnau, G., Serra, O.: Rainbow matchings: existence and counting. arXiv preprint arXiv:1104.2702 (2011)

23. Scarlett, J., Teh, N., Zick, Y.: For one and all: individual and group fairness in the allocation of indivisible goods. In: Proceedings of the 8th International Workshop on Computational Social Choice (COMSOC) (2021)

24. Schrijver, A.: Combinatorial Optimization: Polyhedra and Efficiency. Springer, Heidelberg (2003)

25. Schwarzenberg-Czerny, A.: On matrix factorization and efficient least squares solution. Astron. Astrophys., Suppl. Ser. **110**, 405 (1995)

26. Suksompong, W., Teh, N.: On maximum weighted Nash welfare for binary valuations. Math. Soc. Sci. **117**, 101–108 (2022)

27. Zippel, R.: Interpolating polynomials from their values. J. Symb. Comput. **9**(3), 375–403 (1990)

Gehrlein Stable Committee
with Multi-modal Preferences

Sushmita Gupta[1], Pallavi Jain[2], Daniel Lokshtanov[3], Sanjukta Roy[4(✉)],
and Saket Saurabh[1,5]

[1] Institute of Mathematical Sciences, HBNI, Chennai, India
{sushmitagupta,saket}@imsc.res.in
[2] Indian Institute of Technology Jodhpur, Jodhpur, India
pallavi@iitj.ac.in
[3] University of California, Santa Barbara, Santa Barbara, USA
daniello@ucsb.edu
[4] Czech Technical University in Prague, Prague, Czech Republic
sanjukta.roy@fit.cvut.cz
[5] University of Bergen, Bergen, Norway

Abstract. Inspired by Gehrlein stability in multiwinner election, in this paper, we define several notions of stability that are applicable in multi-winner elections with multimodal preferences, a model recently proposed by Jain and Talmon [ECAI, 2020]. In this paper we take a two-pronged approach to this study: we introduce several natural notions of stability that are applicable to multiwinner multimodal elections (MME) and show an array of hardness and algorithmic results.

In a multimodal election, we have a set of candidates, $\mathcal{C}$, and a multi-set of ℓ different preference profiles, where each profile contains a multi-set of strictly ordered lists over $\mathcal{C}$. The goal is to find a committee of a given size, say k, that satisfies certain notions of stability. In this context, we define the following notions of stability: global-strongly (weakly) stable, individual-strongly (weakly) stable, and pairwise-strongly (weakly) stable. In general, finding any of these committees is an intractable problem, and hence motivates us to study them for restricted domains, namely single-peaked and single-crossing, and when the number of voters is odd. Besides showing that several of these variants remain computationally intractable, we present several efficient algorithms for certain parameters and restricted domains.

SG received funding from MATRICS Grant (MTR/2021/000869) and SERB-SUPRA Grant(SPR/2021/000860).
PJ received funding from Seed Grant (IITJ/R&D/2022-23/07) and SERB-SUPRA Grant(SPR/2021/000860).
SR is supported by the CTU Global postdoc fellowship program.
SS received funding from European Research Council (ERC) under the European Union's Horizon 2020 research and innovation programme (grant no. 819416), and Swarnajayanti Fellowship grant DST/SJF/MSA-01/2017-18.

© The Author(s), under exclusive license to Springer Nature Switzerland AG 2022
P. Kanellopoulos et al. (Eds.): SAGT 2022, LNCS 13584, pp. 508–525, 2022.
https://doi.org/10.1007/978-3-031-15714-1_29

Keywords: Multiwinner Election · Multi-modal · Stability · Parameterized Complexity

1   Introduction

In social choice theory, *multiwinner election* is an important problem as many real-life problems such as the selection of the members of a Parliament, research papers for a conference, restaurant menu, a team of players for a team sports competition, a catalogue of movies for an airline, locations for police or fire stations in a city, etc., can be viewed as a "multiwinner election" problem. Mathematically modelled as a problem where the input consists of a set of alternatives (called candidates), a set of voters such that every voter submits a ranking (a total order) over the candidates, called the preference list of the voter[1], and a positive integer k. The goal is to choose a k-sized subset of candidates (called a *committee*) that satisfy certain acceptability conditions.

This model has an obvious limitation in that in real-life scenarios, rarely does one factor decide the desirability of a subset of candidates. In fact, in complex decision making scenarios, e.g., selecting research papers for a conference, a team of astronauts for a space mission, hors-d'oeuvres for a banquet, a team of players for a basketball competition, a catalogue of movies for an airline, etc., multiple competing factors (call them attributes) come into play. Certain candidates may rank highly with respect to some attributes and lowly with respect to others. In choosing a solution, the goal is to balance all these factors and choose a committee that scores well on as many factors as possible. In our modelling of the committee selection problem, the multiple attributes under consideration can be modelled by submitting ℓ different preference profiles, where each profile is a set of strict rankings of the candidates based on a specific attribute. Such a model has been studied recently for various problems in computational social choce theory, including voting theory [9,26,35,36] and the importance of such a model is also highlighted in [4]. How we aggregate all these information to produce a high quality solution with desirable properties is the context of this work. We use the term MULTIMODAL COMMITTEE SELECTION (as opposed to the unimodal setting where $\ell = 1$), introduced by Jain and Talmon [26], to refer to the problem under consideration.

Of the many notions of a good solution, the one that comes readily to mind is the one closely associated to "popularity", i.e., a solution that is preferred by at least half of the voters, known as the Condorcet winner. Fishburn [21] generalized Condorcet's idea for a single winner election (when $k = 1$) to a multiwinner election (when $k > 1$). Darmann [12] defined two notions of a Condorcet committee: *weak* and *strong*, where the ranking over the committees is based on some *scoring rules*. Gehrlein [24] proposed a new notion of a Condorcet committee that compares the popularity of each committee member to every non-member.

In this paper, we extend the notion of Gehrlein-stability in the unimodal setting [24] to the multimodal setting. Gehrlein-stability has been studied quite

---

[1] There are several other ways to submit a ballot.

extensively for the committee selection problem in recent years [2,10,25,28,32]. It has been argued by Aziz et al. [2] that Gehrlein-stable committees are natural choice for shortlisting of candidates in situations that mirror multiwinner elections to avoid controversy surrounding inclusion of some candidate and exclusion of others as noted previously by [17,34]. Hence, there are good reasons to believe that a Gehrlein-stable committee for multimodal preferences will ably model scenarios described above. There are two notions of Gehrlein-stable committee in the unimodal setting, namely, *Strongly Gehrlein-stable committee*, and *Weakly Gehrlein-stable committee*, depending on margin of victory between two candidates. A committee is *strongly (weakly) Gehrlein-stable*, if each committee member, v, is preferred by more than (at least) half of the voters over any non-committee member, u, in the pairwise election between u and v. The problem of finding strongly (weakly) Gehrlein stable committee is called STRONGLY (WEAKLY) GEHRLEIN STABLE COMMITTEE SELECTION or S(W)GSCS in short. In the multimodal setting, we extend these definitions in a way that will capture our goal that the winning committee is "great across several attributes". Naturally, there may be several ways of achieving this. Chen et al. [9] undertakes one such study in the context of the stable matching problem, where instead of a committee, the goal is to pick a matching that satisfied some notion of stability in multiple preference profiles. In this paper, we use similar ideas to motivate notions of desirable solutions for the MULTIMODAL COMMITTEE SELECTION problem that we believe are compelling, namely: *global stability*, *individual stability*, and *pairwise stability*, where each notion may be further refined in terms of strong or weak stability.

Our Model. Formally stated, for a positive integer ℓ, a *multimodal election $\mathscr{E}$* with ℓ attributes (called *layers*) is defined by a set $\mathcal{C}$ of candidates, and a multiset of ℓ preference profiles $(\mathcal{L}_i)_{i \in [\ell]}$, where each $\mathcal{L}_i$ is a multi-set of strict rankings of the candidate set, representing the voters (model is oblivious to voter set). The input instance of the MULTIMODAL COMMITTEE SELECTION problem is a multimodal election $\mathscr{E} = (\mathcal{C}, (\mathcal{L}_i)_{i \in [\ell]})$, and two integers $\alpha, k \geq 1$ where $\alpha \in [\ell]$.[2] The goal is to find a k-sized committee that satisfies certain stability criteria, defined below, in α layers. We say that

– a committee S is *globally-strongly (weakly) stable* if there exist α layers in which S is strongly (weakly) Gehrlein-stable.
– a committee S is *individually-strongly (weakly) stable* if for each (committee member) $c \in S$, there exist α layers in which c is preferred by more than (at least) half of the voters over every (non-committee member) $d \in \mathcal{C} \setminus S$ in the pairwise election between c and d. We say that these layers provide stability to the candidate c, and c is *individually-strongly (weakly) stable* in these layers.
– a committee S is *pairwise-strongly (weakly) stable* if for each pair of candidates $\{c, d\} \subseteq \mathcal{C}$, where $c \in S$ and $d \in \mathcal{C} \setminus S$, there exist α layers in which c is preferred by more than (at least) half of the voters in the pairwise election between c

---

[2] For any $x \in \mathbb{N}$, $[x]$ denotes the set $\{1, 2, \ldots, x\}$.

and d. We say that these layers provide stability to the pair $\{c, d\}$, and the pair $\{c, d\}$ is *pairwise-strongly (weakly) stable* in these layers.

In our model, we do not assume that α is a function of ℓ. However, when there exists a relationship, we are able to exploit it (e.g., Theorem 15). In fact, it is very well possible that ℓ is large and $\alpha = 1$, for example, suppose the committee to be selected is a panel of experts to adjudicate fellowships. Each member of the panel is an expert in one field and while the panel size is k, there are some ℓ different subjects under consideration. In situations like these $\alpha = 1$.

We call a stable committee as a solution of the multimodal committee selection problem.

Problem Names

We denote the problems of computing a globally-strongly (weakly) stable solution by G-SS (G-WS); an individually-strongly (weakly) stable solution by I-SS (I-WS); and a pairwise-strongly (weakly) stable solution by P-SS (P-WS). Additionally, for any $X \in \{G, I, P\}$, we will use X-YS to refer to both X-SS and X-WS.

For $X \in \{G, I, P\}$ and $Y \in \{S, W\}$, the formal definition of the problem is presented below.

X-YS

Input: A multimodal election $\mathscr{E} = (\mathcal{C}, (\mathcal{L}_i)_{i \in [\ell]})$, and two integers $\alpha, k \geq 1$, where $\alpha \in [\ell]$.
Question: Does there exist a committee of size k that is a solution for X-YS?

Remark 1. All of the definitions coincide with that of Strongly (Weakly) Gehrlein-stability when $\ell = \alpha = 1$.

Remark 2. The notion of strong and weak stability are equivalent for the odd number of voters.

Remark 3. A committee that is globally stable is also individually and pairwise stable; a committee which is individually stable is also pairwise stable.

Example 1. We explain our model using the following example containing 3 voters $\{v_1, v_2, v_3\}$, 4 layers $\{\mathcal{L}_1, \mathcal{L}_2, \mathcal{L}_3, \mathcal{L}_4\}$, and 4 candidates $\{a, b, c, d\}$.

$$
\begin{array}{cccc}
 & v_1 & v_2 & v_3 \\
\mathcal{L}_1: & b \succ a \succ d \succ c; & a \succ b \succ d \succ c; & d \succ b \succ a \succ c \\
\mathcal{L}_2: & b \succ a \succ d \succ c; & a \succ d \succ c \succ b; & b \succ c \succ a \succ d \\
\mathcal{L}_3: & c \succ b \succ d \succ a; & c \succ a \succ d \succ b; & d \succ c \succ a \succ b \\
\mathcal{L}_4: & c \succ b \succ a \succ d; & d \succ c \succ b \succ a; & c \succ a \succ b \succ d
\end{array}
$$

Let $\alpha = 2, k = 2$. Let $S = \{a, b\}$. In $\mathcal{L}_1$, v_1 and v_2 prefers a and b over c and d. Thus, S is strongly Gehrlein-stable in $\mathcal{L}_1$. In $\mathcal{L}_2$, v_1 and v_2 prefer a over c and d, and v_1 and v_3 prefer b over c and d. Thus, there exist 2 layers in which

S is strongly Gehrlein-stable. Hence, S is globally-strongly stable. Next, let us consider a committee $S = \{b, c\}$. Note that S is not strongly Gehrlein-stable in any layer, thus, it is not a globally-strongly stable committee. However, b is more preferred than non-committee members a and d in layers $\mathcal{L}_1$ and $\mathcal{L}_2$, c is more preferred than a and d in the layers $\mathcal{L}_3$ and $\mathcal{L}_4$. Thus, b is individually-strongly stable in the layers $\mathcal{L}_1$ and $\mathcal{L}_2$, and c is individually-strongly stable in the layers $\mathcal{L}_3$ and $\mathcal{L}_4$. Hence, $S = \{b, c\}$ is individually-strongly stable. Let us consider a committee $S = \{b, d\}$. Note that S is neither globally-strongly stable nor individually-strongly stable as d is not more preferred than both a and c in any layer. However, d is more preferred than a in layers $\mathcal{L}_3$ and $\mathcal{L}_4$, and d is more preferred than c in layers $\mathcal{L}_1$ and $\mathcal{L}_2$. Furthermore, b prefers a and c both in $\mathcal{L}_1$ and $\mathcal{L}_2$. Hence, $S = \{b, d\}$ is pairwise-strongly stable.

Differences Between the Notions. Note that for an instance of a MULTI-MODAL COMMITTEE SELECTION, it may be the case that it has no globally stable solution but has an individually stable solution. Moreover, it may also be the case that an instance may not have a globally stable or an individually stable solution but has a pairwise stable solution. We explain it using an example in Example 1.

Graph-Theoretic Formulation. Similar to Gehrlein-stable model, all the models of stability that we study for multimodal election can be transformed to graph-theoretic problems on directed graphs. Using each of ℓ preference profiles, we create ℓ directed graphs with $\mathcal{C}$ as the vertex set, where in the ith *layer*, denoted by the directed graph $G_i = (\mathcal{C}, \mathcal{A}_i)$, there is an arc from vertex a to b in $\mathcal{A}_i$ if and only if in $\mathcal{L}_i$ the candidate[3] a is preferred by more than half of the voters over b in the pairwise election between a and b. These directed graphs are known as *majority graphs* in the literature [2].

Let $S \subseteq \mathcal{C}$. In the language of the majority graph, S is strongly Gehrlein-stable in the ith layer if for every pair of vertices u, v such that $u \in S$ and $v \in \mathcal{C} \setminus S$, v is an out-neighbor of u in G_i, which demonstrates that u is preferred over v by more than half of the voters. The set S is weakly Gehrlein-stable in the ith layer if for every pair of vertices u, v such that $u \in S$ and $v \in \mathcal{C} \setminus S$, v is not an in-neighbor of u in G_i (i.e., either (u, v) is an arc or there is no arc between u and v), which demonstrates that u is preferred over v by at least half of the voters. We say that for the committee S, the vertex $u \in S$ is individually-strongly stable in the ith layer if every $v \in \mathcal{C} \setminus S$ is an out-neighbor of u in G_i, and is individually-weakly stable if every in-neighbor of u in G_i is in S. Analogously, for the set S, a pair of vertices $u \in S$ and $v \in \mathcal{C} \setminus S$ is pairwise-strongly stable in the ith layer if v is an out-neighbor of u in G_i, and is pairwise-weakly stable if v is not an in-neighbor of u in G_i. Note that when the numbers of voters is odd, all the graphs are *tournaments* (a directed graph in which there is an arc between every pair of vertices) and strongly and weakly stable definitions coincides to be the same. We will use graph-theoretic formulation for deriving our results.

---

[3] In the graph-theoretic formulation, we will refer to the candidates as vertices.

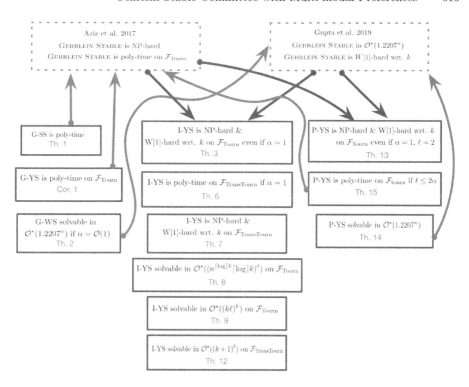

Fig. 1. Our Contributions. The green arrows to the dashed boxes represent reductions that led to an algorithm, and the **red arrows** from the dashed boxes represent reductions that led to a hardness result. (Color figure online)

Our Contributions. Due to Remark 1, and NP-hardness and W[1]-hardness of WGSCS[4] with respect to k [2,25], G-WS, I-WS, and P-WS are NP-hard and W[1]-hard with respect to k. We list our contributions here. The notation $\mathcal{O}^\star(f(k))$ suppresses factors polynomial in input size. Here, $\mathcal{F}_{\mathsf{Tourn}}$ and $\mathcal{F}_{\mathsf{TransTourn}}$ denote the sets of graphs that contain tournaments and transitive tournaments, respectively.

- G-SS can be solved in polynomial time and G-WS in $\mathcal{O}^\star(1.2207^n)$ time for constant α, where n is the number of vertices in each layer. Furthermore, when all the layers are tournament graphs, G-WS can be solved in polynomial time due to Remark 2. Both the results are due to the reduction to unimodal case.
- I-WS is NP-hard and W[1]-hard with respect to k even when all the graphs are tournaments and $\alpha = 1$. This result is in contrast to unimodal case. Furthermore, it remains intractable even for transitive tournaments (an acyclic tournament), but in this reduction α is not constant. When all the graphs are transitive tournaments and $\alpha = 1$, it is solvable in polynomial time.
- When all the graphs are tournaments, we give following algorithms for I-WS:

---

[4] GSCS is used in [25] as they only considered the weak stability notion.

- solvable in $\mathcal{O}^\star((n^{\lceil \log k \rceil} \lceil \log k \rceil)^\ell)$ time. Thus, for $\ell \le \log n$, the problem is unlikely to be NP-hard unless $\mathsf{NP} \subseteq \mathsf{QP}^5$.
  - solvable in $\mathcal{O}^\star((k\ell)^k)$ time.
- When all the graphs are transitive tournaments, I-WS can be solved in $\mathcal{O}^\star((k+1)^\ell)$ time.
- P-WS is NP-hard and W[1]-hard with respect to k even when all the graphs are tournaments, $\ell = 2$, and $\alpha = 1$. However, it can be solved in polynomial time when all the graphs are tournaments and $\ell < 2\alpha$.
- P-YS can be solved in $\mathcal{O}^\star(1.2207^n)$ time.

Figure 1 explain the interplay of results and their relations with each other. We skip the motivation for the considered parameters here as it is same as in [26].

Next, we highlight the significance of our study on tournaments and transitive tournaments.

Restrictions on Layers. Aziz et al. [2] show that in the unimodal case a Gehrlein-stable committee can be found in polynomial time when the number of voters is odd, which corresponds to the case when majority graph is a tournament. Moreover, they also show that additionally if the preference lists satisfy *single-peaked* or *single-crossing* properties, then the corresponding majority graph is a transitive tournament (the graph can be a tournament or transitive tournament even in some other scenarios). Such domain restrictions are also studied by [26]. This motivates us to study the MULTIMODAL COMMITTEE SELECTION problem when each layer is a tournament or a transitive tournament.

Related Works. Jain and Talmon [26] studied committee selection under some *mulimodal voting rules*. They discussed the significance of this problem, proposed generalisation of known committee scoring rules [20] to the multimodal setting, and studied computational and parameterized complexity of the multimodal variants of k-Borda and Chamberlin-Courant (CC). Recently, Wen et al. [36] studied matching problem with multimodal preferences under position scoring rules. Chen et al. [9] gave similar definitions for stability for matching with multimodal preferences. Steindl and Zehavi [35] studied pareto optimal allocations of indivisible goods with multi-modal preferences. Boehmer and Niedermeier [4] also highlighted the importance of multimodal preferences. There has been many works on multiwinner elections where the preference profile is attribute-based [1,6,8,14,27,29,33]. G-SS in a restricted setting of transitive tournaments can be viewed as an instance of diverse committee [6] since only top k candidates from each layer can be in a stable committee for transitive tournaments, but it doesn't generalize to our other cases.

For the committee selection problem, extensive research has been conducted to study voting rules and their stability in the context of selecting a committee [10,17,19,28,34]. We refer to some surveys for application of parameterized complexity in social choice theory [5,15,18].

---

2   Preliminaries

Standard definitions and notations of graph theory in [13] apply. Let $G = (V, A)$ be a directed graph. For a vertex $v \in V(G)$, $N_G^-(v) = \{u : (u, v) \in A(G)\}$ denote the in-neighborhood of the vertex v. We drop the subscript G when it is clear from the context. For a subset $X \subseteq V(G)$, $N^-(X)$ is the set of all in-neighbors of the vertices in X. Unless explicitly specified, for two vertices u and v, both (u, v) and (v, u) are not arcs together in a directed graph. We use n to denote the number of vertices in a graph. *Topological ordering* of a directed graph G is a linear ordering of $V(G)$ where u precedes v for each arc (u, v). From the stability definitions, we have the following.

Proposition 1. *For any* $X \in \{G, I, P\}$, *an* X-*strongly stable and* X-*weakly stable solution are the same on* $\mathcal{F}_{\mathsf{Tourn}}$.

The following will be used for some of our algorithms.

Proposition 2. [25, Theorem 3] *WGSCS can be solved in time* $\mathcal{O}^*(1.2207^n)$ *where* n *is the number of vertices in the majority graph.*

We wish to point out that all our hardness reductions produce an instance where each layer is a directed graph (with arcs in only one direction). Thus, due to the following theorem, we can construct an election as well.

Proposition 3. [30] *Given a directed graph, there exists a corresponding election with size polynomial in the size of the given graph.*

Parameterized Complexity. Here, each problem instance is associated with an integer, k called *parameter*. A problem is said to be *fixed-parameter tractable* (**FPT**) with parameter k if it can be solved in $f(k)n^{\mathcal{O}(1)}$ time for some computable function f, where n is the input size. W-hardness captures the parameterized intractability with respect to a parameter. We refer the reader to [11, 16, 22] for further details.

When referring to a solution that is strongly(weakly) Gehrlein-stable, we may just say strongly(weakly) stable.

3   Global Stability

Here, we present results pertaining to G-YS, $Y \in \{S, W\}$. We begin with G-SS and show it is in P and then follow it with G-WS which is NP-hard.

Note that since each layer has a unique strongly stable committee [3, Theorem 1][6], we can "guess" a layer in which the solution is stable and then compute the strongly stable committee in that layer. Next, we verify if there are $\alpha - 1$ other layers in which that committee is also stable. Thus, we have the following:

---

[6] In [2], the term "strict" is used instead of "strong" (Def. 1 and first para in Sec 5 of [2]).

Theorem 1. $(\spadesuit)^7$ G-SS *is solvable in polynomial time.*

Remark 4. Note that the strongly stable committee is unique in a unimodal election [3, Theorem 1], however the same is not true for a multimodal election as seen by the following example: Consider two majority graphs G_1 and G_2 on the vertex set $\{u, v, w\}$. Let arc sets be $E(G_1) = \{(u, v), (v, w), (u, w)\}$ and $E(G_2) = \{(v, u), (v, w), (w, u)\}$. For $k = 2$ and $\alpha = 1$, $S_1 = \{u, v\}$ and $S_2 = \{v, w\}$, both are globally-strongly stable.

Remark 5. Unlike strong stability, weak stable committee need not be unique, even for a unimodal election.

Next, we study parameterized complexity and a tractable case of G-WS. The hardness results, NP-hardness and W[1]-hardness with respect to k, which follows from intractability of WGSCS [2,25], motivates us to study parameterization with respect to n. In the following discussions, we will adopt the following terminology about G-WS: For an instance $((G_i)_{i\in[\ell]}, \alpha, k)$ and a subset of vertices S, we say that the ith layer *provides stability* to S if for any $u \in S$ and any $v \in V(G) \setminus S$ there is no arc (v, u) in the graph G_i.

The following algorithm works on the same idea as Theorem 1, the difference being that in light of Remark 5, it may not be sufficient to guess one layer and proceed as in Theorem 1. Here, we would need to know the solution in the layer it is stable and then verify if there are other layers which provide stability to the committee is also stable. An exhaustive search of such a committee would look through $\binom{n}{k}$ possibilities. Instead, if we guess the α layers, then we would have to find a solution that is weakly stable in those layers only, captured by a graph which is the union of the arc set in each of those layers. This gives an improvement in time if α is a constant.

Theorem 2. $(\spadesuit)$ G-WS *can be solved in* $\mathcal{O}^\star(1.2207^n)$ *time, for* $\alpha = \mathcal{O}(1)$.

Proposition 1 and Theorem 1 imply the following result.

Corollary 1. G-YS *is solvable in polynomial time on* $\mathcal{F}_{\mathsf{Tourn}}$.

4   Individual Stability

In this section, we will discuss results pertaining to I-YS, where $Y \in \{S, W\}$.

4.1   Intractable Cases

We begin with an intractability result for tournaments. This is a sharp contrast to the unimodal case which is polynomial time solvable for $\mathcal{F}_{\mathsf{Tourn}}$.

Theorem 3. I-YS *is* NP-*hard and* W[1]-*hard with respect to* k *on* $\mathcal{F}_{\mathsf{Tourn}}$ *even when* $\alpha = 1$.

---

[7] The proofs marked by $\spadesuit$ are deferred to the full version.

Proof. We give a parameter-preserving reduction from the WGSCS problem, which is known to be W[1]-hard with respect to k [25], to I-WS. Moreover, this being a polynomial time reduction will also prove that I-WS is NP-hard. Let $\mathcal{I} = (G, k')$ be an instance of WGSCS, where G is not a tournament; otherwise the instance is polynomial-time solvable. Let Z denote the set of vertices in G whose total degree (sum of in-degree and out-degree) is less than $n - 1$.

Construction. We will construct an instance of I-WS with $|Z|$ layers and $\alpha = 1$. For each vertex $u \in Z$, we create a graph G_u as follows. Initialize $G_u = G$, i.e., every arc in G also exists in each layer of $(G_u)_{u \in Z}$. Consider a vertex v which is neither an in-neighbor nor an out-neighbor of u. Then, we add an arc from u to v in G_u. We make G_u a tournament by adding the remaining missing arcs in an arbitrary direction. Clearly, this construction takes polynomial time.

   Due to Proposition 3, G_u is a majority graph for an appropriately defined election. Note that the vertex set of G_u is same for each $u \in Z$. Hence, $\mathcal{J} = ((G_u)_{u \in Z}, \alpha = 1, k = k')$ is an instance of I-WS, where each directed graph G_u is a tournament. The next observations follow directly from the construction.

Observation 4. *Any vertex $u \in Z$ has the same set of in-neighbors in G and G_u.*

Observation 5. *Let $G' \in \{G_u : u \in Z\}$. Then, any vertex $v \in V(G) \setminus Z$ has the same in-neighbors in G and G'.*

   The following shows the correctness of the reduction.

Lemma 1. *(♠) S is a solution for WGSCS in $\mathcal{I}$ iff S is a solution for I-WS in $\mathcal{J}$.*

Since the constructed graph is a tournament, we can conclude the intractability of I-YS.   □

   In contrast with the above intractability result, we note that when the layers are transitive tournaments and $\alpha = 1$, we have a tractable case for I-YS.

Theorem 6. *I-YS is solvable in polynomial time on $\mathcal{F}_{\mathsf{TransTourn}}$ if $\alpha = 1$; and a solution always exists.*

Proof. Let $\mathcal{I} = ((G_i)_{i \in [\ell]}, \alpha, k)$ be an instance of I-YS. Since each layer is a transitive tournament, we may assume that the vertices in the ith layer, for $i \in [\ell]$, are ordered in terms of the topological ordering in G_i. Thus, We can find a solution by picking the first k vertices from G_1.

   Unsurprisingly perhaps, for any arbitrary $\alpha > 1$ the problem is again intractable.

Theorem 7. *I-YS is NP-hard and W[1]-hard with respect to k on $\mathcal{F}_{\mathsf{TransTourn}}$.*

Proof. We prove this hardness result by showing a polynomial time reduction from CLIQUE on regular graphs, in which given a regular undirected graph G and an integer k, the goal is to decide if there is a subset $S \subseteq V(G)$ of size k such that for every pair of vertices $u, v \in S$, uv is an edge in G. The CLIQUE problem for regular graphs is NP-hard and W[1]-hard with respect to k [7,23]. Due to Proposition 1, we use I-SS in the rest of the proof.

We explain the construction along with the intuition behind the gadget. The precise construction of the transitive tournaments is in the **black** box below.

Construction: Let $(G, \tilde{k})$ be an instance of CLIQUE, where degree of every vertex in G is d. For the ease of explanation, we assume that d is even. Let n and m denote the number of vertices and edges in G, respectively. We construct an instance of I-SS as follows: For every edge $e = uv$ in G, we have two directed graphs, say $\mathcal{M}_{e_u}$ and $\mathcal{M}_{e_v}$. For every edge $e \in E(G)$ and every vertex $u \in V(G)$, we add vertices u and e in every directed graph. We call these vertices as the *real vertices* of the directed graphs. For every directed graph $\mathcal{M}$ (constructed so far), we also add a set of dummy vertices, denoted by $D_{\mathcal{M}} = \{d_{\mathcal{M}}^1, \dots, d_{\mathcal{M}}^j\}$, where the value of j will be specified later (at the end of the construction). We call these vertices as *dummy vertices* of the directed graphs.

The purpose of adding the dummy vertices is that a real vertex e corresponding to the edge $e \in E(G)$ should get the stability only from the corresponding directed graphs, and the real vertex u corresponding to the vertex $u \in V(G)$ should get stability only from the directed graphs $\mathcal{M}_{e_u}$, where e is an edge incident to u.

Since every transitive tournament has a unique topological ordering, we explain this ordering of vertices in every directed graph. Then, the arc set is self-explanatory. For the directed graph $\mathcal{M}_{e_u}$, the ordering is $(u, e, D_{\mathcal{M}_{e_u}}, \langle \text{remaining vertices} \rangle)$. The notation $\langle \cdot \rangle$ denote that the vertices in this set can be ordered in any arbitrary order. Intuitively, the goal is that if the vertex e is in the committee, then to provide it stability in the required number of layers (the number of layers will be defined later), u and v must also be in the solution (i.e., a vertex corresponding to an edge of G pulls vertices that correspond to its endpoints in G in the committee).

Next, we want to prevent more than $\tilde{k}$ vertices in the committee corresponding to vertices in $V(G)$, so that these vertices corresponds to clique vertices. Towards this, for every vertex $u \in V(G)$, we add a set of $\tilde{k}^2 - 1$ vertices, denoted by $T_u = (t_u^1, \dots, t_u^{\tilde{k}^2 - 1})$, in every directed graph. We call these vertices *indicator vertices*. Let $\overleftarrow{T_u}$ denote the set of vertices in the reverse order of T_u, i.e., $\overleftarrow{T_u} = (t_u^{\tilde{k}^2 - 1}, \dots, t_u^1)$. Let $E(u)$ denote the set of edges incident to u. Let $E_1(u)$ and $E_2(u)$ be two disjoint sbsets of $E(u)$, each of size $|E(u)|/2$. In the ordering of the vertices of the directed graph $\mathcal{M}_{e_u}$, where $e \in E_1(u)$, we add T_u in front of the ordering constructed above, i.e., the new ordering of $\mathcal{M}_{e_u}$ is $(T_u, u, e, D_{\mathcal{M}_{e_u}}, \langle \text{remaining vertices} \rangle)$. For $e \in E_2(u)$, the ordering of the vertices of $\mathcal{M}_{e_u}$ is $(u, \overleftarrow{T_u}, e, D_{\mathcal{M}_{e_u}}, \langle \text{remaining vertices} \rangle)$, i.e., $\overleftarrow{T_u}$ is after u.

Additionally, for every edge $e \in E(G)$, we add $d/2 - 1$ *dummy layers*, $\mathcal{M}_{e^i}$, $i \in [d/2 - 1]$, in which e is the first vertex in the ordering. Next, to ensure that no other real vertex get stability from these dummy layers, for every $\mathcal{M}_{e^i}$, $i \in [d/2 - 1]$, we add a new set of j dummy vertices, denoted by $D_{\mathcal{M}_{e^i}}$. The ordering of the vertices in these directed graphs is $(e, \langle D_{\mathcal{M}_{e^i}} \rangle, \langle \text{remaining vertices} \rangle)$. Note that for every $i \in [d/2 - 1]$, $\mathcal{M}_{e^i}$ provide stability to vertex e as it does not have any in-neighbors in these directed graphs. Note that the number of layers in the constructed instance is $m(d/2 + 1)$.

Finally, we set $k = \tilde{k}^3 + \binom{\tilde{k}}{2}$, $\alpha = d/2 + 1$, and the value of j as k so that no dummy vertex can be part of the solution.

Precisely, the construction is as follows.

Construction of an instance in the proof of Theorem 7

- For every $u \in V(G)$ and $e \in E(G)$, we add vertices u and e to directed graphs.
- For every $e(= uv) \in E(G)$, we add $d/2 + 1$ directed graphs, $\mathcal{M}_{e_u}, \mathcal{M}_{e_v}, \mathcal{M}_{e^1}, \mathcal{M}_{e^2}, \ldots, \mathcal{M}_{e^{d/2-1}}$.
- For every directed graph $\mathcal{M}$, we add a set of $\tilde{k}^3 + \binom{\tilde{k}}{2}$ dummy vertices $D_{\mathcal{M}} = d_{\mathcal{M}}^1, \ldots, d_{\mathcal{M}}^{\tilde{k}^3 + \binom{\tilde{k}}{2}}$.
- For every vertex $u \in V(G)$, we add a set of indicator vertices $T_u = \{t_u^1, \ldots, t_u^{\tilde{k}^2 - 1}\}$.
- To define the edge set of a directed graph, we define its topological ordering. Let $E(u)$ denote the set of edges incident to u, and $E_1(u)$ and $E_2(u)$ be two disjoint subsets of $E(u)$ such that size of both the sets is $|E(u)|/2$.
  - For every $e \in E_1(u)$, the ordering of vertices in $\mathcal{M}_{e_u}$ is $(T_u, u, e, \langle D_{\mathcal{M}_{e_u}} \rangle, \langle \text{remaining vertices} \rangle)$
  - For every $e \in E_2(u)$, the ordering of vertices in $\mathcal{M}_{e_u}$ is $(u, \overleftarrow{T_u}, e, \langle D_{\mathcal{M}_{e_u}} \rangle, \langle \text{remaining vertices} \rangle)$
- For every $i \in [d/2 - 1]$, the ordering of vertices in $\mathcal{M}_{e^i}$ is $(e, \langle D_{\mathcal{M}_{e^i}} \rangle, \langle \text{remaining vertices} \rangle)$.
- $k = \tilde{k}^3 + \binom{\tilde{k}}{2}$ and $\alpha = d/2 + 1$.

Let $\mathcal{Z} = \{e_u, e_v : e(= uv) \in E(G)\} \cup \{e^i : e \in E(G), i \in [d/2 - 1]\}$. Since the set of vertices is same in all the directed graphs, we denote it by $V_{\mathcal{M}}$.

Next, we prove the correctness in the following lemma.

Lemma 2. $\mathcal{I}$ *is a yes-instance of* CLIQUE *iff* $\mathcal{J}$ *is a yes-instance of* I-SS.

Proof. In the forward direction, let S be a solution to $(G, \tilde{k})$. Let $S' = \{\{u, T_u\} \subseteq V_{\mathcal{M}} : u \in S\} \cup \{e \in V_{\mathcal{M}} : e \in E(G[S])\}$, i.e., S' contains real and indicator vertices corresponding to the vertices and edges in $G[S]$. We claim that S' is a solution for $((\mathcal{M}_\ell)_{\ell \in \mathcal{Z}}, \alpha, k)$. Since for every $u \in V(G)$, $|T_u| = \tilde{k}^2 - 1$, and S is a $\tilde{k}$-sized clique, we have that $|S'| = \tilde{k} + \tilde{k}(\tilde{k}^2 - 1) + \binom{\tilde{k}}{2} = k$. Next, we argue that S' is individually stable for $\alpha = d/2 + 1$. Note that there are $d/2$ directed graphs in which the vertex u corresponding to the vertex $u \in V(G)$ does not have any in-neighbor, and there are $d/2$ directed graphs in which the in-neigbor of u is T_u. Since if $u \in S'$, $T_u \subseteq S'$, we have that there are at least $d/2 + 1$ directed graphs that provides individual stability to the vertex $u \in S'$. Similarly, there are at least $d/2 + 1$ directed graphs that provides individual stability to every vertex in T_u, where $T_u \subseteq S'$. Next, we argue about the vertex $e \in S'$ corresponding to the edge $e(= uv) \in E(G)$. Note that there are $d/2 - 1$ directed graphs (in particular, $\mathcal{M}_{e^i}$, where $i \in [d/2 - 1]$) in which e does not have any in-neighbor. Furthermore, in the directed graph $\mathcal{M}_{e_u}$, the set of in-neighbors of e is $T_u \cup \{u\}$ which is a subset of S' as $u \in S$. Similarly, all the in-neighbors of e in $\mathcal{M}_{e_v}$ belong to S'. Thus, S' is individually stable for $\alpha = d/2 + 1$.

In the backward direction, let S be an individually stable committee for $((\mathcal{M}_\ell)_{\ell \in \mathcal{Z}}, \alpha, k)$. We observe some properties of the set S.

Claim 1 (♠) S does not contain any dummy vertex.

Claim 2 (♠) If $u \in S$, then $T_u \subseteq S$.

Claim 3 (♠) If $|T_u \cap S| \neq \emptyset$, then $u \in S$.

Claim 4 (♠) If the vertex e corresponding to the edge $e(= uv) \in E(G)$ is in S, then the vertices $\{u, v\} \subseteq S$.

Let $V^\star = \{v \in V(G) : v \in S\}$ and $E^\star = \{e \in E(G) : e \in S\}$.

Claim 5 (♠) $|V^\star| = \tilde{k}$ and $|E^\star| = \binom{\tilde{k}}{2}$.

Next, we argue that the vertices are consistent with the edges, i.e., if $uv \in E^\star$, then $\{u, v\} \subseteq V^\star$. This follows from Claim 4. Moreover, since $|V^\star| = \tilde{k}$ and $|E^\star| = \binom{\tilde{k}}{2}$, it follows that the graph $G^\star = (V^\star, E^\star)$ is a complete graph on the vertex set $V^\star$, and thus $V^\star$ is a clique of size $\tilde{k}$ in G. This completes the proof of the theorem. $\qquad\square$

4.2   Tractable Cases

The intractability results of Theorems 3 and 7 notwithstanding, motivate us to look for parameters beyond α and k. Specifically, we look for combined parameters and in doing so we show that for $Y \in \{S, W\}$, I-YS is FPT parameterized by $k + \ell$. We note that the parameterized complexity with parameter ℓ eludes us. However, Theorem 8 implies that when $\ell \leq \log n$, we have an algorithm with running time $2^{\text{poly}(\log n)}$. Thus, we cannot hope for an NP-hardness result when $\ell \leq \log n$, unless NP $\subseteq$ QP. Therefore, the complexity when $\ell > \log n$ remains unknown.

At the heart of the parameterized algorithm, Theorem 8, is the notion of an *out-dominating set*, defined as follows. For any graph $G = (V, A)$, a set $S \subseteq V(G)$ is called an out-dominating set if every vertex $v \in V \setminus S$ has an out-neighbor in the set S.

Before we present the algorithm, we can explain the intuition as follows. Any solution S for I-YS can be viewed as $S = S_1 \cup \ldots \cup S_\ell$, where each S_i denotes the set of vertices (possibly empty) that receive individual stability from the layer i. (Clearly, every vertex in S must be in at least α different S_is.) Moreover, we know that in the graph G_i the in-neighbors of any vertex in S_i are also present in S_i. Thus, S_i can be viewed as the union of a set X_i and the set of its in-neighbors in G_i, i.e., $S_i = X_i \cup N_{G_i}^-(X_i)$. The set X_i here is the out-dominating set of the subgraph induced by S_i in G_i, denoted by T_i. While we do not know the set S_i, we know that its size is at most k. Hence, the subgraph $T_i = G_i[S_i]$ has at most k vertices and has an out-dominating set of size at most $\lceil \log k \rceil$, due to Lemma 3. This allows us to enumerate all possible subsets of size $\lceil \log k \rceil$ and from that find its in-neighborhood. This process allows us to find X_i, $N^-(X_i)$, and thus S_i for each $i \in [\ell]$, and from there the set S. We use the next lemma to find the out-dominating set.

Lemma 3. *[31, Fact 2.5] A tournament $G = (V, A)$ has an out-dominating set of size at most $\lceil \log |V| \rceil$. Additionally, if G is a transitive tournament, then G has a unique out-dominating set of size one.*

Theorem 8. *I-YS is solvable in time $\mathcal{O}^\star((n^{\lceil \log k \rceil})^\ell)$ on $\mathcal{F}_{\mathsf{Tourn}}$.*

Proof. Let $\mathcal{I} = ((G_i)_{i\in[\ell]}, \alpha, k)$ be an instance of I-YS. Our algorithm works as follows. For each $i \in [\ell]$, our algorithm guesses a vertex subset of size at most $\lceil \log k \rceil$ in G_i and finds its in-neighborhood set in G_i. The union of these two sets is denoted by Y_i. If $N_{G_i}^-(Y_i) \setminus Y_i \neq \emptyset$ or $|Y_i| > k$, then we set $Y_i = \emptyset$. Else, the algorithm checks if $\cup_{i\in[\ell]} Y_i$ is a solution for $\mathcal{I}$. If the algorithm fails to find a subset of vertices that is a solution for $\mathcal{I}$, then it returns "no".

Correctness. Any solution returned by the algorithm will quite obviously be a solution for $\mathcal{I}$ since at the end the algorithm checks if $\cup_{i\in[\ell]} Y_i$ is a solution. Thus, we only need to prove the other direction. That is, we prove that if there exists an individual stable solution, the algorithm generates it. Suppose that $\mathcal{I}$ is a *yes*-instance and S is a solution. We may view S as a union of ℓ (possibly empty) sets S_i where S_i are the vertices of G_i that are stable in the layer i i.e., all those vertices whose in-neighbors in G_i are also in S_i. We show that we generate the set S_i by enumerating $\lceil \log k \rceil$ size subsets in G_i for each layer i. For each $i \in [\ell]$, let $T_i = G_i[S_i]$ be the tournament induced by the vertices in S_i. For each $i \in [\ell]$, let X_i denote an out-dominating set of the graph T_i. Due to Lemma 3, $|X_i| \leq \lceil \log k \rceil$ since $|S_i| \leq k$ (because $|S| = k$). Recall that $N_{G_i}^-(X_i)$ denotes the set of in-neighbors of X_i in G_i. From the definition of individual stability, $N_{G_i}^-(X_i) \subseteq S_i$ and $S_i = X_i \cup N_{G_i}^-(X_i)$.

Hence, our algorithm generates the set X_i by trying all possible subsets of size at most $\lceil \log k \rceil$, and from that construct the set S_i. Thus, for some choice of X_i we will have $Y_i = S_i$ for each $i \in [\ell]$ and then the algorithm will return $\cup_{i\in[\ell]} Y_i$ which is the solution S.

Time Complexity. This results in an algorithm that has to verify at most $\left(\sum_{0 \leq i \leq \lceil \log k \rceil} \binom{n}{i} \right)^\ell$ different subsets of vertices since in any layer there are

$\sum_{0 \le i \le \lceil \log k \rceil} \binom{n}{i}$ different subsets of size at most $\lceil \log k \rceil$. The first $\lceil \log k \rceil$ terms of binomial coefficients sum up to $O(n^{\lceil \log k \rceil})$. The last verification step can be carried out in $\mathcal{O}(k\ell)$ steps by checking for each vertex in $\cup_{i \in [\ell]} Y_i$ if there are α layers in which it is stable. □

Next, we discuss an FPT algorithm for the parameter $k + \ell$. We begin with the following result that may be of independent interest.

Lemma 4. (♠) *In any tournament there are at most $2k + 1$ vertices with in-degree at most k.*

The next result is inspired by the above lemma as there are only $\mathcal{O}(k\ell)$ vertices that can be part of solution, $\mathcal{O}(k)$ from each layer.

Theorem 9. (♠) I-YS *is solvable in time* $\mathcal{O}^\star(\ell^k)$ *on* $\mathcal{F}_{\mathsf{Tourn}}$.

Remark 6. Comparing Theorem 8 vs Theorem 9. Note that neither algorithm subsumes the other. Each works better than the other in certain situations as described below

- For a constant value of k, Theorem 9 gives a polynomial time algorithm while Theorem 8 gives an $n^{\mathcal{O}(\ell)}$ time algorithm, (i.e., it does not run in polynomial time if ℓ is not a constant.)
- For a constant value of ℓ, Theorem 9 gives an FPT-algorithm with respect to k (i.e., it runs in polynomial time if k is also a constant), while Theorem 8 gives a quasi-polynomial time algorithm.

Notwithstanding the hardness of Theorem 7 on transitive tournaments, we note that the problem does admit polynomial time algorithm if the total number of layers is a constant, which is an improvement over the running times given by Theorems 8 and 9.

Theorem 10. (♠) I-YS *is solvable in* $\mathcal{O}^\star((k+1)^\ell)$ *time on* $\mathcal{F}_{\mathsf{TransTourn}}$.

Due to Theorem 10, we have the following.

Corollary 11. I-YS *is solvable in polynomial time on* $\mathcal{F}_{\mathsf{TransTourn}}$ *if* $\ell = \mathcal{O}(\log_k n)$.

Theorem 12. (♠) I-YS *is solvable in polynomial time on* $\mathcal{F}_{\mathsf{TransTourn}}$ *if* $\ell = \alpha$.

5   Pairwise Stability

In this section, we will discuss results pertaining to P-YS, where $Y \in \{S, W\}$. We begin by showing that P-YS is hard for two layers even for restricted domains. Note that for $\ell = 1$, P-YS can be solved in polynomial time on $\mathcal{F}_{\mathsf{Tourn}}$, however, for $\ell = 2$, we have the following intractability result.

Theorem 13. P-YS *is* NP-*hard and* W[1]-*hard with respect to* k *on* $\mathcal{F}_{\mathsf{Tourn}}$ *even when* $\alpha = 1$ *and* $\ell = 2$.

Proof. We give a reduction from an instance of WGSCS. Since WGSCS is W[1]-hard with respect to parameter k [25], this will prove that P-YS is also W[1]-hard with respect to k. Let $\mathcal{I} = (G, k')$ be an instance of WGSCS. We will create an instance of P-YS with two layers G_1 and G_2. Initialize $G_1 = G_2 = G$. Next, for every pair of vertices $\{u, v\}$ that do not have an arc between them in G, we add the arc (u, v) in G_1, and add the arc (v, u) in G_2. We define $\mathcal{J} = (G_1, G_2, \alpha = 1, k = k')$ to be an instance of P-YS. Note that G_1 and G_2 both are tournaments.

Since we can construct G_1 and G_2 in polynomial time, the following result proves the theorem.

Lemma 5. (♠) S *is solution for* $\mathcal{I}$ *iff* S *is a solution for* $\mathcal{J}$.

This completes the proof.   □

The next result is an FPT algorithm for P-YS with respect to n. We prove it by showing reductions to WGSCS.

Theorem 14. (♠) P-YS *is solvable in time in* $\mathcal{O}^{\star}(1.2207^n)$.

By focusing our attention towards structural parameters pertaining to the layers in the instance of P-YS, we obtain the following result.

Theorem 15. (♠) P-YS *is solvable in polynomial time on* $\mathcal{F}_{\mathsf{Tourn}}$ *if* $\ell < 2\alpha$.

We conclude our discussions with the following result about weak stability that follows due to the relationship between I-WS and P-WS, and Theorem 6.

Corollary 16. P-WS *is solvable in polynomial time on* $\mathcal{F}_{\mathsf{TransTourn}}$ *if* $\alpha = 1$.

6   Conclusion

We extend the study of stable committee to the multimodal elections. In fact, in [26], the authors considered the same set of voters and candidates across the layers. We generalize this to the scenario, where voters need not be the same across the layers, and justified this model in Introduction. We defined three notions of stability and studied their computational and parameterized complexity.

The following questions elude us so far for transitive tournaments: (i) the computational complexity of I-YS for constant $\alpha > 1$, (ii) the parameterized complexity of I-YS with parameter ℓ, (iii) the computational complexity of P-YS.

Jain and Talmon [26] initiated the study of scoring rules for multimodal multiwinner election. We believe that it would be interesting to extend the notion of stability given by Darmann [12] to multimodal preferences. In general, it would be interesting to extend the extensive study of multiwinner election for unimodal case to multimodal preferences.

References

1. Aziz, H.: A rule for committee selection with soft diversity constraints. Group Decis. Negot. **28**(6), 1193–1200 (2019)
2. Aziz, H., Elkind, E., Faliszewski, P., Lackner, M., Skowron, P.: The condorcet principle for multiwinner elections: from shortlisting to proportionality. In: IJCAI, pp. 84–90 (2017)
3. Aziz, H., Elkind, E., Faliszewski, P., Lackner, M., Skowron, P.: The condorcet principle for multiwinner elections: from shortlisting to proportionality. arXiv preprint arXiv:1701.08023 (2017)
4. Boehmer, N., Niedermeier, R.: Broadening the research agenda for computational social choice: multiple preference profiles and multiple solutions. In: AAMAS 2021, pp. 1–5 (2021)
5. Bredereck, R., Chen, J., Faliszewski, P., Guo, J., Niedermeier, R., Woeginger, G.: Parameterized algorithmics for computational social choice. Tsinghua Sci. Technol. **19**(4), 358 (2014)
6. Bredereck, R., Faliszewski, P., Igarashi, A., Lackner, M., Skowron, P.: Multiwinner elections with diversity constraints. In: AAAI (2018)
7. Cai, L.: Parameterized complexity of cardinality constrained optimization problems. Comput. J. **51**(1), 102–121 (2008)
8. Celis, L.E., Huang, L., Vishnoi, N.K.: Multiwinner voting with fairness constraints, pp. 144–151 (2018)
9. Chen, J., Niedermeier, R., Skowron, P.: Stable marriage with multi-modal preferences. In: EC, pp. 269–286 (2018)
10. Coelho, D.: Understanding, evaluating and selecting voting rules through games and axioms. Ph.D. thesis, Universitat Autònoma de Barcelona (2005)
11. Cygan, M., et al.: Parameterized Algorithms. Springer, Cham (2015). https://doi.org/10.1007/978-3-319-21275-3
12. Darmann, A.: How hard is it to tell which is a condorcet committee? Math. Soc. Sci. **66**(3), 282–292 (2013)
13. Diestel, R.: Graph Theory. Graduate Texts in Mathematics, 4th edn, vol. 173. Springer, Heidelberg (2012)
14. Do, V., Atif, J., Lang, J., Usunier, N.: Online selection of diverse committees. In: IJCAI, pp. 154–160 (2021)
15. Dorn, B., Schlotter, I.: Having a hard time? Explore parameterized complexity. In: Endriss, U. (ed.) Trends in Computational Social Choice. AI Access (2017)
16. Downey, R.G., Fellows, M.R.: Fundamentals of Parameterized Complexity. Springer, London (2013). https://doi.org/10.1007/978-1-4471-5559-1
17. Elkind, E., Faliszewski, P., Skowron, P., Slinko, A.: Properties of multiwinner voting rules. Soc. Choice Welfare **48**(3), 599–632 (2017). https://doi.org/10.1007/s00355-017-1026-z
18. Faliszewski, P., Niedermeier, R.: Parameterization in computational social choice. In: Encyclopedia of Algorithms, pp. 1516–1520 (2016)
19. Faliszewski, P., Skowron, P., Slinko, A., Talmon, N.: Multiwinner voting: a new challenge for social choice theory. Trends Comput. Soc. Choice **74**, 27–47 (2017)
20. Faliszewski, P., Skowron, P., Slinko, A., Talmon, N.: Committee scoring rules: axiomatic characterization and hierarchy. TEAC **7**(1), 3:1–3:39 (2019)
21. Fishburn, P.C.: An analysis of simple voting systems for electing committees. SIAM J. Appl. Math. **41**(3), 499–502 (1981)

22. Flum, J., Grohe, M.: Parameterized Complexity Theory. Springer, Heidelberg (2006). https://doi.org/10.1007/3-540-29953-X

23. Garey, M.R., Johnson, D.S.: Computers and Intractability: A Guide to the Theory of NP-Completeness. W. H. Freeman, New York (1979)

24. Gehrlein, W.V.: The condorcet criterion and committee selection. Math. Soc. Sci. **10**(3), 199–209 (1985)

25. Gupta, S., Jain, P., Roy, S., Saurabh, S., Zehavi, M.: Gehrlein stability in committee selection: parameterized hardness and algorithms. Auton. Agent. Multi-Agent Syst. **34**(1), 1–21 (2020). https://doi.org/10.1007/s10458-020-09452-z

26. Jain, P., Talmon, N.: Committee selection with multimodal preferences. In: ECAI, pp. 123–130 (2020)

27. Kagita, V.R., Pujari, A.K., Padmanabhan, V., Aziz, H., Kumar, V.: Committee selection using attribute approvals. In: AAMAS, pp. 683–691 (2021)

28. Kamwa, E.: On stable rules for selecting committees. J. Math. Econ. **70**, 36–44 (2017)

29. Lang, J., Skowron, P.: Multi-attribute proportional representation. Artif. Intell. **263**, 74–106 (2018)

30. McGarvey, D.C.: A theorem on the construction of voting paradoxes. Econometrica J. Econometric Soc. 608–610 (1953)

31. Megiddo, N., Vishkin, U.: On finding a minimum dominating set in a tournament. Theoret. Comput. Sci. **61**(2), 307–316 (1988)

32. Ratliff, T.C.: Some startling inconsistencies when electing committees. Soc. Choice Welf. **21**(3), 433–454 (2003)

33. Relia, K.: Dire committee: diversity and representation constraints in multiwinner elections. arXiv preprint arXiv:2107.07356 (2021)

34. Barberá, S., Coelho, D.: How to choose a non-controversial list with k names. Soc. Choice Welf. **31**(1), 79–96 (2008)

35. Steindl, B., Zehavi, M.: Parameterized analysis of assignment under multiple preferences. In: Rosenfeld, A., Talmon, N. (eds.) EUMAS 2021. LNCS (LNAI), vol. 12802, pp. 160–177. Springer, Cham (2021). https://doi.org/10.1007/978-3-030-82254-5_10

36. Wen, Y., Zhou, A., Guo, J.: Position-based matching with multi-modal preferences. In: AAMAS 2022, pp. 1373–1381 (2022)

Online Max-min Fair Allocation

Yasushi Kawase[1]([⊠]) and Hanna Sumita[2]

[1] University of Tokyo, Tokyo, Japan
`kawase@mist.i.u-tokyo.ac.jp`
[2] Tokyo Institute of Technology, Tokyo, Japan
`sumita@c.titech.ac.jp`

Abstract. We study an online version of the max-min fair allocation problem for indivisible items. In this problem, items arrive one by one, and each item must be allocated irrevocably on arrival to one of n agents, who have additive valuations for the items. Our goal is to maximize the egalitarian social welfare, which is the minimum happiness among the agents. In research on the topic of online allocation, this is a fundamental and natural problem. Our main result is to reveal the asymptotic competitive ratios of the problem for both the adversarial and i.i.d. input models. For the adversarial case, we design a polynomial-time deterministic algorithm that is asymptotically $1/n$-competitive, and we show that this guarantee is optimal. Moreover, the algorithm satisfies proportionality in an asymptotic sense, that is, each agent receives a bundle of value at least nearly $1/n$ of the whole. For the case when the items are drawn from an unknown identical and independent distribution, we construct a simple polynomial-time deterministic algorithm that outputs a nearly optimal allocation. We analyze the strict competitive ratio and show almost tight bounds for the solution. We further mention some implications of our results on variants of the problem.

1 Introduction

In this paper, we study the problem of allocating indivisible items so that the minimum happiness among agents is maximized. Let us consider a toy instance. Suppose that Alice and Bob are trying to share bite-sized snacks that arrive sequentially. As soon as each snack arrives, one of them will receive and eat it. If each snack is picked by the one who values it more than the other, the outcome will become an imbalanced one (Table 1). In contrast, if they pick the items alternately, the outcome will become an inefficient one (Table 2). The question then arises as to what kind of rule would satisfy fairness and efficiency simultaneously, and moreover, what would be the best possible rule.

The fair allocation of resources or items to agents has been a central problem in economic theory for several decades. In classical fair allocation problems, we

The first author was supported by JSPS KAKENHI Grant Number 20K19739, JST PRESTO Grant Number JPMJPR2122, and Value Exchange Engineering, a joint research project between R4D, Mercari, Inc. and the RIISE. The second author was supported by JSPS KAKENHI Grant Numbers 17K12646 and 21K17708.

© The Author(s), under exclusive license to Springer Nature Switzerland AG 2022
P. Kanellopoulos et al. (Eds.): SAGT 2022, LNCS 13584, pp. 526–543, 2022.
https://doi.org/10.1007/978-3-031-15714-1_30

Table 1. Outcome when the snack is picked by the one who values it more

	1	2	3	4	5	6	$\cdots$
Alice's value	0.7	1.0	0.8	0.9	0.7	0.8	$\cdots$
Bob's value	0.5	0.1	0.7	0.2	0.6	0.0	$\cdots$

Table 2. Outcome when the snack is picked alternately

	1	2	3	4	5	6	$\cdots$
Alice's value	0.7	1.0	0.8	0.9	0.7	0.8	$\cdots$
Bob's value	0.5	0.1	0.7	0.2	0.6	0.0	$\cdots$

are given all the items in advance. Recently, the problem of allocating items in an online fashion has been studied in the areas of combinatorial optimization, algorithmic game theory, and artificial intelligence. In online problems, indivisible items arrive one by one, and they need to be allocated immediately and irrevocably to agents. The study of online fair allocation is motivated by its wide range of applications such as the allocation of donor organs to patients, donated food to charities, electric vehicles to charging stations; we refer the reader to the survey [4] for details.

Let $N = \{1, 2, \ldots, n\}$ and $M = \{e_1, e_2, \ldots, e_m\}$ be the sets of agents and indivisible items, respectively. Suppose that each agent $i \in N$ has an additive valuation function v_i. Our goal is to find an allocation A that maximizes the minimum utility among the agents $\min_{i \in N} v_i(A_i)$. The value $\min_{i \in N} v_i(A_i)$ is called the *egalitarian social welfare* of allocation A. The problem of maximizing the egalitarian social welfare when items arrive one by one is called the *online max-min fair allocation problem*. Here, we assume that the number of items is unknown in advance. The max-min fairness (that is, the egalitarian social welfare is maximized) is one of the most commonly used notions for measuring fairness and efficiency, and it has been studied extensively in the area of fair allocation [6,16,24,26,29]. Thus, our problem naturally models the above applications using the notion of max-min fairness. We measure the performance of online algorithms using the *competitive ratio*, which is the ratio of the egalitarian social welfare obtained by an online algorithm to that of the offline optimal value. Furthermore, we consider two types of competitive ratio: *strict* and *asymptotic*. In the strict setting, we consider the worst-case ratio for every possible input sequence, whereas in the asymptotic setting, we consider the worst-case ratio for input sequences with sufficiently large optimal values. Section 2 presents the formal definitions for these terms. Note that the asymptotic competitive ratio represents an intrinsic performance ratio that does not depend on initial behavior. We consider two arrival models: *adversarial*, in which the items are chosen arbitrarily, and *independent and identically distributed (i.i.d.)*, in which the value vectors of the items are drawn independently from an unknown/known distribution.

1.1   Related Work

A class of the online max-min fair allocation problem with identical agents (i.e., $v_1 = \cdots = v_n$) has also been studied as the *online machine covering problem* in the context of scheduling [7,18,22,23,32,33]. Here, an agent's utility corresponds to a machine load. The problem of maximizing the minimum machine load was initially motivated by modeling the sequencing of maintenance actions for modular gas turbine aircraft engines [18]. For this identical agents case in the adversarial model, it is known that any online deterministic algorithm has a strict competitive ratio of at most $1/n$ and that the greedy algorithm is strictly $1/n$-competitive [33]. Besides, there exists a strictly $\Omega(\frac{1}{\sqrt{n}\log n})$-competitive randomized algorithm, which is a best possible algorithm up to logarithmic factors [7]. Note that the greedy algorithm is asymptotically 1-competitive since $\max_{i \in N} v_i(A_i) - \min_{i \in N} v_i(A_i) \le 1$ in its allocation A.

In addition, other settings of online fair allocation problems have been actively studied recently [1–4,8,10,12,14,31,34]. Ma et al. [30] studied the problem of maximizing the minimum of the expected utilities over agents in the known i.i.d. arrival model when $v_i(e) \in \{0,1\}$ for all $I \in N$ and $e \in M$. They proposed a strict 0.725-competitive online algorithm. Note that their setting is easier than ours in two points: their objective is at least the expected value of the minimum utility (i.e., expected egalitarian social welfare), and their algorithm fully uses the prior knowledge. Barman et al. [10] provided online algorithms for maximizing the p-mean welfare $(\frac{1}{n}\sum_{i \in N} v_i(A_i)^p)^{1/p}$ when the items are *divisible*. The p-mean welfare with $p \to -\infty$ corresponds to the egalitarian welfare, and their algorithm is strictly $\Omega(\frac{1}{\sqrt{n}\log n})$-competitive for the egalitarian welfare. Though, their algorithm is hard to apply in our setting because it heavily relies on the assumption that the items are divisible and the number of items are known in advance. Benade et al. [12] focused on an online problem of allocating all the indivisible items to minimize the maximum envy. They designed a deterministic online algorithm such that the maximum envy asymptotically vanishes over time, that is, the algorithm outputs an allocation A such that $v_i(A_i) \ge v_i(A_j) - O(\sqrt{m \log m})$ for any $i, j \in N$. Unlike our setting, they assumed that the number of items is known in advance. Their algorithm is based on a random allocation, where each item is allocated to an agent chosen uniformly at random. In [12], the authors first prove that the maximum envy asymptotically vanishes in the allocation obtained by the random allocation algorithm. Then, they derandomized the algorithm by using a potential function that pessimistically estimates the future allocation. For more models of online fair allocation, see [4] for a comprehensive survey.

The offline version of the max-min allocation problem has also been studied under the name of the *Santa Claus problem* [13,17,21,24,25]. The problem is NP-hard even to approximate within a factor of better than $1/2$ [28]. Bansal and Sviridenko [9] proposed an $\Omega(\log\log\log n/\log\log n)$-approximation algorithm for the restricted case when $v_i(e) \in \{0, v(e)\}$ for all $i \in N$ and $e \in M$. Asadpour and Saberi [6] provided the first polynomial-time approximation algorithm for the general problem, which was improved by Haeupler et al. [25].

1.2   Our Results

Although the online max-min fair allocation problem is a fundamental problem, almost nothing is known about the competitive analysis for nonidentical agents to the best of our knowledge.

Table 3. Summary of our results for the online max-min fair allocation problem. All values in the table represent both upper and lower bounds of the competitive ratios of optimal online algorithms, where $\tilde{\Theta}$ is a variant of big-Theta notation ignoring logarithmic factors.

	Adversarial (det.)	Adversarial (rand.)	Unknown i.i.d.	Known i.i.d.
Asympt.	$1/n$ (Thms. 3, 5)	$1/n$ (Thms. 3, 5)	1 (Thm. 4)	1 (Thm. 4)
Strict	0 (Thm. 7)	$1/n^{\Theta(n)}$ (Thms. 2, 8)	$1/e^{\tilde{\Theta}(n)}$ (Thms. 2, 9)	$1/e^{\tilde{\Theta}(n)}$ (Thms. 2, 9)

Our main results show the asymptotic competitive ratios of optimal online algorithms for the adversarial and i.i.d. arrival models. In addition, we roughly identified the strict competitive ratios of optimal online algorithms, which are much smaller than those of the asymptotic ones. We summarize our results in Table 3.

Adversarial Arrival Model. A main result for the adversarial arrival model is a polynomial-time deterministic algorithm with an asymptotic competitive ratio of nearly $1/n$ (Theorem 3), which is the best possible.

We first observe that the asymptotic competitive ratio is at most $1/n$ (Theorem 5). Thus, our aim is to construct an asymptotically $1/n$-competitive algorithm. If randomization is allowed, we can achieve it by simply allocating each item to an agent chosen uniformly at random. We refer to this randomized algorithm as RANDOM. Note that RANDOM is *not* strictly $1/n$-competitive because the expected value of the minimum of random variables is *not* equal to the minimum of the expected values of random variables. We show that RANDOM guarantees $\mathrm{Opt}/n - O(\sqrt{\mathrm{Opt}\log\mathrm{Opt}})$ even for the adaptive-offline[1] adversary, where Opt is the offline optimal value (Theorem 1). Interestingly, this fact implies the existence of a *deterministic* algorithm with the same guarantee [11]. However, the construction is not obvious. In fact, natural greedy algorithms are far from asymptotically $1/n$-competitive (see full version). Moreover, the natural round-robin procedure[2] fails. One disadvantage of these algorithms is that they output allocations that are too imbalanced and too balanced, respectively. Moreover, it is unclear whether such a deterministic algorithm can be implemented to run in polynomial time.

We propose a novel derandomization method to obtain a polynomial-time deterministic algorithm with almost the same performance as RANDOM. Our algorithm is based on the spirit of giving way to each other. Upon the arrival of an item, our algorithm gives agents a chance to take it in ascending order with

---

[1] The adaptive-offline adversary chooses the next item based on the allocation chosen by the online algorithm thus far, and it obtains an offline optimal value for the resulting request items.

[2] In a round-robin procedure under the offline setting, agents take turns and choose their most preferred unallocated item. In the online setting, we use this term to refer to a procedure in which the jth item is taken by agent j (mod n).

respect to the valuation of the item. Each agent generously passes the chance in consideration of the agent's past assigned units. Then, we can achieve the golden mean between allocations that are too balanced or too imbalanced, and we obtain the main result. We believe that this technique is novel and will have further applications. The advantage of our algorithm is that it does not require the information of the number of items nor an upper bound on the value of the items. In addition, our analysis produces a consequence on another fairness notion called *proportionality* (each of the n agents receives a fraction at least $1/n$ of the entire items according to her valuation) in an asymptotic sense.

As an impossibility result, we prove a stronger bound for deterministic algorithms: no deterministic online algorithm can attain $\text{Opt}/n - \Omega((\text{Opt})^{\frac{1}{2}-\varepsilon})$ for any $\varepsilon > 0$ where Opt is the offline optimal value (Theorem 6). This bound implies that the performance of RANDOM is nearly optimal even when additive terms are taken into consideration.

We also show that the strict competitive ratio of any deterministic algorithm is 0 (Theorem 7) and the strict competitive ratio of the best randomized algorithm is $1/n^{\Theta(n)}$ (Theorems 2 and 8).

Unknown/Known i.i.d. Arrival Models. Our main result for the i.i.d. arrival models is to provide an algorithm that outputs an asymptotically near-optimal allocation. Our algorithm is the following simple one: upon the arrival of each item, allocate the item to the agent with the highest discounted value, where each agent's value of the item is exponentially discounted with respect to the total value received so far. We prove that this algorithm with exponential base $(1 - \varepsilon/2)$ is $(1 - \varepsilon)$-competitive if the expected optimal value is larger than a certain value (Theorem 4).

We remark that our algorithm is based on a similar idea found in Devanur et al. [19], but this is not a naive application. They provided an asymptotically $(1 - \varepsilon)$-competitive algorithm for a wide class of resource allocation problems. However, we have two difficulties when applying their algorithm to our problem. One is that their algorithm requires the number m of items to estimate the expected optimal value, but m is unknown in our setting. The other is that they deal with finite types of online items (i.e., each item is drawn from a discrete distribution) and their algorithm utilizes an LP solution; by contrast, in our setting, there may exist infinite types of value vectors (i.e., a distribution can be continuous). Our contribution is to resolve the above difficulties. In fact, we do not use the LP in the algorithm; we use it only in the analysis. This makes our algorithm quite simple. Note that our algorithm requires no information about the total number of items nor an upper bound on the value of the items.

In addition, our algorithm can be viewed as an application of the *multiplicative weight update method* [5], which is used to solve the experts problem. However, the goals of the experts problem and the online max-min fair allocation problem are different, and no direct relationship can be found between them. We also note that our algorithm is applicable to the mode of Ma et al. [30], and our algorithm has asymptotically higher competitive ratio.

For the strict competitive ratio, we show that even for the known i.i.d. setting, the strict competitive ratio of any algorithm must be exponentially small in the number of agents (Theorem 9). Due to space limitation, some proofs are omitted (see full version [27]).

2   Preliminaries

We denote the sets of agents and indivisible items by $N = \{1, 2, \ldots, n\}$ and $M = \{e_1, e_2, \ldots, e_m\}$, respectively. We use the symbol $[n]$ to denote $\{1, 2, \ldots, n\}$. Each agent has a valuation function $v_i \colon M \to [0, 1]$ that assigns a value to each item. For simplicity, unless otherwise stated, we assume that the value of each item is normalized to $[0, 1]$. We assume that each agent has an additive preference over the items, and we write $v_i(X) := \sum_{e \in X} v_i(e)$ to denote the utility of agent i when i obtains $X \subseteq M$. For an item $e \in M$, we call $(v_1(e), \ldots, v_n(e))$ the *value vector* of e. An allocation $A = (A_1, \ldots, A_n)$ is a partition of M (i.e., $\bigcup_i A_i = M$ and $A_i \cap A_j = \emptyset$ for any distinct $i, j \in N$). For $j \in [m]$, we denote $M^{(j)} = \{e_1, \ldots, e_j\}$ and $A^{(j)} = (A_1 \cap M^{(j)}, \ldots, A_n \cap M^{(j)})$.

To evaluate the performance of online algorithms, we use strict and asymptotic competitive ratios. For an input sequence σ, let $\mathrm{ALG}(\sigma)$ and $\mathrm{OPT}(\sigma)$ respectively denote the egalitarian social welfares of the allocations obtained by an online algorithm ALG and an optimal offline algorithm OPT (here, $\mathrm{ALG}(\sigma)$ is a random variable if ALG is a randomized algorithm). Then, the *strict competitive ratio* and the *asymptotic competitive ratio* for the adversarial arrival model are respectively defined as

$$\inf_{\sigma} \frac{\mathbb{E}[\mathrm{ALG}(\sigma)]}{\mathrm{OPT}(\sigma)} \quad \text{and} \quad \liminf_{\mathrm{OPT}(\sigma) \to \infty} \frac{\mathbb{E}[\mathrm{ALG}(\sigma)]}{\mathrm{OPT}(\sigma)}.$$

Here, the competitive ratios for randomized algorithms are defined by using an oblivious adversary. The competitive ratios are at most 1, and the larger values indicate better performance. By the definition, the asymptotic competitive ratio of ALG is at least ρ if $\mathbb{E}[\mathrm{ALG}(\sigma)] \geq \rho \cdot \mathrm{OPT}(\sigma) - o(\mathrm{OPT}(\sigma))$ for any input sequence σ. Note that, in some literature (e.g., [15]), the asymptotic competitive ratio of ALG is at least ρ only when there is a constant $\alpha \geq 0$ such that $\mathbb{E}[\mathrm{ALG}(\sigma)] \geq \rho \cdot \mathrm{OPT}(\sigma) - \alpha$ for any input sequence σ. We refer to this as the classical definition.

For the i.i.d. arrival model, we consider the distribution of input sequences $R(m, \mathcal{D})$ determined by a number of items m and a distribution of value vectors for each item $\mathcal{D}$. The *strict competitive ratio* and the *asymptotic competitive ratio* for the i.i.d. arrival model are respectively defined as

$$\inf_{m, \mathcal{D}} \frac{\mathbb{E}_{\sigma \sim R(m, \mathcal{D})}[\mathbb{E}[\mathrm{ALG}(\sigma)]]}{\mathbb{E}_{\sigma \sim R(m, \mathcal{D})}[\mathrm{OPT}(\sigma)]} \quad \text{and} \quad \liminf_{\mathrm{OPT}(\sigma) \to \infty} \frac{\mathbb{E}_{\sigma \sim R(m, \mathcal{D})}[\mathbb{E}[\mathrm{ALG}(\sigma)]]}{\mathbb{E}_{\sigma \sim R(m, \mathcal{D})}[\mathrm{OPT}(\sigma)]}.$$

3   Algorithms for Adversarial Arrival

In this section, we provide algorithms for the adversarial arrival model. We first show a randomized algorithm that is asymptotically $1/n$-competitive in Sect. 3.1

and then provide a deterministic algorithm with the same competitive ratio in Sect. 3.2.

3.1 Randomized Algorithm

A simple way to allocate items "fairly" is to allocate each item uniformly at random among all the agents. We refer to this randomized algorithm as RANDOM. One might think that it would be better to choose an agent who has a high valuation for an item. However, this does not perform better than RANDOM in the worst case scenario. Furthermore, it turns out that RANDOM is a nearly optimal algorithm for the adversarial arrival model.

First, we prove that the asymptotic competitive ratio of RANDOM is at least $1/n$ by showing a slightly stronger statement.

Theorem 1. *For any adaptive adversary,* RANDOM *satisfies*

$$\mathbb{E}[\mathrm{RANDOM}(\sigma)] \geq \frac{\mathrm{Opt}}{n} - O\left(\sqrt{\mathrm{Opt} \cdot \log \mathrm{Opt}}\right),$$

where σ is the probabilistic input sequence chosen by the adversary (depending on the stochastic behavior of RANDOM*) and* $\mathrm{Opt} = \mathbb{E}[\mathrm{OPT}(\sigma)]$.

Proof. The adaptive adversary decides to request the next item or terminates depending on the sequence of allocation at each time so far. We use the symbol e^π to denote the next item when the allocation sequence at the moment is $\pi = (a_1, a_2, \ldots, a_k)$, i.e., there are k requested items and ℓth item ($\ell \in [k]$) is allocated to $a_\ell \in N$. Let Π denote the set of all allocation sequences such that the adversary requests the next item. For each $\pi \in \Pi$, let X_i^π be a random variable such that $X_i^\pi = 1$ if RANDOM allocates e^π to agent $i \in N$, and $X_i^\pi = 0$ otherwise. In addition, let Y^π be a random variable such that $Y^\pi = 1$ if e^π is requested (i.e., the allocation sequence chosen by RANDOM is π at some moment), and $Y^\pi = 0$ otherwise. As the allocation is totally uniformly at random, we have $\Pr[X_i^\pi = 1 \mid Y^\pi = 1] = 1/n$ for all $i \in N$, and $\Pr[Y^\pi = 1] = 1/n^{|\pi|}$, where $|\pi|$ denotes the length of π (i.e., the number of items allocated so far).

The total utility of agent i is $S_i = \sum_{\pi \in \Pi} v_i(e^\pi) X_i^\pi Y^\pi$, and the expected utility of i is $\mathbb{E}[S_i] = \sum_{\pi \in \Pi} \frac{v_i(e^\pi)}{n^{|\pi|+1}}$. Let $\mu_i = \mathbb{E}[S_i]$ for each $i \in N$, and let $\mu_{\min} = \min_{i \in N} \mu_i$. Then, the expected optimal value Opt is at most $\mathrm{Opt} \leq \mathbb{E}\left[\min_{i \in N} \sum_{\pi \in \Pi} v_i(e^\pi) Y^\pi\right] \leq \min_{i \in N} \mathbb{E}\left[\sum_{\pi \in \Pi} v_i(e^\pi) Y^\pi\right] \leq \min_{i \in N} \sum_{\pi \in \Pi} \frac{v_i(e^\pi)}{n^{|\pi|}} = \min_{i \in N} n \cdot \mu_i = n \cdot \mu_{\min}$, where the first inequality holds since the utility of i is at most $\sum_{\pi \in \Pi} v_i(e^\pi) Y^\pi$ (which is attained when all items are allocated to i).

We apply the Chernoff–Hoeffding bound (see, e.g., [20]): since $0 \leq v_i(e^\pi) \leq 1$ for each $i \in N$ and $\pi \in \Pi$, we have

$$\Pr\left[S_i \leq (1 - \delta) \cdot \mu_i\right] \leq \exp(-\mu_i \delta^2/2), \qquad (1)$$

for all $\delta > 0$. By setting $\delta = \sqrt{(2\log(n\mu_i))/\mu_i}$ in (1), we see that $\Pr\left[S_i \leq \mu_i - \sqrt{2\mu_i \log(n\mu_i)}\right] = \Pr\left[S_i \leq (1 - \sqrt{(2\log(n\mu_i))/\mu_i}) \cdot \mu_i\right] \leq \exp\left(-\mu_i \cdot \frac{2\log(n\mu_i)/\mu_i}{2}\right) = \frac{1}{n\mu_i}$.

Furthermore, by the union bound, the probability that $S_i \leq \mu_i - \sqrt{2\mu_i \log(n\mu_i)}$ holds for some i is at most $\sum_{i \in N} \frac{1}{n\mu_i} \leq \frac{1}{\mu_{\min}}$. By the definition of the big-O notation, it is sufficient to consider the case where $\mu_{\min} \geq 4n$. As $x - \sqrt{2x \log(nx)}$ is monotone increasing for $x \geq 4n$, we obtain

$$
\mathbb{E}\left[\min_{i \in N} S_i\right] \geq \min_{i \in N}\left(\mu_i - \sqrt{2\mu_i \log(n\mu_i)}\right)\left(1 - \frac{1}{\mu_{\min}}\right)
$$
$$
= \left(\mu_{\min} - \sqrt{2\mu_{\min} \log(n\mu_{\min})}\right)\left(1 - \frac{1}{\mu_{\min}}\right)
$$
$$
\geq \mu_{\min} - \sqrt{2\mu_{\min} \log(n\mu_{\min})} - 1 \geq \mu_{\min} - 3\sqrt{\mu_{\min} \log(n\mu_{\min})}
$$
$$
\geq \frac{\mathrm{Opt}}{n} - 3\sqrt{\frac{\mathrm{Opt} \cdot \log \mathrm{Opt}}{n}} = \frac{\mathrm{Opt}}{n} - O\left(\sqrt{\mathrm{Opt} \cdot \log \mathrm{Opt}}\right).
$$

$\square$

Note that, in the classical definition of the asymptotic competitive ratio, RANDOM is at least $(1 - \varepsilon)/n$-competitive for any constant $\varepsilon > 0$ against adaptive-offline adversaries.

We also analyze the strict competitive ratio of RANDOM. For the strict competitive ratio, a deterministic algorithm can do almost nothing, but RANDOM attains $1/n^{O(n)}$ fraction of the optimal value. Intuitively, this is because each agent obtains $\Omega(1/n)$ fraction of the value received in the optimal allocation with probability $\Omega(1/n)$.

Theorem 2. *The strict competitive ratio of* RANDOM *is at least* $\frac{1}{n^{O(n)}}$ *in the adversarial arrival model.*

3.2 Derandomization

It is well-known that there is no advantage to use randomization against adaptive-offline adversaries with respect to the competitive ratio [11]. This implies the existence of a deterministic algorithm with the same guarantee as RANDOM. However, the proof is not constructive, and hence it is not straightforward to obtain such a deterministic algorithm. Moreover, there is no implication about running time.

A natural way to derandomize RANDOM is a simple round-robin. However, this fails due to the example in the Introduction (see Table 2). Another approach is to estimate the optimal value, but this is impossible in the adversarial setting. Moreover, we can prove that allocating new arriving item e to the agent who maximizes $\phi(v_i(A_i \cup \{e\})) - \phi(v_i(A_i))$ is not asymptotically $1/n$-competitive for any monotone increasing function ϕ (see full version).

Our approach is to classify items into (infinitely many) types and aim to allocate almost the same number of items of each type to each agent. Fixing a positive real $\varepsilon \in (0,1)$, we denote $\mathrm{ind}(x) = \lfloor \log_{1-\varepsilon} x \rfloor$ for $x \in [0,1]$, where $\mathrm{ind}(0) = \infty$. We define a *type* of an item e as a vector $(\mathrm{ind}(v_1(e)), \ldots, \mathrm{ind}(v_n(e)))$. Note that an agent with a smaller $\mathrm{ind}(x)$ has a higher valuation. Now, our task is to schedule the order of allocation for each type of items. If there are only 2 agents, applying the round-robin procedure independently for each type (in which the first item is allocated to the agent who wants it more than the other) is asymptotically $(1-\varepsilon)/2$-competitive. However, in general, such a simple round-robin in a particular type may result in a too unbalanced allocation as shown in Table 4. Thus, we introduce a sophisticated procedure to avoid such an unbalanced allocation.

Table 4. Too unbalanced allocation ($n = 3$)

j	1	2	3	4	5	6	$\cdots$
$\mathrm{ind}(v_1(e_j))$	0	0	0	0	0	0	$\cdots$
$\mathrm{ind}(v_2(e_j))$	1	2	1	3	1	4	$\cdots$
$\mathrm{ind}(v_3(e_j))$	2	1	3	1	4	1	$\cdots$

Table 5. Our allocation ($n = 3$)

j	1	2	3	4	5	6	$\cdots$
$\mathrm{ind}(v_1(e_j))$	0	0	0	0	0	0	$\cdots$
$\mathrm{ind}(v_2(e_j))$	1	2	1	3	1	4	$\cdots$
$\mathrm{ind}(v_3(e_j))$	2	1	3	1	4	1	$\cdots$

We describe our novel technique of derandomization. Suppose that the type of an arriving item e is $(w_1, w_2, \ldots, w_n)$ with $w_1 \leq w_2 \leq \cdots \leq w_n$. By the definition of ind, we have $(1 - \varepsilon)^{w_i+1} < v_i(e) \leq (1 - \varepsilon)^{w_i}$. Our algorithm gives agent n, who has the smallest value for e, a chance to receive e. She obtains e if she has passed previous $n - 1$ chances to receive items of type $(w_1, \ldots, w_n)$, and passes the chance otherwise. If agent n passed the chance, then the algorithm gives agent $n - 1$ a chance. Agent $n - 1$ obtains e if she has passed previous $n - 2$ chances to receive items of type $(w_1, \ldots, w_{n-1}, w_n')$ with some $w_n' \geq w_{n-1}$. Note that w_n' can vary. For example, $n = 3$ and if agent 2 passes an item of type (w_1, w_2, α), and agent 3 passes a next item that has type (w_1, w_2, β), then agent 2 obtains the item. Our algorithm repeats this procedure. In general, if agents $n, n-1, \ldots, i+1$ passed the chances, then the algorithm gives agent i a chance to receive e. Agent i obtains e if she has passed the previous $i-1$ chances to receive items of type $(w_1, \ldots, w_i, w_{i+1}', \ldots, w_n')$ with some $w_i \leq w_{i+1}' \leq \cdots \leq w_n'$. Note that the item e is allocated to some agent. At least, agent 1 obtains e if she receives the chance. See Table 5 for an example of allocation by our algorithm. We present a formal description in Algorithm 1.

It is not difficult to see that Algorithm 1 can be implemented to run in polynomial-time. We prove the following statement.

Theorem 3. *For any positive real $\varepsilon < 1$ and any input sequence σ, Algorithm 1 returns an allocation A such that $v_i(A_i) \geq \frac{1-\varepsilon}{n} v_i(M) - \frac{(n!)^2}{\varepsilon^n}$ for all $i \in N$ where M is the set of items requested in σ.*

This theorem implies that Algorithm 1 is asymptotically $(1 - \varepsilon)/n$-competitive because $\min_{i \in N} v_i(A_i) \geq \min_{i \in N} \frac{1-\varepsilon}{n} v_i(M) - \frac{(n!)^2}{\varepsilon^n} \geq \frac{1-\varepsilon}{n} \mathrm{OPT}(\sigma) - \frac{(n!)^2}{\varepsilon^n}$.

The theorem also indicates that Algorithm 1 finds a nearly proportional allocation, i.e., each agent receives a bundle of value at least nearly $1/n$ of the whole. In contrast, RANDOM cannot guarantee such a proportionality in the ex post sense.

Algorithm 1: Asymptotically $(1 - \varepsilon)/n$-competitive deterministic algorithm (adversarial model)

---

1 Let $A_i \leftarrow \emptyset$ for each $i \in N$;

2 foreach $e_j \leftarrow e_1, e_2, \dots, e_m$ **do**

3   Let τ^j be a permutation over N such that

       $v_{\tau^j(1)}(e_j) \geq v_{\tau^j(2)}(e_j) \geq \cdots \geq v_{\tau^j(n)}(e_j)$;

4   Let $w_i^j \leftarrow \mathrm{ind}(v_{\tau^j(i)}(e_j))$ for each $i \in N$;

5   **for** $i \leftarrow n, n-1, \dots, 1$ **do**

6   Increment $x(\tau^j; w_1^j, w_2^j, \dots, w_i^j)$ by 1 (if the variable is undefined, then set it as 1);

7   **if** $x(\tau^j; w_1^j, w_2^j, \dots, w_i^j) = i$ **then**

8   Allocate e_j to agent $\tau^j(i)$ (i.e., $A_{\tau^j(i)} \leftarrow A_{\tau^j(i)} \cup \{e_j\}$);

9   Set $x(\tau^j; w_1^j, w_2^j \dots, w_i^j) \leftarrow 0$;

10   **Break**;

To prove the theorem, we show that the allocation is almost balanced regarding the number of items. For a permutation τ, index $k \in [n]$, and $\boldsymbol{w} = (w_1, w_2, \dots, w_k) \in \mathbb{Z}_+^k$ with $w_1 \leq w_2 \leq \cdots \leq w_k$, we denote $E^{\tau,k}(\boldsymbol{w}) = \{e_j : \tau^j = \tau \text{ and } (w_1^j, \dots, w_k^j) = \boldsymbol{w}\}$. We remark that $\{E^{\tau,k}(\boldsymbol{w})\}_{\tau,\boldsymbol{w}}$ forms a partition of the entire item set for every $k \in [n]$.

Lemma 1. *For any permutation τ, index $k \in [n]$, and $\boldsymbol{w} = (w_1, \dots, w_k) \in \mathbb{Z}_+^k$ with $w_1 \leq w_2 \leq \cdots \leq w_k$, it holds that $|A_{\tau(k)} \cap E^{\tau,k}(\boldsymbol{w})| \geq |E^{\tau,k}(\boldsymbol{w})|/n - 1$.*

Now we are ready to prove Theorem 3.

Proof (Proof of Theorem 3). Let i be an agent, τ be a permutation, and $k \in [n]$ be an index such that $i = \tau(k)$. Also, let $\boldsymbol{w} = (w_1, \dots, w_k) \in \mathbb{Z}_+^k$ with $w_1 \leq w_2 \leq \cdots \leq w_k$. Note that $(1-\varepsilon)^{w_k+1} < v_i(e) \leq (1-\varepsilon)^{w_k}$ for every $e \in E^{\tau,k}(\boldsymbol{w})$. By Lemma 1, we have

$$
\begin{aligned}
v_i(A_i \cap E^{\tau,k}(\boldsymbol{w})) &\geq |A_i \cap E^{\tau,k}(\boldsymbol{w})| \cdot (1-\varepsilon)^{w_k+1} \\
&\geq \left(\frac{1}{n} |E^{\tau,k}(\boldsymbol{w})| - 1 \right) \cdot (1-\varepsilon)^{w_k+1} \\
&= \frac{1-\varepsilon}{n} \cdot |E^{\tau,k}(\boldsymbol{w})|(1-\varepsilon)^{w_k} - (1-\varepsilon)^{w_k+1} \\
&\geq \frac{1-\varepsilon}{n} v_i(E^{\tau,k}(\boldsymbol{w})) - (1-\varepsilon)^{w_k+1}.
\end{aligned} \tag{2}
$$

By summing up (2) for all $\boldsymbol{w}' = (w'_1, \ldots, w'_{k-1}, w_k)$ with $w'_1 \le \cdots \le w'_{k-1} \le w_k$, we have

$$\sum_{\boldsymbol{w}'} v_i(A_i \cap E^{\tau,k}(\boldsymbol{w}')) \ge \sum_{\boldsymbol{w}'} \left(\frac{1-\varepsilon}{n} v_i(E^{\tau,k}(\boldsymbol{w}')) - (1-\varepsilon)^{w_k+1} \right)$$

$$\ge \frac{1-\varepsilon}{n} \sum_{\boldsymbol{w}'} v_i(E^{\tau,k}(\boldsymbol{w}')) - (w_k+1)^{k-1}(1-\varepsilon)^{w_k+1}.$$

Finally, by summing up for all τ, k and $\boldsymbol{w}$, we obtain

$$v_i(A_i) = \sum_{\tau,k,\boldsymbol{w}} v_i(A_i \cap E^{\tau,k}(\boldsymbol{w}))$$

$$\ge \frac{1-\varepsilon}{n} \sum_{\tau,k,\boldsymbol{w}} v_i(E^{\tau,k}(\boldsymbol{w})) - \sum_{k\in N} \sum_{\tau:\tau(i)=k} \sum_{w_k=0}^{\infty} (w_k+1)^{k-1}(1-\varepsilon)^{w_k+1}$$

$$\ge \frac{1-\varepsilon}{n} v_i(M) - n! \cdot \sum_{\ell=0}^{\infty} (\ell+1)^{n-1}(1-\varepsilon)^{\ell+1}$$

$$\ge \frac{1-\varepsilon}{n} v_i(M) - n! \cdot \sum_{\ell=0}^{\infty} (\ell+1)(\ell+2)\cdots(\ell+n-1)(1-\varepsilon)^{\ell+1}$$

$$= \frac{1-\varepsilon}{n} v_i(M) - \frac{n! \cdot (n-1)!}{\varepsilon^n} \cdot (1-\varepsilon) \ge \frac{1-\varepsilon}{n} v_i(M) - \frac{(n!)^2}{\varepsilon^n}.$$

Here, the second last equality holds because, for any r with $|r| < 1$, $\frac{1}{(1-r)^n} = (1+r+r^2+\cdots)^n = \sum_{\ell=0}^{\infty} \binom{\ell+n-1}{n-1} r^\ell = \frac{1}{(n-1)!} \cdot \sum_{\ell=0}^{\infty} (\ell+1)(\ell+2)\cdots(\ell+n-1)r^\ell$. $\quad\square$

We remark that Algorithm 1 works even if the upper bound of valuations is more than one and the algorithm does not know the upper bound. Let $\eta = \max_{i' \in N, e \in M} v_{i'}(e)$. Note that $\mathrm{ind}(\eta)$ is a negative integer if $\eta > 1$. Then, by summing up (2) for all types $\boldsymbol{w} \in \mathbb{Z}^n$ with $w_i \ge \mathrm{ind}(\eta)$ for all $i \in N$, we obtain

$$v_i(A_i) = \sum_{\tau,k,\boldsymbol{w}} v_i(A_i \cap E^{\tau,k}(\boldsymbol{w}))$$

$$\ge \frac{1-\varepsilon}{n} \sum_{\tau,k,\boldsymbol{w}} v_i(E^{\tau,k}(\boldsymbol{w})) - \sum_{k\in N} \sum_{\tau:\tau(i)=k} \sum_{w_k=\mathrm{ind}(\eta)}^{\infty} (w_k+1-\mathrm{ind}(\eta))^{k-1}(1-\varepsilon)^{w_k+1}$$

$$\ge \frac{1-\varepsilon}{n} v_i(M) - n! \sum_{\ell=0}^{\infty} (\ell+1)^{n-1}(1-\varepsilon)^\ell (1-\varepsilon)^{\mathrm{ind}(\eta)+1} \ge \frac{1-\varepsilon}{n} v_i(M) - \frac{(n!)^2}{\varepsilon^n} \eta$$

for each $i \in N$. Note that this bound is also useful for the case when $\eta \le 1$ because it implies a better guarantee.

One may expect to design better performing algorithms by dynamically changing the value ε according to the current objective value. However, such a method does not work for the online max-min fair allocation problem. In fact, if an agent evaluates 0 for the items that come for a while at first, we essentially need to solve the problem for the other $n-1$ agents with a static ε.

If $\text{OPT}(\sigma)$ is known in advance (semi-online setting), Algorithm 1 can output an allocation A such that $\min_i v_i(A_i) \geq \frac{1}{n}\text{OPT}(\sigma) - O((\text{OPT}(\sigma))^{\frac{n}{n+1}})$ by setting $\varepsilon = (\text{OPT}(\sigma))^{1/(n+1)}$, i.e., Algorithm 1 is asymptotically $1/n$-competitive in this setting.

Finally, we discuss the difference between our results and the results of Benade et al. [12]. Recall that their deterministic algorithm outputs an allocation A such that $v_i(A_i) \geq v_i(A_j) - O(\sqrt{m \log m})$ $(\forall i, j \in N)$. This implies $v_i(A_i) \geq \frac{1}{n}v_i(M) - O(\sqrt{m \log m})$ for each $i \in N$, and hence $\min_{i \in N} v_i(A_i) \geq \frac{1}{n}\text{OPT}(\sigma) - O(\sqrt{m \log m})$. However, their algorithm requires fine-tuned parameters that depend on the number of items m and an upper bound on the value of the items. In contrast, our algorithm can be run independently of the number of items and the upper bound of the value of items, and our evaluation is independent of m.

4   Algorithm for i.i.d. Arrival

In this section, we provide an algorithm for the i.i.d. arrival model, i.e., the value vector v of each item is drawn independently from a given distribution $\mathcal{D}$. We assume that the distribution $\mathcal{D}$ and the total number m of items are unknown to the algorithm. For the strict competitive ratio, we can carry Theorem 2 for this case. In what follows, we will analyze the asymptotic case.

One may expect that the round-robin procedure works well, but unfortunately it does not because, even if $n = 2$ and $\mathcal{D}$ is a distribution that takes $(1, \frac{1}{2})$ with probability 1, the optimal value is $\frac{1}{3}m$ but the round-robin can achieve only $\frac{1}{4}m$. We provide a simple algorithm that is asymptotically near-optimal. Let $\varepsilon > 0$ be a fixed small constant. When a new item e_j arrives, our algorithm virtually discounts its value $v_i(e_j)$ for each agent i by a factor $(1 - \varepsilon)^{v_i(A_i^{(j-1)})}$, where $A_i^{(j-1)}$ is the set of items allocated to i so far. Then, the algorithm allocates the item e_j to the agent $i^{(j)}$ with the highest among discounted values, i.e., $i^{(j)} \in \arg\max_i (1 - \varepsilon)^{v_i(A_i^{(j-1)})} v_i(e_j)$. The discount factor leads to give a priority to an agent who has small utility at the moment. We formally describe our algorithm in Algorithm 2.

Theorem 4. *For any positive $\varepsilon < 1$, the expected egalitarian social welfare of the allocation obtained by Algorithm 2 is at least $(1 - 2\varepsilon)$ fraction of the expected optimal value if the expected optimal value is at least $\frac{2}{\varepsilon^2} \log \frac{n}{\varepsilon}$.*

We prepare to prove Theorem 4. We evaluate the performance of Algorithm 2 by using a linear programming problem that gives an upper bound of the optimal value. For any realization of an input sequence σ, the optimal value $\text{OPT}(\sigma)$ is equivalent to the optimal value of the following integer linear program:

$$\begin{aligned}
\max \; & \lambda \\
\text{s.t.} \; & \lambda \leq \textstyle\sum_{j=1}^m v_{ij}^\sigma \cdot x_{ij} \quad (\forall i \in N), \\
& \textstyle\sum_{i \in N} x_{ij} = 1 \qquad (\forall j \in [m]), \\
& x_{ij} \in \{0, 1\} \qquad (\forall i \in N, \; \forall j \in [m]),
\end{aligned}$$

Algorithm 2: Asymptotically $(1-2\varepsilon)$-competitive deterministic algorithm (unknown i.i.d. model)

---

1 Let $A_i^{(0)}$ be the emptyset for each $i \in N$;

2 **foreach** $e_j \leftarrow e_1, e_2, \ldots, e_m$ **do**

3 $\quad$ Let $i^{(j)}$ be an agent in $\arg\max_i \left((1-\varepsilon)^{v_i(A_i^{(j-1)})} \cdot v_i(e_j) \right)$;

4 $\quad$ Allocate jth item to $i^{(j)}$, i.e., $A_i^{(j)} \leftarrow \begin{cases} A_i^{(j-1)} \cup \{e_j\} & (i = i^{(j)}) \\ A_i^{(j-1)} & (i \neq i^{(j)}) \end{cases}$ $(\forall i \in N)$;

---

where we write $\boldsymbol{v}_j^\sigma = (v_{1j}^\sigma, \ldots, v_{nj}^\sigma)$ to denote the value vector of the jth item in the instance σ. The variable x_{ij} corresponds whether agent i receives the jth item. Let Opt denote the expected optimal value $\mathbb{E}[\text{OPT}(\sigma)]$. Without loss of generality, we may assume that $\text{Opt} > 0$ because any algorithm is 1-competitive if $\text{Opt} = 0$.

We first prove Theorem 4 for the case where $\mathcal{D}$ is a discrete distribution with finite support and then modify the proof for the general case. Thus, we focus on the former case. To analyze the performance of our algorithm, we consider an expected instance of the problem where everything happens as per expectation, which is defined as follows:

$$
\begin{aligned}
\max \ & \lambda \\
\text{s.t.} \ & \lambda \leq \sum_{\boldsymbol{u} \in \text{supp}(\mathcal{D})} m \cdot \Pr_{U \sim \mathcal{D}}[\boldsymbol{U} = \boldsymbol{u}] \cdot u_i \cdot x_{i\boldsymbol{u}} \quad (\forall i \in N), \\
& \sum_{i \in N} x_{i\boldsymbol{u}} = 1 \qquad\qquad\qquad\qquad\qquad (\forall \boldsymbol{u} \in \text{supp}(\mathcal{D})), \\
& x_{i\boldsymbol{u}} \geq 0 \qquad\qquad\qquad\qquad\qquad (\forall i \in N, \ \forall \boldsymbol{u} \in \text{supp}(\mathcal{D})).
\end{aligned}
\tag{LP}
$$

We denote the optimal value of (LP) by $\overline{\text{Opt}}$. We prove that $\overline{\text{Opt}}$ is at least Opt.

Lemma 2. $\overline{\text{Opt}} \geq \text{Opt}$.

Fix $\varepsilon > 0$. Let $X_{i,j}$ be random variables representing the values that agent i obtains from the jth item in Algorithm 2, i.e., $X_{i,j} = v_i(e_j)$ if agent i receives the jth item, and $X_{i,j} = 0$ otherwise. The egalitarian social welfare of the allocation obtained by Algorithm 2 is $\min_{i \in N} \sum_{j=1}^m X_{i,j}$. By the union bound and Markov's inequality, we have

$$
\begin{aligned}
\Pr\left[\min_{i \in N} \sum_{j=1}^m X_{i,j} \leq (1-\varepsilon)\overline{\text{Opt}}\right] &\leq \sum_{i \in N} \Pr\left[\sum_{j=1}^m X_{i,j} \leq (1-\varepsilon)\overline{\text{Opt}}\right] \\
&= \sum_{i \in N} \Pr\left[(1-\varepsilon)^{\sum_{j=1}^m X_{i,j}} \geq (1-\varepsilon)^{(1-\varepsilon)\overline{\text{Opt}}}\right] \\
&\leq \sum_{i \in N} \mathbb{E}\left[(1-\varepsilon)^{\sum_{j=1}^m X_{i,j}}\right] / (1-\varepsilon)^{(1-\varepsilon)\overline{\text{Opt}}}.
\end{aligned}
\tag{3}
$$

In what follows, we prove that the rightmost value in (3) is sufficiently small. For $s = 0, 1, \ldots, m$, let us define $\Phi(s)$ as follows:

$$\Phi(s) := \sum_{i \in N} \mathbb{E}\left[(1 - \varepsilon)^{\sum_{j=1}^{s} X_{i,j}}\right] \cdot \left(1 - \frac{\varepsilon \overline{\mathrm{Opt}}}{m}\right)^{m-s}.$$

Note that the rightmost value in (3) is equal to $\Phi(m)/(1 - \varepsilon)^{(1-\varepsilon)\overline{\mathrm{Opt}}}$.

Lemma 3. $\Phi(s)$ *is monotone decreasing in* s.

Lemma 4. $\Phi(0)/(1 - \varepsilon)^{(1-\varepsilon)\overline{\mathrm{Opt}}} \leq n \cdot e^{-\frac{\varepsilon^2}{2}\overline{\mathrm{Opt}}}$

We are ready to prove Theorem 4.

Proof (Proof of Theorem 4). We first prove the theorem for the case when $\mathcal{D}$ has a finite support. By applying Lemmas 3 and 4 to (3), we see that $\Pr\left[\min_{i \in N} \sum_{j=1}^{m} X_{i,j} \leq (1-\varepsilon)\overline{\mathrm{Opt}}\right] \leq \frac{\Phi(m)}{(1-\varepsilon)^{(1-\varepsilon)\overline{\mathrm{Opt}}}} \leq \frac{\Phi(0)}{(1-\varepsilon)^{(1-\varepsilon)\overline{\mathrm{Opt}}}} \leq n \cdot e^{-\frac{\varepsilon^2}{2}\overline{\mathrm{Opt}}}$. Hence, we obtain $\mathbb{E}\left[\min_{i \in N} \sum_{j=1}^{m} X_{i,j}\right] \geq (1-\varepsilon) \cdot (1 - n \cdot e^{-\frac{\varepsilon^2}{2}\overline{\mathrm{Opt}}}) \cdot \overline{\mathrm{Opt}} \geq (1-\varepsilon) \cdot (1 - n \cdot e^{-\frac{\varepsilon^2}{2}\mathrm{Opt}}) \cdot \mathrm{Opt}$ by Lemma 2. By the assumption that $\mathrm{Opt} \geq \frac{2}{\varepsilon^2} \log \frac{n}{\varepsilon}$, we obtain $\mathbb{E}\left[\min_{i \in N} \sum_{j=1}^{m} X_{i,j}\right] \geq (1-\varepsilon) \cdot (1 - n \cdot e^{-\frac{\varepsilon^2}{2}\mathrm{Opt}}) \cdot \mathrm{Opt} \geq (1-\varepsilon) \cdot (1-\varepsilon)\mathrm{Opt} \geq (1 - 2\varepsilon)\mathrm{Opt}$.

Now, we modify the above discussion for the general case. Let $\delta > 0$ be a sufficiently small positive real. For a real $x \in [0, 1]$, define

$$\kappa(x) = \begin{cases} \lceil \log_{1-\delta} x \rceil & \text{if } x \geq \delta \cdot \mathrm{Opt}/m, \\ \infty & \text{if } x < \delta \cdot \mathrm{Opt}/m. \end{cases}$$

Note that $\kappa(x)$ is in a finite set $\{0, 1, \ldots, \lceil \log_{1-\delta}(\delta \cdot \mathrm{Opt}/m) \rceil\} \cup \{\infty\}$, and we have

$$x \geq (1 - \delta)^{\kappa(x)} \geq (1 - \delta)x \geq (1 - \delta)x - \delta \cdot \mathrm{Opt}/m. \tag{4}$$

Let $\mathcal{D}^{(\delta)}$ be the discrete distribution obtained from $\mathcal{D}$ by modifying a value vector $\boldsymbol{u}$ to $((1 - \delta)^{\kappa(u_i)})_{i \in N}$. Here, the cardinality of $\mathrm{supp}(\mathcal{D}^{(\delta)})$ is at most $(\lceil \log_{1-\delta}(\delta \mathrm{Opt}/m) \rceil + 2)^n$, and hence it is finite. Define $\overline{\mathrm{Opt}}^{(\delta)}$ to be the optimal value of (LP) for the distribution $\mathcal{D}^{(\delta)}$.

In the same way as in the proof for the former case, we can obtain the following inequality:

$$\mathbb{E}\left[\min_{i \in N} \sum_{j=1}^{m} X_{i,j}\right] \geq (1 - \varepsilon) \cdot (1 - n \cdot e^{-\frac{\varepsilon^2}{2}\overline{\mathrm{Opt}}^{(\delta)}}) \overline{\mathrm{Opt}}^{(\delta)}. \tag{5}$$

In addition, by (4) and Lemma 2, we get $\overline{\mathrm{Opt}}^{(\delta)} \geq (1 - \delta)\overline{\mathrm{Opt}} - \delta \cdot \mathrm{Opt} \geq (1 - 2\delta)\mathrm{Opt}$.

As the inequality (5) holds for any $\delta > 0$, we have $\mathbb{E}\left[\min_{i \in N} \sum_{j=1}^{m} X_{i,j}\right] \geq (1 - \varepsilon) \cdot (1 - n \cdot e^{-\frac{\varepsilon^2}{2}\mathrm{Opt}}) \cdot \mathrm{Opt} \geq (1 - \varepsilon) \cdot (1 - \varepsilon)\mathrm{Opt} \geq (1 - 2\varepsilon)\mathrm{Opt}$. $\qquad\square$

We remark that Algorithm 2 works even if the upper bound of valuations is more than one and the algorithm does not know the upper bound. Let η be an upper bound of the value of the items, i.e., $\Pr_{u \sim \mathcal{D}}[\max_{i \in N} u_i \leq \eta] = 1$. Also, let $\hat{v}_i(e) = v_i(e)/\eta$ for each agent $i \in N$ and item $e \in M$. Then, by considering $\hat{\varepsilon}$ such that $(1 - \hat{\varepsilon}) = (1 - \varepsilon)^\eta$, Algorithm 2 can be interpreted as allocating each item e_j to an agent in $\arg\max_{i \in N} (1 - \hat{\varepsilon})^{\hat{v}_i(A_i^{(j-1)})} \cdot \hat{v}_i(e_j)$. Hence, we can conclude that Algorithm 2 is $(1 - 2\hat{\varepsilon})$-competitive if the expected optimal value is at least $\eta \cdot \frac{2}{\hat{\varepsilon}^2} \log \frac{n}{\hat{\varepsilon}}$. Note that this bound is also useful for the case when $\eta \leq 1$ because it implies a better guarantee.

The analysis in Theorem 4 implies the following *regret* bounds. If Opt is known in advance (semi-online setting), Algorithm 2 can attain $\mathbb{E}\left[\min_i \sum_{j=1}^m X_{i,j}\right] = \text{Opt} - O(\sqrt{\text{Opt} \log \text{Opt}})$ by setting $\varepsilon = 2\sqrt{\frac{\log \text{Opt}}{\text{Opt}}}$. If the number of items m is known in advance, Algorithm 2 can attain $\mathbb{E}\left[\min_i \sum_{j=1}^m X_{i,j}\right] = \text{Opt} - O(\sqrt{m \log m})$ by setting $\varepsilon = 2\sqrt{\frac{\log m}{m}}$ because $\text{Opt} \leq m/n$.

5   Impossibilities for Adversarial Arrival

In this section, we provide upper bounds of competitive ratios for the adversarial arrival model.

We provide the upper bound of the asymptotic competitive ratio, which implies that the asymptotic competitive ratio of RANDOM is the best possible.

Theorem 5. *The asymptotic competitive ratio of any randomized algorithm is at most $1/n$ in the adversarial arrival model.*

We show a stronger upper bound of the asymptotic competitive ratio for deterministic algorithms. The upper bound implies that, for any positive real ε ($< 1/10$), there exists input sequences σ such that $\text{ALG}(\sigma) \leq \frac{1}{n}\text{OPT}(\sigma) - \Omega((\text{OPT}(\sigma))^{\frac{1}{2}-\varepsilon})$. (This bound can be obtained by setting $\frac{1}{2} - \varepsilon = \frac{1}{3-r}$.) We construct an adversarial item sequence based on the idea inspired by Benade et al. [12]. The sequence indicates that the competitive ratio of an algorithm will be far from $1/n$ if it tries to allocate in an overly balanced way.

Theorem 6. *Suppose that $n \geq 2$. Let r be a real such that $1/2 < r < 1$. For any deterministic algorithm ALG and a positive real c, there exists an input sequence σ such that $\text{ALG}(\sigma) \leq \text{OPT}(\sigma)/n - c$ and $\text{OPT}(\sigma) = O(c^{3-r})$.*

We also discuss the strict competitive ratio. First, the strict competitive ratio is 0 for any deterministic algorithm.

Theorem 7. *For any $n \geq 2$, the strict competitive ratio of any deterministic algorithm is 0 in the adversarial arrival model.*

Next, we observe that, for any randomized algorithm, the strict competitive ratio could be positive but at most $1/n!$ ($= 1/n^{\Theta(n)}$). This upper bound means that the strict competitive ratio of RANDOM is (almost) tight. The proof is based on Yao's principle.

Theorem 8. *The strict competitive ratio of any randomized algorithm is at most $1/n!$ in the adversarial arrival model.*

6   Impossibilities for i.i.d. Arrival

In this section, we provide an upper bound of competitive ratios for the i.i.d. arrival model. As we show an asymptotic $(1 - O(\varepsilon))$-competitive algorithm in Sect. 4 for the unknown case, we only need to discuss the strict competitive ratio, and show that the strict competitive ratio is at most $\frac{1}{e^{\Omega(n)}}$ even if the algorithm knows the distribution of value vectors and the number of items.

Theorem 9. *There exist a distribution over value vectors and a number of items such that the strict competitive ratio is at most $\frac{1}{e^{\Omega(n)}}$ for any algorithm in the i.i.d. arrival model.*

7   Concluding Remarks

In this paper, we have revealed asymptotic and strict competitive ratios of the online max-min fair allocation problem for the adversarial and i.i.d arrival models. Specifically, we designed polynomial-time deterministic algorithms that achieve asymptotically $\frac{1-\varepsilon}{n}$-competitive for the adversarial arrival model and $(1 - \varepsilon)$-competitive for the i.i.d. arrival model, respectively, for any $\varepsilon > 0$.

We would like to mention a partial information model of our problem. We have focused on the case where the values of agents for the current item are revealed before allocation. The model where the values are revealed *after* allocation (like the expert problem or the multi-armed bandit problem) also seems reasonable, but such a model is too restrictive. In fact, by considering a distribution that takes χ_i with probability $1/n$ for each i, we can see that the asymptotic competitive ratio is at most $1/n$ even for the i.i.d. arrival model. Even worse, by considering an adversarial arrival where the value vector of every item allocated to agent i turns out to be $1 - (1 - \varepsilon)\chi_i$ with $\varepsilon > 0$, we can see that the asymptotic competitive ratio of any deterministic algorithm is at most ε.

References

1. Aleksandrov, M., Aziz, H., Gaspers, S., Walsh, T.: Online fair division: analysing a food bank problem. In: Proceedings of IJCAI, pp. 2540–2546 (2015)
2. Aleksandrov, M., Walsh, T.: Expected outcomes and manipulations in online fair division. In: Kern-Isberner, G., Fürnkranz, J., Thimm, M. (eds.) KI 2017. LNCS (LNAI), vol. 10505, pp. 29–43. Springer, Cham (2017). https://doi.org/10.1007/978-3-319-67190-1_3
3. Aleksandrov, M., Walsh, T.: Strategy-proofness, envy-freeness and pareto efficiency in online fair division with additive utilities. In: Nayak, A.C., Sharma, A. (eds.) PRICAI 2019. LNCS (LNAI), vol. 11670, pp. 527–541. Springer, Cham (2019). https://doi.org/10.1007/978-3-030-29908-8_42

4. Aleksandrov, M., Walsh, T.: Online fair division a survey. In: Proceedings of AAAI, vol. 34, pp. 13557–13562 (2020)
5. Arora, S., Hazan, E., Kale, S.: The multiplicative weights update method: a meta algorithm and applications. Theory Comput. **8**(1), 121–164 (2012)
6. Asadpour, A., Saberi, A.: An approximation algorithm for max-min fair allocation of indivisible goods. SIAM J. Comput. **39**(7), 2970–2989 (2010)
7. Azar, Y., Epstein, L.: On-line machine covering. J. Sched. **1**(2), 67–77 (1998)
8. Banerjee, S., Gkatzelis, V., Gorokh, A., Jin, B.: Online Nash social welfare maximization with predictions. In: Proceedings SODA, pp. 1–19 (2022)
9. Bansal, N., Sviridenko, M.: The Santa Claus problem. In: Proceedings of STOC, pp. 31–40 (2006)
10. Barman, S., Khan, A., Maiti, A.: Universal and tight online algorithms for generalized-mean welfare (2021). https://doi.org/10.48550/ARXIV.2109.00874
11. Ben-David, S., Borodin, A., Karp, R., Tardos, G., Wigderson, A.: On the power of randomization in on-line algorithms. Algorithmica **11**(1), 2–14 (1994)
12. Benade, G., Kazachkov, A.M., Procaccia, A.D., Psomas, C.A.: How to make envy vanish over time. In: Proceedings of EC, pp. 593–610 (2018)
13. Bezáková, I., Dani, V.: Allocating indivisible goods. SIGecom Exchanges **5**(3), 11–18 (2005)
14. Bogomolnaia, A., Moulin, H., Sandomirskiy, F.: On the fair division of a random object. Manag. Sci. **68**, 1174–1194 (2021)
15. Borodin, A., El-Yaniv, R.: Online Computation and Competitive Analysis. Cambridge (1998)
16. Bouveret, S., Chevaleyre, Y., Maudet, N.: Fair allocation of indivisible goods. In: Brandt, F., Conitzer, V., Endriss, U., Lang, J., Procaccia, A.D. (eds.) Handbook of Computational Social Choice, chap. 12, pp. 284–310. Cambridge University Press (2016)
17. Chakrabarty, D., Chuzhoy, J., Khanna, S.: On allocating goods to maximize fairness. In: Proceedings of FOCS, pp. 107–116 (2009)
18. Deuermeyer, B.L., Friesen, D.K., Langston, M.A.: Scheduling to maximize the minimum processor finish time in a multiprocessor system. SIAM J. Algebraic Discret. Methods **3**(2), 190–196 (1982)
19. Devanur, N.R., Jain, K., Sivan, B., Wilkens, C.A.: Near optimal online algorithms and fast approximation algorithms for resource allocation problems. J. ACM **66**(1) (2019)
20. Dubhashi, D.P., Panconesi, A.: Concentration of Measure for the Analysis of Randomized Algorithms. Cambridge University Press (2009). https://doi.org/10.1017/CBO9780511581274
21. Feige, U.: On allocations that maximize fairness. In: Proceedings of SODA, vol. 8, pp. 287–293 (2008)
22. Gálvez, W., Soto, J.A., Verschae, J.: Improved online algorithms for the machine covering problem with bounded migration. In: Proceedings of Workshop on Models and Algorithms for Planning and Scheduling Problems, vol. 21 (2015)
23. Gálvez, W., Soto, J.A., Verschae, J.: Symmetry exploitation for online machine covering with bounded migration. ACM Trans. Algorithms **16**(4), 1–22 (2020)
24. Golovin, D.: Max-min fair allocation of indivisible goods. Technical Report CMU-CS-05-144, Carnegie Mellon University (2005)
25. Haeupler, B., Saha, B., Srinivasan, A.: New constructive aspects of the Lovász local lemma. J. ACM **58**(6), 28:1–28:28 (2011)
26. Kawase, Y., Sumita, H.: On the max-min fair stochastic allocation of indivisible goods. In: Proceedings of AAAI, vol. 34, pp. 2070–2078 (2020)

27. Kawase, Y., Sumita, H.: Online max-min fair allocation (2021). https://doi.org/10.48550/ARXIV.2111.07235
28. Lenstra, J.K., Shmoys, D.B., Tardos, É.: Approximation algorithms for scheduling unrelated parallel machines. Math. Program. **46**(1), 259–271 (1990)
29. Li, Y., et al.: Max-min fair allocation for resources with hybrid divisibilities. Expert Syst. Appl. **124**, 325–340 (2019)
30. Ma, W., Xu, P., Xu, Y.: Fairness maximization among offline agents in online-matching markets. In: Proceedings of WINE, p. 547 (2021)
31. Mattei, N., Saffidine, A., Walsh, T.: Mechanisms for online organ matching. In: Proceedings of IJCAI, pp. 345–351 (2017)
32. Tan, Z., Zhang, A.: Online and semi-online scheduling. In: Pardalos, P.M., Du, D.-Z., Graham, R.L. (eds.) Handbook of Combinatorial Optimization, pp. 2191–2252. Springer, New York (2013). https://doi.org/10.1007/978-1-4419-7997-1_2
33. Woeginger, G.J.: A polynomial-time approximation scheme for maximizing the minimum machine completion time. Oper. Res. Lett. **20**(4), 149–154 (1997)
34. Zeng, D., Psomas, A.: Fairness-efficiency tradeoffs in dynamic fair division. In: Proceedings of EC, pp. 911–912 (2020)

Incomplete List Setting
of the Hospitals/Residents Problem
with Maximally Satisfying Lower Quotas

Kazuhisa Makino[1], Shuichi Miyazaki[2] (ID), and Yu Yokoi[3(✉)] (ID)

[1] Kyoto University, Kyoto 606-8502, Japan
makino@kurims.kyoto-u.ac.jp
[2] University of Hyogo, Hyogo 651-2197, Japan
shuichi@sis.u-hyogo.ac.jp
[3] National Institute of Informatics, Tokyo 101-8430, Japan
yokoi@nii.ac.jp

Abstract. To mitigate the imbalance in the number of assignees in the Hospitals/Residents problem, Goko et al. [Goko et al., Maximally Satisfying Lower Quotas in the Hospitals/Residents Problem with Ties, Proc. STACS 2022, pp. 31:1–31:20] studied the Hospitals/Residents problem with lower quotas whose goal is to find a stable matching that satisfies lower quotas as much as possible. In their paper, preference lists are assumed to be complete, that is, the preference list of each resident (resp., hospital) is assumed to contain all the hospitals (resp., residents). In this paper, we study a more general model where preference lists may be incomplete. For four natural scenarios, we obtain maximum gaps of the best and worst solutions, approximability results, and inapproximability results.

Keywords: Stable matching · Hospitals/Residents problem · Lower quota · Approximation algorithm · Hardness of approximation

1 Introduction

The Hospitals/Residents problem is a many-to-one generalization of the stable marriage model of Gale and Shapley [6], which is widely used as a base for many real-world assignment systems, such as assigning residents to hospitals [18] and students to schools [1,2]. In applications, one of the major drawbacks is the imbalance in the number of assignees. For example, in the hospitals-residents assignment, hospitals in urban areas are popular and are likely to receive many residents, while those in rural areas suffer from a shortage of doctors. To cope with this problem, several approaches have been proposed. One of them is to introduce regional caps, where hospitals in the same district are put into the same set, called a region, and each region as well as each hospital has an upper quota [12]. Another example is to let each hospital h declare not only an upper quota $u(h)$ but also a lower quota $\ell(h)$, and require the number of assignees for

© The Author(s), under exclusive license to Springer Nature Switzerland AG 2022
P. Kanellopoulos et al. (Eds.): SAGT 2022, LNCS 13584, pp. 544–561, 2022.
https://doi.org/10.1007/978-3-031-15714-1_31

each hospital to be between its upper and lower quotas [3,10]. In general, there does not exist a stable matching satisfying all the upper and lower quotas, so Biró et al. [3] allows some hospitals to be closed (i.e., to accept no resident) while Hamada et al. [10] allows a matching to be unstable and tries to minimize the number of blocking pairs. However, in reality, it is too pessimistic to regard lower quotas as hard constraints. In some cases, fewer residents than a lower quota may still be able to keep a hospital in operation, by sacrificing service level to some degree.

Taking this observation into account, recently Goko et al. [9] (including the authors of the present paper) investigated an optimization problem that considers lower quotas as soft constraints. The problem is called *the Hospitals/Residents problem with Ties to Maximally Satisfy Lower Quotas* (HRT-MSLQ for short). In this problem, preference lists of agents may contain ties and the *satisfaction ratio* (or the *score*) of a hospital h in a stable matching M is defined as $s_M(h) = \min\{1, \frac{|M(h)|}{\ell(h)}\}$, where $|M(h)|$ is the number of residents assigned to h in M and $s_M(h) = 1$ if $\ell(h) = 0$. That is, each hospital h is assumed to have $\ell(h)$ seats corresponding to the lower quota, and the satisfaction ratio reflects the fraction of occupied seats among them. The *total satisfaction ratio* (also called *the score*) of a stable matching M is the sum of the scores of all hospitals, and the goal of HRT-MSLQ is to maximize it among all the stable matchings. (See Sect. 2 for the formal definition.) Note that if the preference lists of agents are strict, the problem is trivial because each hospital receives the same number of residents in any stable matching due to the *rural hospitals theorem* [7,18,19], and hence all the stable matchings have the same score. As the problem HRT-MSLQ turns out to be NP-hard in general, Goko et al. proposed an approximation algorithm called DOUBLE PROPOSAL and compared the worst approximation factors of this algorithm and a baseline algorithm that first breaks ties arbitrarily and then applies the ordinary Gale–Shapley algorithm. They showed tight approximation factors of these two algorithms for the following four scenarios: (i) *general model*, which consists of all problem instances, (ii) *uniform model*, in which all hospitals have the same upper and lower quotas, (iii) *marriage model*, in which each hospital has an upper quota of 1 and a lower quota of either 0 or 1, and (iv) resident-side master list model (*R-side ML model*), in which there is a *master preference list* over hospitals and a preference list of every resident coincides with it. Their algorithm DOUBLE PROPOSAL solves the problem exactly for instances of *R-side ML model* and, for each of the other three models, it attains a better approximation factor than that of the baseline algorithm.

Throughout Goko et al.'s paper [9], it is assumed that all preference lists are complete. That is, the preference list of each resident (resp., hospital) is assumed to contain all the hospitals (resp., residents). Under this assumption, all stable matchings have the same cardinality, and hence the objective value is affected only by the *balance* of the numbers of residents assigned to hospitals. Therefore, to obtain a better objective value, we can focus on rectifying the imbalance.

In reality, however, preference lists of agents can be incomplete. In real medical residency matching schemes, there are huge numbers of residents and hospitals participating, and the length of preference lists of residents tend to be much smaller than the number of hospitals. This motivates us to study a more natural but challenging incomplete list setting. When preference lists are incomplete and contain ties, the problem becomes harder since the stable matchings vary on their cardinalities and hence the objective value depends not only on balance but also on size. In fact, a special case of our problem where $\ell(h) = u(h) = 1$ for every hospital h reduces to MAX-SMTI [17], a well-studied NP-hard problem that asks to find a maximum size stable matching in the stable marriage model with ties and incomplete lists.

For instances with incomplete lists, the algorithm DOUBLE PROPOSAL in [9] is still well-defined and finds a stable matching in linear time. However, the analyses of the approximation factors do not work anymore. Indeed, the algorithm fails to attain the approximation factors shown there for this generalized setting. In this paper, we propose a new algorithm TRIPLE PROPOSAL, which is based on DOUBLE PROPOSAL and equipped with additional operations to increase the number of matched residents, which leads to a larger objective value. As mentioned above, our problem is a common generalization of the problem of Goko et al. [9] and MAX-SMTI. Our algorithm TRIPLE PROPOSAL can be regarded as a natural integration of DOUBLE PROPOSAL and Király's algorithm [15] for MAX-SMTI.

Our results are summarized in Table 1, where n denotes the number of residents in an input instance. For each of the four models mentioned above, the first row shows the maximum gap, i.e., the ratio of objective values of the best and worst stable matchings. The maximum gap can be regarded as the worst-case approximation factor of the baseline algorithm. (This fact follows from the rural hospitals theorem and is proved formally in [8], which is a full version of [9].) The second row shows lower bounds of the approximation factors of DOUBLE PROPOSAL in our incomplete list setting. It can be observed that in the uniform and marriage models, DOUBLE PROPOSAL performs as badly as the baseline algorithm, in contrast to the fact that it performs better than the baseline algorithm in all of the four models in the complete list setting [9]. The third row gives the approximation factors of TRIPLE PROPOSAL, which are the main results of this paper. Here, $\phi(n)$ is a function on n that is approximately $\frac{n+2}{3}$; its formal definition is given just before Theorem 4.7 in Sect. 4.3. Note that, in all four models, the approximation factors are improved from DOUBLE PROPOSAL. Finally, the last row shows inapproximability results under the assumption that P$\neq$NP. It is worth emphasizing that, as a byproduct of our inapproximability result, lower bounds on the approximation factor of MAX-SMTI (under P$\neq$NP) can be improved (see Remark 5.3).

Note that, in the incomplete list setting, the R-side ML model means that each resident's preference list is obtained by deleting unacceptable hospitals from the master preference list. This model shows a remarkable difference between complete list setting and incomplete list setting: the model is solved exactly by DOUBLE PROPOSAL in the former case [9], while it has the same inapproximability as the general model in the latter case.

Because of the space constraints, some proofs are roughly sketched or completely omitted. For missing proofs, refer to the full version [16].

Table 1. The maximum gap, a lower bound of the approximation factor of DOUBLE PROPOSAL, the approximation factor of TRIPLE PROPOSAL, and inapproximability (under P≠NP) for four models of HRT-MSLQ. In the uniform model, $\theta = u/\ell$, where u and ℓ are respectively an upper quota and a lower quota common to all the hospitals.

	General	Uniform	Marriage	R-side ML
Maximum gap (i.e., approx. factor of arbitrary tie-break+GS)	$n+1$ (Thm.4.5)	$\theta + 1$ (Thm.4.3)	2 (Thm.4.1)	$n+1$ (Thm.4.5)
LB of approx. factor of DOUBLE PROPOSAL	$\lfloor \frac{n}{2} \rfloor + 1$ (Rem.4.1+Thm.4.6)	$\theta + 1$ (Rem.4.1+Thm.4.3)	2 (Rem.4.1+Thm.4.1)	$\lfloor \frac{n}{2} \rfloor + 1$ (Rem.4.1+Thm.4.6)
Approx. factor of TRIPLE PROPOSAL	$\phi(n)$ $(\sim \frac{n+2}{3})$ (Thm.4.7)	$\frac{\theta}{2} + 1$ (Thm.4.4)	1.5 (Thm.4.2)	$\phi(n)$ (Thm.4.7)
Inapproximability	$n^{\frac{1}{4}-\epsilon}$ ([9])	$\frac{2-\sqrt{2}}{3}\theta + 1 - \epsilon\theta^2$ (Thm.5.1)	$\frac{5-\sqrt{2}}{3} - \epsilon$ (Prop.5.2)	$n^{\frac{1}{4}-\epsilon}$ ([9]+ Rem.5.2)

2   Problem Definition

Let $R = \{r_1, r_2, \ldots, r_n\}$ be a set of residents and $H = \{h_1, h_2, \ldots, h_m\}$ be a set of hospitals. Each hospital h has a lower quota $\ell(h)$ and an upper quota $u(h)$ such that $\ell(h) \leq u(h) \leq n$. We sometimes denote h's quota pair as $[\ell(h), u(h)]$ for simplicity. Each resident (resp., hospital) has a preference list over hospitals (resp., residents), which may be incomplete and may contain ties. A hospital h is *acceptable* to a resident r if h appears in r's list. Similarly, r is *acceptable* to h if r appears in h's list. A resident-hospital pair (r, h) is called *acceptable* if r and h are acceptable to each other. We denote by E the set of all acceptable pairs (r, h). In this paper, we assume without loss of generality that acceptability is mutual, i.e., r is acceptable to h if and only if h is acceptable to r.

In this paper, a preference list is denoted by one row, from left to right according to the preference order. Two or more agents with equal preference is included in parentheses. For example, "r_1: h_3 (h_1 h_6) h_4" is a preference list of resident r_1 such that h_3 is the top choice, h_1 and h_6 are the second choice with equal preference, and h_4 is the last choice. Hospitals not appearing in the list are unacceptable to r_1.

If hospitals h_i and h_j are both acceptable to a resident r and r prefers h_i to h_j, we write $h_i \succ_r h_j$. We also write $h \succ_r \varnothing$ for any hospital h acceptable to r, where $\varnothing$ means r being unmatched. If r is indifferent between acceptable hospitals h_i and h_j (including the case that $h_i = h_j$), we write $h_i =_r h_j$. We write $h_i \succeq_r h_j$ to mean that $h_i \succ_r h_j$ or $h_i =_r h_j$ holds. We use the same notations for the preference of each hospital.

An *assignment* is a subset of the set E of acceptable pairs. For an assignment M and a resident r, let $M(r)$ be the set of hospitals h such that $(r, h) \in M$. Similarly, for a hospital h, let $M(h)$ be the set of residents r such that $(r, h) \in M$. An assignment M is called a *matching* if $|M(r)| \leq 1$ for each resident r and $|M(h)| \leq u(h)$ for each hospital h. For a matching M, a resident r is called *matched* if $|M(r)| = 1$ and *unmatched* otherwise. If $(r, h) \in M$, we say that r is *assigned to* h and h is *assigned* r. For a matching M, we abuse the notation $M(r)$ to denote a unique hospital to which r is assigned, if any. In addition, we denote $M(r) = \varnothing$ to mean that r is unmatched in M. A hospital h is called *deficient* if $|M(h)| < \ell(h)$ and *sufficient* if $\ell(h) \leq |M(h)| \leq u(h)$. Additionally, a hospital h is called *full* if $|M(h)| = u(h)$ and *undersubscribed* otherwise.

An acceptable pair $(r, h) \in E$ is called a *blocking pair* for a matching M (or we say that (r, h) *blocks* M) if (i) r is either unmatched in M or prefers h to $M(r)$ and (ii) h is either undersubscribed in M or prefers r to at least one resident in $M(h)$. A matching is called *stable* if it admits no blocking pair.

Recall from Sect. 1 that the *satisfaction ratio* (also called *the score*) of a hospital h in a matching M is defined by $s_M(h) = \min\{1, \frac{|M(h)|}{\ell(h)}\}$, where we define $s_M(h) = 1$ if $\ell(h) = 0$. The *total satisfaction ratio* (also called *the score*) of a matching M is the sum of the scores of all hospitals, that is, $s(M) = \sum_{h \in H} s_M(h)$. The Hospitals/Residents problem with Ties to Maximally Satisfy Lower Quotas, denoted by *HRT-MSLQ*, is to find a stable matching M that maximizes the score $s(M)$. (In Goko et al. [9], HRT-MSLQ is formulated for the complete list setting. We use the same name HRT-MSLQ to mean the generalized setting with incomplete lists.)

3   Algorithm

In this section, we present our algorithm TRIPLE PROPOSAL for HRT-MSLQ along with a few of its basic properties. TRIPLE PROPOSAL is regarded as a generalization of the algorithm DOUBLE PROPOSAL, which was designed for a special case of HRT-MSLQ with complete preference lists [9].

We first briefly explain DOUBLE PROPOSAL. It is based on the resident-oriented Gale–Shapley algorithm but allows each resident r to make proposals twice to each hospital. DOUBLE PROPOSAL starts with an empty matching $M := \emptyset$ and repeatedly updates M by a proposal-acceptance/rejection process. In each iteration, the algorithm takes a currently unassigned resident r and lets her propose to the hospital at the top of her current list. If the head of r's preference list is a tie when r makes a proposal, then the hospitals to which r has not proposed yet are prioritized. If there are more than one hospital with the same priority, one with the smallest $\ell(h)$ is prioritized. For the acceptance/rejection decision of h, we use $\ell(h)$ as a dummy upper quota. Whenever $|M(h)| < \ell(h)$, a hospital h accepts any proposal. If h receives a new proposal from r when $|M(h)| \geq \ell(h)$, then h checks whether there is a resident in $M(h) \cup \{r\}$ who has not been rejected by h so far. If such a resident exists, h rejects that resident regardless of the preference of h (at this point, the rejected resident does not

delete h from her list). If there is no such resident, we apply the usual accep-
tance/rejection operation, i.e., h accepts r if $|M(h)| < u(h)$ and otherwise h
replaces the worst resident r' in $M(h)$ with r (at this point, r' deletes h from
her list). Roughly speaking, the first proposals are used to prioritize deficient
hospitals and the second proposals are used to guarantee the stability.

In the setting in Goko et al. [9], it is assumed that the preference lists of all
agents are complete and $|R| \leq \sum_{h \in H} u(h)$ holds. With these assumptions, all
residents are matched in M at the end of DOUBLE PROPOSAL. In out setting,
however, some residents are left unmatched at the end, after proposing twice to
each hospital. TRIPLE PROPOSAL gives the second round of proposals for those
unmatched residents, in which a resident has the *third* chance for the proposal
to the same hospital. This idea originates from the algorithm of Király [15] for
another NP-hard problem MAX-SMTI. In TRIPLE PROPOSAL, each resident r
is associated with a value $\mathsf{state}(r) \in \{0, 1, 2\}$, which is initialized as $\mathsf{state}(r) = 0$
at the beginning. Each r behaves as DOUBLE PROPOSAL until her list becomes
empty for the first time (i.e., until r is rejected twice by all hospitals on her list).
When her list becomes empty, $\mathsf{state}(r)$ turns from 0 to 1 and her list is recovered.
Note that at this point, every hospital h in r's list is full with residents that are
no worse than r and have been rejected by h at least once, because r was rejected
by h at the second proposal. When r with $\mathsf{state}(r) = 1$ proposes to a hospital
h and $M(h)$ contains a resident r' such that $r =_h r'$ and $\mathsf{state}(r') = 0$, then h
replaces r' with r. If r exhausts her list for the second time, then $\mathsf{state}(r)$ turns
from 1 to 2, and r becomes inactive.

Formally, our algorithm TRIPLE PROPOSAL is described in Algorithm 1. For
convenience, in the preference list, a hospital h not included in a tie is regarded
as a tie consisting of h only.

We say that a resident is *rejected* by a hospital h if she is chosen as r' in
Lines 12 or 17. Note that the conditions in Lines 9, 11, and 14 never hold for r
with $\mathsf{state}(r) = 1$ because such r has already been rejected by all hospitals in her
list twice. Therefore, whenever r with $\mathsf{state}(r) = 1$ is rejected by h, it must be
at line 17, so r deletes h. Hence, each resident proposes to each hospital at most
three times (at most twice with $\mathsf{state}(r) = 0$ and at most once with $\mathsf{state}(r) = 1$).

We first provide two basic properties of TRIPLE PROPOSAL, which are shown
for DOUBLE PROPOSAL in [9, Lemmas 1, 2]. The first one states that the algorithm finds a stable matching in linear time.

Lemma 3.1. *Algorithm* TRIPLE PROPOSAL *runs in linear time and outputs a
stable matching.*

In addition to the stability, the output of TRIPLE PROPOSAL satisfies the
following property, which is used in the approximation factor analysis in Sect. 4.

Algorithm 1. TRIPLE PROPOSAL

Input: An instance I of HRT-MSLQ where each $h \in H$ has quotas $[\ell(h), u(h)]$.
Output: A stable matching M.

1: $M := \emptyset$.
2: **while** there is an unmatched resident r with nonempty list and $\mathsf{state}(r) \leq 1$ **do**
3:     Let r be such a resident and T be the top tie of r's list.
4:     **if** T contains a hospital to which r has not proposed yet **then**
5:         Let h be such a hospital with minimum $\ell(h)$.
6:     **else**
7:         Let h be a hospital with minimum $\ell(h)$ in T.
8:     **end if**
9:     **if** $|M(h)| < \ell(h)$ **then**
10:        Let $M := M \cup \{(r, h)\}$.
11:    **else if** there is a resident in $M(h) \cup \{r\}$ who has not been rejected by h **then**
12:        Let r' be such a resident (possibly $r' = r$).
13:        Let $M := (M \cup \{(r, h)\}) \setminus \{(r', h)\}$.
14:    **else if** $|M(h)| < u(h)$ **then**
15:        $M := M \cup \{(r, h)\}$.
16:    **else** {i.e., when $|M(h)| = u(h)$ and all residents in $M(h) \cup \{r\}$ have been rejected by h at least once}
17:        Let r' be any resident worst in $M(h) \cup \{r\}$ for h (possibly $r' = r$). If there are multiple worst residents, take anyone with the minimum state value.
18:        Let $M := (M \cup \{(r, h)\}) \setminus \{(r', h)\}$.
19:        Delete h from r''s list.
20:    **end if**
21:    **if** r''s list becomes empty **then**
22:        Increment $\mathsf{state}(r)$ by 1 and recover the original r''s list.
23:    **end if**
24: **end while**
25: Output M and halt.

Lemma 3.2. *Let M be the output of* TRIPLE PROPOSAL, *r be a resident, and h and h' be hospitals such that $h =_r h'$ and $M(r) = h$. Then, we have the following:*

(i) If $\ell(h) > \ell(h')$, then $|M(h')| \geq \ell(h')$.
(ii) If $|M(h)| > \ell(h)$, then $|M(h')| \geq \ell(h')$.

Since the above two properties hold also for DOUBLE PROPOSAL [9], they are insufficient to obtain the approximation factors shown in the third row of Table 1. The main advantage of TRIPLE PROPOSAL is that we can prohibit length-3 augmenting paths, which are defined as follows.

For a stable matching M in an HRT-MSLQ instance, a *length-3 M-augmenting path* is a sequence (r_1, h_1, r_2, h_2) of residents r_1, r_2 and hospitals h_1, h_2 satisfying the following conditions:

- $M(r_1) = \emptyset$,
- $(r_1, h_1), (r_2, h_2) \in E \setminus M$, $(r_2, h_1) \in M$, and
- $|M(h_2)| < \ell(h_2)$.

The output of TRIPLE PROPOSAL satisfies the following property, which can be regarded as a generalization of the property of the output of Király's algorithm [15] for MAX-SMTI.

Lemma 3.3. *Let M be an output of* TRIPLE PROPOSAL *and N be an arbitrary stable matching. Then, there is no length-3 M-augmenting path (r_1, h_1, r_2, h_2) such that $(r_1, h_1), (r_2, h_2) \in N$.*

Proof. Suppose, to the contrary, that there is such an augmenting path. Then, $(r_1, h_1), (r_2, h_2) \in N \setminus M$ and $(r_2, h_1) \in M \setminus N$. Because $M(r_1) = \varnothing$ while $(r_1, h_1) \in E$, resident r_1 was rejected by h_1 three times in the algorithm. Just after the third rejection, h_1 is full with residents each of whom is either (i) better than r_1 and rejected by h_1 at least once or (ii) tied with r_1 in h_1's list and rejected by h_1 twice. Since the assignment of h_1 is monotonically improving, this also holds for the output M.

In case $r_2 \in M(h_1)$ satisfies (i), the stability of N implies $h_2 \succeq_{r_2} h_1$. Because the stability of M with $|M(h_2)| < \ell(h_2)$ implies $h_1 \succeq_{r_2} h_2$, we have $h_2 =_{r_2} h_1$. Since r_2 is assigned to h_1 at her second or third proposal, $h_2 =_{r_2} h_1$ implies that r_2 proposed to and was rejected by h_2 at least once. This implies $|M(h_2)| \geq \ell(h_2)$, which contradicts our assumption $|M(h_2)| < \ell(h_2)$.

In case r_2 satisfies (ii), r_2 was rejected at least twice by all hospitals in her list. This implies that h_2 is full in M, which contradicts $|M(h_2)| < \ell(h_2)$.   □

Remark 3.1. It is shown in Goko et al. [9] that DOUBLE PROPOSAL is strategy-proof for residents. In case where (i) the preference lists are all complete or (ii) the preference lists of hospitals are strict, our algorithm TRIPLE PROPOSAL is also strategy-proof, because its output coincides with that of DOUBLE PROPOSAL (where arbitrariness in the algorithm is removed using some pre-specified order over agents). However, in case neither (i) nor (ii) holds, TRIPLE PROPOSAL is not strategy-proof anymore. Actually, in such a setting, it seems difficult to attain approximation factors better than that of the arbitrary tie-breaking Gale–Shapley algorithm, while preserving strategy-proofness. This is true at least for the marriage model because no strategy-proof algorithm can attain an approximation factor better than 2, which easily follows from Hamada et al. [11].

4   Maximum Gaps and Approximation Factors

In this section, we analyze the approximation factors of TRIPLE PROPOSAL, together with the maximum gaps for the four models mentioned in Sect. 1.

For an instance I of HRT-MSLQ, let $\mathrm{OPT}(I)$ and $\mathrm{WST}(I)$ respectively denote the maximum and minimum scores over all stable matchings of I, and let $\mathrm{ALG}(I)$ be the score of the output of TRIPLE PROPOSAL. For a model $\mathcal{I}$ (i.e., subfamily of problem instances of HRT-MSLQ), let

$$\Lambda(\mathcal{I}) = \max_{I \in \mathcal{I}} \frac{\mathrm{OPT}(I)}{\mathrm{WST}(I)} \quad and \quad \mathrm{APPROX}(\mathcal{I}) = \max_{I \in \mathcal{I}} \frac{\mathrm{OPT}(I)}{\mathrm{ALG}(I)}.$$

The maximum gap $\Lambda(\mathcal{I})$ coincides with the worst approximation factor of a naive algorithm that first breaks ties arbitrarily and then applies the resident-oriented Gale–Shapley algorithm. This equivalence is obtained by combining the following two facts: (1) for any stable matching M of I, there exists an instance I' with strict preferences such that I' is obtained from I via some tie-breaking and M is a stable matching of I', (2) for any instance I' with strict preferences, the number of residents assigned to each hospital is invariant over all stable matchings. (For a more precise proof, see [8, Proposition 20].)

In subsequent subsections, we tightly prove the values of the maximum gap $\Lambda(\mathcal{I})$ and the approximation factor $\mathrm{APPROX}(\mathcal{I})$ of TRIPLE PROPOSAL for the general, uniform, and marriage models. The results for the resident-side master list model follow from those for the general model.

Remark 4.1. Let $\mathcal{I}$ be a model of HRT-MSLQ and $\mathcal{I}'$ be the subfamily of $\mathcal{I}$ consisting of all the instances in which preference lists of residents are strict. The algorithm DOUBLE PROPOSAL applied to an instance $I' \in \mathcal{I}'$ has arbitrariness in the choice of a resident to be rejected at each rejection step because hospitals' lists can contain ties. Any choice in this arbitrariness can be viewed as a tie-breaking of hospitals' preference lists; more precisely, for any way of breaking the ties of hospitals' preference lists in I', which results in an instance I without ties, there is an execution of DOUBLE PROPOSAL for I' in such a way that the output of DOUBLE PROPOSAL for I' coincides with the output of the Gale–Shapley algorithm for I. Therefore, any output of the arbitrary tie-breaking Gale–Shapley algorithm for an instance in $\mathcal{I}'$ can be an output of some execution of DOUBLE PROPOSAL for $\mathcal{I}'$. This implies that the maximum gap for $\mathcal{I}'$ gives a lower bound on the approximation factor of DOUBLE PROPOSAL for $\mathcal{I}$. The results in the second row of Table 1 are obtained in this manner.

4.1   Marriage Model

We start with the model easiest to analyze. Let $\mathcal{I}_{\mathrm{Marriage}}$ denote the family of instances of HRT-MSLQ, in which each hospital has an upper quota of 1. We call $\mathcal{I}_{\mathrm{Marriage}}$ the *marriage model*. By definition, $[\ell(h), u(h)]$ in this model is either $[0, 1]$ or $[1, 1]$ for each $h \in H$. For this simple one-to-one matching case, we can show the maximum gap and the approximation factor of TRIPLE PROPOSAL using standard techniques.

Theorem 4.1. *The maximum gap for the marriage model satisfies* $\Lambda(\mathcal{I}_{\mathrm{Marriage}})$ $= 2$. *This holds even if preference lists of residents are strict.*

Proof. For any $I \in \mathcal{I}_{\mathrm{Marriage}}$, let N and M be stable matchings with $s(N) = \mathrm{OPT}(I)$ and $s(M) = \mathrm{WST}(I)$. Consider a bipartite graph $G = (R, H; N \cup M)$, where an edge used in both N and M is regarded as a length-two cycle in G. Then, each connected component C of G is either an alternating cycle or an alternating path (possibly of length 0). Let $s_N(C)$ and $s_M(C)$, respectively, be the scores of N and M on the component C. Then it suffices to show that

$\frac{s_N(C)}{s_M(C)} \leq 2$ holds for any C. If C is an alternating cycle, then $s_N(h) = s_M(h) = 1$ for every hospital h on C, so $s_N(C) = s_M(C)$. Suppose then that C is an alternating path. Note that a hospital h on C satisfies $s_N(h) = 1$ and $s_M(h) = 0$ only if $\ell(h) = 1$ and h is matched only in N (and hence h is an end terminal of a path). At most one hospital in C can satisfy this condition. Note also that other hospitals h on C satisfy $s_M(h) = 1$. Now, let k be the number of hospitals in C. By the above argument, we have $\frac{s_N(C)}{s_M(C)} \leq \frac{k}{k-1}$, so if $k \geq 2$, we are done. When $k = 1$, there are three cases. If C is a length-two path with a hospital h being a midpoint, then h is matched in both N and M, so $s_N(C) = s_M(C) = 1$. If C is an isolated vertex, then clearly $s_N(C) = s_M(C) = 0$. If C is a length-one path (r, h) of an edge of N (resp. M), then (r, h) blocks M (resp. N), a contradiction. Hence, $\Lambda(\mathcal{I}_{\mathrm{Marriage}}) \leq 2$.

An instance demonstrating the other inequality is given in the full version [16]. $\qquad\square$

Theorem 4.2. *The approximation factor of* TRIPLE PROPOSAL *for the marriage model satisfies* APPROX$(\mathcal{I}_{\mathrm{Marriage}}) = 1.5$.

Proof. For any $I \in \mathcal{I}_{\mathrm{Marriage}}$, let M be the output of TRIPLE PROPOSAL and N be an optimal stable matching. By arguments in the proof of Theorem 4.1, it suffices to show that there is no component of $G = (R, H; N \cup M)$ that forms an alternating path containing exactly two hospitals h_1 and h_2 with $s_N(h_1) = 1$, $s_M(h_1) = 0$, $s_N(h_2) = 1$, and $s_M(h_2) = 1$. Suppose on the contrary that there is such a path. Then, $\ell(h_1) = 1$, h_1 is matched only in N, and there exists a resident r_1 such that $N(r_1) = h_1$ and $M(r_1) = h_2$. Since the path consists of only two hospitals, there are two cases: (i) h_2 is unmatched in N and $\ell(h_2) = 0$ and (ii) there exists a resident r_2 such that $N(r_2) = h_2$ and $M(r_2) = \varnothing$. However, (ii) is impossible since otherwise (r_2, h_2, r_1, h_1) is a length-3 M-augmenting path, which contradicts Lemma 3.3. Hence, assume (i). As h_1 is assigned no resident in M, we have $h_2 = M(r_1) \succeq_{r_1} h_1$ by the stability of M. Similarly, as h_2 is unmatched in N, the stability of N implies $h_1 = N(r_1) \succeq_{r_1} h_2$, and hence $h_1 =_{r_1} h_2$. Since $|M(h_2)| = 1 > \ell(h_2)$, Lemma 3.2(ii) implies $|M(h_1)| \geq \ell(h_1) = 1$, which contradicts $|M(h_1)| = 0$. Thus we obtain $\frac{s(N)}{s(M)} \leq 1.5$ and hence APPROX$(\mathcal{I}_{\mathrm{Marriage}}) \leq 1.5$.

An instance demonstrating the other inequality is given in the full version [16]. $\qquad\square$

4.2   Uniform Model

Let $\mathcal{I}_{\mathrm{Uniform}}$ denote the family of uniform problem instances of HRT-MSLQ, where an instance is called *uniform* if all hospitals have the same upper quotas and the same lower quotas. In the rest of this subsection, we assume that ℓ and u are nonnegative integers to represent the common lower and upper quotas, respectively, and let $\theta := \frac{u}{\ell}$ (≥ 1). We call $\mathcal{I}_{\mathrm{Uniform}}$ the *uniform model*.

Analysing this model is not so easy as the marriage model. Observe that, in the marriage model, our objective can be regarded as a weight maximization

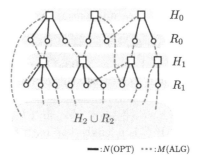

Fig. 1. An example of a connected component in $N \cup M$ for the case $[\ell, u] = [2, 3]$. Hospitals and residents are represented by squares and circles, respectively. The matchings N and M are represented by solid (black) lines and dashed (red) lines, respectively. (Color figure online)

where the weight of each edge in E is 1 if it is incident to a hospital with quotas $[1, 1]$ and 0 otherwise. In the uniform model, however, such an interpretation is impossible and our objective function $\sum_{h \in H} \min\{1, \frac{|M(h)|}{\ell}\}$ is non-linear, which makes the analysis harder. We analyze this model by extending the techniques proposed in Goko et al. [9].

We first provide the maximum gap.

Theorem 4.3. *The maximum gap for the uniform model satisfies* $\Lambda(\mathcal{I}_{\text{Uniform}}) = \theta + 1$. *This holds even if preference lists of residents are strict.*

We next show the approximation factor of our algorithm.

Theorem 4.4. *The approximation factor of* TRIPLE PROPOSAL *for the uniform model satisfies* $\text{APPROX}(\mathcal{I}_{\text{uniform}}) = \frac{\theta}{2} + 1$.

The framework of the proof is similar to that of Theorem 9 of Goko et al. [8]. Here we explain an outline of the proof of $\text{APPROX}(\mathcal{I}_{\text{uniform}}) \leq \frac{\theta}{2} + 1$ putting emphasis on the difference from [8].

Let M be the output of the algorithm and N be an optimal stable matching. Consider a bipartite (multi-)graph $(R, H; M \cup N)$. To complete the proof, it suffices to show that the approximation factor is attained in each connected component. Take any connected component and let H_0 be the set of all hospitals h with $s_N(h) > s_M(h)$ in the component. That is, hospitals in H_0 get larger scores in N than in M, which implies that those hospitals are deficient in M. We then categorize hospitals and residents using a breadth-first search as follows (see Fig. 1): consider NM-alternating paths that start at H_0 with edges in N. Let R_0 and R_1 be the sets of residents reachable from H_0 via those paths of length 1 and 3, respectively and let H_1 be the set of hospitals reachable from H_0 via those paths of length 2. The set of remaining residents (resp., hospitals) in the component is denoted as R_2 (resp., H_2).

In Goko et al. [8], the authors upper bound the ratio of the score of N to that of M by a kind of counting argument on the number of residents in the component: they estimate this number in two ways using the stability of N and M and the property in Lemma 3.2. In the estimations, they use the fact that all residents in the component are matched in M, which is not true for the current incomplete list setting. However, thanks to the nonexistence of length-3 M-augmenting paths shown in Lemma 3.3, we can guarantee that all residents in $R_0 \cup R_1$ are matched in M (residents in R_0 are matched by the stability of M). Utilizing this fact, we can obtain the required upper bound.

4.3   General Model and R-side ML Model

Let $\mathcal{I}_{\mathrm{Gen}}$ denote the family of all instances of HRT-MSLQ, which we call the *general model*. In addition, let $\mathcal{I}_{\mathrm{R\text{-}ML}}$ denote the subfamily of $\mathcal{I}_{\mathrm{Gen}}$ representing the *resident-side master list model*. That is, in an instance in $\mathcal{I}_{\mathrm{R\text{-}ML}}$, there exists a master preference list from which each resident's list is obtained by deleting unacceptable hospitals. In this section, we mainly work on the general model and obtain results on the resident-side master list model as consequences.

As in the case of the uniform model, the non-linearity of the objective function $\sum_{h \in H} \min\{1, \frac{|M(h)|}{\ell(h)}\}$ prevents us from applying the standard techniques used for the marriage model. Furthermore, due to the non-uniformness of the quotas, we cannot apply the counting argument used for the uniform model. It appears, however, that the techniques used in Goko et al. [8] can apply even for the current incomplete list setting.

We first provide two theorems on the maximum gap.

Theorem 4.5. *The maximum gaps for the general and resident-side master list models are $n + 1$, i.e., $\Lambda(\mathcal{I}_{\mathrm{Gen}}) = \Lambda(\mathcal{I}_{\mathrm{R\text{-}ML}}) = n + 1$.*

Theorem 4.6. *If the preference lists of residents are strict, the maximum gaps for the general and resident-side master list models are $\lfloor \frac{n}{2} \rfloor + 1$.*

We next show that the approximation factor of our algorithm is $\phi(n)$, where ϕ is a function of $n = |R|$ defined by

$$\phi(n) = \begin{cases} 1 & n = 1, \\ \frac{3}{2} & n = 2, \\ \frac{n(1 + \lfloor \frac{n}{2} \rfloor)}{n + \lfloor \frac{n}{2} \rfloor} & n \geq 3. \end{cases}$$

Theorem 4.7. *The approximation factor of* TRIPLE PROPOSAL *for the general model satisfies* $\mathrm{APPROX}(\mathcal{I}_{\mathrm{Gen}}) = \phi(n)$. *The same statement holds for the resident-side master list model, i.e.,* $\mathrm{APPROX}(\mathcal{I}_{\mathrm{R\text{-}ML}}) = \phi(n)$.

The proof is in large part the same as that of Theorem 7 of Goko et al. [8], which shows that the approximation factor of DOUBLE PROPOSAL is $\phi(n)$ in the complete list setting. As shown in the second row of Table 1, DOUBLE PROPOSAL fails to attain this factor in the current incomplete list setting. To show the approximation factor $\phi(n)$ of TRIPLE PROPOSAL, we need to use Lemma 3.3, i.e., the nonexistence of length-3 augmenting path. Here, we present a proof outline of $\text{APPROX}(\mathcal{I}_{\text{Gen}}) \le \phi(n)$.

Let M be the output of the algorithm and N be an optimal stable matching. We define vectors p_M and p_N on R, which distribute the scores to residents. For each $h \in H$, among residents in $M(h)$, we set $p_M(r) = \frac{1}{\ell(h)}$ for $\min\{\ell(h), |M(h)|\}$ residents and $p_M(r) = 0$ for the remaining ones. We also set $p_M(r) = 0$ for residents r unmatched in M. Similarly, we define p_N from N. Then, we have $s(M) = \sum_{r \in R} p_M(r)$ and $s(N) = \sum_{r \in R} p_N(r)$.

In the proof of Theorem 7 in [8], the authors upper bound $\frac{s(N)}{s(M)}$ by comparing the vectors p_M and p_N. Their argument still works for the current incomplete list setting if $s(M) \ge 2$ or there is no resident matched only in N.

We need a separate analysis for the remaining case, i.e., the case when $s(M) < 2$ holds and there exists a resident r^* with $N(r^*) \neq \varnothing = M(r^*)$. Denote $h^* := N(r^*)$. Since (r^*, h^*) belongs to E and r^* is unmatched in M, the stability of M implies that the hospital h^* is full in M. By the same argument, for any resident r with $N(r) \neq \varnothing = M(r)$, the hospital $N(r)$ is full in M, which implies $N(r) = h^*$ because there is at most one sufficient hospital in M by $s(M) < 2$. Therefore, any resident r with $N(r) \neq \varnothing = M(r)$ satisfies $r \in N(h^*)$. Since h^* is the unique sufficient hospital, any resident r with $M(r) \neq \varnothing$ and $p_M(r) = 0$ satisfies $r \in M(h^*)$. Thus, every resident r with $p_M(r) = 0$ belongs to $N(h^*) \cup M(h^*)$ unless $r \in S := \{r' \in R \mid M(r') = N(r') = \varnothing\}$. In other words, all residents in $R \setminus (N(h^*) \cup M(h^*) \cup S)$ have positive p_M-values.

Since all hospitals other than h^* are deficient in M, any $r \in M(h^*) \setminus N(h^*)$ satisfies $N(r) = \varnothing$, because otherwise $(r^*, h^*, r, N(r))$ forms a length-3 M-augmenting path, which contradicts Lemma 3.3. Therefore, all residents r in $M(h^*) \setminus N(h^*)$, as well as all residents in S, satisfy $p_N(r) = 0$. Hence, the summation of p_N-values over $N(h^*) \cup M(h^*) \cup S$ is at most 1, while that of p_M-values over $N(h^*) \cup M(h^*) \cup S$ is at least 1 because h^* is full in M.

Combining these observations with others, we upper bound $\frac{\sum_{r \in R} p_N(r)}{\sum_{r \in R} p_M(r)} = \frac{s(N)}{s(M)}$.

5   Inapproximability Results

We provide inapproximability results for HRT-MSLQ. The first subsection investigates the uniform model and the second one investigates the other models.

5.1   Uniform Model

This section shows the following inapproximability results for the uniform model.

Theorem 5.1. *HRT-MSLQ in the uniform model with $\theta = \frac{u}{\ell}$ is*

(i) *inapproximable within a factor $\frac{1}{3}\theta + 1 - \epsilon\theta^2$ for any $\epsilon > 0$ under UGC, and*

(ii) *inapproximable within a factor $\frac{2-\sqrt{2}}{3}\theta + 1 - \epsilon\theta^2$ for any $\epsilon > 0$ unless P=NP.*

We prove Theorem 5.1 by extending the idea of Yanagisawa [20], who provided inapproximability results for MAX-SMTI by a reduction from the Vertex Cover problem (VC for short). VC is a well-studied NP-hard problem that asks to find a minimum size vertex cover in a given graph. We denote by VC-PM the restricted version of VC where an input graph is imposed to have a perfect matching.

Yanagisawa [20] used inapproximability results for VC-PM under UGC [4,14] and under P≠NP [5] to obtain inapproximability results for MAX-SMTI. To prove Theorem 5.1(i), we use the following result as in [20].

Theorem 5.2 (Chlebík and Chlebíková [4], Khot and Regev [14]).
Under UGC, VC-PM is inapproximabile within a factor $2 - \epsilon$ for any $\epsilon > 0$.

To prove Theorem 5.1(ii), we show the following hardness result for VC-PM, which can be obtained by a recent result for VC [13], together with the reduction from VC to VC-PM in [4]. For a graph G, we denote by $\tau(G)$ the size of a minimum vertex cover of G.

Theorem 5.3. *For any $\epsilon > 0$, it is NP-hard for graphs $G = (V, E)$ with perfect matchings to distinguish between the following two cases:*

(1) $\tau(G) \leq (\frac{\sqrt{2}}{2} + \epsilon)|V|$.
(2) $\tau(G) \geq (1 - \epsilon)|V|$.

To transform the above two hardness results for VC-PM into those for HRT-MSLQ, we provide a method to transform VC-PM instances to HRT-MSLQ instances satisfying the following properties.

Proposition 5.1. *Let ℓ and u be positive integers with $\ell \leq u$ and set $\theta = \frac{u}{\ell}$. There is a polynomial-time reduction from VC-PM instances $G = (V, F)$ to HRT-MSLQ instances I in the uniform model with quotas $[\ell, u]$ such that*

(a) for any stable matching M in I, there exists a vertex cover C of G satisfying
    $s(M) \leq (1.5 + \theta)|V| - \theta|C|$, and
(b) $\mathrm{OPT}(I) = (1.5 + \theta)|V| - \theta\tau(G)$.

We now complete the proof of Theorem 5.1 relying on this proposition.

Proof of Theorem 5.1. We show the statements (i) and (ii) in Theorem 5.1, which are inapproximability of HRT-MSLQ under UGC and under P≠NP, respectively. Let G be a VC-PM instance and I be an HRT-MSLQ instance satisfying the conditions (a) and (b) in Proposition 5.1.

We first show (i). For any $\epsilon > 0$, let $r = \frac{\theta}{3} + 1 - \epsilon\theta^2$ and let M be a stable matching in I with $s(M) \geq \frac{\mathrm{OPT}(I)}{r}$. By Proposition 5.1(a), there exists a vertex cover C of G such that $s(M) \leq (1.5 + \theta)|V| - \theta|C|$. Thus we have

$$|C| \leq \frac{1.5 + \theta}{\theta}|V| - \frac{\mathrm{OPT}(I)}{r\theta} \leq \left(1 - \frac{1}{r}\right)\frac{1.5 + \theta}{\theta}|V| + \frac{\tau(G)}{r},$$

where the second inequality follows from $\mathrm{OPT}(I) = (1.5 + \theta)|V| - \theta\tau(G)$ by Proposition 5.1(b). This implies that

$$
\begin{aligned}
\frac{|C|}{\tau(G)} &\leq \frac{1}{r} + \left(1 - \frac{1}{r}\right)\frac{1.5 + \theta}{\theta}\frac{|V|}{\tau(G)} \\
&\leq \frac{1}{r} + 2\left(1 - \frac{1}{r}\right)\frac{1.5 + \theta}{\theta} \\
&= 2 + \frac{3}{\theta} - \frac{\theta + 3}{r\theta} \\
&\leq 2 - \frac{9\epsilon\theta}{\theta + 3} && \text{(by } \tfrac{1}{r} \geq \tfrac{3(\theta+3+3\epsilon\theta^2)}{(\theta+3)^2}) \\
&\leq 2 - \epsilon && \text{(by } \theta \geq 1),
\end{aligned}
$$

where the second inequality follows from $\tau(G) \geq 0.5|V|$, since G has a perfect matching. Therefore, by Theorem 5.2, the uniform model of HRT-MSLQ is inapproximable within a factor $\frac{\theta}{3} + 1 - \epsilon\theta^2$ for any positive ϵ under UGC.

We next show (ii). By Proposition 5.1(b), we have $\mathrm{OPT}(I) = (1.5 + \theta)|V| - \theta\tau(G)$. If $\tau(G) \leq (\frac{\sqrt{2}}{2} + \delta)|V|$ for some positive δ, then $\mathrm{OPT}(I) \geq \frac{1}{2}((2 - \sqrt{2} - 2\delta)\theta + 3)|V|$ holds. On the other hand, if $\tau(G) \geq (1 - \delta)|V|$ for some positive δ, we have $\mathrm{OPT}(I) \leq \frac{1}{2}(3 + 2\delta\theta)|V|$.

By Theorem 5.3, it is NP-hard for HRT-MSLQ in the uniform model to approximate within a factor

$$
\frac{(2 - \sqrt{2} - 2\delta)\theta + 3}{3 + 2\delta\theta} > \frac{2 - \sqrt{2}}{3}\theta + 1 - 2\delta\theta^2,
$$

where the inequality follows from that $\theta \geq 1$. Thus by setting $\epsilon = 2\delta$, we obtain the desired inapproximation factor of the problem. □

Remark 5.1. By modifying the gadget construction in the proof of Proposition 5.1, we can improve a lower bound on the approximation factor of the complete list setting of HRT-MSLQ in the uniform model from constant [8] to linear in θ.

5.2   Other Models

Here we present some inapproximability results on models other than the uniform model. The inapproximability results in Table 1 for the general and resident-side master list models are consequences of a result in [9] as can be seen from Remark 5.2.

Remark 5.2. It is shown in Goko et al. [9] that, even in the complete list setting, HRT-MSLQ is inapproximable within a factor $n^{\frac{1}{4}-\epsilon}$ for any $\epsilon > 0$ unless P=NP. This immediately gives the result in the bottom-left corner of Table 1. We can modify their proof to obtain the same inapproximability result in the resident-side master list model with incomplete lists. In the proof of Theorem 10 in [9], agents denoted by "$\cdots$" are added to preference lists in Fig. 3 in [9]. They are actually added only to make the preference lists complete and do not play any role in the reduction. Actually, removing them still retains the correctness of the reduction, and as a result, we can define a master list from which any resultant resident's preference list can be derived. The result in the bottom-right corner of Table 1 is obtained in this manner.

We then move to the marriage model. Since the marriage model is a special case of the uniform model where $u = 1$ and ℓ is either 0 or 1, we can obtain inapproximability results for the marriage model by letting $u = \ell = 1$ (i.e., $\theta = 1$) in Theorem 5.1.

Proposition 5.2. *HRT-MSLQ in the marriage model is*

(i) *inapproximable within a factor $\frac{4}{3} - \epsilon$ for any $\epsilon > 0$ under UGC, and*

(ii) *inapproximable within a factor $\frac{5-\sqrt{2}}{3} - \epsilon$ for any $\epsilon > 0$ unless P=NP.*

Remark 5.3. Observe that the marriage model when $\ell = u = 1$ is equivalent to MAX-SMTI. Therefore, Proposition 5.2(ii) implies a lower bound $\frac{5-\sqrt{2}}{3}$ (≈ 1.1952) on the approximation factor of MAX-SMTI, which improves the best known lower bound $\frac{33}{29}$ (≈ 1.1379) [20]. We note that the same lower bound can also be obtained by directly applying Theorem 5.3 to Yanagisawa's reduction [20]. We also note that, by the same observation, a lower bound on the approximation factor of MAX-SMTI with one-sided-ties can be improved from $\frac{21}{19}$ (≈ 1.1052) to $\frac{6-\sqrt{2}}{4}$ (≈ 1.1464).

Remark 5.4. As mentioned above, MAX-SMTI is a special case of HRT-MSLQ in the marriage model. In fact, we can show that the two problems are polynomially equivalent in approximability by the following reduction: Let I be an instance of HRT-MSLQ in the marriage model, where R and H are respectively the sets of residents and hospitals. For each $r_i \in R$, construct a man m_i and for each $h_j \in H$, construct a woman w_j. A man m_i's preference list is that of r_i in which a hospital h_j is replaced by a woman w_j. Similarly, a woman m_j's preference list is that of h_j in which a resident r_i is replaced by a man m_i. Furthermore, for each $[0, 1]$-hospital h_j, we construct a man a_j who includes only w_j in the preference list, and we append a_j to w_j's preference list as the last choice. This completes the reduction and let I' be the reduced instance.

For a stable matching M of I, define a matching M' of I' as $M' = \{(m_i, w_j) \mid (r_i, h_j) \in M\} \cup \{(a_j, w_j) \mid h_j$ is a $[0,1]$-hospital unmatched in $M\}$. It is easy to see that M' is stable. We can also see that any stable matching of I' can be obtained in this manner because a woman w_j corresponding to a $[0, 1]$-hospital h_j is always matched in a stable matching. Hence this is a one-to-one correspondence between the stable matchings of I and those in I'. Since the score of M is the same as the size of M', the correctness of the reduction follows.

6 Conclusion

There remain several open questions and future research directions for HRT-MSLQ. Clearly, it is a major open problem to close a gap between the upper and lower bounds on the approximation factor for each scenario. Next, as mentioned in Remark 3.1, TRIPLE PROPOSAL is not strategy-proof in general. It would be an important task to clarify approximability of HRT-MSLQ when we restrict ourselves to strategy-proof (instead of polynomial-time) algorithms. Finally, in our setting, the score of each hospital is piecewise linear in the number of assignees. A possible extension is to consider more general functions, such as convex ones.

Acknowledgements. The authors would like to thank the anonymous reviewers for reading the submitted version carefully and giving useful comments, which improved the quality of the paper. This work was partially supported by the joint project of Kyoto University and Toyota Motor Corporation, titled "Advanced Mathematical Science for Mobility Society". The first author is supported by JSPS KAKENHI Grant Numbers JP20H05967, JP19K22841, and JP20H00609. The second author is supported by JSPS KAKENHI Grant Number JP20K11677. The last author is supported by JSPS KAKENHI Grant Number JP18K18004 and JST, PRESTO Grant Number JPMJPR212B.

References

1. Abdulkadiroğlu, A., Pathak, P.A., Roth, A.E.: The New York city high school match. Am. Econ. Rev. **95**(2), 364–367 (2005)
2. Abdulkadiroğlu, A., Pathak, P.A., Roth, A.E., Sönmez, T.: The Boston public school match. Am. Econ. Rev. **95**(2), 368–371 (2005)
3. Biró, P., Fleiner, T., Irving, R.W., Manlove, D.F.: The College Admissions problem with lower and common quotas. Theor. Comput. Sci. **411**(34–36), 3136–3153 (2010)
4. Chlebík, M., Chlebíková, J.: Minimum 2SAT-DELETION: inapproximability results and relations to minimum vertex cover. Discrete Appl. Math. **155**(2), 172–179 (2007)
5. Dinur, I., Safra, S.: On the hardness of approximating minimum vertex cover. Ann. Math. **162**(1), 439–485 (2005)
6. Gale, D., Shapley, L.S.: College admissions and the stability of marriage. Am. Math. Mon. **69**(1), 9–15 (1962)
7. Gale, D., Sotomayor, M.: Some remarks on the stable matching problem. Discrete Appl. Math. **11**(3), 223–232 (1985)
8. Goko, H., Makino, K., Miyazaki, S., Yokoi, Y.: Maximally satisfying lower quotas in the hospitals/residents problem with ties. CoRR abs/2105.03093 (2021)
9. Goko, H., Makino, K., Miyazaki, S., Yokoi, Y.: Maximally satisfying lower quotas in the hospitals/residents problem with ties. In: Berenbrink, P., Monmege, B. (eds.) 39th International Symposium on Theoretical Aspects of Computer Science (STACS 2022). Leibniz International Proceedings in Informatics (LIPIcs), vol. 219, pp. 31:1–31:20. Schloss Dagstuhl - Leibniz-Zentrum für Informatik, Dagstuhl, Germany (2022)

10. Hamada, K., Iwama, K., Miyazaki, S.: The hospitals/residents problem with lower quotas. Algorithmica **74**(1), 440–465 (2016). https://doi.org/10.1007/s00453-014-9951-z

11. Hamada, K., Miyazaki, S., Yanagisawa, H.: Strategy-proof approximation algorithms for the stable marriage problem with ties and incomplete lists. In: Lu, P., Zhang, G. (eds.) 30th International Symposium on Algorithms and Computation, ISAAC 2019, 8–11 December 2019, Shanghai University of Finance and Economics, Shanghai, China. LIPIcs, vol. 149, pp. 9:1–9:14. Schloss Dagstuhl - Leibniz-Zentrum für Informatik (2019)

12. Kamada, Y., Kojima, F.: Efficiency in matching markets with regional caps: the case of the Japan Residency Matching Program. Discussion Papers 10–011, Stanford Institute for Economic Policy Research (2010)

13. Khot, S., Minzer, D., Safra, M.: Pseudorandom sets in Grassmann graph have near-perfect expansion. In: 2018 IEEE 59th Annual Symposium on Foundations of Computer Science (FOCS), pp. 592–601. IEEE (2018)

14. Khot, S., Regev, O.: Vertex cover might be hard to approximate to within $2 - \varepsilon$. J. Comput. Syst. Sci. **74**(3), 335–349 (2008)

15. Király, Z.: Linear time local approximation algorithm for maximum stable marriage. Algorithms **6**(3), 471–484 (2013)

16. Makino, K., Miyazaki, S., Yokoi, Y.: Maximally satisfying lower quotas in the hospitals/residents problem with ties and incomplete lists. CoRR abs/2203.06660 (2022)

17. Manlove, D.F., Irving, R.W., Iwama, K., Miyazaki, S., Morita, Y.: Hard variants of stable marriage. Theor. Comput. Sci. **276**(1–2), 261–279 (2002)

18. Roth, A.: The evolution of the labor market for medical interns and residents: a case study in game theory. J. Polit. Econ. **92**(6), 991–1016 (1984)

19. Roth, A.: On the allocation of residents to rural hospitals: a general property of two-sided matching markets. Econometrica **54**(2), 425–27 (1986)

20. Yanagisawa, H.: Approximation algorithms for stable marriage problems. Ph.D. thesis, Kyoto University (2007)

Strategic Voting in the Context
of Stable-Matching of Teams

Leora Schmerler[1], Noam Hazon[1(✉)], and Sarit Kraus[2]

[1] Department of Computer Science, Ariel University, Ariel, Israel
{leoras,noamh}@ariel.ac.il
[2] Department of Computer Science, Bar-Ilan University, Ramat Gan, Israel
sarit@cs.biu.ac.il

Abstract. In the celebrated stable-matching problem, there are two sets of agents M and W, and the members of M only have preferences over the members of W and vice versa. It is usually assumed that each member of M and W is a single entity. However, there are many cases in which each member of M or W represents a team that consists of several individuals with common interests. For example, students may need to be matched to professors for their final projects, but each project is carried out by a team of students. Thus, the students first form teams, and the matching is between teams of students and professors.

When a team is considered as an agent from M or W, it needs to have a preference order that represents it. A voting rule is a natural mechanism for aggregating the preferences of the team members into a single preference order. In this paper, we investigate the problem of strategic voting in the context of stable-matching of teams. Specifically, we assume that members of each team use the Borda rule for generating the preference order of the team. Then, the Gale-Shapley algorithm is used for finding a stable-matching, where the set M is the proposing side. We show that the single-voter manipulation problem can be solved in polynomial time, both when the team is from M and when it is from W. We show that the coalitional manipulation problem is computationally hard, but it can be solved approximately both when the team is from M and when it is from W.

1 Introduction

Matching is the process in which agents from different sets are matched with each other. The theory of matching originated with the seminal work of Gale and Shapley [9], and since then intensive research has been conducted in this field. Notably, the theory of matching has also been successfully applied to many real-world applications including college admissions and school matching [1], matching residents to hospitals [16], and kidney exchange [17]. A very common

This research has been partly supported by the Israel Science Foundation under grant 1958/20, by the EU Project TAILOR under grant 952215, and by the Ministry of Science, Technology & Space (MOST), Israel.

© The Author(s), under exclusive license to Springer Nature Switzerland AG 2022
P. Kanellopoulos et al. (Eds.): SAGT 2022, LNCS 13584, pp. 562–579, 2022.
https://doi.org/10.1007/978-3-031-15714-1_32

matching problem, which is also the problem that was studied by Gale and Shapley in their original paper, is the *stable-matching* problem. In this problem there are two equally sized disjoint sets of agents, M and W, and the members of M have preferences over only the members of W, and vice versa. The goal is to find a stable bijection (i.e., matching) from the agents of M to the agents of W, where the stability requirement is that no pair of agents prefers a match with each other over their matched partners. Many works have analyzed this setting, and they assume that each member of the sets M and W represents a single agent. However, there are many cases in which each member of M or W represents more than one individual [13].

For example, suppose that teams of students need to be matched with professors who will serve as their advisors in their final projects. It is common that students form their teams based on friendship connections and common interests and then approach the professors. Therefore, each team is considered to be a single agent for the matching process: the professors may have different preferences regarding which team they would like to mentor, and the teams may have preferences regarding which professor they would like as their mentor. Clearly, even though the team is considered to be a single agent for the matching process, it is still composed of several students, and they may have different opinions regarding the appropriate mentor for their team. Thus, every team needs a mechanism that aggregates the students' opinions and outputs a single preference order that represents the team for the matching process, and a voting rule is a natural candidate.

Indeed, voters might benefit from reporting rankings different from their true ones, and this problem of manipulation also exists in the context of matching. For example, suppose that there are 4 possible professors, denoted by p_1, p_2, p_3 and p_4 and 4 teams. Now, suppose that one of the students, denoted r, who is a member of one of the teams, prefers p_1 over p_2, p_2 over p_3, and p_3 over p_4. It is possible that r will gain an (unauthorized) access to the preferences of the professors and to the preferences of the other teams. Since the matching algorithm is usually publicly known, r might be able to reason that p_3 is matched with his team, but if r votes strategically and misreports his preferences then p_2 will be matched with his team.

In this paper, we investigate the problem of strategic voting in the context of stable-matching of teams. We assume that the members of each team use the Borda rule as a *social welfare function (SWF)*, which outputs a complete preference order. This preference order represents the team for the matching process. The agents then use the Gale-Shapley (GS) algorithm for finding a stable-matching. In the GS algorithm, one set of agents makes proposals to the other set of agents, and it is assumed that M is the proposing side and W is the proposed-to side. The proposing side and proposed-to side are commonly referred to as men and women, respectively. Note that the GS algorithm treats the men and women differently. Therefore, every manipulation problem in the context of stable-matching has two variants: one in which the teams are from the men's side, and another one in which the teams are from the women's side. Moreover, we analyze both manipulation by a single voter and coalitional manipulation. In a single voter manipulation, the goal is to find a preference order for a single manipulator such that his team will be matched by the GS algorithm with a specific preferred agent. In the coalitional manipulation setting, there are several voters who collude and coordinate their votes so that an agreed upon agent will be matched with their team.

We begin by studying manipulation from the men's side, and show that the single voter manipulation problem can be solved in polynomial time. We then analyze the coalitional manipulation problem, and show that the problem is computationally hard. However, we provide a polynomial-time algorithm with the following guarantee: given a manipulable instance with $|R|$ manipulators, the algorithm finds a successful manipulation with at most one additional manipulator. We then study manipulation from the women's side. Manipulation here is more involved, and we propose different algorithms, but with the same computational complexity as in manipulation from the men's side.

The contribution of this work is twofold. First, it provides an analysis of a voting manipulation in the context of stable-matching of teams, a problem that has not been investigated to date. Second, our work concerns the manipulation of Borda as an SWF, which has scarcely been investigated.

2   Related Work

The computational analysis of voting manipulation has been vastly studied in different settings. We refer the reader to the survey provided by Faliszewski and Procaccia [8], and the more recent survey by Conitzer and Walsh [4]. However, most of the works on voting manipulation analyze the problem with no actual context, and where a voting rule is used to output one winning candidate or a set of tied winning candidates (i.e., a social choice function). In this work, we investigate manipulation of Borda as a SWF, which outputs a complete preference order of the candidates, and analyze it within the context of stable-matching.

Indeed, there are a few papers that investigate the manipulation of SWFs. The first work that directly deals with the manipulation of SWF was by Bossert and Storcken [3], who assumed that a voter prefers one order over another if the former is closer to her own preferences than the latter according to the Kemeny distance. Bossert and Sprumont [2] assumed that a voter prefers one order over another if the former is strictly between the latter and the voter's own preferences. Built on this definition, their work studies three classes of SWF that are not prone to manipulation (i.e., strategy-proof). Dogan and Lainé [6] characterized the conditions to be imposed on SWFs so that if we extend the preferences of the voters to preferences over orders in specific ways, the SWFs will not be prone to manipulation. Our work also investigates the manipulation of SWF, but we analyze the SWF in the specific context of stable-matching. Therefore, unlike all of the above works, the preferences of the manipulators are well-defined and no additional assumptions are needed. The work that is closest to ours is that of Schmerler and Hazon [18]. They assume that a positional scoring rule is used as a SWF, and study the manipulation of the SWF in the context of negotiation.

The strategic aspects of the GS algorithm have previously been studied in the literature. It was first shown that reporting the true preferences is a weakly dominant strategy for men, but women may have an incentive to misreport their preferences [7,15]. Teo et al. [21] provided a polynomial-time algorithm for computing the optimal manipulation by a woman. Shen et al. [20] generalized this result to manipulation by a coalition of women. For the proposing side, Dubins and Freedman [7] investigated the strategic actions of a coalition of men, and proved that there is no manipulation that is a strict improvement for every member of the coalition. Huang [12] studied manipulation that is a weak improvement for every member of a coalition of men. Hosseini et al. [10] introduced a new type of strategic action: manipulation through an accomplice. In this manipulation, a man misreports his preferences in behalf of a woman, and Hosseini et al. provided a polynomial time algorithm for computing an optimal accomplice manipulation, and they further generalized this model in [11]. All of these works consider the manipulation of the GS algorithm, while we study the manipulation of Borda as a SWF. Indeed, the output of the SWF is used (as part of the input) for the GS algorithm. As an alternative to the GS algorithm, Pini et al. [14] show how voting rules which are NP-hard to manipulate can be used to build stable-matching procedures, which are themselves NP-hard to manipulate.

3   Preliminaries

We assume that there are two equally sized disjoint sets of agents, M and W. Let $k = |M| = |W|$. The members of M have preferences over only the members of W, and vice versa. The preference of each $m \in M$, denoted by $\succ_m$, is a strict total order over the agents in W. The preference profile $\succ_M$ is a vector $(\succ_{m_1}, \succ_{m_2}, \ldots, \succ_{m_k})$. The preference order $\succ_w$ and the preference profile $\succ_W$ are defined analogously. We will refer to the agents of M as men and to the agents of W as women.

A matching is a mapping $\mu : M \cup W \rightarrow M \cup W$, such that $\mu(m) \in W$ for all $m \in M$, $\mu(w) \in M$ for all $w \in W$, and $\mu(m) = w$ if and only if $\mu(w) = m$. A stable-matching is a matching in which there is no blocking pair. That is, there is no man m and woman w such that $w \succ_m \mu(m)$ and $m \succ_w \mu(w)$. The GS algorithm finds a stable-matching, and it works as follows. There are multiple rounds, and each round is composed of a proposal phase followed by a rejection phase. In a proposal phase, each unmatched man proposes to his favorite woman from among those who have not yet rejected him (regardless of whether the woman is already matched). In the rejection phase, each woman tentatively accepts her favorite proposal and rejects all of the other proposals. The algorithm terminates when no further proposals can be made. Let $o(w)$ be the set of men that proposed to w in one of the rounds of the GS algorithm.

In our setting, (at least) one of the agents of M (W) is a team that runs an election for determining its preferences. That is, there is a man $\hat{m}$ (woman $\hat{w}$), which is associated with a set of voters, V. The preference of each $v \in V$, denoted by ℓ_v, is a strict total order over W (M). The preference profile $\mathcal{L}$ is a vector $(\ell_{v_1}, \ell_{v_2}, \ldots, \ell_{v_{|V|}})$. The voters use the *Borda* rule as a SWF, denoted by $\mathcal{F}$, which is a mapping of the set of all preference profiles to a single strict preference order. Specifically, in the Borda rule, each voter v awards the candidate that is placed in the top-most position in ℓ_v a score of $k-1$, the candidate in the second-highest position in ℓ_v a score of $k-2$, etc. Then, for the output of $\mathcal{F}$, the candidate with the highest aggregated score is placed in the top-most position, the candidate with the second-highest score is placed in the second-highest position, etc. Since ties are possible, we assume that a lexicographical tie-breaking rule is used. Note that the output of $\mathcal{F}$ is the preference order of $\hat{m}$ ($\hat{w}$). That is, $\succ_{\hat{m}} = \mathcal{F}(\mathcal{L})$, and $\succ_{\hat{w}}$ is defined analogously.

Recall that the GS algorithm finds a stable matching, given $\succ_M$ and $\succ_W$. Given a man $m \in M$, let $\succ_{M-m}$ be the preference profile of all of the men besides m, and $\succ_{W-w}$ is defined analogously. We consider a setting in which the input for the GS algorithm is $\succ_{M-\hat{m}}, \succ_{\hat{m}}$, and $\succ_W$, and thus $\mu(\hat{m})$ is the spouse that is the match of $\hat{m}$ according to the output of the GS algorithm. We also consider a setting in which the input for the GS algorithm is $\succ_{W-\hat{w}}, \succ_{\hat{w}}$ and $\succ_M$, and thus $\mu(\hat{w})$ is the spouse that is the match of $\hat{w}$ according to the output of the GS algorithm. In some circumstances, we would like to examine the output of the GS algorithm for different possible preference orders that represent a man $m \in M$. We denote by $\mu_x(m, \succ)$ the spouse that is the match of m when the input for the GS algorithm is $\succ_{M-m}, \succ$ (instead of $\succ_m$), and $\succ_W$. We define $\mu_x(w, \succ)$ and $o_x(w, \succ)$ similarly.

We study the setting in which there exists a manipulator r among the voters associated with a man $\hat{m}$ (woman $\hat{w}$), and her preference order is ℓ_r. The preference order that represents $\hat{m}$ ($\hat{w}$) is thus $\mathcal{F}(\mathcal{L} \cup \{\ell_r\})$. We also study the setting in which there is a set $R = \{r_1, \ldots, r_n\}$ of manipulators, their preference profile is $\mathcal{L}_R = \{\ell_{r_1}, \ell_{r_2}, \ldots, \ell_{r_n}\}$, and preference order that represents $\hat{m}$ ($\hat{w}$) is thus $\mathcal{F}(\mathcal{L} \cup \mathcal{L}_R)$. For clarity purposes we slightly abuse notation, and write $\mu(\hat{m}, \ell_r)$ for denoting the spouse that is the match of $\hat{m}$ according to the output of the GS algorithm, given that its input is $\succ_{M-\hat{m}}, \mathcal{F}(\mathcal{L} \cup \{\ell_r\})$, and $\succ_W$. We define $\mu(\hat{w}, \ell_r)$, $o(\hat{w}, \ell_r)$, $\mu(\hat{m}, \mathcal{L}_R)$, $\mu(\hat{w}, \mathcal{L}_R)$ and $o(\hat{w}, \mathcal{L}_R)$ similarly.

Let $s(c, \ell_v)$ be the score of candidate c from ℓ_v. Similarly, let $s(c, \mathcal{L})$ be the total score of candidate c from $\mathcal{L}$, i.e., $s(c, \mathcal{L}) = \sum_{v \in V} s(c, \ell_v)$. Similarly, $s(c, \mathcal{L}, \ell_r) = \sum_{v \in V} s(c, \ell_v) + s(c, \ell_r)$, and $s(c, \mathcal{L}, \mathcal{L}_R) = \sum_{v \in V} s(c, \ell_v) + \sum_{r \in R} s(c, \ell_r)$. Since we use a lexicographical tie-breaking rule, we write that $(c, \ell) > (c', \ell')$ if $s(c, \ell) > s(c', \ell')$ or $s(c, \ell) = s(c', \ell')$ but c is preferred over c' according to the lexicographical tie-breaking rule. We define $(c, \mathcal{L}, \ell) > (c', \mathcal{L}, \ell')$ and $(c, \mathcal{L}, \mathcal{L}_R) > (c', \mathcal{L}, \mathcal{L}'_R)$ similarly.

Due to space constraint, many proofs are deferred to the full version of the paper [19].

4   Men's Side

We begin by considering the variant in which a specific voter, or a coalition of voters, are associated with an agent $\hat{m}$, and they would like to manipulate the election so that a preferred spouse w^* will be the match of $\hat{m}$.

4.1   Single Manipulator

With a single manipulator, the Manipulation in the context of Matching from the Men's side (MnM-m) is defined as follows:

Definition 1 (MnM-m). *We are given a man $\hat{m}$, the preference profile $\mathcal{L}$ of the honest voters that associate with $\hat{m}$, the preference profile $\succ_{M-\hat{m}}$, the preference profile $\succ_W$, a specific manipulator r, and a preferred woman $w^* \in W$. We are asked whether a preference order ℓ_r exists such that $\mu(\hat{m}, \ell_r) = w^*$.*

We show that MnM-m can be decided in polynomial time by Algorithm 1, which works as follows. The algorithm begins by verifying that a preference order exists for $\hat{m}$, which makes w^* the match of $\hat{m}$. It thus iteratively builds a temporary preference order for $\hat{m}$, $\succ_x$ in lines 4–7. Moreover, during the iterations in lines 4–7 the algorithm identifies a set B, which is the set of women that might prevent w^* from being $\hat{m}$'s match. Specifically, $\succ_x$, is initialized as the original preference order of $\hat{m}$, $\succ_{\hat{m}}$. In each iteration, the algorithm finds the woman b, which is the match of $\hat{m}$ given that $\succ_x$ is the preference order of $\hat{m}$. If b is placed higher than w^* in $\succ_x$, then b is added to the set B, it is placed in $\succ_x$ immediately below w^*, and the algorithm proceeds to the next iteration (using the updated $\succ_x$).

Now, if $b = \mu_x(\hat{m}, \succ_x)$ is positioned lower than w^* in $\succ_x$, then no preference order exists that makes w^* the match of $\hat{m}$, and the algorithm returns false. If $b = w^*$, then the algorithm proceeds to build the preference order for the manipulator, ℓ_r. Clearly, w^* is placed in the top-most position in ℓ_r. Then, the algorithm places all the women that are not in B in the highest available positions. Finally, the algorithm places all the women from B in the lowest positions in ℓ_r, and they are placed in a reverse order with regard to their order in $\mathcal{F}(\mathcal{L})$.

For proving the correctness of Algorithm 1 we use the following known results:

Theorem 1 (due to [15]). *In the Gale-Shapley matching procedure which always yields the optimal stable outcome for the set of the men agents, M, truthful revelation is a dominant strategy for all the agents in that set.*

Lemma 1 (due to [12]). *For man m, his preference list is composed of $(P_L(m), \mu(m), P_R(m))$, where $P_L(m)$ and $P_R(m)$ are respectively those women ranking higher and lower than $\mu(m)$. Let $A \subseteq W$ and let $\pi_r(A)$ be a random permutation from all $|A|!$ sets. For a subset of men $S \subseteq M$, if every member $m \in S$ submits a falsified list of the form $(\pi_r(P_L(m)), \mu(m), \pi_r(P_R(m)))$, then $\mu(m)$ stays m's match.*

ALGORITHM 1: Manipulation by a single voter from the men's side

---

1 $B \leftarrow \emptyset$
2 set $\succ_x$ to be $\succ_{\hat{m}}$
3 $b \leftarrow \mu_x(\hat{m}, \succ_x)$
4 **while** $b \succ_x w^*$ **do**
5   add b to B
6   move b in $\succ_x$ immediately below w^*
7      $b \leftarrow \mu_x(\hat{m}, \succ_x)$
8 **if** $b \neq w^*$ **then**
9   **return** false
10 $\ell_r \leftarrow$ empty preference order
11 place w^* in the highest position in ℓ_r
12 **for each** $w \in W \setminus (B \cup \{w^*\})$ **do**
13   place w in the next highest available position in ℓ_r
14 **while** $B \neq \emptyset$ **do**
15     $b \leftarrow$ the least preferred woman from B according to $\mathcal{F}(\mathcal{L})$
16   place b in the highest available position in ℓ_r
17   remove b from B
18 **if** $\mu(\hat{m}, \ell_r) = w^*$ **then**
19   **return** ℓ_r
20 **return** false

We begin by showing that the set B, which is identified by the algorithm in lines 4–7, is a set of woman that might prevent w^* from being $\hat{m}$'s match. The intuition is as follows. If $b = \mu_x(\hat{m}, \succ_x)$ in a given iteration does not equal w^*, then changing the order of the women ranking higher (or lower) than w^* in $\succ_t$ will not make w^* the match of $\hat{m}$ due to Lemma 1. Moreover, moving a woman that is above b to a position below w^* (or moving a woman that is below w^* to a position above b) will not make w^* the match of $\hat{m}$, due to Theorem 1.

Lemma 2. *Given a preference order $\succ_t$ for $\hat{m}$, if there exists $b \in B$ such that $b \succ_t w^*$ then $\mu_x(\hat{m}, \succ_t) \neq w^*$.*

Using Lemma 2, we show that it is possible to verify (in polynomial time) whether a preference order exists for $\hat{m}$, which makes w^* the match of $\hat{m}$. We do so by showing that it is sufficient to check whether $w^* = \mu_x(\hat{m}, \succ_x)$, where $\succ_x$ is the preference order that is built by Algorithm 1 in lines 4–7.

Lemma 3. *A preference order $\succ_t$ for $\hat{m}$ exists such that $w^* = \mu_x(\hat{m}, \succ_t)$ if and only if $w^* = \mu_x(\hat{m}, \succ_x)$.*

That is, if Algorithm 1 returns false in line 9 then there is no preference order for $\hat{m}$ that makes w^* the match of $\hat{m}$ (and thus no manipulation is possible for r).

Theorem 2. *Algorithm 1 correctly decides the MnM-m problem in polynomial time.*

Proof. Clearly, the algorithm runs in polynomial time since there are three loops, where the three loops together iterate at most $2k$ times, and the running time of the GS matching algorithm is in $O(k^2)$. In addition, if the algorithm returns a preference order, which is a manipulative vote for the manipulator r, then w^* will be the match of $\hat{m}$ by the GS algorithm. We need to show that if there exists a preference order for the manipulator r that makes w^* the match of $\hat{m}$, then our algorithm will find such a preference order for r. Assume that a manipulative vote, ℓ_t, exists, which makes w^* the match of $\hat{m}$. That is, $\mu(\hat{m}, \ell_t) = w^*$. Then, by Lemma 3, the algorithm finds a preference order for $\hat{m}$ that makes w^* his match (i.e., the preference order $\succ_x$), and thus it does not return false in line 9. We show that Algorithm 1 returns ℓ_r in line 19.

We now proceed to build the preference order ℓ_r. By Theorem 1, since each man should be truthful, then r should position w^* as high as possible, and thus w^* is positioned in the highest position in ℓ_r. Therefore, $s(w^*, \ell_r) \geq s(w^*, \ell_t)$, and consequently, w^* is positioned higher in $\mathcal{F}(\mathcal{L} \cup \{\ell_r\})$ than in $\mathcal{F}(\mathcal{L} \cup \{\ell_t\})$ or in the same position. That is, after line 11, $\mu(\hat{m}, \ell_r) = w^*$.

Note that $\succ_x$ is different from $\succ_{\hat{m}} = \mathcal{F}(\mathcal{L})$, but $\succ_x$ does not change the position of all $w \in W \setminus B$. Now, let $w \in W \setminus B$ be such that $w^* \succ_x w$. w is not preferred over w^* in $\mathcal{F}(\mathcal{L} \cup \{\ell_r\})$, since $w^* \succ_{\hat{m}} w$ and $s(w^*, \ell_r) > s(w, \ell_r)$. According to the GS algorithm, the women that are positioned below $\mu(m)$ for some man m do not affect m's match. Thus, placing w in ℓ_r does not change $\hat{m}$'s match, which is w^*. Let $w \in W \setminus B$ be such that $w \succ_x w^*$, but w^* is preferred over w in $\mathcal{F}(\mathcal{L} \cup \{\ell_r\})$. Due to Theorem 1, placing w in ℓ_r does not change $\hat{m}$'s match, which is w^*. Finally, let $w \in W \setminus B$ be such that $w \succ_x w^*$, and w is also preferred over w^* in $\mathcal{F}(\mathcal{L} \cup \{\ell_r\})$. Due to Lemma 1, placing w in ℓ_r does not change $\hat{m}$'s match, which is w^*.

According to Lemma 2, if $b \in B$ is positioned higher than w^* in $\mathcal{F}(\mathcal{L} \cup \{\ell_r\})$, w^* will not be $\hat{m}$'s match. We thus show that Algorithm 1 (lines 14–17) can assign scores to all the women $w \in B$ such that ℓ_r is a successful manipulation. According to Lemma 1 the order of the set B in $\hat{m}$'s preference order does not prevent w^* being the match (as long as each woman of the set B is placed below w^* in $\hat{m}$'s preference order). For any $w \in B$, if $s(w, \ell_r) \leq s(w, \ell_t)$ then $s(w, \mathcal{L}, \ell_r) \leq s(w, \mathcal{L}, \ell_t)$. Since $(w^*, \mathcal{L}, \ell_t) > (w, \mathcal{L}, \ell_t)$ then $(w^*, \mathcal{L}, \ell_r) > (w, \mathcal{L}, \ell_r)$. Otherwise, let $w \in B$ be a woman such that $s(w, \ell_r) > s(w, \ell_t)$ and let $s = s(w, \ell_r)$. There are s women from B below w in ℓ_r. According to the pigeonhole principle, at least one of the women from B, denoted w', gets a score of at least s from ℓ_t. That is, $s(w', \ell_t) \geq s(w, \ell_r)$. By the algorithm construction, all of the women $w'' \in B$ that are positioned lower than w in ℓ_r are positioned higher than w in $\mathcal{F}(\mathcal{L})$. That is, $(w', \mathcal{L}) > (w, \mathcal{L})$. However, $(w', \mathcal{L}, \ell_t) < (w^*, \mathcal{L}, \ell_t)$ and thus $(w, \mathcal{L}, \ell_r) < (w^*, \mathcal{L}, \ell_r)$. Overall, after placing the women from B in ℓ_r, $\forall w \in B$, $(w, \mathcal{L}, \ell_r) < (w^*, \mathcal{L}, \ell_r)$. That is, $\mu(\hat{m}, \ell_r) = w^*$.   □

4.2   Coalitional Manipulation

We now study manipulation by a coalition of voters. The coalitional manipulation in the context of matching from the men's side is defined as follows:

Definition 2 (coalitional MnM-m). *We are given a man $\hat{m}$, the preference profile $\mathcal{L}$ of the honest voters that associate with $\hat{m}$, the preference profile
$\succ_{M-\hat{m}}$, the preference profile $\succ_W$, a coalition of manipulators R, and a preferred
woman $w^* \in W$. We are asked whether a preference profile $\mathcal{L}_R$ exists such that
$\mu(\hat{m}, \mathcal{L}_R) = w^*$.*

We show that the coalitional MnM-m problem is computationally hard. The
reduction is from the Permutation Sum problem (as defined by Davies et al. [5])
that is NP-complete [23].

Definition 3 (Permutation Sum). *Given q integers $X_1 \leq \ldots \leq X_q$ where
$\sum_{i=1}^q X_i = q(q+1)$, do two permutations σ and π of 1 to q exist such that
$\sigma(i) + \pi(i) = X_i$ for all $1 \leq i \leq q$?*

Theorem 3. *Coalitional MnM-m is NP-Complete.*

Even though coalitional MnM-m is NP-complete, it might still be possible to
develop an efficient heuristic algorithm that finds a successful coalitional manipulation. We use Algorithm 2, which is a generalization of Algorithm 1, that
works as follows. Similar to Algorithm 1, Algorithm 2 identifies a set B, which

---

ALGORITHM 2: Manipulation by a coalition of voters from the men's side

1 $B \leftarrow \emptyset$
2 set $\succ_x$ to be $\succ_{\hat{m}}$
3 $b \leftarrow \mu_x(\hat{m}, \succ_x)$
4 **while** $b \succ_x w^*$ **do**
5 $\quad$ add b to B
6 $\quad$ place b in $\succ_x$ immediately below w^*
7 $\quad$ $b \leftarrow \mu_x(\hat{m}, \succ_x)$
8 **if** $b \neq w^*$ **then**
9 $\quad$ **return** false
10 **for** *each* $r \in R$ **do**
11 $\quad$ $\ell_r \leftarrow$ empty preference order
12 $\quad$ place w^* in the highest position in ℓ_r
13 $\quad$ **for** *each* $w \in W \setminus (B \cup \{w^*\})$ **do**
14 $\quad\quad$ place w in the next highest available position in ℓ_r
15 $\quad$ $B' \leftarrow B$
16 $\quad$ **while** $B' \neq \emptyset$ **do**
17 $\quad\quad$ $b \leftarrow$ the least preferred woman from B' according to $\mathcal{F}(\mathcal{L} \cup \mathcal{L}_R)$
18 $\quad\quad$ place b in the highest available position in ℓ_r
19 $\quad\quad$ remove b from B'
20 $\quad$ add ℓ_r to $\mathcal{L}_R$
21 **if** $\mu(\hat{m}) = w^*$ **then**
22 $\quad$ **return** $\mathcal{L}_R$
23 **return** false

---

is the set of women that might prevent w^* from being $\hat{m}$'s match. In addition, it verifies that a preference order for $\hat{m}$ exists, which makes w^* the match of $\hat{m}$. Then, Algorithm 2 proceeds to build the preference order of every manipulator $r \in R$ similarly to how Algorithm 1 builds the preference order for the single manipulator. Indeed, Algorithm 2 builds the preference order of each manipulator r in turn, and the order in which the woman in B are placed depends on their order according to $\mathcal{F}(\mathcal{L} \cup \mathcal{L}_R)$. That is, the order in which the woman in B are placed in each ℓ_r is not the same for each r, since $\mathcal{L}_R$ is updated in each iteration. We refer to each of the iterations in Lines 10–20 as a *stage* of the algorithm. We now show that Algorithm 2 is an efficient heuristic that also has a theoretical guarantee. Specifically, the algorithm is guaranteed to find a coalitional manipulation in many instances, and we characterize the instances in which it may fail. Formally,

Theorem 4. *Given an instance of coalitional MnM-m,*

1. *If there is no preference profile making w^* the match of $\hat{m}$, then Algorithm 2 will return false.*
2. *If a preference profile making w^* the match of $\hat{m}$ exists, then for the same instance with one additional manipulator, Algorithm 2 will return a preference profile that makes w^* the match of $\hat{m}$.*

That is, Algorithm 2 will succeed in any given instance such that the same instance but with one less manipulator is manipulable. Thus, it can be viewed as a 1-additive approximation algorithm (this approximate sense was introduced by Zuckerman et al. [24] when analyzing Borda as a social choice function (SCF)).

5   Women's Side

We now consider the second variant, in which a specific voter, or a coalition of voters, are associated with an agent $\hat{w}$, and they would like to manipulate the election so that a preferred spouse m^* will be the match of $\hat{w}$. This variant is more involved, since manipulation of the GS algorithm is also possible by a single woman or a coalition of women. Indeed, there are notable differences between manipulation from the women's side and manipulation from the men's side. First, the manipulators from the women's side need to ensure that **two** men are positioned "relatively" high. In addition, the set B, which is the set of agents that are placed in low positions, is defined differently, and it is not built iteratively. Finally, in manipulation from the women's side, it is not always possible to place all the agents from B in the lowest positions.

5.1   Single Manipulator

With a single manipulator, the Manipulation in the context of Matching from the Women's side (MnM-w) is defined as follows:

ALGORITHM 3: Manipulation by a single voter from the women's side

---

 1 **for** *each* $m_{nd} \in M \setminus \{m^*\}$ **do**
        // stage 1:
 2      $\ell_r \leftarrow$ empty preference order
 3   place m_{nd} in the highest position in ℓ_r
 4   place m^* in the second-highest position in ℓ_r
 5   **if** $(m_{nd}, \mathcal{L}, \ell_r) > (m^*, \mathcal{L}, \ell_r)$ **then**
 6   place m^* in the highest position in ℓ_r
 7   place m_{nd} in ℓ_r in the highest position such that
            $(m^*, \mathcal{L}, \ell_r) > (m_{nd}, \mathcal{L}, \ell_r)$, if such position exists
 8   **if** *no such position exists* **then**
 9   **continue** to the next iteration
10   **if** $\mu(\hat{w}, \ell_r) \neq m^*$ *or* $m_{nd} \notin o(\hat{w}, \ell_r)$ **then**
11   **continue** to the next iteration
        // stage 2:
12   **for** *each* $m \notin o(\hat{w}, \ell_r)$ **do**
13   place m in the highest available position in ℓ_r
        // stage 3:
14      $B \leftarrow o(\hat{w}, \ell_r) \setminus \{m^*, m_{nd}\}$
15   **while** $B \neq \emptyset$ **do**
16          $b \leftarrow$ the least preferred man from B according to $\mathcal{F}(\mathcal{L})$
17   place b in the highest available position in ℓ_r
18   remove b from B
19   **if** $\mu(\hat{w}, \ell_r) = m^*$ **then**
20   **return** ℓ_r
21 **return** false

Definition 4 (MnM-w). *We are given a woman $\hat{w}$, the preference profile $\mathcal{L}$ of the honest voters that associate with $\hat{w}$, the preference profile $\succ_M$, the preference profile $\succ_{W-\hat{w}}$, a specific manipulator r, and a preferred man $m^* \in M$. We are asked whether a preference order ℓ_r exists such that $\mu(\hat{w}, \ell_r) = m^*$.*

Clearly, if $\mu(\hat{w}) = m^*$ then finding a preference order ℓ_r such that $\mu(\hat{w}, \ell_r) = m^*$ is trivial. We thus henceforth assume that $\mu(\hat{w}) \neq m^*$. The MnM-w problem can be decided in polynomial-time, using Algorithm 3. The algorithm tries to identify a man $m_{nd} \in M$, and to place him and m^* in ℓ_r such that m_{nd} is ranked in $\mathcal{F}(\mathcal{L} \cup \{\ell_r\})$ as high as possible while m^* is still preferred over m_{nd} according to $\mathcal{F}(\mathcal{L} \cup \{\ell_r\})$. In addition, the algorithm ensures (at the end of stage 1) that $\mu(\hat{w}, \ell_r) = m^*$ and $m_{nd} \in o(\hat{w}, \ell_r)$. Note that we compute $\mathcal{F}(\mathcal{L} \cup \{\ell_r\})$ even though ℓ_r is not a complete preference order, since we assume that all the men that are not in ℓ_r get a score of 0 from ℓ_r. If stage 1 is successful (i.e., $\mu(\hat{w}, \ell_r) = m^*$ and $m_{nd} \in o(\hat{w}, \ell_r)$), the algorithm proceeds to stage 2, where it fills the preference order ℓ_r by placing all the men that are not in $o(\hat{w}, \ell_r)$ in the highest available positions. Finally, in stage 3, the algorithm places all the men from $o(\hat{w}, \ell_r)$ (except for m^* and m_{nd} that are already placed in ℓ_r) in the lowest positions in ℓ_r, and they are placed in a reverse order with regard to their order in $\mathcal{F}(\mathcal{L})$. If $\mu(\hat{w}, \ell_r) = m^*$ then we are done; otherwise, the algorithm iterates and considers another man.

For proving the correctness of Algorithm 3 we need the following result.

Lemma 4 (Swapping lemma, due to [22]). *Given a woman $w \in W$, let $\succ'_w$ be a preference order that is derived from $\succ_w$ by swapping the positions of an adjacent pair of men (m_i, m_j) and making no other changes. Then,*

1. *if $m_i \notin o(w)$ or $m_j \notin o(w)$, then $\mu_x(w, \succ'_w) = \mu(w)$.*
2. *if both m_i and m_j are not one of the two most preferred proposals among $o(w)$ according to $\succ_w$, then $\mu_x(w, \succ'_w) = \mu(w)$.*
3. *if m_i is the second preferred proposal among $o(w)$ according to $\succ_w$ and m_j is the third preferred proposal among $o(w)$ according to $\succ_w$, then $\mu_x(w, \succ'_w) \in \{\mu(w), m_j\}$.*
4. *if $m_i = \mu(w)$ and m_j is the second preferred proposal among $o(w)$ according to $\succ_w$, then the second preferred proposal among $o(w)$ according to $\succ'_w$ is m_i or m_j.*

If we use the swapping lemma sequentially, we get the following corollary.

Corollary 1. *Given a woman $w \in W$, let $\succ'_w$ be a preference order for w such that $\succ_w \neq \succ'_w$. Let $m^* \in M$ be the most preferred man among $o(w)$ according to $\succ_w$. That is, $\mu(w) = m^*$. Let $m_{nd} \in M$ be the second most preferred man among $o(w)$ according to $\succ_w$. If m_{nd} is the most preferred man among $o(w) \setminus \{m^*\}$ according to $\succ'_w$, and $m^* \succ'_w m_{nd}$, then $o(w) = o_x(w, \succ'_w)$ and thus $\mu_x(w, \succ'_w) = \mu(w) = m^*$.*

Proof. We construct the preference order $\succ'_w$ by starting from $\succ_w$ and performing a sequence of swaps of two adjacent men till the resulting preference order is $\succ'_w$. We show that each swap does not change the set of proposals, by repeatedly invoking Lemma 4.

We begin by positioning the most preferred man according to $\succ'_w$, using swaps of two adjacent men. That is, if m_{st} is the most preferred man according to $\succ'_w$, we swap pairs $(m, m_{st}), m \in M$, until m_{st} is placed in the first position in $\succ'_w$. We call these swaps the swaps of m_{st}. We then position the second preferred man using his swaps, and so on. Clearly, this process terminates since the number of men is finite. Let $\succ_w^{(t)}$ be $\succ_w$ after t swaps. That is, $\succ_w^{(0)}$ is $\succ_w$, $\succ_w^{(1)}$ is $\succ_w$ after one swap, and $\succ_w^{(t+1)}$ is $\succ_w^{(t)}$ after one swap. We show that for every $t \geq 0$, $o_x(w, \succ_w^{(t)}) = o_x(w, \succ_w^{(t+1)})$ and thus $o(w) = o_x(w, \succ_w^{(0)}) = o_x(w, \succ'_w)$. Let (m_i, m_j) be the pair of adjacent men that swap their positions when moving from $\succ_w^{(t)}$ to $\succ_w^{(t+1)}$. That is, $m_i \succ_w^{(t)} m_j$ and $m_j \succ_w^{(t+1)} m_i$. Recall that for every $m_1, m_2 \in M$, if $m_1 \succ'_w m_2$, then all the swaps of m_1 are executed before all the swaps of m_2. In addition, since m_{nd} is the most preferred man among $o(w) \setminus \{m^*\}$ according to $\succ'_w$ and $m^* \succ'_w m_{nd}$, then the following cases are not possible:

1. $m_i = m^*$ and $m_j \in o_x(w, \succ_w^{(t)})$.

2. $m_i \in o_x(w, \succ_w^{(t)})$ and $m_j = m^*$.

3. $m_i = m_{nd}$ and $m_j \in o_x(w, \succ_w^{(t)})$.

4. $m_i \in o_x(w, \succ_w^{(t)})$ and $m_j = m_{nd}$.

5. $m_i = m^*$ and $m_j = m_{nd}$.

We thus need to consider only the following two cases:

1. $m_i \notin o_x(w, \succ_w^{(t)})$ or $m_j \notin o_x(w, \succ_w^{(t)})$. According to the GS algorithm, a swap of such m_i and m_j cannot change the response of w (either an acceptance or rejection). Therefore, $o_x(w, \succ_w^{(t)}) = o_x(w, \succ_w^{(t+1)})$.

2. $m_i, m_j \in o_x(w, \succ_w^{(t)}) \setminus \{m^*, m_{nd}\}$. We use case 2 of Lemma 4 for this case. Assume to contradiction that $o_x(w, \succ_w^{(t)}) \neq o_x(w, \succ_w^{(t+1)})$. There are two possible cases:

   (a) There exists a man $o \in o_x(w, \succ_w^{(t)})$ such that $o \notin o_x(w, \succ_w^{(t+1)})$. By case 2 of Lemma 4, $m^* = \mu_x(w, \succ_w^{(t)}) = \mu_x(w, \succ_w^{(t+1)})$. Let $\succ^o$ be $\succ_w^{(t+1)}$ such that o is positioned above m^*. We can construct $\succ^o$ from $\succ_w^{(t+1)}$ by swaps of o. Since $o \notin o_x(w, \succ_w^{(t+1)})$, then by case 1 of Lemma 4, $\mu_x(w, \succ_w^{(t+1)}) = \mu_x(w, \succ^o)$. We now swap m_j and m_i in $\succ^o$, and thus $m_i \succ^o m_j$ as in $\succ_w^{(t)}$. Let $Pre^o \subset o_x(w, \succ_w^{(t)})$ be the set of proposals that w receives before she receives the proposal o. Note that all the men $o \in Pre^o$ are in the same order in $\succ_w^{(t)}$ and in $\succ^o$. Therefore, the response of woman w is the same for all the proposals $o \in Pre^o$ and thus $o \in o_x(w, \succ^o)$. Therefore, $m^* \neq \mu_x(w, \succ^o)$, which is a contradiction.

   (b) There exists a man $o \notin o_x(w, \succ_w^{(t)})$ such that $o \in o_x(w, \succ_w^{(t+1)})$. Using a similar argument to case (a) above (i.e., we now construct $\succ^o$ from $\succ_w^{(t)}$) we get that in this case also $o_x(w, \succ_w^{(t)}) = o_x(w, \succ_w^{(t+1)})$

□

Corollary 1 is the basis of our algorithm. Intuitively, the manipulator needs to ensure that m^* is among the set of proposals $o(\hat{w}, \ell_r)$, and that m^* is the most preferred men, according to $\mathcal{F}(\mathcal{L} \cup \{\ell_r\})$, among this set. That is, $m^* = \mu(\hat{w}, \ell_r)$. Thus, the algorithm searches for a man, denoted by m_{nd}, that serves as the second-best proposal. If such a man exists, then, according to Corollary 1, the position of every man $m \in o(\hat{w}, \ell_r)$ does not change $\hat{w}$'s match (which is currently m^*) if m_{nd} is preferred over m in $\mathcal{F}(\mathcal{L} \cup \{\ell_r\})$. In addition, the position of every man $m \notin o(\hat{w}, \ell_r)$ does not change $\hat{w}$'s match at all.

Theorem 5. *Algorithm 3 correctly decides the MnM-w problem in polynomial time.*

Proof. Clearly, the algorithm runs in polynomial time since there are three loops, where the three loops together iterate at most k^2 times, and the running time of the GS matching algorithm is in $O(k^2)$. In addition, if the algorithm returns a preference order, which is a manipulative vote for the manipulator r, then m^* will be the match of $\hat{w}$ by the GS algorithm. We need to show that if there exists a preference order for the manipulator r that makes m^* the match of $\hat{w}$, then our algorithm will find such a preference order for r. Assume that a manipulative vote, ℓ_t, exists, which makes m^* the match of $\hat{w}$. That is, $\mu(\hat{w}, \ell_t) = m^*$. We show that Algorithm 3 returns ℓ_r in line 20. Let $\ell_{r(1)}$ be the preference order ℓ_r after stage 1 of the algorithm. $\ell_{r(2)}$ and $\ell_{r(3)}$ are defined similarly. Note that $\ell_{r(3)}$ is the preference order ℓ_r that is returned by the algorithm in line 20.

Algorithm 3 iterates over all $m_{nd} \in M \setminus \{m^*\}$, and thus there exists an iteration in which m_{nd} is the second preferred proposal among $o(\hat{w}, \ell_t)$ according to $\mathcal{F}(\mathcal{L} \cup \{\ell_t\})$. Let $\ell_{t(1)}$ be the preference order ℓ_t where m^* and m_{nd} are placed in the same positions as in $\ell_{r(1)}$. Note that m^* and m_{nd} are placed in $\ell_{r(1)}$ such that m^* is preferred over m_{nd} according to $\mathcal{F}(\mathcal{L} \cup \{\ell_{r(1)}\})$, and thus m^* is preferred over m_{nd} according to $\mathcal{F}(\mathcal{L} \cup \{\ell_{t(1)}\})$. In addition, m_{nd} is positioned in $\mathcal{F}(\mathcal{L} \cup \{\ell_{t(1)}\})$ not lower than in $\mathcal{F}(\mathcal{L} \cup \{\ell_t\})$. Therefore, m_{nd} is the most preferred man among $o(\hat{w}, \ell_t) \setminus \{m^*\}$ according to $\mathcal{F}(\mathcal{L} \cup \{\ell_{t(1)}\})$. By Corollary 1, $o(\hat{w}, \ell_t) = o(\hat{w}, \ell_{t(1)})$ and $\mu(\hat{w}, \ell_{t(1)}) = m^*$. Thus, m_{nd} is the second preferred proposal among $o(\hat{w}, \ell_{t(1)})$ according to $\mathcal{F}(\mathcal{L} \cup \{\ell_{t(1)}\})$.

Let $\ell_{t(2)}$ be the preference order $\ell_{t(1)}$ where the men $m \notin o(\hat{w}, \ell_{t(1)})$ are placed in the highest positions in $\ell_{t(2)}$ without changing the positions of m^* and m_{nd} (similar to the positioning of the men $m \notin o(\hat{w}, \ell_{r(2)})$ after stage 2 of the algorithm). That is, m^* is preferred over m_{nd} according to $\mathcal{F}(\mathcal{L} \cup \{\ell_{t(2)}\})$ and m_{nd} is the most preferred man among $o(\hat{w}, \ell_{t(1)}) \setminus \{m^*\}$ according to $\mathcal{F}(\mathcal{L} \cup \{\ell_{t(2)}\})$. We can thus use (again) Corollary 1 to get that $o(\hat{w}, \ell_{t(1)}) = o(\hat{w}, \ell_{t(2)})$ and $\mu(\hat{w}, \ell_{t(2)}) = m^*$.

Recall that at the end of stage 1 of Algorithm 3, m^* and m_{nd} are placed in $\ell_{r(1)}$ such that m^* is preferred over m_{nd} according to $\mathcal{F}(\mathcal{L} \cup \{\ell_{r(1)}\})$. In addition, m_{nd} is positioned in $\mathcal{F}(\mathcal{L} \cup \{\ell_{r(1)}\})$ not lower than in $\mathcal{F}(\mathcal{L} \cup \{\ell_{t(2)}\})$, since they are placed in the same position in $\ell_{r(1)}$ and $\ell_{t(2)}$ and the other men in $\ell_{r(1)}$ get a score of 0 from $\ell_{r(1)}$. Specifically, the men $m \in o(\hat{w}, \ell_{t(2)})$ also get a score of 0 from $\ell_{r(1)}$ and thus m_{nd} is the most preferred man among $o(\hat{w}, \ell_{t(2)}) \setminus \{m^*\}$ according to $\mathcal{F}(\mathcal{L} \cup \{\ell_{r(1)}\})$. By Corollary 1, $o(\hat{w}, \ell_{t(2)}) = o(\hat{w}, \ell_{r(1)})$ and $\mu(\hat{w}, \ell_{r(1)}) = m^*$. Since in stage 2 of Algorithm 3 we place only men $m \notin o(\hat{w}, \ell_{r(1)})$, then, we can (again) use Corollary 1 to show that $o(\hat{w}, \ell_{t(2)}) = o(\hat{w}, \ell_{r(2)})$, $\mu(\hat{w}, \ell_{r(2)}) = m^*$, and m_{nd} is the second preferred proposal among $o(\hat{w}, \ell_{r(2)})$ according to $\mathcal{F}(\mathcal{L} \cup \{\ell_{r(2)}\})$.

We now show that Algorithm 3 (lines 14–18) can assign scores to all the men $m \in B$ such that ℓ_r is a successful manipulation. For any $m \in B$, if $s(m, \ell_{r(3)}) \leq s(m, \ell_{t(2)})$ then $s(m, \mathcal{L}, \ell_{r(3)}) \leq s(m, \mathcal{L}, \ell_{t(2)})$. Since $(m_{nd}, \mathcal{L}, \ell_{t(2)}) > (m, \mathcal{L}, \ell_{t(2)})$ and $s(m_{nd}, \mathcal{L}, \ell_{t(2)}) = s(m_{nd}, \mathcal{L}, \ell_{r(3)})$ then $(m_{nd}, \mathcal{L}, \ell_{r(3)}) > (m, \mathcal{L}, \ell_{r(3)})$. Otherwise, let $m \in B$ be a man such that $s(m, \ell_{r(3)}) > s(m, \ell_{t(2)})$ and let $s = s(m, \ell_{r(3)})$. By the algorithm construction, there are s men from B below m in $\ell_{r(3)}$. According to the pigeonhole principle, at least one of the men from B, denoted m', gets a score of at least s from $\ell_{t(2)}$. That is, $s(m', \ell_{t(2)}) \geq s(m, \ell_{r(3)})$. By the algorithm construction, all the men $m'' \in B$ that are positioned lower than m in $\ell_{r(3)}$ are positioned higher than m in $\mathcal{F}(\mathcal{L})$. That is, $(m', \mathcal{L}) > (m, \mathcal{L})$. However, $(m', \mathcal{L}, \ell_{t(2)}) < (m_{nd}, \mathcal{L}, \ell_{t(2)})$ and thus $(m, \mathcal{L}, \ell_{r(3)}) < (m_{nd}, \mathcal{L}, \ell_{r(3)})$.

Overall, after placing the men from B in $\ell_{r(3)}$, $\forall m \in B$, $(m, \mathcal{L}, \ell_{r(3)}) < (m_{nd}, \mathcal{L}, \ell_{r(3)})$. That is, m_{nd} is the most preferred man among $o(\hat{w}, \ell_{r(2)}) \setminus \{m^*\}$ according to $\mathcal{F}(\mathcal{L} \cup \{\ell_{r(2)}\})$. In addition $(m_{nd}, \mathcal{L}, \ell_{r(3)}) < (m^*, \mathcal{L}, \ell_{r(3)})$ and thus by Corollary 1, $\mu(\hat{w}, \ell_{r(3)}) = m^*$.   □

5.2   Coalitional Manipulation

Finally, We study manipulation by a coalition of voters from the women's side.

Definition 5 (coalitional MnM-w). *We are given a woman $\hat{w}$, the prefer- ence profile $\mathcal{L}$ of the honest voters that associate with $\hat{w}$, the preference profile $\succ_M$, the preference profile $\succ_{W-\hat{w}}$, a coalition of manipulators R, and a pre- ferred man $m^* \in M$. We are asked whether a preference profile $\mathcal{L}_R$ exists such that $\mu(\hat{w}, \mathcal{L}_R) = m^*$.*

Similar to the single manipulator setting, if $\mu(\hat{w}) = m^*$ then finding a pref- erence profile $\mathcal{L}_R$ such that $\mu(\hat{w}, \ell_R) = m^*$ is trivial. We thus henceforth assume that $\mu(\hat{w}) \neq m^*$. The coalitional MnM-w problem is computationally hard, and we again reduce from the Permutation Sum problem (Definition 3).

Theorem 6. *Coalitional MnM-w is NP-Complete.*

Similar to the coalitional MnM-m, the coalitional MnM-w also has an efficient heuristic algorithm that finds a successful manipulation. We use Algorithm 4, which works as follows. Similar to Algorithm 3, Algorithm 4 needs to identify a man $m_{nd} \in M$, such that m_{nd} is ranked in $\mathcal{F}(\mathcal{L} \cup \mathcal{L}_R)$ as high as possible while m^* is still preferred over m_{nd} according to $\mathcal{F}(\mathcal{L} \cup \mathcal{L}_R)$. In addition, the algorithm needs to ensure that $\mu(\hat{w}, \mathcal{L}_R) = m^*$ and $m_{nd} \in o(\hat{w}, \mathcal{L}_R)$, which is done at the end of stage 1. Indeed, finding such a man $m_{nd} \in M$, and placing him and m^* in every $\ell_r \in \mathcal{L}_R$ is not trivial. The algorithm considers every $m \in M \setminus \{m^*\}$, and computes the difference between the score of m from $\mathcal{L}$ and the score of m^* from $\mathcal{L}$. Clearly, if this gap is too big, m cannot be m_{nd} (line 6). Otherwise, there are two possible cases. If there are many manipulators, specifically, $|R| \geq gap$, then the algorithm places m^* and m in the two highest positions in every ℓ_r (lines 8–10). On the other hand, if $|R| < gap$, then the algorithm places m^* in the highest position in every ℓ_r. The algorithm places m in the second highest position or in the lowest position in every ℓ_r, except for $\ell_{|R|}$; in this preference order the algorithm places m in the highest position such that m^* is preferred over m according to $\mathcal{F}(\mathcal{L} \cup \mathcal{L}_R)$. If stage 1 is successful, the algorithm proceeds to fill the preference orders of $\mathcal{L}_R$ iteratively in stage 2. In every $\ell_r \in \mathcal{L}_R$, the algorithm places all the men that are not in $o(\hat{w}, \mathcal{L}_R)$ in the highest available positions. The algorithm places all the men from $o(\hat{w}, \mathcal{L}_R)$ (except for m^* and m_{nd} that are already placed in $\mathcal{L}_R$) in the lowest positions in $\mathcal{L}_R$, and they are placed in a reverse order in each manipulator with regard to their current order in $\mathcal{F}(\mathcal{L} \cup \mathcal{L}_R)$. Note that since $\mathcal{L}_R$ is updated in every iteration, the men from $o(\hat{w}, \mathcal{L}_R) \setminus \{m^*, m_{nd}\}$ may be placed in different order in each ℓ_r.

ALGORITHM 4: Manipulation by a coalition of voters from the women's side

---

1 **for** *each* $m_{nd} \in M \setminus \{m^*\}$ **do**

   // **stage 1**:

2 $\quad gap \leftarrow s(m_{nd}, \mathcal{L}) - s(m^*, \mathcal{L})$

3 $\quad$ **if** m_{nd} *is preferred over* m^* *according to the lexicographical tie breaking rule* **then**

4 $\quad\quad gap = gap + 1$

5 $\quad$ **if** $|R| \cdot (k-1) < gap$ **then**

6 $\quad\quad$ **continue** to the next iteration

7 $\quad \mathcal{L}_R \leftarrow \{\ell_{r_1}, ..., \ell_{r_{|R|}}\}$ where each preference order is an empty one

8 $\quad$ **if** $|R| \geq gap$ **then**

9 $\quad\quad$ place m^* in in the highest position and m_{nd} in the second highest position, in $\max(gap + \lceil(|R| - gap)/2\rceil, 0)$ preference orders of $\mathcal{L}_R$

10 $\quad\quad$ place m^* in the second highest position and m_{nd} in the highest position in all of the other preference orders of $\mathcal{L}_R$

11 $\quad$ **else**

12 $\quad\quad$ place m^* in the highest position in each $\ell_r \in \mathcal{L}_R$

13 $\quad\quad$ place m_{nd} in the lowest position in $\lfloor(gap - |R|)/(k-2)\rfloor$ preference orders of $\mathcal{L}_R \setminus \{\ell_{r_{|R|}}\}$

14 $\quad\quad$ place m_{nd} in the second-highest position in all of the other preference orders of $\mathcal{L}_R \setminus \{\ell_{r_{|R|}}\}$

15 $\quad\quad$ in $\ell_{r_{|R|}}$, place m_{nd} in the highest position such that $(m^*, \mathcal{L} \cup \mathcal{L}_R) > (m_{nd}, \mathcal{L} \cup \mathcal{L}_R)$

16 $\quad$ **if** $\mu(\hat{w}, \mathcal{L}_R) \neq m^*$ *or* $m \notin o(\hat{w}, \mathcal{L}_R)$ **then**

17 $\quad\quad$ **continue** to the next iteration

   // **stage 2**:

18 $\quad B \leftarrow o(\hat{w}, \mathcal{L}_R) \setminus \{m^*, m_{nd}\}$

19 $\quad$ **for** *each* $r \in R$ **do**

20 $\quad\quad$ **for** *each* $m \notin B$ **do**

21 $\quad\quad\quad$ place m in the next highest available position in ℓ_r

22 $\quad\quad M^B \leftarrow B$

23 $\quad\quad$ **while** $M^B \neq \emptyset$ **do**

24 $\quad\quad\quad b \leftarrow$ the least preferred man from M^B according to $\mathcal{F}(\mathcal{L} \cup \mathcal{L}_R)$

25 $\quad\quad\quad$ place b at the highest available position in ℓ_r

26 $\quad\quad\quad$ remove b from M^B

27 $\quad$ **if** $\mu(\hat{w}, \mathcal{L}_R) = m^*$ **then**

28 $\quad\quad$ **return** $\mathcal{L}_R$

29 **return** false

We now show that Algorithm 4 will succeed in any given instance such that the same instance but with one less manipulator is manipulable. That is, the coalitional MnM-w admits also a 1-additive approximation algorithm. Formally,

Theorem 7. *Given an instance of coalitional MnM-w,*

1. *If there is no preference profile making m^* the match of $\hat{w}$ exists, then Algorithm 4 will return false.*

2. *If a preference profile making* m^* *the match of* $\hat{w}$, *then for the same instance with one additional manipulator, Algorithm 4 will return a preference profile that makes* m^* *the match of* $\hat{w}$.

6   Conclusion

In this paper, we initiate the analysis of strategic voting in the context of stable matching of teams. Specifically, we assume that the Borda rule is used as a SWF, which outputs an order over the agents that is used as an input in the GS algorithm. Note that in the standard model of manipulation of Borda, the goal is that a specific candidate will be the winner. In our setting, the algorithms need also to ensure that a specific candidates will not be ranked too high. Similarly, in the standard model of manipulation of the GS algorithm, the goal is simply to achieve a more preferred match. In our setting, the algorithms for manipulation need also to ensure that a less preferred spouse is matched to a specific agent. Therefore, even though the manipulation of the Borda rule and the manipulation of the GS algorithm have already been studied, our analysis of the manipulation of Borda rule in the context of GS stable matching provides a better understanding of both algorithms.

Interestingly, our algorithms for the single manipulator settings are quite powerful. They provide exact solutions for the single manipulator case, and their generalizations provide approximate solutions to the coalitional manipulation settings, both when the manipulators are on the men's side or on the women's side.

References

1. Abdulkadiroğlu, A., Pathak, P.A., Roth, A.E.: The New York city high school match. Am. Econ. Rev. **95**(2), 364–367 (2005)
2. Bossert, W., Sprumont, Y.: Strategy-proof preference aggregation: possibilities and characterizations. Games Econom. Behav. **85**, 109–126 (2014)
3. Bossert, W., Storcken, T.: Strategy-proofness of social welfare functions: the use of the Kemeny distance between preference orderings. Soc. Choice Welfare **9**(4), 345–360 (1992)
4. Conitzer, V., Walsh, T.: Barriers to manipulation in voting. In: Brandt, F., Conitzer, V., Endriss, U., Lang, J., Procaccia, A.D. (eds.) Handbook of Computational Social Choice, pp. 127–145. Cambridge University Press (2016)
5. Davies, J., Katsirelos, G., Narodytska, N., Walsh, T.: Complexity of and algorithms for Borda manipulation. In: The Twenty-Fifth AAAI Conference on Artificial Intelligence, pp. 657–662 (2011)
6. Dogan, O., Lainé, J.: Strategic manipulation of social welfare functions via strict preference extensions. In: The 13th Meeting of the Society for Social Choice and Welfare, p. 199 (2016)
7. Dubins, L.E., Freedman, D.A.: Machiavelli and the Gale-Shapley algorithm. Am. Math. Mon. **88**(7), 485–494 (1981)
8. Faliszewski, P., Procaccia, A.D.: Ai's war on manipulation: are we winning? AI Mag. **31**(4), 53–64 (2010)

 9. Gale, D., Shapley, L.S.: College admissions and the stability of marriage. Am. Math. Mon. **69**(1), 9–15 (1962)
10. Hosseini, H., Umar, F., Vaish, R.: Accomplice manipulation of the deferred acceptance algorithm. In: The Thirtieth International Joint Conference on Artificial Intelligence, pp. 231–237 (2021)
11. Hosseini, H., Umar, F., Vaish, R.: Two for one & one for all: two-sided manipulation in matching markets. arXiv preprint arXiv:2201.08774 (2022)
12. Huang, C.-C.: Cheating by men in the Gale-Shapley stable matching algorithm. In: Azar, Y., Erlebach, T. (eds.) ESA 2006. LNCS, vol. 4168, pp. 418–431. Springer, Heidelberg (2006). https://doi.org/10.1007/11841036_39
13. Perach, N., Anily, S.: Stable matching of student-groups to dormitories. Eur. J. Oper. Res. **302**, 50–61 (2022)
14. Pini, M.S., Rossi, F., Venable, K.B., Walsh, T.: Manipulation complexity and gender neutrality in stable marriage procedures. Auton. Agent. Multi-Agent Syst. **22**(1), 183–199 (2011)
15. Roth, A.E.: The economics of matching: stability and incentives. Math. Oper. Res. **7**(4), 617–628 (1982)
16. Roth, A.E.: The NRMP as a labor market: understanding the current study of the match. J. Am. Med. Assoc. **275**(13), 1054–1056 (1996)
17. Roth, A.E., Sönmez, T., Ünver, M.U.: Kidney exchange. Q. J. Econ. **119**(2), 457–488 (2004)
18. Schmerler, L., Hazon, N.: Strategic voting in negotiating teams. In: Fotakis, D., Ríos Insua, D. (eds.) ADT 2021. LNCS (LNAI), vol. 13023, pp. 209–223. Springer, Cham (2021). https://doi.org/10.1007/978-3-030-87756-9_14
19. Schmerler, L., Hazon, N., Kraus, S.: Strategic voting in the context of stable-matching of teams. arXiv preprint arXiv:2207.04912 (2022)
20. Shen, W., Deng, Y., Tang, P.: Coalitional permutation manipulations in the Gale-Shapley algorithm. Artif. Intell. **301**, 103577 (2021)
21. Teo, C.P., Sethuraman, J., Tan, W.P.: Gale-Shapley stable marriage problem revisited: strategic issues and applications. Manag. Sci. **47**(9), 1252–1267 (2001)
22. Vaish, R., Garg, D.: Manipulating Gale-Shapley algorithm: preserving stability and remaining inconspicuous. In: The Twenty-Sixth International Joint Conference on Artificial Intelligence, pp. 437–443 (2017)
23. Yu, W., Hoogeveen, H., Lenstra, J.K.: Minimizing makespan in a two-machine flow shop with delays and unit-time operations is NP-hard. J. Sched. **7**(5), 333–348 (2004)
24. Zuckerman, M., Procaccia, A.D., Rosenschein, J.S.: Algorithms for the coalitional manipulation problem. Artif. Intell. **173**(2), 392–412 (2009)

Abstracts

Competition and Recall in Selection Problems

Fabien Gensbittel[1], Dana Pizarro[1,2(✉)], and Jérôme Renault[1]

[1] Toulouse School of Economics, Université Toulouse 1 Capitole, Toulouse, France
{fabien.gensbittel,dana.pizarro,jerome.renault}@tse-fr.eu
[2] Institute of Engineering Sciences, Universidad de O'Higgins, Rancagua, Chile

Abstract. We extend the prophet inequality problem to a competitive setting. At every period $t \in \{1, \ldots, n\}$, a new sample X_t from a known distribution F arrives and is publicly observed. Then two players simultaneously decide whether to pick an available value or to pass and wait until the next period (ties are broken uniformly at random). As soon as a player gets one sample, he leaves the market and his payoff is the value of the sample. In a first variant, namely *no recall* case, the agents can only bid in period t for the current value X_t. In a second variant, the *full recall* case, the agents can also bid at period t for any of the previous samples with values $X_1,...,X_{t-1}$ which has not been already selected. For each variant, we study the subgame-perfect Nash equilibrium payoffs of the corresponding game, as a function of the number of periods n and the distribution F. More specifically, we give a full characterization in the full recall case, and show in particular that both players always get the same payoff at equilibrium, whereas in the no recall case the set of equilibrium payoffs typically has full dimension. Regarding the welfare at equilibrium, surprisingly it is possible that the best equilibrium payoff a player can have is strictly higher in the no recall case than in the full recall case. However, symmetric equilibrium payoffs are always better when the players have full recall. Finally, we show that in the case of 2 arrivals and arbitrary distributions, the prices of Anarchy and Stability in the no recall case are at most 4/3, and this bound is tight.

Keywords: Optimal stopping · Competing agents · Recall · Prophet inequalities · Price of anarchy · Price of stability · Subgame-perfect equilibria · Game theory

A full version of this paper can be found on arXiv:2108.04501. The authors gratefully acknowledge funding from ANITI ANR-3IA Artificial and Natural Intelligence Toulouse Institute, grant ANR-19-PI3A-0004, and from the ANR under the Investments for the Future program, grant ANR-17-EURE-0010. J. Renault also acknowledges the support of ANR MaSDOL-19-CE23-0017-01.

© The Author(s), under exclusive license to Springer Nature Switzerland AG 2022
P. Kanellopoulos et al. (Eds.): SAGT 2022, LNCS 13584, pp. 583–584, 2022.
https://doi.org/10.1007/978-3-031-15714-1_33

References

1. Ezra, T., Feldman, M., Kupfer, R.: Prophet inequality with competing agents. In: Caragiannis, I., Hansen, K.A. (eds.) SAGT 2021. LNCS, vol. 12885, pp. 112–123. Springer, Cham (2021). https://doi.org/10.1007/978-3-030-85947-3_8
2. Immorlica, N., Kleinberg, R., Mahdian, M.: Secretary problems with competing employers. In: Spirakis, P., Mavronicolas, M., Kontogiannis, S. (eds.) WINE 2006. LNCS, vol. 4286, pp. 389–400. Springer, Heidelberg (2006). https://doi.org/10.1007/11944874_35

Optimality of the Coordinate-Wise Median Mechanism for Strategyproof Facility Location in Two Dimensions

Sumit Goel$^{(\boxtimes)}$ and Wade Hann-Caruthers

California Institute of Technology, Pasadena, CA 91125, USA
{sgoel,whanncar}@caltech.edu

In this paper, we consider the facility location problem in two dimensions. In particular, we consider a setting where agents have Euclidean preferences, defined by their ideal points, for a facility to be located in $\mathbb{R}^2$. A central planner would like to locate the facility so as to minimize the social cost given by the p-norm of vector of Euclidean distances $sc(y, \mathbf{x}) = [\sum \|y - x_i\|^p]^{\frac{1}{p}}$. Our problem is to find a strategyproof mechanism that best approximates the optimal social cost, as measured by the worst-case approximation ratio (AR), and quantify how well it does. We assume that the number of agents n is odd.

Result 1: *The coordinate-wise median mechanism (CM) has the smallest worst-case AR among all deterministic, anonymous, and strategyproof mechanisms.*

Using the characterization of unanimous, anonymous, and strategyproof mechanisms in this domain [2], we only need to demonstrate optimality of CM among generalized coordinate-wise median mechanisms with $n - 1$ phantom peaks. In this class of mechanisms, we first show that for any social cost function that is translation invariant, the lowest worst-case AR must be achieved by a coordinate-wise quantile mechanism (mechanism for which all of the $n - 1$ phantom peaks are at $(\pm\infty, \pm\infty)$). We then show that for any quasi-convex social cost function, the lowest worst-case AR among coordinate-wise quantile mechanisms must be achieved by the CM. This follows from observing that for any quantile mechanism, there are other quantile mechanisms that are isomorphic to it and the coordinate-wise median always lies in the convex hull of the locations chosen by these mechanisms. The result then follows from the fact that the p-norm objective is translation invariant and quasi-convex.

Result 2: *For the minisum objective ($p = 1$), the CM has a worst-case AR of* $\sqrt{2}\frac{\sqrt{n^2+1}}{n+1}$.

The proof of this result is rather involved and the key is to reduce the search space for the worst-case profile from $(\mathbb{R}^2)^n$ to a smaller space of profiles that have a simple structure via a sequence of transformations. For instance, one particularly important transformation involves moving an ideal point directly towards the optimal facility location (geometric median) as long as it doesn't change the coordinate-wise median or the geometric median. We can show this transformation leads to a profile with a higher approximation ratio and allows us to focus on profiles where every ideal point is either on the horizontal or vertical

© The Author(s), under exclusive license to Springer Nature Switzerland AG 2022
P. Kanellopoulos et al. (Eds.): SAGT 2022, LNCS 13584, pp. 585–586, 2022.
https://doi.org/10.1007/978-3-031-15714-1_34

line through the coordinate-wise median or at the geometric median. This and other such transformations eventually lead us to a worst-case profile and thus, the worst-case AR.

Result 3: *For the $p - norm$ objective with $p \geq 2$, the CM has a worst-case AR of at most $2^{\frac{3}{2}-\frac{2}{p}}$.*

[1] showed that for the one-dimensional facility location problem, the median mechanism has an asymptotic AR of $2^{1-\frac{1}{p}}$. This provides a lower bound on the asymptotic AR of the CM mechanism in two dimensions. The lower bound is tight for the cases where $p = 2$ and $p = \infty$, and we conjecture that it is tight for all p. The full version of the paper is available at https://arxiv.org/abs/2007.00903.

References

1. Feigenbaum, I., Sethuraman, J., Ye, C.: Approximately optimal mechanisms for strategyproof facility location: Minimizing L_p norm of costs. Math. Oper. Res. **42**(2), 434–447 (2017)
2. Peters, H., van der Stel, H., Storcken, T.: Range convexity, continuity, and strategy-proofness of voting schemes. Z. Oper. Res. **38**(2), 213–229 (1993). https://doi.org/10.1007/BF01414216

Nash, Conley, and Computation: Impossibility and Incompleteness in Game Dynamics

Jason Milionis[1]([✉])(iD), Christos Papadimitriou[1], Georgios Piliouras[2](iD), and Kelly Spendlove[3](iD)

[1] Columbia University, New York, NY 10027, USA
jm@cs.columbia.edu
[2] SUTD, Singapore, SG, Singapore
[3] Google, Mountain View, CA, USA

Abstract. Under what conditions do the behaviors of players, who play a game repeatedly, converge to a Nash equilibrium? If one assumes that the players' behavior is a discrete-time or continuous-time rule whereby the current mixed strategy profile is mapped to the next, this becomes a problem in the realm of dynamical systems. We apply this theory, and in particular the concepts of chain recurrence, attractors, and Conley index, to prove a general impossibility result: *there exist games that do not admit any game dynamics.* Here, our notion of game dynamics is that the set of Nash equilibria is precisely the chain recurrent set, implying that the Nash equilibria account for all recurrent behavior of the dynamics. Therefore our impossibility result implies for such games any dynamics must either admit recurrent behavior (e.g., cycling) outside of the set of Nash equilibria, or must abandon some Nash equilibrium. In our proof of our main theorem, we first establish a general principle for dynamical systems stated in the framework of Conley theory: if the Conley index of an attractor and that of the entire space are not isomorphic, then there is a non-empty dual repeller, and hence some trajectories are trapped away from the attractor. We then apply this principle to a classical degenerate two-player game g with three strategies for each player, whose Nash equilibria form a continuum, namely a six-sided closed walk in the 4-dimensional space. We then consider an arbitrary dynamics on g assumed to converge to the Nash equilibria, and show that the Conley index of the Nash equilibria attractor is not isomorphic to that of the whole space, which implies the existence of a nonempty dual repeller. We also show that, in some sense, degeneracy is necessary for the impossibility to hold; in fact, we give an algorithm which, given any nondegenerate game, specifies a somewhat trivial game dynamics, but we conjecture that impossibility still holds under complexity assumptions for non-degenerate games. Finally, we exhibit a family of games, in fact with nonzero measure (in particular, perturbations of the game used for our main result), for which any dynamics will fail to converge (in the above sense) to the set of ϵ-approximate Nash equilibria, for some fixed additive $\epsilon > 0$. Our results establish that, although the notions of

© The Author(s), under exclusive license to Springer Nature Switzerland AG 2022
P. Kanellopoulos et al. (Eds.): SAGT 2022, LNCS 13584, pp. 587–588, 2022.
https://doi.org/10.1007/978-3-031-15714-1_35

Nash equilibrium and its computation-inspired approximations are universally applicable in all games, they are also fundamentally incomplete as predictors of long-term behavior, regardless of the choice of dynamics. The full version of this paper is available at: https://arxiv.org/abs/2203.14129.

Author Index